Scottish Rugby

Scottish Rugby

Game by Game

KENNETH R BOGLE

Luath Press Limited

EDINBURGH

www.luath.co.uk

In memory of Dad

James Elliot Bogle 1924–2008

Who loved the game of Rugby Football

First published 2013

ISBN: 978-1-908373-88-5

The paper used in this book is recyclable. It is made from
low chlorine pulps produced in a low energy, low emissions manner
from renewable forests.

Printed and bound by
ScandBook AB, Sweden

Typeset in 9.5 point Sabon by 3btype.com

Contents

This is my country,
The land that begat me.
These windy spaces
Are surely my own.
And those who here toil
In the sweat of their faces
Are flesh of my flesh
And bone of my bone.
Hard is the day's task –
Scotland, stern Mother –
Yet do thy children
Honour and love thee.
Harsh is thy schooling,
Yet great is the gain:
True hearts and strong limbs,
The beauty of faces,
Kissed by the wind
And caressed by the rain.

Adapted from 'Scotland' by Sir Alexander Gray
with kind permission of the Gray estate.

Introduction

IT IS A WELL KNOWN fact that as you get older time seems to pass more quickly. I can hardly believe that it is over 30 years since the forerunner of this book first appeared. Sandy Thorburn's *The History of Scottish Rugby* was published in 1980. The book summarised every match played by the Scotland rugby team from 1871 to the end of season 1979–80, a total of well-over 350 games including some unofficial internationals and war-time matches. For many years it was the bible of the Scottish game. It is incredible to think that Sandy compiled his book in the days before the internet or indeed video recorders or DVDs. He couldn't look-up a fact at the touch of a button or replay old matches at home, but instead had to go to libraries and laboriously trawl through mounds of rapidly decaying newspapers. His book was published by the London firm Johnson and Bacon who have long since disappeared. It was a beautifully produced volume, a fine example of the art of typography.

I was pleased to discover that Sandy Thorburn was, like me, a proud son of Hawick. He was born in 1911 and educated at Hawick High School, which is a good start in life for anybody, and at Edinburgh University, sensible man, where he gained a Physics degree in 1934. He followed a career in teaching and ultimately became deputy headmaster of Broughton High School, Edinburgh, until his retirement in 1974. During the war, he was a civilian radio officer attached to the Royal Artillery, working on radar stations in the Edinburgh area, and later served in the War Office, including a spell in Washington. Sandy didn't play much rugby himself, in part due to injury at school, but he was an enthusiastic cricketer. He became honorary historian and librarian to the Scottish Rugby Union and also looked after the records of Royal High School FP, the Co-optimists and the Scottish Cricket Union. He passed away in October 1988.

I was 15 years old when Sandy's book came out and already had the first stirrings of becoming a rugby-loving anorak, a lifelong affliction for which there is no known cure. I remember the excitement of coming across the book for the first time in the local branch of John Menzies. I see by my original copy that it cost £9.95 which was a lot of money in those days and ours was not the type of house that ever went out and bought new hardbacks. I had to wait until Christmas to finally get my own copy and thereafter I read it almost to death. A second edition of Sandy's book was compiled by John Davidson and continued the story until 1994.

The trouble with books of this kind is that they are no sooner published than they are out of date, although don't let that put you off buying this one. Since 1980 I have kept my own records, on and off, of the Scottish rugby team. I have a terrible memory for most things in life, but for some reason I find that I can recall rugby matches and players quite easily. Perhaps there was something in the Hawick water supply. My original intention was simply to update Sandy's book, but my enthusiasm got the better of me and I ended-up rewriting the whole thing. So this book is a completely new version with lots of new material although it follows the model of Sandy's original. Researching and writing this book took me over eight years to complete. I don't really know why I did it, probably just to keep me out of mischief on the dark winter nights. At times I thought the book would kill me and that I would never finish, but I loved every second of it, reliving all the old matches and learning about the greats of long ago. My intention was to produce the kind of reference book that you pick up to check one thing and still find yourself reading hours later.

Sometimes following Scotland is like the classical myth of Sisyphus. The poor man was condemned by the Gods to spend eternity pushing a boulder up a mountain only to see it roll back down again. But as this book shows, it's not all bad and there are plenty of days when your heart swells and the tears start to flow. *Play up Scotland!*

Edinburgh 2013

Explanatory note

THIS BOOK LISTS every international played by Scotland since 1871, including non-cap and war-time matches which were internationals in all but name. Team line-ups are given in the following order: full-back, right wing, centre, centre, left wing, stand-off, scrum-half, loose-head prop, hooker, tight-head prop, lock, lock, flanker, flanker and Number eight. Formations have changed over time and I have used semi-colons to show the parts of a team, for example between the three-quarters and the half-backs. Until the early 1920s forwards packed in a 'first-up, first-down' formation so they are listed in alphabetical order to then. This is also the case for the half-backs (or quarter-backs as they were known in Scotland) who originally played a left and right position either side of the scrum. Early players often represented more than one club at the same time, such as their old school, university or local side, and in these cases I have used the clubs listed in the official programme when available. Regarding the names of players, I have, of course, tried to be as accurate as possible, but there were many variations of spellings, especially with the 'Macs' and hyphenated surnames, and some individuals changed their names during their lifetimes. In the old days people weren't terribly fussy about spelling and wrote their names as they saw fit. It's all very confusing. And that's before we get to the South Sea islanders and their immensely long names. Don't get me started on them.

Inevitably, there are contradictions between different newspaper accounts about players and scorers. Being a winter game, rugby was often played in murky conditions and poor light. The action was instantaneous and sometimes it was difficult for onlookers to see what had happened. A try might be scored at the other end of the field under a pile of bodies and Scottish players didn't wear numbered shirts until the late 1920s. Also there were no television replays or floodlights to brighten the gloom. When confusion arises I have erred on the side of the Scottish reports, assuming that the home journalists recognised their own players better. In addition, there are a few tour matches when the scoring sequence was not reported in English-language newspapers.

The point-scoring values have changed over the years. Before the early 1890s matches were decided on the numbers of goals scored, which included converted tries, drop goals and goals from a mark. For international matches, a uniform points scoring system was introduced in season 1890–1. After some early tinkering, the value of the try was 3 points until 1971, when it was increased to 4 points, eventually reaching its current value of 5 points in 1992. Conversions and penalties have remained fairly constant at 2 and 3 points respectively, but the drop goal value was 4 points until 1948 when it was reduced to 3. There was another method of scoring available to players in the early days – a goal from a mark, made when a clean catch was awarded and the catcher could drop a goal worth 3 points. Changes to the laws have made the goal from a mark impossible since 1977. All of this means, incidentally, that some matches would have had a completely different outcome if played under the modern scoring system.

At the beginning of each section I have included a summary of the main events of a particular era, both on and off the pitch. I have also indicated the prominent players of the day although obviously I can't mention everybody and don't come moaning to me if your favourite isn't there, especially if you're a big bad forward.

Acknowledgements

IT IS IMPOSSIBLE to produce a book of this kind on your own and I would like to thank the following people who helped make it happen.

First I am grateful to Gavin MacDougall and the team at Luath Press Limited who agreed to produce the book. Any publisher which takes its name after a dog belonging to Robert Burns has to be good.

I would like to thank my friends in the Rugby Memorabilia Society whose membership might be described as 'the nicest kind of nutter'. Thanks to Gary Alexander, Norman Anderson, Dave Fox and Ray 'Four Scoops' Ruddick, the only man I know with a rugby museum in his own home. Special thanks to Tony Lewis of Bridgend who regularly sent mysterious brown envelopes containing information about Scottish players. Sincere thanks to the wonderful John Jenkins of Ceredigion. John, a retired librarian, gave me an enormous amount of help on the list of Scottish players that forms an appendix to the book. They like their rugby, those Welshmen.

This book is adorned with some excellent illustrations I would like the following people who kindly provided them: David Mackie of Orkney Museums and Libraries; Michael Rowe, curator of the RFU Museum of Rugby; Mark Vivian at the Mary Evans Picture Library; George Herringshaw at Sporting-Heroes.net; and the trustees of the Robert D Clapperton Photographic Trust, Selkirk. The Scottish Rugby Union were supportive of the project and kindly allowed me to use some of their historic images. Thanks to Graham Ireland, Graham Law and Isobel Irvine. Special thanks to Kerry Black of *The Scotsman* who kindly supplied many images that have featured in Scotland's premier rugby paper over the years. The author and publishers have made every effort to contact the holders of copyright material and we apologise in advance if we have inadvertently infringed copyright. We will be happy to acknowledge proper ownership of images any future editions of the book.

I need hardly add that this book is my own work and none of the good folk mentioned here are responsible for what follows. Any errors are mine and I apologise in advance for my own fallibility.

Two important thanks to finish. For too long my wife and friend Alison has had to put up with old rugby books strewn across the living room floor and constant excuses from her hapless husband for not doing more useful things. She has accompanied me to rugby grounds around the world and knows a lot more about the current Scottish team than I do. Finally, I would like to dedicate my work in this book to the memory of my father James Elliot Bogle who passed away during its early stages. Dad watched rugby all his life and when I was a wee boy he fired my imagination with tales of Peter Kininmonth's drop goal, Tommy Gray's boot and the Springbok massacre. Like many fathers and sons, we communicated with each other through a mutual love of sport. I'm sorry Dad that I never wore the green jersey, or the navy blue one come to that, but hopefully this book is compensation.

Abbreviations

*	Captain
†	First cap (Scotland only)
Acs	Academicals
Alb	Albion
Ath	Athletic
CS	Civil Service
Coll	College
FP	Former Pupils
Gnrs	Gunners
GS	Grammar School
H	Hospital
HS	High School
Inst	Institution
OB	Old Boys
Rgrs	Rangers
RL	Rugby League
Rov	Rovers
Rvrs	Reivers
Sch	School
Servs	Services
TC	Training College
U	University
Wdrs	Wanderers
Wrs	Warriors

Teams

Scotland

F-Ls	Fettesians-Lorettonians
GH-K	Glasgow High-Kelvinside
Glasgow Cal	Glasgow Caledonian Reds
Scot Borders	Scottish Borders
W of Scot	West of Scotland

England

Leicester Tgrs	Leicester Tigers
London Scot	London Scottish
Newcastle F	Newcastle Falcons
Northampton Sts	Northampton Saints
OMT	Old Merchant Taylors
RA	Royal Artillery
RAF	Royal Air Force
RE	Royal Engineers

RIE	Royal Indian Engineering
RMA	Royal Military Academy
RN	Royal Navy
RNE	Royal Naval Engineering
Utd Servs	United Services

Ireland

CIYMS	Church of Ireland Young Men's Society
Cork Const	Cork Constitution
DLSP	De La Salle Palmerston
NIFC	North of Ireland Football Club

Wales

NG Dragons	Newport-Gwent Dragons
NS Ospreys	Neath-Swansea Ospreys

France

Clermont Auv	Clermont-Auvergne
CASG	Club Athlétique des Sports Généraux
EC	(Bordeaux) Etudiants Club
RCF	Racing Club de France
SBUC	Stade Bordelais Université Club
SCUF	Sporting Club Universitaire de France
TOEC	Toulouse Olympique Employés Club

South Africa

OFS	Orange Free State
SWA	South West Africa

Australia

ACT	Australian Capital Territory
NSW	New South Wales

Argentina

CUBA	Club Universitario Buenos Aires

Rugby in the 1870s

BY THE TIME OF Scotland's first international match in March 1871 rugby football was already a well-established pastime in Edinburgh and Glasgow and also in the Scottish universities. Some form of primitive ball game had been played in towns and villages across Scotland for many centuries, perhaps since Roman times. There were many local variations in the styles of play, but in general street football was played with a small hard ball between two sets of villagers or townspeople. Sides were often composed of men living in different parts of their community, perhaps at the top and bottom of a hill (traditionally known as Uppies and Doonies) or on opposite banks of a river. There were no written rules for street football and it was notoriously violent, but in some cases it had ritual significance and was associated with Shrove Tuesday, which was known in Scotland as Fastern's Een. Urban authorities were rarely enthusiastic about these events because they were difficult to control and a threat to life and property. Street football largely died out in the 19th century, but there are still a few survivals in modern Scotland. Jethart Ba' is still played annually in Jedburgh around Shrovetide and in the Orkney Islands Kirkwall Ba' takes place on New Year's Day, including separate matches for boys and men. Similar to street football, Scottish schools and universities had their own ball games. Pupils and students used them for recreation and to keep fit, and they were also a means of controlling the natural exuberance of adolescents and young men who otherwise might cause trouble. Once again there were many different versions of football. Schools tended to use a larger

Kirkwall Ba' Game in the Orkney Islands is a rare survival of the type of
pre-industrial street football once played all over Britain.
Orkney Museums and Libraries

air-filled ball which players were allowed to catch and kick but they most likely were not allowed to run with it in their hands.

Modern rugby has deep links with both of these traditions, but the game would never have taken off in Scotland without two distinct 19th century phenomena. The first was the growth of a private or independent school system. The new burgeoning middle classes placed great emphasis on the values of a good education, preferably one that brought access to the elite world of the universities, professions and the Empire. The demand for education led to the creation of many new schools, especially in the Edinburgh area, including the Edinburgh Academy (1824), Loretto (1827), Merchiston Castle (1833) and Fettes College (1870). Schools were also established in other areas such as Dollar Institution (1819), Glasgow Academy (1845) and Trinity College, Glenalmond (1847). Secondly, these types of schools enthusiastically adopted the 19th century cult of organised team games and healthy outdoor exercise. The theory was that vigorous exertion encouraged greater discipline and self-control, and that team games nurtured team spirit, courage in the face of adversity and self-sacrifice for the greater good.

All of this meant that the schools were very receptive to a new brand of football that emerged from Rugby School in England in the 1840s and 1850s. The story that the game was invented by a pupil at Rugby called William Webb Ellis in 1823 is now regarded as mythology, but the school definitely played a handling game and produced its own set of rules for play. Knowledge of this game was gradually spread by former pupils, some of whom moved to Scotland. By the early 1850s, 'Rugby Rules' had been adopted by several schools in the Edinburgh area. These schools were situated close to each other and inter-school matches were a natural development, the earliest taking place in the 1850s. Originally therefore, organised rugby as we know it today was only played amongst schoolboys, but quite soon former pupils started to form clubs and to organise matches of their own. Edinburgh Academicals, an exclusive club for former pupils of the Academy, started in 1857 and is the oldest senior club in Scotland. West of Scotland was formed in 1865, Glasgow Academicals in 1866, Royal High School FP, 1867, and Kilmarnock and Edinburgh Wanderers in 1868. By the early 1870s, there was string of rugby clubs across Scotland and mutual fixtures had been established between many of them, including matches between clubs from Edinburgh and Glasgow. The first inter-city match between sides selected from Edinburgh and Glasgow clubs took place in Glasgow in December 1872 with a return game in Edinburgh in January 1873. These games were organised by an ad-hoc Scottish football committee which in turn led to the formation of a new Scottish Football Union in March 1873. The new organisation, which stubbornly clung onto the word 'Football' until the mid-1920s, was composed of a secretary and representatives from eight senior clubs. It was designed to ensure co-operation between member clubs and to organise the selection of the Scottish international team. Meanwhile, the game was beginning to spread beyond its original boundaries and in particular into the Scottish Borders. A football club was established at Langholm in 1871 and neighbouring Border towns soon followed their lead. Rugby was always more socially inclusive in the Borders than the cities. Patronised and encouraged by local industrialists and manufacturers, it became popular amongst the working classes in Border mill towns, but it was not until the 1890s that Border players gained recognition in the national team.

The style of game played in the 1870s was, of course, very different from modern rugby. The first international matches were played twenty-a-side with 13 forwards in each team. Most of the players were concentrated in the scrums, and games were dominated by long periods of static mauling. It was customary to play two quarter-backs, later known as half-backs, who would patrol either side of the scrum. The backs were largely used as defenders, to stop runners and field kicks. At this time, most kicks were taken as a drop and punting was frowned upon as being a bit soft. Unsurprisingly, there were often stoppages as there was regular confusion about what was permissible, especially over the vexed question of 'hacking', the right to be able to trip up an opponent. Players could appeal to an umpire, as in cricket, and play would stop until an appeal was considered and a decision made. Referees were not mandatory in the early days and it was only in the 1880s that they were equipped with a whistle. Slowly, rugby adopted a more recognisable shape. In 1877, the number of players in a team was reduced to 15. Around the same time, the passing game began to take root. There is some debate about where it started, but Scottish schools were certainly pioneers, in particular Loretto and Fettes. Initially, many traditionalists considered passing to be a sign of weakness, but its values were soon recognised and it became commonplace in the 1880s.

The nature of rugby in its early days meant that there were few stars or personalities, although a handful of players stand out. In the first-ever Scotland team Robert Irvine was a powerful forward who was known as 'Bulldog' for his aggression and exceptional strength. He was only 17 when he made his debut and he played for the next nine years. A graduate of Edinburgh University, he practised medicine in Pitlochry and was a superb all-round athlete. Ninian Finlay was one of the youngest players ever to play international rugby. He was only 36 days past his 17th birthday when he won his first cap in 1875 alongside his elder brothers Jim and Alec. Although a back, he was as big as some of the forwards and difficult to put down in full flight. He was renowned for his ability to drop goals and one of his best efforts secured a draw in the match against England in 1879. He was a Writer to the Signet in Edinburgh and died in 1936. Gordon Petrie was another big man for his era, standing at well over six feet tall. A forward with Royal High School FP, he won 11 caps between 1873 and 1880. An Edinburgh lawyer, he was a very strong and excelled in other strenuous sports. Nat Brewis won six caps between 1876 and 1880. A product of Edinburgh Institution, he was a solid forward and like many early internationalists had a successful career in medicine.

| **1** | 1871 | ENGLAND |

Raeburn Place · Monday 27 March 1871 · Won 1 goal, 1 try to 1 try

SCOTLAND †WD Brown (*Glasgow Acs*), T Chalmers (*Glasgow Acs*), † A Clunies-Ross (*St Andrews U*), †TR Marshall (*Edinburgh Acs*), †JW Arthur (*Glasgow Acs*), †W Cross (*Merchistonians*), †A Buchanan (*Royal HSFP*), †AG Colville (*Merchistonians*), †D Drew (*Glasgow Acs*), †JF Finlay (*Edinburgh Acs*), †J Forsyth (*Edinburgh U*), †RW Irvine (*Edinburgh Acs*), †WJC Lyall (*Edinburgh Acs*), †JLH Macfarlane (*Edinburgh U*), †JAW Mein (*Edinburgh Acs*), †FJ Moncreiff* (*Edinburgh Acs*), †R Munro (*St Andrews U*), †G Ritchie (*Merchistonians*), †AH Robertson (*W of Scot*), †JS Thomson (*St Andrews U*)

ENGLAND   A Lyon (*Liverpool*), AG Guillemard (*West Kent*), RR Osborne (*Manchester*), W McLaren (*Manchester*), F Tobin (*Liverpool*), JE Bentley (*Gipsies*), JF Green (*West Kent*), RH Birkett (*Clapham Rov*), BH Burns (*Blackheath*), JH Clayton (*Liverpool*), CA Crompton (*Blackheath*), A Davenport (*Ravenscourt Park*), JM Dugdale (*Ravenscourt Park*), AS Gibson (*Manchester*), A StG Hamersley (*Marlborough Nomads*), JH Luscombe (*Gipsies*), CW Sherrard (*Blackheath*), F Stokes* (*Blackheath*), DP Turner (*Richmond*), HJC Turner (*Manchester*)

SCORING   No scoring in the first half. Buchanan, try; Cross, con; Birkett, try; Cross, try

The inspiration for the world's first rugby international seems to have come from football. In March and November 1870, two matches were held at the Oval cricket ground in London between teams representing England and Scotland. On both occasions, the Scottish 11 was composed of players who happened to live in the London area, some of whom had only tenuous links with Scotland. Subsequently in December 1870, the captains of five Scottish rugby clubs wrote a letter to the press challenging their English counterparts to a match between the two countries to be played under Rugby rules. The Scottish challenge was accepted by clubs in England and both countries formed committees to select their best players and make the necessary arrangements, including travel and players' outfits. The two sides agreed on the rules and that there would be 20 players on each side. The match was fixed for Monday 27 March 1871 to be played on the Edinburgh Academy cricket field at Raeburn Place, Edinburgh.

The Scots took their preparations seriously and organised two trial matches in Edinburgh and Glasgow before finally naming their side. Players were expected to train hard and to be fit. The Scottish xx consisted of players from former pupils clubs in Edinburgh and Glasgow and two each from Edinburgh and St Andrews Universities. The side was captained by Francis Jeffrey Moncreiff, known to his friends as Frank, the fifth son of Lord Moncrieff of Tulliebole. Aged 22, he was a former pupil of Edinburgh Academy, captain of the Academicals and apprenticed to become a chartered accountant. Amongst the Scottish side, Andrew Colville, a back, played for Blackheath in London and might be thought of as the first in a long line of Anglo-Scottish players. Colville has been asked to play for England but wisely chose Scotland. Two members of the Scottish side were born overseas, reflecting Scotland's strong links with the colonies. John MacFarlane, a forward, was born in Jamaica but educated in Scotland and at the time was a medical student at Edinburgh University. Alfred Clunies-Ross, a back, came from the Cocos Islands in the Indian Ocean and was of mixed race, Scottish and Malaysian. He spent seven years at Madras College before studying at St Andrews and Edinburgh Universities. Several of the Scottish team played at half-back for their clubs, but on this occasion were selected amongst the forwards. The English side was made-up of 12 players from the London area with four each from the two main northern clubs, Liverpool and Manchester. A late change in the England side brought in Benjamin H Burns of Blackheath, who had been born and educated in Scotland before moving to London to work in banking.

Although the game was played on a Monday afternoon, it created considerable interest and it was estimated that around 2,000 spectators were present. At this time, the ground at Raeburn Place was broadly similar to that which is still in use at the beginning of the 21st century. The pitch was in roughly the same position and measured 120 yards in length and 55 yards wide which was quite narrow by English standards and caused the visitors some problems as they were used to playing on a wider field. The playing area was bounded on the west and north by an open burn which ran to the Water of Leith. North Park Terrace and Inverleith pond had not yet been constructed and there was an area of slopping ground to the west and north of the pitch that was used by spectators. The east touchline, which included a prominent mound that was used for archery practice, was reserved for members of Edinburgh Academicals and their guests. Spectators probably entered the ground at the south west corner where there was a small footbridge over the burn. The entrance fee was one shilling and it is not known if there was any kind of official programme.

The Scotland side wore blue jerseys with a big thistle badge sewn on, light coloured trousers and a range of socks, some of which were brightly striped. England wore white jerseys with a rose emblem, white flannels and brown stockings. The visitors, who looked much bigger than the Scots, were measured before the match and had an average weight of around 12st 3lbs. The teams agreed to play 50 minutes each way. Shortly after 3pm, Scotland kicked off from the north of the ground with the slight breeze behind them. Play was fairly even in the first half. Scotland carried the ball over the English line on one occasion, but the umpires did not allow the try. In one incident, Finlay, the Scottish forward, broke away and looked certain to score until Osborne, the English back, with his arms folded across his chest, ran at him 'after the fashion of a bull charging a gate'. The collision shook the ground, but both men simply picked themselves up and carried on. Early in the second half, a maul formed close to the English line and Ritchie, the Scottish forward, was pushed over with several players on top of him. Both sides claimed the touchdown so the umpires decided on a 'hack off' at five yards (although Ritchie maintained throughout his life that he had scored). This meant that the game was restarted with a kind of scrum. The two groups of forwards stood upright and pushed against each other whilst trying to kick or force the ball forward. The Scottish forwards drove over the line again and Angus Buchanan of Royal High School FP was credited with having

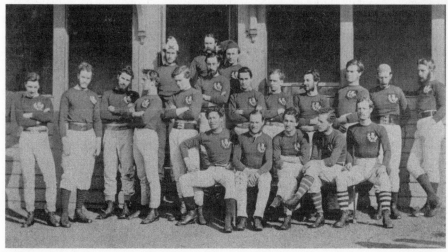

This famous photograph shows the Scottish twenty that played England in March 1871, the world's first-ever rugby international.

SRU

grounded the ball for a try, the first ever scored in international rugby (although at this time tries did not count for anything and only gave a 'try' at goal). The English players disputed the score vociferously and claimed that the ball had been carried over the line without having been first played on the ground in the scrum, as the rules demanded. The umpires, Mr Almond of Scotland and Mr Ward of England, decided that a try had been scored, although with so many forwards involved they probably couldn't tell either way. In any case, Cross converted with a magnificent kick from near the east touchline. As the ball flew between the posts, James Carmichael, a teacher at the Edinburgh Academy, excitedly threw up his tall hat and shouted: 'Flodden is at last revenged!' England now put together some good attacks and came close to scoring only to be held out by courageous Scottish defence. Eventually, Birkett scored far out but England captain Fred Stokes missed the difficult conversion attempt across the wind. The superior fitness and technique of the Scottish forwards started to tell as the match drew on. From a lineout near the English line, the ball was thrown long to Scottish half-back John Arthur, who accidentally knocked it forwards past the defenders. Cross followed-up quickly and touched down for a try. Once again the English players objected, but unintentional knock-ons were not illegal at this time and the try was allowed to stand. Cross failed to convert against the wind and the game ended a few minutes later, Scotland winning by the only goal. The Scots were exultant and for many years after the match ball, adorned with ribbons, hung in the window of a Stockbridge shop near the ground. Whatever happened to it?

---

2   **1872**   ENGLAND

Kennington Oval, London · Monday 5 February 1872
Lost 1 drop goal to 1 goal, 2 tries, 1 drop goal

SCOTLAND WD Brown (*Glasgow Acs*), T Chalmers (*Glasgow Acs*), †LM Balfour (*Edinburgh Acs*), TR Marshall (*Edinburgh Acs*), †RP Maitland (*RA*), JW Arthur (*Glasgow Acs*), W Cross (*Merchistonians*), FJ Moncreiff* (*Edinburgh Acs*), †JW Anderson (*W of Scot*), †EM Bannerman (*Edinburgh Acs*), †CW Cathcart (*Edinburgh U*), AG Colville (*Merchistonians*), JF Finlay (*Edinburgh Acs*), RW Irvine (*Edinburgh Acs*), †JH McClure (*W of Scot*), JLH Macfarlane (*Edinburgh U*), †W Marshall (*Edinburgh Acs*), †FT Maxwell (*RE*), JAW Mein (*Edinburgh Acs*), †RW Renny-Tailyour (*RE*)

ENGLAND AG Guillemard (*West Kent*), FW Mills (*Marlborough Nomads*), WO Moberly (*Ravenscourt Park*), H Freeman (*Marlborough Nomads*), JE Bentley (*Gipsies*), S Finney (*RIE Coll*), P Wilkinson (*Law Club*), T Batson (*Blackheath*), JA Body (*Gipsies*), JA Bush (*Clifton*), FI Currey (*Marlborough Nom*), FBG D'Aguilar (*RE*), A StG Hamersley (*Marlborough Nomads*), FW Isherwood (*Ravenscourt Park*), F Luscombe (*Gipsies*), JEH Mackinlay (*St George's H*), WW Pinching (*Guy's H*), CW Sherrard (*RE*), F Stokes* (*Blackheath*), DP Turner (*Richmond*)

SCORING Cathcart, drop; Hamersley, try; Isherwood, con (half-time) Freeman, drop; D'Aguilar, try; Finney, try

After the success of the first match, it was agreed to hold an annual fixture which would alternate between the two countries. Both teams were selected after a series of trial matches. Frank Moncreiff captained Scotland once again and the Scots included three players who were based south of the border, all in the military. This match was

An artist's impression of the England v Scotland match at the Kennington Oval in February 1872.
RFU Museum of Rugby

played at the Oval cricket ground in London and kicked off at 2.30pm. The pitch was about 15 yards wider than the previous encounter and was firm but wet after recent heavy rain. After their success the previous year, the Scots were quietly confident, but England had selected some very big forwards who dominated throughout and the Scottish runners were starved of ball. Scotland started well and within the first 15 minutes Cathcart, a forward, took the ball from a maul, dodged two opponents and dropped a goal. Then the English forwards started to take control and, after a period of sustained pressure, Hamersley touched down from a maul in goal. Isherwood kicked a fine conversion. The second half was largely dominated by England and after about 15 minutes Freeman, a three-quarter, dropped a goal. Soon after D'Aguilar scored a try, but Isherwood missed the kick. Scotland came close to scoring again when Balfour was wide with a drop at goal from a 'fair catch'. Just before the finish, Finney, the English half-back, capped a good display with another try, but Ishwerwood narrowly failed to convert. In the evening, the two sides were entertained at a grand dinner at St James's Hall in London.

3	1873	ENGLAND

Hamilton Crescent, Glasgow · Monday 3 March 1873
Drawn no scoring

SCOTLAND WD Brown (*Glasgow Acs*), T Chalmers (*Glasgow Acs*), †JLP Sanderson (*Edinburgh*

The official card for the Scotland v England match at Hamilton Crescent, Glasgow in March 1873, the oldest known international rugby programme in existence.

RFU Museum of Rugby

Acs), TR Marshall (*Edinburgh Acs*), †W StC Grant (*Craigmount Sch*), †GB McClure (*W of Scot*), JLH Macfarlane (*Edinburgh U*), †HW Allen (*Glasgow Acs*), †P Anton (*St Andrews U*), EM Bannerman (*Edinburgh Acs*), †CC Bryce (*Glasgow Acs*), CW Cathcart (*Edinburgh U*), †JP Davidson (*RIE Coll*), RW Irvine (*Edinburgh Acs*), JAW Mein (*Edinburgh Acs*), FJ Moncreiff* (*Edinburgh Acs*), †AG Petrie (*Royal HSFP*), †TP Whittington (*Merchistonians*), †RW Wilson (*W of Scot*), †A Wood (*Royal HSFP*)

ENGLAND FW Mills (*Marlborough Nomads*), CHR Vanderspar (*Richmond*), WRB Fletcher (*Marlborough Nomads*), H Freeman (*Marlborough Nomads*), CW Boyle (*Oxford U*), S Finney (*RIE Coll*), S Morse (*Law Club*), JA Body (*Gipsies*), JA Bush (*Clifton*), EC Cheston (*Law Club*), A StG Hamersley (*Marlborough Nomads*), HA Lawrence (*Richmond*), F Luscombe (*Gipsies*), JEH Mackinlay (*St George's H*), H Marsh (*RIE Coll*), MW Marshall (*Blackheath*), CH Rickards (*Gipsies*), ER Still (*Ravenscourt Park*), F Stokes* (*Blackheath*), DP Turner (*Richmond*)

The third encounter between the two sides took place at the West of Scotland cricket ground at Hamilton Crescent (now Fortrose Street) in the west of Glasgow (strictly speaking in Partick which was then an independent burgh). The same ground had staged the world's first association football international the previous November and the rugby authorities seem to have used their game as a kind of missionary effort. Heavy rain had fallen on the morning of the game and the pitch was quite soft. According to an account written by Peter Anton, one of the Scottish forwards, some of the English players sent their boots to a local cobbler to have leather bars hammered onto the soles to get a better grip. When the boots were returned it was found that several of them had gone missing and the English players had to play wearing an odd boot and a shoe, a clever piece of Scottish gamesmanship. Conditions were awkward with a Scotch mist blowing in from the west, although at times the sun tried to break through. Curiously, both sides played better when facing into the elements. Scotland opted to play with an extra forward, but they were under a lot pressure from the heavier English pack. The visitors came perilously close to scoring at times, especially towards the end of the first half, only to be denied by tenacious Scottish defence. In the second half, Harold Freeman, the English three-quarter, who was described as 'one of the best drop-kickers in England', took an enormous drop at goal which was so high in the air that the umpires had to declare it a 'poster'. This meant that they could not tell if it had passed between the upward line of the posts or not. (At this time rugby posts extended only a foot or so above the crossbar.) A drawn match was probably a fair result. In the evening, the two sides were entertained in a local hotel. The Scottish hospitality was too much for one English visitor who later stole a mail carriage and drove it around the streets of Glasgow.

---

4   **1874**   **ENGLAND**

Kennington Oval, London   ·   Monday 23 February 1874

Lost 1 try to 1 drop goal

SCOTLAND WD Brown* (*Glasgow Acs*), T Chalmers (*Glasgow Acs*), TR Marshall (*Edinburgh Acs)*, †WH Kidston (*W of Scot*), †HM Hamilton (*W of Scot*), W StC Grant (*Craigmount Sch*), †AK Stewart (*Edinburgh U*), CC Bryce (*Glasgow Acs*), JP Davidson (*RIE Coll*), JF Finlay (*Edinburgh Acs*), †G Heron (*Glasgow Acs*), RW Irvine (*Edinburgh Acs*), JAW Mein (*Edinburgh Acs*), †T Neilson (*W of Scot*) , AG Petrie(*Royal HSFP*), †J Reid (*Edinburgh Wdrs*), †JK Todd (*Glasgow Acs*), RW Wilson (*W of Scot*), A Wood (*Royal HSFP*), †AH Young (*Edinburgh Acs*)

ENGLAND JM Batten (*Cambridge U*), MJ Brooks (*Oxford U*), H Freeman (*Marlborough Nomads*), WH Milton (*Marlborough Nomads*), S Morse (*Marlborough Nomads*), WE Collins (*Old Cheltonians*), T Batson (*Blackheath*), HA Bryden (*Clapham Rov*), EC Cheston (*Richmond*), CW Crosse (*Oxford U*), FL Cunliffe (*RMA*), JSM Genth (*Manchester*), A StG Hamersley* (*Marlborough Nomads*), E Kewley (*Liverpool*), HA Lawrence (*Richmond*), MW Marshall (*Blackheath*), S Parker (*Liverpool*), WFH Stafford (*RE*), DP Turner (*Richmond*), R Walker (*Manchester*)

SCORING Finlay, try (half-time) Freeman, drop

Like the previous encounter, this match was played on a sodden pitch and in persistent drizzle. The conditions hampered the Scottish backs who were potentially very good. Scotland had the better of the first half and forced England to touch down behind their line early on. Finlay, the Scottish forward, scored a try after a run inside the English 25, but it was too far out for Chalmers to convert. Then Stewart, the Scottish quarter-back, crossed at the posts, but the umpire judged, perhaps wrongly, that he had played a 'dead ball' (a ball on the ground) illegally. Stewart had two good runs, but was tackled before he managed to break away from the defence. England were much more prominent in the second half and the Scots had to touch down twice. Morse, the English half-back, missed two attempts at drop goals and with about ten minutes left Harold Freeman dropped a splendid left footed goal to put England into the lead. Scotland fought hard to save the match, but the home side held out for a rather fortuitous win. One feature of the game was some 'excellent chucking' amongst the Scottish backs. At this time, passing amongst the backs was still something of a novelty and was frowned upon by traditionalists.

---

5   1875   ENGLAND

Raeburn Place · Monday 8 March 1875 · Drawn no scoring

SCOTLAND WD Brown* (*Glasgow Acs*), T Chalmers (*Glasgow Acs*), †NJ Finlay (*Edinburgh Acad*), †M Cross (*Merchistonians*), HM Hamilton (*W of Scot*), †JR Hay Gordon (*Edinburgh Acs*), JK Tod (*Glasgow Acs*), †A Arthur (*Glasgow Acs*), †JW Dunlop (*W of Scot*), †AB Finlay (*Edinburgh Acs*), JF Finlay (*Edinburgh Acs*), †GR Fleming (*Glasgow Acs*), G Heron (*Glasgow Acs*), RW Irvine (*Edinburgh Acs*), †A Marshall (*Edinburgh Acs*), JAW Mein (*Edinburgh Acs*), AG Petrie (*Royal HSFP*), J Reid (*Edinburgh Wdrs*), †D Robertson (*Edinburgh Acs*), A Wood (*Royal HSFP*)

ENGLAND LH Birkett (*Clapham Rov*), S Morse (*Marlborough Nomads*), AW Pearson (*Guy's H*), WAD Evanson (*CS*), WE Collins (*Old Cheltonians*), AT Michell (*Oxford U*), FR Adams (*Richmond*), RH Birkett (*Clapham Rov*), JA Bush (*Clifton*), EC Cheston (*Richmond*), WRB Fletcher (*Oxford U*), JSM Genth (*Manchester*), HJ Graham (*Wimbledon Hornets*), E Kewley (*Liverpool*), HA Lawrence* (*Richmond*), F Luscombe (*Gipsies*), MW Marshall (*Blackheath*), S Parker (*Liverpool*), JE Paul (*RIE Coll*), DP Turner (*Richmond*)

This match attracted the largest crowd to date for an international, estimated at around 6,000 people. The teams adopted different formations amongst the backs and the Scots opted to play with one less forward. However, the English backs changed their formation several times during the game. Ninian Finlay, a new cap in the Scottish half-backs (three-quarters), was still a schoolboy at the Edinburgh Academy and joined his two brothers Alec and James, both of whom played in the forwards. For England, full-back Louis Birkett and forward Reginald Birkett were brothers. The playing field was increased in breadth to 85 yards which made for some exciting attacking play. Conditions were excellent and Scotland played with the breeze in the first half. This was a close and well contested game with plenty of scoring chances. Both sides were forced to touch down behind their own line on several occasions and both narrowly missed drop goal attempts. The English backs, in particular, had numerous shots at goal from all sorts of positions, but it was the Scots who came closest to scoring. In the first half, Ninian Finlay dropped a clear goal 'amid tremendous cheering and waving of hats and handkerchiefs' only to have his effort disallowed because of an earlier infringement.

---

6   1876   ENGLAND

Kennington Oval, London · Monday 6 March 1876

Lost to 1 goal, 1 try

SCOTLAND †JS Carrick (*W of Scot*), T Chalmers (*Glasgow Acs*), M Cross (*Glasgow Acs*), NJ Finlay (*Edinburgh Acs*), †GQ Paterson (*Edinburgh Acs*), AK Stewart (*Edinburgh U*), A Arthur (*Merchistonians*), †WH Bolton (*W of Scot*), †NT Brewis (*Edinburgh Inst FP*), CW Cathcart

(*Edinburgh U*), D Drew (*Glasgow Acs*), GR Fleming (*Glasgow Acs*), †JHS Graham (*Edinburgh Acs*), RW Irvine* (*Edinburgh Acs*), †JE Junor (*Glasgow Acs*), †D Lang (*Paisley*), AG Petrie (*Royal HSFP*), J Reid (*Edinburgh Wdrs*), †C Villar (*Edinburgh Wdrs*), †DH Watson (*Glasgow Acs*)

ENGLAND AH Heath (*Oxford U*), AW Pearson (*Blackheath*), TS Tetley (*Bradford*), L Stokes (*Blackheath*), RH Birkett (*Clapham Rov*), WE Collins (*Old Cheltonians*), WC Hutchinson (*RIE Coll*), FR Adams (*Richmond*), JA Bush (*Clifton*), EC Cheston (*Richmond*), HJ Graham (*Wimbledon Hornets*), W Greg (*Manchester*), WH Hunt (*Preston Grasshoppers*), E Kewley (*Liverpool*), FH Lee (*Oxford U*), F Luscombe* (*Gipsies*), MW Marshall (*Blackheath*), WCW Rawlinson (*Blackheath*), GR Turner (*St George's H*), R Walker (*Manchester*)

REFEREE A Rutter (*England*)

SCORING No scoring in the first half. Lee, try; Stokes, con; Collins, try

There were some controversial selections for this game, especially George 'Quinty' Paterson at quarter-back. Paterson weighed only 8st 12lbs in his playing kit and, even at the time, he was considered too small and light for the rigours of international football. A large crowd was present at the Oval cricket ground on a fine chilly afternoon. Play kicked off about 3.10pm with England facing into a strong sun and wind. The first half was evenly balanced with both sides having spells of pressure and some scoring opportunities, mainly drop goal attempts that went wide. In the second half, a Scottish attack broke down near the English line. Collins, the English half-back, beat his opposite number Paterson and passed to Hutchinson who made a long diagonal run up the field. He was eventually tackled by Stewart, but Lee, the English forward, gathered the loose ball and ran round behind the posts. Stokes kicked the conversion, the ball hitting the crossbar before going over. England now had a lot of the play and Collins scored a second try, but Stokes was unable to convert. The Scottish forwards, who played well throughout, tried hard to save the game, but England, the pre-match favourites, were worthy winners.

| 7 | 1877 | IRELAND |

Ormeau Park, Belfast · Monday 19 February 1877

Won 4 goals, 2 drop goals, 2 tries to nil

SCOTLAND †HH Johnston (*Edinburgh Collegians*), M Cross (*Glasgow Acs*), †RC Mackenzie (*Glasgow Acs*), JR Hay Gordon (*Edinburgh Acs*), †EJ Pocock (*Edinburgh Wdrs*), JHS Graham (*Edinburgh Acs*), RW Irvine* (*Edinburgh Acs*), JE Junor (*Glasgow Acs*), D Lang (*Paisley*), †HM Napier (*W of Scot*), AG Petrie (*Royal HSFP*), J Reid (*Edinburgh Wdrs*), †SH Smith (*Glasgow Acs*), C Villar (*Edinburgh Wdrs*), DH Watson (*Glasgow Acs*)

IRELAND H Moore (*Windsor*), GM Shaw (*Windsor*), RB Walkington (*NIFC*), FW Kidd (*Lansdowne*), J Heron (*NIFC*), TG Gordon (*NIFC*), WH Ash (*NIFC*), T Brown (*Windsor*), HL Cox (*Dublin U*), J Currell (*NIFC*), W Finlay (*NIFC*), HC Kelly (*NIFC*), JA Macdonald (*Methodist Coll*), HW Murray (*Dublin U*), WH Wilson* (*Dublin U*)

REFEREE A Buchanan

SCORING Pocock, try; Mackenzie, drop; Mackenzie, try; Cross, con; Mackenzie, drop (half-time) Mackenzie, try; Irvine, try; Cross, con; Mackenzie, try; Cross, con; Reid, try; Cross, con

This was the inaugural match between the two countries and, for the first time, Scotland played with 15 players and a single full-back: Henry Halcro Johnston, an Edinburgh medical student who came from a distinguished Orkney family. A sizeable crowd assembled at Ormeau Park, the home of the North of Ireland Cricket Cub, but the weather broke down just after the start of the match and there was heavy rain in the second half. Ireland were full of enthusiasm, but they were very inexperienced and Scotland won a comfortable victory, scoring six goals and two tries to nil. On average the Scots were around a stone-per-man heavier than the Irish and they outplayed them in all respects. The Scottish forwards combined well, their footwork was good and the innovative Scottish passing game was very effective. Robert Mackenzie, a three-quarter from Glasgow Academicals, scored three tries and two drops, Pocock had some strong runs and Malcolm Cross, the Scottish quarter-back, gave a fine display of place-kicking.

---

8   1877   ENGLAND

Raeburn Place · Monday 5 March 1877 · Won 1 drop goal to nil

SCOTLAND JS Carrick (*Glasgow Acs*), HH Johnston (*Edinburgh Collegians*), M Cross (*Glasgow Acs*), RC Mackenzie (*Glasgow Acs*), JR Hay Gordon (*Edinburgh Acs*), EJ Pocock (*Edinburgh Wdrs*), JHS Graham (*Edinburgh Acs*), RW Irvine* (*Edinburgh Acs*), JE Junor (*Glasgow Acs*), HM Napier (*W of Scot*), AG Petrie (*Royal HSFP*), J Reid (*Edinburgh Wdrs*), †TJ Torrie (*Edinburgh Acs*), C Villar (*Edinburgh Wdrs*), DH Watson (*Glasgow Acs*)

ENGLAND L Birkett (*Clapham Rov*), AW Pearson (*Blackheath*), AN Hornby (*Preston Grasshoppers*), L Stokes (*Blackheath*), WAD Evanson (*Richmond*), PLA Price (*RIE Coll*), CC Bryden (*Clapham Rov*), HWT Garnett (*Bradford*), G Harrison (*Hull*), WH Hunt (*Preston Grasshoppers*), E Kewley* (*Liverpool*), AF Law (*Richmond*), MW Marshall (*Blackheath*), R Todd (*Manchester*), CJC Touzell (*Cambridge U*)

REFEREE W Cross (*Scotland*)

SCORING No scoring in the first half. Cross, drop

Scotland reverted to six players behind the scrum to counter the threat of the English backs. Conditions were almost ideal and there was a big crowd estimated at between 3–4,000 people, 'including a large number of ladies'. They were entertained before the match by the pipes and drums of the 75th Highlanders. Both sides played with 15 men for the first time. In a closely fought struggle which had a dramatic conclusion, the heavier Scottish forwards dominated tight play but the English backs were always dangerous and the Scots had to defend stubbornly to contain them. The Scots held their own when playing into the wind in the first half and after the break they were able to put England under some pressure. The winning score came a few minutes before the end. Malcolm Cross, the Scottish three-quarter, dropped a long goal from the centre of the field which the wind carried between the posts. The goal was greeted with an enormous cheer and Cross was lifted shoulder-high by some of his fellow players. England did not have enough time to respond and the Scots won their second victory of the series. Amongst some good performances, Hay Gordon, a big and strong player, was always in the thick of the action, Cross and Mackenzie, the half-backs, played well and Torrie's dribbling was to the fore. This was a famous win for Scotland that did much to encourage the growth of the game throughout the country.

---

9   1878   ENGLAND

Kennington Oval, London · Monday 4 March 1878
Drawn no scoring

SCOTLAND †WE Maclagan (*Edinburgh Acs*), M Cross (*Glasgow Acs*), NJ Finlay (*Edinburgh Acs*), †JA Campbell (*Merchiston Sch*), †JA Neilson (*Glasgow Acs*), †LJ Auldjo (*Abertay*), NT Brewis (*Edinburgh Inst FP*), JHS Graham (*Edinburgh Acs*), †DR Irvine (*Edinburgh Acs*), RW Irvine* (*Edinburgh Acs*), JE Junor (*Glasgow Acs*), †GWL MacLeod (*Edinburgh Acs*), HM Napier (*W of Scot*), AG Petrie (*Royal HSFP*), SH Smith (*Glasgow Acs*)

ENGLAND AW Pearson (*Blackheath*), HE Kayll (*Sunderland*), L Stokes (*Blackheath*), AN Hornby (*Preston Grasshoppers*), PLA Price (*RIE Coll*), WAD Evanson (*Richmond*), FR Adams (*Richmond*), JM Biggs (*UC Hospital*), H Fowler (*Oxford U*), FD Fowler (*RIE Coll*), ET Gurdon (*Richmond*), E Kewley* (*Liverpool*), MW Marshall (*Blackheath*), GT Thomson (*Halifax*), GF Vernon (*Blackheath*)

REFEREE AG Guillemard (*England*)

Scotland had the wind and sun behind them in the first half and looked the better of the two sides. Play was rather loose throughout the game and both teams missed scoring chances. In the first half, Kewley, the English forward, made a long run from inside his own half, but was brought down near halfway. Napier of Scotland was held-up over the English line and in the ensuing maul the whistle went for half-time. England were more lively in the second half and both sides had spells of pressure. Stokes, the English back, was always prominent and Adams had a try disallowed because the Scots had already stopped for an infringement. The English players disputed the decision, but Kewley, the captain, was courteous enough to accept it. Similarly, Neilson had a try disallowed because of an infringement. The Scottish forwards played well together, but both sets of backs were only mediocre and the game ended in a no scoring draw.

---

10   1879   IRELAND

Ormeau Park, Belfast · Monday 17 February 1879
Won 1 goal, 1 drop goal, 1 try to nil

SCOTLAND WE Maclagan (*Edinburgh Acs*), M Cross (*Glasgow Acs*), NJ Finlay (*Edinburgh Acs*), †WH Masters (*Edinburgh Inst FP*), JA Campbell (*Merchistonians*); †R Ainslie (*Edinburgh Inst FP*), NT Brewis (*Edinburgh Inst FP*), †JB Brown (*Glasgow Acs*), JHS Graham (*Edinburgh Acs*), DR Irvine (*Edinburgh Acs*), RW Irvine* (*Edinburgh Acs*), HM Napier (*W of Scot*), AG Petrie (*Royal HSFP*), †ER Smith (*Edinburgh Acs*), †D Somerville (*Edinburgh Inst FP*)

IRELAND RB Walkington (*NIFC*), T Harrison (*Cork*), RN Matier (*NIFC*), JC Bagot (*Dublin U*), AM Whitestone (*Dublin U*), WJ Goulding (*Cork*); AM Archer (*Dublin U*), WEA Cummins

(*QC Cork*), W Finlay (*NIFC*), HC Kelly (*NIFC*), JA Macdonald (*Methodist Coll*), WC Neville*
(*Dublin U*), H Purdon (*NIFC*), G Scriven (*Dublin U*), JW Taylor (*NIFC*)

REFEREE Dr Chiene (*Scotland*)

SCORING Brown, try; Somerville, try; Cross, con (half-time) Cross, drop

There was no match against Ireland in 1878 because of a lack of agreement between the two Irish unions (the Irish Football Union and the Northern Football Union of Ireland), but the fixture was resumed the following year. A large crowd saw a well contested game that was played in fine conditions on a heavy pitch. The Irish had improved since the previous encounter, but the Scots had too much experience and technique, especially amongst the forwards. In the first half, both Masters and Smith came close to scoring only to be denied by desperate Irish defence. Graham crossed the line after a break by Masters, but he was called back for an infringement. After a good run and punt by Maclagan, the Scots forced play to the Irish line and Brown snatched the ball out of an Irishman's hands to score near the posts. Then followed a controversial incident typical of the sort that occurred the rules were still ambiguous. Cross was preparing for the conversion when the Irish players ran out and hacked the ball away, claiming that they were entitled to make a charge as soon as the ball had been placed on the ground in preparation for the kick. At this time players did not dig a hole with their heel or use a kicking tee, but instead relied on a colleague to place or hold the ball for them, as sometimes still happens in the modern game when there's a strong wind. There was then a lengthy argument about who was correct and eventually Cross was allowed to take his kick (which he put over). Subsequently, the matter was referred to the Rugby Football Union who confirmed that the Irish action

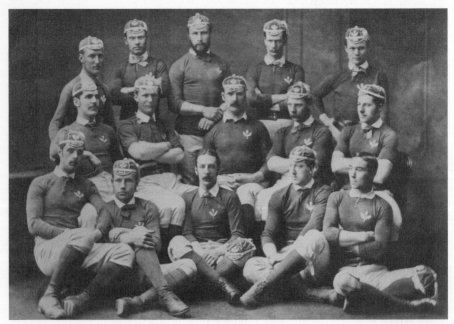

The Scottish team that played England in March 1879, the first contest for the Calcutta Cup.
SRU

SCOTTISH RUGBY

was permissible and that the conversion should not stand. It seemed that Cross had inadvertently let the ball touch the ground when showing his placer, Irvine, where to hold it. Later, Somerville broke a tackle to score a try and on this occasion Cross kicked the conversion from an awkward angle. The second half was more evenly contested and the Scots sealed victory with a drop goal by Cross. Scottish quarterback Masters had an excellent game and was prominent throughout.

| **11** | 1879 | ENGLAND |

Raeburn Place · Monday 10 March 1879

Drawn 1 drop goal to 1 goal

SCOTLAND WE Maclagan (*Edinburgh Acs*), M Cross (*Glasgow Acs*), NJ Finlay (*Edinburgh Acs*), JA Campbell (*Glasgow Acs*), JA Neilson (*Glasgow Acs*); R Ainslie (*Edinburgh Inst FP*), NT Brewis (*Edinburgh Inst FP*), JB Brown (*Glasgow Acs*), †EN Ewart (*Glasgow Acs*), JHS Graham (*Edinburgh Acs*), DR Irvine (*Edinburgh Acs*), RW Irvine* (*Edinburgh Acs*), JE Junor (*Glasgow Acs*), HM Napier (*W of Scot*), AG Petrie (*Royal HSFP*)

ENGLAND H Huth (*Huddersfield*), WJ Penney (*Utd Hs*); L Stokes (*Blackheath*), WAD Evanson (*Richmond*), HH Taylor (*St George's H*), FR Adams* (*Richmond*), A Budd (*Blackheath*), GW Burton (*Blackheath*), FD Fowler (*Manchester*), G Harrison (*Hull*), NF McLeod (*RIE Coll*), S Neame (*Old Cheltonians*), HC Rowley (*Manchester*), HH Springmann (*Liverpool*), R Walker (*Manchester*)

REFEREE GR Fleming (*Scotland*)

SCORING Burton, try; Stokes, con (half-time) Finlay, drop

This was the first match for the Calcutta Cup which had been presented to the Rugby Football Union after the dissolution of the Calcutta Football Club in India. A huge crowd packed into Raeburn Place and at one point the match was stopped when spectators spilled onto the playing field. On a dull afternoon, England had the stiff wind behind them in the first half. The visitors were a good side with powerful forwards and fleet-footed backs. Stokes's long and accurate drop kicking kept most of the action near the Scottish line, although the Scottish forwards were always ready to counterattack. From one maul, Cross missed a clearing kick and Burton, the English forward, gathered the ball for an easy run-in. In the second half, the Scottish forwards drove to the line, but they were thwarted by a defender who carried the ball behind and touched it down. Although a legal move, this was considered bad form and was loudly barracked by the crowd because, in *The Scotsman*'s words, 'it lost a rare chance for Scotland [and] showed a want of pluck not usual with Britons'. In later incidents, Stokes and Maclagan were both cheered when they attacked from behind their own lines rather than taking the easier defensive option. After a strong charge by the Scottish forwards, Finlay found just enough space to drop a goal. Both sides had spells of pressure and Stokes hit a post with a drop goal attempt, but there was no further scoring. Maclagan's ferocious tackling was a feature of the game and he prevented several scores with his uncompromising approach.

Hamilton Crescent, Glasgow · Saturday 14 February 1880

Won 1 goal, 2 drop goals, 2 tries to nil

SCOTLAND WE Maclagan (*Edinburgh Acs*), M Cross (*Glasgow Acs*), NJ Finlay (*Edinburgh Acs*), WH Masters (*Edinburgh Inst FP*), †WS Brown (*Edinburgh Inst FP*), R Ainslie (*Edinburgh Inst FP*), NT Brewis (*Edinburgh Inst FP*), JB Brown (*Glasgow Acs*), EN Ewart (*Glasgow Acs*), JHS Graham (*Edinburgh Acs*), RW Irvine* (*Edinburgh Acs*), †D McCowan (*W of Scot*), AG Petrie (*Royal HSFP*), †CR Stewart (*W of Scot*), †JG Tait (*Edinburgh Acs*)

IRELAND RB Walkington (*NIFC*), JC Bagot (*Dublin U*), T Harrison (*Cork*), WT Heron (*NIFC*), M Johnston (*Dublin U*), AP Cronyn (*Lansdowne*), JL Cuppaidge (*Dublin U*), W Finlay (*NIFC*), AJ Forrest (*Wdrs*), RW Hughes (*NIFC*), HC Kelly* (*NIFC*), A Millar (*Kingstown*), G Scriven (*Dublin U*), JW Taylor (*NIFC*), WA Wallis (*Wdrs*)

REFEREE A Buchanan (*Scotland*)

SCORING Finlay, drop; Finlay, drop; Masters, try; Cross, con (half-time) Ewart, try; Ewart, try

Scotland played on a Saturday for the first time. The previous month Ireland had given England a real fright in Dublin and this was expected to be a close match, but Scotland were comfortable winners in a one-sided encounter. The Scottish forwards showed good teamwork, and their footwork and handling were very effective. Playing in fine conditions before a large crowd, the Scots had the advantage of the notorious Hamilton Crescent slope in the first half. After about ten minutes, Finlay dropped a goal and then Ainslie crossed the Irish line but was recalled for an infringement. Finlay dropped a second goal which was disputed by the Irish who claimed that the umpires had been unsighted and the referee should not have awarded it. Shortly before the interval, the Scottish forwards displayed 'some of the prettiest chucking probably ever seen in Scotland' and Masters rounded the defence for a great try. In the second half, Ewart scored two tries for Scotland, but Cross failed with both conversion attempts. His second went over the bar but it was touched in flight by an Irish hand and disallowed.

Whalley Range, Manchester · Monday 28 February 1880

Lost 1 goal to 2 goals, 3 tries

SCOTLAND WE Maclagan (*Edinburgh Acs*), NJ Finlay (*Edinburgh Acs*), M Cross (*Glasgow Acs*), WH Masters (*Edinburgh Inst FP*), WS Brown (*Edinburgh Inst FP*), R Ainslie (*Edinburgh Inst FP*), NT Brewis (*Edinburgh Inst FP*), JB Brown (*Glasgow Acs*), †DY Cassels (*W of Scot*), EN Ewart (*Glasgow Acs*), JHS Graham (*Edinburgh Acs*), RW Irvine* (*Edinburgh Acs*), D McCowan (*W of Scot*), AG Petrie (*Royal HSFP*), CR Stewart (*W of Scot*)

ENGLAND TW Fry (*Queen's House*); L Stokes* (*Blackheath*), CM Sawyer (*Broughton*); RT Finch (*Cambridge U*), HH Taylor (*St George's H*); GW Burton (*Blackheath*), CH Coates (*Cambridge U*), C Gurdon (*Richmond*), ET Gurdon (*Richmond*), G Harrison (*Hull*), S Neame (*Old Cheltonians*), C Phillips (*Oxford U*), HC Rowley (*Manchester*), GF Vernon (*Blackheath*), R Walker (*Manchester*)

SCORING Taylor, try; Taylor, try (half-time) Fry, try; Stokes, con; WS Brown, try; Cross, con; Gurdon, try; Burton, try; Stokes, con

In an attempt to spread the rugby gospel to a wider audience, this match was played at Whalley Range in the south of Manchester. A large crowd saw an excellent contest played in bright and breezy conditions on a slippery pitch. Scotland were quietly confident, but they were outclassed and some of their defence was fatally weak. A few minutes after the start, Taylor, the English half-back, beat several opponents for a solo try and later he added a second. Scotland had some pressure and Masters dropped a pass with the line in front of him. Cross and Finlay narrowly missed four attempted drop goals between them, the strong wind taking the ball away from the posts. In the second half, there was little between the two packs, but the English backs were more dangerous. Fry, the English full-back, scored a converted try and the Scots responded with a try by Sorley Brown who took a pass from Masters inside the English 25 and ran behind the posts. Cross kicked the easy goal, but in the closing stages England scored another two tries to underline their superiority. For Scotland, Masters defended strongly and Irvine, playing in his tenth and final match against England, was always prominent.

---

14 1881 IRELAND

Ormeau Park, Belfast · Saturday 19 February 1881
Lost 1 try to 1 drop goal

SCOTLAND †TA Begbie (*Edinburgh Wdrs*); WE Maclagan (*Edinburgh Acs*), NJ Finlay (*Edinburgh Acs*), RC Mackenzie (*Glasgow Acs*); JA Campbell (*Glasgow Acs*), †PW Smeaton (*Edinburgh Acs*); †RB Allan (*Glasgow Acs*), JB Brown (*Glasgow Acs*), DY Cassels (*W of Scot*), JHS Graham* (*Edinburgh Acs*), JE Junor (*Glasgow Acs*), D McCowan (*W of Scot*), †C Reid (*Edinburgh Acad*), †GH Robb (*Glasgow U*), †A Walker (*W of Scot*)

IRELAND RE McLean (*Dublin U*); JC Bagot (*Dublin U*), WW Pike (*Kingstown*); M Johnston (*Dublin U*), HF Spunner (*Wdrs*); DR Browning (*Wdrs*), AJ Forrest* (*Wdrs*), RW Hughes (*NIFC*), J Johnston (*Belfast Alb*), JA Macdonald (*Methodist Coll*), AR McMullan (*Cork*), HB Morell (*Dublin U*), H Purdon (*NIFC*), JW Taylor (*NIFC*), WA Wallis (*Wdrs*)

SCORING No scoring in the first half. Graham, try; Bagot, drop

There was great controversy in Scotland about the original selection for this match. John Graham, the Edinburgh Academicals forward, was chosen as Scottish captain, but many felt that it should have been Gordon Petrie of Royal High School FP who was the more senior player. There were calls for the selection committee to resign because of their perceived bias towards the Academicals. Feelings ran so high that several players withdrew from the side and Scotland sent a weakened team to Belfast. Scotland experimented with three three-quarters for the first time and this was the first appearance of Charles Reid, one of the truly great Scottish forwards, who was then still a schoolboy. In a vigorously contested match, Ireland played with great determination and snatched their first-ever win in international rugby with a dramatic late drop goal. In the first half, both sides had spells of pressure and were close to scoring. A drop goal attempt by Bagot slipped under the bar and the Scottish forwards twice forced their opponents to touch down in defence. In the second half, a drop kick by Maclagan was touched in-flight by an Irish player. Graham, the Scottish captain, who had been standing well in front of the kicker, collected the ball, as he entitled to do, and touched down between the posts. Unfortunately, Begbie missed the simple conversion. Roared on by their excited supporters, Ireland sensed victory and made some frantic late attacks. They missed a glorious chance because of a loose pass, but after a quickly taken lineout Bigot dropped the winning goal amidst wildly ecstatic scenes.

---

15   1881   ENGLAND

Raeburn Place · Saturday 19 March 1881

Drawn 1 goal, 1 try to 1 drop goal, 1 try

SCOTLAND TA Begbie (*Edinburgh Wdrs*), WE Maclagan (*Edinburgh Acs*), NJ Finlay (*Edinburgh Acs*), RC Mackenzie (*Glasgow Acs*), †AR Don Wauchope (*Cambridge U*), JA Campbell (*Glasgow Acs*); R Ainslie (*Edinburgh Inst FP*), †T Ainslie (*Edinburgh Inst FP*), JB Brown (*Glasgow Acs*), †JW Fraser (*Edinburgh Inst FP*), JHS Graham* (*Edinburgh Acs*), D McCowan (*W of Scot*), †R Maitland (*Edinburgh Inst FP*), †WA Peterkin (*Edinburgh U*), C Reid (*Edinburgh Acad*)

ENGLAND AN Hornby (*Manchester*), R Hunt (*Manchester*), L Stokes* (*Blackheath*), FT Wright (*Edinburgh Acad*), HC Rowley (*Manchester*); A Budd (*Blackheath*), GW Burton (*Blackheath*), CH Coates (*Leeds*), CWL Fernandes (*Leeds*), H Fowler (*Walthamstow*), C Gurdon (*Richmond*), ET Gurdon (*Richmond*), WW Hewitt (*Queen's House*), C Phillips (*Birkenhead Park*), H Vassall (*Oxford U*)

REFEREE DH Watson (*Scotland*)

SCORING R Ainslie, try (half-time) Stokes, drop; Rowley, try; Brown, try; Begbie, con

Originally scheduled for Saturday 5 March 1881, this match was twice postponed because of frost and snow. Scotland had to make two changes from the original selection, one of whom, JE Junor, the Glasgow Academicals forward, had gone to India on business. For England, Henry Herbert Taylor, the original choice at half-back, missed the train north and his place was hurriedly filled by 18-year-old Frank Wright, 'a bright fair-haired Lancashire boy' who was still a pupil at the Edinburgh Academy. This gave the school the unusual distinction of having two players on the same field with Charles Reid playing for Scotland. A large crowd saw a thrilling match and the result in doubt until the end. With the sun and wind behind them, Scotland had the better of the first half. Bob Ainslie, who was prominent throughout, scored the opening try, but Begbie's conversion rebounded off one of the uprights. At this time, the rules allowed play to continue (similar to the modern game when a penalty kick hits a post and the ball comes back into play). Reid gathered and forced his way over the English line, but lost possession at a maul in the English goal area. Near the interval, Campbell made a strong run and crossed at the corner, but he was adjudged to have been in touch. England, who played with an extra man in the forwards, dominated the second half and forced the Scots onto the defensive. Stokes dropped an enormous goal from near halfway, 'amid tremendous cheering and waving of hats and handkerchiefs, which lasted fully a minute'. England half-back Rowley scored an unconverted try near the corner and in the dying minutes the Scots, roared on by the home crowd, fought their way back into the game. Play moved into English territory and Brown scored at the posts amidst great excitement. Some of the English players disputed the try because Brown had been in an offside position, but the match officials, two of whom were Scottish, had no doubts. Begbie kicked the simple conversion and the match ended in a draw. Afterwards, Arthur George Guillemard, the president of the Rugby Football Union, claimed that his side had been denied a rightful victory by biased officials. This in turn led to a flurry of heated correspondence between the two unions. The outcome was that a neutral referee was appointed for the next match between the sides.

---

16   1882   IRELAND

Hamilton Crescent, Glasgow · Saturday 18 February 1882
Won 2 tries to nil

SCOTLAND †T Anderson (*Merchiston Sch*); WE Maclagan (*Edinburgh Acs*), †F Hunter (*Edinburgh U*); WS Brown (*Edinburgh Inst FP*), †AGG Asher (*Oxford U*); R Ainslie* (*Edinburgh Inst FP*), T Ainslie (*Edinburgh Inst FP*), JB Brown (*Glasgow Acs*), DY Cassels (*W of Scot*), †AFC Gore (*London Scot*), D McCowan (*W of Scot*), GWL McLeod (*Edinburgh Wdrs*), R Maitland (*Edinburgh Inst FP*), C Reid (*Edinburgh Acs*), D Somerville (*Edinburgh Inst FP*)

IRELAND RB Walkington (*NIFC*); RE McLean (*Dublin U*), JR Atkinson (*Dublin U*), RW Morrow (*QC Belfast*); WW Fletcher (*Kingstown*), J Pedlow (*Bessbrook*); JB Buchanan (*Dublin U*), W Finlay (*NIFC*), RW Hughes (*NIFC*), J Johnston (*Albion*), JA Macdonald (*Methodist Coll*), R Nelson (*QC Belfast*), AC O'Sullivan (*Dublin U*), G Scriven (*Dublin U*), JW Taylor* (*NIFC*)

REFEREE AG Petrie (*Scotland*)

SCORING WS Brown, try (half-time) McCowan, try

Conditions were difficult with a cold, stiff wind and a heavy pitch. Two weeks earlier Ireland had fought out a spirited draw against England and, although their team was weakened by many withdrawals, they put up a good fight and at times had the Scots under pressure. However, the Scottish forwards combined better and their footwork was very effective. Scotland opened the scoring when the forwards made a classic rush to take play into the Irish 25 and William Sorley Brown, the quarter-back, wriggled through for an unconverted try. The Scots played with the elements in the second half, but they could only manage one further try because of stout Irish defence. Right at the end, Sorley Brown was caught just short. Scottish full-back Tom Anderson was still a pupil at Merchiston Castle School and gave a solid display after early nerves. He narrowly missed both conversions, his second taken from an awkward angle went just under the bar. This was his only cap, but later he represented Scotland at cricket.

Whalley Range, Manchester · Saturday 4 March 1882

Won 2 tries to nil

SCOTLAND †JP Veitch (*Royal HSFP*); WE Maclagan (*Edinburgh Acs*), †A Philp (*Edinburgh Inst FP*); WS Brown (*Edinburgh Inst FP*), AR Don Wauchope (*Cambridge U*); R Ainslie (*Edinburgh Inst FP*), T Ainslie (*Edinburgh Inst FP*), JB Brown (*Glasgow Acs*), DY Cassels* (*W of Scot*), D McCowan (*W of Scot*), R Maitland (*Edinburgh Inst FP*), C Reid (*Edinburgh Acs*), A Walker (*W of Scot*), †JG Walker (*W of Scot*), †WA Walls (*Glasgow Acs*)

ENGLAND AN Hornby* (*Manchester*); E Beswick (*Swinton*), WN Bolton (*Blackheath*); HH Taylor (*Blackheath*), JH Payne (*Broughton*); CH Coates (*Yorkshire Wdrs*), HG Fuller (*Cambridge U*), C Gurdon (*Richmond*), ET Gurdon (*Richmond*), JT Hunt (*Manchester*), PA Newton (*Blackheath*), HC Rowley (*Manchester*), WM Tatham (*Oxford U*), GT Thomson (*Halifax*), H Vassall (*Oxford U*)

REFEREE HL Robinson (*Ireland*)

SCORING R Ainslie, try (half-time) R Ainslie, try

This game became known as 'Bob Ainslie's match' because of an outstanding display by the Edinburgh Institution forward Robert Ainslie. A farmer from Lasswade, he scored two tries and was the best player on the field. The pitch was heavy after a week of heavy rain and at one point the game was almost transferred to London. An enormous crowd estimated at around 15,000 spectators squeezed into the Manchester ground. The game was disrupted several times when spectators spilled onto the playing field. Scotland won on English territory for the first time thanks to a stirring effort by the forwards. Their teamwork was very effective and their aggressive defence upset the English backs. After an uneventful opening, Don Wauchope made a strong run deep into English territory and Ainslie was on hand to score his first try. Soon afterwards, Maclagan dropped a goal from a fair catch, but it was disallowed because he had not marked the ball properly. In the second half, Ainslie scored his second try and Payne, the English half-back, was denied a score when he was impeded on his way to the line by encroaching spectators.

The Modern Game Emerges
1883–1898

IN RETROSPECT, 1883 can be seen as a significant year in the development of international rugby. In January, Scotland played Wales for the first time, winning by three goals to one. This meant that Scotland had three matches in a season and also that Scotland, England, Ireland and Wales now played each other in a regular cycle of games (although the latter two did not have a fixture in 1883). In other words, this was the tentative beginnings of the International Rugby Championship which subsequently became the Five Nations when France joined in 1910 and then the Six Nations after Italy's accession in 2000.

Rugby has always been suspicious of innovation and the fledgling Championship had plenty of early teething troubles. The authorities were slow to recognise it or to give it official sanction because of the fear that it would lead to a win-at-all-costs attitude and push the game towards full-blooded professionalism. It is difficult for us to conceive of a time when excessive competition was regarded as problematic, but in its early days rugby, even at the highest level, was supposed to be a game for gentlemen played for fun and fraternity rather than money and success. It was only in the 1890s that the concept of an international championship was accepted and then only because newspapers, rather than the powers-that-be, issued league tables and declared an annual champion. Rugby was still in its formative stages at this time and countries played to their own sets of rules, which led to regular disagreements. In 1884, there was a major dispute between England and Scotland because of a controversial incident that occurred in the Calcutta Cup match at Blackheath. England took advantage of a fumble by a Scottish player to score the winning try, but the Scots claimed that it should not have been allowed under Scottish laws and refused to accept the outcome of the match. The dispute, which in retrospect seems like a proverbial storm in a teacup, was very bitter and the Scots were so incensed that they refused to play against England in 1885. Ultimately, this led to the formation of the International Rugby Football Board in 1886 whose aim was to standardise the rules of the game and settle disputes. But even then England refused to recognise the new Board and pulled out of the Championship in 1887 and 1888. Arguments between the countries continued and six of the 14 Championships to 1898 were curtailed because of disagreements.

However, amidst all the rancour and confusion, there were also some significant developments. After years of confusion, a standard system of scoring was introduced in season 1890–1. From then on, internationals would be decided by the number of points scored rather than goals or tries. Gradually, rugby was becoming a more open and attractive game both to play and watch. The early 1890s saw the introduction of the four three-quarters system which was pioneered in Wales and then adopted by the other countries. Forward packs were reduced to eight men and teams played with two centre three-quarters giving them more options in attack. The Welsh innovation aroused fierce debate in Scotland and was opposed by conservative rugby thinkers.

The traditional Scottish game was built around an aggressive forward pack that kept the ball tight and worked as a single unit, only bringing the backs into play when the opposition had been cleared out of the way. It was feared that the concentration on back play would undermine traditional forward skills, an argument that would run in Scotland until the 1950s.

Two further developments of the '80s and '90s are worth mentioning. The first was the beginning of seven-a-side rugby in Scotland. The story goes that in season 1882-3 the Melrose club was short of funds and hit upon the idea of holding a sports day that would include a rugby tournament with teams reduced to seven men and ties limited to 15 minutes each way. The world's first-ever sevens tournament was held at The Greenyards in April 1883. Appropriately, it was won by the host club who defeated local rivals Gala by scoring the first try in extra-time and thereby introducing the notion of sudden death. Sevens were an immediate success and other Border clubs quickly followed the Melrose lead. Another significant development of this period was the first contacts with overseas teams. In 1888, a British team made a 35-match tour of Australia and New Zealand with an additional 18 matches played under Australian Rules. The touring side included three players from Hawick, the Burnet brothers, Willie and Rob, and Alex 'Lal' Laing, and also two from Edinburgh University, Herbert Brooks and John Smith. The Scottish Football Union was deeply concerned that players taking part in the tour, which was organised by two professional cricketers, were being paid to play and therefore in breach of the amateur code. On their return, the Hawick contingent were interviewed by the SFU and asked to give assurances that they had not received any material benefits. Their case was eventually dropped, but tellingly none of them were ever capped. The same year a team of New Zealand Natives, who were popularly known as the Maoris, made an arduous 74 match tour of the British Isles. They played only one game in Scotland, beating Hawick at Mansfield Park by three goals to one. Thus the pattern of rugby touring was established. Bill Maclagan, a former Scottish wing and captain, led a British team to South Africa in 1891. Further British tours followed to South Africa in 1896 and to Australia in 1899, the latter including Scottish players Alec Timms, Alf Bucher and the uncapped trialist HGS Gray.

On the field, the late 1880s was a period of considerable success for Scotland. They lost only one match between 1885 and 1899 and won the Championship three times. Entering the new decade, Scotland achieved their first-ever clean sweep in 1891, a feat they repeated four years later. In rugby terms, the early 1890s were dominated by arguments over professionalism and whether or not players should be paid for playing rugby. The game was attracting growing interest from the working classes, especially in the north and west of England, South Wales and southern Scotland. At this time, most people still worked on a Saturday morning and it was difficult for working men to find the time to play rugby without taking unpaid leave from their employers, something that few working class people could afford to do. In England, an acrimonious dispute over financial compensation or 'Broken Time' payments led many northern clubs to break away from the ultra-conservative Rugby Football Union and form their own Northern Union which ultimately became the Rugby Football League. The established authorities, which were under the exclusive control of the middle and upper classes, treated the rebel code with utter contempt.

Anybody with the slightest involvement received a life ban from the amateur game. The impact of the new code was less pronounced in Scotland than in other countries because rugby was largely played by the professional and middle classes. However, some players did make the change. Alec Laidlaw, a Hawick stonemason, became the first Scottish international player to turn professional when he moved to Bradford in season 1898–9.

Amongst the leading Scottish players of the 1880s, Andrew Don Wauchope was a great attacking quarterback. A small man with a low centre of gravity, he had a devastating sidestep and was famous for his elusive breaks around the fringes of the scrums and mauls. He partnered his younger brother, Patrick Don Wauchope, in three internationals, but was most effective when playing with Augustus Grant Asher. Born in India into a military family, Asher was one the great Victorian sporting all-rounders and was once described as the 'Achilles of Scottish Athleticism'. He was a brilliant footballer and had an important role in establishing the passing game at Oxford University in the 1880s. He was a triple Blue at Oxford, Scottish pole-vault champion and represented Scotland at cricket. He also had a successful law career and was knighted in 1927. Bill Maclagan had a long and illustrious career that stretched over 13 years, first as a full-back and then as a three-quarter. Standing at well over six foot tall, he was a very determined runner and renowned for his aggressive defence. As Robert Irvine, one of the 1871 originals, wrote: 'I would rather fall into the hands of any back in the three kingdoms than into those of W.E. Maclagan when roused.' A stockbroker in London, Maclagan was one of the founders of the London Scottish club.

Although back play and the passing game became more prominent in the '80s and '90s, Scottish rugby remained firmly wedded to a traditional forward style. The Scots were renowned for producing hard, powerful, even ferocious forwards who combined together into formidable fighting units, both in tight and open play. Charles Reid was one of the best known rugby players of the 1880s. He won his first cap whilst a schoolboy at Edinburgh Academy and was unusually large for his era, standing at 6ft 3in and weighing in at between 15–16 stones. He was known as 'Hippo' not because of his extraordinary physique, but apparently because in one of his classes he could not remember the Greek word for a horse. Reid moved around the field quickly, handled well and was a destructive tackler. Like many early international players, he pursued a medical career, practising in Selkirk and Swindon where he died in 1909 aged only 45. Two other notable forwards of the 1880s were the Ainslie brothers, Robert and Tom. Bob Ainslie was not a big man, but he was very fast in the loose, a good dribbler and a devastating tackler. His younger brother Tom was solid in the scrums and a useful all-rounder. The brothers came from farming stock in Lasswade, Bob later becoming a sheep farmer in Australia.

Another pair of brothers, Matthew and Bill McEwan maintained the tradition of powerful Scottish forwards into the '90s. Like Charles Reid before him, Matthew McEwan was capped as a schoolboy whilst at Edinburgh Academy. Raw-boned, vigorous and hard, McEwan had the splendid nickname of 'Saxon' because of his fair hair and powerful build. He became a chartered accountant and died only in his 30s in Chicago. His younger brother Bill McEwan (16 caps 1894–1900) was described by the *Rugby Football Annual* as 'the finest Scots forward of his age ... though no tapping parlour forward he was good at all points and untiring.' He emigrated to South Africa and played twice for his adopted country against the British touring side in 1903. Herbert Leggatt was a very tall man whose great height and reach made him invaluable in the lineout and scrum, and also at charging down opposition kicks. John Boswell was a rotund and heavy player who was surprisingly light on his feet and a master of the snap drop goal, often from the unlikeliest positions. Gala's Adam Dalgleish was the first member of a Border club to be capped for Scotland. Although a light man, he was sturdy, strong and had great footwork. He was highly versatile and often called upon to replace an injured back, leading to the claim that he played in every position except full-back. The 1890s also saw the emergence of Mark Morrison who is regarded as one of greatest Scottish forwards of any era. Morrison came from farming stock and was first capped as a teenager. He was an extremely hard and physical player who handled well and was a destructive tackler. He captained Scotland to two Triple Crowns (1901 and 1903) and also led the British team to South Africa in 1903.

Amongst the backs, Harry Stevenson played both at centre and full-back. He was a firm tackler and a thrilling runner with his sudden twists and dummy passes. A fine all-rounder, he also represented Scotland at cricket and was a noted lob bowler. William Neilson, the second of the four Neilson brothers, was a brilliant centre. In 1895, *Famous Footballers* described him as 'the finest halfback [three-quarter] that Scotland has produced of late years... he is full of resource, and with plenty of judgement is equally good as an offensive or defensive player.' George Campbell was a skilful three-quarter and, like Stevenson, a good cricketer. Scotland also had some very fast wings in the 1890s including Langholm's Tom Scott and Henry Gedge who, like several other early Scottish international players, followed a career in religion.

---

18   INTERNATIONAL CHAMPIONSHIP 1883   WALES

Raeburn Place · Monday 8 January 1883

Won 3 goals to 1 goal

SCOTLAND †DW Kidston (*Glasgow Acs*); WE Maclagan (*London Scot*), †DJ Macfarlan (*London Scot*); AR Don Wauchope (*Cambridge U*), WS Brown (*Edinburgh Inst FP*); T Ainslie (*Edinburgh Inst FP*), JB Brown (*Glasgow Acs*), DY Cassels* (*W of Scot*), †J Jamieson (*W of Scot*), †JG Mowat (*Glasgow Acs*), C Reid (*Edinburgh Acs*), D Somerville (*Edinburgh Inst FP*), A Walker (*W of Scot*), JG Walker (*W of Scot*), WA Walls (*Glasgow Acs*)

WALES CP Lewis* (*Llandovery*); CH Newman (*Newport*), WB Norton (*Cardiff*); WF Evans (*Rhymney & Oxford U*), GF Harding (*Newport*); A Cattell (*Llanelli*), TJS Clapp (*Newport*), R Gould (*Newport*), J Griffin (*Edinburgh U*), JA Jones (*Cardiff*), TB Jones (*Newport*), TH Judson (*Llanelli*), HS Lyne (*Newport*), GLB Morris (*Swansea*), FT Purdon (*Swansea*)

REFEREE G Rowland Hill (*England*)

SCORING Macfarlan, try; Maclagan, con (half-time) Don Wauchope, try; Maclagan, con; Macfarlan, try; Maclagan, con; Judson, try; Lewis, con

This was the first match between Scotland and Wales, and Scotland's first match in the International Championship. Wales had some problems raising a team and drafted in John Griffin of Edinburgh University who apparently had no Welsh connections, apart from a Welsh-sounding surname. Conditions were fine but the pitch was hard after overnight frost. Play was vigorously contested, but Scotland benefitted from greater experience and were fairly easy winners, despite playing much of the game a man short after Walker went off early with a twisted knee. In the first half, both sides had spells of pressure and Macfarlan scored a try following good combined play by the Scottish backs. After the break, Don Wauchope, who had played a club match two days earlier, scored a try and Macfarlan completed his brace. Maclagan converted all three scores. Wales never gave in and near the finish Clapp made a strong run before giving a scoring pass to Judson for a consolation try.

19   INTERNATIONAL CHAMPIONSHIP 1883   IRELAND

Ormeau, Belfast · Saturday 17 February 1883

Won 1 goal, 1 try to nil

SCOTLAND JP Veitch (*Royal HSFP*); WE Maclagan (*London Scot*), †MF Reid (*Loretto Sch*); PW Smeaton (*Edinburgh Acs*), †GR Aitchison (*Edinburgh Wdrs*); T Ainslie (*Edinburgh Inst FP*), JB Brown (*Glasgow Acs*), DY Cassels* (*W of Scot*), J Jamieson (*W of Scot*), D McCowan (*W of Scot*), WA Peterkin (*Edinburgh U*), C Reid (*Edinburgh Acs*), D Somerville (*Edinburgh Inst FP*), A Walker (*W of Scot*), WA Walls (*Glasgow Acs*)

IRELAND JWR Morrow (*QC Belfast*); WW Pike (*Kingstown*), RE McLean (*NIFC*); SR Collier (*QC Belfast*), AM Whitestone (*Dublin U*); SAM Bruce (*NIFC*), FS Heuston (*Kingstown*), RW Hughes (*NIFC*), H King (*Dublin U*), JA Macdonald (*Methodist Coll Belfast*), DF Moore (*Wdrs*), R Nelson (*QC Belfast*), G Scriven* (*Dublin U*), JW Taylor (*NIFC*), WA Wallis (*Wdrs*)

SCORING No scoring in the first half. C Reid, try; Somerville, try; Maclagan, con

Marshall Frederick Reid, a pupil at Loretto School, was a late replacement for DJ Macfarlan. This match was played in heavy rain and the pitch quickly became a sea of mud. There was little open play and by the closing stages both sides had resorted to wild kicks at the ball rather than trying to handle it. Ireland started strongly and forced the Scots onto the defensive. Unfortunately, the home side were badly handicapped by injuries. They lost three players before the interval and several others were hurt but soldiered on. The Scots had the better of the second half, and Charles Reid and Somerville scored tries, the second converted by Maclagan who was also strong in defence.

20   INTERNATIONAL CHAMPIONSHIP 1883   ENGLAND

Raeburn Place · Saturday 3 March 1883 · Lost 1 try to 2 tries

SCOTLAND DW Kidston (*Glasgow Acs*); WE Maclagan (*London Scot*), MF Reid (*Loretto Sch*); PW Smeaton (*Edinburgh Acs*), WS Brown (*Edinburgh Inst FP*); T Ainslie (*Edinburgh Inst FP*), JB Brown (*Glasgow Acs*), DY Cassels* (*W of Scot*), J Jamieson (*W of Scot*), D McCowan (*W of Scot*), JG Mowat (*Glasgow Acs*), C Reid (*Edinburgh Acs*), D Somerville (*Edinburgh Inst FP*), A Walker (*W of Scot*), WA Walls (*Glasgow Acs*)

ENGLAND HB Tristram (*Oxford U*); WN Bolton (*Blackheath*), AM Evanson (*Oxford U*),

CG Wade (*Oxford U*); A Rotherham (*Oxford U*), JH Payne (*Broughton*); HG Fuller (*Cambridge U*), C Gurdon (*Richmond*), ET Gurdon* (*Richmond*), RSF Henderson (*Blackheath*), EJ Moore (*Oxford U*), RM Pattisson (*Cambridge U*), WM Tatham (*Oxford U*), GT Thomson (*Halifax*), CS Wooldridge (*Oxford U*)

REFEREE HC Kelly (*Ireland*)

SCORING Rotherham, try (half-time) Reid, try; Bolton, try

England won in Scotland for the first time. This was a fine, evenly balanced match played in near perfect conditions. Rugby was still evolving at this time and becoming more open and attractive thanks to the development of back play and a 'scientific' handling game. Oxford University were amongst the pioneers of the new style and with seven Oxford men in their side England produced, in *The Scotsman*'s words, 'an exhibition of passing, the like of which has never previously been seen here... a better opportunity of displaying the art of passing could not have been wished.' The conservatively-minded Scots played with an extra forward and mainly relied on their traditional kick-and-rush tactics and fast following-up. Scotland were missing some key men due to injury, in particular the influential quarter-back Andrew Don Wauchope. London Scot Bill Maclagan played but was not fully fit and the Scottish back division was rather makeshift. In a well-contested first half, both sides had chances, but were denied by strong defence. England scored a solitary try by Rotherham, the Oxford half-back, although this was disputed by the Scots because of a forward pass. The second half was largely a forward battle and early on Charlie Reid scored an equal-ising try for Scotland, although this was also disputed. Play was fast and swung from end-to-end. Bolton, the powerful English wing, settled the issue with a try between the posts after a great solo run past several defenders. Evanson missed the simple conversion during which he was 'most ungraciously hissed' by a section of spectators. England's victory encouraged the reluctant Scots to adopt the new style of three three-quarter backs the following season.

21 INTERNATIONAL CHAMPIONSHIP 1884 WALES

Rodney Parade, Newport · Saturday 12 January 1884
Won 1 drop goal, 1 try to nil

SCOTLAND JP Veitch (*Royal HSFP*); WE Maclagan* (*London Scot*), DJ Macfarlan (*London Scot*), †GC Lindsay (*F-Ls*); AR Don Wauchope (*F-Ls*), AGG Asher (*Oxford U*); T Ainslie (*Edinburgh Inst FP*), JB Brown (*Glasgow Acs*), J Jamieson (*W of Scot*), R Maitland (*Edinburgh Inst FP*), WA Peterkin (*Edinburgh U*), C Reid (*Edinburgh Acs*), D Somerville (*Edinburgh Inst FP*), †J Tod (*Watsonians*), WA Walls (*Glasgow Acs*)

WALES CP Lewis (*Llandovery Coll*); CP Allen (*Beaumaris & Oxford U*), WB Norton (*Cardiff*), CG Taylor (*Ruabon & Blackheath*); CH Newman* (*Newport*), WH Gwynn (*Swansea*); FG Andrews (*Swansea*), TJS Clapp (*Newport*), R Gould (*Newport*), TB Jones (*Newport*), HS Lyne (*Newport*), FL Margrave (*Llanelli*), GLB Morris (*Swansea*), WD Phillips (*Cardiff*), HJ Simpson (*Cardiff*)

REFEREE JS McLaren (*England*)

SCORING No scoring in the first half. Asher, drop; Ainslie, try

Originally scheduled for the previous Monday, this was a well contested match and both sides had spells of pressure although Scotland, who had to make several late changes, had better technique and combination. Asher and Don Wauchope, the Scottish quarter-backs, were in good form and the forwards made some stirring rushes. Wales started and finished the first half very strongly, but the Scottish defence was firm. In the second half, Asher dropped an excellent goal to give Scotland the lead. Then Don Wauchope made a good run and Ainslie was in support to score wide out.

22 INTERNATIONAL CHAMPIONSHIP 1884 IRELAND

Raeburn Place · Saturday 16 February 1884

Won 2 goals, 2 tries to 1 try

SCOTLAND JP Veitch (*Royal HSFP*); WE Maclagan* (*London Scot*), †ET Roland (*Edinburgh Wdrs*), DF Macfarlan (*London Scot*); AR Don Wauchope (*F-Ls*), AGG Asher (*Oxford U*); T Ainslie (*Edinburgh Inst FP*), †CW Berry (*F-Ls*), JB Brown (*Glasgow Acs*), J Jamieson (*W of Scot*), D McCowan (*W of Scot*), WA Peterkin (*Edinburgh U*), C Reid (*Edinburgh Acs*), J Tod (*Watsonians*), WA Walls (*Glasgow Acs*)

IRELAND JM O'Sullivan (*Limerick*); RE McLean (*NIFC*), GH Wheeler (*QC Belfast*), LM McIntosh (*Dublin U*); M Johnson (*Dublin U*), WW Higgins (*NIFC*); JBW Buchanan (*Dublin U*), A Gordon (*Dublin U*), THM Hobbs (*Dublin U*), RW Hughes (*NIFC*), J Johnston (*NIFC*), W Kelly (*Wdrs*), JA Macdonald* (*Methodist Coll Belfast*), JF Maguire (*Cork*), WG Rutherford (*Lansdowne*)

REFEREE G Rowland Hill (*England*)

SCORING McIntosh, try; Peterkin, try; Tod, try (half-time) Don Wauchope, try; Berry, con; Asher, try; Berry, con

Played in cold and dry conditions, this was an entertaining match that Scotland deserved to win by virtue of having greater speed and skill. Asher and Don Wauchope, the Scottish quarter-backs, were too fast and clever for their opponents. Ireland had to make numerous changes to their original selection, but they were always competitive and their handling was assured. The visitors opened the scoring after about ten minutes when Johnson made a break before giving a scoring pass to McIntosh. Peterkin, a Scottish athletics champion, had a long solo run to score a try wide out and Berry narrowly missed the awkward conversion. Then Don Wauchope made an elusive run to the line and Tod was on hand to score. Scotland dominated in the second half and Don Wauchope and Asher scored tries between the posts. Berry converted both to cap a fine all-round performance and Maclagan was also prominent.

23 INTERNATIONAL CHAMPIONSHIP 1884 ENGLAND

Rectory Field, Blackheath · Saturday 1 March 1884

Lost 1 try to 1 goal

SCOTLAND JP Veitch (*Royal HSFP*); WE Maclagan* (*London Scot*), ET Roland (*Edinburgh Wdrs*), DJ Macfarlan (*London Scot*); AGG Asher (*F-Ls*), AR Don Wauchope (*F-Ls*); T Ainslie

(*Edinburgh Inst FP*), CW Berry (*F-Ls*), JB Brown (*Glasgow Acs*), J Jamieson (*W of Scot*), D McCowan (*W of Scot*), WA Peterkin (*Edinburgh U*), C Reid (*Edinburgh Acs*), J Tod (*Watsonians*), WA Walls (*Glasgow Acs*)

ENGLAND HB Tristram (*Oxford U*); WN Bolton (*Blackheath*), AM Evanson (*Richmond*), CG Wade (*Oxford U*); A Rotherham (*Oxford U*), HT Twynam (*Richmond*); C Gurdon (*Richmond*), ET Gurdon* (*Richmond*), RSF Henderson (*Blackheath*), RS Kindersley (*Exeter & Oxford U*), CJB Marriott (*Blackheath & Cambridge U*), EL Strong (*Oxford U*), WM Tatham (*Oxford U*), GT Thomson (*Halifax*), CS Wooldridge (*Blackheath*)

REFEREE G Scriven (*Ireland*)

SCORING Jamieson, try (half-time) Kindersley, try; Bolton, con

On its return to London the fixture created great interest and special trains for spectators were run from Yorkshire and from Oxford and Cambridge. On a cold, sunny day the big crowd saw an exciting match that created some controversy. The Scottish forwards made many devastating dribbling rushes, but the English backs were good in defence and always ready to attack. Both sides had some scoring chances and play was vigorously contested. Scotland's try in the first half came after sustained pressure on the English line and Jamieson followed-up a short kick ahead to score out wide. After the interval, Kindersley, the English forward, scored between the posts after a good handling movement. The match was then held up for some time as Scotland claimed that one of the Scottish players had knocked (or 'fisted') the ball forwards and in such cases it was customary to stop play immediately rather than play advantage, a term that was not then in use. After a lengthy debate, which included consultation of the rule book by the RFU secretary, the try was awarded and Bolton converted to give England the lead. A disgruntled Scotland fought hard to save the match but to no avail. The dispute over Kindersley's try led to the cancellation of the fixture the following season and ultimately to the formation of the International Rugby Board.

---

24   **INTERNATIONAL CHAMPIONSHIP 1885**   **WALES**

Hamilton Crescent, Glasgow · Saturday 10 January 1885
Drawn no score

SCOTLAND †PR Harrower (*London Scot*); WE Maclagan* (*London Scot*), †AE Stephen (*W of Scot*), †G Maitland (*Edinburgh Inst FP*); AR Don Wauchope (*F-Ls*), AGG Asher (*F-Ls*); T Ainslie (*Edinburgh Inst FP*), CW Berry (*F-Ls*), J Jamieson (*W of Scot*), R Maitland (*Edinburgh Inst FP*), †JG Mitchell (*W of Scot*), WA Peterkin (*Edinburgh U*), C Reid (*Edinburgh Acs*), GH Robb (*Glasgow Acs*), J Tod (*Watsonians*)

WALES AJ Gould (*Newport*); CG Taylor (*Ruabon & Blackheath*), FE Hancock (*Cardiff*), HM Jordan (*Newport*); CH Newman* (*Newport*), WH Gwyn (*Swansea*); EP Alexander (*Camridge U*), TJS Clapp (*Newport*), SJ Goldsworthy (*Swansea*), R Gould (*Newport*), AF Hill (*Cardiff*), TB Jones (*Newport*), D Morgan (*Swansea*), LC Thomas (*Cardiff*), WH Thomas (*Llandovery & Cambridge U*)

REFEREE G Rowland Hill (*England*)

The sides were hampered by a soft pitch and wet conditions, and as a result there was little open play. The game was strenuously contested and Scotland had the greater share of possession and territory, but Wales defended strongly and deserved at least a draw. Both sides came close to scoring with drops at goal and on occasion forced the other to touch down behind their own line. The respective captains, Bill Maclagan and Charlie Newman, were both prominent.

25   INTERNATIONAL CHAMPIONSHIP 1885   IRELAND

Ormeau, Belfast · Saturday 21 February 1885 · Match abandoned

SCOTLAND JP Veitch (*Royal HSFP*); WE Maclagan* (*London Scot*), GC Lindsay (*Oxford U*) †HL Evans (*Edinburgh U*); AR Don Wauchope (*F-Ls*), †PH Don Wauchope (*F-Ls*); T Ainslie (*Edinburgh Inst FP*), CW Berry (*Oxford U*), JB Brown (*Glasgow Acs*), †TW Irvine (*Edinburgh Acs*), J Jamieson (*W of Scot*), JG Mitchell (*W of Scot*), WA Peterkin (*Edinburgh U*), C Reid (*Edinburgh Acs*), J Tod (*Watsonians*)

IRELAND RW Morrow (*Belfast Alb*); RE McLean (*NIFC*), JP Ross (*Lansdowne*), DJ Ross (*Belfast Alb*); EC Crawford (*Dublin U*), RG Warren (*Lansdowne*); TC Allen (*NIFC*), HM Brabazon (*Dublin U*), RM Bradshaw (*Wdrs*), J Johnson (*Belfast Alb*), TR Lyle (*Dublin U*), HJ Neil (*NIFC*), WG Rutherford* (*Tipperary*), T Shanahan (*Lansdowne*), RG Thompson (*Cork*)

REFEREE HC Kelly (*Ireland*)

SCORING Jamieson scored a try before the game was abandoned

Play started in a ferocious storm of rain and sleet, and it soon became apparent that no sensible football could be played on the heavily waterlogged pitch. Ireland kicked off into the wind which was so strong that the ball barely got into the Scottish half. Inevitably, Scotland had all of the territory and forced Ireland to touch down behind their own line several times. After about 20 minutes Jamieson, the Scottish forward, scored the only try of the match. A few minutes later, it was reluctantly agreed to abandon the game and replay it at a later date.

26   INTERNATIONAL CHAMPIONSHIP 1885   IRELAND

Raeburn Place · Saturday 7 March 1885 · Won 1 goal, 2 tries to nil

SCOTLAND JP Veitch (*Royal HSFP*); WE Maclagan* (*London Scot*), G Maitland (*Edinburgh Inst FP*), HL Evans (*Edinburgh U*); AR Don Wauchope (*F-Ls*), PH Don Wauchope (*F-Ls*); T Ainslie (*Edinburgh Inst FP*), JB Brown (*Glasgow Acs*), TW Irvine (*Edinburgh Acs*), J Jamieson (*W of Scot*), JG Mitchell (*W of Scot*), WA Peterkin (*Edinburgh U*), C Reid (*Edinburgh Acs*), JG Tait (*Cambridge U*), J Tod (*Watsonians*)

IRELAND JWR Morrow (*Belfast Alb*); JP Ross (*Lansdowne*), DJ Ross (*Belfast Alb*), EH Greene (*Dublin U*); RG Warren (*Lansdowne*), DV Hunter (*Dublin U*); RM Bradshaw (*Wdrs*), AJ Forrest* (*Wdrs*), W Hogg (*Dublin U*), J Johnstone (*Belfast Alb*), TR Lyle (*Dublin U*), FW Moore (*Wdrs*), HJ Neill (*NIFC*), T Shanahan (*Lansdowne*), JA Thompson (*QC Belfast*)

REFEREE HC Kelly (*Ireland*)

SCORING Reid, try (half-time) Peterkin, try; AR Don Wauchope, try; Veitch, con

Played in fine conditions, Scotland were slightly flattered by the final score, but their forwards combined well and some of the Irish handling was wayward. At quarter-back, the Don Wauchope brothers were in great form and both of them had elusive runs. After about 15 minutes, Reid forced his way over the line although the Irish disputed the score because of a forward pass. In the second half, the Scottish forwards made a dribbling rush and Jamieson passed left to Peterkin who used his great speed to reach the line. Near the finish, Andrew Don Wauchope made a long dodging run past numerous defenders and sprinted round under the posts, amidst 'tremendous cheering and waving of hats and handkerchiefs, which lasted for some time'. For Scotland, Veitch was almost faultless at full-back and Maclagan was again prominent.

27   INTERNATIONAL CHAMPIONSHIP 1886   WALES

Cardiff Arms Park · Saturday 9 January 1886

Won 2 goals, 1 try to nil

SCOTLAND †F McIndoe (*Glasgow Acs*); †WF Holms (*London Scot*), DJ Macfarlan (*London Scot*), †RH Morrison (*Edinburgh U*); AR Don Wauchope (*F-Ls*), PH Don Wauchope (*F-Ls*); JB Brown* (*Glasgow Acs*), †AT Clay (*Edinburgh Acs*), †J French (*Glasgow Acs*), TW Irvine (*Edinburgh Acs*), †WM Macleod (*Edinburgh Wdrs*), †CJB Milne (*W of Scot*), C Reid (*Edinburgh Acs*), J Tod (*Watsonians*), WA Walls (*Glasgow Acs*)

WALES DH Bowen (*Llanelli*); WM Douglas (*Cardiff*), FE Hancock* (*Cardiff*), AJ Gould (*Newport*), CG Taylor (*Ruabon & Blackheath*); AA Matthews (*Lampeter*), WH Stadden (*Cardiff*); EP Alexander (*Cambridge U*), WA Bowen (*Swansea*), TJS Clapp (*Newport*), AF Hill (*Cardiff*), DH Lewis (*Cardiff*), D Morgan (*Swansea*), WH Thomas (*Llandovery & Cambridge U*), GA Young (*Cardiff*)

REFEREE DF Moore (*Ireland*)

SCORING Clay, try; Macleod, con (half-time) Tod, try; AR Don Wauchope, try; Macleod, con

The pitch had been protected by straw but it was still hard in places. Scotland were more experienced and were comfortable winners. The Welshmen put up a good fight, but they faded badly in the second half. After the early exchanges, Wales were forced to touch down and from the ensuing play Clay scored a try and Macleod added the conversion. Wales had started the game with four three-quarters, but the nine-man Scottish pack was so dominant that early in the second half Bowen was moved into the forwards and Gould switched to full-back. Tod scored an unconverted try and Holms went close but was forced into touch-in-goal. Andrew Don Wauchope made a long run to score a brilliant solo try and Macleod kicked a fine conversion. Taylor, the Welsh wing, managed to cross the Scottish line, but he was unable to ground the ball before being thrown into touch.

28   INTERNATIONAL CHAMPIONSHIP 1886   IRELAND

Raeburn Place · Saturday 20 February 1886

Won 3 goals, 1 drop goal, 2 tries to nil

SCOTLAND F McIndoe (*Glasgow Acs*); AE Stephen (*W of Scot*), DJ Macfarlan (*London Scot*), RH Morrison (*Edinburgh U*); AR Don Wauchope (*F-Ls*), AGG Asher (*F-Ls*); JB Brown* (*Glasgow Acs*), AT Clay (*Edinburgh Acs*), TW Irvine (*Edinburgh Acs*), †DA Macleod (*Glasgow U*), WM Macleod (*F-Ls*), CJB Milne (*W of Scot*), C Reid (*Edinburgh Acs*), J Tod (*Watsonians*), WA Walls (*Glasgow Acs*)

IRELAND JWR Morrow (*Lisburn*); JP Ross* (*Lansdowne*), DJ Ross (*Belfast Alb*), MJ Carpendale (*Monkstown*); RW Herrick (*Dublin U*), JF Ross (*NIFC*); J Chambers (*Dublin U*), J McMordie (*QC Belfast*), FH Miller (*Wdrs*), FW Moore (*Wdrs*), VC le Fanu (*Cambridge U*), HJ Neill (*NIFC*), R Nelson (*QC Belfast*), FO Stoker (*Wdrs*), J Waites (*Bective Rgrs*)

REFEREE G Rowland Hill (*England*)

SCORING Don Wauchope, try; Don Wauchope, try; Morrison, try; Macfarlan, con; Morrison, try; Macfarlan, con (half-time) Asher, drop; Macfarlan, try; Macfarlan, con

Played in continuous rain and sleet, Scotland were convincing winners against an under-strength Irish side. The Scottish backs were full of running and scored five exciting tries, two in the early stages. After about 12 minutes, the forwards rushed to the Irish 25 and Don Wauchope made one his famous 'deer-like runs' through the defence for a fine solo score. Macleod's conversion attempt was charged down. A few minutes later, Don Wauchope scored again between the posts and Macleod's kick hit the crossbar. Before the interval, Morrison used his electric pace to score a brace of tries and Macfarlan converted both. In the second half, Asher dropped a goal and then Macfarlan made a weaving run through the defence for a try that he also converted. Scotland came close to scoring on several other occasions only to be thwarted by errors and desperate Irish defence.

29   INTERNATIONAL CHAMPIONSHIP 1886   ENGLAND

Raeburn Place · Saturday 13 March 1886 · Drawn no score

SCOTLAND JP Veitch (*Royal HSFP*); WF Holms (*RIE Coll*), †GR Wilson (*Royal HSFP*), RH Morrison (*Edinburgh U*); AR Don Wauchope (*F-Ls*), AGG Asher (*F-Ls & Edinburgh Wdrs*); JB Brown* (*Glasgow Acs*), AT Clay (*Edinburgh Acs*), TW Irvine (*Edinburgh Acs*), †MC McEwan (*Edinburgh Acs*), DA MacLeod (*Glasgow U*), CJB Milne (*W of Scot*), C Reid (*Edinburgh Acs*), J Tod (*Watsonians*), WA Walls (*Glasgow Acs*)

ENGLAND CH Sample (*Cambridge U*); AE Stoddart (*Blackheath*), AR Robertshaw (*Bradford*), EB Brutton (*Cambridge U*); A Rotherham (*Richmond*), F Bonsor (*Bradford*); WG Clibborn (*Richmond*), C Gurdon (*Richmond*), ET Gurdon* (*Richmond*), RE Inglis (*Blackheath*), GL Jeffery (*Cambridge U*), CJB Marriott (*Blackheath*), N Spurling (*Blackheath*), A Teggin (*Broughton Rgrs*), E Wilkinson (*Bradford*)

REFEREE HG Cook (*Ireland*)

This match, which was postponed for a week because of the wintery weather, attracted a large crowd and special trains for spectators were run from around the country. For the first time at a Scotland game, mounted police officers were used to control the crowd. This was a hard and fiercely contested encounter between two determined sides. Both of them had scoring opportunities, but the defences remained intact. Facing into a strong northerly wind, the Scots had the better of the first half. Twice they forced their opponents to touch down and George Wilson, the Scottish three-quarter, got over the English line only to be recalled for an infringement. Likewise, Morrison almost scored but was unable to put the ball down before he was bundled into touch. Play was more even in the second half. Reid broke clear, but instead of running on he passed out and the ball did not go to hand. Towards the finish England crossed the line, but the try was disallowed after a Scottish appeal. Don Wauchope was in great form and made one searing break, and Reid was also prominent.

30   INTERNATIONAL CHAMPIONSHIP 1887   IRELAND

Ormeau, Belfast · Saturday 19 February 1887

Won 1 goal, 1 mark goal, 2 tries to nil

SCOTLAND WF Holms (*London Scot*); †AN Woodrow (*Glasgow Acs*), WE Maclagan (*London Scot*), DJ Macfarlan (*London Scot*); PH Don Wauchope (*F-Ls*), †CE Orr (*W of Scot*); CW Berry (*Edinburgh Wdrs*), AT Clay (*Edinburgh Acs*), J French (*Glasgow Acs*), TW Irvine (*Edinburgh Acs*), †HT Ker (*Glasgow Acs*), MC McEwan (*Edinburgh Acs*), †RG McMillan (*W of Scot*), †DS Morton (*W of Scot*), C Reid* (*Edinburgh Acs*)

IRELAND JM O'Sullivan (*Cork*); R Montgomery (*Cambridge U*), DF Rambant (*Dublin U*), CR Tillie (*Dublin U*); RG Warren* (*Lansdowne*), JH McLaughlin (*Derry*); J Chambers (*Dublin U*), JS Dick (*QC Cork*), J Johnston (*Belfast Alb*), TR Lyle (*Dublin U*), J Macaulay (*Limerick*), CM Moore (*Dublin U*), HJ Neill (*NIFC*), R Stevenson (*Lisburn*), EJ Walsh (*Lansdowne*)

REFEREE G Rowland Hill (*England*)

SCORING Berry, mark; Maclagan, try; Berry, con (half-time) McEwan, try; Morton, try

Played in fine conditions, this was a well-contested match although Scotland had the better of the play. After about 15 minutes, Macfarlan made a fair catch from which Berry kicked a good goal. Then McEwan put Maclagan away for a try and Berry added the conversion. Ireland had some pressure and forced the Scots to touch down, but the Scottish tackling was very firm. The second half was fast and exciting, and both sides had some good runs. McEwan scored a try from a scrum and soon after Morton added another, but neither score was converted.

31   INTERNATIONAL CHAMPIONSHIP 1887   WALES

Raeburn Place · Saturday 26 February 1887

Won 4 goals and 8 tries to nil

SCOTLAND †AW Cameron (*Watsonians*); WE Maclagan (*London Scot*), GC Lindsay (*London Scot*), AN Woodrow (*Glasgow Acs*); PH Don Wauchope (*Edinburgh Wdrs*), CE Orr (*W of Scot*); CW Berry (*Edinburgh Wdrs*), AT Clay (*Edinburgh Acs*), J French (*Glasgow Acs*), TW Irvine (*Edinburgh Acs*), HT Ker (*Glasgow Acs*), MC McEwan (*Edinburgh Acs*), RG Macmillan (*W of Scot*), DS Morton (*W of Scot*), C Reid* (*Edinburgh Acs*)

WALES H Hughes (*Cardiff*); D Gwynn (*Swansea*), AJ Gould (*Newport*), WM Douglas (*Cardiff*); GE Bowen (*Swansea*), OJ Evans (*Cardiff*); AF Bland (*Cardiff*), WA Bowen (*Swansea*), TJS Clapp (*Newport*), R Gould* (*Newport*), TW Lockwood (*Newport*), D Morgan (*Swansea*), ES Richards (*Swansea*), WH Thomas (*Llandovery & Cambridge U*), WEO Williams (*Cardiff*)

SCORING Don Wauchope, try; Lindsay, try; Berry, con; Orr, try; Berry, con; Lindsay, try (half-time) Reid, try; Lindsay, try; Macmillan, try; Woodrow, con; McEwan, try; Lindsay, try; Maclagan, try; Morton, try; Lindsay, try

This one-sided match was postponed from January because of frost and both sides had to make changes to their original selections. Lindsay, a very fast runner, came in at three-quarter for Macfarlan and he ended the day with five tries. As the score suggests, Scotland completely outclassed their opponents and scored a total of 12 tries. The forwards dominated throughout, and their footwork and handling were devastating. The backs were full of running and their brilliant passing movements bewildered the Welsh defence. Inside the first ten minutes, Don Wauchope made one of his elusive runs to score the first Scottish try. Lindsay made a strong run to score a second and then Orr was credited with a try after a rush by the forwards. Scotland made waves of attacks and shortly before the interval Lindsay eluded the defence for his second try. Play continued in a similar fashion in the second half and eventually the hapless Welshmen were completely swamped. Scotland's victory would have been much greater if they had not missed a series of easy conversions.

32   INTERNATIONAL CHAMPIONSHIP 1887   ENGLAND

Whalley Range, Manchester · Saturday 5 March 1887

Drawn 1 try each

SCOTLAND WF Holms (*London Scot*); WE Maclagan (*London Scot*), GC Lindsay (*London Scot*), AN Woodrow (*Glasgow Acs*); PH Don Wauchope (*Edinburgh Wdrs*), CE Orr (*W of Scot*); CW Berry (*Edinburgh Wdrs*), AT Clay (*Edinburgh Acs*), J French (*Glasgow Acs*), TW Irvine (*Edinburgh Acs*), HT Ker (*Glasgow Acs*), MC McEwan (*Edinburgh Acs*), RG Macmillan (*London Scot*), DS Morton (*W of Scot*), C Reid* (*Edinburgh Acs*)

ENGLAND HB Tristram (*Richmond*); WN Bolton (*Blackheath*), R Robertshaw (*Bradford*), RE Lockwood (*Dewsbury*); A Rotherham* (*Richmond*), F Bonsor (*Bradford*); CR Cleveland (*Oxford U*), WG Clibborn (*Richmond*), JH Dewhurst (*Cambridge U*), JL Hickson (*Bradford*), GL Jeffery (*Blackheath*), RL Seddon (*Broughton Rgrs*), HH Springmann (*Liverpool*), A Teggin (*Broughton Rgrs*), E Wilkinson (*Bradford*)

REFEREE J Lyle (*Ireland*)

SCORING Jeffrey, try (half-time) Morton, try

This game became known as the 'foggy international' because a thick mist enveloped the ground and at times it was difficult for spectators to see any of the play. Scotland started confidently and came close to scoring on several occasions, but then the English forwards began to assert themselves and after a series of scrums Jeffrey ran in for a try. Play was fairly even in the second half with the English backs eager to run the ball and the Scottish forwards making attacks with their carefully controlled footwork. Holms, the Scottish full-back, had a great run through the defence, but his drop goal attempt fell narrowly shortly. Then Maclagan escaped and grounded the ball only to be recalled for an infringement. Finally Morton scored the equalising try, but Berry failed to convert. England defended well throughout and at one point Tristram, the full-back, saved a certain score when he flattened Maclagan who was going at full tilt for the line.

33   INTERNATIONAL CHAMPIONSHIP 1888   WALES

Rodney Parade, Newport · Saturday 4 February 1888

Lost nil to 1 try

SCOTLAND †HFT Chambers (*Edinburgh U*); WE Maclagan (*London Scot*), †HJ Stevenson (*Edinburgh Acs*), †MM Duncan (*Cambridge U*); CE Orr (*W of Scot*), †CFP Fraser (*Glasgow U*); CW Berry (*F-Ls*), AT Clay (*Edinburgh Acs*), †A Duke (*Royal HSFP*), TW Irvine (*Edinburgh Acs*), MC McEwan (*Edinburgh Acs*), DS Morton (*W of Scot*), C Reid* (*Edinburgh Acs*), †LE Stevenson (*Edinburgh U*), †TB White (*Edinburgh Acs*)

WALES EJ Roberts (*Llanelli*); GE Bowen (*Swansea*), AJ Gould (*Newport*), TJP Jenkins (*London Welsh*); OJ Evans (*Cardiff*), WH Stadden (*Cardiff*); AF Bland (*Cardiff*), TJS Clapp* (*Newport*), AF Hill (*Cardiff*), WH Howell (*Swansea*), QD Kedzlie (*Cardiff*), J Meredith (*Swansea*), RW Powell (*Newport*), WH Thomas (*Llandovery*), T Williams (*Swansea*)

REFEREE J Chambers (*Ireland*)

SCORING Jenkins, try (half-time)

Playing in dull but fine conditions, Wales unexpectedly beat Scotland for the first time. Play was well-contested and both sides had their moments in attack. There was some controversy about the winning try by Tom Jenkins. He made a strong run up the touchline, but several defenders seemed to think he had gone into touch and allowed him to carry on only for the referee to award a try. Scotland had a lot of pressure for the rest of the game and forced the ball over the Welsh line on several occasions, but could not get the vital score. The final whistle was greeted with great enthusiasm by the crowd. Welsh three-quarter Arthur Gould was the outstanding player on the field whilst Chambers, Stevenson and Reid had good matches for Scotland.

34   INTERNATIONAL CHAMPIONSHIP 1888   IRELAND

Raeburn Place · Saturday 10 March 1888 · Won 1 goal to nil

SCOTLAND HFT Chambers (*Edinburgh U*); WE Maclagan (*London Scot*); HJ Stevenson (*Edinburgh Acs*), DJ Macfarlan (*London Scot*); AR Don Wauchope* (*F-Ls*), CE Orr (*W of Scot*); CW Berry (*Edinburgh Wdrs*), A Duke (*Royal HSFP*), TW Irvine (*Edinburgh Acs*), HT Ker (*Glasgow Acs*), MC McEwan (*Edinburgh Acs*), †AG Malcolm (*Glasgow U*), DS Morton (*W of Scot*), C Reid (*Edinburgh Acs*), TB White (*Edinburgh Acs*)

IRELAND JWR Morrow (*Lisburn*); CR Tillie (*Dublin U*), A Walpole (*Dublin U*), MJ Carpendale (*Monkstown*); RG Warren (*Lansdowne*), JH McLaughlin (*Derry*); W Ekin (*QC Belfast*), VC le Fanu (*Lansdowne*), RH Mayne (*Belfast Albion*), J Moffatt (*Belfast Alb*), CM Moore (*Dublin U*), WA Morton (*Dublin U*), HJ Neill* (*NIFC*), T Shanahan (*Lansdowne*), EW Stoker (*Wdrs*)

REFEREE J McLaren (*England*)

SCORING Macfarlan, try; Berry, con (half-time)

Played in fine conditions, this was a sternly-contested match between two strong packs. Both sides were keen to run the ball, but the defences were very strong. In the first half, both Maclagan and Don Wauchope got over the Irish line only to be recalled for infringements. After about 25 minutes Don Wauchope started a run and Stevenson cut through the defence to give Macfarlan a clear run to the line. Berry kicked the difficult conversion. Orr had to retire with an injury and White took his place at quarter-back. Play continued in a similar fashion in the second half and Scotland finished strongly, but there was no further scoring. For Scotland, White and Don Wauchope were courageous at the feet of the Irish forwards and Stevenson had a fine match. Reid was also prominent and at one point, according to *The Scotsman*, he 'had a run with the bulk of the Irish forwards hanging on to him, this feat exciting great laughter'.

35   INTERNATIONAL CHAMPIONSHIP 1889   WALES

Raeburn Place · Saturday 2 February 1889 · Won 2 tries to nil

SCOTLAND HFT Chambers (*Edinburgh U*); WF Holms (*Edinburgh Wdrs*), HJ Stevenson (*Edinburgh Acs*), †J Marsh (*Edinburgh Inst FP*); CE Orr (*W of Scot*), CFP Fraser (*Glasgow U*): †W Auld (*W of Scot*), †JD Boswell (*W of Scot*), A Duke (*Royal HSFP*), HT Ker (*Glasgow Acs*), MC McEwan (*Edinburgh Acs*), †WA Macdonald (*Glasgow U*), †A Methuen (*Cambridge U*), DS Morton* (*W of Scot*), TB White (*Edinburgh Acs*)

WALES H Hughes (*Cardiff*); RM Garrett (*Penarth*), JE Webb (*Newport*), EH Bishop (*Swansea*), HM Jordan (*Newport & London Welsh*); CJ Thomas (*Newport*), GR Evans (*Cardiff*); WA Bowen (*Swansea*), DW Evans (*Cardiff*), J Hannan (*Newport*), CT Harding (*Newport*), AF Hill* (*Cardiff*), SH Nicholls (*Cardiff*), RL Thomas (*London Welsh*), WEO Williams (*Cardiff*)

REFEREE A McAllister (*Ireland*)

SCORING Orr, try (half-time) Ker, try

Heavy snow showers fell on the morning of the game and the pitch was slippery. It was agreed to play two halves of only 30 minutes each. Both sides were under-strength and some leading Welsh players chose to stay at home and play for their clubs rather than travel north. Scotland were the better side and should have won more easily, but the forwards did not combine very well. Facing into a stiff wind, Scotland opened the scoring when McEwan made a good run from midfield to put Orr over. In the second half, Fraser escaped and Ker scored a try that the Welsh players disputed. McEwan missed the simple conversion from in front of the posts. Scotland crossed the line several times during the match only to be recalled for infringements or because they were unable to ground the ball. The Welshmen, who played with only eight forwards, had some good dribbling rushes, but the Scottish defence was firm.

36   INTERNATIONAL CHAMPIONSHIP 1889   IRELAND

Ormeau, Belfast · Saturday 16 February 1889
Won 1 drop goal to nil

SCOTLAND HFT Chambers (*Edinburgh U*); WF Holms (*London Scot*), HJ Stevenson (*Edinburgh Acs*), J Marsh (*Edinburgh Inst FP*); CE Orr (*W of Scot*), †DG Anderson (*London Scot*); †AI Aitken (*Edinburgh Inst FP*), JD Boswell (*W of Scot*), A Duke (*Royal HSFP*), TW Irvine (*Edinburgh Acs*), MC McEwan (*Edinburgh Acs*), †JG McKendrick (*W of Scot*), A Methuen (*Cambridge U*), DS Morton* (*W of Scot*), †JE Orr (*W of Scot*)

IRELAND LJ Holmes (*Lisburn*); RA Yeates (*Dublin U*), TB Pedlow (*QC Belfast*), DC Woods (*Bessbrook*); J Stevenson (*Lisburn*), RG Warren* (*Lansdowne*); HW Andrews (*NIFC*), TM Donovan (*QC Cork*), EG Forrest (*Wdrs*), JS Jameson (*Lansdowne*), J Moffatt (*Belfast Alb*), LC Nash (*QC Cork*), CRR Stack (*Dublin U*), R Stevenson (*Lisburn*), FO Stoker (*Wdrs*)

REFEREE WD Phillips (*Wales*)

SCORING Stevenson, drop (half-time)

Both sides had to make some late changes. Heavy rain had fallen during the week and the pitch was very soft. This was a strenuously fought match and both teams had some good dribbling rushes, but the defences were to the fore. Scotland played with the elements in their favour in the first half and after only a few minutes Anderson passed to Stevenson who dropped a goal down wind, the only score of the game. Later in the half Holms had to go off with an injury and Boswell took his place on the wing. Ireland made a stirring late rally, but Scotland held them out.

 37 INTERNATIONAL CHAMPIONSHIP 1890 WALES

Cardiff Arms Park · Saturday 1 February 1890 · Won 8–2

SCOTLAND †G MacGregor (*Cambridge U*); WE Maclagan* (*London Scot*), HJ Stevenson (*Edinburgh Acs*), GR Wilson (*Royal HSFP*); CE Orr (*W of Scot*), DG Anderson (*London Scot*); W Auld (*W of Scot*), JD Boswell (*W of Scot*), †A Dalgleish (*Gala*), A Duke (*Royal HSFP*), †FWJ Goodhue (*London Scot*), MC McEwan (*Edinburgh Acs*), †I McIntyre (*Edinburgh Wdrs*), RG Macmillan (*W of Scot*), JE Orr (*W of Scot*)

WALES WJ Bancroft (*Swansea*); CJ Thomas (*Newport*), AJ Gould (*Newport*), RM Garrett (*Penarth*), DPM Lloyd (*Llanelli*), E James (*Swansea*), WT Stadden (*Cardiff*); AF Bland (*Cardiff*), WA Bowen (*Swansea*), WR Evans (*Swansea*), J Hannan (*Newport*), AF Hill* (*Cardiff*), J Meredith (*Swansea*), S Thomas (*Llanelli*), WEO Williams (*Cardiff*)

REFEREE A McAllister (*Ireland*)

SCORING Anderson, try (2–0); Duke, try (4–0); Maclagan, try (6–0); McEwan, con (8–0) (half-time) Gould, try (8–2)

The weather was dull and the ground was in deplorable condition but the rain held off. The nine-man Scottish pack largely held the upper-hand although the Welsh backs were full of running and always threatening. The Scots made an early rush and Anderson scored an unconverted try, Scotland's first under the new points scoring system. Shortly afterwards, the forwards dribbled over the Welsh line for a second score, which was credited to Duke although several players fell on the ball at once. Close to the interval Maclagan missed a drop goal attempt, but from the restart he made a dodging run to score wide out and McEwan landed the awkward conversion. In the second half, both sides had spells of pressure, but the defences were strong. The Welsh forwards made a strong dribbling rush which Anderson stopped courageously.

From the scrum Garrett broke through before passing to Gould who just made it to the corner with Maclagan hanging onto him.

38   INTERNATIONAL CHAMPIONSHIP 1890   IRELAND

Raeburn Place · Saturday 22 February 1890 · Won 5–0

SCOTLAND G MacGregor (*Cambridge U*); WE Maclagan (*London Scot*), HJ Stevenson (*Edinburgh Acs*), GR Wilson (*Royal HSFP*); CE Orr (*W of Scot*), DG Anderson (*London Scot*); JD Boswell (*W of Scot*), A Duke (*Royal HSFP*), FWJ Goodhue (*London Scot*), HT Ker (*Glasgow Acs*), MC McEwan* (*Edinburgh Acs*), I MacIntyre (*Edinburgh Wdrs*), RG Macmillan (*W of Scot*), DS Morton (*W of Scot*), JE Orr (*W of Scot*)

IRELAND HP Gifford (*Wdrs*); RW Dunlop (*Dublin U*), RW Johnstone (*Dublin U*), T Edwards (*Lansdowne*); RG Warren* (*Lansdowne*), AC McDonnell (*Dublin U*); WJN Davis (*Bessbrook*), EF Doran (*Lansdowne*), EG Forest (*Wdrs*), J Moffatt (*Belfast Alb*), JH O'Conor (*Bective Rgrs*), HA Richey (*Dublin U*), J Roche (*Wdrs*), R Stevenson (*Dungannon*), J Waites (*Bective Rgrs*)

REFEREE HL Ashmore (*England*)

SCORING Boswell, drop (3–0); JE Orr, try (5–0) (half-time)

On a fine afternoon, much of the play took place in midfield and was largely confined to the forwards. Wilson hacked on a loose pass which took play to the Irish line and Boswell kicked one of his trademark drop goals. Stevenson, who was in great form, almost scored a try, but he was collared on the Irish line and from the ensuing maul-in-goal Ireland stole the ball. The only try of the game came after a good handling movement by the Scottish backs although the final pass to Jack Orr may have been forward. The Irish improved in the second half and made several promising attacks, but there was no further scoring.

39   INTERNATIONAL CHAMPIONSHIP 1890   ENGLAND

Raeburn Place · Saturday 1 March 1890 · Lost 0–6

SCOTLAND G MacGregor (*Cambridge U*); WE Maclagan* (*London Scot*), HJ Stevenson (*Edinburgh Acs*), GR Wilson (*Royal HSFP*); CE Orr (*W of Scot*), DG Anderson (*London Scot*); JD Boswell (*W of Scot*), A Dalgleish (*Gala*), FWJ Goodhue (*London Scot*), HT Ker (*Glasgow Acs*), MC McEwan (*Edinburgh Acs*), I Macintyre (*Edinburgh Wdrs*), RG Macmillan (*W of Scot*), DS Morton (*W of Scot*), JE Orr (*W of Scot*)

ENGLAND WG Mitchell (*Richmond*); PH Morrison (*Cambridge U*), RL Aston (*Cambridge U*), JW Dyson (*Huddersfield*); MT Scott (*Northern*), FH Fox* (*Wellington*); H Bedford (*Morley*), F Evershed (*Burton*), JL Hickson (*Bradford*), E Holmes (*Manningham*), D Jowett (*Heckmondwike*), A Robinson (*Blackheath*), JH Rogers (*Moseley*), JT Toothill (*Bradford*), SMJ Woods (*Cambridge U*)

REFEREE J Chambers (*Ireland*)

SCORING Evershed, try (0–2) (half-time) Dyson, try (0–4); Jowett, con (0–6)

The resumption of fixtures with England saw a well-contested match that was played on a wintery afternoon. The visiting forwards were bolstered by a hard core of rugged

Yorkshire players and they combined together effectively. The English backs were also a good outfit and produced some exciting handling movements and defended well. Aston, a long-legged, straight-running centre, was outstanding and the two English wings, Morrison and Dyson, were very fast. Scotland fought hard and Stevenson was prominent in all aspects, but their teamwork was not as good and a couple of the players were not fully fit. Play was fairly even until Evershed beat several half-hearted tackles on an unstoppable run to the line. In the second half, Aston put the Dyson away up the touchline and nobody could catch him as he sprinted to the corner. Jowett kicked a fine conversion and at the finish the sporting crowd warmly applauded England as worthy winners.

40   INTERNATIONAL CHAMPIONSHIP 1891   WALES

Raeburn Place · Saturday 7 February 1891 · Won 15–0

SCOTLAND HJ Stevenson (*Edinburgh Acs*); †W Neilson (*Merchiston*), G MacGregor (*Cambridge U*), †PR Clauss (*Oxford U*); CE Orr (*W of Scot*), DG Anderson (*London Scot*); JD Boswell (*W of Scot*), A Dalgleish (*Gala*), FWJ Goodhue (*London Scot*), †HTO Leggatt (*Watsonians*), MC McEwan* (*Edinburgh Acs*), I Mcintyre (*Edinburgh Wdrs*), RG Macmillan (*London Scot*), †GT Neilson (*W of Scot*), JE Orr (*W of Scot*)

WALES WJ Bancroft (*Swansea*); RM Garrett (*Penarth*), D Gwynn (*Swansea*), G Thomas (*Newport*), WM McCutcheon (*Swansea*); RB Sweet-Escott (*Cardiff*), HM Ingledew (*Cardiff*); P Bennett (*Cardiff Harlequins*), WA Bowen (*Swansea*), DJ Daniel (*Llanelli*), TC Graham (*Newport*), SH Nicholls (*Cardiff*), WR Evans (*Swansea*), RL Thomas (*Llanelli*), WH Thomas* (*Llanelli*)

REFEREE HL Ashmore (*England*)

SCORING CE Orr, try (1–0); JE Orr, try (2–0); Goodhue, try (3–0); Clauss, try (4–0) (half-time) W Neilson, drop (7–0); Leggatt, try (8–0); Gordon, con (10-0); Stevenson, drop (13–0); Clauss, try (14–0); Boswell, try (15–0)

Harry Stevenson, who had played at centre for the last three years, was selected at full-back and Gregor McGregor, a more attacking player, took his place in midfield. Both players were outstanding in a fine Scottish display. The nine-man Scottish pack completely overwhelmed their opponents and gave the backs a plentiful supply of ball. Anderson had a good match at the heels of his rampant pack, McGregor used his wings effectively and Stevenson was solid in defence. The Scots scored four unconverted tries in the first half, the Orr brothers, Charles and Jack, completing a family double for the first two. Then after a rush to the Welsh line, Anderson and Goodhue touched down simultaneously, the latter being credited with the score. Towards the interval McGregor made a strong run before giving a scoring pass to Clauss. In the second half, new wing Willie Neilson dropped a magnificent goal and straightaway Goodhue put Leggatt in for a try. Stevenson dropped a goal from a scrum and towards the finish Clauss and Boswell scored unconverted tries against a rapidly-tiring defence. Gordon also had a try disallowed for being offside.

Ballynafeigh, Belfast · Saturday 21 February 1891 · Won 14–0

SCOTLAND HJ Stevenson (*Edinburgh Acs*); PR Clauss (*Oxford U*), G MacGregor (*Cambridge U*),GR Wilson (*Royal HSFP*); CE Orr (*W of Scot*), †W Wotherspoon (*Cambridge U*); JD Boswell (*W of Scot*), A Dalgleish (*Gala*), †WR Gibson (*Royal HSFP*), FWJ Goodhue (*London Scot*), HTO Leggatt (*Watsonians*), MC McEwan* (*Edinburgh Acs*), I McIntyre (*Edinburgh Wdrs*), GT Neilson (*W of Scot*), JE Orr (*W of Scot*)

IRELAND DB Walkington* (*NIFC*); HG Wells (*Bective Rgrs*), S Lee (*NIFC*), RW Dunlop (*NIFC*); BB Tuke (*Bective Rgrs*), ED Cameron (*Bective Rgrs*); G Collopy (*Bective Rgrs*), WJN Davis (*Bessbrook*), EF Fraser (*Bective Rgrs*), JN Lytle (*NIFC*), J Moffatt (*Belfast Alb*), LC Nash (*QC Cork*), JH O'Conor (*Bective Rgrs*), J Roche (*Wdrs*), RD Stokes (*QC Cork*)

REFEREE G Rowland Hill (*England*)

SCORING Wotherspoon, try (1–0); Boswell, con (3–0); Clauss, try (4–0); McEwan, drop (7–0) (half-time) Wotherspoon, try (8–0); Boswell, con (10–0); Wotherspoon, try (11–0); MacGregor, try (12–0); Boswell, con (14–0)

Played in fine weather before a crowd of about 3,000 people, Scotland were convincing winners of an open match that had lots of action. The Scottish forwards kept a tight grip and their handling was very effective. Ireland played with plenty of spirit and had some scoring chances, but they were largely outclassed. In the first half, McGregor made a strong burst before passing to Wotherspoon, the Scottish quarter-back, who scored a try. Soon afterwards, Clauss had an elusive run for a second try and McEwan, snatching some loose possession, dropped a goal. Play continued in a similar fashion in the second half. Wotherspoon completed his hat-trick before Wells, the Irish wing, ran the length of the field and touched down only to be recalled for an infringement. Just before the finish McGregor slipped through for a try and Boswell converted.

Athletic Ground, Richmond · Saturday 7 March 1891 · Won 9–3

SCOTLAND HJ Stevenson (*Edinburgh Acs*); PR Clauss (*Oxford U*), G MacGregor (*Cambridge U*), W Neilson (*Merchiston*); CE Orr (*W of Scot*), DG Anderson (*London Scot*); JD Boswell (*W of Scot*), WR Gibson (*Royal HSFP*), FWJ Goodhue (*London Scot*), HTO Leggatt (*Watsonians*), MC McEwan* (*Edinburgh Acs*), I McIntyre (*Edinburgh Wdrs*), RG Macmillan (*London Scot*), GT Neilson (*W of Scot*), JE Orr (*W of Scot*)

ENGLAND WG Mitchell (*Richmond*); P Christopherson (*Blackheath*), FHR Alderson* (*Hartlepool Rovers*), RE Lockwood (*Heckmondwike*); J Berry (*Tyldesley*), WRM Leake (*Harlequins*); E Bonham-Carter (*Oxford U*), RTD Budworth (*Blackheath*), D Jowett (*Heckmondwike*), T Kent (*Salford*), EHG North (*Oxford U*), J Richards (*Bradford*), JH Rogers (*Moseley*), RP Wilson (*Liverpool OB*), SMJ Woods (*Cambridge U*)

REFEREE J Chambers (*Ireland*)

SCORING Clauss, drop (3–0) (half-time) JE Orr, try (4–0); MacGregor, con (6–0); W Neilson, try (7–0); Macgregor, con (9–0); Lockwood, try (9–1); Alderson, con (9–3)

This Scottish team won the Triple Crown against England in March 1891.
SRU

A rampant Scotland clinched their first Triple Crown in emphatic style. The Scottish forwards were full of dash and vigour, and denied the English backs much possession. Anderson and Orr, the Scottish quarter-backs, played astutely and the three-quarters were always dangerous. By contrast, Arthur Budd, the great English forward of the 1870s, described this as 'the very worst display which any English team ever gave'. Boswell missed an early penalty attempt and after about eight minutes Clauss dropped a goal from in front of the posts, although he might just as easily have scored a try. England had a spell of pressure towards the end of the half, but the Scottish defence was firm. At one point Lockwood crossed the line only to be recalled for an infringement. Soon after the restart, a good passing movement put Jack Orr away down the left and he sprinted away to the posts. England seemed to lose heart after this and Scotland dominated the rest of the game. Anderson and McGregor combined to put Willie Neilson over for a try. Lockwood scored a late consolation try for a sorry-looking England.

43 INTERNATIONAL CHAMPIONSHIP 1892   WALES

St Helen's, Swansea · Saturday 6 February 1892 · Won 7–2

SCOTLAND HJ Stevenson (*Edinburgh Acs*); W Neilson (*Cambridge U*), †GT Campbell (*London Scot*), PR Clauss (*Oxford U*); CE Orr* (*W of Scot*), DG Anderson (*London Scot*); JD Boswell (*W of Scot*), A Dalgleish (*Gala*), WR Gibson (*Royal HSFP*), FWJ Goodhue (*London Scot*), HTO Leggatt (*Watsonians*), RG Macmillan (*London Scot*), †JN Millar (*W of Scot*), GT Neilson (*W of Scot*), JE Orr (*W of Scot*)

WALES WJ Bancroft (*Swansea*); TW Pearson (*Cardiff*) AJ Gould* (*Newport*), J Conway Rees (*Llanelli*), W McCutcheon (*Swansea*); D James (*Swansea*), E James (*Swansea*); P Bennett (*Cardiff Harlequins*), AW Boucher (*Newport*), JT Deacon (*Swansea*), TC Graham (*Newport*), J Hannan (*Newport*), FM Mills (*Swansea*), CB Nicholl (*Llanelli*), WH Watts (*Newport*)

REFEREE JR Hodgson (*England*)

SCORING Hannan, try (0–2); Boswell, try (2–2); Campbell, try (4–2); Boswell, con (7–2) (half-time)

The pitch was sodden after heavy rain and undoubtedly this favoured the heavier Scottish pack. Nevertheless this was a stubbornly contested match with lots of movement and incident. Wales, who played with four three-quarters, opened the scoring when the forwards made a dribbling rush and Hannan raced onto a kick ahead to touch down. Straight from the restart, the Scots charged into Welsh territory and after several attempts Boswell burst through and scored. Close to the interval, Anderson made a break and passed to Campbell who scored a try at the posts. In the second half, play swung from end-to-end, but there was no further scoring.

44 — INTERNATIONAL CHAMPIONSHIP 1892 — IRELAND

Raeburn Place · Saturday 20 February 1892 · Won 2–0

SCOTLAND HJ Stevenson (*Edinburgh Acs*); GT Campbell (*London Scot*), W Neilson (*Cambridge U*), †JC Woodburn (*Kelvinside Acs*); CE Orr* (*W of Scot*), W Wotherspoon (*Cambridge U*); JD Boswell (*W of Scot*), WR Gibson (*Royal HSFP*), FWJ Goodhue (*London Scot*), †NF Henderson (*London Scot*), HTO Leggatt (*Watsonians*), WA Macdonald (*Glasgow U*), RG Macmillan (*London Scot*), JN Millar (*W of Scot*), JE Orr (*W of Scot*)

IRELAND T Peel (*Bective Rgrs*); RW Dunlop (*Dublin U*), S Lee (*NIFC*), W Gardiner (*NIFC*); T Thornhill (*Wdrs*), FE Davies (*Lansdowne*); AD Clinch (*Dublin U*), G Collopy (*Bective Rgrs*) WJN Davis (*Edinburgh U*), EF Frazer (*Bective Rgrs*), TJ Johnston (*QC Belfast*), VC le Fanu* (*Lansdowne*), CV Rooke (*Dublin U*), AK Wallis (*Wdrs*), EJ Walsh (*Lansdowne*)

REFEREE HL Ashmore (*England*)

SCORING Millar, try (2–0) (half-time)

The pitch was heavy underfoot and the closing stages were played in a blinding snow storm that made the action nearly invisible. Scotland were slightly fortunate to win against a determined Irish side although neither side was at full strength because of injuries and withdrawals. This was a game of limited quality and mainly a strenuous forward battle, although Thornhill, the Irish quarter-back, had some dangerous runs. Scotland defended soundly and Stevenson at full-back kicked and tackled well. Scotland made a slow start, but gradually worked their way into contention. Boswell had a drop goal disallowed before Millar scored the only try of the match after a lineout near the Irish line. Both sides had their moments in attack, but could not make the vital breakthrough.

Raeburn Place · Saturday 5 March 1892 · Lost 0–5

SCOTLAND HJ Stevenson (*Edinburgh Acs*); PR Clauss (*Oxford U*), W Neilson (*Cambridge U*), GT Campbell (*London Scot*); CE Orr* (*W of Scot*), DG Anderson (*London Scot*); JD Boswell (*W of Scot*), WR Gibson (*Royal HSFP*), FWJ Goodhue (*London Scot*), WA Macdonald (*Glasgow U*), MC McEwan (*Edinburgh Acs*), RG Macmillan (*London Scot*), JN Millar (*W of Scot*), GT Neilson (*W of Scot*), JE Orr (*W of Scot*)

ENGLAND T Coop (*Leigh*); RE Lockwood (*Heckmondwike*), FHR Alderson* (*Hartlepool Rov*), JW Dyson (*Huddersfield*); A Briggs (*Bradford*), H Varley (*Liversedge*); H Bradshaw (*Bramley*), WE Bromet (*Todcaster*), E Bullough (*Wigan*), F Evershed (*Blackheath*), T Kent (*Salford*), W Nichol (*Brighouse Rgrs*), JT Toothill (*Bradford*), SMJ Woods (*Wellington*), W Yiend (*Hartlepool Rov*)

REFEREE RG Warren (*Ireland*)

SCORING Bromet, try (0–3); Lockwood, con (0–5) (half-time)

After the rout of their pack the previous year, England had stiffened their side by including 13 players from northern clubs who were renowned for their rugged approach. The result was a tough and uncompromising encounter mainly confined to the forwards. Play was evenly contested and Scotland were a little unfortunate not to win as several marginal decisions went against them. Some onlookers felt that the referee had given England considerable leniency, especially in applying the offside law, and after the match indignant letters appeared in the Scottish press about his handling of the game. Playing in fine conditions, both sides had their moments in attack, but the

An artist's impression from the weekly magazine *Black and White* of the England match at Raeburn Place in 1892. The newly-built tenements at Comely Bank Road are visible in the background and some cheapskate spectators get a free view of the match from the roof of the local bus.

defences were very good. Bromet scored the only try of the game after about 30 minutes and Lockwood added the simple conversion. The latter was the outstanding player on the English side and for Scotland Stevenson was good in all aspects.

46   INTERNATIONAL CHAMPIONSHIP 1893   WALES

Raeburn Place · Saturday 4 February 1893 · Lost 0–9

SCOTLAND AW Cameron (*Watsonians*); †DD Robertson (*Cambridge U*), G MacGregor (*London Scot*), †JJ Gowans (*Cambridge U*); †RC Greig (*Glasgow Acs*), W Wotherspoon (*W of Scot*); †WB Cownie (*Watsonians*), A Dalgleish (*Gala*), WR Gibson (*Royal HSFP*), †TL Hendry (*Clydesdale*), HTO Leggatt (*Watsonians*), RG Macmillan* (*London Scot*), †HF Menzies (*W of Scot*), JN Millar (*W of Scot*), GT Neilson (*W of Scot*)

WALES WJ Bancroft (*Swansea*); NW Biggs (*Cardiff*), AJ Gould* (*Newport*), GH Gould (*Newport*), WM McCutcheon (*Swansea*); FC Parfitt (*Newport*), HP Phillips (*Newport*); AW Boucher (*Newport*), HT Day (*Newport*), TC Graham (*Newport*), J Hannan (*Newport*), AF Hill (*Cardiff*), FM Mills (*Swansea*), CB Nicholl (*Llanelli*), WH Watts (*Newport*)

REFEREE WH Humphreys (*England*)

SCORING No scoring in the first half. GH Gould, try (0–2); Biggs, try (0–4); Bancroft, pen (0–7); McCutcheon, try (0–9)

Scotland were under-strength and a little out of condition as Wales, with nine players from Newport, won on Scottish soil for the first time. On a bright and windy day, the virtues of the Welsh four three-quarters system were clearly apparent and the visitors made many spectacular runs and passing movements. Scotland, in contrast, played their traditional forward game and, although they had spells of pressure, they were unable to pierce the Welsh defence. There was no scoring in the first half and it was generally expected that Wales would fade away as the game wore on. Instead, play became more open and Wales ran away with the match. The great Welsh centre Arthur Gould controlled much of the play and one good movement by the Welsh backs led to an unconverted try by Gould's younger brother Bert, the first ever scored by a Welshman in Scotland. The home side almost crossed after a rush by the forwards and then Biggs, a fast wing, scored a try for Wales. Bancroft failed with the conversion attempt and then drop kicked a goal from a penalty award. Later, another good move by the Welsh backs gave McCutcheon enough space to run round behind the posts and firmly plant the ball down.

47   INTERNATIONAL CHAMPIONSHIP 1893   IRELAND

Ballynafeigh, Belfast · Saturday 20 February 1893 · Drawn 0–0

SCOTLAND HJ Stevenson (*Edinburgh Acs*); GT Campbell (*London Scot*), G MacGregor (*London Scot*), W Neilson (*Cambridge U*); †JW Simpson (*Royal HSFP*), †WP Donaldson (*Oxford U*); †JM Bishop (*Glasgow Acs*), JD Boswell* (*W of Scot*), WB Cownie (*Watsonians*), †D Fisher (*W of Scot*), †JR Ford (*Gala*), WR Gibson (*Royal HSFP*), TL Hendry (*Clydesdale*), HF Menzies (*W of Scot*), JE Orr (*W of Scot*)

IRELAND S Gardiner (*Belfast Alb*); W Gardiner (*NIFC*), S Lee* (*NIFC*), LH Gwynn (*Dublin U*); WS Brown (*Dublin U*), FE Davies (*Lansdowne*); EG Forrest (*Wdrs*), H Forrest (*Wdrs*), TJ Johnston (*QC Belfast*), JS Jameson (*Lansdowne*), H Lindsay (*Dublin U*), B O'Brien (*Derry*), JH O'Conor (*Bective Rgrs*), CV O'Rooke (*Dublin U*), R Stevenson (*Dungannon*)

REFEREE G Rowland Hill (*England*)

The pitch was in a poor condition because of heavy rain and by the end of the first half it was little more than a quagmire. The result was a hard forward battle with little back play. The Irish forwards held a definite edge, but lacked composure at crucial moments and several scoring chances were lost. Scottish forward Jack Orr was withdrawn from the pack and played as an extra back to stop the Irish charges. For Scotland, Campbell and Neilson defended courageously, Donaldson was active at quarter-back and amongst the forwards Boswell and Menzies worked tirelessly.

48　　INTERNATIONAL CHAMPIONSHIP 1893　　ENGLAND

Headingley, Leeds · Saturday 4 March 1893 · Won 8–0

SCOTLAND HJ Stevenson (*Edinburgh Acs*); GT Campbell (*London Scot*), G MacGregor (*London Scot*), W Neilson (*Cambridge U*); JW Simpson (*Royal HSFP*), W Wotherspoon (*W of Scot*); JD Boswell* (*W of Scot*), WB Cownie (*Watsonians*), †RS Davidson (*Royal HSFP*), WR Gibson (*Royal HSFP*), TL Hendry (*Clydesdale*), HTO Leggatt (*Watsonians*), RG Macmillan (*London Scot*), JE Orr (*W of Scot*), †TM Scott (*Melrose*)

ENGLAND WG Mitchell (*Richmond*); JW Dyson (*Huddersfield*), AE Stoddart* (*Blackheath*), FP Jones (*New Brighton*); H Duckett (*Bradford*), CM Wells (*Cambridge U*); H Bradshaw (*Bramley*), T Broadley (*Bingley*), WE Bromet (*Richmond*), F Evershed (*Burton*), LJ Percival (*Rugby*), JJ Robertson (*Cambridge U*), F Soane (*Bath*), JT Toothill (*Bradford*), W Yiend (*Hartlepool Rov*)

REFEREE W Wilkins (*Wales*)

SCORING Boswell, drop (4–0) (half-time) Campbell, drop (8–0)

Scotland were in great form and deserved to win by more than two drop goals. The Scottish forwards were formidable in tight play and their footwork was devastating. Simpson and Wotherspoon, the Scottish quarter-backs, linked well and the three-quarters were full of enterprise. Conditions were fine although there was a strong breeze and the pitch was slippery. Soon after the start, a drop goal attempt by Neilson hit one of the uprights and seemed to go over, but the referee did not allow the score. Scotland had most of the game although England defended well and had a couple of breakouts. Towards the end of the half, Boswell landed one of his trademark drop goals to give the Scots a well deserved lead. After the resumption, Campbell took the ball from a scrum and dropped a goal. There was no further scoring although both sides had their moments in attack.

Rodney Parade, Newport · Saturday 3 February 1894 · Lost 0–7

SCOTLAND †J Rogerson (*Kelvinside Acs*); GT Campbell (*London Scot*), G MacGregor (*London Scot*), JJ Gowans (*Cambridge U*), †HTS Gedge (*London Scot*); W Wotherspoon (*W of Scot*), JW Simpson (*Royal HSFP*); WB Cownie (*Watsonians*), A Dalgleish (*Gala*), WR Gibson (*Royal HSFP*), †WMC McEwan (*Edinburgh Acad*); RG Macmillan* (*London Scot*), HF Menzies (*W of Scot*), GT Neilson (*W of Scot*), †JB Wright (*Watsonians*)

WALES WJ Bancroft (*Swansea*); TW Pearson (*Cardiff*), D Fitzgerald (*Cardiff*), AJ Gould* (*Newport*), WL Thomas (*Newport*); FC Parfitt (*Newport*), HP Phillips (*Newport*); DJ Daniel (*Llanelli*), HT Day (*Newport*), TC Graham (*Newport*), J Hannan (*Newport*), AF Hill (*Cardiff*), FM Mills (*Swansea*), CB Nicholl (*Llanelli & Cambridge U*), WH Watts (*Newport*)

REFEREE EB Holmes (*England*)

SCORING Fitzgerald, try (0–3) (half-time) Fitzgerald, drop (0–7)

Scotland adopted the four three-quarter system for the first time. The side was weakened by several withdrawals, including Boswell, the captain-elect, whilst McEwan, who had a fine match, was still a schoolboy at Edinburgh Academy. This was a spirited encounter between two hard-working packs. Scotland went about their task with pluck and determination, but Wales held a definite advantage up front and their backs were given plenty of scope in attack. Playing on a soft ground, Scotland started strongly and had the ball over the Welsh line forcing the home side to touchdown. Soon however, the Welshmen began to press and after one move Fitzgerald, the Cardiff centre, scored an unconverted try. The rest of the play was quite even and both sides were near to scoring on several occasions. In the second half, Fitzgerald dropped a goal for Wales and although the Scots made a great final flourish they could not break through.

Lansdowne Road, Dublin · Saturday 24 February 1894 · Lost 0–5

SCOTLAND AW Cameron (*Watsonians*); GT Campbell (*London Scot*), G MacGregor (*London Scot*), W Wotherspoon (*W of Scot*), HTS Gedge (*Edinburgh Wdrs*); JW Simpson (*Royal HSFP*), WP Donaldson (*Oxford U*); †AH Anderson (*Glasgow Acs*), JD Boswell* (*W of Scot*), WB Cownie (*Watsonians*), A Dalgleish (*Gala*), WR Gibson (*Royal HSFP*), HTO Leggatt (*Watsonians*), RG Macmillan (*London Scot*), GT Neilson (*W of Scot*)

IRELAND PJ Grant (*Bective Rgrs*); W Gardiner (*NIFC*), S Lee (*NIFC*), LH Gwynn (*Dublin U*), HG Wells (*Bective Rgrs*); WS Brown (*Dublin U*), BB Tuke (*Bective Rgrs*); ATW Bond (*Derry*), TJ Crean (*Wdrs*), EG Forrest* (*Wdrs*), H Lindsay (*Dublin U*), JH Lytle (*NIFC*), JN Lytle (*NIFC*), JH O'Conor (*Bective Rgrs*), CV Rooke (*Dublin U*)

REFEREE HL Ashmore (*England*)

SCORING No scoring in the first half. Wells, try (0–3); Lytle, con (0–5)

There was heavy rain before kick-off and the pitch was sodden, but there was lots of entertainment for the large and enthusiastic crowd to enjoy. The Irish forwards were in fine form and Tuke gave his backs plenty of ball. The Scots, who were without several key players, defended courageously and the forwards were always ready to counter-attack. Playing with the wind in their favour, Ireland had the better of the first half. Curiously, during the interval the two captains were introduced to the Lord Lieutenant of Ireland, who, in *The Scotsman*'s words, 'chatted with them for a few minutes while the spectators waxed impatient'. Both sides had chances in the second half and Boswell, who was renowned for the snap drop shot, missed two attempts at goal. The Irish had greater stamina and some of the Scots faded badly towards the finish. Just when it seemed that the match would end in a draw, Tuke broke away and Wells ran-in for the winning score, much to the delight of the ecstatic home crowd.

51   INTERNATIONAL CHAMPIONSHIP 1894   ENGLAND

Raeburn Place · Saturday 17 March 1894 · Won 6–0

SCOTLAND G MacGregor (*London Scot*); GT Campbell (*London Scot*), W Neilson (*Cambridge U*),HTS Gedge (*Edinburgh Wdrs*), JJ Gowans (*Cambridge U*); W Wotherspoon (*W of Scot*), JW Simpson (*Royal HSFP*); JD Boswell* (*W of Scot*), WB Cownie (*Watsonians*), WR Gibson (*Royal HSFP*), HTO Leggatt (*Watsonians*), WMC McEwan (*Edinburgh Acad*), RG Macmillan (*London Scot*), HF Menzies (*W of Scot*), †WG Neilson (*Merchiston Sch*)

ENGLAND JF Byrne (*Moseley*); CA Hooper (*Middlesex Wdrs*), WJ Jackson (*Halifax*), S Morfitt (*West Hartlepool*), F Firth (*Halifax*); EW Taylor* (*Rockcliff*), CM Wells (*Harlequins*); A Allport (*Blackheath*), H Bradshaw (*Bramley*), T Broadley (*Bingley*), AE Elliot (*St Thomas's H*), J Hall (*North Durham*), F Soane (*Bath*), H Speed (*Castleford*), W Walton (*Castleford*)

An attractive menu for the dinner after the England match in 1894. *RFU Museum of Rugby*

REFEREE W Wilkins (*Wales*)

SCORING No scoring in the first half. Boswell, try (3–0); Boswell, try (6–0)

Scotland fielded two schoolboys in the pack: Willie McEwan and Gordon Neilson, who came in for his injured brother George. On a perfect day, Scotland deservedly won their first home victory over England since 1877. The Scottish forwards were largely in control and much of the play took place inside the English 25. The Scottish backs shone individually, but they did not combine well and the English defence was mostly sound. Scotland played with a strong sun behind them in the first half. Gowans made two good runs that almost brought tries, Leggatt was held-up on the line and a couple of drop kicks just missed. Wotherspoon, the Scottish quarter-back, hurt his arm and had to leave the field temporarily. He resumed in the second half, but moved to the left wing forcing a reorganisation of the Scottish back division. After the break, the Scots again missed several drop shots and eventually Boswell forced his way over for a try. Towards the finish, Boswell scored a second to complete a good win for the Scots.

52   INTERNATIONAL CHAMPIONSHIP 1895   WALES

Raeburn Place · Saturday 26 January 1895 · Won 5–4

SCOTLAND †AR Smith (*Oxford U*); JJ Gowans (*London Scot*), GT Campbell (*London Scot*), W Neilson (*London Scot*), †R Welsh (*Watsonians*); JW Simpson (*Royal HSFP*), †M Elliot (*Hawick*); WB Cownie (*Watsonians*), †JH Dods (*Edinburgh Acs*), WR Gibson* (*Royal HSFP*), WMC McEwan (*Edinburgh Acs*), RG Macmillan (*London Scot*), GT Neilson (*W of Scot*), T Scott (*Hawick*), †HO Smith (*Watsonians*)

WALES WJ Bancroft (*Swansea*); TW Pearson (*Cardiff*), AJ Gould* (*Newport*), O Badger (*Llanelli*), E Lloyd (*Llanelli*); FC Parfitt (*Newport*), SH Biggs (*Cardiff*); AW Boucher (*Newport*), EE George (*Pontypridd*), TC Graham (*Newport*), J Hannan (*Newport*), FM Mills (*Cardiff*), CB Nicholl (*Llanelli*), H Packer (*Newport*), TR Pook (*Newport*)

REFEREE EB Holmes (*England*)

SCORING No scoring in the first half. Gowans, try (3–0); HO Smith, con (5–0); Bancroft, drop (5–4)

It is doubtful if this match should have taken place because the country was in the grip of freezing conditions and the pitch was barely fit for play. Protective straw was removed just before the start but the northern end of the ground was frozen. The Welshmen refused to play until the pitch was shortened by some 18 yards and even then the players found it difficult to hold their footing. Despite the conditions, there was plenty of open play and incident. Scotland deserved to win thanks to a good display by the forwards who were the better combination. Simpson and Elliot, the Scottish half-backs, played cleverly and kept a tight grip on the game. Both sides had promising attacks in the first half, but were unable to break through. After the break, Gowans scored a try and Smith converted from an awkward angle. Wales pressed heavily and Smith, the Scottish full-back, saved several times on his own line. Then McEwan made a lofty clearing kick which was collected by Bancroft who ran into midfield and dropped a goal. In an exciting finish, Gould made a great break but slipped on the icy surface, Gowans also had a promising run and Bancroft narrowly missed another shot at goal.

53   INTERNATIONAL CHAMPIONSHIP 1895   IRELAND

Raeburn Place · Saturday 2 March 1895 · Won 6–0

SCOTLAND AR Smith (*Oxford U*); JJ Gowans (*London Scot*), GT Campbell (*London Scot*), W Neilson (*London Scot*), R Welsh (*Watsonians*); JW Simpson (*Royal HSFP*), PR Clauss (*Birkenhead Park*); WB Cownie (*Watsonians*), JH Dods (*Edinburgh Acs*), WR Gibson (*Royal HSFP*), TL Hendry (*Clydesdale*), RG Macmillan* (*London Scot*), JN Millar (*W of Scot*), GT Neilson (*W of Scot*), TM Scott (*Hawick*)

IRELAND J Fulton (*NIFC*); W Gardiner (*NIFC*), JT Magee (*Bective Rgrs*), A Montgomery (*NIFC*), J O'Connor (*Garryowen*); LM Magee (*Bective Rgrs*), BB Tuke (*Bective Rgrs*); AD Clinch (*Wdrs*), TJ Crean (*Wdrs*), WJN Davis (*Edinburgh U*), MS Egan (*Garryowen*), HC McCoull (*Belfast Alb*), EH McIlwaine (*NIFC*), W O'Sullivan (*QC Cork*), CV Rooke* (*Monkstown*)

REFEREE HL Ashmore (*England*)

SCORING No scoring in the first half. Welsh, try (3–0); Campbell, try (6–0).

This match was postponed from January because of frost and both sides were forced to make changes because of a flu epidemic. The crowd was very small, but conditions were good. Scotland were the better side although the Irish defence was very strong. In the first half, the Scottish forwards made their trademark rushes and Tom Scott twice narrowly missed kicks at goal. Ireland started the second half purposefully and Magee made a long run before Smith hunted him down. Neilson missed a drop goal and then the Scots made a great handling move and Welsh scored in the corner. Scott missed the awkward conversion, but from this point Scotland were firmly in control. After another good move, Campbell thundered through the defence and dived underneath the posts. Cownie's conversion cleared the bar, but it was touched in flight and therefore disallowed.

---

54   INTERNATIONAL CHAMPIONSHIP 1895   ENGLAND

Athletic Ground, Richmond · Saturday 9 March 1895 · Won 6–3

SCOTLAND AR Smith (*Oxford U*); R Welsh (*Watsonians*), W Neilson (*London Scot*), JJ Gowans (*London Scot*), GT Campbell (*London Scot*); JW Simpson (*Royal HSFP*), WP Donaldson (*W of Scot*); WB Cownie (*Watsonians*), JH Dods (*Edinburgh Acs*), WR Gibson (*Royal HSFP*), WMC McEwan (*Edinburgh Acs*), RG Macmillan* (*London Scot*), JN Millar (*W of Scot*), GT Neilson (*W of Scot*), TM Scott (*Hawick*)

The Scottish team that beat Wales at Raeburn Place in January 1895. *SRU*

The Scottish team that won the Triple Crown against England in March 1895.

ENGLAND JF Byrne (*Moseley*); WB Thomson (*Blackheath*), EM Baker (*Oxford U*), TH Dobson (*Bradford*), JHC Fegan (*Blackheath*); RHB Cattell (*Moseley*), EW Taylor (*Rockcliff*); WE Bromet (*Richmond*), GM Carey (*Oxford U*), WH Finlinson (*Blackheath*), FMitchell (*Cambridge U*), FO Poole (*Oxford U*), C Thomas (*Barnstaple*), WE Tucker (*Cambridge U*), SMJ Woods* (*Blackheath*)

REFEREE W Wilkins (*Wales*)

SCORING Byrne, pen (0–3); GT Neilson, pen (3–3); GT Neilson, try (6–3) (half-time)

A big crowd saw Scotland clinch the Triple Crown in largely a forward battle. The Scottish pack combined effectively and kept a tight grip on the game so the English backs had few opportunities. Willie Donaldson, the Scottish half-back, did well at the heels of his pack and his accurate kicking kept the Scots on the front foot. The Scottish backs were not often seen in attack, but Smith was solid at full-back. Scotland started purposefully, but after about 15 minutes Byrne kicked a penalty for England. Soon afterwards George Neilson replied in kind, the first penalty goal ever scored by Scotland in an international. The game then degenerated into a series of scrums until Campbell fly-hacked to the English line. Byrne, the English full-back, took too long to clear and Neilson charged down his kick for an unconverted try. In the second half, Scotland were well on top and Donaldson nursed the touchline to good effect. England made a few breaks, but the Scottish defence was firm. Neilson missed a couple of penalty attempts and the Scots almost scored a couple of tries in the last minutes.

54   INTERNATIONAL CHAMPIONSHIP 1896   WALES

Cardiff Arms Park · Saturday 25 January 1896 · Lost 0–6

SCOTLAND AR Smith (*Oxford U*); GT Campbell (*London Scot*), †AB Timms (*Edinburgh Wdrs*),

†T Scott (*Langholm*), R Welsh (*Watsonians*); JW Simpson (*Royal HSFP*), †D Patterson (*Hawick*); †A Balfour (*Watsonians*), †JH Couper (*W of Scot*), JH Dods (*London Scot*), WMC McEwan (*Edinburgh Acs*), †MC Morrison (*Royal HSFP*), GT Neilson* (*W of Scot*), T Scott (*Hawick*), HO Smith (*Watsonians*)

WALES WJ Bancroft (*Swansea*); CA Bowen (*Llanelli*), EG Nicholls (*Cardiff*), AJ Gould* (*Newport*), FH Dauncey (*Newport*); SH Biggs (*Cardiff*), FC Parfitt (*Newport*); W Cope (*Blackheath*), W Davies (*Cardiff*), D Evans (*Penygraig*), J Evans (*Llanelli*), FO Hutchinson (*Neath*), W Morris (*Llanelli*), CB Nicholl (*Llanelli*), H Packer (*Newport*)

REFEREE GH Harnett (*England*)

SCORING No scoring in the first half. Bowen, try (0–3); Gould, try (0–6)

Two of the greatest players in rugby history made their debuts: Scottish forward Mark Morrison and mercurial Welsh centre Gwyn Nicholls. Despite a morning of heavy rain, this was an entertaining and keenly fought encounter that Wales deserved to win. The home side held an advantage in the loose and their backs were full of running and outclassed their rather hapless opponents. Biggs and Parfitt, the Welsh half-backs, were very impressive and they defended courageously at the feet of the Scottish forwards. Both sides had spells of pressure in the first half and Wales came closest to scoring. On one occasion, Packer was over the line but was bundled into touch. Wales continued to press in the second half and after a good movement Bowen scored in the corner. The home side held the upper hand and eventually Gould scored a try after some brilliant combined play. The Scots made a great effort to score in the closing stages, but to no avail.

56 INTERNATIONAL CHAMPIONSHIP 1896 IRELAND

Lansdowne Road, Dubin · Saturday 15 February 1896 · Drawn 0–0

SCOTLAND AR Smith (*Oxford U*); W Neilson (*London Scot*), GT Campbell (*London Scot*), JJ Gowans (*London Scot*), †CJN Fleming (*Edinburgh Wdrs*); JW Simpson (*Royal HSFP*), WP Donaldson (*W of Scot*); A Balfour (*Watsonians*), JH Couper (*W of Scot*), JH Dods (*London Scot*), WMC McEwan (*Edinburgh Acs*), MC Morrison (*Royal HSFP*), GT Neilson* (*W of Scot*), HD Smith (*Watsonians*), †GO Turnbull (*W of Scot*)

IRELAND GH McAllan (*Dungannon*); W Gardiner (*NIFC*), S Lee* (*NIFC*), TH Stevenson (*Edinburgh U*), LQ Bulger (*Dublin U*); LM Magee (*Bective Rgrs*), GG Allen (*Derry*); WG Byron (*NIFC*), AD Clinch (*Wdrs*), TJ Crean (*Wdrs*), H Lindsay (*Armagh*), JH Lytle (*NIFC*), JH O'Conor (*Bective Rgrs*), CV Rooke (*Monkstown*), JW Sealy (*Dublin U*)

REFEREE EB Holmes (*England*)

This was a spirited encounter and a draw was probably a fair result. Both sides dominated at times and missed several scoring chances, including some kicks at goal. The two sets of backs played well and their tackling was very firm. The forward exchanges were evenly balanced and the Irish showed plenty of fire in the loose. Scottish half-back Willie Donaldson was courageous at the feet of the Irish pack and he also made several breaks. In the second half, Allen, the Irish half-back, broke through and looked set to score, but he passed out to Gardiner who missed the ball. Later, Gowans had a strong run before being pushed into touch. Ireland made a desperate late effort to snatch the game, but the Scottish defence was resolute.

Hampden Park, Glasgow · Saturday 14 March 1896 · Won 11–0

SCOTLAND G MacGregor (*London Scot*); HTS Gedge (*London Scot*), GT Campbell (*London Scot*), CJN Fleming (*Edinburgh Wdrs*), JJ Gowans (*London Scot*); M Elliot (*Hawick*), WP Donaldson (*W of Scot*); A Balfour (*Watsonians*), JH Dods (*London Scot*), WMC McEwan (*Edinburgh Acs*), MC Morrison (*Royal HSFP*), GT Neilson (*W of Scot*), TM Scott (*Hawick*), HO Smith (*Watsonians*), GO Turnbull (*W of Scot*)

ENGLAND RW Poole (*Hartlepool Rov*); EF Fookes (*Sowerby Bridge*), J Valentine (*Swinton*), EM Baker (*Oxford U*), S Morfitt (*W Hartlepool*); RHB Cattell (*Blackheath*), CM Wells (*Harlequins*); JH Barron (*Bingley*), T Broadley (*Bingley*), GE Hughes (*Barrow*), E Knowles (*Millom*), F Mitchell* (*Cambridge U*), J Rhodes (*Castleford*), H Speed (*Castleford*), JW Ward (*Castleford*)

REFEREE WM Douglas (*Wales*)

SCORING Gedge, try (3–0) (half-time) Gowans, try (6–0); Fleming, try (9–0); Scott, con (11–0)

By season 1895–96, the Scottish Football Union and the Edinburgh Academy had fallen out about the use of Raeburn Place for international matches. The result was that Scotland were temporarily homeless and this match was played at the second Hampden Park in Glasgow. The ground had been home to Queen's Park Football Club since 1884 and was situated a little to the north of the current stadium. 'The Scottish are a splendid race of footballers,' declared *The Times* in its match report, 'and on Saturday their brilliant victory of a goal and two tries to nothing over England was in every sense the triumph of better-class football.' Playing in ideal conditions, the Scottish forwards dominated throughout, Donaldson and Elliot, the half-backs, were both excellent and the back line showed plenty of attacking flair. Both sides had scoring opportunities in the opening stages and at one point Gedge missed a drop goal attempt. Near the interval, the Scottish backs combined to put Gedge away for a picture-book try near the posts. In the second half, Gedge almost scored his second try after a blunder by Poole. England, with five Yorkshire forwards, never stopped trying, but their backs tended to crab across the field and were easily contained. Gowans and Fleming scored tries in quick succession to clinch a memorable Scottish victory.

Powderhall, Edinburgh · Saturday 20 February 1897 · Won 8–3

SCOTLAND AR Smith (*Oxford U*); GT Campbell (*London Scot*), W Neilson (*London Scot*), CJN Fleming (*Edinburgh Wdrs*), T Scott (*Hawick*); M Elliot (*Hawick*), RC Greig (*Glasgow Acs*); JH Dods (*Edinburgh Acs*), †A Laidlaw (*Hawick*), WMC McEwan (*Edinburgh Acs*), RG Macmillan* (*London Scot*), MC Morrison (*Royal HSFP*), TM Scott (*Hawick*), †RC Stevenson (*London Scot*), GO Turnbull (*London Scot*)

IRELAND PE O'Brien-Butler (*Monkstown*); W Gardiner (*NIFC*), LQ Bulger (*Dublin U*), TH Stevenson (*Belfast Alb*), LH Gwynn (*Dublin U*); LM Magee (*Bective Rgrs*), GG Allen (*Derry*); WG Byron (*NIFC*), AD Clinch (*Wdrs*), EF Forrest* (*Wdrs*), JH Lytle (*NIFC*), JE McIlwaine (*NIFC*), CV Rooke (*Monkstown*), M Ryan (*Rockwell Coll*), J Sealey (*Dublin U*)

Famous Footballers was produced by the *News of the World* in 1895
and featured portraits of the leading footballers of the day, including several Scots.
Clockwise from top left:
AR Smith, JW Simpson, GT Campbell and Paul Clauss.

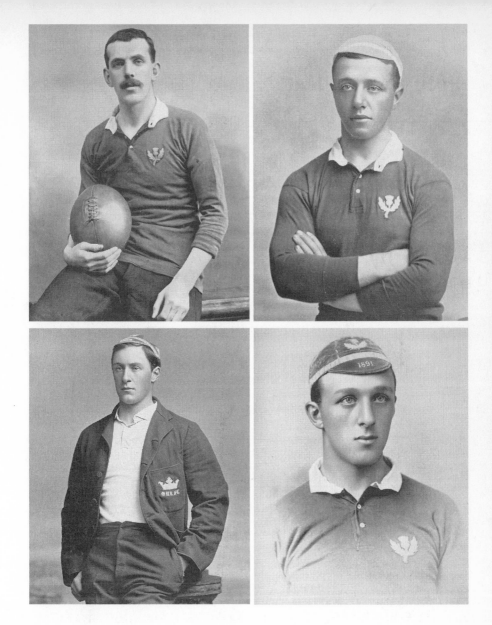

Clockwise from top left:
WB Cownie, W Neilson, G Neilson and WP Donaldson.

REFEREE EB Holmes (*England*)

SCORING Bulger, try (0–3) (half-time) Turnbull, try (3–3); TM Scott, con (5–3); TM Scott, pen (8–3)

There was no Welsh match in 1897 because of allegations of professionalism against Arthur Gould, the famous Welsh player, who was given a testimonial fund at the end of his playing career, much to the abhorrence of the Scottish Football Union. This game was played at the Powderhall stadium in the north-east of Edinburgh. Ireland had the benefit of a strong wind in the first half, but they could only manage a single try by Bulger who took advantage of an error by Fleming. Earlier, Tom M Scott missed a penalty against the wind and on one occasion the Scottish forwards rushed the ball over the Irish line only to be beaten to the touchdown. Just before the break, Gwynn, the Irish wing, punted the ball between the posts, but it was not a drop kick so no score was awarded. In the second half, Morrison seemed to have scored a try which the referee mysteriously disallowed and then Scott kicked a penalty goal which also was not given. Finally, Turnbull scored an undisputed try and Tom M Scott landed the goal. From then on, Scotland were largely in control and Scott kicked a late penalty to seal the win.

59 INTERNATIONAL CHAMPIONSHIP 1897   ENGLAND

Fallowfield, Manchester · Saturday 13 March 1897 · Lost 3–12

SCOTLAND AR Smith (*Oxford U*); †AM Bucher (*Edinburgh Acs*), W Neilson (*London Scot*), T Scott (*Hawick*), †AW Robertson (*Edinburgh Acs*); M Elliot (*Hawick*), JW Simpson (*Royal HSFP*); A Balfour (*Cambridge U*), JH Dods (*Edinburgh Acs*), WMC McEwan (*Edinburgh Acs*), RG Macmillan* (*London Scot*), MC Morrison (*Royal HSFP*), TM Scott (*Hawick*), RC Stevenson (*London Scot*), GO Turnbull (*London Scot*)

ENGLAND JF Byrne (*Moseley*); EF Fookes (*Sowerby Bridge*), WL Bunting (*Richmond*), OG Mackie (*Cambridge U*), GC Robinson (*Percy Park*); EW Taylor* (*Rockcliff*), CM Wells (*Harlequins*); J Davidson (*Aspatria*), HW Dudgeon (*Richmond*), LF Giblin (*Cambridge U*), F Jacob (*Cambridge U*), E Knowles (*Millom*), RF Oakes (*Hartlepool Rov*), J Pinch (*Lancaster*), WB Stoddart (*Liverpool*)

REFEREE JT Magee (*Ireland*)

SCORING No scoring in the first half. Fookes, try (0–3); Byrne, con (0–5); Robinson, try (0–8); Bucher, try (3–8); Byrne, drop (3–12)

Scotland were firm favourites, but on the day they were completely outplayed. The English forwards rose to the occasion and gave their backs a steady supply of ball. Taylor and Wells, the English half-backs, controlled the game and it was only strong Scottish defence that kept the score down. Smith, the Scottish full-back, tackled well and at several points Macmillan withdrew from the Scottish pack to bolster the defence. In a hard fought encounter, both sides showed plenty of enterprise in the first half, but there was no scoring before the interval. Eventually, the English backs made a good passing movement and Fookes scored a try. The momentum swung towards England and after another good move Robinson scored a second English try. Scotland responded when Boucher made a dribbling run and won the race for the touchdown after he had hacked on. Right at the finish, Byrne dropped a goal to seal England's first win over Scotland since 1892. Unfortunately, England weren't able to receive the Calcutta Cup at the after-match dinner because the Scots, whether by accident or over-confidence, had left it in Edinburgh.

Balmoral Showgrounds, Belfast · Saturday 19 February 1898

Won 8–0

SCOTLAND †JM Reid (*Edinburgh Acs*); AR Smith* (*Oxford U*), †E Spencer (*Clydesdale*), †RT Neilson (*W of Scot*), T Scott (*Hawick*); M Elliot (*Hawick*), †JT Mabon (*Jed-Forest*); †JM Dykes (*Clydesdale*), †GC Kerr (*Durham*), WMC McEwan (*Edinburgh Acs*), †A Mackinnon (*London Scot*), MC Morrison (*Royal HSFP*), †R Scott (*Hawick*), TM Scott (*Hawick*), HO Smith (*Watsonians*)

IRELAND PE O'Brien-Butler (*Monkstown*); FC Purser (*Dublin U*), FFS Smithwick (*Monkstown*), LH Gwynn (*Monkstown*), LQ Bulger (*Lansdowne*); GG Allen* (*Derry*), LM Magee (*Bective Rgrs*); WG Byron (*NIFC*), JL Davis (*Monkstown*), JG Franks (*Dublin U*), H Lindsay (*Wdrs*), JH Lytle (*NIFC*), JE McIlwaine (*NIFC*), J Ryan (*Rockwell Coll*), M Ryan (*Rockwell Coll*)

REFEREE ET Gurdon (*England*)

SCORING No scoring in the first half. T Scott, try (3–0); TM Scott, con (5–0); T Scott, try (8–0)

Scotland fielded eight new caps and Smithwick, a last-minute replacement for Ireland, was aged only 17. A big Belfast crowd witnessed a vigorous and occasionally rough encounter. There were several stoppages for injuries with, in the words of *The Scotsman*, 'the opposing players handling one another in anything but a gentle manner'. Scotland had the benefit of a strong wind in the first half, but their efforts were very disjointed and strong Irish defence prevented any scoring before the interval. The Irish had some pressure early in the second period and a great tackle by Reid, the Scottish full-back, prevented a certain score. McEwan injured his back in a heavy fall and was largely ineffective from then on. Around the hour mark, Tom Scott, the flying winger from Langholm, latched onto a loose ball and sprinted away to score between the posts. Scott's try, which was easily converted by his namesake Tom M Scott, was greeted by a stony silence from the Irish spectators who had been confident of victory until this point. Scotland continued to defend well and just before the finish Scott escaped again for his second try.

Powderhall Stadium, Edinburgh · Saturday 12 March 1898

Drawn 3–3

SCOTLAND JM Reid (*Edinburgh Acs*); AR Smith* (*Oxford U*), †TA Nelson (*Oxford U*), RT Neilson (*W of Scot*), T Scott (*Hawick*); M Elliot (*Hawick*), JT Mabon (*Jed-Forest*); JM Dykes (*Clydesdale*), GC Kerr (*Durham*), WMC McEwan (*Edinburgh Acs*), A MacKinnon (*London Scot*), MC Morrison (*Royal HSFP*), TM Scott (*Hawick*), HO Smith (*Watsonians*), RC Stevenson (*London Scot*)

ENGLAND JF Byrne* (*Moseley*); WN Pilkington (*Cambridge U*), WL Bunting (*Richmond*), PMR Royds (*Blackheath*), PW Stout (*Gloucester*); GT Unwin (*Blackheath*), A Rotherham (*Richmond*); W Ashford (*Exeter*), J Davidson (*Aspatria*), HW Dudgeon (*Richmond*), F Jacob (*Richmond*), RF Oakes (*Hartlepool Rov*), HE Ramsden (*Bingley*), JF Shaw (*RIE Coll*), FM Stout (*Gloucester*)

REFEREE J Dodds (*Ireland*)

SCORING No scoring in the first half. Royds, try (0–3); McEwan, try (3–3)

For the first time Scotland fielded Border half-backs, Hawick's Matthew Elliot and Jed-Forest's Joe Mabon. This was a hard fought but rather unspectacular contest that Scotland should have won. They had the better of the game, but the back division never got into its stride and the English defence was almost impenetrable. The Scottish forwards played with their usual fire and their footwork brought out some courageous saves from the English half-backs, Unwin and Rotherham. Playing with the wind against them, the Scots started purposefully and England were unlucky to lose Unwin who had to go off temporarily. Both sides had spells of pressure and missed some scoring opportunities. Tom Scott, the Langholm wing, had a couple of dangerous runs, Neilson intercepted a pass and almost escaped, and English winger Pilkington dropped a pass with the line in front of him. Early in the second half, Royds, the English centre, charged down a kick for a fortuitous try against the run of play. The Scottish forwards continued to press and eventually McEwan broke away and scored at the posts. Unfortunately, the normally reliable Tom M Scott missed the easy conversion. In the closing stages, the Scottish forwards twice rushed over the English line, but Bryne beat them to the touchdown. England almost scored with a late breakout, but the match ended in stalemate.

The Inverleith Years 1899–1919

BY THE 1890s Scotland's traditional home at Raeburn Place, which was then little more than an open field with some temporary stands, was unable to meet the burgeoning demands of international rugby. Matches were attracting large numbers of spectators and the old ground was simply unable to cope. Moreover, the governors of Edinburgh Academy, the owners of Raeburn Place, were dissatisfied about the burden being placed on their property, especially because school pupils wanted to use the ground on the morning of internationals. Clearly, it was time for Scotland to find a permanent home that they owned. The Irish game in March 1895 was the last international to be played at Raeburn Place and for the next four years Scotland lived a nomadic existence. In 1896, the English match was played at the second Hampden Park in Glasgow, the home of the Queen's Park Football Club. The following two years, Scotland played at the Powderhall stadium in the north-east of Edinburgh. In the meantime, the Scottish Football Union purchased land at Inverleith and set about building a new stadium. The first international there took place in February 1899 when Ireland spoiled the party, winning 9–3. The new ground had a spacious grandstand on the west touchline (which still exists and is now used by Stewart's-Melville FP). There were raised earthen banks for standing spectators around the rest of the ground and opposite the main stand was a large wooden hut for newspaper reporters. The players made their final preparations in a separate pavilion behind the main stand, but, as was common in rugby at this time, they changed their clothes at a local hotel and were driven to the ground by horse-drawn carriage.

The opening decade of the new century was a golden era for Wales, but it was also a successful one for Scotland. Between 1901 and 1907, the Scots won the International Championship four times, including three Triple Crowns (1901, 1903 and 1907). They beat England eight times between 1899 and 1910 and had six wins in succession on English soil, a record that now seems the stuff of fantasy. Scotland did less well in the 1910s, although they unexpectedly beat a resurgent England in 1912. International rugby was starting to expand in these years and several new opponents appeared on the scene. Scotland played their first match against France in January 1910, thereby completing the annual cycle of matches that became the Five Nations Championship. Initially, the Scottish Football Union, which never liked anything new, was largely dismissive of the French. They did not award caps and treated the game, which was always played in early January, as a trial for more important challenges to come. The Scots got their comeuppance in 1911 when they sent an under-strength side to Paris and became the first team to lose against the newcomers.

In the first decade of the 20th century, the balance of power in world rugby moved to the southern hemisphere where it has been ever since. In 1903, a British team under the captaincy of Scottish forward Mark Morrison lost a test series in South Africa for the first time. The following year, another British team, led by Scotsman David Bedell-Sivright, lost a one-off test against New Zealand. Teams from the southern hemisphere started to make tours of the British Isles where they played provincial and test matches. Undoubtedly, the most important of the early tourists was the legendary

New Zealand side of 1905–6. They played 35 games in Europe and North America and lost only once. Tactically, they were very innovative and swept aside the best that British rugby had to offer, including a narrow victory over Scotland in November 1905. The following year South Africa made their first tour of Europe. They did not have the same impact as the New Zealanders, but they set a pattern for future Springbok tours by combining big mobile forwards and strong running backs. However, they lost to a rampant Scotland in the mud at Hampden Park in November 1906. Australia made a tour in 1908–9, but they did not play any games in Scotland or Ireland. The South Africans returned in 1912 and revenged their defeat by Scotland six years earlier. The pupils were becoming the masters.

During these years, Scottish rugby maintained its reputation for producing formidable forward packs. Without question, the outstanding player of the time was David Bedell-Sivright who won 22 caps between 1900 and 1908. Known as 'Darkie' for his swarthy skin colour, he was an extremely hard player who was fearless and uncompromising, but also a skilful footballer who had good hands. A Fettesian, he played for Cambridge and Edinburgh Universities, and later became a Scottish amateur boxing champion. He qualified as a doctor and died at Gallipoli in 1915. Other celebrated Scottish forwards of the early 1900s included Bill Scott, who won 21 caps between 1900 and 1907 and toured with the British team in 1903, and Jimmy Dykes, a stalwart of Glasgow High School FP and a solid scrummager. The leading Border forward was Bill Kyle of Hawick who was a great all-rounder and appeared in many winning sides in the local sevens circuit. The development of loose forward play and the increasingly open nature of the game favoured more mobile players, such as Watsonian John MacCallum, who was a man of few words but a much respected captain, and John Scott of Edinburgh Accies. David Bain, another Academical, and Liverpool's Fred Turner where coming to the fore when war intervened.

At half-back, John Gillespie, Ernie 'Kemo' Simson, who died of cholera in India aged only 28, and Pat Munro were always dangerous in attack and ready to make a quick break. The Royal High duo of John 'Jenny' Hume and Sandy Gunn appear to have been the first Scottish players selected as a scrum-half and stand-off. Eric 'Puss' Milroy of Watsonians, a reserved and deeply intelligent man, was an excellent link player and one of the first specialist scrum-halves in Scotland. In the three-quarter line, the unusually named Phipps Turnbull was a superb athlete who read the game astutely and had the ability to glide through defences. Turnbull had a great mathematical brain and worked as an actuary, but died in his late 20s. Australian-born Alec Timms, who was a medical student at Edinburgh University, was a powerful runner and strong in defence. Later, Alexander 'Gus' Angus and Jimmy Pearson formed a brilliant partnership for Watsonians, and it was rare for a Scottish team not to include one or both of them in the years immediately before the First World War. Australian-born Angus was a strong runner with good hands and excellent awareness. He was an intense and aloof person in contrast to his partner 'Jimmy P' who was a natural extrovert and full of fun. A small and slight man, Pearson was a good ball player with a devastating body swerve.

Scotland had a succession of wingers of genuine pace and real ability. Pre-eminent amongst these was Ken MacLeod who won ten caps between 1905 and 1908, most as a teenager. Educated at Fettes College and Cambridge University, 'KG' was a brilliant attacking three-quarter who possessed a sprinter's speed and great all-round ability. He agreed to give up the game after the premature death of his older brother Lewis and instead turned to cricket. Slightly earlier, William Welsh won eight caps between 1900 and 1902, and he was also a Scottish sprint champion. Educated at Edinburgh University, he served with distinction in the Great War and, like many early internationalists, followed a medical career. Other prominent wingers of this time included Australian-born Bill Stewart, who scored seven tries in his first three internationals, the trim little George Will, and the fair-haired Hawick favourite Walter Sutherland who, like William Welsh, was a Scottish sprint champion. At full-back there was Harry Rottenburg, Sandy Duncan (another medic), Douglas Schulze and Mike Dickson, but probably the most colourful was Walter Forrest, a Kelso man who turned out for Hawick. Forrest was often guilty of committing dreadful blunders and then escaping from them by an inspired piece of virtuosity.

Rugby football came to a shuddering halt with the outbreak of the First World War in August 1914. Clubs closed their doors and players were strongly encouraged to join the armed forces. Rugby players of all nations were at the forefront of the struggle and the game paid an enormous and terrible price for their enthusiasm and bravery. Thirty Scottish internationalists lost their lives in the war, more than any other nation, and these included such greats as the aforementioned David Bedell-Sivright, Eric Milroy, Jimmy Pearson, Walter Sutherland and Walter Forrest.

---

62   INTERNATIONAL CHAMPIONSHIP 1899   IRELAND

Inverleith · Saturday 18 February 1899 · Lost 3–9

SCOTLAND JM Reid (*Edinburgh Acs*); GT Campbell (*London Scot*), †DB Monypenny (*London Scot*), RT Neilson (*W of Scot*), T Scott (*Langholm*); WP Donaldson (*W of Scot*), JT Mabon (*Jed-Forest*); JH Couper (*W of Scot*), †L Harvey (*Greenock Wdrs*), GC Kerr (*Durham*), WMC McEwan (*Edinburgh Acs*), A Mackinnon (*London Scot*), MC Morrison (*Royal HSFP*), HO Smith (*Watsonians*), RC Stevenson (*London Scot*)

IRELAND PE O'Brien-Butler (*Monkstown*); GP Doran (*Lansdowne*), JB Allison (*Campbell Coll*), C Reid (*NIFC*), EF Campbell (*Monkstown*); LM Magee* (*Bective Rgrs*), A Barr (*Methodist Coll*); WG Byron (*NIFC*), TJ Little (*Bective Rgrs*), JH Lytle (*NIFC*), TMW McGown (*NIFC*), AWD Meares (*Dublin U*), J Ryan (*Rockwell Coll*), M Ryan (*Rockwell Coll*), J Sealy (*Dublin U*)

REFEREE ET Gurdon (*England*)

SCORING Campbell, try (0–3); Lytle, try (0–6) (half-time) Sealy, try (0–9); Donaldson, pen (3–9)

The match against Wales was postponed so this was the opening game at the new ground at Inverleith. Both sides had to make numerous changes to their original selections. Drizzling rain set-in just before kick-off and the pitch cut-up during the match, but this was an entertaining encounter between two strong packs. Ireland confounded the predictions by winning on Scottish soil for the first time. The Irish forwards were superior and their back division played effectively. Magee, the Irish half-back, made several elusive runs and was always prominent. Early on, Magee made a break from a scrum and after some quick passing Campbell had a clear run-in. Soon afterwards, Magee escaped again, Barr carried on and found Reid who

The Scottish team that lost to Ireland in February 1899, the opening match at the new SFU ground at Inverleith. *SRU*

scored Ireland's second try. Early in the second half, Irish forward Sealy scored between the posts, but Magee missed the simple goal kick. Reid, the Scottish full-back, had to leave the field with a damaged shoulder and Monypenny was tackled illegally when racing for a touchdown. Donaldson drop-kicked the resulting penalty, but Ireland were clear winners.

63   INTERNATIONAL CHAMPIONSHIP 1899   WALES

Inverleith · Saturday 4 March 1899 · Won 21–10

SCOTLAND †H Rottenburg (*Cambridge U*); HTS Gedge (*F-Ls*), †GAW Lamond (*Kelvinside Acs*), DB Monypenny (*London Scot*), T Scott (*Langholm*); RT Neilson (*W of Scot*), JW Simpson (*Royal HSFP*); JM Dykes (*London Scot*), GC Kerr (*Durham*), WMC McEwan (*Edinburgh Acs*), A Mackinnon (*London Scot*), MC Morrison (*Royal HSFP*), HO Smith (*Watsonians*), RC Stevenson (*London Scot*), †WJ Thomson (*W of Scot*)

WALES WJ Bancroft* (*Swansea*); HVP Huzzey (*Cardiff*), EG Nicholls (*Cardiff*), RT Skirmshire (*Newport*), WM Llewellyn (*Llwynypia*); SH Biggs (*Cardiff*), GL Lloyd (*Newport*); WH Alexander (*Llwynypia*), J Blake (*Cardiff*), AB Brice (*Aberavon*), T Dobson (*Cardiff*), R Hellings (*Llwynypia*), JJ Hodges (*Newport*), WJ Parker (*Swansea*), FG Scrine (*Swansea*)

REFEREE MG Delaney (*Ireland*)

SCORING Gedge, try (3–0); Lloyd, try (3–3); Bancroft, con (3–5); Llewellyn, try (3–8); Bancroft, con (3–10) (half-time) Monypenny, try (6–10); Thomson, mark (10–10); Lamond, drop (14–10); Smith, try (17–10); Gedge, drop (21–10)

This match was postponed four times because of frost. Wales were firm favourites and had already demolished England (26–3), but the Scottish forwards were in rare form and the home side were decisive winners. Playing an old-fashioned type of game, the

Scots were solid in the scrums and used their feet well in the loose. They tackled strongly and never allowed Wales to find their natural rhythm. On a bright afternoon with occasional flurries of snow, Neilson and Lamond combined to put Gedge away on a weaving run for a try near the posts. The Scots had the better of the play, but the visitors scored two converted tries close to the interval. According to *The Times*, the first half was extended by some ten minutes because of a timekeeping error by the referee. Scotland restarted with great energy and after about five minutes Monypenny beat the defence for a fine solo try. The forwards continued to press and about ten minutes later Thomson kicked a mark goal to level the scores. The crowd began to sense an unlikely victory and Lamond dropped a goal to put Scotland in front. Then, after several near misses, Smith scored an unconverted try after a charge-down. Shortly before the finish, Gedge dropped a huge goal to seal a memorable win for Scotland.

64   INTERNATIONAL CHAMPIONSHIP 1899   ENGLAND

Rectory Field, Blackheath · Saturday 11 March 1899 · Won 5–0

SCOTLAND H Rottenburg (*London Scot*); HTS Gedge (*F-Ls*), DB Monypenny (*London Scot*), GAW Lamond (*Kelvinside Acs*), T Scott (*Langholm*); †JI Gillespie (*Edinburgh Acs*), JW Simpson (*Royal HSFP*); JM Dykes (*London Scot*), GC Kerr (*Edinburgh Wdrs*), WMC McEwan (*Edinburgh Acs*), A Mackinnon (*London Scot*), MC Morrison* (*Royal HSFP*), HO Smith (*Watsonians*), RC Stevenson (*London Scot*), WJ Thomson (*W of Scot*)

ENGLAND HT Gamlin (*Devonport Alb*); EF Fookes (*Sowerby Bridge*), WL Bunting (*Richmond*), JC Matters (*RNE Coll, Keyham*), PW Stout (*Gloucester*); A Rotherham* (*Richmond*), RO Schwarz (*Richmond*); James Davidson (*Aspatria*), Joseph Davidson (*Aspatria*), AO Dowson (*Moseley*), HW Dudgeon (*Richmond*), RFA Hobbs (*Blackheath*), RF Oakes (*Hartlepool Rov*), JP Shooter (*Morley*), FM Stout (*Gloucester*)

REFEREE JT Magee (*Ireland*)

SCORING No scoring in the first half. Gillespie, try (3–0); Thomson, con (5–0)

Scotland were weakened by several injuries but were deserved winners. The Scottish forwards were much livelier than their lumbering opponents whom *The Times* dismissed as northern 'delinquents'. The Scottish footwork was very effective and put the English half-backs under a lot of pressure. Playing in fine conditions with a slight breeze, this game was dominated by the forwards and lacked real spectacle. Both sides wasted some opportunities in the first half. Langholm wing Tom Scott broke away with only one man to beat, but Gedge, who was at his side, dropped the ball with the line in front of him. Later Scott made another great run, but Gamlin, the English fullback, caught him with a superb try-saving tackle. Similarly, Bunting made a clear break for England, but the supporting player knocked-on. Before the break, Simpson, the Scottish half-back, injured his leg and had to drop back as an auxiliary full-back. Smith came out of the pack and performed heroically in his new role at half-back. The only score of the match came around the fiftieth minute. The Scottish forwards rushed the ball over the ball over the line and Gillespie just managed to touch it down before it ran out of play. Thomson kicked the conversion from a difficult angle. The rest of the game was strenuously contested but largely uneventful and many spectators were seen to leave the ground long before the final whistle.

St Helen's, Swansea · Saturday 27 January 1900 · Lost 3–12

SCOTLAND H Rottenburg (*London Scot*); †JE Crabbie (*Edinburgh Acs*), AB Timms (*Edinburgh U*), †WH Morrison (*Edinburgh Acs*), T Scott (*Langholm*); JI Gillespie (*Edinburgh Acs*), †FH Fasson (*London Scot*); †DR Bedell-Sivright (*Cambridge U*), JM Dykes (*London Scot*), †FW Henderson (*London Scot*), GC Kerr (*Durham*), WMC McEwan (*Edinburgh Acs*), MC Morrison* (*Royal HSFP*), TM Scott (*Hawick*), WJ Thomson (*W of Scot*)

WALES WJ Bancroft* (*Swansea*); WM Llewellyn (*Llwynypia*), EG Nicholls (*Cardiff*), G Davies (*Swansea*), WJ Trew (*Swansea*); LA Phillips (*Newport*), GL Lloyd (*Newport*); J Blake (*Cardiff*), JG Boots (*Newport*), A Brice (*Aberavon*), G Dobson (*Cardiff*), JJ Hodges (*Newport*), F Miller (*Mountain Ash*), R Thomas (*Swansea*), WH Williams (*Pontyminster*)

REFEREE A Hartley (*England*)

SCORING Llewellyn, try (0–3); Dykes, try (3–3); Nicholls, try (3–6) (half-time) Llewellyn, try (3–9); Williams, try (3–12)

Against some expectations, this was a one-sided match and Wales should have won more easily. Scotland started strongly, but soon Wales gained the upper-hand. The Scottish pack did some good work in the loose, but their foot-rushes lacked their usual vigour and were easily contained. The Welsh backs were full of adventure and made many dangerous attacks. Wing Willie Llewellyn used his speed to great effect and he was well served by his partner Gwyn Nicholls. It was only good defence by the Scottish backs that prevented a worst defeat. Wing Tom Scott and Harry Rottenburg, a late replacement at full-back, repeatedly saved the Scots with their brave tackling. Playing in favourable conditions, Llewellyn opened the scoring with a classic break and for awhile it seemed that Wales would run away with it. Then the Scottish forwards made a strong charge and Dykes scored an unconverted try. A few minutes later, the ball was kicked over the Scottish line and Nicholls won the scramble for the touchdown. In the second half, play was almost entirely in the Scottish part of the field. Llewellyn scored his second try and in the dying minutes Williams took advantage of a rare mistake by Scott to complete the scoring.

David Bedell-Sivright won 22 caps between 1900 and 1908 and was one the greatest ever Scottish forwards.

Lansdowne Road, Dublin · Saturday 24 February 1900 · Drawn 0–0

SCOTLAND H Rottenburg (*London Scot*); T Scott (*Langholm*), AR Smith (*London Scot*), AB Timms (*Edinburgh U*), †WH Welsh (*Edinburgh U*); RT Neilson (*W of Scot*), JT Mabon (*Jed-Forest*); †JA Campbell (*Cambridge U*), JM Dykes (*London Scot*), †JRC Greenlees (*Cambridge U*), FW Henderson (*London Scot*), GC Kerr (*Durham*), R Scott (*Hawick*), TM Scott* (*Hawick*), †WP Scott (*W of Scot*)

IRELAND CA Boyd (*Dublin U*); GP Doran (*Lansdowne*), BRW Doran (*Lansdowne*), JB Allison (*QC Belfast*), IG Davidson (*NIFC*); LM Magee* (*Bective Rgrs*), JH Ferris (*QC Belfast*); CE Allen (*Liverpool*), F Gardiner (*NIFC*), ST Irwin (*QC Belfast*), TJ Little (*Bective Rgrs*), PC Nicholson (*Dublin U*), J Ryan (*Rockwell Coll*), M Ryan (*Rockwell Coll*), J Sealy (*Dublin U*)

REFEREE Dr Badger (*England*)

The country was in the grip of a cold snap so this match was postponed for one week and both teams were short of match practice, but on the day conditions were almost ideal. Play was mainly confined to the forwards and was vigorously contested with several lengthy stoppages for injuries. In the first half, Boyd, the Irish full-back, twisted his knee and had to retire. Also in the half, Tom Scott, the Scottish forward and captain, had a penalty attempt charged down. Both sides had some good attacks, but they were unable to break through. Scottish wing Willie Welsh made an encouraging debut and half-back Joe Mabon used his touch-kicking to good effect. Ireland finished strongly and Doran almost snatched a late try, but the Scots managed to hold out.

67   INTERNATIONAL CHAMPIONSHIP 1900   ENGLAND

Inverleith · Saturday 10 March 1900 · Drawn 0–0

SCOTLAND H Rottenburg (*London Scot*); T Scott (*Langholm*), GT Campbell (*London Scot*), AR Smith (*London Scot*), WH Welsh (*Edinburgh U*); RT Neilson (*W of Scot*), JI Gillespie (*Edinburgh Acs*); †LHI Bell (*Edinburgh Acs*), GC Kerr (*Edinburgh Wdrs*), WMC McEwan (*Edinburgh Acs*), A Mackinnon (*London Scot*), MC Morrison (*Royal HSFP*), R Scott (*Hawick*), WP Scott (*W of Scot*), HO Smith (*Watsonians*)

ENGLAND HT Gamlin (*Blackheath*); GC Robinson (*Percy Park*), GW Gordon-Smith (*Blackheath*), WL Bunting (*Richmond*), R Forrest (*Wellington*); GH Marsden (*Morley*), JC Marquis (*Birkenhead Park*); H Alexander (*Birkenhead Park*), J Baxter (*Birkenhead Park*), RW Bell (*Cambridge U*), J Daniell* (*Cambridge U*), AFCC Luxmore (*Richmond*), S Reynolds (*Richmond*), JH Shooter (*Morley*), AF Todd (*Blackheath*)

REFEREE MG Delaney (*Ireland*)

Played in ideal conditions, England held the edge in tight play, but the Scots were better in the loose. The visitors had the greater share of the game in the first half when they wasted two great chances. Both Robinson and Bunting made breaks and had the line in front of them, but they mistakenly passed inside and the cover arrived in the nick of time. The Scottish forwards made some good rushes and England full-back Gamlin defended courageously. The second half was delayed because several players were receiving treatment for injuries and also because the match ball was temporarily mislaid. Most of the play was in English territory and the Scottish forwards put the visitors under a lot of pressure. Both Welsh and Gillespie went close to scoring, the latter knocking down the corner flag as he was thrown into touch. Gillespie also narrowly missed a late penalty attempt. Amongst several fine performances, Gillespie, Neilson and Tom Scott were prominent for Scotland, and Bunting and Marsden were good on the English side.

Inverleith · Saturday 9 February 1901 · Won 18–8

SCOTLAND †AW Duncan (*Edinburgh U*); WH Welsh (*Edinburgh U*), AB Timms (*Edinburgh U*), †P Turnbull (*Edinburgh Acs*), †AN Fell (*Edinburgh U*); JI Gillespie (*Edinburgh Acs*), FH Fasson (*Edinburgh U*); DR Bedell-Sivright (*Cambridge U*), †JA Bell (*Clydesdale*), JM Dykes (*Glasgow HSFP*), †AB Flett (*Edinburgh U*), †A Frew (*Edinburgh U*), MC Morrison* (*Royal HSFP*), †J Ross (*London Scot*), †RS Stronach (*Glasgow Acs*)

WALES WJ Bancroft* (*Swansea*); WM Llewellyn (*London Welsh*), EG Nicholls (*Cardiff*), G Davies (*Swansea*), WJ Trew (*Swansea*); LA Phillips (*Newport*), GL Lloyd (*Newport*); WH Alexander (*Llwynypia*), J Blake (*Cardiff*), JG Boots (*Newport*), A Brice (*Aberavon*), H Davies (*Swansea*), R Hellings (*Llwynypia*), JJ Hodges (*Newport*), F Millar (*Mountain Ash*)

REFEREE RW Jeffares (*Ireland*)

SCORING Gillespie, try (3–0); Gillespie, con (5–0); Flett, try (8–0); Gillespie, con (10–0) (half-time) Gillespie, try (13–0); Flett, con (15–0); Turnbull, try (18–0); Lloyd, try (18–3); Bancroft, con (18–5); Boots, try (18–8)

Scotland fielded eight new caps and seven players from the successful Edinburgh University side. Playing in fine conditions, a youthful Scotland were comfortable winners and never allowed their more experienced opponents to settle down. The heavy Welsh forwards did well in the scrums, but the Scots were much faster in loose play and they defended brilliantly. Fasson and Gillespie, the Scottish half-backs, easily outplayed their rivals and the Scottish three-quarters were always dangerous, in particular Phipps Turnbull who made some thrilling solo runs. This was an uncompromising encounter and several players were laid out with injuries during the game. Scotland almost scored in the opening minutes when a loose pass was hacked over the Welsh line and Fell was just beaten by Llewellyn in a race to the ball. Wales had better of early stages and twice Duncan, the Scottish full-back, made courageous last-ditch tackles to prevent certain tries. The game turned Scotland's way when the forwards made a charge into the Welsh 25 and from the ensuing maul Gillespie dummied past two defenders and dived over the line with a tackler hanging onto him. Soon after, Turnbull made a brilliant weaving run from near midway and Flett was in support for a great score. Scotland continued to dominate in the second half. Turnbull made another elusive run to the Welsh line and from the maul Gillespie dashed over at the corner and Flett kicked the difficult conversion. Then a long kick found touch on the Welsh 25 and from the lineout the ball was passed out to Turnbull who raced over wide out. Wales made a strong late rally and Lloyd and Boots scored consolation tries, the first of which was converted by Bancroft.

Inverleith · Saturday 23 February 1901 · Won 9–5

SCOTLAND AW Duncan (*Edinburgh U*); WH Welsh (*Edinburgh U*), AB Timms (*Edinburgh U*), P Turnbull (*Ebinburgh Acs*), AN Fell (*Edinburgh U*); JI Gillespie (*Edinburgh Acs*), FH Fasson (*Edinburgh U*); DR Bedell-Sivright (*F-Ls*), JA Bell (*Clydesdale*), †FP Dods (*Edinburgh Acs*),

JM Dykes (*Glasgow HSFP*), AB Flett (*Edinburgh U*), A Frew (*Edinburgh U*), MC Morrison* (*Royal HSFP*), J Ross (*London Scot*)

IRELAND CA Boyd (*Wdrs*); AE Freear (*Lansdowne*), BRW Doran (*Lansdowne*), JB Allison (*Edinburgh U*), IG Davidson (*NIFC*); LM Magee* (*Bective Rgrs*), A Barr (*Methodist Coll*); CE Allan (*Derry*), TA Harvey (*Dublin U*), P Healey (*Limerick*), HAS Irvine (*Belfast Collegians*), TJ Little (*Bective Rgrs*), TMW McGowan (*NIFC*), J Ryan (*Rockwell Coll*), M Ryan (*Rockwell Coll*)

REFEREE G Harnett (*England*)

SCORING Gillespie, try (3–0); Welsh, try (6–0); Welsh, try (9–0); Doran, try (9–3); Irvine, con (9–5) (half-time)

There was little to choose between the two sets of forwards, but the Scottish backs were much livelier and inventive. Edinburgh University supplied seven of the Scottish team and another University player, JB Allison, was in the Irish side. On a dull but dry afternoon, Scotland scored three tries inside the first ten minutes. Boyd, the Irish full-back, was caught inside his own 25 and Fell and Dykes combined to put Gillespie over. The Scottish backs kept up the attack and good handling allowed Welsh to run round the defence for a fine solo try. Straight from the kick-off, Welsh scored again from a similar movement. Ireland finally got into the game and after a forwards charge into the Scottish 25 Doran scored between the posts and Irvine converted. There was plenty more attacking play, but both sides defended well and there was no further scoring. Towards the finish, Duncan, the Scottish full-back, made a heroic last-gasp tackle on John Ryan, the powerful Irish forward, which saved the day for Scotland.

---

70   INTERNATIONAL CHAMPIONSHIP 1901   ENGLAND

Blackheath · Saturday 9 March 1901 · Won 18–3

SCOTLAND AW Duncan (*Edinburgh U*); WH Welsh (*Edinburgh U*), AB Timms (*Edinburgh U*), P Turnbull (*Edinburgh Acs*), AN Fell (*Edinburgh U*); JI Gillespie (*Edinburgh Acs*), †RM Neill (*Edinburgh Acs*); DR Bedell-Sivright (*F-Ls*), JA Bell (*Clydesdale*), JM Dykes (*Glasgow HSFP*), AB Flett (*Edinburgh U*), A Frew (*Edinburgh U*), MC Morrison* (*Royal HSFP*), J Ross (*London Scot*), RS Stronach (*Glasgow Acs*)

ENGLAND HT Gamlin (*Blackheath*); GC Robinson (*Percy Park*), WL Bunting* (*Richmond*), NS Cox (*Sunderland*), EW Elliot (*Sunderland*), PD Kendall (*Birkenhead Park*), B Oughtred (*Hartlepool Rov*); H Alexander (*Birkenhead Park*), CS Edgar (*Birkenhead Park*), NC Fletcher (*OMT*), GR Gibson (*Northern*), C Hall (*Gloucester*), BC Hartley (*Blackheath*), A O'Neill (*Torquay Ath*), HTF Weston (*Northampton*)

REFEREE RW Jeffares (*Ireland*)

SCORING Gillespie, try (3–0); Gillespie, con (5–0); Welsh, try (8–0); Gillespie, con (10–0); Timms, try (13–0); Gillespie, con (15–0) (half-time) Robinson, try (15–3); Fell, try (18–3)

In a one-sided encounter Scotland's young team were decisive winners and set the seal on a magnificent Triple Crown. The English forwards held a slight advantage in tight play, but the Scots were much faster in the loose and their footwork was very effective. The real difference between the sides was at half-back where the Scottish pair Gillespie and Neill easily outplayed their rather hapless opponents, who struggled to gain any

Captained by Mark Morrison, this Scottish team won the Triple Crown
against England in March 1901. *SRU*

sort of understanding. The Scottish three-quarters were in brilliant form and were
much too fast and skilful for England. As *The Times* put it: 'Their combined runs,
when going at full speed, could not have been surpassed... not often has finer back
play been seen in an international match.' On a firm but slippery pitch, Scotland
scored three tries in quick succession. After about 15 minutes, the backs combined to
put Gillespie over and then Welsh used his great pace to beat the defence and score a
second. Timms scored a third Scottish try after quick and accurate passing. In the
second half, Robinson, the England wing, brushed past some weak defence for a try,
but Scotland had the final say when swift passing put Fell over near the corner.

71 · INTERNATIONAL CHAMPIONSHIP 1902 · WALES

Cardiff Arms Park · Saturday 1 February 1902 · Lost 5–14

SCOTLAND AW Duncan (*Edinburgh U*); AN Fell (*Edinburgh U*), P Turnbull (*Edinburgh Acs*),
AB Timms (*Edinburgh U*), WH Welsh (*Edinburgh U*); JI Gillespie (*Edinburgh Acs*), FH Fasson
(*Edinburgh U*); DR Bedell-Sivright (*Cambridge U*), †JV Bedell-Sivright (*Cambridge U*), JA Bell
(*Clydesdale*), AB Flett (*Edinburgh U*), JRC Greenlees (*Cambridge U*), †WE Kyle (*Hawick*),
MC Morrison* (*Royal HSFP*), J Ross (*London Scot*)

WALES J Strand-Jones (*Llanelli*); WM Llewellyn (*Llwynypia*), EG Nicholls* (*Cardiff*), RT Gabe
(*London Welsh*), E Morgan (*London Welsh*); GL Lloyd (*Newport*), RM Owen (*Swansea*);
JG Boots (*Newport*), A Brice (*Aberavon*), AF Harding (*Cardiff*), JJ Hodges (*Newport*), D Jones
(*Aberdare*), H Jones (*Penygraig*), WW Joseph (*Swansea*), WT Osborne (*Mountain Ash*)

REFEREE P Gilliard (*England*)

SCORING Llewellyn, try (0–3); Llewellyn, try (0–6); Gabe, try (0–9); Gabe, try (0–12); Strand-
Jones, con (0–14); Welsh, try (3–14); Gillespie, try (5–14) (half-time)

Against expectations, Wales were convincing winners. The Welsh forwards were in control throughout and their backs played confidently and at great pace. Nolan Fell, the Scottish wing, was injured in the opening minutes. He played on with a bandaged head but he was always a weak link. Playing in fine conditions, Wales attacked immediately and after some five minutes Llewellyn had a clear run-in. Ten minutes later, Llewellyn scored his second try after a break by Nicholls. Wales showed no signs of slackening and Gabe finished off a good handling movement with an unconverted score. Soon after, Morgan made a long run from the Welsh half and Gabe was in support for his second try of the game. Strand-Jones added the conversion to give the home side a commanding lead. Just before the

Bill Kyle won 21 caps between 1902 and 1910.

break, the Scots made a good passing move and Welsh used his strength and pace to round the defence. Scotland had the wind behind them in the second half and both sides had spells of pressure, but there was no further scoring.

72   INTERNATIONAL CHAMPIONSHIP 1902   IRELAND

Balmoral Showgrounds, Belfast · Saturday 22 February 1902

Lost 0–5

SCOTLAND   AW Duncan (*Edinburgh U*); WH Welsh (*Edinburgh U*), †AS Drybrough (*Edinburgh Wdrs*), P Turnbull (*Edinburgh Acs*), JE Crabbie (*Oxford U*); JI Gillespie (*Edinburgh Acs*), RM Neill (*Edinburgh Acs*); DR Bedell-Sivright (*Cambridge U*), JA Bell (*Clydesdale*), †HH Bullmore (*Edinburgh U*), AB Flett (*Edinburgh U*), JRC Greenlees (*Cambridge U*), WE Kyle (*Hawick*), MC Morrison* (*Royal HSFP*), WP Scott (*W of Scot*)

IRELAND   J Fulton* (*NIFC*); IG Davidson (*NIFC*), JB Allison (*Edinburgh U*), BRW Doran (*Lansdowne*), GP Doran (*Lansdowne*); LM Magee (*Bective Rgrs*), HH Corley (*Dublin U*); JJ Coffey (*Lansdowne*), F Gardiner (*NIFC*), GT Hamlet (*Old Wesley*), TA Harvey (*Dublin U*), P Healey (*Limerick*), ST Irwin (*QC Belfast*), JC Pringle (*RIE Coll*), A Tedford (*Malone*)

REFEREE   A Hill (*England*)

SCORING   No scoring in the first half. Doran, try (0–3); Corley, con (0–5)

This was mainly a forward battle and both sides had some good loose rushes. Ireland deserved to win because their pack held a slight edge and they had greater stamina. Conditions were awkward with a slippery pitch and a gusty wind. Scotland kicked-off against the elements, but the wind was so strong that it blew the ball back into their half of the field. Play was mainly in Scottish territory and Ireland had a lot of pressure, but the Scots defended very well, especially centre Andrew Drybrough, and there was no scoring in the first half. With the wind behind them, Scotland restarted strongly and after a great dribbling rush they got over the Irish line and claimed a try, but the referee ruled that the ball had gone out of play. Welsh made a dangerous break, but Fulton, the Irish full-back, caught him with a great tackle. Shortly after, Welsh escaped again and set-up Drybrough for a clear run-in, but the centre dropped the ball with the line at his mercy. Gradually, the Scots ran out of steam and Ireland became more prominent. With about 12 minutes to go, the home side won a scrum near the Scottish 25 and a quick bout of passing put Doran over for the winning try. Scotland tried hard to save the game, but the Irishmen had no problems holding out.

73   INTERNATIONAL CHAMPIONSHIP 1902   ENGLAND

Inverleith · Saturday 15 March 1902 · Lost 3–6

SCOTLAND AW Duncan (*Edinburgh U*); AN Fell (*Edinburgh U*), P Turnbull (*Edinburgh Acs*), AB Timms (*Edinburgh U*), WH Welsh (*Edinburgh U*); FH Fasson (*Edinburgh U*), †ED Simson (*Edinburgh U*); DR Bedell-Sivright (*Cambridge U*), JA Bell (*Clydesdale*), JM Dykes (*Glasgow HSFP*), JRC Greenlees (*Cambridge U*), WE Kyle (*Hawick*), MC Morrison* (*Royal HSFP*), WP Scott (*W of Scot*), HO Smith (*Watsonians*)

ENGLAND HT Gamlin (*Devonport Alb*); T Simpson (*Rockcliff*), JT Taylor (*West Hartlepool*), JE Raphael (*Oxford U*), R Forrest (*Blackheath*); B Oughtred (*Hartlepool Rov*), EJ Walton (*Castleford & Oxford U*); J Daniell* (*Richmond*), DD Dobson (*Oxford U*), G Fraser (*Richmond*), PF Hardwick (*Percy Park*), BC Hartley (*Blackheath*), JJ Robinson (*Headingley*), LR Tosswill (*Exeter*), SG Williams (*Devonport Alb*)

REFEREE FM Hamilton (*Ireland*)

SCORING Williams, try (0–3); Taylor, try (0–6) (half-time) Fell, try (3–6)

This was a hard fought and exciting contest between two fully committed sides. England won their first victory over Scotland for five years and the Scots, having won the Triple Crown the previous season, ended-up with a whitewash. Oughtred and Walton, the English halves, played very astutely and full-back Gamlin defended like a lion. His opposite number, Duncan, was very hesitant and both English tries were due in part to his errors. The forward exchanges were fairly even, but the English backs were more resourceful and their marking was tight. Both sides had spells of pressure in the first half and after about 20 minutes Williams, the English forward, scored an unconverted try. Taylor added a second after good combined play with Raphael. In the second half, Fell scored near the corner after a splendid passing by the three-quarters. Scotland controlled the rest of the half, but were unable to break the English defence. Fell almost scored a late try but Gamlin caught him short of the line.

74   INTERNATIONAL CHAMPIONSHIP 1903   WALES

Inverleith · Saturday 7 February 1903 · Won 6–0

SCOTLAND †WT Forrest (*Hawick*); AN Fell (*Edinburgh U*), AB Timms (*Edinburgh U*), †HJ Orr

(*London Scot*), JE Crabbie (*Oxford U*); ED Simson (*Edinburgh U*), †J Knox (*Kelvinside Acs*);
DR Bedell-Sivright (*Cambridge U*), †AG Cairns (*Watsonians*), JRC Greenless (*Kelvinside Acs*),
†N Kennedy (*W of Scot*), WE Kyle (*Hawick*), MC Morrison* (*Royal HSFP*), WP Scott (*W of Scot*),
†L West (*Edinburgh U*)

WALES J Strand-Jones (*Llanelli*); WR Arnold (*Llanelli*), RT Gabe (*Llanelli*), D Rees (*Swansea*),
WJ Trew (*Swansea*); GL Lloyd* (*Newport*), RM Owen (*Swansea*); JG Boots (*Newport*), AB Brice
(*Aberavon*), AF Harding (*Cardiff & London Welsh*), JJ Hodges (*Newport*), D Jones (*Treherbert*),
W Joseph (*Swansea*), WT Osborne (*Mountain Ash*), G Travers (*Pill Harriers*)

REFEREE A Martelli (*Ireland*)

SCORING Timms, drop (3–0) (half-time) Kyle, try (6–0)

This match was played in appalling conditions with a vicious wind and blinding rain
sweeping in from the south west. The pitch was cleared just before the start, but it
was sodden underfoot and very slippery. The leather ball absorbed so much water
that it was difficult to kick it any great distance, especially against the wind. Inevitably,
the match lacked spectacle and was largely a kick-and-rush affair littered with errors.
Wales were expected to win, but mistakenly they tried to play too much open rugby
and Scotland adapted to the conditions much better. The forward exchanges were
fairly even although the home side were stronger in the loose and their footwork was
excellent. Scotland played with the elements in the first half and, after early pressure,
Timms used the wind to drop kick a penalty from near halfway. Wales took their time
to settle and then made some promising moves, but the home defence was secure. The
visitors had the better of the second half and threatened several times. Once again,
the Scottish defence was very sharp, especially Forrest at full-back, and the Scottish
forwards, who showed great stamina, made some stirring rushes out of defence.
Towards the finish Scotland took play the length of the field, Morrison lost the ball
near the Welsh line but Kyle was on hand to pick up and score.

75 INTERNATIONAL CHAMPIONSHIP 1903 IRELAND

Inverleith · Saturday 28 February 1903 · Won 3–0

SCOTLAND WT Forrest (*Hawick*); †C France (*Kelvinside Acs*), AS Drybrough
(*Edinburgh Wdrs*), HJ Orr (*London Scot*), JE Crabbie (*Oxford U*); J Knox (*Kelvinside Acs*)
ED Simson (*Edinburgh U*); DR Bedell-Sivright (*Cambridge U*), AG Cairns (*Watsonians*),
JRC Greenless (*Kelvinside Acs*), N Kennedy (*W of Scot*), WE Kyle (*Hawick*), MC Morrison*
(*Royal HSFP*), WP Scott (*W of Scot*), L West (*Edinburgh U*)

IRELAND J Fulton (*NIFC*); CC Fitzgerald (*Glasgow U*), AD Harvey (*Wdrs*), JB Allison
(*Edinburgh U*), HJ Anderson (*Old Wesley*); LM Magee (*Bective Rgrs*), HH Corley* (*Wdrs*);
CE Allen (*Derry*), JJ Coffey (*Lansdowne*), GT Hamlet (*Old Wesley*), P Healy (*Garryowen*),
ST Irwin (*NIFC*), RS Smyth (*Dublin U*), A Tedford (*Malone*), J Wallace (*Wdrs*)

REFEREE F R Alderson (England)

SCORING No scoring in the first half. Crabbie, try (3–0)

The Irish players had experienced a rough crossing of the Irish Channel two days
earlier. As a result, some of them were not at their best and they faded badly in the

second half. This match was mainly a hard forward battle and each pack had some good rushes and dribbles. Both sides tackled firmly and there were only limited opportunities for the backs to show their paces. On a dull but fair afternoon, Ireland started with plenty of dash and the Scots had to defend well. Corley made a good solo run and looked set to score, but Forrest, who was at his erratic best, collared him and replied with a fine clearance. The Irish backs put Anderson into the clear until Simson, who was also in great from, sprinted across and stopped him with a great piece of defence. In the second half, the Scottish forwards got on top with Mark Morrison leading from the front. Eventually, Knox took the ball from a maul and Orr passed to Crabbie who flew in at the corner. This was the only score of the match although the Scots made several more promising attacks and Forrest missed a lengthy penalty attempt.

---

76 INTERNATIONAL CHAMPIONSHIP 1903   ENGLAND

Athletic Ground, Richmond · Saturday 21 March 1903 · Won 10–6

SCOTLAND WT Forrest (*Hawick*); AN Fell (*Edinburgh U*), HJ Orr (*London Scot*), AB Timms (*Edinburgh U*), †JS Macdonald (*Edinburgh U*); ED Simson (*Edinburgh U*), J Knox (*Kelvinside Acs*); AG Cairns (*Watsonians*), †JD Dallas (*Watsonians*), JRC Greenlees* (*Kelvinside Acs*), N Kennedy (*W of Scot*), WE Kyle (*Hawick*), J Ross (*London Scot*), WP Scott (*W of Scot*), L West (*Edinburgh U*)

ENGLAND HT Gamlin (*Devonport Alb*); T Simpson (*Rockcliff*), AT Brettargh (*Liverpool OB*), EIM Barrett (*Lennox*), R Forrest (*Blackheath*); WV Butcher (*Streatham & Croydon*), PD Kendall* (*Birkenhead Park*); VH Cartwright (*Oxford U*), DD Dobson (*Newton Abbot*), NC Fletcher (*OMT*), PF Hardwick (*Percy Park*), BA Hill (*Blackheath*), R Pierce (*Liverpool*), FM Stout (*Richmond*), SG Williams (*Devonport Alb*)

This cigarette card shows action from an England v Scotland match in the early 1900s.

SCORING Forrest, try (0–3); Timms, drop (4–3); Dallas, try (7–3) (half-time) Dobson, try (7–6); Simson, try (10–6)

Playing in summer-like conditions, Scotland clinched the Triple Crown despite missing their two best forwards, Mark Morrison and David Bedell-Sivright, who were both injured. The entire Scottish three-quarter line were from the colonies: Timms and Orr were Australians, Fell from New Zealand, and Macdonald a South African. This was an undistinguished and scrambling encounter with an exciting finish. The forward exchanges were keenly contested, both sides tackled firmly and the match was played at a fast pace, but the handling and back play was not of a high standard. England started well and winger Forrest scored an early try. The Scots responded with a strong charge by the pack following which Timms dropped a goal. Play was fairly even until the Scots put together a good passing movement giving Dallas a clear run to the English line. Scotland opened the second half very brightly and Fell almost scored twice, but each time he was stopped by the veteran English full-back Gamlin. Scotland continued to have the better of the game, but then a good run by Brettargh took play to the Scottish line and from the ensuing scrum Dobson scored a soft try. With only a single point in it, the two sides tried desperately hard for the decisive score. The Scots kept their heads and showed greater stamina and control. Near the finish, Gamlin, who otherwise had a fine match, was caught in possession inside his 25. The Scottish forwards robbed the ball and Simson romped home to seal the game.

---

77 INTERNATIONAL CHAMPIONSHIP 1904 WALES

St Helen's, Swansea · Saturday 6 February 1904 · Lost 3–21

SCOTLAND WT Forrest (*Hawick*); HJ Orr (*London Scot*), †GE Crabbie (*Edinburgh Acs*), †LM MacLeod (*Cambridge U*), JS Macdonald (*Edinburgh U*); ED Simson (*Edinburgh U*), †AA Bisset (*RIE Coll*); DR Bedell-Sivright (*W of Scot*), LHI Bell (*Edinburgh Acs*), AG Cairns (*Watsonians*), WE Kyle (*Hawick*), MC Morrison* (*Royal HSFP*), †EJ Ross (*London Scot*), WP Scott (*W of Scot*), GO Turnbull (*Edinburgh Wdrs*)

WALES HB Winfield (*Cardiff*); WM Llewellyn* (*Newport*), CC Pritchard (*Newport*), RT Gabe (*Cardiff*), E Morgan (*London Welsh*); RH Jones (*Swansea*), RM Owen (*Swansea*); AB Brice (*Aberavon*), DH Davies (*Neath*), AF Harding (*Cardiff*), JJ Hodges (*Newport*), W Joseph (*Swansea*), W O'Neil (*Cardiff*), E Thomas (*Newport*), HV Watkins (*Llanelli*)

REFEREE FW Nicholls (*England*)

SCORING Winfield, pen (0–3); Gabe, try (0–6); Winfield, con (0–8); Jones, try (0–11); Winfield, con (0–13) (half-time) Morgan, try (0–16); Orr, try (3–16); Brice, try (3–19); Winfield, try (3–21)

Wales won an unexpectedly easy victory and were clearly the better side. They played with great confidence, combined well and eagerly grasped their opportunities. On the left, Gabe and Morgan formed an effective partnership, and the Welsh backs were purposeful and ready to attack. By contrast, their Scottish opponents, as *The Times* said, 'wandered about the field in an aimless way'. The Scottish forwards were largely outplayed and the half-backs were always under pressure, although Simson defended well. At full-back, Walter Forrest was the best of a disappointing side and his tackling prevented a much heavier defeat. The afternoon was bright, but the pitch was slippery from morning rain. After some 15 minutes, Scotland were penalised for foot-up in a scrum and Winfield kicked a fine goal. Then, from a series of mauls near the Scottish line, Jones and Morgan combined to send Gabe over at the posts and Winfield added the simple conversion. In another attack, Gabe tried to jump over a tackle by Forest but landed awkwardly on his head and play had to be stopped to allow him to recover. Just before the interval, Jones scored a try converted by Winfield and with the home side leading 13–0 the match was as good as over. Playing with the breeze behind them in the second half, Scotland were unlucky not score when Macdonald put a foot into touch just before he crossed the line. Wales worked play back up the field and Morgan scored an unconverted try after a clever movement. Scotland's only score came from a scrum inside Welsh territory and Bisset gave Orr a clear run-in. Wales replied with a similar effort by Brice and Winfield added the extras. The Scots rallied strongly in the closing stages, but their attacks were too laboured and the home side had few problems holding out for a handsome victory.

78   INTERNATIONAL CHAMPIONSHIP 1904   IRELAND

Lansdowne Road, Dublin · Saturday 28 February 1904 · Won 19–3

SCOTLAND WT Forrest (*Hawick*); HJ Orr (*London Scot*), AB Timms (*Cardiff*), LM MacLeod (*Cambridge U*), JS Macdonald (*Edinburgh U*); ED Simson (*Edinburgh U*), JI Gillespie (*Edinburgh Acs*); DR Bedell-Sivright (*W of Scot*), LHI Bell (*Edinburgh Acs*), AG Cairns (*Watsonians*), WE Kyle (*Hawick*), †WM Milne (*Glasgow Acads*), MC Morrison* (*Royal HSFP*), WP Scott (*W of Scot*), †JB Waters (*Cambridge U*)

IRELAND J Fulton (*NIFC*); JE Moffatt (*Old Wesley*), JC Parke (*Dublin U*), HH Corley* (*Wdrs*), CG Robb (*QC Belfast*); TTH Robinson (*Dublin U*), ED Caddell (*Dublin U*); CE Allen (*Derry*), F Gardiner (*NIFC*), GT Hamlet (*Old Wesley*), P Healey (*Limerick*), M Ryan (*Rockwell Coll*), A Tedford (*Malone*), J Wallace (*Wdrs*), J Wallace (*Wdrs*)

REFEREE W Williams (*England*)

SCORING Bedell-Sivright, try (3–0) (half-time) Timms, try (6–0); Macdonald, con (8–0); Sivright, try (11–0); Macdonald, con (13–0); Moffatt, try (13–3); Macdonald, try (16–3); Simson, try (19–3)

Most of this match was played in drizzling rain, but the pitch was in good order. Scotland were rather fortunate to be in the lead at the interval as Ireland had the better of the first half. However, the visitors were well on top after the break and ran out comfortable winners, scoring five tries to one. The two sets of forwards were fairly evenly matched, but the Scottish backs combined well and took their chances. Ireland made a strong start and seemed to have scored a try after only a few minutes. They dribbled the ball over the Scottish line, but the referee ruled that a defender had reached it first. Shortly afterwards, play moved into the Irish 25 and after a scramble near the line Fulton, the Irish full-back, lost control of the ball and Bedell-Sivright and Kyle dived on it simultaneously, the former being credited with the score. Ireland then had a lot of pressure, but could not penetrate the tight Scottish defence. They lost a great chance when Parke broke away with support close at hand, but his final pass went to ground. Early in the second half, Macdonald made a weaving run before finding Timms who eluded the last defender to score between the posts. The Scottish forwards then began to assert themselves. Fulton once again failed to deal with a ball near his own line and Bedell-Sivright pounced on it for another try. The Irish backs put together a good move inside the Scottish 25 and Moffatt scored an unconverted try in the corner. The Scots replied with a similar move of their own which ended with Macdonald dashing around behind the posts. Near the finish, Simson dummied his way through the defence for a fine solo try. At full-back, Walter Forrest had another excellent display, and Morrison and Bedell-Sivright were prominent amongst the forwards.

---

79   INTERNATIONAL CHAMPIONSHIP 1904   ENGLAND

Inverleith · Saturday 19 March 1904 · Won 6–3

SCOTLAND WT Forrest (*Hawick*); JE Crabbie (*Edinburgh Acs*), LM MacLeod (*Cambridge U*), AB Timms (*Cardiff*), JS Macdonald (*Edinburgh U*); JI Gillespie (*Edinburgh Acs*), ED Simson (*Edinburgh U*); DRB Sivright (*W of Scot*), AG Cairns (*Watsonians*), †HN Fletcher (*Edinburgh U*), WE Kyle (*Hawick*), WM Milne (*Glasgow As*), MC Morrison* (*Royal HSFP*), WP Scott (*W of Scot*), JB Waters (*Cambridge U*)

ENGLAND HT Gamlin (*Blackheath*); T Simpson (*Rockcliff*), AT Brettargh (*Liverpool OB*), EW Dillon (*Harlequins*), EJ Vivyan (*Devonport Alb*); PS Hancock (*Richmond*), WV Butcher (*Bristol*); VH Cartwright (*Oxford U*), J Daniell* (*Richmond*), PF Hardwick (*Percy Park*), GH Keeton (*Richmond*), JG Milton (*Bedford GS*), NJNH Moore (*Bristol*), CJ Newbold (*Blackheath*), FM Stout (*Richmond*)

REFEREE S Lee (*Ireland*)

SCORING Crabbie, try (3–0) (half-time) Vivyan, try (3–3); Macdonald, try (6–3)

Conditions were favourable despite a strong south-westerly wind. This was a keenly contested and exciting match between two well balanced sides. The Scottish forwards were strong in the scrums and fast in the loose. Gillespie and Simson, the Scottish half-backs, had the better of their opponents and the Scottish backs combined well. Playing with the wind behind them, Scotland opened the scoring after 13 minutes. Taking the ball from a scrum, Gillespie drew the defence and McLeod linked with Crabbie who scored a try at the corner. Shortly afterwards, Macdonald crossed the line but was recalled for putting a foot in touch. England lost their inspirational captain John Daniell because of a head injury. Against doctor's orders, he returned for the second half but he was never quite the same. Scotland were close to scoring on several occasions, but the English defence was very strong. Ten minutes after the restart, Vivyan, the English wing, intercepted a loose pass and from the ensuing maul he ran round behind the posts. His conversion attempt rebounded off the crossbar. England made good use of the wind and put the Scots under pressure for a spell, and Timms had to go off temporarily. Scotland finished strongly and with a few minutes to go an English clearing kick was charged down and Macdonald pounced for a try which the referee awarded after consultation with the touch-judge. Macdonald missed the difficult conversion, but it was Scotland's day.

Inverleith · Saturday 4 February 1905 · Lost 3–6

SCOTLAND WT Forrest (*Hawick*); JS Macdonald (*Edinburgh U*), †JL Forbes (*Watsonians*), LM MacLeod (*Cambridge U*), JE Crabbie (*Oxford U*); †P Munro (*Oxford U*), ED Simson (*Edinburgh U*); AG Cairns (*Watsonians*), HN Fletcher (*Edinburgh U*), WE Kyle (*Hawick*), †AW Little (*Hawick*), WM Milne (*Glasgow Acs*), †A Ross (*Royal HSFP*), WP Scott* (*W of Scot*), RS Stronach (*Glasgow Acs*)

WALES G Davies (*Swansea*); WM Llewellyn* (*Newport*), D Rees (*Swansea*), RT Gabe (*Cardiff*), E Morgan (*London Welsh*); WJ Trew (*Swansea*), RM Owen (*Swansea*); AF Harding (*London Welsh*), JJ Hodges (*Newport*), D Jones (*Treherbert*), W Joseph (*Swansea*), W O'Neil (*Cardiff*), CM Pritchard (*Newport*), G Travers (*Pill Harriers*), HW Watkins (*Llanelli*)

REFEREE H Kennedy (*Ireland*)

SCORING Little, try (3–0); Llewellyn, try (3–3) (half-time) Llewellyn, try (3–6)

The weather was favourable apart from a strong cross wind. A very good Welsh team won their first victory on Scottish soil for 12 years. The forward exchanges were evenly balanced, but the Welsh backs had more speed and guile. It was only a great defensive display by Forrest, the Scottish full-back, which prevented a heavier defeat. Playing with the wind behind them in the first half, Scotland made a lot of attacks and forward Ned Little powered his way over from close range. Near the interval, Rees made a weaving run and Llewellyn scored at the corner. Wales had most of the play in the second half and towards the finish Rees created another a gap for Llewellyn to score the winning try. Straight after the game, Little, the Scottish try-scorer, turned professional with Wigan.

Inverleith · Saturday 25 February 1905 · Lost 5–11

SCOTLAND WT Forrest (*Hawick*); †WT Ritchie (*Cambridge U*), LM MacLeod (*Cambridge U*), AB Timms (*Cardiff*), †RH McCowat (*Glasgow Acs*); ED Simson (*Edinburgh U*), P Munro (*Oxford U*); AG Cairns (*Watsonians*), †MR Dickson (*Edinburgh U*), WE Kyle (*Hawick*), WM Milne (*Glasgow Acs*), A Ross (*Royal HSFP*), WP Scott* (*W of Scot*), RS Stronach (*Glasgow Acs*), L West (*Carlisle*)

IRELAND MF Landers (*Cork Const*); JE Moffatt (*Old Wesley*), B Maclear (*Cork Const*), GAD Harvey (*Wdrs*), H Thrift (*Dublin U*); TTH Robinson (*Dublin U*), ED Caddell (*Dublin U*); CE Allen* (*Derry*), JJ Coffey (*Lansdowne*), GT Hamlet (*Old Wesley*), HJ Knox (*Dublin U*), HJ Millar (*Monkstown*), A Tedford (*Malone*), J Wallace (*Wdrs*), HG Wilson (*Malone & Glasgow U*)

REFEREE P Coles (*England*)

SCORING Tedford, try (0–3); Maclear, con (0–5) (half-time) Wallace, try (0–8); Moffatt, try (0–11); Timms, try (3–11); Forrest, con (5–11)

Playing in perfect conditions, the Irish forwards were in an aggressive mood and never allowed the Scots to settle down. Their fast, bustling tactics were almost irresistible and they had great stamina and determination. The Scots were out on their feet long before the finish. Irish centre Basil Maclear was always dangerous and his strong running was very hard to stop. Munro and Simson, the Scottish half-backs, played well behind a beaten pack, but the three-quarters made too many errors. At full-back, Walter Forrest gave another excellent display and his firm tackling saved the Scots numerous times. Both sides had early spells of pressure before the Irish forwards made a thunderous charge and Tedford, who may have been offside, scored near the posts. Soon after the interval, Wallace scored a second try and later Maclear drew the defence to create a simple run-in for Moffatt. Near the finish, Munro broke away and cross-kicked to Timms who scored a consolation try for the jaded Scots.

---

82   INTERNATIONAL CHAMPIONSHIP 1905   ENGLAND

Richmond · Saturday 18 March 1905 · Won 8–0

SCOTLAND †DG Schulze (*London Scot*); WT Ritchie (*Cambridge U*), GAW Lamond (*Bristol*), AB Timms* (*Cardiff*), †T Elliot (*Gala*); ED Simson (*Edinburgh U*), P Munro (*Oxford U*); AG Cairns (*Watsonians*), WE Kyle (*Hawick*), †JC MacCallum (*Watsonians*), †HG Monteith (*Cambridge U*), A Ross (*Royal HSFP*), WP Scott (*W of Scot*), RS Stronach (*Glasgow Acs*), L West (*Carlisle*)

ENGLAND JT Taylor (*W Hartlepool*); SF Cooper (*Blackheath*), JE Raphael (*OMT*), AT Brettargh (*Liverpool OB*), T Simpson (*Rockcliff*); AD Stoop (*Oxford U*), WV Butcher (*Streatham*); VH Cartwright (*Nottingham*), TA Gibson (*Northern*), CEL Hammond (*Harlequins*), JL Mathias (*Bristol*), JG Milton (*Camborne*), CJ Newbold (*Blackheath*), SH Osborne (*St Bees*), FM Stout (*Richmond*)

REFEREE HD Bowen (*Wales*)

SCORING No scoring in the first half. Simson, try (3–0); Stronach, try (6–0); Scott, con (8–0)

Both sides were playing to avoid the wooden spoon. The first half was evenly balanced and there were some good individual efforts and near misses. For Scotland, Ritchie and Timms both knocked-on with the try-line beckoning. Timms also missed a drop goal attempt and Cairns charged the ball down over the English line, but a defender beat him to the touchdown. The Scottish forwards gained the upper-hand in the second half. Munro and Simpson, the Scottish halves, played astutely and the three-quarters were very sound. All of the points were scored in the first ten minutes of the second half. In a brilliant piece of opportunism, Simson sent a high kick into the English 25 and followed-up so quickly that he was able to snatch the ball and score in the corner before the defence could react. Then the Scots made a great attack from midway and Stronach ran away to the line. Both sides had further chances and England made a strong late rally, but there was no more scoring.

---

83   TOUR MATCH   NEW ZEALAND

Inverleith · Saturday 18 November 1905 · Lost 7–12

SCOTLAND †JG Scoular (*Cambridge U*); †JT Simson (*Watsonians*), †KG MacLeod (*Cambridge U*), LM MacLeod (*Cambridge U*), †T Sloan (*Glasgow Acs*); †LL Greig (*Utd Servs*);

ED Simson (*Edinburgh U*), P Munro (*London Scot*); DR Bedell-Sivright* (*Edinburgh U*), WE Kyle (*Hawick*), JC MacCallum (*Watsonians*), †JM Mackenzie (*Edinburgh U*), †WL Russell (*Glasgow U*),
WP Scott (*W of Scot*), L West (*Carlisle*)

NEW ZEALAND GA Gillett (*Canterbury*); WJ Wallace (*Wellington*), RG Deans (*Canterbury*), GW Smith (*Auckland*); J Hunter (*Taranaki*), JW Stead (*Southland*); F Roberts (*Wellington*); ST Casey (*Otago*), GA Tyler (*Auckland*), W Cunningham (*Auckland*), FT Glasgow (*Taranaki*), A McDonald (*Otago*), JM O'Sullivan (*Taranaki*), CE Seeling (*Auckland*), D Gallaher* (*Auckland*)

REFEREE W Kennedy (*Ireland*)

SCORING Simson, drop (4–0); Glasgow, try (4–3); Smith, try (4–6); MacCallum, try (7–6) (half-time) Smith, try (7–9); Cunningham, try (7–12)

The first All Blacks of 1905–6 are regarded as the most important tourists in rugby history. They were still unbeaten when they played Scotland, which was the 20th match of the tour and also New Zealand's first-ever test match in the British Isles. The Scottish Football Union was rather disdainful about the brash newcomers and their fancy ways. They did not award caps and only finalised the Scottish team shortly before kick-off. To make matters worse, quarter-back Nolan Fell withdrew from the original selection. A medical student at Edinburgh University, Fell was born in New Zealand and had already won seven Scottish caps, but he refused to play against the land of his birth. Needless to say, he was never selected for Scotland again. His place went to Louis Greig who, on this occasion, played as a third quarter-back in an attempt to counter the New Zealanders' extra roving player, the tourists fielding seven forwards and a kind of free-ranging wing forward. The experiment was not successful and the Scottish back play was often disorganised and uncertain. In a tense encounter played on a hard pitch, Scotland relied on their traditional dribbling rushes and the New Zealanders favoured a handling game. The Scots opened the scoring when Simson dropped a goal from a scrum. New Zealand replied with a brace of tries by the Scottish-sounding Glasgow and Smith, and then John MacCallum scored for the Scots after a forward charge. Early in the second half, Lewis MacLeod, the elder brother of Ken, went off with an ankle injury and could only resume with a bad limp. New Zealand had the better of the play, but they made unforced errors and struggled to get through the Scottish defence. The closing stages were very exciting and the tourists came close to losing their unbeaten record. With only minutes to go, Smith, the Auckland winger, took the ball at full speed near the Scottish 25 and rounded Scoular to score at the corner. The New Zealanders were ecstatic and Smith was warmly embraced by his team-mates, breaking an unwritten rule that players were not supposed to show their emotions. Wallace missed the awkward conversion, but a few minutes later Cunningham made certain with another try. The final whistle was greeted in stony silence by the parsimonious crowd apart from some visiting colonial students who made their feelings all too clear. In the evening, the SFU did not give any hospitality to the New Zealand side, as was traditional, and instead the tourists were entertained by a local Australasian society. There was also considerable rancour over the division of the gate receipts, the outcome of which was that the Scots refused to play New Zealand when they next visited the British Isles in 1924.

THE FIRST TEST MATCH OF THE RUGBY TOUR.—NEW ZEALAND BEAT SCOTLAND.

PLAYED AT EDINBURGH ON SATURDAY LAST, AND WON BY THE COLONIALS DURING THE LAST FIVE MINUTES' PLAY.

Piping the Scotch team on to the ground.   *Scotland get into the Colonial twenty-five.*

2. D. Gallaher, the New Zealand captain and forward.   1. The New Zealand Maori dance and song.   3. The brakes arriving outside the ground.   4. G. W. Smith, the speedy New Zealand three-quarter.

Wallace takes a place kick.   *Scotland nearly score.—Collared within two yards of the line.*

In November 1905, *The Illustrated Sporting and Dramatic News* reported on the first-ever match between Scotland and New Zealand.

Cardiff Arms Park · Saturday 3 February 1906 · Lost 3–9

SCOTLAND JG Scoular (*Cambridge U*); †WC Church (*Glasgow Acs*), T Sloan (*Glasgow Acs*), KG MacLeod (*Cambridge U*), †ABHL Purves (*London Scot*); ED Simson (*Edinburgh U*), P Munro (*Oxford U*); DR Bedell-Sivright (*Edinburgh U*), AG Cairns (*Watsonians*), WE Kyle (*Hawick*), JC MacCallum (*Watsonians*), HG Monteith (*Cambridge U*), WL Russell (*Glasgow Acs*), WP Scott (*W of Scot*), L West* (*Hartlepool Rov*)

WALES HB Winfield (*Cardiff*); HT Maddock (*London Welsh*), EG Nicholls* (*Cardiff*), CC Pritchard (*Pontypool*), E Morgan (*London Welsh*); WJ Trew (*Swansea*), RA Gibbs (*Cardiff*); RM Owen (*Swansea*); AF Harding (*London Welsh*), JJ Hodges (*Newport*), D Jones (*Aberdare*), W Joseph (*Swansea*), CM Pritchard (*Newport*), G Travers (*Pill Harriers*), JF Williams (*London Welsh*)

REFEREE JW Allen (*Ireland*)

SCORING Hodges, try (0–3); Pritchard, try (0–6) (half-time) Maddock, try (0–9); MacLeod, pen (3–9)

Conditions were fair but the pitch was heavy underfoot. Following the example of New Zealand, Wales experimented with seven forwards and an extra half-back. The Scottish forwards and half-backs were in good form, especially in loose play, but with the exception of Ken MacLeod, the three-quarters made too many errors. Scotland were unfortunate not to be awarded an early try. The forwards rushed the ball over the line where it rebounded off a policeman standing inside the goal area. Bedell-Sivright touched it down, but the referee disallowed the score. Both sides had some pressure and, at times, MacCallum came out of the pack to counter the extra Welsh player. Wales opened the scoring when Morgan kicked across the field and Hodges followed-up for a try. Then Nicholls missed a drop goal attempt and Pritchard raced-up to claim the touchdown. In the second half, Maddock gathered the ball near midfield and made a swerving run through several weak tackles for the third Welsh try. Inside the last ten minutes MacLeod dropped kicked a penalty.

Lansdowne Park · Saturday 24 February 1906 · Won 13–6

SCOTLAND JG Scoular (*Cambridge U*); KG MacLeod (*Cambridge U*), JL Forbes (*Watsonians*), †MW Walter (*London Scot*), ABHL Purves (*London Scot*); ED Simson (*Edinburgh U*), P Munro (*Oxford U*); DR Bedell-Sivright (*Edinburgh U*), AG Cairns (*Watsonians*), WE Kyle (*Hawick*), JC MacCallum (*Watsonians*), HG Monteith (*London Scot*), WL Russell (*Glasgow Acs*), WP Scott (*W of Scot*), L West* (*London Scot*)

IRELAND GJ Henebrey (*Garryowen*); CG Robb (*QU Belfast*), JC Parke (*Dublin U*), F Casement (*Dublin U*), HJ Anderson (*Old Wesley*); B Maclear (*Cork Const*), ED Caddell (*Dublin U*), WB Purdon (*QC Belfast*); CE Allen* (*Derry*), JJ Coffey (*Lansdowne*), F Gardiner (*NIFC*), HJ Knox (*Lansdowne*), A Tedford (*Malone*), M White (*QC Cork*), HG Wilson (*Malone*)

REFEREE VH Cartwright (*England*)

SCORING Bedell-Sivright, try (3–0); MacCallum, con (5–0); Munro, try (8–0); MacCallum, con (10–0) (half-time) MacLeod, mark (13–0); Parke, try (13–3); Robb, try (13–6)

Like Wales three weeks earlier, Ireland played with seven forwards and an extra roving player, but in this case the experiment was not very successful. The Scottish forwards exploited their weight advantage in the scrums, and Simson and Munro, the Scottish half-backs, were in fine form. It was only after Scotland had built-up a big lead that Maclear, the Irish half-back, joined his forwards. Playing on a greasy surface, both sides had some early chances and the Scots made several strong rushes to the Irish line. After 15 minutes, Russell made a good dribbling run and Bedell-Sivright picked-up and dashed through for a try. Ten minutes later, MacLeod was caught just short, but Munro followed-up to score a try. Ireland were much livelier in the second half and both sides came close to scoring, but the defences were firm. MacLeod dropped a goal from a mark and in a late surge Ireland scored two tries in the closing minutes.

86   INTERNATIONAL CHAMPIONSHIP 1906   ENGLAND

Inverleith · Saturday 17 March 1906 · Lost 3–9

SCOTLAND JG Scoular (*Cambridge U*); KG MacLeod (*Cambridge U*), JL Forbes (*Watsonians*), MW Walter (*London Scot*), ABHL Purves (*London Scot*); ED Simson (*Edinburgh U*), P Munro (*Oxford U*); DR Bedell-Sivright (*Edinburgh U*), AG Cairns (*Watsonians*), WE Kyle (*Hawick*), JC MacCallum (*Watsonians*), HG Monteith (*London Scot*), WL Russell (*Glasgow Acs*), WP Scott (*W of Scot*), L West* (*London Scot*)

ENGLAND EJ Jackett (*Falmouth*); JE Raphael (*OMT*), HE Shewring (*Bristol*), JGG Birkett (*Harlequins*), T Simpson (*Rockcliff*); J Peters (*Plymouth*), AD Stoop (*Harlequins*); VH Cartwright* (*Nottingham*), R Dibble (*Bridgwater & Alb*), J Green (*Skipton*), CEL Hammond (*Harlequins*), TS Kelly (*Exeter*), AL Kewney (*Rockcliff*), WA Mills (*Devonport Alb*), CH Shaw (*Moseley*)

REFEREE JW Allen (*Ireland*)

SCORING Raphael, try (0–3); Purves, try (3–3) (half-time) Simson, try (3–6); Mills, try (3–9)

England surprised their critics by winning quite convincingly. The English forwards had been dismissed as 'beefy, slow and cumbersome', but they held a definite edge and Peters and Stoop, the English half-backs, were in great form. Stoop, in particular, was dangerous in attack, courageous in defence and his long passes gave his three-quarter line plenty of time and scope. By contrast, the Scottish backs were mostly disappointing. Their passing was slow and inaccurate, their kicking wayward and some of their tackling was weak. The pitch was heavy and Scotland faced into a strong wind in the first half. They started promisingly with the forwards making their traditional rushes, but MacLeod and Bedell-Sivright were both injured early on. After about 15 minutes, Raphael picked-up a loose ball and made a long run up the touchline for a rather soft try. Scotland equalised when Munro broke away from a scrum and made an opening for Purves. Early in the second half, Simson, the English wing, claimed a loose ball and made a long diagonal run past several tackles for a great solo try. Both sides had some opportunities and Raphael was just stopped with the line in front of him. Forbes, the Scottish centre, just managed to catch Raphael who had the line at his mercy. Both sides continued to press, but there was no further scoring.

Hampden Park, Glasgow · Saturday 17 November 1906 · Won 6–0

SCOTLAND JG Scoular (*Cambridge U*); KG MacLeod (*Cambridge U*), T Sloan (*Glasgow Acs*), MW Walter (*London Scot*), ABHL Purves (*London Scot*); P Munro (*Oxford U*), LL Greig* (*Utd Servs*); DR Bedell-Sivright (*Edinburgh U*), †GM Frew (*Glasgow HSFP*), †IC Geddes (*London Scot*), JC MacCallum (*Watsonians*), HG Monteith (*London H*), WP Scott (*W of Scot*), †LM Spiers (*Watsonians*), †WH Thomson (*W of Scot*)

SOUTH AFRICA AFW Marsburg (*Griqualand W*); AC Stegmann (*W Province*), HA de Villiers (*W Province*), JD Krige (*W Province*), JA Loubser (*W Province*); HW Carolin* (*W Province*), FJ Dobbin (*Griqualand W*); DJ Brink (*W Province*), D Brooks (*Border*), AF Burdett (*W Province*), WA Burger (*Border*), H Daneel (*W Province*), DS Mare (*Transvaal*), WS Morkel (*Transvaal*), JWE Raaff (*Griqualand W*)

REFEREE HH Chorley (*Ireland*)

SCORING No scoring in the first half. MacLeod, try (3–0); Purves, try (6–0)

This was a third home game of the season so it was decided to play it at Hampden Park, which had recently opened. The First Springboks were making a 28 match tour of the British Isles and were still unbeaten by the time they faced Scotland, the 16th match of the tour. The pitch was very soft after several days of continuous rain, which suited the home side perfectly. The Scottish forwards rose to the occasion. Their footwork was excellent and they controlled both the scrums and loose play. Behind them Greig and Munro, the Scottish quarter-backs, played a canny game and the rest of the Scottish backs defended courageously. The South Africans were never allowed to settle into their normal pattern, but they were hampered by a series of injuries. In

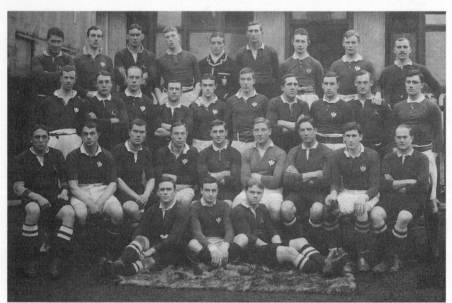

The combined Scotland and South Africa teams photographed together before Scotland's famous win at Hampden Park in November 1906. *SRU*

the first half, Brink had to leave the field for a spell and was reduced to a passenger when he returned. Mare broke several bones in his hand and had to move to the wing. In the second half Marsburg had to retire for good after a head wound. There was no scoring in the first half, although Scotland completely dominated play. As *The Scotsman* reported: 'At the interval the Scottish half of the field presented a stretch of beautifully green swath practically unmarked, and the other half was worn quite black as the result of constant scrummaging and contesting.' Playing with the wind in the second half, Scotland scored in sensational style. Munro punted high across the field to the right and MacLeod, running at top speed, caught the ball on the full and scored at the corner before the defence had time to react. Shortly afterwards, the South Africans made their only break of the day, but Loubser was hunted down by Scoular. Towards the finish, the Scottish forwards made a strong rush to the line and Purves scored a try to seal a historic win for Scotland. The South Africans accepted their defeat in good spirits and it was reported that Scottish exiles in South Africa were absolutely ecstatic.

---

88   INTERNATIONAL CHAMPIONSHIP 1907   WALES

Inverleith · Saturday 2 February 1907 · Won 6–3

SCOTLAND   T Sloan (*Glasgow Acs*); KG MacLeod (*Cambridge U*), †DG MacGregor (*Pontypridd*), WM Walter (*London Scot*), ABHL Purves (*London Scot*); ED Simson (*London Scot*), LL Greig* (*Utd Servs*); DR Bedell-Sivright (*Edinburgh U*), GM Frew (*Glasgow HSFP*), IC Geddes (*London Scot*), JC MacCallum (*Watsonians*), HG Monteith (*London Scot*), †GA Sanderson (*Royal HSFP*), WP Scott (*W of Scot*), LM Spiers (*Watsonians*)

WALES   HB Winfield (*Cardiff*); JL Williams (*Cardiff*), RT Gabe (*Cardiff*), JH Evans (*Pontypool*), HT Maddock (*London Welsh*); RM Owen (*Swansea*), WJ Trew* (*Swansea*); RA Gibbs (*Cardiff*); JA Brown (*Cardiff*), WH Dowell (*Newport*), TH Evans (*Llanelli*), CM Pritchard (*Newport*), G Travers (*Pill Harriers*), J Watts (*Llanelli*), AJ Webb (*Abertillery*)

REFEREE   J Lefevre (*Ireland*)

SCORING   Winfield, pen (0–3) (half-time) Purves, try (3–3); Monteith, try (6–3)

David MacGregor won his first cap. He was born in Wales to a Scottish father and had been asked to be a reserve for Wales, but instead opted for Scotland. Played on a cold afternoon, this was an ordinary match that had an exciting ending. After a good win over England, Wales reverted to playing seven forwards with Gibbs acting as a rover. The forward exchanges were fairly even and the Scots used their traditional rush tactics to good effect. Both defences were strong and the only score in the first half was a penalty goal by Welsh full-back Bert Winfield. Early in the second half, the Scots won a scrum near the Welsh line and Purves brushed-off several defenders to score. A few minutes later, Winfield was injured when trying to stop a rush and had to leave the field. Scotland had a lot of pressure, but it seemed that the game would end in stalemate until they conjured a late try. Purves made a strong run before punting towards goal. MacGregor carried on and Monteith collected the ball and scrambled over. Wales made a strong finish and Gibbs touched down only to be called back for putting his foot in touch just short of the line.

Inverleith · Saturday 23 February 1907 · Won 15–3

SCOTLAND DG Schulze (*London Scot*); KG McLeod (*Cambridge U*), DG MacGregor
(*Pontypridd*), MW Walter (*London Scot*), ABHL Purves (*London Scot*); ED Simson (*London Scot*),
P Munro* (*London Scot*); DR Bedell-Sivright (*Edinburgh U*), GM Frew (*Glasgow HSFP*),
IC Geddes (*London Scot*), JC MacCallum (*Watsonians*), HG Monteith (*London Scot*),
GA Sanderson (*Royal HSFP*), WP Scott (*W of Scot*), LM Spiers (*Watsonians*)

IRELAND C Thompson (*Belfast Collegians*); HB Thrift (*Dublin U*), JC Parke (*Dublin U*),
TJ Greeves (*NIFC*), B MacLear (*Cork Const*); ED Cadell (*Wdrs*), TTH Robinson (*Wdrs*);
CE Allen* (*Derry*), W St J Cogan (*QC Cork*), F Gardiner (*NIFC*), GT Hamlet (*Old Wesley*),
HS Sugars (*Dublin U*), JA Sweeny (*Blackrock Coll*), A Tedford (*Malone*), HG Wilson (*Malone*)

REFEREE AD Jones (*England*)

SCORING Parke, pen (0–3) (half-time) Sanderson, try (3–3); MacLeod, con (5–3); Purves, try
(8–3); Geddes, con (10–3); Frew, try (13–3); Geddes, con (15–3)

This match was keenly fought but unspectacular. Scotland had greater stamina and
deserved to win, but the game was still in the balance until the closing stages. Playing
with a strong breeze behind them, the Irish forwards started vigorously and their
backs had several chances, but the Scottish defence was firm, especially Schulze who
made several try-saving tackles. The Scottish forwards were more assertive in the
second half and around the hour mark MacLeod sprinted into the Irish 25 and kicked
over the line. Unluckily for Ireland, the ball got stuck in some straw that had been
used to protect the pitch and Sanderson dashed up quickly to score a try. Ireland had
a spell of pressure before Walter broke away and fed Purves who raced under the
posts. Then the Scottish forwards made a strong charge and Frew scored a try. Geddes
converted both tries, ponderously removing his 'maul cap' before each kick.

Rectory Field, Blackheath · Saturday 16 March 1907 · Won 8–3

SCOTLAND DG Schulze (*London Scot*); ABHL Purves (*London Scot*), T Sloan (*Glasgow Acs*),
DG MacGregor (*Pontypridd*), KG McLeod (*Cambridge U*); P Munro* (*London Scot*), ED Simson
(*London Scot*); DR Bedell-Sivright (*Edinburgh U*), GM Frew (*Glasgow HSFP*), IC Geddes
(*London Scot*), JC MacCallum (*Watsonians*), GA Sanderson (*Royal HSFP*), †JMB Scott
(*Edinburgh Acs*), WP Scott (*W of Scot*), LM Spiers (*Watsonians*)

ENGLAND EJ Jackett (*Falmouth*); WC Wilson (*Richmond*), HE Shewring (*Bristol*), JGG Birkett
(*Harlequins*), AW Newton (*Blackheath*); J Peters (*Plymouth*), SP Start (*Utd Servs*); J Green
(*Skipton*), TS Kelly (*Exeter*), WA Mills (*Devonport Alb*), E Roberts* (*RNE Coll*), GD Roberts
(*Harlequins & Oxford U*), CH Shaw (*Moseley*), LAN Slocock (*Liverpool*), SG Williams
(*Devonport Alb*)

REFEREE TD Schofield (*Wales*)

SCORING No scoring in the first half. Simson, try (3–0); Purves, try (6–0); Geddes, con (8–0);
Peters, try (8–3)

Scotland completed their fourth win of the season and a clean-sweep in the Champion-

Captained by Pat Munro, this Scottish team won the Triple Crown at Blackheath in March 1907.
SRU

ship. They had a stiff breeze behind them in the first half, but the nearest that they came to scoring was a long drop kick by Ken MacLeod which hit an upright and rebounded back into play. The renowned Scottish pack took a long time to wear their opponents down and it was only in the second half that they gained the upper-hand. MacCallum knocked-on with the line beckoning and a few minutes later Simson powered away from a scrum for a fine solo try. The Scottish forwards had greater stamina and finished strongly. A few minutes before the end, a speculative kick to the English line bounced kindly for Purves who scored unopposed, his fourth try in four matches. Peters scored a late consolation try for England, the only try conceded by the Scots in the season.

---

91 INTERNATIONAL CHAMPIONSHIP 1908 WALES

St Helen's, Swansea · Saturday 1 February 1908 · Lost 5–6

SCOTLAND DG Schulze (*Dartmouth RN Coll*); †HG Martin (*Oxford U*), T Sloan (*London Scot*), MW Walter (*London Scot*), ABHL Purves (*London Scot*); LL Greig* (*Utd Servs*), †G Cunningham (*Oxford U*); DR Bedell-Sivright (*Edinburgh U*), †JA Brown (*Glasgow Acs*), GM Frew (*Glasgow HSFP*), IC Geddes (*London Scot*), †GC Gowlland (*London Scot*), JC MacCallum (*Watsonians*), JMB Scott (*Edinburgh Acs*), LM Spiers (*Watsonians*)

WALES HB Winfield (*Cardiff*); JL Williams (*Cardiff*), RT Gabe (*Cardiff*), WJ Trew (*Swansea*), RA Gibbs (*Cardiff*); PF Bush (*Cardiff*), TH Vile (*Newport*); JA Brown (*Cardiff*), WH Dowell (*Pontypool*), AF Harding (*London Welsh*), G Hayward (*Swansea*), W O'Neil (*Cardiff*), G Travers* (*Pill Harriers*), J Watts (*Llanelli*), AJ Webb (*Abertillery*)

REFEREE W Williams (*England*)

SCORING Trew, try (0–3); Purves, try (3–3); Geddes, con (5–3) (half-time) Williams, try (5–6)

This was a hard struggle, but play did not reach a high standard. The Scottish forwards held a slight advantage, especially in the open, but the back line, which was only finalised shortly before kick-off, was disappointing in attack. The Welsh backs were more dangerous and their half-backs, Bush and Vile, were outstanding. Both sides defended well and made many handling errors. Conditions were favourable and the crowd was estimated at around 40,000 people. After about 12 minutes, Gabe beat the defence and Trew had a clear run-in. Ten minutes later, the Scots made a long dribbling rush and Purves scored a try. Early in the second half, Bush put Gabe away and Williams was in support to complete the best move of the game. Both sides had chances towards the end and Greig, the Scottish captain, made a last desperate effort only to be stopped inches short. He claimed that he had grounded the ball before being dragged backwards, but the referee awarded a scrum.

---

92   INTERNATIONAL CHAMPIONSHIP 1908   IRELAND

Lansdowne Road, Dublin · Saturday 29 February 1908 · Lost 11–16

SCOTLAND DG Schulze (*London Scot*); H Martin (*Oxford U*), KG MacLeod (*Cambridge U*), MW Walter (*London Scot*), ABHL Purves (*London Scot*); LL Greig* (*Utd Servs*), G Cunningham (*Oxford U*); DR Bedell-Sivright (*Edinburgh U*), JA Brown (*Glasgow Acs*), GM Frew (*Glasgow HSFP*), JC MacCallum (*Watsonians*), GA Sanderson (*Royal HSFP*), JMB Scott (*Edinburgh Acs*), LM Spiers (*Watsonians*), †JS Wilson (*London Scot*)

IRELAND WP Hinton (*Old Wesley*); H Thrift* (*Dublin U*), JC Parke (*Monkstown*), GGP Beckett (*Dublin U*), C Thompson (*Belfast Collegians*); ED Caddell (*Wdrs*), FNB Smartt (*Dublin U*); F Gardiner (*NIFC*), GT Hamlet (*Old Wesley*), TG Harpur (*Dublin U*), HJ Knox (*Lansdowne*), T Smyth (*Malone*), B Solomons (*Dublin U*), A Tedford (*Malone*), HG Wilson (*Malone*)

REFEREE W Williams (*England*)

SCORING Thrift, try (0–3); Parke, con (0–5); MacLeod, try (3–5); Thompson, try (3–8); Beckett, try (3–11); Hinton, con (3–13) (half-time) Martin, try (6–13); MacLeod, con (8–13); MacLeod, pen (11–13); Thrift, try (11–16)

Scotland were favourites, but never looked like winning on the day. On a cold and breezy afternoon, centre Walter broke his collar-bone in the opening stages and the Scots had to play most of the game with only 14 men. Sanderson came out of the pack in the first half and MacCallum in the second, but the back-line was disorganised and the forwards struggled against the fiery Irish pack. Once again, Ken MacLeod was in outstanding form. Thrift, the Irish wing, opened the scoring with a try near the corner which was brilliantly converted by Parke. After a spell of Irish pressure, Martin intercepted a pass and ran away before linking with MacLeod who outwitted the remaining defenders and sprinted round behind the posts. His conversion attempt hit an upright. A few minutes later, the Irish backs combined to create a score for Thompson. Then Parke made a long run and drew the defence before giving a scoring pass to Beckett. Hinton converted to put Ireland 13–3 ahead at the break. With the wind behind, the Scots started to claw back the Irish lead. Martin intercepted another loose pass, chipped over the head of Hinton, the Irish full-back, and re-gathered the ball to score at the posts. MacLeod converted and later drop-kicked a penalty to bring the Scots back to within two points, but straight from the restart Thrift scored a try in the corner to seal the game for Ireland. A few minutes before the finish, MacLeod had to leave the field with cramp.

93   INTERNATIONAL CHAMPIONSHIP 1908   ENGLAND

Inverleith · Saturday 21 March 1908 · Won 16–10

SCOTLAND DG Schulze (*London Scot*); H Martin (*Oxford U*), KG MacLeod (*Cambridge U*), †CM Gilray (*London Scot*), ABHL Purves (*London Scot*); †J Robertson (*Clydesdale*), †AL Wade (*London Scot*); GM Frew (*Glasgow HSFP*), IC Geddes* (*London Scot*), WE Kyle (*Hawick*), JC MacCallum (*Watsonians*), HG Monteith (*London Scot*), †AL Robertson (*London Scot*), JMB Scott (*Edinburgh Acs*), LM Spiers (*Watsonians*)

ENGLAND GHD Lyon (*Utd Servs*); D Lambert (*Harlequins*), JGG Birkett (*Harlequins*), WN Lapage (*Utd Servs*), A Hudson (*Gloucester*); J Davey (*Redruth*), RH Williamson (*Oxford U*); F Boylen (*Hartlepool Rov*), R Dibble (*Bridgwater & Alb*), R Gilbert (*Devonport Alb*), TS Kelly (*Exeter*), WL Oldham (*Coventry*), LAN Slocock* (*Liverpool*), FB Watson (*Utd Servs*), T Woods (*Bridgwater & Alb*)

REFEREE HH Corley (*Ireland*)

SCORING Birkett, try (0–3); Lambert, con (0–5); MacLeod (3–5); Slocock, try (3–8); Lambert, con (3–10); Purves, drop (7–10) (half-time) MacLeod, try (10–10); Geddes, con (12–10); Schulze, drop (16–10)

In perfect conditions, both sides played open, attacking rugby and the result was a hugely entertaining match, one of the best between the two old rivals to date. The Scottish forwards had greater stamina and Ken MacLeod, on his final appearance, was outstanding. England scored a sensational try inside the first five minutes. From a scrum in midfield, the half-backs created an opening for Birkett who made a long run around Schulze, the Scottish full-back, to score between the posts. Lambert added the simple conversion. Soon after, MacLeod created space for Martin who in turn gave him an inside pass and MacLeod beat the last defenders for a thrilling try. Later, Wilkinson made a break from a maul before feeding Slocock who sprinted away to the line. Lambert converted and Purves dropped a goal to leave England 10–7 ahead at the interval. Scotland had the better of the second half, but they missed several clear chances. As the match wore on, it seemed that England would win until the Scottish three-quarters made a great handling movement and MacLeod scored his second try. Geddes converted to put the Scots in the lead for the first time. Lambert narrowly missed a penalty attempt and with a few minutes remaining Schulze dropped a goal to seal a memorable victory for the Scots.

94   INTERNATIONAL CHAMPIONSHIP 1909   WALES

Inverleith · Saturday 6 February 1909 · Lost 3–5

SCOTLAND DG Schulze (*London Scot*); H Martin (*Edinburgh Acs*), †AW Angus (*Watsonians*), CM Gilray (*London Scot*), JT Simson (*Watsonians*); G Cunningham (*London Scot*), †JM Tennent

(*W of Scot*); GM Frew (*Glasgow HSFP*), GC Gowlland (*London Scot*), WE Kyle (*Hawick*),
JC MacCallum (*Watsonians*), JM Mackenzie (*Edinburgh U*), A Ross (*Royal HSFP*), JMB Scott*
(*Edinburgh Acs*), JS Wilson (*London Scot*)

WALES J Bancroft (*Swansea*); AM Baker (*Newport*), JP Jones (*Newport*), WJ Trew* (*Swansea*),
JL Williams (*Cardiff*); RH Jones (*Swansea*), RM Owen (*Swansea*); TH Evans (*Llanelli*),
WI Morgan (*Swansea*), E Thomas (*Newport*), EJ Thomas (*Mountain Ash*), G Travers
(*Pill Harriers*), PD Waller (*Newport*), J Watts (*Llanelli*), AJ Webb (*Abertillery*)

REFEREE JW Jeffares (*Ireland*)

SCORING No scoring in the first half. Cunningham, pen (3–0); Trew, try (3–3); Bancroft,
con (3–5)

Played in ideal conditions, this was a fiercely contested but scrappy match between
two mediocre teams. The Scottish forwards were marginally better, but the backs did
little in attack and their handling was slow and inaccurate. After about 15 minutes,
Gilray, the Scottish centre, had to leave with a head knock. He returned in the second
half, but he was not quite right and later he was found to have been suffering from
concussion. Both sides missed chances in the first half. Simson dribbled over the line,
but was held back in the act of touching down. The Welsh players were in the habit
of killing the ball on the ground, much to the displeasure of the referee, and Bancroft,
the famous Welsh full-back, received 'a severe mauling' by the Scottish forwards. The
quality of play did not improve much in second half. Cunningham kicked a penalty
for Scotland and towards the end Wales made a strong rally and Trew scored a
converted try. Simson almost scored for Scotland, but he was hauled into touch
before he could put the ball down. Tennent was also denied when Bancroft made a
courageous save at his feet. In the dying seconds, Scotland were awarded a penalty
and amidst great tension Cunningham attempted the kick but the ball curled outside
of the post.

---

95   INTERNATIONAL CHAMPIONSHIP 1909   IRELAND

Inverleith · Saturday 27 February 1909 · Won 9–3

SCOTLAND DG Schulze (*London Scot*); JT Simson (*Watsonians*), †J Pearson (*Watsonians*),
T Sloan (*London Scot*), †RH Lindsay-Watson (*Hawick*); †JR MacGregor (*Edinburgh U*), JM
Tennent (*W of Scot*); GM Frew (*Glasgow HSFP*), WE Kyle (*Hawick*), WG Lely (*London Scot*),
JC MacCallum (*Watsonians*), JM Mackenzie (*Edinburgh U*), A Ross (*Royal HSFP*), JMB Scott*
(*Edinburgh Acs*), †CD Stuart (*W of Scot*)

IRELAND WP Hinton (*Old Wesley*); HB Thrift (*Dublin U*), JC Parke (*Monkstown*), C Thompson
(*Collegians*), RM Magrath (*Cork Const*); G Pinion (*Collegians*), F Gardiner* (*NIFC*); JC Blackham
(*QC Cork*), MG Garry (*Bective Rgrs*), T Halpin (*Garryowen*), GT Hamlet (*Old Wesley*), OJS Piper
(*Cork Const*), T Smyth (*Malone*), BA Solomons (*Dublin U*), HG Wilson (*Malone*)

REFEREE VH Cartwright (*England*)

SCORING Lindsay-Watson, try (3–0) (half-time) Parke, pen (3–3); McGregor, try (6–3); Kyle,
try (9–3)

Heavy rain before the match made the pitch soft and it cut up during the game.
Ireland had the better of the first half, but Scottish tackling was very firm. McGregor

and Tennent, the Scottish half-backs, were under a lot of pressure from the Irish marauders. Tennent started the match as scrum-half or 'scrum-worker', but switched position with his partner and played as a 'rover'. Just before the interval, Scotland opened the scoring against the run of play. Pearson drew the Irish defence and new cap Lindsay-Watson flew over on the left. In the second half, Parke equalised with a penalty for Ireland. The Scottish forwards slowly took charge and from a scrum near the Irish line MacGregor nipped through for a solo try. Then from a scrum in midfield the Scottish forwards rushed away and Kyle and MacCallum touched down simultaneously, the try being credited to Kyle. Both sides made some late attacks, but there was no further scoring.

---

96   INTERNATIONAL CHAMPIONSHIP 1909   ENGLAND

Athletic Ground, Richmond · Saturday 20 March 1909 · Won 18–8

SCOTLAND DG Schulze (*London Scot*); H Martin (*Oxford U*), J Pearson (*Watsonians*), CM Gilray (*Oxford U*), JT Simson (*Watsonians*); JM Tennent (*W of Scot*), G Cunningham* (*Oxford U*); GM Frew (*Glasgow HSFP*), GC Gowlland (*London Scot*), †JR Kerr (*Greenock Wdrs*), WE Kyle (*Hawick*), JC MacCallum (*Watsonians*), JM Mackenzie (*Edinburgh U*), †AR Moodie (*St Andrews U*), JMB Scott (*Edinburgh Acs*)

ENGLAND EJ Jackett (*Falmouth*); AC Palmer (*London H*), CCG Wright (*Cambridge U*), RW Poulton (*Oxford U*), ER Mobbs (*Northampton*); F Hutchinson (*Headingley*), HJH Sibree (*Harlequins*); R Dibble* (*Bridgwater & Alb*), FG Handford (*Manchester*), HC Harrison (*RN*), ED Ibbitson (*Headingley*), WA Johns (*Gloucester*), AL Kewney (*Leicester*), HJS Morton (*Cambridge U*), FB Watson (*RN*)

REFEREE EG Nicholls (*Wales*)

SCORING Simson, try (3–0); Mobbs, try (3–3); Watson, try (3–6); Palmer, con (3–8) (half-time) Gilray, try (6–8); Cunningham, con (8–8); Tennent, try (11–8); Cunningham, con (13–8); Tennent, try (16–8); Cunningham, con (18–8)

This was Scotland's sixth win in succession on English soil and England's final international before the move to Twickenham. The match was played before the Prince of Wales and around 20,000 spectators. The forward exchanges were evenly contested, but the Scottish half-backs, Tennent and Cunningham, were much better than their English opponents. They played with great determination and intelligence, and did some excellent spoiling at the heels of their aggressive pack. Scotland opened the scoring when Simson escaped up the touchline, evaded a last-ditch tackle and ran round behind the posts only for Cunningham to miss the simple conversion. Almost immediately, Mobbs responded with a try, but Palmer hooked the goal kick. England had a long spell of pressure and Palmer crossed the line only to be called back for an infringement. Later in the half, Watson scored from a lineout and Palmer converted to give England the lead at the interval. The Scottish forwards started the second half purposefully and after a few minutes Gilray feinted his way through the English defence to dot down between the posts. Then Mackenzie led a classic Scottish charge into English territory and Tennent slipped through for a try. With about 15 minutes left the Scottish forwards made another charge and Tennent scored his second try, despite a strong tackle by Jackett. Cunningham kicked the conversion from an awkward angle. England made a furious attempt to save the game, but the Scottish defence held out for a great victory. This was the only international match refereed by the famous Welsh three-quarter Gwyn Nicholls, who afterwards admitted that he had not been very good.

Inverleith · Saturday 22 January 1910 · Won 27–0

SCOTLAND †FG Buchanan (*Oxford U*); †IPM Robertson (*Watsonians*), AW Angus (*Watsonians*), J Pearson (*Watsonians*), JT Simson (*Watsonians*); G Cunningham* (*Oxford U*), JM Tennent (*W of Scot*); GM Frew (*Glasgow HSFP*), GC Gowlland (*London Scot*), JC MacCallum (*Watsonians*), AR Moodie (*St Andrews U*), JMB Scott (*Edinburgh Acs*), LM Spiers (*Watsonians*), †RC Stevenson (*St Andrews U*), CD Stuart (*W of Scot*)

FRANCE J Combe (*Stade Français*); E Lesieur (*Stade Français*), J Dedet (*Stade Français*), M Burgun (*RCF*), C Vareilles (*Stade Français*); C Martin (*Lyon*), A Theuriet (*SCUF*); P Guillemin (*RCF*), P Mauriat (*Lyon*), R Boudreaux (*SCUF*), A Hourdebaigt (*SBUC*), J Cadenat (*SCUF*), R Laffitte (*SCUF*), M Communeau* (*Stade Français*), A Massé (*SBUC*)

REFEREE GA Harris (*Ireland*)

SCORING Robertson, try (3–0); Angus, try (6–0); MacCallum, con (8–0); Tennent, try (11–0) (half-time) Tennent, try (14–0); Robertson, try (17–0); Gowlland, try (20–0); MacCallum, con (22–0); Tennent, try (25–0); MacCallum, con (27–0)

This was Scotland's first match against France, but the SFU treated it as a trial game for the rest of the Championship and did not award caps. The Scots played in white shirts and dark shorts so that the visitors could wear their light blue. The entire

Resplendent in their change white jerseys, this Scotland team played France in January 1910, the first fixture against the French. *SRU*

Scottish three-quarter line came from Watsonians, the leading Scottish club at this time. Conditions were clear and almost windless, and it was estimated that around 12,000 spectators were present. Scotland had too much experience for the international newcomers and the result was never in any doubt although the home side played well within themselves. Despite being raw at this level, France showed lots of potential and eagerness. They defended wholeheartedly, but they did not combine well and they were inclined to stray offside and obstruct opponents who did not have the ball. The referee, Mr Harris of Ireland, gave them considerable latitude in order to keep the game flowing. Scotland made a strong start and within the opening ten minutes Robertson and Angus scored tries. Then France came into the game and there was no more scoring until shortly before the interval when scrum-half Jim Tennent made a strong run for Scotland's third. A few minutes after the restart, Tennent stole round a scrum near the French line for another try. Later on, Scotland scored three tries in quick succession as the Frenchmen started to tire, including a third for Tennent who rounded off a dribbling rush with a neat pick-up and score.

98   INTERNATIONAL CHAMPIONSHIP 1910   WALES

Cardiff Arms Park · Saturday 5 February 1910 · Lost 0–14

SCOTLAND DG Schulze (*London Scot*); †WR Sutherland (*Hawick*), AW Angus (*Watsonians*), J Pearson (*Watsonians*), JT Simson (*Watsonians*); JM Tennent (*W of Scot*), †E Milroy (*Watsonians*); GM Frew* (*Glasgow HSFP*), GC Gowlland (*London Scot*), WE Kyle (*Hawick*), JC MacCallum (*Watsonians*), JM Mackenzie (*Edinburgh U*), JMB Scott (*Edinburgh Acs*), LM Spiers (*Watsonians*), CD Stuart (*W of Scot*)

WALES J Bancroft (*Swansea*); RA Gibbs (*Cardiff*), W Spiller (*Cardiff*), WJ Trew* (*Swansea*), AM Baker (*Newport*); PF Bush (*Cardiff*), WL Morgan (*Cardiff*); TH Evans (*Llanelli*), B Gronow (*Bridgend*), H Jarman (*Newport*), E Jenkins (*Newport*), WI Morgan (*Swansea*), J Pugsley (*Cardiff*), DJ Thomas (*Swansea*), AJ Webb (*Abertillery*)

REFEREE GHB Kennedy (*Ireland*)

SCORING Pugsley, try (0–3); Spiller, try (0–6); Bancroft, con (0–8) (half-time) Baker, try (0–11); J Morgan, try (0–14)

Persistent drizzle fell throughout the match and the playing field was quickly reduced to a deplorable state. There was little handling by either side, but the Welsh forwards adapted well to the conditions. Much of their footwork was devastatingly effective, outdoing the Scots at their own game. By contrast, the Scottish forwards were never comfortable in the thick and clinging mud. After some early forays, the Scottish backs were rarely seen in attack and some of their defensive work was weak. Fortunately for Scotland, full-back Douglas Schulze was in excellent form and his kicking, tackling and positional play helped save his side from a heavier defeat. Scotland were hampered when their stand-off Jim Tennent had to leave the field before half-time with an injured elbow. He returned to the field, but straight after the interval he was badly hurt again and had to retire for good, MacCallum coming out of the pack to replace him. Tennent's injuries were caused by old-fashioned pointed studs which led to new rules about footwear being introduced the following season. Joe Pugsley, the Cardiff

1. A line out.
3. A corner of the crowd.
4. Wiping the mud from a Scotchman's eyes.
2. The mud-covered players at half-time.
5. A try to Wales.

WALES BEAT SCOTLAND AT CARDIFF BY 14 POINTS TO NIL.

The Illustrated Sporting and Dramatic News reports on the Wales v Scotland match at Cardiff in February 1910.

forward, scored the first try after a dribbling rush and Spiller burst through the defence for Wales's second which Bancroft converted with a fine kick. In the second half, the short-handed Scots fought hard, but were mostly on the defensive. Gibbs and Baker broke through with a dribbling run which ended with the latter scoring out wide. Then after some loose play close to the Scottish line Ivor Morgan crossed to complete the scoring.

99   INTERNATIONAL CHAMPIONSHIP 1910   IRELAND

Balmoral Showgrounds, Belfast · Saturday 26 February 1910

Won 14–0

SCOTLAND DG Schulze (*Northampton*); †DG Macpherson (*London H*), MW Walter (*London Scot*), J Pearson (*Watsonians*), †JD Dobson (*Glasgow Acs*); G Cunningham* (*Oxford U*), †AB Lindsay (*London H*); †CH Abercrombie (*Utd Servs*), GM Frew (*Glasgow HSFP*), GC Gowlland (*London Scot*), JC MacCallum (*Watsonians*), JM Mackenzie (*Edinburgh U*), JMB Scott (*Edinburgh Acs*), RC Stevenson (*St Andrews U*), CD Stuart (*W of Scot*)

IRELAND WP Hinton (*Old Wesley*); JP Quinn (*Dublin U*), AR Foster (*QU Belfast*), AS Taylor (*QU Belfast*), C Thompson (*Collegians*); RA Lloyd (*Dublin U*), HM Read (*Dublin U*); JC Blackham (*Wdrs*), T Halpin (*Garryowen*), GT Hamlet* (*Old Wesley*), G McIldowie (*Malone*), H Moore (*QU Belfast*), OJS Piper (*Cork Const*), T Smyth (*Newport*), B Solomons (*Wdrs*)

REFEREE VH Cartwright (*England*)

SCORING Dobson, try (3–0) (half-time) Walter, try (6–0); Walter, try (9–0); Stuart, try (12–0); MacCallum, con (14–0)

Scotland made several changes after the defeat in Wales, including a first cap for wing Donald Macpherson who had played for his native New Zealand against Australia in 1905 before moving to London to continue his medical studies. In contrast to the Welsh match, conditions were almost perfect and the pitch was firm. Scotland played into a stiff headwind in the first half. There was little to choose between the two packs in the early stages. Both sides made errors and defended stoutly. Scotland began the scoring when Pearson made a dodging run from midfield before being caught near the corner, but Dobson was in close support to touch the ball down. With the wind behind them in the second half, Scotland applied more pressure. Good Scottish handling and support play created a score for Walter and after this the Irish seemed to lose heart. Walter scored his second try after a spirited attack by the Scottish forwards and a few minutes from time Stuart scored near the corner and MacCallum kicked the angled conversion. The Scottish forwards were a better combination and had greater stamina. New wing Jimmy Dobson made a splendid debut and half-back George Cunningham was courageous in defence, frustrating numerous Irish rushes with his speed. Irish full-back Hinton also had an impressive match and saved his side from a heavier defeat with his fierce tackling and long touch finders.

100   INTERNATIONAL CHAMPIONSHIP 1910   ENGLAND

Inverleith · Saturday 19 March 1910 · Lost 5–14

SCOTLAND DG Schulze (*London Scot*); WR Sutherland (*Hawick*), J Pearson (*Watsonians*), AW Angus (*Watsonians*), DG Macpherson (*London H*); G Cunningham* (*Oxford U*), JM Tennent (*W of Scot*); CH Abercrombie (*Utd Servs*), GC Gowlland (*London Scot*), JC MacCallum (*Watsonians*), JM Mackenzie (*Edinburgh U*), JMB Scott (*Edinburgh Acs*), LM Spiers (*Watsonians*), RC Stevenson (*St Andrews U*), CD Stuart (*W of Scot*)

ENGLAND WR Johnston (*Bristol*); FE Chapman (*Westoe*), JGG Birkett* (*Harlequins*), FM Stoop (*Harlequins*), PW Lawrie (*Leicester*); AD Stoop (*Harlequins*), ALH Gotley (*Oxford U*); LE Barrington-Ward (*Edinburgh U*), H Berry (*Gloucester*), R Dibble (*Bridgwater & Albion*), RHM Hands (*Oxford U*), L Haigh (*Manchester*), GR Hind (*Guy's H*), CH Pillman (*Blackheath*), JAS Ritson (*Northern*)

REFEREE GHB Kennedy (*Ireland*)

SCORING Macpherson, try (3–0); MacCallum, con (5–0); Birkett, try (5–3); Chapman, con (5–5) (half-time) Birkett, try (5–8); Berry, try (5–11); Ritson, try (5–14)

In an open and entertaining encounter, England deservedly won their first championship since 1892. The Scottish forwards were outstanding in the first half when their scrummaging and footwork was very effective, but gradually they fell away and the visitors ended up in total control. The Scottish half-backs were under a lot of pressure and as a result the three-quarters were only moderate in attack. Played in near perfect conditions and in front of a large crowd, both sides had some early opportunities. The Scottish forwards were full of their usual fire, but the talented English backs were denied several times only by desperate defence. Pearson made one great tap-tackle on

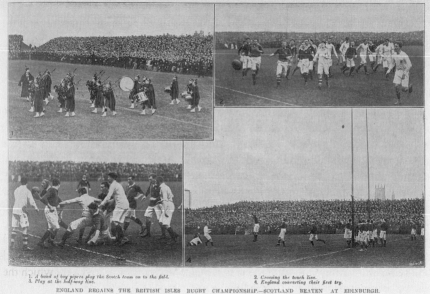

1. *A band of boy pipers play the Scotch team on to the field.* 2. *Crossing the touch line.*
3. *Play at the half-way line.* 4. *England converting their first try.*

ENGLAND REGAINS THE BRITISH ISLES RUGBY CHAMPIONSHIP.—SCOTLAND BEATEN AT EDINBURGH.

By beating Scotland by 14 points to 5 at Inverleith last Saturday before a record crowd for Edinburgh, England regained the Calcutta Cup and Championship.

The Illustrated Sporting and Dramatic News reports on England's victory at Inverleith in March 1910.

Lawrie as the Englishman looked certain to score. Sutherland, who was Scotland's best player, had a long solo run that took play into the English 25, and after some pressure Macpherson wriggled his way over at the posts. Soon afterwards, Macpherson was bundled into touch at the corner flag and then the Stoop brothers, Adrian and Freddie, combined to give Birkett a clear run to the Scottish line. Chapman converted to level the scores at half-time. The English forwards were much livelier in the second half and their backs enjoyed a steady supply of good possession. Birkett completed his brace and then Berry and Ritson both scored unconverted tries. A late move by Angus and Pearson set Sutherland away on a thrilling long run, but he was caught inches short of the English line.

---

101   INTERNATIONAL CHAMPIONSHIP 1911   FRANCE

Stade Colombes, Paris · Monday 2 January 1911 · Lost 15–16

SCOTLAND †HB Tod (*Gala*); WR Sutherland (*Hawick*), †TEB Young (*Durham U*),
FG Buchanan (*Oxford U*), J Pearson (*Watsonians*); P Munro* (*London Scot*), †FL Osler
(*Edinburgh U*); CH Abercrombie (*Utd Servs*), †R Fraser (*Cambridge U*), JC MacCallum
(*Watsonians*), AR Moodie (*St Andrews U*), JMB Scott (*Edinburgh Acs*), †AM Stevenson
(*Glasgow U*), RC Stevenson (*St Andrews U*), †FH Turner (*Oxford U*)

FRANCE J Combe (*Stade Français*); P Failliot (*RCF*), M Burgun (*RCF*), A Francquenelle
(*Vaugirard*), G Lane (*RCF*); G Peyroutou (*Périgueux*), G Laterrade (*Tarbes*); P Mouniq (*Toulouse*),
P Mauriat (*Lyon*), P Guillemin (*RCF*), P Decamps (*RCF*), F Forgues (*Bayonne*), M Legrain
(*Stade Français*), J Bavozet (*Lyon*), M Communeau* (*Stade Français*)

REFEREE MAS Jones (*England*)

SCORING MacCallum, try (3–0); Laterrade, try (3–3); Decamps, con (3–5); Failliot, try (3–8); Peyroutou, try (3–11); Munro, try (6–11); Turner, con (8–11) (half-time) Pearson, drop (12–11); Failliot, try (12–14); Decamps, con (12–16); Abercrombie, try (15–16)

The Scots fielded an experimental side with six newcomers, still treating the fixture as a trial match. They got their just deserts as France won an international for the first time. Despite the wet conditions, this was an open and exciting encounter with seven tries and a thrilling conclusion. The French were better than expected and their big three-quarters proved quite a handful for the lightweight Scots. Incredibly, the home side started a man short as one of their players, André Francquenelle, turned up late and had to join the game after it had started. MacCallum scored an early try for Scotland, but France responded with three tries in quick succession. The Scots managed to steady their ship and just before the interval Munro scored a converted try. In the second half, Scotland had a long spell of pressure, but the French defence held firm until Pearson dropped a goal to put the visitors into the lead. Then wing Pierre Failliot, who was known as 'La Locomotive' for his strong running, collected a loose kick and powered his way through the defence for his second try. Scotland made a desperate attempt to save the match and Abercrombie scored a try which the French players contested. Tod missed the conversion to leave Scotland trailing by a point. The closing stages were almost unbearable for the French crowd who were on the verge of seeing their team create history. In the closing minutes, Tom Young, a Durham University student, knocked-on with the line at his mercy and Scotland's great chance had gone. The final whistle was greeted with 'wild enthusiasm' by the spectators and both sides were warmly applauded as they left the field.

102   INTERNATIONAL CHAMPIONSHIP 1911   WALES

Inverleith · Saturday 4 February 1911 · Lost 10–32

SCOTLAND DG Schulze (*London Scot*); †DM Grant (*Elstow Sch*), AW Angus (*Watsonians*), FG Buchanan (*Kelvinside Acs*), †JM Macdonald (*Edinburgh Wdrs*); P Munro* (*London Scot*), F Osler (*Edinburgh U*); CH Abercrombie (*London Scot*), R Fraser (*Cambridge U*), JM Mackenzie (*Edinburgh U*), L Robertson (*London Scot*), †AR Ross (*Edinburgh U*), JMB Scott (*Edinburgh Acs*), RC Stevenson (*St Andrews U*), FH Turner (*London Scot*)

WALES FW Birt (*Newport*); RA Gibbs (*Cardiff*), W Spiller (*Cardiff*), LM Dyke (*Cardiff*), JL Williams (*Cardiff*); WJ Trew* (*Swansea*), RM Owen (*Swansea*); J Birch (*Neath*), AP Coldrick (*Newport*), TH Evans (*Llanelli*), J Pugsley (*Cardiff*), DJ Thomas (*Swansea*), R Thomas (*Pontypool*), G Travers (*Newport*), AJ Webb (*Abertillery*)

REFEREE JG Davidson (*Ireland*)

SCORING Spiller, drop (0–4); Williams, try (0–7); Munro, drop (4–7) (half-time) R Thomas, try (4–10); Gibbs, try (4–13); Spiller, try (4–16); Spiller, try (4–19); Williams, try (4–22); Dyke, con (4–24); Gibbs, try (4–27); Dyke, con (4–29); Scott, try (7–29); Turner, try (10–29); Gibbs, try (10–32)

Donald Grant, a new cap on the right wing, was still a schoolboy at Elstow School in Bedfordshire although he also played senior rugby for London Scottish and the East Midlands. Scotland's season went from bad to worse as Wales inflicted their heaviest defeat to date. Playing in near perfect conditions, the Scots held their own in the first half and trailed by only three points at the break. Around the 12th minute, Spiller opened the scoring with a drop goal and a few minutes later Williams scored in the corner after a good bout of passing. Munro responded with a well taken drop goal and at half-time there was little indication of the rout to follow. Early in the second half, Rhys Thomas scored a try for Wales and Macdonald, the Scottish left wing, was carried off the field with a leg injury, one of the Scottish forwards coming out of the pack in his place. Wales then took complete control and scored five tries in a brilliant spell. The Scottish forwards were completely outplayed and the defence was fatally weak. Welsh scrum-half Dicky Owen was full of tricks and left his opponents grasping at air with his famous twisting runs and reverse passes. Wales raced to a huge lead before losing their concentration towards the end. Angus made a good run and linked with Scott who ploughed over for a try. Scotland continued to press and Turner scored from a lineout. In the final minute, Gibbs scored the eighth try for the visitors.

103   INTERNATIONAL CHAMPIONSHIP 1911   IRELAND

Inverleith · Saturday 25 February 1911 · Lost 10–16

SCOTLAND †A Greig (*Glasgow HSFP*); DM Grant (*Elstow Sch*), †C Ogilvy (*Hawick*), AW Angus (*Watsonians*), JT Simson (*Watsonians*); P Munro* (*London Scot*), AB Lindsay (*London H*); R Fraser (*Cambridge U*), GM Frew (*Glasgow HSFP*), JC MacCallum (*Watsonians*), JM Mackenzie (*Edinburgh U*), JMB Scott (*Edinburgh Acs*), RC Stevenson (*St Andrews U*), CD Stuart (*W of Scot*), FH Turner (*Oxford U*)

IRELAND WP Hinton (*Old Wesley*); CT O'Callaghan (*OMT*), AR Foster (*QU Belfast*), ARV Jackson (*Wdrs*), JP Quinn (*Dublin U*); RA Lloyd (*Dublin U*), HM Read (*Dublin U*); C Adams (*Old Wesley*), SBB Campbell (*Derry*), MG Garry (*Bective Rgrs*), T Halpin (*Garryowen*), GT Hamlet* (*Old Wesley*), MR Heffernan (*Cork Const*), PJ Smyth (*Collegians*), T Smyth (*Malone*)

REFEREE VH Cartwright (*England*)

SCORING O'Callaghan, try (0–3); Hinton, con (0–5); Foster, try (0–8); Simson, try (3–8) (half-time) Adams, try (3–11); Lloyd, con (3–13); Munro, drop (7–13); Angus, try (10–13); Quinn, try (10–16)

Ireland played with a strong northerly wind in their favour and scored two tries in the first ten minutes. Scotland gradually settled and after some promising attacks Simson made a determined run and forced his way over the line, taking several defenders with him. The rest of the half was evenly balanced and Scotland might have scored again, but their attacks lacked precision. After the interval, the Irish forwards made an irresistible break and Adams scored a try. Scotland had a spell of pressure near the Irish line and Munro dropped a goal. They continued to attack and from a close range scrum the halves combined cleverly to put Angus over. The match was still in the balance inside the final ten minutes, but the Irish made a quick breakaway and Lloyd drew the defence before giving Quinn a clear run in. Ireland finished strongly and deserved to win. Scotland made too many handling errors in the awkward conditions and several players were too selfish with the ball. Pat Munro, one of the leading Scottish players of this era, made his final appearance in this match. Almost immediately after the game, he went back to his post as a district commissioner in the Sudan.

Later in his career Munro presented his Scottish cap to a local tribal chief who was so pleased with it that he always wore it on state occasions instead of the traditional fez.

---

104 INTERNATIONAL CHAMPIONSHIP 1911 ENGLAND

Twickenham · Saturday 18 March 1911 · Lost 8–13

SCOTLAND C Ogilvy (*Hawick*); WR Sutherland (*Hawick*), G Cunningham (*London Scot*), †RF Simson (*London Scot*), †SSL Steyn (*London Scot*); E Milroy (*Watsonians*), †JYM Henderson (*Watsonians*); †DM Bain (*Oxford U*), †J Dobson (*Glasgow Acs*), R Fraser (*Cambridge U*), GM Frew (*Glasgow HSFP*), †WR Hutchison (*Glasgow HSFP*), JC MacCallum* (*Watsonians*), CD Stuart (*W of Scot*), FH Turner (*Oxford U*)

ENGLAND SH Williams (*Newport*); AD Roberts (*Northern*), JGG Birkett (*Harlequins*), RW Poulton (*Oxford U*), PW Lawrie (*Leicester*); AD Stoop (*Harlequins*), ALH Gotley* (*Blackheath*); LG Brown (*Oxford U*), R Dibble (*Bridgwater & Alb*), L Haigh (*Manchester*), AL Kewney (*Rockcliff*), JA King (*Headingley*), RO Lagden (*Oxford U*), CH Pillman (*Blackheath*), NA Wodehouse (*RN*)

REFEREE TD Schofield (*Wales*)

SCORING Sutherland, try (3–0); Wodehouse, try (3–3); Lagden, con (3–5); Lawrie, try (3–8) (half-time) Birkett, try (3–11); Lagden, con (3–13); Simson, try (6–13); Cunningham, con (8–13)

This was Scotland's first visit to the new RFU ground at Twickenham, never the happiest of hunting grounds for them. Apparently, some of the Scottish players could not find their way inside and had to tramp over neighbouring allotments to get in. After their dismal season, the Scots were underdogs, but they put up a gallant fight against a better side. The match kicked-off in a 'Scotch mist' so that the ground was slippery and the ball wet. Nevertheless, this was an exciting and strenuous encounter with lots of open play. England started in a lively fashion, but the Scottish defence was firm. Cunningham made a break and from the ensuing play Sutherland raced past the defence and threw himself over at the corner. Soon afterwards Wodehouse scored between the posts with a defender clinging to his heels. Both sides were eager to run the ball and had several scoring chances. Lawrie scored a try wide out after some good English handling. In the second half, Henderson injured his arm and moved to full-back, Cunningham took over at half and Ogilvy moved to the centre. Stoop and Birkett, the Harlequins midfield, made a break and the latter easily rounded Henderson to score between the posts. England continued to press, but then Scotland had a stroke of luck. From a loose English pass, Simson collected a rebound when going at full speed, kicked over the head of Williams, the full-back, and won the ensuing scramble at the posts. Cunningham's conversion brought Scotland back to within a converted try, but they were unable to close the gap.

---

105 INTERNATIONAL CHAMPIONSHIP 1912 FRANCE

Inverleith · Saturday 20 January 1912 · Won 31–3

SCOTLAND †WM Dickson (*Blackheath*); WR Sutherland (*Hawick*), AW Angus (*Watsonians*),

J Pearson (*Watsonians*), †JG Will (*Cambridge U*); †AW Gunn (*Royal HSFP*), †J Hume (*Royal HSFP*); DM Bain (*Oxford U*), J Dobson (*Glasgow Acs*), †CCP Hill (*St Andrews U*), †DD Howie (*Kirkcaldy*), JC MacCallum* (*Watsonians*), †WDCL Purves (*Cambridge U*), †RD Robertson (*London Scot*), FH Turner (*Oxford U*)

FRANCE FX Dutour (*Toulouse*); P Failliot (*RCF*), D Ihingoué (*Bordeaux EC*), J Dufau (*Biarritz*), M Burgun (*RCF*); J Dedet* (*Stade Français*), L Larribau (*Périgueux*); R Monier (*SBUC*), C Vallot (*SCUF*), JJ Conilh de Beyssac (*SBUC*), P Mauriat (*Lyon*), R Simonpaoli (*Stade Français*), M Boyau (*SBUC*), J Domercq (*Bayonne*), M Communeau (*Beauvais*)

REFEREE JJ Coffey (*Ireland*)

SCORING Pearson, pen (3–0); Gunn, try (6–0); Turner, con (8–0); Communeau, try (8–3); Pearson, try (11–3); Turner, con (13–3) (half-time) Will, try (16–3); Turner, con (18–3); Turner, try (21–3); Sutherland, try (24–3); Turner, con (26–3); Sutherland, try (29–3); Turner, con (31–3)

Scotland, in their changed strip, took revenge for their shock defeat by France the previous year. Played in dull and misty conditions, this was an entertaining match and both sides were eager to attack. Scotland were comfortable winners, but France had clearly made huge strides. The first 20 minutes were evenly balanced and both sides scored a try. The Scottish forwards asserted themselves and used their traditional footwork to good effect. Both sides made some promising attacks and defended strongly. Shortly before the interval, the Watsonians duo Angus and Pearson made a smart break and the latter scored in the corner. Turner kicked a fine goal from near the touchline. The Scots had much the better of the second half and the backs put together some attractive moves. Will slipped through the defence for a try which Turner converted. Then after a forwards' charge, Gunn escaped and MacCallum gave a scoring pass to Turner. Scotland finished firmly in control and Sutherland, who had been quiet up to now, scored a brace of tries. The first came from an interception and sprint to the corner, the second an opportunist score against a rapidly tiring defence. French fullback François Dutour had an excellent match and his courageous defensive work prevented a heavier defeat.

---

106 INTERNATIONAL CHAMPIONSHIP 1912 WALES

St Helen's, Swansea · Saturday 3 February 1912 · Lost 6–21

SCOTLAND WM Dickson (*Blackheath*); WR Sutherland (*Hawick*), AW Angus (*Watsonians*), J Pearson (*Watsonians*), JG Will (*Cambridge U*); AW Gunn (*Royal HSFP*), E Milroy (*Watsonians*); DM Bain (*Oxford U*), J Dobson (*Glasgow Acs*), DD Howie (*Kirkcaldy*), JC MacCallum* (*Watsonians*), WDCL Purves (*London Scot*), L Robertson (*London Scot*), JMB Scott (*Edinburgh Acs*), FH Turner (*Liverpool*)

WALES J Bancroft (*Swansea*); RCS Plummer (*Newport*), FW Birt (*Newport*), WA Davies (*Aberavon*), GL Hirst (*Newport*); WJ Trew (*Swansea*), RM Owen* (*Swansea*); AP Coldrick (*Newport*), HJ Davies (*Neath*), WI Morgan (*Swansea*), G Stephens (*Neath*), R Thomas (*Pontypool*), LC Trump (*Newport*), H Uzzell (*Newport*), AJ Webb (*Abertillery*)

REFEREE FC Potter-Irwin (*England*)

SCORING Hirst, try (0–3); Trew, drop (0–7); Will, try (3–7) (half-time) Milroy, try (6–7); Morgan, try (6–10); Bancroft, con (6–12); Birt, drop (6–16); Plummer, try (6–19); Bancroft, con (6–21)

Despite the wintery conditions, the pitch was in excellent order and the big crowd was treated to a fast match. Wales always looked likely winners, but they were flattered by the final score, eight of their points coming from drop goals (then worth four each). The Scottish backs were faster than their opponents, but less imaginative and penetrative. The Scottish forwards held their own against a heavier pack and their dribbling was as good as always. After a cautious start, play opened out and both sides had some promising attacks, but there was no scoring until a few minutes before the interval. Owen deceived Milroy with a dummy pass and shot down the blind before feeding his wing Hurst who squeezed in at the corner. Trew dropped a neat goal and Scotland responded with a brilliant try by Will who broke clean away. Early in the second period, Gunn burst through and Scott was in support to give the scoring pass to Milroy. Wales replied with a try by Ivor Morgan after a forwards' rush that had started near the Welsh line. Turner missed an easy penalty chance before Birt dropped a goal. Shortly before the finish, Trew made a great run and linked with Plummer who scored a try. At the finish, Trew and Owen, the famous Swansea half-backs, were chaired off the field by their supporters. After the match David Bain, the Scottish forward, collapsed from the effects of concussion and had to be left overnight in Swansea rather than accompanying the rest of the team back to London.

107 INTERNATIONAL CHAMPIONSHIP 1912 IRELAND

Lansdowne Road, Dublin · Saturday 24 February 1912 · Lost 8–10

SCOTLAND C Ogilvy (*Hawick*); SSL Steyn (*Oxford U*), AW Angus (*Watsonians*), CM Gilray (*London Scot*), JG Will (*Cambridge U*); AW Gunn (*Royal HSFP*), E Milroy (*Watsonians*); J Dobson (*Glasgow Acs*), CCP Hill (*St Andrews U*), DD Howie (*Kirkcaldy*), JC MacCallum* (*Watsonians*), WDCL Purves (*London Scot*), L Robertson (*London Scot*), JMB Scott (*Edinburgh Acs*), FH Turner (*Liverpool*)

IRELAND RA Wright (*Monkstown*); CV MacIvor (*Dublin U*), M Abraham (*Bective Rgrs*), AR Foster (*QU Belfast*), JP Quinn (*Dublin U*); RA Lloyd* (*Dublin U*), HM Read (*Dublin U*); C Adams (*Old Wesley*), GS Brown (*Monkstown*), SBB Campbell (*Derry*), T Halpin (*Garryowen*), R Hemphill (*Dublin U*), GV Killeen (*Garryowen*), H Moore (*QU Belfast*), R d'A Patterson (*Wdrs*)

REFEREE F Potter-Irwin (*England*)

SCORING Lloyd, pen (0–3); Lloyd, drop (0–7); Will, try (3–7) (half-time) Turner, try (6–7); MacCallum, con (8–7); Foster, try (8–10)

This was a fast and exciting match, but much of the play was scrappy and scrambling. The Scottish forwards held the edge and won a lot of possession, but the backs did not combine well in attack. Mercurial Irish stand-off Dickie Lloyd was the match-winner for his side. His tactical kicking and defence were excellent and he was always dangerous in attack. Wright, the Irish full-back, also had a fine match. Lloyd kicked an early penalty and a drop goal before Gilray punted to the Irish line, the ball bounced awkwardly for the defence and Will pounced on it. Playing with the slight breeze in their favour in the second half, the Scots scored again when Angus made an elusive run, Will kicked ahead and Turner followed up fast for a try that he also converted. With about ten minutes remaining, Lloyd put up a high kick into the

Scottish 25, the defence let it bounce, and Foster kicked on and won the race to the touchdown. Lloyd's conversion attempt hit one of the uprights.

108 INTERNATIONAL CHAMPIONSHIP 1912 ENGLAND

Inverleith · Saturday 16 March 1912 · Won 8–3

SCOTLAND WM Dickson (*Blackheath*); WR Sutherland (*Hawick*), †W Burnet (*Hawick*), AW Angus (*Watsonians*), JG Will (*Cambridge U*); †JL Boyd (*Utd Servs*), E Milroy (*Watsonians*); DM Bain (*Oxford U*), J Dobson (*Glasgow Acs*), DD Howie (*Kirkcaldy*), JC MacCallum* (*Watsonians*), L Robertson (*London Scot*), JMB Scott (*Edinburgh Acs*), FH Turner (*Liverpool*), †CM Usher (*London Scot*)

ENGLAND WR Johnston (*Bristol*); AD Roberts (*Northern*), RW Poulton (*Harlequins*), JGG Birkett (*Harlequins*), H Brougham (*Harlequins*); AD Stoop (*Harlequins*), JA Pym (*Blackheath*); R Dibble* (*Newport*), JH Eddison (*Headingley*), D Holland (*Devonport & Alb*), AL Kewney (*Rockcliff*), JA King (*Headingley*), AH MacIlwaine (*Utd Servs*), RC Stafford (*Bedford*), NA Wodehouse (*Utd Servs*)

REFEREE F Gardiner (*Ireland*)

SCORING No scoring in the first half. Sutherland, try (3–0); Holland, try (3–3); Usher, try (6–3); MacCallum, con (8–3)

Scotland deserved to win thanks to a stirring display by the forwards, although England were badly hampered by injuries. In near perfect conditions, this was a hard and uncompromising battle between two determined sides. Early on the visitors lost one of their forwards, John King, who broke two ribs at a scrum. Later, Bill Johnston, the England full-back, was twice knocked out by heavy tackles. Scotland had much the better of the first half, but there was no scoring at the interval. About five minutes after the restart, the ball was fed out to Sutherland who shot down the touchline and scored in the corner. Boyd and Will narrowly missed drop goals, and one Scottish forward missed a great chance with Sutherland standing next to him unmarked. Holland scored an unconverted try for England and play went from end-to-end. Towards the finish, Scotland were encamped on the English line and after heavy pressure Usher dived over for the winning try. As the Edinburgh *Evening Dispatch* put it; 'What was to have been a glorious Flodden Field turned out to be a veritable Bannockburn.'

109 TOUR MATCH SOUTH AFRICA

Inverleith · Saturday 23 November 1912 · Lost 0–16

SCOTLAND WM Dickson (*Oxford U*); WR Sutherland (*Hawick*), AW Gunn (*Royal HSFP*), AW Angus (*Watsonians*), J Pearson (*Watsonians*); JL Boyd (*Utd Servs*), E Milroy (*Watsonians*); DM Bain (*Oxford U*), †PCB Blair (*Cambridge U*), J Dobson (*Glasgow Acs*), DD Howie (*Kirkcaldy*), WDCL Purves (*London Scot*), L Robertson (*London Scot*), JMB Scott (*Edinburgh Acs*), FH Turner (*Liverpool*)

SOUTH AFRICA PG Morkel (*W Province*); JA Stegmann (*W Province*), RR Luyt (*W Province*), JWH Morkel (*W Province*), E McHardy (*OFS*); FP Luyt (*W Province*), FJ Dobbin*

(*Griqualand W*); JAJ Francis (*Transvaal*),
AS Knight (*Transvaal*), SH Ledger
(*Griqualand W*), JD Luyt (*E Province*),
DFT Morkel (*Transvaal*), WH Morkel
(*W Province*), G Thompson (*W Province*),
TF van Vuuren (*E Province*)

REFEREE FC Potter-Irwin (*England*)

SCORING McHardy, try (0–3) (half-time)
Stegmann, try (0–6); PG Morkel, con (0–8);
Stegmann, try (0–11); WH Morkel, try (0–14);
DTF Morkel, con (0–16)

International Football Match

Scotland

VERSUS

South Africa

At Inverleith, Edinburgh
Saturday, 23rd November 1912
KICK-OFF AT 2.30 P.M.

Music by Dr Guthrie's Pipe and Brass Bands

PRICE ONE PENNY

PUBLISHED WITH AUTHORITY OF
THE SCOTTISH FOOTBALL UNION
(ENTERED AT STATIONERS' HALL)

In 1912, South Africa made a 27-match tour of the British Isles and France. The tourists arrived in Scotland determined to avenge their defeat at Hampden Park six years earlier. Curiously, their side included two sets of brothers: Gerhard and Jackie Morkel, and Freddie, John and Richard Luyt. This was the first time that three brothers had played together in an international since the Finlay boys appeared for Scotland way back in 1875. The South Africans fulfilled their ambition and were decisive winners. To a man, they were superb physical specimens and used their strength and athleticism to control the game throughout. The Scots played with their usual determination, but they were no match for their burly opponents. The first half was fairly even during which the heavyweight South African forwards gradually subdued the Scottish pack. Just before the interval, Jackie Morkel, the South African centre,

The official match programme for the game against South Africa in 1912. This style of programme was introduced in that year and lasted almost unchanged for the next 40 years.
Dave Fox

made a cross-kick which confused the defence and McHardy dashed up for the opening try. In the second half, the talented South African backs began to open out. Jan Stegmann, the powerful right wing, scored a brace of tries and towards the finish 'Boy' Morkel added a late try. Several of the South African players were chaired off the field by a small but enthusiastic group of their supporters, some of whom wept openly with joy. Scotland were well beaten on the day although Walter Dickson was sound at full-back and right wing Walter Sutherland had an excellent match, using his speed to great effect and defending courageously.

Parc des Princes, Paris · Wednesday 1 January 1913 · Won 21–3

SCOTLAND WM Dickson (*Oxford U*); †WA Stewart (*London H*), AW Angus (*Watsonians*), †RE Gordon (*Utd Servs*), WR Sutherland (*Hawick*); AW Gunn (*Royal HSFP*), E Milroy (*Watsonians*); CH Abercrombie (*Utd Servs*), DM Bain (*Oxford U*), PCB Blair (*Cambridge U*), DD Howie (*Kirkcaldy*), †GA Ledingham (*Aberdeen GSFP*), †JB McDougall (*Greenock Wdrs*), FH Turner* (*Liverpool*), CM Usher (*London Scot*)

FRANCE FX Dutour (*Toulouse*); L Larribau (*Périgueux*), G Lane* (*RCF*), J Sentilles (*Tarbes*), P Jauréguy (*Toulouse*), M Burgun (*RCF*), M Hedembaigt (*Bayonne*); P Mauriat (*Lyon*), JR Pascarel (*TOEC*), J Sébédio (*Tarbes*), P Mouniq (*Toulouse*), H Tilh (*Nantes*), M Legrain (*RCF*), F Forgues (*Bayonne*), M Leuvielle (*SBUC*)

REFEREE J Baxter (*England*)

SCORING Sébédio, try (0–3); Stewart, try (3–3); Turner, con (5–3); Stewart, try (8–3), (half-time) Gordon, try (11–3); Turner, con (13–3); Stewart, try (16–3); Gordon, try (19–3); Turner, con (21–3)

This encounter became known as the 'riot match' or the match of *la bagarre* because of an incident of crowd disorder at the end of it. The original venue at Colombes Stadium was unplayable due to flooding so the game was switched to the Parc des Princes velodrome at short notice. France did much better than the score suggests and did not deserve to lose by such a big margin. There was little to choose between the forwards although the Scots held the edge in the loose. The Scottish backs combined well and made the most of their opportunities. On a bright and windless afternoon, France scored the opening try after about 20 minutes. The Scots replied with a quick brace by new winger Bill Stewart, a Scottish sprint champion who was raised in Tasmania. In the second half, Gordon made a long solo run for a try. Sutherland was caught just short and Abercrombie hit a post with a penalty attempt. In the closing stages, Stewart completed his hat-trick after a good passing movement and right at the death Gordon, who had a fine game, scored between the posts. During the match, some sections of the French crowd became dissatisfied with the English referee John Baxter who did not allow the home side any leniency. After the final whistle, one irate Frenchman, an army officer, tried to reach Mr Baxter to remonstrate with him. He was stopped by police, but then released as some of the crowd had invaded the pitch and threatened to turn ugly. Several Scottish players were jostled in the crush and there were reports of stones being thrown. The trouble quickly died down and no real harm was done, but the outcome of the incident was that the SFU refused to play the fixture the following season and it was not resumed until 1920.

Inverleith · Saturday 1 February 1913 · Lost 0–8

SCOTLAND WM Dickson (*Oxford U*); WA Stewart (*London H*), RE Gordon (*Utd Servs*), AW Angus (*Watsonians*), WR Sutherland (*Hawick*); †JH Bruce Lockhart (*London Scot*), E Milroy (*Watsonians*); CH Abercrombie (*Utd Servs*), DM Bain (*Oxford U*), PCB Blair (*Cambridge U*),

DD Howie (*Kirkcaldy*), L Robertson (*London Scot*), JMB Scott (*Edinburgh Acs*), FH Turner* (*Liverpool*), CM Usher (*London Scot*)

WALES RF Williams (*Cardiff*); GL Hirst (*Newport*), JP Jones (*Pontypool*), WJ Trew* (*Swansea*), H Lewis (*Swansea*); JMC Lewis (*Cardiff*), RA Lloyd (*Pontypool*); F Andrews (*Pontypool*), JA Davies (*Swansea*), WJ Jenkins (*Cardiff*), PL Jones (*Newport*), FL Perrett (*Neath*), R Richards (*Aberavon*), G Stephens (*Neath*), H Uzzell (*Newport*)

REFEREE SH Crawford (*Ireland*)

SCORING JMC Lewis, try (0–3) (half-time) JP Jones, try (0–6); JMC Lewis, con (0–8)

Wales had been heavily beaten by England two weeks earlier and did not finalise their team until the Friday evening. Scotland were expected to win, but they were strangely out-of-sorts and the match fell a long way short of expectations. Snow had been cleared off the pitch in the morning and a freezing wind blew from the south. The Scottish forwards struggled in the scrums and had none of their traditional fire in the loose. The backs had few chances in attack, but they defended strongly. The match was marred by a whistle-happy referee who called back several promising moves. After some early pressure, Wales opened the scoring around the eighth minute. Clem Lewis, the Welsh stand-off, pounced on a loose pass near the Scottish line and was quickest to the touchdown. The rest of the half was fairly evenly balanced, but the second period was largely one-sided and play was mainly in Scottish territory. Towards the finish, Clem Lewis was wide with a drop goal attempt, but the defence was beaten by the wickedly bouncing ball and centre Tuan Jones followed-up to score. The weather affected the attendance which was estimated at around 17,000 people. As *The Times* put it, 'the majority of whom, cold and disheartened, were glad to see the game over'.

---

112 INTERNATIONAL CHAMPIONSHIP 1913 IRELAND

Inverleith · Saturday 22 February 1913 · Won 29–14

SCOTLAND WM Dickson (*Oxford U*); WA Stewart (*London H*), RE Gordon (*Utd Servs*), J Pearson (*Watsonians*), WR Sutherland (*Hawick*); †TC Bowie (*Watsonians*), E Milroy (*Watsonians*); DM Bain (*Oxford U*), PCB Blair (*Cambridge U*), †GHHP Maxwell (*Edinburgh Acs*), WDCL Purves (*London Scot*), L Robertson (*London Scot*), JMB Scott (*Edinburgh Acs*), FH Turner* (*Liverpool*), CM Usher (*London Scot*)

IRELAND JW McConnell (*Lansdowne*); CV MacIvor (*Dublin U*), GW Holmes (*Dublin U*), JB Minch (*Bective Rgrs*), F Bennett (*Collegians*); RA Lloyd* (*Liverpool*), HM Read (*Dublin U*); SBB Campbell (*Edinburgh U*), JE Finlay (*QU Belfast*); EW Jeffares (*Wdrs*), GV Killeen (*Garryowen*), R d'A Patterson (*Wdrs*), FG Schute (*Dublin U*), P Stokes (*Blackrock Coll*), W Tyrrell (*QU Belfast*)

REFEREE J Baxter (*England*)

SCORING Stewart, try (3–0); Turner, con (5–0); Schute, try (5–3); Lloyd, con (5–5); Stewart, try (8–5); Turner, con (10–5); Stewart, try (13–5); Turner, con (15–5); Usher, try (18–5) (half-time) Bowie, try (21–5); Turner, con (23–5); Stewart, try (26–5); Stokes, try (26–8); Lloyd, con (26–10); Lloyd, drop (26–14); Purves, try (29–14)

This was an exciting match that was full of open play and incident. Scotland out-classed a poor Irish side and scored seven tries. The forwards won the bulk of posse-ssion and gave the backs plenty of scope in attack. Left wing Bill Stewart was much too fast for his opponents and scored four tries. About midway through the first half, Scotland were reduced to 14 men when their full-back Dickson injured his shoulder, Scott joining the back division. This seemed to inspire the Scots and the depleted pack had no problems containing the Irish eight. Scotland made a strong start and Stewart scored his first try after about five minutes. Turner converted from the touchline. Ireland drew level with a converted try before Stewart made a spectacular run from midfield for a brilliant solo score. Turner converted and then Dickson went off. Stewart scored again after a breakaway by Gordon and, shortly before the interval, Usher touched down after a rush by the forwards. The prolific scoring continued at the start of the second half. The Scottish backs made a great handling movement which ended with Bowie going over for a try which Turner converted. Stewart crashed over at the corner flag for his fourth try after some neat passing amongst the three-quarters. Scotland then eased off and the visitors staged a short revival. Stokes scored a try converted by Lloyd who then dropped a goal before Purves replied with another try for the Scots. This ended the scoring, but both sides continued to attack and had several near misses.

---

113   INTERNATIONAL CHAMPIONSHIP 1913   ENGLAND

Twickenham · Saturday 15 March 1913 · Lost 0–3

SCOTLAND †WM Wallace (*Cambridge U*); †JB Sweet (*Glasgow HSFP*), J Pearson (*Watsonians*), †EG Loudoun-Shand (*Oxford U*), WR Sutherland (*Hawick*); TC Bowie (*Watsonians*), E Milroy (*Watsonians*); DM Bain (*Oxford U*), PCB Blair (*Cambridge U*), GHHP Maxwell (*Edinburgh Acs*), WDCL Purves (*London Scot*), L Robertson (*London Scot*), JMB Scott (*Edinburgh Acs*), FH Turner* (*Oxford U*), CM Usher (*London Scot*)

ENGLAND WR Johnston (*Bristol*); CN Lowe (*Cambridge U*), FN Tarr (*Leicester*), RW Poulton (*Harlequins*), VHM Coates (*Bath*); WJA Davles (*RN Coll*), FE Oakeley (*RN*); LG Brown (*Oxford U*), JE Greenwood (*Cambridge U*), JA King (*Headingley*), CH Pillman (*Blackheath*), JAS Ritson (*Northern*), S Smart (*Gloucester*), G Ward (*Leicester*), NA Wodehouse* (*RN*)

REFEREE TD Schofield (*Wales*)

SCORING Brown, try (0–3) (half-time)

Played in front of the Prince of Wales, England won their first-ever Grand Slam thanks to a scrambled try by the Oxford forward Bruno Brown towards the end of the first half. The English pack was well on top, but their backs squandered many opportunities with indifferent and unimaginative play. Twice England players were over the line but were thrown into touch and one England forward dropped the ball with the line at his mercy. Both sides defended strongly and the Scottish effort was outstanding, especially that of the Hawick wing Walter Sutherland who was the man of the match. Always dangerous in attack, he achieved miracles in defence after new cap Eric Louden-Shand hurt his leg and became a passenger for most of the second half. Sutherland moved to centre and used all of his speed, tactical sense and raw courage to successfully cancel out the joint threat of Poulton and Coates. Reportedly,

A rare surviving match ticket for the England game in 1913. *Dave Fox*

he was punch-drunk after the match because of his exertions. Sutherland had one long run that almost brought a try, but he was caught at the corner by Johnston. On the other wing, Sweet also had a fine game and Willie Wallace was solid at full-back.

114   INTERNATIONAL CHAMPIONSHIP 1914   WALES

Cardiff Arms Park · Saturday 7 February 1914 · Lost 5–24

SCOTLAND WM Wallace (*London Scot*); JG Will (*Cambridge U*), WR Sutherland (*Hawick*), †RM Scobie (*London Scot*), WA Stewart (*London H*); †AS Hamilton (*Headingley*), †AT Sloan (*Edinburgh Acs*); DM Bain* (*Oxford U*), †DG Donald (*Oxford U*), †AD Laing (*Royal HSFP*), GHHP Maxwell (*Edinburgh Acs*), AR Ross (*Edinburgh U*), †AM Stewart (*Edinburgh Acs*), †AW Symington (*Cambridge U*), †A Wemyss (*Gala*)

WALES J Bancroft (*Swansea*); GL Hirst (*Newport*), JJ Wetter (*Newport*), WH Evans (*Llwynypia*), IT Davies (*Llanelli*); JMC Lewis (*Cardiff*), RA Lloyd (*Pontypool*); JA Davies (*Llanelli*), JL Jones (*Abertillery*), PL Jones (*Pontypool*), TJ Lloyd (*Neath*), E Morgan (*Swansea*), H Uzzell (*Newport*), D Watts (*Maesteg*), T Williams (*Swansea*)

REFEREE V Drennon (*Ireland*)

SCORING Stewart, try (3–0); Laing, con (5–0); Hirst, drop (5–4); Bancroft, pen (5–7) (half-time) IT Davies, try (5–10); Wetter, try (5–13); Bancroft, con (5–15); Lewis, drop (5–19); Hirst, try (5–22); Bancroft, con (5–24)

Wales won the match as expected, their seventh victory in succession against the Scots, but the visitors had bad luck with injuries. Towards the end of the first half, Sutherland, who had been superb until then, hurt his ankle and was reduced to a passenger for the second period. On a cold and dry afternoon, Scotland started promisingly and within three minutes Stewart powered round two defenders to score at the posts. Laing added the simple conversion. Wales slowly came into the game, but they were frustrated by a determined Scottish defence. Play was vigorous and hotly contested. *The Scotsman* observed that 'it was no kid battle that was being waged'. Laing, for one, suffered 'a severe gruelling' from a Welsh forward who was given a good ticking-off by the referee. Eventually Hirst dropped a goal from a tight angle. He was later carried off, but returned for the second half. Following Sutherland's injury, Bancroft landed a penalty goal and the game slowly turned. In the second half, Sutherland and Will changed places, but this unsettled the Scottish defence and Wales targeted this weakness. The visitors were further hampered by an eye-injury to their captain David Bain. After six minutes, Lloyd set-up Ivor Davies for an easy run-in. Then Wetter charged down a kick, gathered the ball and eluded the defence for a try between the posts. Lewis added a drop goal and Hirst scored a try in the corner which was converted by Bancroft from the touchline. The final score flattered Wales, but they were worthy winners. The Scots played with less cohesion and purpose, and their lighter forwards were gradually worn down by the powerful Welsh eight.

115   INTERNATIONAL CHAMPIONSHIP 1914   IRELAND

Lansdowne Road, Dublin · Saturday 28 February 1914 · Lost 0–6

SCOTLAND WM Wallace (*Cambridge U*); JB Sweet (*Glasgow HSFP*), RM Scobie (*RMA*), †JR Warren (*Glasgow Acs*), JG Will (*Cambridge U*); TC Bowie (*Watsonians*), E Milroy* (*Watsonians*); DM Bain (*Oxford U*), DG Donald (*Oxford U*), AD Laing (*Royal HSFP*), JB McDougall (*Greenock Wdrs*), GHHP Maxwell (*Edinburgh Acs*), AR Ross (*Edinburgh U*), FH Turner (*Liverpool*), A Wemyss (*Gala*)

IRELAND FP Montgomery (*QU Belfast*); JP Quinn* (*Dublin U*), ARV Jackson (*Wdrs*), JB Minch (*Bective Rgrs*), AR Foster (*NIFC*); HW Jack (*UC Cork*), V McNamara (*UC Cork*); C Adams (*Old Wesley*), WP Collopy (*Bective Rgrs*), JCA Dowse (*Monkstown*), GV Killeen (*Garryowen*), P O'Connell (*Bective Rgrs*), JS Parr (*Wdrs*), J Taylor (*Collegians*), W Tyrrell (*QU Belfast*)

REFEREE J Baxter (*England*)

SCORING No scoring in the first half. Quinn, try (0–3); McNamara, try (0–6)

Both sides were forced to make late changes. For Scotland, winger Bill Stewart, who had scored four tries against Ireland the previous season, was replaced by JB Sweet of Glasgow High. Persistent drizzle began before kick-off and the second half was played in a torrential downpour turning the pitch to a quagmire long before the finish. Naturally, the Irish forwards revelled in the conditions. They struggled in the set scrums, but they were ferocious in loose play and around the fringes, using their traditional rush tactics to great effect. In fact, Ireland might have won by more if they had managed to harness their own impetuosity and enthusiasm. The Scots were brave in defence, but the forwards faded away as the game progressed. The first hour of the match was mainly a dour forward struggle. Then around the hour mark an Irish rush ended with Quinn scoring an unconverted try. Will made a clean break for Scotland, but slipped on the wet turf and a great chance was lost. Ireland finished strongly and McNamara scored after heavy pressure on the Scottish line. Right at the death Will might have scored a consolation try, but he knocked-on with the line at his mercy.

116 INTERNATIONAL CHAMPIONSHIP 1914 ENGLAND

Inverleith · Saturday 21 March 1914 · Lost 15–16

SCOTLAND WM Wallace (*Cambridge U*); †JL Huggan (*London Scot*), RM Scobie (*Utd Servs*), AW Angus (*Watsonians*), JG Will (*Cambridge U*); TC Bowie (*Watsonians*), E Milroy* (*Watsonians*); AD Laing (*Royal HSFP*), GHHP Maxwell (*Edinburgh Acs*), †IM Pender (*London Scot*), AR Ross (*Edinburgh U*), AW Symington (*Cambridge U*), FH Turner (*Liverpool*), CM Usher (*London Scot*), †ET Young (*Glasgow Acs*)

ENGLAND WR Johnston (*Bristol*); CN Lowe (*Cambridge U*), JHD Watson (*Blackheath*), RW Poulton* (*Liverpool*), AJ Dingle (*Hartlepool Rov*); WJA Davies (*RN*), FE Oakeley (*RN*); LG Brown (*Blackheath*); J Brunton (*N Durham*), JE Greenwood (*Cambridge U*), HC Harrison (*RN*), AF Maynard (*Cambridge U*), CH Pillman (*Blackheath*), S Smart (*Gloucester*), G Ward (*Leicester*)

REFEREE TD Schofield (*Wales*)

SCORING Will, try (3–0); Lowe, try (3–3) (half-time) Huggan, try (6–3); Lowe, try (6–6); Harrison, con (6–8); Lowe, try (6–11); Harrison, con (6–13); Poulton, try (6–16); Bowie, drop (10–16); Will, try (13–16); Turner, con (15–16)

This was a wonderfully exciting game that was played in tremendous spirit. England were the better team, but Scotland refused to be beaten and the outcome was in the

This Scottish team lost narrowly to England in March 1914, the final international before the Great War. *SRU*

balance until the end. Before the match, opposing wingers George Will and Cyril Lowe, who were friends at Cambridge University, made a bet that neither would allow the other to score. It turned out that they shared five tries between them. The pitch was heavy after recent rain, but conditions were ideal apart from a strong north-westerly which favoured the Scots in the first half. After some early scares, Scotland opened the scoring after 20 minutes. From a drop-out, Maxwell dribbled up field and the ball reached Will who went at full tilt to the corner with Lowe unable to stop him. Just before the interval, English centre 'Bungy' Watson, who once almost played for Scotland, created an opening for Lowe who went over with Will hanging onto him. A minute after the restart, the Scottish forwards made the best rush of the match which ended with Huggan scoring a debut try. The English back division then began to show their paces. At times Watson and Poulton seemed to dance through the Scottish defence. Will completed his hat-trick and Poulton added a fourth for England. Towards the finish Scotland made a furious revival. Bowie dropped a goal and then Will beat several defenders on a long run before diving under the posts. Turner's conversion brought the Scots back to a single point. Roared on by the enraptured crowd, the Scots battled hard for the winning score, but England held out to win a memorable encounter.

Between the Wars

RUGBY FOOTBALL RECOVERED surprisingly quickly after the First World War and Scotland played their first post-war international match a little over a year after the signing of the Armistice. The inter-war period was a golden age for rugby and many legendary encounters took place at this time. Leading rugby matches attracted great interest, both at club and international level. Indeed, as these reports show, the size of the crowds was so enormous at some games, especially in Wales, that the stadiums became dangerously overcrowded. Several matches were almost abandoned because of the press of numbers.

The Scottish Football Union, which was renamed Scottish Rugby Union in 1924, recognised that their old home at Inverleith was no longer adequate to handle the size of the crowds attending games. In 1922, the SFU bought an area of land in the Murrayfield area of Edinburgh that previously had belonged to the Edinburgh polo club. The construction of the new stadium was partly financed by the issue of debentures, as it had been at Inverleith. The first issue of these was quickly over-subscribed, further proof of the enormous interest in rugby football at this time.

AERIAL PHOTO-
GRAPH OF THE
SCOTTISH RUGBY
UNION FIELD AT
MURRAYFIELD
This photograph is the
copyright of the Scottish
Rugby Union. Mounted
Prints may be obtained
on application to Messrs
R. W. Forsyth, Ltd.,
Princes Street, Edin-
burgh . . . . . Price
2/6

This aerial view of Murrayfield was included in the match programme for the opening game at the new stadium in March 1925. *SRU*

Originally, the new stadium had a single large grandstand and terrace embankments around the other three sides. Murrayfield, as it became known, was opened on 21 March 1925 in the best of all possible circumstances when Scotland defeated England to win the Grand Slam. On the day, it was estimated that around 70,000 people came to see the match which took the organisers completely by surprise and created problems about crowd control. Some spectators were locked out and kick-off had to be delayed. Over the years, Murrayfield was further developed in an effort to keep pace with the changing nature of spectator demands. In 1936, two extensions were added to the grandstand which more than doubled the seating capacity.

On the field, the inter-war period was very successful for Scotland, although for most of time they had to play second fiddle to England, the dominant side of the era. The greatest achievement was, of course, the Grand Slam in 1925. The Scots also won the Championship outright in 1929 and shared the title in 1926 and 1927. Results were a little more inconsistent in the 30s. Scotland won the Triple Crown in 1933 and 1938, at a time when France had been expelled, but they were whitewashed in 1932, 1936 and 1939. Away from the Championship, tours from the Dominions were no more frequent than they had been before the war. The New South Wales Waratahs toured in 1927, captained by the former Scotland wing Johnny Wallace, although Scotland did not award caps for the international. They were followed by South Africa in season 1931–2 under the guidance of the brilliant half-back Bennie Osler and then by Jack Manchester's New Zealand side in 1935–6. The All Blacks had also toured the British Isles and France in season 1924–5, but Scotland were still unhappy about payments made to their predecessors way back 1905 and refused to play them.

In rugby terms at least, the inter-war period was one of social conservatism and resistance to change. Both at club and international level, fixtures were long established and repeated in a regular routine. At club level, there was little or no interest in organised league or cup competitions. The unofficial club championship was created by the newspapers and received no official recognition by the authorities. The Border League and Border Sevens were tolerated, but prize-giving was frowned upon and strictly controlled. Any suspicion of professionalism or somebody making money out of the game was quickly and ruthlessly suppressed. In the most notorious case from this time, Neil Macpherson, a three-quarter who had won seven caps for Scotland in the early 1920s, was suspended *sine die* for accepting a gold watch from his club Newport. He was eventually reinstated, but was never asked to play for his country again. Former players who turned their hand to journalism were treated with similar disdain. Anybody who switched to rugby league was considered an untouchable outcast and forbidden to have any contact with the amateur game. Their pariah status was so extreme that they were even being barred from entering grounds or clubhouses.

However, there were a few signs of change. Scotland finally adopted numbered jerseys, first as an experiment against France in 1928 and then permanently from the Wales game in 1933. Forward play became increasingly specialist and moved away from the traditional 'first-up-and-down' approach of the pre-war era to more clearly defined positions, such as hookers and back-row men. Rugby also started to benefit from coverage by what we would now describe as new media. As early as 1927, the fledgling BBC provided a live radio broadcast of the Scotland v England match from Murrayfield. In March 1938, the corresponding fixture at Twickenham became the first rugby international in the world to be shown live on television, although only a handful of homes in the London area had access to the new marvel. But for most people the only way to see rugby was either by going to a game or watching the newsreels at their local cinema, which often featured a brief report from international matches.

The outstanding Scottish full-back of the inter-war period was Dan Drysdale who was the first of a dynasty of full-backs from Heriot's FP. Drysdale was a neat and careful player who had an excellent positional sense and was always willing to run with the ball. He was also a good defender and kicked accurately. In the 1930s, Jimmy Kerr, another Herioter, and Kenneth Marshall of Edinburgh Accies were both solid and reliable. Scotland benefitted from several outstanding partnerships in the inter-war period. First, there was winger Eric Liddell and centre Leslie Gracie. Liddell was born in China and Gracie in Ceylon, and both attended Eltham College in south London, a school for the sons of missionaries (as did Ernest Fahmy who won four Scottish caps in 1920). Liddell was determined, intelligent and, of course, extremely fast. He prematurely gave up rugby to concentrate on athletics and famously won the gold medal for the 400 metres at the Paris Olympic Games in 1924. Gracie was an unorthodox player who was quick off the mark and liked to experiment and take chances. He ran with his head well back and swung the ball in front of him to confuse his opponents. Gracie scored a famous match-winning try against Wales in 1923 for which he was chaired off the field.

Undoubtedly, the most celebrated partnership of this time was the Oxford three-quarter line of Johnny Wallace, George Aitken, GPS 'Phil' Macpherson and Ian Smith. They were all at one time students at Oxford University and played together five times for Scotland. Curiously, only Macpherson was born in Scotland, in this case Newtonmore. Wallace and Smith were both from Australia, and Aitken was a New Zealander who won two caps for the All Blacks in 1922 before coming to Britain. Smith had the nickname the 'Flying Scotsman' for his long, leggy stride and his high knee action which made him difficult to stop. He was a prolific scorer and ended his career with 24 tries in internationals, a world record that lasted until 1987. Smith was partnered by Phil Macpherson who is regarded as one of the greatest centres in the history of the game. He was very fast and had a devastating range of attacking skills, including the ability to swerve, side-step and dummy his way past the tightest of defences. An intelligent man who was partly educated at Yale University, he was a great theorist and tactical thinker, and later in life became a highly successful business-man. Sometimes he was criticised for his tendency to shadow-tackle and his reluctance to go down on the ball. Max Simmers of Glasgow Accies, who played around the same time, was said to have been the better all-rounder. Other prominent three-quarters of this era were Ken Fyfe and Charlie Dick, both elusive wingers from Cambridge University, and Duncan Macrae, a strong running centre from St Andrews University.

John 'Jenny' Hume, who played either side of the First World War, and Willie Bryce were the leading scrum-halves of the early 1920s. Bryce made 11 appearances before his career was halted by injury, but he later became a Scottish hockey inter-nationalist. The outstanding half-back partnership of the 1920s was the Glasgow Accies pair of Jimmy Nelson and Herbert Waddell. Nelson was an aggressive scrum-half with a strong hand-off. Waddell had a keen eye for a gap and was a good link with his three-quarters. His finest moment was dropping the winning goal against

England in the Grand Slam match in 1925. Waddell, whose career was also disrupted by injury, became president of the Barbarians and a successful stockbroker. In the 1930s, Ross Logan formed an effective half-back partnership with Wilson Shaw. Logan, a heavily built man, was a strong defensive player with a powerful break from the base of the scrum. Shaw was the most talented Scottish back to emerge in the thirties. He won his early caps as a wing and there was great debate about his best position. Shaw could hit top speed almost immediately and side-step off either foot, but his defence was said to be suspect. Harry Lind was also a fine player either at stand-off or centre. In a tense match against Ireland in 1933, Lind calmly landed a late drop goal to win the Triple Crown for Scotland.

The greatest forward of this era was John Bannerman who won 37 caps in succession between 1921 and 1929, a remarkable achievement for the time and one not bettered until the 1960s. With his characteristic dark hair and bushy eyebrows, Bannerman was a tireless and aggressive player who had great mobility and footwork. The Borders continued the tradition of producing rugged forwards, including Hawick's Doug Davies and Jock Beattie, Jimmie Graham, the first Kelso player to be capped, Selkirk's Jack Waters and Melrose's Jock Allan. Both Davies and Waters toured with British teams overseas whilst Allan was a reliable placekicker even though he was rarely first choice kicker for his club. Stewart's FP also produced several prominent forwards at this time, including Rankin 'Buckie' Buchanan, James 'Jumbo' Scott, who was surprisingly fast and mobile for a man of enormous stature, and Finlay Kennedy, the first player to be capped from the club and who was also a good kicker. Sandy Gillies of Watsonians was another forward who kicked goals and he was also a renowned dribbler. He landed a superb touchline conversion against Wales in 1927 that helped to win the match. Another Watsonian David Bertram was one of the first specialist hookers. He was a small muscular man who was extremely fast in the loose. His efficient striking technique helped the Scots to monopolise scrum ball in their big win over Wales in 1924. Bertam was followed by Jimmie Ireland who was principal hooker in the 1925 Grand Slam. Ireland, whose initials 'JCH' earned him the nickname 'Jimmie Cannae Hook', became one of the Grand Old Men of Scottish rugby and was the last survivor of the original Grand Slam team, passing away in 1998 at the age of 94.

117   INTERNATIONAL CHAMPIONSHIP 1920   FRANCE

Parc des Princes, Paris · Thursday 1 January 1920 · Won 5–0

SCOTLAND †GL Pattullo (*Panmure*); AT Sloan (*Edinburgh Acs*), †EC Fahmy (*Abertillery*), AW Angus* (*Watsonians*), †GB Crole (*Oxford U*); J Hume (*Royal HSFP*), AS Hamilton (*Headingley*); †DD Duncan (*Oxford U*), †RA Gallie (*Glasgow Acs*), †F Kennedy (*Stewart's FP*), AD Laing (*Royal HSFP*), †WAK Murray (*London Scot*), †G Thom (*Kirkcaldy*), CM Usher (*London Scot*), A Wemyss (*Edinburgh Wdrs*)

FRANCE A Chilo (*RCF*); P Serre (*Perpignan*), R Crabos (*RCF*), R Lasserre (*Bayonne*), A Jauréguy (*RCF*); E Billac (*Bayonne*), P Struxiano* (*Toulouse*); J Sébédio (*Béziers*), P Pons (*Toulouse*), M-F Lubin-Lebrère (*Toulouse*), A Cassayet-Armagnac (*Tarbes*), L Puech (*Toulouse*), R Thierry (*RCF*), J Laurent (*Bayonne*), R Marchand (*Poitiers*)

This Scottish team played France in January 1920, the first international after the Great War. *SRU*

REFEREE FC Potter-Irwin (*England*)

SCORING No scoring in the first half. Crole, try (3–0); Laing, con (5–0)

The International Championship resumed after an interval of five years and the Scots played their first match against France since 1913. Seven of the Scottish team had been capped before the war. This became known as *le match des borgnes* because no less than five players had lost an eye in the war: Hume, Laing and Wemyss for Scotland and Thierry and Lubin-Lebrère for France. Charlie Usher, who had interrupted his honeymoon in Paris to play in the match, led the Scottish team onto the field playing the bagpipes and wearing a kilt (which he took off for the game). Played in front of a very large crowd, conditions were difficult with drizzling rain, a muddy pitch and a slippery ball. The Scots lasted the pace better and deserved their narrow win, but both teams were rather makeshift and the standard of play was not very high. Midway through the second half, new winger Gerard Crole scored the only try of the match after a kick-and-chase from the centre of the field. At the end of the game, some of the crowd invaded the pitch to escort the players and referee back to the grandstand.

---

118   INTERNATIONAL CHAMPIONSHIP 1920   WALES

Inverleith · Saturday 7 February 1920 · Won 9–5

SCOTLAND GL Pattullo (*Panmure*); †EB Mackay (*Glasgow Acs*), AW Angus (*Watsonians*), EC Fahmy (*Abertillery*), GB Crole (*Oxford U*); AT Sloan (*Edinburgh Acs*), †JAR Selby (*Watsonians*); DD Duncan (*Oxford U*), RA Gallie (*Glasgow Acs*), F Kennedy (*Stewart's FP*), AD Laing (*Royal HSFP*), †N Macpherson (*Newport*), GHHP Maxwell (*RAF*), G Thom (*Kirkcaldy*), CM Usher* (*London Scot*)

WALES J Rees (*Swansea*); WJ Powell (*Cardiff*), J Shea (*Newport*), AE Jenkins (*Llanelli*), B Williams (*Llanelli*); B Beynon (*Swansea*), JJ Wetter (*Newport*); CW Jones (*Bridgend*), J Jones (*Aberavon*), S Morris (*Cross Keys*), G Oliver (*Pontypool*), ET Parker (*Swansea*), JJ Whitfield (*Newport*), JL Williams (*Blaina*), H Uzzell* (*Newport*)

SCORING Jenkins, try (0–3); Jenkins, con (0–5) (half-time) Kennedy, pen (3–5); Sloan, try (6–5); Kennedy, pen (9–5)

There were several changes after the win in Paris, including three new caps. Curiously, two of the Scottish team played their club rugby in Wales: Ernest Fahmy of Abertillery and Edinburgh University, and forward Neil Macpherson who was born in Cardiff and played for Newport. Wales had already beaten England at Swansea (19–5) and arrived full of confidence. In a thrilling game played in perfect conditions, the Scots unexpectedly won their first victory over Wales since 1907, despite playing much of the second half with a depleted side. Fahmy hurt his ankle and had to be switched to the wing whilst newcomer EB Mackay was carried-off with a leg injury, Macpherson coming out of the forwards. Wales also lost two players during the game. The Welsh pack was very strong, good at heeling and fast in the open, but several of their backs, in particular centre Jerry Shea, were too selfish with the ball and conceded a lot of penalties. Wales opened the scoring after 23 minutes when Albert Jenkins finished off a good three-quarter movement. In the second half, Finlay Kennedy kicked a long-range penalty and then Allen Sloan, who shortly before had been limping, scored an electrifying solo try. The Scottish forwards latched onto a loose pass near their own 25 and the ball reached Sloan who made a long diagonal run to the corner. Kennedy missed the conversion, but later kicked another awkward penalty and doubt started to enter the Welsh minds. The match had a thrilling conclusion as Wales tried desperately to snatch the winning score, but the weakened Scottish forwards were resolute and Usher gave a fine lead. At the close some of the crowd invaded the field and several players were carried off shoulder-high.

119   INTERNATIONAL CHAMPIONSHIP 1920   IRELAND

Inverleith · Saturday 28 February 1920 · Won 19–0

SCOTLAND GL Pattullo (*Panmure*); †A Browning (*Glasgow HSFP*), AW Angus (*Watsonians*), AT Sloan (*Edinburgh Acs*), GB Crole (*Oxford U*); EC Fahmy (*Abertillery*), JAR Selby (*Watsonians*); DD Duncan (*Oxford U*), RA Gallie (*Glasgow Acs*), F Kennedy (*Stewart's FP*), AD Laing (*Royal HSFP*), N Macpherson (*Newport*), WAK Murray (*London Scot*), G Thom (*Kirkcaldy*), CM Usher* (*London Scot*)

IRELAND WE Crawford (*Lansdowne*); CH Bryant (*Cardiff*), TH Wallace (*Cardiff*), PJ Roddy (*Bective Rgrs*), BAT McFarland (*Derry*); W Duggan (*UC Cork*), JB O'Neill (*QU Belfast*); HH Coulter (*QU Belfast*), AW Courtney (*UC Dublin*), RY Crichton (*Dublin U*), WO Doherty* (*Guy's H*), JE Finlay (*Cardiff*), AH Price (*Dublin U*), WJ Roche (*UC Cork*), P Stokes (*Garryowen*)

REFEREE J Baxter (*England*)

SCORING Crole, try (3–0); Kennedy, con (5–0); Kennedy, pen (8–0); Crole, try (11–0); Kennedy, con (13–0) (half-time) Angus, try (16–0); Browning, try (19–0)

After the excitement of the Welsh game this was a disappointing encounter that lacked tension or great interest. The Scots were always winners against a lacklustre Irish side whose forwards played without their traditional fervour and submitted too easily. By contrast, the Scottish backs played with lots of imagination and unpredictability. Winger Gerard Crole caused endless trouble to the defence and twice scored a try by punting over his opponent's head and using his great speed to regain the ball. Switched from centre to stand-off, his club position, Ernie Fahmy showed good handling skills and twice broke through with outrageous dummies, the second of which created a try for Angus who ran onto the stand-off's cross-kick. Towards the end, Arthur Browning, who had come in for the injured EB Mackay, scored a debut try after good passing down the line.

120 INTERNATIONAL CHAMPIONSHIP 1920 ENGLAND

Twickenham · Saturday 20 March 1920 · Lost 4–13

SCOTLAND GL Pattullo (*Panmure*); AT Sloan (*Edinburgh Acs*), AW Angus (*Watsonians*), JH Bruce Lockhart (*London Scot*), GB Crole (*Oxford U*); EC Fahmy (*Abertillery*), †CS Nimmo (*Watsonians*); DD Duncan (*Oxford U*), RA Gallie (*Glasgow Acs*), F Kennedy (*Stewart's FP*), N Macpherson (*Newport*), GHHP Maxwell (*RAF*), G Thom (*Kirkcaldy*), CM Usher* (*London Scot*), A Wemyss (*Edinburgh Wdrs*)

ENGLAND BS Cumberlege (*Blackheath*); CN Lowe (*Blackheath*), E Myers (*Bradford*), EDG Hammett (*Newport*), SW Harris (*Blackheath*); WJA Davies (*Utd Servs*), CA Kershaw (*Utd Servs*); AF Blakiston (*Northampton*), GS Conway (*Cambridge U*), JE Greenwood* (*Cambridge U*), FW Mellish (*Blackheath*), S Smart (*Gloucester*), AT Voyce (*Gloucester*), WW Wakefield (*Harlequins*), T Woods (*RN*)

REFEREE TD Schofield (*Wales*)

SCORING Lowe, try (0–3); Greenwood, con (0–5); Harris, try (0–8); Greenwood, con (0–10); Bruce Lockhart, drop (4–10) (half-time) Kershaw, try (4–13)

The teams were presented to King George V in front of a crowd estimated at some 40,000 people, a record for the ground. Scotland were playing for a clean sweep, but had to concede to faster and more enterprising opponents. Led from the front by Charlie Usher, the Scottish forwards worked hard and won their fare share of possession, but the backs were too slow and predictable. The new half-back partnership of Fahmy and Nimmo did not combine well and the three-quarters were easily contained. England opened the scoring after five minutes with some typical opportunism. Nimmo missed his partner with a loose pass, Davies intercepted and cross-kicked to Lowe who gathered at full speed to score at the posts. Both sides narrowly missed chances before Harris, the Blackheath wing, scored his side's second try after a good handling move and strong running. Bruce Lockhart reduced the deficit with a drop goal before the interval. In the second half, Scotland had most of the possession, but were unable to make anything of it. Then around the 25th minute, Kershaw picked up from a scrum and dummied his way through the bemused defence for a splendid solo try.

121 INTERNATIONAL CHAMPIONSHIP 1921 FRANCE

Inverleith · Saturday 22 January 1921 · Lost 0–3

SCOTLAND †HH Forsayth (*Oxford U*); †IJ Kilgour (*RMA Sandhurst*), †AE Thomson (*Utd Servs*), †AL Gracie (*Harlequins*), †JH Carmichael (*Watsonians*); AT Sloan (*Edinburgh Acs*), J Hume* (*Royal HSFP*); †JM Bannerman (*Glasgow HSFP*), †RS Cumming (*Aberdeen U*), RA Gallie (*Glasgow Acs*), AD Laing (*Royal HSFP*), GHHP Maxwell (*London Scot*), JB McDougall (*Wakefield*), NC Macpherson (*Newport*), WAK Murray (*Kelvinside Acs*)

FRANCE J Clément (*RCF*); R Got (*Perpignan*), R Crabos* (*RCF*), F Borde (*RCF*), J Lobies (*RCF*); E Billac (*Bayonne*), R Piteu (*Pau*); M Biraben (*Dax*), P Pons (*Toulouse*), M-F Lubin-Lebrère (*Toulouse*), E Soulié (*CASG*), G Coscolla (*Béziers*), J Boubée (*Tarbes*), R Lasserre (*Bayonne*), F Vaquer (*Perpignan*)

REFEREE WP Hinton (*Ireland*)

SCORING Billac, try (o-3) (half-time)

France had to make numerous changes from their original selection because of illness and injuries but still managed to record their first victory on Scottish soil. Playing on a cold day and in a difficult swirling wind, the visitors were highly impressive and probably should have won more easily. They showed plenty of speed, stamina and inventiveness, and defended stubbornly, especially at the end of the match when the Scots were pressing hard. The two sets of forwards were fairly evenly matched, but the Scottish back division lacked any penetration and was shaky in defence. The only try of the match was scored just before half-time. The Scottish backs fumbled the ball and François Borde, the French centre, picked it up on the run and broke through. He could easily have scored himself but unselfishly passed to Eugène Billac, the stand-off, who ran over at the posts. Crabos's conversion attempt hit the woodwork. The second half was mainly a laborious forward scramble although Hume and Maxwell had good runs for Scotland. Lobies did the same for France with, according to one report, 'disastrous results to his wearing apparel'.

122 INTERNATIONAL CHAMPIONSHIP 1921 WALES

St Helen's, Swansea · Saturday 5 February 1921 · Won 14–8

SCOTLAND HH Forsayth (*Oxford U*); AT Sloan (*Edinburgh Acs*), AL Gracie (*Harlequins*), AE Thomson (*Utd Servs*), JH Carmichael (*Watsonians*); †RLH Donald (*Glasgow HSFP*), J Hume* (*Royal HSFP*); JM Bannerman (*Glasgow HSFP*), †JCR Buchanan (*Stewart's FP*), RS Cumming (*Aberdeen U*), †G Douglas (*Jed-Forest*), RA Gallie (*Glasgow Acs*), GHHP Maxwell (*RAF*), †JN Shaw (*Edinburgh Acs*), CM Usher (*Edinburgh Wdrs*)

WALES J Rees (*Swansea*); F Evans (*Llanelli*), AE Jenkins (*Llanelli*), PER Jones (*Newport*), BMG Thomas (*Bart's H*); WE Bowen (*Swansea*), TH Vile* (*Newport*); JL Williams (*Blaina*), S Winmill (*Cross Keys*), T Roberts (*Risca*), W Hodder (*Pontypool*), SL Attewell (*Newport*), ET Parker (*Swansea*), J Jones (*Aberavon*), DE Morgan (*Llanelli*)

REFEREE J Baxter (*England*)

SCORING Thomson, try (3-0); Buchanan, try (6-0); Maxwell, con (8-0); Maxwell, pen (11-0) (half-time) Jenkins, drop (11-4); Jenkins, drop (11-8); Sloan, try (14-8)

The Scots were a huge improvement on the previous match and unexpectedly won in Wales for the first time since 1892. The game was marred by serious crowd problems and play was interrupted on several occasions by careless and over-enthusiastic spectators invading the field. At one point, the players had to retire to the pavilion until order was restored and the game was under threat of being abandoned. Arguably, these problems cost Wales the match because some of their players seemed to be unnerved by the crowd's behaviour and lost their concentration at crucial moments. However, the Scots deserved to win thanks to a spirited forward effort in the first half. Playing with the wind, the visitors raced to a big early lead. Thomson intercepted a loose pass and dashed away, Sloan was in support before feeding back to Thomson for the opening score. Then Buchanan finished off a devastating forwards charge that sliced through the Welsh defence for Scotland's second. Maxwell converted and later kicked a huge penalty from near halfway. Wales dominated in the second half and fought back to within three points with a brace of drop goals by centre Albert Jenkins. In a tense finale, Wales looked more likely to score until the Scottish forwards broke away; Sloan gathered the loose ball and crossed amongst a throng of spectators for the decisive try. The victorious Scottish team was cheered from the field by the crowd and had to fight their way out of the ground to catch their train back to London.

123   INTERNATIONAL CHAMPIONSHIP 1921   IRELAND

Lansdowne Road, Dublin · Saturday 26 February 1921 · Lost 8–9

SCOTLAND HH Forsayth (*Oxford U*); †JWS McCrow (*Edinburgh Acs*), AL Gracie (*Harlequins*), AT Sloan (*Edinburgh Acs*), JH Carmichael (*Watsonians*); RLH Donald (*Glasgow HSFP*), J Hume*(*Royal HSFP*); JM Bannerman (*Glasgow HSFP*), JCR Buchanan (*Stewart's FP*), RA Gaille (*Glasgow Acs*), JB McDougall (*Wakefield*), GHHP Maxwell (*London Scot*), †GM Murray (*Glasgow Acs*), †JL Stewart (*Edinburgh Acs*), JN Shaw (*Edinburgh Acs*)

IRELAND WE Crawford (*Lansdowne*); DJ Cussen (*Dublin U*), GV Stephenson (*QU Belfast*), AR Foster (*Derry*), HST Cormac (*Clontarf & W of Scot*); W Cunningham (*Lansdowne*), T Mayne (*NIFC*); JJ Bermingham (*Blackrock Coll*), WP Collopy (*Bective Rgrs*), AW Courtney (*UC Dublin*), WD Doherty* (*Cambridge U*), CFGT Hallaran (*RN*), TA McClelland (*QU Belfast*), NM Purcell (*Lansdowne*), P Stokes (*Blackrock Coll*)

REFEREE J Baxter (*England*)

SCORING Hume, try (3–0); Maxwell, con (5–0); Cussen, try (5–3); Hume, try (8–3) (half-time) Stephenson, try (8–6); Cunningham, try (8–9)

Against expectations, the Irish won their first international victory since before the First World War. The Scottish forwards were weakened by the late withdrawals of Usher and Macpherson, and they had to give second best in tight play. Their opponents were a more robust combination and, in the words of *The Scotsman*, 'certainly did not stand on ceremony'. The Scottish half-backs played well under pressure and scrum-half Hume was courageous at the feet of the rampaging Irish pack. The backs had only limited opportunities in attack and were hampered by several injuries, but they stuck manfully to their task and good tackling prevented a much heavier defeat. The Irish backs had most of the possession, but largely were unimaginative and made many errors. Ireland started strongly but the Scots opened the scoring within five minutes. McCrow intercepted and broke away from his own half, and Hume was in support to run in between the posts. Ireland missed several penalty and drop kicks before Cussen scored an unconverted try. Soon afterwards,

Hume scored a blindside try from a scrum near the Irish line. A few minutes into the second half, Stephenson scored the best try of the game after a lovely penetrating movement by the Irish backs. Ten minutes later, Cunningham and Courtney combined for Ireland's third try, which turned out to be the winning score. The Scots tried unsuccessfully to save the game and Forsayth, who was excellent throughout, was just short with a drop goal attempt.

124   INTERNATIONAL CHAMPIONSHIP 1921   ENGLAND

Inverleith · Saturday 19 March 1921 · Lost 0–18

SCOTLAND HH Forsayth (*Oxford U*); AT Sloan (*Edinburgh Acs*), AE Thomson (*Utd Servs*), †CJG Mackenzie (*Utd Servs*), AL Gracie (*Harlequins*); RHL Donald (*Glasgow HSFP*), J Hume* (*Royal HSFP*); JM Bannerman (*Glasgow HSFP*), JCR Buchanan (*Stewart's FP*), RA Gallie (*Glasgow Acs*), F Kennedy (*Stewart's FP*), JB McDougall (*Wakefield*), NC Macpherson (*Newport*), CM Usher (*Edinburgh Wdrs*), GHHP Maxwell (*London Scot*)

ENGLAND BS Cumberlege (*Blackheath*); CN Lowe (*Blackheath*), AM Smallwood (*Leicester*), EDG Hammett (*Newport*), QEMA King (*Blackheath & Army*); WJA Davies* (*Utd Servs*); CA Kershaw (*Utd Servs*); R Edwards (*Newport*), ER Gardner (*RN*), LG Brown (*Blackheath*), T Woods (*Devonport Servs*), R Cove-Smith (*Cambridge U*), AF Blakiston (*Northampton*), AT Voyce (*Gloucester*), WW Wakefield (*Harlequins*)

REFEREE JC Crawford (*Ireland*)

SCORING Gardner, try (0–3); Woods, try (0–6); Hammett, con (0–8) (half-time) Brown, try (0–11); Hammett, con (0–13); King, try (0–16); Hammett, con (0–18)

On the 50th anniversary of the first meeting between the two sides, a very good England side were decisive winners, scoring four tries to none and clinching the Triple Crown. The Scottish forwards had parity in the scrums, but were no match for their opponents in the loose. The English handling and support play was very impressive, and Brown and Wakefield were prominent throughout. Scottish scrum-half Hume had another courageous match, but otherwise the backs were disappointing and they made too many errors. Played in drizzling rain and the infamous Inverleith swirl, this match started promisingly before degenerating into a rather featureless and drab encounter. The early exchanges were evenly balanced, and after 18 minutes Gardner took the ball at a lineout near the Scottish line and crossed for an unconverted try. England continued to press and Woods took advantage of some poor Scottish marking to score a simple try which Hammett converted from an easy position. Early in the second half, Hume and Gardner were injured in the same incident and had to leave the field temporarily. The English half-backs, Davies and Kershaw, started to show their potential with some slippery runs and a series of teasing kicks that kept Scotland under pressure, but the home side responded with some forward rushes. England were fortunate when Davies kicked ahead and the ball rebounded off the crossbar straight into the arms of Brown who playfully dotted down underneath the posts. The try was awarded even though Brown seemed to be in an offside position. England scored a fourth try when a Scottish movement broke down. King scooped up the loose ball and raced away to the posts for Hammett to convert.

Stade Colombes, Paris · Monday 2 January 1922 · Draw 3–3

SCOTLAND †WC Johnston (*Glasgow HSFP*); A Browning (*Glasgow HSFP*), †GPS Macpherson (*Oxford U*), AL Gracie (*Harlequins*), †EH Liddell (*Edinburgh U*); †JC Dykes (*Glasgow Acs*), J Hume (*Royal HSFP*), A Wemyss (*Edinburgh Wdrs*), †DM Bertram (*Watsonians*), †AK Stevenson (*Glasgow Acs*), †DS Davies (*Hawick*), JM Bannerman (*Glasgow HSFP*), †JR Lawrie (*Melrose*), GHHP Maxwell (*London Scot*), CM Usher* (*Edinburgh Wdrs*)

FRANCE J Clément (*Valence*); R Got (*Perpignan*), R Crabos* (*St Sever*), F Borde (*Toulouse*), A Jauréguy (*Toulouse*); J Pascot (*Perpignan*), R Piteu (*Pau*); M Biraben (*Dax*), P Pons (*Toulouse*), M-F Lubin-Lebrère (*Toulouse*), A Cassayet-Armagnac (*St Gaudens*), P Moureu (*Béziers*), F Cahuc (*St Girons*), R Lasserre (*Cognac*), J Sébédio (*Carcassone*)

REFEREE HC Harrison (*England*)

SCORING Jauréguy, try (0–3); Browning, try (3–3) (half-time)

Eric Liddell, the famous athlete, made his first appearance on the left wing, two years before he won an Olympic gold medal in the same stadium. Interest in this match was so great that barriers were torn down long before kick-off and some of the crowd had to be removed from the pitch. Played under a dark and lowering sky, the first half was fairly open and fast, and both sides scored a try. France opened the scoring when Clément set his backs away and Jauréguy used his speed and strength to power over near the posts. Scotland responded with a good passing movement and Macpherson gave Browning just enough space to slip in. Persistent heavy rain fell during the second half and the pitch turned in a quagmire. Play was rather featureless and mainly a relentless struggle between the forwards. The Scottish pack held the upper hand and the exciting French runners had few opportunities in attack.

Inverleith · Saturday 4 February 1922 · Drawn 9–9

SCOTLAND HH Forsayth (*Oxford U*); A Browning (*Glasgow HSFP*), †RC Warren (*Glasgow Acs*), AL Gracie (*Harlequins*), EH Liddell (*Edinburgh U*); GPS Macpherson (*Oxford U*), †WE Bryce (*Selkirk*); A Wemyss (*Edinburgh Wdrs*), DM Bertram (*Watsonians*), †WG Dobson (*Heriot's FP*), DS Davies (*Hawick*), JM Bannerman (*Glasgow HSFP*), JR Lawrie (*Melrose*), JCR Buchanan (*Stewart's FP*), CM Usher* (*Edinburgh Wdrs*)

WALES TF Samuel (*Mountain Ash*); FC Palmer (*Swansea*), HI Evans (*Swansea*), BS Evans (*Llanelli*), WC Richards (*Pontypool*); WE Bowen (*Swansea*), WJ Delahay (*Bridgend*); ET Parker* (*Swansea*), JJ Whitfield (*Newport*), T Jones (*Newport*), S Morris (*Cross Keys*), T Roberts (*Risca*), JG Stephens (*Llanelli*), W Cummins (*Treorchy*), DD Hiddlestone (*Neath*)

REFEREE RA Lloyd (*England*)

SCORING No scoring in the first half. Bowen, try (0–3); Samuel, con (0–5); Browning, try (3–5); Browning, pen (6–5); Browning, try (9–5); I Evans, drop (9–9)

On a wintery afternoon, Scotland were deprived of victory by a last minute drop goal. This was a rather disappointing game mainly confined to the forwards. The Scottish pack showed-up well and Bryce at scrum-half was resolute and courageous. However, much of the Scottish back play lacked flair or imagination, and the potentially dangerous Gracie-Liddell combination was largely neglected. There was no scoring in the first half and the first points came from a Scottish error. Forsayth, the Scottish fullback, gathered a loose ball deep inside his own 25, but hesitated when making his clearance. Bowen charged down with a resounding thud and scored near the posts, and Samuel added the conversion. Scotland responded with great determination and Bryce made a sniping run near the Welsh line to create a simple run-in for Browning. Bertram missed the conversion and, with 13 minutes to go, Browning kicked a penalty to give Scotland a one-point advantage. Then the home side put together the best move of the match which ended with Browning running around an openmouthed Samuel to score a fine winger's try. Browning missed the conversion, but the game looked as good as won until the Welshmen made a late surge and Islwyn Evans dropped an opportunist goal to tie the scores. The final whistle sounded a few moments later and the largely Scottish crowd left the ground in stunned silence.

127   INTERNATIONAL CHAMPIONSHIP 1922   IRELAND

Inverleith · Saturday 25 February 1922 · Won 6–3

SCOTLAND HH Forsayth (*Oxford U*); A Browning (*Glasgow HSFP*), RC Warren (*Glasgow Acs*), AL Gracie (*Harlequins*), EH Liddell (*Edinburgh U*); GPS Macpherson (*Oxford U*), WE Bryce (*Selkirk*); A Wemyss (*Edinburgh Wdrs*), DM Bertram (*Watsonians*), WG Dobson (*Heriot's FP*), DS Davies (*Hawick*), JM Bannerman (*Glasgow HSFP*), JR Lawrie (*Melrose*), CM Usher* (*Edinburgh Wdrs*), JCR Buchanan (*Stewart's FP*)

IRELAND WE Crawford (*Lansdowne*); HWV Stephenson (*Utd Servs*), GV Stephenson (*QU Belfast*), DB Sullivan(*UC Dublin*), TG Wallis (*Wdrs*); JR Wheeler (*QU Belfast*), JAB Clarke (*Bective Rgrs*); WP Collopy* (*Bective Rgrs*), MJ Bradley (*Dolphin*), I Popham (*Cork Const*), CFGT Hallaran (*Utd Servs*), S McVicker (*QU Belfast*), RH Owens (*Dublin U*), JD Egan (*Bective Rgrs*), JKS Thompson (*Dublin U*)

REFEREE TD Schofield (*Wales*)

SCORING Clarke, try (0–3) (half-time) Bryce, try (3–3); Liddell, try (6–3)

Edinburgh was in the grip of an almighty gale which made this match something of a lottery. Passing and kicking were difficult and unpredictable, and both sides struggled for any sort of control in the wild conditions. There was little to choose between two enthusiastic and hard-working packs. Both had spells of supremacy although the Scots had greater stamina, and Usher and Bannerman were always prominent. At scrum-half, the diminutive Willie Bryce had another excellent game and was in the thick of the action from the start. The speedy Scottish backs had their chances, but too often they were hesitant and strong Irish tackling held them out. Twice in the first half, Liddell was set free but the defence managed to catch him. Near the interval, the Irish forwards made a rush into the Scottish 25 and scrum-half Clark dodged over at the corner flag. The Scots started the second half strongly and from a maul inside the Irish 25 Bryce made an elusive run to score a fine solo try. Then from a kick ahead, Liddell followed up and used his remarkable pace to beat Crawford for the winning score. The Scottish forwards kept a tight grip on the rest of the game and, apart from a couple of shaky moments, the home side held on to win.

128   INTERNATIONAL CHAMPIONSHIP 1922   ENGLAND

Twickenham · Saturday 18 March 1922 · Lost 5–11

SCOTLAND HH Forsayth (*Oxford U*); †JM Tolmie (*Glasgow HSFP*), AL Gracie (*Harlequins*), GPS Macpherson (*Oxford U*), EB Mackay (*Glasgow Acs*); JC Dykes (*Glasgow Acs*), WE Bryce (*Selkirk*); JCR Buchanan (*Stewart's FP*), DM Bertram (*Watsonians*), WG Dobson (*Heriot's FP*), DS Davies (*Hawick*), JM Bannerman (*Glasgow HSFP*), JR Lawrie (*Melrose*), GHHP Maxwell (*Edinburgh Acs*), CM Usher* (*Edinburgh Wdrs*)

ENGLAND JA Middleton (*Richmond*); CN Lowe (*Blackheath*), E Myers (*Bradford*), AM Smallwood (*Leicester*), IJ Pitman (*Oxford U*); WJA Davies* (*Utd Servs*), CA Kershaw (*Utd Servs*); PBRW Williams-Powlett (*Utd Servs*), HL Price (*Oxford U*), RFH Duncan (*Guy's H*), R Cove-Smith (*Cambridge U*), WW Wakefield (*Harlequins*), AT Voyce (*Gloucester*), JE Maxwell-Hyslop (*Oxford U*), GS Conway (*Cambridge U*)

REFEREE RA Lloyd (*Ireland*)

SCORING Dykes, try (3–0); Bertram, con (5–0) (half-time) Lowe, try (5–3); Lowe, try (5–6); Conway, con (5–8); Davies, try (5–11)

On a warm afternoon the two sides were presented to King George V. Scotland were very impressive in the first half against a strangely out-of-sorts England, but the home side recovered after the interval and were convincing winners in the end. Playing with the wind behind them, Scotland began strongly and opened the scoring after some 30 minutes. From a lineout on the English 25, the ball was whipped left to Mackay who dashed past a weak tackle before passing inside to Dykes who had an easy run-in for Bertram to convert. After about ten minutes of the second half, a rejuvenated English side suddenly found its best form. Kershaw and Davies, the half-backs, took play into Scottish territory, and Lowe gathered his own kick ahead and made a flying leap over the line. Conway missed the awkward conversion but England were in the ascendancy. A few minutes later, a break by Davies and a bout of clever handling put Myers away on a penetrating run almost to the goal-line and Lowe was in support to take the scoring pass. Conway's conversion gave England a two-point lead. The home side continued to press but then Maxwell, the Scottish forward, hit the post with a penalty attempt. Davies relieved the pressure with a long touch-finder and a few minutes later the mercurial stand-off made an elusive run through the startled Scottish defence for the clinching try.

129   INTERNATIONAL CHAMPIONSHIP 1923   FRANCE

Inverleith · Saturday 20 January 1923 · Won 16–3

SCOTLAND †D Drysdale (*Heriot's FP*); †AC Wallace (*Oxford U*), †E McLaren (*Royal HSFP*), AL Gracie* (*Harlequins*), EH Liddell (*Edinburgh U*); †SB McQueen (*Waterloo*), WE Bryce (*Selkirk*); †DS Kerr (*Heriot's FP*), DM Bertram (*Watsonians*), AK Stevenson (*Glasgow Acs*), †LM Stuart (*Glasgow HSFP*), JM Bannerman (*Glasgow HSFP*), JR Lawrie (*Melrose*), JCR Buchanan (*Stewart's FP*), DS Davies (*Hawick*)

FRANCE J Clément (*Valence*); M Lalande (*RCF*), R Crabos* (*St Sever*), F Borde (*Toulouse*), A Jauréguy (*Toulouse*); J Pascot (*Perpignan*), C Dupont (*Lourdes*); J Bernon (*Lourdes*), J Bayard (*Toulouse*), L Béguet (*RCF*), A Cassayet-Armagnac (*St Gaudens*), P Moureu (*Béziers*), J Larrieu (*Tarbes*), A Guichemerre (*Dax*), J Sébédio (*Carcassone*)

REFEREE TH Vile (*Wales*)

SCORING McLaren, try (3–0); Drysdale, con (5–0) (half-time) Bryce, try (8–0); Drysdale, con (10–0); McLaren, try (13–0); Béguet, mark (13–3); Liddell, try (16–3)

Conditions were good with a firm pitch and a sharp northerly wind. Scotland scored four tries and were the superior side, but this was an uninspiring match and play did not reach a high standard. *The Scotsman* reported: 'There have been many club matches this season in which much better rugby has been witnessed.' Scotland lost a couple of early chances before McLaren made a break and scored a try in the corner which Drysdale converted. France were handicapped by several injuries and for a time had to play with seven forwards. The Scottish backs made several good handling moves and Wallace got over the line, but carelessly lost hold of the ball when running around to the posts. The Scots improved in the second half and scored three further tries. The French team did not combine well and were largely outplayed although they defended wholeheartedly and Béguest kicked a drop goal from a mark. The Scots finished strongly, but there was no further scoring. Bannerman and Lawrie were prominent in the loose and the backs always looked dangerous.

Cardiff Arms Park · Saturday 3 February 1923 · Won 11–8

SCOTLAND D Drysdale (*Heriot's FP*); A Browning (*Glasgow HSFP*), E McLaren (*Royal HSFP*), AL Gracie* (*Harlequins*), EH Liddell (*Edinburgh U*); SB McQueen (*Waterloo*), WE Bryce (*Selkirk*); DS Kerr (*Heriot's FP*), DM Bertram (*Watsonians*), AK Stevenson (*Glasgow Acs*), LM Stuart (*Glasgow HSFP*), JM Bannerman (*Glasgow HSFP*), JR Lawrie (*Melrose*), DS Davies (*Hawick*), JCR Buchanan (*Stewart's FP*)

WALES BO Male (*Pontypool*); TAW Johnson (*Cardiff*), RA Cornish (*Cardiff*), AE Jenkins (*Llanelli*), WR Harding (*Swansea*); JMC Lewis* (*Cardiff*), WJ Delahay (*Bridgend*); A Baker (*Neath*), S Morris (*Cross Keys*), DG Davies (*Cardiff*), ET Parker (*Swansea*), GM Michael (*Swansea*), SG Thomas (*Llanelli*), JL Jenkins (*Aberavon*), T Roberts (*Newport*)

REFEREE JW Baxter (*England*)

SCORING A Jenkins, pen (0–3) (half-time) Liddell, try (3–3); Lewis, try (3–6); A Jenkins, con (3–8); Stuart, try (6–8); Gracie, try (9–8); Drysdale, con (11–8)

This became known as 'Gracie's match' because of a dramatic late try by Scottish centre and captain Leslie Gracie that won the game right at the death. Cardiff Arms Park was almost overwhelmed with the size of the crowd and during the game spectators lined the touchlines. Several people were hurt in the crush and part of the grandstand collapsed, injuring three men. The ground was heavy after recent rain and had been drained with the help of the local fire brigade. Scotland took a long time to settle down and Wales, the favourites, had much the better of the first half, but they could only score a penalty goal by Albert Jenkins. The home side applied tremendous pressure just before the interval, but the Scottish defence stood firm. Early in the second half, Liddell showed his great speed when he rushed onto a kick ahead and scored an unconverted try in the left corner. Wales responded with a try by stand-off Clem Lewis and Jenkins added the simple conversion. The Scottish forwards grew stronger as the game went on and after a spell of pressure Stuart raced away from a scrum and scored a try. Browning missed the conversion to leave Wales two points in the lead. The closing stages were almost unbearably exciting as the Scots battled for the winning score and the Welsh defence refused to yield. The Scottish forwards repeatedly hammered on the line and both Liddell and Gracie looked certain to score but were caught with courageous last-ditch tackles. Then, in the dying seconds, Scotland won a scrum near the Welsh 25 and the ball was passed out to Gracie going at full tilt with Liddell in close support. Aware of the threat of Liddell, the Welsh defenders were momentarily caught in two minds and Gracie slipped between them and ran around behind the posts. In his excitement, he almost put a foot over the dead-ball line and his flying boot struck a small boy on the face and knocked out a few of his teeth. Drysdale's successful conversion finished a memorable encounter. This was Scotland's first win in Cardiff since 1890 and at the end of the game several Scottish players, including Gracie, were chaired off the field by sporting Welsh spectators.

131   INTERNATIONAL CHAMPIONSHIP 1923   IRELAND

Lansdowne Road, Dublin   ·   Saturday 24 February 1923   ·   Won 13–3

SCOTLAND D Drysdale (*Heriot's FP*); A Browning (*Glasgow HSFP*), E McLaren (*London Scot*), AL Gracie* (*Harlequins*), EH Liddell (*Edinburgh U*); SB McQueen (*Waterloo*), WE Bryce (*Selkirk*); N Macpherson (*Newport*), DM Bertram (*Watsonians*), JCR Buchanan (*Stewart's FP*), LM Stuart (*Glasgow HSFP*), JM Bannerman (*Glasgow HSFP*), JR Lawrie (*Melrose*), DS Davies (*Hawick*), †RS Simpson (*Glasgow Acs*)

IRELAND WE Crawford (*Lansdowne*); DJ Cussen (*Dublin U*), GV Stephenson (*QU Belfast*), JB Gardiner (*NIFC*), RO McClenahan (*Instonians*); WH Hall (*Instonians*), WA Cunningham (*Lansdowne*); MJ Bradley (*Dolphin*), R Collopy (*Bective Rgrs*), WP Collopy (*Bective Rgrs*), DM Cunningham (*NIFC*), PEF Dunn (*Bective Rgrs*), RD Gray (*Old Wesley*), JKS Thompson* (*Dublin U*), TA McClelland (*QU Belfast*)

REFEREE TH Vile (*Wales*)

SCORING Cussen, try (0–3); Liddell, try (3–3); Browning, con (5–3); Browning, try (8–3) (half-time) McQueen, try (11–3); Browning, con (13–3)

Scotland continued their winning ways in a dour defensive struggle played in wet conditions. The visitors were the better side, but Ireland played an enthusiastic spoiling game and fought right to the end. The Scottish backs were tightly marked and only once managed an orthodox handling movement, which led to a try by Browning. The Irish defence was very aggressive and both Bryce and Gracie, the Scottish captain, were on the receiving end of some heavy tackles. Gracie, in particular, was badly dazed after a tackle by Cussen in the first half. Both sides started cautiously until the Irish seized their chance after 20 minutes. The backs made a good handling movement which ended with a try by Cussen. Soon afterwards, Liddell scored a try and Browning added the conversion. Browning scored a second try before the interval.

Ireland started the second period purposefully and twice were denied by courageous defence from Drysdale, who was in his best form. Liddell used his great speed to round the Irish defence before giving an inside pass to McQueen who scored between the posts. Scotland had several chances late in the game, but could not escape the defence. McQueen broke through but his kick ahead was too heavy and the ball went dead. Both Scottish wings earned plaudits and Liddell showed growing confidence and awareness to match his searing pace.

132 INTERNATIONAL CHAMPIONSHIP 1923 ENGLAND

Inverleith · Saturday 17 March 1923 · Lost 6–8

SCOTLAND D Drysdale (*Heriot's FP*); A Browning (*Glasgow HSFP*), E McLaren (*London Scot*), AL Gracie* (*Harlequins*), EH Liddell (*Edinburgh U*); SB McQueen (*Waterloo*), WE Bryce (*Selkirk*); N Macpherson (*Newport*), DM Bertram (*Watsonians*), AK Stevenson (*Glasgow Acs*), LM Stuart (*Glasgow HSFP*), JM Bannerman (*Glasgow HSFP*), JR Lawrie (*Melrose*), JCR Buchanan (Stewart's FP), DS Davies (*Hawick*)

ENGLAND TE Holliday (*Aspatria*); CN Lowe (*Blackheath*), E Myers (*Bradford*), HM Locke (*Birkenhead Park*), AM Smallwood (*Leicester*); WJA Davies* (*Utd Servs*), CA Kershaw (*Utd Servs*); ER Gardner (*Devonport Servs*), FW Sanders (*Plymouth Alb*), WGE Luddington (*Devonport Servs*), R Cove-Smith (*OMT*), WW Wakefield (*Cambridge U*), AF Blakiston (*Northampton*), AT Voyce (*Gloucester*), GS Conway (*Rugby*)

REFEREE TH Vile (*Wales*)

SCORING Smallwood, try (0–3); McLaren, try (3–3) (half-time) Gracie, try (6–3); Voyce, try (6–6); Luddington, con (6–8)

Interest and enthusiasm for this match was enormous as both sides were playing for the Championship. On a beautiful spring afternoon, the teams were fairly evenly matched, but England were more enterprising and took their opportunities. With the prospect of a Grand Slam before them, some of the Scottish play was nervous and the home side never found their best form. The forwards did well enough, especially in the lineout, and Lawrie was prominent in the loose. Bryce had another great game at scrum-half, but his partner, McQueen, kicked too much and his handling was often erratic. Liddell showed plenty of resolve on the rare occasions when he had the ball. Both sides had some early chances and Lawrie crossed the English line only to be called back for a forward pass. Then, on the 23rd minute, Smallwood, the Leicester winger, took everybody by surprise when he made a dodging run from 40 yards to open the scoring. Scotland responded shortly before the interval when McLaren made a midfield break and cut inside to scramble over the line. Scotland seemed to have the game under control for much of the second half and around the hour mark Gracie scored a brilliant solo try. Instead of trying to pick-up a low pass, he twice kicked on past the defence and just managed to reach the ball before it bounced out of play. Drysdale missed the conversion and from a Scottish attack Locke intercepted a loose pass, play swept up field and Voyce was in support to score near the corner. Luddington, under considerable pressure, landed the awkward conversion. The Scots fought desperately to save the match but to no avail.

Stade Pershing, Paris · Tuesday 1 January 1924 · Lost 10–12

SCOTLAND D Drysdale (*Heriot's FP*); AC Wallace (*Oxford U*), AL Gracie (*Harlequins*), E McLaren (*London Scot*), †CEWC Mackintosh (*London Scot*); †H Waddell (*Glasgow Acs*), WE Bryce (*Selkirk*); DS Kerr (*Heriot's FP*), †A Ross (*Kilmarnock*), †RA Howie (*Kirkcaldy*), LM Stuart (*Glasgow HSFP*), JM Bannerman (*Glasgow HSFP*), JCR Buchanan* (*Stewart's FP*), †KGP Hendrie (*Heriot's FP*), DS Davies (*Hawick*)

FRANCE E Besset (*Grenoble*); L Cluchague (*Biarritz*), R Crabos* (*St Sever*), A Béhotéguy (*Bayonne*), A Jauréguy (*Stade Français*); H Galau (*Toulouse*), C Dupont (*Rouen*); L Lepatey (*Mazamet*), C-A Gonnet (*RCF*), L Béguet (*RCF*), A Cassayet-Armagnac (*St Gaudens*), P Moureu (*Béziers*), J Etcheberry (*Cognac*), R Lasserre (*Grenoble*), E Piquiral (*RCF*)

REFEREE E Roberts (*Wales*)

SCORING Jauréguy, try (0–3); Piquiral, try (0–6); Wallace, try (3–6) (half-time) Davies, pen (6–6); Waddell, drop (10–6); Galau, try (10–9); Moureu, try (10–12)

The pitch at Colombes Stadium was flooded so this match was switched to Stade Pershing at short notice. Scotland were expected to win, but France raised their game and thoroughly outplayed their rather hapless opponents. The French forwards were strong and determined, and the backs showed plenty of enterprise and eagerness to run the ball. Scotland lacked composure in the face of the French maelstrom and made too many errors, especially McLaren in the centre who barely caught a pass all day. France could have won by a lot more if they had taken their chances. In the first half, France scored two tries in quick succession. McLaren dropped a pass, the ball was hacked on by a French back, and Galau passed to Jauréguy who ran away to the line. Shortly afterwards, Piquiral scored a try following a solid French attack. Curiously, the conversion was signalled as a goal and it was only after the game that the referee confirmed that he had not awarded it. Scotland responded when Wallace made a swerving run for a brilliant solo try and early in the second half Davies, a back-row forward, kicked a penalty. The Scottish forwards began to assert themselves and from one attack Waddell dropped a goal to give Scotland the lead. France refused to give in and Galau scored a try after an excellent passing movement. France finished very strongly, and inside the final minutes Lasserre broke away from a lineout and in the ensuing scramble Moureu managed to get his hand on the bouncing ball for the winning score.

Inverleith · Saturday 2 February 1924 · Won 35–10

SCOTLAND D Drysdale (*Heriot's FP*); †IS Smith (*Oxford U*), GPS Macpherson (*Oxford U*), †GG Aitken (*Oxford U*); AC Wallace (*Oxford U*); H Waddell (*Glasgow Acs*), WE Bryce (*Selkirk*); A Ross (*Kilmarnock*), DM Bertram (*Watsonians*), RA Howie (*Kirkcaldy*), JCR Buchanan* (*Stewart's FP*), JM Bannerman (*Glasgow HSFP*), JR Lawrie (*Leicester*), KGP Hendrie (*Heriot's FP*), †AC Gillies (*Watsonians*)

WALES BO Male (*Cardiff*); HJ Davies (*Newport*), JE Evans (*Llanelli*), MA Rosser (*Penarth*),

The famous Oxford University and Scotland three-quarter line of Johnny Wallace, George Aitken, Phil Macpherson and Ian Smith. *Mary Evans Picture Library*

TAW Johnson (*Cardiff*); VM Griffiths (*Newport*), E Watkins (*Neath*); JJ Whitfield* (*Newport*), S Morris (*Cross Keys*), JIT Morris (*Swansea*), T Jones (*Newport*), CH Pugh (*Maesteg*), IE Jones (*Llanelli*), WJ Ould (*Cardiff*), DG Francis (*Llanelli*)

REFEREE JB McGowan (*Ireland*)

SCORING Smith, try (3–0); Drysdale, con (5–0); Drysdale, pen (8–0); Bryce, try (11–0); Drysdale, con (13–0); Bertram, try (16–0); Smith, try (19–0); Wallace, try (22–0) (half-time) Waddell, try (25–0); Macpherson, try (28–0); Drysdale, con (30–0); Smith, try (33–0); Drysdale, con (35–0); Griffiths, try (35–3); Male, con (35–5); IE Jones, try (35–8); Male, con (35–10)

Scotland fielded the famous Oxford University three-quarter line, including first caps for Australian-born Ian Smith and New Zealander George Aitken. In an extraordinary encounter, a rampant Scotland completely outclassed a lethargic Welsh team, scoring eight tries and dominating every aspect. The Scottish forwards won most of the possession and the backs were much too fast and accurate for their hapless opponents. Wales showed little confidence and some of their defence was very weak. Playing with the wind behind them, the visitors almost scored an early try, but soon the Scottish forwards made a rush to the Welsh line and quick passing allowed Smith to run round the defence and behind the posts. Drysdale converted and then kicked an angled penalty against the wind. Scotland continued to press and scored three tries in quick succession. Bryce slipped over from a scrum near the Welsh line and a few minutes later Aitken made a strong run which led up to a scrambled try by Bertram. Two minutes later, the backs combined to give Smith his second try, but Drysdale's conversion attempt hit one of the posts. Towards the interval, Aitken made another direct run and Wallace just managed to squeeze over at the corner. Early in the second half, Bryce passed to Waddell who powered to the line. Aitken made another break and gave Macpherson an easy run-in and with ten minutes remaining Bryce and Macpherson combined to put Smith away for his hat-trick. Scotland eased up towards the end and Wales scored two late tries to bring at least some respectability to the extraordinary score-line.

135   INTERNATIONAL CHAMPIONSHIP 1924   IRELAND

Inverleith · Saturday 23 February 1924 · Won 13–8

SCOTLAND D Drysdale (*Heriot's FP*); IS Smith (*Oxford U*), GG Aitken (*Oxford U*), JC Dykes (*Glasgow Acs*), †RK Millar (*London Scot*); H Waddell (*Glasgow Acs*), WE Bryce (*Selkirk*); †RG Henderson (*Northern*), DM Bertram (*Watsonians*), RA Howie (*Kirkcaldy*), JCR Buchanan* (*Stewart's FP*), JM Bannerman (*Glasgow HSFP*), JR Lawrie (*Leicester*), KGP Hendrie (*Heriot's FP*), AC Gillies (*Watsonians*)

IRELAND WJ Stewart (*QU Belfast*); HWV Stephenson (*Utd Servs*), GV Stephenson (*QU Belfast*), JB Gardiner (*NIFC*), AC Douglas (*lnstonians*); WH Hall (*lnstonians*), JAB Clarke (*Bective Rgrs*); JD Clinch (*Dublin U*), WP Collopy* (*Bective Rgrs*), R Collopy (*Bective Rgrs*), RY Crichton (*Dublin U*), CFGT Hallaran (*Utd Servs*), TA McClelland (*QU Belfast*), IMB Stuart (*Dublin U*), J McVicker (*Collegians*)

REFEREE TH Vile (*Wales*)

SCORING Waddell, try (3–0); Drysdale, con (5–0); Bertram, try (8–0); Drysdale, con (10–0); GV Stephenson, try (10–3); GV Stephenson, con (10–5) (half-time) GV Stephenson, try (10–8); Waddell, try (13–8)

This was an entertaining and lively match played in near perfect conditions. Much of the action was in the Scottish half of the field and Ireland did very well for the first hour before fading away in the closing stages. Scotland made two changes in the three-quarter line: Millar, usually a right wing, came in on the left, and Dykes at centre although he played stand-off for his club. The Scottish backs struggled to combine effectively and the Irish tackling and spoiling work were very good. The forward exchanges were vigorously contested with Scotland slowly gaining the upper-hand. Ireland had some early pressure before the Scots scored against the run of play. Smith broke to the Irish 25 and passed to Aitken who just managed to hold onto the ball before giving Waddell a clear run to the line. Scotland's second try, which was scored after 20 minutes, came from a stirring forward rush up to the Irish line and Bertram picked up and dived across. Ireland kept up the pressure and George Stephenson slipped inside several defenders for a try that he also converted. In the second half, the Stephenson brothers, Henry and George, combined to create a second try for the latter. Scotland's superior fitness told towards the end and after pressure on the Irish line Waddell, who was in great form, made a dodging run around the blindside for the final score.

136 INTERNATIONAL CHAMPIONSHIP 1924 ENGLAND

Twickenham · Saturday 15 March 1924 · Lost 0–19

SCOTLAND D Drysdale (*Heriot's FP*); IS Smith (*Oxford U*), GPS Macpherson (*Oxford U*), GG Aitken (*Oxford U*), AC Wallace (*Oxford U*); H Waddell (*Glasgow Acs*), WE Bryce (*Selkirk*); DS Davies (*Hawick*), DM Bertram (*Watsonians*), RA Howie (*Kirkcaldy*), RG Henderson (*Northern*), JM Bannerman (*Glasgow HSFP*), JR Lawrie (*Leicester*), JCR Buchanan* (*Stewart's FP*), AC Gillies (*Watsonians*)

SCOTLAND BS Chantrill (*Bristol*); HC Catcheside (*Percy Park*), LJ Corbett (*Bristol*), HM Locke (*Birkenhead Park*), HP Jacob (*Oxford U*); E Myers (*Bradford*), AT Young (*Cambridge U*); R Edwards (*Newport*), A Robson (*Northern*), R Cove-Smith (*OMT*), WGE Luddington (*Devonport Servs*), CS Conway (*Rugby*), AF Blakiston (*Liverpool*), AT Voyce (*Gloucester*), WW Wakefield* (*Leicester*)

REFEREE TH Vile (*Wales*)

SCORING Wakefield, try (0–3); Conway, con (0–5) (half-time) Myers, drop (0–9); Myers, try (0–12); Conway, con (0–14); Catcheside, try (0–17); Conway, con (0–19)

On a fine spring day, England made a late burst of scoring to win their second Grand Slam in two seasons. There was little between the sides for the first hour and at this stage no suggestion about the final result. Scotland fought hard, but the English forwards held an advantage in the scrums and were much faster in loose play. In the first half, the Scots narrowly missed several chances because of wayward passing and determined English tackling. Near to the interval, Corbett made a strong run and crosskicked into midfield. The ball bounced awkwardly for the Scottish defence and Wakefield gathered to score near the posts. Play continued in a similar vein in the second half. Scotland again made some promising attacks and Macpherson missed a drop goal attempt. Waddell almost scored twice, but dropped the ball at the end of a great attack and then was caught at the last moment by Wakefield. Moving into the final quarter and with match still in the balance, England made a rush to the line and from the ensuing scrum Myers dropped a goal that broke Scottish hearts. Soon afterwards, the same player made an angled run through the rapidly-tiring defence for a try at the posts. Conway converted and the match ended with England firmly in control. In the last minutes, Catcheside collected a loose pass inside his own half and none of the exhausted Scottish defenders could stop him on a long run to the line.

137 INTERNATIONAL CHAMPIONSHIP 1925 FRANCE

Inverleith · Saturday 24 January 1925 · Won 25–4

SCOTLAND D Drysdale (*Heriot's FP*); IS Smith (*Oxford U*), GPS Macpherson (*Oxford U*), GG Aitken (*Oxford U*), AC Wallace (*Oxford U*); JC Dykes (*Glasgow Acs*), †JB Nelson

(*Glasgow Acs*); JCR Buchanan (*Exeter*), †J Gilchrist (*Glasgow Acs*), †WH Stevenson (*Glasgow Acs*), †DJ MacMyn (*Cambridge U*), JM Bannerman (*Glasgow HSFP*), †JW Scott (*Stewart's FP*), †JR Paterson (*Birkenhead Park*), AC Gillies (*Carlisle*)

FRANCE J Ducousso (*Tarbes*); R Halet (*Strasbourg*), J Ballarin (*Toulouse*), M Baillette (*Perpignan*), F Raymond (*Toulouse*); Y du Manoir (*RCF*), C Dupont (*Rouen*); C Montadé (*Perpignan*), J Marcet (*Albi*), A Maury (*Toulouse*), A Cassayet-Armagnac* (*Narbonne*), A Laurent (*Biarritz*), E Ribère (*Perpignan*), A Bioussa (*Toulouse*), J Boubée (*Agen*)

REFEREE E de Courcy Wheeler (*Ireland*)

SCORING Gillies, try (3–0); Gillies, con (5–0); du Manoir, drop (5–4) (half-time) Wallace, try (8–4); Smith, try (11–4); Drysdale, con (13–4); Wallace, try (16–4); Smith, try (19–4); Smith, try (22–4); Smith, try (25–4)

Scotland said goodbye to Inverleith with a comprehensive defeat of a lacklustre French side. Conditions were almost perfect, but in the second half there was a partial eclipse of the sun and the light faded a little although the game carried on regardless. Scotland started in unconvincing style and the first half lacked any real excitement. Gillies scored a try after a rush by the forwards and soon afterwards du Manoir dropped an excellent goal. The French played a tight game and kept the ball amongst their obstinate pack. It took a long time for the Scots to wrestle the initiative and it was only well into the second half that the Scottish back division began to find some space. Ian Smith ended the day with four tries and Johnny Wallace two. Centre Phil Macpherson was involved in almost every score and Nelson had an excellent game at scrum-half. There was plenty of room for improvement, but the 1925 campaign was off to a winning start.

138 INTERNATIONAL CHAMPIONSHIP 1925 WALES

Saturday 7 February 1925 · St Helen's, Swansea · Won 24–14

SCOTLAND D Drysdale (*Heriot's FP*); IS Smith (*Oxford U*), GPS Macpherson* (*Oxford U*), GG Aitken (*Oxford U*), AC Wallace (*Oxford U*); JC Dykes (*Glasgow Acs*), JB Nelson (*Glasgow Acs*); DS Davies (*Hawick*), †JCH Ireland (*Glasgow HSFP*), RA Howie (*Kirkcaldy*), DJ MacMyn (*Cambridge U*), JM Bannerman (*Glasgow HSFP*), JW Scott (*Stewart's FP*), AC Gillies (*Carlisle*), JR Paterson (*Birkenhead Park*)

WALES TAW Johnson (*Cardiff*); WP James (*Aberavon*), E Williams (*Aberavon*), RA Cornish (*Cardiff*), CR Thomas (*Bridgend*); WJ Hopkins (*Aberavon*), WJ Delahay (*Cardiff*); CH Pugh (*Maesteg*), S Morris* (*Cross Keys*), RC Herrara (*Cross Keys*), B Phillips (*Aberavon*), WI Jones (*Llanelli*), DS Parker (*Swansea*), EI Richards (*Cardiff*), SD Lawrence (*Bridgend*)

REFEREE J Baxter (*England*)

SCORING Smith, try (3–0); Drysdale, con (5–0); Smith, try (8–0); Smith, try (11–0); Drysdale, drop (15–0); Wallace, try (18–0) (half-time) Wallace, try (21–0); Hopkins, try (21–3); Parker, con (21–5); Smith, try (24–5); Jones, try (24–8); Cornish, try (24–11); Parker, pen (24–14)

Played in brilliant sunshine, Scotland won on Welsh soil for the third time in succession. The speedy Scottish backs were quite irrepressible in the first half when they scored four tries and a drop goal without reply, but towards the end of the game Wales restored some of their battered pride. Scotland started in whirlwind fashion and, after only a couple of minutes, a swift handling movement gave Smith the first of his four tries. Shortly afterwards Macpherson cut through to create another try for Smith and then a few minutes later Smith completed his hat-trick. The Welsh crowd were momentarily dumbfounded before giving the scorer a tumultuous cheer as he walked back to his position. Next Drysdale dropped a goal and then Wallace scored an unconverted try to give the Scots an 18 points lead at the interval. Wallace completed his brace with a strong run up the touchline before Hopkins scored against the run of play and Parker converted. Once again Macpherson set-up Smith for another try before the Welshmen made their storming finish. Jones scored a try after a rush by the Welsh forwards and then Cornish crossed from a lineout near the Scottish line. Neither try was converted, but Parker kicked a late penalty to end the scoring in a remarkable game.

139   INTERNATIONAL CHAMPIONSHIP 1925   IRELAND

Lansdowne Road, Dublin · Saturday 28 February 1925 · Won 14–8

SCOTLAND D Drysdale* (*Heriot's FP*); IS Smith (*Oxford U*), JC Dykes (*Glasgow Acs*), GG Aitken (*Oxford U*), AC Wallace (*Oxford U*); H Waddell (*Glasgow Acs*), JB Nelson (*Glasgow Acs*); DS Davies (*Hawick*), JCH Ireland (*Glasgow HSFP*), RA Howie (*Kirkcaldy*), DJ MacMyn (*Cambridge U*), JM Bannerman (*Glasgow HSFP*), JW Scott (*Stewart's FP*), JCR Buchanan (*Exeter*), JR Paterson (*Birkenhead Park*)

IRELAND WE Crawford* (*Lansdowne*); HWV Stephenson (*Utd Servs*), GV Stephenson (*QU Belfast*), JB Gardiner (*NIFC*), TR Hewitt (*QU Belfast*); FS Hewitt (*Instonians*), M Sugden (*Dublin U*); GR Beamish (*Coleraine & RAF*), WF Browne (*Utd Servs*), JD Clinch (*Dublin U*), WRF Collis (*Wdrs*), R Collopy (*Bective Rgrs*), RY Crichton (*Dublin U*), MJ Bradley (*Dolphin*), J McVicker (*Collegians*)

REFEREE AE Freethy (*Wales*)

SCORING Wallace, try (3–0); Drysdale, con (5–0) (half-time) Crawford, pen (5–3); MacMyn, try (8–3); Dykes, con (10–3); HWV Stephenson, try (10–6); Crawford, con (10–8); Waddell, drop (14–8)

Despite the heavy ground, this was a strenuously contested match that had many exciting incidents. Scotland were the better side, but Ireland fought hard all the way and the result was in doubt until the closing minutes. Once again the speed and handling of the Scottish backs was outstanding and they also defended well. Ireland started in a determined mood, but slowly the Scottish forwards began to assert themselves. Dykes made a break and Aitken was in support to put Wallace over for a try and Drysdale converted. Ireland had a long spell of concerted pressure after the interval and eventually Crawford kicked a penalty. Then from a scrum near the Scottish 25, the ball was passed to Wallace who made a long run before finding support from the forwards and MacMyn went over at the posts with two defenders clinging to him. Inside the final ten minutes, Stephenson, the Irish wing, caught the defence by surprise when he threw the ball to himself at a lineout and dived over the line. Crawford converted from the touchline. With match in the balance, the Scottish forwards made a late rally and Smith escaped twice, but was caught both times by magnificent last-ditch tackles. Then after a series of mauls on the Irish line, Waddell scooped over a drop goal from almost under the Irish posts.

Murrayfield · Saturday 21 March 1925 · Won 14–11

SCOTLAND D Drysdale (*Heriot's FP*); IS Smith (*Oxford U*), GPS Macpherson* (*Oxford U*), GG Aitken (*Oxford U*), AC Wallace (*Oxford U*); H Waddell (*Glasgow Acs*), JB Nelson (*Glasgow Acs*); DS Davies (*Hawick*), JCH Ireland (*Glasgow HSFP*), RA Howie (*Kirkcaldy*), DJ MacMyn (*London Scot*), JM Bannerman (*Glasgow HSFP*), JW Scott (*Stewart's FP*), JR Paterson (*Birkenhead Park*), AC Gillies (*Carlisle*)

ENGLAND TE Holliday (*Aspatria*); RH Hamilton-Wickes (*Harlequins*), LJ Corbett (*Bristol*), HM Locke (*Birkenhead Park*), AM Smallwood (*Leicester*); E Myers (*Bradford*), EJ Massey (*Leicester*); WGE Luddington (*RN*), JS Tucker (*Bristol*), RRF MacLennan (*OMT*), R Cove-Smith (*OMT*), WW Wakefield* (*Harlequins*), AF Blakiston (*Liverpool*), AT Voyce (*Gloucester*), DC Cumming (*Cambridge U*)

REFEREE AE Freethy (*Wales*)

SCORING Luddington, pen (0–3); Nelson, try (3–3); Drysdale, con (5–3); Hamilton-Wickes, try (5–6); Luddington, con (5–8) (half-time) Wakefield, try (5–11); Wallace, try (8–11); Gillies, con (10–11); Waddell, drop (14–11)

This legendary match marked the opening of Murrayfield stadium and attracted the largest crowd ever seen at a rugby match in Scotland to date. Scotland were playing for their first-ever Grand Slam and their first victory over England since 1912. Both sides were nervous and the standard of play was not high, but the match was fast-moving and unparalleled in terms of excitement and tension. The forward exchanges were stubbornly contested and occasionally fractious. Twice the referee had to warn the players about their behaviour. Luddington, the Royal Navy prop-forward, kicked an early penalty for England against the run of play. Then Macpherson made a typical break and Waddell passed to Nelson who handed-off a defender to score under the

Under the captaincy of Phil Macpherson, this Scottish team won the Grand Slam against England in March 1925. *SRU*

SCOTLAND TRIUMPHS AT LAST: ENGLAND JUST BEATEN.

(Photographs by Sport and General and Central News.)

THE BREAK-UP OF A SCRUM: SCOTLAND PASSES OUT.

CLEVER CLOSE PASSING BY THE SCOTS STARTS A MOVEMENT.

A. C. WALLACE SCORING THE TRY FOR SCOTLAND BY THE CORNER FLAG WHICH WAS SPLENDIDLY CONVERTED BY A. C. GILLIES: A GENERAL VIEW.

WINNING THE MATCH FOR SCOTLAND: H. WADDELL, THE STAND-OFF
HALF-BACK, DROPS A GOAL AFTER JUST PREVIOUSLY FAILING.

UNWILLING TO BE OUT OF THE STRUGGLE: A TERRIER, WHO RAN
ON THE FIELD, HAD TO BE "FORCIBLY REMOVED."

With their removal from Inverleith to their monster new ground at Murrayfield, Scotland have broken the long series of defeats at the hands of England. After one of the most thrilling and tremendous struggles in the history of these encounters, the Scottish XV prevailed over the Englishmen on Saturday last by 14 points (two goals and a dropped goal) to 11 points (a goal, a penalty goal and try) and thus secured a clear win in the Calcutta Cup Championship for the first time since 1907. A full account of the game will be found in Mr. F. J. Sellicks' article on the opposite page.

The Illustrated London News reports on the opening match at Murrayfield in March 1925.
Mary Evans Picture Library

posts and Drysdale converted. Scotland continued to attack, but could not penetrate the tight English defence. Shortly before the interval, Smith misfielded a high ball. The rapacious Tom Voyce gathered and raced up to Drysdale before sending Hamilton-Wickes over at the posts. In the second half, Corbett made a clever cross-kick and Wakefield was up quickly to grab the ball from the startled defence and dive over. In a strange incident that had some bearing on the final outcome, the Englishmen dithered over taking the conversion attempt and MacMyn rushed up and kicked the ball away from the mark, as he was entitled to do. Scotland slowly gained the upper-hand and hit back with a superb try. A crisp handling movement put Wallace away and he eluded several tackles to crash over in the right corner. Gillies kicked a brilliant conversion from the touchline. With only one point between the sides, play was wonderfully exciting and both teams narrowly missed some scoring opportunities. Waddell was wide with a drop goal attempt and the Scottish forwards made a rush to the line only for the ball to rebound of one of the posts. Then with only a few minutes remaining, Waddell dropped a goal to put Scotland into the lead. There was still enough time for England to make some desperate final attacks, but Scotland held out for a historic win. At the finish of this gruelling encounter, some of the players were so exhausted that they staggered off the field.

141   INTERNATIONAL CHAMPIONSHIP 1926   FRANCE

Stade Colombes, Paris · Saturday 2 January 1926 · Won 20–6

SCOTLAND D Drysdale (*Oxford U*); IS Smith (*Edinburgh U*), †RM Kinnear (*Heriot's FP*), JC Dykes (*Glasgow Acs*), AC Wallace (*Oxford U*); H Waddell (*Glasgow Acs*), JB Nelson (*Glasgow Acs*); DS Davies (*Hawick*), JCH Ireland (*Glasgow HSFP*), †WV Berkley (*Oxford U*), DJ MacMyn (*London Scot*), JM Bannerman (*Glasgow HSFP*), JW Scott (*Stewart's FP*), AC Gillies (*Watsonians*), JR Paterson (*Birkenhead Park*)

FRANCE L Destarac (*Tarbes*); M Besson (*CASG*), C Magnanou (*RCF*), M Chapuy (*Stade Français*), A Jauréguy (*Stade Français*); Y du Manoir (*RCF*), R Llari (*Carcassone*); J Etcheberry (*Vienne*), CA Gonnet (*RCF*), A Maury (*Toulouse*), A Cassayet-Armagnac* (*Narbonne*), A Puig (*Perpignan*), E Ribère (*Perpignan*), A Bioussa (*Toulouse*), E Piquiral (*RCF*)

REFEREE WM Llewellyn (*Wales*)

SCORING Gillies, pen (3–0); Wallace, try (6–0); Wallace, try (9–0) (half-time) MacMyn, try (12–0); Wallace, try (15–0); Gonnet, pen (15–3); Piquiral, try (15–6); Bannerman, try (18–6); Drysdale, con (20–6)

Scotland were slightly flattered by the final score but they were worthy winners thanks to a strong forward effort and better combined play. The pitch was heavy after rain and the Scottish forwards adapted to the conditions very effectively. Behind the scrum, the Glasgow Academicals trio of Nelson, Waddell and Dykes dominated midfield, Smith and Wallace were always dangerous on the wings and at full-back Dan Drysdale was almost faultless. The Frenchmen played with plenty of spirit and won their fare share of ball, but they lacked technique and cleverness. Gillies kicked an early penalty for Scotland and soon afterwards Dykes put Wallace away on a long run for a brilliant solo try. Both sides missed some chances before Wallace scored his second try when he cleverly anticipated a kick ahead. Straight after the interval, a rush by the Scottish forwards ended with a try by MacMyn and later Wallace completed his hat-trick after a good handling movement. France fought back with a penalty by Gonnet and a try by Piquiral, but the Scots kept their composure and right at the finish Bannerman scored a try after some classic Scottish dribbling.

142   INTERNATIONAL CHAMPIONSHIP 1926   WALES

Murrayfield · Saturday 6 February 1926 · Won 8–5

SCOTLAND D Drysdale* (*Oxford U*); IS Smith (*Edinburgh U*), RM Kinnear (*Heriot's FP*), JC Dykes (*Glasgow Acs*), †WM Simmers (*Glasgow Acs*); H Waddell (*Glasgow Acs*), JB Nelson (*Glasgow Acs*); DS Davies (*Hawick*), JCH Ireland (*Glasgow HSFP*), GM Murray (*Glasgow Acs*), DJ MacMyn (*London Scot*), JM Bannerman (*Glasgow HSFP*), JW Scott (*Stewart's FP*), AC Gillies (*Watsonians*), JR Paterson (*Birkenhead Park*)

WALES WA Everson (*Newport*); GE Andrews (*Newport*), A Stock (*Newport*), RA Cornish* (*Cardiff*), WC Powell (*London Welsh*); R Jones (*Northampton*), WJ Delahay (*Cardiff*); SD Lawrence (*Bridgend*), JH John (*Swansea*), D Jones (*Newport*), S Hinam (*Cardiff*), RC Herrera (*Cross Keys*), T Hopkins (*Swansea*), E Watkins (*Blaina*), DM Jenkins (*Treorchy*)

REFEREE D Hellewell (*England*)

SCORING Herrera, try (0–3); Everson, con (0–5) (half-time) Gillies, pen (3–5); Waddell, try (6–5); Drysdale, con (8–5)

Scotland were slightly fortunate to win as the Welsh forwards were very strong, but their three-quarter line was disappointing and made little of their opportunities. The Scottish backs were well marked and it was only a piece of individual brilliance by Herbert Waddell that won the day. Playing on a wet pitch, the Scots missed a few early chances, including a drop kick by Waddell, before the Welshmen opened the scoring. Scrum-half Delahay made a break into the Scottish 25 and from the ensuing scrum the Welsh forwards made a rush and Herrera scored a try. Early in the second half, Gillies kicked a long angled penalty and a few minutes later Waddell beat the defence with an intuitive cut back inside before triumphantly touching down behind the posts. Drysdale added the simple conversion. Both sides had a few half-chances and Welsh centre Stock looked set to score until he was floored near the line by Waddell. The Welsh pack made a great effort at the end but the Scots cleverly wheeled a scrum under their own posts to relieve the pressure. For Scotland, Waddell and Drysdale kicked very well, Bannerman had another fine match, and Scott and MacMyn were prominent in the loose.

143   INTERNATIONAL CHAMPIONSHIP 1926   IRELAND

Murrayfield · Saturday 27 February 1926 · Lost 0–3

SCOTLAND D Drysdale* (*Oxford U*); IS Smith (*Edinburgh U*), JC Dykes (*Glasgow Acs*), RM Kinnear (*Heriot's FP*), WM Simmers (*Glasgow Acs*); H Waddell (*Glasgow Acs*), JB Nelson (*Glasgow Acs*); DS Davies (*Hawick*), JCH Ireland (*Glasgow HSFP*), DS Kerr (*Heriot's FP*), DJ MacMyn (*London Scot*), JM Bannerman (*Glasgow HSFP*), †J Graham (*Kelso*), JR Paterson (*Birkenhead Park*), JW Scott (*Stewart's FP*)

IRELAND WE Crawford* (*Lansdowne*); DJ Cussen (*Dublin U*), GV Stephenson (*NIFC*), TR Hewitt (*QU Belfast*), JH Gage (*QU Belfast*); EO Davy (*UC Dublin*), M Sugden (*Dublin U*); MJ Bradley (*Dolphin*), WF Browne (*Army*), AM Buchanan (*Dublin U*), SJ Cagney (*London Irish*), JD Clinch (*Wdrs*), JL Farrell (*Bective Rgrs*), J McVicker (*Collegians*), CJ Hanrahan (*Dolphin*)

REFEREE BS Cumberlege (*England*)

SCORING No scoring in the first half. Gage, try (0–3)

Ireland scored a last-second try to win at Murrayfield for the first time. The pitch was sodden after heavy rain and it cut up badly during the game. This was a hard struggle between two evenly matched sides. The forward exchanges were uncompromising and handling was difficult. Both sets of backs were seen largely in defence. Scotland started in stirring fashion and missed several scoring chances before Ireland took control and ended the half as the stronger side. Scotland did most of the attacking in the second half and twice Simmers crossed the line only to be called back for infringements. Cussen and Gage almost scored for Ireland but were thwarted by desperate last-ditch defence. Towards the finish, Waddell was taken off with concussion and Paterson came out of the pack onto the wing. Then in the dying seconds, Ireland made one last attack and Gage did just enough to squeeze over for the winning try. Stephenson missed the conversion, the final whistle sounded and the delirious Irish supporters rushed onto the pitch to acclaim their heroes.

---

144   INTERNATIONAL CHAMPIONSHIP 1926   ENGLAND

Twickenham · Saturday 20 March 1926 · Won 17–9

SCOTLAND D Drysdale* (*Oxford U*); IS Smith (*Edinburgh U*), JC Dykes (*Glasgow Acs*), WM Simmers (*Glasgow Acs*), †GM Boyd (*Glasgow HSFP*); H Waddell (*Glasgow Acs*), JB Nelson (*Glasgow Acs*); DS Davies (*Hawick*), JCH Ireland (*Glasgow HSFP*), DS Kerr (*Heriot's FP*), DJ MacMyn (*London Scot*), JM Bannerman (*Glasgow HSFP*), JW Scott (*Stewart's FP*), J Graham (*Kelso*), JR Paterson (*Birkenhead Park*)

ENGLAND TE Holliday (*Aspatria*); RH Hamilton-Wickes (*Harlequins*), AR Aslett (*Richmond & Army*), TES Francis (*Blackheath*), HLV Day (*Leicester*); HJ Kittermaster (*Harlequins*), AT Young (*Blackheath*); CKT Faithful (*Harlequins*), JS Tucker (*Bristol*), RJ Hanvey (*Aspatria*), WW Wakefield* (*Harlequins*), E Stanbury (*Plymouth Alb*), HG Periton (*Waterloo*), AT Voyce (*Gloucester*), JWG Webb (*Northampton*)

REFEREE WH Acton (*Ireland*)

SCORING Dykes, drop (4–0); Waddell, try (7–0); Waddell, con (9–0); Smith, try (12–0); Waddell, con (14–0); Voyce, try (14–3) (half-time) Tucker, try (14–6); Smith, try (17–6); Stanbury, try (17–9)

In the presence of King George V, Scotland became the first away side to win a championship match at Twickenham. England held a slight advantage in tight play, but their back three lacked speed and decisiveness which the Scots were able to exploit. Holliday, in particular, had a miserable afternoon and his uncertainty under the high ball was compounded by Smith's determination in following-up. The Scottish forwards did some stirring footwork and the whole team tackled very securely. Playing in chilly conditions with the odd shower, Scotland surprised everybody when they forged away to a big lead in the first half. After 15 minutes, Dykes dropped goal from a scrum in front of the posts. England had a spell of pressure, but then Smith broke away from his own 25 and kicked ahead. Holliday was beaten by an awkward bounce, and Smith, tearing up at great speed, re-gathered and found Waddell who ran in at the posts. A few minutes later, Holliday was caught in two minds by a punt across and he was enveloped by several Scottish forwards. The ball was kicked over the line and Smith was first to the touchdown. Waddell converted both tries and just before the interval Voyce broke away from a lineout for England's first score. Early in the second half, Tucker also scored from a lineout, but neither try was converted. Hopes of an English revival were dashed when Simmers made a diagonal kick to the corner and Smith flew up at top speed to score, the winger going so fast that he almost ended up in the crowd. England went down fighting and Webb scored a late consolation try, but this did not detract from a great win for Scotland.

145　　　INTERNATIONAL CHAMPIONSHIP 1927　　　FRANCE

Murrayfield · Saturday 22 January 1927 · Won 23–6

SCOTLAND D Drysdale (*Heriot's FP*); IS Smith (*Edinburgh U*), GPS Macpherson* (*Edinburgh Acs*), JC Dykes (*Glasgow Acs*), WM Simmers (*Glasgow Acs*); H Waddell (*Glasgow Acs*), JB Nelson (*Glasgow Acs*); DS Davies (*Hawick*), JCH Ireland (*Glasgow HSFP*), †JW Allan (*Melrose*), JM Bannerman (*Glasgow HSFP*), JW Scott (*Stewart's FP*), J Graham (*Kelso*), JR Paterson (*Birkenhead Park*), AC Gillies (*Watsonians*)

FRANCE M Piquemal (*Tarbes*); R Houdet (*Stade Français*), R Graciet (*SBUC*), V Graule (*Perpignan*), J Revillon (*CASG*); Y du Manoir* (*RCF*), E Bader (*Primevères*); J Etcheberry (*Vienne*), CA Gonnet (*RCF*), R Hutin (*CASG*), A Cassayet-Armagnac (*Narbonne*), R Bousquet (*Albi*), E Ribère (*Quillan*), A Prévost (*Albi*), E Piquiral (*Lyon*)

REFEREE BS Cumberlege (*England*)

SCORING Waddell, try (3–0); Gillies, con (5–0); Smith, try (8–0); Gillies, con (10–0); Waddell, try (13–0); Drysdale, con (15–0); Hutin, try (15–3); Smith, try (18–3); Gillies, con (20–3) (half-time) Gillies, pen (23–3); Piquiral, try (23–6)

The Scottish backs were in great attacking form and were too fast and clever for their opponents. The Scots scored four converted tries in the first half and the game was as good as over by the interval, but to their credit the Frenchmen did not crumble away. Their forwards put up a lively fight and more than held their own in the second period. As *The Scotsman* put it: 'To the strongly biased Scottish spectator the first half must have seemed like wine; the second water.' In favourable conditions, the Scots opened the scoring after only four minutes when Nelson broke through and Waddell was at his side to take the scoring pass. A few minutes later, the Scottish backs combined to put Smith away on a strong run around Piquemal, the French full-back. Next Macpherson confused the defence to put Waddell in at the posts. The French responded with a try by Hutin, and just before the break Smith took a pass from Nelson and brushed aside the last defender for his second try. The second half was a rather featureless scramble between the forwards. The visitors had more of the game and slowly got on top, but they were unable to break the Scottish defence. Gillies increased the Scottish lead with a penalty goal and ten minutes before time Piquiral scored a consolation try for the plucky French.

Cardiff Arms Park · Saturday 5 February 1927 · Won 5–0

SCOTLAND D Drysdale (*Heriot's FP*); †EG Taylor (*Oxford U*), GPS Macpherson* (*Edinburgh Acs*), JC Dykes (*Glasgow Acs*), WM Simmers (*Glasgow Acs*); H Waddell (*Glasgow Acs*), JB Nelson (*Glasgow Acs*); DS Davies (*Hawick*), JCH Ireland (*Glasgow HSFP*), DS Kerr (*Heriot's FP*), JW Scott (*Stewart's FP*), JM Bannerman (*Glasgow HSFP*), J Graham (*Kelso*), AC Gillies (*Watsonians*), JR Paterson (*Birkenhead Park*)

WALES BO Male* (*Cardiff*); JD Bartlett (*Llanelli & London Welsh*), BR Turnbull (*Cardiff*), J Roberts (*Cardiff*), WR Harding (*Cambridge U & Swansea*); EG Richards (*Cardiff*), WJ Delahay (*Cardiff*); TW Lewis (*Cardiff*), JH John (*Swansea*), HT Phillips (*Newport*), T Arthur (*Neath*), EM Jenkins (*Aberavon*), WA Williams (*Crumlin*), IE Jones (*Llanelli*), WG Thomas (*Llanelli*)

REFEREE WH Jackson (*England*)

SCORING Kerr, try (3–0); Gillies, con (5–0) (half-time)

The teams were introduced to the Prince of Wales and the crowd responded with a spontaneous rendition of 'For He's a Jolly Good Fellow'. This match took place in steady rain and the pitch quickly turned into a sea of clinging mud. Against some expectations, the Scottish forwards adapted to the conditions successfully and never let themselves to be intimidated. They kept the ball tight and their wheeling and footwork was in the best Scottish traditions. The backs stuck to their task and defended heroically. Wales dominated play in the first half, but their attacks were too predictable and Scotland opened the scoring just before the interval. A defender was caught dithering over a high kick, the Scottish forwards dribbled on and Kerr scooped-up the loose ball to score wide out. The conversion was very awkward, but Gillies kicked it with great aplomb. In the second half, Wales were twice reduced to 14 men when Arthur, a forward, had to go off for running repairs. Both sides had some scoring chances, but the defences were too strong and the Scots held on for their fourth win in succession over Wales.

Lansdowne Road, Dublin · Saturday 26 February 1927 · Lost 0–6

SCOTLAND D Drysdale (*Heriot's FP*); IS Smith (*Edinburgh U*), GPS Macpherson* (*Edinburgh Acs*), JC Dykes (*Glasgow Acs*), WM Simmers (*Glasgow Acs*); H Waddell (*Glasgow Acs*), JB Nelson (*Glasgow Acs*); DS Davies (*Hawick*), JCH Ireland (*Glasgow HSFP*), DS Kerr (*Heriot's FP*), JW Scott (*Stewart's FP*), JM Bannerman (*Glasgow HSFP*), J Graham (*Kelso*), AC Gillies (*Watsonians*), JR Paterson (*Birkenhead Park*)

IRELAND WE Crawford* (*Lansdowne*); JB Ganly (*Monkstown*), FS Hewitt (*Instonians*), GV Stephenson (*NIFC*), JH Gage (*QU Belfast*); EO Davy (*Lansdowne*), M Sugden (*Wdrs*); AM Buchanan (*Dublin U*), WF Browne (*Army*), TO Pike (*Lansdowne*), H McVicker (*Richmond*), JL Farrell (*Bective Rgrs*), J McVicker (*Collegians*), CF Hanrahan (*Dolphin*), CT Payne (*NIFC*)

REFEREE BS Cumberlege (*England*)

SCORING Pike, try (0–3); Ganly, try (0–6) (half-time)

The weather was even worse than the previous match with a strong wind and icy rain sweeping down the field. The pitch quickly became a quagmire and the players were indistinguishable from each other. Inevitably, kick-and-rush tactics were the order of the day. The Irish forwards adapted to the conditions quite effectively and did not stand on ceremony. Playing with the wind behind them in the first half, Ireland opened the scoring after 12 minutes when Pike, lying unmarked, took the ball from a lineout and dived over. Ten minutes later, the Irish forwards made a typical charge and Ganly picked-up smartly on the run and scored near the corner. In the second half, the Scots had periods of ascendency and there were several close calls, but the home side had greater stamina and held onto their lead tenaciously. At one point, Stephenson, the Irish centre, almost collapsed from exposure and had to be helped from the field. After the match, the referee and many of the players took a long time to regain any feeling in their numb and frozen bodies.

148   INTERNATIONAL CHAMPIONSHIP 1927   ENGLAND

Murrayfield · Saturday 19 March 1927 · Won 21–13

SCOTLAND D Drysdale* (*Heriot's FP*); IS Smith (*Edinburgh U*), GPS Macpherson (*Edinburgh Acs*), JC Dykes (*Glasgow Acs*), WM Simmers (*Glasgow Acs*); H Waddell (*Glasgow Acs*), JB Nelson (*Glasgow Acs*); JW Scott (*Stewart's FP*), JCH Ireland (*Glasgow HSFP*), DS Kerr (*Heriot's FP*), DJ MacMyn (*London Scot*), JM Bannerman (*Glasgow HSFP*), J Graham (*Kelso*), JR Paterson (*Birkenhead Park*), AC Gillies (*Watsonians*)

ENGLAND KA Sellar (*RN*); HC Catcheside (*Percy Park*), LJ Corbett* (*Bristol*), HM Locke (*Birkenhead Park*), JC Gibbs (*Harlequins*); HCC Laird (*Harlequins*), AT Young (*Blackheath*); E Stanbury (*Plymouth Alb*), JS Tucker (*Bristol*), KJ Stark (*Old Alleynians*), WE Pratten (*Blackheath*), R Cove-Smith (*OMT*), J Hanley (*Plymouth Alb*) HG Periton (*Waterloo*), WW Wakefield (*Harlequins*)

REFEREE NM Purcell (*Ireland*)

SCORING Macpherson, try (3–0); Gibbs, try (3–3); Stanbury, con (3–5); Smith, try (6–5); Smith, try (9–5); Stark, pen (9–8) (half-time) Waddell, drop (13–8); Dykes, try (16–8); Gillies, con (18–8); Laird, try (18–11); Stark, con (18–13); Scott, try (21–13)

An enormous crowd estimated at around 70,000 people, including many English visitors, witnessed a thrilling game that was played at great pace. The action swung from end-to-end and Scotland won the try count 5–2. It was said that the cheering of the crowd could be heard in the Edinburgh suburbs of Grange and Newington, two-and-a-half miles away from Murrayfield. On a fresh afternoon, Scotland were the more enterprising side and the backs were full of running. Macpherson was always penetrative, Smith used his speed to great effect and Waddell was a master tactician at stand-off. The Scottish forwards were full of fire and their opponents were rather sluggish until the closing stages. The Scots showed their intentions straightaway when Macpherson scored an early try. A few minutes later, Corbett engineered a break to give Gibbs a simple run-in. Waddell was wide with a drop kick, but Smith won the race to the touchdown. Gillies' conversion attempt rebounded off one of the uprights. Play was fairly even and both sides missed some scoring opportunities before Smith swept past the cover for his second try. Stark replied with a penalty for England and it was anybody's game at the break. Early in the second half, England were unlucky to lose Catcheside with a leg injury and they had to soldier on with 14 men, Hanley coming out of the pack. Waddell dropped a goal, although Wakefield claimed that he had touched the ball in flight. Dykes scored a brilliant solo try when he slipped past the defence and Gillies converted to give Scotland a ten-point advantage. The English forwards made a strenuous effort to save the match, despite being short-handed. Wakefield made a break to put Laird over between the posts and Stark kicked the simple conversion. The closing stages took place in almost unbearable excitement and just before the end Macpherson made a break to put Scott over for the clinching try.

---

149   TOUR MATCH   NEW SOUTH WALES

Murrayfield · Saturday 17 December 1927 · Won 10–8

SCOTLAND D Drysdale* (*London Scot*); EG Taylor (*Oxford U*), †RF Kelly (*Watsonians*), JC Dykes (*Glasgow Acs*), WM Simmers (*Glasgow Acs*); †HD Greenlees (*Leicester*), †PS Douty (*London Scot*); JW Scott (*Stewart's FP*), †WN Roughead (*London Scot*), †WG Ferguson (*Royal HSFP*), DJ MacMyn (*London Scot*), JM Bannerman (*Glasgow HSFP*), J Graham (*Kelso*), †WB Welsh (*Hawick*), JR Paterson (*Birkenhead Park*)

NEW SOUTH WALES AW Ross (*Sydney U*); EE Ford (*Glebe-Balmain*), WBJ Sheehan (*Sydney U*), SC King (*W Suburbs*), AC Wallace* (*Glebe-Balmain*); T Lawton (*W Suburbs*), SJ Malcolm (*Newcastle*); HF Woods (*YMCA*), JG Blackwood (*E Suburbs*), BP Judd (*W Suburbs*), AN Finlay (*Sydney U*), GP Storey (*W Suburbs*), JW Breckenridge (*Glebe-Balmain*), J Ford (*Glebe-Balmain*), AJ Tancred (*Glebe-Balmain*)

REFEREE WJ Llewellyn (*Wales*)

SCORING E Ford, try (0–3); Lawton, con (0–5); Graham, try (3–5); Drysdale, con (5–5) (half-time) Welsh, try (8–5); Drysdale, con (10–5); J Ford, try (10–8)

In season 1927–8, the New South Wales Waratahs made a 31-match tour of the British Isles and France. Rugby Union was barely played in the other Australian states at this time and in 1986 that this tour was awarded full Australian cap status. The tourists were captained by winger Johnny Wallace who earlier in the decade had won nine caps for Scotland whilst a student at Oxford University. The Scotland test was the 24th game of the tour and the Waratahs had already beaten the three Scottish District sides and Ireland and Wales. Heavy snow fell during the week and the pitch was protected by straw, but it hardened up as the afternoon wore on. This was a memorable match played at great pace and with a thrilling conclusion. Despite fielding six newcomers, the Scots knitted together well, making some fine attacks and defending stoutly. The lighter Scottish forwards held their own until the closing stages and the backs were equally impressive. Simmers, in particular, had a fine match with his elusive running. The Waratahs, who played in light blue shirts, were perhaps feeling the effects of their long tour, but they were always ready to attack and looked capable of scoring from anywhere. After an exciting first quarter when both sides had chances, the tourists opened the scoring against the run of play. Jack Ford made a strong run down the touchline before finding his namesake Eric who ran around between the posts. Three minutes later, Simmers made a dodging run and then punted back infield where Graham touched down. Drysdale converted from an awkward angle. Play swung from end-to-end in the second half and with about 13 minutes remaining Simmers made another strong run and crosskicked to new cap Willie Welsh who scored between the posts. Drysdale added the simple conversion. The tourists fought desperately hard to rescue the game. Wallace made a great run, but was stopped at the corner by Drysdale. Eventually, the gigantic Jack Ford brushed past several tackles and scored wide out, but Lawton's conversion attempt just failed. Amidst great excitement, Wallace made another break right at the finish, but he slipped on the icy surface and the Scots escaped with a narrow victory in a great match.

150   INTERNATIONAL CHAMPIONSHIP 1928   FRANCE

Stade Colombes, Paris · Monday 2 January 1928 · Won 15–6

SCOTLAND D Drysdale* (*Heriot's FP*); GPS Macpherson (*Edinburgh Acs*), RF Kelly (*Watsonians*), JC Dykes (*Glasgow HSFP*), WM Simmers (*Glasgow Acs*); HD Greenlees (*Leicester*), PS Douty (*London Scot*), WB Welsh (*Hawick*), WN Roughead (*London Scot*), WG Ferguson (*Royal HSFP*), DJ MacMyn (*London Scot*), JM Bannerman (*Glasgow HSFP*), J Graham (*Kelso*), JR Paterson (*Birkenhead Park*), JW Scott (*Stewart's FP*)

FRANCE L Magnol (*Toulouse*); C Dulaurens (*Toulouse*), E Coulon (*Grenoble*), G Gérald (*RCF*), A Jauréguy* (*Stade Français*); H Haget (*CASG*), G Daudignon (*Stade Français*); A Loury (*RCF*), F Camicas (*Tarbes*), J Morère (*Marseilles*), J Galia (*Quillan*), A Camel (*Toulouse*), E Ribère (*Quillan*), A Cazenave (*Pau*), G Branca (*Stade Français*)

REFEREE RM McGrath (*Ireland*)

SCORING Simmers, try (3–0); Haget, try (3–3); Paterson, try (6–3); Dykes, try (9–3) (half-time) Douty, try (12–3); Scott, try (15–3); Camel, try (15–6)

The forward exchanges were strenuously contested, but the Scots combined better and their finishing was more accurate. The French produced some brilliant play at times, but they were let down by some poor handling and a lack of composure. The Scottish tackling was also very sound. Drysdale was imperturbable at full-back and Simmers ran strongly and defended well. This match was marred by a whistle-happy referee who incurred the wrath of the crowd on more than one occasion. Playing in cold conditions, the white-shirted French started strongly and they almost scored an early try. After some six minutes, the Scots forwards took play to the French 25 and the ball was quickly passed to Simmers who went over in fine style. France again missed several chances before Haget charged down a kick and followed-up for a score. The Scots responded almost immediately with a try by Paterson. France continued to press, but near the end of the half Dykes scored a try from a maul near the French line. Play for much of the second half was rather undistinguished and largely confined to the forwards. From a scrum, the Scots rushed over the line and Douty was awarded a try, although some spectators felt that the ball had been knocked forward. Then Drysdale picked up a loose pass and punted ahead. Magnol, the French full-back, was caught in possession and from the ensuing maul Scott took the ball and scored a try. The Scots grew tired in the closing stages, which were played in gathering darkness, and home side finished with a series of attacks, one of which produced one consolation score. Curiously, there were seven tries in total but no conversions.

Murrayfield · Saturday 4 February 1928 · Lost 0–13

SCOTLAND D Drysdale (*London Scot*); †J Goodfellow (*Langholm*), GPS Macpherson (*Edinburgh Acs*), RF Kelly (*Watsonians*), WM Simmers (*Glasgow Acs*); HD Greenlees (*Leicester*), PS Douty (*London Scot*); †JH Ferguson (*Gala*), WN Roughead (*London Scot*), WG Ferguson (*Royal HSFP*), JW Scott (*Stewart's FP*), JM Bannerman* (*Glasgow HSFP*), J Graham (*Kelso*), WB Welsh (*Hawick*), JR Paterson (*Birkenhead Park*)

WALES BO Male* (*Cardiff*); JD Bartlett (*London Welsh*), J Roberts (*Cardiff*), AE Jenkins (*Llanelli*), WC Powell (*London Welsh*); DE John (*Llanelli*), DA John (*Llanelli*); FA Bowdler (*Cross Keys*), CC Pritchard (*Pontypool*), HT Phillips (*Newport*), EM Jenkins (*Aberavon*), A Skym (*Llanelli*), TI Jones (*Llanelli*), T Hollingdale (*Neath*), I Jones (*Llanelli*)

REFEREE RW Harland (*Ireland*)

SCORING A Jenkins, try (0–3); Male, con (0–5); DE John, try (0–8); Male, con (0–10); Roberts, try (0–13) (half-time)

Wales deservedly beat Scotland for the first time since 1914. Their play was purposeful and vigorous whilst the Scots were too disjointed. The Scottish forwards made some good dribbling rushes, but they were outclassed in tight play and the backs had few chances. Conditions were difficult with a strong wind and rain blowing down the field, which cut-up badly as the game progressed. Wales made a storming start and raced to ten-point lead within the first 15 minutes. Drysdale, who was badly off-form, let the ball roll into touch near the corner flag and from the ensuing lineout Llanelli centre Albert Jenkins barged his way over near the posts. Wales continued to press and some eight minutes later Dai John made a swerving run from a scrum on the Scottish 25 to reach the line. Male converted both tries and just before the interval Roberts raced onto a kick ahead by Powell to score a third Welsh try. With the elements in their favour in the second half, the Scots tried hard, but they could make little headway against a stout Welsh defence and there was no further scoring.

Murrayfield · Saturday 25 February 1928 · Lost 5–13

SCOTLAND D Drysdale* (*London Scot*); J Goodfellow (*Langholm*), †JWG Hume (*Oxford U*), JC Dykes (*Glasgow Acs*), WM Simmers (*Glasgow Acs*); †H Lind (*Dunfermline*), JB Nelson (*Glasgow Acs*); JW Allan (*Melrose*), WN Roughead (*London Scot*), DS Kerr (*Heriot's FP*), WG Ferguson (*Royal HSFP*), JM Bannerman (*Glasgow HSFP*), J Graham (*Kelso*), JR Paterson (*Birkenhead Park*), WB Welsh (*Hawick*)

IRELAND WJ Stewart (*NIFC*); RM Byers (*NIFC*), GV Stephenson* (*NIFC*), JB Ganly (*Monkstown*), AC Douglas (*Instonians*); EO Davy (*Lansdowne*), M Sugden (*Wdrs*); TO Pike (*Lansdowne*), SJ Cagney (*London Irish*), WF Browne (*Utd Servs*), CT Payne (*NIFC*), CJ Hanrahan (*Dolphin*), JL Farrell (*Bective Rgrs*), GR Beamish (*RAF*), JD Clinch (*Wdrs*)

REFEREE BS Cumberlege (*England*)

SCORING Ganly, try (0–3); Kerr, try (3–3); Drysdale, con (5–3) (half-time) Davy, try (5–6); Stephenson, con (5–8); Stephenson, try (5–11); Stephenson, con (5–13)

A nervous and error-prone Scottish side were well beaten by a better team and the losing margin could have far higher. The Irish forwards more than held their own in the scrums and loose play, and their back division, blessed with some seasoned veterans, easily outplayed the rather hapless Scots. In near perfect conditions, Scotland started promisingly but Ireland settled down and began to test the Scottish defence. Around the 20th minute, Ganly, who was always dangerous, took a loose pass, combined with Douglas and raced away for the opening score. The Scots made a slight recovery towards the end of the half and Kerr scored a try after a stirring dribble by Bannerman. Drysdale converted to give the home side an undeserved lead at the interval. Ireland quickly recovered in the second half with tries by Davy and Stephenson, the latter adding both conversions. The visitors stayed in control for the rest of the game and the outcome was clear long before the finish, although the Scottish defence was quite resolute. *The Scotsman* concluded: 'Abandoning hope of a Scottish recovery, many of the onlookers began to troop out of the ground. The mood created two hours before by sunshine and hope was followed by one of joyless resignation.'

Harry Lind won his first cap against Ireland in 1928 and was one of the great half-backs of his era.

153 INTERNATIONAL CHAMPIONSHIP 1928 ENGLAND

Twickenham · Saturday 17 March 1928 · Lost 0–6

SCOTLAND D Drysdale* (*London Scot*); J Goodfellow (*Langholm*), GPS Macpherson (*Edinburgh Acs*), WM Simmers (*Glasgow Acs*), RF Kelly (*Watsonians*); †AH Brown (*Heriot's FP*), JB Nelson (*Glasgow Acs*); LM Stuart (*Glasgow HSFP*), WN Roughead (*London Scot*), DS Kerr (*Heriot's FP*), WG Ferguson (*Royal HSFP*), JM Bannerman (*Glasgow HSFP*), J Graham (*Kelso*), JR Paterson (*Birkenhead Park*), JW Scott (*Stewart's FP*)

ENGLAND TW Brown (*Bristol*); WJ Taylor (*Blackheath*), CD Aarvold (*Cambridge U*), JV Richardson (*Birkenhead Park*), GV Palmer (*Richmond*); HCC Laird (*Harlequins*), AT Young (*Blackheath*); RHW Sparkes (*Plymouth Alb*), JS Tucker (*Bristol*), E Stanbury (*Plymouth Alb*), KJ Stark (*Old Alleynians*), R Cove-Smith* (*OMT*), J Hanley (*Plymouth Alb*), HG Periton (*Waterloo*), FD Prentice (*Leicester*)

REFEREE TH Vile (*Wales*)

SCORING Laird, try (0–3) (half-time) Hanley, try (0–6)

Match programme for the England v Scotland match in March 1928.
Dave Fox

Played on a perfect spring afternoon, this match attracted enormous interest. The gates were closed before kick-off and spectators had to be moved off the field of play. The teams were presented to King George V. England secured the Grand Slam by virtue of having a better pack and rock solid defence. Despite conceding an early score, the Scots played much better than their previous two games and battled right to the end, but they could not escape the stranglehold of the English forwards. Brown and Nelson, the Scottish half-backs, toiled bravely behind a beaten pack, and Macpherson and Simmers were enterprising when they did have the ball. England opened the scoring after some 12 minutes. Taylor made a break and play was taken to the Scottish line from where Laird picked-up and dived over in the corner. Scotland had a few scoring chances in the first half. Drysdale missed a couple of drop kicks, Macpherson and Simmers went close, and Kelly ought to have scored, but he lost his footing with only one man to beat. The second half was largely a struggle between the forwards. The Scottish pack broke loose once or twice, but never in combination and their opponents became more dominant as the game went on. About ten minutes from time, Young, the English scrum-half who had a superb match, broke away from a scrum near the Scottish 25 and Hanley was up in support to take the scoring pass.

Murrayfield · Saturday 19 January 1929 · Won 6–3

SCOTLAND D Drysdale* (*London Scot*); IS Smith (*Edinburgh U*), GG Aitken (*London Scot*), JC Dykes (*Glasgow Acs*), WM Simmers (*Glasgow Acs*); AH Brown (*Heriot's FP*), JB Nelson (*Glasgow Acs*); JW Allan (*Melrose*), †HS Mackintosh (*W of Scot*), †RT Smith (*Kelso*), †JA Beattie (*Hawick*), JM Bannerman (*Glasgow HSFP*), †KM Wright (*London Scot*), JR Paterson (*Birkenhead Park*), WV Berkley (*London Scot*)

FRANCE L Magnol (*Toulouse*); R Houdet (*Stade Français*), A Béhotéguy (*Cognac*), G Gérald (*RCF*), A Jauréguy*(*Stade Français*); C Magnanou (*Bayonne*), C Lacazedieu (*Dax*); J Hauc (*Toulon*), F Camicas (*Tarbes*), J Sayrou (*Perpignan*), R Majérus (*Stade Français*), A Camel (*Toulouse*), J Augé (*Dax*), A Bioussa (*Toulouse*), G Branca (*Stade Français*)

REFEREE BS Cumberlege (*England*)

SCORING Brown, pen (3–0) (half-time) Paterson, try (6–0) Béhotéguy, try (6–3)

This was a rather undistinguished match that Scotland were fortunate to win. The two sides were evenly matched and all aspects of play were vigorously contested. The French gave a good account of themselves, especially towards the finish, and the Scottish three-quarters could make little headway against some sturdy French tackling. Playing in winter sunshine, Scotland made a promising start and after only a few minutes Brown kicked a penalty goal. The Scottish forwards dominated the early stages but France won more possession as the game went on. There was no further scoring until about midway through the second half when Paterson dived over from a scrum near the French line. Some ten minutes later, the veteran French winger Jauréguy made an opening and Béhotéguy scored a try. The Frenchmen rallied after this and the closing stages were very tense as they tried everything to save the game. They made several dangerous runs and Houdet got over the line but was adjudged to have been in touch. Both sides were very tired at the finish and the Scots just managed to hang on. Magnol, the French full-back, earned many plaudits for his great all-round display and acrobatic fielding.

St Helen's, Swansea · Saturday 2 February 1929 · Lost 7–14

SCOTLAND †TG Aitchison (*Gala*); IS Smith (*Edinburgh U*), JC Dykes (*Glasgow Acs*), WM Simmers (*Glasgow Acs*), †TG Brown (*Heriot's FP*); AH Brown (*Heriot's FP*), JB Nelson (*Glasgow Acs*); JW Allan (*Melrose*), HS Mackintosh (*Glasgow U*), RT Smith (*Kelso*), JA Beattie (*Hawick*), JM Bannerman* (*Glasgow HSFP*), KM Wright (*London Scot*), WV Berkley (*London Scot*), JR Paterson (*Birkenhead Park*)

WALES JA Bassett (*Penarth*); J Roberts (*Cardiff*), HM Bowcott (*Cardiff*), WG Morgan* (*Swansea*), JC Morley (*Newport*); FL Williams (*Cardiff*), WC Powell (*London Welsh*); FA Bowdler (*Cross Keys*), CC Pritchard (*Pontypool*), RJ Barrell (*Cardiff*), T Arthur (*Neath*), HJ Jones (*Neath*), H Peacock (*Newport*), AS Broughton (*Treorchy*), IE Jones (*Llanelli*)

REFEREE D Helliwell (*England*)

SCORING Roberts, try (0–3); AH Brown, pen (3–3) (half-time) AH Brown, drop (7–3); Peacock, try (7–6); I Jones, con (7–8); Roberts, try (7–11); Morgan, try (7–14)

Scotland put up a hard fight and made a courageous late rally, but Wales were worthy winners and scored four tries to none. The Scottish forwards were outplayed in the tight and the Welsh backs had a generous supply of ball which they used to good effect. The Scottish backs spent most of the game in defence and their attacking play was ordinary when compared to the brilliant efforts of the Welshmen. The match was played in a fine Scotch mist, the pitch was heavy and the ball treacherous to handle. Wales started purposely and after 12 minutes Roberts scored an unconverted try near the corner. The Scots missed two penalty attempts, and Nelson made a clean break, but his kick past the full-back went harmlessly over the dead ball line. Five minutes before the interval, Brown kicked a penalty to level the scores. A few minutes into the second half, the same player dropped a goal to give Scotland an unlikely lead, but straight from the restart the Welsh forwards made a thunderous charge to the line and Peacock secured the touchdown. Ten minutes later, Roberts scored his second try and shortly afterwards Welsh captain Guy Morgan, who was always prominent, added another to settle the issue. To their credit, the Scots made great efforts in the closing stages. The Scottish forwards took control and had some strong rushes, but the backs handled poorly and several individual efforts were easily contained. In the final act of the game, which took place amidst gathering gloom, Simmers made a strong break and put Smith away, but the winger was bundled into touch at the corner flag.

---

156   INTERNATIONAL CHAMPIONSHIP 1929   IRELAND

Lansdowne Road, Dublin · Saturday 23 February 1929 · Won 16–7

SCOTLAND TG Aitchison (*Gala*); IS Smith (*Edinburgh U*), GPS Macpherson (*Edinburgh Acs*), JC Dykes (*Glasgow Acs*), WM Simmers (*Glasgow Acs*); HD Greenlees (*Leicester*), JB Nelson (*Glasgow Acs*); RT Smith (*Kelso*), HS Mackintosh (*Glasgow U*), JW Allan (*Melrose*), WV Berkley (*London Scot*), JM Bannerman* (*Oxford U*), JR Paterson (*Birkenhead Park*), WB Welsh (*Hawick*), KM Wright (*London Scot*)

IRELAND JW Stewart (*NIFC*); RM Byers (*NIFC*), JB Ganly (*Monkstown*), PF Murray (*Wdrs*), JE Arigho (*Lansdowne*); EO Davy* (*Lansdowne*), M Sugden (*Wdrs*); GR Beamish (*RAF*), HC Browne (*Utd Servs*), SJ Cagney (*London Irish*), JD Clinch (*Wdrs*), MJ Dunne (*Lansdowne*), JL Farrell (*Bective Rgrs*), JS Synge (*Lansdowne*), CJ Hanrahan (*Dolphin*)

REFEREE BS Cumberlege (*England*)

SCORING Macpherson, try (3–0); Dykes, con (5–0); Davy, drop (5–4); Arigho, try (5–7) (half-time) Bannerman, try (8–7); Allan, con (10–7); Smith, try (13–7); Simmers, try (16–7)

Ireland had already beaten France and England, and this match created enormous interest. A huge crowd crammed into Lansdowne Road which was far too small to accommodate everybody. Spectators regularly spilled onto the field of play and the game was stopped several times to force them back. The Scots were under pressure for most of the game, but they had great stamina and they made a remarkable recovery towards the end. The visitors had a fortunate start when Dykes intercepted a dropped pass and gave Macpherson a clear run to the line. After some 20 minutes, Davy dropped a goal for Ireland and play was held up as the referee and players tried to force excited spectators back off the field. A good handling movement put left wing

Arigho over for a try, but he was unable to run behind the posts because of the crowd standing in the in-goal area and Murray missed the conversion. Ireland had by far the best of the play until the closing stages, but their attacks were too individualistic and the Scottish defence was very strong. Then with some 15 minutes to go, Nelson and Berkley combined to put Bannerman away and the veteran Scottish captain made an unstoppable charge for a try which came against the run of play. Allan converted to silence the crowd and knock much of the heart out of the Irish effort. Simmers ignited a good movement from his own 25 which ended with Smith flying over for a try. Another Scottish attack against some dejected Irish defence gave Simmers a try with the last move of the game.

157 INTERNATIONAL CHAMPIONSHIP 1929 ENGLAND

Murrayfield · Saturday 16 March 1929 · Won 12–6

SCOTLAND TG Aitchison (*Gala*); IS Smith (*Edinburgh U*), GPS Macpherson (*Edinburgh Acs*), WM Simmers (*Glasgow Acs*), †CHC Brown (*Dunfermline*); HD Greenlees (*Leicester*), JB Nelson (*Glasgow Acs*); RT Smith (*Kelso*), HS Mackintosh (*Glasgow U*), JW Allan (*Melrose*), JW Scott (*Bradford*), JM Bannerman* (*Oxford U*), JR Paterson (*Birkenhead Park*), KM Wright (*London Scot*), WB Welsh (*Hawick*)

ENGLAND TW Brown (*Bristol*); RW Smeddle (*Cambridge U*), AR Aslett (*Richmond*), GM Sladen (*RN*); AL Novis (*Army*); SCC Meikle (*Waterloo*), EE Richards (*Plymouth Alb*); E Stanbury (*Plymouth Alb*), RHW Sparks (*Plymouth Alb*), JWG Webb (*Northampton*), TW Harris (*Northampton*), H Rew (*Army*), H Wilkinson (*Halifax*), HG Periton* (*Waterloo*), D Turquand-Young (*Richmond*)

REFEREE JR Wheeler (*Ireland*)

SCORING Novis, try (0–3) (half-time) Nelson, try (3–3); Meikle, try (3–6); Brown, try (6–6); Smith, try (9–6); Smith, try (12–6)

Scotland clinched the Championship in a memorable encounter that had six tries and an exciting finish. The two sides were evenly matched, but once again the Scottish forwards showed great stamina and determination to win in the last 15 minutes. Playing in cold and dull conditions, the game had a lively start and after seven minutes Novis scored an unconverted try in the corner. Both sides had some promising breaks in the first half and the Scottish handling gradually improved. The veteran wing Ian Smith was almost clean away on one occasion, but was just pushed into touch by Brown, the England full-back. The Scots continued to press after the interval and eventually Jimmy Nelson slipped over from a scrum near the line. Four minutes later, Aslett took the defence by surprise when he made a swift dash and cross-field kick, and Meikle won the race for the touchdown. Scotland responded almost immediately and the backs combined to put Brown over in the corner. The outcome was decided with a brace of tries by Ian Smith, the first scored with a quarter-of-an-hour left for play. Running at full tilt but with no room to manoeuvre, Smith thundered up to Brown, the English full-back, and used every ounce of his strength and will-power to squeeze over the line. Both players required treatment before resuming. Right at the finish, Smith scored again in a similar fashion to seal a handsome win for Scotland. This was John Bannerman's last game for Scotland and at the finish he was chaired off the field by jubilant Scottish supporters.

Stade Yves du Manoir, Colombes, Paris · Wednesday 1 January 1930
Lost 3–7

SCOTLAND †RW Langrish (*London Scot*); IS Smith (*London Scot*), GPS Macpherson* (*Edinburgh Acs*), JWG Hume (*Edinburgh Wdrs*), WM Simmers (*Glasgow Acs*); †WD Emslie (*Royal HSFP*), JB Nelson (*Glasgow Acs*); JW Allan (*Melrose*), HS Mackintosh (*Glasgow U*), RT Smith (*Kelso*), JW Scott (*Waterloo*), †J Stewart (*Glasgow HSFP*), WB Welsh (*Hawick*), †FH Waters (*Cambridge U*), †R Rowand (*Glasgow HSFP*)

FRANCE M Piquemal (*Tarbes*); R Houdet (*Stade Français*), M Baillette (*Quillan*), G Gérald (*RCF*), RR Samatan (*Agen*); C Magnanou (*Bayonne*), L Serin (*Béziers*); A Ambert (*Toulouse*), C Bigot (*Quillan*), J Choy (*Narbonne*), R Majérus (*Stade Français*), A Camel (*TOEC*), E Ribère* (*Quillan*), A Bioussa (*Toulouse*), J Galia (*Quillan*)

REFEREE D Helliwell (*England*)

SCORING Bioussa, try (0–3); Simmers, try (3–3) (half-time) Magnanou, drop (3–7)

Scotland fielded five new caps, including Cambridge University back-row FH Waters whose father JB Waters had won two caps in 1904. The Scots were chasing their third win in succession in Paris, but France were deserved winners because of their greater speed and excellent loose forward play. Stand-off Christian Magnanou was always dangerous, making the opening for Alex Bioussa's try in the first five minutes and then winning the match near the end with a splendid drop goal. The French pack struggled in the scrums, but handled brilliantly in the loose and were as fierce and tough as their opponents. The Scottish backs could not penetrate a speedy defence although Macpherson cut through beautifully several times only to find his passes go astray. Both packs were depleted in the second half. Allan had to go off before half-time and a collision laid out two French players for a spell.

Max Simmers on the charge against France in January 1930. *SRU*

Murrayfield · Saturday 1 February 1930 · Won 12–9

SCOTLAND RC Warren (*Glasgow Acs*); IS Smith (*London Scot*), GPS Macpherson*
(*Edinburgh Acs*), †TM Hart (*Glasgow U*), WM Simmers (*Glasgow Acs*); H Waddell
(*Glasgow Acs*), JB Nelson (*Glasgow Acs*); RT Smith (*Kelso*), HS Mackintosh (*Glasgow Acs*),
†RA Foster (*Hawick*), JA Beattie (*Hawick*), FH Waters (*London Scot*), †WCC Agnew
(*Stewart's FP*), WB Welsh (*Hawick*), R Rowand (*Glasgow HSFP*)

WALES JA Bassett (*Penarth*); EG Davies (*Cardiff*), BR Turnbull (*Cardiff*), GG Jones (*Cardiff*),
RW Boon (*Cardiff*); FL Williams (*Cardiff*), WC Powell (*London Welsh*); T Arthur (*Neath*),
HC Day (*Newport*), A Skym (*Cardiff*), EM Jenkins (*Aberavon*), DJ Thomas (*Swansea*), AW Lemon
(*Neath*), H Peacock (*Newport*), IE Jones* (*Llanelli*)

REFEREE JR Wheeler (*Ireland*)

SCORING Simmers, try (3–0); Waters, con (5–0); G Jones, try (5–3); I Jones, con (5–5); G Jones,
drop (5–9); Simmers, try (8–9) (half-time) Waddell, drop (12–9)

Glasgow Accies full-back RC Warren was recalled after eight years and Herbert
Waddell returned after three. In a rather dour struggle, Scotland had to do a lot of
defending in the first half, but they were only one point behind at the interval. Wales
had most of the early pressure, but the Scots opened the scoring against the run of
play. Hart made a crosskick to the corner and Welsh picked up and gave a scoring pass
to Simmers. A few minutes later, new Welsh centre Graham Jones scored a try and
later dropped a goal. Shortly before the interval, Macpherson started a move from
his own half that led to a second try for Simmers. The second half was more equally
contested. At one point Hart was hurt and Rowand came out of the pack to act as an
extra defender. The game had a sensational finish when Waddell dropped a goal
following a scrum in front of the posts. Wales could easily have won this match, but
their backs did not turn a plentiful supply of possession into points.

Murrayfield · Saturday 22 February 1930 · Lost 11–14

SCOTLAND RC Warren (*Glasgow Acs*); IS Smith (*London Scot*), GPS Macpherson*
(*Edinburgh Acs*), WM Simmers (*Glasgow Acs*), †D StC Ford (*Utd Servs*); TM Hart (*Glasgow U*),
JB Nelson (*Glasgow Acs*); HS Mackintosh (*Glasgow U*), WN Roughmead (*London Scot*),
RT Smith (*Kelso*), WCC Agnew (*Stewart's FP*), LM Stuart (*Glasgow HSFP*), WB Welsh (*Hawick*),
FH Waters (*London Scot*), J Graham (*Kelso*)

IRELAND FW Williamson (*Dolphin*); GV Stephenson* (*London H*), EO Davy (*Lansdowne*),
MF Crowe (*Lansdowne*), JE Arigho (*Lansdowne*); PF Murray (*Wdrs*), M Sugden (*Wdrs*);
HO O'Neill (*QU Belfast*), TC Casey (*Young Munster*), CJ Hanrahan (*Dolphin*), CT Payne
(*NIFC*), MJ Dunne (*Lansdowne*), JL Farrell (*Bective Rgrs*), GR Beamish (*Leicester & RAF*),
JD Clinch (*Wdrs*)

REFEREE BS Cumberlege (*England*)

SCORING Ford, try (3–0); Davy, try (3–3); Davy, try (3–6); Murray, con (3–8); Davy, try (3–11)
(half-time) Macpherson, try (6–11); Waters, con (8–11); Crowe, try (8–14); Waters, try (11–14)

Once again the Scottish forwards failed to match their opponents who held their own in the scrums and were very fast in the loose. Scotland were the better team in the opening stages. Nelson sent Ford away for a good try inside five minutes, but two further scores were lost when the ball was knocked on at the crucial moment. Then Ireland came to life and centre Eugene Davy scored three tries in a devastating ten minute spell before the interval. Soon after the restart, Smith made a good run and his crosskick was collected by Macpherson for a try. The visitors replied when Crowe scored after a forward rush. The Scottish pack rallied in the last ten minutes, but could only manage a solitary try by Waters.

161   INTERNATIONAL CHAMPIONSHIP 1930   ENGLAND

Twickenham · Saturday 15 March 1930 · Drew 0–0

SCOTLAND RC Warren (*Glasgow Acs*); WM Simmers (*Glasgow Acs*), GPS Macpherson* (*Edinburgh Acs*), †JE Hutton (*Harlequins*), D StC Ford (*Utd Servs*); HD Greenlees (*Leicester*), JB Nelson (*Glasgow Acs*); HS Mackintosh (*W of Scot*), WN Roughead (*London Scot*), JW Allan (*Melrose*), WB Welsh (*Hawick*), LM Stuart (*Glasgow HSFP*), †AH Polson (*Gala*), FH Waters (*London Scot*), J Graham (*Kelso*)

ENGLAND JC Hubbard (*Harlequins*); CC Tanner (*Richmond*), M Robson (*Oxford U*), FWS Malir (*Otley*), JSR Reeve (*Harlequins*); RS Spong (*Old Millhillians*), WH Sobey (*Old Millhillians*); H Rew (*Exeter & Army*), JS Tucker* (*Bristol*), AH Bateson (*Otley*), JW Forrest (*Utd Servs*), BH Black (*Oxford U*), HG Periton (*Waterloo*), PWP Brook (*Cambridge U*), PD Howard (*Oxford U*)

REFEREE RW Jeffares (*Ireland*)

A no-scoring draw was a fairly accurate reflection of this close and rather uninspiring match. Both sides were guilty of some aimless kicking and disappointing back play. England scrum-half Sobey was the best back on the field and had one splendid solo run in the first half which narrowly failed to bring a score. Macpherson, playing at the unaccustomed position of left centre, made a typical sidestepping run and his crosskick found Waters unmarked, but the referee judged that latter was offside. Both sides earned a point from the drawn match which was enough to give England the title, but it could not save Scotland, the previous year's winners, from the wooden spoon.

162   INTERNATIONAL CHAMPIONSHIP 1931   FRANCE

Murrayfield · Saturday 24 January 1931 · Won 6–4

SCOTLAND RW Langrish (*London Scot*); IS Smith (*London Scot*), JE Hutton (*Harlequins*), †AW Wilson (*Dunfermline*), WM Simmers (*Glasgow Acs*); H Lind (*Dunfermline*), JB Nelson (*Glasgow Acs*); JW Allan (*Melrose*), WN Roughead* (*London Scot*), HS Mackintosh (*W of Scot*), JA Beattie (*Hawick*), †DA McLaren (*Durham*), †JS Wilson (*St Andrews U*), WB Welsh (*Hawick*), †AW Walker (*Cambridge U*)

FRANCE M Savy (*Montferrand*); S Samatan (*Agen*), M Baillette (*Toulon*), G Gérald (*RCF*), L Augras-Fabre (*Agen*); L Servole (*Toulon*), M Rousié (*Villeneuve*); J Duhau (*SA Bordeaux*), R Scohy (*Bordeaux EC*), A Duclos (*Lourdes*), J Galia (*Villeneuve*), A Clady (*Lézignan*), E Ribère* (*Quillan*), C Bigot (*Lézignan*), E Camo (*Villeneuve*)

REFEREE RW Jeffares (*Ireland*)

SCORING Allan, pen (3–0); Allan, pen (6–0) (half-time) Servole, drop (6–4)

Conditions were favourable, but this match was not a great spectacle. The Scottish forwards were superior at set-piece play, but France, who wore numbered shirts, were very strong in defence and quick and dangerous in the loose. In the first half, the visitors were penalised regularly for their spoiling tactics and prop John Allan kicked two goals from long range. Towards the finish of the game, Scotland were temporarily reduced when Langrish had to go off and Servole dropped a goal. The Scots had to defend stoutly, but managed to prevent any further scoring. This was the last match between the two sides for 16 years as the Home Unions refused to play against France because of alleged professionalism in the French game.

163 INTERNATIONAL CHAMPIONSHIP 1931 WALES

Cardiff Arms Park · Saturday 7 February 1931 · Lost 8-13

SCOTLAND RW Langrish (*London Scot*); IS Smith (*London Scot*), GPS Macpherson (*Edinburgh Acs*), WM Simmers (*Glasgow Acs*), †G Wood (*Gala*); H Lind (*Dunfermline*), JB Nelson (*Glasgow Acs*); JW Allan (*Melrose*), WM Roughead* (*London Scot*), HS Mackintosh (*W of Scot*), AW Walker (*Cambridge U*), JA Beattie (*Hawick*), WB Welsh (*Hawick*), JS Wilson (*St Andrews U*), †D Crichton-Miller (*Gloucester*)

WALES JA Bassett* (*Penarth*); JC Morley (*Newport*), EC Davey (*Swansea*), TE Jones-Davies (*London Welsh*), RW Boon (*Cardiff*); HM Bowcott (*Cardiff*), WC Powell (*London Welsh*); A Skym (*Cardiff*), HC Day (*Newport*), TB Day (*Swansea*), T Arthur (*Neath*), EM Jenkins (*Aberavon*), AW Lemon (*Neath*), WG Thomas (*Swansea*), NH Fender (*Cardiff*)

REFEREE JE Bott (*England*)

SCORING Morley, try (0–3); Crichton-Miller, try (3–3) (half-time) Crichton-Miller, try (6–3); Allan, con (8–3); Thomas, try (8–6); Bassett, con (8–8); Boon, try (8–11); Bassett, con (8–13)

This match was preceded by a minute's silence in respect of James Aikman Smith, the former SFU secretary, who died accompanying the Scottish team on the way to the game. Played in fine weather, this was a relentless struggle between the forwards, but the three-quarter play was not of a high standard. Morley opened the scoring for Wales after only three minutes and around a quarter of an hour later new Scottish back-row Crichton-Miller scored the first of his brace of tries. Wood gathered a kick ahead by Simmers, but lost his footing when trying to beat Bassett. Crichton-Miller was in support and hacked the ball on to score. Early in the second half, Lind made a break and found support from Macpherson who was tackled by Bassett, but Crichton-Miller was on hand to score again. Allan converted and then Watcyn Thomas, who played most of the game with a broken collarbone, scored a try which Bassett converted to tie the scores. Scotland defended heroically and looked set to draw the game, only to be undone with a controversial late try by Welsh winger Ronnie Boon. The move that led to Boon's try seemed to include a forward pass and some of the Scottish players hesitated, but Boon kept going and was allowed to follow-up his kick ahead and touch the ball down unchallenged. It was hard lines on the plucky Scots who had done enough to deserve a draw.

Ian Smith looks on anxiously as the forwards battle it out during the Irish match in 1931.

Lansdowne Road · Saturday 28 February 1931 · Lost 5–8

SCOTLAND RW Langrish (*London Scot*); IS Smith (*London Scot*), WM Simmers (*Glasgow Acs*), AW Wilson (*Dunfermline*), G Wood (*Gala*); H Lind (*Dunfermline*), JB Nelson (*Glasgow Acs*); JW Allan (*Melrose*), WN Roughead* (*London Scot*), HS Mackintosh (*W of Scot*), AW Walker (*Cambridge U*), JA Beattie (*Hawick*), WB Welsh (*Hawick*), D Crichton-Miller (*Gloucester*), JS Wilson (*St Andrews U*)

IRELAND JC Entrican (*QU Belfast*); EJ Lightfoot (*Lansdowne*), EO Davy (*Lansdowne*), MP Crowe (*Lansdowne*), JE Arigho (*Lansdowne*); PF Murray (*Wdrs*), M Sugden* (*Wdrs*); HCC Withers (*NIFC*), JAE Siggins (*Collegians*), J Russell (*UC Cork*), NF Murphy (*Cork Const*), VJ Pike (*Lansdowne*), JL Farrell (*Bective Rgrs*), GR Beamish (*London Irish*), JD Clinch (*Wdrs*)

REFEREE BS Cumberlege (*England*)

SCORING Sugden, try (0–3); Mackintosh, try (3–3); Allan, con (5–3) (half-time) Pike, try (5–6); Murray, con (5–8)

Conditions were very difficult with a strong bitingly cold wind and several snow showers. Ireland fielded an entire three-quarter line from the Lansdowne club. Playing with the elements in their favour, it took the home side some 30 minutes to open the scoring when their lively scrum-half Mark Sugden made a typical dart and dummy from a scrum near the Scottish line. Then Lind made a break and threw a long pass inside. Mackintosh grabbed the ball and despite being brought down just short of the line he managed to scramble his way. Allan converted into the wind. After all of their heroics in defence, the Scots were very fatigued in the second half and were unable to take advantage of the conditions. Ian Smith made one good run, but the wind carried his kick ahead out of play before Walker could reach the ball. Ireland's winning try was scored by Pike after a rush by the forwards.

Murrayfield · Saturday 21 March 1931 · Won 28–19

SCOTLAND AW Wilson (*Dunfermline*); IS Smith (*London Scot*), GPS Macpherson* (*Edinburgh Acs*), D StC Ford (*RN*), WM Simmers (*Glasgow Acs*); H Lind (*Dunfermline*), †WR Logan (*Edinburgh U*); JW Allan (*Melrose*), WN Roughead (*London Scot*), HS Mackintosh

(*W of Scot*), AW Walker (*Cambridge U*), JA Beattie (*Hawick*), WB Welsh (*Hawick*), D Crichton-Miller (*Gloucester*), JS Wilson (*St Andrews U*)

ENGLAND   ECP Whiteley (*Old Alleynians*); JSR Reeve (*Harlequins*), JA Tallent (*Cambridge U*), CD Aarvold* (*Headingley*), AC Harrison (*Hartlepool Rov*); TC Knowles (*Birkenhead Park*), EB Pope (*Blackheath*); H Rew (*Blackheath & Army*), RHW Sparkes (*Plymouth Alb & CS*), GG Gregory (*Taunton & Reading U*), JW Forrest (*RN*), BH Black (*Blackheath*), PC Hordern (*Blackheath*), PE Dunkley (*Harlequins*), PD Howard (*Old Millhillians & Oxford U*)

REFEREE   JR Wheeler (*Ireland*)

SCORING   Ford, try (3–0); Allan, con (5–0); Mackintosh, try (8–0); Allan, con (10–0); Tallent, try (10–3); Black, con (10–5); Tallent, try (10–8); Black, con (10–10); Logan, try (13–10); Allan, con (15–10); Reeve, try (15–13); Mackintosh, try (18–13); Allan, con (20–13) (half-time) Smith, try (23–13); Smith, try (26–13); Allan, con (28–15); Black, pen (28–16); Reeve, try (28–19)

It was estimated that around 75,000 spectators saw this spectacular and unusually high scoring match. Both sides were keen to run the ball at all times and both were guilty of some weak tackling which led to a flood of tries, ten in total. GPS Macpherson was in great form and his bewildering running created many difficulties for his opponents. Scrum-half Ross Logan had an excellent debut, Ian Smith and HS Mackintosh scored a brace of tries each and John Allan kicked five conversions, most from difficult angles. Scotland opened the scoring after ten minutes when Macpherson kicked a high ball to the English 25 and Simmers took it at full pace. He was stopped right at the line, but Ford was in support to touch the ball down. Allan converted and then followed a hectic 20 minute spell when the teams ran up an astonishing 28 points between them. Mackintosh scored Scotland's second try after a crosskick and then England replied with a brace of tries by the speedy Cambridge centre Tallent, both converted by Black. Before the interval, Logan and Mackintosh scored for Scotland and Reeve replied for the visitors. In the second half, Smith scored two tries in quick succession, Black replied with a penalty goal from in front of the posts and near the end Reeve scored in the corner to conclude the scoring. The English team wore numbered shirts.

166   TOUR MATCH   SOUTH AFRICA

Murrayfield · Saturday 16 January 1932 · Lost 3–6

SCOTLAND   †THB Lawther (*Old Millhillians*); IS Smith (*London Scot*), GPS Macpherson (*Edinburgh Acs*), WM Simmers* (*Glasgow Acs*), †JE Forrest (*Glasgow Acs*); H Lind (*Dunfermline*), WR Logan (*Edinburgh U*); JW Allan (*Melrose*), HS Mackintosh (*W of Scot*), RA Foster (*Hawick*), †MS Stewart (*Stewart's FP*), JA Beattie (*Hawick*), J Graham (*Kelso*), FH Waters (*London Scot*), WB Welsh (*Hawick*)

SOUTH AFRICA   GH Brand (*W Province*); M Zimmerman (*W Province*), BG Gray (*W Province*), JH van der Westhuizen (*W Province*), FD Venter (*Transvaal*)); BL Osler* (*W Province*), DH Craven (*W Province*); PJ Mostert (*W Province*), HG Kipling (*Griqualand West*), MM Louw (*W Province*), WF Bergh (*SW Districts*), PJ Nel (*Natal*), LC Strachan (*Transvaal*), JAJ McDonald (*W Province*), GM Daneel (*W Province*)

REFEREE   BS Cumberlege (*England*)

SCORING   Lind, try (3–0) (half-time) Osler, try (3–3); Craven, try (3–6)

In season 1931-2, the third Springboks, under the captaincy of stand-off and tactical genius Bennie Osler, made a 26-match tour of the British Isles. The South Africans had already beaten the other three Home Unions and had lost only one match against the Midland Counties at Leicester. Their final game was against Scotland at Murrayfield, which drew a very large crowd despite being played in treacherous conditions with a gale and icy rain raging down the field. Conditions dictated that this was a terrific forward battle with the heavy and experienced South Africans having a narrow advantage over the doughty Scots who had five Borderers in the pack. Early in the first half, Harry Lind pounced on a loose pass around the halfway line and raced away with full-back Brand unable to stop him near the posts. Scotland, who played in white unnumbered jerseys, held the lead until about the 50th minute when Osler scored from a maul near the Scottish line. The prolific Osler missed the conversion attempt when the strong wind blew the ball away from its position. Scotland began to fade as the match went on and with a quarter of an hour remaining Craven broke away from a scrum and beat several defenders for a match-winning opportunist try.

167 · INTERNATIONAL CHAMPIONSHIP 1932 · WALES

Murrayfield · Saturday 6 February 1932 · Lost 0–6

SCOTLAND THB Lawther (*Old Millhillians*); IS Smith (*London Scot*), D StC Ford (*Utd Servs*), WM Simmers* (*Glasgow Acs*), G Wood (*Gala*); H Lind (*Dunfermline*), WR Logan (*Edinburgh U*); JW Allan (*Melrose*), WN Roughead (*London Scot*), HS Mackintosh (*W of Scot*), MS Stewart (*Stewart's FP*), JA Beattie (*Hawick*), J Graham (*Kelso*), WB Welsh (*Hawick*), FH Waters (*London Scot*)

WALES JA Bassett* (*Penarth*); JC Morley (*Newport*), EC Davey (*Swansea*), FL Williams (*Cardiff*), RW Boon (*Cardiff*); AR Ralph (*Newport*), WC Powell (*London Welsh*); A Skym (*Cardiff*), FA Bowdler (*Cross Keys*), TB Day (*Swansea*), DJ Thomas (*Swansea*), EM Jenkins (*Aberavon*), W Davies (*Swansea*), AW Lemon (*Neath*), WG Thomas (*Swansea*)

REFEREE T Bell (*Ireland*)

SCORING Boon, try (0–3) (half-time) Bassett, pen (0–6)

Approximately 60,000 spectators saw a scrappy and unattractive match played in near perfect conditions. The first half was fairly even, but gradually the forceful Welsh pack subdued their lighter opponents and finished the game well on top. Wales opened the scoring after some 20 minutes when winger Ronnie Boon raced over at the corner flag for an unconverted try. In the second half, the visitors were able to apply a lot of pressure and it was only committed Scottish defence that prevented further scoring. Around seven minutes from the finish, Welsh captain Jack Bassett kicked a penalty goal from an awkward angle. The Welsh team were identified by letters on their shirts.

168 · INTERNATIONAL CHAMPIONSHIP 1932 · IRELAND

Murrayfield · Saturday 27 February 1932 · Lost 8–20

SCOTLAND †AHM Hutton (*Dunfermline*); IS Smith (*London Scot*), G Wood (*Gala*), D StC Ford

(*Utd Servs*), WM Simmers* (*Glasgow Acs*); WD Emslie (*Royal HSFP*), WR Logan (*Edinburgh U*);
JW Allan (*Melrose*), HS Mackintosh (*W of Scot*), RA Foster (*Hawick*), MS Stewart (*Stewart's FP*),
JA Beattie (*Hawick*), AW Walker (*Birkenhead Park*), WB Welsh (*Hawick*), FH Waters
(*London Scot*)

IRELAND EC Ridgeway (*Wdrs*); SL Waide (*NIFC*), EWF de V Hunt (*Wdrs & Army*),
MP Crowe (*Lansdowne*), EJ Lightfoot (*Lansdowne*); EO Davy (*Lansdowne*), PF Murray (*Wdrs*);
GR Beamish* (*London Irish & RAF*), MJ Dunne (*Lansdowne*), JL Farrell (*Bective Rgrs*),
N Murphy (*Cork Const*), VJ Pike (*Lansdowne*), WM Ross (*QU Belfast*), CJ Hanrahan (*Dolphin*),
JAE Siggins (*Collegians*)

REFEREE BS Cumberlege (*England*)

SCORING Lightfoot, try (0–3); Murray, con (0–5) (half-time) Wood, try (3–5); Hunt, try (3–8);
Murray, con (3–10); Lightfoot, try (3–13); Murray, con (3–15); Waide, try (3–18); Murray, con
(3–20); Simmers, try (6–20); Allan, con (8–20)

The opening stages were fairly evenly balanced, but Scotland were badly handicapped
around the 25th minute when stand-off Emslie had to leave the field with an ankle
injury. Simmers took his place and Welsh was withdrawn from the pack to play at
wing three-quarter. Gradually, the Irish forwards took advantage of their numerical
superiority and played with increasing confidence and control. Ireland opened the
scoring shortly before the interval. From a scrum near the Scottish line, scrum-half
Murray made enough space for Lightfoot to squeeze in at the corner, the winger
knocking over the flag as he crossed. Murray converted from the touchline, the first
of four successful goals. Scotland had an encouraging spell just after the restart and
centre Dod Wood instigated a movement that ended with him scoring Scotland's first
try. Welsh made a great break down the touchline and kicked past Ridgeway, the Irish
full-back, but he was just beaten in the race for the touchdown. Then the Irish
forwards exerted their dominance and the visitors scored three converted tries. The
Scots rallied at the end and Simmers scored a consolation try following a rush by Ford
and Smith. Allan converted and the final whistle sounded.

167 INTERNATIONAL CHAMPIONSHIP 1932 ENGLAND

Twickenham · Saturday 19 March 1932 · Lost 3–16

SCOTLAND †AS Dykes (*Glasgow Acs*); IS Smith (*London Scot*), GPS Macpherson*
(*Edinburgh Acs*), G Wood (*Gala*), WM Simmers (*Glasgow Acs*); H Lind (*Dunfermline*),
†JP McArthur (*Waterloo*); RA Foster (*Hawick*), HS Mackintosh (*W of Scot*), R Rowand
(*Glasgow HSFP*), †FA Wright (*Edinburgh Acs*), JA Beattie (*Hawick*), WB Welsh (*Hawick*),
JS Wilson (*St Andrews U*), †GF Ritchie (*Dundee HSFP*)

ENGLAND TW Brown (*Bristol*); CC Tanner (*Gloucester*), DW Burland (*Bristol*), RA Gerrard
(*Bath*), CD Aarvold* (*Blackheath*); W Elliot (*Utd Servs*), BC Gadney (*Leicester*); RJ Longland
(*Northampton*), GG Gregory (*Bristol*), NL Evans (*RNE Coll*), CSH Webb (*Devonport Servs*),
RGS Hobbs (*Richmond*), A Vaughan-Jones (*Utd Servs*), JM Hodgson (*Northern*), BH Black
(*Blackheath*)

REFEREE JR Wheeler (*Ireland*)

SCORING Smith, try (3–0); Tanner, try (3–3); Aarvold, try (3–6) (half-time) Aarvold, try (3–9);
Burland, con (3–11); Black, try (3–14); Burland, con (3–16)

The teams were presented to the Duke of York, the future George VI. Playing in brilliant weather, Scotland were convincingly defeated by an on-form English side that was superior in all aspects. After some 15 minutes and against the run of play, Beattie broke clean away from a lineout and Mackintosh carried on before finding Smith who showed great resolution to make it to the corner. Ten minutes later, Bristol centre Don Burland, who was very prominent, pounced on a fumble by Macpherson and made a strong run to put Tanner clear. Then from a scrum near the Scottish line, Gadney and Elliot combined to create a simple run-in for Aarvold. In the second half, the English forwards dominated and Burland was a constant threat to the Scottish defence. Both of England's second half tries resulted from his powerful direct running.

170   INTERNATIONAL CHAMPIONSHIP 1933   WALES

St Helen's, Swansea · Saturday 4 February 1933 · Won 11–3

SCOTLAND †DI Brown (*Cambridge U*); IS Smith* (*London Scot*), †HDB Lorraine (*Oxford U*), H Lind (*Dunfermline*), †KC Fyfe (*Cambridge U*); †KLT Jackson (*Oxford U*), WR Logan (*Edinburgh Wdrs*); †JA Waters (*Selkirk*), †JM Ritchie (*Watsonians*), †JR Thom (*Watsonians*), JA Beattie (*Hawick*), MS Stewart (*Stewart's FP*), WB Welsh (*Hawick*), †JM Henderson (*Edinburgh Acs*), R Rowand (*Glasgow HSFP*)

WALES G Bayliss (*Pontypool*); A Hickman (*Neath*), EC Davey (*Swansea*), W Wooller (*Rydal Sch & Colwyn Bay*), AH Jones (*Cardiff*); RR Morris (*Swansea*), DB Evans (*Swansea*); EL Jones (*Llanelli*), B Evans (*Llanelli*), A Skym (*Cardiff*), RB Jones (*Cambridge U*), DJ Thomas (*Swansea*), T Arthur (*Neath*), I Isaacs (*Cardiff*), WG Thomas* (*Swansea*)

REFEREE JG Bott (*Ireland*)

SCORING Smith, try (3–0); Fyfe, pen (6–0) (half-time) Jackson, try (9–0); Fyfe, con (11–0); Arthur, try (11–3)

Scotland reintroduced numbered jerseys, this time as a permanent feature unlike the previous attempt against France in 1928. Two weeks earlier Wales had beaten England at Twickenham for the first time, but their team was unsettled by some late changes and Scotland won an unexpected victory. The Welsh forwards held a slight advantage at the scrums, but the Scots were faster and cleverer in loose play. They never allowed their opponents to settle and lasted the furious pace much better. Veteran captain Ian Smith led from the front and the new caps, eight in total, were full of youthful enthusiasm and not overawed by the occasion. David Brown, the new full-back, dropped his first ball, but thereafter he never put a foot wrong and was courageous in defence. Playing with the wind, the visitors opened the scoring after about 15 minutes. Lind rescued a poor pass and fed Lorraine who made ground before giving the ball to Smith about 20 yards out. The Scottish winger used his pace to round Bayliss, the new Welsh full-back, and slammed the ball down joyously at the corner flag. Fyfe missed the conversion, but shortly before the interval he kicked a long range penalty. Wales lost second row Dai Thomas with a damaged shoulder and had to play the second half with only seven forwards. Smith was also instrumental in Scotland's second try which was scored about the 60th minute. Taking a pass from Ritchie, Smith, after juggling with the ball, made a typical determined run before finding Jackson who followed-up at top speed and raced over the line. Heavy rain started to fall during the second half and many spectators drifted away, but shortly before the end Arthur scored a consolation try after a rush by the forwards. At the finish, Ian Smith was chaired off the field by a small band of Scottish supporters.

Murrayfield · Saturday 18 March 1933 · Won 3–0

SCOTLAND DI Brown (*Cambridge U*); IS Smith* (*London Scot*), HDB Lorraine (*Oxford U*), H Lind (*Dunfermline*), KC Fyfe (*Cambridge U*); KLT Jackson (*Oxford U*), WR Logan (*Edinburgh Wdrs*); JA Waters (*Selkirk*), JR Thom (*Watsonians*), JM Ritchie (*Watsonians*), WB Welsh (*Hawick*), JM Henderson (*Edinburgh Acs*), MS Stewart (*Stewart's FP*), JA Beattie (*Hawick*), R Rowand (*Glasgow HSFP*)

ENGLAND TW Brown (*Bristol*); LA Booth (*Headingley*), DW Burland (*Bristol*), RA Gerrard (*Bath*), AL Novis* (*Blackheath & Army*); W Elliot (*RN*), BC Gadney (*Leicester*); DA Kendrew (*Woodford*), GG Gregory (*Bristol*), RJ Longland (*Northampton*), CSH Webb (*Devonport Servs*), ADS Roncoroni (*Richmond*), WH Weston (*Northampton*), EH Sadler (*Army*), CL Troop (*Army*)

REFEREE JR Wheeler (*Ireland*)

SCORING Fyfe, try (3–0) (half-time)

In a rather lacklustre match, the Scottish forwards did well enough in the loose, but the backs produced a lot of aimless and ineffective play. Burland and Gerrard, the English centres, were hampered by injury and as a result the Scottish defence was rarely stretched. The only score of the match came a few minutes before the interval. Lind kicked ahead and Fyfe harried Brown, the English full-back, before kicking the ball over the line to score. England staged a late revival as the Scots started to tire but they were unable to make anything of it.

The Scottish team that played England in 1933, a Triple Crown year. *SRU*

Lansdowne Road, Dublin · Saturday 1 April 1933 · Won 8–6

SCOTLAND DI Brown (*Cambridge U*); IS Smith* (*London Scot*), HDB Lorraine (*Oxford U*), H Lind (*Dunfermline*), †PMS Gedge (*Edinburgh Wdrs*); KLT Jackson (*Oxford U*), WR Logan (*Edinburgh Wdrs*); JA Waters (*Selkirk*), JR Thom (*Watsonians*), JM Ritchie (*Watsonians*), JA Beattie (*Hawick*), MS Stewart (*Stewart's FP*), WB Welsh (*Hawick*), JM Henderson (*Edinburgh Acs*), R Rowand (*Glasgow HSFP*)

IRELAND RH Pratt (*Dublin U*); JJ O'Connor (*UC Cork*), PB Coote (*Leicester*), MP Crowe (*Lansdowne*), EJ Lightfoot (*Lansdowne*); EO Davy* (*Lansdowne*), PF Murray (*Wdrs*); GR Beamish (*Leicester*), MJ Dunne (*Lansdowne*), H O'Neill (*UC Cork*), J Russell (*UC Cork*), JAE Siggins (*Collegians*), CE StJ Beamish (*Harlequins*), WM Ross (*QU Belfast*), VJ Pike (*Lansdowne*)

REFEREE BS Cumberlege (*England*)

SCORING Crowe, try (0–3); Jackson, drop (4–3) (half-time) Murray, try (4–6); Lind, drop (8–6)

This game had been postponed from 25 February because a terrible blizzard had covered Lansdowne Road in snow and the boat carrying the Scottish team was forced to lie off Dublin Bay for many hours unable to land. The team were in no condition to play rugby when they finally made it ashore on the morning of the game. Scotland had to make one change for the rescheduled match. Gedge came in for Fyfe who had been injured in a car accident the day before the game. This was a bruising encounter played on a very hard pitch. Both sides tackled fiercely at one stage or another and several players were injured, including all of the Scottish three-quarter line. Scotland led at half time thanks to a drop goal by Jackson, but they fell behind immediately after the restart. Davy put in a long kick to the corner which the officials failed to notice went into touch after hitting the corner flag. From the lineout and scrum, Murray slipped over for a try to put Ireland in the lead. The Scottish forwards then took charge and good work by the half-backs gradually moved play into the Irish 25. With around ten minutes remaining, Logan threw out a long pass from a scrum to Lind who had just enough time to drop the winning goal. This was Ian Smith's final match for Scotland after a playing career of nine years and it was appropriate that he should end by leading his side to the Triple Crown.

Murrayfield · Saturday 3 February 1934 · Lost 6–13

SCOTLAND †KW Marshall (*Edinburgh Acs*); †RW Shaw (*Glasgow HSFP*), †RCS Dick (*Cambridge U*), H Lind* (*Dunfermline*), †J Park (*Royal HSFP*); KLT Jackson (*Oxford U*), WR Logan (*Edinburgh Wdrs*); †WA Burnet (*W of Scot*), †LB Lambie (*Glasgow HSFP*), JM Ritchie (*Watsonians*), †JD Lowe (*Heriot's FP*), MS Stewart (*Stewart's FP*), †DA Thom (*London Scot*), R Rowand (*Glasgow HSFP*), JA Waters (*Selkirk*)

WALES VGJ Jenkins (*Bridgend*); BTV Cowey (*Newport*), EC Davey* (*Swansea & Sale*), JI Rees (*Swansea & Edinburgh Wdrs*), GR Rees-Jones (*London Welsh*); CW Jones (*Cambridge U*), WH Jones (*Llanelli*); TB Day (*Swansea*), I Evans (*London Welsh*), DR Prosser (*Neath*), G Hughes (*Penarth*), WS Ward (*Cross Keys*), IG Prosser (*Neath*), AG Fear (*Newport*), J Lang (*Llanelli*)

REFEREE HLV Day (*England*)

SCORING Rees, try (0–3); Jenkins, con (0–5) (half-time) Cowey, try (0–8); Jenkins, con (0–10); Ritchie, pen (3–10); Logan, try (6–10); Cowey, try (6–13)

Scotland had to make some last minute changes and fielded eight new caps. Playing in near perfect conditions, Wales held the initiative for most of the game and were deserved winners. Their combined play was superior to Scotland's and their backs were much livelier and more assured. Vivian Jenkins gave had an almost faultless display at full-back, Cliff Jones was intelligent at stand-off, and wing forward Bert Fear was very conspicuous and constantly hampered Scottish scrum-half Ross Logan. Wales built a comfortable lead with tries by Idwal Rees and Bunny Cowey, both converted by Jenkins, but midway through the second half the Scots staged a stirring revival. Ritchie kicked a penalty and after a rush by the forwards Logan darted through a wall of defenders for a try. Jackson was unable to convert and Wales regained control. A couple of minutes before the end, Cowey scored in the corner to make the match safe for the visitors.

174   INTERNATIONAL CHAMPIONSHIP 1934   IRELAND

Murrayfield · Saturday 24 February 1934 · Won 16–9

SCOTLAND KW Marshall (*Edinburgh Acs*), RW Shaw (*Glasgow HSFP*), RCS Dick (*Cambridge U*), H Lind (*Dunfermline*), †JA Crawford (*Army*); †JL Cotter (*Hillhead HSFP*), WR Logan (*Edinburgh Wdrs*); JW Allan (*Melrose*), †GS Cottington (*Kelso*), JM Ritchie (*Watsonians*), JA Beattie (*Hawick*), MS Stewart* (*Stewart's FP*), LB Lambie (*Glasgow HSFP*), †JG Watherston (*Edinburgh Wdrs*), JA Waters (*Selkirk*)

IRELAND RH Pratt (*Dublin U*); D Lane (*UC Cork*), NH Lambert (*Lansdowne*), JV Reardon (*Cork Const*), JJ O'Connor (*UC Cork*); JL Reid (*London Irish*), GJ Morgan (*Clontarf*); VJ Pike (*Lansdowne & Army*), WM Ross (*QU Belfast*), CRA Graves (*Wdrs*), S Walker (*Instonians*), JAE Siggins* (*Collegians*), CE StJ Beamish (*NIFC & RAF*), J Russell (*UC Cork*), MJ Dunne (*Lansdowne*)

REFEREE BS Cumberlege (*England*)

SCORING Russell, try (0–3); Dick, try (3–3); Shaw, con (5–3); Allan, pen (8–3); Crawford, try (11–3) (half-time) Dick, try (14–3); Shaw, con (16–3); O'Connor, try (16–6); Russell, try (16–9)

This was Scotland's first win over Ireland at Murrayfield, the visitors having won four successive matches at the new stadium. On a blustery afternoon, the Scots played with more confidence and dash than the previous game against Wales. The Irish pack was heavier and held the edge in the scrums, but the Scots were good in the loose and the backs were more resourceful. Ireland made their usual hurricane start and Russell scored a try within eight minutes. Gradually, Scotland settled down and after 22 minutes they scored an audacious try. Cotter gave an awkward low pass to Lind who confused the defence by quickly flicking the ball back between his legs to Dick. The Scottish centre raced away and dummied past Pratt, the Irish full-back, for a memorable score. Shaw converted and a few minutes later Allan kicked a penalty from an awkward angle. Then Crawford made a stirring run down the wing and beat two defenders to squeeze in at the corner. Scotland had several other chances to score and Shaw was over the line but unable to put the ball down properly. In the second half, Dick took a pass from Cotter and raced between the posts for a try converted by Shaw. Scotland were out of reach, but the Irish put in a rousing finish and scored two consolation tries from close range.

175   INTERNATIONAL CHAMPIONSHIP 1934   ENGLAND

Twickenham · Saturday 17 March 1934 · Lost 3–6

SCOTLAND KW Marshall (*Edinburgh Acs*); RW Shaw (*Glasgow HSFP*), RCS Dick (*Cambridge U*), H Lind (*Dunfermline*), KC Fyfe (*Cambridge U*); JL Cotter (*Hillhead HSFP*) WR Logan (*Edinburgh Wdrs*); JW Allan (*Melrose*), GS Cottington (*Kelso*), JM Ritchie (*Watsonians*), JA Beattie (*Hawick*), MS Stewart* (*Stewart's FP*), LB Lambie (*Glasgow HSFP*), JG Watherston (*Edinburgh Wdrs*), JA Waters (*Selkirk*)

ENGLAND HG Owen-Smith (*St Mary's H*); LA Booth (*Headingley*), P Cranmer (*Oxford U*), RA Gerrard (*Bath*), GWC Meikle (*Waterloo*): CF Slow (*Leicester*), BC Gadney* (*Leicester*); H Rew (*Blackheath*), GG Gregory (*Bristol*), RJ Longland (*Northampton*), JW Forrest (*RN*), J Dicks (*Northampton*), WH Weston (*Northampton*), HA Fry (*Liverpool*), DA Kendrew (*Leicester*)

REFEREE FW Haslett (*Ireland*)

SCORING Shaw, try (3–0); Meikle, try (3–3) (half-time) Booth, try (3–6)

This was an exciting game played at a tremendous pace. Scotland held the upper hand in the first half, but could only manage a single try because of solid English tackling. Five minutes before the interval, Dick made a lovely break and was tackled just short of the line. Lind carried on before sending Shaw over in the corner. Soon after, England equalised with a rather bizarre try. Forrest miscued a penalty attempt and ball hit a Scottish forward and bounced high into the air. England reacted quickly and Fry started a move which sent Meikle away up the touchline to score. In a tense climax, Lind made several good breaks, but could not escape the English defence. One such Scottish attack broke down and the loose ball was gathered by Booth near the centre line. The England winger made a long swerving run and side-stepped Marshall for a dramatic winning score. Scotland tried desperately to save the game in dying stages, but to no avail.

176   INTERNATIONAL CHAMPIONSHIP 1935   WALES

Cardiff Arms Park · Saturday 2 February 1935 · Lost 6–10

SCOTLAND KW Marshall (*Edinburgh Acs*); †WGS Johnston (*Cambridge U*), RCS Dick (*Guy's H*), RW Shaw (*Glasgow HSFP*), KC Fyfe* (*Cambridge U*); †CF Grieve (*Oxford U*), WR Logan (*Edinburgh Wdrs*); †RO Murray (*Cambridge U*), GS Cottington (*Kelso*), †RM Grieve (*Kelso*), JA Beattie (*Hawick*), WA Burnet (*W of Scot*), DA Thom (*London Scot*), JA Waters (*Selkirk*), LB Lambie (*Glasgow HSFP*)

WALES VGJ Jenkins (*Bridgend*); JI Rees (*Swansea*), W Wooller (*Cambridge U*), EC Davey* (*Swansea*), A Bassett (*Aberavon*); CW Jones (*Cambridge U*), WC Powell (*Northampton*); TJ Rees (*Newport*), CD Murphy (*Cross Keys*), TB Day (*Swansea*), DJ Thomas (*Swansea*), TG Williams (*Cross Keys*), AM Rees (*Cambridge U*), J Lang (*Llanelli*), AG Fear (*Newport*)

SCORING Jones, try (0–3); Wooller, try (0–6); Thom, try (3–6) (half-time) Shaw, try (6–6); Jenkins, drop (6–10)

Scotland won the toss and chose to play with a strong wind behind them. Welsh stand-off and playmaker Cliff Jones showed tremendous form in the early stages. He opened with a spectacular solo try and a few minutes later drew the defence to send Wooller in for a second. The Scottish forwards asserted themselves with Jock Beattie setting a fine example. Jones injured his arm when bravely trying to stop a rush and had to leave the field. Idwal Rees moved to stand-off and Bert Fear onto the wing. Towards the interval, the Scots applied pressure on the Welsh line before Thom picked-up and dropped over for an unconverted try. Five minutes after the restart, Scotland drew level. From a Dick crosskick, Beattie snatched-up the ball and fed a long pass to Shaw who ran over. Then the depleted Welsh forwards roused themselves and the half-backs used the wind to keep the Scots pinned down and slowly tire them out. The crowd started to sense victory and with around ten minutes remaining full-back Vivian Jenkins won the game in spectacular style. He raced back and collected the ball just before a Scottish player dived on it, turned on his heel and dropped a magnificent goal from about 40 yards.

---

177   INTERNATIONAL CHAMPIONSHIP 1935   IRELAND

Lansdowne Road, Dublin · Saturday 23 February 1935 · Lost 5–12

SCOTLAND KW Marshall (*Edinburgh Acs*); WGS Johnston (*Cambridge U*), RCS Dick (*Guy's H*), H Lind (*London Scot*), KC Fyfe (*Cambridge U*); RW Shaw* (*Glasgow HSFP*), WR Logan (*Edinburgh Wdrs*); †ASB McNeil (*Watsonians*), GS Cottington (*Kelso*), RM Grieve (*Kelso*), JA Beattie (*Hawick*), WA Burnet (*W of Scot*), DA Thom (*London Scot*), LB Lambie (*Glasgow HSFP*), JA Waters (*Selkirk*)

IRELAND DP Morris (*Bective Rgrs*); JJ O'Connor (*UC Cork*), EC Ridgeway (*Wdrs*), AH Bailey (*UC Dublin*), D Lane (*UC Cork*); VA Hewitt (*Instonians*), GJ Morgan (*Clontarf*); SJ Deering (*Bective Rgrs*), J Russell (*UC Cork*), PJ Lawlor (*Bective Rgrs*), CRA Graves (*Wdrs*), S Walker (*Instonians*), JAE Siggins* (*Collegians*), HJM Sayers (*Army*), CE StJ Beamish (*Leicester & RAF*)

REFEREE J Hughes (*England*)

SCORING O'Connor, try (0–3); Shaw, try (3–3); Fyfe, con (5–3) (half-time) Lawlor, try (5–6); Bailey, try (5–9); Ridgeway, try (5–12)

On an afternoon of misty rain, the heavier Irish pack dominated throughout and eventually the Scottish defence was worn down. The defeat would have been greater if Ireland had possessed a reliable place-kicker and more penetrative three-quarters. Play did not reach a high standard, but there were plenty of incidents and the game took place at a furious pace. Ireland's opening try after 24 minutes showed typical opportunism. From a scrum inside the Scottish 25, Morgan threw out a poor pass that trundled along the ground to left wing O'Connor who hacked the ball over the line and just beat the defence to the touchdown before sliding into the crowd behind the dead-ball line. Ten minutes later, and against the run of play, the Scots scored their only try which turned out to be the highlight of the match. Dick made a strong break

Bill Johnston, the Cambridge and Scotland wing but wearing number 8, is pushed into touch during the Irish match in 1935.

into the Irish half and when he was tackled Lind stabbed the ball forwards. Then Shaw racing up at top speed kicked towards the line and won a breathtaking race for the touch against three defenders. Fyfe converted to give the Scots a narrow lead at the interval, but in the second half Ireland's unrelenting pressure was too great and the home side scored three unconverted tries to win the match decisively. Waters and Beattie were the best in a beaten pack.

178   INTERNATIONAL CHAMPIONSHIP 1935   ENGLAND

Murrayfield · Saturday 16 March 1935 · Won 10–7

SCOTLAND KW Marshall (*Edinburgh Acs*); JE Forrest (*Glasgow Acs*), RCS Dick (*Guy's H*), †WCW Murdoch (*Hillhead HSFP*), KC Fyfe (*Cambridge U*); RW Shaw* (*Glasgow HSFP*), WR Logan (*Edinburgh Wdrs*); RO Murray (*Cambridge U*), †PW Tait (*Royal HSFP*), RM Grieve (*Kelso*), JA Beattie (*Hawick*), WA Burnet (*W of Scot*), DA Thom (*London Scot*), LB Lambie (*Glasgow HSFP*), JA Waters (*Selkirk*)

ENGLAND HJ Boughton (*Gloucester*); LA Booth (*Headingley*), P Cranmer (*Richmond*), J Heaton (*Liverpool U*), R Leyland (*Waterloo*); JR Auty (*Headingley*), BC Gadney* (*Leicester*); J Dicks (*Northampton*), ES Nicholson (*Oxford U*), RJ Longland (*Northampton*), AJ Clark (*Coventry*), CSH Webb (*Devonport Servs*), WH Weston (*Northampton*), AG Cridlan (*Blackheath*), AT Payne (*Bristol*)

REFEREE RW Jeffares (*Ireland*)

SCORING Cranmer, drop (0–4); Fyfe, try (3–4); Fyfe, con (5–4); Lambie, try (8–4); Fyfe, con (10–4) (half-time) Booth, try (10–7)

Playing in ideal conditions, the big English forwards won a lot of ball, but the Scots were more active in the loose and they defended very well. England took the lead against the run of play when Cranmer dropped a goal. Then Scotland conjured two tries in quick succession. Murdoch intercepted an English pass and from the ensuing play Fyfe kicked over the defence and just made it to the touchdown before the ball ran out of play. Shaw made a great run down the line before kicking ahead and Lambie was in support to score. Both tries were converted by Fyfe. The only score of the second half was a try by Booth, although he might have hit the corner flag before putting the ball down. Right at the finish, Beattie went over after a handling attack only to be called back for a forward pass. For Scotland, Wilson Shaw and Ross Logan formed an effective half-back partnership.

---

179   TOUR MATCH   NEW ZEALAND

Murrayfield · Saturday 23 November 1935 · Lost 8–18

SCOTLAND †JM Kerr (*Heriot's FP*); JE Forrest (*Glasgow Acs*), RCS Dick (*Guy's H*), WCW Murdoch (*Hillhead HSFP*), KC Fyfe (*Cambridge U*); RW Shaw* (*Glasgow HSFP*), WR Logan (*Edinburgh Wdrs*); RM Grieve (*Kelso*), †GL Gray (*Gala*), †GD Shaw (*Sale*), JA Beattie (*Hawick*), WA Burnet (*W of Scot*), LB Lambie (*Glasgow HSFP*), JA Waters (*Selkirk*), DA Thom (*London Scot*)

NEW ZEALAND GDM Gilbert (*West Coast*); GF Hart (*Canterbury*), CJ Oliver (*Canterbury*), NA Mitchell (*Southland*); THC Caughey (*Auckland*), JL Griffiths (*Wellington*), BS Sadler (*Wellington*); J Hore (*Otago*), WE Hadley (*Auckland*), A Lambourn (*Wellington*), RR King (*West Coast*), ST Reid (*Hawke's Bay*), RM McKenzie (*Manawatu*), JE Manchester* (*Canterbury*), A Mahoney (*Bush Districts*)

REFEREE CH Gadney (*England*)

SCORING Fyfe, try (3–0); Caughey, try (3–3); Gilbert, con (3–5); Hadley, try (3–8); Gilbert, con (3–10); Caughey, try (3–13) (half-time) Dick, try (6–13); Murdoch, con (8–13); Caughey, try (8–16); Gilbert, con (8–18)

In season 1935–6, New Zealand made a 30-match tour of the British Isles and Canada, including four games in Scotland. Captained by the Canterbury forward Jack Manchester, the tourists had managed only narrow wins in some of their provincial games, including those against the South of Scotland (11–8) and the Combined Cities (9–8). Scotland approached the test match, the first of the tour, with some optimism. The Cites provided five of the back division, including the new full-back Jimmy Kerr and captain Wilson Shaw, whilst the South supplied four forwards, including newcomers Dod Gray and Duncan Shaw. In a fast and exciting game played in near perfect conditions, the New Zealanders rose to the occasion and gave one of the best performances of their tour. The Scots competed well, but they could not match the superior speed and power of their opponents. Scotland opened the scoring after ten minutes when Shaw and Dick made a break and winger Ken Fyfe beat the defence to the corner. Soon afterwards, Copey Murdoch had to leave the field temporarily and in his absence Pat Caughey scored the first of his three tries. Hadley and Caughey added further tries to put the visitors 13–3 ahead at the interval. In the second half Shaw cut through to send Dick racing in at the posts. Murdoch's conversion brought the Scots back into the game, but they lost a great chance when Fyfe dropped a scoring pass after a fine break by Murdoch. The visitors sealed the match when Sadler, who played well at full-back, went blind and fed Mitchell who threw out a long pass to Caughey for his third try. This was a well deserved win for the New Zealanders who showed some excellent teamwork. For Scotland, Dick and Shaw were good in attack whilst Beattie and Burnett were the best of the forwards

---

180   INTERNATIONAL CHAMPIONSHIP 1936   WALES

Murrayfield · Saturday 1 February 1936 · Lost 3–13

SCOTLAND KW Marshall (*Edinburgh Acs*); WCW Murdoch (*Hillhead HSFP*), RCS Dick* (*Guy's H*), †HM Murray (*Glasgow U*), KC Fyfe (*Cambridge U*); RW Shaw (*Glasgow HSFP*), WR Logan (*Edinburgh Wdrs*); RM Grieve (*Kelso*), †WAH Druitt (*London Scot*), JA Waters (*Selkirk*), JA Beattie (*Hawick*), WA Burnet (*W of Scot*), †MMG Cooper (*Oxford U*), GD Shaw (*Sale & Gala*), †PL Duff (*Glasgow Acs*)

WALES VGJ Jenkins (*London Welsh*); JI Rees (*Swansea & Edinburgh Wdrs*), W Wooller (*Cambridge U*), EC Davey* (*Swansea*), BEW McCall (*Welch Regt & Newport*); CW Jones (*Cambridge U*), H Tanner (*Swansea*); TJ Rees (*Newport*), B Evans (*Llanelli*), TG Williams (*Cross Keys*), HW Thomas (*Neath*), GM Williams (*Aberavon*), AM Rees (*London Welsh*), EC Long (*Swansea*), J Lang (*Llanelli*)

REFEREE CH Gadney (*England*)

SCORING Wooller, try (0–3); Davey, try (0–6); Jenkins, con (0–8) (half-time) Murray, try (3–8); Jones, try (3–11); Jenkins, con (3–13)

Scotland fielded three new caps amongst the forwards: WAH Druitt, a surprise choice at hooker; New Zealander and Oxford Blue Malcolm 'Mac' Cooper; and back-row man Peter Duff, who was simply described as a 'big fellow'. Centre Harry Lind withdrew from the original selection and was replaced by HM Murray of Glasgow University. Wales had beaten New Zealand earlier in the season and arrived at Murrayfield in confident mood. The Scottish forwards held their own against a powerful Welsh eight but the backs struggled to cope with the brilliant skills of Cliff Jones and Wilf Wooller, both of whom became more prominent as the game went on. The Welsh tackling was very firm and the visitors deserved their victory. On a gloomy afternoon with a thin drizzle of rain, the first half consisted largely of Welsh pressure and occasional Scottish rushes. After 15 minutes, Jones received the ball from a scrum near the Scottish 25, drew two defenders before passing to Wooller who tore through the remaining cover for a fine score. Shortly before the interval, Claude Davey, the Welsh captain, collected the ball from a scrum near the Scottish line and scrambled over with Dick hanging onto him. Three minutes after the break, Dick kicked ahead and caught Jenkins in possession, Murray pounced on the loose ball and scored an unconverted try at the corner. The rest of the game was exciting and evenly balanced. The Scots exerted a lot of pressure, but towards the end Jones made a bewildering run from just outside the Scottish 25 for a great solo try.

---

181   INTERNATIONAL CHAMPIONSHIP 1936   IRELAND

Murrayfield · Saturday 22 February 1936 · Lost 4–10

SCOTLAND JM Kerr (*Heriot's FP*); WCW Murdoch (*Hillhead HSFP*), RCS Dick* (*Guy's H*),

A SMALL BOY SUMS UP THE SCOTS AT MURRAYFIELD

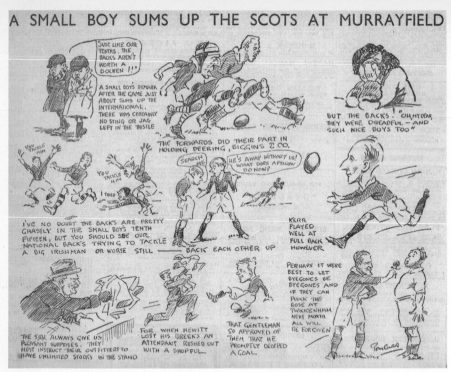

Cartoonist Tom Kerr of the *Evening News* sums up Scotland's 10–4 defeat by Ireland at Murrayfield in 1936. *Scotsman Publications Ltd*

HM Murray (*Glasgow U*), †RJE Whitworth (*London Scot*); RW Shaw (*Glasgow HSFP*), WR Logan (*Edinburgh Wdrs*); RM Grieve (*Kelso*), WAH Druitt (*London Scot*), JA Waters (*Selkirk*), JA Beattie (*Hawick*), WA Burnet (*W of Scot*), MM Cooper (*Oxford U*), †VG Weston (*Kelvinside Acs*), PL Duff (*Glasgow Acs*)

IRELAND GL Malcolmson (*NIFC*); JJ O'Connor (*UC Cork*), AH Bailey (*UC Dublin*), LB McMahon (*Blackrock Coll*), CV Boyle (*Dublin U*); VA Hewitt (*Instonians*), GJ Morgan (*Clontarf*); R Alexander (*NIFC*), S Walker (*Instonians*), CE StJ Beamish (*NIFC & RAF*), HJM Sayers (*Lansdowne & Army*), SJ Deering (*Bective Rgrs*), JAE Siggins* (*Collegians*), J Russell (*UC Cork*), CRA Graves (*Wdrs*)

REFEREE JW Faull (*Wales*)

SCORING Walker, try (0–3); McMahon, try (0–6); Hewitt, drop (0–10) (half-time) Murdoch, drop (4–10)

Played in perfect conditions in front of a small crowd, the Scottish forwards competed well and had some stirring foot rushes but the backs were disappointing. The visitors were stronger, more resolute and better at taking their chances. After ten minutes, Ireland opened the scoring against the run of play. They pounced on a loose ball and after a bout of passing Walker crossed at the corner. Ireland's second try came after a spell of pressure near the Scottish line. Larry McMahon, the Blackrock College centre, took the ball in midfield just outside the Scottish 25 and had enough speed to reach the corner. Shortly before the interval, Hewitt put over a snap drop goal. In the second half, Scotland improved but the Irish defence was firm and all that the home side could manage was a late Murdoch drop goal. Dick had one long run from his own 25, but he was tackled by Boyle just a few yards short of the Irish line.

182 INTERNATIONAL CHAMPIONSHIP 1936 ENGLAND

Twickenham · Saturday 21 March 1936 · Lost 8–9

SCOTLAND JM Kerr (*Heriot's FP*); RW Shaw (*Glasgow HSFP*), H Lind (*London Scot*), RCS Dick (*Guy's H*), KC Fyfe (*Sale*); CF Grieve (*Oxford U*), WR Logan (*Edinburgh Wdrs*); RM Grieve (*Kelso*), GS Cottington (*Headingley*), WAH Druitt (*London Scot*), JA Beattie* (*Hawick*), WA Burnet (*W of Scot*), †RW Barrie (*Hawick*), VG Weston (*Kelvinside Acs*), JA Waters (*Selkirk*)

ENGLAND HG Owen-Smith (*St Mary's H*); A Obolensky (*Oxford U*), RA Gerrard (*Bath*), P Cranmer (*Richmond*), HS Sever (*Sale*); PL Candler (*St Bart's H*), BC Gadney* (*Leicester*); RJ Longland (*Northampton*), HB Toft (*Waterloo*), J Dicks (*Northampton*), CSH Webb (*Devonport Servs*), PE Dunkley (*Harlequins*), R Bolton (*Harlequins*), WH Weston (*Northampton*), PWP Brook (*Harlequins*)

REFEREE TH Phillips (*Wales*)

SCORING Bolton, try (0–3); Fyfe, pen (3–3); Candler, try (3–6); Sever, try (3–9); Shaw, try (6–9); Fyfe, con (8–9) (half-time)

Hawick's Rob Barrie was a late replacement for Mac Cooper. On a lovely spring afternoon, Scotland fought hard, but they were well beaten and the final score flattered them. The Scots defended valiantly and England were guilty of some poor finishing and hugging the touchlines too much, especially scrum-half Gadney who kicked away a lot of possession. England took an early lead with a try by Bolton, but two minutes later Fyfe kicked a penalty from around midway. England scored two unconverted tries in quick succession before Scotland responded with a well-worked try. Logan switched play and kicked diagonally across the field. Shaw raced ahead, hacked the ball over the line and just managed to reach it before it ran out of play. Fyfe kicked a great conversion from near the touchline. There was no scoring in the second half although both sides had some chances and the game wound down with England camped on the Scottish line.

183 INTERNATIONAL CHAMPIONSHIP 1937 WALES

St Helen's, Swansea · Saturday 6 February 1937 · Won 13–6

SCOTLAND JM Kerr (*Heriot's FP*); WGS Johnston (*Richmond*), RCS Dick (*Guy's H*), †DJ Macrae (*St Andrews U*), RW Shaw (*Glasgow HSFP*); †WA Ross (*Hillhead HSFP*), WR Logan* (*Edinburgh Wdrs*); †MM Henderson (*Dunfermline*), GL Gray (*Gala*), †WM Inglis (*Cambridge U*), †GB Horsburgh (*London Scot*), †CL Melville (*Army*), †WB Young (*Cambridge U*), GD Shaw (*Gala & Sale*), JA Waters (*Selkirk*)

WALES TO James (*Aberavon*); WH Hopkin (*Newport*), JI Rees* (*Edinburgh Wdrs*), W Wooller (*Cardiff*), WH Clement (*Llanelli*); RR Morris (*Bristol*), H Tanner (*Swansea*); TG Williams

(*Cross Keys*), W Travers (*Newport*), TJ Rees (*Newport*), HT Rees (*Cardiff*), HW Thomas (*Neath*),
EC Long (*Swansea*), AM Rees (*London Welsh*), EV Watkins (*Cardiff*)

REFEREE CH Gadney (*England*)

SCORING Wooller, try (0–3); Dick, try (3–3) (half-time) Dick, try (6–3); GD Shaw, con (8–3);
RW Shaw, try (11–3); GD Shaw, con (13–3); Wooller, try (13–6)

Scotland fielded no less than seven new caps, five amongst the forwards. Curiously, both captains, Ross Logan and Idwal Rees, played for Edinburgh Wanderers. It was customary at this time for spectators to arrive at the ground hours before kick-off. To while away the time, they indulged in community singing and other 'preliminary antics', which usually involved somebody trying to shin-up one of the goalposts. On this occasion, the mean-spirited WRU had applied fresh paint to the posts, but this did not discourage one hardy spectator who climbed up and planted a saucepan on the top despite ruining his suit in the process. On a firm pitch and with a dry ball, the Scots gave one of their best displays for some time. The big Scottish forwards struggled in tight play, but were excellent in the loose. The backs were enterprising and sound in defence, especially Charlie Dick who kept a grip on the Welsh maestro Wilf Wooller. Playing with the elements behind them, Wales made a determined start and Wooller collected a lucky bounce to run in for the opening try. The Scots worked their way into the game and after 25 minutes Macrae swerved past two defenders and passed to Dick for a try. Seven minutes after the break, the Scots created a fine handling move which led to Dick's second try. Then Jimmy Kerr fielded a loose kick, ran-up the left wing and drew the cover before releasing Wilson Shaw who had just enough speed to reach the corner. Duncan Shaw landed the tricky conversion and just before the finish a defiant Wooller outstripped Johnston to score a consolation try for Wales. This was to be Scotland's last win in Wales until 1962.

184   INTERNATIONAL CHAMPIONSHIP 1937   IRELAND

Lansdowne Road, Dublin · Saturday 27 February 1937 · Lost 4–11

SCOTLAND JM Kerr (*Heriot's FP*); WGS Johnston (*Richmond*), DJ Macrae (*St Andrews U*),
†I Shaw (*Glasgow HSFP*), RW Shaw (*Glasgow HSFP*); †RB Bruce Lockhart (*Cambridge U*),
WR Logan* (*Edinburgh Wdrs*); MM Henderson (*Dunfermline*), GL Gray (*Gala*), WM Inglis
(*Cambridge U*), GB Horsburgh (*London Scot*), CL Melville (*Army*), WB Young (*Cambridge U*),
JA Waters (*Selkirk*), GD Shaw (*Gala & Sale*)

IRELAND GL Malcolmson (*NIFC & RAF*); CV Boyle (*Dublin U*), AH Bailey (*UC Dublin*),
LB McMahon (*Blackrock Coll*), FG Moran (*Clontarf*); GE Cromey (*QU Belfast*), GJ Morgan*
(*Clontarf*); CRA Graves (*Dublin Wdrs*), TS Corken (*Belfast Collegians*), S Walker (*Instonians*),
SJ Deering (*Bective Rgrs*), J Russell (*UC Cork*), PJ Lawlor (*Bective Rgrs*), R Alexander (*NIFC*),
JAE Siggins (*Belfast Collegians*)

REFEREE CH Gadney (*England*)

SCORING Alexander, try (0–3) (half-time) McMahon, try (0–6); Moran, try (0–9); Bailey, con
(0–11); I Shaw, drop (4–11)

There were two enforced changes after the great win at Swansea, both new caps. The slightly-built Rab Bruce Lockhart, son of former cap John, came in at stand-off and

Ian Shaw, the brother of Wilson, took the place of Charlie Dick who withdrew because of a family bereavement. Played at times in blizzard conditions, Ireland deserved to win after their fine defensive effort in the first half when they faced into the elements. The Scottish backs did not combine very well and Ireland played an effective spoiling game. This was a hard and vigorous match and several players were injured in the course of it. Wilson Shaw had to withdraw during the second half because of concussion, his place being taken by Henderson. Ireland's first two tries came from handling errors near the Scottish line. Their third was scored in unusual circumstances. Fred Moran, an Irish sprint champion, punted speculatively and the wind carried the ball half the length of the field. In the ensuing race, Wilson Shaw managed to catch the Irishman near the line and push him to one side. Shaw, still suffering from concussion, plunged on the bouncing ball, but only managed to knock it further ahead. He tried again to reach it, but stumbled and Moran, having regained his feet, went past to touch down inches from the dead ball line. Ian Shaw, winning his only cap, dropped a goal against the wind and the depleted Scottish pack finished strongly, but there was no further scoring.

185   INTERNATIONAL CHAMPIONSHIP 1937   ENGLAND

Murrayfield · Saturday 20 March 1937 · Lost 3–6

SCOTLAND KW Marshall (*Edinburgh Acs*); WGS Johnston (*Richmond*), RW Shaw (*Glasgow HSFP*), DJ Macrae (*St Andrews U*), †RH Dryden (*Watsonians*); WA Ross (*Hillhead HSFP*), WR Logan* (*Edinburgh Wdrs*); MM Henderson (*Dunfermline*), GL Gray (*Gala*), WM Inglis (*Cambridge U*), GB Horsburgh (*London Scot*), CL Melville (*Black Watch Regt*), WB Young (*Cambridge U*), GD Shaw (*Gala & Sale*), JA Waters (*Selkirk*)

ENGLAND HG Owen-Smith* (*St Mary's H*); EJ Unwin (*Army*), PL Candler (*St Bart's H*), P Cranmer (*Richmond*), HS Sever (*Sale*); FJ Reynolds (*Old Cranleighans & Army*), BC Gadney (*Leicester*); HF Wheatley (*Coventry*), HB Toft (*Waterloo*), RJ Longland (*Northampton*), TF Huskisson (*OMT*), A Wheatley (*Coventry*), JG Cook (*Bedford*), WH Weston (*Northampton*), R Bolton (*Harlequins*)

REFEREE S Donaldson (*Ireland*)

SCORING Unwin, try (0–3) (half-time) Sever, try (0–6); GD Shaw, pen (3–6)

In a rather featureless match, England won at Murrayfield for the first time. The English forwards dominated and the winning margin might have been greater but for some stout Scottish defence. England had to wait almost until the interval for their first try, Unwin swerving around the defence after a quick bout of passing. In the second half, the ball reached Sever from a scrum inside the Scottish 25 and the big winger from Sale side-stepped his way over the line. Duncan Shaw kicked a penalty for Scotland, but the visitors finished strongly and Sever was denied another try only by an awkward bounce.

186   INTERNATIONAL CHAMPIONSHIP 1938   WALES

Murrayfield · Saturday 5 February 1938 · Won 8–6

SCOTLAND †G Roberts (*Watsonians*); †AH Drummond (*Kelvinside Acs*), RCS Dick (*Guy's H*), DJ Macrae (*St Andrews U*), †JGS Forrest (*Cambridge U*); RW Shaw* (*Glasgow HSFP*), †TF Dorward (*Gala*); †JB Borthwick (*Stewart's FP*), †JD Hastie (*Melrose*), WM Inglis (*Royal Engineers*), GB Horsburgh (*London Scot*), †A Roy (*Waterloo*), WB Young (*Cambridge U*), †WH Crawford (*Utd Servs*), PL Duff (*Glasgow Acs*)

WALES VGJ Jenkins (*London Welsh*); WH Clement (*Llanelli*), JI Rees (*Edinburgh Wdrs*), W Wooller (*Cardiff*), A Bassett (*Cardiff*); CW Jones* (*Cardiff*), H Tanner (*Swansea*); ME Morgan (*Swansea*), W Travers (*Newport*), HT Rees (*Cardiff*), EV Watkins (*Cardiff*), FL Morgan (*Llanelli*), AM Rees (*London Welsh*), A McCarley (*Neath*), WE Vickery (*Aberavon*)

REFEREE CH Gadney (*England*)

SCORING McCarley, try (o–3); McCarley, try (o–6) (half-time) Crawford, try (3–6); Crawford, con (5–6); Crawford, pen (8–6)

In a dramatic finale, Scotland won this match with a penalty goal in the dying minutes. Play was fairly even in the first half and the Scots did not deserve to trail by six points at the interval. Stand-off Wilson Shaw proved himself to be the equal of Welsh maestro Cliff Jones and showed his speed when he made one saving touch-down from 30 yards. Macrae and Dick, the Scottish centres, were always dangerous and the latter had few problems containing the genius of Wilf Wooller. In the first half, Welsh forward Eddie Morgan was forced to retire with a rib injury. Undeterred, McCarley scored a brace of tries, the first after a run and crosskick by Jones and the second from a wayward pass by Dorward. In the second half, Scotland were able apply almost continuous pressure on depleted Wales. The Scots missed several scoring attempts until Macrae and Forrest combined to put Crawford over for a try which he also converted. Wooler sustained an injury so McCarley withdrew from the Welsh pack, leaving them with only six forwards. To their credit, the visitors held their own and the match degenerated into a rather heated affair with Dorward coming in for some harsh treatment. With less than five minutes to go and the Scots still one point adrift, Drummond was short with a penalty attempt, but the Scots hammered away the Welsh defence and eventually were awarded a penalty after a maul on the line. Following a lengthy and nervous delay to allow several injured players to recover, Crawford stepped-up and coolly kicked the winning goal.

187   INTERNATIONAL CHAMPIONSHIP 1938   IRELAND

Murrayfield · Saturday 26 February 1938 · Won 23–14

SCOTLAND G Roberts (*Watsonians*); AH Drummond (*Kelvinside Acs*), RCS Dick (*Guy's H*), DJ Macrae (*St Andrews U*), JGS Forrest (*Cambridge U*); RW Shaw* (*Glasgow HSFP*), TF Dorward (*Gala*); JB Borthwick (*Stewart's FP*), JD Hastie (*Melrose*), WM Inglis (*Royal Engineers*), GB Horsburgh (*London Scot*), A Roy (*Waterloo*), WB Young (*Cambridge U*), WH Crawford (*Utd Servs*), PL Duff (*Glasgow Acs*)

IRELAND RG Craig (*QU Belfast*); FG Moran (*Clontarf*), AH Bailey (*UC Dublin*), LB McMahon (*Blackrock Coll*), JJ O'Connor (*Blackrock Coll*); GE Cromey (*QU Belfast*), GJ Morgan* (*Old Belvedere*); E Ryan (*Dolphin*), CRA Graves (*Wdrs*), H Kennedy (*Bradford*), DB O'Loughlin (*UC Cork*), D Tierney (*UC Cork*), R Alexander (*NIFC*), JWS Irwin (*NIFC*), S Walker (*Instonians*)

REFEREE CH Gadney (*England*)

SCORING Forrest, try (3–0); Forrest, try (6–0); Crawford, con (8–0); Cromey, try (8–3); Dorward, drop (12–3); Drummond, pen (15–3) (half-time) O'Loughlin, try (15–6); Moran, try (15–9); Macrae, try (18–9); Crawford, con (20–9); Drummond, try (23–9); Morgan, try (23–12); Walker, con (23–14)

Both sides scored four tries in a high-scoring and entertaining match, but Scotland had the advantage of superior goal-kicking and greater pace and opportunism. The Scottish backs were full of running, although some of their handling was erratic. Stand-off Wilson Shaw was at his brilliant best and always asking questions of the defence without doing anything rash. The Irish forwards played with plenty of early fire, but gradually they were subdued. Ireland dominated the opening stages, during which a dog had to be removed from the pitch, but after some fifteen minutes Shaw made a break before throwing out a long and high pass to the supporting Forrest who had a clear run-in. On the 28th minute, Shaw passed to Macrae who chipped ahead and gathered the ball to put Forrest over for his second try. Crawford's conversion hit an upright before going over. The Irish forwards made a rush and Morgan gave a scoring pass to Cromey. Dick missed a drop goal attempt, but moments later Dorward was successful with a similar kick and then Drummond landed a long penalty to. Ireland came back into the match in the second half and O'Loughlin scored a try after a charge down. Both sides wasted some clear chances before Morgan escaped from a scrum and fed Moran who made a strong run up the touchline to score in the corner. The Scottish forwards roused themselves and Shaw put Macrae away at top speed to score between the posts. Scotland continued to press and after a good movement Shaw sent in Drummond wide out. Then in the most thrilling incident of the game, Roberts started a great Scottish handling move and Horsburgh almost scored but he was bundled into touch at the corner flag. Morgan added a late consolation try for Ireland which completed the scoring in an excellent match.

188   INTERNATIONAL CHAMPIONSHIP 1938   ENGLAND

Twickenham · Saturday 19 March 1938 · Won 21–16

SCOTLAND G Roberts (*Watsonians*); †WN Renwick (*London Scot*), RCS Dick (*Guy's H*), DJ Macrae (*St Andrews U*), JGS Forrest (*Cambridge U*); RW Shaw* (*Glasgow HSFP*), TF Dorward (*Gala*); †WF Blackadder (*W of Scot*), JD Hastie (*Melrose*), WM Inglis (*Army*), GB Horsburgh (*London Scot*), A Roy (*Waterloo*), WB Young (*Cambridge U*), WH Crawford (*Utd Servs*), PL Duff (*Glasgow Acs*)

ENGLAND GW Parker (*Blackheath*); EJ Unwin (*Rosslyn Park*), PL Candler (*St Bart's H*), P Cranmer (*Moseley*), HS Sever (*Sale*); FJ Reynolds (*Old Cranleighans*), JL Giles (*Coventry*); RJ Longland (*Northampton*), HB Toft* (*Waterloo*), HF Wheatley (*Coventry*), RM Marshall (*Oxford U*), A Wheatley (*Coventry*), WH Weston (*Northampton*), AA Brown (*Exeter*), DLK Milman (*Bedford*)

REFEREE I David (*Wales*)

SCORING Renwick, try (3–0); Parker, pen (3–3); Parker, pen (3–6) Renwick, try (6–6); Dick, try (9–6); Unwin, try (9–9); Shaw, try (12–9) (half-time) Reynolds, drop (12–13); Crawford, pen (15–13); Crawford, pen (18–13); Parker, pen (18–16); Shaw, try (21–16)

On a fine spring afternoon, King George VI and Queen Elizabeth were amongst a capacity crowd who witnessed one of the greatest rugby matches ever played. Scotland scored five tries to one and clinched the Triple Crown in a thrilling encounter. This became known as 'Wilson Shaw's match' for a brilliant performance by the Scottish captain and stand-off. He scored two wonderful solo tries and was full of incisive running. Shaw was chaired him off in triumph at the end and in its match report *The Scotsman* described him as 'the greatest Rugby player of his generation'. Shaw was well supported by his three-quarter line who defended aggressively and cut through almost at will. The Scottish forwards struggled in the scrums, but the back-row were untiring spoilers in the loose and snapped up anything that came their way. England had a much greater share of possession, but their backs were too hesitant and lacked pace. The home side started purposefully and the opening stages of the game were rather scrappy until Renwick hacked on and collected a fortunate bounce to score Scotland's first try. Parker responded with two penalties before Crawford made a powerful run to put Renwick over again. Then the Scottish back-row stole possession and made a sweeping counter-attack up-field. Macrae carried on at top speed before giving a scoring pass to Dick. Two minutes later Unwin, the English wing, made a determined run and, although he was caught short of the line, he managed to make a secondary dive and score. Next came the first of Shaw's great tries. He collected the ball from a retreating scrum, dummied and shot off down the narrow side before making a long, jinking run to score at the left corner. Play continued in a similarly exciting fashion in the second half. Early on, Shaw had another 'electric dash' that almost brought a try before Reynolds, the English stand-off, dropped a goal. Crawford recaptured the lead for Scotland with two penalties,

Captained by Wilson Shaw, this Scottish team won the Triple Crown against England in March 1938.
SRU

SCOTTISH RUGBY

THE CALCUTTA CUP: R. C. S. DICK TOUCHING DOWN WIDE OUT TO SCORE SCOTLAND'S THIRD TRY; AND (LEFT) THE KING AND QUEEN IN THE ROYAL BOX—THE FIRST OCCASION ON WHICH THE CONSORT OF A REIGNING KING OF ENGLAND HAS BEEN PRESENT AT THE MATCH.

THE OPENING SCORE IN THE ENGLAND v. SCOTLAND INTERNATIONAL RUGBY FOOTBALL MATCH: W. N. RENWICK (SCOTLAND), WHO WAS WELL SUPPORTED, DIVING OVER THE LINE FOR A TRY, AN ADVANTAGE NULLIFIED A MOMENT LATER WITH A PENALTY GOAL KICKED BY PARKER (ENGLAND).

The King and Queen were present at the Rugby football match between England and Scotland for the Calcutta Cup on March 19. This was the first occasion on which the Consort of a reigning King of England had seen an international and the first at which King George has been present since succeeding. His Majesty was televised walking out on to the field, before the match started, by means of one of the B.B.C.'s new super-sensitive cameras, which was used to follow the actual play. Scotland beat England in an exciting game by 21 points to 16 and thus won the Calcutta Cup—presented to the Rugby Union by the original Calcutta F.C. on their disbandment in 1879 and competed for annually by England and Scotland—the international championship (52 points to 36), and the Triple Crown of legend by beating Wales, England and Ireland. This was the first occasion on which Scotland had won at Twickenham since 1926. (Sport and General.)

The Illustrated London News reports on the famous Triple Crown match at Twickenham in March 1938.

Mary Evans Picture Library

Parker kicked one for England and Sever almost scored a try but was hampered by one of the goalposts. In a breathtaking conclusion, England fought hard for the winning score, but with a few minutes left Shaw made a long diagonal run and dived over in the left corner to seal the game for Scotland. At the final whistle, the exhausted crowd still had enough energy to burst into a spontaneous rendition of the National Anthem before ecstatic Scottish supporters invaded the pitch to acclaim their heroes.

---

189   INTERNATIONAL CHAMPIONSHIP 1939   WALES

Cardiff Arms Park · Saturday 4 February 1939 · Lost 3–11

SCOTLAND G Roberts (*Watsonians*); †JB Craig (*Heriot's FP*), DJ Macrae (*St Andrews U*), †JRS Innes (*Aberdeen U*), WN Renwick (*Edinburgh Wdrs*); RW Shaw* (*Glasgow HSFP*), †WRC Brydon (*Heriot's FP*); †GH Gallie (*Edinburgh Acs*), †RWF Sampson (*London Scot*), †W Purdie (*Jed-Forest*), GB Horsburgh (*London Scot*), A Roy (*Waterloo*), WB Young (*King's Coll H*), WH Crawford (*Utd Servs*), PL Duff (*Glasgow Acs*)

WALES CH Davies (*Swansea*); EL Jones (*Llanelli*), MJ Davies (*Oxford U*), W Wooller* (*Cardiff*), SA Williams (*Aberavon*); WTH Davies (*Swansea*), H Tanner (*Swansea*); L Davies (*Swansea*), W Travers (*Newport*), WEN Davis (*Cardiff*), EV Watkins (*Cardiff*), ER Price (*Weston-super-Mare*), E Evans (*Llanelli*), EC Long (*Swansea*), L Manfield (*Otley & Mountain Ash*)

REFEREE AS Bean (*England*)

SCORING MJ Davies, try (0–3); Wooller, pen (0–6) (half-time) Crawford, pen (3–6); Travers, try (3–9); Wooller, con (3–11)

The 50th meeting between the sides and both fielded six new caps. Willie Bryce came in at scrum-half after Tommy Dorward withdrew because of injury. This was a surprise choice because 'Wee Willie' was a brilliant sevens player but wasn't even first choice for his club, Heriot's FP. In a rather dull game, the Scottish forwards were disappointing and a methodical Welsh side emerged as worthy winners. The talismanic Wilson Shaw had been unwell during the train journey south and was not in his best form although he did manage one good break at the start of the match that almost brought a try. After some ten minutes, Welsh stand-off Willie Davies fooled the defence with a neat diagonal kick and his namesake Mickey hurtled through and picked-up the ball to score. Wooller missed the conversion, but later kicked a penalty goal. In the second half, Wales lost scrum-half Haydn Tanner temporarily with a wrist injury, but the Scots could only manage a penalty by Crawford. Near the end, Bunner Travers broke away from a lineout and ran between two defenders for a simple try to seal the match.

---

190   INTERNATIONAL CHAMPIONSHIP 1939   IRELAND

Lansdowne Road, Dublin · Saturday 25 February 1939 · Lost 3–12

SCOTLAND †WM Penman (*Utd Servs*); JRS Innes (*Aberdeen U*), DJ Macrae (*St Andrews U*), RW Shaw* (*Glasgow HSFP*), KC Fyfe (*London Scot*); RB Bruce Lockhart (*Cambridge U*), TF Dorward (*Gala*); †IC Henderson (*Edinburgh Acs*), †IN Graham (*Edinburgh Acs*), W Purdie (*Jed-Forest*), GB Horsburgh (*London Scot*), A Roy (*Waterloo*), GD Shaw (*Sale*), †DKA Mackenzie (*Edinburgh Wdrs*), WB Young (*King's Coll H*)

IRELAND CJ Murphy (*Lansdowne*); VJ Lyttle (*Bedford*), JD Torrens (*Bohemians*), HR McKibbin (*Instonians*), FG Morran (*Clontarf*); GE Cromey (*QU Belfast*), GJ Morgan* (*Old Belvedere*); TA Headon (*UC Dublin*), C Teehan (*UC Cork*), HJM Sayers (*Lansdowne & Army*), JG Ryan (*UC Dublin*), DB O'Loughlin (*Garryowen*), RB Mayne (*Malone*), R Alexander (*RUC*), JWS Irwin (*NIFC*)

REFEREE CH Gadney (*England*)

SCORING Moran, try (0–3); McKibbin, pen (0–6); Sayers, mark (0–9) (half-time) Innes, try (3–9); Torrens, try (3–12)

In the first half Scotland faced into pelting showers of rain and sleet. The field churned-up badly and the players became barely distinguishable from each other. The Scots gave a fighting display and were a little unlucky to lose, but the fiery Irish forwards revelled in the conditions and the game was largely one of tearaway rushes and courageous defence. The Scots made a promising start, but very soon the Irish forwards began to assert themselves. After some 15 minutes, winger Moran followed-up a forward rush to score out wide. McKibbin added a penalty and just before the interval Sayers, the Irish flanker, marked the ball from a poor clearance and kicked an unlikely goal. In the second half, Macrae missed a long penalty attempt, having first wiped the ball and his boot with a clean handkerchief that he kept in his pocket. From the ensuing scramble, Bruce Lockhart attempted a drop goal that seemed to be going over until a gust of wind swirled it against the post. The Scots absorbed more pressure and with 15 minutes left they scored the best try of the game. Wilson Shaw broke between the Irish centres and fed Macrae who gave a perfect pass to Innes and the winger raced over. The Irish forwards continued to press and Torrens scored the clinching try after a kick ahead.

191 INTERNATIONAL CHAMPIONSHIP 1939 ENGLAND

Murrayfield · Saturday 18 March 1939 · Lost 6–9

SCOTLAND G Roberts (*Watsonians*); JRS Innes (*Aberdeen U*), DJ Macrae (*St Andrews U*), RW Shaw* (*Glasgow HSFP*), WCW Murdoch (*Hillhead HSFP*); RB Bruce Lockhart (*London Scot*), TF Dorward (*Gala*); IC Henderson (*Edinburgh Acs*), IN Graham (*Edinburgh Acs*), W Purdie (*Jed-Forest*), GB Horsburgh (*London Scot*), A Roy (*Waterloo*), WB Young (*King's Coll H*), WH Crawford (*Utd Servs*), DKA Mackenzie (*Edinburgh Wdrs*)

ENGLAND EI Parsons (*RAF*); RH Guest (*Waterloo & Liverpool U*), J Heaton (*Waterloo*), GE Hancock (*Birkenhead Park*), RSL Carr (*Old Cranleighans*); TA Kemp (*St Mary's H*), J Ellis (*Wakefield*); DE Teden (*Richmond*), HB Toft* (*Waterloo*), RE Prescott (*Harlequins*), HF Wheatley (*Coventry*), TF Huskisson (*OMT*), JK Watkins (*RN*), JTW Berry (*Leicester*), RM Marshall (*Harlequins & Oxford U*)

REFEREE I David (*Wales*)

SCORING Murdoch, try (3–0); Shaw, try (6–0); Heaton, pen (6–3); Heaton, pen (6–6) (half-time) Heaton, pen (6–9)

In a rather dreary match, Scotland scored two tries to none, but England deserved to win. The English forwards controlled possession, although their backs were unimaginative and easily contained. The Scots, by contrast, were alert and full of running,

This Scottish team lost to England at Murrayfield in March 1939, the last rugby international before the Second World War. *SRU*

especially Murdoch, Macrae and Shaw who moved to stand-off in the second half. Murdoch scored a brilliant opening try when he pounced on a crosskick by Innes near halfway and made a long run to the line. Crawford's conversion was disallowed as he was adjudged to have touched the ball illegally once he had set it up. Shaw also scored a great try when he accelerated and dummied through the defence before hurling himself over the line with his confused opponents running into each other. Then Heaton kicked two long range penalties to level the score and early in the second half added the winning goal. Murdoch narrowly missed a drop goal attempt and at the finish Bruce Lockhart made a good break, but fatally delayed his pass to Innes. This was the final championship match before the outbreak of the Second World War and Scotland's last full international for eight years.

XV ∙ SERVICES INTERNATIONAL ∙ ENGLAND SERVICES

Inverleith · Saturday 21 March 1942 · Won 21–6

SCOTLAND SERVICES WCW Murdoch (*Army & Hillhead HSFP*); JRS Innes (*Army & Aberdeen GSFP*), WH Munro (*Army & Glasgow HSFP*), EC Hunter (*RAF & Watsonians*), ECK Douglas (*Edinburgh U*); T Gray (*Army & Heriot's FP*), MR Dewar (*Fleet Air Arm & Watsonians*); J Maltman (*Army & Hawick*), RM Grieve (*Army, Kelso & Acs-Wdrs*), NW Ramsay (*Army*), SGA Harper (*RN & Watsonians*), CL Melville* (*Army & London Scot*), AWB Buchanan (*Army & London Scot*), GD Shaw (*Army, Gala & Sale*), PL Duff (*Army & Glasgow Acs*)

ENGLAND SERVICES GW Parker (*Army, Gloucester & Cambridge U*); EJH Williams (*Army & Cambridge U*), S Brogden (*Army & Hull RL*), H Kenyon (*RAF & Coventry*), GA Hollis (*RN & Oxford U*); J Ellis (*Army & Wakefield*), GA Walker (*RAF & Blackheath*); RE Prescott* (*Army & Harlequins*), CG Gilthorpe (*RAF & Coventry*), RJ Longland (*RAF & Northampton*), TF Huskisson (*Army & OMTs*), RJL Hammond (*RN*), JK Watkins (*RN*), WT Reynolds (*RAF & Bristol*), CL Newton-Thompson (*Army & Cambridge U*)

REFEREE AM Buchanan (*Ireland*)

SCORING Shaw, try (3–0); Dewar, try (6–0); Murdoch, con (8–0) (half-time) Parker, pen (8–3); Murdoch, drop (12–3); Ellis, try (12–6); Gray, try (15–6); Murdoch, con (17–6); Murdoch, drop (21–6)

The outbreak of the Second World War in September 1939 brought an end to meaningful rugby. Unlike the First World War, when rugby came to an almost complete stop, clubs were encouraged to continue as best they could. It was felt that sports could help to maintain morale and provide a welcome respite from the rigours of war as well as keeping young men fit and active. Some Scottish clubs amalgamated temporarily, such the Academicals-Wanderers in Edinburgh or Kelvinside-West in Glasgow. Equipment was very scarce and the majority of players were unavailable. Murrayfield was taken over as a military supply depot. International rugby was, of course, also curtailed, including an Australian tour of the British Isles which was scheduled for season 1939–40 but never took place. During the war, Scotland played a series of 'Services Internationals' against England with home and away fixtures at the end of each season. International caps were not awarded for these matches, but both countries took them seriously and tried to field strong sides, including pre-war internationalists, foreign guests and leading rugby league professionals, the old antagonisms between the two codes having been temporarily forgotten. For the first match of the series, which was played at Inverleith, the old international ground, England included Stan Brogden, the Leeds, Huddersfield and Great Britain Rugby League three-quarter. Scotland, with six pre-war caps, won a surprisingly large victory thanks to spirited forward play and plenty of enterprise by the back division. Two drop goals by Murdoch, still worth four points at this time, slightly flattered the Scots, but they were worthy winners. The forwards stood-up well in the scrums, especially hooker Bob Grieve, and were much livelier in the loose. England defended well, but their backs were unimaginative in attack. Scotland had most of the early pressure and after 26 minutes the three-quarters combined to send wing forward Shaw galloping over for the first try. Towards the interval, the Scottish forwards made a rousing rush which ended with a try by Dewar. In the second half, Parker kicked a penalty for England before Murdoch dropped his first goal around the hour mark. England responded with a try by stand-off Ellis and then his opposite number Gray weaved his way through the defence for a try. Just before the final whistle Murdoch dropped another goal. *The Scotsman* concluded: 'With the play always of a high standard and exciting there was plenty of noise from the crowd. Indeed, many a full-scale international has been less entertaining.'

 XV   SERVICES INTERNATIONAL   ENGLAND SERVICES

Wembley Stadium, London · Saturday 11 April 1942 · Won 8–5

SCOTLAND SERVICES WCW Murdoch (*Army & Hillhead HSFP*); JB Craig (*Army & Heriot's FP*), DA Roberts (*Acs-Wdrs*), EC Hunter (*RAF & Watsonians*), ECK Douglas (*Edinburgh U*); T Gray (*Army & Heriot's FP*), MR Dewar (*Fleet Air Arm & Watsonians*); J Maltman (*Army & Hawick*), RM Grieve (*Army, Kelso & Acs-Wdrs*), NW Ramsay (*Army*), JB McNeil (*Glasgow HSFP*), CL Melville* (*Army & London Scot*), AWB Buchanan (*London Scot*), GD Shaw (*Army, Gala & Sale*), PL Duff (*Army & Glasgow Acs*)

Scotland attempt to escape from their own line during the Services International at Wembley Stadium in 1942.

ENGLAND SERVICES R Rankin (*RAF & NSW*); GA Hollis (*RN & Oxford U*), AC Simmonds (*RN*), PRH Hastings (*Army & Oxford U*), AL Evans (*Army, Cambridge U & Rosslyn Park*); J Ellis (*Army & Wakefield*), H Kenyon (*RAF & Coventry*); RE Prescott* (*Army & Harlequins*), CG Gilthorpe (*RAF & Coventry*), RJ Longland (*RAF & Northampton*), TF Huskisson (*Army & OMTs*), J Mycock (*RAF & Harlequins*), E Hodgson (*Army & Broughton Rgrs*), WT Reynolds (*RAF & Bristol*), W Fallowfieid (*RAF & Northampton*)

REFEREE CH Gadney (*England*)

SCORING Ellis, try (0–3); Rankin, con (0–5); Shaw, try (3–5); Murdoch, con (5–5) (half-time) Dewar, try (8–5)

The return match of the series was played at Wembley Stadium in front of around 20,000 enthusiastic spectators. England probably should have won this match, as their forwards dominated the scrums, but their backs were too individualistic and did not combine very well. By contrast, the Scottish backs, who had much less ball to work with, were always lively, especially Gray and Dewar, the nippy half-backs. At full-back, Murdoch's anticipation, defence and touch-kicking were first class. The Scottish forwards were aggressive in the loose and they won their share of ball at the lineout. However, the star of the show was England full-back Ron Rankin, an Australian international, who used his power and weight to great advantage, once leaving three Scottish forwards prostrate on the ground before him. England opened the scoring after about 25 minutes when scrum-half Ellis broke away from a scrum and raced 30 yards for a try converted by Rankin. Shortly before the interval, Scotland drew level against the run of play. Gray made a swerving run before passing to Hunter who was tackled a few yards short of the line, but managed to find Shaw who scored near the posts. Murdoch converted and at the beginning of the second half the Scots made several attacks which ended with Dewar dashing through for an unconverted try. England fought hard to save the game, but the Scots, after some close shaves, managed to hold out.

Inverleith · Saturday 27 February 1943 · Lost 6–29

SCOTLAND SERVICES WCW Murdoch (*Hillhead HSFP*); TGH Jackson (*Army & Cheltenham*), ECK Douglas (*Edinburgh U*), WH Munro (*Army & Glasgow HSFP*), JRS Innes (*Aberdeen GSFP*); T Gray (*Army & Heriot's FP*), JM Blair (*Acs-Wdrs & Oxford U*); WF Blackadder (*W of Scot*), IN Graham (*Army & Acs-Wdrs*), NW Ramsay (*Army*), D Maltman (*Army & Hawick*), R Cowe (*Melrose*), C McLay (*Acs-Wdrs*), GD Shaw (*Gala & Sale*), CL Melville* (*Army & London Scot*)

ENGLAND SERVICES E Ward (*Army & Bradford Northern RL*); EJ Unwin (*Army & Rosslyn Park*), J Lawrenson (*RAF & Wigan RL*), MM Walford (*Army & Oxford U*), RL Francis (*Army & Dewsbury RL*); FJC Reynolds (*Army & Old Cranleighans*), J Ellis (*Army & Wakefield*); RJ Longland (*RAF & Northampton*), BJ McMaster (*RAF & Bedford*), RE Prescott* (*Army & Harlequins*), J Mycock (*RAF & Harlequins*), RS Hall (*St Bart's H*), EH Sadler (*RAF & Castleford RL*), G Hudson (*RAF & Gloucester*), CL Newton-Thompson (*Army & Cambridge U*)

REFEREE AM Buchanan (*Ireland*)

SCORING Munro, try (3–0); Newton-Thompson, try (3–3); Ward, con (3–5); Munro, try (6–5); Walford, try (6–8) (half-time) In the second half, Lawrenson (3), Francis and Saddler scored tries and Ward converted three of them.

England fielded five rugby league players, four in the back division. The first half was evenly contested, but after the interval England stretched away and won a convincing victory. The English forwards were well on top in the scrums and lively in loose play. Blessed with a plentiful supply of ball, their backs were full of pace and made the most of their opportunities. Reynolds and Ellis, the English half-backs were very prominent and the rugby league imports brought thrust and dynamism to the attack. Centre Johnny Lawrenson, an England league international, scored three tries in the second half, and his hard straight running caused nightmares for the Scottish defence. Powerful Dewsbury winger Roy Francis was always dangerous and Ernest Ward, the Bradford Northern favourite, was intrusive from full-back. The Scots fought courageously, but were outplayed. Their cause was not helped by a leg injury to winger Jackson who could only limp about in the second half.

Action from a Services International at Inverleith in the 1940s. Note the attractive press box in the background, a feature of the old ground.

Welford Road, Leicester · Saturday 10 April 1943 · Lost 19–24

SCOTLAND SERVICES WG Biggart (*Army & Glasgow Acs*); E Grant (*RNZAF*), ECK Douglas (*Army & Edinburgh U*), CR Bruce* (*Army & Glasgow Acs*), JRS Innes (*Army & Aberdeen GSFP*); T Gray (*Army & Heriot's FP*), JM Blair (*Army & Acs-Wdrs*); J Maltman (*Army & Hawick*), IN Graham (*Army & Acs-Wdrs*), MD Kennedy (*Army & Acs-Wdrs*), CL Melville (*Army & London Scot*), J McNeill (*Army & Glasgow HSFP*), PL Duff (*Army & Glasgow Acs*), GD Shaw (*Army, Sale & Gala*), JA Waters (*Army & Selkirk*)

ENGLAND SERVICES RT Campbell (*St Mary's H*); G Hollis (*RN*), J Lawrenson (*RAF & Wigan RL*), J Stott (*Army & St Helens RL*), RL Francis (*Army & Barrow RL*); PRH Hastings (*Army*), J Parsons (*RAF & Leicester*); GT Dancer (*RAF & Bedford*), RJ Longland (*RAF & Northampton*), RE Prescott* (Army & *Harlequins*), GPC Vallance (*Army & Leicester*), RL Hall (*RN & St Bart's H*), EH Sadler (*RAF & Castleford RL*), G Hudson (*RAF & Gloucester*), DLK Milman (*Army & Bedford*)

REFEREE I David (*Wales*)

SCORING Hollis, try (0–3); Lawrenson, try (0–6); Stott, con (0–8); Innes, try (3–8); Shaw, con (5–8); Bruce, try (8–8) (half-time) Hastings, try (8–11); Parsons, try (8–14); Stott, try (8–17); Stott, drop (8–21); Innes, try (11–21); Shaw, try (14–21); Shaw, con (16–21); Kennedy, try (19–21); Francis, try (19–24)

This was a fast and open encounter played at a hectic pace. The English forwards had the better of the game, but the Scots showed lots of enterprise, especially in midfield, and did well to make two strong recoveries. Both sides lost a player to injury in the first half and had only 14 men for much of the game. Scottish forward McNeill was hurt straight away and after 25 minutes Lawrenson, the England wing, was injured in a tackle and had to go off. Hollis, the other wing, was reduced to a passenger for most of the second half. Once again England included several rugby league players and raced to an early lead, but Scotland recovered well and the scores were even at the interval. In the second half, England seized the initiative and scored three unconverted tries and a drop goal. Scotland made another heroic recovery and pulled back to within two points, but a late try by Francis sealed a deserved win for England.

Murrayfield · Saturday 26 February 1944 · Lost 13–23

SCOTLAND SERVICES WCW Murdoch (*Army & Hillhead HSFP*); JRS Innes (*Aberdeen GSFP*), WH Munro (*Army & Glasgow HSFP*), CR Bruce (*Army & Glasgow Acs*), AE Murray (*Oxford U*); T Gray (*Army & Heriot's FP*), JM Blair (*Oxford U*); HH Campbell (*Cambridge U*), JDH Hastie (*Melrose*), R Cowe (*Army & Melrose*), CL Melville (*Army & London Scot*), FH Coutts (*Army & Melrose*), GD Shaw (*Army & Gala*), JR McClure (*Ayr & Wasps*), JA Waters* (*Army & Selkirk*)

ENGLAND SERVICES E Ward (*Bradford Northern RL & Army*); G Hollis (*RN & Sale*), J Lawrenson (*RAF & Wigan RL*), J Stott (*Army & St Helens RL*), RL Francis (*Army & Dewsbury RL*); PR Hastings (*Army*), J Parsons (*RAF & Leicester*); RE Prescott* (*Army & Harlequins*), RJ Longland (*RAF & Northampton*), I Dustin (*RNZAF*), J Mycock (*RAF & Harlequins*),

JB Doherty (*RN & Manchester*), G Hudson (*RAF & Gloucester*), RGH Weighill (*RAF & Waterloo*), GT Dancer (*RAF & Bedford*)

REFEREE AM Buchanan (*Ireland*)

SCORING Gray, pen (3–0); Parsons, try (3–3); Hudson, try (3–6); Lawrenson, con (3–8); Stott, drop (3–12); Hudson, try (3–15); Hudson, try (3–18); Lawrenson, con (3–20) (half-time) Hudson, try (3–23); Gray, try (6–23); Murdoch, con (8–23); Blair, try (11–23); Murdoch, con (13–23)

In the first international match at Murrayfield for five years, England fielded several rugby league professionals in their back division and were comfortable winners. Their forwards gained an early mastery and built-up a big lead before a late Scottish revival. Blessed with a plentiful supply of ball, the English backs had many opportunities to show their paces and they exposed some weak Scottish tackling, especially in midfield. Hudson, the Gloucester back-row player, scored four tries and his roving work about the field was reminiscent of the great Kingsholm marauder Tom Voyce. Scotland opened the scoring with a Gray penalty goal and the visitors responded with a scoring blitz to lead 20–3 at the interval. Hudson scored another try for England early in the second half and a cricket score looked likely, but then the Scots made a spirited fight-back. Gray scored a try after a strong run by Munro and right at the finish Blair crossed for a try. Murdoch added the extras with the last kick of the game.

  SERVICES INTERNATIONAL   **ENGLAND SERVICES**

Welford Road, Leicester · Saturday 18 March 1944 · Lost 15–27

SCOTLAND SERVICES WCW Murdoch (*Army & Hillhead HSFP*); JRS Innes (*Army & Aberdeen GSFP*), WH Munro (*Army & Glasgow HSFP*), E Grant (*RNZAF*), HG Uren (*Glasgow Acs*); CR Bruce (*Army & Glasgow Acs*), E Anderson (*Stewart's FP & Cambridge U*); HH Campbell (*Cambridge U*), JR McClure (*Ayr & Wasps*), R Cowe (*Army & Melrose*), CL Melville (*Army & London Scot*), FH Coutts (*Army & Melrose*), JB Lees (*Gala*), GD Shaw (*Gala & Sale*), JA Waters* (*Army & Selkirk*)

ENGLAND SERVICES E Ward (*Army & Bradford Northern RL*); G Hollis (*RN & Sale*), LE Oakley (*Army & Bedford*), J Stott (*Army & St Helens RL*), RL Francis (*Army & Dewsbury RL*); PR Hastings (*Army*), J Parsons (*RAF & Leicester*); GT Dancer (*RAF & Bedford*), RJ Longland (*RAF & Northampton*), RE Prescott* (*Army & Harlequins*), J Mycock (*RAF & Harlequins*), JB Doherty (*RN & Sale*), G Hudson (*RAF & Gloucester*), FW Gilbert (*Army & Coventry*) RGH Weighill (*RAF & Waterloo*)

REFEREE CH Gadney (*England*)

SCORING Ward, pen (0–3); Hudson, try (0–6); Stott, con (0–8); Innes, try (3–8); Hollis, try (3–11) (half-time) Cowe, pen (6–11); Oakley, try (6–14); Stott, con (6–16); Murdoch, drop (10–16); Hastings, try (10–19); Francis, try (10–22); Stott, con (10–24); Francis, try (10–27); Coutts, try (13–27); Cowe, con (15–27)

The English forwards were well on top both in the scrums and in loose play. The Scottish defence was generally solid and it was only late in the game that England stretched away as the Scots grew tired. Bruce and Anderson, the new Scottish halves, combined well and the three-quarters looked dangerous, but they were starved of possession. A crowd of around 18,000 saw England take an early lead with a Ward penalty goal from midfield. Then Hudson scored his fifth try in two matches against Scotland. Innes replied with a try, but a minute later Hollis dashed over in the corner. There was no more scoring in the first half. *The Leicester Mercury* reported: 'It was like old times at Tigers' Ground when Tom Goodrich brought out the oranges at the interval, amid great cheering.' Ten minutes after the restart, Cowe kicked a penalty for Scotland which was followed by a converted English try. Scotland had a spell of pressure on the English line and Murdoch dropped a goal, but the Scots faded away badly and the home side ran in three further tries. Towards the end, Coutts dribbled over for a consolation try.

SERVICES INTERNATIONAL   ENGLAND SERVICES

Welford Road, Leicester · Saturday 24 February 1945 · Won 18–11

SCOTLAND SERVICES KI Geddes (*Wasps & RAF*); JB Nicholls (*NSW & RAAF*), JR Henderson (*Army & Glasgow Acs*), WD MacLennan (*RN & Watsonians*), E Grant (*RNZAF*); DD Mackenzie (*RAF & Merchistonians*), AW Black (*Edinburgh U*); JR McClure (*Army & Ayr*), JDH Hastie (*Army & Melrose*), TPL McGlashan (*Army & Royal HSFP*), C Wilhelm (*SA Services*), RM McKenzie (*NZ Servs*), JH Orr (*RAF & Heriot's FP*), JAD Thom (*Army, Hawick & London Scot*), FAL Barcroft (*RAF & Heriot's FP*)

ENGLAND SERVICES E Ward (*Army & Bradford Northern RL*); RJ Forbes (*RAF & Heaton Park*), MP Goddard (*RNZAF*), E Ruston (*RN*), G Hollis (*RN & Sale*); RE Bibby (*RN*), J Parsons (*RAF & Leicester*); RJ Longland (*RAF & Northampton*), CG Gilthorpe (*RAF*), FP Dunkley (*Army*), J Mycock (*RAF & Harlequins*), JB Docherty (*RN & Sale*), E Bedford (*RAF*), RGH Weighill (*Waterloo & RAF*), JD Robins (*RN*)

REFEREE I Jones (*Wales*)

SCORING RM Mackenzie, try (3–0); Geddes, con (5–0); Ward, pen (5–3); Grant, try (8–3); Geddes, con (10–3) (half-time) MacLennan, try (13–3); Ward, try (13–6); Orr, try (16–6); Geddes, con (18–6); Goddard, try (18–9); Gilthorpe, con (18–11)

After four successive defeats in the war-time series, Scotland won an unexpected but well deserved victory over a lacklustre English side. Scotland fielded a youthful and enthusiastic team that included All Black forward Rod McKenzie and several colonial players. They were forced to make some late changes and play Australian JB Nicholls on the right wing although he was usually a forward. The Scottish pack matched their more experienced opponents up-front and some of their dribbling was very effective. The Scottish backs were a better combination and showed plenty of speed and adventure in attack. Mackenzie and Black, the Scottish halves, had a fine game, and full-back Geddes was solid in defence and put in some enormous touch-finders. Scotland opened the scoring after ten minutes when Mackenzie took advantage of an English handling error. Geddes converted and Ward responded with a penalty. Shortly before the interval, Geddes and Henderson made a counter-attack to send Grant away up the right and his powerful side-step and pace beat the defence. Geddes converted to give the Scots a 10–3 lead at the break. Early in the second half, MacLennan scored after a good bout of passing. England then applied a lot of pressure and full-back Ward came up in support to score a try. There was no further scoring until the dying minutes when Orr and Goddard crossed for their respective sides.

Murrayfield · Saturday 17 March 1945 · Lost 5–16

SCOTLAND SERVICES KI Geddes* (*RAF & Wasps*); E Grant (*RNZAF*), JR Henderson (*Army & Glasgow Acs*), WD MacLennan (*RN & Watsonians*), DWC Smith (*Army & Aberdeen U*); DD McKenzie (*RAF & Merchistonians*), AW Black (*Army & Edinburgh U*); JR McClure (*Army & Ayr*), JDH Hastie (*Army & Melrose*), TPL McGlashan (*Army & Royal HSFP*), EA Melling (*Army & Old Sedberghians*), RM McKenzie (*NZ Servs*), JH Orr (*RAF & Heriot's FP*), AL Barcroft (*RAF & Heriot's FP*), JB Nicholls (*RAAF*)

ENGLAND SERVICES MTA Ackermann (*SAAF*); RJ Forbes (*RAF & Heaton Park*), MP Goddard (*RNZAF*), E Ward (*Bradford Northern RL & Army*), G Hollis* (*RN & Sale*); E Ruston (*RN*), PW Sykes (*RAF & Cambridge U*); RJ Longland (*RAF & Northampton*), CG Gilthorpe (*RAF & Wasps*), P Plumpton (*RAF & Downside Sch*), J Mycock (*RAF & Harlequins*), JB Doherty (*RN & Sale*), GA Hudson (*RAF & Gloucester*), E Bedford (*RAF & Hull KR RL*), RGH Weighill (*RAF & Waterloo*)

REFEREE AM Buchanan (*Ireland*)

SCORING Hollis, try (0–3); Hollis, try (0–6); Ward, con (0–8); MacLennan, try (3–8); Geddes, con (5–8) (half-time) Hollis, try (5–11); Hudson, try (5–14); Gilthorpe, con (5–16)

An experienced England side were convincing winners of the final match of the series. They were a better balanced team and their forwards held an advantage in the scrums and in the loose. England had to make a late change with Sykes coming in at scrum-half, but their half-backs combined effectively. Ernest Ward, the Bradford Northern league player, revelled in his new role at centre where he showed a sharp eye for an opening and had some strong runs. Both full-backs, Ackermann and Geddes, gave excellent displays and their long raking touch-finders were one of the best features of the match. Scotland lacked cohesion in attack and their backs were always under pressure, but they worked hard in defence. Hollis scored two early tries for England, the second converted by Ward, before the Scots responded with a fine try of their own. Geddes fielded a kick and made a long diagonal run before finding MacLennan who cut back inside and forced his way over the line. The Scots were under increasing pressure as the game progressed and made only the occasional flurry in attack. England scored two further tries and should have won by more but for stout Scottish defending.

XV   VICTORY INTERNATIONAL   NEW ZEALAND ARMY

Murrayfield · Saturday 19 January 1946 · Won 11–6

SCOTLAND KI Geddes* (*London Scot*); J Anderson (*London Scot*), WH Munro (*Glasgow HSFP & Army*), CR Bruce (*Glasgow Acs & Army*), DWC Smith (*Aberdeen U*); IJM Lumsden (*Watsonians*), AW Black (*Edinburgh U*); IC Henderson (*Acs-Wdrs*), GG Lyall (*Gala*), R Aitken (*London Scot*), AGM Watt (*Acs-Wdrs*), J Kirk (*Acs-Wdrs*), WID Elliot (*Acs-Wdrs*), JH Orr (*Edinburgh City Police*), DW Deas (*Heriot's FP*)

NEW ZEALAND ARMY HE Cooke (*Hawkes Bay*); JR Sherratt (*Wellington*), JB Smith (*N Auckland*), WG Argus (*Canterbury*); FR Allen (*Canterbury*), JC Kearney (*Otago*); CK Saxton* (*Southland*); NJ McPhail (*Canterbury*), FN Haigh (*Wellington*), JG Simpson (*Auckland*),

Captained by Keith Geddes, this Scottish XV defeated the New Zealand Army at Murrayfield in January 1946. *SRU*

KD Arnold (*N Auckland*), SW Woolley (*Marlborough*), SL Young (*N Auckland*), J Finlay (*Manawatu*), AW Blake (*Hawkes Bay*)

REFEREE GD Gadney (*England*)

SCORING Woolley, try (0–3) (half-time) Anderson, try (3–3); Munro, try (6–3); Smith, con (8–3); Cooke, pen (8–6); Anderson, try (11–6)

With hostilities over, rugby slowly came back to life and resumed its familiar pre-war pattern. The International Championship was not held in 1946, but instead there were a series of 'Victory Internationals' between the Home Unions, France and a touring New Zealand Army side. These were regarded as unofficial matches and the Scots did not award caps, but they attracted big crowds who were eager for some colour and normality, and did much to revive interest in the game. Scotland had some outstanding victories in these matches, in particular in their opening encounter against the New Zealand 'Kiwis'. The tourists were drawn from New Zealand soldiers serving in Europe and included some past or future All Blacks. Their captain and scrum-half Charlie Saxton had won three caps back in 1938. Playing in the famous black strip, the New Zealanders were unbeaten after 16 matches in Britain and were expected to win, but the Scots rose to the occasion. In a hard and exciting encounter, the Scottish forwards were fast and lively, their footwork was very effective and they stood-up well in the scrums against bigger opponents. Douglas Elliot was, in the words of *The Times*, 'a veritable demon of destructiveness' and always ready to break with the ball at his feet or join in the handling movements. The Scottish backs showed plenty of confidence and fighting spirit. Keith Geddes gave a fine display at full-back, the three-quarters were always threatening and defended soundly, and scrum-half Black was excellent against the experienced Saxton. New Zealand started strongly and about midway through the first half Woolley scored an unconverted try from a forward rush. Scotland had some pressure, but there was no further scoring before the interval. Against expectations, the Scots kept firm control in the second period and around the hour mark Bruce made a break to send Hawick's Darcy Anderson, a professional sprinter, over at the corner. A few minutes later, Munro drew the defence before dashing over for a try converted by Smith. Cooke responded with a penalty goal and in the dying minutes Anderson raced onto a crosskick by Bruce to seal a historic victory for the Scots. Immediately after the match, Anderson, the two-try hero, signed professional forms with Huddersfield.

VICTORY INTERNATIONAL   WALES

St Helen's, Swansea · Saturday 2 February 1946 · Won 25–6

SCOTLAND KI Geddes* (*London Scot*); CW Drummond (*Melrose*), WH Munro (*Glasgow HSFP & Army*), CR Bruce (*Glasgow Acs & Army*), DWC Smith (*Aberdeen U*); IJM Lumsden (*Watsonians*), AW Black (*Edinburgh U*); IC Henderson (*Acs-Wdrs*), GG Lyall (*Gala*), R Aitken (*London Scot*), AGM Watt (*Acs-Wdrs*), J Kirk (*Acs-Wdrs*), WID Elliot (*Acs-Wdrs*), JH Orr (*Heriot's FP*), DW Deas (*Heriot's FP*)

WALES RF Trott (*Penarth*); WLT Williams (*Llanelli & Devonport Servs*), J Matthews* (*Cardiff*), BL Williams (*Cardiff*), WE Williams (*Newport*); GR Davies (*Pontypridd Co Sch*), W Davies (*Cardiff U & Pontypridd*); G Bevan (*Llanelli*), M James (*Cardiff*), FE Morris (*Pill Harriers & Newport*), R Hughes (*Aberavon*), G Hughes (*Neath*), DH Steer (*Abercarn & Taunton*), L Manfield (*Cardiff*), JRG Stephens (*Neath*)

REFEREE HLV Day (*England*)

SCORING Elliot, try (3–0); Bruce, try (6–0); Geddes, con (8–0); Drummond, try (11–0); Orr, try (14–0); Geddes, con (16–0) (half-time) G Davies, try (16–3); Elliot, try (19–3); G Bevan, try (19–6); Black, try (22–6); Geddes, pen (25–6)

In one of their best performances for years, Scotland followed-up their surprise win over the Kiwis with this resounding six try victory in Swansea. The Scottish forwards took control from the start and the whole side was full of brilliant running and adventure. On a wet pitch and with the elements in their favour, the Scots completely outplayed their opponents in the first half and scored four well-taken tries to lead 16–0 at the interval. In the second half, Wales, to their credit, made something of a recovery and for a spell put the Scots under pressure. The Welsh forwards, who had been well beaten in the opening period, started to win more possession and after ten minutes schoolboy stand-off Glyn Davies broke away for a thrilling solo try. However, the Scots never quite lost their grip on the game and their courageous defence kept the dangerous Welsh backs firmly in check. Inside the last quarter, Black made a neat run and Elliot supported him to score. Wales responded with a try in the corner by Bevan, but the Scots had the last word with a fine individual try by Black and a late penalty goal by Geddes. This was a great team effort by Scotland for whom scrum-half Black had an excellent match and Elliot was always in the thick of the action.

VICTORY INTERNATIONAL   IRELAND

Murrayfield · Saturday 23 February 1946 · Won 9–0

SCOTLAND KI Geddes* (*London Scot*); CW Drummond (*Melrose*), WH Munro (*Glasgow*

HSFP & Army), CR Bruce (*Glasgow Acs & Army*), DWC Smith (*Aberdeen U*); IJM Lumsden (*Watsonians*), AW Black (*Edinburgh U*); IC Henderson (*Acs-Wdrs*), GG Lyall (*Gala*), R Aitken (*London Scot*), JR McClure (*Ayr*), J Kirk (*Acs-Wdrs*), WID Elliott (*Acs-Wdrs*), JH Orr (*Heriot's FP*), DW Deas (*Heriot's FP*)

IRELAND   CJ Murphy* (*Lansdowne*); FG Moran (*Clontarf*), T Coveney (*St Mary's Coll*), KJ Quinn (*Old Belvedere*), BT Quinn (*Old Belvedere*); EA Carry (*Old Wesley*), E Strathdee (*QU Belfast*); JC Corcoran (*UC Cork*), KD Mullen (*Old Belvedere*), MR Neely (*RN*), CP Callan (*Lansdowne*), E Keeffe (*Sunday's Well*), D McCourt (*Instonians*), DJ Hingerty (*Lansdowne*), HG Dudgeon (*Collegians*)

REFEREE   I Jones (*Wales*)

SCORING   Munro, try (3–0); Geddes, con (5–0) (half-time) Lumsden, drop (9–0)

In a strenuously fought encounter, Ireland were much stronger than expected and almost managed to put the Scots off their stride. The spirited Irish forwards held the advantage almost throughout, but their backs were unimaginative and laboured in attack. They kicked away too much possession and were unable to escape from a sound Scottish defence. Scotland played into a strong and troublesome wind in the first half and, after weathering some early Irish attacks, took the lead around the tenth minute. Elliot made a long run from inside his own half before kicking ahead. The ball was quickly recycled and Munro cut inside in for a try which Geddes converted. Ireland were persistent and caused the Scots some anxious moments, but were unable to score. Around the hour mark, Geddes hit the crossbar with a long penalty attempt and soon after Lumsden dropped a goal following a swift heel from a scrum.

 XV   VICTORY INTERNATIONAL   ENGLAND

Twickenham · Saturday 16 March 1946 · Lost 8–12

SCOTLAND   KI Geddes* (*London Scot*); CW Drummond (*Melrose*), WH Munro (*Glasgow HSFP & Army*), CR Bruce (*Glasgow Acs & Army*), JRS Innes (*Aberdeen GSFP*): IJM Lumsden (*Watsonians*), KSH Wilson (*Watsonians & London Scot*); IC Henderson (*Acs-Wdrs*), GG Lyall (*Gala*), R Aitken (*London Scot*), AGM Watt (*Acs-Wdrs*), J Kirk (*Acs-Wdrs*), WID Elliot (*Acs-Wdrs*), JH Orr (Heriot's FP), DW Deas (*Heriot's FP*)

ENGLAND   HJM Uren (*Waterloo*); RSL Carr (*Manchester*), J Heaton* (*Waterloo*), EK Scott (*St Mary's H*), HF Greasley (*Coventry*); NM Hall (*St Mary's H*), WKT Moore (*Devonport Servs & Leicester*); TW Price (*Gloucester*), FCH Hill (*Bristol*), GA Kelly (*Bedford*), J Mycock (*Sale*), HR Peel (*Headingley*), DB Vaughan (*RNE Coll*), JW Thornton (*Gloucester*), E Bole (*Cambridge U*)

REFEREE   I David (*Wales*)

SCORING   Innes, try (3–0); Bruce, try (6–0); Geddes, con (8–0) (half-time) Heaton, pen (8–3); Carr, try (8–6); Heaton, con (8–8); Scott, drop (8–12)

Scotland's winning run in the Victory Internationals came to end on a cold afternoon at Twickenham. After the traumas of the war, rugby was returning to its old self and the large crowd saw an exciting match with lots of open play, three well-taken tries and a dramatic conclusion. The Scots had by far the better of the first half and led 8–0 at the interval, but after that England were firmly in control. Scotland's two tries were classics. After about 16 minutes, Bruce sold a dummy and broke away from his own half. He passed to Innes on the English 10-yards line and the Aberdeen winger outstripped two defenders on his way to score. Shortly afterwards, Elliot kicked ahead outside the English 25 and Bruce raced onto the bouncing ball for a try near the posts. Near the end of the half, Wilson made a break and put Lumsden away, but a Heaton tackle prevented a certain score. Early in the second half, Heaton, who had won the corresponding match with three goal kicks in 1939, kicked a fine angled penalty. Then England won a lineout deep in the Scottish 25 and slick passing put right winger Carr over in the corner. Heaton kicked a touchline conversion to level the scores. The English forwards were well on top and inside the last ten minutes Scott kicked the winning drop goal. Scotland fought bravely to save the game and near the end a mammoth drop goal attempt by Geddes fell just under the crossbar. At the finish of a great match a draw would have been a fairer result.

 XV VICTORY INTERNATIONAL WALES

Murrayfield · Saturday 30 March 1946 · Won 13–11

SCOTLAND KI Geddes (*London Scot*); CW Drummond (*Melrose*), WH Munro (*Glasgow HSFP & Army*), CR Bruce (*Glasgow Acs & Army*), JRS Innes (*Aberdeen GSFP*); IJM Lumsden (*Watsonians*), AW Black (*Edinburgh U*); IC Henderson (*Acs-Wdrs*), GG Lyall (*Gala*), R Aitken (*London Scot*), AGM Watt (*Acs-Wdrs*), FH Coutts (*Melrose*), WID Elliot (*Acs-Wdrs*), JH Orr (*Heriot's FP*), DW Deas* (*Heriot's FP*)

WALES T Griffiths (*Newport*); WLT Williams (*Devonport Servs*), BL Williams (*Cardiff*), J Matthews (*Cardiff*), WE Williams (*Newport*); WB Cleaver (*Cardiff*), H Tanner* (*Swansea*); JH Bale (*Newport*), WJ Evans (*Pontypool*), C Davies (*Cardiff*), DJ Davies (*Swansea*), GW Parsons (*Abertillery*), L Manfield (*Cardiff*), H Jones (*Cardiff*), RT Evans (*Newport*)

REFEREE JBG Whittaker (*England*)

SCORING Jones, try (0–3); Cleaver, con (0–5); Drummond, try (3–5); Geddes, con (5–5) (half-time) WE Williams, try (5–8); Geddes, pen (8–8); WLT Williams, try (8–11); Bruce, try (11–11); Geddes, con (13–11)

In a tense struggle, Scotland trailed three times but eventually overhauled a depleted Wales who made a great effort in the closing stages and probably deserved at least a draw. The visitors started strongly and wing forward Hubert Jones scored an early try after Geddes misjudged a high kick. After about 13 minutes, Wales lost full-back Griffiths with a rib injury. Manfield took his place, but he was immediately dispossessed in a bruising Scottish forward rush from which Drummond scored a try. Wales again reshuffled and Cleaver moved to full-back, Jones, the try scorer, to the wing and Bleddyn Williams to stand-off where he played very effectively. Wales dictated the pace for the rest of the half, but were unable to score. Both sides made mistakes and the match only came to life inside the last 30 minutes. WE Williams intercepted a pass and ran in for a try, but Tanner's conversion rebounded off an upright. Geddes, who again had a good match, kicked a long penalty before Bleddyn Williams swerved through the defence and sent his namesake Les between the posts. Tanner kicked the simple conversion wide. Geddes came close to scoring after a long run from midfield and a neat kick ahead only to be beaten by an awkward bounce.

Lumsden sliced a drop goal attempt, but Bruce followed-up fast to score a try and Geddes converted to give Scotland the lead. Wales put in a storming finish, but the Scottish defence held on for a slightly fortuitous victory.

VICTORY INTERNATIONAL ENGLAND

Murrayfield · Saturday 13 April 1946 · Won 27–0

SCOTLAND KI Geddes (*London Scot*); TGH Jackson (*London Scot*), WH Munro (*Glasgow HSFP*), CR Bruce (*Glasgow Acs*), WD MacLennan (*Watsonians*); IJM Lumsden (*Watsonians*), AW Black (*Edinburgh U*); IC Henderson (*Acs-Wdrs*), GG Lyall (*Gala*), R Aitken (*London Scot*), AGM Watt (*Acs-Wdrs*), FH Coutts (*Melrose*), WID Elliot (*Acs-Wdrs*), JH Orr (*Heriot's FP*), DW Deas* (*Heriot's FP*)

ENGLAND HJM Uren (*Waterloo*); RH Guest (*Waterloo*), J Heaton* (*Waterloo*), EK Scott (*St Mary's H*), RSL Carr (*Manchester*); NM Hall (*St Mary's H*), WKT Moore (*Devonport Serv*); TW Price (*Gloucester*), FCH Hill (*Bristol*), GA Kelly (*Bedford*), J Mycock (*Sale*), HR Peel (*Headingley*), E Bole (*Cambridge U*), JW Thornton (*Gloucester*), DB Vaughan (*RNE Coll*)

REFEREE H Lambert (*Ireland*)

SCORING Watt, try (3–0); Geddes, pen (6–0); Bruce, try (9–0) (half-time) Lumsden, try (12–0); Geddes, con (14–0); Watt, try (17–0); Geddes, con (19–0); Munro, try (22–0); Geddes, con (24–0); MacLennan, try (27–0)

Scotland ended their series of Victory Internationals with a resounding six try victory over the Auld Enemy. Playing on a bright afternoon in front of a big crowd, England lost full-back Uren with a knee injury early on and Thornton came out of the forwards to take his place. The depleted English pack fought hard, but gradually faded away and the closing stages of the game were completely one-sided. The Scottish breakaway forwards were in devastating form and Douglas Elliot was again outstanding. Geddes was intrusive from full-back and the two new wingers, Jackson and MacLennan, were full of dangerous running. Scotland did not have everything their own way, but the English backs were ineffective and the normally reliable Heaton had an off-day with his kicking, although he had some good touches in attack. After five minutes, Jackson made a strong run down the right before kicking ahead. Uren lost the ball and Watt, who was always prominent, was up fast to score the opening try. Just before the interval, Carr, the English wing, was caught in possession and Bruce picked-up the loose ball and dashed over the line. Shortly after the restart, Lumsden scored a try converted by Geddes. The Scots imposed themselves towards the end and Watt scored his second try after a strong run by MacLennan. In the dying minutes, Munro and MacLennan scored further tries to complete the rout.

After the War 1947–1959

SCOTLAND'S RECORD IN the late 1940s was not too bad. They were whitewashed in the 1947 championship, the first after the war, and then won a couple of matches in each of the next three giving them mid-table respectability. Early in 1951, it seemed that Scottish rugby might have finally turned a corner. They lost their first match in Paris, but then beat a star-studded Welsh team 19–0 at Murrayfield, one of the most unexpected results in the history of the game. This should have been the start of a new era for Scotland, but instead they narrowly lost their next games against Ireland and England and finished joint bottom of the table. Nobody knew it at the time, of course, but this was the beginning of a depressing sequence of 17 games without a win for Scotland that lasted from February 1951 to February 1955. The Scottish team hit rock bottom in November 1951 when they lost 0–44 against the touring South Africans, an unprecedented score at the time. It was clear that Scottish rugby was seriously out-of-date and lagging behind rest of the world. The selectors did not help matters by some wildly inconsistent selections and never allowing the team to settle and develop. Over 30 different players were picked for the 1953 championship, including 14 new caps. Thankfully, in the following year, 1954, some there were some hopeful signs. Scotland did not win a game, but they had some close results and managed to hold Bob Stuart's All Blacks to a single penalty goal. Moreover, some new forwards emerged that would go on to form the basis of a strong pack in the second half of the 1950s, such as Hugh McLeod, Hamish Kemp, Ernie Michie and Adam Robson. The turning point came in February 1955 when Scotland beat Wales at Murrayfield thanks to a brilliant display by new winger Arthur Smith. They then beat Ireland for the first time since 1938 and, remarkably after all their recent travails, went to Twickenham to play for the Triple Crown only to lose narrowly. For the rest of the 1950s Scotland managed to win at least one game per season, hardly earth-shattering, but at least they managed to re-establish their credibility on the international scene.

Although the results were generally mediocre in the '40s and '50s, Scotland did benefit from some outstanding individual players. At full-back Ken Scotland won his first cap in 1957 and is rightly regarded as one of the greatest Scottish players of all. Slim and lightly built, he had a fine positional sense, kicked beautifully off either foot, tackled securely and fielded well. He was also a wonderful passer of the ball and pioneered the round-the-corner style of place-kicking rather than the traditional toe-bashers. He loved to attack and make perfectly-timed intrusions into the line. Scotland toured with the British Lions in 1959 and was versatile enough to play at centre in the fourth test against the All Blacks. He also played cricket for his country. Melrose's Robin Chisholm was unlucky to play around the same time as Scotland. He was a fine full-back who was known for his fearsome tackling and the ability to kick well with either foot.

Undoubtedly, the leading three-quarter of this period was Arthur Smith who burst onto the international scene with a sensational solo try against Wales in 1955. A man of many clubs, Smith was a natural athlete and a beautifully balanced runner. He captained Scotland from the wing and toured with the Lions in 1955 and 1962, the second time as captain. A highly intelligent person, he had a flourishing business career, but died aged only 42. Grant Weatherstone and Ian Swan were talented wingers who would have achieved greater things in a more successful era. Swan won 17 caps between 1953 and 1957 and was never dropped. Hawick's wayward genius George Stevenson started his career at centre before being shunted out to the wing. He had some brilliant moments, including a killer sidestep, but was too erratic and inconsistent for international level.

Scotland struggled for consistency at half-back during these years. Probably the best stand-off was Gordon Waddell who won 18 caps between 1957 and 1962, and also toured twice with the Lions. He was a gifted player and had great coolness under pressure, but he was very much a kicking stand-off and was never universally popular with the Scottish support. Earlier Glasgow High's Angus Cameron was versatile enough to play at full-back, centre and stand-off. He was renowned for his mighty boot and as a skilful handler and a forthright captain. At scrum-half, Aberdeen's Dally Allardice won eight caps between 1947 and 1949. A teacher of physical education, Allardice was short in stature, but muscular and hard. He had a flying dive-pass and loved to drop goals. He was followed by Gala's Arthur Dorward, who was the best scrum-half of the fifties, and then by Tremayne Rodd and Stan Coughtrie. Rodd was a multi-talented sportsman who had a quick break and a fearless approach to the game. At club level he turned out for London Scottish with whom he won the Middlesex Sevens five times in the 1960s.

Amongst the forwards Hawick prop Hugh McLeod was a permanent fixture in the Scottish side between 1954 and 1962. He was not a big man, but he was immensely strong with powerful legs, a high standard of fitness and strong opinions. He toured twice with the Lions and became the first Scottish player to achieve the milestone of 40 caps, breaking John Bannerman's record which had stood since the 1920s. McLeod forged a formidable partnership with Gala prop Tom Elliot who won 14 caps between 1955 and 1958. A Border livestock farmer, the craggy-faced Elliot was an intimidating presence on the field. He played hard and had seemingly limitless energy. Slightly earlier, Hamish Dawson made his debut in 1947 and won 20 caps, initially at lock before moving into the front-row. An accountant, he had a splendid physique and scored one try in Scotland's famous win over Wales in 1951. The best hooker of this period was Norman Bruce who won 31 caps between 1958 and 1964. Brought up in Galashiels, 'Bonzo' was a professional soldier and played most of his rugby in England for Blackheath, London Scottish and the Army. A tall man, he was a secure striker of the ball and, unusually for the time, had exceptional mobility. In the second-row, Ernie Michie and Hamish Kemp played together for three seasons in the mid-50s. Aberdonian Michie toured with the British Lions in 1955 and won 15 caps. His partner Kemp, who won 27 caps between 1954 and 1960, was a great line-out exponent even though he was quite light and short by the standards of an international lock.

There was never a shortage of good back-row men and the best of them all was Douglas Elliot who played 29 times between 1947 and 1954. A natural predator who breathed aggression, his long stride and destructive tackling wrecked havoc about the field. He was ideally built for a wing forward, had great footballer's skills and was rarely far from the action. Elliot was a Border sheep farmer and, in Bill McLaren's words, 'a man who made you proud to be Scottish'. Richmond's Peter Kinimonth, who always wore an old-fashioned scrum-cap, is forever identified with his glorious drop goal in the 19–0 defeat of Wales in 1951. He won 21 caps between 1949 and 1954, and toured New Zealand with the Lions in 1950 where he played in three tests. Dunfermline's Jim Greenwood, who first appeared in 1952, had great mobility and footwork, and was a great reader of the game. After his playing days, he became a leading figure in the nascent coaching movement and later wrote a seminal book *Total Rugby* which had a huge influence on modern rugby. Finally, the bald-headed Adam Robson won 22 caps between 1954 and 1960. He was a very fit player, a strong tackler and Scottish rugby's Renaissance Man. As well as playing rugby at the highest level, he wrote several history books and was a successful artist and teacher.

192   INTERNATIONAL CHAMPIONSHIP 1947   FRANCE

Stade Yves du Manoir, Colombes, Paris · Wednesday 1 January 1947
Lost 3–8

SCOTLAND †KI Geddes* (*London Scot*); †TGH Jackson (*London Scot & Army*), †CR Bruce (*Glasgow Acs*), †CW Drummond (*Melrose*), †WD MacLennan (*Utd Servs & Watsonians*); †IJM Lumsden (*Bath & Watsonians*), †AW Black (*Edinburgh U*); †AGM Watt (*Acs-Wdrs*), IC Henderson (*Acs-Wdrs*), †TPL McGlashan (*Royal HSFP*), †GL Cawkwell (*Oxford U*), †JM Hunter (*London Scot*), †WID Elliot (*Acs-Wdrs*), †JH Orr (*Edinburgh City Police*), †DW Deas (*Heriot's FP*)

FRANCE A Alvarez (*Tyrosse*); E Pebeyre (*Brive*), L Junquas* (*Bayonne*), M Sorondo (*Montauban*), J Lassègue (*Toulouse*); M Terreau (*Bressane*), Y Bergougnan (*Toulouse*); E Buzy (*Lourdes*), M Jol (*Biarritz*), J Prin-Clary (*Brive*), R Soro (*Romans*), A Moga (*Bègles*), J Prat (*Lourdes*), J Matheu-Cambas (*Castres*), G Basquet (*Agen*)

REFEREE CH Gadney (*England*)

SCORING Geddes, pen (3–0); Terreau, try (3–3); Prat, con (3–5), Lassègue, try (3–8); (half-time)

The International Championship resumed on New Year's Day 1947 after an absence of eight years. France had been re-admitted to the Championship and this was Scotland's first game in Paris since 1930. After their good showing in the Victory

This Scottish team played France on New Year's Day 1947, the first international after the war for which caps were awarded. *SRU*

Internationals, Scotland were expected to win, but they were outplayed by much livelier opponents. In bright and sunny conditions, Scotland started well and Geddes kicked an early penalty goal. Then France took a firm grip on the game which they barely relinquished until the final whistle. The French forwards were good in all aspects and the French tackling was quick and effective. From a scrum near the Scottish line, Terreau, the stand-off, broke through for a try converted by Prat. Soon afterwards, Geddes, who was otherwise very impressive, misjudged a kick ahead and Lassègue, following up at top speed, grabbed the ball and scored a try. France dominated in the second half, but they were unable to break the tight Scottish defence. The closing stages were hectic and exciting, and both sides had some scoring opportunities. Drummond made a long run from his own half and in the final minutes Geddes kicked over the French line, but the cover defence beat him to the touchdown.

193   INTERNATIONAL CHAMPIONSHIP 1947   WALES

Murrayfield · Saturday 1 February 1947 · Lost 8–22

SCOTLAND KI Geddes* (*London Scot*); TGH Jackson (*Army*), CW Drummond (*Melrose*), CR Bruce (*Glasgow Acs*), †DD Mackenzie (*Edinburgh U*); IJM Lumsden (*Bath*), AW Black (*Edinburgh U*); IC Henderson (*Acs-Wdrs*), RW Sampson (*London Scot*), †R Aitken (*RN*), †FH Coutts (*Melrose*), DW Deas (*Heriot's FP*), WID Elliot (*Acs-Wdrs*), JH Orr (*Edinburgh City Police*), AGM Watt (*Acs-Wdrs*)

WALES CH Davies (*Llanelli*); KJ Jones (*Newport*), BL Williams (*Cardiff*), WB Cleaver (*Cardiff*), WLT Williams (*Llanelli*); G Davies (*Pontypridd*), H Tanner* (*Cardiff*); WJ Evans (*Pontypool*), W Gore (*Newbridge*), C Davies (*Cardiff*), WE Tamplin (*Cardiff*), S Williams (*Llanelli*), O Williams (*Llanelli*), G Evans (*Cardiff*), JRG Stephens (*Neath*)

REFEREE MJ Dowling (*Ireland*)

SCORING BL Williams, try (0–3); Tamplin, pen (0–6); Geddes, pen (3–6); Elliot, try (6–6); Geddes, con (8–6) (half-time) Cleaver, try (8–9); Tamplin, con (8–11); KJ Jones, try (8–14); Cleaver, con (8–16); KJ Jones, try (8–19); WLT Williams, try (8–22)

Murrayfield presented a very wintery appearance and the pitch had been protected by straw. Scotland held their own until half-time, but then faded badly against a buoyant and talented Welsh team who exceeded all expectations. The Scottish forwards were lacklustre and failed to match their opponents in loose play. Similarly, the backs were slow and predictable against a Welsh three-quarter line which was full of zest and skill. Wales opened the scoring after some six minutes when Bleddyn Williams intercepted a slow pass near halfway and raced away to the line. Tamplin hit a post with his conversion attempt, but then kicked a penalty and Geddes replied in kind with a superb long effort. Close to the interval, Cleaver fumbled a wild pass behind his own goal-line and Elliot was up quickly to snatch a try. Geddes converted to give Scotland a fortuitous lead at the interval. The Welsh forwards began the second half purposefully. After a few minutes, Bleddyn Williams forced an opening with a strong hand-off and fed Cleaver who, although partly stopped, managed to roll over the line for a try converted by Tamplin. Wales were well on top, but there was no further scoring until the last ten minutes when the visiting wingers, Ken Jones and Les Williams, scored three tries between them to underline Welsh superiority.

Murrayfield · Saturday 22 February 1947 · Lost 0–3

SCOTLAND KI Geddes (*London Scot*); WD MacLennan (*Utd Servs*), CW Drummond (*Melrose*), CR Bruce (*Glasgow Acs*), DD Mackenzie (*Edinburgh U*); †WH Munro* (*Glasgow HSFP*), †E Anderson (*Stewart's FP*); TPL McGlashan (*Royal HSFP*), †AT Fisher (*Waterloo*), †HH Campbell (*Cambridge U & London Scot*), FH Coutts (*Melrose*), AGM Watt (*Acs-Wdrs*), †DD Valentine (*Hawick*), †DI McLean (*Royal HSFP*), †JB Lees (*Gala*)

IRELAND JAD Higgins (*Ulster CS*); B O'Hanlon (*Dolphin*), JDE Monteith* (*QU Belfast*), J Harper (*Instonians*), B Mullan (*Clontarf*); JW Kyle (*QU Belfast*), E Strathdee (*QU Belfast*); MR Neely (*Collegians*), KD Mullen (*Old Belvedere*), JC Daly (*London Irish*), CP Callan (*Lansdowne*), E Keefe (*Sunday's Well*), JW McKay (*QU Belfast*), DJ Hingerty (*UC Dublin*) RD Agar (*Malone*)

REFEREE CH Gadney (*England*)

SCORING No scoring in the first half. Mullan, try (0–3)

Following the heavy defeat against Wales, only Frank Coutts retained his place in the pack. Douglas Elliot had to drop out at the 11th hour and was replaced by debutant Duncan McLean which meant that the Scots fielded an entirely new back-row. Scotland also introduced new half-backs in Bill Munro and Ernie Anderson with the former taking over the captaincy on the occasion of his first cap. There was some doubt if the match would go ahead and snow had to be cleared off the pitch in the morning. The ground was in reasonable condition, but there were further snow showers during the game. Scotland were a big improvement on their previous showing, but Ireland, who two weeks earlier had beaten England resoundingly (22–0), were superior in the loose and did just enough to scrape through. Scotland defended very strongly, but made one fatal lapse around the 65th minute. From a scrum near halfway, Strathdee, the Irish scrum-half, picked-up, hesitated for a moment and then broke clean away down the blindside. Winger Barney Mullan was in support and cleverly cut inside for the winning score. The Scots fought hard to save the game, but were hampered when they lost Watt through injury in the closing ten minutes. For Scotland, Drummond threatened at times with his strong running and Munro had a very competent debut.

Twickenham · Saturday 15 March 1947 · Lost 5–24

SCOTLAND KI Geddes (*London Scot*); TGH Jackson (*London Scot*), CW Drummond (*Melrose*), WH Munro (*Glasgow HSFP*), DD Mackenzie (*Edinburgh U*); CR Bruce* (*Glasgow Acs*), E Anderson (*Stewart's FP*); TPL McGlashan (*Royal HSFP*), AT Fisher (*Waterloo*), HH Campbell (*Cambridge U & London Scot*), FH Coutts (*Army & Melrose*), IC Henderson (*Acs-Wdrs*), DD Valentine (*Hawick*), WID Elliot (*Acs-Wdrs*), DI McLean (*Royal HSFP*)

ENGLAND A Gray (*Otley*); CB Holmes (*Manchester*), NO Bennett (*St Mary's H*), J Heaton* (*Waterloo*), RH Guest (*Waterloo*); NM Hall (*St Mary's H*), JO Newton-Thompson (*Oxford U*); HW Walker (*Coventry*), AP Henderson (*Cambridge U*), GA Kelly (*Bedford*), JT George

(*Falmouth*), J Mycock (*Sale*), MR Steele-Bodger (*Cambridge U*), DF White (*Army & Northampton*), RHG Weighill (*RAF & Harlequins*)

REFEREE I David (*Wales*)

SCORING Hall, drop (0–4); Holmes, try (0–7); Heaton, con (0–9); Guest, try (0–12); Heaton, con (0–14) (half-time) Henderson, try (0–17); Heaton, con (0–19); Bennett, try (0–22); Heaton, con (0–24); Jackson, try (3–24); Geddes, con (5–24)

The winter of 1947 was particularly severe and both sides were short of match practice. Travel was difficult and many of the players, especially the Scottish ones, had to endure long and tortuous journeys just to reach the ground. Some of them did not arrive in London until the morning of the match. Snow showers fell regularly during the afternoon and the pitch was frozen. Unsurprisingly, the match was marred by a spate of injuries and at one stage both sides were reduced to 13 men. England had the best of the forward battle and their backs took their chances with relish. Blessed with a good supply of ball, Hall and Newton-Thompson, the English half-backs, easily outshone their opposite numbers Bruce and Anderson, who, in the words of *The Scotsman*, 'looked like a partnership that were shaking hands for the first time'. The Scots spent a lot of the game on the defensive and in truth they never quite recovered from two injuries in the first half. The inspirational Douglas Elliot had to leave the field with a leg injury after only a few minutes and during his absence Hall dropped a right-footed goal. England extended their lead when Holmes intercepted a pass near halfway and sprinted all the way to the Scottish line. Elliot returned to the fray, but then Jackson and Drummond had to go off, the latter with a broken collarbone, leaving the Scots with only six forwards for a period. Hall kicked into the Scottish half and the fast running Guest gathered a lucky bounce at full pace for an easy try at the posts. Jackson returned after the interval and Kelly, the English prop, had to leave with damaged ribs. Holmes was also stretchered off with severe cramp although he came back on again later. Henderson and Bennett both scored from Scottish defensive errors and Heaton converted all four English tries. Both sets of players got very tired in the closing stages, which took place in blizzard conditions, and play became very loose. Eventually, Munro beat the defence and put the long-striding Jackson away on a run up the right touchline for a fine consolation score.

---

196 TOUR MATCH AUSTRALIA

Murrayfield · Saturday 22 November 1947 · Lost 7–16

SCOTLAND IJM Lumsden (*Watsonians & Bath*); TGH Jackson (*London Scot*), JRS Innes* (*Aberdeen GSFP*), †T Wright (*Hawick*), †C McDonald (*Jed-Forest*); †DP Hepburn (*Woodford*), †WD Allardice (*Aberdeen GSFP*); †JC Dawson (*Glasgow Acs*), †GG Lyall (*Gala*), IC Henderson (*Edinburgh Acs*), †RM Bruce (*Gordonians*), †L Currie (*Dunfermline*), WID Elliot (*Edinburgh Acs*), JB Lees (*Gala*), AGM Watt (*Edinburgh Acs & Army*)

AUSTRALIA BJC Piper (*NSW*); AEJ Tonkin (*NSW*), T Allan* (*NSW*), ML Howell (*NSW*), JWT MacBride (*NSW*); NA Emery (NSW), CT Burke (*NSW*); E Tweedale (*NSW*), KH Kearney (*NSW*), EH Davis (*Victoria*), DF Kraefft (*NSW*), GM Cooke (*Queensland*), DH Keller (*NSW*), CJ Windon (*NSW*), AJ Buchan (*NSW*)

REFEREE NH Lambert (*Ireland*)

SCORING McDonald, pen (3–0); Kearney, try (3–3) (half-time) Hepburn, drop (7–3); Tonkin, try (7–6); Piper, con (7–8); Howell, try (7–11); Piper, con (7–13); Cooke, try (7–16)

In season 1947–48, Australia made a 35-match tour of the British Isles and France. In October, the Australians defeated the North of Scotland (14–0), the South of Scotland (15–6) and the Combined Cities (23–9) before moving onto the test match at Murrayfield, the first of their tour. Scotland fielded eight new caps, including Woodford stand-off Peter Hepburn, a player almost unknown north of the border, and Aberdeen scrum-half Dally Allardyce. In the forwards, CM Bruce and Hamish Dawson, chosen at prop and lock respectively, switched positions with each other before the start of the match, unbeknown to the selectors. On a heavy pitch and with a wet ball, this was a vigorous and evenly contested match until midway through the second half when new cap Tommy Wright, the Hawick centre, was injured and had to be withdrawn. Until this point, Scotland had stood-up well to their physically imposing opponents and held a four-point lead. The Scots started the game purposively and Bruce should have scored an early try, but he dropped the ball with the line at his mercy. Shortly afterwards, Charlie McDonald, the new wing, kicked a long penalty and later Kearney took advantage of some weak Scottish defence to score a soft try for Australia. In the second half, Hepburn dropped a goal after a scrum in front of the posts and then came Wright's injury. Elliot went onto the wing and a few minutes later Allan and Piper combined to give Tonkin a clear run-in. Piper converted to put the visitors in front for the first time. Australia's numerical and physical superiority told as the match wore on and they added further tries by Howell and Cooke, the first converted by Piper. Undaunted, Scotland made some spirited but ultimately unsuccessful attacks before the close of an excellent match.

197   INTERNATIONAL CHAMPIONSHIP 1948   FRANCE

Murrayfield · Saturday 24 January 1948 · Won 9–8

SCOTLAND WCW Murdoch (*Hillhead HSFP*); TGH Jackson (*London Scot*), JRS Innes* (*Aberdeen GSFP*), CW Drummond (*Melrose*), DD Mackenzie (*Edinburgh U*); DP Hepburn (*Woodford*), WD Allardice (*Aberdeen GSFP*); RM Bruce (*Gordonians*), GG Lyall (*Gala*), †WP Black (*Glasgow HSFP*), LR Currie (*Dunfermline*), JC Dawson (*Glasgow Acs*), WID Elliot (*Edinburgh Acs*), JB Lees (*Gala*), AGM Watt (*Army*)

FRANCE A Alvarez (*Tyrosse*); M Pomathios (*Agen*), L Junquas (*Bayonne*), P Dizabo (*Tyrosse*), R Lacaussade (*Bègles*); L Bordenave (*Toulon*), Y Bergougnan (*Toulouse*); E Buzy (*Lourdes*), L Martin (*Pau*), L Aristouy (*Pau*), R Soro (*Romans*), A Moga (*Bègles*), J Prat (*Lourdes*), J Matheu-Cambas (*Castres*), G Basquet* (*Agen*)

REFEREE AS Bean (*England*)

SCORING Lacaussade, try (0–3); Alvarez, con (0–5); Murdoch, pen (3–5); Prat, drop (3–8) (half-time) Jackson, try (6–8); Murdoch, pen (9–8)

Scotland fielded two pre-war veterans: Innes and Murdoch, the latter of whom had won his first cap way back in 1935. Murdoch was a late call-up as third choice full-back and turned out to be a match-winner. Played in bright but cold conditions, this was an exciting and fast game where Scottish grit and determination triumphed

Lineout action from Scotland v France at Murrayfield in January 1948.

narrowly over French *joie de vivre*. In the first half, France were the better side and deserved to lead at the interval, but afterwards Scotland made some splendid counter-attacks and defended courageously for a hard-earned victory. The match started disastrously for the home side when Drummond was laid out after being tackled by Junquas and had to leave the field for ten minutes. Shortly after his return, Bergougnan was wide with a drop goal attempt, but the Scottish defence got themselves into a tangle and Lacaussade raced onto the rolling ball for a soft try. Alvarez added the simple conversion. A similar incident occurred shortly afterwards, but this time Hepburn managed to kick the ball dead. Murdoch kicked a penalty and just before the interval Prat drop-kicked a penalty from 40 yards, the ball bouncing off the crossbar before it went over. France started the second half briskly, but then the Scots came to life and made several promising attacks of their own. After some 15 minutes, Alvarez, who otherwise was excellent, failed to gather a kick ahead, Innes regained the ball and passed to Jackson who sprinted powerfully to the line. Murdoch missed the conversion, but later kicked a second penalty from in front of the posts to give Scotland a slender lead. The closing stages were very tense and in the last act of the game Prat missed another lengthy drop-kick much to Scotland's relief.

198   INTERNATIONAL CHAMPIONSHIP 1948   WALES

Cardiff Arms Park · Saturday 7 February 1948 · Lost 0–14

SCOTLAND WCW Murdoch (*Hillhead HSFP*); TGH Jackson (*London Scot*), JRS Innes*
(*Aberdeen GSFP*), †A Cameron (*Glasgow HSFP*), DD Mackenzie (*Edinburgh U*); DP Hepburn
(*Woodford*), WD Allardice (*Aberdeen GSFP*); RM Bruce (*Gordonians*), GG Lyall (*Gala*),
LR Currie (*Dunfermline*), JC Dawson (*Glasgow Acs*), WP Black (*Glasgow HSFP*), WID Elliot
(*Edinburgh Acs*), JB Lees (*Gala*), AGM Watt (*Edinburgh Acs*)

WALES RF Trott (*Cardiff*); KJ Jones (*Newport*), BL Williams (*Cardiff*), WB Cleaver (*Cardiff*),
J Matthews (*Cardiff*); G Davies (*Pontypridd*), H Tanner* (*Cardiff*); L Anthony (*Neath*), DM James

(*Cardiff*), C Davies (*Cardiff*), WE Tamplin (*Cardiff*), S Williams (*Llanelli*), O Williams (*Llanelli*), GW Evans (*Cardiff*), L Manfield (*Cardiff*)

REFEREE TN Pearce (*England*)

SCORING No scoring in the first half. BL Williams, try (0–3); Tamplin, con (0–5); Matthews, try (0–8); Tamplin, pen (0–11); Jones, try (0–14)

Playing on a heavy pitch and in a ferocious wind, Scotland were outclassed by a good Welsh side that was never in any danger of losing. Fielding ten players from the Cardiff club, Wales displayed much greater cohesiveness, invention and strength. The belligerent Welsh forwards were always in the ascendancy, especially in the scrums, and gave their backs a plentiful supply of ball. The Welsh half-backs were in fine form and the three-quarter line produced some lively movements. Scotland played with the wind behind them in the first half, but failed to take advantage. The game was mainly in Welsh territory, but the Welsh defence was very effective and Murdoch missed several penalty attempts. Wales quickly asserted themselves after the change of ends. Cleaver made an opening to send Bleddyn Williams streaking down the left touchline for a fine try. Tamplin converted from a wide angle and later added a penalty. Soon afterwards, Tanner broke away down the left wing and cleverly drew the defence to give Matthews an easy run-in. Ken Jones used his electrifying pace to exploit a Scottish defensive mix-up and score a third Welsh try. Scottish scrum-half Dally Allardice was always courageous and determined in a losing cause.

199   INTERNATIONAL CHAMPIONSHIP 1948   IRELAND

Lansdowne Road, Dublin · Saturday 28 February 1948 · Lost 0–6

SCOTLAND WCW Murdoch (*Hillhead HSFP*); TGH Jackson (*London Scot*), CW Drummond (*Melrose*), JRS Innes* (*Aberdeen GSFP*), DD Mackenzie (*Edinburgh U*); DP Hepburn (*Woodford*), WD Allardice (*Aberdeen GSFP*); IC Henderson (*Edinburgh Acs*), GG Lyall (*Gala*), †S Coltman (*Hawick*), LR Currie (*Dunfermline*), HH Campbell (*London Scot*), RM Bruce (*Gordonians*), WID Elliot (*Edinburgh Acs*), WP Black (*Glasgow HSFP*)

IRELAND JAD Higgins (*Ulster CS*); BR O'Hanlon (*Dolphin*), M O'Flanagan (*Lansdowne*), WD McKee (*NIFC*), B Mullan (*Clontarf*); JW Kyle (*QU Belfast*), H de Lacy (*Harlequins & Garryowen*); AAM McConnell (*Collegians*), KD Mullen* (*Old Belvedere*), JC Daly (*London Irish*), CP Callan (*Lansdowne*), JE Nelson (*Malone*), JW McKay (*QU Belfast*), JS McCarthy (*Dolphin*), DJ O'Brien (*London Irish*)

REFEREE CH Gadney (*England*)

SCORING No scoring in the first half. Mullan, try (0–3); Kyle, try (0–6)

In near perfect conditions, the Irish forwards laid the foundation for a well-earned victory which would have been greater but for some poor play by the Irish midfield and stout Scottish tackling. The first half was regularly interrupted by injuries and was largely without incident, Mullan missing three kicks at goal for Ireland. The second half belonged almost entirely to the home side and after some ten minutes McKee made the opening for a try by Mullan. Murdoch was wide with a penalty attempt and soon afterwards Kyle, the best back on the field, cut through the defence for a great solo try. The Irish pack combined in some formidable rushes and in one of these Allardice, the Scottish scrum-half, was involuntarily swept along for some 25 yards.

Murrayfield · Saturday 20 March 1948 · Won 6–3

SCOTLAND WCW Murdoch (*Hillhead HSFP*); TGH Jackson (*London Scot*), JRS Innes* (*Aberdeen GSFP*), †L Bruce Lockhart (*London Scot*), CW Drummond (*Melrose*); DP Hepburn (*Woodford*), AW Black (*Edinburgh U*); IC Henderson (*Edinburgh Acs*), GG Lyall (*Gala*), HH Campbell (*London Scot*), WP Black (*Glasgow HSFP*), †R Finlay (*Watsonians*), WB Young (*London Scot*), WID Elliot (*Edinburgh Acs*), JB Lees (*Gala*)

ENGLAND R Uren (*Waterloo*); RH Guest (*Waterloo*), NO Bennett (*Utd Servs*), EK Scott* (*Redruth*), MF Turner (*Blackheath*); I Preece (*Coventry*), RJP Madge (*Exeter*); HW Walker (*Coventry*), AP Henderson (*Cambridge U & Edinburgh Wdrs*), TW Price (*Gloucester*), SV Perry (*Cambridge U*), HF Luya (*Headingley*), MR Steele-Bodger (*Edinburgh U*), DB Vaughan (*Devonport Servs*), RHG Weighill (*RAF*)

REFEREE NH Lambert (*Ireland*)

SCORING Uren, pen (0–3) (half-time) Drummond, try (3–3); Young, try (6–3)

Scotland completed the 1948 Championship with their first win against England for a decade, but this was not a match of any real quality. England were unlucky to lose scrum-half Madge with a knee injury early on. His place was taken by wing forward Steele-Bodger who had a lively and effective game. England showed great resilience to lead at the interval despite having faced into a troublesome wind. Uren kicked a penalty after about 20 minutes, but this was an awkward day for the kickers and both sides missed several chances, including a few sitters. The Scots began to assert themselves in the second half. After about ten minutes, Drummond finished off a good attack when he scored at the corner flag. The English forwards started to tire inside the final quarter and Scotland back-rower Young shot away from a lineout inside the English 25 and barged through several defenders for the winning try. Both sides had opportunities towards the end, but there was no further scoring. After the match it was discovered that Scott, the English captain, had fractured his jaw during the second half but played on unperturbed.

Stade Yves du Manoir, Colombes, Paris · Saturday 15 January 1949 Won 8–0

SCOTLAND IJM Lumsden (*Bath*); TGH Jackson (*London Scot*), †LG Gloag (*Cambridge U*), DP Hepburn (*Woodford*), †DWC Smith (*London Scot & Army*); CR Bruce (*Glasgow Acs*), WD Allardice (*Aberdeen GSFP*); JC Dawson (*Glasgow Acs*), †JC Abercrombie (*Edinburgh U*), S Coltman (*Hawick*), LR Currie (*Dunfermline*), †GA Wilson (*Oxford U*), †DH Keller* (*London Scot*), WID Elliot (*Edinburgh Acs*), †PW Kininmonth (*Oxford U*)

FRANCE N Baudry (*Montferrand*); M Pomathios (*Lyon*), P Dizabo (*Tyrosse*), M Terreau (*Bressane*), M Siman (*Castres*); L Bordenave (*Toulon*), Y Bergougnan (*Toulouse*); E Buzy (*Lourdes*), M Jol (*Biarritz*), L Caron (*Lyon*), R Soro (*Romans*), A Moga (*Bégles*), J Prat (*Lourdes*), J Matheu-Cambas (*Castres*), G Basquet* (*Agen*)

REFEREE TN Pearce (*England*)

SCORING Elliot, try (3–0) (half-time) Kininmonth, try (6–0); Allardice, con (8–0)

Scotland fielded six new caps including new captain Douglas Keller, a controversial choice because two years earlier he had played for the touring Australians against Scotland. France were firm favourites, but the Scots managed to pull off an unlikely victory thanks to their spirit, tenacious defence and alertness as well as French ineptitude. The Scottish forwards were under a huge amount of pressure and at times looked like being swept away, but the whole team stood firm against the French battering-rams. Although France did most of the attacking, their tactics and back play were unimaginative and they rarely looked like crossing the Scottish line. Scotland opened the scoring after some ten minutes with a fine breakaway try by Elliot. France were unlucky to lose their scrum-half Yves Bergougnan in the first half with a broken collar-bone. His place was taken by back-row man Jean Prat who did an admirable job although, in *The Scotsman*'s words, he was 'one of the heaviest forwards, whose bulging waistline hardly suggested his ability to perform acrobatics'. The second half followed much the same course as the first with France doing most of the attacking, but the Scots scoring the only points. Allardice, who had a superb match, broke from inside his own half and the ball was kicked inside for the chasing Kininmonth to collect and score. Allardice converted and although France kept up the pressure they were unable to make anything of it, much to the disgust of the partisan crowd.

202 · INTERNATIONAL CHAMPIONSHIP 1949 · WALES

Murrayfield · Saturday 5 February 1949 · Won 6–5

SCOTLAND IJM Lumsden (*Bath*); TGH Jackson (*London Scot*), LG Gloag (*Cambridge U*), DP Hepburn (*Woodford*), DWC Smith (*London Scot*); CR Bruce (*Glasgow Acs*), WD Allardice (*Aberdeen GSFP*); JC Dawson (*Glasgow Acs*), JG Abercrombie (*Edinburgh U*), S Coltman (*Hawick*), LR Currie (*Dunfermline*), GA Wilson (*Oxford U*), DH Keller* (*London Scot*), WID Elliot (*Edinburgh Acs*), PW Kininmonth (*Oxford U*)

WALES RF Trott (*Cardiff*); KJ Jones (*Newport*), J Matthews (*Cardiff*), BL Williams (*Cardiff*), TJ Cook (*Cardiff*); G Davies (*Cambridge U*), H Tanner* (*Cardiff*); EO Colman (*Newport*), W Travers (*Newport*), DCJ Jones (*Swansea*), JA Gwilliam (*Cambridge U*), A Meredith (*Devonport Servs*), WR Cale (*Newbridge*), G Evans (*Cardiff*), JRG Stephens (*Neath*)

REFEREE NH Lambert (*Ireland*)

SCORING Gloag, try (3–0) (half-time) Smith, try (6–0); Williams, try (6–3); Trott, con (6–5)

This exciting match was threatened by a thick fog which hung over Murrayfield and only lifted shortly before kick-off although much of the play was shrouded in gloom. Amongst the huge crowd were a party of uniformed sailors from the Soviet Union who were returning a ship to Rosyth that had been loaned to their country during the Second World War. The Scots won another remarkable victory against the odds, just as they had done in Paris. They were inferior in most of the forward battles and limited in attack, but their defence was outstanding. The fiendishly aggressive Scottish back-row repeatedly hammered the Welsh midfield and knocked them out of their stride. Douglas Elliot had one of his best games for Scotland and he was well supported by the rest of the pack. The visitors, for all their possession and effort, only managed to score near the end. In the first half, Allardice, who had a fine match, broke away from a lineout inside Welsh territory, and Elliot and Hepburn supported

Lineout action from the Wales game at Murrayfield in 1949.
Scotsman Publications Ltd

to put Gloag over for an unconverted try. After the interval, Wales continued to attack, but their passing became increasingly over-anxious and wayward as time slipped by. On several occasions, the Scots came close to scoring from interceptions. Smith made two long runs only to be hunted down by Ken Jones, the Welsh Olympic sprinter. With around 12 minutes to go, the Scots kicked down the touchline, Trott, the Welsh full-back, slipped, Dawson picked up and gave Smith a clear run. The Scottish left winger just beat the desperate pursuit of Jones and dived over in the corner. In the last five minutes, Bleddyn Williams took a miss-pass from Tanner and side-stepped his way over at the posts. Trott's conversion made the score 6–5 in favour of Scotland and amidst breathless excitement the Scots managed to hold on for a deserved victory.

203   INTERNATIONAL CHAMPIONSHIP 1949   IRELAND

Murrayfield · Saturday 26 February 1949 · Lost 3–13

SCOTLAND IJM Lumsden (*Bath*); TGH Jackson (*London Scot*), LG Gloag (*Cambridge U*), DP Hepburn (*Woodford*), DWC Smith (*London Scot*); CR Bruce (*Glasgow Acs*), WD Allardice (*Aberdeen GSFP*); JC Dawson (*Glasgow Acs*), JG Abercrombie (*Edinburgh U*), S Coltman (*Hawick*), LR Currie (*Dunfermline*), †AM Thomson (*St Andrews U*), DH Keller* (*London Scot*), WID Elliot (*Edinburgh Acs*), PW Kininmonth (*Oxford U*)

IRELAND GW Norton (*Bective Rgrs*); MF Lane (*UC Cork*), WD McKee (*NIFC*), NJ Henderson (*QU Belfast*), B O'Hanlon (*Dolphin*); JW Kyle (*QU Belfast*), E Strathdee (*QU Belfast*); JT Clifford (*Young Munster*), KD Mullen* (*Old Belvedere*), LJ Griffin (*Wdrs*), JE Nelson (*Malone*), RD Agar (*Malone*), JW McKay (*QU Belfast*), JS McCarthy (*Dolphin*), DJ O'Brien (*London Irish*)

SCORING   McCarthy, try (0–3); Norton, con (0–5) (half-time) Norton, pen (0–8); McCarthy, try (0–11); Norton, con (0–13); Allardice, pen (3–13)

Scotland's hopes of winning a championship clean-sweep were dashed by the lively Irish forwards. The visitors dominated the scrums, their support play was very good and they were fast in the loose. Behind the scrum, the Irish half-backs were very astute and Norton, the Irish full-back, never put a foot wrong despite the swirling wind. Scotland started well, but gradually Ireland forced their way into the game. On the 23rd minute, after a spell of pressure on the Scottish line, McCarthy slipped over from a lineout almost unopposed. Both sides missed some opportunities and Elliot might have scored from a breakaway, but he was obstructed by Norton just after he had kicked ahead and left prostrate on the turf for several minutes. The referee, however, judged that Norton's challenge was fair and there was no further action. In the second half, Norton, who always took an age over his kicks, landed a penalty goal and then converted a second try by McCarthy after good support work by the Irish forwards. Ireland finished strongly and Allardice's late penalty goal was no more than compensation for the weary Scots.

---

204   INTERNATIONAL CHAMPIONSHIP 1949   ENGLAND

Twickenham · Saturday 19 March 1949 · Lost 3–19

SCOTLAND   IJM Lumsden (*Bath*); TGH Jackson (*London Scot*), LG Gloag (*Cambridge U*), DP Hepburn (*Woodford*), WDC Smith (*Army*); CR Bruce (*Glasgow Acs*), WD Allardice (*Aberdeen GSFP*); †STH Wright (*Stewart's FP*), †JAR Macphail (*Edinburgh Acs*), S Coltman (*Hawick*), LR Currie (*Dunfermline*), GA Wilson (*Oxford U*), DH Keller* (*London Scot*), WID Elliot (*Edinburgh Acs*), PW Kininmonth (*Oxford U*)

ENGLAND   WB Holmes (*Cambridge U*); RH Guest (*Waterloo*), LB Cannell (*Oxford U*), CB van Ryneveld (*Oxford U*), RD Kennedy (*Camborne Sch of Mines*); I Preece* (*Coventry*), WKT Moore (*Leicester*); TW Price (*Cheltenham*), JH Steeds (*Middlesex H*), JMK Kendall-Carpenter (*Oxford U*), JRC Matthews (*Harlequins*), GRD'A Hosking (*Devonport Servs*), BH Travers (*Harlequins*), VG Roberts (*Penryn*), DB Vaughan (*Headingley*)

REFEREE   NH Lambert (*Ireland*)

SCORING   Kennedy, try (0–3) (half-time) van Rynevald, try (0–6); Travers, con (0–8); Wilson, pen (3–8); van Rynefeld, try (3–11); Hosking, try (3–14); Travers, con (3–16); Guest, try (3–19)

Both sides had something to play for. Scotland, despite losing to Ireland, still had a chance of sharing the championship and England needed at least a draw to avoid the wooden spoon. The teams were introduced to the Duke of Edinburgh. In perfect conditions, the first half was evenly contested until around the 25th minute when Tom Jackson, the Scottish right wing who had been troubled before the game, started to limp badly because of an injury to his right knee. The Scots tried to compensate by switching wings whenever possible, but Jackson was reduced to a mere passenger and England were quick to exploit his weakness. Roberts, the liveliest forward on the field, broke clean away and found van Ryneveld who gave Kennedy a clear run up the touchline for England's first try. The second half was largely one-way traffic as

England showed plenty of enterprise and scored four more tries. Preece played with great authority at stand-off and the English forwards became increasingly dominant. Van Ryneveld, a South African, weaved his way through the bemused defence and dived over the line for a great try converted by Travers. Wilson raised Scottish hopes with a fine angled penalty and then the ever-alert van Ryneveld scored his second try. Scotland's defence deteriorated as the match moved on, and Hosking and the veteran Guest added further tries to complete the rout.

205 · INTERNATIONAL CHAMPIONSHIP 1950 · FRANCE

Murrayfield · Saturday 14 January 1950 · Won 8–5

SCOTLAND †G Burrell (*Gala*); DWC Smith (*Army*), †R Macdonald (*Edinburgh U*), †DA Sloan (*Edinburgh Acs*), CW Drummond (*Melrose*); L Bruce Lockhart (*London Scot*), †AF Dorward (*Cambridge U*); JC Dawson (*Glasgow Acs*), JG Abercrombie (*Edinburgh U*), †GM Budge (*Edinburgh Wdrs*), †DE Muir (*Heriot's FP*), †R Gemmill (*Glasgow HSFP*), WID Elliot* (*Edinburgh Acs*), DH Keller (*London Scot*), PW Kininmonth (*Richmond*)

FRANCE R Arcalis (*Brive*): M Siman (*Castres*), P Dizabo (*RCF*), J Merquey (*Toulon*), M Pomathios (*Lyon*); P Lauga (*Vichy*), G Dufau (*RCF*); P Lavergne (*Limoges*), L Martin (*Pau*), R Ferrien (*Tarbes*), P Aristouy (*Pau*), F Bonnus (*Toulon*), J Prat (*Lourdes*), R Biénès (*Cognac*), G Basquet* (*Agen*)

REFEREE T Jones (*Wales*)

SCORING Macdonald, try (3–0); Budge, try (6–0); Bruce Lockhart, con (8–0) (half-time) Merquey, try (8–3); Prat, con (8–5)

Both sides fielded seven new caps each and Scotland a new captain, Douglas Elliot. The Scots were more emphatic winners than the final score suggests thanks to a great effort by the forwards, but France improved as the match went on and came close to snatching a draw. On a fine and chilly afternoon play was full of errors but open and vigorous. At one stage in the second half several players were laid out on the turf, one of whom, Dod Burrell, the hefty Scottish full-back, had to go off temporarily, Kininmonth taking his place. Likewise, France had to play the last five minutes without their captain Guy Basquet. After a largely uneventful opening, Bruce Lockhart and Sloan created an opening for new cap Ranald Macdonald, an Edinburgh University medical student, who made a strong run to score in the right corner. Three minutes later, Budge, the new prop, forced his way over for a try which was converted by Bruce Lockhart. The French were much livelier and dangerous after the interval. During Burrell's absence, Siman broke away and kicked across field, Smith failed to gather the ball and Merquey was up in a flash to score in the corner. Prat kicked a superb conversion from the touchline and a few minutes later he narrowly missed a huge drop kick from a penalty, an unearthly silence falling over Murrayfield as the ball fell just under the crossbar. Towards the end, Lauga missed a drop goal attempt and Arcalis, the diminutive French full-back, made a heroic tackle on Elliot to prevent a certain score. For Scotland, the powerfully built Grahame Budge was always in the thick of the action and showed great mobility for a prop forward.

St Helen's, Swansea · Saturday 4 February 1950 · Lost 0–12

SCOTLAND G Burrell (*Gala*); DWC Smith (*Army*), R Macdonald (*Edinburgh U*), DA Sloan (*Edinburgh Acs*), CW Drummond (*Melrose*); L Bruce Lockhart (*London Scot*), AW Black (*Edinburgh U*); JC Dawson (*Glasgow Acs*), JG Abercrombie (*Edinburgh U*), GM Budge (*Edinburgh Wdrs*), DE Muir (*Heriot's FP*), R Gemmill (*Glasgow HSFP*), WID Elliot* (*Edinburgh Acs*), DH Keller (*London Scot*), PW Kininmonth (*Richmond*)

WALES BL Jones (*Devonport Servs*); KJ Jones (*Newport*), J Matthews (*Cardiff*), MC Thomas (*Newport*), WC Major (*Maesteg*); WB Cleaver (*Cardiff*), WR Willis (*Cardiff*); C Davies (*Cardiff*), DM Davies (*Somerset Police*), JD Robins (*Birkenhead Park*), ER John (*Neath*), DJ Hayward (*Newbridge*), WR Cale (*Pontypool*), RT Evans (*Newport*), JA Gwilliam* (*Edinburgh Wdrs*)

REFEREE MJ Dowling (*Ireland*)

SCORING Thomas, try (0–3) (half-time) BJ Jones, pen (0–6); KJ Jones, try (0–9); Cleaver, drop (0–12)

The final score was a reasonably accurate reflection of the play. Scotland had the better of the first half, but they were unable to penetrate a solid Welsh defence. Both sides missed several penalty kicks at goal and on the 38th minute Matthews created an opening for Thomas who had just enough speed and determination to reach the line. The Scots kept their fighting spirit, but they were largely outplayed in the second half and their attacks gradually petered out. Five minutes after the restart, Welsh full-back Lewis Jones landed the only successful penalty of the day, a fine kick from 35 yards. A few minutes later, the opportunistic Matthews kicked into the right corner where Ken Jones dribbled over the goal-line and just beat several defenders to the touchdown. Play continued to be hard and vigorous, and both sides grew tired towards the end. In the closing stages Cleaver dropped a goal to seal a good win for Wales, the second of their Grand Slam season. For Scotland, Budge and Gemmill were always industrious and Elliot led from the front.

Lansdowne Road, Dublin · Saturday 25 February 1950 · Lost 0–21

SCOTLAND G Burrell (*Gala*); †DM Scott (*Langholm*), CW Drummond (*Melrose*), R Macdonald (*Edinburgh U*), DWC Smith (*London Scot & Army*); A Cameron (*Glasgow HSFP*), AW Black (*Edinburgh U*); JC Dawson (*Glasgow Acs*), JG Abercrombie (*Edinburgh U*), GM Budge (*Edinburgh Wdrs*), DE Muir (*Heriot's FP*), R Gemmill (*Glasgow HSFP*), WID Elliot* (*Edinburgh Acs*), DH Keller (*Sheffield*), PW Kininmonth (*Richmond*)

IRELAND GW Norton (*Bective Rgrs*); MF Lane (*UC Cork*), R Uprichard (*RAF & NIFC*), J Blayney (*Wdrs*), LC Crowe (*Old Belvedere*); JW Kyle (*QU Befast*), R Carroll (*Lansdowne*); T Clifford (*Young Munster*), KD Mullen* (*Old Belvedere*), D McKibbin (*Instonians*), JE Nelson (*Malone*), J Maloney (*UC Dublin*), AB Curtis (*Oxford U*), JW McKay (*QU Belfast*), DJ O'Brien (*London Irish*)

REFEREE T Pearce (*England*)

SCORING Norton, pen (0–3); Norton, pen (0–6) (half-time) Blayney, try (0–9); Norton, con (0–11); Curtis, try (0–14); Norton, con (0–16); Crowe, try (0–19); Norton, con (0–21)

Ireland were an unknown quantity and surprised everybody with their biggest win over Scotland to date. The Irish were flattered by the final score, but they were worthy winners thanks to superior cohesion, opportunism and stamina. Once again Scotland competed well, but they faded away in the second half and Ireland scored three tries in the later stages, all converted by full-back George Norton who never put a foot wrong. Scotland failed to take their own chances and missed six kicks at goal. Playing into the breeze in the first half, the Scots should have had an early try when the backs put together a superb passing movement that was halted only a few yards from the Irish line. Instead, the home side took the lead with two Norton penalties. In the second half the Irish forwards played with great fire in the loose and gradually subdued the heavier Scottish pack. Ireland's first try was one of the brightest ever seen at Lansdowne Road. From a scrum some 40 yards out, Kyle made a beautiful opening and Blayney cut through the defence on a long run to the line. The second try came from a forward rush and Curtis was on hand to pick up short of the line and dive over at the posts. With the Scots in disarray, Burrell was caught in possession by Kyle who sent Crowe racing away to the corner. Norton kicked a fine conversion from near the touchline. Lane almost scored another try only to be caught by Macdonald and the game ended with the Irish forwards in complete control.

208 INTERNATIONAL CHAMPIONSHIP 1950 ENGLAND

Murrayfield · Saturday 18 March 1950 · Won 13–11

SCOTLAND †T Gray (*Heriot's FP & Northampton*); CW Drummond (*Melrose*), R Macdonald (*Edinburgh U*), DA Sloan (*Edinburgh Acs*), DM Scott (*Langholm*); A Cameron (*Glasgow HSFP*), AW Black (*Edinburgh U*); JC Dawson (*Glasgow Acs*), JG Abercrombie (*Edinburgh U*), GM Budge (*Edinburgh Wdrs*), DE Muir (*Heriot's FP*), R Gemmill (*Glasgow HSFP*), WID Elliot (*Edinburgh Acs*), †H Scott (*St Andrews U*), PW Kininmonth* (*Richmond*)

ENGLAND MB Hofmeyr (*Oxford U*); JP Hyde (*Northampton & Army*), B Boobbyer (*Oxford U*), LB Cannell (*Oxford U*), JV Smith (*Cambridge U*); I Preece* (*Coventry*), WKT Moore (*Leicester*); JL Baume (*Northern & Army*), JH Steeds (*Saracens*), WA Holmes (*Nuneaton*), JRC Matthews (*Harlequins*), SJ Adkins (*Coventry*), HD Small (*Oxford U*), VG Roberts (*Penryn*), JM Kendall-Carpenter (*Oxford U*)

REFEREE MJ Dowling (*Ireland*)

SCORING Sloan, try (3–0); Smith, try (3–3); Abercrombie, try (6–3); Gray, con (8–3) (half-time) Hofmeyr, pen (8–6); Smith, try (8–9); Hofmeyr, con (8–11); Sloan, try (11–11); Gray, con (13–11)

The silver jubilee of Murrayfield was celebrated with an exciting contest that was only decided in the closing minutes. Scotland fielded a surprise choice at full-back in the shape of Tommy Gray. A versatile all-rounder, Gray continued the great tradition of the Heriot's full-back factory although at the time he was playing stand-off for Northampton. His selection was all the more remarkable because he had lost part of his left foot during the Second World War and had to play with specially designed boots. Playing in wet and slippery conditions throughout, Gray and Hofmeyr, the English full-back, had excellent games. The Scottish forwards were well beaten in the scrums, but they were very good in loose play. Unlike their previous two outings, they lasted the pace well and finished strongly. Budge was very prominent and Elliot, who had lost the captaincy to Kininmonth, returned to his best form. Cameron and Black, the Scottish half-backs, did not have an easy match, but they defended well and at times were lively in attack. Sloan showed plenty of enterprise to score a brace of tries. In front of a huge crowd, the Scots opened the scoring after some 15 minutes. England lost control of the ball inside their own 25, and Scott and Sloan dribbled it over the line for the latter to be credited with the try. England soon equalised when their forwards made a strong rush. Gray was bundled off the ball which rolled over the Scottish goal-line and Smith reacted quickly to beat two defenders and win the touchdown. Hofmeyr narrowly missed an angled drop goal and Smith might have scored but for a delayed pass. Shortly before the interval, Black made two breaks, the second of which ended with Abercrombie diving over near the posts. Gray converted to give Scotland the lead against the run of play. England started the second half purposefully. Hofmeyr kicked an early penalty and then Smith raced onto a kick to score wide out. Hofmeyr added the extra points with a superb low place-kick. Play continued to be fast and exciting despite the conditions and both sides came close to scoring. The Scottish forwards launched a series of attacks and a few minutes from time Sloan scored a try midway between the touchline and the posts. In pelting rain and amidst unbearable tension, Gray kicked the angled conversion to win both the match and immortality.

209 INTERNATIONAL CHAMPIONSHIP 1951 FRANCE

Stade Yves du Manoir, Colombes, Paris · Saturday 13 January 1951
Lost 12–14

SCOTLAND T Gray (*Northampton*); †AD Cameron (*Hillhead HSFP*), †IDF Coutts (*Old Alleynians*), †FO Turnbull (*Kelso*), †DM Rose (*Jed-Forest*); A Cameron (*Glasgow HSFP*), †IA Ross (*Hillhead HSFP*); JC Dawson (*Glasgow Acs*), †NGR Mair (*Edinburgh U*), †RL Wilson (*Gala*), †HM Inglis (*Edinburgh Acs*), R Gemmill (*Glasgow HSFP*), WID Elliot (*Edinburgh Acs*), †JJ Hegarty (*Hawick*), PW Kininmonth* (*Richmond*)

FRANCE A Alvarez (*Tyrosse*); A Porthault (*RCF*), M Terreau (*Bressane*), G Brun (*Vienne*), M Pomathios (*Lyon*); J Carabignac (*Agen*), G Dufau (*RCF*); R Biénès (*Cognac*), P Pascalin (*Mont-de-Marsan*), R Bernard (*Bergerac*), L Mias (*Mazamet*), H Fourès (*Toulouse*), J Prat (*Lourdes*), J Matheu (*Castres*), G Basquet* (*Agen*)

REFEREE TN Pearce (*England*)

SCORING Prat, pen (0–3); Gray, pen (3–3); Mias, try (3–6); Gray, pen (6–6) (half-time) Rose, try (9–6); Rose, try (12–6); Porthault, try (12–9); Prat, con (12–11); Prat, pen (12–14)

For the opening match of the 1951 Championship, Scotland fielded nine new caps and France five. Played in fine conditions, this was an exciting encounter full of unexpected twists and turns. Scotland made an encouraging start, but France opened the scoring with a lengthy penalty goal by Prat. Around the 30th minute Gray levelled with a penalty, having earlier missed two attempts. Shortly before the interval, France attacked down the left and from a crosskick the ball bounced luckily for Mias who grabbed it and scored a try. Alvarez narrowly missed the conversion although one touch-judge signalled that it had been successful. For the rest of the game, the scoreboard and stadium announcer gave the wrong score and the confusion even continued into some newspaper reports after the match. In the second half, Scotland forged ahead with a brace of tries by new left wing David Rose. Coutts made a break to set-up Rose for his first score and then from a counter-attack Turnbull and Elliot created space to give him a long run-in. Scotland were now six points in front, but they fell away towards the finish and the French forwards dramatically raised their game. A kick ahead put the defence into a tangle and Porthault raced up to snatch the touchdown. Prat kicked a magnificent conversion to reduce the lead to a single point. In a nail-biting conclusion, the Scots conceded a penalty and Prat kicked the vital goal.

210   INTERNATIONAL CHAMPIONSHIP 1951   WALES

Murrayfield · Saturday 3 February 1951 · Won 19–0

SCOTLAND †IHM Thomson (*Heriot's FP*); †R Gordon (*Edinburgh Wdrs*), DA Sloan (*Edinburgh Acs*), DM Scott (*Langholm*), DM Rose (*Jed-Forest*); A Cameron (*Glasgow HSFP*), IA Ross (*Hillhead HSFP*); JC Dawson (*Glasgow Acs*), NGR Mair (*Edinburgh U*), RL Wilson (*Gala*), HM Inglis (*Edinburgh Acs*), R Gemmill (*Glasgow HSFP*), WID Elliot (*Edinburgh Acs*), †RC Taylor (*Kelvinside-West*), PW Kininmonth* (*Richmond*)

WALES G Williams (*Llanelli*); KJ Jones (*Newport*), J Matthews (*Cardiff*), BL Jones (*Devonport Servs*), MC Thomas (*Devonport Servs*); G Davies (*Cambridge U*), WR Willis (*Cardiff*); JD Robins (*Birkenhead Park*), DM Davies (*Somerset Police*), C Davies (*Cardiff*), ER John (*Neath*), DJ Hayward (*Newbridge*), A Forward (*Pontypool*), RT Evans (*Newport*), JA Gwilliam* (*Edinburgh Wdrs*)

REFEREE MJ Dowling (*Ireland*)

SCORING Thomson, pen (3–0) (half-time) Kininmonth, drop (6–0); Gordon, try (9–0); Inglis, con (11–0); Gordon, try (14–0); Dawson, try (17–0); Thomson, con (19–0)

The Scotland team that defeated Wales 19–0 in February 1951. *SRU*

This famous match was one of the most remarkable and unexpected results in the history of rugby and one of Scotland's greatest ever victories. A confident and multi-talented Welsh team, which included eleven British Lions, had already demolished England at Swansea (23–5) and were firm favourites against a youthful Scottish side. None of the Scottish back division was over 22-years-old. The pitch was soft after recent snow and cut-up during the match, but there was plenty of open play. The game was watched by an enormous crowd estimated at around 80,000 people, perhaps a quarter of whom were travelling supporters. Wales began with natural confidence, but the Scottish forwards held their own and were quick to counter-attack. The Scottish back-row put the Welsh backs under a lot of pressure, forcing them into errors and not allowing them to play with their normal fluency. Douglas Elliot relentlessly harried Glyn Davies, the Welsh stand-off who, it was rumoured, did not relish hard tackles. The Scottish centres, Donald Scott and Donald Sloan, never allowed their wily opponents to get the better of them. Both sides had some near misses in the first half and just before the interval Scotland's new full-back Ian Thomson, a late replacement for Tommy Gray, kicked a penalty to give his side the lead at the interval. The first 20 minutes of the second half were fairly evenly balanced. The Scottish forwards played with all of their traditional fire and it was only good defence by the Welshmen that prevented the Scots from scoring. The defining moment of the game came around the hour mark. Gerwyn Williams, the Welsh full-back, made a hurried clearance that failed to find touch. The ball was caught by Peter Kininmonth standing close to the left touchline about 30-yards from goal. The Scottish captain steadied himself before letting fly with an enormous drop kick which soared between the posts, one of the most extraordinary things ever seen at Murrayfield. Wales tried to recover and Lewis Jones was brought up to stand-off in place of the battered Davies, but still they could not break through the Scottish defence. The home side continued to play with great pace and determination, and they were rewarded when Scott made a break to let new cap Bob Gordon over for try on the right. Inglis added the extra points and from then on Scotland were rampant. Elliot made a dribbling rush into the Welsh 25, Gordon hacked on and was first to the touchdown. Inglis's conversion attempt hit a post. Finally, the ball was kicked into the Welsh 25, Cameron brought down Lewis Jones with a hefty tackle, and Dawson gathered and forced his way over. Thomson added the conversion to finish a memorable encounter. This was to be Scotland's final victory for four years and now began a long, dark period of 17 defeats in succession.

211   INTERNATIONAL CHAMPIONSHIP 1951   IRELAND

Murrayfield · Saturday 24 February 1951 · Lost 5–6

SCOTLAND IHM Thomson (*Heriot's FP*); †KJ Dalgleish (*Edinburgh Wdrs*), DA Sloan (*Edinburgh Acs*), DM Scott (*Langholm*), DM Rose (*Jed-Forest*); A Cameron (*Glasgow HSFP*), IA Ross (*Hillhead HSFP*); JC Dawson (*Glasgow Acs*), NGR Mair (*Edinburgh U*), RL Wilson (*Gala*), HM Inglis (*Edinburgh Acs*), R Gemmill (*Glasgow HSFP*), WID Elliot (*Edinburgh Acs*), RC Taylor (*Kelvinside-West*), PW Kininmonth* (*Richmond*)

IRELAND GW Norton (*Bective Rgrs*); WHJ Millar (*QU Belfast*), NJ Henderson (*QU Belfast*), RR Chambers (*Instonians*), MF Lane (*UC Cork*); JW Kyle (*QU Belfast*), JA O'Meara (*UC Cork*);

JH Smith (*QU Belfast*), KD Mullen* (*Old Belvedere*), D McKibbin (*Instonians*), PJ Lawlor (*Clontarf*), JR Brady (*CIYMS*), JS McCarthy (*Dolphin*), JW McKay (*QU Belfast*), DJ O'Brien (*London Irish*)

REFEREE TN Pearce (*England*)

SCORING Sloan, try (3–0); Thomson, con (5–0); Henderson, drop (5–3) (half-time) O'Brien, try (5–6)

Despite having a man advantage for most of the game, the Scots were unable to repeat the heroics of the Welsh match. Ireland lost their full-back Norton with a shoulder injury after some 15 minutes and McKay had to come out of the pack. Undaunted, the visitors were superior in most respects and controlled much of the play. The fiery Irish forwards never allowed the Scots to settle and the Scottish half-backs were always under pressure. In contrast, Kyle's touch-kicking and positional play was excellent. It was only at the lineout that the Scots held the upper-hand thanks to Inglis and Kininmonth. On a perfect pitch, Scotland started with a flourish. Thomson hit a post with an easy penalty attempt and Cameron had a drop goal disallowed because of a knock-on. Five minutes before the interval, Cameron made an elusive run near the Irish 25 and found a gap to put Sloan over for a try near the posts. Thomson converted and a few minutes later Henderson dropped a goal. Ireland completely dominated the second half. The depleted Irish pack set a cracking pace that the Scots could not match and Kyle's tactical genius was much to the fore. McKibbin hit a post with a penalty from an awkward angle and Lane almost made it to the corner several times. With some ten minutes remaining, Kyle cut through on a diagonal run and McCarthy gave a scoring pass to O'Brien who powered over at the posts. McKibbin, to his obvious disgust, missed the simple conversion. In a pulsating conclusion, Scotland had some unsuccessful drops at goal, but the Irish forwards and Kyle remained masters of the situation. At the finish, the visitors were given a heart-felt ovation for their stirring victory against the odds.

212   INTERNATIONAL CHAMPIONSHIP 1951   ENGLAND

Twickenham · Saturday 17 March 1951 · Lost 3–5

SCOTLAND T Gray (*Northampton*); KJ Dalgleish (*Edinburgh Wdrs*), DA Sloan (*Edinburgh Acs*), DM Scott (*Langholm*), DM Rose (*Jed-Forest*); A Cameron (*Glasgow HSFP*), IA Ross (*Hillhead HSFP*); JC Dawson (*Glasgow Acs*), NGR Mair (*Edinburgh U*), RL Wilson (*Gala*), WP Black (*Glasgow HSFP*), HM Inglis (*Edinburgh Acs*), WID Elliot (*Edinburgh Acs*), PW Kininmonth* (*Richmond*), RC Taylor (*Kelvinside-West*)

ENGLAND WG Hook (*Gloucester*); CG Woodruff (*Harlequins*), AC Towell (*Bedford*), JM Williams (*Penzance & Newlyn*), VR Tindall (*Liverpool U*); EMP Hardy (*Blackheath & Army*), DW Shuttleworth (*Blackheath & Army*); RV Stirling (*Leicester*), E Evans (*Sale*), WA Holmes (*Nuneaton*), DT Wilkins (*RN*), BA Neale (*Army*), DF White (*Northampton*), VG Roberts (*Penryn*), JM Kendall-Carpenter* (*Oxford U*)

REFEREE MJ Dowling (*Ireland*)

SCORING White, try (0–3); Hook, con (0–5) (half-time) Cameron, try (3–5)

Played in the presence of Queen Elizabeth and Princess Margaret, this was a hard and fast game on a heavy pitch. Conditions deteriorated as the game went on and heavy showers fell in the second half. England were the livelier side and salvaged their disappointing season with a narrow but deserved victory, although the Scots were close to snatching a draw at the finish. The English forwards paved the way with their solid scrummaging and enthusiastic work in the loose. Despite the slippery ball, the home backs had some good passing movements only to be let down by poor finishing. For Scotland, Angus Cameron played an excellent game behind a losing pack. Both sides had promising attacks in the first half, but there was no scoring until shortly before the interval. Don White, the English back-row, pounced on a loose heel inside the Scottish 25, slipped a tackle and dummied over for a try that Hook converted into a goal. The second half was keenly contested with missed opportunities on both sides. Williams, the English centre, made a fine save on his own line after a kick ahead by Elliot. At the other end, Gray narrowly beat Roberts to a touchdown. Scotland gained the upper-hand towards the finish. The forwards charged to the English posts, Cameron took the ball and used all of his weight and momentum to score in the left corner. Inglis made a great effort with the awkward conversion but his kick drifted past the wrong side of the upright.

213 TOUR MATCH SOUTH AFRICA

Murrayfield · Saturday 24 November 1951 · Lost 0–44

SCOTLAND G Burrell (*Gala*); †JGM Hart (*London Scot*), DM Scott (*Langholm*), FO Turnbull (*Kelso*), DM Rose (*Jed-Forest*); A Cameron* (*Glasgow HSFP*), AF Dorward (*Gala*); JC Dawson (*Glasgow Acs*), JAR Macphail (*Edinburgh Acs*), RL Wilson (*Gala*), HM Inglis (*Edinburgh Acs*), †J Johnston (*Melrose*), WID Elliot (*Edinburgh Acs*), RC Taylor (*Kelvinside Acs*), PW Kininmonth (*Richmond*)

SOUTH AFRICA JU Buchler (*Transvaal*); FP Marais (*Boland*), RAM van Schoor (*Rhodesia*), MT Lategan (*W Province*), PGA Johnstone (*W Province*); JD Brewis (*N Transvaal*), PA du Toit (*N Transvaal*); A Geffin (*Transvaal*), WH Delport (*E Province*), AC Koch (*Boland*), J du Rand (*Rhodesia*), E Dinkelman (*N Transvaal*), CJ van Wyk (*Transvaal*), SP Fry (*W Province*), HSV Muller* (*Transvaal*)

REFEREE MJ Dowling (*Ireland*)

SCORING Du Rand, try (0–3); van Schoor, try (0–6); Geffin, con (0–8); Koch, try (0–11); Geffin, con (0–13); Brewis, drop (0–16); Koch, try (0–19) (half-time) Delport, try (0–22); Geffin, con (0–24); van Wyk, try (0–27); Geffin, con (0–29); Muller, try (0–32); Geffin, con (0–34); Lategan, try (0–37); Geffin, con (0–39); Dinkelman, try (0–42); Geffin, con (0–44)

This infamous match became known as the 'Murrayfield Massacre', a devastating defeat for Scotland and one that inflicted an inferiority complex on Scottish rugby for many years to come. In the professional era results of this kind are not uncommon, but in the 1950s it was without precedent. Captained by the great back-row Basil Kenyon, who missed this match because of injury, the South Africans were on a 31-match tour of the British Isles and France. They were expected to win although nobody could have guessed at the outcome. Playing in near perfect conditions, Scotland's deficiencies were ruthlessly exposed. The South Africans were a wonderfully fit and physically imposing side, especially up-front, and their speed of thought and combination in attack made

SCOTLAND (White Jerseys)   SOUTH AFRICA (Green Jerseys)

<table>
<tr><td colspan="2">

FULL BACK
(15)   G. Burrell (Gala)

</td><td colspan="2">

FULL BACK
(1)   J. Buchler (Transvaal)

</td></tr>
</table>

SCOTLAND (White Jerseys)

FULL BACK
(15)   G. Burrell (Gala)

THREE-QUARTERS
(11)   J. G. M. Hart (London Scottish), *Right Wing*
(12)   D. M. Scott (London Scottish)
(13)   F. O. Turnbull (Kelso)
(14)   D. M. Rose (Jedforest) *Left Wing*

HALF BACKS
(10)   A. Cameron, *Capt.* (Glasgow H.S. F.P.), *Stand-off*
(9)   A. F. Dorward (Gala), *Scrum*

FORWARDS
(1)   J. C. Dawson (Glasgow Academicals)
(2)   J. A. R. Macphail (Edinburgh Academicals)
(3)   R. L. Wilson (Gala)
(4)   H. M. Inglis (Edinburgh Academicals)
(5)   J. Johnston (Melrose)
(6)   W. I. D. Elliot (Edinburgh Academicals)
(7)   P. W. Kininmonth (Richmond)
(8)   R. C. Taylor (Kelvinside Academicals)

SOUTH AFRICA (Green Jerseys)

FULL BACK
(1)   J. Buchler (Transvaal)

THREE-QUARTERS
(4)   F. Marais (Boland), *Right Wing*
(7)   R. van Schoor (Rhodesia)
(8)   M. T. Lategan (Western Province) OR
(12)   D. J. Fry (Western Province)
(6)   P. Johnstone (Western Province), *Left Wing*

HALF BACKS
(11)   J. D. Brewis (Northern Transvaal), *Stand-off*
(15)   P. A. du Toit (Northern Transvaal), *Scrum*

FORWARDS
(18)   A. Geffin (Transvaal)
(17)   W. Delport (Eastern Province)
(20)   C. Koch (Boland)
(26)   C. J. van Wyk (Transvaal)
(29)   J. du Rand (Rhodesia)
(24)   E. Dinkelmann (Northern Transvaal)
(27)   S. P. Fry (Western Province)
(30)   H. Muller (Transvaal), *Captain*

Touch Judge—R. W. Shaw (S.R.U.)   *Referee*—M. J. Dowling (IRELAND)   S. S. Viviers (O.F.S.)—*Touch Judge*

The Ball for this match is made and supplied by Walter S. Machenzie, Sports Outfitter, Tollcross, Edinburgh.

PROGRAMME OF MUSIC

The Band of THE SEAFORTH HIGHLANDERS
(72nd Duke of Albany's Own - 78th Ross-shire Buffs)

(By kind permission of Lieut.-Col. P. J. JOHNSTON, Commanding Officer, and Officers)

Conductor—Bandmaster A. BRUNSDEN, A.R.C.M.

1. **Quick March** . . . . " Imperial Echoes " . . . . . *Safroni*
2. **Selection** . . . . "Oklahoma" . . . . . *Rodgers*
3. **Medley** . . . "Tunes of the Commonwealth" . . . *Somers*
4. **Selection** . . . . "Kiss Me Kate" . . . . . *Ellis*
5. **March Medley** " Passing of the Regiments" . . . *arr. Winter*
6. **Selection** . . . "Scottish Country Dances" . . . . *Campbell*

" God Save the King "

QUEEN VICTORIA SCHOOL PIPE & BUGLE BANDS

Band President—Major D. G. WASHBELL, R.A.E.C.
Drum and Bugle-Major—Mr W. DUNGLISON   *Pipe-Major*—Mr J. SANDERSON

Pipe Band :
March . . *Farewell to the Creeks*   Reel . . *The Piper o' Drummond*
Strathspey . *Captain Horn*   March . . *Atholl and Broadalbane Gathering*

Bugle Band :
Fanfare . . *Normandie*   Slow March *Cawnpore*
Quick March *Nuts in May*   Quick March *60th Rifles*

Pipe Band :
March . . *Scotland the Brave*   Strathspey . *Inverness Rant*
Slow March *Loch Laven Castle*   Reel . . *The Highway to Linton*
March . . *The Rhodesian Regiment*   March . . *Dovecola Park*

Bugle Band :
Quick March *Anon*   Slow March *Band Master*
Quick Step . *Pop goes the Weasel*   Quick March *Bangalore*
Quick March *Three Parts Fall In*

Pipe Band :
March . . *The Siege of Delhi*   March . . *Bonnie Highlanders*
Slow March *Road to the Isles*

Military Band and Bugles . . . . . *Marching through Georgia*
Interval March . . . . *The Barren Rocks of Aden*

The team line-ups for the South Africa match in November 1951, a dark day for Scotland.

---

the Scottish approach seem hopelessly old fashioned and pedestrian. Scotland fielded nine of the side that had sensationally beaten Wales earlier in the year, but their preparation for the match was almost non-existent, much of their tackling was woefully weak and they had no idea how to counter the brilliant interplay of the Springboks. Curiously, Scotland started quite strongly and almost scored an early try, but the South Africans quickly got into their stride. After 17 minutes, du Rand forced his way over the line and soon after van Schoor added a second try. Prop forward Okey Geffin, one of the great personalities of the tour, converted the latter, one of seven successful conversions for the man known appropriately as 'The Boot'. Two tries by prop forward Chris Koch, who was the outstanding figure in the pack, and an angled drop goal by Hannes Brewis gave the tourists a 19–0 lead at the interval and the match was all over bar the shouting. Angus Cameron missed a penalty attempt, but the Scots never looked like scoring apart from their early foray. The second half developed into a complete rout with the South Africans scoring another five tries, all converted by the inimitable Geffin. Their hunger and opportunism was demonstrated with their eighth try. Centre Tjol Lategan picked-up a loose pass and showed the defence a clean pair of heels with a spectacular run to the posts. The Scottish crowd had never seen anything like it and at the final whistle they courteously gave their conquerors a rousing ovation. Hennie Muller, the stand-in captain, was chaired from the field by his delirious teammates. It was hard to single out any of the South Africans from such an awesome display of teamwork. Jonny Buchler was almost faultless at full-back, Brewis the ideal link at stand-off, and his partner Fonnie du Toit played with snap and intelligence at scrum-half. It said much that six of the eight forwards scored tries, including a brace for Koch who repeatedly bulldozed his way through the hapless Scots. There was little compensation for the home side, although full-back Dod Burrell kicked and handled well whilst Douglas Elliott seemed to stand alone against a relentless tide of green and gold.

---

214   INTERNATIONAL CHAMPIONSHIP 1952   FRANCE

Murrayfield · Saturday 12 January 1952 · Lost 11–13

SCOTLAND IHM Thomson (*Heriot's FP*); R Gordon (*Edinburgh Wdrs*), †IF Cordial (*Edinburgh Wdrs*), †JL Allan (*Melrose*), DM Scott (*London Scot*); †JNG Davidson (*Edinburgh U*), †AK Fulton (*Edinburgh U*); JC Dawson (*Glasgow Acs*), †NM Munnoch (*Watsonians*), †J Fox (*Gala*), †M Walker (*Oxford U*), J Johnston (*Melrose*), WID Elliot (*Edinburgh Acs*), †JT Greenwood (*Dunfermline*), PW Kininmonth* (*Richmond*)

FRANCE R Labarthète (*Pau*); G Brun (*Vienne*), M Prat (*Lourdes*), R Martine (*Lourdes*), F Cazenave (*Mont-de-Marsan*); R Furcade (*Perpignan*), P Lasaosa (*Dax*); R Bréjassou (*Tarbes*), P Labadie (*Bayonne*), R Biénès (*Cognac*), B Chevallier (*Montferrand*), F Varenne (*RCF*), J Prat (*Lourdes*), R Bourdeu (*Lourdes*), G Basquet* (*Agen*)

REFEREE I David (*Wales*)

SCORING Thomson, pen (3–0); J Prat, pen (3–3); J Prat, try (3–6); J Prat, con (3–8) (half-time) Thomson, pen (6–8); Basquet, try (6–11); J Prat, con (6–13); Cordial, try (9–13); Thomson, con (11–13)

Scotland made drastic changes after the South African debacle, including eight new caps. France also fielded eight newcomers and managed to win at Murrayfield for the first time. On a fine but cold afternoon, Thomson, who was easily Scotland's best player, kicked a long angled penalty in the first minutes, although the goal was only awarded after a consultation between the officials. The Scots had a lot of possession in the opening stages, but failed to make it count and after some 20 minutes Jean Prat equalised with a penalty. France improved as the game went on and before the interval Prat's younger brother Maurice made a break which Jean finished off at the posts. Early in the second half, Thomson kicked a second penalty and then Gordon made a long run down the touchline but was forced into touch by Jean Prat near from the line. The closing stages were the most exciting of the match. Scrum-half Lasaosa slipped away down the blind side, Jean Prat was in support and Basquet, taking an inside pass, bulldozed his way over the line. Jean Prat converted and the match looked won and lost, but the Scottish forwards rallied and new cap Ian Cordial raced through for a try. Thomson's conversion left Scotland two points in arrears, but France managed to hang on for a narrowly deserved win. Douglas Elliot had another fine match and veteran French back-row and captain Jean Prat was outstanding.

Cardiff Arms Park · Saturday 2 February 1952 · Lost 0–11

SCOTLAND IHM Thomson (*Heriot's FP*); R Gordon (*Edinburgh Wdrs*), IF Cordial (*Edinburgh Wdrs*), JL Allan (*Melrose*), DM Scott (*London Scot*); JNG Davidson (*Edinburgh U*), AF Dorward (*Gala*); JC Dawson (*Glasgow Acs*), NM Munnoch (*Watsonians*), J Fox (*Gala*), J Johnston (*Melrose*), DE Muir (*Heriot's FP*), WID Elliot (*Edinburgh Acs*), PW Kininmonth* (*Richmond*), HM Inglis (*Edinburgh Acs*)

WALES G Williams (*Llanelli*); KJ Jones (*Newport*), MC Thomas (*Newport*), BL Williams (*Cardiff*), AG Thomas (*Cardiff*); CI Morgan (*Cardiff*), WR Willis (*Cardiff*); WOG Williams (*Swansea*), DM Davies (*Somerset Police*), DJ Hayward (*Newbridge*), ER John (*Neath*), JRG Stephens (*Neath*), L Blyth (*Swansea*), A Forward (*Pontypool*), JA Gwilliam* (*Edinburgh Wdrs*)

REFEREE MJ Dowling (*Ireland*)

SCORING MC Thomas, pen (0–3); Jones, try (0–6); MC Thomas, con (0–8) (half-time) MC Thomas, pen (0–11)

An enormous crowd estimated at around 56,000 spectators, then a record for the Arms Park, saw an unspectacular encounter that was played on a treacherous surface. Scotland gave a creditable display against a strong Welsh side that had already beaten England (8–6) and were on their way to another Grand Slam. The Scottish forwards held up well and made some spirited rushes, but once again the backs lacked scoring power and decisiveness. Wales did enough to win but little more and perhaps they were flattered by the outcome. The home side opened the scoring inside ten minutes when Malcolm Jones kicked an angled penalty goal. Scotland then had their best chance of the game. Scott started a run from midfield and Davidson carried on and beat several defenders before finding Kininmonth. The Scottish captain broke clean away and seemed certain to score only to be overhauled in the nick of time by Welsh flyer Ken Jones. After some 30 minutes, Wales scored the only try of the match. From a lineout on the left, Willis, who played part of the match with a broken jaw, fed Alun Thomas who made an incisive diagonal run to the Scottish 25 before lobbing out a pass to Ken Jones and the right wing, using all of his Olympic speed, did the rest. Both sides made some attacking forays in the second half, but the defences were well on top. Shortly before the finish, Thomas kicked a second penalty goal to seal the game for Wales.

Lansdowne Road, Dublin · Saturday 23 February 1952 · Lost 8-12

SCOTLAND IHM Thomson (*Heriot's FP*); R Gordon (*Edinburgh Wdrs*), IF Cordial (*Edinburgh Wdrs*), JL Allan (*Melrose*), DM Scott (*London Scot*); JNG Davidson (*Edinburgh U*), AF Dorward (*Gala*); JC Dawson (*Glasgow Acs*), NM Munnoch (*Watsonians*), J Fox (*Gala*), J Johnston (*Melrose*), DE Muir (*Heriot's FP*), WID Elliot (*Edinburgh Acs*), PW Kininmonth* (*Richmond*), HM Inglis (*Edinburgh Acs*)

IRELAND JGMW Murphy (*Dublin U*); WHJ Millar (*QU Belfast*), NJ Henderson (*QU Belfast*), JR Notley (*Wanderers*), MF Lane (*UC Cork*); JW Kyle (*QU Belfast*), JA O'Meara (*UC Cork*);

T Clifford (*Young Munster*), KD Mullen (*Old Belvedere*), JH Smith (*Collegians*), PJ Lawlor (*Clontarf*), AF O'Leary (*Cork Const*), M Dargan (*Old Belvedere*), JS McCarthy (*Dolphin*), DJ O'Brien* (*Cardiff*)

REFEREE I David (*Wales*)

SCORING Thomson, pen (3–0); Henderson, pen (3–3); Lane, try (3–6); Kyle, try (3–9); Davidson, try (6–9); Thomson, con (8–9) (half-time) Henderson, try (8–12)

Scotland retained the side that had done well in Wales. This was a hard fought match with both sides suffering numerous injuries. After some 20 minutes, Irish left wing Lane had to leave the field with a broken wrist and the versatile McCarthy came out of the pack. Despite their numerical advantage, the heavier Scottish forwards struggled to contain their fiery and determined opponents. The Irish forwards were strong in the scrums and loose play, causing the Scottish halves many problems. The talented Irish half-backs, Kyle and O'Meara, were a constant menace in attack and the reno-wned tactical genius of Kyle was very apparent. On a perfect winter afternoon, Thomson and Henderson exchanged early penalties and then Ireland scored two excellent tries, the first a few minutes after Henderson's goal. The elusive O'Meara, who was outstanding throughout, made a blindside break and O'Brien was in support to send in the unmarked Lane, who had to depart shortly afterwards. Kyle scored a second try after a brilliant solo run. Shortly before the interval, Kininmonth tore himself away in the loose and passed to Davidson who sprinted over near the posts. Thomson's conversion reduced the lead to a single point. Ten minutes after the restart, Gordon made a hurried clearance from behind his own line which went straight into Millar's hands. He passed to Henderson who used all of his momentum to dive over at the right-hand corner. The rest of the game was a stern struggle in which the under-strength Irish forwards more than held their own. Scotland always had a chance of snatching victory, but they flagged towards the end and Ireland held on a well deserved win.

217 INTERNATIONAL CHAMPIONSHIP 1952   ENGLAND

Murrayfield · Saturday 15 March 1952 · Lost 3–19

SCOTLAND †NW Cameron (*Glasgow U*); R Gordon (*Edinburgh Wdrs*), IF Cordial (*Edinburgh Wdrs*), IDF Coutts (*Old Alleynians*), †TG Weatherstone (*Stewart's FP*); JNG Davidson (*Edinburgh U*), AF Dorward* (*Gala*); JC Dawson (*Glasgow Acs*), J Fox (*Gala*), †JM Inglis (*Selkirk*), J Johnston (*Melrose*), DE Muir (*Heriot's FP*), WID Elliot (*Edinburgh Acs*), †DS Gilbert-Smith (*London Scot*), †JP Friebe (*Glasgow HSFP*)

ENGLAND PJ Collins (*Camborne Sch of Mines*); JE Woodward (*Wasps*), AE Agar (*Harlequins*), B Boobyer (*Rosslyn Park*), CE Winn (*Rosslyn Park*); NM Hall* (*Richmond*), PW Sykes (*Wasps*); WA Holmes (*Nuneaton*), E Evans (*Sale*), RV Stirling (*Leicester & RAF*), JRC Matthews (*Harlequins*), DT Wilkins (*RN*), DF White (*Northampton*), AO Lewis (*Bath*), JM Kendall-Carpenter (*Penzance & Newlyn*)

REFEREE MJ Dowling (*Ireland*)

SCORING Winn, try (0–3); Hall, con (0–5) (half-time) Evans, try (0–8); Woodward, try (0–11); Kendall-Carpenter, try (0–14); Hall, con (0–16); Johnston, try (3–16); Agar, drop (3–19)

Scotland fielded five new caps, making 15 for the season. In fine conditions, the Scottish forwards worked hard but lacked cohesiveness. Much of the Scottish handling was wayward and as a result England prospered in loose play. Only the Scottish half-backs, Davidson and Dorward, shone in adversity and gave any hope for the future. England were the better side and coasted to a comfortable victory. The visitors opened the scoring almost immediately. Pouncing on a fumble near the Scottish 25, Agar broke through a confused defence and, when checked, cross-kicked over to the left. Winn collected the ball and shook off two weak tackles to score a try that Hall converted. Both sides had some chances, but there was no further scoring in the first half. Scotland continued to struggle in the second period as England gave glimpses of their prowess in attack. Boobyer had a couple of exciting runs and from a lineout near the Scottish line Evans, the English hooker, took the loose ball and touched down. Evans was injured in the process and had to leave the field temporarily. England continued to press and excellent combined play led to further tries by Woodward and Kendall-Carpenter, the latter converted by Hall. Near the finish, Johnston lifted Scottish spirits when he scored a try after a scramble near the English line, but Agar promptly replied with surprise drop goal to complete Scotland's misery.

<hr>

218   INTERNATIONAL CHAMPIONSHIP 1953   FRANCE

Stade Yves du Manoir, Colombes, Paris · Saturday 10 January 1953

Lost 5–11

SCOTLAND NW Cameron (*Glasgow U*); KJ Dalgleish (*Cambridge U*), DA Sloan (*London Scot*), DM Scott (*Watsonians*), DM Rose (*Jed-Forest*); JNG Davidson (*Edinburgh U*), AF Dorward* (*Gala*); †BE Thomson (*Oxford U*), †JHF King (*Selkirk*), RL Wilson (*Gala*), †JH Henderson (*Oxford U*), JJ Hegarty (*Hawick*), †AR Valentine (*RNAS*), †DC Macdonald (*Edinburgh U*), †KHD McMillan (*Sale*)

FRANCE J Rouan (*Narbonne*); A Porthault (*RCF*), J Dauger (*Bayonne*), M Prat (*Lourdes*), M Pomathios (*Bressane*); G Carabignac (*Agen*), G Dufau (*RCF*); P Bertrand (*Bressane*), P Labadie (*Bayonne*), A Sanac (*Perpignan*), L Mias (*Mazamet*), P Tignol (*Toulouse*), J Prat* (*Lourdes*), R Bourdeu (*Lourdes*), R Biénès (*Cognac*)

REFEREE OB Glasgow (*Ireland*)

SCORING Bertrand, pen (0–3); Carabignac, drop (0–6); Rose, try (3–6); Cameron, con (5–6) (half-time) Bourdeu, try (5–9); Bertrand, con (5–11)

The pitch was treacherous after frost, snow and sleet. The Scottish forwards, with six new caps, did well against heavier and more experienced opponents, but the three-quarters were largely disappointing both in attack and defence, apart from the strong running of David Rose on the left wing. France played their traditional fast-paced game and deserved to win, but they also lacked penetration in midfield and missed several scoring opportunities because of their inaccurate handling. Before a smaller crowd than normal, play was not of the highest standard but there were some moments of excitement. France lost no time in settling into Scottish territory. Bertrand landed an early penalty goal and a few minutes later Carabignac dropped a goal from long range. Scotland stuck to their task and after a charge by the forwards Dorward passed out to Rose who easily beat two defenders for a good score. Cameron kicked a fine conversion, but missed a long penalty attempt before the interval. Both sides had several promising attacks in the second half. France made a great passing movement which ended with Bourdeu scoring a splendid try. Rose was agonisingly close to a second try for Scotland, but he was bundled into touch-in-goal at the corner flag. Amongst several good performances for Scotland, scrum-half Arthur Dorward was always lively and tackled courageously, second-row Jack Hegarty played with intelligence and alacrity, and new hooker Jock King earned his first cap with a combative display.

219   INTERNATIONAL CHAMPIONSHIP 1953   WALES

Murrayfield · Saturday 7 February 1953 · Lost 0–12

SCOTLAND NW Cameron (*Glasgow U*); R Gordon (*Edinburgh Wdrs*), KJ Dalgleish (*Cambridge U*), JL Allan (*Melrose*), DM Rose (*Jed-Forest*); JNG Davidson (*Edinburgh U*), AF Dorward* (*Gala*); BE Thomson (*Oxford U*), IHF King (*Selkirk*), RL Wilson (*Gala*), JH Henderson (*Oxford U*), JJ Hegarty (*Hawick*), AR Valentine (*RNAS Anthorn*), KHD McMillan (*Sale*), DC Macdonald (*Edinburgh U*)

WALES TJ Davies (*Devonport Servs & Swansea*); KJ Jones (*Newport*), AG Thomas (*Cardiff*), BL Williams* (*Cardiff*), GM Griffiths (*Cardiff*); CI Morgan (*Cardiff*), WR Willis (*Cardiff*); WOG Williams (*Devonport Servs & Swansea*), G Beckingham (*Cardiff*), CC Meredith (*Neath*), ER John (*Neath*), JRG Stephens (*Neath*), S Judd (*Cardiff*), RCC Thomas (*Coventry & Swansea*), RJ Robins (*Royal Signals & Pontypridd*)

REFEREE PF Cooper (*England*)

SCORING Davies, pen (0–3); Jones, try (0–6) (half-time) BL Williams, try (0–9); BL Williams, try (0–12)

In near perfect conditions the Scottish forwards fought hard, but there was no repeat of the great victory of two years earlier. Wales deserved to win by virtue of having the heavier pack and more opportunistic backs, although they were slightly flattered by the final outcome. The Scots might easily have done better with a more accurate goal-kicker. Wales had most of the early pressure and after some 20 minutes Davies kicked a fine angled penalty. The Scottish defence stood up well to the Welsh attack, but six minutes before the interval Morgan put in a well-judged cross-kick. The ball fell awkwardly for the steady, if rather slow-footed Cameron and before he could reach it Jones had dribbled over the line for a try. On the stroke of half-time, Cameron missed a relatively simple penalty chance and Wales led 6–0 at the break. In the second half, Welsh scrum-half Rex Willis had to go off for a period with a damaged shoulder and Morgan took his place. Willis returned, but later had to retire for good. Cameron missed another penalty attempt, and almost immediately a Scottish handling movement broke down and the Welsh backs seized their fleeting opportunity. Griffiths and Jones combined to put Bleddyn Williams, the Welsh captain, away and he beat the last defender to score at the corner. Towards the finish, Williams intercepted another loose pass and raced away for his second try.

Murrayfield · Saturday 28 February 1953 · Lost 8–26

SCOTLAND IHM Thomson (*Heriot's FP & Army*); TG Weatherstone (*Stewart's FP*),
A Cameron* (*Glasgow HSFP*), †D Cameron (*Glasgow HSFP*), DWC Smith (*London Scot*);
L Bruce Lockhart (*London Scot*), †KM Spence (*London Scot*); BE Thomson (*Oxford U*),
†GC Hoyer-Millar (*Oxford U*), †JH Wilson (*Watsonians*), JH Henderson (*Oxford U*), JJ Hegarty
(*Hawick*), AR Valentine (*RNAS*), KHD McMillan (*Sale*), †EH Henriksen (*Royal HSFP*)

IRELAND RJ Gregg (*QU Belfast*); SJ Byrne (*Lansdowne*), NJ Henderson (*QU Belfast*),
K Quinn (*Old Belvedere*), M Mortell (*Bective Rgrs*); JW Kyle* (*NIFC*), JA O'Meara (*UC Cork*);
FE Anderson (*QU Belfast*), R Roe (*Dublin U*), WA O'Neill (*UC Dublin*), JR Brady (*CIYMS*),
TE Reid (*Garryowen*), WE Bell (*Collegians*), JS McCarthy (*Dolphin*), JR Kavanagh (*UC Dublin*)

REFEREE I David (*Wales*)

SCORING McCarthy, try (0–3); Gregg, con (0–5); Byrne, try (0–8); Gregg, con (0–10) (half-time)
Byrne, try (0–13); Gregg, con (0–15); Thomson, pen (3–15); Kavanagh, try (3–18); Henderson, try
(6–18); Thomson, con (8–18); Mortell, try (8–21); Byrne, try (8–24); Gregg, con (8–26)

Ireland were too fast and lively for a disappointing Scottish side that leaked six tries.
The forward exchanges were fairly evenly balanced, but the visitors held an advantage
in the lineout and loose play where flanker Jim McCarthy, who sometimes looked
more like a half-back than a forward, was very prominent. Stand-off Jackie Kyle was
well marked, but the Irish three-quarters were much superior, especially on the right.
By comparison, the Scottish centres were slow and cumbersome and the wings had
few opportunities. However, Weatherstone and Henderson were both outstanding in
a lost cause. Scotland opened nervously and Ireland set the early pace. On the 16th
minute McCarthy scored a try converted by Gregg. Scotland made some spasmodic
attacks but there was no teamwork behind them. Further weak tackling let Ireland
in again. Kavanagh broke away from a lineout and instead of being pulled down he
was allowed to pass out to Byrne for an easy try in the corner. Gregg converted from
the touchline to give Ireland a 10–0 lead at the interval. The visitors restarted very
purposefully and soon went further ahead. Quinn pick-up a dropped pass and sent
Byrne racing in for his second score. Thomson kicked a penalty and Weatherstone made
a long and promising run, but he was pulled down. From the counter-attack, Ireland
made a good passing movement which Kavanagh finished off with an unconverted
try. Scotland then made a brief but stirring revival. Bruce Lockhart had a drop goal
attempt charged down, but he re-gathered the ball and after some swift passing
Henderson hurled himself over the line. Thomson kicked the goal, but Ireland were
not finished. Kyle made a great run that led to a try for Mortell in the corner. Then a
fine bout of passing set the sprightly Byrne away on the Scottish 25 and he powered
round behind the posts to complete his hat-trick.

Twickenham · Saturday 21 March 1953 · Lost 8–26

SCOTLAND IHM Thomson (*Heriot's FP & Army*); TG Weatherstone (*Stewart's FP*),

A Cameron* (*Glasgow HSFP*), D Cameron (*Glasgow HSFP*), †JS Swan (*St Andrews U*); L Bruce Lockhart (*London Scot*), AF Dorward (*Gala*); JC Dawson (*Glasgow Acs*), JHF King (*Selkirk*), RL Wilson (*Gala*), JH Henderson (*Oxford U*), JJ Hegarty (*Hawick*), †W Kerr (*London Scot*), KHD McMillan (*Sale*), †WLK Cowie (*Edinburgh Wdrs*)

ENGLAND NM Hall* (*Richmond*); RC Bazley (*Waterloo*), WPC Davies (*Harlequins*), J Butterfield (*Northampton*), JE Woodward (*Wasps*); M Regan (*Liverpool*), DW Shuttleworth (*Headingley & Army*); RV Stirling (*Leicester & RAF*), E Evans (*Sale*), WA Holmes (*Nuneaton*), DT Wilkins (*RN*), SJ Adkins (*Coventry*), AO Lewis (*Bath*), DF White (*Northampton*), JMK Kendall-Carpenter (*Bath*)

REFEREE MJ Dowling (*Ireland*)

SCORING Bazley, try (0–3); Hall, con (0–5); Weatherstone, try (3–5); Bazley, try (3–8); Adkins, try (3–11) (half-time) Stirling, try (3–14); Hall, con (3–16); Butterfield, try (3–19); Hall, con (3–21); Henderson, try (6–21); Thomson, con (8–21); Woodward, try (8–24); Hall, con (8–26)

Scotland's miserable championship came to a sorry end with this big defeat at the Twickenham graveyard. Played in fine conditions, the Scots contributed fully to a fast and open match, but much of their defence and marking was very poor and a rampant England ran in six tries, the most that they had scored in the fixture to date. The English midfield was dangerous and full of enterprise, and Martin Regan had a marvellous match at stand-off. The Scots opened promisingly, but the backs did little in attack and Thomson missed two kickable penalty attempts. After some 15 minutes, White made a tremendous break from his own half and fed Reagan who raced almost to the line before he was cut down by Swan's last-ditch tackle. From a lineout inside the Scottish 25, Regan punted across to Bazley who easily beat the defence for the opening try. Thomson missed another penalty and England continued to press. After some 32 minutes, Dorward drew the defence with a run in front of the English posts and fed Cameron who put Weatherstone over in the right-hand corner. Shortly before the interval, England scored twice in quick succession. Regan set-up Bazley who swerved through some weak defence to the line, and then Regan and Lewis made a breakaway and Adkins grounded the ball on the whitewash despite a strong tackle by Dorward. The English forwards took control in the second half and the home side scored another brace within 12 minutes of the restart. Stirling pilfered a ball near the line and thundered over, and then White and Davies put Butterfield away on a mazy run to the right corner. Angus Cameron switched to stand-off and Scotland conjured a thrilling consolation score. Bruce Lockhart, now at centre, made a long run from his own half, Dawson carried on into the English 25 and Henderson was up in support to score near the posts. The Scottish recovery quickly faded away and Woodward, from a standing start near halfway, worked his way down the touchline past some feeble defence to the corner and Hall converted from wide out.

222 INTERNATIONAL CHAMPIONSHIP 1954 FRANCE

Murrayfield · Saturday 9 January 1954 · Lost 0–3

SCOTLAND †JC Marshall (*London Scot*); JS Swan (*London Scot*), AD Cameron (*Hillhead HSFP*), D Cameron (*Glasgow HSFP*), TG Weatherstone (*Stewart's FP*); JNG Davidson* (*Edinburgh U*), AK Fulton (*Dollar Acs*); TPL McGlashan (*Royal HSFP*), †RKG MacEwen

(*Cambridge U*), †HF McLeod (*Hawick*), †EAJ Fergusson (*Oxford U*), †EJS Michie (*Aberdeen U*), †A Robson (*Hawick*), JH Henderson (*Richmond*), PW Kininmonth (*Richmond*)

FRANCE M Vannier (*RCF*); M Pomathios (*Bressane*), J Bouquet (*Bourgoin-Jallieu*), R Martine (*Lourdes*), L Rogé (*Béziers*); A Labazuy (*Lourdes*), G Dufau (*RCF*); R Bréjassou (*Tarbes*), P Labadie (*Bayonne*), R Biénès (*Cognac*), L Mias (*Mazamet*), B Chevallier (*Montferrand*), J Prat* (*Lourdes*), H Domec (*Lourdes*), R Baulon (*Vienne*)

REFEREE I David (*Wales*)

SCORING No scoring in the first half. Bréjassou, try (0–3)

Scotland were a little unlucky to lose this game. The new-look forwards, with five new caps, showed potential and worked hard, especially in loose play, but the back division was largely disappointing. The half-backs were under a lot of pressure from the marauding French back-row and the three-quarter line was limited in attack and kicked too much. France were an adequate side whose main strengths were their slick passing, good support play and speed about the field. Scotland opened purposefully and Weatherstone came close to scoring. The French began to assert themselves after the early storm. Pomathios was denied a try by a forward pass and later Domec knocked-on with the way ahead open. Scotland then came agonisingly close to scoring a brilliant try. Weatherstone, going at top speed, took a pass from Fulton near halfway, rounded Pomathios with a determined run and was almost at the French line when he stumbled and lost the ball. The decisive move came 12 minutes into the second half. Labazuy broke away from some loose play, and Prat and Pomathios leant their support to give Bréjassou a clear run to the line.

---

223 TOUR MATCH NEW ZEALAND

Murrayfield · Saturday 13 February 1954 · Lost 0–3

SCOTLAND JC Marshall (*London Scot*), JS Swan (*London Scot*), †MK Elgie (*London Scot*), D Cameron (*Glasgow HSFP*), TG Weatherstone (*Stewart's FP*); †GT Ross (*Watsonians*), †LP MacLachlan (*Oxford U*); TPL McGlashan (*Royal HSFP*), RKG MacEwen (*Cambridge U*), HF McLeod (*Hawick*), EAJ Fergusson (*Oxford U*), EJS Michie (*Aberdeen U*), WID Elliot* (*Edinburgh Acs*), JH Henderson (*Richmond*), PW Kininmonth (*Richmond*)

NEW ZEALAND RWH Scott (*Auckland*); RA Jarden (*Wellington*), CJ Loader (*Wellington*), MJ Dixon (*Canterbury*); DD Wilson (*Canterbury*), LS Haig (*Otago*), K Davis (*Auckland*); KL Skinner (*Otago*), RC Hemi (*Waikato*), P Eastgate (*Canterbury*), RA White (*Poverty Bay*), GN Dalzell (*Canterbury*), WH Clark (*Wellington*), PFH Jones (*North Auckland*), RC Stuart* (*Canterbury*)

REFEREE I David (*Wales*)

SCORING No scoring in the first half. Scott, pen (0–3)

Scotland fielded three new caps, but the main talking point was the selection of Douglas Elliot as captain. Elliot had just returned after injury and there were concerns about his fitness. The arrival of another touring side brought back bitter memories of the Springbok debacle three years earlier, but in the event New Zealand scraped home with the only score of the game, a penalty goal by Bob Scott after 47 minutes. Scotland

Bob Stuart's All Blacks of 1953–54 were one of the most popular touring sides to visit the British Isles. They played four games in Scotland including a 32–0 win over the South of Scotland at Netherdale. Here the players take the field and the All Blacks perform the pre-match haka.

Robert D Clapperton Photographic Trust

produced a stirring performance and probably deserved a draw. The forwards stood their ground and the tackling was very sound. Both sides came close to scoring on several occasions only to be denied by last ditch defence or an unlucky bounce. For Scotland, Douglas Elliot made his critics eat their words with an inspirational and determined display. The new half-backs combined well, Ross showing coolness and good hands whilst MacLachlan was sharp enough to beat the All Black back-row at times. Full-back Marshall was excellent and Swan never loosened his grip on the mighty All Black winger Ron Jarden.

224 INTERNATIONAL CHAMPIONSHIP 1954 IRELAND

Ravenhill, Belfast · Saturday 27 February 1954 · Lost 0–6

SCOTLAND JC Marshall (*London Scot*); JS Swan (*London Scot*), MK Elgie (*London Scot*), D Cameron (*Glasgow HSFP*), TG Weatherstone (*Stewart's FP*); GT Ross (*Watsonians*), LP MacLachlan (*London Scot*); TPL McGlashan (*Royal HSFP*), RKG MacEwen (*Cambridge U*), HF McLeod (*Hawick*), EAJ Fergusson (*Oxford U*), EJS Michie (*Aberdeen U*), WID Elliot* (*Edinburgh Acs*), JH Henderson (*Richmond*), PW Kininmonth (*Richmond*)

IRELAND RJ Gregg (*QU Belfast*); M Mortell (*Bective Rgrs*), NJ Henderson (*NIFC*), RP Godfrey (*UC Dublin*), JT Gaston (*Dublin U*); S Kelly (*Lansdowne*), JA O'Meara (*Dolphin*); FE Anderson (*QU Belfast*), R Roe (*Dublin U*), BGM Wood (*Garryowen*), RH Thompson (*Instonians*), PJ Lawler (*Clontarf*), GF Reidy (*Lansdowne*), JS McCarthy* (*Dolphin*), JR Kavanagh (*Wdrs*)

SCORING Mortell, try (o–3) (half-time) Mortell, try (3–3)

This was a disappointing game between two mediocre teams and Scotland were a shadow of the side that had done so well against New Zealand. The forwards played well at times, but as individuals rather than a unit and there was none of the fiery enthusiasm that they had shown against the All Blacks. The half-backs did not combine effectively and in fact Scotland never looked like winning. The Irish forwards heeled quickly and cleanly and their backs were always ready to attack, but they made little ground. Both sides kicked too much, made a lot of errors and conceded penalties. There were only two really notable incidents in the game, both leading to Irish tries. After seven minutes, Gaston, the Irish left wing, made a long run from deep inside his own half before kicking ahead. The defence failed to gather the ball; the Irishmen regained it and sent Mortell, the other wing, over for a try. Scotland never really recovered from this early blow. Towards the finish, they lost their hooker MacEwan with a damaged knee and a few minutes later Ireland scored again. Kelly, the stand-off, went off down the blind side before drawing the defence with a timely pass to put Mortell over in the right corner for his second score.

225   INTERNATIONAL CHAMPIONSHIP 1954   ENGLAND

Murrayfield · Saturday 20 March 1954 · Lost 3–12

SCOTLAND JC Marshall (*London Scot*); JS Swan (*London Scot*), MK Elgie (*London Scot*), D Cameron (*Glasgow HSFP*), TG Weatherstone (*Stewart's FP*); GT Ross (*Watsonians*), LP MacLachlan (*Oxford U*); TPL McGlashan (*Royal HSFP*), JHF King (*Selkirk*), HF McLeod (*Hawick*), EAJ Fergusson (*Oxford U*), EJS Michie (*Aberdeen U*), WID Elliot* (*Edinburgh Acs*), JH Henderson (*Richmond*), PW Kininmonth (*Richmond*)

ENGLAND N Gibbs (*Harlequins*); JE Woodward (*Wasps*), J Butterfield (*Northampton*), JP Quinn (*New Brighton*), CE Winn (*Rosslyn Park*); M Regan (*Liverpool*), G Rimmer (*Waterloo*); RV Stirling* (*Wasps & RAF*), E Robinson (*Coventry*), DL Sanders (*Harlequins*), PD Young (*Dublin Wdrs*), JF Bance (*Bedford*), DS Wilson (*Met Police*), R Higgins (*Army & Liverpool*), VH Leadbetter (*Edinburgh Wdrs*)

REFEREE OB Glasgow (*Ireland*)

SCORING Young, try (o–3); Gibbs, con (o–5) (half-time) Wilson, try (o–8); Gibbs, con (o–10); Elgie, try (3–10); Wilson, try (3–13)

Scotland made a worthy effort but in the end they were outclassed by a useful English side that won the Triple Crown for the first time since 1937. The visitors had a superior back division and their forwards improved as the match progressed. Scotland held their own for the first 15 minutes and Elgie missed an early penalty chance, then England made a counter-attack which ended with second-row Peter Young running in for a try. Gibbs, who played steadily in his first international, added the conversion. Elgie missed another penalty before the Scots had their best attacks of the game. The ball was hacked over the English line, but Winn, the English winger, won the race to the touchdown. Then Cameron put Weatherstone away down the touchline, but the wing was tackled by Young a few yards short. In between, Woodward made a strong run and set-up Butterfield who looked certain to score until Cameron brought him down with a magnificent tackle. Elgie missed another shot at goal and England led 5–0 at the break. Both sides came close to scoring early in the second half. Elliot broke away but his kick ahead bounced into touch and the chance was lost. Butterfield made a long solo run and actually crossed the line only to be bundled into touch-in-goal. Around the 65th minute, the visitors made a fast attack and Wilson scored behind the posts. Gibbs converted to effectively end the contest. England then lost concentration momentarily. Cameron caught Quinn in possession and Elgie successfully chased a long kick ahead for an opportunist score, Scotland's first try of the season. This reawakened the crowd, but England never really looked threatened. Shortly before the finish, Wilson intercepted a lazy pass near the Scottish line and ran in for his second try before the defence could react.

---

226   INTERNATIONAL CHAMPIONSHIP 1954   WALES

St Helen's, Swansea · Saturday 10 April 1954 · Lost 3–15

SCOTLAND JC Marshall (*London Scot*); JS Swan (*London Scot*), MK Elgie (*London Scot*), AD Cameron (*Hillhead HSFP*), TG Weatherstone (*Stewart's FP*); GT Ross (*Watsonians*), LP MacLachan (*Oxford U*); TPL McGlashan (*Royal HSFP*), RKG MacEwen (*Cambridge U*), HF McLeod (*Hawick*), EAJ Fergusson (*Oxford U*), †JWY Kemp (*Glasgow HSFP*), WID Elliot* (*Edinburgh Acs*), JH Henderson (*Richmond*), PW Kininmonth (*Richmond*)

WALES V Evans (*Neath*); KJ Jones* (*Newport*), GM Griffiths (*Cardiff*), BL Williams (*Cardiff*), R Williams (*Llanelli*); CI Morgan (*Cardiff*), WR Willis (*Cardiff*); WOG Williams (*Swansea*), BV Meredith (*St Luke's Coll*), CC Meredith (*Neath*), RJ Robins (*Pontypridd*), RH Williams (*Llanelli*), L Davies (*Llanelli*), RCC Thomas (*Swansea*), S Judd (*Cardiff*),

REFEREE PF Cooper (*England*)

SCORING RH Williams, try (0–3); BV Meredith, try (0–6) (half-time) R Williams, try (0–9); Evans, pen (0–12); Morgan, try (0–15); Henderson, try (3–15)

This match was postponed from late January because of frost and was the last championship match to be played at the historic St Helen's ground in Swansea. Before a large crowd, Wales were comfortable winners and scored four tries to Scotland's one, but they were never wholly convincing in attack. Their backs tended to over-elaborate in midfield instead of running hard and straight. Playing with the sun behind them, Wales had most of the pressure in the first half, but it was only close to the interval that they opened the scoring, lock Rhys Williams going over from a short lineout near the corner flag. A few minutes later, hooker Meredith added a second. At the start of the second half, Elliot almost scored a try after he had kicked ahead, but the last defender cleared in the nick of time. After the best passing movement of the game, Ray Williams, the Welsh left wing, squeezed in at the corner. Evans missed the difficult kick, but later added a penalty. Cliff Morgan, the mercurial Welsh stand-off, scored the fourth Welsh try with a typical piece of determined genius. Around halfway he kicked hard along the ground and just managed to win the race for the touchdown. In the final ten minutes, and with the game out of reach, Scotland started to play more expansively. After several close things, Marshall and Elgie combined to put Henderson over for a consolation score.

Stade Yves du Manoir, Colombes, Paris · Saturday 8 January 1955

Lost 0–15

SCOTLAND A Cameron (*Glasgow HSFP*); JS Swan (*London Scot*), MK Elgie (*London Scot*), †ML Grant (*Harlequins*), T G Weatherstone (*Stewart's FP*); †JT Docherty (*Glasgow HSFP*), AF Dorward (*Gala*); HF McLeod (*Hawick*), †WKL Relph (*Stewart's FP*), †IR Hastie (*Kelso*), JWY Kemp (*Glasgow HSFP*), †H Duffy (*Jed-Forest*), JJ Hegarty (*Hawick*), JT Greenwood* (*Dunfermline*), A Robson (*Hawick*)

FRANCE M Vannier (*RCF*); A Boniface (*Mont-de-Marsan*), M Prat (*Lourdes*), L Rogé (*Béziers*), J Lepatey (*Mazamet*); R Martine (*Lourdes*), G Dufau (*RCF*); A Domenech (*Vichy*), J Labadie (*Bayonne*), R Bréjassou (*Tarbes*), J Barthe (*Lourdes*), B Chevallier (*Montferrand*), J Prat* (*Lourdes*), H Domec (*Lourdes*), M Celaya (*Biarritz*)

REFEREE HB Elliot (*England*)

SCORING Boniface, try (0–3); Vannier, pen (0–6); J Prat, try (0–9) (half-time) Domenech, try (0–12); Dufau, try (0–15)

Scotland were no match for an adventurous and free-running French team who should have won by more, but they made errors at crucial moments and their goal-kicking was lamentable. France had a big weight advantage and their forwards were in control throughout. The French breakaways were very prominent, Jean Prat was in superb form and hardly needed to push in the scrums, and Dufau had an easy ride at scrum-half. Some of the French handling and attacking play was wonderfully exciting, backs and forwards knitting together as one, although at times they were guilty of over-elaboration. The Scots never lost heart, but they spent most of the game trying to contain opponents who were faster, more powerful and more skilful. Docherty, the new stand-off, and Elgie made occasional breaks, but there was nobody supporting them. Conditions were near perfect and the pitch was firm, but the weather grew bitterly cold as the afternoon wore on. Scotland were in trouble almost from the start and within six minutes Rogé made an opening and Vannier gave out an overhead pass to Boniface who crossed in the right corner. France continued to attack and around the thirtieth minute Vannier kicked a simple penalty from in front of the posts. Just before the break, Martine, the stand-off, made a break and Jean Prat scored a try. Early in the second period, Boniface looked to have added another only to be recalled for an infringement, much to the crowd's displeasure. However, there was little doubt about the next try which was a French classic. From a scrum inside the French half, Rogé made a brilliant weaving run to the Scottish 25 and Celaya was in support to give a scoring pass to prop forward Domenech. Towards the finish, France made an attack from a lineout and the ball was passed through several pairs of hands before Dufau finished off in the right corner.

Murrayfield · Saturday 5 February 1955 · Won 14–8

SCOTLAND A Cameron* (*Glasgow HSFP*); †AR Smith (*Cambridge U*), MK Elgie (*London*

Scot), †RG Charters (*Hawick*), JS Swan (*London Scot*); JT Docherty (*Glasgow HSFP*), †JA Nichol (*Royal HSFP*); HF McLeod (*Hawick*), WKL Relph (*Stewart's FP*), †T Elliot (*Gala*), EJS Michie (*Aberdeen U*), JWY Kemp (*Glasgow HSFP*), †WS Glen (*Edinburgh Wdrs*), A Robson (*Hawick*), JT Greenwood (*Dunfermline*)

WALES AB Edwards (*London Welsh*); KJ Jones (*Newport*), GT Wells (*Cardiff*), AG Thomas (*Llanelli*), TJ Brewer (*London Welsh*); CI Morgan (*Bective Rgrs*), WR Willis* (*Cardiff*); WOG Williams (*Swansea*), BV Meredith (*Newport*), CC Meredith (*Neath*), RJ Robins (*Pontypridd*), RH Williams (*Llanelli*), S Judd (*Cardiff*), RCC Thomas (*Swansea*), JRG Stephens (*Neath*)

REFEREE MJ Dowling (*Ireland*)

SCORING Brewer, try (0–3) (half-time) Smith, try (3–3); Docherty, drop (6–3); Elgie, pen (9–3); Brewer, try (9–6); Stephens, con (9–8); Nichol, try (12–8); Elgie, con (14–8)

In an unforgettable and emotional encounter Scotland finally brought to an end their long run of defeats that stretched back for four years. Wales were favourites to win and they started in ominous fashion. After a few minutes, Morgan punted diagonally into the Scottish 25, the defence was caught in two minds and Brewer gathered the ball to score an easy try. The visitors dominated the rest of the half and looked set for victory if they could change their tactics. Morgan, in particular, kicked too much and largely ignored the men outside him. Brewer nearly scored a second try and imme-diately after Jones had the line at his mercy, but the scoring pass was thrown at his toes. The Scottish forwards began the second half vigorously and after some ten minutes the home side conjured a wonderful try that turned the game in their favour. Inside the Scottish half, Robson lobbed out a pass to the new right wing Arthur Smith who was standing near the touchline. Smith escaped from two tackles, made a long run up the stand side before twice kicking ahead and then re-gathered the bouncing ball to score in the right corner, one the greatest solo efforts ever seen at Murrayfield. Elgie missed the awkward conversion, but a few minutes later Jim Docherty, another

The Scotland team that beat Wales in 1955, the first win in four years. *SRU*

new cap, dropped a left-footed goal from a scrum inside the Welsh 25 and then Elgie added a penalty. Stung into action, Wales fought back desperately hard and after several close shaves Brewer scored a well-worked try and Stephens added a fine conversion. With a single point in it and time fading, Scottish hearts were in their mouths when Olympic sprinter Ken Jones made a dash for the line, but he was caught just short by a brilliant tackle by Swan. The Scots fought their way out of trouble and when Wales mishandled the ball behind their own line Nichol pounced on it for the decisive try which Elgie converted. At the final whistle, the ecstatic crowd invaded the pitch to congratulate their heroes. The beaten Welsh team warmly applauded the Scots off the field and at long last the darkest era in the story of Scottish rugby was at an end.

229   INTERNATIONAL CHAMPIONSHIP 1955   IRELAND

Murrayfield · Saturday 26 February 1955 · Won 12–3

SCOTLAND †RWT Chisholm (*Melrose*); AR Smith (*Cambridge U*), MK Elgie (*London Scot*), RG Charters (*Hawick*), JS Swan (*Coventry*); A Cameron* (*Glasgow HSFP*), JA Nichol (*Royal HSFP*); HF McLeod (*Hawick*), WKL Relph (*Stewart's FP*), T Elliot (*Gala*), EJS Michie (*Aberdeen U*), JWY Kemp (*Glasgow HSFP*), †IAA MacGregor (*Hillhead HSFP*), A Robson (*Hawick*), JT Greenwood (*Dunfermline*)

IRELAND WR Tector (*Wdrs*); AC Pedlow (*QU Belfast*), AJF O'Reilly (*Old Belvedere*), NJ Henderson (*NIFC*), RE Roche (*UC Galway*); S Kelly (*Lansdowne*), SJ McDermott (*London Irish*); PJ O'Donoghue (*Bective Rgrs*), R Roe (*Lansdowne*), FE Anderson (*NIFC*), TE Reid (*London Irish*), MN Madden (*Sunday's Well*), DA McSweeney (*Blackrock Coll*), MJ Cunningham (*UC Cork*), RH Thompson* (*London Irish*)

REFEREE LM Boundy (*England*)

SCORING Kelly, pen (0–3); Elgie, pen (3–3); Swan, try (6–3) (half-time) Cameron, drop (9–3); Elgie, pen (12–3)

Angus Cameron was restored at stand-off after Jim Docherty made a late call-off. Scotland, although by no means the finished article, were more emphatic winners than the final score suggests and their victory would have been greater if Elgie's placekicking had been more accurate. The Scottish forwards recaptured much of their old fire and determination; they held their own at the set-pieces despite a weight dis-advantage and they were masters in the loose. McLeod and Kemp were in particularly fine form. Behind the scrum, Nicol played courageously and Cameron, despite suspicions about his lack of speed, rose to the occasion splendidly. Although rarely using his back line, his adroit tactical kicking and committed tackling were inspirational. The Scottish backs defended well and new full-back Chisholm recovered from a shaky start to make a confident debut. Playing in excellent conditions, Kelly kicked a simple penalty after eight minutes but later hit an upright with a drop goal attempt. Elgie missed two kicks but equalised with a penalty on the 26th minute. Near the interval, Swan, who had come into the centre, intercepted a pass and made a long diagonal run to score a try on the right. Scotland dominated the second half and, after fielding a loose kick, Cameron dropped a goal. MacGregor very nearly scored when he chased onto a kick-ahead, but the ball went out of play. Elgie kicked a second penalty to seal Scotland's first victory over Ireland since 1938 and astonishingly, after so many years of disappointment, Scotland were heading to Twickenham to challenge for the Triple Crown and the Championship.

---

230 INTERNATIONAL CHAMPIONSHIP 1955   ENGLAND

Twickenham · Saturday 19 March 1955 · Lost 6–9

SCOTLAND RWT Chisholm (*Melrose*); AR Smith (*Cambridge U*), MK Elgie (*London Scot*), RG Charters (*Hawick*), JS Swan (*Coventry*); A Cameron* (*Glasgow HSFP*), JA Nichol (*Royal HSFP*); HF McLeod (*Hawick*), WKL Relph (*Stewart's FP*), T Elliot (*Gala*), EJS Michie (*Aberdeen U*), JWY Kemp (*Glasgow HSFP*), IAA MacGregor (*Hillhead HSFP*), A Robson (*Hawick*), JT Greenwood (*Dunfermline*)

ENGLAND NSD Estcourt (*Blackheath*); FD Sykes (*Northampton*), J Butterfield (*Northampton*), WPC Davies (*Harlequins*), RC Bazley (*Waterloo*); DGS Baker (*OMTs*), JE Williams (*Old Millhillians*); GWD Hastings (*Gloucester*), NA Labuschagne (*Guy's H*), D StG Hazell (*Leicester*), PD Young* (*Dublin Wdrs*), PG Yarranton (*Wasps*), DS Wilson (*Met Police*), R Higgins (*Liverpool*), IDS Beer (*Harlequins*)

REFEREE DC Joynson (*Wales*)

SCORING Hazell, pen (0–3); Sykes, try (0–6); Cameron, pen (3–6); Beer, try (3–9) (half-time) Cameron, try (6–9)

The Scots were optimistic that they could win their first Triple Crown since 1938, but once again Twickenham proved their bogey ground. Encouraged by a large travelling support, they showed lots of fighting spirit and it was touch-and-go to the finish, but England, seeking their first win of the season, just deserved their victory by virtue of having a stronger pack and a speedier and more creative back division. The marauding English back-row put the Scottish halves under a lot of pressure although Angus Cameron kicked effectively and played a real captain's role. The ground was firm despite a brief flurry of snow shortly before kick-off. Elgie missed two long shots at goal before Hazell kicked a penalty to give England the lead after 16 minutes. A few moments later Wilson picked up a ball in his own half and set his backs moving, before Butterfield lobbed a pass to Sykes and the winger handed off Charters to score an excellent try. At this stage Scotland looked in danger of being swept away, but Cameron dropped a monumental goal from a penalty award to reduce the gap. England regained the initiative, and after a break by Estcourt and good combined play between backs and forwards, Beer thundered his way over festooned by defenders. The Scottish forwards started the second half with great vigour, but their efforts went unrewarded. Chisholm, the slight Scottish full-back, made a perfectly-executed tackle on Butterfield to prevent a certain try. On the 64th minute, Cameron kicked over to the left and scored a try in the follow-up. Elgie missed the conversion and, despite their best efforts, Scotland were unable to score again.

---

231 INTERNATIONAL CHAMPIONSHIP 1956   FRANCE

Murrayfield · Saturday 14 January 1956 · Won 12–0

SCOTLAND RWT Chisholm (*Melrose*); AR Smith (*Cambridge U*), A Cameron*

(*Glasgow HSFP*), †KR Macdonald (*Stewart's FP*), JS Swan (*Coventry*); ML Grant (*Harlequins*), †NM Campbell (*London Scot*); HF McLeod (*Hawick*), RKG MacEwen (*London Scot*), T Elliot (*Gala*), EJS Michie (*Aberdeen GSFP*), JWY Kemp (*Glasgow HSFP*), IAA MacGregor (*Llanelli*), A Robson (*Hawick*), JT Greenwood (*Dunfermline*)

FRANCE   M Vannier (*RCF*); J Dupuy (*Tarbes*), G Stener (*Paris U*), A Boniface (*Mont-de-Marsan*), S Torreilles (*Perpignan*); J Bouquet (*Vienne*), G Dufau* (*RCF*); A Domenech (*Brive*), R Vigier (*Montferrand*), R Biénès (*Cognac*), G Roucariès (*Perpignan*), B Chevallier (*Montferrand*), J Carrère (*Vichy*), R Baulon (*Bayonne*), M Celaya (*Biarritz*)

REFEREE   MJ Dowling (*Ireland*)

SCORING   Smith, pen (3–0); Cameron, pen (6–0) (half-time) Kemp, try (9–0); Kemp, try (12–0)

On a wet and cold afternoon, Scotland played their traditional forward tactics to great effect. Their fierce but carefully controlled dribbling rushes upset the French defence and the visitors, who were missing several key players, never looked comfortable in the miserable conditions. Smith landed an early penalty for Scotland but missed two other attempts on a difficult day for the kickers. Both sides had several scoring opportunities and right at the end of the half of the Cameron kicked a second goal for the Scots. In the second half, Domenech, the French prop, was almost over in the left corner. Play was keenly contested and both sides were full of fight, but gradually the Scottish forwards got on top. Around the hour mark the Scots scored a push-over try from a scrum near the French line, the score being awarded to Hamish Kemp. The rest of the play was vigorous and mainly in the French half of the field. Shortly before the end, Grant made a surprise dash and Kemp was left with the simple job of dotting the ball down near the posts. Cameron missed both relatively simple conversions, but Scotland emerged emphatic winners.

232   INTERNATIONAL CHAMPIONSHIP 1956   WALES

Cardiff Arms Park · Saturday 4 February 1956 · Lost 3–9

SCOTLAND   RWT Chisholm (*Melrose*); AR Smith (*Cambridge U*), A Cameron* (*Glasgow HSFP*), KR Macdonald (*Stewart's FP*), JS Swan (*Coventry*); ML Grant (*Harlequins*), NM Campbell (*London Scot*); HF McLeod (*Hawick*), RKG MacEwen (*London Scot*), T Elliot (*Gala*), EJS Michie (*Aberdeen GSFP*), JWY Kemp (*Glasgow HSFP*), IAA MacGregor (*Llanelli*), A Robson (*Hawick*), JT Greenwood (*Dunfermline*)

WALES   G Owen (*Newport*); KJ Jones (*Newport*), HP Morgan (*Newport*), MC Thomas (*Newport*), CL Davies (*Cardiff*); CI Morgan* (*Cardiff*), DO Brace (*Newport*); WOG Williams (*Swansea*), BV Meredith (*Newport*), R Prosser (*Pontypool*), RH Williams (*Llanelli*), JRG Stephens (*Neath*), B Sparks (*Neath*), RCC Thomas (*Swansea*), LH Jenkins (*Newport*)

REFEREE   LM Boundy (*England*)

SCORING   HP Morgan, try (0–3); Cameron, pen (3–3); Davies, try (3–6) (half-time) CI Morgan, try (3–9)

The country was in the grip of icy weather and braziers and straw were used to keep the pitch fit for play. The surface was still treacherous and a misty rain, which started soon after kick-off, added to the problems. The Scottish effort was robust and determined, but Wales were the better side. The two sets of forwards were fairly evenly matched, but the Scottish backs found the conditions difficult. By contrast, their Welsh opponents adapted well, especially half-backs Cliff Morgan and Onllwyn Brace. The mercurial Morgan was near his sparkling best. His tactical kicking was very accurate and he was always ready to attack, even when under pressure. After 19 minutes, Morgan got away in his stride and the ball reached his namesake Harry, the Welsh centre, who scored wide-out. Ten minutes later, Cameron equalised with a penalty goal. Wales were looking very impressive and, after some close shaves, good combined play between the backs and forwards put Lynn Davies down the left for an unconverted try. Scotland had spells of pressure in the second half, but the Welsh defence gave nothing away. The highlight of the match came about 12 minutes from the finish. Morgan and Brace made a clever switch move and the former shot clear through the bewildered defence for a magnificent try. For Scotland, Greenwood and Kemp were prominent in loose play.

233   INTERNATIONAL CHAMPIONSHIP 1956   IRELAND

Lansdowne Road, Dublin · Saturday 25 February 1956 · Lost 10–14

SCOTLAND RWT Chisholm (*Melrose*); AR Smith (*Cambridge U*), †T McClung (*Edinburgh Acs*), KR Macdonald (*Stewart's FP*), JS Swan (*Coventry*); A Cameron* (*Glasgow HSFP*), AF Dorward (*Gala*); HF McLeod (*Hawick*), RKG MacEwen (*London Scot*), T Elliot (*Gala*), EJS Michie (*Aberdeen GSFP*), JWY Kemp (*Glasgow HSFP*), IAA McGregor (*Llanelli*), A Robson (*Hawick*), JT Greenwood (*Dunfermline*)

IRELAND PJ Berkery (*Lansdowne*); AC Pedlow (*QU Belfast*), AJF O'Reilly (*Old Belvedere*), NJ Henderson* (*NIFC*), WJ Hewitt (*Instonians*); JW Kyle (*NIFC*), JA O'Meara (*Dolphin*); WB Fagan (*Moseley & Wdrs*), R Roe (*London Irish*), BGM Wood (*Garryowen*), BM Guerin (*Galwegians*), LM Lynch (*Lansdowne*), CTJ Lydon (*Galwegians*), MJ Cunningham (*Cork Const*), JR Kavanagh (*Wdrs*)

REFEREE HB Elliott (*England*)

SCORING Henderson, try (0–3); O'Reilly, try (0–6); Michie, try (3–6); McClung, con (5–6) (half-time) O'Meara, try (5–9); Pedlow, con (5–11); Smith, try (8–11); McClung, con (10–11); Kyle, try (10–14)

Played in fine conditions, this was an exciting and open match with six well-taken tries. Scotland were unlucky to lose their stand-off Angus Cameron early on and had to play most of the match with only 14 men. The under-strength Scottish forwards held their own throughout the game but the cover defence was fatally weakened. Ireland showed their intent immediately and Hewitt looked to have scored an early try after a brilliant movement only to be called back for a forward pass. After 12 minutes, Cameron attempted a break from his own half but was heavily tackled and had to leave the field with concussion. The Scots reorganised with McClung moving to stand-off, Swan to centre and MacGregor coming out of the pack and onto the wing. Soon afterwards, Ireland scored their first try. O'Reilly stopped a Scottish attack with a thunderous tackle in midfield. Henderson re-gathered the ball and powered down the right touchline breaking Chisholm's tackle to score in the corner. Henderson then sent O'Reilly away down the left and the big Irish centre ran round to the posts, but Pedlow missed the simple conversion. Just before the interval, Smith took play into the Irish 25, Kemp kicked on and Michie only had to fall on the ball as it rolled over the line. McClung's conversion made the score 6–5 to Ireland at half-time. Pedlow and Cunningham combined to give O'Meara a clear run to the line for a try converted by Pedlow and Scotland responded with the best try of the game. Macdonald made a mazy run from halfway and found support from Swan who weaved his way to the Irish line. Swan could probably have scored himself, but unselfishly passed to Smith who crossed near the posts and McClung converted. The match was now finely balanced and shortly before the end Jackie Kyle squeezed through on the blind side of a maul to seal Ireland's win.

234   INTERNATIONAL CHAMPIONSHIP 1956   ENGLAND

Murrayfield · Saturday 17 March 1956 · Lost 6–11

SCOTLAND RWT Chisholm (*Melrose*); AR Smith (*Cambridge U*), JT Docherty (*Glasgow HSFP*), †GD Stevenson (*Hawick*), JS Swan (*Coventry*); T McClung (*Edinburgh Acs*), AF Dorward (*Gala*); HF McLeod (*Hawick*), RKG MacEwen (*London Scot*), T Elliot (*Gala*), EJS Michie (*Aberdeen GSFP*), JWY Kemp (*Glasgow HSFP*), IAA MacGregor (*Llanelli*), A Robson (*Hawick*), JT Greenwood* (*Dunfermline*)

ENGLAND DF Allison (*Coventry*); JE Woodward (*Wasps*), J Butterfield (*Northampton*), LB Cannell (*St Mary's H*), PH Thompson (*Headingley*); M Regan (*Liverpool*), JE Williams (*Old Millhillians*); DL Sanders (*Harlequins*), E Evans (*Sale*), CR Jacobs (*Northampton*), RWD Marques (*Cambridge U*), JD Currie (*Oxford U*), PGD Robbins (*Oxford U*), VG Roberts (*Harlequins*), A Ashcroft (*Waterloo*)

REFEREE MJ Dowling (*Ireland*)

SCORING Currie, pen (0–3); Williams, try (0–6); Currie, con (0–8); Smith, pen (3–8); Currie, pen (3–11); Stevenson, try (6–11) (half-time)

In near perfect conditions, England looked the more accomplished side but Scotland might have won with a better goal-kicker and a more penetrative back division. England made a flying start and Currie kicked a penalty after 12 minutes. Williams scored a classic scrum-half try down the blind side and Currie added the extras. Smith and Currie exchanged penalties and shortly before the interval Scotland scored with the best move of the match. The forwards worked down the right and then the backs switched the direction of attack. McClung seemed to be crowded out, but threw out a long and high pass to Stevenson, the new centre, who did well to take the ball and thunder over near the posts. McClung missed the simple conversion. There was no further scoring in the second half which was largely a dour forward battle with both sets of defences to the fore. Scotland had the better of the play, but they missed four penalty kicks that might have turned the game. Arthur Smith was unlucky not to score when he raced onto a diagonal kick and had the line at his mercy but the ball bounced away from him. Amongst several good performances, Greenwood was superb as Scottish pack leader, Dorward supported his forwards well and McClung was sound in defence. For England, Marques and Currie dominated the lineouts, and Ashcroft and Robbins were fast in the loose.

Stade Yves du Manoir, Colombes, Paris · Saturday 12 January 1957
Won 6–0

SCOTLAND †KJF Scotland (*Army & Heriot's FP*); AR Smith (*Cambridge U*), †E McKeating (*Heriot's FP*), GD Stevenson (*Hawick*), JS Swan (*Coventry*); ML Grant (*Harlequins*), AF Dorward (*Gala*); HF McLeod (*Hawick*), RKG MacEwan (*London Scot*), T Elliot (*Gala*), EJS Michie (*London Scot*), JWY Kemp (*Glasgow HSFP*), IAA MacGregor (*Llanelli*), A Robson (*Hawick*), JT Greenwood* (*Perthshire Acs*)

FRANCE M Vannier (*RCF*); A Boniface (*Mont-de-Marsan*), M Prat (*Lourdes*), L Rogé (*Béziers*), J Dupuy (*Tarbes*); J Bouquet (*Vienne*), G Dufau (*RCF*); A Domenech (*Brive*), R Vigier (*Montferrand*), H Laziès (*Toulouse*), B Chevallier (*Montferrand*), A Sanac (*Perpignan*), R Baulon (*Bayonne*), J Barthe (*Lourdes*), M Celaya* (*Biarritz*)

REFEREE LM Boundy (*England*)

SCORING No scoring in the first half. Scotland, drop (3-0); Scotland, pen (6-0)

France made a strong start and after only a few minutes MacEwan was stretchered off with a leg injury, McLeod taking over as temporary hooker. The depleted Scottish forwards managed to hold out until MacEwan returned and France were unable to capitalise. After about 15 minutes, heavy, billowing rain began and continued to the end of the match, gradually turning the pitch into a swampy morass and making the ball heavy. Conditions undoubtedly favoured the Scots who wanted to play a tight game. The lighter Scottish forwards were in superb form and knocked the French out of their stride. The Scots combined very effectively and were relentless in their tackling and foraging work. They never conceded an inch in the sometimes boisterous forward exchanges. Behind them, the Scottish halves kept the French pinned down, rarely, if ever, bringing the Scottish three-quarters into action. Unable to play their normal handling game, the French were drawn into a dogfight and at times seemed to lack leadership and direction. There was no scoring in the first half and about ten minutes after the interval Ken Scotland, the new full-back, fielded a clearing kick, steadied himself like a seasoned veteran and calmly dropped a goal. Soon afterwards, he added a penalty against the din of the crowd. France launched a few handling moves but they never looked like winning. It seemed out of spite that the rain went off almost as soon as the final whistle sounded.

Murrayfield · Saturday 2 February 1957 · Won 9–6

SCOTLAND KJF Scotland (*Army & Heriot's FP*); AR Smith (*Cambridge U*), E McKeating (*Heriot's FP*), KR: Macdonald (*Stewart's FP*), JS Swan (*Coventry*); T McClung (*Edinburgh Acs*), AF Dorward (*Gala*); HF McLeod (*Hawick*), RKG MacEwen (*London Scot*), T Elliot (*Gala*), EJS Michie (*London Scot*), JWY Kemp (*Glasgow HSFP*), IAA MacGregor (*Hillhead HSFP*), A Robson (*Hawick*), JT Greenwood* (*Perthshire Acs*)

WALES TJ Davies (*Llanelli*); KJ Jones (*Newport*), GM Griffiths (*Cardiff*), MC Thomas* (*Newport*), G Howells (*Llanelli*); CI Morgan (*Cardiff*), LH Williams (*Cardiff*); CC Meredith

(*Neath*), BV Meredith (*London Welsh*), R Prosser (*Pontypool*), RH Williams (*Llanelli*), JRG Stephens (*Neath*), RH Davies (*Oxford U*), B Sparks (*Neath*), RJ Robins (*Pontypridd*)

REFEREE   RC Williams (*Ireland*)

SCORING   TJ Davies, pen (0–3); Scotland, pen (3–3); RH Davies, try (3–6); Smith, try (6–6) (half-time) Dorward, drop (9–6)

On a dry and sunny afternoon, an enormous crowd that included many thousands of Welsh supporters saw a hard, fast and exciting match. The outcome was uncertain until the end and it took one act of genius to separate the sides. There was plenty of open play and an uncompromising forward battle in which both teams gave their all. In the first half the two full-backs, Terry Davies and Ken Scotland, kicked penalty goals before Robin Davies, the new Welsh flanker, was bundled over the line after an irresistible drive from a lineout. Close to the interval, McClung, who played maturely throughout, put in a perfect diagonal kick to the right corner and Smith raced up to score a try. The second half was fairly evenly balanced and full of incident. Welsh maestro Cliff Morgan always looked dangerous, but he was tightly policed by the Scottish back-row and midfield. Close to the hour mark, Ken Scotland missed a penalty attempt, but Terry Davies failed to find touch with his clearing kick from a mark. Scrum-half Arthur Dorward took the ball and, completely unexpectedly, dropped a prodigious goal from a long and difficult angle. It was said that the cheers of the astonished crowd were heard in Princes Street. Wales fought hard to save the game, but the Scots deserved to win for their courage and tenacity.

237   INTERNATIONAL CHAMPIONSHIP 1957   IRELAND

Murrayfield · Saturday 23 February 1957 · Lost 3–5

SCOTLAND   KJF Scotland (*Army & Heriot's FP*); AR Smith* (*Cambridge U*), T McClung (*Edinburgh Acs*), KR Macdonald (*Stewart's FP*), †JLF Allan (*Cambridge U*); †JM Maxwell (*Langholm*), AF Dorward (*Gala*); HF McLeod (*Hawick*), RKG MacEwen (*London Scot*), T Elliot (*Gala*), EJS Michie (*London Scot*), JWY Kemp (*Glasgow HSFP*), IAA MacGregor (*Hillhead HSFP*), A Robson (*Hawick*), †GK Smith (*Kelso*)

IRELAND   PJ Berkery (*Lansdowne*); RE Roche (*Galwegians*), AJF O'Reilly (*Old Belvedere*), NJ Henderson* (*NIFC*), AC Pedlow (*QU Belfast*); JW Kyle (*NIFC*), AA Mulligan (*Cambridge U*); BGM Wood (*Garryowen*), R Roe (*London Irish*), JI Brennan (*CIYMS*), TE Reid (*London Irish*), JR Brady (*CIYMS*), JR Kavanagh (*Wdrs*), HS O'Connor (*Dublin U*), PJA O'Sullivan (*Galwegians*)

REFEREE   LM Boundy (*England*)

SCORING   O'Sullivan, try (0–3); Berkery, con (0–5) (half-time) Scotland, pen (3–5)

Jim Greenwood was a late withdrawal because of a leg injury and was replaced by new cap Ken Smith. After a fine morning, a windswept snowstorm started shortly before kick-off and continued for the rest of the afternoon. The conditions ruined any hope of an open, handling game and instead this was a test of stamina rather than skill, the players slipping about on the wet surface and struggling with the sodden ball and frozen fingers. Many spectators standing on the open terraces left long before the end. Scotland were expected to win, but the Irish adapted to the conditions much better and ought to have won by more. They were safer, quicker and more decisive than Scotland, and showed no traces of self-doubt. The Irish forwards were full of fire, Jack Kyle, the old master at stand-off, kicked astutely and the big Irish centres, Henderson and O'Reilly, were physically well-equipped for the treacherous conditions. With the weather behind them in the first half, Ireland had the best of the play and opened the scoring after some 27 minutes. Kyle kicked diagonally to the left corner and O'Sullivan was up fast to get the touchdown. Berkley converted from a tight angle. In the second half, the big-kicking McClung switched places with new stand-off Jimmy Maxwell who earlier had taken a heavy tackle. Ken Scotland kicked a late penalty when the Scots might have gambled on an all-or-nothing attack, but there was no doubt that Ireland deserved to win.

---

238 INTERNATIONAL CHAMPIONSHIP 1957 ENGLAND

Twickenham · Saturday 16 March 1957 · Lost 3–16

SCOTLAND KJF Scotland (*Royal Signals & Heriot's FP*); AR Smith (*Cambridge U*), T McClung (*Edinburgh Acs*), KR Macdonald (*Stewart's FP*), JLF Allan (*Cambridge U*); †GH Waddell (*London Scot*), AF Dorward (*Gala*); HF McLeod (*Hawick*), RKG MacEwen (*London Scot*), T Elliot (*Gala*), EJS Michie (*London Scot*), JWY Kemp (*Glasgow HSFP*), GK Smith (*Kelso*), A Robson (*Hawick*), JT Greenwood* (*Perthshire Acs*)

ENGLAND R Challis (*Bristol*); PB Jackson (*Coventry*), J Butterfield (*Northampton*), WPC Davies (*Harlequins*), PH Thompson (*Headingley*); RM Bartlett (*Harlequins*), REG Jeeps (*Northampton*); CR Jacobs (*Northampton*), E Evans* (*Sale*), GWD Hastings (*Gloucester*), RWD Marques (*Cambridge U*), JD Currie (*Oxford U*), PGD Robbins (*Oxford U*), R Higgins (*Liverpool*), A Ashcroft (*Waterloo*)

REFEREE R Mitchell (*Ireland*)

SCORING Davies, try (0–3) (half-time) Challis, pen (0–6); Scotland, pen (3–6); Thompson, try (3–9); Challis, con (3–11); Higgins, try (3–14); Challis, con (3–16)

This match was played in the presence of Her Majesty the Queen and Prince Philip. England were the best team of the year and duly clinched their first clean-sweep since 1928. Scotland did not play particularly badly, but they were under a lot of pressure and rarely looked capable of scoring. They spent most of the game on the defensive and their resolve was gradually worn down, England crossing for two converted tries towards the end. The home side opened the scoring around the 35th minute when Butterfield took a loose kick on the Scottish 25 and ghosted through the defence before putting Davies over at the right-hand corner. In the second half, Challis and Scotland exchanged lengthy penalties, the latter a huge effort from near halfway. England were constantly on the attack and eventually from a scrum near the Scottish line Higgins fed Thompson who thundered over in the corner. Challis converted from the left-hand touchline. Finally from a scrum in front of the Scottish posts, wing forward Higgins, who had an outstanding match, charged through the exhausted defence for a try converted by Challis.

Murrayfield · Saturday 11 January 1958 · Won 11–9

SCOTLAND RWT Chisholm (*Melrose*); AR Smith* (*Cambridge U*), GD Stevenson (*Hawick*), JT Docherty (*Glasgow HSFP*), JS Swan (*Leicester*); GH Waddell (*Devonport Servs*), †JAT Rodd (*US Portsmouth*); HF McLeod (*Hawick*), †NS Bruce (*Blackheath*), IR Hastie (*Kelso*), †MW Swan (*Oxford U*), JWY Kemp (*Glasgow HSFP*), GK Smith (*Kelso*), †MA Robertson (*Gala*), JT Greenwood (*Perthshire Acs*)

FRANCE M Vannier (*RCF*); J Dupuy (*Tarbes*), J Bouquet (*Vienne*), A Boniface (*Mont-de-Marsan*), G Mauduy (*Périgueux*); C Vignes (*RCF*), P Danos (*Béziers*); A Domenech (*Brive*), R Vigier (*Montferrand*), A Quaglio (*Mazamet*), M Celaya* (*Biarritz*), L Mias (*Mazamet*), J Carrère (*Toulon*), M Crauste (*RCF*), J Barthe (*Lourdes*)

REFEREE LM Boundy (*England*)

SCORING Chisholm, pen (3–0); Vannier, pen (3–3); Stevenson, try (6–3); Chisholm, con (8–3); Dupuy, try (8–6) (half-time) Vannier, pen (8–9); Hastie, try (11–9)

Playing in dry and still conditions, Scotland made an encouraging start to the 1958 Championship with their third win in succession against France. This was an evenly balanced and hard fought encounter that could have gone either way. There was little to choose between the forwards, although the Scots did slightly better at the set-pieces. Behind the scrum, the home side were a more effective combination. The French backs showed plenty of flair and adventure, but often they were too individualistic and made a lot of errors. Both sides kicked early penalties, and then Waddell broke through and fed Stevenson who side-stepped his way over for a try converted by Chisholm. The Scots made some further attacks before the game swung to the French. The visitors narrowly missed several chances, including a long drop goal attempt by Vannier. Just before the interval, Boniface kicked diagonally to the left and the flying Dupuy collected the ball and dived over in the corner. France continued to press in the second half and Vannier kicked a penalty to put France into the lead. The Scots might easily have lost heart at this point, but instead the forwards led a ferocious revival. Ken Smith and Stevenson were within inches of scoring tries and then from a lineout Arthur Smith made a clever short throw to Hastie who bundled his way over for the winning try.

Cardiff Arms Park · Saturday 1 February 1958 · Lost 3–8

SCOTLAND RWT Chisholm (*Melrose*); AR Smith* (*Cambridge U*), GD Stevenson (*Hawick*), JT Docherty (*Glasgow HSFP*), TG Weatherstone (*Stewart's FP*); GH Waddell (*Devonport Servs*), JAT Rodd (*US Portsmouth*); HF McLeod (*Hawick*), RKG MacEwen (*Lansdowne*), T Elliot (*Gala*), MW Swan (*Oxford U*); JWY Kemp (*Glasgow HSFP*), GK Smith (*Kelso*), A Robson (*Hawick*), JT Greenwood (*Perthshire Acs*)

WALES TJ Davies (*Llanelli*); JR Collins (*Aberavon*), MC Thomas (*Newport*), CAH Davies (*Llanelli*), GT Wells (*Cardiff*); CI Morgan (*Cardiff*), LH Williams (*Cardiff*); R Prosser (*Pontypool*), BV Meredith (*Newport*), D Devereux (*Neath*), RH Williams (*Llanelli*), WR Evans (*Cardiff*), RCC Thomas* (*Swansea*), HJ Morgan (*Abertillery*), J Faull (*Swansea*)

REFEREE NM Parkes (*England*)

SCORING Wells, try (0–3); TJ Davies, con (0–5) (half-time) AR Smith, pen (3–5); Collins, try (3–8)

Scotland made a gallant fight of it, but the strength of the Welsh forwards was eventually decisive. The Scottish half-backs were under a lot of pressure from the Welsh back-row and the three-quarters had only limited usable ball. Both sides defended stubbornly, but the Welsh backs were better in attack and grew in confidence as the match progressed. Welsh stand-off Cliff Morgan was close to his brilliant best with his accurate tactical kicking and ghost-like ability to draw defenders and create space. Scotland started strongly and in the opening stages Chisholm and Arthur Smith missed penalty chances, Docherty was only just beaten in a desperate race for a touchdown and the same player was off the mark with a drop at goal. The Welsh also had a few moments and just before the interval they scored their first try. From a scrum inside the Scottish 25, the ball was whipped left to wing Gordon Wells. Although the final pass was at his feet, Wells skilfully flicked past Arthur Smith and ran onto score in the left corner. Terry Davies capped the move with a superb conversion. After some five minutes of the second half, Arthur Smith kicked a long, straight penalty. The rest of the half largely belonged to the home side, but it was only inside the final 15 minutes that they made certain of victory. From a scrum on halfway, Williams and Collins made a slick passing movement, albeit with one pass that was glaringly forward, and the latter finished it off by diving over in the right-hand corner. Arthur Smith made a late desperate assault for the Scots but to no avail.

---

241   TOUR MATCH   AUSTRALIA

Murrayfield · Saturday 15 February 1958 · Won 12–8

SCOTLAND RWT Chisholm (*Melrose*); AR Smith* (*Gosforth*), GD Stevenson (*Hawick*), JT Docherty (*Glasgow HSFP*), TG Weatherstone (*Stewart's FP*); GH Waddell (*Devonport Servs*), JAT Rodd (*Utd Servs*); HF McLeod (*Hawick*), NS Bruce (*Blackheath*), T Elliot (*Gala*), MW Swan (*Oxford U*), JWY Kemp (*Glasgow HSFP*), GK Smith (*Kelso*), A Robson (*Hawick*), JT Greenwood (*Perthshire Acs*)

AUSTRALIA TGP Curley (*NSW*); KJ Donald (*Queensland*), JK Lenehan (*NSW*), SW White (*NSW*), R Phelps (*NSW*); AJ Summons (*NSW*), DM Connor (*Queensland*); GN Vaughan (*Victoria*), JV Brown (*NSW*), RAL Davidson* (*NSW*), AR Miller (*NSW*), DM Emanuel (*NSW*), EM Purkiss (*NSW*), JE Thornett (*NSW*), NM Hughes (*NSW*)

REFEREE RC Williams (*Ireland*)

SCORING Donald, try (0–3); Lenehan con (0–5); Weatherstone, try (3–5); Thornett, try (3–8); Smith, pen (6–8) (half-time) Smith, penalty (9–8); Stevenson, try (12–8)

In season 1957–8, Australia made a 34-match tour of the British Isles and France. The tourists had only mixed success and by the time they reached Murrayfield in February 1958 they had already lost three international matches. Conditions were ideal and Scotland played in white jerseys to avoid a clash with the dark green of Australia. As in their previous test matches, the Australians started confidently and played some attractive and uninhibited rugby, but gradually the match slipped away from them. Centre Lenehan, who was otherwise excellent, missed five penalty attempts which might have been decisive. Australia took an early lead when Donald, a very fast wing, collected a kick ahead by Curley and powered his way to the right corner. Lenehan converted from a wide angle. Scotland replied some ten minutes later. From a scrum on the Wallaby 25, Docherty put in a deft cross-kick to the left, and Weatherstone gathered the ball and slithered over the line. Within minutes Summons made a break and Thornett supported to score Australia's second try. Smith kicked penalty goals either side of the interval, the second a towering effort from near halfway. Smith's second goal proved the turning point in the game. After one or two attacks, the Australian forwards seemed to lose heart and their Scottish opponents took control, using their traditional foot-rushes to disrupt the Australians and throw them onto the defensive. Around 15 minutes before the finish, the tourists were unlucky to lose their centre White, who was injured when trying to stop a forward rush. A few minutes from time, Stevenson scored the winning try although there was a hint of a forward pass in the movement leading up to it. The Australians were naturally disappointed at the outcome, but as they left the field they were given a great ovation by the crowd.

242   INTERNATIONAL CHAMPIONSHIP 1958   IRELAND

Lansdowne Road, Dublin · Saturday 1 March 1958 · Lost 6–12

SCOTLAND RWT Chisholm (*Melrose*); AR Smith* (*Gosforth*), GD Stevenson (*Hawick*), JT Docherty (*Glasgow HSFP*), TG Weatherstone (*Stewart's FP*); GH Waddell (*Devonport Servs*), JAT Rodd (*US Portsmouth*); HF McLeod (*Hawick*), NS Bruce (*Blackheath*), T Elliot (*Gala*), MW Swan (*Oxford U*), JWY Kemp (*Glasgow HSFP*), DC Macdonald (*Edinburgh U*), A Robson (*Hawick*), JT Greenwood (*Perthshire Acs*)

IRELAND PJ Berkery (*London Irish*); AC Pedlow (*CIYMS*), D Hewitt (*QU Belfast*), NJ Henderson* (*NIFC*), AJF O'Reilly (*Old Belvedere*); JW Kyle (*NIFC*), AA Mulligan (*Wdrs*); PJ O'Donoghue (*Bective Rgrs*), AR Dawson (*Wdrs*), BGM Wood (*Garryowen*), JB Stevenson (*Instonians*), WA Mulcahy (*UC Dublin*), JA Donaldson (*Collegians*), NAA Murphy (*Cork Const*), JR Kavanagh (*Wdrs*)

REFEREE WN Gillmore (*England*)

SCORING Smith, try (3–0); Weatherstone, try (6–0) (half-time) Henderson, pen (6–3); Pedlow, try (6–6); Berkery, pen (6–9); Pedlow, try (6–12)

Ireland held a slight edge up-front and probably deserved to win, but the Scottish effort was badly disrupted when Chisholm went off with a head injury after some 32 minutes. At this point, the visitors had snatched two tries and looked comfortable enough although there were signs that Irish pressure was mounting. Scotland then lost the initiative and Ireland bungled their way to an untidy victory. In near perfect conditions, the home side had some early pressure that almost brought scores. Around the 12th minute, an attack broke down and the ball reached Arthur Smith who made a spectacular dash from halfway to score near the right-hand corner. A few minutes later, Rodd weaved through the Irish 25 before throwing out an overhead pass to the lonely Weatherstone who pounded over for Scotland's second try. Both sides had some scoring chances and Waddell missed two drop goal attempts in quick succession. Following Chisholm's injury, Arthur Smith took his place at full-back and Adam Robson came out of the pack. Ireland were on level terms within ten minutes of the restart. Henderson kicked a penalty and then the same player made a great break into the Scottish 25 before lobbing out a pass to Pedlow who raced over on the left. After 62 minutes, Berkery kicked an angled penalty to put Ireland into the lead. Towards the finish, O'Reilly swept through the centre and threw out an overhead pass to Pedlow who streaked over for the clinching try.

243   INTERNATIONAL CHAMPIONSHIP 1958   ENGLAND

Murrayfield · Saturday 15 March 1958 · Drawn 3–3

SCOTLAND KJF Scotland (*Heriot's FP*); †C Elliot (*Langholm*), GD Stevenson (*Hawick*), JT Docherty (*Glasgow HSFP*), TG Weatherstone (*Stewart's FP*); GH Waddell (*Devonport Servs*), JAT Rodd (*US Portsmouth*); HF McLeod (*Hawick*), NS Bruce (*Blackheath*), IR Hastie (*Kelso*), MW Swan (*London Scot*), JWY Kemp (*Glasgow HSFP*), DC Macdonald (*Edinburgh U*), A Robson (*Hawick*), JT Greenwood* (*Perthshire Acs*)

ENGLAND DF Allison (*Coventry*); PB Jackson (*Coventry*), J Butterfield (*Northampton*), MS Phillips (*Oxford U*), PH Thompson (*Headingley*); RM Bartlett (*Harlequins*), REG Jeeps (*Northampton*); CR Jacobs (*Northampton*), E Evans* (*Sale*), GWD Hastings (*Gloucester*), RWD Marques (*Cambridge U*), JD Currie (*Oxford U*), PGD Robbins (*Oxford U*), AJ Herbert (*Wasps*), A Ashcroft (*Waterloo*)

REFEREE RC Williams (*Ireland*)

SCORING No scoring in the first half. Elliot, pen (3–0); Hastings, pen (3–3)

On paper England held an advantage in most areas and were expected to win quite easily, but in the event they displayed a lack of leadership and purpose. Their much-vaunted three-quarter line never got into their stride and their play was often mean-

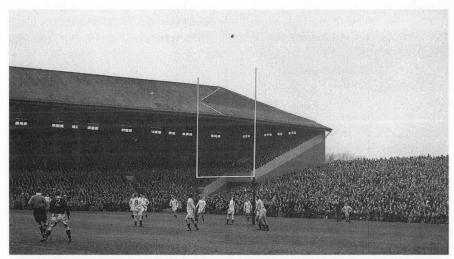

With the Murrayfield West Stand and North Terrace in the background, Langholm's Christie Elliot kicks a penalty in the drawn match against England in 1958.
Scotsman Publications Ltd

Resplendent in their latest gear, Ken Scotland, Arthur Smith, Edward McKeating, Keith Macdonald and Ian Swan take a break from training in 1958.
Scotsman Publications Ltd

dering and lacking in purpose. By comparison, the Scots gave their best performance of the season and were unlucky to be held to a draw. The Scottish forwards were full of fire and determination, and at times shoved their heavier opponents backwards in the scrums and mauls. The Scots worked hard in the loose and were always disruptive. Conditions were ideal for a fast and open game, but the first half was a dreary affair and both sides seemed wary of each other. There was no scoring and most of the chances came from kicks at goal. In the best move of the game, Jackson made a counter-attack from deep inside his own half and the ball was passed downfield until Hastings was hunted down by Ken Scotland inside the Scottish 25. Scotland dominated the second half with the forwards playing like terriers and the backs trying to force some openings. Langholm's Christie Elliot, a late replacement for flu-stricken Arthur Smith, kicked a penalty to a resounding cheer. England were temporarily reduced when Jeeps went off and Weatherstone came agonisingly close to a try. With about 15 minutes remaining, England made a rare incursion into Scottish territory and Hastings kicked a penalty. The Scots threw everything into the closing stages, but England withstood the onslaught and the match ended in stalemate.

244   INTERNATIONAL CHAMPIONSHIP 1959   FRANCE

Stade Yves du Manoir, Colombes, Paris · Saturday 10 January 1959
Lost 0–9

SCOTLAND KJF Scotland (*Cambridge U*); AR Smith (*Gosforth*), T McClung (*Edinburgh Acs*), †IHP Laughland (*London Scot*), C Elliot (*Langholm*); GH Waddell (*Cambridge U*), †S Coughtrie (*Edinburgh Acs*); HF McLeod (*Hawick*), NS Bruce (*Blackheath*), IR Hastie (*Kelso*), MW Swan (*London Scot*), JWY Kemp (*Glasgow HSFP*), GK Smith (*Kelso*), A Robson (*Hawick*), JT Greenwood* (*Perthshire Acs*)

FRANCE P Lacaze (*Lourdes*); H Rancoule (*Lourdes*), A Marquesuzaa (*RCF*), J Bouquet (*Vienne*), J Dupuy (*Tarbes*); A Labazuy (*Lourdes*), P Danos (*Béziers*); A Quaglio (*Mazamet*), R Vigier (*Monteferrand*), A Roques (*Cahors*), B Mommějat (*Cahors*), L Mias* (*Mazamet*), M Celaya (*Biarritz*), J Barthe (*Lourdes*), F Moncla (*RCF*)

REFEREE G Walters (*Wales*)

SCORING Lacaze, drop (0–3); Moncla, try (0–6) (half-time) Lacaze, drop (0–9)

Playing on a firm surface, France were more decisive winners than the final score suggests. The French forwards were almost entirely on top, despite an injury to their tight-head prop and man-mountain Alfred Roques after some 20 minutes. France showed plenty of confidence, enterprise and traditional *joie de vivre*, but they were restricted to a solitary try because of some over-exuberant back play and doughty Scottish defence. At times the visitors looked in danger of being over-run, but they stuck to their task courageously. The new scrum-half Stan Coughtrie, a tall, wispy player for his position, did particularly well behind a beaten pack. Scotland were limited in attack and their few intrusions were too slow. Their only real chance came early in the match when Waddell lofted a punt to the left and Elliot almost managed to gather the ball and score. Soon afterwards, French full-back Pierre Lacaze, who was outstanding, dropped a goal after the Scots had failed to find touch. Then, following a spell of French pressure, No 8 Moncla drove over near the right-hand corner. Early in the second half, Lacaze dropped his second goal. Ken Scotland narrowly missed a penalty attempt, Bouquet a drop goal and Dupuy nearly forced his way over on the left, but there was no further scoring.

245   INTERNATIONAL CHAMPIONSHIP 1959   WALES

Murrayfield · Saturday 7 February 1959 · Won 6–5

SCOTLAND KJF Scotland (*Cambridge U*); AR Smith (*Gosforth*), T McClung (*Edinburgh Acs*), GD Stevenson (*Hawick*), TG Weatherstone (*Stewart's FP*); GH Waddell (*Cambridge U*), S Coughtrie (*Edinburgh Acs*); HF McLeod (*Hawick*), NS Bruce (*Blackheath*), IR Hastie (*Kelso*), MW Swan (*London Scot*), JWY Kemp (*Glasgow HSFP*), GK Smith (*Kelso*), A Robson (*Hawick*), JT Greenwood* (*Perthshire Acs*)

WALES TE Davies (*Llanelli*); JR Collins (*Aberavon*), HJ Davies (*Cambridge U*), MJ Price (*Pontypool*), DI Bebb (*Carmarthen TC*); C Ashton (*Aberavon*), LH Williams (*Cardiff*); R Prosser (*Pontypool*), BV Meredith (*Newport*), DR Main (*London Welsh*), RH Williams (*Llanelli*), I Ford (*Newport*), RCC Thomas (*Swansea*), J Leleu (*London Welsh*), J Faull (*Swansea*)

REFEREE RC Williams (*Ireland*)

SCORING Price, try (0–3); TE Davies, con (0–5); Scotland, pen (3–5); Bruce, try (6–5) (half-time)

Despite conceding almost a stone-per-man, the Scottish forwards held their own in the scrums and were ferocious in loose play, going about their opponents, as *The*

Times put it, 'like furious hornets attacking an angry bull'. The back-row trio was very prominent and the half-backs, Waddell and Coughtrie, linked effectively. By comparison, the heavier Welsh forwards were exposed for their lack of pace and mobility. Playing on a firm pitch, Wales took the lead inside five minutes when centre Malcolm Price made a long solo run to score a try converted by Terry Davies. The Scots did not allow their heads to drop and the rest of the half was fairly evenly balanced, the Scottish forwards gradually running the Welshmen off their feet. After some 35 minutes, Ken Scotland kicked a fine angled penalty. Then on the stroke of half-time, the Scottish forwards made a stirring, old-fashioned charge down the field. Waddell snatched the ball inside the Welsh 25 and fed Bruce who crashed over in the right-hand corner, the Scottish hooker being knocked unconscious in the act of scoring. The Scots were the better side in the second half and only desperate defence by the visitors prevented them from scoring again. To their credit, Wales made a late revival and Ashton almost snatched victory in the last seconds with a long drop goal attempt, but his kick fell just under the bar.

246 INTERNATIONAL CHAMPIONSHIP 1959 IRELAND

Murrayfield · Saturday 28 February 1959 · Lost 3–8

SCOTLAND KJF Scotland (*Cambridge U*); AR Smith (*Ebbw Vale*), T McClung (*Edinburgh Acs*), GD Stevenson (*Hawick*), TG Weatherstone (*Stewart's FP*); GH Waddell (*Cambridge U*), S Coughtrie (*Edinburgh Acs*); HF McLeod (*Hawick*), NS Bruce (*Blackheath*), IR Hastie (*Kelso*), MW Swan (*London Scot*), JWY Kemp (*Glasgow HSFP*), GK Smith (*Kelso*), A Robson (*Hawick*), JT Greenwood* (*Perthshire Acs*)

IRELAND NJ Henderson (*NIFC*); NH Brophy (*UC Dublin*), D Hewitt (*QU Belfast*), JF Dooley (*Galwegians*), AJF O'Reilly (*Old Belvedere*); MAF English (*Bohemians*), AA Mulligan (*London Irish*); BGM Wood (*Garryowen*), AR Dawson* (*Wdrs*), S Millar (*Ballymena*), WA Mulcahy (*UC Dublin*), MG Culliton (*Wdrs*), NAA Murphy (*Cork Const*), JR Kavanagh (*Wdrs*), PJA O'Sullivan (*Galwegians*)

REFEREE LM Boundy (*England*)

SCORING Hewitt, pen (0–3); Dooley, try (0–6); Hewitt, con (0–8) (half-time) Scotland, pen (3–8)

Scotland were under pressure, especially at half-back, from the Irish marauders and they never recaptured the spirit that they had shown in their victory over Wales. The home side suffered an early set-back when their captain and inspiration Jim Greenwood went off with a dislocated shoulder. Greenwood bravely returned to the fray with his left arm tucked across his chest, but he had to pack down and tackle with only one arm. The Scottish forwards fought bravely, especially Kemp and Robson, but Ireland had the edge at the set-pieces and in the loose. Scotland started strongly before Hewitt kicked a fine angled penalty for the visitors. Close to the interval, Ireland won a heel on the right and O'Reilly came inside quickly and passed to Hewitt who put Dooley over near the corner. Hewitt converted with another fine kick. Both sides showed plenty of adventure in the second half although Ireland always looked more threatening and the Scottish attack was easily contained. Close to the end, Ken Scotland kicked a penalty goal and the Scots made a storming finish, but they were unable to make it count. This was Ireland's 12th win in 13 matches against Scotland since the end of the Second World War.

Twickenham · Saturday 21 March 1959 · Drawn 3–3

SCOTLAND KJF Scotland (*Cambridge U*); AR Smith (*Ebbw Vale*), †JAP Shackleton (*London Scot*), GD Stevenson (*Hawick*), TG Weatherstone (*Stewart's FP*); GH Waddell* (*Cambridge U*), S Coughtrie (*Edinburgh Acs*); †DMD Rollo (*Howe of Fife*), NS Bruce (*Blackheath*), HF McLeod (*Hawick*), †FH ten Bos (*Oxford U*), JWY Kemp (*Glasgow HSFP*), GK Smith (*Kelso*), A Robson (*Hawick*), †JA Davidson (*London Scot*)

ENGLAND JGG Hetherington (*Northampton*); PB Jackson (*Coventry*), MS Phillips (*Oxford U*), J Butterfield* (*Northampton*), PH Thompson (*Waterloo*); ABW Risman (*Manchester U*), SR Smith (*Cambridge U*); StLH Webb (*Bedford*), HO Godwin (*Coventry*), GJ Bendon (*Wasps*), RWD Marques (*Harlequins*), JD Currie (*Harlequins*), AJ Herbert (*Wasps*), JW Clements (*Old Cranleighans*), A Ashcroft (*Waterloo*)

REFEREE G Walters (*Wales*)

SCORING Risman, pen (0–3) (half-time) Scotland, pen (3–3)

After a disappointing Championship, Scotland went south with little to lose. Jim Shackleton and David Rollo won their first caps, George Stevenson was a last minute replacement for Keith Macdonald, and Gordon Waddell took over the captaincy. Conditions were ideal and both sides attempted to play an open game, but they made too many basic errors and neither was able to conjure a try. The heavyweight English forwards did well at the set-pieces, but their lighter opponents stood-up well and were

Laying the famous electric blanket at Murrayfield in 1959. The blanket was a gift by Dr C A Hepburn and allowed matches to go ahead despite the winter weather.
Scotsman Publications Ltd

much faster in loose play. Scotland started in a lively fashion and in the first 30 minutes Ken Scotland, who was always ready to attack from full-back, missed three shots at goal. Near the interval, Risman kicked a towering penalty to give England the lead against the run of play. In the second half, Ken Scotland kicked an equalising penalty and both sides had several scoring chances only to be denied by strong tackling or mistakes. The Scots had a spell of pressure near the England line and Waddell had a drop goal attempt charged down. There was plenty of movement from both sides right to the finish, but no further scoring and in truth neither side deserved to win.

In the Sixties 1960–1971

THE 1950S WERE often a traumatic time for Scottish rugby, but the subsequent decade was much brighter and more successful. Twice Scotland narrowly missed out on a Triple Crown, losing 6–0 to England at Twickenham in 1961 and a frustrating 3–3 draw at Murrayfield the following year. In 1964, Scotland won three matches out of four, their best showing in the championship since way back in 1938. Furthermore, Scotland had an excellent record against touring sides from the southern hemisphere. They fought out a creditable draw against New Zealand in 1964 and twice beat Australia (1966 and 1968) and South Africa (1965 and 1969).

At full-back, Ken Scotland, first capped in 1957, played until 1965, including a couple of caps at stand-off. The other outstanding full-back of this era was Stewart Wilson, who held the position from 1964 to 1968. He was a sound, polished player and a reliable goal-kicker who was good enough to play test rugby for the British Lions. On the wing, Arthur Smith played until 1962 and George Stevenson to 1965. They were followed by Langholm's Christie Elliot, David Whyte, Sandy Hinshelwood and Alastair Biggar, who were all honest, serviceable players. In the early '70s, Billy Steele, another Langholm man, was fast and elusive with a devastating side-step. David Shedden was a classic flying winger who was a good tackler despite his fragile appearance. In the centre, Iain Laughland won 31 caps between 1959 and 1967, including several at stand-off. He was always dependable, but it was felt that he never quite lived up to his club reputation as a brilliant runner. Brian Henderson and John Frame were big and powerful centres, and the latter formed an effective partnership with Chris Rea who had explosive acceleration off the mark. Probably the best centre of this time was Gala's Jock Turner. He won 20 caps between 1965 and 1971 and retired when he was still at his peak. Turner, who also played at stand-off, was a beautifully balanced runner and a fine all-rounder.

Scotland struggled to find a really outstanding stand-off in this period. Gordon Waddell played his last international in 1962 and two years later Melrose's David Chisholm made his debut. At club and international level, Chisholm formed a successful partnership with scrum-half Alec Hastie and it is almost impossible to think of one without the other. Chisholm could kick well off either foot and was a drop goal expert. He had the ability to create openings and to do the unexpected. Both Chisholm and Hastie were hard tacklers who linked well with their forwards. Colin Telfer was a good club stand-off with Hawick and won 17 caps between 1968 and 1976. He was tactically astute and a clever kicker, but never quite fulfilled his early potential. Ian Robertson, who won eight caps between 1968 and 1970, was much more of a cavalier. He had an electrifying break and was an exciting runner, but his defence and kicking skills were sometimes lacking. Scotland experimented with numerous scrum-halves in the early sixties, including Stan Coughtrie and Tremayne Rodd, before the arrival of Alec Hastie. Towards the end of the decade, Gala's Duncan Paterson was a great sevens player and deserved to win more than his ten caps.

Amongst the forwards, David Rollo continued the tradition of long serving front-row men. A Fife farmer, Rollo, who always played with his socks rolled down to his ankles, was vigorous and unyielding. It was typical of his character that he played most of his debut against England in 1959 with a broken nose. He was good enough to play on either side of the scrum and also to equal Hugh McLeod's record of 40 caps. Loose-head Ian McLauchlan made his first appearance in 1969 and became one of the legendary figures of Scottish rugby. Known as 'Mighty Mouse' for his diminutive stature, he was a magnificent scrummager who burrowed under larger opponents whilst at the same time giving his own second-row a solid platform to shove against. He was forceful character and revelled in the roll of captain, inspiring his side to some notable successes in the '70s. His partner, Sandy Carmichael, was the first Scottish player to reach the milestone of 50 caps. Technically proficient at the scrums, he was surprisingly fast in the loose, and often covered and tackled like an auxiliary flank forward, but perhaps lacked enough assertiveness. At hooker, Norman Bruce played until 1964 and was followed directly by Frank Laidlaw of Melrose who played until 1971. He toured twice with the British Lions and played in two tests on the 1966 tour of New Zealand.

Scotland unearthed some truly enormous second-row players in the '60s. Army officer Mike Campbell-Lamerton was once memorably described as resembling a runaway battleship. He had a strange galumphing stride and was not the most skilful of players, but he was effective in the lineout and always played wholeheartedly. Famously, he captained the British Lions on their tour in 1966, but dropped himself from the test team. Another giant, Frans ten Bos was of Dutch ancestry and won 17 caps between 1959 and 1963. Peter Stagg, who played his club rugby for Sale, was even taller at around six foot ten inches. Peter Brown was dubbed 'the man on the coat-hanger' because of his unusually broad shoulders. He was an eccentric individualist whose play was full of surprises. He had great ability and his own unique style of goal-kicking. He started at lock before moving back to No 8 where his idiosyncratic talents were better employed. His younger brother Gordon was arguably Scotland's greatest-ever second-row. First capped in 1969, 'Broon frae Troon' was a larger-than-life figure and the ultimate player's player. He was solid in the scrums, unfailingly sure of winning his own ball at the lineout and mobile about the field. A big man, he had problems maintaining peak fitness and undoubtedly was at his best on his three Lions tours, especially on the hard grounds in South Africa in 1974. Finally, there was hugely unorthodox Alastair McHarg who partnered Gordon Brown in the early '70s. McHarg was a tough and abrasive Ayrshireman who won 44 caps over 11 years. Tall and rangy but a little too light for a modern lock, he was an exceptional ball winner at the lineout and liked to rove about the field, sometimes playing like an extra three-quarter.

Scotland were never short of good back-row men in this era. They included the Hawick hard man Derrick Grant, who later was Scottish coach, the superbly athletic Pringle Fisher, the fair-haired Rodger Arneil and the much travelled Nairn MacEwan who also coached the national side. Dunfermline's Ron Glasgow was a destructive tackler who harried the opposition ceaselessly and had a great will to win. Finally, Melrose No 8 Jim Telfer was supremely fit, completely fearless and as hard as nails. He was not a natural ball-player, but he was good at the tail of the lineout and in the scrums, an intelligent all-rounder whose innate air of quiet authority made him a natural leader and captain. Subsequently, he became one of the most respected coaches in the game with Melrose, Scotland and the British and Irish Lions.

Murrayfield · Saturday 9 January 1960 · Lost 11–13

SCOTLAND KJF Scotland (*Cambridge U*); AR Smith* (*Ebbw Vale*), †JJ McPartlin (*Harlequins*), IHP Laugland (*London Scot*), C Elliot (*Langholm*); †G Sharp (*Stewart's FP*), JAT Rodd (*Utd Servs*); HF McLeod (*Hawick*), NS Bruce (*London Scot*), DMD Rollo (*Howe of Fife*), FH ten Bos (*Oxford U*), JWY Kemp (*Glasgow HSFP*), GK Smith (*Kelso*), A Robson (*Hawick*), †KRF Bearne (*Cambridge U*)

FRANCE M Vannier (*RCF*); L Rogé (*Béziers*), J Bouquet (*Vienne*), A Marquesuzaa (*Lourdes*), S Méricq (*Agen*); R Martine (*Lourdes*), P Danos (*Béziers*); A Domenech (*Brive*), J De Grégorio (*Grenoble*), A Roques (*Cahors*), B Momméjat (*Cahors*), M Celaya (*SBUC*), S Meyer (*Périgueux*), F Moncla* (*Pau*), M Crauste (*Lourdes*)

REFEREE G Walters (*Wales*)

SCORING Meyer, try (0–3); Vannier, con (0–5) (half-time) Méricq, try (0–8); Moncla, try (0–11); Vannier, con (0–13); AR Smith, try (3–13); Elliot, con (5–13); Elliot, pen (8–13); AR Smith, try (11–13)

This was an exciting match which Scotland might have won had they changed their tactics early on. After some ten minutes, French right wing Lucien Rogé fractured his hand making a tackle. He stayed on the field as an extra back and flanker Sylvain Meyer went onto the wing. The depleted French pack held their own in all phases, except in the scrums, and their ferocious tackling and speed in defence stifled all Scottish attacks. Near half-time, centre Jacques Bouquet intercepted a pass at midway and when Arthur Smith ran him down he passed to Meyer who scored at the posts. France started the second half in tremendous fashion, scoring two tries within three minutes. Then Scotland began to play on the injured Rogé. He missed a fly-kick at a bouncing ball allowing Arthur Smith to pick-up and score. Elliot converted and almost at once kicked a penalty for offside. From a scrum, Gregor Sharp kicked ahead, two defenders collided and Arthur Smith picked-up and ran round the full-back to score far out. Elliot was unable to convert and time ran out for Scotland.

Cardiff Arms Park · Saturday 6 February 1960 · Lost 0–8

SCOTLAND KJF Scotland (*Cambridge U*); AR Smith* (*Ebbw Vale*), JJ McPartlin (*Harlequins*), IHP Laughland (*London Scot*), GD Stevenson (*Hawick*); T McClung (*Edinburgh Acs*), JAT Rodd (*Utd Servs*); HF McLeod (*Hawick*), NS Bruce (*London Scot*), DMD Rollo (*Howe of Fife*), FH ten Bos (*Oxford U*), JWY Kemp (*Glasgow HSFP*), GK Smith (*Kelso*), †CEB Stewart (*Kelso*), KRF Bearne (*Cambridge U*)

WALES N Morgan (*Newport*); FC Coles (*Pontypool*), MJ Price (*RAF & Pontypool*), GW Lewis (*Richmond*), DIE Bebb (*Carmarthen TC & Swanea*); C Ashton (*Aberavon*), DO Brace (*Llanelli*); R Prosser (*Pontypool*), BV Meredith* (*Newport*), LJ Cunningham (*Aberavon*), GW Payne (*Army & Pontypridd*), DJE Harris (*Cardiff*), B Cresswell (*Newport*), G Whitson (*Newport*), GD Davidge (*Newport*)

REFEREE K Kelleher (*Ireland*)

No scoring in the first half. Bebb, try (o–3); Morgan, con (o–5); Morgan, pen (o–8)

Both sets of backs gave a disappointing display. Playing behind beaten forwards, Scottish scrum-half Tommy McClung had to rely mainly on making diagonal kicks to his wing Arthur Smith, who was the best back on the field. One long run by Smith almost made a try for Ken Smith, but the final pass was too wide. Welsh scrum-half Onllwyn Brace did relatively well behind a strong pack, but the home backs were off form with their handling. The only try came early in the second half when a kick ahead by Brace was fumbled and left wing Dewi Bebb nipped in to score.

250   INTERNATIONAL CHAMPIONSHIP 1960   IRELAND

Lansdowne Road, Dublin · Saturday 27 February 1960 · Won 6–5

SCOTLAND KJF Scotland (*Cambridge U*); AR Smith (*Ebbw Vale*), GD Stevenson (*Hawick*), IHP Laughland (*London Scot*), †RH Thomson (*London Scot*); GH Waddell* (*Cambridge U*), †RB Shillinglaw (*KOSB*); DMD Rollo (*Howe of Fife*), NS Bruce (*London Scot*), HF McLeod (*Hawick*), †TO Grant (*Hawick*), JWY Kemp (*Glasgow HSFP*), GK Smith (*Kelso*), †DB Edwards (*Heriot's FP*), JA Davidson (*Edinburgh Wdrs*)

IRELAND TJ Kiernan (*UC Cork*); AC Pedlow (*CIYMS*), D Hewitt (*QU Belfast*), JC Walsh (*UC Cork*), WW Bornemann (*Wdrs*); MAF English (*Bohemians*), AA Mulligan* (*London Irish*); BGM Wood (*Lansdowne*), B McCallan (*Ballymena*), S Millar (*Ballymena*), WA Mulcahy (*UC Dublin*), MG Culliton (*Wdrs*), NAA Murphy (*Cork Const*), JR Kavanagh (*Wdrs*), T McGrath (*Garryowen*)

REFEREE DG Walters (*Wales*)

SCORING Wood, try (o–3); Hewitt, con (o–5); Thomson, try (3–5); Scotland, drop (6–5) (half-time)

This was Scotland's first win in Ireland since 1933. The Scottish team had some changes and showed welcome signs of improvement. At scrum-half, Brian Shillinglaw made an excellent debut and his long service allowed Gordon Waddell to dictate play, especially towards the finish when Ireland were battling hard to save the game. The Scottish three-quarters were limited in attack, but defended well even though both centres had been injured. After an early Irish try, Ken Scotland, who fielded beautifully all afternoon, came up into the line and put Thomson over for a great score. Scotland missed the conversion, but shortly afterwards he dropped a goal from a scrum in front of the posts.

251   INTERNATIONAL CHAMPIONSHIP 1960   ENGLAND

Murrayfield · Saturday 19 March 1960 · Lost 12–21

SCOTLAND KJF Scotland (*Cambridge U*); AR Smith (*Ebbw Vale*), GD Stevenson (*Hawick*), IHP Laughland (*London Scot*), RH Thomson (*London Scot*); GH Waddell* (*Cambridge U*), RB Shillinglaw (*KOSB*); DMD Rollo (*Howe of Fife*), NS Bruce (*London Scot*), HF McLeod (*Hawick*), TO Grant (*Hawick*), JWY Kemp (*Glasgow HSFP*), GK Smith (*Kelso*), DB Edwards (*Heriot's FP*), JA Davidson (*Edinburgh Wdrs*)

ENGLAND D Rutherford (*Percy Park*); JRC Young (*Harlequins*), MS Phillips (*Oxford U*), MP Weston (*Richmond*), J Roberts (*Old Millhillians*); RAW Sharp (*Oxford U*), REG Jeeps* (*Northampton*); CR Jacobs (*Northampton*), SAM Hodgson (*Durham City*), TP Wright (*Blackheath*), RWD Marques (*Harlequins*), JD Currie (*Harlequins*), PGD Robbins (*Moseley*), RE Syrett (*Wasps*), WGD Morgan (*Medicals*)

REFEREE RC Williams (*Ireland*)

SCORING Sharp, drop (0–3); Syrett, try (0–6); Rutherford, con (0–8); Roberts, try (0–11); Rutherford, con (0–13); Rutherford, pen (0–16); Scotland, pen (3–16); Scotland, pen (6–16) (half-time) Scotland, pen (9–16); Young, try (9–19); Rutherford, con (9–21); AR Smith, try (12–21)

This was a spectacular game full of exciting action. England were well served by Richard Sharp at stand-off and Malcolm Phillips at centre. For Scotland, Brian Shillinglaw did well under pressure from his opposite number Dickie Jeeps and the English back-row, but there was no penetration further back and the potentially dangerous Scottish wings saw little of the ball. England made a great start, going 13 points up in as many minutes. Sharp opened the scoring with a long drop goal and then Syrett and Roberts scored tries, both converted by Don Rutherford who followed with a penalty. Before half-time, Ken Scotland reduced the deficit with two long range penalties and ten minutes after the interval he added a third from around 40 yards. Scotland seemed to be fighting their way back, but then Phillips made a break to send John Young racing away for the decisive try. Late in the game, Ken Scotland created space for Arthur Smith to show his pace and score.

252 TOUR OF SOUTH AFRICA 1960   SOUTH AFRICA

Boet Erasmus Stadium, Port Elizabeth · Saturday 30 April 1960

Lost 10–18

SCOTLAND RWT Chisholm (*Melrose*); AR Smith (*Ebbw Vale*), †PJ Burnet (*London Scot*), GD Stevenson (*Hawick*), RH Thomson (*London Scot*); GH Waddell* (*Cambridge U*), RB Shillinglaw (*Gala*); HF McLeod (*Hawick*), NS Bruce (*London Scot*) DMD Rollo (*Howe of Fife*), FH ten Bos (*Oxford U*), JWY Kemp (*Glasgow HSFP*), DB Edwards (*Heriot's FP*), †W Hart (*Melrose*), TO Grant (*Hawick*)

SOUTH AFRICA MC Gerber (*E Province*); JP Engelbrecht (*W Province*), AI Kirkpatrick (*Griqualand W*), JL Gainsford (*W Province*), RJ Twigge (*N Transvaal*); DA Stewart (*W Province*), FW Gericke (*Transvaal*); DN Holton (*E Province*), AJ van der Merwe (*Boland*), MJ Bekker (*N Transvaal*), JT Claassen (*W Transvaal*), PB Allen (*E Province*), DC van Jaarsveldt* (*Rhodesia*), GH van Zyl (*W Province*), DJ Hopwood (*W Province*)

REFEREE EA Strasheim

SCORING Bruce, try (3–0); Smith, con (5–0); van Zyl, try (5–3); Gerber, con (5–5) (half-time) van Zyl, try (5–8); Gerike, try (5–11); Gerber, con (5–13); van Jaarsveldt, try (5–16); Gerber, con (5–18); Smith, try (8–18); Smith, con (10–18)

At the end of season 1959–60, Scotland made a three-match tour of South Africa, their first ever in the southern hemisphere. The tour opened with a test match against South Africa in Port Elizabeth. The home side were firm favourites, but the Scots exceeded expectations especially in the forwards. The lighter Scottish pack more than held their own in the set-pieces and did well in the loose although they were vulnerable around the edge of the scrums. Stand-off Gordon Waddell had an outstanding match. He made some dangerous breaks down the centre, showed great tactical awareness and kicked astutely. The Scottish backs tackled solidly and were always ready to attack although Stevenson was handicapped by an injury early on. The game had barely started when Bruce scored at the posts and Smith converted. South Africa equalised after some 25 minutes. Gericke went blind from a scrum and gave a scoring pass to van Zyl. Scotland started the second half purposefully before the South Africans scored twice. Van Zyl scored a similar try to his first and then Gericke barged his way over. The best score of the day came when van Jaarsveld, the Springbok captain, grabbed the ball in midfield and made a spectacular long run to the line. In the closing minutes, Shillinglaw, who was excellent throughout, made a break and sent Smith in for a try. After this game, Scotland won provincial matches against Griqualand West (21–11) and East Transvaal (30–16).

---

253   INTERNATIONAL CHAMPIONSHIP 1961   FRANCE

Stade Yves du Manoir, Colombes, Paris · Saturday 7 January 1961

Lost 0–11

SCOTLAND KJF Scotland (*London Scot*); AR Smith (*Edinburgh Wdrs*), †RC Cowan (*Selkirk*), GD Stevenson (*Hawick*), RH Thomson (*London Scot*); GH Waddell* (*Cambridge U*), RB Shillinglaw (*KOSB*); HF McLeod (*Hawick*), NS Bruce (*London Scot*), DMD Rollo (*Howe of Fife*), FH ten Bos (*Oxford U*), †MJ Campbell-Lamerton (*Blackheath*), GK Smith (*Kelso*), CEB Stewart (*Kelso*), †J Douglas (*Stewart's FP*)

FRANCE R Martine (*Lourdes*); J Gachassin (*Lourdes*), G Boniface (*Mont-de-Marsan*), J Bouquet (*Vienne*), J Dupuy (*Tarbes*); P Albaladéjo (*Dax*), P Lacroix (*Agen*); A Domenech (*Brive*), J De Grégorio (*Grenoble*), A Roques (*Cahors*), L Echavé (*Agen*), M Celaya (*SBUC*), M Crauste (*Lourdes*), F Moncla* (*Pau*), R Crancée (*Lourdes*)

REFEREE RC Williams (*Ireland*)

SCORING No scoring in the first half. Albaladéjo, drop (0–3); Albaladéjo, pen (0–6); Boniface, try (0–9); Albaladéjo, con (0–11)

Flanker Charlie Stewart injured his leg in the opening minute and, although he remained on the field, he was little more than a passenger for the rest of the game. Although the match was played in early January, conditions were ideal and France adopted their traditional handling game. The depleted Scottish forwards did well to prevent any scoring in the first half, but the physical strain told eventually and the home side ran out deserved winners. Albaladéjo opened the scoring with a trademark drop goal and then he kicked a magnificent long penalty. The only try of the match was scored on the right by Guy Boniface and converted from near the touchline by Albaladéjo. Scotland came close to scoring twice in the second half. Waddell made a spirited break, but was held almost underneath the posts and then Thomson dived over in the left-hand corner only to be recalled for an earlier infringement. The Scottish half-backs, Waddell and Shillinglaw, were very impressive and new second-row Mike Campbell-Lamerton used his considerable presence to good effect.

Murrayfield · Saturday 21 January 1961 · Lost 5–12

SCOTLAND KJF Scotland (*London Scot*); AR Smith* (*Edinburgh Wdrs*), E McKeating (*Heriot's FP*), GD Stevenson (*Hawick*), RH Thomson (*London Scot*); IHP Laughland (*London Scot*), RB Shillinglaw (*Gala*); HF McLeod (*Hawick*), NS Bruce (*London Scot*), DMD Rollo (*Howe of Fife*), FH ten Bos (*Oxford U*), MJ Campbell-Lamerton (*Blackheath*), GK Smith (*Kelso*), †KI Ross (*Boroughmuir FP*), J Douglas (*Stewart's FP*)

SOUTH AFRICA DA Stewart (*W Province*); JP Engelbrecht (*W Province*), JL Gainsford (*W Province*), AI Kirkpatrick (*OFS*), HJ Van Zyl (*Transvaal*); K Oxlee (*Natal*), P de W Uys (*N Transvaal*); SP Kuhn (*Transvaal*), GF Malan (*W Province*), PS du Toit (*Boland*), AS Malan* (*Transvaal*), JT Claassen (*W Transvaal*), GH Van Zyl (*W Province*), FC Du Preez (*N Transvaal*), DJ Hopwood (*W Province*)

REFEREE LM Boundy (England)

SCORING Hopwood, try (0–3); Claassen, try (0–6) (half-time) AR Smith, try (3–6); Scotland, con (5–6); Du Preez, pen (5–9); Du Preez, pen (5–12)

In season 1960–1, South Africa made a 34-match tour of the British Isles and France under the captaincy of second-row Avril Malan. The Springboks were still unbeaten by the time they reached Murrayfield and had already defeated the other three home nations. This was an entertaining match with both sides playing fast and open rugby. The South African forwards produced some great handling and support work, and they held the upper-hand in the set-pieces. The lighter Scots showed plenty of fighting spirit and did well in the loose. At full-back, Ken Scotland's positional play and touch-kicking were excellent. The South Africans scored their first try after 24 minutes when the ever-alert Hopwood picked up from a scrum near the Scottish line and darted through to score. Near the interval, Hopwood found another opening at a close-range scrum and Claassen was on hand to claim the try. Scotland withstood a lot of pressure in the second half and around the 60th minute they scored an exciting try of their own. Laughland was wide with a drop goal attempt, but Arthur Smith followed up fast and just managed to reach the ball before it went out of play. Ken Scotland kicked a fine conversion to raise Scottish hopes, but du Preez responded with two long range penalties to seal a deserved win for the visitors.

Murrayfield · Saturday 11 February 1961 · Won 3–0

SCOTLAND KJF Scotland (*London Scot*); AR Smith* (*Edinburgh Wdrs*), E McKeating (*Heriot's FP*), GD Stevenson (*Hawick*), RH Thomson (*London Scot*); IHP Laughland (*London Scot*), †AJ Hastie (*Melrose*); HF McLeod (*Hawick*), NS Bruce (*London Scot*), DMD Rollo (*Howe of Fife*), FH ten Bos (*London Scot*), MJ Campbell-Lamerton (*Halifax*), KI Ross (*Boroughmuir FP*), GK Smith (*Kelso*), J Douglas (*Stewart's FP*)

WALES TJ Davies* (*Llanelli*); PM Rees (*Newport*), G Britton (*Newport*), HM Roberts (*Cardiff*), DI Bebb (*Swansea*); K Richards (*Bridgend*), A O'Connor (*Aberavon*); PEJ Morgan (*Aberavon*), BV Meredith (*Newport*), KD Jones (*Cardiff*), WR Evans (*Bridgend*), DJE Harris (*Cardiff*), GD Davidge (*Newport*), HJ Morgan (*Abertillery*), D Nash (*Ebbw Vale*)

SCORING AR Smith, try (3–0) (half-time)

This was mainly a hard, slogging forward battle played in wind and rain. The Scottish eight held their own in the scrums and were superior in the open. The three-quarters tackled well and gave their dangerous opponents limited opportunity. The only score of the match came after some 31 minutes when Ken Scotland breached the Welsh defence before giving a perfectly timed pass to Arthur Smith who powered over at the corner. Scotland missed the conversion and several penalty attempts, but otherwise he played immaculately. In the second half, he saved a certain score when he felled Dewi Bebb at the corner flag after the Welsh wing had made a long run up the touch-line. For Scotland, scrum-half Alex Hastie played manfully on his debut.

---

256   INTERNATIONAL CHAMPIONSHIP 1961   IRELAND

Murrayfield · Saturday 25 February 1961 · Won 16–8

SCOTLAND KJF Scotland (*London Scot*); AR Smith* (*Edinburgh Wdrs*), E McKeating (*Heriot's FP*), GD Stevenson (*Hawick*), RH Thomson (*London Scot*); IHP Laughland (*London Scot*), AJ Hastie (*Melrose*); HF McLeod (*Hawick*), NS Bruce (*London Scot*), DMD Rollo (*Howe of Fife*), FH ten Bos (*London Scot*), MJ Campbell-Lamerton (*Halifax*), KI Ross (*Boroughmuir FP*), GK Smith (*Kelso*), J Douglas (*Stewart's FP*)

IRELAND TJ Kiernan (*UC Cork*); AC Pedlow (*CIYMS*), D Hewitt (*QU Belfast*), JC Walsh (*UC Cork*), NH Brophy (*Blackrock Coll*); MAF English (*Bohemians*), JW Moffett (*Ballymena*); BGM Wood (*Lansdowne*), AR Dawson* (*Wdrs*), S Millar (*Ballymena*), WA Mulcahy (*UC Dublin*), MG Culliton (*Wdrs*), IR Kavanagh (*Wdrs*), NAA Murphy (*Garryowen*), PJA O'Sullivan (*Galwegians*)

REFEREE MHR King (*England*)

SCORING Kavanagh, try (0–3); Moffett, con (0–5); Scotland, pen (3–5); Douglas, try (6–5); Scotland, con (8–5) (half-time) Ross, try (11–5); Scotland, con (13–5); Hewitt, try (13–8); Ross, try (16–8)

This was a fast and entertaining match with both sets of forwards throwing everything into the fray. Hugh McLeod led the Scottish pack from the front, Mike Campbell-Lamerton did well at the lineout and the back-row trio were very prominent, especially in their support play. The Irish had more threat behind the scrum, especially centre Dave Hewitt, but the Scots did enough to hold them. After an early Irish score, Ken Scotland kicked a penalty goal and then converted a try by No 8 John Douglas before the interval. In the second half, Scotland was again involved when he broke into the line and made a strong run to set-up a try for Ken Ross. Scotland kicked a fine conversion from near the touchline. Ireland started to play more expansively and test the Scottish defence. The visitors scored a lovely try from a flowing movement by their three-quarters although Hewitt, the try scorer, seemed to knock-on before he touched the ball down. Eight minutes from the end Ross completed an excellent display when he scored his second try.

Twickenham · Saturday 18 March 1961 · Lost 0–6

SCOTLAND KJF Scotland (*Heriot's FP*); AR Smith* (*Edinburgh Wdrs*), E McKeating (*Heriot's FP*), GD Stevenson (*Hawick*), RH Thomson (*London Scot*); IHP Laughland (*London Scot*), AJ Hastie (*Melrose*); HF McLeod (*Hawick*), NS Bruce (*London Scot*), DMD Rollo (*Howe of Fife*), FH ten Bos (*London Scot*), J Douglas (*Stewart's FP*), KI Ross (*Boroughmuir FP*), †JC Brash (*Cambridge U*), GK Smith (*Kelso*)

ENGLAND JG Willcox (*Harlequins & Oxford U*); PB Jackson (*Coventry*), WM Patterson (*Sale*), MP Weston (*Richmond*), J Roberts (*Sale*); JP Horrocks-Taylor (*Leicester*), REG Jeeps* (*Northampton*); CR Jacobs (*Northampton*), E Robinson (*Coventry*), TP Wright (*Blackheath*), RJ French (*St Helens*), VSJ Harding (*Saracens & Cambridge U*), LI Rimmer (*Bath*), DP Rogers (*Bedford*), WGD Morgan (*Medicals*)

REFEREE KD Kelleher (Ireland)

SCORING Roberts, try (0–3) (half-time) Horrocks-Taylor, pen (0–6)

Once again Scotland failed to win the Triple Crown at Twickenham. The Scots were favourites but gave their worst performance of the season and England, although hardly brilliant, deserved to win. The absence of the bulky Mike Campbell-Lamerton severely weakened the Scottish forwards and the back division was only moderate at best. Even full-back Ken Scotland was out of sorts and missed several penalty chances well within his range. By contrast, English stand-off Phil Horrocks-Taylor, deputising for the injured Richard Sharp, had a great match. This was a scrappy and rather dull encounter with only brief flurries of excitement. Around midway in the first half, England centre Paterson made a break inside the Scottish 22, kicked towards the corner and Roberts raced onto the ball to touchdown. There was no further scoring until shortly before the end when Horrocks-Taylor kicked a penalty. The Scots missed a great chance for a grandstand finish when Douglas, who otherwise was very good, knocked on near the English line when he only needed to tap the ball over for a certain score.

Murrayfield · Saturday 13 January 1962 · Lost 3–11

SCOTLAND KJF Scotland (*Leicester*); AR Smith* (*Edinburgh Wdrs*), JJ McPartlin (*Oxford U*), IHP Laughland (*London Scot*), RC Cowan (*Selkirk*); GH Waddell (*London Scot*), JAT Rodd (*London Scot*); HF McLeod (*Hawick*), NS Bruce (*London Scot*), DMD Rollo (*Howe of Fife*), FH ten Bos (*London Scot*), MJ Campbell-Lamerton (*Halifax*), †RJC Glasgow (*Dunfermline*), KI Ross (*Boroughmuir FP*), J Douglas (*Stewart's FP*)

FRANCE L Casaux (*Tarbes*); H Rancoule (*Tarbes*), J Piqué (*Pau*), J Bouquet (*Vienne*), J Dupuy (*Tarbes*); P Albaladéjo (*Dax*), P Lacroix* (*Agen*); A Domenech (*Brive*), J De Grégorio (*Grenoble*), A Roques (*Cahors*), B Momméjat (*Albi*), JP Saux (*Pau*), R Gensane (*Béziers*), M Crauste (*Lourdes*), H Romero (*Montauban*)

REFEREE RC Williams (*Ireland*)

SCORING Smith, pen (3–0); Albaladéjo, pen (3–3) (half-time) Albaladéjo, pen (3–6); Rancoule, try (3–9); Albaladéjo, con (3–11)

Playing in perfect conditions, the Scottish forwards were in fine form, but back division lacked pace and imagination. Stand-off Gordon Waddell adopted a very cautious approach and gave his three-quarters little opportunity to attack. Arthur Smith opened the scoring with a penalty goal after some 15 minutes, but the Scots missed four other kickable chances during the match. Albaladéjo equalised with a penalty from near the touchline shortly before the interval. Scotland dominated territorially and, despite wasting several scoring opportunities, they looked likely winners until the closing stages. With around 15 minutes left, Campbell-Lamerton was penalised for foul play and Albaladéjo kicked a magnificent long angled penalty. Up to this point, France had been grimly hanging on, but now took charge. Ken Scotland missed another penalty and then Crauste and Gensane, the French flank forwards, made a dribbling rush from a lineout. Ken Scotland fumbled the ball on the ground allowing right wing Rancoule to outpace the Scottish defence and score. Albaladéjo converted and late in the game the same player, who was known as 'Monsieur Drop', narrowly missed two drop goal attempts.

---

259   INTERNATIONAL CHAMPIONSHIP 1962   WALES

Cardiff Arms Park · Saturday 3 February 1962 · Won 8–3

SCOTLAND KJF Scotland (*Leicester*); AR Smith* (*Edinburgh Wdrs*), JJ McPartlin (*Oxford U*), IHP Laughland (*London Scot*), RC Cowan (*Selkirk*); GH Waddell (*London Scot*), S Coughtrie (*Edinburgh Acs*); HF McLeod (*Hawick*), NS Bruce (*London Scot*), DMD Rollo (*Howe of Fife*), FH ten Bos (*London Scot*), MJ Campbell-Lamerton (*Halifax*), RJC Glasgow (*Dunfermline*), KI Ross (*Boroughmuir FP*), J Douglas (*Stewart's FP*)

WALES K Coslett (*Aberavon*); DRR Morgan (*Llanelli*), DK Jones (*Llanelli*), HM Roberts (*Cardiff*), DIE Bebb (*Swansea*); A Rees (*Maesteg*), LH Williams* (*Cardiff*); LJ Cunningham (*Aberavon*), BV Meredith (*Newport*), D Greenslade (*Newport*), B Price (*Newport*), WR Evans (*Bridgend*), RH Davies (*London Welsh*), HJ Morgan (*Abertillery*), A Pask (*Abertillery*)

REFEREE NM Parkes (*England*)

SCORING Glasgow, try (3–0); ten Bos, try (6–0); Scotland, con (8–0) (half-time) Rees, drop (8–3)

In miserable conditions, Scotland won at Cardiff for the first time since 1927. The veteran Hugh McLeod led from the front and the Scottish forwards responded magnificently, especially in the scrums. Stan Coughtrie, a late replacement at scrum-half, used his long and accurate kicking to great effect. The Scots opened the scoring after 17 minutes when the forwards held the ball at an advancing scrum before Douglas and ten Bos broke away and put Glasgow over on the left. A few minutes later, Waddell put up a high kick into the Welsh 22, ten Bos gathered the rebound and used his considerable momentum to get over the line. Ken Scotland converted. The Scots did not score again, but they always held the upper-hand even when playing into the elements in the second-half. They defended courageously and showed great stamina and determination in the face of the Welsh onslaught. Wales tried everything they knew, but could only manage a late drop goal by Rees.

Lansdowne Road, Dublin · Saturday 24 February 1962 · Won 20–6

SCOTLAND KJF Scotland (*Leicester*); AR Smith* (*Edinburgh Wdrs*), JJ McPartlin (*Oxford U*), IHP Laughland (*London Scot*), RC Cowan (*Selkirk*); GH Waddell (*London Scot*), S Coughtrie (*Edinburgh Acs*); HF McLeod (*Hawick*), NS Bruce (*London Scot*), †R Steven (*Edinburgh Wdrs*), FH ten Bos (*London Scot*), MJ Campbell-Lamerton (*Halifax*), RJC Glasgow (*Dunfermline*), KI Ross (*Boroughmuir FP*), J Douglas (*Stewart's FP*)

IRELAND FG Gilpin (*QU Belfast*); WR Hunter (*CIYMS*), MK Flynn (*Wdrs*), D Hewitt (*Instonians*), NH Brophy (*Blackrock Coll*); GG Hardy (*Bective Rgrs*), JTM Quirke (*Blackrock Coll*); S Millar (*Ballymena*), AR Dawson (*Wdrs*), RJ McLoughlin (*UC Dublin*), WJ McBride (*Ballymena*), WA Mulcahy* (*Bohemians*), D Scott (*Malone*), ML Hipwell (*Terenure*), MG Culliton (*Wdrs*)

REFEREE NM Parkes (*England*)

SCORING Scotland, pen (3–0); Smith, try (6–0); Cowan, try (9–0) (half-time) Hunter, pen (9–3); Hunter, try (9–6); Scotland, pen (12–6); Smith, try (15–6); Scotland, con (17–6); Coughtrie, drop (20–6)

Scotland were a little flattered by the final score, but they were deserved winners. The Scottish forwards had to fight hard, but the backs played very soundly, especially Waddell and Coughtrie at half-back. Facing into the wind, Ireland started strongly and came close to scoring before Ken Scotland kicked a fine penalty goal after 11 minutes. Then from a scrum near the Irish line, Waddell made a break and Scotland gathered his pass on the bounce to send Smith over on the right. Seven minutes before the interval, Cowan scored in the opposite corner after Waddell worked his way into the Irish 22 and Laughland provided the link. In the second half, Irish right wing Hunter kicked a penalty and scored a try after the Scots had failed to deal with a high ball. The home side were always threatening, but the Scottish forwards mounted a late rally and Scotland kicked his second penalty. Then Coughtrie broke into the Irish 22, and Waddell and McLeod were in support to put Smith racing over for his second try. Scotland converted and at the end Coughtrie kicked an angled left-footed drop goal to seal Scotland's victory.

Murrayfield · Saturday 17 March 1962 · Drawn 3–3

SCOTLAND KJF Scotland (*Leicester*); AR Smith* (*Edinburgh Wdrs*), JJ McPartlin (*Oxford U*), IHP Laughland (*London Scot*), RC Cowan (*Selkirk*); GH Waddell (*London Scot*), S Coughtrie (*Edinburgh Acs*); HF McLeod (*Hawick*), NS Bruce (*London Scot*), DMD Rollo (*Howe of Fife*), FH ten Bos (*London Scot*), MJ Campbell-Lamerton (*Halifax*), RJC Glasgow (*Dunfermline*), KI Ross (*Boroughmuir FP*), J Douglas (*Stewart's FP*)

ENGLAND JG Willcox (*Oxford U*); ACB Hurst (*Wasps*), AM Underwood (*Northampton*), JM Dee (*Hartlepool Rovers*), J Roberts (*Sale*); JP Horrocks-Taylor (*Leicester*), REG Jeeps* (*Northampton*); PE Judd (*Coventry*), SAM Hodgson (*Durham City*), TP Wright (*Blackheath*), TA Pargetter (*Coventry*), VSJ Harding (*Sale*), SJ Purdy (*Rugby*), PGD Robbins (*Coventry*), PJ Taylor (*Northampton*)

SCORING Willcox, pen (0–3); Scotland, pen (3–3) (half-time)

Scotland were trying to win their first Triple Crown since 1938, but were denied in a disappointing draw. Playing in front of an enormous crowd, the Scots fought hard and could have won, but just did not take their chances. They kept the ball tight when they should have tried to run the heavy English pack off its feet. The Scottish backs were unable to escape a watchful defence and at times they looked uncertain and lacking invention. Ken Scotland narrowly missed three penalty attempts and in the second half both Smith and Cowan were thrown into touch just inches from the goal-line. England were never able to control play and had few scoring chances, but they were always ready to turn defence into attack. The visitors took the lead after 25 minutes when Oxford's John Willcox kicked a long angled penalty. Ken Scotland equalised with a similar score just before the interval. In the second half, Underwood went off with a dislocated shoulder and Purdy took his place on the wing. Scotland players Arthur Smith, Gordon Waddell and Hugh McLeod made their final appearances in this game. Curiously, despite their long careers, none of them played in a winning side against England.

262 INTERNATIONAL CHAMPIONSHIP 1963 FRANCE

Stade Yves du Manoir, Colombes, Paris · Saturday 12 January 1963
Won 11–6

SCOTLAND KJF Scotland* (*Leicester*); RH Thomson (*London Scot*), JAP Shackleton (*London Scot*), †DM White (*Kelvinside Acs*), GD Stevenson (*Hawick*); IHP Laughland (*London Scot*), S Coughtrie (*Edinburgh Acs*); †ACW Boyle (*London Scot*), NS Bruce (*London Scot*) DMD Rollo (*Howe of Fife*), FH ten Bos (*London Scot*), MJ Campbell-Lamerton (*Halifax*), KI Ross (*Boroughmuir FP*), †WRA Watherston (*London Scot*), J Douglas (*Stewart's FP*)

FRANCE J-P Razat (*Agen*); P Besson (*Brive*), G Boniface (*Mont-de-Marsan*), A Boniface (*Mont-de-Marsan*), C Darrouy (*Mont-de-Marsan*); P Albaledéjo (*Dax*), P Lacroix* (*Agen*); F Mas (*Béziers*), J De Gregorio (*Grenoble*), A Roques (*Cahors*), B Momméjat (*Albi*), J-P Saux (*Pau*), R Gensane (*Béziers*), M Crauste (*Lourdes*), J Fabre (*Toulouse*)

REFEREE RC Williams (*Ireland*)

SCORING A Boniface, drop (0–3); Albaladéjo, pen (0–6) (half-time) Scotland, drop (3–6); Scotland, pen (6–6); Thomson, try (9–6); Scotland, con (11–6)

The pitch had been protected by straw which was set alight in an attempt to thaw out the ground, making the playing surface look brown instead of green. Nevertheless, it was still very hard despite the strong winter sunshine. France, the reigning champions, played with the wind behind them in the first half, but could only manage a drop goal by André Boniface and a penalty goal by Pierre Albaladéjo. In the second half, the Scottish forwards, who were heavier than their opponents, took a firm grip of the game. At the hour mark, Ken Scotland collected a poor clearance and dropped a beautiful goal from around 40 yards. He then equalised with a simple penalty goal after a French defender had passed off the ground near his own line. It seemed that the match was heading for a draw until a dramatic late score. Laughland attempted a long speculative drop goal, but the ball bounced harmlessly towards the French goal-line. The defence were slow to react and Ronnie Thomson, who appeared out of nowhere, grabbed the ball and dived over. Ken Scotland, who proved an inspirational leader throughout, converted with the last kick of the game.

263   INTERNATIONAL CHAMPIONSHIP 1963   WALES

Murrayfield · Saturday 2 February 1963 · Lost 0–6

SCOTLAND KJF Scotland* (*Heriot's FP*); RH Thomson (*London Scot*), JAP Shackleton (*London Scot*), DM White (*Kelvinside Acs*), GD Stevenson (*Hawick*); IHP Laughland (*London Scot*), S Coughtrie (*Edinburgh Acs*); ACW Boyle (*London Scot*), NS Bruce (*London Scot*), DMD Rollo (*Howe of Fife*), FH ten Bos (*London Scot*), MJ Campbell-Lamerton (*Halifax*), KI Ross (*Boroughmuir FP*), WRA Watherston (*London Scot*), J Douglas (*Stewart's FP*)

WALES GTR Hodgson (*Neath*); DRR Morgan (*Llanelli*), DB Davies (*Llanelli*), R Evans (*Bridgend*), WJ Morris (*Pontypool*); D Watkins (*Newport*), DCT Rowlands* (*Pontypool*); D Williams (*Ebbw Vale*), NR Gale (*Llanelli*), KD Jones (*Cardiff*), B Price (*Newport*), BE Thomas (*Cambridge U*), G Jones (*Ebbw Vale*), HJ Morgan (*Abertillery*), AEI Pask (*Abertillery*)

REFEREE RC Williams (*Ireland*)

SCORING Hodgson, pen (0–3) (half-time) Rowlands, drop (0–6)

This infamous match has gone down as one of the dreariest internationals ever played. The Welsh forwards won the bulk of possession, but their scrum-half, Clive Rowlands, kicked most of it into touch and did nothing exciting or daring. The Scots, living on thinner rations, largely followed suit and the result was an utterly boring spectacle without any open play. On a cold afternoon with snow lying around the pitch, Wales dominated the opening stages and after about 16 minutes full-back Graham Hodgson kicked a good penalty into the breeze. Towards the end of the half, the Scots made some unsuccessful forays into the Welsh 25 and Ken Scotland missed two penalty attempts, the second of which struck a post. The second half followed a similar story. Towards the hour mark, Wales won yet another lineout and Rowlands had plenty of time to set himself up for a splendid drop goal from an acute angle. The Scots staged a desperate late rally and Stevenson was stopped just short of the line in the final minute.

264   INTERNATIONAL CHAMPIONSHIP 1963   IRELAND

Murrayfield · Saturday 23 February 1963 · Won 3–0

SCOTLAND †CF Blaikie (*Heriot's FP*); RH Thomson (*London Scot*), IHP Laughland (*London Scot*), DM White (*Kelvinside Acs*), GD Stevenson (*Hawick*); KJF Scotland* (*Heriot's FP*), S Coughtrie (*Edinburgh Acs*); ACW Boyle (*London Scot*), NS Bruce (*London Scot*), DMD Rollo (*Howe of Fife*), FH ten Bos (*London Scot*), MJ Campbell-Lamerton (*Halifax*), RJC Glasgow (*Dunfermline*), WRA Watherston (*London Scot*), J Douglas (*Stewart's FP*)

IRELAND TJ Kiernan (*UC Cork*); WR Hunter (*CIYMS*), JC Walsh (*UC Cork*), PJ Casey (*UC Dublin*), AJF O'Reilly (*Old Belvedere*); MAF English (*Lansdowne*), JC Kelly (*UC Dublin*);

S Millar (*Ballymena*), AR Dawson (*Wdrs*), RJ McLoughlin (*Gosforth*), WA Mulcahy* (*Bective Rgrs*), WJ McBride (*Ballymena*), EP McGuire (*UC Galway*), MD Kiely (*Lansdowne*), CJ Dick (*Ballymena*)

REFEREE GJ Treharne (*Wales*)

SCORING Coughtrie, pen (3–0) (half-time)

New cap Colin Blaikie continued the tradition of the Heriot's full-back factory and Ken Scotland made his first start at stand-off. Played in ideal conditions, this was an undistinguished match decided by a solitary Coughtrie penalty goal just before the interval. Ireland were a little unlucky to lose as they ran the ball more often and came close to scoring a try on several occasions. The Scottish forwards played well enough, but were never able to exert any control. After half-time, an injury to prop Cameron Boyle forced him to switch places with ten Bos whose gigantic frame was not suited to the front-row. Ron Glasgow tackled fiercely and was prominent in open play. Ken Scotland was greatly troubled by the marauding Irish forwards and had to kick more than usual.

265   INTERNATIONAL CHAMPIONSHIP 1963   ENGLAND

Twickenham · Saturday 16 March 1963 · Lost 8–10

SCOTLAND CF Blaikie (*Heriot's FP*); C Elliot (*Langholm*), †BC Henderson (*Edinburgh Wdrs*), DM White (*Kelvinside Acs*), RH Thomson (*London Scot*); KJF Scotland* (*Heriot's FP*), S Coughtrie (*Edinburgh Acs*); †JB Neill (*Edinburgh Acs*), NS Bruce (*London Scot*), DMD Rollo (*Howe of Fife*), FH ten Bos (*London Scot*), MJ Campbell-Lamerton (*Halifax*), RJC Glasgow (*Dunfermline*), KI Ross (*Boroughmuir FP*), †JP Fisher (*Royal HSFP*)

ENGLAND JG Willcox (*Harlequins*); PB Jackson (*Coventry*), MS Phillips (*Fylde*), MP Weston (*Durham City*), J Roberts (*Sale*); RAW Sharp* (*Wasps*), SJS Clarke (*Cambridge U*); PE Judd (*Coventry*), HO Godwin (*Coventry*), NJ Drake-Lee (*Cambridge U*), AM Davis (*Torquay Ath*), JE Owen (*Coventry*), DC Manley (*Exeter*), DP Rogers (*Bedford*), DG Perry (*Bedford*)

REFEREE G Walters (*Wales*)

SCORING Glasgow, try (3–0); Coughtrie, con (5–0); Scotland, drop (8–0); Drake-Lee, try (8–5); Willcox, con (8–5) (half-time) Sharp, try (8–8); Willcox, con (8–10)

The teams were introduced to the Prime Minister Harold Macmillan. England's fair-haired stand-off Richard Sharp stamped his name on this match with a classic individual try that turned the game England's way. Early in the second half, he received the ball from a scrum on the right and feinted and dummied his way through the Scottish defence on a long angled run to the line. Willcox converted to give England a lead that they never relinquished. This was a very exciting match played at great pace. Both sides made handling errors, but also showed a lot of enterprise and the result was in doubt until the end. Scotland had the gusty wind behind them in the first half and raced to an early lead. After some eight minutes, Ron Glasgow scored a try from a long throw to the back of a lineout on the English goal-line. Coughtrie converted and a few minutes later Ken Scotland kicked a left-footed drop goal. England responded with a try by prop forward Drake-Lee which was brilliantly converted by Willcox from the touchline. Shortly before the interval, Coughtrie missed a long penalty attempt. Sharp's wonderful effort gave England the advantage and, try as they might, the Scots were unable to create the winning score.

---

266   INTERNATIONAL CHAMPIONSHIP 1964   FRANCE

Murrayfield · Saturday 4 January 1964 · Won 10–0

SCOTLAND †S Wilson (*Oxford U*); C Elliot (*Langholm*), BC Henderson (*Edinburgh Wdrs*), IHP Laughland (*London Scot*), RH Thomson (*London Scot*); G Sharp (*Stewart's FP*); JAT Rodd (*London Scot*); JB Neill* (*Edinburgh Acs*), NS Bruce (*London Scot*), DMD Rollo (*Howe of Fife*), †WJ Hunter (*Hawick*), †PC Brown (*W of Scot*), †JW Telfer (*Melrose*), JP Fisher (*Royal HSFP*), TO Grant (*Hawick*)

FRANCE C Lacaze (*Angoulême*); J Gachassin (*Lourdes*), G Boniface (*Mont-de-Marsan*), A Boniface (*Mont-de-Marsan*), J Dupuy (*Tarbes*); P Albaladéjo (*Dax*), J-C Lasserre (*Dax*); J-C Berejnoï (*Tulle*), J-M Cabanier (*Montauban*), J Bayardon (*Chalon*), J Le Droff (*Auch*), B Dauga (*Mont-de-Marsan*), J-J Rupert (*Tyrosse*), M Crauste (*Lourdes*), J Fabre* (*Toulouse*)

REFEREE RC Williams (*Ireland*)

SCORING Laughland, try (3–0); Wilson, con (5–0) (half-time) Thomson, try (8–0); Wilson, con (10–0)

Scotland fielded four new caps and France six, including five in the pack. David Rollo was an 11th hour replacement for Cameron Boyle. Heavy rain in the morning restricted the attendance to only around 25,000 people and the match was played in continuous drizzle with surface water lying on the pitch. Scotland kept it tight whilst the French were more enterprising and tried to play their traditional handling style. This made for some fast and entertaining rugby, especially in the second half as the French tried to chase the game, but it also contributed to their downfall. After 17 minutes, Albaladéjo failed to collect a pass and the Scots were up fast to make a dribbling rush that ended with Laughland scoring a try. There was no further scoring until near the end when Thomson intercepted a pass on the French 25 and raced away to the posts. Scotland's new full-back Stewart Wilson converted both tries and made an encouraging debut. The Scottish forwards were solid at the set-piece and the defence performed well against lively opponents.

---

267   TOUR MATCH   NEW ZEALAND

Murrayfield · Saturday 18 January 1964 · Drawn 0–0

SCOTLAND S Wilson (*Oxford U*); C Elliot (*Langholm*), JAP Shackleton (*London Scot*), IHP Laughland (*London Scot*), RH Thomson (*London Scot*); G Sharp (*Stewart's FP*), JAT Rodd (*London Scot*); JB Neill* (*Edinburgh Acs*), NS Bruce (*London Scot*), DMD Rollo (*Howe of Fife*), WJ Hunter (*Hawick*), PC Brown (*W of Scot*), JW Telfer (*Melrose*), JP Fisher (*Royal HSFP*), TO Grant (*Hawick*)

NEW ZEALAND DB Clarke (*Waikato*); RW Coulton (*Wellington*), PF Little (*Auckland*), MJ Dick (*Auckland*); MA Herewini (*Auckland*), BA Watt (*Canterbury*), KC Briscoe (*Taranaki*); KF Gray (*Wellington*), D Young (*Canterbury*), WJ Whineray* (*Auckland*), AJ Stewart (*Canterbury*),

CE Meads (*King Country*), BJ Lochore (*Wairarapa*), DJ Graham (*Canterbury*), KR Tremain (*Hawkes Bay*)

REFEREE RC Williams (*Ireland*)

On their 36 match tour, the New Zealanders had already beaten Ireland, Wales and England, and were confident of completing their first Grand Slam in the British Isles. The Scots had other ideas and put up an excellent performance to deprive the visitors of their prize. Indeed, with a little luck, Scotland might easily have won as they came close to scoring on three occasions. The lighter Scottish forwards were beaten in the scrums, but were quicker in the loose and their backing-up and cover defence were exemplary. Pringle Fisher produced one crunching tackle on Colin Meads that knocked the mighty All Black flat out. Sharp and Rodd were an effective pairing at half-back, the former opting for a tight, kicking game that reduced the danger of counter-attacks. Towards the end, the visitors made much use of speculative high kicks only to find that Stewart Wilson was secure and more than willing to run the ball back at them. At the final whistle, the ecstatic crowd demanded a lap of honour with shouts of 'We want Scotland! We want Scotland!' but the players were too exhausted. Scotland had won a moral victory and achieved their best, and most unexpected result since the famous Welsh match in 1951.

---

268   INTERNATIONAL CHAMPIONSHIP 1964   WALES

Cardiff Arms Park · Saturday 1 February 1964 · Lost 3–11

SCOTLAND S Wilson (*Oxford U*); C Elliot (*Langholm*), JAP Shackleton (*London Scot*), IHP Laughland (*London Scot*), RH Thomson (*London Scot*); G Sharp (*Stewart's FP*), JAT Rodd (*London Scot*); JB Neill* (*Edinburgh Acs*), NS Bruce (*London Scot*), DMD Rollo (*Howe of Fife*), WJ Hunter (*Hawick*),PC Brown (*W of Scot*), JW Telfer (*Melrose*), JP Fisher (*Royal HSFP*), TO Grant (*Hawick*)

WALES GTR Hodgson (*Neath*); SJ Watkins (*Newport*), DK Jones (*Llanelli*), K Bradshaw (*Bridgend*), DIE Bebb (*Swansea*); D Watkins (*Newport*), DCT Rowlands* (*Pontypool*); D Williams (*Ebbw Vale*), NR Gale (*Llanelli*), LJ Cunningham (*Aberavon*), B Price (*Newport*), BE Thomas (*Neath*), GJ Prothero (*Bridgend*), DJ Hayward (*Cardiff*), AIE Pask (*Abertillery*)

REFEREE PG Brook (*England*)

SCORING Laughland, try (3–0) (half-time) Bradshaw, try (3–3); Bradshaw, con (3–5); Bradshaw, pen (3–8); Thomas, try (3–11)

Scotland played far below the standard that they had reached in the New Zealand game and the score did not exaggerate the all-round supremacy of their opponents. The only compensation was that the Scots did not disintegrate under heavy pressure in the second half. The visitors played with the elements in the first period and made a lively start. After six minutes, Sharp hoisted an up-and-under, Hodgson, the Welsh full-back, fumbled his catch and Laughland was up fast to score. Wilson missed the conversion and a penalty attempt, and both half-backs had abortive drops at goal. Wales had a good ten minute spell and although they did not score the signs were ominous for Scotland. In the second half, Wales scored their points almost easily. From a scrum five minutes after the restart, Rowlands broke clean away and sent in

Bradshaw for a try. The scorer converted his own try and a few minutes later added a penalty goal. Towards the end, Thomas plunged over from a lineout to seal the game.

269   INTERNATIONAL CHAMPIONSHIP 1964   IRELAND

Lansdowne Road, Dublin · Saturday 22 February 1964 · Won 6–3

SCOTLAND S Wilson (*Oxford U*); C Elliot (*Langholm*), BC Henderson (*Edinburgh Wdrs*), IHP Laughland (*London Scot*), †WD Jackson (*Hawick*); †DH Chisholm (*Melrose*), AJ Hastie (*Melrose*); JB Neill* (*Edinburgh Acs*), NS Bruce (*London Scot*), DMD Rollo (*Howe of Fife*), PC Brown (*W of Scot*), MJ Campbell-Lamerton (*London Scot*), JW Telfer (*Melrose*), RJC Glasgow (*Dunfermline*), JP Fisher (*Royal HSFP*)

IRELAND TJ Kiernan (*Cork Const*); PJ Casey (*UC Dublin*), MK Flynn (*Wdrs*), JC Walsh (*UC Cork*), KJ Houston (*QU Belfast*); CMH Gibson (*Cambridge U*), JC Kelly (*UC Dublin*); PJ Dwyer (*UC Dublin*), AR Dawson (*Wdrs*), RJ McLoughlin (*Gosforth*), WA Mulcahy* (*Bective Rgrs*), WJ McBride (*Ballymena*), EP McGuire (*UC Galway*), NAA Murphy (*Cork Const*), MG Culliton (*Wdrs*)

REFEREE AC Luff (*England*)

SCORING Wilson, pen (3–0); Wilson, pen (6–0) (half-time) Kiernan, pen (6–3)

Ireland had beaten England convincingly at Twickenham two weeks earlier (18–5) and were firm favourites, but the Scottish forwards showed a lot more spirit and cohesion than their previous match against Wales. Scotland played with the rain and wind in their favour in the first half and Stewart Wilson kicked two penalties from long range for a 6–0 lead at the interval. Early in the second half, Kiernan kicked a penalty, having taken almost two minutes in preparation, but missed two other attempts during the game, including one sitter. Playing into the elements, the Scots closed the game down and managed to grind out an unspectacular and hard-earned victory. Both centres Laughland and Henderson tackled very solidly and Ron Glasgow did a good job of containing the dangerous Mike Gibson. In fairness, Ireland's cause was seriously weakened by an early leg injury to prop Ray McLoughlin.

270   INTERNATIONAL CHAMPIONSHIP 1964   ENGLAND

Murrayfield · Saturday 21 March 1964 · Won 15–6

SCOTLAND S Wilson (*Oxford U*); C Elliot (*Langholm*), BC Henderson (*Edinburgh Wdrs*), IHP Laughland (*London Scot*), GD Stevenson (*Hawick*); DH Chisholm (*Melrose*), AJ Hastie (*Melrose*); JB Neill* (*Edinburgh Acs*), NS Bruce (*London Scot*), DMD Rollo (*Howe of Fife*), PC Brown (*W of Scot*), MJ Campbell-Lamerton (*London Scot*), JP Fisher (*Royal HSFP*), RJC Glasgow (*Dunfermline*), JW Telfer (*Melrose*)

ENGLAND JG Willcox (*Harlequins*); RW Hosen (*Northampton*), MS Phillips (*Fylde*), MP Weston (*Durham City*), JM Ranson (*Rosslyn Park*); TJ Brophy (*Liverpool*), SI Smith (*Blackheath*); CR Jacobs* (*Northampton*), HO Godwin (*Coventry*), DFB Wrench (*Harlequins*), CM Payne (*Harlequins*), AM Davis (*Torquay Ath*), PJ Ford (*Gloucester*), DP Rogers (*Bedford*), TGAH Peart (*Hartlepool Rov*)

SCORING Glasgow, try (3–0); Wilson, con (5–0); Bruce, try (8–0); Wilson, con (10–0) (half-time) Hosen, pen (10–3); Telfer, try (13–3); Wilson, con (15–3); Rogers, try (15–6)

Scotland rose to the occasion to defeat the auld enemy for the first time in 14 years. In so doing, they became joint international champions with Wales, their best performance since 1938. Scotland's comprehensive victory was down to a magnificent effort by the forwards. They were solid in the scrums despite conceding a lot of poundage, much faster in loose play than their lumbering opponents and their handling was very secure. The back-row put the English midfield under great pressure and the Scottish backs also tackled sternly. The opening stages of the match, which was played on a soft surface, were balanced and largely uneventful. After 30 minutes, Jim Telfer picked-up from a scrum and fed Glasgow who stormed over for a try which Wilson converted from a tight angle. Near the interval, Brown broke away from a lineout and Telfer was in support to put Bruce over for a try. This was a great moment for the Scotland hooker, a professional solider, who was making his 31st and final appearance before going abroad on military service. Wilson added the conversion and early in the second half Hosen kicked a penalty for the visitors. The veteran wing George Stevenson, who had been recalled in place of Ronnie Thomson, almost scored at the corner, but just put his foot into touch. With a couple of minutes left, Hastie made a great break which was finished off by Telfer scoring at the posts, prompting ecstatic spectators to make an unprecedented pitch invasion. Wilson converted once the field had been cleared and right at the end England managed a pushover try credited to Rogers. Thus, the Scots ended their most successful season since the war in fine style.

271 INTERNATIONAL CHAMPIONSHIP 1965 FRANCE

Stade Yves du Manoir, Colombes, Paris · Saturday 9 January 1965
Lost 8–16

SCOTLAND KJF Scotland (*Aberdeenshire*); C Elliot (*Langholm*), BC Henderson (*Edinburgh Wdrs*), IHP Laughland (*London Scot*), GD Stevenson (*Hawick*); †BM Simmers (*Glasgow Acs*), JAT Rodd (*London Scot*); JB Neill* (*Edinburgh Acs*), †FAL Laidlaw (*Melrose*), DMD Rollo (*Howe of Fife*), †PK Stagg (*Sale*), MJ Campbell-Lamerton (*London Scot*), †D Grant (*Hawick*), JP Fisher (*London Scot*), JW Telfer (*Melrose*)

FRANCE P Dedieu (*Béziers*); J Gachassin (*Lourdes*), G Boniface (*Mont-de-Marsan*), J Piqué (*Pau*), C Darrouy (*Mont-de-Marsan*); J Capdouze (*Pau*), L Camberabero, (*La Voulte*); J-C Berejnoï (*Tulle*), J-M Cabanier (*Montauban*), A Gruarin (*Toulon*), W Spanghero (*Narbonne*), B Dauga (*Mont-de-Marsan*), M Lira (*La Voulte*), M Crauste* (*Lourdes*), A Herrero (*Toulon*)

REFEREE KD Kelleher (*Ireland*)

SCORING Gachassin, try (0–3); Dedieu, con (0–5); Henderson, try (3–5); Scotland, con (5–5) (half-time) Darrouy, try (5–8); Piqué, try (5–11); Henderson, try (8–11); Darrouy, try (8–14); Dedieu, con (8–16)

Scotland fielded four new caps: stand-off Brian Simmers, the son of inter-war star Max; Melrose hooker Frank Laidlaw; gigantic lock Peter Stagg; and Hawick flanker Derrick Grant. All four went on to have encouraging debuts. France were deserved winners of an entertaining match that featured six well-taken tries. Playing with a dry ball on a firm pitch, the French had greater pace, imagination and discipline, but Scotland were brave and often skilful. Within a few minutes of the kick-off, Capdouze hoisted an evil kick to the Scottish posts. Ken Scotland failed to reach the ball and it bounced back into the grateful hands of Piqué who sent in Gachassin. Dedieu converted, but soon the Scots drew level with a great try. Laugland dummied past a defender and found support from Fisher who passed to Henderson, and the big centre made a powerful 40-yard run through the heart of the defence to the line. Scotland's conversion tied the scores at the interval, but early in the second half the same player fired a clearing kick straight at Darrouy who was as surprised as anyone to score a try. Worse was to follow when France launched a slick passing move from the halfway line and Piqué burst through two weak tackles for his second try. The brave Scots retaliated with a superb second try by Henderson. Simmers counter-attacked from his own half and after some accurate combined play and switches of direction Henderson took a pass from Simmers and crashed over on the right. France sealed the match when Laughland was caught in possession by Crauste and the ball was worked to Darrouy for his second try.

272   INTERNATIONAL CHAMPIONSHIP 1965   WALES

Murrayfield · Saturday 6 February 1965 · Lost 12-14

SCOTLAND S Wilson (*London Scot*); C Elliot (*Langholm*), BC Henderson (*Edinburgh Wdrs*), IHP Laughland (*London Scot*), †DJ Whyte (*Edinburgh Wdrs*); BM Simmers (*Glasgow Acs*), JAT Rodd (*London Scot*); †N Suddon (*Hawick*), FAL Laidlaw (*Melrose*), DMD Rollo (*Howe of Fife*), PK Stagg (*Sale*), MJ Campbell-Lamerton* (*London Scot*), JP Fisher (*London Scot*), RJC Glasgow (*Dunfermline*), JW Telfer (*Melrose*)

WALES TG Price (*Llanelli*); SJ Watkins (*Newport*), JR Uzzell (*Newport*), SJ Dawes (*London Welsh*), DI Bebb (*Swansea*); D Watkins (*Newport*), DCT Rowlands* (*Pontypool*); D Williams (*Ebbw Vale*), NR Gale (*Llanelli*), R Waldron (*Neath*), B Price (*Newport*), WJ Morris (*Newport*), GJ Prothero (*Bridgend*), HJ Morgan (*Abertillery*), AIE Pask (*Abertillery*)

REFEREE RW Gilliland (*Ireland*)

SCORING Simmers, drop (3–0); T Price, pen (3–3); Wilson, pen (6–3); Watkins, try (6–6); T Price, con (6–8) (half-time) T Price, pen (6–11); Wilson, pen (9–11); Simmers, drop (12–11); Gale, try (12–14)

This was an exciting game that Wales snatched with a late try. Scotland started brightly and a long drop goal by Simmers gave them an early lead. Soon afterwards, the same player had to leave the field temporarily with a knee injury. He returned to the fray, but was never quite the same and the Scottish back play was hampered as result. After an exchange of penalties, Wales scored the game's first try near the interval. David Watkins broke blind and kicked to the corner, Simmers, on his injured leg, was unable to clear the loose ball near his own line and Stuart Watkins gathered a lucky bounce to run behind the posts. In the second half, Price and Wilson exchanged early penalties before Simmers dropped his second goal after a scrum in front of the Welsh posts. Play was fairly even until the closing stages when Wales, showing admirable composure, made a late surge to win the game. With around nine minutes remaining, the visitors stole a lineout on the Scottish line and hooker Norman Gale barrelled his way over at the corner. Wales held onto their two-point lead for the nervous closing minutes and their ecstatic supports invaded the pitch at the final whistle.

Murrayfield · Saturday 27 February 1965 · Lost 6–16

SCOTLAND S Wilson (*London Scot*); C Elliot (*Langholm*), BC Henderson (*Edinburgh Wdrs*), JAP Shackleton (*London Scot*), DJ Whyte (*Edinburgh Wdrs*); IHP Laughland (*London Scot*), JAT Rodd (*London Scot*); N Suddon (*Hawick*), FAL Laidlaw (*Melrose*), DMD Rollo (*Howe of Fife*), PC Brown (*W of Scot*), MJ Campbell-Lamerton* (*London Scot*), JP Fisher (*London Scot*), RJC Glasgow (*Dunfermline*), JW Telfer (*Melrose*)

IRELAND TJ Kiernan (*Cork Const*); PJ Casey (*Lansdowne*), JC Walsh (*UC Cork*), MK Flynn (*Wdrs*), PJ McGrath (*UC Cork*); CMH Gibson (*Cambridge U*), RM Young (*QU Belfast*); S MacHale (*Lansdowne*), KW Kennedy (*QU Belfast*), RJ McLoughlin* (*Gosforth*), WJ McBride (*Ballymena*), WA Mulcahy (*Bective Rgrs*), MG Doyle (*UC Dublin*), NAA Murphy (*Cork Const*), H Wall (*Dolphin*)

REFEREE DG Walters (Wales)

SCORING Laughland, drop (3–0); McGrath, try (3–3); Young, try (3–6); Kiernan, con (3–8) (half-time) Gibson, drop (3–11); Murphy, try (3–14); Kiernan, con (3–16); Wilson, pen (6–16)

Ireland were worthy winners against a sluggish Scotland. The forward exchanges were fairly evenly contested, but Ireland played a more confident and controlled game all-round. The delivery and distribution of the ball by the Scottish pack was largely of poor quality and put the half-backs under a lot of pressure. Scotland opened the scoring with an early drop goal by Laughland from a scrum in front of the posts. Ireland drew level when they won a lineout deep inside the Scottish 22, the ball was moved swiftly left and McGrath dashed over near the corner. Ireland's second try came from a quick heel close to the Scottish line. Breaking to the open-side, scrum-half Young made a neat dummy scissors move with Flynn which confused the defence and let him to slip under the posts. Kiernan converted and in the second half Gibson increased the lead with a splendid drop goal. The Scots started to play with more purpose, but Ireland scored a third try when Murphy took a blind side pass from a scrum and ran past a hesitant defence. A late penalty goal by Wilson did not detract from a substantial Irish victory.

Twickenham · Saturday 20 March 1965 · Drawn 3–3

SCOTLAND S Wilson* (*London Scot*); DJ Whyte (*Edinburgh Wdrs*), BC Henderson (*Edinburgh Wdrs*), IHP Laughland (*London Scot*), WD Jackson (*Hawick*); DH Chisholm (*Melrose*), AJ Hastie (*Melrose*); N Suddon (*Hawick*), FAL Laidlaw (*Melrose*), DMD Rollo (*Howe of Fife*), PK Stagg (*Sale*), MJ Campbell-Lamerton (*London Scot*), JP Fisher (*London Scot*), D Grant (*Hawick*) PC Brown (*W of Scot*)

ENGLAND D Rutherford (*Gloucester*); EL Rudd (*Oxford U*), DWA Rosser (*Cambridge U*), GP Frankcom (*Cambridge U*), AW Hancock (*Northampton*); MP Weston (*Durham City*), SJS Clarke (*Blackheath*); AL Horton (*Blackheath*), SB Richards (*Richmond*), PE Judd (*Coventry*), JE Owen (*Coventry*), CM Payne (*Harlequins*), N Silk (*Harlequins*), DP Rogers (*Bedford*), DG Perry* (*Bedford*)

REFEREE DG Walters (*Wales*)

SCORING No scoring in the first half. Chisholm, drop (3–0); Hancock, try (3–3)

The match was played in the presence of Her Majesty the Queen. Once again a classic individual try denied the Scots an elusive win at Twickenham. In the dying moments of a less than spectacular game and with Scotland leading 3–0, England won possession deep inside their own 25. The ball was passed to Andy Hancock, the solid Northampton left wing, who swerved around the Scottish back-row and set-off up the touchline. He evaded several tackles on an incredible run and just managed to beat the pursuing Laughland before lunging exhausted over the line. It was little compensation for the disbelieving Scots that Rutherford missed the conversion and the match ended in a draw. Scotland were much the better team and victory had been snatched from them in the most extraordinary fashion. Playing on a soggy pitch, the Scots had contained their lacklustre opponents during the first half and held the upper-hand during the second spell. They took the lead just after half-time when Chisholm dropped a goal from the left touchline. Hastie seemed to have scored a try when he dived over the line, but his effort was ruled out for an earlier infringement. The same player almost scored in the right corner only to be bundled out at the flag. Then came Hancock and his long run into rugby history.

---

275   TOUR MATCH   SOUTH AFRICA

Murrayfield · Saturday 17 April 1965 · Won 8–5

SCOTLAND S Wilson* (*London Scot*); DJ Whyte (*Edinburgh Wdrs*), JAP Shackleton (*London Scot*), IHP Laughland (*London Scot*), WD Jackson (*Hawick*); DH Chisholm (*Melrose*), AJ Hastie (*Melrose*); N Suddon (*Hawick*), FAL Laidlaw (*Melrose*), DMD Rollo (*Howe of Fife*), PK Stagg (*Sale*), MJ Campbell-Lamerton (*London Scot*), JP Fisher (*London Scot*), D Grant (*Hawick*), PC Brown (*W of Scot*)

SOUTH AFRICA LG Wilson (*W Province*); JP Engelbrecht (*W Province*), WJ Mans (*W Province*), JL Gainsford (*W Province*), CW Dirksen (*N Transvaal*); JH Barnard (*Transvaal*), DJ de Vos (*W Province*); SP Kuhn (*Transvaal*), DC Walton (*Natal*), JFK Marais (*W Province*), AS Malan* (*Transvaal*), G Carelse (*E Province*), J Schoeman (*W Province*), MR Suter (*Natal*), DJ Hopwood (*W Province*)

REFEREE DG Walters (*Wales*)

SCORING Shackleton, try (3–0); Wilson, con (5–0) (half-time) Englebrecht, try (5–3); Mans, con (5–5); Chisholm, drop (8–5)

In April 1965, South Africa made an experimental five match tour of Ireland and Scotland under the captaincy of lock Avril Malan. By the high standards of South African rugby, the tour was nothing short of a disaster. It took place at the beginning of their season and many of their players were not fully fit. The South Africans failed to win any of their games, including defeat to a Scottish Districts XV at Hawick (16–8). In the test match, Scotland were narrow but deserved winners, their first over the mighty Springboks since 1906. The Scottish forwards matched their burly opponents in all aspects and the gigantic Peter Stagg dominated the lineout. The Melrose half-backs, Chisholm and Hastie, had very good games. The former made several penetrating breaks which faltered because of a lack of support. Scotland opened the scoring after some ten minutes. From a strike against the head, Chisholm sent up a high ball which Wilson fumbled and Shackleton was on hand to pick-up and dive over at the posts. Soon after the interval, de Vos broke away from a ruck and the ball went from Gainsford to Engelbrecht who rounded Stewart Wilson easily for a try in the corner. Mans kicked a fine conversion to level the scores. Both sides had opportunities and near the finish Chisholm dropped the winning goal from in front of the posts. South Africa had one last attack, but Shackleton made a timely interception and kicked the ball into touch to finish the game.

276　　INTERNATIONAL CHAMPIONSHIP 1966　　　　FRANCE

Murrayfield　·　Saturday 15 January 1966　·　Drawn 3–3

SCOTLAND S Wilson* (*London Scot*); †AJW Hinshelwood (*London Scot*), BC Henderson (*Edinburgh Wdrs*), IHP Laughland (*London Scot*), DJ Whyte (*Edinburgh Wdrs*); DH Chisholm (*Melrose*), AJ Hastie (*Melrose*); †JD Macdonald (*London Scot*), FAL Laidlaw (*Melrose*), DMD Rollo (*Howe of Fife*), PK Stagg (*Sale*), MJ Campbell-Lamerton (*London Scot*), JP Fisher (*London Scot*), D Grant (*Hawick*), JW Telfer (*Melrose*)

FRANCE C Lacaze (*Angoulême*); J Gachassin (*Lourdes*), G Boniface (*Mont-de-Marsan*), A Boniface (*Mont-de-Marsan*), C Darrouy (*Mont-de-Marsan*); J-C Roques (*Brive*), M Puget (*Brive*); J-C Berejnoï (*Tulle*), J-M Cabanier (*Montauban*), A Gruarin (*Toulon*), W Spanghero (*Narbonne*), E Cester (*TOEC*), J-J Rupert (*Tyrosse*), M Crauste* (*Lourdes*), B Dauga (*Mont-de-Marsan*)

REFEREE DM Hughes (*Wales*)

SCORING Lacaze, pen (0–3); Whyte, try (3–3) (half-time)

Scotland were the better side by some margin, but failed to turn their superiority into points and had to settle for a frustrating draw. The Scottish forwards were well on top and denied France their usual attacking platform. The half-backs controlled the game effectively and, in contrast, their opposite numbers looked very ordinary. Playing with the wind behind them, France took the lead with a Lacaze penalty goal after 13 minutes. Stung into action, Chisholm ignited a spectacular handling movement from his own half which Whyte and Fisher continued into the French 25. Play swung quickly to the left and Whyte, with little room to manoeuvre, gathered a lobbed pass to dive over at the corner. Wilson missed the long conversion against the wind and new prop MacDonald narrowly failed with a penalty attempt. In the second half, Wilson missed two further penalties and Chisholm two drop goal attempts. Whyte knocked-on with the line at his mercy and later was stopped just short. France showed little of their traditional flair and swift handling skills although flank forward Jean-Joseph Rupert was unlucky to have a try chalked-off for an earlier infringement.

The gigantic Peter Stagg dominates the lineout against France in 1966.
Scotsman Publications Ltd

Cardiff Arms Park · Saturday 5 February 1966 · Lost 3–8

SCOTLAND S Wilson* (*London Scot*); AJW Hinshelwood (*London Scot*), BC Henderson (*Edinburgh Wdrs*), IHP Laughland (*London Scot*), DJ Whyte (*Edinburgh Wdrs*); †JWC Turner (*Gala*), AJ Hastie (*Melrose*); JD Macdonald (*London Scot*), FAL Laidlaw (*Melrose*), DMD Rollo (*Howe of Fife*), PK Stagg (*Sale*), MJ Campbell-Lamerton (*London Scot*), JP Fisher (*London Scot*), D Grant (*Hawick*), JW Telfer (*Melrose*)

WALES TGR Hodgson (*Neath*); SJ Watkins (*Newport*), DK Jones (*Cardiff*), K Bradshaw (*Bridgend*), L Davies (*Bridgend*); D Watkins (*Newport*), AR Lewis (*Abertillery*); D Williams (*Ebbw Vale*), NR Gale (*Llanelli*), DJ Lloyd (*Bridgend*), B Price (*Newport*), BE Thomas (*Neath*), GJ Prothero (*Bridgend*), HJ Morgan (*Abertillery*), AIE Pask* (*Abertillery*)

REFEREE MH Titcomb (*England*)

SCORING Jones, try (0–3) (half-time) Jones, try (0–6); Bradshaw, con (0–8); Wilson, pen (3–8)

Gala's Jock Turner won his first cap as a late replacement for David Chisholm. Conditions were truly dreadful with a sodden and glutinous field swept by driving rain. Wales won more convincingly than the final score suggests, although the Scots were always in the game until the end. Scotland faced into the elements in the first half and did well to hold the score to 3–0 at the interval thanks to a solid forward effort. After some 15 minutes, Wales won a scrum on the Scottish 25 and the ball was passed out to Stuart Watkins on the right wing. He was brought down by Whyte, but quickly got to his feet and gave a one-handed pass inside to Ken Jones who swerved past the rest of the cover to score far out. At the start of the second half, Scotland looked set to take control and Hinshelwood came close to scoring. The Welsh forwards rallied despite playing into the wind, and from a scrum near the Scottish line the light-footed and elusive David Watkins made a break to put Jones over for his second try. Bradshaw converted and later Wilson kicked a consolation penalty for the well-beaten visitors.

278 INTERNATIONAL CHAMPIONSHIP 1966 IRELAND

Lansdowne Road · Saturday 26 February 1966 · Won 11–3

SCOTLAND S Wilson (*London Scot*); AJW Hinshelwood (*London Scot*), BC Henderson (*Edinburgh Wdrs*), IHP Laughland* (*London Scot*), DJ Whyte (*Edinburgh Wdrs*); DH Chisholm (*Melrose*), AJ Hastie (*Melrose*); JD Macdonald (*London Scot*), FAL Laidlaw (*Melrose*), DMD Rollo (*Howe of Fife*), PK Stagg (*Sale*), MJ Campbell-Lamerton (*London Scot*), JP Fisher (*London Scot*), D Grant (*Hawick*), JW Telfer (*Melrose*)

IRELAND TJ Kiernan (*Cork Const*); WR Hunter (*CIYMS*), MK Flynn (*Wdrs*) JC Walsh (*Sunday's Well*), PJ McGrath (*UC Cork*); CMH Gibson (*Cambridge U*) RM Young (*QU Belfast*); S MacHale (*Lansdowne*), AM Brady (*Dublin U*), RJ McLoughlin* (*Gosforth*), WJ McBride (*Ballymena*), OC Waldron (*Oxford U*) NAA Murphy (*Cork Const*), MG Doyle (*Cambridge U*), RA Lamont (*Instonians*)

REFEREE DM Hughes (*Wales*)

SCORING Hinshelwood, try (3–0); Wilson, con (5–0); Kiernan, pen (5–3) (half-time) Hinshelwood, try (8–3); Grant, try (11–3)

Scotland delivered an efficient and workmanlike performance for their fourth win in succession at Lansdowne Road. The Scottish forwards had a fresh urgency and cohesion with the restoration of Jim Telfer as pack leader. They dominated the scrums and the back-row put Ireland under a lot of pressure, especially their scrum-half Roger Young. The return of Chisholm at stand-off made an obvious improvement and his half-back partner Hastie was very industrious, giving the final pass for all three tries. Scotland played with the blustery wind behind them in the first half. An early Scottish attack was stopped near the goal-line and Hunter, the Irish right wing, had to leave the field temporarily after accidentally colliding with a goal post. In his absence, the Scots won a scrum inside the Irish 25; Hastie broke to the right and made a dummy scissors with Henderson before putting Hinshelwood over at the corner. Wilson kicked a fine conversion almost from the touchline and later hit a post with a penalty attempt. Before the interval, Kiernan kicked a good penalty against the wind, but Ireland's second half surge never materialised. Instead, the Scots played the conditions wisely and made good use of shortened lineouts. From one of these, the forwards combined well to create a gap for Hastie who put Hinshelwood over at the corner for his second try. Near the end, Hastie made a break which ended with Grant crashing over the Irish line.

279 INTERNATIONAL CHAMPIONSHIP 1966 ENGLAND

Murrayfield · Saturday 19 March 1966 · Won 6–3

SCOTLAND CF Blaikie (*Heriot's FP*); AJW Hinshelwood (*London Scot*), BC Henderson (*Edinburgh Wdrs*), IHP Laughland* (*London Scot*), DJ Whyte (*Edinburgh Wdrs*); DH Chisholm (*Melrose*), AJ Hastie (*Melrose*); JD Macdonald (*London Scot*), FAL Laidlaw (*Melrose*), DMD Rollo (*Howe of Fife*), PK Stagg (*Sale*), MJ Campbell-Lamerton (*London Scot*), JP Fisher (*London Scot*), D Grant (*Hawick*), JW Telfer (*Melrose*)

ENGLAND D Rutherford (*Gloucester*); EL Rudd (*Liverpool*), RD Hearn (*Bedford*), CW McFadyean (*Moseley*), KF Savage (*Northampton*); MP Weston (*Durham City*), TC Wintle (*Northampton*); AL Horton (*Blackheath*), WT Treadwell (*Wasps*), PE Judd (*Coventry*), JE Owen (*Coventry*), CM Payne (*Harlequins*), JRH Greenwood (*Waterloo*), DP Rogers* (*Bedford*), GA Sherriff (*Saracens*)

REFEREE KD Kelleher (*Ireland*)

SCORING Blaikie, pen (3–0) (half-time) McFadyean, drop (3–3); Whyte, try (6–3)

On a lovely spring afternoon, Scotland deservedly retained the Calcutta Cup in a fragmented encounter that was less than memorable. Full-back Colin Blaikie was recalled after three years for the injured Stewart Wilson and he proved himself an accomplished deputy, dealing comfortably with a series of high kicks and tackling soundly. In the first half, he saved a certain try when he made a great stop on Keith Savage as the Northampton wing powered towards the line. Blaikie opened the scoring after some 30 minutes with a penalty goal via the far post. McFadyean equalised with a snap drop goal early in the second half and a few minutes later the Scots conjured the only try of the game. From a lineout inside English territory, Chisholm cut through, both centres carried on and Grant was in support to give a scoring pass to Whyte who had just enough speed to reach the corner. Amongst several good performances for Scotland, Campbell-Lamerton and Grant were always prominent and Chisholm and Hastie, the Melrose half-backs, played astutely.

280   TOUR MATCH   AUSTRALIA

Murrayfield · Saturday 17 December 1966 · Won 11–5

SCOTLAND S Wilson (*London Scot*); AJW Hinshelwood (*London Scot*), JWC Turner (*Gala*), BM Simmers (*Glasgow Acs*), DJ Whyte (*Edinburgh Wdrs*); DH Chisholm (*Melrose*), AJ Hastie (*Melrose*); N Suddon (*Hawick*), FAL Laidlaw (*Melrose*), DMD Rollo (*Howe of Fife*), PK Stagg (*Sale*), PC Brown (*W of Scot*), JP Fisher* (*London Scot*), D Grant (*Hawick*), †AHW Boyle (*St Thomas's H*)

AUSTRALIA JK Lenehan (*NSW*); S Boyce (*NSW*), RJ Marks (*Queensland*), JE Brass (*NSW*), AM Cardy (*NSW*); PR Gibbs (*Victoria*), KW Catchpole* (*NSW*); JM Miller (*NSW*), PG Johnson (*NSW*), AR Miller (*NSW*), RG Teitzel (*Queensland*), PC Crittle (*NSW*), MP Purcell (*Queensland*), GV Davis (*NSW*), JF O'Gorman (*NSW*)

REFEREE M Joseph (*Wales*)

SCORING Wilson, pen (3–0); Brass, try (3–3); Leneharn, con (3–5); Chisholm, try (6–5); Wilson, con (8–5) (half-time) Boyle, try (11–5)

Two weeks earlier, the touring Australians had beaten Wales for the first time and were quietly confident, but they were hampered by injuries and never recaptured their best form. Under a threatening sky and in a cold swirling wind, this was an entertaining and fast-moving match, although play did not reach a high standard. The forward exchanges were evenly balanced, but Scotland held an edge at half-back with the Melrose pair Chisholm and Hastie combining very well. Chisholm, in particular, had an excellent match with his accurate kicking, good distribution and sniping runs. Scotland, playing with the wind, made a great start and Wilson kicked a lengthy penalty inside the first two minutes. Midway through the half, Brass, the Australian centre, charged down a delayed clearance near the Scottish line and scored a soft try that Lenehan converted. Ten minutes later, the Scots made a great charge to the left corner and from the ensuing maul Chisholm wrong-footed two defenders to go over for a brilliant solo score. Just before the interval, Australia ought to have scored a try after a rush by the forwards, but Davis, who otherwise was excellent, dropped the ball short of the line. In the second half both sides had some scoring chances and Scotland missed two kickable penalties. Towards the finish Australian stand-off Gibbs was injured and O'Gorman withdrew from the pack, which helped to encourage the Scots. In the final minute, Simmers made a great run almost to the line and Boyle capped a great debut when he grabbed the ball and dived over for the winning score.

---

281   INTERNATIONAL CHAMPIONSHIP 1967   FRANCE

Stade Yves du Manoir, Colombes, Paris · Saturday 14 January 1967
Won 9–8

SCOTLAND S Wilson (*London Scot*); AJW Hinshelwood (*London Scot*), JWC Turner (*Gala*), BM Simmers (*Glasgow Acs*), DJ Whyte (*Edinburgh Wdrs*); DH Chisholm (*Melrose*), AJ Hastie (*Melrose*); JD MacDonald (*London Scot*), FAL Laidlaw (*Melrose*), DMD Rollo (*Howe of Fife*), PK Stagg (*Sale*), WJ Hunter (*Hawick*), JP Fisher* (*London Scot*), D Grant (*Hawick*) AHW Boyle (*St Thomas's H*)

FRANCE C Lacaze (*Angoulême*); B Duprat (*Bayonne*), C Dourthe (*Dax*), J Maso (*Perpignan*), C Darrouy* (*Mont-de-Marsan*); J Gachassin (*Lourdes*), J-C Lasserre (*Dax*); J-C Berejnoï (*Tulle*), J-M Cabanier (*Montauban*), A Gruarin (*Toulon*), W Spanghero (*Narbonne*), B Dauga (*Mont-de-Marsan*), J Salut (*Toulouse*), C Carrère (*Toulon*), A Herrero (*Toulon*)

REFEREE KD Kelleher (*Ireland*)

SCORING Wilson, pen (3–0); Duprat, try (3–3); Wilson, pen (6–3) (half-time) Simmers, drop (9–3); Gruarin, try (9–6); Gachassin, con (9–8)

In a frantic encounter played in fine conditions, Scotland showed great team spirit and composure to record a narrow victory against a skilful French side. Stewart Wilson kicked an early penalty goal, but Scotland were under a lot of pressure in the first half and had to defend vigorously against a tidal wave of French attacks. From a scrum in the French half, Dourthe broke past the defence and made a long run before giving a perfectly timed pass to Duprat who streaked over in the right corner. Gachassin missed the awkward conversion and a few minutes later Wilson kicked his second penalty. Just before the interval, Maso twisted his knee badly and spent the rest of the game hobbling about as an auxiliary full-back. The fair-haired flanker Salut moved into the centre, but inevitably the French rhythm was disrupted. Eight minutes into the second half the Scots went further ahead when Simmers dropped a goal after a lineout take by Stagg. Around the hour mark, France made a swift handling move in the Scottish 25 and Duprat was stopped near the corner after a superb cover tackle by Wilson. From the ensuing lineout, prop Gruarin surged around the tail to score a try although there was some doubt if he had managed to get the ball over the line. Gachassin kicked the simple conversion and France fought hard to get the winning score, but the Scottish forwards used their numerical advantage to deny an increasingly frustrated home side.

282   INTERNATIONAL CHAMPIONSHIP 1967   WALES

Murrayfield · Saturday 4 February 1967 · Won 11–5

SCOTLAND S Wilson (*London Scot*); AJW Hinshelwood (*London Scot*), JWC Turner (*Gala*), BM Simmers (*Glasgow Acs*), DJ Whyte (*Edinburgh Wdrs*); DH Chisholm (*Melrose*), AJ Hastie (*Melrose*); JD MacDonald (*London Scot*), FAL Laidlaw (*Melrose*), DMD Rollo (*Howe of Fife*), PK Stagg (*Sale*), WJ Hunter (*Hawick*), JP Fisher* (*London Scot*), D Grant (*Hawick*), JW Telfer (*Melrose*)

WALES TG Price (*Leicester U*); DIE Bebb (*Swansea*), TGR Davies (*Cardiff*), WH Raybould (*Cambridge U*), SJ Watkins (*Newport*); B John (*Llanelli*), WG Hullin (*Cardiff*); JP O'Shea (*Cardiff*), BI Rees (*London Welsh*), DJ Lloyd (*Bridgend*), B Price (*Newport*), WT Mainwaring (*Aberavon*), KJ Braddock (*Newbridge*), J Taylor (*London Welsh*), AEI Pask* (*Abertillery*)

REFEREE KD Kelleher (*Ireland*)

SCORING Watkins, try (0–3); Price, con (0–5) (half-time) Hinshelwood, try (3–5); Chisholm, drop (6–5); Telfer, try (9–5); Wilson, con (11–5)

Wales fielded six new caps and dominated territory in the first half, but they wasted a lot of possession with some aimless kicking and unimaginative tactics. A few minutes before the interval, Whyte went off temporarily with an injured hand and in his absence Wales opened the scoring. Stuart Watkins grabbed a loose ball at lineout inside the Scottish 25 and ran unopposed to the corner. Terry Price kicked a magnificent conversion from the touchline. In the second half, Scotland began a slow comeback and around the 55th minute they scored a thrilling try. From a lineout inside the Welsh 25, the ball was passed crisply along the line and Wilson made a timely intrusion to send Hinshelwood thundering away to the corner. Inside the last ten minutes, Chisholm dropped a goal to put the Scots in front and the inexperienced Welsh side were unable to respond. Right at the end, Hastie pinched an untidy ball from a scrum near the Welsh line and flipped it to Telfer who barged his way over.

283   INTERNATIONAL CHAMPIONSHIP 1967   IRELAND

Murrayfield · Saturday 25 February 1967 · Lost 3–5

SCOTLAND S Wilson (*London Scot*); AJW Hinshelwood (*London Scot*), JWC Turner (*Gala*), †RB Welsh (*Hawick*), DJ Whyte (*Edinburgh Wdrs*); BM Simmers (*Glasgow Acs*), AJ Hastie (*Melrose*); JD MacDonald (*London Scot*), FAL Laidlaw (*Melrose*), †AB Carmichael (*W of Scot*), PK Stagg (*Sale*), WJ Hunter (*Hawick*), JP Fisher* (*London Scot*), D Grant (*Hawick*), JW Telfer (*Melrose*)

IRELAND TJ Kiernan (*Cork Const*); NH Brophy (*Blackrock Coll*), JC Walsh (*Sunday's Well*),
FPK Bresnihan (*UC Dublin*), ATA Duggan (*Lansdowne*); CMH Gibson (*NIFC*), BF Sherry
(*Terenure Coll*); S MacHale (*Lansdowne*), KW Kennedy (*CIYMS*), SA Hutton (*Malone*),
WJ McBride (*Ballymena*), MG Malloy (*UC Galway*), NAA Murphy* (*Cork Const*), KG Goodhall
(*Newcastle U*), MG Doyle (*Edinburgh Wdrs*)

REFEREE DM Hughes (*Wales*)

SCORING No scoring in the first half. Murphy, try (0–3); Kiernan, con (0–5); Wilson, pen (3–5)

David Chisholm was injured and his place at stand-off was taken by Brian Simmers
with Rob Welsh coming in at centre. Sandy Carmichael won his first cap as a late
replacement for David Rollo. Scotland had more than enough possession to win the
match, but Chisholm's absence was keenly felt and the backs played without conviction or sparkle. In contrast, Irish stand-off Mike Gibson showed great authority and
orchestrated his side very effectively. The Irish forwards were quick about the field
and veteran full-back Tom Kiernan acted as a solid last line of defence. In a largely
disappointing encounter, there was no scoring until the 15th minute of the second
half. Kiernan kicked to the right corner and from the lineout the Irish forwards
bundled over, the try being credited to flanker Noel Murphy. Kiernan kicked a fine
conversion and all that Scotland could manage in reply was a long penalty by Stewart
Wilson. Once again, Pringle Fisher was very productive at the tail of the lineout and
Peter Stagg used his height to good effect. Carmichael made a sound debut, showing
impressive mobility and combative tackling.

284   INTERNATIONAL CHAMPIONSHIP 1967   ENGLAND

Twickenham · Saturday 18 March 1967 · Lost 14–27

SCOTLAND S Wilson (*London Scot*); AJW Hinshelwood (*London Scot*), JWC Turner (*Gala*),
RB Welsh (*Hawick*), DJ Whyte (*Edinburgh Wdrs*); IHP Laughland (*London Scot*), †IG McCrae
(*Gordonians*); JD MacDonald (*London Scot*), FAL Laidlaw (*Melrose*), DMD Rollo (*Howe of Fife*),
PK Stagg (*Sale*), WJ Hunter (*Hawick*), JP Fisher* (*London Scot*), D Grant (*Hawick*) JW Telfer
(*Melrose*)

ENGLAND RW Hosen (*Bristol*); KF Savage (*Northampton*), RD Hearn (*Bedford*),
CW McFadyean (*Moseley*), RC Webb (*Coventry*); JF Finlan (*Moseley*), RDA Pickering (*Bradford*);
PE Judd* (*Coventry*), SB Richards (*Richmond*), MJ Coulman (*Moseley*), JN Pallant (*Nottingham*),
DEJ Watt (*Bristol*), DP Rogers (*Bedford*), RB Taylor (*Northampton*), DM Rollitt (*Bristol*)

REFEREE DP D'Arcy (*Ireland*)

SCORING Hosen, pen (0–3); Turner, try (3–3); Hinshelwood, try (6–3); Wilson, con (8–3);
McFadyean, try (8–6); Hosen, con (8–8); Wilson, pen (11–8) (half-time) Taylor, try (11–11);
Hosen, con (11–13); Wilson, pen (14–13); Hosen, pen (14–16); Webb, try (14–19); McFadyean,
try (14–22); Hosen, con (14–24); Finlan, drop (14–27)

Ian McCrae, a stalwart of rugby in the north-east of Scotland, won his first cap. Played
in fine conditions, this high scoring match was one of the most entertaining between
the two countries for some time. The Scottish forwards were largely outplayed and the
backs could not match the attacking skills of their opponents. Nevertheless, Scotland
held a narrow lead inside the last ten minutes only for them to crumble away and

England to emerge as comfortable and deserved winners. After an early English penalty, Turner and Hinshelwood scored tries in the right-hand corner, the second of which was converted by Wilson. England drew level with a try by the powerful Colin McFadyen and then Scotland seemed to have scored again when Whyte crossed the line only to be called back for a forward pass. Shortly before the interval, Wilson kicked a penalty to put the Scots back in front. In the second half, England regained the lead with another converted try and then Wilson kicked his second penalty. Play remained tense until England mounted their late surge. They scored 14 points in the closing minutes, including a wonderful second try by McFadyen, and the Scots were left shaking their heads in disbelief at the finish.

---

285 TOUR MATCH NEW ZEALAND

Murrayfield · Saturday 2 December 1967 · Lost 3–14

SCOTLAND S Wilson (*London Scot*); AJW Hinshelwood (*London Scot*), JWC Turner (*Gala*), †JNM Frame (*Edinburgh U*), †RR Keddie (*Watsonians*); DH Chisholm (*Melrose*), AJ Hastie (*Melrose*); AB Carmichael (*W of Scot*), FAL Laidlaw (*Melrose*), DMD Rollo (*Howe of Fife*), PK Stagg (*Sale*), †GWE Mitchell (*Edinburgh Wdrs*), JP Fisher* (*London Scot*), D Grant (*Hawick*), AHW Boyle (*London Scot*)

NEW ZEALAND WF McCormick (*Canterbury*); AG Steel (*Canterbury*), IR MacRae (*Hawkes Bay*), WL Davis (*Hawkes Bay*), WM Birtwistle (*Waikato*); EW Kirton (*Otago*), CR Laidlaw (*Otago*); KF Gray (*Wellington*), BE McLeod (*Counties*), AE Hopkinson (*Canterbury*), SC Strahan (*Manawatu*), CE Meads (*King County*), KR Tremain (*Hawkes Bay*), GC Williams (*Wellington*), BJ Lochore* (*Wairarapa*)

REFEREE Kevin Kelleher (*Ireland*)

SCORING Chisholm, drop (3–0); McCormick, pen (3–3); MacRae, try (3–6); McCormick, pen (3–9) (half-time) Davis, try (3–12); McCormick, con (3–14)

All Black Colin Meads heads disconsolately to the dressing room after being sent off at Murrayfield in 1967. *Scotsman Publications Ltd*

This match was overshadowed by the sending-off of the legendary Colin Meads who became the first man to be dismissed in an international match since 1925. Late in the second half, Meads took a reckless kick at the ball just as it had been gathered by Scottish scrum-half David Chisholm. Both players over-balanced, although neither was injured. The incident took place right in front of referee Kevin Kelleher who had already warned Meads for rough play and therefore felt that he had no option but to send him off. It was a brave and controversial decision against the most revered rugby player in the world at the time. Meads was guilty of dangerous play, but Kelleher seemed to have been unduly harsh. The game itself was hard and vigorous, but largely unspectacular. The Scots put up a good show against a much stronger side, but lacked sufficient resources to create an upset. The tackling and covering was tight, especially Turner and Frame in the centres, and Fisher was prominent in the loose. The tactic of shortened lineouts was successful and hooker Frank Laidlaw took the only strike against the head. Deprived of their usual share of possession and in the face of a determined defence, the New Zealanders rarely produced the attacking flair that was their trademark. After some ten minutes, Chisholm opened the scoring with a left-footed drop goal from an awkward angle and then McCormack equalised with a penalty. From a lineout peel, Ken Gray made a storming charge and fed Ian MacRae who dashed past the defence for the first try. McCormick missed the conversion, but later added a second penalty to give the visitors a 9–3 lead at the interval. The only score of the second half came from a lineout on the Scottish 25. Kirton made a great break from a loop move with MacRae and sent Keith Davis over for a try. McCormick converted to seal New Zealand's win.

---

286   INTERNATIONAL CHAMPIONSHIP 1968   FRANCE

Murrayfield · Saturday 13 January 1968 · Lost 6–8

SCOTLAND S Wilson (*London Scot*); AJW Hinshelwood (*London Scot*), JWC Turner (*Gala*), JNM Frame (*Edinburgh U*), †GJ Keith (*Wasps*); DH Chisholm (*Melrose*), AJ Hastie (*Melrose*); AB Carmichael (*W of Scot*), FAL Laidlaw (*Melrose*), DMD Rollo (*Howe of Fife*), PK Stagg (*Sale*), GWE Mitchell (*Edinburgh Wdrs*), JP Fisher* (*London Scot*), D Grant (*Hawick*), AHW Boyle (*London Scot*)

FRANCE C Lacaze (*Angoulême*); B Duprat (*Bayonne*), J Trillo (*Bègles*), J Maso (*Perpignan*), A Campaès (*Lourdes*); G Camberabero (*La Voulte*), L Camberabero (*La Voulte*); A Abadie (*Graulhet*), J-M Cabanier (*Montauban*), A Gruarin (*Toulon*), E Cester (*TOEC*), B Dauga (*Mont-de-Marsan*), J-J Rupert (*Tyrosse*), C Carrère* (*Toulon*), W Spanghero (*Narbonne*)

REFEREE KD Kelleher (*Ireland*)

SCORING Duprat, try (0–3); Keith, try (3–3) (half-time) Wilson, pen (6–3); Campaès, try (6–6); Camberabero, con (6–8)

Both sides wore black armbands in respect of two French players, Guy Boniface and Jean-Michel Capendeguy, who had been killed in separate traffic accidents early in 1968. Capendeguy had been selected to play in this match, his place on the right wing being taken by Bernard Duprat. France took an early lead when Guy Camberabero sliced a drop goal attempt. The ball bounced around in the Scottish in-goal area and Duprat, following-up like an express train, just beat Stewart Wilson to the touchdown.

This incident seemed to unsettle the normally dependable Wilson who had a poor game, especially with his goal-kicking. Play was largely confined to the French half of the field, but the visiting backs handled well and on occasion launched counter-attacks from behind their own line. Shortly before the interval, Scotland conjured a great try. From a lineout, Chisholm made a good burst before passing to Turner who tore through the defence. Frame carried on and new cap Hamish Keith, the Wasps winger, hurled himself over at the corner. Wilson missed the awkward conversion, but kicked a penalty early in the second-half. Around 15 minutes later, Dauga picked up a bad pass and made a strong run which ended with Campaès scoring in the corner. Guy Camberabero kicked a superb match-winning conversion, his brother Lilian placing the ball because of the strong wind. Scotland pressed, but could not break the speedy defence. Right at the end, Wilson missed a penalty attempt that would have won the match. Scotland were unlucky to lose a well balanced match and France went on to win their first-ever Grand Slam later in the season.

287   INTERNATIONAL CHAMPIONSHIP 1968   WALES

Cardiff Arms Park · Saturday 3 February 1968 · Lost 0–5

SCOTLAND S Wilson (*London Scot*); AJW Hinshelwood (*London Scot*), JWC Turner (*Gala*), JNM Frame (*Edinburgh U*), GJ Keith (*Wasps*); DH Chisholm (*Melrose*), AJ Hastie (*Melrose*); AB Carmichael (*W of Scot*), FAL Laidlaw (*Melrose*), DMD Rollo (*Howe of Fife*), PK Stagg (*Sale*), GWE Mitchell (*Edinburgh Wdrs*), JP Fisher* (*London Scot*), †TG Elliot (*Langholm*), AHW Boyle (*London Scot*)

WALES D Rees (*Swansea*); SJ Watkins (*Newport*), KS Jarrett (*Newport*), TGR Davies (*Cardiff*), WK Jones (*Cardiff*); B John (*Cardiff*), GO Edwards* (*Cardiff*); J O'Shea (*Cardiff*), J Young (*Harrogate*), DJ Lloyd (*Bridgend*), M Wiltshire (*Aberavon*), WD Thomas (*Llanelli*), WD Morris (*Neath*), AJ Gray (*London Welsh*), RE Jones (*Coventry*)

REFEREE GC Lamb (*England*)

SCORING WK Jones, try (0–3); Jarrett, con (0–5) (half-time)

Langholm flank forward Tom Elliot came in for Derrick Grant who withdrew because of injury. Wales made five changes amongst their forwards after struggling in a drawn match against England. This was a rather poor quality game decided by a single score in the first half. The opening exchanges were mainly confined to the forwards with both sets of half-backs kicking to touch. The rejuvenated Welsh pack was quick onto the loose ball and held their own in the lineout. The only try of the match came around 20 minutes from the start. Following a scrum on the Scottish 25, Jarrett made a half-break and fed Davies, albeit with a pass that looked forward, who then put Keri Jones over towards the left-hand corner. Jarrett converted, but otherwise had an off-day with his kicking. For Scotland, Wilson, who had a much happier game than against France, missed with his only penalty attempt, an ambitious effort from around 50 yards. Both sides had several scoring opportunities only to be narrowly denied. Gareth Edwards made one lovely break up the left touchline, but his kick over Wilson's head beat him to the dead ball line. Pringle Fisher played very well and was held up more than once on the line.

Lansdowne Road, Dublin · Saturday 24 February 1968 · Lost 6–14

SCOTLAND S Wilson (*London Scot*); AJW Hinshelwood (*London Scot*), JWC Turner (*Gala*), JNM Frame (*Edinburgh U*), †CG Hodgson (*London Scot*); DH Chisholm (*Melrose*), IG McCrae (*Gordonians*); AB Carmichael (*W of Scot*), FAL Laidlaw (*Melrose*), DMD Rollo (*Howe of Fife*), PK Stagg (*Sale*), †AF McHarg (*W of Scot*), JP Fisher* (*London Scot*), †RJ Arneil (*Edinburgh Acs*), AHW Boyle (*London Scot*)

IRELAND TJ Kiernan (*Cork Const*); ATA Duggan (*Lansdowne*), BAP O'Brien (*Shannon*), FPK Bresnihan (*UC Dublin*), RD Scott (*QU Belfast*); CMH Gibson (*NIFC*), J Quirke (*Blackrock Coll*); S Millar (*Ballymena*), AM Brady (*Malone*), P O'Callaghan (*Dolphin*), MG Malloy (*UC Galway*), WJ McBride (*Ballymena*), MG Doyle (*Blackrock Coll*), TJ Doyle (*Wdrs*), KG Goodall (*City of Derry*)

REFEREE M Joseph (*Wales*)

SCORING Kiernan, pen (0–3); Duggan, try (0–6) (half-time) Wilson, pen (3–6); Bresnihan, try (3–9); Wilson, pen (6–9); Duggan, try (6–12); Kiernan, con (6–14)

David Rollo won his 40th cap, equalling the Scottish cap record held by Hugh McLeod. Scrum-half Ian McCrae was recalled in place of Alex Hastie. The Scottish pack was disappointing once again and the new half-back combination was not a success. The backs mishandled too often and Wilson missed several penalty attempts. Ireland, on the other hand, took their opportunities very well and scored three tries to none. Tom Kieran, who had a great match, kicked a penalty before Duggan scored a try when he caught a crosskick by O'Brien and managed to fall over the line despite being tackled. Early in the second-half, Wilson kicked a penalty to raise Scottish hopes, but then a clearing kick was charged down and the ball broke to Bresnihan who scored a gift try. Wilson kicked a second penalty and the Scots put in a fighting finish until Quirke robbed the ball at a ruck and kicked downfield for Duggan to score. Kiernan converted to seal a good win for Ireland.

Murrayfield · Saturday 16 March 1968 · Lost 6–8

SCOTLAND S Wilson (*London Scot*); AJW Hinshelwood (*London Scot*), JWC Turner (*Gala*), JNM Frame (*Edinburgh U*), CG Hodgson (*London Scot*); †I Robertson (*London Scot*), †GC Connell (*Trinity Acs*); N Suddon (*Hawick*), †DT Deans (*Hawick*), AB Carmichael (*W of Scot*), PK Stagg (*Sale*), AF McHarg (*W of Scot*), JP Fisher (*London Scot*), RJ Ameil (*Edinburgh Acs*), JW Telfer* (*Melrose*)

ENGLAND RB Hiller (*Harlequins*); KF Savage (*Northampton*), TJ Brooke (*Richmond*), RH Lloyd (*Harlequins*), RE Webb (*Coventry*); MP Weston* (*Durham City*), RDA Pickering (*Bradford*); BW Keen (*Newcastle U*), JV Pullin (*Bristol*), MJ Coulman (*Moseley*), PJ Larter (*Northampton*), MJ Parsons (*Northampton*), PJ Bell (*Blackheath*), BR West (*Loughborough Coll*), DJ Gay (*Bath*)

REFEREE DP d'Arcy (*Ireland*)

SCORING Wilson, pen (3–0); Connell, drop (6–0) (half-time) Coulman, try (6–3); Hiller, con (6–5); Hiller, pen (6–8)

This match took place in wind and rain which made control of the ball very difficult. Consequently, the standard of play was only mediocre and both sides adopted unimaginative tactics. Scotland had the elements in their favour in the first half and after around 15 minutes Wilson kicked a penalty. Towards the end of the half, Gordon Connell, the new scrum-half, increased the lead with an unusual drop goal almost from under the English posts. Scotland ought to have been further head at the interval, but Wilson missed a few kickable penalty chances. England had barely reached the Scottish 25 in the first half, but 12 minutes after the interval, with the wind behind them, they scored a well worked try from a planned move. Taking a short lineout about 30 yards from the Scottish line, the ball was thrown into midfield where it was gathered by prop Mike Coulman who, showing a rare turn of speed, burst through the startled defence with a straight run to the line. He was tackled just short, but his momentum took him over for a try. Hiller converted and near the end kicked the winning penalty goal. Thus Scotland ended the season without a win and their first championship whitewash since 1954.

---

290 · TOUR MATCH · AUSTRALIA

Murrayfield · Saturday 2 November 1968 · Won 9–3

SCOTLAND CF Blaikie (*Heriot's FP*); AJW Hinshelwood (*London Scot*), JWC Turner (*Gala*), †CWW Rea (*W of Scot*), WD Jackson (*Hawick*); †CM Telfer (*Hawick*), GC Connell (*Trinity Acs*); N Suddon (*Hawick*), FAL Laidlaw (*Melrose*), AB Carmichael (*W of Scot*), PK Stagg (*Sale*), AF McHarg (*London Scot*), TG Elliot (*Langholm*), RJ Ameil (*Edinburgh Acs*), JW Telfer* (*Melrose*)

AUSTRALIA BD Honan (*Queensland*); TR Forman (*NSW*), PV Smith (*NSW*), JE Brass (*NSW*), JW Cole (*NSW*); JP Ballesty (*NSW*), JNB Hipwell (*NSW*); KR Bell (*Queensland*), PG Johnson* (*NSW*), RB Prosser (*NSW*), PNP Reilly (*Queensland*), SC Gregory (*Queensland*), HA Rose (*NSW*), GV Davis (*NSW*), DA Taylor (*Queensland*)

REFEREE MH Titcomb (*England*)

SCORING Blaikie, pen (3–0); Hinshelwood, try (6–0); Brass, pen (6–3); Blaikie, pen (9–3) (half-time)

In the autumn of 1968 Australia made a short tour of Ireland and Scotland, including two games in Scotland. Centre Chris Rea and stand-off Colin Telfer made their debuts. Played in a bitingly cold wind, this was an entertaining match that Scotland deserved to win although the visitors might have snatched it with a better goal-kicker and greater composure at critical moments. The Scottish forwards, led by the fiery Jim Telfer, held the upper hand throughout and Colin Telfer played well in his first game. The Australians missed three early penalty attempts before Blaikie put one over for Scotland. Rea made a break with Jim Telfer and Arneil in support and Hinshelwood cut inside the defence for a great Scottish try. Brass and Blaikie exchanged penalties to complete the scoring. The second half was one of cut and thrust and both sides had some chances, but their finishing was poor. At one point, Hinshelwood crossed the line only to be recalled for an infringement.

Stade Yves du Manoir, Colombes, Paris · Saturday 11 January 1969
Won 6–3

SCOTLAND CF Blaikie (*Heriot's FP*); AJW Hinshelwood (*London Scot*), JWC Turner (*Gala*), CWW Rea (*W of Scot*), WD Jackson (*Hawick*); CM Telfer (*Hawick*), GC Connell (*London Scot*); N Suddon (*Hawick*), FAL Laidlaw (*Melrose*), AB Carmichael (*W of Scot*), PK Stagg (*Sale*), AF McHarg (*London Scot*), TG Elliot (*Langholm*), RJ Arneil (*Edinburgh Acs*), JW Telfer* (*Melrose*) … Replacement: IG McCrae (*Gordonians*) for Connell (11)

FRANCE P Villepreux (*Toulouse*); J-M Bonal (*Toulouse*), J-P Lux (*Tyrosse*), J Maso (*Narbonne*), A Campaès (*Lourdes*); J Gachassin (*Lourdes*), J-L Bérot (*Toulouse*); J lraçabal (*Bayonne*), M Yachvili (*Tulle*), J-M Esponda (*Perpignan*), E Cester (*TOEC*), M Lasserre (*Agen*), W Spanghero (*Narbonne*), C Carrère* (*Toulon*), B Dauga (*Mont-de-Marsan*)

REFEREE GC Lamb (*England*)

SCORING Blaikie, pen (3–0) (half-time) Villepreux, pen (3–3); Telfer, try (6–3)

Scotland won an extraordinary victory in a match that was full of incident. As the teams were taking the field, Jean Salut, the French flanker, fell over and twisted his ankle. France had to quickly reshuffle their team with Jean Iraçabal coming on at prop, Michel Lasserre moving to the second-row and Benoit Dauga to the back-row. Colin Blaikie kicked an early penalty before Ian McCrae made history when he came on for the injured Gordon Connell, the first ever replacement in international rugby. France, the reigning champions, dominated this match and should have won comfortably. They had the bulk of possession and launched many dangerous attacks. Time and again they broke through and a try seemed inevitable, but the Scots held them out with some desperate last-ditch defence. France were over the line several times only to be called back for infringements or because the referee was unsighted. At times their attacks were over-elaborate, bringing the ball back inside into the heart of the cover defence when they should have run straight. To make matters worse, the normally reliable Pierre Villepreux missed five penalty attempts, although he did land a long goal early in the second half. About ten minutes from the end, McCrae disrupted an untidy French heel at a scrum inside the French 25; Elliot gathered the ball and passed to Telfer who barged his way over in the corner. Blaikie missed the conversion, but the Scots held out for an improbable victory. A French spectator was heard to ask if the Scottish team would fly home or just walk back over the Channel! Subsequently, Telfer's try became part of Scottish rugby folklore. Grainy footage of it was replayed biennially for the next 26 years until Scotland won again in Paris.

Murrayfield · Saturday 1 February 1969 · Lost 3–17

SCOTLAND CF Blaikie (*Heriot's FP*); AJ W Hinshelwood (*London Scot*), JNM Frame (*Gala*), CWW Rea (*W of Scot*), WD Jackson (*Hawick*); CM Telfer (*Hawick*), IG McCrae (*Gordonians*); N Suddon (*Hawick*), FAL Laidlaw (*Melrose*), AB Carmichael (*W of Scot*), PK Stagg (*Sale*), AF McHarg (*London Scot*), TG Elliot (*Langholm*), RJ Arneil (*Edinburgh Acs*), JW Telfer* (*Melrose*)

WALES JPR Williams (*London Welsh*); MCR Richards (*Cardiff*), TGR Davies (*Cardiff*),
KS Jarrett (*Newport*), SJ Watkins (*Newport*); B John (*Cardiff*), GO Edwards (*Cardiff*); D Williams
(*Ebbw Vale*), J Young (*Harrogate*), DJ Lloyd (*Bridgend*), B Price* (*Newport*), BE Thomas (*Neath*),
WD Morris (*Neath*), J Taylor (*London Welsh*), TM Davies (*London Welsh*)

REFEREE KD Kelleher (*Ireland*)

SCORING Jarrett, pen (0–3); Jarrett, pen (0–6) (half-time) Edwards, try (0–9); Blaikie, pen (3–9);
Richards, try (3–12); John, try (3–15); Jarrett, con (3–17)

The famous Welsh full-back JPR Williams won his first cap. Scotland were well
beaten by a confident Welsh side that was alert and quick to capitalise on Scottish
errors. The Welsh forwards combined together effectively and were stronger at the
set-pieces. Playing on a soft pitch and into a difficult wind, Keith Jarrett kicked two
early penalties that set the tone for the rest of the match. By contrast, Blaikie narrowly
missed three attempts from long range. In the second half, McCrae spilled the ball at
a scrum near the Scottish line and Gareth Edwards pounced for the opening try. Then
Richards collected a tap down at a lineout and had a clear run-in. Finally, the elusive
John charged down a kick, gathered the ball and sped away from the defence to score
underneath the posts.

293   INTERNATIONAL CHAMPIONSHIP 1969   IRELAND

Murrayfield · Saturday 22 February 1969 · Lost 0–16

SCOTLAND CF Blaikie (*Heriot's FP*); AJW Hinshelwood (*London Scot*), JNM Frame (*Gala*),
CWW Rea (*W of Scot*), WD Jackson(*Hawick*); CM Telfer (*Hawick*), †RC Allan (*Hutchesons'
GSFP*); N Suddon (*Hawick*), FAL Laidlaw (*Melrose*), AB Carmichael (*W of Scot*), PC Brown
(*Gala*), AF McHarg (*London Scot*), †W Lauder (*Neath*), RJ Arneil (*Edinburgh Acs*), JW Telfer*
(*Melrose*) ... Replacements: PK Stagg (*Sale*) for Telfer (18), †WG Macdonald (*London Scot*) for
Rea (78)

IRELAND TJ Kiernan* (*Cork Const*); ATA Duggan (*Lansdowne*), FPK Bresnihan (*UC Dublin*),
CMH Gibson (*NIFC*), JCM Moroney (*London Irish*); BJ McGann (*Lansdowne*), RM Young
(*QU Belfast*); S Millar (*Ballymena*), KW Kennedy (*London Irish*), P O'Callaghan (*Dolphin*),
WJ McBride (*Ballymena*), MG Molloy (*London Irish*), JC Davidson (*Dungannon*), NAA Murphy
(*Cork Const*), KG Goodall (*Derry*) ... Replacement: ML Hipwell (*Terenure Coll*) for Goodall (65)

REFEREE M Joseph (*Wales*)

SCORING Duggan, try (0–3) (half-time) McGann, try (0–6); Gibson, try (0–9); Moroney, con
(0–11); Bresnihan, try (0–14); Moroney, con (0–16)

Conditions were difficult with a bustling wind and surface water lying on top of a
hard pitch. An experienced Irish side had already beaten France and England and
were superior to Scotland in all respects, winning the try count four to none. The
visitors were more aggressive, combined better and were faster about the field.
Scotland were unlucky to lose their captain Jim Telfer early in the game, but at best
they were only a moderate side who were well beaten on the day. They squandered
18 points through missed goal kicks and made several costly errors in defence. Ireland
opened the scoring after some 27 minutes when Duggan raced onto a perfect diagonal
chip by McGann after pressure near the Scottish line. Five minutes into the second

half, McGann jigged his way through the dishevelled defence for a fine solo try. Further tries by Gibson and Bresnihan, both converted by Moroney, sealed a great day for Ireland. Towards the end, the auburn-haired WG MacDonald won his first and only cap when he replaced Chris Rea. MacDonald played for less than five minutes, the shortest international career of any Scottish player.

294 · INTERNATIONAL CHAMPIONSHIP 1969 · ENGLAND

Twickenham · Saturday 15 March 1969 · Lost 3–8

SCOTLAND CF Blaikie (*Heriot's FP*); †WCC Steele (*Langholm & RAF*), JNM Frame (*Gala*), I Robertson (*Watsonians*), WD Jackson (*Hawick*); CM Telfer (*Hawick*), GC Connell (*London Scot*); †J McLauchlan (*Jordanhill*), FAL Laidlaw (*Melrose*), AB Carmichael (*W of Scot*), PC Brown (*Gala*), AF McHarg (*London Scot*), W Lauder (*Neath*), RJ Arneil (*Edinburgh Acs*), JW Telfer* (*Melrose*)

ENGLAND RB Hiller (*Harlequins*); KJ Fielding (*Moseley*), JS Spencer (*Cambridge U*), DJ Duckham (*Coventry*), RE Webb (*Coventry*); JF Finlan (*Moseley*), TC Wintle (*Northampton*); DL Powell (*Northampton*), JV Pullin (*Bristol*), KE Fairbrother (*Coventry*), NE Horton (*Moseley*), PJ Larter (*Northampton*), RB Taylor (*Northampton*), DP Rogers* (*Bedford*), DM Rollitt (*Bristol*) ... Replacement: TJ Dalton (*Coventry*) for Fielding

REFEREE C Durand (*France*)

SCORING Duckham, try (0–3); Hiller, con (0–5) (half-time) Duckham, try (0–8); Brown, pen (3–8)

Billy Steel and Ian McLauchlan won their first caps. Scotland gave a more spirited performance than their previous two matches and the lightweight forward pack stood-up well. Once again, the three-quarters were ineffective in attack and the Scots might have won if they had kicked their goals. Playing in a swirling wind, Blaikie and Lauder missed four kickable penalties between them before Peter Brown nonchalantly hammered one over towards the end of the game. England, however, deserved to win if only for their two splendid tries, both scored by exciting fair-haired centre David Duckham. Close to half-time, Blaikie failed to deal with a high kick by Finlan and Duckham plucked the ball out of his grasp and blazed away to the line. Midway through the second half, Spencer and Dalton combined to put Duckham away near the Scottish 25 and the Coventry centre beat the defence with a devastating sidestep for a fine try.

XV · TOUR OF ARGENTINA · ARGENTINA

Buenos Aires · Saturday 13 September 1969 · Lost 3–20

SCOTLAND XV CF Blaikie (*Heriot's FP*); MA Smith (*London Scot*), IR Murchie (*W of Scot*), AV Orr (*London Scot*), AD Gill (*Gala*); I Robertson (*Watsonians*), DS Paterson (*Gala*); J McLauchlan (*Jordanhill*), FAL Laidlaw (*Melrose*), AB Carmichael (*W of Scot*), PK Stagg (*Sale*), AF McHarg (*London Scot*), RJ Arneil (*Edinburgh Acs*), W Lauder (*Neath*), JW Telfer* (*Melrose*)

ARGENTINA D Morgan (*Old Georgian*); M Pascual (*Pucara*), A Travaglini (*San Isidro*), AR Jurado (*San Isidro*), M Walther (*San Isidro*); T Harris-Smith (*Old Georgian*), A Etchegaray (*San*

Isidro); M Farina (*San Isidro*), R Handley (*Old Georgian*), LG Yanez (*San Fernando*), B Otano (*Pucara*), A Anthony (*San Isidro*), R Loyola (*Belgrano*), H Miguens (*CUBA*), H Silva* (*Los Tilos*)

REFEREE R Colombo

SCORING Jurado, try (0–3); Harris-Smith, con (0–5); Walther, try (0–8) (half-time) Harris-Smith, pen (0–11); Harris-Smith, drop (0–14); Smith, try (3–14); Travaglini, try (3–17); Harris-Smith, drop (3–20)

In September 1969, Scotland made a six-match tour of Argentina, including two non-cap test matches. Despite fielding a strong side with ten full internationalists, the Scots were well beaten in the first test against lively and passionate opponents. Playing on a bone-hard pitch and in scorching temperatures, the Scots started promisingly, but were handicapped when centre Ian Murchie damaged a shoulder early on. He had to leave the field with a broken collarbone after only 28 minutes and Lauder was withdrawn from the pack to take his place. Scotland never really recovered and Argentina ran out comfortable winners. Stand-off Thomas Harris-Smith kicked 11 points and the Pumas scored 3 tries. In the second half, Mike Smith scored a consolation try for Scotland, but the heat took its toll and the short-handed tourists wilted badly towards the end of the game.

| XV | TOUR OF ARGENTINA | ARGENTINA |

Buenos Aires · Saturday 27 September 1969 · Won 6–3

SCOTLAND XV CF Blaikie (*Heriot's FP*); MA Smith (*London Scot*), B Laidlaw (*Royal HSFP*), CWW Rea (*W of Scot*), WCC Steele (*Langholm*); I Robertson (*Watsonians*), DS Paterson (*Gala*); J McLauchlan (*Jordanhill*), FAL Laidlaw (*Melrose*), AB Carmichael (*W of Scot*), PK Stagg (*Sale*), AF McHarg (*London Scot*), RJ Ameil (*Edinburgh Acs*), W Lauder (*Neath*), JW Telfer* (*Melrose*)

ARGENTINA D Morgan (*Old Georgian*); M Pascual (*Pucara*), A Travaglini (*San Isidro*), D Benzi (*Duendez*), M Walther (*San Isidro*); T Harris-Smith (*Old Georgian*), A Etchegaray (*San Isidro*); M Farini (*San Isidro*), R Handley (*Old Georgian*), LG Yanez (*San Fernando*), A Otano (*Pucara*), A Anthony (*San Isidro*), R Loyola (*Belgrano*), H Miguens (*CUBA*), H Silva* (*Los Tilos*)

REFEREE CA Pozzi

SCORING Otano, try (0–3); Carmichael, try (3–3); Blaikie, pen (6–3) (half-time)

In a fast and rugged encounter, Scotland shrugged off an early score to produce their best rugby of the tour. Playing on a soft and muddy pitch which suited their style, the Scots were superior in all aspects. Their tackling was very strong and Argentinean stand-off Harris-Smith, who booted 11 points in the first test, was given a rough time by the Scottish back-row. The Argentineans missed several penalties and drop kicks, and some of their handling and finishing was weak. The home side quickly took the lead when Blaikie was caught near his own line and tried to pass backwards, but the ball rolled into the goal area and Otano pounced on it for an unconverted try. Seven minutes later, Telfer set-off down the wing from midfield and at least ten Scottish players handled the ball before Carmichael crashed over at the corner. Blaikie missed the conversion, but later kicked a penalty to give Scotland a lead that they held for the rest of the game. Tempers flared amongst the forwards in the second half and blows were traded several times.

Murrayfield · Saturday 6 December 1969 · Won 6–3

SCOTLAND †ISG Smith (*London Scot*); †AG Biggar (*London Scot*), JNM Frame (*Gala*), CWW Rea (*W of Scot*), AJW Hinshelwood (*London Scot*); I Robertson (*Watsonians*), †DS Paterson (*Gala*); J McLauchlan (*Jordanhill*), FAL Laidlaw (*Melrose*), AB Carmichael (*W of Scot*), PK Stagg (*Sale*), †GL Brown (*W of Scot*), W Lauder (*Neath*), RJ Arneil (*Leicester*), JW Telfer* (*Melrose*)

SOUTH AFRICA HO de Villiers (*W Province*); SH Nomis (*Transvaal*), OA Roux (*N Transvaal*), E Olivier (*W Province*), GH Muller (*W Province*); PJ Visagie (*Griqualand W*), DJJ de Vos (*W Transvaal*); JB Neethling (*W Province*), CH Cockrell (*W Province*), JFK Marais (*NE Cape*), FCH du Preez (*N Transvaal*), G Carelse (*E Province*), PJF Greyling (*Transvaal*), JH Ellis (*SWA*), TP Bedford* (*Natal*) ... Replacement: AE van der Watt (*W Province*) for Muller (70)

REFEREE M Joseph (*Wales*)

SCORING Visagie, pen (0–3) (half-time) Smith, pen (3–3); Smith, try (6–3)

The 1969–70 South Africans were one of the most controversial tours in the history of rugby. The tourists were continually harassed by anti-apartheid demonstrators and some matches were interrupted by pitch invasions and fighting between spectators and activists. There was a huge candlelit demonstration on Princes Street the evening before the Scotland test and the local police mounted a big operation to make sure that the game went ahead. Both end terraces at Murrayfield were closed and the pitch was enclosed by a ring of policemen and stewards. There were 27 arrests at the game and afterwards there were reports of violent behaviour both by the police and demonstrators. Away from politics, Scotland fielded four new caps, including scrum-half Duncan Paterson and baby-faced lock Gordon Brown. South Africa were handicapped

Ian Smith is congratulated by Wilson Lauder after scoring his match-winning try against South Africa in 1969. Note the empty south terrace and ring of policemen in the background.
Scotsman Publications Ltd

by the late withdrawal of their captain Dawie de Villiers whose skill and calming influence were greatly missed by his team. Perhaps because of the tense atmosphere, this was a rather featureless encounter with both sets of defences well on top. Scotland deserved to win thanks to great effort by the forwards. Orchestrated by Jim Telfer, they held their own at the scrums and combined well in the loose. The gigantic Peter Stagg dominated at the lineout and the quick-thinking Scots cleverly rotated their main lineout jumpers to good effect. Both sides missed numerous kicks at goal and also half chances to score tries because of handling errors and stout defence. Shortly before the interval, Visagie gave South Africa the lead with a penalty and early in the second half Ian 'Sid' Smith equalised in kind. The game seemed to be heading for stalemate until the Scots scored a classic try towards the finish. Robertson gave a long pass to Frame and the big centre burst through the defence before finding the intruding Smith who had a clear run to the line.

296 INTERNATIONAL CHAMPIONSHIP 1970 FRANCE

Murrayfield · Saturday 10 January 1970 · Lost 9–11

SCOTLAND Ian Smith (*London Scot*); Alastair Biggar (*London Scot*), John Frame (*Gala*), Chris Rea (*W of Scot*), Sandy Hinshelwood (*London Scot*); Ian Robertson (*Watsonians*), Gordon Connell (*London Scot*); Ian McLauchlan (*Jordanhill*), Frank Laidlaw (*Melrose*), Sandy Carmichael (*W of Scot*), Peter Stagg (*Sale*), Gordon Brown (*W of Scot*), Wilson Lauder (*Neath*), Rodger Arneil (*Leicester*), Jim Telfer* (*Melrose*)

FRANCE Pierre Villepreux (*Toulouse*); Roger Bourgarel (*Toulouse*), Jean-Pierre Lux (*Tyrosse*), Alain Marot (*Brive*), Jean Sillières (*Tarbes*); Lucien Pariès (*Biarritz*), Gérard Sutra (*Narbonne*); Jean Iraçabal (*Bayonne*), René Bénésis (*Narbonne*), Jean-Louis Azarète (*Dax*), Jean-Pierre Bastiat (*Dax*), Elie Cester (*TOEC*), Gérard Viard (*Narbonne*), Christian Carrère* (*Toulon*), Benoit Dauga (*Mont-de-Marsan*)

REFEREE GC Lamb (*England*)

SCORING Dauga, try (0–3); Pariès, con (0–5); Smith, try (3–5); Pariès, drop (3–8); Lauder, pen (6–8); Lux, try (6–11) (half-time) Lauder, pen (9–11)

Scrum-half Duncan Paterson made a late withdrawal and was replaced by Gordon Connell. France selected a mixture of experience and youth, including five new caps. After their victory over South Africa the previous month, Scotland were cautiously optimistic, but France were a useful side and deserved their victory. After 18 minutes, Dauga picked-up from a scrum near the line and bulldozed his way past Ian Smith for a score. Smith responded with a try of his own, bursting into the line as he had done against the Springboks. Pariès missed a penalty attempt, but then retrieved the poorly hit clearance kick and dropped a goal. After a skirmish in front of the referee, Wilson Lauder, a flank forward, kicked a long penalty and near the interval France scored a spectacular try. Slick passing amongst the French backs created space for Sillières who raced up the field. When confronted by Smith, he slipped a perfectly timed pass to Lux for a classic French score. Play was fairly even in the second-half and with 20 minutes left Lauder kicked his second penalty. Scotland continued to press, but they missed several scoring chances and the visitors held on.

Cardiff Arms Park · Saturday 7 February 1970 · Lost 9–18

SCOTLAND Ian Smith (*London Scot*); †Mike Smith (*London Scot*), John Frame (*Gala*), Chris Rea (*W of Scot*), Sandy Hinshelwood (*London Scot*); Ian Robertson (*Watsonians*), †Bob Young (*Watsonians*); Ian McLauchlan (*Jordanhill*), Frank Laidlaw (*Melrose*), Sandy Carmichael (*W of Scot*), Peter Stagg (*Sale*), Peter Brown (*Gala*), Wilson Lauder (*Neath*), Rodger Arneil (*Leicester*), Jim Telfer* (*Melrose*) ... Replacement: Gordon Brown (*W of Scot*) for Brown

WALES JPR Williams (*London Welsh*); Laurie Daniel (*Newport*), John Dawes (*London Welsh*), Phil Bennett (*Llanelli*), Ian Hall (*Aberavon*); Barry John (*Cardiff*), Gareth Edwards* (*Cardiff*); Barry Llewelyn (*Newport*), Vic Perrins (*Newport*), Denzil Williams (*Ebbw Vale*), Delme Thomas (*Llanelli*), Geoff Evans (London Welsh), Dave Morris (*Neath*), Dennis Hughes (*Newbridge*), Mervyn Davies (*London Welsh*)

REFEREE DP D'Arcy (*Ireland*)

SCORING Robertson, drop (3–0); Lauder, pen (6–0); Robertson, try (9–0); Daniel, try (9–3); Daniel, con (9–5) (half-time) Llewelyn, try (9–8); Dawes, try (9–11); Edwards, con (9–13); Morris, try (9–16); Edwards, con (9–18)

Winger Mike Smith and scrum-half Bob Young were awarded their first caps, the latter joining his club partner Ian Robertson at half-back. Playing with a strong wind behind them, Scotland began to build a lead when Robertson dropped a goal from a scrum in front of the Welsh posts and then Lauder kicked a penalty. Robertson, playing a fine game, collected a loose kick and, after a bout of passing, he beat the defence with an imperious dummy. Gradually, the Welsh forwards gained the upper-hand and Scotland's early advantage was whittled away. Just before the interval, Daniel scored in the corner and he also converted. In the second half, Llewelyn crashed over from a ruck and then Dawes charged down a kick to put Wales in front. Later, Morris, who had a great match, scored when the Scottish scrum was driven backwards over its own line. A curiosity of this match occurred when Gordon Brown replaced his elder brother Peter early in the second half: Gordon had been left out in favour of Peter in the original selection.

Lansdowne Road, Dublin · Saturday 28 February 1970 · Lost 11–16

SCOTLAND Ian Smith (*London Scot*); Mike Smith (*London Scot*), John Frame (*Gala*), Chris Rea (*W of Scot*), Alastair Biggar (*London Scot*); Ian Robertson (*Watsonians*), Duncan Paterson (*Gala*); Norman Suddon (*Hawick*), Frank Laidlaw (*Melrose*), Sandy Carmichael (*W of Scot*), Peter Stagg (*Sale*), Gordon Brown (*W of Scot*), Wilson Lauder (*Neath*), Rodger Arneil (*Leicester*), Jim Telfer* (*Melrose*)

IRELAND Tom Kiernan* (*Cork Const*); Alan Duggan (*Lansdowne*), Barry Bresnihan (*London Irish*), Mike Gibson (*NIFC*), William Brown (*Malone*); Barry McGann (*Cork Const*), Roger Young (*Collegians*); Sid Millar (*Ballymena*), Ken Kennedy (*London Irish*), Philip O'Callaghan (*Dolphin*), Willie John McBride (*Ballymena*), Mick Malloy (*London Irish*), Ronnie Lamont (*Instonians*), Fergus Slattery (*UC Dublin*), Ken Goodall (*City of Derry*)

REFEREE C Durand (*France*)

SCORING Malloy, try (0–3); Robertson, drop (3–3); Goddall, try (3–6); Kiernan, con (3–8); Gibson, try (3–11); Kiernan, con (3–13) (half-time) Brown, try (3–16); Lauder, try (6–16); I Smith, con (8–16); M Smith, try (11–16)

Scotland made four changes from the side that had lost in Cardiff. Ireland dominated the game and at one point looked set to run up a big score, but the Scots made a late rally and scored two tries. Playing with the wind behind them in the first half, the Irish forwards were in a dominant mood and their marauding back-row gave the Scottish half-backs an uncomfortable time. Ireland scored three first half tries, including a brilliant effort by centre Mike Gibson who took a crosskick at top speed and cut through the defence. A try by Brown in the second half gave Ireland a commanding lead, but then Lauder scored a disputed try and Ian Smith intruded into the line to create a try for his namesake Mike.

299 INTERNATIONAL CHAMPIONSHIP 1970   ENGLAND

Murrayfield · Saturday 21 March 1970 · Won 14–5

SCOTLAND Ian Smith (*London Scot*); Mike Smith (*London Scot*), John Frame (*Gala*), Jock Turner (*Gala*), Alastair Biggar (*London Scot*); Ian Robertson (*Watsonians*), Duncan Paterson (*Gala*); Norman Suddon (*Hawick*), Frank Laidlaw* (*Melrose*), Sandy Carmichael (*W of Scot*), Peter Stagg (*Sale*), Gordon Brown (*W of Scot*), Tom Elliot (*Langholm*), Rodger Arneil (*Leicester*), Peter Brown (*Gala*)

ENGLAND Bob Hiller* (*Harlequins*); Michael Novak (*Harlequins*), John Spencer (*Cambridge U*), David Duckham (*Coventry*), Mike Bulpitt (*Blackheath*); Ian Shackleton (*Cambridge U*), Nigel Starmer-Smith (*Harlequins*); Stack Stevens (*Penzance & Newlyn*), John Pullin (*Bristol*), Keith Fairbrother (*Coventry*), Mike Davis (*Harlequins*), Peter Larter (*Northampton*), Tony Bucknall (*Richmond*), Bob Taylor (*Northampton*), Bryan West (*Northampton*)

Replacement: Barry Jackson (*Broughton Park*) for West

REFEREE M Joseph (*Wales*)

SCORING P Brown, pen (3–0); Biggar, try (6–0) (half-time) P Brown, pen (9–0); Spencer, try (9–3); Hiller, con (9–5); Turner, try (12–5); P Brown, con (14–5)

Scotland made several changes and Frank Laidlaw took over the captaincy from Jim Telfer. The Scottish forwards were well on top, especially at the rucks, and supplied the backs with plenty of ball. Scotland started briskly and raced to a 6–0 lead within ten minutes. Peter Brown opened the scoring with a long range penalty. Then Robertson made a midfield break and passed to Frame who put Biggar away to the corner. There was no further scoring in the first half, although England full-back Bob Hiller was unlucky to miss four huge kicks at goal. Brown's second penalty gave Scotland a comfortable lead until seven minutes from time when Spencer made a long run to score at the corner. Hiller kicked a wonderful conversion to raise English hopes, but Turner scored in the final minutes after taking a well-timed reverse pass from Robertson. At the end, Laidlaw was chaired off the field by ecstatic Scottish supporters.

Murrayfield · Saturday 9 May 1970 · Lost 17–33

SCOTLAND XV Ian Smith (*London Scot & Army*); Mike Smith (*London Scot*), John Frame (*Gala*), Jock Turner (*Gala*), Alastair Biggar (*London Scot*); Ian Robertson (*Watsonians*), Duncan Paterson (*Gala*); Norman Suddon (*Hawick*), Frank Laidlaw* (*Melrose*), Sandy Carmichael (*W of Scot*), Peter Stagg (*Sale*), Gordon Brown (*W of Scot*), Tom Elliot (*Langholm*), Rodger Arneil (*Leicester*), Peter Brown (*Gala*)

BARBARIANS JPR Williams (*London Welsh & Wales*); Alan Duggan (*Lansdowne & Ireland*), John Spencer* (*Cambridge U & England*), David Duckham (*Coventry & England*), Keith Fielding (*Moseley & England*); Barry John (*Cardiff & Wales*), Gareth Edwards (*Cardiff & Wales*); Barry Llewelyn (*Newport & Wales*), John Pullin (*Bristol & England*), Phil O'Callaghan (*Dolphin & Ireland*), Mick Molloy (*London Irish & Ireland*), Stuart Gallacher (*Llanelli & Wales*), Mick Hipwell (*Terenure Coll & Ireland*), Fergus Slattery (*UC Dublin & Ireland*), Mervyn Davies (*London Welsh & Wales*)

REFEREE Bob Burrell (*Gala*)

SCORING P Brown, pen (3–0); P Brown, pen (6–0); Fielding, try (6–3); Williams, con (6–5); Duckham, try (6–8) (half-time) Duckham, try (6–11); Williams, con (6–13); Spencer, try (6–16); Williams, con (6–18); Molloy, try (6–21); Williams, con (6–23); Edwards, try (6–26); Williams, con (6–28); Elliot, try (9–28); P Brown, con (11–28); Llewelyn, try (11–31); Williams, con (11–33); P Brown, pen (14–33); P Brown, pen (17–33)

This non-cap match was staged to raise funds for the Commonwealth Games which were due to be held in Edinburgh in July 1970. Murrayfield had been considered as a venue for the athletics events, but was too small to accommodate a running track. In a fast and open game, the Scots were soundly beaten by an all-star Barbarians team who outscored them by seven tries to one. The home side were immediately hampered when Mike Smith went off with an injury after only three minutes. Replacements were not allowed in this exhibition game so flanker Tom Elliot was moved to the wing. After an undistinguished opening, the Barbarians clicked into gear and produced some spectacular play. The Scots competed well at the set-pieces, but they could not match the Barbarians in attack. Leggy England winger David Duckham made some elusive runs and scored two tries. Near the finish, Peter Brown, who stood at six foot four inches, was moved to scrum-half for the injured Duncan Paterson.

300 TOUR OF AUSTRALIA 1970 AUSTRALIA

Sydney Cricket Ground · Saturday 6 June 1970 · Lost 3–23

SCOTLAND Jock Turner (*Gala*); Mike Smith (*London Scot*), John Frame (*Gala*), Chris Rea (*W of Scot*), Alastair Biggar (*London Scot*); Ian Robertson (*Watsonians*), Duncan Paterson (*Gala*); Norman Suddon (*Hawick*), Frank Laidlaw* (*Melrose*), Sandy Carmichael (*W of Scot*), Peter Stagg (*Sale*), Gordon Brown (*W of Scot*), Wilson Lauder (*Neath*), Rodger Arneil (*Leicester*), †Ken Oliver (*Gala*)

AUSTRALIA Arthur McGill (*NSW*); John Cole (*NSW*), Stephen Knight (*NSW*), Geoff Shaw (*NSW*), Rod Batterham (*NSW*); Rubie Rosenblum (*NSW*), John Hipwell (*NSW*); James Roxburgh (*NSW*), Peter Johnson (*NSW*), Jake Howard (*NSW*), Owen Butler (*NSW*), Alan Skinner (*NSW*), Barry McDonald (*NSW*), Greg Davis* (*NSW*), Hugh Rose (*NSW*)

SCORING Hipwell, try (0–3); McGill, con (0–5); Batterham, try (0–8); Lauder, pen (3–8) (half-time) Rosenblum, try (3–11); McGill, pen (3–14); Cole, try (3–17); Batterham, try (3–20); Cole, try (3–23)

Captained by hooker Frank Laidlaw, Scotland made a six-match tour of Australia in early summer 1970. They had mixed fortunes in their provincial games, winning three but losing to New South Wales (14–28) and Queensland (13–16). The Scots were heavily beaten in the only test match when they conceded six tries. The tourists started well, but made a series of defensive mistakes and the Australians were quick to capitalise. Hipwell and Batterham scored tries, the first was converted by McGill, and Scotland's only response was a penalty goal by flanker Wilson Lauder shortly before the interval. Playing with the wind in the second half, the Australian backs enjoyed a plentiful supply of the ball and scored four unconverted tries to finish as convincing winners.

301 INTERNATIONAL CHAMPIONSHIP 1971 FRANCE

Stade Yves du Manoir, Colombes, Paris · Saturday 16 January 1971

Lost 8–13

SCOTLAND Ian Smith (*London Scot*); Alastair Biggar (*London Scot*), John Frame (*Gala*), Chris Rea (*Headingley*), Billy Steele (*Bedford*); Jock Turner (*Gala*), Duncan Paterson (*Gala*); Ian McLauchlan (*Jordanhill*), Frank Laidlaw (*Melrose*), Sandy Carmichael (*W of Scot*), Alastair McHarg (*London Scot*), Gordon Brown (*W of Scot*), †Nairn MacEwan (*Gala*), Rodger Arneil (Leicester), Peter Brown* (*Gala*) ... Replacement: Brain Simmers (*Glasgow Acs*) for Smith (42)

FRANCE Pierre Villepreux (*Toulouse*); Jean Sillières (*Tarbes*), Jean Trillo (*Bégles*), Jean-Pierre Lux (*Tyrosse*), Jack Cantoni (*Béziers*); Jean-Louis Bérot (*Toulouse*), Max Barrau (*Beaumont*); Marc Etcheverry (*Pau*), René Bénésis (*Narbonne*), Jean-Louis Azarète (*St-Jean-de-Luz*), Jean-Pierre Bastiat (*Dax*), Jean Le Droff (*Auch*), Gérard Viard (*Narbonne*), D Dubois (*Bègles*), Benoit Dauga* (*Mont-de-Marsan*)

REFEREE KD Kelleher (*Ireland*)

SCORING Villepreux, pen (0–3); Smith, pen (3–3) (half-time) Steele, try (6–3); P Brown, con (8–3); Sillières, try (8–6); Villepreux, con (8–8); Villepreux, try (8–11); Villepreux, con (8–13)

Scotland gave their opponents a real fright only to lose out in the closing stages. The first half was evenly contested with Villepreux and Smith exchanging penalties. At half-time, Smith had to leave the field with an injury, the victim of a late tackle. He was replaced by Brian Simmers who went to stand-off and Jock Turner moved to full-back. In retrospect, this rearrangement was a mistake because it split up the Gala half-back pairing of Turner and Paterson who had combined well together in the first half. Scotland took the lead when Steele made a long run, chipped ahead and caught the bouncing ball to score in the corner. Peter Brown converted with a fine curling kick. The Scots held their lead until the final 15 minutes when Sillières and Villepreux scored tries, both of which were converted by Villepreux who had an outstanding match.

Murrayfield · Saturday 6 February 1971 · Lost 18–19

SCOTLAND Ian Smith (*London Scot*); Billy Steele (*Bedford*), John Frame (*Gala*), Chris Rea (*Headingley*), Alastair Biggar (*London Scot*); Jock Turner (*Gala*), Duncan Paterson (*Gala*); Ian McLauchlan (*Jordanhill*), Frank Laidlaw (*Melrose*), Sandy Carmichael (*W of Scot*), Alastair McHarg (*London Scot*), Gordon Brown (*W of Scot*), Nairn MacEwan (*Gala*), Rodger Arneil (*Leicester*), Peter Brown* (*Gala*)

WALES JPR Williams (*London Welsh*); Gerald Davies (*Cambridge U*), John Dawes* (*London Welsh*), Arthur Lewis (*Ebbw Vale*), John Bevan (*Cardiff CE*); Barry John (*Cardiff*), Gareth Edwards (*Cardiff*); Barry Llewelyn (*Llanelli*), Jeff Young (*Harrogate*), Denzil Williams (*Ebbw Vale*), Delme Thomas (*Llanelli*), Mike Roberts (*London Welsh*), Dave Morris (*Neath*), John Taylor (*London Welsh*), Mervyn Davies (*London Welsh*)

REFEREE MH Titcomb (*England*)

SCORING P Brown, pen (3–0); John, pen (3–3); P Brown, pen (6–3); Taylor, try (6–6); John, con (6–8) (half-time) Edwards, try (6–11); Carmichael, try (9–11); P Brown, pen (12–11); John, try (12–14); P Brown, pen (15–14); Rea, try (18–14); G Davies, try (18–17); Taylor, con (18–19)

This match was one of the greatest internationals ever played and had everything in terms of excitement and drama. Scotland were firm underdogs, but they pushed a brilliant Welsh team right to the end. The lead changed hands six times and in truth neither side deserved to lose. Three weeks earlier, the Welsh forwards had torn England to ribbons (22–6), but the Scots rose to the occasion and gave their opponents as good as they got. Peter Brown proved an inspirational leader and his eccentric goal-kicking kept his side in contention. The Scottish midfield worked very hard with Rea making some crunching tackles. The famous Welsh half-backs, Gareth Edwards

Prop Sandy Carmichael has just scored Scotland's first try in their epic encounter against Wales in 1971.
Scotsman Publications Ltd

and Barry John, displayed all of their abundant talent; the latter bobbing and weaving his way around the field like a red phantom. In the first half, Peter Brown kicked two penalties and John one before the visitors scored their opening try on the stroke of half-time. From a lineout, the ball was passed swiftly left, JPR Williams intruded into the line and John Taylor streaked diagonally to the posts. In the second half, Edwards collected from a ruck on the Scottish 25 and powered to the corner. Ten minutes later, Carmichael snatched a wayward Welsh tap-down near the line and bundled his way over. Brown kicked his third penalty to put Scotland in front before John picked-up a loose ball on the Scottish 25 and ghosted past three defenders for a try. Brown kicked another long penalty to recapture the lead and with seven minutes remaining the Scots seemed to have scored the winning try. From a lineout inside the Scottish half, Paterson put up a high kick and Steele, following-up quickly, charged down Bevan's ponderous clearance. JPR Williams was flattened by Arneil and the loose ball was grasped by Rea who thundered his way from the Welsh 25 to the posts. The conversion should have been a formality, but Peter Brown's kick struck an upright and the door was still open for Wales. With injury-time looming, Wales won a lineout deep in the Scottish 25, the ball was passed left, JPR Williams intruded into the line, and Gerald Davies had just enough speed to beat Smith's despairing dive and race over in the right corner. It all depended on the conversion and Taylor, under enormous pressure, kicked a superb left-footed goal to win a memorable encounter.

303 INTERNATIONAL CHAMPIONSHIP 1971 IRELAND

Murrayfield · Saturday 27 February 1971 · Lost 5–17

SCOTLAND Ian Smith (*London Scot*); Billy Steele (*Bedford*), John Frame (*Gala*), Alastair Biggar (*London Scot*), †Ronald Hannah (*W of Scot*); Jock Turner (*Gala*), Duncan Paterson (*Gala*); Ian McLauchlan (*Jordanhill*), Frank Laidlaw (*Melrose*), Sandy Carmichael (*W of Scot*), Alastair McHarg (*London Scot*), Gordon Brown (*W of Scot*), Nairn MacEwan (*Gala*), Rodger Arneil (*Leicester*), Peter Brown* (*Gala*)

IRELAND Barry O'Driscoll (*Manchester*); Alan Duggan (*Lansdowne*), Barry Bresnihan (*London Irish*), Mike Gibson* (*NIFC*), Eddie Grant (*CIYMS*); Barry McGann (*Cork Const*), Roger Young (*Collegians*); Ray McLoughlin (*Blackrock Coll*), Ken Kennedy (*London Irish*), Sean Lynch (*St Mary's Coll*), Willie John McBride (*Ballymena*), Mick Molloy (*London Irish*), Mick Hipwell (*Terenure Coll*), Fergus Slattery (*UC Dublin*), Dennis Hickie (*St Mary's Coll*)

REFEREE WKM Jones (*Wales*)

SCORING Gibson, pen (0–3); Duggan, try (0–6); Gibson, pen (0–9) (half-time) Frame, try (3–9); P Brown, con (5–9); Grant, try (5–12); Duggan, try (5–15); Gibson, con (5–17)

After their good showing against Wales, the Scots were quietly confident, but Ireland were convincing winners even though two of their tries came in the closing stages when the Scots were chasing the game. The Irish forwards were superior in all aspects and gave their talented back division a good supply of ball. Gibson opened the scoring with a long penalty goal and then Young and McGann combined down the blind side to put Duggan over. Gibson kicked his second penalty on the stroke of half-time. Scotland improved in the second half and, after some pressure, Frame crashed over for a try converted by Peter Brown. Scotland fought hard only to concede two soft tries near the end. The first came when Young pounced on a poor Scottish heel from a scrum and gave Grant a clear run in. Then Duggan intercepted a loose pass and made a long sprint to the line. Gibson converted to seal a great win for Ireland.

Twickenham · Saturday 20 March 1971 · Won 16–15

SCOTLAND †Arthur Brown (*Gala*); Billy Steele (*Bedford*), John Frame (*Gala*), Chris Rea (*Headingley*), Alastair Biggar (*London Scot*); Jock Turner (*Gala*), Duncan Paterson (*Gala*); Ian McLauchlan (*Jordanhill*), †Quintin Dunlop (*W of Scot*), Sandy Carmichael (*W of Scot*), Alastair McHarg (*London Scot*), Gordon Brown (*W of Scot*), Nairn MacEwan (*Gala*), Rodger Arneil (*Leicester*), Peter Brown* (*Gala*) ... Replacement: †Stephen Turk (*Langholm*) for Frame

ENGLAND Bob Hiller (*Harlequins*); Jeremy Janion (*Bedford*), Chris Wardlow (*Northampton*), John Spencer* (*Headingley*), David Duckham (*Coventry*); Dick Cowman (*Loughborough Coll*), Jacko Page (*Bedford*); David Powell (*Northampton*), John Pullin (*Bristol*), Fran Cotton (*Loughborough Coll*), Peter Larter (*Northampton*), Nigel Horton (*Moseley*), Tony Bucknall (*Richmond*), Tony Neary (*Broughton Park*), Bob Taylor (*Northampton*) ... Replacement: Ian Wright (*Northampton*) for Cotton

REFEREE C Durand (*France*)

SCORING Hiller, try (0–3); P Brown, try (3–3); P Brown, con (5–3); Hiller, pen (5–6); Hiller, pen (5–9) (half-time) Paterson, drop (8–9); Neary, try (8–12); Hiller, pen (8–15); Paterson, try (11–15); Rea, try (14–15); P Brown, con (16–15)

In a legendary encounter, Scotland won at Twickenham for the first time in 33 years. England opened the scoring when Janion broke away from his own 25 and found support from Cowman who jinked back inside. The ball was passed through several pairs of hands to Spencer who put Hiller over at the right corner. From a retreating scrum on the English 25, Rea went left and made a scissors movement with Biggar who burst through. MacEwan was in support and found Peter Brown who dived over the line. Brown converted his own try and Hiller kicked two long penalties to give England the lead at the interval. In the second half, from a lineout and ruck inside the English 25, Paterson dropped a goal. Scotland lost control of the ball at a scrum near halfway, Page picked-up and put Janion away down the right. Neary was in support and ran through some weak tackles to score in the corner. Hiller missed the awkward conversion, but inside the final ten minutes kicked another penalty and England seemed to be heading for yet another victory. Rea set-up a ruck on the English 25 and Paterson chipped towards the goal-line. Cowman let the ball slip from his grasp and Paterson gathered and threw himself over. Then in the dying seconds, McLauchlan thundered to the English 25 from a short lineout. Paterson made a darting run before finding Peter Brown who gave out a one-handed overhead pass to Rea. The centre juggled with the ball and just managed to make the line with Spencer hanging onto him. The outcome hinged on Peter Brown's conversion attempt. From a position about halfway between the posts and the touchline he put the ball straight between the uprights and all of Scotland rejoiced.

Murrayfield · Saturday 27 March 1971 · Won 26–6

SCOTLAND Arthur Brown (*Gala*); Billy Steele (*Bedford*), John Frame (*Gala*), Chris Rea (*Headingley*), Alastair Biggar (*London Scot*); John Turner (*Gala*), Duncan Paterson (*Gala*); Ian McLauchlan (*Jordanhill*), Quintin Dunlop (*W of Scot*), Sandy Carmichael (*W of Scot*), Alastair McHarg (*London Scot*), Gordon Brown (*W of Scot*), Nairn MacEwan (*Gala*), Rodger Arneil (*Leicester*), Peter Brown* (*Gala*) … Replacement: †Gordon Strachan (*Jordanhill*) for G Brown

ENGLAND Bob Hiller (*Harlequins*); Jeremy Janion (*Bedford*), Chris Wardlow (*Northampton*), John Spencer* (*Headingley*), David Duckham (*Coventry*); Dick Cowman (*Loughborough Coll*), Nigel Starmer-Smith (*Harlequins*), David Powell (*Northampton*), John Pullin (*Bristol*), Fran Cotton (*Loughborough Coll*), Peter Larter (*Northampton*), Chris Ralston (*Richmond*), Tony Bucknall (*Richmond*), Tony Neary (*Broughton Park*), Bob Taylor (*Northampton*)

REFEREE M Joseph (*Wales*)

SCORING Frame, try (3–0); A Brown, con (5–0); P Brown, pen (8–0); Cowman, drop (8–3); P Brown, try (11–3) (half-time) Frame, try (14–3); A Brown, con (16–3); Hiller, pen (16–6); Steele, try (19–6); A Brown, con (21–6); Rea, try (24–6); A Brown, con (26–6)

Caps were awarded for this extra game which was played to mark the centenary of the first international between the two countries on the corresponding date in 1871.

Scottish players celebrate in the dressing room after thumping England in the Centenary International in March 1971.
Scotsman Publications Ltd

The teams were presented to the Prince of Wales and Edward Heath, the Prime Minister. Scotland were in rampant form and scored five tries to none. Straight from the kick-off, England tried to attack from deep, but dropped the ball and Frame, moving up for the tackle, was on hand to score. Frame's try was estimated to have taken around ten seconds, one of the quickest ever scored in an international match. Peter Brown kicked a penalty and Cowman dropped a goal for England. Then Dunlop pinched a scrum against the head, Paterson chipped ahead and gathered the rebound before flipping the ball to Peter Brown who crashed over the line. In the second half, Rea made a strong diagonal run to create a score for Frame. The Scottish forwards had a thunderous series of drives and from a ruck Paterson fed Steele on the blind side for the wing to nip over at the corner. Finally, Wardlow was caught behind his forwards and Rea, with a huge overlap outside him, raced away to the line. Arthur Brown kicked four conversions on an immensely satisfying afternoon for Scotland.

Irvine and the Second Grand Slam
1972–1985

IF THE 1960s was a rather drab era for rugby then the 1970s was a golden age. The game was open and attractive to watch, and it achieved greater popularity than ever before. In 1975, it was estimated that over 100,000 people crammed into Murrayfield to see the Welsh match with thousands more shut outside. Thereafter, internationals at Murrayfield became all-ticket. Rugby also benefitted from increased coverage on television. In the 1970s, colour television became increasingly affordable and live coverage of international matches were one of the mainstays of the winter schedules, attracting millions of viewers, many of whom were not traditional rugby supporters. They were fortunate to have a hugely knowledgeable commentator in the BBC's Bill McLaren, a former Scottish trialist whose steady authority and easily accessible style turned him into a broadcasting legend.

One of the biggest and most influential changes at this time was the advent of coaching and new attitudes towards training, preparation and fitness. Traditionally, international teams had been left to their own affairs. At best, one or two senior players might take their side for a run around before a big game, but anything else was frowned upon as it had connotations of professionalism. The coaching revolution began in Wales in the mid-1960s and gradually was adopted by other countries, sometimes reluctantly. In 1971, the Scottish Rugby Union appointed Bill Dickinson as the first official coach to the national side (or, as he was quaintly described, 'adviser to the captain'). Dickinson was a former player with Hillhead High School FP and a lecturer in Physical Education at Jordanhill College in Glasgow. He made an enormous contribution to Scottish rugby in the seventies, especially in forward play. In 1977, Dickinson was replaced by the former Scotland flanker Nairn MacEwan, a surprise choice who struggled to emulate the success of his predecessor.

It is also worth mentioning that in the early 1970s Scottish rugby had enough foresight and wisdom to introduce official club leagues. For over a hundred years the club game in Scotland had been loosely based on a series of long-established friendly fixtures, although clubs in the Borders had a league of their own. By the late 1960s, it had become apparent that the game needed a competitive club structure to bring out the best from a limited pool of players and thus benefit the international team. There was some reluctance to adopt the new leagues, but they were introduced in season 1973–74 and undoubtedly they helped to raise the standard of Scottish rugby. It was no coincidence that ten years after the start of the leagues Scotland won their second Grand Slam with a side largely composed of players from Scottish clubs.

The period between 1973 and 1985 was, as always, one of mixed fortunes for Scottish rugby. In the early and mid-70s, Scotland had a strong scrummaging pack, including such redoubtable stalwarts as Sandy Carmichael, Iain McLauchlan, Gordon Brown and Alastair McHarg. Between 1972 and 1975 they won eight Championship matches in a row at home, including two victories over Wales, the outstanding side of the seventies, and twice against England. Curiously, they were never able to repeat their form away from home. Taking the 1970s as a whole, Scotland won only twice

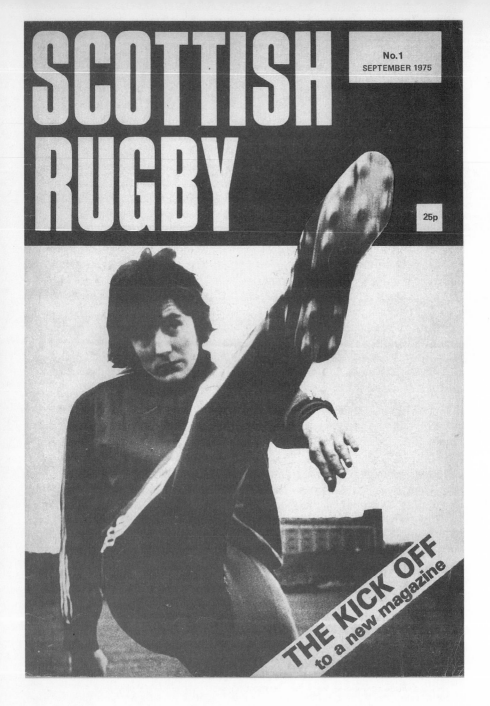

SCOTTISH RUGBY

No.1
SEPTEMBER 1975

25p

THE KICK OFF
to a new magazine

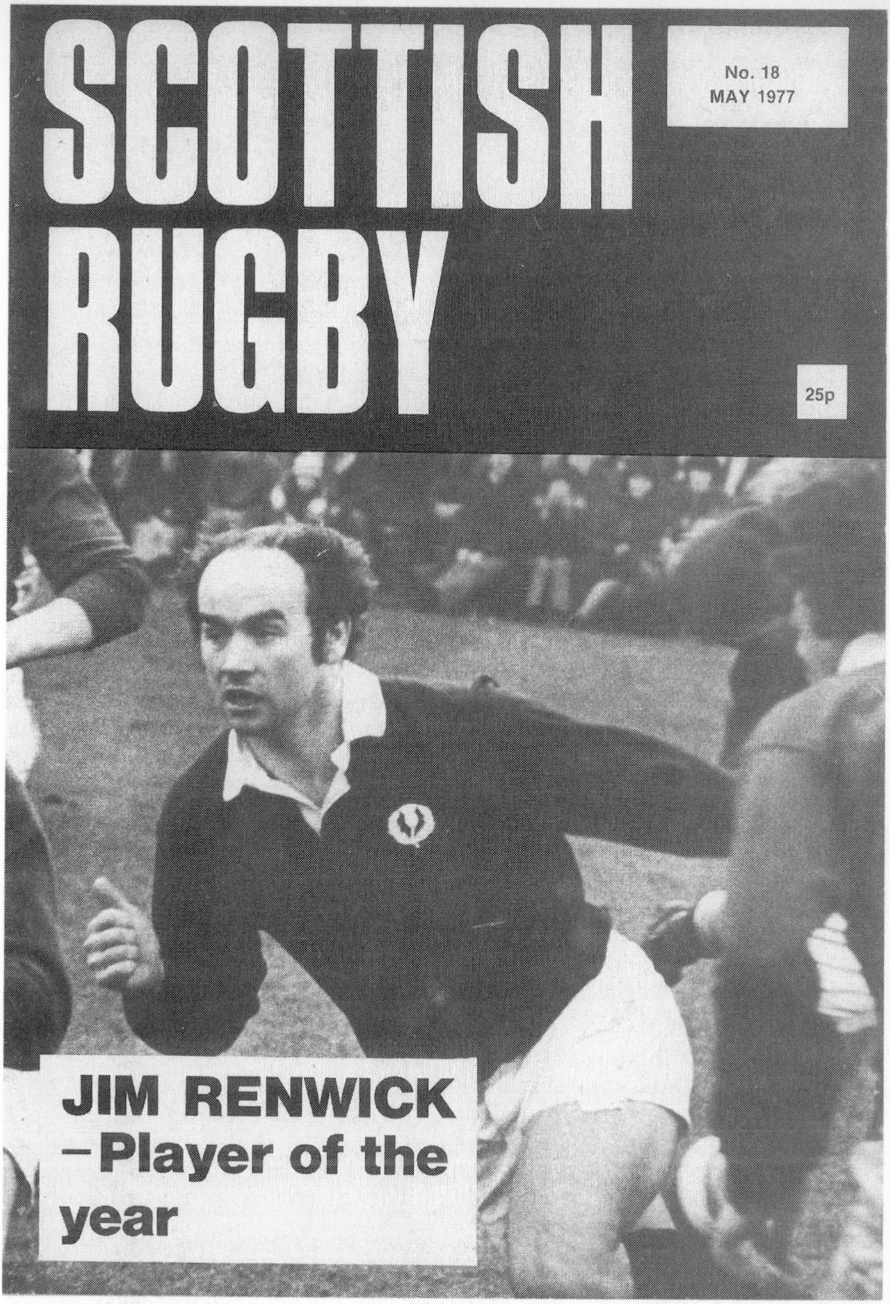

SCOTTISH RUGBY

No. 18
MAY 1977

25p

**JIM RENWICK
– Player of the
year**

Andy Irvine and Jim Renwick, shown here on the cover of the short-lived
Scottish Rugby magazine, were the two most popular and charismatic players of the 1970s.

on the road, famously against England in 1971 and also in a dreary match against Ireland in 1976. Otherwise, although some of their results were close, the Scots did not manage an away victory until the famous win in Cardiff in 1982. In the second half of the seventies, the great pack started to age and break-up, and Scottish success slowly evaporated. Scotland defeated Ireland in 1977, but they did not win again until they beat France in 1980, a depressing run of 13 games without a victory. Results started to improve when Jim Telfer, the former Scottish No.8 and captain, took over as coach for season 1980–1. Scotland won both home matches in the 1981 Championship and the following year they won in Wales for the first time for 20 years. Under Telfer's inspirational guidance, the side grew in confidence and strength, and his reign culminated in season 1983–4 when Scotland drew against the All Blacks before going on to win their first Grand Slam for 59 years.

Without question, the face of Scottish rugby in the 1970s was Andy Irvine. A glamorous swashbuckling full-back from Heriot's FP, Irvine won 51 caps between 1972 and 1982 and toured three times with the British Lions. He had great pace, could kick goals from long range and loved to counter-attack from deep, although there were always doubts about his defence and ability under the high ball. Irvine was one of those rare players who could turn a game with an instinctive touch of genius. Playing against France at Murrayfield in 1980, he did little right for much of the time, but in the closing stages he scored two spectacular tries to win the match. Boroughmuir's tough little full-back Bruce Hay, first capped in 1975, spent much of the time in Irvine's shadow, but he was too good to leave out of the side and appeared on the wing even though he lacked genuine pace. Grand Slam full-back Peter Dods was a smooth runner, solid in defence and a steady placekicker. Scotland had several good wingers at this time, including the lightly built Dave Shedden, Louis Dick, the long striding Bill Gammell and the Ayr flyer Steve Munro, but probably the best of them was Kelso's Roger Baird who won 27 caps between 1981 and 1988. Baird had natural attacking flair and tackled well, but, surprisingly, he never scored a try for Scotland.

In the centres, Jim Renwick was an irrepressible man of Hawick. He had a devastating jink and swerve, wonderful acceleration, steady nerves and could read the game instinctively. A laid back character with quick wits, he played for Scotland over 12 years and was one of the most popular players of his generation. Headingley's Ian McGeechan appeared both at centre and stand-off, and was skilful and sound. He later became a highly respected coach, including two spells with Scotland, and in 2010 he was knighted for his services to rugby. Keith Robertson, like McGeechan, was a versatile and clever footballer who won his early caps on the wing before making a successful switch to centre. David Johnston was a smooth runner who had a great pace and work rate although his passing was sometimes unreliable. He scored a marvellous try against Wales in 1982 when he glided through the defence without a hand being laid on him.

Selkirk stand-off John Rutherford won his first cap in 1979 and made 42 appearances in total, missing only a couple games because of injury. He was a raw talent at first, but matured into one of the best in the world. He had good hands, pace, elusiveness, a prodigious boot and superb tactical awareness. For most of the 1970s, the scrum-half position was either held by Alan Lawson, who was first capped in 1972, or Douglas Morgan, who appeared the following year. They were both fine players, but they had very different styles. Lawson had an electrifying break and a long spin pass, but was not so good in defence or with his tactical kicking. Morgan, by contrast, was much more of a spoiler who liked to chivvy his forwards and harass his opposite number. Jed-Forest's Roy Laidlaw won his first cap in 1980 and was never dropped until his retirement eight years later. Laidlaw was a small man, but he had enormous courage and never hesitated to deal with bad ball or take on the opposition back-row. He had a sharp change of direction and could wrong-foot a defence to devastating effect. He scored some brilliant solo tries, including a classic scrum-half effort behind a retreating scrum against England in 1983 and twice in the Triple Crown match against Ireland in 1984.

Prop forwards Ian McLauchlan and Sandy Carmichael played until the late 1970s and they were followed by the fiery Gala loose-head Jim Aitken, who captained Scotland to the Grand Slam in 1984, and the Heriot's bulwark Iain Milne. Nicknamed 'The Bear' because of his sheer size and strength, Milne was first of three brothers to play for Scotland, all in the front-row, and was the cornerstone of the Scottish pack for 11 years. At hooker, Colin Deans was in a class of his own. A smallish man, he was extremely fit and mobile, and a master at the seemingly simple art of throwing the ball into the lineout. He won his first cap in 1978 and at his peak was the best hooker in world rugby. In the second row, Gordon Brown played his last game in 1976, the same year that Alan Tomes made his debut. The bearded Hawick lock played for 11 years, and ended his career at the inaugural World Cup in 1987. 'Toomba' was a great lineout exponent and was surprisingly mobile for a big man, often acting as the link in some spectacular Scottish tries. Kilmarnock's Bill Cuthbertson, the Gala giant Tom Smith, who scored the clinching try on his debut against England in 1983, and the fair-haired Alister Campbell were workhorses who never let their side down. Scotland benefitted from some outstanding back-row players in this era. David Leslie's career was blighted by injury, but he was a key factor in the 1984 Grand Slam. He was fearless in the loose and highly skilful with the ball in hand, intuitively taking the correct option time after time. The bald-headed London Scot Mike Biggar was almost ever-present in the late 1970s and captained the side in 1980. Jim Calder, one of four rugby playing brothers from Stewart's-Melville, won his first 23 caps in succession and famously scored the Grand Slam-winning try against France in 1984. In the early '80s, Scotland had two excellent players vying with each other for the No 8 jersey. Dunfermline-born Iain Paxton was a fine athlete who also won caps at lock forward. Memorably, he made a long run out of defence in the lead-up to Jim Calder's great try against Wales in 1982 and he also ran the length of the field in a spectacular kick-and-chase effort against Wales in 1985. John Beattie, who was born in North Borneo, was more of a maverick character, but good enough to win 25 caps and tour twice with the Lions before becoming a successful journalist and broadcaster.

306   INTERNATIONAL CHAMPIONSHIP 1972   FRANCE

Murrayfield · Saturday 15 January 1972 · Won 20–9

SCOTLAND Arthur Brown (*Gala*); Billy Steele (*Bedford*), John Frame (*Gala*), †Jim Renwick (*Hawick*), Alastair Biggar (*London Scot*); Colin Telfer (*Hawick*), Ian McCrae (*Gordonians*); Ian McLauchlan (*Jordanhill*), †Bobby Clark (*Edinburgh Wdrs*), Sandy Carmichael (*W of Scot*),

A youthful Jim Renwick scores a debut try against France in 1972.
Touch judge Eric Grierson shows his impartiality.
Scotsman Publications Ltd

Alastair McHarg (*London Scot*), Gordon Brown (*W of Scot*), Nairn MacEwan (*Gala*), Rodger Arneil (*Northampton*), Peter Brown* (*Gala*) ... Replacement: †Alan Lawson (*Edinburgh Wdrs*) for McCrae (50)

FRANCE Pierre Villepreux (*Toulouse*); Roland Bertranne (*Bagnéres*), Jean Trillo (*Bègles*), Jean-Pierre Lux (*Dax*), Jack Cantoni (*Béziers*); Jean-Louis Bérot (*Toulouse*), Jean-Michel Aguirre (*Bagnéres*); Armand Vacquerin (*Béziers*), René Bénésis (*Agen*), Jean-Louis Martin (*Béziers*), Jean-Pierre Bastiat (*Dax*), Benoit Dauga* (*Mont-de-Marsan*), Olivier Saïsset (*Béziers*), Victor Boffelli (*Aurillac*), Claude Spanghero (*Narbonne*)

REFEREE M Joseph (*Wales*)

SCORING Telfer, try (4–0); Telfer, drop (7–0); P Brown, pen (10–0) (half-time) Villepreux, pen (10–3); Renwick, try (14–3); Dauga, try (14–7); Villepreux, con (14–9); Frame, try (18–9); A Brown, con (20–9)

In perfect conditions, Scotland made a great start to the 1972 Championship with this comprehensive win. The Scots played with flair and adventure, and they scored three glorious tries. The Scottish forwards were superior in all aspects apart from the scrums, where France won five strikes against the head. New cap Jim Renwick showed his potential and his Hawick colleague Colin Telfer had an outstanding match. The Scots started at great pace and on the 11th minute Telfer scored the opening try. Telfer added a drop goal and just on half-time Peter Brown kicked a penalty. In the second half, McCrae was carried off with rib damage after making a strong tackle. Arthur Brown acted as a temporary scrum-half and Villepreux kicked a huge penalty just before Alan Lawson came on to win his first cap. Scotland put together a fine handling movement and Renwick scored a debut try in the corner, much to the delight of touch-judge Eric Grierson, who was supposed to be neutral. A pushover try by Dauga and conversion by Villepreux brought France back to within striking distance, but Scotland had the final say when Frame took a reverse pass from Telfer and smashed his way over the line. Some excited spectators invaded the pitch at this point and it took several minutes to clear them away before Arthur Brown nonchalantly converted.

307　INTERNATIONAL CHAMPIONSHIP 1972　WALES

Cardiff Arms Park　·　Saturday 5 February 1972　·　Lost 12–35

SCOTLAND Arthur Brown (*Gala*); Billy Steele (*Bedford*), John Frame (*Gala*), Jim Renwick (*Hawick*), Alastair Biggar (*London Scot*); Colin Telfer (*Hawick*), Duncan Paterson (*Gala*); Ian McLauchlan (*Jordanhill*), Bobby Clark (*Edinburgh Wdrs*), Sandy Carmichael (*W of Scot*), †Ian Barnes (*Hawick*), Gordon Brown (*W of Scot*), Nairn MacEwan (*Gala*), Rodger Arneil (*Northampton*), Peter Brown* (*Gala*) ... Replacement: †Lewis Dick (*Loughborough Coll*) for Biggar (46)

WALES JPR Williams (*London Welsh*); Gerald Davies (*London Welsh*), Roy Bergiers (*Cardiff CE*), Arthur Lewis (*Ebbw Vale*), John Bevan (*Cardiff*); Barry John (*Cardiff*), Gareth Edwards (*Cardiff*); John Lloyd* (*Bridgend*), Jeff Young (*RAF*), Barrie Llewelyn (*Llanelli*), Delme Thomas (*Llanelli*), Geoff Evans (*London Welsh*), Dave Morris (*Neath*), John Taylor (*London Welsh*), Mervyn Davies (*London Welsh*) ... Replacement: Phil Bennett (*Llanelli*) for Williams (20)

REFEREE GA Jamieson (*Ireland*)

SCORING Renwick, pen (3–0); John, pen (3–3); G Davies, try (3–7); P Brown, pen (6–7); John, pen (6–10) (half-time) Clark, try (10–10); P Brown, con (12–10); Edwards, try (12–14); John, con (12–16); Edwards, try (12–20); John, pen (12–23); Bergiers, try (12–27); John, con (12–29); Taylor, try (12–33); John, con (12–35)

Scotland stuck with a hugely talented Wales for about 50 minutes and then the home side powered away like a classic racehorse. The Scots made some good forays and worked tirelessly, but their kicking was often inaccurate and the side lacked mobility. Early in the second half, Clark scored a try and Peter Brown kicked a fine conversion from the touchline. This gave the Scots a narrow lead and raised temporary hopes, but then Wales took control. Gareth Edwards scored a brace of tries, the second of which was one of the greatest individual efforts in rugby history. Taking the ball on the Welsh 25, Edwards brushed off the fringe defence and powered away up the touchline. After looking for support and finding none, he chipped over the head of Arthur Brown, the Scottish full-back, hacked on from the Scottish 25 and just beat Renwick to the touchdown in the corner. Pure genius. John added a penalty and Bergiers and Taylor scored tries, both converted by John. Scotland were left to wonder where it had all gone wrong.

Scotland's next match was scheduled to be against Ireland in Dublin on 26 February 1972, but the Scots declined to send a team because of the volatile political situation in Northern Ireland and the possible threat of violence to the Scottish players and supporters. This controversial decision divided opinion and it was suggested that the match be played at a neutral venue, possibly in Belgium or at a later date, but in the event it never took place.

Murrayfield · Saturday 18 March 1972 · Won 23–9

SCOTLAND Arthur Brown (*Gala*); Billy Steele (*Bedford*), John Frame (*Gala*), Jim Renwick (*Hawick*), Lewis Dick (*Loughborough Coll*); Colin Telfer (*Hawick*), Alan Lawson (*Edinburgh Wdrs*); Ian McLauchlan (*Jordanhill*), Bobby Clark (*Edinburgh Wdrs*), Sandy Carmichael (*W of Scot*), Alastair McHarg (*London Scot*), Gordon Brown (*W of Scot*), Nairn MacEwan (*Gala*), Rodger Arneil (*Northampton*), Peter Brown* (*Gala*)

ENGLAND Peter Knight (*Bristol*); Keith Fielding (*Moseley*), Jeremy Janion (*Bedford*), Geoff Evans (*Coventry*), David Duckham (*Coventry*); Alan Old (*Middlesbrough*), Lionel Weston (*W of Scot*); Stack Stevens (*Harlequins*), John Pullin (*Bristol*), Mike Burton (*Gloucester*), Alan Brinn (*Gloucester*), Chris Ralston (*Richmond*), Peter Dixon* (*Harlequins*), Tony Neary (*Broughton Park*), Andy Ripley (*Rosslyn Park*)

REFEREE M Joseph (*Wales*)

SCORING MacEwan, try (4–0); Old, pen (4–3); P Brown, pen (7–3); P Brown, try (11–3); Telfer, drop (14–3) (half-time) Old, pen (14–6); Old, pen (14–9); A Brown, pen (17–9); P Brown, pen (20–9); P Brown, pen (23–9)

Scotland finished their campaign with this comfortable win, but otherwise this was a largely forgettable encounter. The Scottish forwards held their own at the scrums and were much faster in the loose, and in truth the Scots never looked like losing. Peter Brown scored a try and three penalties and dominated at the tail of the lineout. Nairn MacEwan also had a fine match and scored a try after only three minutes. Following an exchange of penalties, Brown scored a try from a lineout on the English goal-line. Telfer dropped a goal to give Scotland a good lead at the interval. In the second half, Old kicked two penalties to pull England back into contention and then the two Browns, Arthur and Peter, kicked three penalties between them to seal the match. This was Scotland's fourth win in succession against England, something they had last achieved way back in the 1890s. England's defeat meant that for the first time they lost all of their championship games in a single season.

---

309   TOUR MATCH   NEW ZEALAND

Murrayfield · Saturday 16 December 1972 · Lost 9–14

SCOTLAND †Andy Irvine (*Heriot's FP*); Billy Steele (*Bedford*), †Ian Forsyth (*Stewart's FP*), Jim Renwick (*Hawick*), †David Shedden (*W of Scot*); †Ian McGeechan (*Headingley*), Ian McCrae (*Gordonians*); Ian McLauchlan (*Jordanhill*), Bobby Clark (*Edinburgh Wdrs*), Sandy Carmichael (*W of Scot*), Alastair McHarg (*London Scot*), Gordon Brown (*W of Scot*), Nairn MacEwan (*Gala*), Rodger Arneil (*Northampton*), Peter Brown* (*Gala*)

NEW ZEALAND Joe Karam (*Wellington*); Bryan Williams (*Auckland*), Bruce Robertson (*Counties*), Mike Parkinson (*Poverty Bay*), Grant Batty (*Wellington*); Ian Stevens (*Wellington*), Sid Going (*North Auckland*); Jeff Matheson (*Otago*), Tane Norton (*Canterbury*), Graham Whiting (*King Country*), Peter Whiting (*Auckland*), Hamish McDonald (*Canterbury*), Ian Kirkpatrick* (*Poverty Bay*), Alister Scown (*Taranaki*), Alex Wyllie (*Canterbury*) ... Replacement: Kent Lambert (*Manawatu*) for Matheson (5)

REFEREE G Domercq (*France*)

Ian McCrae sends out a perfect dive pass against New Zealand in 1972.
Scotsman Publications Ltd

SCORING Wyllie, try (0–4); Karam, con (0–6) (half-time) Irvine, pen (3–6); Batty, try (3–9); McGeechan, drop (6–10); Irvine, pen (9–10); Going, try (9–14)

Scotland fielded four new caps in the back division. On a mild and windless day, most of the first half was played in Scottish territory with the home side making occasional breakouts. Both sides were reluctant to use their backs and the game was largely a series of set-pieces. Deep into injury-time, Going slipped round a scrum near the Scottish line and fed Wyllie who bolted through a big gap for a try. Karam kicked a fine conversion to put the visitors 6–0 ahead at the interval. After a penalty goal by Irvine, Robertson made a long weaving run and kicked perfectly to the corner for Batty to race on and score. McGeechan replied with a left-footed drop goal and Irvine kicked a huge penalty to set-up an exciting conclusion. As the gloom descended, Scotland made a gallant effort to save the match only to be undone by some typical New Zealand opportunism. Anxious to keep the ball alive, McHarg lobbed a careless pass inside, but it was intercepted by Going who scampered away up the left touchline to the line. Scotland were unlucky at the end, but New Zealand had been able to exert more pressure and forced the Scots into making errors. Both Irvine and McGeechan played solidly and showed great promise.

310   INTERNATIONAL CHAMPIONSHIP 1973   FRANCE

Parc des Princes, Paris · Saturday 13 January 1973 · Lost 13–16

SCOTLAND Andy Irvine (*Heriot's FP*); Billy Steele (*Bedford*), Ian Forsyth (*Stewart's FP*), Jim Renwick (*Hawick*), David Shedden (*W of Scot*); Ian McGeechan (*Headingley*), Alan Lawson (*Edinburgh Wdrs*); Ian McLauchlan (*Jordanhill*), Bobby Clark (*Edinburgh Wdrs*), Sandy Carmichael (*W of Scot*), Alastair McHarg (*London Scot*), †Ronald Wright (*Edinburgh Wdrs*), Nairn MacEwan (*Gala*), Wilson Lauder (*Neath*), Peter Brown* (*Gala*)

FRANCE Jack Cantoni (*Béziers*); Jean-Pierre Lux (*Dax*), Claude Dourthe (*Dax*), Jean Trillo (*Bègles*), Roger Bourgarel (*Toulouse*); Jean-Pierre Romeu (*Montferrand*), Max Barrau (*Toulouse*); Armand Vaquerin (*Béziers*), André Lubrano (*Béziers*), Jean Iraçabal (*Bayonne*), Elie Cester (*Valence*), Alain Estève (*Béziers*), Olivier Saïsset (*Béziers*), Pierre Biémouret (*Agen*), Walter Spanghero* (*Narbonne*)

REFEREE Ken Pattinson (*England*) replaced after 15 minutes by François Palmade (*France*)

SCORING Romeu, pen (0–3); Romeu, pen (0–6); Brown, pen (3–6); Dourthe, try (3–10); McGeechan, drop (6–10) (half-time) Lawson, try (10–10); Romeu, pen (10–13); Romeu, drop (10–16); Brown, pen (13–16)

Scotland were the first-foots at the new, multi-purpose Parc des Princes stadium, a great concrete bowl in the west of Paris. The occasion demanded a free-flowing celebratory match, but instead it was a disjointed encounter punctuated by penalty awards and aimless kicking. The game was held-up in the first half because of an injury to referee Ken Pattinson who was replaced by touch-judge François Palmade. France were the better of two mediocre sides although they were strangely cautious, perhaps overawed by their new surroundings. Scotland won plenty of possession, especially at the line-out, but their inexperienced back division made little headway. McGeechan kicked too much, although he dropped a brilliant left-footed goal in the first half. Scotland showed considerable spirit to draw level soon after the interval. France misfielded a high kick and Clark gathered to put Lawson over. Romeu restored the French lead with a penalty and a drop goal, and in injury-time Peter Brown kicked a penalty.

311 INTERNATIONAL CHAMPIONSHIP 1973 WALES

Murrayfield · Saturday 3 February 1973 · Won 10–9

SCOTLAND Andy Irvine (*Heriot's FP*); Billy Steele (*Bedford*), Ian McGeechan (*Headingley*), Ian Forsyth (*Stewart's FP*), David Shedden (*W of Scot*); Colin Telfer (*Hawick*), †Douglas Morgan (*Melville Coll*); Ian McLauchlan* (*Jordanhill*), Bobby Clark (*Edinburgh Wdrs*), Sandy Carmichael (*W of Scot*), Alastair McHarg (*London Scot*), Peter Brown (*Gala*), Nairn MacEwan (*Gala*), †Jock Millican (*Edinburgh U*), Gordon Strachan (*Jordanhill*)

WALES JPR Williams (*London Welsh*); Gerald Davies (*London Welsh*), Roy Bergiers (*Llanelli*), Arthur Lewis* (*Ebbw Vale*), John Bevan (*Cardiff*); Phil Bennet (*Llanelli*), Gareth Edwards (*Cardiff*); Glyn Shaw (*Neath*), Jeff Young (*London Welsh*), John Lloyd (*Bridgend*), Delme Thomas (*Llanelli*), Derek Quinnell (*Llanelli*), Dave Morris (*Neath*), John Taylor (*London Welsh*), Mervyn Davies (*Swansea*)

REFEREE MF Palmade (*France*)

SCORING Telfer, try (4–0); Morgan, con (6–0); Steele, try (10–0); Bennett, pen (10–3); Taylor, pen (10–6) (half-time) Bennett, pen (10–9)

Scotland ripped-up the form book and deservedly won their first victory over Wales for six years. The Scottish forwards created the platform for success with a passionate but controlled performance. They held the edge in the scrums, Brown and McHarg dominated at the lineout, and the back-row constantly harried the Welsh half-backs and midfield. The Scots tackled aggressively and the visitors were never able to find their natural rhythm. Fired-up by new captain Ian McLauchlan, Scotland scored twice from set-pieces in the opening quarter. From a five yards scrum in the right-hand corner, Forsyth acted a decoy runner to draw the Welsh defence and Telfer, who was sometimes criticised for his lack of acceleration, shot through a gap to score at the posts. Morgan kicked the goal and then from a similar position Telfer made a dummy run, Steele took the ball in the stand-off position and skipped past three defenders to score. Bennett and Taylor kicked penalties, and Bennett reduced the lead to a single point with a penalty towards the finish. Wales fought hard to save the game, but the Scots never let-up. They tackled and covered courageously and held out for a satisfying win. Amongst many good performances, McGeechan tackled superbly and new scrum-half Douglas Morgan grew in confidence as the game progressed. His persistent niggling of Gareth Edwards put the Welsh maestro out of his stride and was a crucial factor in Scotland's success.

312   INTERNATIONAL CHAMPIONSHIP 1973   IRELAND

Murrayfield · Saturday 24 February 1973 · Won 19–15

SCOTLAND Andy Irvine (*Heriot's FP*); Billy Steele (*Bedford*), Ian McGeechan (*Headingley*), Ian Forsyth (*Stewart's FP*), David Shedden (*W of Scot*); Colin Telfer (*Hawick*), Douglas Morgan (*Melville Coll*); Ian McLauchlan* (*Jordanhill*), Bobby Clark (*Edinburgh Wdrs*), Sandy Carmichael (*W of Scot*), Alastair McHarg (*London Scot*), Peter Brown (*Gala*), Nairn MacEwan (*Gala*), Jock Millican (*Edinburgh U*), Gordon Strachan (*Jordanhill*) ... Replacement: †Hamish Bryce (*W of Scot*) for McLauchlan

IRELAND Tom Kiernan* (*Cork Const*); Tom Grace (*St Mary's Coll*), Dick Milliken (*Bangor*), Mike Gibson (*NIFC*), Wallace McMaster (*Ballymena*); Barry McGann (*Cork Const*), John Maloney (*St Mary's Coll*); Ray McLoughlin (*Blackrock Coll*), Ken Kennedy (*London Irish*), Sean Lynch (*St Mary's Coll*), Kevin Mays (*UC Dublin*), Willie John McBride (*Ballymena*), Fergus Slattery (*Blackrock Coll*), Jim Buckley (*Sunday's Well*), Terry Moore (*Highfield*)

REFEREE R Lewis (*Wales*)

SCORING Morgan, pen (3–0); McGann, pen (3–3); McGann, pen (3–6); Morgan, drop (6–6); Morgan, pen (9–6); McMaster, try (9–10) (half-time) McGeechan, drop (12–10); Kiernan, try (12–14); Forsyth, try (16–14); Morgan, drop (19–14)

Scotland lost their inspirational captain Ian McLauchlan just before the interval, but still managed to defeat Ireland for the first time since 1966. The lead changed hands six times and the Scots were behind inside the final five minutes, but they made a late rally and pulled off a dramatic win. The forward exchanges were uncompromising and neither side conceded an inch. The set-pieces were evenly contested, but the Scots had greater mobility in the loose. The Scottish backs threatened more and Ireland did not make enough of their talented three-quarter line, despite the presence of Mike Gibson and Dick Milliken. Scotland held a narrow lead when McLauchlan cracked his right fibula around the 30th minute. He soldiered on for a few minutes before being replaced by Hamish Bryce. McMaster scored a try just before the interval and a few minutes after the restart McGeechan recaptured the lead for Scotland with a drop goal. Ireland made a great sweeping move and Kiernan scored in the left corner although he seemed to have been knocked in touch before grounding the ball. Scotland made a rousing finish and a few minutes before time Forsyth crashed over in the corner. Morgan missed the difficult conversion, but kicked a last-second drop goal to secure Scotland's win. This was, incidentally, the 54th and final cap for Tom Kiernan, Ireland's veteran full-back and one of the great players of his, or any, era.

313   INTERNATIONAL CHAMPIONSHIP 1973   ENGLAND

Twickenham · Saturday 17 March 1973 · Lost 13–20

SCOTLAND Andy Irvine (*Heriot's FP*); Billy Steele (*Bedford*), Ian McGeechan (*Headingley*), Ian Forsyth (*Stewart's FP*), David Shedden (*W of Scot*); Colin Telfer (*Hawick*), Douglas Morgan (*Melville FP*); Ian McLauchlan* (*Jordanhill*), Bobby Clark (*Edinburgh Wdrs*), Sandy Carmichael (*W of Scot*), Alastair McHarg (*London Scot*), Peter Brown (*Gala*), Nairn MacEwan (*Gala*), Jock Millican (*Edinburgh U*), Gordon Strachan (Jordanhill) ... Replacement: Gordon Brown (*W of Scot*) for Millican

ENGLAND Tony Jorden (*Blackheath*); Peter Squires (*Harrogate*), Geoff Evans (*Coventry*), Peter Preece (*Coventry*), David Duckham (*Coventry*); Martin Cooper (*Moseley*), Steve Smith (*Sale*); Stack Stevens (*Penzance & Newlyn*), John Pullin* (*Bristol*), Fran Cotton (*Loughborough Coll*), Roger Uttley (*Gosforth*), Chris Ralston (*Richmond*), Peter Dixon (*Gosforth*), Tony Neary (*Broughton Park*), Andy Ripley (*Rosslyn Park*)

REFEREE JC Kelleher (*Wales*)

SCORING Squires, try (0–4); Dixon, try (0–8) (half-time) Dixon, try (0–12); Jorden, con (0–14); Morgan, pen (3–14); Steele, try (7–14); Steele, try (11–14); Irvine, con (13–14); Evans, try (13–18); Jorden, con (13–20)

Scotland's dream of winning the Triple Crown in their centenary season foundered at the Twickenham graveyard. The English forwards were superior in all aspects. Ralston and Uttley dominated at the lineout and the English back-row foraged well in the loose. In fact, England would have won more easily if Cooper, the English stand-off, had not kicked so much. Controversially, Ian McLauchlan decided to play despite having broken his leg against Ireland three weeks earlier. The gamble did not really pay off and he was far from his normal self. Indeed, several of the Scottish players did not look fully fit. After England had built a 14 points lead, Scotland did well to claw back to within a single point, but it would have been an injustice if the Scots had managed to snatch a win. In the first half, Squires and Dixon scored tries in quick succession and Dixon added a third soon after the interval. England lost their concentration and the Scots made a late revival. Morgan kicked a long penalty and Steele charged down a clearance and won the race for the touchdown. Towards the finish, Scotland stole a scrum ball and Peter Brown flipped a one-handed pass to Steele who just made it to the line. Irvine kicked a touchline conversion, but almost immediately a diagonal kick by Preece bounced awkwardly over the Scottish line and Evans followed-up fast to score the clinching try.

314   CENTENARY MATCH   SRU PRESIDENT'S OVERSEAS XV

Murrayfield · 31 March 1973 · Won 27–16

SCOTLAND Andy Irvine (*Heriot's FP*); †Drew Gill (*Gala*), Ian McGeechan (*Headingley*),

Ian Forsyth (*Stewart's FP*), David Shedden (*W of Scot*); Colin Telfer (*Hawick*), Douglas Morgan (Melville Coll); Ian McLauchlan* (*Jordanhill*), Bobby Clark (*Edinburgh Wdrs*), Sandy Carmichael (*W of Scot*), Alastair McHarg (*London Scot*), Gordon Brown (*W of Scot*), Nairn MacEwan (*Gala*), Gordon Strachan (*Jordanhill*), Peter Brown (*Gala*) ... Replacement: John Frame (*Gala*) for McGeechan (13)

SRU PRESIDENT'S XV Ray Carlson (*South Africa*); Jeff McLean (*Australia*), David Burnet (*Australia*), Duncan Hales (*New Zealand*), Grant Batty (*New Zealand*); Ian Stevens (*New Zealand*), Lin Colling (*New Zealand*); Jean Iracabal (*France*), René Benesis (*France*), David Dunworth (*Australia*), Benoit Dauga (*France*), Alan Sutherland (*New Zealand*), Jan Ellis (*South Africa*), Piet Greyling (*South Africa*), Alex Wyllie* (*New Zealand*)

REFEREE M Joseph (*Wales*)

SCORING Shedden, try (4–0); McLean, try (4–4); McLean, con (4–6); Gill, try (8–6); Irvine, con (10–6) (half-time) Gill, try (14–6); McHarg, try (18–6); Hales, try (18–10); Burnet, try (18–14); McLean, con (18–16); Irvine, pen (21–16); Telfer, try (25–16); Irvine, con (27–16)

Caps were awarded for this special celebration match which was one of the highlights of the SRU centenary season. Composed of some of the leading players from France and the southern hemisphere, the President's Overseas XV had only come together a few days before the match and many of them were playing out of season. They still managed to put up a good fight although the Scots were a stronger combination and always likely winners. Played in blustery and wet conditions before a sparse crowd, this was an entertaining and fluid game that featured eight tries. Once again Andy Irvine showed himself to be the find of the season. He fielded the wet ball securely and lit up the match with his brilliant attacking play, beating world class defenders with consummate ease. On the right wing, Gala's Drew Gill, a late replacement for Billy Steele, had a fine debut and scored two tries with his fast and determined running. The Brown brothers, Gordon and Peter, did well at the lineout and Alastair McHarg, as always, showed great mobility in the loose.

 XV TOUR MATCH ARGENTINA

Murrayfield · Saturday 24 November 1973 · Won 12–11

SCOTLAND XV Andy Irvine (*Heriot's FP*); Billy Steele (*Bedford*), Jim Renwick (*Hawick*), Mike Hunter (*Glasgow HSFP*), Drew Gill (*Gala*); Colin Telfer (*Hawick*), Douglas Morgan (*Stew-Mel FP*); Ian McLauchlan* (*Jordanhill*), Duncan Madsen (*Gosforth*), Sandy Carmichael (*W of Scot*), Alastair McHarg (*London Scot*), Gordon Brown (*W of Scot*), Nairn MacEwan (*Highland*), Bill Watson (*Boroughmuir*), Gordon Strachan (*Jordanhill*)

ARGENTINA Martin Alonzo (*San Isidro*), Roberto Matarazzo (*San Isidro*), Alejandro Travaglini (*San Isidro*), Arturo Jurado (*San Isidro*), Eduardo Morgan (*Old Georgians*); Hugo Porta (*Banco Nación*), Luis Gradin (*Belgrano*); Fernando Insua (*San Isidro*), Juan Dumas (*CUBA*), Roberto Fariello (*Mendoza*), Jose Virasoro (*San Martin*), Jose Fernandez (*Deportiva Francesa*), Nestor Carbone (*Puchara*), Jorge Carracedo (*San Isidro*), Hugo Miguens* (*CUBA*)

REFEREE JSP Evans (*Wales*)

SCORING Porta, try (0–4); Travaglini, try (0–8); Morgan, pen (3–8); Morgan, pen (6–8); Porta, drop (6–11) (half-time) Morgan, pen (9–11); Telfer, drop (12–11)

In the autumn of 1973, Argentina, one of rugby's 'developing nations', made an eight match tour of Ireland and Scotland. The Scots did not award caps for the test match, but fielded a near full strength side and were fortunate to win. The Argentineans gave their best performance of the tour and scored two tries to none. They defended well and their forwards were good in the loose, but they struggled at the set-pieces. Argentina's downfall was their lack of discipline, a problem that had dogged their other games on tour. They were repeatedly penalised for various offences, including several violent incidents, and Morgan kept the Scots in contention with three penalty goals. Argentina looked likely winners until the closing stages when Telfer dropped a goal to put Scotland into the lead. The visitors made a brave late rally, but they also allowed their frustrations got the better of them and an ugly brawl erupted on the Scottish line that left Duncan Madsen with a badly cut head. Worse still, as the players were leaving the field at the end, Gordon Brown was knocked to the ground by a cowardly assault from behind, an unsavoury incident that was contrary to all of the best traditions of rugby.

315   INTERNATIONAL CHAMPIONSHIP 1974   WALES

Cardiff Arms Park · Saturday 19 January 1974 · Lost 0–6

SCOTLAND Andy Irvine (*Heriot's FP*); Drew Gill (*Gala*), Jim Renwick (*Hawick*), Ian McGeechan (*Headingley*), Lewis Dick (*Jordanhill*); Colin Telfer (*Hawick*), Alan Lawson (*Edinburgh Wdrs*); Ian McLauchlan* (*Jordanhill*), †Duncan Madsen (*Gosforth*), Sandy Carmichael (*W of Scot*), Alastair McHarg (*London Scot*), Gordon Brown (*W of Scot*), Nairn MacEwan (*Highland*), Wilson Lauder (*Neath*), †Bill Watson (*Boroughmuir*)

WALES JPR Williams (*London Welsh*); Gerald Davies (*London Welsh*), Keith Hughes (*London Welsh*), Ian Hall (*Aberavon*), JJ Williams (*Llanelli*); Phil Bennett (*Llanelli*), Gareth Edwards* (*Cardiff*); Glyn Shaw (*Neath*), Bobby Windsor (*Pontypool*), Barry Llewellyn (*Swansea*), Allan Martin (*Aberavon*), Derek Quinnell (*Llanelli*), Dave Morris (*Neath*), Terry Cobner (*Pontypool*), Mervyn Davies (*Swansea*)

REFEREE RF Johnson (*England*)

SCORING Cobner, try (0–4); Bennett, con (0–6) (half-time)

Scotland deserved at least a draw in a hard but rather undistinguished encounter. The billowing wind seemed to trouble the Welsh back division, but on the 23rd minute they scored the only try. Wales pilfered a scrum on the Scottish 25 and switched to the right. Gerald Davies side-stepped past two defenders before being caught, but he managed to pop the ball to Cobner who ran over the line and Bennett converted. The Scottish forwards were in good form, but the backs could not quite reach their standard. McHarg and Brown dominated at the lineout, the Scottish scrum exerted a lot of pressure, and McLauchlan and the back-row were very conspicuous. Both sides launched a series of attacks in the second half, but the defences were impenetrable. JPR Williams made at least two try-saving tackles and, like his opposite number Andy Irvine, was always ready to come forward.

Murrayfield · Saturday 2 February 1974 · Won 16–14

SCOTLAND Andy Irvine (*Heriot's FP*); Drew Gill (*Gala*), Jim Renwick (*Hawick*), Ian McGeechan (*Headingley*), Lewis Dick (*Jordanhill*); Colin Telfer (*Hawick*), Alan Lawson (*Edinburgh Wdrs*); Ian McLauchlan* (*Jordanhill*), Duncan Madsen (*Gosforth*), Sandy Carmichael (*W of Scot*), Alastair McHarg (*London Scot*), Gordon Brown (*W of Scot*), Nairn MacEwan (*Highland*), Wilson Lauder (*Neath*), Bill Watson (*Boroughmuir*)

ENGLAND Peter Rossborough (*Coventry*); Peter Squires (*Harrogate*), David Roughley (*Liverpool*), Geoff Evans (*Coventry*), David Duckham (*Coventry*); Alan Old (*Leicester*), Jan Webster (*Moseley*); Stack Stevens (*Penzance & Newlyn*), John Pullin* (*Bristol*), Fran Cotton (*Coventry*), Chris Ralston (*Richmond*), Nigel Horton (*Moseley*), Peter Dixon (*Gosforth*), Tony Neary (*Broughton Park*), Andy Ripley (*Rosslyn Park*)

REFEREE MJ Saint Guilhem (*France*)

SCORING Irvine, pen (3–0); Lauder, try (7–0); Irvine, con (9–0); Cotton, try (9–4); Old, pen (9–7) (half-time) Neary, try (9–11); Irvine, try (13–11); Rossborough, drop (13–14); Irvine, pen (16–14)

In a pulsating encounter, the lead changed hands four times in the final quarter and the outcome was not settled until the last kick of the game. Scotland started strongly and raced to an early lead. Man-of-the match Andy Irvine kicked a long penalty before Madsen pounced on a loose ball at a lineout and fed Lauder for a simple try. Irvine converted from a wide angle. Later in the half, England started to put their game together. Squires made a chip-and-chase, the English forwards carried on and Cotton battered his way over for an unconverted try. Near the interval, Old kicked a long penalty to reduce Scotland's lead to only two points. In the second half, the visitors made some dangerous attacks, but were frustrated by brave Scottish defence in which McGeechan was outstanding. The final quarter had barely begun when England conjured a great score. From a tap penalty move inside the English half, No 8 Andy Ripley made a powerful charge deep into the Scottish 25 and Neary stormed up to take the scoring pass. Then from a lineout near the English 25, Telfer switched from left to right and fed Irvine who side-stepped past one defender, accelerated away and had just enough momentum to reach the corner. Irvine missed the difficult conversion and a few minutes before the end Rossborough seemed to have won the game for England when he collected a poor clearance and dropped a long goal. Then in the final minute of injury-time, Scotland were awarded a penalty on the right touchline about 40 yards out. Under the greatest pressure, Irvine coolly kicked the goal, the final whistle went and the stadium erupted.

Lansdowne Road · Saturday 2 March 1974 · Lost 6–9

SCOTLAND Andy Irvine (*Heriot's FP*); Drew Gill (*Gala*), Jim Renwick (*Hawick*), Ian McGeechan (*Headingley*), Lewis Dick (*Jordanhill*); Colin Telfer (*Hawick*), Douglas Morgan (*Stew-Mel FP*); Ian McLauchlan* (*Jordanhill*), Duncan Madsen (*Gosforth*), Sandy Carmichael (*W of Scot*), Alastair McHarg (*London Scot*), Gordon Brown (*W of Scot*), Nairn MacEwan (*Highland*), Wilson Lauder (*Neath*), Bill Watson (*Boroughmuir*)

IRELAND Tony Ensor (*Lansdowne*); Tom Grace (*UC Dublin*), Dick Milliken (*Bangor*), Mike Gibson (*NIFC*), Wallace McMaster (*Ballymena*); Mick Quinn (*Lansdowne*), John Moloney (*St Mary's Coll*); Ray McLoughlin (*Blackrock Coll*), Ken Kennedy (*London Irish*), Sean Lynch (*St Mary's Coll*), Moss Keane (*Lansdowne*), Willie John McBride* (*Ballymena*), Stewart McKinney (*Dungannon*), Fergus Slattery (*Blackrock Coll*), Terry Moore (*Highfield*)

REFEREE F Palmade (*France*)

SCORING McKinney, pen (0–3) Milliken, try (0–7) Gibson, con (0–9) (half-time) Irvine, pen (3–9) Irvine, pen (6–9)

Ireland started as if they meant to sweep the Scots away and on the tenth minute McKinney kicked a lengthy penalty. The lead was increased after 30 minutes when Slattery broke through from a long throw-in and took play deep into the Scottish 25. Milliken was in support and was driven over by a swarm of Irish forwards. Gibson converted and the home side led 9–0 at the break. Ireland had short spell of pressure early in the second half and then the Scottish forwards took a firm grip. They won a lot of territory and possession, but the backs were ineffective against a tight Irish defence. McGeechan dropped a pass a few yards from the line and later Renwick was caught just short by Gibson. The Scots could manage only two Irvine penalty goals and Ireland held on.

---

318 INTERNATIONAL CHAMPIONSHIP 1974 FRANCE

Murrayfield · Saturday 16 March 1974 · Won 19–6

SCOTLAND Andy Irvine (*Heriot's FP*); Drew Gill (*Gala),* Jim Renwick (*Hawick*), †Mike Hunter (*Glasgow HSFP*), Lewis Dick (*Jordanhill*); Ian McGeechan (*Headingley*), Douglas Morgan (*Stew-Mel FP*); Ian McLauchlan* (*Jordanhill*), Duncan Madsen (*Gosforth*), Sandy Carmichael (*W of Scot*), Alastair McHarg (*London Scot*), Gordon Brown (*W of Scot*), Nairn MacEwan (*Highland*), Wilson Lauder (*Neath*), Bill Watson (*Boroughmuir*) … Replacement: Ian Barnes (*Hawick*) for MacEwan (62)

FRANCE Michel Droitecourt (*Montferrand*); Jean-François Gourdon (*RCF*), Joel Pécune (*Tarbes*), Jean-Pierre Lux (*Dax*), Roland Bertranne (*Bagnères*); Jean-Pierre Romeu (*Montferrand*), Max Barrau (*Agen*); Jean Iraçabal (*Bayonne*), René Bénésis (*Agen*), Armand Vaquerin (*Béziers*), Elie Cester* (*Valence*), Alain Estève (*Béziers*), Jean-Claude Skréla (*Toulouse*), Victor Boffelli (*Aurillac*), Claude Spanghéro (*Narbonne*)

REFEREE KH Clark (*Ireland*)

SCORING Romeu, pen (0–3); Morgan, pen (3–3); McHarg, try (7–3); Irvine, con (9–3) (half-time) Romeu, drop (9–6) Irvine, pen (12–6); Irvine, pen (15–6); Dick, try (19–6)

Scotland were full of adventure and running, and swept aside French championship aspirations. The Scottish forwards were in rousing form and knocked their opponents completely off their stride. Duncan Madsen won three strikes against the head, Gordon Brown took a lot of ball at the lineout and Alastair McHarg showed outstanding mobility and support play. As one onlooker put it, he was never where should have been, but always exactly where he was needed. McHarg scored Scotland's first try in injury-time at the end of the first half. Irvine intruded into a sweeping movement and cut inside before giving a one-handed pass to McHarg who plunged joyfully over the

This painting by W H Overend and L P Smythe shows the Calcutta Cup match at Raeburn Place in 1886. *Edinburgh Academicals*

PLAYER'S CIGARETTES.

I. S. SMITH.
SCOTLAND.

PLAYER'S CIGARETTES.

E. G. TAYLOR. (SCOTLAND)

PLAYER'S CIGARETTES.

G. P. S. MACPHERSON
SCOTLAND.

PLAYER'S CIGARETTES

H. WADDELL.

PLAYER'S CIGARETTES

D. DRYSDALE.

PLAYER'S CIGARETTES

J. M. BANNERMAN.

WILLS'S CIGARETTES

J. B. NELSON.

WILLS'S CIGARETTES

R. T. SMITH.

WILLS'S CIGARETTES

J. W. ALLAN.

Cigarette card heroes of the twenties and thirties. Did Scotland play in red socks?
On the next page try to spot the club.

W. A. BURNET

W. C. W. MURDOCH

R. W. SHAW

A. S. B. McNEIL

J. H. BEATTIE

G. S. COTTINGTON

J. E. FORREST

H. LIND

W. R. LOGAN

Above:

This Victorian postcard shows Jed-Forest's John Mabon playing against England in 1898, apparently in the middle of the countryside.
RFU Museum of Rugby

Left:

Produced by the Edinburgh department store, Forsyth's Rugby Record was issued annually from 1919 to the 1980s.

Adam Robson, who won 22 caps between 1954 and 1960, was an accomplished artist and painted this picture of Arthur Smith scoring a famous try against Wales in 1955. *SRU*

Five Hawick caps and their club president in 1961. Back row: George Stevenson, Oliver Grant and Adam Robson. Front row: Jack Hegarty and Hugh McLeod. *Hawick RFC*

International Football Match

OFFICIAL PROGRAMME

SCOTLAND
versus
FRANCE

At Murrayfield, Edinburgh
Saturday, 24th January 1931

Published with
Authority of the
SCOTTISH
RUGBY
UNION

PRICE
THREE
PENCE

Rugby Football Union
Twickenham

2D.   **2**D.

OFFICIAL 🌹 **PROGRAMME**

Copyright   Photo by Aerofilms Ltd.

ENGLAND v. SCOTLAND
SATURDAY, 19th MARCH, 1938
Kick-off 3 p.m.

FOR HEALTH STRENGTH & VITALITY
Mitchells & Butlers
"Good Honest Beer"
THERE'S AN M&B HOUSE QUITE NEAR TO YOU

WELSH RUGBY UNION
OFFICIAL PROGRAMME, Price **3**d.

Kick-off 3.0 p.m.   Walter E. Rees

SCOTLAND
v.
WALES

CARDIFF ARMS PARK
Saturday, February 7th, 1948

ON COLD DAYS
kick off with
BOVRIL

SCOTTISH RUGBY UNION

SCOTLAND
v
ENGLAND

MURRAYFIELD
SATURDAY 17th MARCH
1956

OFFICIAL PROGRAMME
ONE SHILLING

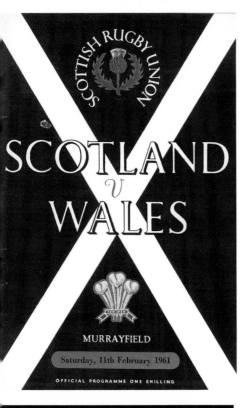

SCOTTISH RUGBY UNION

SCOTLAND
v
WALES

MURRAYFIELD

Saturday, 11th February 1961

OFFICIAL PROGRAMME ONE SHILLING

TOURNOI DES 5 NATIONS

FRANCE
ECOSSE

PROGRAMME OFFICIEL - PRIX : 1 NF

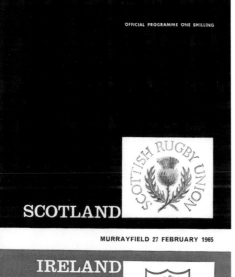

OFFICIAL PROGRAMME ONE SHILLING

SCOTTISH RUGBY UNION

SCOTLAND

MURRAYFIELD 27 FEBRUARY 1965

IRELAND

THE
RUGBY
NEWS

Vol. 48 — No. 16
Price 20 cents

SYDNEY CRICKET
GROUND

SATURDAY,
JUNE 6, 1970

AUSTRALIA
versus
SCOTLAND

Registered at the G.P.O. Sydney, for transmission by post as a periodical

The fruits of compulsive programme collecting!

In 1995, Scotland won in Paris for the first time in 26 years. Here Gregor Townsend gives the 'Toonie flip' pass to Gavin Hastings who powers away for a dramatic last minute try.
Scotsman Publications Ltd

Duncan Hodge celebrates after scoring the winning try against England in 2000.
Scotsman Publications Ltd

The Scotland World Cup squad, and a couple of lucky air hostesses,
wave goodbye before leaving for New Zealand in 2011.
Scotsman Publications Ltd

Richie Gray on the charge with Ross Ford looking on.
Scotsman Publications Ltd

Chris Paterson, the first Scotsman to win over 100 caps, leaves the field
after his final competitive game for Edinburgh in 2012.
Scotsman Publications Ltd

The flying Dutchman Tim Visser races away to score a try against New Zealand in 2012.
Scotsman Publications Ltd

Olympic cyclist Chris Hoy presented the match ball before the Scotland v New Zealand match in 2012.
Scotsman Publications Ltd

Henry Pyrgos scores a spectacular try against South Africa in 2012.
Scotsman Publications Ltd

Matt Scott on the way to a superb solo try against Italy in 2013 with Stuart Hogg in support.
Scotsman Publications Ltd

The Scottish team celebrates after beating Ireland in 2013.
Scotsman Publications Ltd

Greig Laidlaw kicks for goal during the victory over Ireland in 2013.
Scotsman Publications Ltd

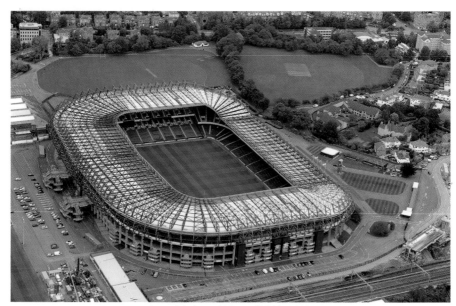

An aerial view of Murrayfield in 2012.
Scotsman Publications Ltd

Scotland Women's team played their first international in 1993. Here they take on Ireland in 2010.
SRU

Alastair McHarg finishes off a great movement against France in 1974.
Scotsman Publications Ltd

line. Towards the finish, Irvine took a high ball in his own half and raced ahead before finding support from McHarg who charged to the French 25. The forwards kept the move alive and the ball was whipped left to Dick who skidded over at the corner.

 TOUR MATCH TONGA

Murrayfield · Saturday 28 September 1974 · Won 44–8

SCOTLAND XV Andy Irvine (*Heriot's FP*); Billy Steele (*London Scot*), Jim Renwick (*Hawick*), Ian McGeechan (*Headingley*), Lewis Dick (*Jordanhill*); Colin Telfer (*Hawick*), Douglas Morgan (*Stew-Mel FP*); Ian McLauchlan* (*Jordanhill*), Duncan Madsen (*Gosforth*), Sandy Carmichael (*W of Scot*), Alastair McHarg (*London Scot*), Gordon Brown (*W of Scot*), Nairn MacEwan (*Highland*), Wilson Lauder (*Neath*), Bill Watson (*Boroughmuir*)

TONGA Valita Ma'ake; 'Isikeli Vave, Sami Latu, Sitafooti 'Aho, Talilotu Ngaluafe; Malakai 'Alatini, Ha'unga Fonua; Siosaia Fifita, Tevita Pulumufila, Ualeni Pahulu, Fa'aleo Tupi, Polutele Tu'ihalamaka, Saimone Vaea, Fakahau Valu, Sione Mafi*

REFEREE Georges Domercq (*France*)

SCORING Irvine, pen (3–0); Irvine, pen (6–0) (half-time) Steele, try (10–0); Irvine, con (12–0); Dick, try (16–0); Steele, try (20–0); Irvine, con (22–0); Fifita, try (22–4); Steele, try (26–4); Irvine, con (28–4); Lauder, try (32–4); Steele, try (36–4); Irvine, con (38–4); McLauchlan, try (42–4); Irvine, con (44–4); Vave, try (44–8)

In the autumn of 1974, the colourful South Sea islanders from Tonga made a ten match tour of the British Isles. Scotland did not award caps, but they fielded a full strength team. The burly Tongans defended well in the first half and Scotland could only manage two Irvine penalties. The visitors started to tire as the game wore on and at times they showed their naivety and inexperience. The Scots put together some lovely handling movements and scored seven tries after the interval, including five by the wings. Tonga were not disgraced and they had enough spirit and flair to score two exciting tries of their own. Fifita grabbed the first after a thrilling counter-attack that started near the Tongan line. In the last few minutes, Vave intercepted a loose pass and ran the length of the field for the biggest cheer of the day.

319   INTERNATIONAL CHAMPIONSHIP 1975   IRELAND

Murrayfield · Saturday 1 February 1975 · Won 20–15

SCOTLAND Andy Irvine (*Heriot's FP*); Billy Steele (*London Scot*), Jim Renwick (*Hawick*), †David Bell (*Watsonians*), Lewis Dick (*Jordanhill*); Ian McGeechan (*Headingley*), Douglas Morgan (*Stew-Mel FP*); Ian McLauchlan* (*Jordanhill*), Duncan Madsen (*Gosforth*), Sandy Carmichael (*W of Scot*), Alastair McHarg (*London Scot*), Gordon Brown (*W of Scot*), †Mike Biggar (*London Scot*), Wilson Lauder (*Neath*), †David Leslie (*Dundee HSFP*)

IRELAND Tony Ensor (*Wdrs*); Tom Grace (*St Mary's Coll*), Dick Milliken (*Bangor*), Mike Gibson (*NIFC*), Seamus Dennison (*Garryowen*); Billy McCombe (*Bangor*), John Maloney (*St Mary's Coll*); Ray McLoughlin (*Blackrock Coll*), Pat Whelan (*Garryowen*), Roger Clegg (*Bangor*), Willie John McBride* (*Ballymena*), Moss Keane (*Lansdowne*), Fergus Slattery (*Blackrock Coll*), Stewart McKinney (*Dungannon*), Willie Duggan (*Blackrock Coll*)

REFEREE RF Johnson (*England*)

SCORING Morgan, drop (3–0); Dennison, try (3–4); McCombe, con (3–6); McGeechan, drop (6–6); Renwick, try (10–6); Steele, try (14–6) (half-time) McCombe, pen (14–9); Irvine, pen (17–9); Grace, try (17–13); Irvine, pen (20–13)

Scotland were convincing winners thanks to a great forward effort and astute tactical play by the half-backs. Scotland made a great start with a drop goal by Morgan in the opening minute. Dennison scored a try for Ireland before McGeechan dropped a goal. Then Renwick scored a try after a beautiful scissors movement between McGeechan and Bell. Just before the interval, Ireland made a hash of a tap-penalty move and the Scots reacted quickly to create try for Steele in the right corner. In the second half, McCombe and Irvine exchanged penalties and both sides continued to attack without success. In the last ten minutes, the Scots lost a lineout near their own line and the Irish backs passed out to Grace who raced over. Just short of time, Irvine made the game safe for Scotland by kicking his second penalty.

320   INTERNATIONAL CHAMPIONSHIP 1975   FRANCE

Parc des Princes, Paris · Saturday 15 February 1975 · Lost 9–10

SCOTLAND Andy Irvine (*Heriot's FP*); Billy Steele (*London Scot*), Jim Renwick (*Hawick*), David Bell (*Watsonians*), Lewis Dick (*Jordanhill*); Ian McGeechan (*Headingley*), Douglas Morgan

(*Stew-Mel FP*); Ian McLauchlan* (*Jordanhill*), Duncan Madsen (*Gosforth*), Sandy Carmichael (*W of Scot*), Alastair McHarg (*London Scot*), Gordon Brown (*W of Scot*), Mike Biggar (*London Scot*), Wilson Lauder (*Neath*), David Leslie (*Dundee HSFP*)

FRANCE Michel Taffary (*RCF*); Jean-François Gourdon (*RCF*), Claude Dourthe* (*Dax*), Roland Bertranne (*Bagnères*), Jean-Luc Averous (*La Voulte*); Lucien Pariès (*Narbonne*), Richard Astre (*Béziers*); Armand Vaquerin (*Béziers*), Jean-Louis Ugartemendia (*St-Jean-de-Luz*), Gérard Cholley (*Castres*), Alain Guilbert (*Toulon*), Claude Spanghero (*Narbonne*), Jean-Pierre Rives (*Toulouse*), Jean-Claude Skréla (*Toulouse*), Victor Boffelli (*Aurillac*)

REFEREE SM Lewis (*Wales*) · ATTENDANCE 43,472

SCORING Irvine, pen (3–0); Astre, drop (3–3) (half-time) Dourthe, try (3–7); Irvine, pen (6–7); Pariès, pen (6–10); Irvine, pen (9–10)

This was a scrappy and bad-tempered match that Scotland could have won if they had kept their discipline. From the kick-off there was fighting amongst the forwards and the antagonism persisted throughout the match. The Scottish half-backs kicked too much rather than using their three-quarters. Andy Irvine was rarely seen in attack and had a poor day with his goal-kicking, managing only three out of nine penalty attempts. The only try of the match came from a lineout break by the French back-row and Dourthe forced off some weak tackles to score. Scotland came close on two occasions, but lacked composure at the critical moments. After one missed opportunity, the Scottish forwards went for a pushover try, but the wily Rives dived-in at their feet, the scrum collapsed and inexplicably France were awarded a penalty.

---

321   INTERNATIONAL CHAMPIONSHIP 1975   WALES

Murrayfield · Saturday 1 March 1975 · Won 12–10

SCOTLAND Andy Irvine (*Heriot's FP*); Billy Steele (*London Scot*), Jim Renwick (*Hawick*), David Bell (*Watsonians*), Lewis Dick (*Jordanhill*); Ian McGeechan (*Headingley*), Douglas Morgan (*Stew-Mel FP*); Ian McLauchlan* (*Jordanhill*), Duncan Madsen (*Gosforth*), Sandy Carmichael (*W of Scot*), Alastair McHarg (*London Scot*), Gordon Brown (*W of Scot*), Mike Biggar (*London Scot*), Nairn MacEwan (*Highland*), Davd Leslie (*Dundee HSFP*)

WALES JPR Williams (*London Welsh*); Gerald Davis (*Cardiff*), Steve Fenwick (*Bridgend*), Ray Gravell (*Llanelli*), JJ Williams (*Llanelli*); John Bevan (*Aberavon*), Gareth Edwards (*Cardiff*); Charlie Faulkner (*Pontypool*), Bobby Windsor (*Pontypool*), Graham Price (*Pontypool*), Allan Martin (*Aberavon*), Mike Roberts (*London Welsh*), Terry Cobner (*Pontypool*), Trevor Evans (*Swansea*) Mervyn Davies* (*Swansea*) … Replacements: Phil Bennett (*Llanelli*) for Bevan (26), Roger Blyth (*Swansea*) for Fenwick (37)

REFEREE JR West (*Ireland*) · ATTENDANCE 104,000

SCORING Morgan, pen (3–0); Fenwick, pen (3–3); Morgan, pen (6–3); Fenwick, pen (6–6); Morgan, pen (9–6) (half-time) McGeechan, drop (12–6); Evans, try (12–10)

Having already beaten France (25–10) and England (20–4), Wales brought a huge number of supporters to Edinburgh. Several hours before the kick-off, Murrayfield (which at this time still had pay-at-the-gate admission) and its immediate vicinity were jammed with people. It was estimated that the game was watched by a then world record crowd of around 104,000 with many others locked outside, including some who had tickets. The match itself was a hard and exciting one, but the standard was not very high. The first half was mainly a tale of brief runs and kicks at goal: three for Scotland and two for Wales, who missed three other attempts. In the second half, McGeechan stretched Scotland's lead with a drop goal. There was little else of note until injury-time when JPR Williams burst into the line and Gerald Davies put Evans over in the corner. Much to Scotland's relief, Martin's conversion attempt went wide and the final whistle went.

322   INTERNATIONAL CHAMPIONSHIP 1975   ENGLAND

Twickenham · Saturday 15 March 1975 · Lost 6–7

SCOTLAND Andy Irvine (*Heriot's FP*); Billy Steele (*London Scot*), Jim Renwick (*Hawick*), David Bell (*Watsonians*), Lewis Dick (*Jordanhill*); Ian McGeechan (*Headingley*), Douglas Morgan (*Stew-Mel FP*); Ian McLauchlan* (*Jordanhill*), Duncan Madsen (*Gosforth*), Sandy Carmichael (*W of Scot*), Alastair McHarg (*London Scot*), Gordon Brown (*W of Scot*), Mike Biggar (*London Scot*), Nairn MacEwan (*Highland*), David Leslie (*Dundee HSFP*) ... Replacement: Ian Barnes (*Hawick*) for MacEwan (4)

ENGLAND Tony Jorden (*Bedford*); Peter Squires (*Harrogate*), Peter Warfield (*Cambridge U*), Keith Smith (*Roundhay*), Alan Morley (*Bristol*); Neil Bennett (*Bedford*), Jacko Page (*Northampton*); Stack Stevens (*Penzance & Newlyn*), John Pullin (*Bristol*), Fran Cotton* (*Coventry*), Roger Uttley (*Gosforth*), Chris Ralston (*Richmond*), Dave Rollitt (*Bristol*), Tony Neary (*Broughton Park*), Andy Ripley (*Rosslyn Park*)

REFEREE DP D'Arcy (*Ireland*)

SCORING Morgan, pen (3–0); Bennett, pen (3–3) (half-time) Morgan, pen (6–3); Morley, try (6–7)

Scotland went to Twickenham hoping to win their first Triple Crown since 1938. In an unspectacular struggle played in damp conditions, the Scottish forwards won plenty of possession, but the backs kicked too much and were guilty of over-elaboration. Consequently, the English line was rarely threatened. Scotland had an early setback when Nairn MacEwan went off after only four minutes with a broken jaw. He was replaced by Ian Barnes with Alastair McHarg dropping back to No 8. Morgan and Bennett exchanged penalties in the first half, and Morgan nudged the Scots ahead with a penalty after the interval. The decisive try came from an English kick ahead near the halfway line. The covering Irvine was beaten by a wicked bounce, Morley booted on and just beat Irvine in a race to the rolling ball. In the dying minutes, Morgan missed two kickable penalty attempts and the Triple Crown was gone once again. In the gloomy Scottish dressing-room after the match, Jim Renwick was heard to say: 'Dougie, I could have kicked over a chest of drawers from there.'

323   TOUR OF NEW ZEALAND 1975   NEW ZEALAND

Eden Park, Auckland · Saturday 14 June 1975 · Lost 0–24

SCOTLAND †Bruce Hay (*Boroughmuir*); Andy Irvine (*Heriot's FP*), Jim Renwick (*Hawick*), †Graham Birkett (*Harlequins*), Lewis Dick (*Jordanhill*); Ian McGeechan (*Headingley*),

Douglas Morgan (*Stew-Mel FP*); Ian McLauchlan* (*Jordanhill*), †Colin Fisher (*Waterloo*), Sandy Carmichael (*W of Scot*), Ian Barnes (*Hawick*), Alastair McHarg (*London Scot*), David Leslie (*Dundee HSFP*), Wilson Lauder (*Neath*), Bill Watson (*Boroughmuir*) ... Replacement: Billy Steele (*London Scot*) for Hay (10)

NEW ZEALAND Joe Karam (*Horowhenua*); Bryan Williams (*Auckland*), Bill Osborne (*Wanganui*), Lyn Jaffray (*Otago*), Grant Batty (*Wellington*); Duncan Robertson (*Otago*), Sid Going (*N Auckland*); Bill Bush (*Canterbury*), Tane Norton (*Canterbury*), Kerry Tanner (*Canterbury*), Hamish Macdonald (*N Auckland*), John Callesen (*Manawatu*), Ian Kirkpatrick (*Poverty Bay*), Ken Stewart (*Southland*), Andy Leslie* (*Wellington*)

REFEREE Peter McDavitt (Wellington)

SCORING Macdonald, try (0–4); Karam, con (0–6) (half-time) Williams, try (0–10); Karam, con (0–12); Robertson, try (0–16); Karam, con (0–18); Williams, try (0–22); Karam, con (0–24)

In May and June 1975, Scotland made a seven match tour of New Zealand. The Scots did reasonably well in their provincial games, winning four out of six, before taking on the mighty All Blacks at their spiritual home at Eden Park, Auckland. Unfortunately, the city was hit by a deluge of tropical rain before kick-off and the downpour continued throughout the match. Conditions were near farcical with deep pools of water lying on the pitch and there was a real possibility that a player might have drowned if they had been caught at the bottom of a pile-up. The match should have been cancelled, but that the Scots were due to fly home the following day and it was not possible to rearrange the game at short notice. In the event, the white-shirted New Zealanders adapted to the conditions with consummate ease. Their forwards were well on top, the backs handled superbly, and Robertson's probing kicks kept the Scots on the back foot. By contrast, the tourists never got into their stride and they made too many errors, especially under the high ball where Andy Irvine had an unhappy afternoon. New Zealand scored their first try after some ten minutes. Debutant Scottish full-back Bruce Hay, who seconds earlier had broken his arm, appeared to call for a mark, but was enveloped by the charging All Black forwards. The ball was quickly recycled and Kirkpatrick put Macdonald over at the posts. Hay then went off and was replaced by Billy Steele with Irvine moving to full-back. It was a minor miracle that the Scots were only six points adrift at the interval, but soon after the restart the home side wrapped up the game. Williams made a strong run from his own half and kicked ahead to the Scottish goal-line where Steele lost the ball and Williams pounced on it for a remarkable solo score. Then Irvine and Dick failed to deal with a high kick inside their own goal area and Robertson made an Olympic-style dive in the water to touch down. Finally, Dick missed touch with a fly hack, and Williams was on hand to pick up the ball and charge through the surprised defence. Karam converted all four tries, a great achievement in the conditions, but this game is only remembered for the dreadful weather rather than any of the play.

324   TOUR MATCH   AUSTRALIA

Murrayfield · Saturday 6 December 1975 · Won 10–3

SCOTLAND Bruce Hay (*Boroughmuir*); Andy Irvine (*Heriot's FP*), Jim Renwick (*Hawick*), Ian McGeechan (*Headingley*), Lewis Dick (*Jordanhill*); Colin Telfer (*Hawick*), Douglas Morgan

(*Stew-Mel FP*); Ian McLauchlan* (*Jordanhill*), Colin Fisher (*Waterloo*), Sandy Carmichael (*W of Scot*), Alastair McHarg (*W of Scot*), Gordon Brown (*W of Scot*), Wilson Lauder (*Neath*), David Leslie (*W of Scot*), †George Mackie (*Highland*)

AUSTRALIA Paul McLean (*Queensland*); Paddy Batch (*Queensland*), Rex L'Estrange (*Queensland*), John Berne (*NSW*), Laurie Monaghan (*NSW*); James Hindmarsh (*NSW*), John Hipwell* (*NSW*); John Meadows (*Victoria*), Peter Horton (*NSW*), Ronald Graham (*NSW*), Garrick Fay (*NSW*), Reginald Smith (*NSW*), Greg Cornelsen (*NSW*), Tony Shaw (*Queensland*), Spider Hillhouse (*Queensland*) … Replacement: Spoon Weatherstone (*ACT*) for Berne

REFEREE RF Johnson (*England*)

SCORING Dick, try (4–0); Renwick, try (8–0); Morgan, con (10–0) (half-time) McLean, pen (10–3)

The sixth Wallabies were making a mammoth 26 match tour of the British Isles and the United States, and on their Scottish leg had already beaten Edinburgh (10–9) and the South of Scotland (10–6). Scotland fielded one new cap in George Mackie, a big-haired No8 from the Highland club. Mackie had been selected for the previous match against New Zealand, but was forced to make a late withdrawal. Sandy Carmichael broke the Scottish cap record and led the team onto the field. Playing in bright sunshine, the Australians dominated the first quarter, but on the 26th minute Scotland scored against the run of play. From a scrum, Morgan improvised a long over-arm pass to McGeechan who sped through a gap. Hay was in support and passed to Dick who just managed to squeeze in at the left corner before being thrown into touch. Shortly before the interval, McGeechan intercepted a wild pass and sent Renwick away on a long run to the line. In the second half, the Scottish pack gradually took control and most of the play was in Australian territory. However, the only score was a fine angled penalty by McLean from about 40 yards.

---

325 INTERNATIONAL CHAMPIONSHIP 1976 FRANCE

Murrayfield · Saturday 10 January 1976 · Lost 6–13

SCOTLAND Bruce Hay (*Boroughmuir*); Andy Irvine (*Heriot's FP*), Jim Renwick (*Hawick*), Ian McGeechan (*Headingley*), Lewis Dick (*Jordanhill*); Colin Telfer (*Hawick*), Douglas Morgan (*Stew-Mel FP*); Ian McLauchlan* (*Jordanhill*), Duncan Madsen (*Gosforth*), Sandy Carmichael (*W of Scot*), Alastair McHarg (*London Scot*), Gordon Brown (*W of Scot*), Wilson Lauder (*Neath*), David Leslie (*W of Scot*), George Mackie (*Highland*)

FRANCE Michel Droitecourt (*Montferrand*); Jean-François Gourdon (*RCF*), Roland Bertranne (*Bagnères*), François Sangalli (*Narbonne*), André Dubertrand (*Montferrand*); Jean-Pierre Romeu (*Montferrand*), Jacques Fouroux* (*La Voulte*); Gérard Cholley (*Castres*), Alain Paco (*Béziers*), Robert Paparemborde (*Pau*), Francis Haget (*Agen*), Michel Palmié (*Béziers*), Jean-Pierre Rives (*Toulouse*), Jean-Claude Skrela (*Toulouse*), Jean-Pierre Bastiat (*Dax*)

REFEREE Ken Pattinson (*England*)

SCORING Morgan, drop (3–0); Romeu, pen (3–3); Dubertrand, try (3–7) (half-time) Romeu, pen (3–10); Renwick, pen (6–10); Romeu (6–13)

Scotland's run of ten successive home wins came to an end in frustrating fashion. They had the game within their grasp, but missed nine out of ten shots at goal, including eight in the first half when they had a fierce wind behind them. They were also unfortunate to have a successful kick by Andy Irvine disallowed because Ken Pattinson, the referee, adjudged that McLauchlan, who was placing the ball for Irvine due to the wind, was lying in an offside position. Pattinson later admitted that he had made a mistake, but the damage had been done. Scotland would have gone into a 6–0 lead which might have been enough of a winning platform. The Scots started well and dominated at the lineout, but their only reward was an early drop goal by Morgan. France took heart from Scotland's continual failures and became more assertive. Romeu kicked a wide-angled penalty and close to the interval Dubertand scored a try after some excellent build-up play. Romeu missed the conversion, but landed two penalties in the second half as opposed to one by Renwick who had taken over the kicking duties from Irvine. Both the Scottish players and the crowd became increasingly disenchanted as the game wore on and France finished the stronger side. The French back-row was prominent in loose play and Romeu's tactical kicking kept the Scots at bay.

---

326   INTERNATIONAL CHAMPIONSHIP 1976   WALES

Cardiff Arms Park · Saturday 7 February 1976 · Lost 6–28

SCOTLAND Andy Irvine (*Heriot's FP*); Billy Steele (*London Scot*), Jim Renwick (*Hawick*), †Alastair Cranston (*Hawick*), David Shedden (*W of Scot*); Ian McGeechan (*Headingley*), Douglas Morgan (*Stew-Mel FP*); Ian McLauchlan* (*Jordanhill*), Colin Fisher (*Waterloo*), Sandy Carmichael (*W of Scot*), Alastair McHarg (*London Scot*), Gordon Brown (*W of Scot*), Mike Biggar (*London Scot*), David Leslie (*W of Scot*), George Mackie (*Highland*)

WALES JPR Williams (*London Welsh*); Gerald Davies (*Cardiff*), Ray Gravell (*Llanelli*), Steve Fenwick (*Bridgend*), JJ Williams (*Llanelli*); Phil Bennett (*Llanelli*), Gareth Edwards (*Cardiff*); Charlie Faulkner (*Pontypool*), Bobby Windsor (*Pontypool*), Graham Price (*Pontypool*), Allan Martin (*Aberavon*), Geoff Wheel (*Swansea*), Terry Cobner (*Pontypool*), Trevor Evans (*Swansea*), Mervyn Davies* (*Swansea*)

REFEREE André Cluny (*France*)

SCORING JJ Williams, try (0–4); Bennett, con (0–6); Irvine, try (4–6); Morgan, con (6–6); Bennett, pen (6–9); Bennett, pen (6–12) (half-time) Bennett, pen (6–15); Fenwick, drop (6–18); Evans, try (6–22); Edwards, try (6–26); Bennett, con (6–28)

Scotland were only six points behind at the interval, but a star-studded Wales were at their commanding best and ran out decisive winners. Long before the finish the only question was how many points they would score. On a greasy, murky day, Wales scored after only three minutes. Bennett kicked to the corner, Steele and Irvine collided with each other, the ball went loose and JJ Williams won the race to the touchdown. Bennett kicked a superb conversion and Scotland replied with the best try of the match. After a long passage of play, a Welsh move broke down near the halfway line and McLauchlan hacked on. Scotland recovered the ball and moved it quickly left. McHarg intrude into the line and gave a scoring pass to Irvine who just managed to squeeze in at the corner flag. Morgan converted from the touchline and Bennett kicked two penalties before the interval. In the second half, the Welsh forwards took a form grip and Scotland never looked like scoring again. Bennett kicked a penalty, Fenwick dropped a goal and Evans and Edwards scored tries. The later stages of the match were marred by the farcical behaviour of French referee André Cluny who tore his calf muscle but stubbornly refused to leave the field. The result was that he could not keep up with the play and run the game properly. Offences went unpunished and there were several outbreaks of punching when the exasperated players tried to take matters into their own hands.

327   INTERNATIONAL CHAMPIONSHIP 1976   ENGLAND

Murrayfield · Saturday 21 February 1976 · Won 22–12

SCOTLAND Andy Irvine (*Heriot's FP*); Billy Steele (*London Scot*), Alastair Cranston (*Hawick*), Ian McGeechan (*Headingley*), David Shedden (*W of Scot*); †Ron Wilson (*London Scot*), Alan Lawson (*London Scot*); Ian McLauchlan* (*Jordanhill*), Colin Fisher (*Waterloo*), Sandy Carmichael (*W of Scot*), †Alan Tomes (*Hawick*), Gordon Brown (*W of Scot*), Mike Biggar (*London Scot*), David Leslie (*W of Scot*), Alastair McHarg (*London Scot*) ... Replacement: Jim Renwick (*Hawick*) for Shedden (32)

ENGLAND Alastair Hignell (*Cambridge U*); Ken Plummer (*Bristol*), Andy Maxwell (*Headingley*), David Cooke (*Harlequins*), David Duckham (*Coventry*); Alan Old (*Middlesbrough*), Mike Lampkowski (*Headingley*); Fran Cotton (*Sale*), Peter Wheeler (*Leicester*), Mike Burton (*Gloucester*), Bill Beaumont (*Fylde*), Bob Wilkinson (*Bedford*), Mark Keyworth (*Swansea*), Tony Neary* (*Broughton Park*), Andy Ripley (*Rosslyn Park*) ... Replacements: Derek Wyatt (*Bedford*) for Duckham (10), Neil Bennett (*Bedford*) for Maxwell (45)

REFEREE DM Lloyd (*Wales*)

SCORING Maxwell, try (0–4); Old, con (0–6); Irvine, pen (3–6); Old, pen (3–9); Lawson, try (7–9); Irvine, con (9–9); Old, pen (9–12) (half-time) Irvine, pen (12–12); Leslie, try (16–12); Lawson, try (20–12); Irvine, con (22–12)

Alan Lawson scores his first try against England in 1976 after a magnificent Scottish breakout.
Scotsman Publications Ltd

The teams were presented to Her Majesty Queen Elizabeth and Prince Philip before the match. This was a fast and furious encounter played in perfect conditions. The Scots were under a lot of pressure in the scrums, but they deserved to win by virtue of taking their chances. They had greater mobility, their handling was secure and they looked positive and relaxed. Returning to the colours after two years, scrum-half Alan Lawson was a match-winner. He scored two memorable tries, displayed an abundance of energy and enthusiasm, and after a shaky start his service gave new stand-off Ron Wilson enough time to settle to his task. England opened strongly and after six minutes Maxwell scored a try which was converted by Old. Irvine and Old exchanged penalties before the Scots scored a brilliant try. England were attacking inside the Scottish 25 and Wyatt hooked a kick backwards. Shedden, on the wrong wing, snatched the ball and broke clear. Three forwards, Biggar, Carmichael and new cap Tomes leant their support and Lawson finished the move with a sprint to the line. Irvine converted and Old regained the lead for England with a penalty. In the second half, Irvine kicked a penalty to level the scores and set-up an exciting finish. The turning point came midway through the second period. Taking a wild pass-back from Burton on his own 25, the otherwise excellent Old tried to clear, but his kick was charged down by Leslie who gathered the bouncing ball and raced away to the line. Although unconverted, Leslie's try seemed to sap the English spirit. The Scots mounted a further attack; Lawson collected a loose pass on the English 25 and sprinted through a gap to score at the posts. Irvine converted and although the visitors rallied in the closing stages some uncompromising defence held them at bay. This was the final appearance of two icons of world rugby: the superbly athletic and utterly eccentric Andy Ripley and blonde-haired winger David Duckham who limped off after ten minutes.

---

328   INTERNATIONAL CHAMPIONSHIP 1976   IRELAND

Lansdowne Road · Saturday 20 March 1976 · Won 15–6

SCOTLAND Andy Irvine (*Heriot's FP*); Billy Steele (*London Scot*), Alastair Cranston (*Hawick*), Ian McGeechan (*Headingley*), David Shedden (*W of Scot*); Ron Wilson (*London Scot*), Alan Lawson (*London Scot*); Ian McLauchlan* (*Jordanhill*), Colin Fisher (*Waterloo*), Sandy Carmichael (*W of Scot*), Alan Tomes (*Hawick*), Gordon Brown (*W of Scot*), Mike Biggar (*London Scot*), David Leslie (*W of Scot*), Alastair McHarg (*London Scot*)

IRELAND Larry Moloney (*Garryowen*); Tom Grace* (*St Mary's Coll*), Joe Brady (*Wdrs*), Mike Gibson (*NIFC*), Steve Blake-Knox (*NIFC*); Barry McGann (*Cork Const*), John Moloney (*St Mary's Coll*); Phil Orr (*Old Wesley*), John Cantrell (*UC Dublin*), Philip O'Callaghan (*Dolphin*), Moss Keane (*Lansdowne*), Ronnie Hakin (*CIYMS*), Seamus Deering (*Garryowen*), Stewart McKinney (*Dungannon*), Willie Duggan (*Blackrock Coll*) ... Replacement: Harry McKibbin (*Instonians*) for Gibson (73)

REFEREE MS Lewis (*Wales*)

SCORING McGann, pen (0–3); Irvine, pen (3–3); Irvine, pen (6–3); McGann, pen (6–6) (half-time) Irvine, pen, (9–6); Irvine, pen (12–6); Wilson, drop (15–6)

Scotland won away from home for the first time since 1971, but otherwise this was a scrappy and uninspiring encounter that was bereft of tries. Continuous drizzle made handling very difficult and play was regularly interrupted by penalties. The main difference between the sides was that the Scots were better at taking their chances. Andy Irvine was successful with four kicks out of eight, but Ireland's Barry McGann could only take two out of six. A drop goal by Ron Wilson in the second half completed the scoring. The Scottish forwards adapted to the conditions better and were solid in the scrums. Wilson's steady if unadventurous tactical kicking helped to keep the Irish at arm's length and Irvine was outstanding at full-back.

XV   TOUR MATCH   JAPAN

Murrayfield · Saturday 25 September 1976 · Won 34–9

SCOTLAND XV Andy Irvine (*Heriot's FP*); Bill Gammell (*Edinburgh Wdrs*), Keith Robertson (*Melrose*), Ian McGeechan* (*Headingley*), David Ashton (*Ayr*); Ron Wilson (*London Scot*), Alan Lawson (*London Scot*); Jim Aitken (*Gala*), Colin Fisher (*Waterloo*), Norman Pender (*Hawick*), Alan Tomes (Hawick), Jim Carswell (*Jordanhill*), Mike Biggar (*London Scot*), David Leslie (*W of Scot*), Bill Watson (*Boroughmuir*) ... Replacement: George Mackie (*Highland*) for Leslie (43)

JAPAN Nobufumi Tanaka; Masaru Fujiwara, Shigetaka Mori, Masao Yoshida, Ken Aruga; Shigekazu Hoshino, Ryozo Imazato; Tsukasa Takata*, Toru Wada, Toshiaki Yasui, Koiichi Shibata, Toshio Terai, Yoshiaki Izawa, Hideo Akama, Ichiro Kobayashi ... Replacement: K Muraguchi for Aruga (63)

REFEREE KH Clark (*Ireland*)

SCORING Tanaka, pen (0–3); Gammell, try (4–3); Irvine, con (6–3); McGeechan, try (10–3); Irvine, try (14–3) (half-time) Fisher, try (18–3); Gammell, try (22–3); Irvine, con (24–3); Fujiwara, try (24–7); Tanaka, con (24–9); Lawson, try (28–9); Irvine, con (30–9); Ashton, try (34–9)

In the autumn of 1976, Japan made a ten match tour of Britain and Italy. The Japanese were popular tourists and great ambassadors for their country, but on the field they were hampered by their lack of height and weight. The tour opened with a heavy defeat against Gloucestershire (62–10) before a non-cap international at Murrayfield. Scotland fielded an experimental side with six newcomers, including wings Bill Gammell and David Ashton, and props Jim Aitken and Norman Pender. Playing in a raw wind and steady rain, the Japanese tackled bravely and took an early lead, but their forwards were largely outgunned and the outcome was never in doubt. The Japanese half-backs were under constant pressure and the midfield had little room to operate. Scotland did what was expected of them and scored seven tries, but at times they tried to play too much rugby when the conditions were against it. Andy Irvine was in great attacking form and his opposite number Tanaka, with much less ball to exploit, defended strongly and was always ready to run out of defence.

329   INTERNATIONAL CHAMPIONSHIP 1977   ENGLAND

Twickenham · Saturday 15 January 1977 · Lost 6–26

SCOTLAND Andy Irvine (*Heriot's FP*); Billy Steele (*London Scot*), Ian McGeechan* (*Headingley*), Alastair Cranston (*Hawick*), Lewis Dick (*Swansea*); Ron Wilson (*London Scot*), Alan Lawson (*London Scot*); †Jim Aitken (*Gala*), Duncan Madsen (*Gosforth*), Sandy Carmichael

(*W of Scot*), Alan Tomes (*Hawick*), Alastair McHarg (*London Scot*), Wilson Lauder (*Neath*), †Alex Brewster (*Stew-Mel FP*), †Donald Macdonald (*Oxford U*)

ENGLAND Alastair Hignell (*Cambridge U*); Peter Squires (*Harrogate*), Barrie Corless (*Moseley*), Charles Kent (*Rosslyn Park*), Mike Slemen (*Liverpool*); Martin Cooper (*Moseley*), Malcolm Young (*Gosforth*); Robin Cowling (*Leicester*), Peter Wheeler (*Leicester*), Fran Cotton (*Sale*), Bill Beaumont (*Fylde*), Nigel Horton (*Moseley*), Peter Dixon (*Gosforth*), Mike Rafter (*Bristol*), Roger Uttley* (*Gosforth*)

REFEREE Meirion Joseph (*Wales*)

SCORING Irvine, pen (3–0); Slemen, try (3–4); Hignell, pen (3–7); Irvine, pen (6–7); Young, try (6–11); Hignell, con (6–13) (half-time) Hignell, pen (6–16); Kent, try (6–20); Uttley, try (6–24); Hignell, con (6–26)

Scotland field three new caps, two in the back-row, but they were without Gordon Brown who had been suspended after being sent off in a District match. This was a day of complete disaster for Scotland as England ran up their biggest winning margin in the fixture to date. The home side scored four tries and would have won by a lot more if Hignell had been in better kicking form. Playing under a lowering sky and in a bitter wind, the Scots gained some parity in the lineout, but the big English forwards dominated all other aspects and gave their backs a solid platform. Cooper and Young controlled the match from half-back. Charles Kent, a new cap in the centre, was devastating on the crash ball and his thunderous runs paved the way for two of England's tries. Starved of possession, the Scottish backs had few opportunities and the dual threats of Irvine or the burly Cranston were easily contained. Scotland could only muster two penalty goals by Irvine, the second a huge kick of over 50 yards, but otherwise this was grim afternoon for the visitors.

330 INTERNATIONAL CHAMPIONSHIP 1977 IRELAND

Murrayfield · Saturday 19 February 1977 · Won 21–18

SCOTLAND Andy Irvine (*Heriot's FP*); †Bill Gammell (*Edinburgh Wdrs*), Ian McGeechan (*Headingley*), Jim Renwick (*Hawick*), David Shedden (*W of Scot*); Ron Wilson (*London Scot*), Douglas Morgan (*Stew-Mel FP*); Jim Aitken (*Gala*), Duncan Madsen (*Gosforth*), †Norman Pender (*Hawick*), Ian Barnes (*Hawick*), Alastair McHarg (*London Scot*), Mike Biggar (*London Scot*), Bill Watson (*Boroughmuir*), Donald McDonald (*London Scot*) ... Replacement: Sandy Carmichael (*W of Scot*) for Pender (15)

IRELAND Frank Wilson (*CIYMS*); Tom Grace* (*St Mary's Coll*), Alistair McKibbin (*Instonians*), Mike Gibson (*NIFC*), Jimmy Bowen (*Cork Const*); Mick Quinn (*Lansdowne*), John Robbie (*Dublin U*); Phil Orr (*Old Wesley*), Pat Whelan (*Garryowen*), Ned Byrne (*Blackrock Coll*), Moss Keane (*Lansdowne*), Charles Munagh (*Portadown*), Seamus McKinney (*Dungannon*), Fergus Slattery (*Blackrock Coll*), Willie Duggan (*Blackrock Coll*)

REFEREE M Joseph (*Wales*)

SCORING Irvine, pen (3–0); Gibson, pen (3–3); Gammell, try (7–3); Quinn, drop (7–6); Gibson, pen (7–9) (half-time) Gammell, try (11–9); Irvine, pen (14–9); Madsen, try (18–9); Quinn, pen (18–12); Morgan, drop (21–12); Gibson, try (21–16); Gibson, con (21–18)

With eight changes and two new caps, Scotland did well to bounce back after their traumatic experience at Twickenham. They were much livelier and showed good invention and teamwork. The wily Alastair McHarg did particularly well in the lineout. On a soft pitch, Irvine and Gibson exchanged early penalties before Norman Pender, the new prop, left the field with a rib injury after only 15 minutes. He was replaced by the old campaigner Sandy Carmichael who received a great ovation. Soon after, the Scots took play deep into the Irish 22 and Gammell snatched a loose pass and dived over at the corner. A drop goal by Quinn and a penalty by Gibson put Ireland in front and the game was wide open at the interval. The long-striding Gammell scored his second try when he grabbed a fortunate bounce and ran away to the corner. Irvine added a penalty and Madsen scored a try after latching onto a loose ball at an Irish lineout. Quinn kicked a penalty, but the Scots lasted the pace better and Morgan put them out-of-sight with a drop goal two minutes before the end. Then in injury-time, Grace made a strong run on the right, the ball was hacked into the Scottish goal area where it skewed awkwardly for Renwick, and the outstanding Gibson pounced for a try that he also converted.

---

331   INTERNATIONAL CHAMPIONSHIP 1977   FRANCE

Parc des Princes, Paris · Saturday 5 March 1977 · Lost 3–23

SCOTLAND Andy Irvine (*Heriot's FP*); Bill Gammell (*Edinburgh Wdrs*), Ian McGeechan* (*Headingley*), Jim Renwick (*Hawick*), David Shedden (*W of Scot*); Ron Wilson (*London Scot*), Douglas Morgan (*Stew-Mel FP*); Jim Aitken (*Gala*), Duncan Madsen (*Gosforth*), Sandy Carmichael (*W of Scot*), Ian Barnes (*Hawick*), Alastair McHarg (*London Scot*), Mike Biggar (*London Scot*), Bill Watson (*Boroughmuir*), Donald Macdonald (*London Scot*)

FRANCE Jean-Michel Aguirre (*Bagnères*); Dominique Harize (*Toulouse*), Roland Bertanne (*Bagnères*), François Sangalli (*Narbonne*), Jean-Luc Averous (*La Voulte*); Jean-Pierre Romeu (*Montferrand*), Jacques Fouroux* (*Auch*); Gérard Cholley (*Castres*), Alain Paco (*Béziers*), Robert Paparemborde (*Pau*), Michel Palmié (*Béziers*), Jean-François Imbernon (*Perpignan*), Jean-Pierre Rives (*Toulouse*), Jean-Claude Skrela (*Toulouse*), Jean-Pierre Bastiat (*Dax*)

REFEREE Merion Joseph (*Wales*)

SCORING Irvine, pen (3–0); Paco, try (3–4); Romeu, con (3–6); Romeu, pen (3–9) (half-time) Harize, try (3–13); Bertranne, try (3–17); Paparemborde, try (3–21); Romeu, con (3–23)

This match was marred by rough play of some of the French forwards, in particular 16 stone prop Gérard Cholley. He flattened Macdonald with a punch straight from the kick-off and committed several other violent acts during the match. It was widely felt that the referee, Welshman Merion Joseph, ought to have been firmer and sent him off the field. Cholley's behaviour detracted from an otherwise excellent performance by the French who were superior to the Scots in all aspects. The home side played some brilliant attacking rugby and at times their speed and handling skills reduced the Scottish defence to ribbons. They scored four tries, had another disallowed and the winning margin might easily have been greater if their finishing had not been so hurried. The Scots competed well at the lineout thanks to Alastair McHarg, but they were under enormous pressure in the scrums and the French back-row was immense in the loose. At stand-off, Ron Wilson's kicking was very wayward and the Scottish backs were barely seen as an attacking force. At the after-match dinner, French president Albert Ferasse apologised for the behaviour of some of his players.

Murrayfield · Saturday 19 March 1977 · Lost 9–18

SCOTLAND Andy Irvine (*Heriot's FP*); Bill Gammell (*Edinburgh Wdrs*), Jim Renwick (*Hawick*), Alastair Cranston (*Hawick*), David Shedden (*W of Scot*); Ian McGeechan* (*Headingley*), Douglas Morgan (*Stew-Mel FP*); Ian McLauchlan (*Jordanhill*), Duncan Madsen (*Gosforth*), Sandy Carmichael (*W of Scot*), Ian Barnes (*Hawick*), Alastair McHarg (*London Scot*), Mike Biggar (*London Scot*), Bill Watson (*Boroughmuir*), Donald Macdonald (*London Scot*)

WALES JPR Williams (*Bridgend*); Gerald Davies (*Cardiff*), Steve Fenwick (*Bridgend*), David Burcher (*Newport*), JJ Williams (*Llanelli*); Phil Bennett* (*Llanelli*), Gareth Edwards (*Cardiff*); Clive Williams (*Aberavon*), Bobby Windsor (*Pontypool*), Graham Price (*Pontypool*), Allan Martin (*Aberavon*), Geoff Wheel (*Swansea*), Terry Cobner (*Pontypool*), Clive Burgess (*Ebbw Vale*), Derek Quinnell (*Llanelli*)

REFEREE Georges Domercq (*France*)

SCORING McGeechan, drop (3–0); Bennett, pen (3–3) (half-time) Irvine, try (7–3); Irvine, con (9–3); Davies, try (9–7); Bennett, con (9–9); Bennett, pen (9–12); Bennett, try (9–16); Bennett, con (9–18)

In a great match, Scotland played their best and most expansive rugby of the championship. They pushed a hugely talented Welsh team all the way and perhaps deserved to draw, but in the end the visitors had too much class and skill. Both sides scored a brilliant try each and Wales did not take the lead until the final quarter when they

Andy Irvine finishes off a great Scottish move against Wales in 1977.
Scotsman Publications Ltd

delivered the *coup de grâce* with a touch of genius. Scotland made a brilliant start and McGeechan kicked an early left-footed drop goal, but Bennett levelled soon afterwards with a penalty. There was no further scoring in the first half although both sides were keen to run the ball. The Scottish forwards were in excellent form and the backs looked sharp and dangerous. Early in the second half, Morgan broke right from a scrum on the Welsh 10 metres line and fed Renwick who burst through at top speed. Irvine supported and although he looked covered he veered inside four defenders to score under the posts. A few minutes later, Wales drew level with a well worked try by JJ Williams. Bennett converted from the touchline and then kicked a penalty. Scotland launched a promising attack and Irvine chipped into space deep in the Welsh 22. Wales worked the ball to Gerald Davies who beat three men before putting Bennett away up the touchline. Burcher carried on before lobbing a pass inside to Fenwick (which looked suspiciously forward) who in turn flicked the ball back to Bennett, and the mercurial stand-off skipped past the last defenders to slide down between the posts, one of the greatest tries ever seen at Murrayfield. The Scots battled right to the end, but were unable to score again.

XV · TOUR OF THE FAR EAST 1977 · JAPAN

Olympic Stadium, Tokyo · Sunday 18 September 1977 · Won 74–9

SCOTLAND XV Colin Mair (*W of Scot*); Bill Gammell (*Edinburgh Wdrs*), Jim Renwick (*Hawick*), Alastair Cranston (*Hawick*), Lewis Dick (*Swansea*); Ron Wilson (*London Scot*), Roy Laidlaw (*Jed-Forest*); Ian McLauchlan (*Jordanhill*), Colin Deans (*Hawick*), Bob Cunningham (*Gala*), Alan Tomes (*Hawick*), Ian Barnes (*Hawick*), Mike Biggar* (London Scot), Gordon Dickson (*Gala*), Donald Macdonald (*London Scot*) ... Replacements: Rob Moffat (*Melrose*), Gerry McGuinness (*W of Scot*)

JAPAN Nobufumi Tanaka; Shigetaka Mori, Masaru Fujiwara, Masao Yoshida, Hirotaka Ujino; Yuji Matsuo, Junya Matsumoto; Takeshi Hatakeyama, Tsukasa Takada*, Toshiaki Yasui, Naoshi Kumagai, Kiyoshi Segawa, Hideo Akama, Ichiro Kobayashi, Hiroshi Ogasawara ... Replacement: Manabu Sasada

REFEREE Peter Hughes (*England*)

SCORING Try scorers for Scotland were Gammell (4), Laidlaw (2), Wilson, Renwick, Cranston, Dickson and McLauchlan. Mair kicked nine conversions and four penalty goals. For Japan, Ujino scored a try converted by Tanaka and Matsuo kicked a penalty.

In September 1977, Scotland, under the captaincy of Mike Biggar, made a five match tour of the Far East. Several leading players were unavailable and the party included 12 newcomers, but they still managed to win all of their games and run up some big scores. The tour started with an exhibition match against Thailand which the Scots won easily (82–3). This was followed by a game against Hong Kong and several provincial matches in Japan before the tour ended with a non-cap international against Japan. Played in intermittent rain, the lighter, smaller Japanese started strongly and were only 16–3 adrift at the interval, but in the second half the weighty Scottish pack asserted itself and eventually the tourists were in complete control. The backs made good use of the plentiful supply of ball and Scotland scored eleven tries in total. New scrum-half Roy Laidlaw impressed with his accurate service and penetrative runs, Jim Renwick was very lively and long-striding wing Bill Gammell scored four tries.

Lansdowne Road, Dublin · Saturday 21 January 1978 · Lost 9–12

SCOTLAND Bruce Hay (*Boroughmuir*); Andy Irvine (*Heriot's FP*), Jim Renwick (*Hawick*), Ian McGeechan (*Headingley*), David Shedden (*W of Scot*); Ron Wilson (*London Scot*), Douglas Morgan* (*Stew-Mel FP*); Ian McLauchlan (*Jordanhill*), Duncan Madsen (*Gosforth*), Sandy Carmichael (*W of Scot*), Alan Tomes (*Hawick*), Alastair McHarg (*London Scot*), Mike Biggar (*London Scot*), †Brian Hegarty (*Hawick*), Donald Macdonald (*W of Scot*)

IRELAND Tony Ensor (*Wdrs*); Tom Grace (*St Mary's Coll*), Alistair McKibben (*London Irish*), Paul McNaughton (*Greystones*), Freddie McLennan (*Wdrs*); Tony Ward (*Garryowen*), John Moloney* (*St Mary's Coll*); Phil Orr (*Old Wesley*), Pat Whelan (*Garryowen*), Michael Fitzpatrick (*Wdrs*), Moss Keane (*Lansdowne*), Donal Spring (*Dublin U*), John O'Driscoll (*London Irish*), Fergus Slattery (*Blackrock Coll*), Willie Duggan (*Blackrock Coll*) … Replacements: Stewart McKinney (*Dungannon*) for O'Driscoll, Lawrence Moloney (*Garryowen*) for Ensor

REFEREE PE Hughes (*England*)

SCORING Morgan, pen (3–0); Ward, pen (3–3); Morgan, pen (6–3); Ward, pen (6–6); McKinney, try (6–10); Ward, con (6–12) (half-time) Morgan, pen (9–12)

In his final appearance, Sandy Carmichael became the first Scot to reach 50 caps. Ireland deserved to win by virtue of scoring the only try, but the Scots should have snatched a draw at the finish. The first half was largely a scrappy affair with Douglas Morgan, the new Scottish captain, and Tony Ward, the exciting Irish stand-off, swapping two penalties each. Close to the interval, Ireland made a terrific charge from their own half almost to the Scottish line. From the resulting scrum, Ireland stole the ball and substitute flanker Stewart McKinney took a pass from Slattery and scored a try. Ward converted to give Ireland a 12–6 lead at half-time. Scotland had the wind advantage in the second half and were able to apply some pressure, but their only score was third penalty goal by Morgan. Irvine, who looked out of place on the right wing, narrowly missed a very long shot at goal. Deep into injury time, the Scots were awarded a kickable penalty which Morgan controversially opted to run in hope of scoring the winning try. The move broke down and Ireland held out. This was an inexplicably long match with lengthy periods of added time at the end of both halves.

Murrayfield · Saturday 4 February 1978 · Lost 16–19

SCOTLAND Andy Irvine (*Heriot's FP*); Bruce Hay (*Boroughmuir*), Jim Renwick (*Hawick*), Ian McGeechan (*Headingley*), David Shedden (*W of Scot*); Ron Wilson (*London Scot*), Douglas Morgan* (*Stew-Mel FP*); Ian McLauchlan (*Jordanhill*), †Colin Deans (*Hawick*), Norman Pender (*Hawick*), Alan Tomes (*Hawick*), Alastair McHarg (*London Scot*), Mike Biggar (*London Scot*), Brian Hegarty (*Hawick*), George Mackie (*Highland*) … Replacements: Alastair Cranston (*Hawick*) for Irvine (43), Graham Hogg (*Boroughmuir*) for Shedden (57)

FRANCE Jean-Michel Aguirre (*Bagnéres*); Jean-François Gourdon (*Bagnéres*), Roland Bertranne (*Bagnéres*), Christian Bélascain (*Bayonne*), Jean-Luc Averous (*La Voulte*); Bernard Vivès (*Agen*), Jérôme Gallion (*Toulon*); Gérard Cholley (*Castres*), Alain Paco (*Béziers*), Robert Paparemborde (*Pau*), Francis Haget (*Agen*), Michel Palmié (*Béziers*), Jean-Pierre Rives (*Toulouse*), Jean-Claude Skrela (*Toulouse*), Jean-Pierre Bastiat* (*Dax*)

SCORING Morgan, pen (3–0); Shedden, try (7–0); Irvine, try (11–0); Morgan, con (13–0); Gallion, try (13–4) (half-time) Aguirre, pen (13–7); Haget, try (13–11); Aguirre, con (13–13); Aguirre, pen (13–16); Morgan, drop (16–16); Aguirre, pen (16–19)

Colin Deans, one of the world's great hookers, won his first cap. This was an exciting and well contested match despite the wet conditions. The Scots were underdogs, but showed plenty of fighting spirit and were unlucky not to earn at least a draw. They led 13–0 at one stage and seemed to have the French in disarray, but conceded a soft try near the interval which let the visitors back into contention and eventual victory. Morgan kicked an early penalty and Shedden scored an unconverted try after he charged down a clearance by Gourdon. Then Hay enveloped Aguirre near the Scottish 22, the Scottish forwards won the ball and Morgan kicked ahead into the space. Irvine followed-up fast, hacked on and won the race to the touchdown despite being impeded. Unfortunately, he hurt his left shoulder in the act of scoring which proved to be the turning point of the match. During his absence for treatment (there were no temporary replacements at this time) Gallion hoisted a high kick to the Scottish line. Hegarty, who had been temporarily withdrawn from the pack, was unable to hold onto the slippery ball and Gallion dived on it to score. In the second half, Aguirre kicked a penalty and converted a try by Haget, and then added a second penalty to snatch the lead. Morgan levelled with a controversial drop goal which was disputed by the French. He was awarded an indirect free-kick and did not tap the ball first before going for goal, as the rules required, but the referee failed to notice. It didn't matter because a few minutes later Aguirre kicked the winning penalty. Scotland tried desperately to save the match, but could not get the crucial score.

---

335   INTERNATIONAL CHAMPIONSHIP 1978   WALES

Cardiff Arms Park · Saturday 18 February 1978 · Lost 14–22

SCOTLAND Bruce Hay (*Boroughmuir*); Bill Gammell (*Edinburgh Wdrs*), Jim Renwick (*Hawick*), Alastair Cranston (*Hawick*), David Shedden (*W of Scot*); Ian McGeechan (*Headingley*), Douglas Morgan* (*Stew-Mel FP*); Ian McLauchlan (*Jordanhill*), Colin Deans (*Hawick*), Norman Pender (*Hawick*), Alan Tomes (*Hawick*), Alastair McHarg (*London Scot*), Mike Biggar (*London Scot*), Brian Hegarty (*Hawick*), Donald Macdonald (*W of Scot*) ... Replacement: Graham Hogg (*Boroughmuir*) for Shedden (8)

WALES JPR Williams (*Bridgend*); Gerald Davies (*Cardiff*), Ray Gravell (*Llanelli*), Steve Fenwick (*Bridgend*), JJ Williams (*Llanelli*); Phil Bennett* (*Llanelli*), Gareth Edwards (*Cardiff*); Charlie Faulkner (*Pontypool*), Bobby Windsor (*Pontypool*), Graham Price (*Pontypool*), Allan Martin (*Aberavon*), Geoff Wheel (*Swansea*), Terry Cobner (*Pontypool*), Jeff Squire (*Newport*), Derek Quinnell (*Llanelli*)

REFEREE John West (*Ireland*)

SCORING Morgan, pen (3–0); Edwards, try (3–4); Renwick, try (7–4); Gravell, try (7–8) (half-time) Bennett, drop (7–11); Fenwick, try (7–15); Bennett, pen (7–18); Quinnell, try (7–22); Morgan, pen (10–22); Tomes, try (14–22)

On a bitterly cold afternoon, the two sides played out a vivid and entertaining contest that did the game credit. The Scots showed plenty of tenacity and spirit, but Wales were at their imperious best and always had something in reserve. The Welsh scrum was very solid and provided a platform for their star-studded back division who happily exploited some Scottish defensive lapses. Playing with the wind, the Scots were dealt an early blow when left wing David Shedden had to leave the field on a stretcher. Boroughmuir centre Graham Hogg acted as replacement for the second match in succession. Douglas Morgan opened with a penalty, but Welsh maestro Gareth Edwards replied with a classic dart-and-dive from a scrum near the Scottish line. Around the half hour mark, the Scots made a superb movement deep into the Welsh 22 and Renwick sidestepped past the defence for a try. Wales hit back with a try by burly centre Ray Gravell, who took the ball from a tap penalty and brushed past several defenders to the line. Bennett missed the conversion on an awkward day for the kickers – none of the six tries were converted – and Wales led 8–7 at the interval. Early in the second half, the home side rattled up 14 points in quick succession. Fenwick and Quinnell scored unconverted tries, the latter from a thundering run up the touchline, and Bennett added a drop goal and a penalty. It seemed that the floodgates might open, but the Scots rallied in the later stages. Morgan, who had a mixed day with his boot, kicked an easy penalty and then set-up a position from which Tomes crashed over. Morgan missed the simple conversion and Wales finished strongly, but there was no further scoring. After the match the winter weather closed in and many Scottish supporters were left stranded in Wales for several days because of heavy snow.

---

336   INTERNATIONAL CHAMPIONSHIP 1978   ENGLAND

Murrayfield · Saturday 4 March 1978 · Lost 0–15

SCOTLAND Andy Irvine (*Heriot's FP*); Bill Gammell (*Edinburgh Wdrs*), Jim Renwick (*Hawick*), Alastair Cranston (*Hawick*), Bruce Hay (*Boroughmuir*); †Richard Breakey (*Gosforth*), Douglas Morgan* (*Stew-Mel FP*); Ian McLauchlan (*Jordanhill*), Colin Deans (*Hawick*), Norman Pender (*Hawick*), Alan Tomes (*Hawick*), †David Gray (*W of Scot*), Mike Biggar (*London Scot*), Brian Hegarty (*Hawick*), Donald Macdonald (*W of Scot*)

ENGLAND David Caplan (*Headingley*); Peter Squires (*Harrogate*), Barrie Corless (*Moseley*), Paul Dodge (*Leicester*), Mike Slemen (*Liverpool*); John Horton (*Bath*), Malcolm Young (*Gosforth*); Barry Nelmes (*Cardiff*), Peter Wheeler (*Leicester*), Fran Cotton (*Sale*), Bill Beaumont* (*Fylde*), Maurice Colclough (*Angoulême*), Peter Dixon (*Gosforth*), Mike Rafter (*Bristol*), John Scott (*Rosslyn Park*)

REFEREE John West (*Ireland*)

SCORING Squires, try (0–4); Young, con (0–6); Dodge, pen (0–9) (half-time) Nelmes, try (0–13); Young, con (0–15)

Gosforth's Richard Breakey was a late replacement at stand-off for McGeechan. England won at Murrayfield for the first time in a decade against a lacklustre Scottish side. The English forwards were stronger and livelier, and it was only in the lineout that the Scots had any parity. England played with a brisk wind behind them in the first half and their new full-back Dave Caplan narrowly missed scoring a try in the opening seconds. Although the visitors were able to apply a lot of pressure, it took them some 30 minutes to open the scoring. Slemen broke away down the left and after some good support by the forwards Peter Squires cut inside for a try near the posts. Young converted and near the interval Dodge kicked a huge penalty. Playing with the wind, Scotland made some promising attacks and both Gammell and Renwick were caught just short. Towards the finish, Dodge made a strong run from which Nelmes powered his way over to seal the game.

| 337 | TOUR MATCH | NEW ZEALAND |

Murrayfield · Saturday 9 December 1978 · Lost 9–18

SCOTLAND Andy Irvine (*Heriot's FP*); †Keith Robertson (*Melrose*), Jim Renwick (*Hawick*), Alastair Cranston (*Hawick*), Bruce Hay (*Boroughmuir*); Ian McGeechan* (*Headingley*), Alan Lawson (*London Scot*); Ian McLauchlan (*Jordanhill*), Colin Deans (*Hawick*), †Bob Cunningham (*Gala*), Alan Tomes (*Hawick*), Alastair McHarg (*London Scot*), Mike Biggar (*London Scot*), †Gordon Dickson (*Gala*), David Leslie (*Gala*) ... Replacement: †Ian Lambie (*Watsonians*) for Leslie

NEW ZEALAND Brian McKechnie (*Southland*); Stu Wilson (*Wellington*), Bruce Robertson (*Counties*), Bill Osborne (*Wanganui*), Bryan Williams (*Auckland*); Doug Bruce (*Canterbury*), Mark Donaldson (*Manawatu*); Brad Johnstone (*Auckland*), Andy Dalton (*Counties*), Gary Knight (*Manawatu*), Andy Haden (*Auckland*), Frank Oliver (*Otago*), Leicester Rutledge (*Southland*), Graham Mourie* (*Taranaki*), Gary Seear (*Otago*)

REFEREE John West (*Ireland*)

SCORING Hay, try (4–0); Irvine, con (6–0); McKechnie, pen (6–3); Seear, try (6–7); McKechnie, con (6–9) (half-time) McKechnie, con (6–12), McGeechan, drop (9–12); Robertson, try (9–16); McKechnie, con (9–18)

Captained by the dynamic flanker Graham Mourie, the 8th All Blacks were making an 18 match tour of the British Isles, including two games in Scotland. Having already defeated the other three home nations, they headed to Scotland in search of their first-ever Grand Slam. Scotland introduced three new caps in Keith Robertson, Bob Cunningham and Gordon Dickson, and recalled the prodigal Alan Lawson at scrum-half and David Leslie at No8. Murrayfield did not have floodlights so the kick-off time was advanced by five minutes to compensate for the lack of winter light. Nevertheless, the closing stages of the game were played in near darkness and the players were barely distinguishable. On a slippery, rain-soaked pitch, the Scots sensationally opened the scoring after nine minutes. Bruce Hay kicked and chased, and after some quick passing near the line the ball rebounded back into Hay's arms for him to dive over. It was the first try conceded by the New Zealanders since their defeat against Munster eleven matches earlier and amazingly Scotland's first try against them since 1935. Irvine converted with a magnificent kick from near the touchline. Fourteen minutes later, McKechnie brought his side back into the game with a penalty. After half an hour, Irvine, who had a disappointing afternoon, fumbled a kick near the Scottish line and from the ensuing scrum Seear picked up and drove over. McKechnie's conversion put New Zealand 9–6 ahead at the interval. Both sides missed several chances in the second half, notably Rutledge, who had the ball knocked out of his hands on the point of scoring after a crunching tackle by Biggar. McKechnie kicked

Scottish captain Ian McGeechan with new caps Bob Cunningham, Keith Robertson and Gordon Dickson before the New Zealand game in 1978.
Scotsman Publications Ltd

a long penalty after 61 minutes, but in response McGeechan dropped a goal to set up a dramatic finish. With the match moving into injury-time, Scotland pressed furiously near the New Zealand line and looked likely to score. McGeechan, opting for the draw, attempted another drop at goal, but the ball was charged down. Osborne hacked down field and in the ensuing kick-and-chase Bruce Robertson outpaced the defence to score between the posts. McKechnie converted to seal New Zealand's Grand Slam and enhance his side's reputation as the 'Last Gasp All Blacks'. Scotland had done much better than expected, but there was no doubt that the New Zealanders deserved their win.

338 INTERNATIONAL CHAMPIONSHIP 1979 WALES

Murrayfield · Saturday 20 January 1979 · Lost 13–19

SCOTLAND Andy Irvine (*Heriot's FP*); Keith Robertson (*Melrose*), Jim Renwick (*Hawick*), Ian McGeechan* (*Headingley*), Bruce Hay (*Boroughmuir*); †John Rutherford (*Selkirk*), Alan Lawson (*London Scot*); Ian McLauchlan (*Jordanhill*), Colin Deans (*Hawick*), Bobby Cunningham (*Gala*), Alan Tomes (*Hawick*), Alastair McHarg (*London Scot*), Mike Biggar (*London Scot*), Gordon Dickson (*Gala*), Ian Lambie (*Watsonians*)

WALES JPR Williams* (*Bridgend*); Elgin Rees (*Neath*), Ray Gravell (*Llanelli*), Steve Fenwick (*Bridgend*), JJ Williams (*Llanelli*); Gareth Davies (*Cardiff*), Terry Holmes (*Cardiff*); Charlie Faulkner (*Pontypool*), Bobby Windsor (*Pontypool*), Graham Price (*Pontypool*), Allan Martin (*Aberavon*), Geoff Wheel (*Swansea*), Paul Ringer (*Llanelli*), Jeff Squire (*Pontypool*), Derek Quinnell (*Llanelli*)

REFEREE F Palmade (*France*)

SCORING Fenwick, pen (o–3); Irvine, pen (3–3); Irvine, pen (6–3); Irvine, try (10–3); Fenwick, pen (10–6); Irvine, pen (13–6) (half-time) Fenwick, pen (13–9); Rees, try (13–13); Holmes, try (13–17); Fenwick, con (13–19)

John Rutherford won his first cap. Scotland played resolutely and scored a great try, but their forwards were under a lot of pressure and Wales came through at the end. The country was in the grip of wintery conditions and a bitterly cold wind blew down the pitch which was to be a decisive factor in the course of the game. The Scots played with the elements in the first half, but soon went behind to a Fenwick penalty goal. Irvine kicked two goals and on the 24th minute he both ignited and finished a superb try. Fielding a kick near halfway, he sidestepped past Rees and found support from Hay who made the ball available as he was tackled. Lawson swept a pass to Rutherford who broke up-field before finding support from McGeechan and Tomes. The big lock floated a long, overhead pass back to Irvine who beat the last defenders for a memorable score. He missed the conversion and penalty goals by Fenwick and Irvine saw the Scots 13–6 ahead at the interval. With the wind behind them, Wales started to dominate and Fenwick kicked a penalty within a minute of the restart. Soon after, JPR Williams intruded into an attack up the right and chip ahead perfectly into the path of the accelerating Rees who scored in the corner. In the last five minutes, Wales had a series of punishing scrums on the Scottish line. The Scots defended heroically, but eventually Holmes dived into the mêlée for the decisive try which was converted by Fenwick. For Scotland, John Rutherford's display was the most promising feature of the match.

---

339   INTERNATIONAL CHAMPIONSHIP 1979   ENGLAND

Twickenham · Saturday 3 February 1979 · Drew 7–7

SCOTLAND Andy Irvine (*Heriot's FP*); Keith Robertson (*Melrose*), Jim Renwick (*Hawick*), Ian McGeechan* (*Headingley*), Bruce Hay (*Boroughmuir*); John Rutherford (*Selkirk*), Alan Lawson (London Scot); Ian McLauchlan (*Jordanhill*), Colin Deans (*Hawick*), Bobby Cunningham (*Gala*), Alan Tomes (*Hawick*), Alastair McHarg (*London Scot*), Mike Biggar (*London Scot*), Gordon Dickson (*Gala*), Ian Lambie (*Watsonians*)

ENGLAND Alastair Hignell (*Bristol*); Peter Squires (*Harrogate*), Tony Bond (*Sale*), Paul Dodge (*Leicester*), Mike Slemen (*Liverpool*); Neil Bennett (*London Welsh*), Malcolm Young (*Gosforth*); Robin Cowling (*Leicester*), Peter Wheeler (*Leicester*), Gary Pearce (Northampton), Bill Beaumont (*Fylde*), Nigel Horton (*Toulouse*), Tony Neary (*Broughton Park*), Mike Rafter (*Bristol*), Roger Uttley* (*Gosforth*) … Replacement: John Scott (*Cardiff*) for Uttley (70)

REFEREE Clive Norling (*Wales*)

SCORING Slemen, try (o–4); Bennett, pen (o–7); Rutherford, try (4–7) (half-time) Irvine, pen (7–7)

The teams were introduced to Prince Philip. England ought to have won this match with something to spare. Their powerful forwards dominated throughout, but their backs failed to capitalise. Bennett and Young, the half-backs, never looked comfortable, in part due to the marauding Scottish back-row and the energetic Lawson, and the English centres cut back inside too much when they would have better using their wings. Playing with a strong wind behind them, England scored a textbook try straightaway. Horton won a lineout, the ball was whipped across the field, Hignell intruded from full-back and made an overlap which Sleman finished off in the left corner. Bennett missed the conversion, but added a long range penalty on the fifteenth minute. From a scrum, the Scots worked the ball to Irvine who cut through at full tilt. He kicked ahead and looked certain to score only for Sleman to take his legs from under him. Rutherford followed-up fast and touched down for the try, but Irvine missed the conversion. The irony was that if Rutherford had not scored then the referee would probably have awarded a penalty try, the conversion would have been a formality and the extra two points would, in theory, have given Scotland victory. The second half was a similar story with England winning the bulk of possession, but the only score was a long penalty by Irvine and the match ended in stalemate.

340　　　INTERNATIONAL CHAMPIONSHIP 1979　　　IRELAND

Murrayfield · Saturday 3 March 1979 · Drew 11–11

SCOTLAND Andy Irvine (*Heriot's FP*); Keith Robertson (*Melrose*), Jim Renwick (*Hawick*), Ian McGeechan* (*Headingley*), Bruce Hay (*Boroughmuir*); John Rutherford (*Selkirk*), Alan Lawson (*London Scot*); Ian McLauchlan (*Jordanhill*), Colin Deans (*Hawick*), †Iain Milne (*Heriot's FP*), Alan Tomes (*Hawick*), David Gray (*W of Scot*), Mike Biggar (*London Scot*), Gordon Dickson (*Gala*), Bill Watson (*Boroughmuir*)

IRELAND Ronnie Elliott (*Bangor*); Mike Gibson (*NIFC*), Alistair McKibbin (*London Irish*), Paul McNaughton (*Greystones*), Freddie McLennan (*Wdrs*); Tony Ward (*Garryowen*), Colin Patterson (*Instonians*); Phil Orr (*Old Wesley*), Pat Whelan (*Garryowen*), Gerry McLoughlin (*Shannon*), Moss Keane (*Lansdowne*), Donal Spring (*Dublin U*), Willie Duggan (*Blackrock Coll*), Fergus Slattery* (*Blackrock Coll*), Michael Gibson (*Lansdowne*)

REFEREE Corris Thomas (*Wales*)

SCORING Rutherford, try (4–0); Patterson, try (4–4); Irvine, pen (7–4) (half-time) Irvine, try (11–4); Ward, pen (11–7); Patterson, try (11–11)

Iain Milne won his first cap. Scotland seemed poised to end their miserable run of nine games without a win only to be denied by a late Irish try. This match was played in a strong, swirling wind which made kicking and throwing-in very treacherous. After some 15 minutes, the Scots deflected the ball at a lineout inside Irish territory. Milne rumbled blind, the fleet-footed Deans reached the Irish 22 before linking with Lawson who put Robertson over in the corner. Ireland responded with a try by Paterson from a scrum near the Scottish line. Near the interval, Irvine, with Dickson placing the ball for him, slotted a penalty to give the Scots a 7–4 lead. Early in the second half, the Scots stole the ball from Elliot, Renwick kicked through to the right where Robertson collected and fed Irvine who beat the remains of the defence for an unconverted score. Scotland should have gone on to win, but the Irish staged a comeback. Ward kicked a penalty and with a few minutes remaining the diminutive Paterson picked-up from a scrum near the Scottish line and sped away to the corner for a classic scrum-half's try. Ward's conversion attempt hit an upright, Rutherford miscued a late drop goal and the match ended in a draw, the first between the two countries since 1900. For

Scotland, Iain Milne had an encouraging debut and flanker Gordon Dickson was very industrious.

Parc des Princes, Paris · Saturday 17 March 1979 · Lost 17–21

SCOTLAND   Andy Irvine (*Heriot's FP*); Keith Robertson (*Melrose*), Jim Renwick (*Hawick*); Ian McGeechan* (*Headingley*), Bruce Hay (*Boroughmuir*); John Rutherford (*Selkirk*), Alan Lawson (*London Scot*); Ian McLauchlan (*Jordanhill*), Colin Deans (*Hawick*), Iain Milne (*Heriot's FP*), Alan Tomes (*Hawick*), David Gray (*W of Scot*), Mike Biggar (*London Scot*), Gordon Dickson (*Gala*), Bill Watson (*Boroughmuir*)

FRANCE   Jean-Michel Aguirre (*Bagnéres*); Jean-François Gourdon (*Bagnéres*), Roland Bertranne (*Bagnéres*), Christian Bélascain (*Bayonne*), Frédéric Costes (*Montferrand*); Roger Aguerre (*Biarritz*), Jérôme Gallion (*Toulon*); Gérard Cholley (*Castres*), Alain Paco (*Béziers*), Robert Paparemborde (*Pau*), Francis Haget (*Biarritz*), Jean-François Marchal (*Lourdes*), Jean-Pierre Rives* (*Toulouse*), Jean-Luc Joinel (*Brive*), Yves Malquier (*Narbonne*)

REFEREE   RC Quittenton (*England*)

SCORING   Bélascain, try (0–4); Robertson, try (4–4); Aguirre, pen (4–7); Aguirre, drop (4–10); Dickson, try (8–10); Irvine, con (10–10) (half-time) Irvine, pen (13–10); Malquier, try (13–14); Irvine, try (17–14); Malquier, try (17–18); Aguirre, pen (17–21)

Played in the Parisian sunshine on a firm pitch, this was an exciting and attractive game with lots of open play and plenty of errors. Both sides scored three tries each and the result could have gone either way, but France scraped home thanks to slightly better goal-kicking and stronger forwards. The Scots did much better than expected and started strongly, but France opened the scoring after 13 minutes. The defence was dragged left before the ball was whipped down the line to Gourdon on the overlap. He was checked by Irvine near the corner flag, but flipped an overhead pass inside to Bélascain who scored. A few minutes later, Lawson, who was in fine form throughout, broke away from a scrum inside his own half and kicked deep into the French 22. Rutherford retrieved possession, Hay gave out a brilliant dive pass and the Scottish centres put Robertson away to the corner. Aguirre restored the French lead with a penalty and a drop goal, and then Renwick made a typical sidestepping run to put Dickson over. Irvine converted and in the second half kicked a penalty before Malquier scored his first try. The Scottish backs made a good attack on the French 22, Renwick chipped through perfectly as he was tackled and Irvine raced on to score. Irvine's conversion attempt hit a post and immediately after Malquier scored his second try when he burst onto a chip ahead by Aguirre. Finally, Aguirre, who had mixed day with the boot, kicked a long penalty to seal a memorable game for France.

342 TOUR MATCH NEW ZEALAND

Murrayfield · Saturday 10 November 1979 · Lost 6–20

SCOTLAND   Andy Irvine (*Heriot's FP*); Keith Robertson (*Melrose*), Jim Renwick (*Hawick*), †David Johnston (*Watsonians*), Bruce Hay (*Boroughmuir*); John Rutherford (*Selkirk*),

Alan Lawson (*Heriot's FP*); Ian McLauchlan* (*Jordanhill*), Colin Deans (*Hawick*), Iain Milne (*Heriot's FP*), Alan Tomes (*Hawick*), David Gray (*W of Scot*), Mike Biggar (*London Scot*), Gordon Dickson (*Gala*), Ian Lambie (*Watsonians*)

NEW ZEALAND Richard Wilson (*Canterbury*); Stu Wilson (*Wellington*), Gary Cunningham (*Auckland*), Murray Taylor (*Waikato*), Bernie Fraser (*Wellington*); Eddie Dunn (*North Auckland*), Dave Loveridge (*Taranaki*); Brad Johnstone (*Auckland*), Andy Dalton (*Counties*), John Spiers (*Counties*), Andy Haden (*Auckland*), John Fleming (*Wellington*), Ken Stewart (*Southland*), Graham Mourie* (*Taranaki*), Murray Mexted (*Wellington*) ... Replacement: Mark Donaldson (*Manawatu*) for Loveridge

REFEREE RC Quittenton (*England*)

SCORING Loveridge, try (0–4) (half-time) Mexted, try (0–8); R Wilson, con (0–10); Irvine, pen (3–10); Irvine, pen (6–10); S Wilson, try (6–14); Dunn, try (6–18); R Wilson, con (6–20)

After their good showing the previous year against the Grand Slam All Blacks, the Scots were optimistic that they could record their first win over New Zealand. Captained by Ian McLauchlan, Scotland introduced one new cap in David Johnston, a smooth-running centre from Watsonians who had once signed as part-time football player with Heart of Midlothian. Touted as the best-ever prepared Scotland xv, the home players were their own worst enemies. The forwards competed at the set-pieces, but the backs made too many errors. Their kicking and handling was highly erratic, and the defence was woeful at times. The game started off at a tremendous pace and after 17 minutes New Zealand opened the scoring. From a ruck on the Scottish line, Loveridge sent four defenders the wrong way with an outrageous dummy. After the interval, Mexted scored a memorable solo try that summed-up the difference between the sides. Taking a simple catch at a short lineout, he stormed 30m through some weak tackling to the line. Irvine briefly rekindled hope with two penalties, but the truth was that New Zealand never looked like losing. Wilson and Dunn sealed the match with well-taken tries. None of the Scots enhanced their reputations and for Ian McLauchlan, one of Scotland's great servants, the match was a sad end to a long and distinguished career.

343   INTERNATIONAL CHAMPIONSHIP 1980   IRELAND

Lansdowne Road, Dublin · Saturday 2 February 1980 · Lost 15–22

SCOTLAND Andy Irvine (*Heriot's FP*); †Steve Munro (*Ayr*), Jim Renwick (*Hawick*), David Johnston (*Watsonians*), Bruce Hay (*Boroughmuir*); John Rutherford (*Selkirk*), †Roy Laidlaw (*Jed-Forest*); †Jim Burnett (*Heriot's FP*), Colin Deans (*Hawick*), Iain Milne (*Heriot's FP*), †Bill Cuthbertson (*Kilmarnock*), David Gray (*W of Scot*), Mike Biggar* (*London Scot*), Alex Brewster (*Stew-Mel FP*), †John Beattie (*Glasgow Acs*)

IRELAND Roddy O'Donnell (*St Mary's Coll*); Terry Kennedy (*St Mary's Coll*), Alistair McKibbin (*London Irish*), Paul McNaughton (*Greystones*), Freddie McLennan (*Wdrs*); Olie Campbell (*Old Belvedere*), Colin Patterson (*Instonians*); Phil Orr (*Old Wesley*), Ciaran Fitzgerald (*St Mary's Coll*), Michael Fitzpatrick (*Wdrs*), Jim Glennon (*Skerries*), Moss Keane (*Lansdowne*), John O'Driscoll (*London Irish*), Fergus Slattery* (*Blackrock Coll*), Donal Spring (*Dublin U*)

REFEREE Guilbert Chevrier (*France*)

SCORING Irvine, pen (3–0); Johnston, try (7–0); Irvine, con (9–0); Campbell, pen (9–3); Campbell, pen (9–6); Keane, try (9–10) (half-time) Kennedy, try (9–14); Campbell, con (9–16); Campbell, pen (9–19); Campbell, drop (9–22); Johnston, try (13–22); Irvine, con (15–22)

Scotland fielded five new caps, including scrum-half Roy Laidlaw and No8 John Beattie. Playing in wet and muddy conditions, this was a match where Scotland flattered to deceive. They raced to an early lead with a penalty by Irvine and try by Johnston, but thereafter it was all Ireland. The home side rattled up 22 points without reply until Johnston scored his second try near the end. The Irish forwards were superior in most aspects and typically aggressive in the loose. Scotland's main advantage lay in the lineout, largely through the gigantic David Gray, but often their possession was spoiled by their opponents pouring through the gaps and winning the ball back again. The Scottish backs looked sharp, but never had enough quality possession. The opening try came from a Rutherford break which Renwick carried on. His pass to Johnston didn't go to hand, but the Watsonian centre smartly booted the ball on and won the race to the touchdown. Ollie Campbell missed his first three penalty attempts before landing two to reduce Scotland's lead. Just before the interval, the diminutive Colin Paterson made a great break from his own half and kicked down field. From the ensuing lineout, Campbell swayed back to the narrow side and Keane was in support to break Irvine's tackle and thunder over. Campbell missed the conversion and Ireland led 10–9 at the break. In the second half, Paterson broke away from a maul to put Kennedy over in the corner. Campbell landed the awkward conversion and added a penalty and a drop goal to put Ireland out of reach. Towards the finish, Johnston showed startling pace to score his second try after Rutherford had made a half-break. For Scotland, Roy Laidlaw had an impressive debut despite being under constant pressure.

344   INTERNATIONAL CHAMPIONSHIP 1980   FRANCE

Murrayfield · Saturday 16 February 1980 · Won 22–14

SCOTLAND Andy Irvine (*Heriot's FP*); Steve Munro (*Ayr*), Jim Renwick (*Hawick*), David Johnston (*Watsonians*), Bruce Hay (*Boroughmuir*); John Rutherford (*Selkirk*), Roy Laidlaw (*Jed-Forest*); Jim Burnett (*Heriot's FP*), Colin Deans (*Hawick*), Iain Milne (*Heriot's FP*), Alan Tomes (*Hawick*) David Gray (*W of Scot*), Mike Biggar* (*London Scot*), Alex Brewster (*Stew-Mel FP*) John Beattie (*Glasgow Acs*) … Replacement: †Ken Lawrie (*Gala*) for Deans

FRANCE Serge Gabernet (*Toulouse*); Daniel Bustaffa (*Carcassonne*), Roland Bertranne (*Bagnéres*), Didier Codorniou (*Narbonne*), Jean-Luc Averous (*La Voulte*); Alain Caussade (*Lourdes*), Jérôme Gallion (*Toulon*); Armand Vaquerin (*Béziers*), Philippe Dintrans (*Tarbes*), Robert Paparemborde (*Pau*), Francis Haget (*Biarritz*), Jean-Francis Marchal (*Lourdes*), Jean-Pierre Rives* (*Toulouse*), Jean-Luc Joinel (*Brive*), Michel Clement (*Oloron*)

REFEREE John West (*Ireland*)

SCORING Gallion, try (0–4); Rutherford, try (4–4); Gabernet, pen (4–7) (half-time) Gabernet, try (4–11); Caussade, drop (4–14); Irvine, try (8–14); Irvine, con (10–14); Irvine, try (14–14); Renwick, con (16–14); Irvine, pen (19–14); Irvine, pen (22–14)

In a legendary turnaround, Scotland brought to an end their dismal run of 13 games without a win. Their play had been laboured and uninspiring until the closing minutes

Andy Irvine scores his second try against France in 1980 to seal a sensational Scottish comeback.
Scotsman Publications Ltd

when suddenly they burst into life and rattled up 18 points without reply, 16 from full-back Andy Irvine. This represented an incredible *volte-face* for the Scottish captain who up to this point had done little right. He had missed seven kicks at goal, including one sitter in front of the posts, and was booed by some of his own supporters. But then his attacking genius came to the fore and he ended up by scoring two tries, a conversion and two penalties. France started the match strongly and for much of the time seemed to be heading for a comfortable, if rather mundane victory. Scrum-half Gallion opened the scoring with a try from close range after the French forwards had driven to the line. Rutherford levelled when Renwick hoisted a high kick and Bustaffa, the French right wing, dropped the ball. The Scottish forwards quickly recycled and the stand-off squeezed through a gap near the corner. Gabernet kicked a long penalty to give France a 7–4 lead at the interval. Two minutes after the restart, the same player fielded a high ball inside his own half and set off on a long run leaving defenders in his wake. He exchanged passes with Averous before scoring the try himself, a classic of its kind. A drop goal by Caussade gave France a ten point lead and a steady platform, or so it seemed. With the game slowly slipping away from them, the Scots started to run from deep and suddenly everything changed. From a scrum inside the Scottish half, the ball was whipped out to Irvine who intruded at full speed. Johnston and Hay were in support and although a French hand put the ball to ground near the line Irvine snatched it for a try in the corner. His splendid conversion put the Scots back in business and the ground lit up. With a few minutes remaining, the otherwise excellent Gabernet lost possession in midfield, and Renwick picked up and darted away. The movement swept up-field with Rutherford and Johnston making ground and Irvine was on hand to dive over at the posts. Renwick converted to put Scotland into the lead and in injury-time Irvine kicked two penalties to finish the game off. Whilst Irvine took the plaudits, this was far from a one-man show. Rutherford, Renwick and Johnston provided great support, the pack drove well at times and No8 John Beattie was always prominent.

Cardiff Arms Park · Saturday 1 March 1980 · Lost 6–17

SCOTLAND Andy Irvine (*Heriot's FP*), Keith Robertson (*Melrose*), Jim Renwick (*Hawick*), David Johnston (*Watsonians*), Bruce Hay (*Boroughmuir*); †Bryan Gossman (*W of Scot*), Roy Laidlaw (*Jed-Forest*); Jim Burnett (*Heriot's FP*), Ken Lawrie (*Gala*), Norrie Rowan (*Boroughmuir*), Alan Tomes (*Hawick*), David Gray (*W of Scot*), Mike Biggar* (*London Scot*), Gordon Dickson (*Gala*), John Beattie (*Glasgow Acs*) ... Replacement: Alan Lawson (*Heriot's FP*) for Laidlaw (28)

WALES Roger Blyth (*Swansea*); Elgin Rees (*Neath*), David Richards (*Swansea*), Steve Fenwick (*Bridgend*), Les Keen (*Aberavon*); Gareth Davies (*Cardiff*), Terry Holmes (*Cardiff*); Clive Williams (*Swansea*), Alan Phillips (*Cardiff*), Graham Price (*Pontypool*), Allan Martin (*Aberavon*), Geoff Wheel (*Swansea*), Stuart Lane (*Cardiff*), Jeff Squire* (*Pontypool*), Eddie Butler (*Pontypool*) ... Replacement: Peter Morgan (*Llanelli*) for Davies (36)

REFEREE LM Prideaux (*England*)

SCORING Fenwick, pen (0–3); Holmes, try (0–7) (half-time) Keen, try (0–11); Richards, try (0–15); Blyth, con (0–17); Renwick, try (4–17); Irvine, con (6–17)

Playing on St David's Day, the sides were introduced to the Prince of Wales. John Rutherford and Ron Wilson were unavailable so third-choice stand-off Bryan Gossman made his debut. Two weeks earlier, Wales had taken part in a brutal match at Twickenham and both sides were on their best behaviour. The result was a rather tame encounter that lacked its usual intensity. Wales took the honours with something to spare, scoring three tries to Scotland's one. The home side might have won more convincingly if their backs had not made so many handling errors. The Scots defended well at times, especially at a series of close-range scrums in the first half, but some of their defence was weak. The Scottish forwards dominated at the lineout, where Gray and Tomes excelled, but in other aspects they were outplayed. Much of Scotland's possession was untidy and put the half-backs under a lot of pressure. Their problems were compounded by an injury to Roy Laidlaw who had to leave the field in the first half. The Scottish goal-kicking was also poor. Although well beaten, the Scots made a final flourish and scored the best try of the game. From a breakdown on their 22, the ball was worked to Robertson who made a long, corkscrew run from his own half before giving a perfectly-timed pass to Renwick and the centre eluded the last defender to score under the posts. Renwick showed excellent judgement and pace throughout, and his partner David Johnston had a fine all-round game. No8 John Beattie used his speed and athleticism to good effect and Bryan Gossman marked his first appearance with a shrewd and sturdy effort behind a struggling pack.

Murrayfield · Saturday 15 March 1980 · Lost 18–30

SCOTLAND Andy Irvine* (*Heriot's FP*), Keith Robertson (*Melrose*), Jim Renwick (*Hawick*), David Johnston (*Watsonians*), Bruce Hay (*Boroughmuir*); John Rutherford (*Selkirk*), Roy Laidlaw (*Jed-Forest*); Jim Burnett (*Heriot's FP*), Ken Lawrie (*Gala*), Norrie Rowan (*Boroughmuir*), Alan Tomes (*Hawick*), David Gray (*W of Scot*), David Leslie (*Gala*), Mike Biggar (*London Scot*), John Beattie (*Glasgow Acs*) ... Replacement: †Jim Gossman (*W of Scot*) for Hay (50)

ENGLAND Dusty Hare (*Leicester*); John Carleton (*Orrell*), Clive Woodward (*Leicester*), Paul Dodge (*Leicester*), Mike Slemen (*Liverpool*); John Horton (*Bath*), Steve Smith (*Sale*); Frank Cotton (*Sale*), Peter Wheeler (*Leicester*), Phil Blakeway (*Gloucester*), Bill Beaumont* (*Fylde*), Maurice Colclough (*Angoulême*), Roger Uttley (*Wasps*), Tony Neary (*Broughton Park*), John Scott (*Cardiff*)

REFEREE Jean-Pierre Bonnet (*France*)

SCORING Carleton, try (0–4); Hare, con (0–6); Slemen, try (0–10); Hare, con (0–12); Carleton, try (0–16); Irvine, pen (3–16); Hare, pen (3–19) (half-time) Irvine, pen (6–19); Smith, try (6–23); Tomes, try (10–23); Irvine, con (12–23); Hare, pen (12–26); Carleton, try (12–30); Rutherford, try (16–30); Irvine, con (18–30)

Under the captaincy of the popular Bill Beaumont, England won their first Grand Slam for 23 years. This was classic encounter with lots of attacking rugby and seven tries in total. The Scots put up a good fight and were always ready to run the ball, but the outcome was never in doubt. The big English forwards took a firm grip early on and by the interval the visitors led 19–3 and were largely out of sight. The Scots were overwhelmed by a powerful English scrum which shoved them backwards and wheeled them off the ball. Blessed with an abundance of possession, the English backs carved out many openings and Woodward's purposeful running exposed frailties in the Scottish defence. In the second half, England stretched to 23–6, but the Scots rallied and scored two tries of their own. After some excellent support play, Jim Renwick jinked his way to the English goal-line and Tomes was on hand to dive over. Irvine converted, but hopes of a comeback were soon dashed when Hare kicked a penalty and Carleton scored his third try of the match after Irvine failed to deal with a high ball. Finally, Rutherford cut through the English defence from close range to dot the ball down at the posts. The closing stages were played at a frantic pace, but despite vociferous backing from the home crowd there was no further scoring.

347 INTERNATIONAL CHAMPIONSHIP 1981 FRANCE

Parc des Princes, Paris · Saturday 17 January 1981 · Lost 9–16

SCOTLAND Andy Irvine* (*Heriot's FP*); Steve Munro (*Ayr*), Jim Renwick (*Hawick*), Keith Robertson (*Melrose*), Bruce Hay (*Boroughmuir*); John Rutherford (*Selkirk*), Roy Laidlaw (*Jed-Forest*); Norrie Rowan (*Boroughmuir*), Colin Deans (*Hawick*), Jim Aitken (*Gala*), Alan Tomes (*Hawick*), David Gray (*W of Scot*), †Jim Calder (*Stew-Mel FP*), Gordon Dickson (*Gala*), John Beattie (*Heriot's FP*)

FRANCE Serge Gabernet (*Toulouse*); Serge Blanco (*Biarritz*), Roland Bertranne (*Bagnéres*), Didier Codorniou (*Narbonne*), Laurent Pardo (*Bayonne*); Bernard Viviès (*Agen*), Pierre Berbizier (*Lourdes*); Pierre Dospital (*Bayonne*), Philippe Dintranes (*Tarbes*), Robert Paparemborde (*Pau*), Daniel Revallier (*Graulhet*), Jean-François Imbernon (*Perpignan*), Jean-Pierre Rives* (*Toulouse*), Jean-Luc Joinel (*Brives*), Manuel Carpentier (*Lourdes*) ... Replacement: Alain Caussade (*Lourdes*) for Viviès (30)

REFEREE Ken Rowlands (*Wales*) · **ATTENDANCE** 44,448

SCORING Blanco, try (0–4); Viviès, pen (0–7); Irvine, pen (3–7); Gabernet, pen (3–10); Bertranne, try (3–14); Caussade, con (3–16) (half-time) Rutherford, try (7–16); Renwick, con (9–16)

Scotland were very nervous in the first half, during which France scored two exciting tries. The visitors improved after the break and Rutherford scored a memorable try when he ghosted through the French defence and round to the posts. Jim Renwick converted to complete the scoring. The Scots never looked like winning, but they might have done better if a controversial decision had gone their way near the end. Renwick charged down a kick and sprinted clear from the French 22. He was tap-tackled just short of the line, but he regained his footing to dive over at the posts. The referee ruled that the ball had touched the ground before the goal-line and gave a penalty to France, but to most onlookers Renwick seemed to have scored a perfectly good try. Immediately afterwards, Irvine missed a simple penalty chance that, had Renwick's try been given, would have put Scotland in the lead. Overall this was a disappointing display by Scotland and much of their play lacked conviction. The forwards were always second best although new cap Jim Calder showed plenty of promise.

348   INTERNATIONAL CHAMPIONSHIP 1981   WALES

Murrayfield · Saturday 7 February 1981 · Won 15–6

SCOTLAND Andy Irvine* (*Heriot's FP*); Steve Munro (*Ayr*), Jim Renwick (*Hawick*), Keith Robertson (*Melrose*), Bruce Hay (*Boroughmuir*); John Rutherford (*Selkirk*), Roy Laidlaw (*Jed-Forest*); Norrie Rowan (*Boroughmuir*), Colin Deans (*Hawick*), Jim Aitken (*Gala*), Alan Tomes (*Hawick*), Bill Cuthbertson (*Kilmarnock*), Jim Calder (*Stew-Mel FP*), David Leslie (*Gala*), John Beattie (*Heriot's FP*)

WALES JPR Williams (*Bridgend*); Robert Ackerman (*Newport*), David Richards (*Swansea*), Steve Fenwick* (*Bridgend*), David Nicholas (*Llanelli*); Gareth Davies (*Cardiff*), Brynmor Williams (*Swansea*); Ian Stephens (*Bridgend*), Allan Phillips (*Cardiff*), Graham Price (*Pontypool*), Clive Davies (*Newbridge*), Geoff Wheel (*Swansea*), Rhodri Lewis (*Cardiff & SGIHE*), Jeff Squire (*Pontypool*), Gareth Williams (*Bridgend*) … Replacement: Gwyn Evans (*Maesteg*) for Nicholas (h-t)

REFEREE David Burnett (*Ireland*)

SCORING Renwick, pen (3–0); Fenwick, pen (3–3); Tomes, try (7–3); Renwick, con (9–3); Fenwick, pen (9–6) (half-time) penalty try (13–6); Renwick, con (15–6)

This comprehensive victory, the first over Wales for six years, marked a turning point in Scottish fortunes. With two changes in the pack, Scotland were unrecognisable from the tentative side that had lost in Paris. Beattie, Tomes and Cuthbertson excelled in the lineout and the marauding Leslie was a constant menace to the Welsh midfield. Playing on a heavy pitch the Welsh back division, which included some legendary players, was never allowed to settle. After an early exchange of penalties, Renwick fed Robertson 'on the pop' and the Melrose centre made a weaving run before finding support from Calder and Deans. The former was caught just short of the line, but Tomes was on hand to pick-up and dive over. Ten minutes before time, Hay hacked on a loose pass and in the ensuing footrace Davies was adjudged to have held back Irvine illegally and the referee awarded a penalty try to Scotland, the first in the history of the championship. Renwick kicked the simple conversion to seal a great Scottish win.

Twickenham · Saturday 21 February 1981 · Lost 17–23

SCOTLAND Andy Irvine* (*Heriot's FP*); Steve Munro (*Ayr*), Jim Renwick (*Hawick*), Keith Robertson (*Melrose*), Bruce Hay (*Boroughmuir*); John Rutherford (*Selkirk*), Roy Laidlaw (*Jed-Forest*); Jim Aitken (*Gala*), Colin Deans (*Hawick*), Norrie Rowan (*Boroughmuir*), Bill Cuthbertson (*Kilmarnock*), Alan Tomes (*Hawick*), Jim Calder (*Stew-Mel FP*), David Leslie (*Gala*), John Beattie (*Heriot's FP*)

ENGLAND Dusty Hare (*Leicester*); John Carleton (*Orrell*), Clive Woodward (*Leicester*), Paul Dodge (*Leicester*), Mike Slemen (*Liverpool*); Huw Davies (*Coventry*), Steve Smith (*Sale*); Colin Smart (*Newport*), Peter Wheeler (*Leicester*), Phil Blakeway (*Gloucester*), Bill Beaumont* (*Fylde*), Maurice Colclough (*Augoulême*), Nick Jeavons (*Moseley*), David Cooke (*Harlequins*), John Scott (*Cardiff*) ... Replacement: Bob Hesford (*Bristol*) for Jeavons (14)

REFEREE David Burnett (*Ireland*)

SCORING Irvine, pen (3–0); Hare, pen (3–3); Munro, try (7–3); Woodward, try (7–7); Hare, con (7–9) (half-time); Munro, try (11–9); Irvine, con (13–9); Hare, pen (13–12); Slemen, try (13–16); Calder, try (17–16); Davies, try (17–20); Hare, pen (17–23)

This was a great championship encounter that was full of incident and open play. Both sides scored three tries, including some spectacular efforts, the lead changed hands five times and the result was in doubt almost until the end. After an early penalty exchange, Renwick hunted for a break before kicking ahead. The bounce beat the defence, Munro hacked on and just got to the ball before it ran out of play. Then from a lineout, Davies, the new English stand-off, made a scissor in midfield with Woodward who weaved his way through the heart of the Scottish defence, wrong-footing Hay as he dived over the line. Hare converted to make it 9–7 to England at the interval. Seven minutes into the second half, Munro scored his second try after some excellent handling by the Scots. England replied with a Hare penalty and a try by Slemen. Scotland recaptured the lead with some ten minutes left. From a wheeled scrum, Laidlaw picked-up and chipped into space, the Scots took the ball on and Calder crashed over the line. For a few minutes, Scotland seemed to be heading for victory, but then England launched a movement from inside their own half and Carleton made a long run before feeding Davies who outstripped the last of the defence. A late penalty by Hare sealed England's win, but neither side deserved to lose a magnificent match.

Murrayfield · Saturday 21 March 1981 · Won 10–9

SCOTLAND Andy Irvine* (*Heriot's FP*); Steve Munro (*Ayr*), Jim Renwick (*Hawick*), Keith Robertson (*Melrose*), Bruce Hay (*Boroughmuir*); John Rutherford (*Selkirk*), Roy Laidlaw (*Jed-Forest*); Jim Aitken (*Gala*), Colin Deans (*Hawick*), Norrie Rowan (*Boroughmuir*), Bill Cuthbertson (*Kilmarnock*), Alan Tomes (*Hawick*), Jim Calder (*Stew-Mel FP*), David Leslie (*W of Scot*), John Beattie (*Heriot's FP*)

IRELAND Hugo MacNeill (*Dublin U*); Kenny Hooks (*QU Belfast*), David Irwin (*QU Belfast*), Ollie Campbell (*Old Belvedere*), Freddie McLennan (*Wdrs*); Tony Ward (*Garryowen*),

John Robbie (*Greystones*); Phil Orr (*Old Wesley*), John Cantrell (*Blackrock Coll*), Michael Fitzpatrick (*Wdrs*), Moss Keane (*Lansdowne*), Brendan Foley (*Shannon*), John O'Driscoll (*London Irish*), Fergus Slattery* (*Blackrock Coll*), Willie Duggan (*Blackrock Coll*)

REFEREE Laurie Prideaux (*England*)

SCORING Rutherford, drop (3–0); Hay, try (7–0); Irvine, pen (10–0) (half-time) Campbell, pen (10–3); Irwin, try (10–7); Campbell, con (10–9)

Miserable weather conditions and a sodden pitch spoiled this match as a spectacle, but Scotland were happy enough with their second win of the season. Rutherford opened the scoring with a drop goal before Hay intercepted a loose pass and ran half the length of the field for a spectacular try. Irvine missed the conversion, but kicked a penalty to give Scotland a 10–0 lead at the interval. Ireland had the better of the second-half and were rewarded with a Campbell penalty and a converted try by Irwin who charged down an Irvine clearance near the Scottish line. Scotland managed to resist a late Irish rally to consign the championship favourites to a whitewash.

351 TOUR OF NEW ZEALAND 1981   NEW ZEALAND

Carisbrook, Dunedin · Saturday 13 June 1981 · Lost 4–11

SCOTLAND Andy Irvine* (*Heriot's FP*); Steve Munro (*Ayr*), Alastair Cranston (*Hawick*), Jim Renwick (*Hawick*), Bruce Hay (*Boroughmuir*); John Rutherford (*Selkirk*), Roy Laidlaw (*Jed-Forest*); Jim Aitken (*Gala*), Colin Deans (*Hawick*), Iain Milne (*Heriot's FP*), Bill Cuthbertson (*Kilmarnock*), Alan Tomes (*Hawick*), David Leslie (*Gala*), Jim Calder (*Stew-Mel FP*), †Iain Paxton (*Selkirk*)

NEW ZEALAND Allan Hewson (*Wellington*); Stu Wilson (*Wellington*), Bruce Robertson (*Counties*), Andy Jefferd (*East Coast*), Bernie Fraser (*Wellington*); Eddie Dunn (*N Auckland*), Dave Loveridge (*Taranaki*); Rod Ketels (*Counties*), Andy Dalton (*Counties*), Gary Knight (*Manawatu*), Haydn Rickit (*Waikato*), Graeme Higginson (*Canterbury*), Mark Shaw (*Manawatu*), Graham Mourie* (*Taranaki*), Murray Mexted (*Wellington*)

REFEREE Dick Byres (*Australia*)

SCORING Hewson, pen (0–3) (half-time) Loveridge, try (0–7); Wilson, try (0–11); Deans, try (4–11)

In the summer of 1981, Scotland made an eight-match tour of New Zealand under the captaincy of Andy Irvine. The First Test at Dunedin was played in an icy cold wind and sweeping sheets of rain. The sides were evenly matched and Scotland might have won if they had taken their chances and had a bit of luck. In the first half, Munro missed a sitter when he failed to gather the ball on the New Zealand line. He was also denied a momentum try when the referee ruled, perhaps mistakenly, that he had made an illegal movement to get over the line. New Zealand led by a solitary penalty goal at the interval and stretched away in a decisive period early in the second half. At a scrum on their own line, the Scots heeled the ball backwards, but the quick-thinking Loveridge dived in at their feet to touch down. A few minutes later, Jeffred sent a long pass to Wilson who scored in the corner. Ten minutes from time, the Scots hacked the ball on from a loose lineout tap and the mobile Deans won the race for the touchdown. Scotland finished strongly, but could not score again and a great chance for a historic win was lost. For Scotland, Hay's tackling was very solid, Rutherford kicked astutely, the front row had the better of their opponents and new No 8 Iain Paxton was not overawed by the big occasion.

352   TOUR OF NEW ZEALAND 1981   NEW ZEALAND

Eden Park, Auckland · Saturday 20 June 1981 · Lost 15–40

SCOTLAND Andy Irvine* (*Heriot's FP*); Steve Munro (*Ayr*), Alastair Cranston (*Hawick*), Jim Renwick (*Hawick*), Bruce Hay (*Boroughmuir*); John Rutherford (*Selkirk*), Roy Laidlaw (*Jed-Forest*); Jim Aitken (*Gala*), Colin Deans (*Hawick*), Iain Milne (*Heriot's FP*), Bill Cuthbertson (*Kilmarnock*), Alan Tomes (*Hawick*), David Leslie (*Gala*), Jim Calder (*Stew-Mel FP*), Iain Paxton (*Selkirk*)

NEW ZEALAND Allan Hewson (*Wellington*); Stu Wilson (*Wellington*), Bruce Robertson (*Counties*), Andy Jefferd (*East Coast*), Bernie Fraser (*Wellington*); Douglas Rollerson (*Manawatu*), David Loveridge (*Taranaki*); Rod Ketels (*Counties*), Andy Dalton (*Counties*), Gary Knight (*Manawatu*), Haydn Rickit (*Waikato*), Andy Haden (*Auckland*), Mark Shaw (*Manawatu*), Graham Mourie* (*Taranaki*), Murray Mexted (*Wellington*)

REFEREE CK Collett (*Australia*)

SCORING Wilson, try (0–4); Hewson, con (0–6); Irvine, pen (3–6); Renwick, drop (6–6); Hewson, try (6–10) (half-time) Mourie, try (6–14); Hewson, con (6–16); Wilson, try (6–20); Hewson, con (6–22); Hay, try (10–22); Irvine, con (12–22); Irvine, pen (15–22); Hewson, try (15–26); Hewson, con (15–28); Wilson, try (15–32); Hewson, con (15–34); Robertson, try (15–38); Hewson, con (15–40)

The final score does not truly reflect the nature of this fast and open encounter. At one stage in the second half, Scotland were only seven points down and had several opportunities to close the gap even further. Munro made an interception on his own 22 and raced away, but was hunted down by Fraser. Then Calder crossed the line only to be recalled because of a forward pass. Scotland lost a little concentration and heart after these incidents and the New Zealanders scored three converted tries in the closing stages to take the game away from the tourists. Earlier, Scotland had shown great self-belief to twice pull back into contention. New Zealand started with an early try by Wilson before Irvine kicked a penalty and Renwick dropped a goal. Just before the interval, Hewson raced onto a kick ahead by Robertson and in the second half Mourie and Wilson scored tries to give New Zealand a comfortable lead. Scotland rallied with a try by Hay who made a scissor with Laidlaw before crashing through several tackles. Irvine converted and kicked a penalty, and for a few moments Scotland seemed poised for victory only for the All Blacks to make their devastating late surge.

353   TOUR MATCH   ROMANIA

Murrayfield · Saturday 26 September 1981 · Won 12–6

SCOTLAND Andy Irvine* (*Heriot's FP*); Steve Munro (*W of Scot*), Jim Renwick (*Hawick*), David Johnston (*Watsonians*), Keith Robertson (*Melrose*); Ron Wilson (*London Scot*),

Roy Laidlaw (*Jed-Forest*); Jim Aitken (*Gala*), Colin Deans (*Hawick*), Iain Milne (*Heriot's FP*), Bill Cuthbertson (*Kilmarnock*), Alan Tomes (*Hawick*), Jim Calder (*Stew-Mel FP*), David Leslie (*Gala*), Iain Paxton (*Selkirk*)

ROMANIA Gheorghe Florea (*Farul Constanta*); Sorin Fuicu (*Steaua*), Adrian Lungu (*Farul Constanta*), Ion Constantin (*Dinamo*), Marian Aldea (*Dinamo*), Dumitru Alexandru (*Steaua*), Mircea Parachiv* (*Dinamo*); Ion Bucan (*Stiinta Petrosani*), Mircea Munteanu (*Steaua*), Octavian Corneliu (*Steaua*), Gheorghe Dumitru (*Farul Constanta*), Gheorghe Caragea (*Dinamo*), Alexandru Radulescu (*Steaua*), Enciu Stoica (*Dinamo*), Pompilie Bors (*Dinamo*)

REFEREE Michael Rea (*Ireland*)

SCORING Irvine, pen (3–0); Irvine, pen (6–0); Constantin, pen (6–3); Irvine, pen (9–3); Constantin, pen (9–6) (half-time) Irvine, pen (12–6)

Romanian rugby was in the ascendancy in the early 1980s and in September 1981 Romania made a three-match tour of Scotland. They beat Edinburgh (18–13) and the South (18–10) before playing Scotland at Murrayfield. The Scots awarded caps against an 'emerging' nation for the first time. Unfortunately, the weather conditions were appalling with a strong wind sweeping heavy rain down the pitch. Even the normally parsimonious SRU showed a little sympathy and midway through the first-half the grandstand was opened for bedraggled spectators on the terraces. The elements were not conducive to a handling game and this was a drab encounter without any tries. Romania were very unimaginative and rarely used their backs whereas Scotland showed at least some willingness to attack. The Scottish forwards were largely in control and some of their rucking was excellent. At full-back, Andy Irvine was secure under the high ball despite the conditions and kicked all of Scotland's points. In so doing, he surpassed the existing world record of points scoring in international matches which previously had been held by New Zealand full-back Don Clarke. London Scottish stand-off Ron Wilson, brought in as a late replacement for John Rutherford, also had a good match.

354   TOUR MATCH   AUSTRALIA

Murrayfield · Saturday 19 December 1981 · Won 24–15

SCOTLAND Andy Irvine* (*Heriot's FP*); Keith Robertson (*Melrose*), Jim Renwick (*Hawick*), David Johnston (*Watsonians*), †Roger Baird (*Kelso*); John Rutherford (*Selkirk*), Roy Laidlaw (*Jed-Forest*); Jim Aitken (*Gala*), Colin Deans (*Hawick*), Iain Milne (*Heriot's FP*), Bill Cuthbertson (*Kilmarnock*), Alan Tomes (*Hawick*), Jim Calder (*Stew-Mel FP*), David Leslie (*Gala*), Iain Paxton (*Selkirk*)

AUSTRALIA Roger Gould (*Queensland*); Mitchell Cox (*NSW*), Andrew Slack (*Queensland*), Paul McLean (*Queensland*), Brendan Moon (*Queensland*); Mark Ella (*NSW*), Phillip Cox (*NSW*); John Meadows (*Victoria*), Chris Carberry (*Queensland*), Tony D'Arcy (*Queensland*), Tony Shaw* (*Queensland*), Peter McLean (*Queensland*), Simon Poidevin (*NSW*), Greg Cornelsen (*NSW*), Mark Loane (*Queensland*)

REFEREE Roger Quittenton (*England*)

SCORING Irvine, pen (3–0); Poidevin, try (3–4); Irvine, pen (6–4); Irvine, pen (9–4); Moon, try (9–8); McLean, pen (9–11); Slack, try (9–15); Irvine, pen (12–15) (half-time) Irvine, pen (15–15); Rutherford, drop (18–15); Renwick, try (22–15); Irvine, con (24–15)

The Australians were making a 23-match tour of the British Isles and spent a week in Scotland where they defeated Glasgow (31–0) and the North and Midlands (36–6) before heading to a snow-bound Murrayfield. Scotland lost the try count, but deserved to win the match because of their superior forward play and Andy Irvine's prodigious kicking, landing five penalties and a conversion. The Scots took precious few risks and relied on an incessant barrage of towering Rutherford up-and-unders. The backs made a few careless errors, but they defended well and the forwards dominated at the set-pieces and in the loose. No 8 Iain Paxton had an outstanding match and he was well supported by Leslie, Calder and Deans. Unable to develop much momentum, the quick-thinking Australians did well to score three tries in the first half. Poidevin charged down a sluggish clearance by Irvine to score the first try and then McLean floated a cross-field kick to Moon standing unmarked at the left corner. Australia's third was the best move of the match. Counter-attacking from deep, the backs combined to release Moon who drew the cover before feeding Slack on the overlap for a try in the corner. McLean missed all three conversions and several other kicks. Australia held a narrow lead at the interval, but the Scots gradually moved ahead in the second period. Towards the end, Rutherford dropped a goal and Renwick scored a try at the posts after the defence completely missed a high kick. Australian frustration boiled over when their captain Tony Shaw flattened Cuthbertson with a vicious punch right in front of the referee. Shaw, who later claimed that he was provoked, was fortunate not to be sent-off, but he apologised for his behaviour immediately after the match.

---

355   INTERNATIONAL CHAMPIONSHIP 1982   ENGLAND

Murrayfield · Saturday 15 January 1982 · Drawn 9–9

SCOTLAND Andy Irvine* (*Heriot's FP*); Keith Robertson (*Melrose*), Jim Renwick (*Hawick*), David Johnston (*Watsonians*), Roger Baird (*Kelso*); John Rutherford (*Selkirk*), Roy Laidlaw (*Jed-Forest*); Jim Aitken (*Gala*), Colin Deans (*Hawick*), Iain Milne (*Heriot's FP*), Alan Tomes (*Hawick*), Bill Cuthbertson (*Kilmarnock*), Jim Calder (*Stew-Mel FP*), David Leslie (*Gala*), Iain Paxton (*Selkirk*)

ENGLAND Marcus Rose (*Cambridge U*); John Carleton (*Orrell*), Clive Woodward (*Leicester*), Paul Dodge (*Leicester*), Mike Slemen (*Liverpool*); Huw Davies (*Cambridge U*), Steve Smith (*Sale*); Colin Smart (*Newport*), Peter Wheeler (*Leicester*), Gary Pearce (*Northampton*), Bill Beaumont* (*Fylde*), Maurice Colclough (*Angoulême*), Nick Jeavons (*Moseley*), Peter Winterbottom (*Headingley*), Bob Hesford (*Bristol*)

REFEREE Keith Rowlands (*Wales*)

SCORING Rutherford, drop (3–0); Dodge, pen (3–3); Irvine, pen (6–3); Dodge, pen (6–6); Rose, pen (6–9) (half-time) Irvine, pen (9–9)

The famous electric blanket at Murrayfield allowed this match to take place despite the country being covered in deep snow. This was an undistinguished encounter remembered only for its exciting conclusion. England held a three-point lead deep in injury-time, but Colin Smart obstructed Paxton off the ball and Scotland were awarded a penalty just inside their own half. Under enormous pressure, Irvine gave the ball 'a real hoof' and his incredible kick salvaged a draw. Playing into a strong wind, Scotland started the match brightly and Rutherford dropped a goal within five minutes. Dodge replied with a penalty before an Irvine goal in the 26th minute. Dodge and Rose kicked further penalties to put England ahead and the rest was Irvine.

356   INTERNATIONAL CHAMPIONSHIP 1982   IRELAND

Lansdowne Road, Dublin · Saturday 20 February 1982 · Lost 12–21

SCOTLAND Andy lrvine* (*Heriot's FP*); Keith Robertson (*Melrose*), Jim Renwick (*Hawick*), David Johnston (*Watsonians*), Roger Baird (*Kelso*); John Rutherford (*Selkirk*), Roy Laidlaw (*Jed-Forest*); Jim Aitken (*Gala*), Colin Deans (*Hawick*), Iain Milne (*Heriot's FP*), Bill Cuthbertson (*Kilmarnock*), Alan Tomes (*Hawick*), Jim Calder (*Stew-Mel FP*), †Eric Paxton (*Kelso*), Iain Paxton (*Selkirk*)

IRELAND Hugo MacNeill (*Dublin U*); Moss Finn (*Cork Const*), Michael Kiernan (*Dolphin*), Paul Dean (*St Mary's Coll*), Keith Crossan (*Instonians*); Ollie Campbell (*Old Belvedere*), Robbie McGrath (*Wanderers*); Phil Orr (*Old Wesley*), Ciaran Fitzgerald* (*St Mary's Coll*), Gerry McLoughlin (*Shannon*), Moss Keane (*Lansdowne*), Donal Lenihan (*UC Cork*), Fergus Slattery (*Blackrock Coll*), John O'Driscoll (*London Irish*), Willie Duggan (*Blackrock Coll*)

REFEREE Clive Norling (*Wales*)

SCORING Campbell, pen (0–3); Campbell, pen (0–6); Rutherford, try (4–6); Irvine, con (6–6); Campbell, pen (6–9); Campbell, drop (6–12); Campbell, pen (6–15) (half-time) Campbell, pen (6–18); Renwick, pen (9–18); Campbell, pen (9–21); Renwick, pen (12–21)

Scotland were the bridesmaids as the jubilant Irish clinched their first Triple Crown for 33 years. Ollie Campbell, the Irish stand-off, kicked all of his side's points and in truth the home side never looked like losing. Under the inspired leadership of Ciaran Fitzgerald, the veteran Irish forwards always had the edge and provided a solid platform for Campbell to work his magic. By contrast, much of the Scottish play was tentative and uncertain. Irvine missed four successive penalty attempts before handing over the kicking duties to Renwick. Scotland could take some consolation from scoring the only try of the match, a brilliantly worked effort by the half-backs. From a shortened lineout just inside the Irish half, Laidlaw dummied and made a searing break before linking with Rutherford who outstripped the rest of the defence on a long run to the line. It was a rare moment of elation for the Scots on a day that belonged firmly to Ireland.

357   INTERNATIONAL CHAMPIONSHIP 1982   FRANCE

Murrayfield · Saturday 6 March 1982 · Won 16–7

SCOTLAND Andy Irvine* (*Heriot's FP*); Keith Robertson (*Melrose*), Jim Renwick (*Hawick*), David Johnston (*Watsonians*), Roger Baird (*Kelso*); John Rutherford (*Selkirk*), Roy Laidlaw (*Jed-Forest*); Jim Aitken (*Gala*), Colin Deans (*Hawick*), Iain Milne (*Heriot's FP*), Bill Cuthbertson (*Kilmarnock*), Alan Tomes (*Hawick*), Jim Calder (*Stew-Mel FP*), †Derek White (*Gala*), Iain Paxton (*Selkirk*)

FRANCE Marc Sallefranque (*Dax*); Serge Blanco (*Biarritz*), Patrick Perrier (*Bayonne*), Christian Bélascain (*Bayonne*), Laurent Pardo (*Bayonne*); Jean-Patrick Lescarboura (*Dax*),

Gerald Martinez (*Toulouse*); Michel Cremaschi (*Lourdes*), Philippe Dintrans (*Tarbes*),
Daniel Dubroca (*Agen*), Daniel Revallier (*Graulhet*), Laurent Rodriguez (*Mont-de-Marsan*),
Jean-Pierre Rives* (*Toulouse*), Jean-Luc Joinel (*Brive*), Manuel Carpentier (*Lourdes*)

REFEREE   Tony Trigg (*England*)

SCORING   Irvine, pen (3–0); Rives, try (3–4); Sallefranque, pen (3–7) (half-time) Irvine, pen (6–7);
Renwick, drop (9–7); Rutherford, try (13–7); Irvine, pen (16–7)

On a wet afternoon, Scotland were worthy winners of a scrappy and undistinguished
match that was marred by a whistle-happy referee. The Scots made a fine start and
Irvine kicked a penalty after two minutes. France responded with a dynamic try by
Rives who somehow escaped from a scrum on the Scottish 22 and made it all the way
to the posts. In the second half, the Scottish forwards took charge and the Frenchmen
became increasingly disorganised and ineffectual. A penalty by Irvine, who earlier
had missed three attempts, and a drop goal by Renwick put the Scots into the lead.
Laidlaw made a break from a ruck in midfield and when the move broke down he
slipped left and passed to Rutherford who found a big enough gap to score out wide.
Towards the finish, Scotland were awarded a penalty, which was advanced a further
ten metres because of French indiscipline, and Irvine kicked the goal from near halfway. Scotland ended firmly in control and perhaps should have won more convincingly. This was the last match played in front of the old east terrace and its famous
scoreboard before the construction of the new east stand.

---

358   INTERNATIONAL CHAMPIONSHIP 1982   WALES

Cardiff Arms Park   ·   Saturday 20 March 1982   ·   Won 34–18

SCOTLAND   Andy Irvine* (*Heriot's FP*); †Jim Pollock (*Gosforth*), Jim Renwick (*Hawick*),
David Johnston (*Watsonians*), Roger Baird (*Kelso*); John Rutherford (*Selkirk*), Roy Laidlaw
(*Jed-Forest*); Jim Aitken (*Gala*), Colin Deans (*Hawick*), Iain Milne (*Heriot's FP*), Bill Cuthbertson
(*Kilmarnock*), Alan Tomes (*Hawick*), Jim Calder (*Stew-Mel FP*), Derek White (*Gala*), Iain Paxton
(*Selkirk*) … Replacement: Gordon Dickson (*Gala*) for Paxton (11)

WALES   Gwyn Evans (*Maesteg*); Robert Ackerman (*Newport*), Ray Gravell (*Llanelli*),
Alun Donovan (*Swansea*), Clive Rees (*London Welsh*); Gareth Davies* (*Cardiff*), Gerald Williams
(*Bridgend*); Ian Stephens (*Bridgend*), Alan Phillips (Cardiff), Graham Price (*Pontypool*),
Robert Norster (*Cardiff*), Richard Moriarty (*Swansea*), Clive Burgess (*Ebbw Vale*), Rhodri Lewis
(*Cardiff*), Eddie Butler (*Pontypool*)

REFEREE   Jean-Pierre Bonnet (*France*)

SCORING   Evans, pen (0–3); Calder, try (3–4); Renwick, drop (7–3); Renwick, try (11–3); Irvine,
con (13–3); Evans, pen (13–6); Evans, pen (13–9) (half-time) Pollock, try (17–9); Irvine, con
(19–9); White, try (23–9); Irvine, con (25–9); Johnston, try (29–9); Irvine, con (31–9); Rutherford,
drop (34–9); Butler, try (34–13); Evans, con (34–15); Evans, pen (34–18)

Gosforth's Jim Pollock, who was known as 'Lucky Jim' because of his happy knack
for appearing on the winning side, came in as a late replacement for flu victim Keith
Robertson. In an astonishing and completely unexpected result, Scotland won at
Cardiff for the first time in 20 years and inflicted on Wales their first Championship
defeat at home since 1968. The Scots scored five sparkling tries and long before the

finish the home crowd were applauding their sense of adventure. After an early penalty, Wales made a promising attack, but Gareth Davies, with a clear overlap outside him, kicked ahead and the ball fell to Roger Baird who escaped up the left touchline. Paxton carried on to the Welsh 22 and Tomes was in support to give Calder a scoring pass. It was a breathtaking try marred only by an injury to Paxton who fell awkwardly in the tackle. Renwick dropped a goal and then scored a great breakout try after Calder had pilfered the ball in midfield. The veteran centre ran half the length of the field and pushed off a tackle from behind to score at the posts. Irvine kicked the simple conversion and Evans landed two penalties to make it 13–9 to Scotland at the interval. Scotland were simply rampant in an awe-inspiring second half. Capitalising on a Welsh mistake, they swept downfield before passing right to Pollock who dived over at the corner. Irvine kicked a touchline conversion and also converted a try by White from a five-metre scrum. Scotland's fifth try came when Rutherford fainted a drop goal before switching right and Johnston floated through the defence. After years of frustration and disappointment, this was a remarkable display by the Scots. The loose forwards were fast to the breakdowns and forced Wales into costly errors. The Scottish rucking and support play was first class and the defence was solid. The irrepressible Jim Renwick orchestrated the three-quarter line with great aplomb and jinked around eagerly looking for gaps. Renwick had played for Scotland for a decade, but this was the first time in his long career that he had won away from home.

---

359   TOUR OF AUSTRALIA 1982   AUSTRALIA

Ballymore, Brisbane · Sunday 4 July 1982 · Won 12–7

SCOTLAND Andy Irvine* (*Heriot's FP*); Keith Robertson (*Melrose*), †Rick Gordon (*London Scot*), David Johnston (*Watsonians*), Roger Baird (*Kelso*); John Rutherford (*Selkirk*), Roy Laidlaw (*Jed-Forest*); †Gerry McGuinness (*W of Scot*), Colin Deans (*Hawick*), Iain Milne (*Heriot's FP*), Bill Cuthbertson (*Kilmarnock*), Alan Tomes (*Hawick*), Jim Calder (*Stew-Mel FP*), Derek White (*Gala*), Iain Paxton (*Selkirk*)

AUSTRALIA Glen Ella (*NSW*); Michael Hawker (*NSW*), Michael O'Connor (*Queensland*), Andrew Slack (*Queensland*), Brendan Moon (*Queensland*); Mark Ella (*NSW*), Phillip Cox (*NSW*); Tony D'Arcy (*Queensland*), Bill Ross (*Queensland*), Stan Pilecki (*Queensland*), Duncan Hall (*Queensland*), Peter McLean (*Queensland*), Tony Shaw (*Queensland*), Chris Roche (*Queensland*), Mark Loane* (*Queensland*)

REFEREE Dick Byres (*Australia*)

SCORING Rutherford, drop (3–0); Hawker, pen (3–3) (half-time) Robertson, try (7–3); Irvine, con (9–3); Hawker, try (9–7); Irvine, pen (12–7)

Captained by Andy Irvine, who won his 50th cap in this game, Scotland made a nine-match tour of Australia in the summer of 1982. The Scots did reasonably well in their provincial games and then made history by winning a full international match in the southern hemisphere for the first time. Play was close and rigorously contested. Both sides made many errors and as a result the match was rather unspectacular. Australia dominated the first half, but they could not penetrate a tight Scottish defence and the scores were level at the interval. Early on Rutherford dropped a goal and a few minutes before half-time Hawker equalised with a penalty, his only successful kick of the game. The Scottish forwards played with greater authority in the second half and started to control the scrums and in loose play. After some 12 minutes, Deans made a strike against the head inside the Australian 22 and the ball was passed quickly to Robertson who scored in the corner. Irvine converted from the touchline. Hawker took advantage of a Scottish defensive error to score an unconverted try and Irvine responded with a long penalty after some Australian foul play. The outcome was uncertain until the finish, but the Scots held on for a historic victory that stunned the Australian crowd.

360 · TOUR OF AUSTRALIA 1982 · AUSTRALIA

Sydney Cricket Ground · Saturday 10 July 1982 · Lost 9–33

SCOTLAND Andy Irvine* (*Heriot's FP*); Keith Robertson (*Melrose*), Rick Gordon (*London Scot*), David Johnston (*Watsonians*), Roger Baird (*Kelso*); John Rutherford (*Selkirk*), Roy Laidlaw (*Jed-Forest*); Gerry McGuinness (*W of Scot*), Colin Deans (*Hawick*), Iain Milne (*Heriot's FP*), Bill Cuthbertson (*Kilmarnock*), Alan Tomes (*Hawick*), Jim Calder (*Stew-Mel FP*), Derek White (*Gala*), Iain Paxton (*Selkirk*) … Replacement: Eric Paxton (*Kelso*) for Iain Paxton (47)

AUSTRALIA Roger Gould (*Queensland*); Peter Grigg (*Queensland*), Michael O'Connor (*Queensland*), Michael Hawker (*NSW*), Brendan Moon (*Queensland*); Paul McLean (*Queensland*), Phillip Cox (*NSW*); Tony D'Arcy (*Queensland*), Bill Ross (*Queensland*), Stan Pilecki (*Queensland*), Duncan Hall (*Queensland*), Peter McLean (*Queensland*), Tony Shaw (*Queensland*), Chris Roche (*Queensland*), Mark Loane* (*Queensland*)

REFEREE Dick Byres (Australia) · **ATTENDANCE** 36,498

SCORING McLean, pen (0–3); McLean, pen (0–6); Irvine, pen (3–6); Gould, try (3–10); McLean, con (3–12); McLean, pen (3–15); Gould, try (3–19); McLean, con (3–21); Irvine, pen (6–21) (half-time) McLean, pen (6–24); McLean, pen (6–27); Irvine, pen (9–27); O'Connor, try (9–31); McLean, con (9–33)

Wounded by their unexpected defeat in the first test, Australia recalled full-back Roger Gould and veteran stand-off Paul McLean. The changes worked a treat and the Australians completely overwhelmed the rather hapless Scots. Both McLean and Gould were inspirational and much of the game revolved around them. McLean kicked eight goals and Gould scored two first half tries. The Australian forwards were full of fire and it was only in the scrums that Scotland were able to match them. Gould scored his first try after 15 minutes and by the interval the Australians had built a comfortable lead. The second half was marred by a torrential downpour that turned much of the pitch into a mud bath. Scotland lost Iain Paxton, one of their main lineout providers, who was replaced by his namesake Eric. McLean's steady kicking and a try by O'Connor eventually gave Australia their biggest test match victory to date. This was Andy Irvine's final appearance for Scotland and Paul McLean made his swansong for Australia.

XV · TOUR MATCH · FIJI

Murrayfield · Saturday 25 September 1982 · Won 32–12

SCOTLAND XV Peter Dods (*Gala*); Keith Robertson (*Melrose*), Jim Renwick (*Hawick*);

David Johnston (*Watsonians*), Roger Baird (*Kelso*); John Rutherford (*Selkirk*), Roy Laidlaw* (*Jed-Forest*); Gerry McGuinness (*W of Scot*), Colin Deans (*Hawick*), Iain Milne (*Heriot's FP*), Bill Cuthbertson (*Harlequins*), Alan Tomes (*Hawick*), Jim Calder (*Stew-Mel FP*), Derek White (*Gala*), John Beattie (*Glasgow Acs*)

FIJI Severo Koroduadua (*Suva*); Sakaraia Nacaka (*Nadi*), Kameli Yacalevu (*Rewa*), Kaiava Salusalu (*Yasawa*), Isikeli Tikoduadua (*Suva*); Elia Rokowailoa (*Suva*), Samisoni Viriviri (*Nadi*); Rusiate Namoro (*Suva*), Mosese Tamata (*Rewa*), Tuimasi Tubananitu (*Suva*), Vilikesa Vatuwaliwali* (*Nadi*), Ilisoni Taoba (*Rewa*), Sunia Nadruku (*Nadroga*), Emosi Tatawaqa (*Labusa*), Esala Teleni (*Suva*) … Replacements: Jone Ratu (*Nadroga*) for Yacalevu (40); Josevata Naikidi (*Dreketi*) for Taoba (79)

REFEREE Clive Norling (*Wales*)

SCORING Dods, pen (3–0); Rutherford, drop (6–0); Koroduadua, pen (6–3); Calder, try (10–3); Nadruku, try (10–7); Koroduadua, con (10–9); Johnston, try (14–9); Dods, con (16–9) (half-time) Dods, try (20–9); Dods, con (22–9); Koroduadua, pen (22–12); Beattie, try (26–12); Dods, con (28–12); Dods, try (32–12)

In autumn 1982, the popular Fijians made a ten-match tour of Scotland and England, their first visit north of the Border. Faced with a demanding schedule, the Fijians showed occasional flashes of improvised brilliance, but in general they were out of their depth, especially in the technical aspects of forward play, and sadly they lost all of their matches. The tour opened with a heavy defeat against Edinburgh (12–47) before improved displays against the South of Scotland (17–23) and the Anglo-Scots (19–29). Scotland did not award caps, but they fielded nearly their best side and Roy Laidlaw took over as captain. The Scots were comfortable winners, but they showed signs of early season rustiness and struggled to breakdown a tough Fijian defence. Much of their play lacked direction and was too loose and careless. At full-back, the uncapped Peter Dods showed lots of potential and scored 17 points, including two tries. It was only in the closing stages that the Scots stretched away. Laidlaw took a quick tap-penalty and the ball was spun down the line to Dods who scored in the corner. The full-back converted from the touchline and late tries by Beattie and Dods brought some respectability to the final score.

361 INTERNATIONAL CHAMPIONSHIP 1983 IRELAND

Murrayfield · Saturday 15 January 1983 · Lost 13–15

SCOTLAND †Peter Dods (*Gala*); Keith Robertson (*Melrose*), Jim Renwick (*Hawick*), David Johnston (*Watsonians*), Roger Baird (*Kelso*); Ron Wilson (*London Scot*), Roy Laidlaw* (*Jed-Forest*); Gerry McGuinness (*W of Scot*), Colin Deans (*Hawick*), Iain Milne (*Heriot's FP*), Bill Cuthbertson (*Harlequins*), Alan Tomes (*Hawick*), Jim Calder (*Stew-Mel FP*), David Leslie (*Gala*), Iain Paxton (*Selkirk*)

IRELAND Hugo MacNeill (*Oxford U*); Trevor Ringland (*Ballymena*), David lrwin (*Instonians*), Michael Kiernan (*Dolphin*), Moss Finn (*Cork Const*); Ollie Campbell (*Old Belvedere*), Robbie McGrath (*Wdrs*); Phil Orr (*Old Wesley*), Ciaran Fitzgerald (*St Mary's Coll*), Gerry McLoughlin (*Shannon*), Moss Keane (*Lansdowne*), Donal Lenihan (*Cork Const*), Fergus Slattery (*Blackrock Coll*), John O'Driscoll (*Manchester*), Willie Duggan (*Blackrock Coll*)

REFEREE Jean-Claude Yché (*France*)

SCORING Campbell, pen (0–3); Laidlaw, try (4–3); Campbell, pen (4–6); Kiernan, try (4–10); Campbell, con (4–12); Campbell, pen (4–15) (half-time) Renwick, drop (7–15); Dods, pen (10–15); Dods, pen (13–15)

Ron Wilson came in for the injured John Rutherford and Peter Dods won his first cap. Played on a windy day in front of the new east stand, Scotland came agonisingly close to snatching a late victory, but it would have been undeserved. Ireland were the better team and their redoubtable 'Dad's Army' pack of seasoned veterans had enough strength and experience to see off a largely disappointing Scotland. Full-back Hugo MacNeill was almost flawless despite the tricky conditions, Donal Lenihan won a lot of lineout possession and Ollie Campbell excelled in everything he did. By contrast, the Scots did not combine so well and their handling was erratic and often hurried. Playing with the wind, Campbell kicked three first half penalties and converted a well-worked try by Kiernan. For Scotland, Roy Laidlaw scored a classic scrum-half's try when he shot off around the side of a scrum and made a wide arcing run to the corner. Dods' conversion attempt hit a post. In the second half, Scotland slowly nibbled away at the Irish lead. Renwick dropped a goal and Dods kicked two penalties. In a rousing conclusion, the Scots tried everything for the winning score, but they had insufficient technique and patience to unlock a tenacious Irish defence. Fergus Slattery, the veteran Irish flanker, made a prodigious leap to charge down a Renwick drop goal attempt, Dods missed a lengthy penalty attempt and the visitors held on.

362   INTERNATIONAL CHAMPIONSHIP 1983   FRANCE

Parc des Princes, Paris · Saturday 5 February 1983 · Lost 15–19

SCOTLAND Peter Dods (*Gala*); Keith Robertson (*Melrose*), Jim Renwick (*Hawick*), David Johnston (*Watsonians*), Roger Baird (*Kelso*); Bryan Gossman (*W of Scot*), Roy Laidlaw* (*Jed-Forest*); Jim Aitken (*Gala*), Colin Deans (*Hawick*), Iain Milne (*Heriot's FP*), Bill Cuthbertson (*Harlequins*), Alan Tomes (*Hawick*), Jim Calder (*Stew-Mel FP*), David Leslie (*Gala*), John Beattie (*Glasgow Acs*)

FRANCE Serge Blanco (*Biarritz*); Philippe Sella (*Agen*), Christian Bélascain (*Bayonne*), Didier Codorniou (*Narbonne*), Patrick Estève (*Narbonne*); Christian Delage (*Agen*), Pierre Berbizier (*Lourdes*); Pierre Dospital (*Bayonne*), Jean-Louis Dupont (*Agen*), Robert Paparemborde (*Pau*), Jean Condom (*Boucau*), Jean-Charles Orso (*Nice*), Jean-Pierre Rives* (*RCF*), Laurent Rodriguez (*Mont-de-Marson*), Jean-Luc Joinel (*Brive*) ... Replacement: Dominique Erbani (*Agen*) for Rodriguez (65)

REFEREE Alan Richards (*Wales*)

SCORING Dods, pen (3–0); Blanco, pen (3–3); Robertson, try (7–3); Dods, con (9–3); Gossman, drop (12–3); Blanco, pen (12–6); Estève, try (12–10); Blanco, con (12–12); Gossman, drop (15–12); Blanco, pen (15–15) (half-time) Estève, try (15–19)

There were several changes after the defeat against Ireland. Bryan Gossman came in at stand-off, John Beattie at No 8 and Jim Aitken at loose-head prop. Aitken also took over as pack leader and perhaps as a result the forwards were a big improvement on the previous match. Scotland crossed the Channel as underdogs, but they played with great courage and determination, especially in the first half, before finally going down to a top quality French side. At one point in the first half they held a nine-point lead only for France to draw level by the interval. Scotland's solitary try came from a back-row movement and Laidlaw drew the cover to send Robertson in at the right corner. Dods converted from the touchline. Gossman defended courageously throughout and dropped two goals. France slowly gained the upper-hand in the second half although towards the end Dods missed a simple penalty chance that would have given Scotland the lead. Then the French backs made a slick handling move and Estève squeezed in at the left, dragging three defenders with him as he crossed for the match-winning try. A draw would have been a fairer result.

---

363   INTERNATIONAL CHAMPIONSHIP 1983   WALES

Murrayfield · Saturday 19 February 1983 · Lost 15–19

SCOTLAND Peter Dods (*Gala*); Keith Robertson (*Melrose*), Jim Renwick (*Hawick*), David Johnston (*Watsonians*), Roger Baird (*Kelso*); Bryan Gossman (*W of Scot*), Roy Laidlaw* (*Jed-Forest*); Jim Aitken (*Gala*), Colin Deans (*Hawick*), Iain Milne (*Heriot's FP*), Bill Cuthbertson (*Harlequins*), Alan Tomes (*Hawick*), Jim Calder (*Stew-Mel FP*), David Leslie (*Gala*), John Beattie (*Glasgow Acs*)

WALES Mark Wyatt (*Swansea*); Elgin Rees (*Neath*), David Richards (*Swansea*), Robert Ackerman (*London Welsh*), Clive Rees (*London Welsh*); Malcolm Dacey (*Swansea*), Terry Holmes (*Cardiff*); Staff Jones (*Pontypool*), Billy James (*Aberavon*), Ian Eidman (*Cardiff*), Robert Norster (*Cardiff*), John Perkins (*Pontypool*), Jeff Squire (*Pontypool*), David Pickering (*Llanelli*), Eddie Butler* (*Pontypool*)

REFEREE Roger Quittenton (*England*)

SCORING Wyatt, pen (0–3); Jones, try (0–7); Wyatt, con (0–9); Dods, pen (3–9); Wyatt, pen (3–12); Dods, pen (6–12); Wyatt, pen (6–15) (half-time) Dods, pen (9–15); Rees, try (9–19); Renwick, try (13–19); Dods, con (15–19)

The scores were the same as the previous game, but Scotland were a shadow of the side that had done so well in Paris. The forwards never recaptured their dynamism and the backs lacked conviction in attack. A much-criticised Welsh side played with great determination and a sense of adventure, and in truth they never looked like losing. After an early penalty by Wyatt, Staff Jones, the new Welsh prop, thundered over from a lineout inside the Scottish 22. Wyatt added the conversion and two further penalties, and Dods kicked three penalties for the Scots. In the second half, Clive Rees made a long mazy run down the left and, after a bout of good handling, Elgan Rees scored in the opposite corner. Scotland made a desperate late rally and Jim Renwick, on the occasion of his 50th cap, scored a try with a nicely-angled run. Dods converted to keep the scores tight and Wales survived an extended period of injury-time for a deserved victory.

---

364   INTERNATIONAL CHAMPIONSHIP 1983   ENGLAND

Twickenham · Saturday 5 March 1983 · Won 22–12

SCOTLAND Peter Dods (*Gala*); Jim Pollock (*Gosforth*), Jim Renwick (*Hawick*), Keith Robertson

(*Melrose*), Roger Baird (*Kelso*); John Rutherford (*Selkirk*), Roy Laidlaw (*Jed-Forest*); Jim Aitken*
(*Gala*) Colin Deans (*Hawick*), Iain Milne (*Heriot's FP*), †Tom Smith (*Gala*), Iain Paxton (*Selkirk*),
Jim Calder (*Stew-Mel FP*), David Leslie (*Gala*), John Beattie (*Glasgow Acs*)

ENGLAND Dusty Hare (*Leicester*); John Carleton (*Orrell*), Huw Davies (*Coventry*), Paul Dodge
(*Leicester*), Tony Swift (*Swansea*); John Horton (*Bath*), Steve Smith (*Sale*); Colin Smart (*Newport*),
Peter Wheeler (*Leicester*), Gary Pearce (*Northampton*), Steve Boyle (*Gloucester*), Steve Bainbridge
(*Gosforth*), Nick Jeavons (*Moseley*), Peter Winterbottom (*Headingley*), John Scott* (*Cardiff*)

REFEREE Tom Doocey (*New Zealand*)

SCORING Horton, drop (0–3); Dods, pen (3–3); Hare, pen (3–6); Dods, pen (6–6); Hare, pen
(6–9); Dods, pen (9–9) (half-time) Laidlaw, try (13–9); Dods, con (15–9); Hare, pen (15–12);
Robertson, drop (18–12); Smith, try (22–12)

There were several changes after the defeat by Wales, including a long-awaited first
cap for the gigantic Gala lock Tom Smith. The fiery Jim Aitken relieved Roy Laidlaw
of the captaincy and the Jed-Forest scrum-half immediately looked more at ease. John
Rutherford returned from injury and brought stability and reassurance to a struggling
back division. Scotland rescued their season with a rare win at Twickenham, their first
since 1971 and only their fourth overall. This was not a match of any great quality,
but Scotland deserved to win. They played with a greater sense of adventure, the
forwards were fast about the field and their ruck work was first rate. England did well
enough at the set-pieces, but they were too ponderous, ill-disciplined and strangely
lacking in passion. The sides were level at the interval although Scotland should have
been awarded a penalty try after Jim Renwick was tackled illegally when he was in a
scoring position. In the second half, Laidlaw gathered the ball from a creaking scrum
in the English 22 and danced his way to the line, a classic scrum-half's try. Later,

Roy Laidlaw scores a classic scrum-half try against England in 1983.
Scotsman Publications Ltd

Robertson dropped a goal and the *coup de grâce* was delivered by Tom Smith, the new lock. From a lineout on the English line, he took a clean two-handed catch and simply fell over the line for the clinching try.

 1983 BARBARIANS

Murrayfield · Saturday 26 March 1983 · Lost 13–26

SCOTLAND Peter Dods (*Gala*); Jim Pollock (*Gosforth*), Jim Renwick (*Hawick*). Keith Robertson (*Melrose*), Roger Baird (*Kelso*); John Rutherford (*Selkirk*), Roy Laidlaw (*Jed-Forest*); Jim Aitken* (*Gala*), Colin Deans (*Hawick*), Norrie Rowan (*Boroughmuir*), Tom Smith (*Gala*), Iain Paxton (*Selkirk*), Jim Calder (*Stew-Mel FP*), David Leslie (*Gala*), John Beattie (*Glasgow Acs*) ... Replacement: David Johnston (*Watsonians*) for Robertson (7)

BARBARIANS Jean-Baptiste Lafond (*RCF*); John Carleton (*Orrell & England*), Danie Gerber (*E Province & SA*), Errol Tobias (*Boland & SA*), Clive Rees (*London Welsh & Wales*); Gareth Davies (*Cardiff & Wales*), Terry Holmes (*Cardiff & Wales*); Paul Rendall (*Wasps*), Philippe Dintrans (*Tarbes & France*), Robert Paparemborde (*Pau & France*), Hennie Bekker (*W Province & SA*), Robert Norster (*Cardiff & Wales*), Peter Winterbottom (*Headingley & England*), Fergus Slattery* (*Blackrock Coll & Ireland*), John Scott (*Cardiff & England*)

REFEREE René Hourquet (*France*)

SCORING Dods, pen (3–0); Bekker, try (3–4); Lafond, try (3–8); Rutherford, try (7–8) (half-time) Carleton, try (7–12); Davies, con (7–14); Gerber, try (7–18); Davies, con (7–20); Rutherford, try (11–20); Dods, con (13–20); Gerber, try (13–24); Davies, con (13–26)

This special match was played to celebrate the opening of the new east stand which was unveiled before the game by Her Royal Highness Princess Anne. The Barbarians fielded a strong team with world class players from six countries. Both sides were committed to attack from the start and played some wonderfully entertaining rugby. Despite being a scratch side, the Barbarians combined effectively and showed plenty of skill and daring, outscoring their hosts by five tries to two. The Scottish forwards started well, but as the match progressed they could not match the superior power and coordination of the Barbarians. Springbok centre Danie Gerber was prominent with his strong, direct running and uncapped French full-back Jean-Baptiste Lafond showed tremendous flair and audacity. Lafond's try was the highlight of the match. He was half-tackled near his own 22, but recovered and ran away down the right wing. There seemed to be plenty of Scottish cover, but he had enough speed and confidence to reach the line for a glorious score.

365 TOUR MATCH NEW ZEALAND

Murrayfield · Saturday 12 November 1983 · Drawn 25–25

SCOTLAND Peter Dods (*Gala*); Jim Pollock (*Gosforth*), †Euan Kennedy (*Watsonians*), David Johnston (*Watsonians*), Roger Baird (*Kelso*); John Rutherford (*Selkirk*), Roy Laidlaw (*Jed-Forest*); Jim Aitken* (*Gala*), Colin Deans (*Hawick*), Iain Milne (*Heriot's FP*), Bill Cuthbertson (*Harlequins*), Tom Smith (*Gala*), Jim Calder (*Stew-Mel FP*), John Beattie (Glasgow Acs), Iain Paxton (*Selkirk*)

NEW ZEALAND: Robbie Deans (*Canterbury*); Stu Wilson* (*Wellington*), Steve Pokere (*Southland*), Warwick Taylor (*Canterbury*), Bernie Fraser (*Wellington*); Wayne Smith (*Canterbury*), Andrew Donald (*Wanganui*); Brian McGrattan (*Wellington*), Hika Reid (*Bay of Plenty*), Scott Crichton (*Wellington*), Gary Braid (*Bay of Plenty*), Albert Anderson (*Canterbury*), Mark Shaw (*Manawatu*), Jock Hobbs (*Canterbury*), Murray Mexted (*Wellington*) ... Replacement: Craig Green (*Canterbury*) for Taylor (h-t)

REFEREE René Hourquet (*France*)

SCORING Rutherford, drop (3–0); Deans, pen (3–3); Rutherford, drop (6–3); Hobbs, try (6–7); Fraser, try (6–11); Deans, con (6–13); Dods, pen (9–13); Deans, pen (9–16); Dods, pen (12–16); Dods, pen (15–16) (half-time) Fraser, try (15–20); Deans, con (15–22); Dods, pen (18–22); Dods, pen (21–22); Deans, pen (21–25); Pollock, try (25–25)

Scotland gave the New Zealanders more than they bargained for and for once the All Blacks let an important match slip through their grasp. New Zealand won the try-count by three to one and enjoyed a greater share of the game, but they gave away too many penalties and made a lot of errors. This allowed a spirited Scottish side to stay in contention and come within a whisker of their first-ever win over the All Blacks. Scotland started purposefully and Rutherford dropped an early goal which Deans cancelled out with a penalty. Rutherford dropped his second goal after some magnificent driving play by the Scottish forwards. Hobbs scored a soft try when the Scots were caught sleeping at a short lineout and then Fraser beat the cover in a kick-and-chase to the Scottish line. In the second half, Fraser scored a copy-cat try to his first, but Dods kept Scotland within striking distance with his accurate goal-kicking. New Zealand held a four-point lead in the closing minutes before the Scots scored a dramatic late try. From a lineout on the New Zealand 22, the ball sped down the line to Johnston who sent a perfectly weighted kick to the corner and Pollock raced on to get the touchdown. Amidst great tension, Dods took the conversion kick from the touchline but missed narrowly. There was still enough time for the New Zealanders to get over the Scottish line, but they were brought back for a penalty which was eminently kickable. However, the touch-judge intervened and the penalty was reversed, much to the visitors' frustration. A draw was probably a fair result. New Zealand had been more creative than Scotland, but they had never showed their usual rhythm or authority. The Scottish forwards played whole-heartedly and at times their rucking and driving play had their illustrious opponents reeling. Peter Dods was excellent at full-back and kicked five goals out of six, and Jim Aitken proved an inspiring captain.

366 INTERNATIONAL CHAMPIONSHIP 1984 WALES

Cardiff Arms Park · Saturday 21 January 1984 · Won 15–9

SCOTLAND Peter Dods (*Gala*); Steve Munro (*Ayr*), David Johnston (*Watsonians*), Euan Kennedy (*Watsonians*), Roger (*Kelso*); John Rutherford (*Selkirk*), Roy Laidlaw (*Jed-Forest*); Jim Aitken* (*Gala*), Colin Deans (*Hawick*), Iain Milne (*Heriot's FP*), Bill Cuthbertson (*Harlequins*), Alan Tomes (*Hawick*), Jim Calder (*Stew-Mel FP*), David Leslie (*Gala*), Iain Paxton (*Selkirk*)

WALES Howell Davies (*Bridgend*); Mark Titley (*Bridgend*), Robert Ackerman (*London Welsh*), Bleddyn Bowen (*South Wales Police*), Adrian Hadley (*Cardiff*); Malcolm Dacey (*Swansea*), Mark Douglas (*Llanelli*); Staff Jones (*Pontypool*), Billy James (*Aberavon*), Rhys Morgan

Scottish captain Jim Aitken is barrelled over the line for the winning try against Wales in 1984.
Scotsman Publications Ltd

(*Newport*), John Perkins (*Pontypool*), Robert Norster (*Cardiff*), Richard Moriarty (*Swansea*), David Pickering (*Llanelli*), Eddie Butler* (*Pontypool*)

REFEREE Owen Doyle (*Ireland*)

SCORING Davies, pen (0–3); Paxton, try (4–3); Dods, con (6–3) (half-time) Titley, try (6–7); Davies, con (6–9); Dods, pen (9–9); Aitken, try (13–9); Dods, con (15–9)

Scotland kicked-off the 1984 championship with their second win in succession in Wales, the first time that this had happened since the 1920s. Unlike the previous encounter, which the Scots had won 34–18, this was a hard fought and frequently abrasive match. Scotland required all of their composure and experience to see them through. The Scottish forwards won a lot of possession and flanker David Leslie gave a vintage display in the loose and at the tail of the lineout. Wales opened the scoring with a penalty goal by newcomer Howell Davies after 30 minutes. In injury-time at the interval, Deans made a quick tap-penalty. The ball was worked to Paxton, albeit with a couple of forward-looking passes, and the No 8 raced away to the line. Dods converted to put Scotland 6–3 ahead. Around the hour mark, Titley squeezed in at the corner after a scrum near the Scottish line. Davies converted from the touchline and soon afterwards Dods kicked a penalty to level the scores. With 12 minutes remaining, Rutherford found touch a few metres from the Welsh line. The Scots stole the lineout and after a couple of thrusts Aitken was driven over the line. Dods kicked the conversion despite playing with a split boot. In a frantic conclusion, Scotland had to mount a desperate rearguard action but the defence held firm.

Murrayfield · Saturday 4 February 1984 · Won 18–6

SCOTLAND Peter Dods (*Gala*); Keith Robertson (*Melrose*), Euan Kennedy (*Watsonians*), David Johnston (*Watsonians*), Roger Baird (*Kelso*); John Rutherford (*Selkirk*), Roy Laidlaw (*Jed-Forest*); Jim Aitken* (*Gala*), Colin Deans (*Hawick*), Iain Milne (*Heriot's FP*), Bill Cuthbertson (*Harlequins*), Alan Tomes (*Hawick*), Jim Calder (*Stew-Mel FP*), David Leslie (*Gala*), Iain Paxton (*Selkirk*) ... Replacements: John Beattie (*Glasgow Acs*) for Cuthbertson (40), Jim Pollock (*Gosforth*) for Kennedy (60)

ENGLAND Dusty Hare (*Leicester*); John Carleton (*Orrell*), Clive Woodward (*Leicester*), Huw Davies (*Wasps*), Mike Slemen (Liverpool); Les Cusworth (*Leicester*), Nick Youngs (*Leicester*); Colin White (*Gosforth*), Peter Wheeler* (*Leicester*), Gary Pearce (*Northampton*), Maurice Colclough (*Wasps*), Steve Bainbridge (*Gosforth*), Paul Simpson (*Bath*), Peter Winterbottom (*Headingley*), John Scott (*Cardiff*) ... Replacement: John Hall (*Bath*) for Winterbottom (50)

REFEREE David Burnett (*Ireland*)

SCORING Johnston, try (4–0); Dods, con (6–0); Hare, pen (6–3) (half-time) Kennedy, try (10–3); Dods, con (12–3); Hare, pen (12–6); Dods, pen (15–6); Dods, pen (18–6)

This was the 100th playing of the fixture and Scotland won as comprehensive a victory as any of the previous games. England had beaten New Zealand the previous November and they were optimistic about their championship prospects. In the event, Scotland were miles faster and had much greater enthusiasm and creativity. Some of the Scottish rucking and driving play was exemplary and stand-off John Rutherford tormented the English defence with his superb tactical kicking. By contrast England lacked enough imagination to change their game plan as things went wrong. Much of the English play was ponderous and lacking in urgency and some of their players did not look fully fit. Scotland conceded many penalties, but the normally reliable Dusty Hare had a miserable day with his kicking and managed only two from eight attempts. Scotland adapted to the wet conditions cleverly and their first try showed their speed of thought and action. A long ball from a lineout inside the English 22 squirted into midfield where it was overran by the English centres. David Johnston, a former professional footballer, skilfully dribbled it over the line and won the race to the touchdown. Dods kicked a fine conversion and just before half-time Hare's persistence was finally rewarded with a penalty goal. The Scots delivered the killer blow within a minute of the restart. The English defence failed to deal with a high kick by Laidlaw, and Calder grabbed the ball and fed the rampaging Tomes who thundered deep into the English 22. The ball was spun left quickly where Rutherford caught a low pass and put Kennedy in at the posts. Dods converted and Hare replied immediately with a penalty, but two further penalties by Dods, the second after an old fashioned kick-and-chase, sealed a memorable win for the Scots.

Lansdowne Road, Dublin · Saturday 3 March 1984 · Won 32–9

SCOTLAND Peter Dods (*Gala*); Jim Pollock (*Gosforth*), Keith Robertson (*Melrose*), David Johnston (*Watsonians*), Roger Baird (*Kelso*); John Rutherford (*Selkirk*), Roy Laidlaw

(*Jed-Forest*); Jim Aitken* (*Gala*), Colin Deans (*Hawick*), Iain Milne (*Heriot's FP*),
†Alister Campbell (*Hawick*), Alan Tomes (*Hawick*), Jim Calder (*Stew-Mel FP*), David Leslie
(*Gala*), Iain Paxton (*Selkirk*) ... Replacement: †Gordon Hunter (*Selkirk*) for Laidlaw (h-t)

IRELAND John Murphy (*Greystones*); Trevor Ringland (*Ballymena*), Michael Kiernan
(*Lansdowne*), Moss Finn (*Cork Const*), Keith Crossan (*Instonians*); Tony Ward (*St Mary's Coll*),
Tony Doyle (*Greystones*); Phil Orr (*Old Wesley*), Harry Harbison (*Bective Rgrs*), Des Fitzgerald
(*Lansdowne*), Moss Keane (*Lansdowne*), Donal Lenihan (*Cork Const*), John O'Driscoll
(*London Irish*), Derek McGrath (*UC Dublin*), Willie Duggan* (*Blackrock Coll*) ... Replacement:
Hugh Condon (*London Irish*) for Ward (55)

REFEREE Fred Howard (*England*)

SCORING Laidlaw, try (4–0); Dods, con (6–0); Dods, pen (9–0); Dods, pen (12–0); penalty try
(16–0); Dods, con (18–0); Laidlaw, try (22–0) (half-time) Murphy, pen (22–3); Kiernan, try (22–7);
Murphy, con (22–9); Robertson, try (26–9); Dods, con (28–9); Dods, try (32–9)

Hawick's Alister Campbell came in as replacement for the injured Bill Cuthbertson.
Scotland went to Lansdowne Road seeking their first Triple Crown since 1938. They
won in majestic style, scoring five tries to one and were never in any danger apart
from a nervy spell in the second half. Playing with a strong wind behind them, the Scots
made a tremendous start and in essence had the game won long before the interval.
After only four minutes, the forwards won a lineout and ruck inside the Irish 22 and
Laidlaw side-stepped through the defence for great solo try. Dods converted and then
kicked two penalties. Scotland's second try came from a scrum near the Irish line. The
Scots drove and wheeled, Irish No 8 Duggan dived in illegally and the referee awarded
a penalty try for the infringement. Then from a scrum in a similar position, Laidlaw
took quick ball and sprinted over at the right corner. Unfortunately, Laidlaw had to
leave the field with concussion at half-time allowing Gordon Hunter to win his long-
awaited first cap. Ireland rallied the second half with a penalty by Murphy and a
superb try by Kiernan, but the Scots regained their composure and finished the match
in complete control. From a lineout inside the Irish 22, Hunter broke into midfield
and fed Rutherford who swept past the defence before giving a scoring pass to
Robertson. Finally, amidst a loud chorus of 'Scotland! Scotland!', the Scots switched
play from a scrum in midfield and Baird unselfishly passed to Dods who dived over
at the corner. The only cloud on a perfect afternoon for Scotland was that Gordon
Hunter fractured his cheekbone in a collision with a spectator at the end of the match
and the injury ruled him out of the next game.

---

369 INTERNATIONAL CHAMPIONSHIP 1984 FRANCE

Murrayfield · Saturday 17 March 1984 · Won 21–12

SCOTLAND Peter Dods (*Gala*); Jim Pollock (*Gosforth*), Keith Robertson (*Melrose*),
David Johnston (*Watsonians*), Roger Baird (*Kelso*); John Rutherford (*Selkirk*), Roy Laidlaw
(*Jed-Forest*); Jim Aitken* (Gala), Colin Deans (*Hawick*), Iain Milne (*Heriot's FP*), Alister Campbell
(*Hawick*), Alan Tomes (*Hawick*), Jim Calder (*Stew-Mel FP*), David Leslie (*Gala*), Iain Paxton
(*Selkirk*)

FRANCE Serge Blanco (*Biarritz*); Jacques Bégu (*Dax*), Philippe Sella (*Agen*), Didier Codorniou
(*Narbonne*), Patrick Estève (*Narbonne*); Jean-Patrick Lescarboura (*Dax*), Jérôme Gallion (*Toulon*);

Pierre Dospital (*Bayonne*), Philippe Dintrans (*Tarbes*), Daniel Dubroca (*Agen*), Francis Haget (*Biarritz*), Jean Condom (*Boucau*), Jean-Pierre Rives* (*RCF*), Jean-Luc Joinel (*Brive*), Jean-Charles Orso (*Nice*) ... Replacement: Pierre Berbizier (*Lourdes*) for Gallion (61)

REFEREE Winston Jones (*Wales*)

SCORING Dods, pen (3–0); Gallion, try (3–4); Lescarboura, con (3–6) (half-time) Lescarboura, pen (3–9); Dods, pen (6–9); Dods, pen (9–9); Lescarboura, drop (9–12); Dods, pen (12–12); Calder, try (16–12); Dods, con (18–12); Dods, pen (21–12)

Scotland had a scrum-half crisis in the run-up to this vital match and even considering recalling veterans Douglas Morgan or Alan Lawson, but fortunately Roy Laidlaw was fit enough in time and uncapped Stuart Johnston sat on the bench. Both sides were playing for the Grand Slam, in Scotland's case their first since 1925. With so much at stake, this was a hard and tense match that had drama, excitement and some controversy. Scotland opened with a penalty goal by Peter Dods, but France dominated the first quarter and at times threatened to sweep the home side away. The Scottish forwards were unable to impose themselves and the backs seemed very nervous, Rutherford temporarily losing all authority with his kicking. And yet France led by only three points at the interval. On the 24th minute, Gallion scored a try after a scrum pick-up by Orso and Lescarboura converted. Apart from this, Scotland's defence was resolute and their self-belief grew as the match wore on. One of the key turning points came around the hour mark when the influential Gallion was knocked senseless in an accidental collision and had to leave the field. The Scottish forwards began to assert their authority, especially in the scrums where Iain Milne was immense, and the French slowly lost their composure. Lescarboura kicked a penalty and Dods levelled the scores with two of his own, having earlier missed two easy chances. Lescarboura restored the French lead with a massive drop goal, but then the visitors stupidly conce-

Jim Calder celebrates scoring the Grand Slam-winning try against France in 1984, one of the greatest photographs in the story of Scottish rugby.
Scotsman Publications Ltd

ded an extra ten metres for dissent and Dods levelled the scores again. Inside the final five minutes, with France reeling and the crowd roaring the Scots on, Rutherford hoisted a high ball into the French 22 and the defence scrambled it away, but only to within a few metres of their own line. Deans threw to the tail of the lineout and a French hand tapped the ball straight to Jim Calder who dived over the line for a historic try. Murrayfield erupted. Peter Dods, playing with one eye almost closed because of injury, converted Calder's try and then kicked his fifth penalty after a late tackle by Blanco. The match ended with Scotland in total control and France in disarray. There were emotional and joyful scenes at the final whistle. After so many false dawns, Scotland's long wait for their second Grand Slam was finally over.

370　　　　　　　TOUR OF ROMANIA 1984　　　　　　ROMANIA

August 23 Stadium Bucharest · Sunday 20 May 1984 · Lost 22–28

SCOTLAND Peter Dods (*Gala*); Jim Pollock (*Gosforth*), Jim Renwick (*Hawick*), David Johnston (*Watsonians*), Keith Robertson (*Melrose*); John Rutherford (*Selkirk*), Roy Laidlaw (*Jed-Forest*); Jim Aitken* (*Gala*), †Gary Callander (*Kelso*), Norrie Rowan (*Boroughmuir*), Alister Campbell (*Hawick*), Alan Tomes (*Hawick*), †Sean McGaughey (*Hawick*), David Leslie (*Gala*), John Beattie (*Glasgow Acs*)

ROMANIA Ion Vasile; Adrian Lungu, Gheorghie Varzaru, Mihai Marghescu, Marian Aldea; Dumitru Alexandru, Mircea Paraschiv*; Ion Bucan, Mircea Munteanu, Gheorghie Leonte, Gheorghie Dumitru, Laurentiu Constantin, Florica Morariu, Stefan Constantin, Alexandru Radulescu

REFEREE Owen Doyle (*Ireland*)

SCORING Leslie, try (4–0); Dods, con (6–0); Dumitru, try (6–4); Alexandru, con (6–6); Alexandru, pen (6–9); Robertson, drop (9–9); Dods, pen (12–9); Dods, try (16–9) (half-time) Alexandru, pen (16–12); Dods, pen (19–12); Alexandru, drop (19–15); Paraschiv, try (19–19); Dods, pen (22–19); Radulescu, try (22–23); Alexandru, con (22–25); Alexandru, pen (22–28)

In May 1984, Scotland made a three-match tour of Romania concluding with a test match against the national side. Gary Callander and Sean McGaughey won their first caps. Hawick stalwart Jim Renwick, who was unlucky to miss out on the Grand Slam because of injury, returned to make his 52nd appearance and break Andy Irvine's Scottish cap record. The match was played in sweltering conditions with temperatures reaching the 90s and unsurprisingly the Scots faded away in the second half. Jim Aitken, the Scottish captain, later revealed that his mouth was so dry that he could barely give the team talk at half-time. To make matters worse, some of the players were suffering from stomach upsets after several days of poor food. The big Romanian forwards dominated the set-pieces, but their backs were dull and unadventurous. Scotland opened the scoring after five minutes when David Leslie intercepted a wayward pass near the line. The second try came from a miss-move in midfield which put Pollock away to the 22. Johnston was in support and drew the remaining cover to put Dods over for an excellent score. Romania's winning try was very controversial. With Scotland clinging to a three-point lead, Alexandru put up a towering kick to the Scottish posts. Dods bravely stood his ground, but seemed to be illegally bowled over before the ball reached him and in the ensuing scramble Radulescu plunged through to score. Alexandru converted and a few minutes later sealed the game with his third penalty.

Murrayfield · Saturday 8 December 1984 · Lost 12–37

SCOTLAND Peter Dods (*Gala*); †Peter Steven (*Heriot's FP*), Euan Kennedy (*Watsonians*), Keith Robertson (*Melrose*), Roger Baird (*Kelso*); †Douglas Wyllie (*Stew-Mel FP*), Roy Laidlaw* (*Jed-Forest*); †Gregor Mackenzie (*Selkirk*), Colin Deans (*Hawick*), Iain Milne (*Harlequins*), Bill Cuthbertson (*Harlequins*), Alan Tomes (*Hawick*), Jim Calder (*Stew-Mel FP*), †John Jeffrey (*Kelso*) John Beattie (*Glasgow Acs*)

AUSTRALIA Roger Gould (*Queensland*); Peter Grigg (*Queensland*), Andrew Slack* (*Queensland*), Michael Lynagh (*Queensland*), David Campese (*ACT*); Mark Ella (*NSW*), Nick Farr-Jones (*NSW*); Enrique Rodriguez (*NSW*), Tom Lawton (*Queensland*), Andy McIntyre (*Queensland*), Steve Williams (*NSW*), Steve Cutler (*NSW*), Simon Poidevin (*NSW*), David Codey (*Queensland*), Steve Tuynman (*NSW*)

REFEREE Stephen Hilditch (*Ireland*)

SCORING Lynagh, pen (0–3); Dods, pen (3–3); Campese, try (3–7); Lynagh, con (3–9); Lynagh, pen (3–12); Dods, pen (6–12); Dods, pen (9–12) (half-time) Lynagh, pen (9–15); Lynagh, pen (9–18); Dods, pen (12–18); Ella, try (12–22); Lynagh, con (12–24); Farr-Jones, try (12–28); Lynagh, pen (12–31); Campese, try (12–35); Lynagh, con (12–37)

Scotland were missing several key players, including John Rutherford and David Leslie, but the main talking point was the omission of Jim Aitken who was deemed too old for international rugby. His place was taken by newcomer Gregor Mackenzie who recently had moved from Highland to Selkirk. Peter Steven, Douglas Wyllie and John Jeffrey won their first caps. Scotland worked hard, but they were simply outclassed by a brilliant Australian side chasing their first Grand Slam in the British Isles. Despite the slippery conditions, the Australians scored four lovely tries, including one by stand-off Mark Ella which meant that he had scored a try in each leg of the Grand Slam. Nick Farr-Jones caught the Scots napping when he collected the ball at the front of a short lineout and went all the way to the line. Australia's final try summed-up all of their attacking brilliance and sense of adventure. Grigg intercepted a loose pass inside his own half and the ball was worked to Campese who made a long mazy run up the left touchline for a breathtaking score. It brought down the curtain on a great day for the Wallabies.

Murrayfield · Saturday 2 February 1985 · Lost 15–18

SCOTLAND Peter Dods (*Gala*); Roger Baird (*Kelso*), †Keith Murray (*Hawick*), Keith Robertson (*Melrose*), †Iwan Tukalo (*Selkirk*); John Rutherford (*Selkirk*), Roy Laidlaw* (*Jed-Forest*); Gerry McGuinness (*W of Scot*), Colin Deans (*Hawick*), Norrie Rowan (*Boroughmuir*), Alister Campbell (*Hawick*), Tom Smith (*Gala*), Jim Calder (*Stew-Mel FP*), John Jeffrey (*Kelso*), John Beattie (*Glasgow Acs*) ... Replacement: Iain Paxton (*Selkirk*) for Beattie (41)

IRELAND Hugo MacNeill (*Oxford U*); Trevor Ringland (*Ballymena*), Brendan Mullin (*Dublin U*), Michael Kiernan (*Lansdowne*), Keith Crossan (*Instonians*); Paul Dean (*St Mary's Coll*), Michael Bradley (*Cork Const*); Phil Orr (*Old Wesley*), Ciaran Fitzgerald* (*St Mary's Coll*), Jimmy McCoy (*Dungannon*), Donal Lenihan (*Cork Const*), Willie Anderson (*Dungannon*), Philip Matthews (*Ards*), Nigel Carr (*Ards*), Brian Spillane (*Bohemians*)

REFEREE Steve Strydom (*South Africa*)

SCORING Dods, pen (3–0); Rutherford, drop (6–0); Kiernan, drop (6–3) (half-time) Ringland, try (6–7); Kiernan, con (6–9); Dods, pen (9–9); Dods, pen (12–9); Kiernan, pen (12–12); Dods, pen (15–12); Ringland, try (15–16); Kiernan, con (15–18)

Scotland made seven changes from the side that had lost to Australia, including first caps for Keith Murray and Iwan Tukalo. Iain Milne withdrew at the 11th hour and was replaced by Norrie Rowan. Scotland were a little out of sorts and Ireland deserved their late victory. The Irish forwards won a lot of quality possession, especially at the lineout, and their youthful back division was enterprising and skilful. Right at the start, new cap Tukalo made a superb cover tackle on MacNeill that saved a certain score. Scotland led 6–3 at half-time. Dods kicked a penalty and Robertson a drop goal, but the Scots missed a great chance just before the break when Beattie seemed to be caught in two minds with the line at his mercy. The second half had barely started when Bradley ran wide from a scrum and made a scissors movement with Ringland for an excellent Irish try. The Scottish forwards asserted themselves and Robertson made some dangerous breaks. Towards the end, Rutherford was driven over the Irish line, but the grounding of the ball was uncertain. A penalty by Dods put Scotland in front, but in the dying seconds Ireland conjured a try fit to win any match. The Irish forwards took play up the left touchline, Dean and Kiernan made a loop movement in midfield and the ball was whipped out to Ringland who dashed over at the corner.

373 INTERNATIONAL CHAMPIONSHIP 1985 FRANCE

Parc des Princes, Paris · Saturday 16 February 1985 · Lost 3–11

SCOTLAND Peter Dods (*Gala*); Peter Steven (*Heriot's FP*), Keith Murray (*Hawick*), Keith Robertson (*Melrose*), Jim Pollock (*Gosforth*); John Rutherford (*Selkirk*), Roy Laidlaw (*Jed-Forest*); Gerry McGuinness (*W of Scot*), Colin Deans (*Hawick*), Iain Milne (*Harlequins*), Alister Campbell (*Hawick*), Tom Smith (*Gala*), Jim Calder (*Stew-Mel FP*), David Leslie* (*Gala*), Iain Paxton (*Selkirk*) ... Replacement: Gordon Hunter (*Selkirk*) for Laidlaw (half-time)

FRANCE Serge Blanco (*Biarritz*); Laurent Pardo (*Monteferrand*), Philippe Sella (*Agen*), Didier Codorniou (*Narbonne*), Patrick Estève (*Narbonne*); Jean-Patrick Lescarboura (*Dax*), Jérôme Gallion (*Toulon*); Pierre Dospital (*Bayonne*), Philippe Dintrans* (*Tarbes*), Jean-Pierre Garuet (*Lourdes*), Francis Haget (*Biarritz*), Jean Condom (*Boucau*), Jacques Gratton (*Agen*), Laurent Rodriguez (*Mont-de-Marsan*), Jean-Luc Joinel (*Brive*)

REFEREE LM Prideaux (*England*)

SCORING Dods, pen (3–0); Blanco, try (3–4); Lescarboura, pen (3–7); Blanco, try (3–11) (half-time)

Grand Slam heroes Iain Milne and David Leslie were recalled, but shortly before the match Scotland had to replace both wings with Peter Steven coming in for Iwan Tukalo and Jim Pollock for Roger Baird. The Scots battled hard against a talented French side, but they had little in attack. Much of their possession was too slow, and their lineout play and tactical kicking were imprecise. The Scottish half-backs were under a lot of pressure although Gordon Hunter played well after he came on for Laidlaw at half-time. Scotland took the lead against the run of play when Dods kicked a penalty, but almost at once Blanco burst through the Scottish defence for a classic French try. Lescarboura kicked a penalty and then made an elusive run before linking with Sella who put Blanco away for his second try. It seemed that France would cut loose after the interval, but there was no further scoring in a meandering second half.

---

374   INTERNATIONAL CHAMPIONSHIP 1985   WALES

Murrayfield · Saturday 2 March 1985 · Lost 21–25

SCOTLAND Peter Dods (*Gala*); Peter Steven (*Heriot's FP*), Keith Murray (*Hawick*), Keith Robertson (*Melrose*), Roger Baird (*Kelso*); John Rutherford (*Selkirk*), Gordon Hunter (*Selkirk*); Gerry McGuinness (*W of Scot*), Colin Deans (*Hawick*), Iain Milne (*Harlequins*), Alister Campbell (*Hawick*), Alan Tomes (*Hawick*), Jim Calder (*Stew-Mel FP*), David Leslie* (*Gala*), Iain Paxton (*Selkirk*) ... Replacement: Douglas Wyllie (*Stew-Mel FP*) for Murray (38)

WALES Mark Wyatt (*Swansea*); Mark Titley (*Bridgend*), Robert Ackerman (*London Welsh*), Mark Ring (*Cardiff*), Phil Lewis (*Llanelli*); Gareth Davies (*Cardiff*), Terry Holmes* (*Cardiff*);

Iain Paxton (with ball) is surrounded by Gerry McGuiness, Alister Campbell, Jim Calder and David Leslie after scoring his second try against Wales in 1985.
Scotsman Publications Ltd

Jeff Whitefoot (*Cardiff*), Billy James (*Aberavon*), Ian Eidman (Cardiff), John Perkins (*Pontypool*), Robert Norster (*Cardiff*), Martyn Morris (*South Wales Police*), David Pickering (*Llanelli*), Richard Moriarty (*Swansea*)

REFEREE R Hourquet (*France*)

SCORING Davies, drop (0–3); Paxton, try (4–3); Dods, con (6–3); Wyatt, pen (6–6); Wyatt, pen (6–9); Dods, pen (9–9) (half-time) Paxton, try (13–9); Dods, con (15–9); Wyatt, pen (15–12); Rutherford, drop (18–12); Pickering, try (18–16); Wyatt, con (18–18); Rutherford, drop (21–18); Pickering, try (21–22); Wyatt, pen (21–25)

Scotland showed signs of improvement, but Wales had stronger forwards and more inventive backs. The highlight for Scotland was a remarkable brace of tries by No 8 Iain Paxton. He scored his first when he broke away from his own 22 and kicked ahead. Lewis got to the ball first, but inadvertently knocked it over his own line and an exultant Paxton dived on it for an amazing score. Straight from the kick-off at the start of the second half, Wales made a defensive mix-up and Paxton grabbed the ball to score his second try. This was a good day for the back-rows and Welsh flanker David Pickering also scored a brace of tries. There was only a single point between the sides when Steven hit a post with an enormous penalty attempt, but then Wyatt won the game with his fourth penalty.

---

375   INTERNATIONAL CHAMPIONSHIP 1985   ENGLAND

Twickenham · Saturday 16 March 1985 · Lost 7–10

SCOTLAND Peter Dods (*Gala*); Peter Steven (*Heriot's FP*), Douglas Wyllie (*Stew-Mel FP*), Keith Robertson (*Melrose*), Roger Baird (*Kelso*); John Rutherford (*Selkirk*), Gordon Hunter (*Selkirk*); Gerry McGuinness (*W of Scot*), Colin Deans (*Hawick*), Iain Milne (*Harlequins*), Alister Campbell (*Hawick*), Alan Tomes (*Hawick*), John Jeffrey (*Kelso*), David Leslie* (*Gala*), Iain Paxton (*Selkirk*)

ENGLAND Chris Martin (*Bath*); Simon Smith (*Wasps*), Kevin Simms (*Cambridge U & Liverpool*), Paul Dodge* (*Leicester*), Rory Underwood (*Leicester*); Rob Andrew (*Cambridge U & Nottingham*), Richard Harding (*Bristol*); Phil Blakeway (*Gloucester*), Steve Brain (*Coventry*), Gary Pearce (*Northampton*), John Orwin (*Gloucester*), Wade Dooley (*Preston Grasshoppers*), John Hall (*Bath*), David Cooke (*Harlequins*), Bob Hesford (*Bristol*)

REFEREE Clive Norling (*Wales*)

SCORING Andrew, pen (0–3); Robertson, try (4–3); Andrew, pen (4–6) (half-time) Dods, pen (7–6); Smith, try (7–10)

The bulky English forwards dominated possession, but their backs achieved little and largely ignored their talented wings. Scotland were more incisive, especially Rutherford and Robertson, but they were starved of possession. Playing with the wind, Andrew kicked an enormous penalty and just before the interval Hunter made a half-break before Robertson carved his way through the defence for a glorious Scottish try. Andrew and Dods exchanged penalties either side of the break. Towards the finish, Dods spilled a high kicked inside his 22 and the ball was whipped out to Smith who easily rounded Baird for a try at the corner. Scotland still had one great chance to snatch victory right at the end. A kick ahead by Dods was followed-up by three Scottish players. It was a simple matter for one of them to pick-up and score, but they all over-ran the ball. Rutherford gathered, but fatally delayed his pass to Paxton who was caught at the line and the chance had gone. Thus Scotland went from Grand Slam to Grand Slump in a single season.

The Hastings Era 1986–1995

A NEW ERA FOR Scottish rugby began with the match against France in January 1986. Colin Deans was appointed as captain, an honour that was overdue, and Derrick Grant, who had won 14 caps in the 1960s, took over as coach with Ian McGeechan, another former player, as his deputy. The 1984 Grand Slam side had started to break-up and the selectors boldly chose six newcomers, including the Hastings brothers, Gavin and Scott, prop David Sole and flanker Finlay Calder, the twin brother of Jim. The injection of new blood made an immediate impact and Scotland won an unexpected victory against the odds. They were unlucky to lose their next game against Wales and then they swept aside England at Murrayfield (33–6) and narrowly beat Ireland (10–9) to finish as joint champions with France.

That success set the tone for an exciting period for Scottish rugby. Ian McGeechan and Jim Telfer took over as head coaches in 1988. Ambitious and innovative, they were adept at getting the best out of their limited resources. Their sides adopted an attractive, rapid style of rugby that made some of the other countries look old-fashioned and slow. With the ongoing malaise of the Scottish football team, the rugby side became the standard bearers for Scottish sporting aspirations and also, to some extent, the focus of national pride and identity. Even the traditionalist SRU cottoned on to the new mood and in 1989 adopted the Corries' song 'The Flower of Scotland' as an unofficial national anthem. International matches at Murrayfield, which had had its capacity gradually reduced in the 1980s, attracted huge interest and tickets were much sought over and highly prized. The Scottish Rugby Union responded with great foresight and undertook an enormous and costly redevelopment of the ground. In 1992, the old terraces at the north and south ends were replaced by towering two-level stands. Shortly afterwards, the historic west stand was demolished and its awe-inspiring replacement completed an atmospheric concrete bowl with an all-seated capacity of over 67,000.

On the field the greatest achievement was, of course, the Grand Slam in 1990 which Scotland won in a famous winner-takes-all match against England. The Scots had stuttered during the campaign and had been largely written-off, but on the day they were deserved winners thanks to astute tactical planning and their self-belief, probably the greatest victory in the history of the Scottish game. Three months later, Scotland toured New Zealand and in the second test match at Auckland they were agonisingly close to beating the All Blacks for the first time ever. The period between 1986 and 1995 was one of 'Fortress Murrayfield' when Scotland were almost un-beatable at home. They won 17 out of 20 championship matches at Murrayfield and England were the only European side to win on Scottish soil. Scotland were much less successful on the road. They played their part in some memorable encounters, but won only five times in ten years: thrice in Ireland (1986, 1990 and 1992) and once each in Cardiff (1990) and Paris (1995). They also drew at Twickenham in 1989 and Dublin in 1994. The former venue retained its reputation as Scotland's graveyard and Scotland lost the Triple Crown there in 1987 and 1993. On a brighter note, in February 1995, Scotland won in Paris for the first time in 26 years with an extra-ordinary last minute try and conversion by the inspirational Gavin Hastings. That famous win set-up Scotland for another Grand Slam decider against England, albeit this time at Twickenham. The Scots defended courageously and played their best, but England were worthy winners.

The most significant innovation of this period was the introduction of the Rugby World Cup. The inaugural tournament was held in Australia and New Zealand in 1987. The World Cup was a leap in the dark for rugby and was not taken entirely seriously in some quarters, but Scotland gave the fledgling competition a great boost when they fought out a thrilling draw with France at the start of the group stages. The Scots went on to reach the quarter-finals where they were lost to New Zealand, the eventual winners. Despite initial misgivings, the World Cup was an unbridled success and a second tournament was held in the British Isles and France in 1991. Scotland benefitted from playing all their matches at Murrayfield and reached the semi-final where they lost a titanic struggle against England. The World Cup caught the public imagination and was a great encouragement to nations outside the traditional elite, such as Samoa, Argentina, Canada and Italy. In the early '90s, South Africa, one of the world's rugby giants, returned to the international stage after years of isolation and boycott. They quickly re-established their old pre-eminence and in November 1994 they won easily at Murrayfield (34–10). The following year, the third Rugby World Cup was held in the new Rainbow Nation. Scotland reached the quarter-finals, but once again lost to New Zealand, the eventual finalists. Two years earlier, New Zealand had been the first side to score more than 50 points against the Scots, winning 51–15 at Murrayfield in November 1993. This defeat sent shockwaves through Scottish rugby and was to have a profound effect on the development of the game in the professional era.

Full-back Gavin Hastings bestrides this era like a colossus. A big man at 6ft 2in and around 14½ stones, he was a solid tackler, secure under the high ball and had a prodigious boot. He burst onto the international scene with six match-winning penalties against France in 1986 and in the course of his nine year career he scored a total of 667 points for Scotland, including 17 tries. A born leader, he was blessed with huge self-confidence and had the rare ability to inspire others. He took over the Scottish captaincy from David Sole in 1992 and the following year led the British Lions in New Zealand. For several years he was the best full-back in world rugby. Gavin won his first cap on the same day as his younger brother Scott who played at outside centre. Scott Hastings had a longer career than Gavin and was known for his strong straight running and rock solid defence. The cocksure Hastings won 64 caps, toured twice with the Lions and, if nothing else, is remembered for a brilliant try-saving tackle on the English flyer Rory Underwood in the 1990 match. Hastings formed an effective centre partnership with Boroughmuir's Sean Lineen, one of a line of 'kilted kiwis' who came from New Zealand to play for the land of their ancestors. Lineen, a classic smooth-running centre, later made a successful move into professional coaching. On the wings, Tony Stanger was a powerful runner who knew the way to the line. He scored five tries in his first two internationals and won immortality for his winning try against England in 1990. Selkirk's Iwan Tukalo made 37 appearances between 1985 and 1992. He was very fast and a great finisher, scoring 15 international tries in the course of his career. Kenny Logan made his debut in 1992 at full-back and was the first player to be capped from Stirling County. A natural extrovert, he won 70 caps over 11 years and became something of a media personality after his move to London Wasps in 1997, one of the first Scottish players to exploit the possibilities of the new professional era.

John Rutherford and Roy Laidlaw retired in the late '80s and they were followed by another Border half-back pairing, Craig Chalmers of Melrose and Gary Armstrong of Jed-Forest. In the early '90s, 'Chick' Chalmers was the pin-up boy of Scottish rugby. He was an astute tactical kicker with a good break and a solid tackler, although he became a more cautious player as he got older. Armstrong was the proverbial Border terrier. He was tenacious and determined with a good long pass and devastating around the fringes. It was Armstrong more than anybody who turned the 1990 Grand Slam match in Scotland's favour. He injured his knee in 1992 which opened the door for Dundee's Andy Nichol who won 23 caps over nine years. Nichol was a very competent scrum-half who captained Scotland to a famous win over England in 2000 and also Bath to the European Cup in 1998.

In the forwards, softly-spoken prop David Sole is forever identified with the slow walk onto Murrayfield before the Grand Slam game in 1990. Educated at Glenalmond College, he won 44 caps, toured with the Lions in 1989 and was an inspirational and thoughtful leader. Unobtrusive tight-head Paul Burnell won 52 caps over ten years, including three World Cups. At hooker Kenny Milne, the younger brother of prop Iain, had a good work-rate and was hard-tackling and courageous. Scotland lacked a world class second-row in this period, but Grand Slam partnership Chris Gray and Damian Cronin were more than competent. Cronin, a larger-than-life figure, was often an erratic performer, but won 45 caps over ten years, including a spell as a professional with London Wasps. Melrose's Doddie Weir was a mainstay of the Scottish boiler-house in the nineties. A tall and angular man, he was a superb lineout player and had great mobility. In season 1992–93, Cornishman Andy Reed had a spectacular rise from obscurity to the British Lions test side. He was the best Scottish lineout player since Gordon Brown although his career was blighted by injury.

In the late '80s Scotland had a superb back-row of Finlay Calder, John Jeffrey and Derek White. Calder was the twin brother of Jim, one of the heroes of the 1984 Grand Slam, but curiously their international careers never overlapped. Finlay was a dynamic flank forward who was good with the ball in hand and fearless in the tackle. He showed great tenacity to win his first cap at the comparatively late age of 28 and went on to captain the Lions to a series win in Australia in 1989. John Jeffrey was one of the most charismatic Scottish players of his generation. A Border farmer, he stood out with his blonde-hair and chiselled face. He was at his best in loose play and was a great sevens player with Kelso. Derek White played both at lock and No 8, and won 42 caps over ten years. He was a big man with great pace and athleticism as well as an uncompromising attitude. Fair-haired Derek Turnbull was an abrasive flanker who was unlucky not to win more than 15 caps. Later, Rob Wainwright, an army doctor, had a quiet and urbane personality that disguised a steely determination. He was not a showy player, but won 37 caps, captained Scotland and was effective at the tail of the lineout and in defence.

One final development of this era was the beginning of competitive women's rugby in Scotland. Women's club sides emerged in the late 1980s principally in the universities or as an offshoot of established men's clubs. In February 1993, the Scotland Women's team played their first international match, beating Ireland 10–0 at Raeburn Place. The following year Scotland hosted the second Women's Rugby World Cup which was won by England. Scotland played in a Home Nations tournament in 1996 and subsequently in the Women's Six Nations Championship where, like their male counterparts, they have endured mixed fortunes. In 2007, Donna Kennedy, a forward with Royal High Corstorphine, became the first Scottish player of either sex to reach the milestone of 100 international caps.

376   INTERNATIONAL CHAMPIONSHIP 1986   FRANCE

Murrayfield · Saturday 18 January 1986 · Won 18–17

SCOTLAND †Gavin Hastings (*Cambridge U*); †Matt Duncan (*W of Scot*), David Johnston (*Watsonians*), †Scott Hastings (*Watsonians*), Roger Baird (*Kelso*); John Rutherford (*Selkirk*), Roy Laidlaw (*Jed-Forest*); †David Sole (*Bath*), Colin Deans* (*Hawick*), Iain Milne (*Harlequins*), Alister Campbell (*Hawick*), †Jeremy Campbell-Lamerton (*London Scot*), John Jeffrey (*Kelso*), †Finlay Calder (*Stew-Mel FP*), John Beattie (*Glasgow Acs*)

FRANCE Serge Blanco (*Biarritz*); Jean-Baptiste Lafond (*RCF*), Philippe Sella (*Agen*), Pierre Chadebech (*Brive*), Patrick Estève (*Narbonne*); Guy Laporte (*Graulhet*), Pierre Berbizier (*Agen*); Philippe Marocco (*Montferrand*) , Daniel Dubroca* (*Agen*), Jean-Pierre Garuet (*Lourdes*), Francis Haget (*Biarritz*), Jean Condom (*Boucau*), Jacques Gratton (*Agen*), Dominique Erbani (*Agen*), Jean-Luc Joinel (*Brive*)

REFEREE David Burnett (*Ireland*)

SCORING Berbizier, try (0–4); G Hastings, pen (3–4); G Hastings, pen (6–4); Laporte, pen (6–7); G Hastings, pen (9–7); G Hastings, pen (12–7) (half-time) Laporte, drop (12–10); G Hastings, pen (15–10); Sella, try (15–14); G Hastings, pen (18–14); Laporte, pen (18–17)

In a famous result, new-look Scotland did not score any tries but they won the game with six penalties by newcomer Gavin Hastings. Arguably, France were the better side but they were let down by poor discipline. In a dramatic opening, Hastings put his kick-off straight out of play and most of the players and the referee retired to the middle of the pitch for the restart. The quick-thinking French took a short lineout, as they were entitled to do, and ran away up the right touchline for a sensational try scored inside the first minute. It said much about Scotland's self-belief and commitment that they recovered from this early blow and went on to victory.

377   INTERNATIONAL CHAMPIONSHIP 1986   WALES

Cardiff Arms Park · Saturday 1 February 1986 · Lost 15–22

SCOTLAND Gavin Hastings (*Cambridge U*); Matt Duncan (*W of Scot*), David Johnston (*Watsonians*), Scott Hastings (*Watsonians*), Roger Baird (*Kelso*); John Rutherford (*Selkirk*), Roy Laidlaw (*Jed-Forest*); David Sole (*Bath*), Colin Deans* (*Hawick*), Iain Milne (*Harlequins*), Alister Campbell (*Hawick*), Iain Paxton (*Selkirk*), John Jeffrey (*Kelso*), Finlay Calder (*Stew-Mel FP*), John Beattie (*Glasgow Acs*)

WALES Paul Thorburn (*Neath*); Phil Lewis (*Llanelli*), John Devereux (*South Glamorgan Inst*), Bleddyn Bowen (*South Wales Police*), Adrian Hadley (*Cardiff*); Jonathan Davies (*Neath*), Robert Jones (*Swansea*); Jeff Whitefoot (*Cardiff*), Billy James (*Aberavon*), Ian Eidman (*Cardiff*), John Perkins (*Pontypool*), David Waters (*Newport*), Mark Brown (*Pontypool*), David Pickering* (*Llanelli*), Phil Davies (*Llanelli*)

REFEREE Bob Francis (*New Zealand*)

SCORING Thorburn, pen (0–3); Thorburn, pen (0–6); Duncan, try (4–6); Jeffrey, try (8–6); Thorburn, pen (8–9); G Hastings, try (12–9) (half-time) Hadley, try (12–13); G Hastings, pen (15–13); J Davies, drop (15–16); Thorburn, pen (15–19); Thorburn, pen (15–22)

The lead changed hands six times in this enthralling encounter. The Scots won the try count and might have taken the honours if it had not been for two freakishly long penalty goals by Welsh full-back Paul Thorburn. With the score delicately balanced, Thorburn blasted over a monumental goal from deep inside his own half which effectively killed off the Scottish challenge. Thorburn's effort was measured at a phenomenal 70 yards 8 inches and was reckoned to be one of the longest goals ever kicked in an international match. Later, he knocked over another huge effort from halfway to seal the game. It was hard lines on the Scots because they played very well and dominated in the loose. John Jeffrey was in outstanding form and scored a great try after a handling movement down the left touchline that he himself had initiated. Scotland's other tries were scored by Matt Duncan following a break by Rutherford and by Gavin Hastings who forced his way over in the corner. In the second half, Hadley scored a try for Wales and then Scotland spent a long period on the Welsh line, but were unable to capitalise. They lost control of the ball at an attempted pushover and twice Sole was driven over the line but the referee was unsighted. Gavin Hastings restored the Scottish lead with a penalty before a Davies drop goal and Thorburn's match-winning heroics.

---

378   INTERNATIONAL CHAMPIONSHIP 1986   ENGLAND

Murrayfield · Saturday 15 February 1986 · Won 33–6

SCOTLAND Gavin Hastings (*Watsonians*); Matt Duncan (*W of Scot*), David Johnston (*Watsonians*), Scott Hastings (*Watsonians*), Roger Baird (*Kelso*); John Rutherford (*Selkirk*), Roy Laidlaw (*Jed-Forest*); Alex Brewster (*Stew-Mel FP*), Colin Deans* (*Hawick*), Iain Milne (*Harlequins*), Alister Campbell (*Hawick*), Iain Paxton (*Selkirk*), John Jeffrey (*Kelso*), Finlay Calder (*Stew-Mel FP*), John Beattie (*Glasgow Acs*)

ENGLAND Huw Davies (*Wasps*); Simon Smith (*Wasps*), Simon Halliday (*Bath*), Jamie Salmon (*Harlequins*), Mike Harrison (*Wakefield*); Rob Andrew (*Nottingham*), Nigel Melville* (*Wasps*); Paul Rendall (*Wasps*), Steve Brain (*Coventry*), Gary Pearce (*Northampton*), Wade Dooley (*Preston Grasshoppers*), Maurice Colclough (*Swansea*), John Hall (*Bath*), Peter Winterbottom (*Headingley*), Graham Robbins (*Coventry*)

REFEREE Bob Francis (*New Zealand*)

SCORING G Hastings, pen (3–0); Andrew, pen (3–3); G Hastings, pen (6–3); G Hastings, pen (9–3); Andrew, pen (9–6); G Hastings, pen (12–6) (half-time) Duncan, try (16–6); G Hastings, con (18–6); G Hastings, pen (21–6); Rutherford, try (25–6); G Hastings, con (27–6); S Hastings, try (31–6); G Hastings, con (33–6)

Alex Brewster was recalled at prop six years after winning his previous cap as a flanker. In this incredible match, Scotland gave their lumbering opponents a lesson in the arts of fitness, mobility and speed of thought. England started the game as favourites, but long before the finish they had completely lost heart and were utterly bedraggled. The Scots recorded their biggest win in the fixture and looked like they could go on all evening. Scotland held a six-point lead at the interval and there were few signs of the impending rout. The Scots scored their first try when Rutherford made a half-break and Duncan powered over at the right corner. Gavin Hastings converted from the touchline and then kicked a penalty. Towards the finish, Calder plundered a loose ball in midfield and some quick handling found Rutherford inside the English 22. The stand-off swerved to the line leaving a trail of defenders in his wake. Then an English attack broke down, Baird picked-up and set-off down the left. The back-row gave their support and the ball was passed infield to Scott Hastings who juggled with it before touching down at the posts. This was a hugely impressive team performance by Scotland. The Hastings brothers, both winning only their third caps, played with enormous confidence and maturity. Gavin Hastings fielded immaculately and landed eight goals. Matt Duncan troubled the defence every time he had the ball. Rutherford and Laidlaw, the old firm at half-back, were at their commanding best and the back-row rampaged about the field to great effect.

---

379   INTERNATIONAL CHAMPIONSHIP 1986   IRELAND

Lansdowne Road, Dublin · Saturday 15 March 1986 · Won 10–9

SCOTLAND   Gavin Hastings (*Watsonians*); Keith Robertson (*Melrose*), David Johnston (*Watsonians*), Scott Hastings (*Watsonians*), Roger Baird (*Kelso*); John Rutherford (*Selkirk*), Roy Laidlaw (*Jed-Forest*); Alex Brewster (*Stew-Mel FP*), Colin Deans* (*Hawick*), Iain Milne (*Harlequins*), Alister Campbell (*Hawick*), Iain Paxton (*Selkirk*), John Jeffrey (*Kelso*), Finlay Calder (*Stew-Mel FP*), John Beattie (*Glasgow Acs*)

IRELAND   Hugo MacNeill (*London Irish*); Trevor Ringland (*Ballymena*), Brendan Mullin (*Dublin U*), Michael Kiernan (*Dolphin*), Keith Crossan (*Instonians*); Tony Ward (*Greystones*), Michael Bradley (*Cork Const*); Phil Orr (*Old Wesley*), Ciaran Fitzgerald* (*St Mary's Coll*), Des Fitzgerald (*Lansdowne*), Donal Lenihan (*Cork Const*), Brian McCall (*London Irish*), Dave Morrow (*Bangor*), Nigel Carr (*Ards*), Willie Anderson (*Dungannon*)

REFEREE   Francis Palmade (*France*)

SCORING   Kiernan, pen (0–3); Ringland, try (0–7); Kiernan, con (0–9) (half-time) G Hastings, pen (3–9); G Hastings, pen (6–9); Laidlaw, try (10–9)

Scotland were firm favourites but they seemed to freeze on the day and were fortunate to escape with a narrow victory. Ireland played with the strong wind behind them in the first half and led 9–0 at the interval. Kiernan kicked a penalty and Ringland scored a well-worked try after a break by Mullen. In the second half, Gavin Hastings kicked two penalties, the second a huge effort from inside his own half. Then from a scrum in midfield, Beattie fed Laidlaw who broke through the defence for a great solo try. Scotland looked poised to run away with the game but somehow they lost their way in the closing stages and Ireland made a stirring comeback. The home side made some wonderful handling attacks, but they could not penetrate a tight Scottish defence. Near the finish Kiernan missed a simple penalty chance that probably would have won the game. Scotland's victory meant that they had won three games out of four in the Championship and finished the season as joint winners with France.

23 August Stadium, Bucharest · Saturday 29 March 1986
Won 33–18

SCOTLAND Gavin Hastings (*Watsonians*); Matt Duncan (*W of Scot*), David Johnston (*Watsonians*), Scott Hastings (*Watsonians*), Roger Baird (*Kelso*); John Rutherford (*Selkirk*), Roy Laidlaw (*Jed-Forest*); Alex Brewster (*Stew-Mel FP*), Colin Deans* (*Hawick*), Iain Milne (*Harlequins*), Alister Campbell (*Hawick*), Iain Paxton (*Selkirk*), John Jeffrey (*Kelso*), Finlay Calder (*Stew-Mel FP*), John Beattie (*Glasgow Acs*)

ROMANIA Liviu Hodorca (*Steaua*); Radoico Vionov (*Timisoara U*) Vasile David (*Steaua*), Adrian Lungu (*Dinamo*), Marcel Toader (*Dinamo*); Gelu Ignat (*CSM Sibiu*), Mircea Parachiv* (*Dinamo*); Vasile Pascu (*Dinamo*), Mircea Munteanu (*Steaua*), Ioan Bucan (*Dinamo*), Laurentiu Constantin (*Steaua*), Gheorghie Caragea (*Dinamo*), Florica Murariu (*Steaua*), Viorel Giuglea (*Farul*), Stefan Constantin (*Farul*) ... Replacements: Nicolae Copil (*Cluj U*) for Toader, Valere Tufa (*Dinamo*) for Munteanu

REFEREE Roger Quittenton (*England*)

SCORING G Hastings, pen (3–0); Ignat, drop (3–3); G Hastings, pen (6–3); Ignat, pen (6–6); G Hastings, pen (9–6); G Hastings, pen (12–6); Ignat, pen (12–9); G Hastings, pen (15–9); Ignat, pen (15–12) (half-time) Jeffrey, try (19–12); G Hastings, con (21–12); Ignat, pen (21–15); S Hastings, try (25–15); G Hastings, con (27–15); Ignat, pen (27–18); Deans, try (32–18); G Hastings, con (34–18)

On a warm afternoon, Scotland avenged their defeat by Romania two years earlier. The Scots were not quite at their best and clearly were affected by the heat, but they did more than enough for a satisfactory win. The Scottish forwards stood-up to the challenge of the burly Romanians and had greater mobility and all-round fitness. The Scottish defence was very strong and full-back Gavin Hastings gave another impressive display. He kicked five penalties in the first half to give Scotland an interval lead. Thereafter Scotland never looked seriously threatened and they scored three second half tries by Jeffrey, Scott Hastings and Deans. This game is best remembered for Roger Baird's try-that-never-was. Baird was a prolific try scorer for Kelso and the South of Scotland, and had scored in a British Lions test match, but had yet to score for Scotland. Midway through the first half, he seemed finally to have broken his duck when he squeezed in at the left corner only for the touch-judge to rule, perhaps mistakenly, that he had put a foot in touch. Baird won a total of 27 caps and was a first class wing, but curiously he never scored a try for Scotland.

TOUR OF SPAIN AND FRANCE 1986   SPAIN

Cornella, Barcelona · Thursday 1 May 1986 · Won 39–17

SCOTLAND XV Peter Dods (*Gala*); Matt Duncan (*W of Scot*), David Johnston (*Watsonians*), Keith Murray (*Hawick*), Iwan Tukalo (*Selkirk*); Richard Cramb (*Harlequins*), Stuart Johnston (*Watsonians*); Alex Brewster (*Stew-Mel FP*), Gary Callander* (*Kelso*), Gary Waite (*Kelso*), Alister Campbell (*Hawick*), Iain Paxton (*Selkirk*), John Jeffrey (*Kelso*), Derek Turnbull (*Hawick*), John Beattie (*Glasgow Acs*)

SPAIN Franciso Puertas (*Canoe NC*); Ricardo Sainz de la Cuesta (*Arquitectura*), Gabriel Rivero (*Hagetmau*), Jon Azkargorta (*Getxo*), J Cubelis; Jorge Moreno (*Arquitectura*), Javier Diaz (*Getxo*); Julio Alvarez (*El Salvador*), Santiago Santos* (*Liceo Francés*), Tomas Pardo (*Valencia*), Francisco Mendez (*Cisneros*), Bosco Abascal (*Ciencias*), Hector Massoni (*Santboiana*), Sergio Loughney (*FC Barcelona*), Alberto Malo (*Santboiana*) ... Replacement: Javier Chocarro (*AS Sebastián*) for Loughney (51)

REFEREE René Hourquet (*France*)

SCORING Scotland's tries were scored by Duncan (2), Cramb, Johnston, Tukalo, Johnston and Murray. Dods kicked four conversions and a penalty. For Spain, Puertas, Ribero and Azcargota scored tries. Diaz converted one and Puertas kicked a penalty. The half-time score was 25–7.

In May 1986, Scotland made a five-match tour of Spain and France, beginning with a non-cap test against the Spanish National XV. Some first choice players were unavailable and the Scots fielded a rather makeshift side, including uncapped half-backs Richard Cramb and Stuart Johnston. Played on a threadbare pitch in front of a small crowd, Scotland were comfortable winners but they were clearly affected by the heat and at times lost their momentum. The Scottish forwards made some stirring drives and the set-piece play was solid. John Beattie's pick-ups from No 8 created tries for Tukalo and Duncan, the latter after a direct pass by Beattie to the narrow side. The Spanish were largely outclassed, but they worked hard and were surprisingly resilient. Following this match, the Scots played four very tough games in the south of France. They won only their final fixture against a Pyrenees XV in Graulhet (26–7). There is, incidentally, some confusion about the status of the third match of the tour against an Armagnac-Bigorre XV at Tarbes, which the Scots did well to draw (16–16). The home side fielded virtually a full French international team and in some quarters the game has been described as a non-cap test match. Officially, this was a provincial game and therefore an account of it does not appear in this book.

XV   TOUR MATCH   JAPAN

Murrayfield · Saturday 27 September 1986 · Won 33–18

SCOTLAND XV Peter Dods (*Gala*); Matt Duncan (*W of Scot*), David Johnston (*Watsonians*), Scott Hastings (*Watsonians*), Iwan Tukalo (*Selkirk*); Douglas Wyllie (*Stew-Mel FP*), Roy Laidlaw (*Jed-Forest*); David Sole (*Bath*), Colin Deans* (*Hawick*), Norrie Rowan (*Boroughmuir*), Alister Campbell (*Hawick*), Iain Paxton (*Selkirk*), John Jeffrey (*Kelso*), Finlay Calder (*Stew-Mel FP*), John Beattie (*Glasgow Acs*) ... Replacement: Andrew Ker (*Kelso*) for Wyllie

JAPAN Katsunori Ishii (*Waseda U*); Nofomuli Taumoefolau (*Sanyo Electric*), Eiji Kutsuki (*Toyota*), Seiji Hirao (*Kobe Steel*), Shinji Onuki (*Suntory*); Katsuhiro Matsuo (*Doshisha U*), Yoshimitsu Konishi (*Suntory*); Osamu Ohta (*Meiji U*), Tsuyoshi Fujita (*Nisshin Steel*), Masaharu Aizawa (*Richo*), Yoshihiko Sakuraba (*Nippon Steel Kamaishi*), Seiji Kurihara (*Waseda U*), Hopoi Taione (*Sanyo Electric*), Toshiyuki Hayashi* (*Kobe Steel*), Michihito Chida (*Nippon Steel Kamaishi*) ... Replacement: Katsufumi Miyamoto (*Doshisha U*) for Taiona

REFEREE LM Prideaux (*England*)

SCORING Tukalo, try (4–0); Dods, con (6–0); Matsuo, pen (6–3); Matsuo, drop (6–6); Dods, pen (9–6); Tukalo, try (13–6) (half-time) Tukalo, try (17–6); Duncan, try (21–6); Dods, con (23–6); Tukalo, try (27–6); Dods, con (29–6); Campbell, try (33–6); Onuki, try (33–10); Chida, try (33–14); Kutsuki, try (33–18)

In autumn 1986, Japan made an eight match tour of Scotland and England. The tour opened in Melrose with a big defeat by the South of Scotland (12–45) followed by a win over the North and Midlands (27–19) and a loss to Edinburgh (14–26). Scotland did not award caps and several regulars were unavailable. This was a memorable afternoon for left wing Iwan Tukalo who had come in for the injured Roger Baird. He scored four tries and threatened every time he had the ball. On the other wing Matt Duncan scored a thrilling solo try from long range. The Scottish scoring was completed by lock Alister Campbell who finished off a superb handling movement that had started in the Scottish 22. To their credit the Japanese made a heroic comeback and scored three late tries. Playing in early season, the Scots were a little rusty, but they were always eager and the forwards made some stirring charges.

---

381   INTERNATIONAL CHAMPIONSHIP 1987   IRELAND

Murrayfield · Saturday 21 February 1987 · Won 16–12

SCOTLAND Gavin Hastings (*Watsonians*); Matt Duncan (*W of Scot*), Douglas Wyllie (*Stew-Mel FP*), Scott Hastings (*Watsonians*), Iwan Tukalo (*Selkirk*); John Rutherford (*Selkirk*), Roy Laidlaw (*Jed-Forest*); David Sole (*Bath*), Colin Deans* (*Hawick*), Iain Milne (*Heriot's FP*), Alan Tomes (*Hawick*), Iain Paxton (*Selkirk*), John Jeffrey (*Kelso*), Finlay Calder (*Stew-Mel FP*), John Beattie (*Glasgow Acs*)

IRELAND Hugo MacNeill (*London Irish*); Trevor Ringland (*Ballymena*), Brendan Mullin (*Oxford U*), Michael Kiernan (*Dolphin*), Keith Crossan (*Instonians*); Paul Dean (*St Mary's Coll*), Michael Bradley (*Cork Const*), Phil Orr (*Old Wesley*), Harry Harbison (*Bective Rgrs*), Des Fitzgerald (*Lansdowne*), Donal Lenihan* (*Cork Const*), Jim Glennon (*Skerries*), Philip Matthews (*Wdrs*), Nigel Carr (*Ards*), Willie Anderson (*Dungannon*)

REFEREE Roger Quittenton (*England*)

SCORING Rutherford, drop (3–0); Rutherford, drop (6–0); Lenihan, try (6–4); Kiernan, con (6–6); Kiernan, drop (6–9); Laidlaw, try (10–9) (half-time) Tukalo, try (14–9); G Hastings, con (16–9); Kiernan, pen (16–12)

Played on a lovely spring afternoon, this was an evenly contested match, but Scotland deserved to win because they had greater mobility and more skilful half-backs. John Rutherford stamped his authority all over proceedings. He gave Scotland the lead with two early drop goals and had a major hand in both of Scotland's tries. He also prevented a certain Irish score by getting his body underneath Kiernan as the Irishman crossed the line. Scotland's first try came in injury-time before the break. Rutherford broke down the blind side and from the ensuing ruck Laidlaw shaped to pass the ball, but wheeled around and slipped over the line. In the final quarter, Rutherford took quick ball from a ruck and put in a little kick along the ground that bounced horribly for the Irish defence. Rutherford flicked the ball on and Tukalo raced onto it and scored. Gavin Hastings, who otherwise kicked poorly, landed the important conversion and although Ireland tried hard they never looked like overhauling the Scottish lead.

Parc des Princes, Paris · Saturday 7 March 1987 · Lost 22–28

SCOTLAND Gavin Hastings (*Watsonians*); Matt Duncan (*W of Scot*), Douglas Wyllie (*Stew-Mel FP*), Scott Hastings (*Watsonians*), Iwan Tukalo (*Selkirk*); John Rutherford (*Selkirk*), Roy Laidlaw (*Jed-Forest*); David Sole (*Bath*), Colin Deans* (*Hawick*), Iain Milne (*Heriot's FP*), Alan Tomes (*Hawick*), Iain Paxton (*Selkirk*), John Jeffrey (*Kelso*), Finlay Calder (*Stew-Mel FP*), John Beattie (*Glasgow Acs*) ... Replacement: Keith Robertson (*Melrose*) for Wyllie (55)

FRANCE Serge Blanco (*Biarritz*); Philippe Bérot (*Agen*), Philippe Sella (*Agen*), Denis Charvet (*Toulouse*), Eric Bonneval (*Toulouse*); Frank Mesnel (*RCF*), Pierre Berbizier (*Agen*); Pascal Ondarts (*Biarritz*), Daniel Dubroca* (*Agen*), Jean-Pierre Garuet (*Lourdes*), Francis Haget (*Biarritz*), Jean Condom (*Biarritz*), Dominique Erbani (*Agen*), Eric Champ (*Toulon*), Laurent Rodriguez (*Montferrand*)

REFEREE Keith Lawrence (*New Zealand*)

SCORING Bonneval, try (0–4); Beattie, try (4–4); Mesnel, drop (4–7); Bonneval, try (4–11); Bérot, try (4–15); G Hastings, pen (7–15); Bérot, pen (7–18) (half-time) Bonneval, try (7–22); G Hastings, pen (10–22); Bérot, pen (10–25); G Hastings, pen (13–25); S Hastings, try (17–25); G Hastings, con (19–25); Bérot, pen (19–28); G Hastings, pen (22–28)

This was a sublime match that showed all the best qualities of the rugby game. The French were in dazzling form and scored four lovely tries, including a hat-trick for wing Eric Bonneval. Scotland were never able to overtake their opponents, but they played with great self-belief and made a stirring comeback when lesser teams might have crumbled. In the first-half, Beattie scored a try when he charged down a clearance and raced away to the line. After the break, France stretched their lead to 15 points before Gavin Hastings kicked a penalty. Then from scrum, Rutherford chipped ahead and Gavin Hastings plucked the ball out of the air to send his brother Scott over for a try. Gavin Hastings converted despite the ball toppling over and Scotland were back within striking distance. The muscular French forwards reasserted themselves, and Bérot and Hastings exchanged penalties to finish the scoring. France deserved to win to match, the third of their Grand Slam season, but the Scots left with their heads held high after a magnificent encounter.

Murrayfield · Saturday 21 March 1987 · Won 21–15

SCOTLAND Gavin Hastings (*Watsonians*); Matt Duncan (*W of Scot*), Keith Robertson (*Melrose*), Scott Hastings (*Watsonians*), Iwan Tukalo (*Selkirk*); John Rutherford (*Selkirk*) Roy Laidlaw (*Jed-Forest*); David Sole (*Bath*), Colin Deans* (*Hawick*), Iain Milne (*Heriot's FP*), Derek White (*Gala*), Iain Paxton (*Selkirk*), John Jeffrey (*Kelso*), Finlay Calder (*Stew-Mel FP*), John Beattie (*Glasgow Acs*)

WALES Mark Wyatt (*Swansea*); Glen Webbe (*Bridgend*), John Devereux (*South Glamorgan Inst*), Kevin Hopkins (*Swansea*), Ieuan Evans (*Llanelli*); Jonathan Davies (*Neath*), Robert Jones (*Swansea*); Jeff Whitefoot (*Cardiff*), Billy James (*Aberavon*), Peter Francis (*Maesteg*), Steve Sutton (*South Wales Police*), Robert Norster (*Cardiff*), Paul Moriarty (*Swansea*), David Pickering* (*Llanelli*), Mark Jones (*Neath*) ... Replacement: Adrian Hadley (*Cardiff*) for Evans (28)

For the Welsh game in 1987, Scotland fielded five players who had played No8 for their clubs: Iain Paxton, John Jeffrey, John Beattie, Finlay Calder and Derek White.

Scotsman Publications Ltd

REFEREE Keith Lawrence (*New Zealand*)

SCORING Beattie, try (4–0); G Hastings, con (6–0); G Hastings, pen (9–0); Davies, drop (9–3); G Hastings, pen (12–3) (half-time) Wyatt, pen (12–6); Wyatt, pen (12–9); Rutherford, drop (15–9); Jeffrey, try (19–9); G Hastings, con (21–9); Jones, try (21–13); Wyatt, con (21–15)

Scotland were more emphatic winners than the final score suggests and they would have won by more if their finishing had been more accurate. In fact, Wales did well to stay within touching distance for so long, such was Scotland's dominance. Famously, this was the match of the five No 8s. The back five of the Scottish scrum had all played at No 8 for their clubs and as a result the home side were much more mobile than their rather lumbering opponents. The Scottish back-row was outstanding in the loose, and their support play and driving were exemplary. Although the Welsh pack was heavier, the Scottish scrum was rock solid and props David Sole and Iain Milne gave their opponents a torrid time. Scotland scored a pushover try after only six minutes when they shunted the Welsh pack backwards over their own line and Beattie touched down. In the second half, Scotland had a major test of character when Wales pulled back to within three points, but they kept their heads and Rutherford dropped a goal. The Scots missed several more chances before Calder escaped up the right and found support from Duncan. The wing was tackled just short of the Welsh line, but the ever-present Jeffrey picked up and dived over at the corner. Gavin Hastings had not been in his best form with his kicking, but he converted from the touchline. Mark Jones scored a late consolation try for Wales and Wyatt converted.

Twickenham · Saturday 4 April 1987 · Lost 12–21

SCOTLAND Gavin Hastings (*Watsonians*); Matt Duncan (*W of Scot*), Keith Robertson (*Melrose*), Roger Baird (*Kelso*), Iwan Tukalo (*Selkirk*); John Rutherford (*Selkirk*), Roy Laidlaw (*Jed-Forest*); David Sole (*Bath*), Colin Deans* (*Hawick*), Iain Milne (*Heriot's FP*), Derek White (*Gala*), Iain Paxton (*Selkirk*), John Jeffrey (*Kelso*), Finlay Calder (*Stew-Mel FP*), John Beattie (*Glasgow Acs*) ... Replacement: Alan Tomes (*Hawick*) for Beattie (44)

ENGLAND Marcus Rose (*Harlequins*); Mike Harrison* (*Wakefield*), Simon Halliday (*Bath*), Jamie Salmon (*Harlequins*), Rory Underwood (*Leicester*); Peter Williams (*Orrell*), Richard Harding (*Bristol*); Paul Rendall (*Wasps*), Brian Moore (*Nottingham*), Gary Pearce (*Northampton*), Nigel Redman (*Bath*), Steve Bainbridge (*Fylde*), John Hall (*Bath*), Gary Rees (*Nottingham*), Dean Richards (*Leicester*)

REFEREE Owen Doyle (*Ireland*)

SCORING Hastings, pen (3–0); Rose, pen (3–3); penalty try (3–7); Rose, con (3–9) (half-time) Rose, pen (3–12); Rose, try (3–16); Rose, con (3–18); Hastings, pen (6–18); Rose, pen (6–21); Robertson, try (10–21); Hastings, con (12–21)

This match should have been played on 17 January, but was postponed because of heavy snow. Scotland went to Twickenham in search of the Triple Crown, but long before the finish they were just trying to keep the score down. Their weaknesses were ruthlessly exposed, in particular their lack of weight up-front and their inability to win lineout possession. Conditions were treacherous with a soft pitch, a slippery ball and incessant rain. England had lost all of their games so far, including a brutal affair in Cardiff, but here, with several newcomers, they were a transformation. The Scots were never allowed to get into their stride and the English forwards kept a tight grip on possession, especially in the lineout where Steve Bainbridge and Nigel Redman ruled supreme. Starved of quality ball, not even John Rutherford and Roy Laidlaw could rescue their side. The new centre pairing of Keith Robertson and Roger Baird did not combine well and in general Scotland had a lack of presence. England's opening try, their first of the championship, came from a Scottish handling error in midfield. Harrison hacked the ball into the Scottish in-goal area and as he tried to reach it he was illegally brought down by Duncan. The referee awarded a penalty try which was converted by Rose. England's other try also came from a Scottish error. Gavin Hastings failed to find touch with a clearance, Rose hoisted a high ball towards the Scottish posts which caused panic amongst the defence and the ball bounced sweetly into Rose's arms who ran over. With the match beyond them, the Scots scored a lovely try when Robertson carved his way through. Gavin Hastings converted, having earlier kicked two penalties, one a huge effort from inside his own half, but this was little consolation for a sorry and bedraggled Scotland.

XV   RUGBY WORLD CUP WARM-UP MATCH   SPAIN

Murrayfield · Sunday 19 April 1987 · Won 25–7

SCOTLAND XV Gavin Hastings (*Watsonians*); Matt Duncan (*W of Scot*), Keith Robertson

(*Melrose*), Douglas Wyllie (*Stew-Mel FP*), Iwan Tukalo (*Selkirk*); Andrew Ker (*Kelso*), Roy Laidlaw (*Jed-Forest*); David Sole (*Bath*), Colin Deans* (*Hawick*), Norrie Rowan (*Boroughmuir*), Derek White (*Gala*), Alan Tomes (*Hawick*), John Jeffrey (*Kelso*), Finlay Calder (*Stew-Mel FP*), Iain Paxton (*Selkirk*)

SPAIN Gabriel Rivero* (*Olimpico*); Enrique Uzquiano (*Canoe*), Jose Tormo (*Valencia*), Jon Azkargorta (*Getxo*), Salvador Torres (*Santboiana*); Francisco Puertas (*Canoe*), Javier Diaz (*Getxo*); Julio Alvarez (*El Salvador*), Arturo Trenzano (*BUC*), Jose del Moral (*CD Universitario*), Bosco Abascal (*Ciencias*), Francisco Mendez (*Cisneros*), Santiago Noriega (*Cisneros*), Jorge Ruiz (*Filosofia*), Alberto Malo (*Santboiana*)

REFEREE Derek Bevan (*Wales*)

SCORING Hastings, pen (3–0); Puertas, pen (3–3); Tukalo, try (7–3) (half-time) Paxton, try (11–3); Hastings, con (13–3); Deans, try (17–3); Hastings, con (19–3); Duncan, try (23–3); Hastings, con (25–3); del Moral, try (27–7)

In April 1987, Spain made a two match tour of Scotland. The tour began against a SRU President's XV at Kelso (17–27) before moving onto a non-cap test at Murrayfield. Scotland used this match as a warm-up for the inaugural World Cup due to begin the following month. They fielded their strongest side, apart from the injured John Rutherford whose place was taken by the uncapped Andrew Kerr. The Scottish players were clearly anxious to avoid injury and much of their play was undistinguished and lacked their normal conviction. The forward struggled to achieve domination, especially at the lineout, and the backs were indecisive and meandering. Scotland scored four tries, but at times found it hard to escape the fierce Spanish tackling. The biggest cheer of the day came right at the end when Spanish No8 Alberto Malo fended off several defenders before releasing his prop Jose del Moral for a short run to the line. This match set several unusual precedents. It was the first international to be played at Murrayfield on a Sunday, the traditional anthem 'God Save the Queen' was replaced by 'Scotland the Brave' (with words in the match programme) and the ball-boys ran on with buckets of sand to supply the mounds for goal kicks.

Rugby World Cup 1987

1987 was a watershed year for rugby union. After years of dithering, the inaugural Rugby World Cup was held in Australia and New Zealand. The new competition was an unknown quantity and was not greeted with universal enthusiasm, but it turned out to be a great success and transformed rugby forever. Sixteen teams were invited to take part and Scotland were drawn in Pool 4 alongside France, Romania and Zimbabwe, who had taken the place of South Africa. After a successful championship, Scotland were optimistic about their chances, but their preparations were disrupted by an injury to John Rutherford who hurt his knee playing in a rugby tournament in Bermuda. Forwards Alister Campbell and John Beattie were also ruled out because of injury.

Lancaster Park, Christchurch · Saturday 23 May 1987 · Drew 20–20

SCOTLAND Gavin Hastings (*Watsonians*); Matt Duncan (*W of Scot*), Keith Robertson (*Melrose*), Douglas Wyllie (*Stew-Mel FP*), Iwan Tukalo (*Selkirk*); John Rutherford (*Selkirk*), Roy Laidlaw (*Jed-Forest*); David Sole (*Bath*), Colin Deans* (*Hawick*), Iain Milne (*Heriot's FP*), Derek White (*Gala*), Alan Tomes (*Hawick*), John Jeffrey (*Kelso*), Finlay Calder (*Stew-Mel FP*) Iain Paxton (*Selkirk*) ... Replacement: †Alan Tait (*Kelso*) for Rutherford (7)

FRANCE Serge Blanco (*Biarritz*); Patrice Lagisquet (*Bayonne*), Philippe Sella (*Agen*), Denis Charvet (*Toulouse*), Patrick Estève (*Lavelanet*); Franck Mesnel (*RCF*), Pierre Berbizier (*Agen*); Pascal Ondarts (*Biarritz*), Daniel Dubroca (*Agen*), Jean-Pierre Garuet (*Lourdes*), Alain Lorieux (*Aix-les-Bains*), Jean Condom (*Biarritz*), Eric Champ (*Toulon*), Dominique Erbani (*Agen*), Laurent Rodriguez (*Montferrand*)

REFEREE Fred Howard (*England*)

SCORING White, try (4–0); Blanco, pen (4–3); Hastings, pen (7–3); Hastings, pen (10–3); Blanco, pen (10–6); Hastings, pen (13–6) (half-time) Hastings, pen (16–6); Sella, try (16–10); Berbizier, try (16–14); Blanco, try (16–18); Blanco, con (16–20); Duncan, try (20–20)

In the unusual surroundings of Lancaster Park, Christchurch, this was a classic encounter that had controversy and drama right to the end. Scotland made a great start and White scored in the opening minutes after Calder had erupted from the tail of a lineout. Soon after, John Rutherford was taken off with knee damage which was the end of his illustrious career. Douglas Wyllie moved to stand-off and Alan Tait came on to win his first cap. Scotland led 13–6 at the interval and early in the second-half Robertson missed a great chance when he knocked on with the line beckoning. After a Hastings penalty, the momentum swung towards France and tries by Lagisquet and Berbezier brought them back to within two points. Towards the finish, France were awarded a penalty and the game seemed to stop to allow treatment to injured players. With everybody else distracted, Blanco took a quick tap-penalty and raced away to score under the posts. He had not broken any laws and the try was awarded, but his behaviour was not in the best spirit. Stung by this reverse, the Scots fought like wounded animals to save the match. They worked up the right touchline and from a ruck Laidlaw slipped blind for White to put Duncan over at the corner. Gavin Hastings made a great attempt at the awkward conversion, but his kick drifted narrowly wide and a great match ended in a draw.

Athletic Park, Wellington · Saturday 30 May 1987 · Won 60–21

SCOTLAND Gavin Hastings (*Watsonians*); Matt Duncan (*W of Scot*), Alan Tait (*Kelso*), Keith Robertson (*Melrose*), Iwan Tukalo (*Selkirk*); Douglas Wyllie (*Stew-Mel FP*), †Greig Oliver (*Hawick*); David Sole (*Bath*), Colin Deans* (*Hawick*), Iain Milne (*Heriot's FP*), Jeremy Campbell-Lamerton (*London Scot*), Alan Tomes (*Hawick*), John Jeffrey (*Kelso*), Finlay Calder (*Stew-Mel FP*), Iain Paxton (*Selkirk*)

ZIMBABWE Andy Ferreira; Shawn Graham, Andre Buitendag, Campbell Graham, Eric Barratt; Marthinus Grobler, Malcolm Jellicoe*; Alex Nicholls, Lance Bray, Andy Tucker, Tom Sawyer, Michael Martin, Rod Gray, Dirk Buitendag, Mark Neill

SCORING Tait, try (4–0); Hastings, con (6–0); Duncan, try (10–0); Hastings, con (12–0); Grobler, pen (12–3); Oliver, try (16–3); Tukalo, try (20–3); Hastings, con (22–3); Hastings, try (26–3); Hastings, con (28–3); Paxton, try (32–3); Hastings, con (34–3); Grobler, pen (34–6); Tait, try (38–6); Hastings, con (40–6) (half-time) Paxton, try (44–6); Hastings, con (46–6); Buitendag, try (46–10); Grobler, con (46–12); Grobler, pen (46–15); Duncan, try (50–15); Grobler, pen (50–18); Grobler, pen (50–21); Jeffrey, try (54–21); Hastings, try (56–21); Tukalo, try (60–21)

Colin Deans won his 50th cap and scrum-half Greig Oliver made his debut. Scotland were comfortable winners and scored 11 tries against a plucky but limited Zimbabwe. The Scots played a tight game and starved their opponents of possession. With the infamous Wellington wind behind them, Scotland raced to a 40–6 lead at the interval. The Scottish scrum was solid and the handling was fast and accurate. With the game won, Scotland lost momentum in the second half and the Zimbabweans made a small comeback, but two late tries by Jeffrey and Tukalo sealed Scotland's first-ever victory in the World Cup.

387 RUGBY WORLD CUP 1987 ROMANIA

Carisbrook, Dunedin · Tuesday 2 June 1987 · Won 55–28

SCOTLAND Gavin Hastings (*Watsonians*); Matt Duncan (*W of Scot*), Alan Tait (*Kelso*), Scott Hastings (*Watsonians*), Iwan Tukalo (*Selkirk*); Douglas Wyllie (*Stew-Mel FP*), Roy Laidlaw (*Jed-Forest*); Norrie Rowan (*Boroughmuir*), Colin Deans* (*Hawick*), David Sole (*Bath*), Derek White (*Gala*), Alan Tomes (*Hawick*), John Jeffrey (*Kelso*), Finlay Calder (*Stew-Mel FP*), Iain Paxton (*Selkirk*) ... Replacements: †Richard Cramb (*Harlequins*) for S Hastings, Jeremy Campbell-Lamerton (*London Scot*) for Tomes

ROMANIA Vasile Ion (*Baia Mare*); Adrian Pilotschi (*Farul Constanta*), Adrian Lungu (*Dinamo*), Stefan Tofan (*Dinamo*), Marcel Toader (*Dinamo*); Dumitru Alexandru (*Steaua*), Mircea Paraschiv* (*Dinamo*); Ion Bucan (*Dinamo*), Emilian Grigore (*Farul Constanta*), Gheorghe Leonte (*Steaua*), Stefan Constantin (*Steaua*), Laurentiu Constantin (*Farul Constanta*), Haralambie Dumitras (*Buzau*), Florica Murariu (*Steaua*), Christian Raducanu (*Dinamo*) ... Replacement: Gheorghie Dumitru (*Farul Constanta*) for Raducanu

REFEREE Stephen Hilditch (*Ireland*)

SCORING Tait, try (4–0); G Hastings, con (6–0); G Hastings, pen (9–0); Jeffrey, try (13–0); G Hastings, con (15–0); Duncan, try (19–0); G Hastings, con (21–0); Tait, try (25–0); G Hastings, con (27–0); Alexandru, pen (27–3); Jeffrey, try (31–3); G Hastings, con (33–3); Murariu, try (33–7) (half-time) Jeffrey, try (37–7); G Hastings, con (39–7); Toader, try (39–11); Alexandru, con (39–13); Alexandru, pen (39–16); Alexandru, pen (39–19); G Hastings, try (43–19); Ion, pen (43–22); Tukalo, try (47–22); G Hastings, con (49–22); G Hastings, try (53–22); G Hastings, con (55–22); Murariu, try (55–26); Ion, con (55–28)

Scotland secured their place in the knock-out stages with a straightforward victory over a rather hapless Romania. This one-sided match was effectively over long before half-time as the Scots raced to a 27–0 lead before Romania scored their first points. Scotland eased off in the second half but were comfortable winners. Unfortunately, several players were injured and Scotland finished the game reduced to 14, only two replacements being permitted under competition rules. Scott Hastings lasted less than a minute before breaking down with a recurrent hamstring injury. He was replaced by new cap Richard Cramb and Douglas Wyllie moved to inside centre. Scotland scored nine tries in total, John Jeffrey three and Alan Tait two. Gavin Hastings gave another commanding display and scored 27 points. Both of Hastings' tries were spectacular efforts. From a scrum, he kicked ahead and despite starting a long way back he beat the cover defence in the ensuing hack-and-chase. His second try came from an interception in his own half when he snatched a loose pass out of the air and raced away to score. Hastings' tally set a new world record for individual points scoring in an international match, but his record lasted only a few hours before it was beaten by Didier Camberabero who scored 30 points for France against Zimbabwe. Thus Scotland finished in second place in Pool 4 behind France, the latter having won the try-count 3–2 when the two countries met in their drawn pool match. The Scots now had the unenviable task of taking on New Zealand in the quarter-final.

388 · RUGBY WORLD CUP 1987 · NEW ZEALAND

Lancaster Park, Christchurch · Saturday 6 June 1987 · Lost 3–30

SCOTLAND Gavin Hastings (*Watsonians*); Matt Duncan (*W of Scot*), Alan Tait (*Kelso*), Keith Robertson (*Melrose*), Iwan Tukalo (*Selkirk*); Douglas Wyllie (*Stew-Mel FP*), Roy Laidlaw (*Jed-Forest*): David Sole (*Bath*), Colin Deans* (*Hawick*), Iain Milne (*Heriot's FP*), Derek White (*Gala*), Alan Tomes (*Hawick*), †Derek Turnbull (*Hawick*), Finlay Calder (*Stew-Mel FP*), Iain Paxton (*Selkirk*)

NEW ZEALAND John Gallagher (*Wellington*); John Kirwan (*Auckland*), Joe Stanley (*Auckland*), Warwick Taylor (*Canterbury*), Craig Green (*Canterbury*); Grant Fox (*Auckland*), David Kirk* (*Auckland*); Steve McDowell (*Auckland*), Sean Fitzpatrick (*Auckland*), John Drake (*Auckland*), Murray Pierce (*Wellington*), Gary Whetton (*Auckland*), Alan Whetton (*Auckland*), Michael Jones (*Auckland*), Wayne Shelford (*North Harbour*) ... Replacement: Bernie McCahill (*Auckland*) for Taylor (20)

REFEREE David Burnett (*Ireland*)

SCORING Fox, pen (0–3); Fox, pen (0–6); Hastings, pen (3–6); Fox, pen (3–9) (half-time) A Whetton, try (3–13); Fox, con (3–15); Fox, pen (3–18); Fox, pen (3–21); Fox, pen (3–24); Gallacher, try (3–28); Fox, con (3–30)

Derek Turnbull won his first cap, and Colin Deans and Alan Tomes made their final appearances. Scotland defended well and gave their opponents a thorough examination, but New Zealand were just too good for them. This match was strenuously contested, but largely unspectacular and marred by a plethora of penalty awards. The prolific Grant Fox kicked six penalties and Gavin Hastings landed one from two attempts. Scotland were still in contention at the interval, but they were under a lot of pressure and started to make errors as the game progressed. Whetton scored New Zealand's first try around the 50th minute, and Fox converted and kicked three penalties to put the result beyond doubt. New Zealand's second try was the highlight of the game. From a lineout, the forwards drove to the Scottish line, Kirk fed a long miss-pass to Stanley, and Gallagher swerved inside for a try at the posts. New Zealand were the best team in the World Cup, but Scotland left with their pride intact. With a little luck in their first match against France, they might easily have reached the semi-finals.

Netherdale, Galashiels · Saturday 26 September 1987 · Won 15–12

SCOTLAND XV Ian Ramsay (*Melrose*); Matt Duncan (*W of Scot*), Tim Exeter (*Moseley*), Euan Kennedy (*Watsonians*), Iwan Tukalo (*Selkirk*); Richard Cramb (*Harlequins*), Greig Oliver (*Hawick*); David Sole (*Bath*), Gary Callander* (*Kelso*), Norrie Rowan (*Boroughmuir*), Chris Gray (*Nottingham*), Damian Cronin (*Bath*), Graham Marshall (*Wakefield*), Derek Turnbull (*Hawick*), Jeremy Macklin (*London Scot*)

FRANCE XV Jérôme Bianchi (*Toulon*); Jean-Baptiste Lafond (*RCF*), Marc Andrieu (*Nîmes*), Alain Gély (*Grenoble*), Pierre Peytavin (*Bayonne*); Franck Mesnel (*RCF*), Pierre Berbizier (*Agen*); Louis Armary (*Lourdes*), Philippe Dintrans* (*Tarbes*), Jean-Pierre Garuet (*Lourdes*), Jean Condom (*Biarritz*), Alain Carminati (*Béziers*), Jacques Gratton (*Agen*), Karl Janik (*Toulouse*), Herve Chaffardon (*Grenoble*)

REFEREE Brian Anderson (*Currie*)

SCORING Ramsay, pen (3–0); Ramsay, pen (6–0); Bianchi, pen (6–3); Mesnel, try (6–7); Bianchi, con (6–9); Bianchi, pen (6–12) (half-time) Ramsay, pen (9–12); Ramsay, pen (12–12); Ramsay, pen (15–12)

In September 1987, France made a short tour of Scotland. The tourists had mixed fortunes in their district games, winning twice in midweek against Glasgow (38–9) and Edinburgh (22–9), but losing their Saturday match against the Anglo Scots (16–19). The tour finished with a match against a Scotland XV at Netherdale, Galashiels. It is questionable if this game can be considered an international match as both sides fielded experimental line-ups and neither awarded caps. This was a disjointed and unspectacular encounter ruined by too much aimless kicking. France scored the only try, but Melrose full-back Ian Ramsey, a late replacement for Keith Robertson, won the match for Scotland with five penalties. The Scottish forwards played well, in particular uncapped locks Damian Cronin and Chris Gray who both showed their potential.

389 INTERNATIONAL CHAMPIONSHIP 1988 IRELAND

Lansdowne Road, Dublin · Saturday 16 January 1988 · Lost 18–22

SCOTLAND Gavin Hastings (*Watsonians*); Matt Duncan (*W of Scot*), Alan Tait (*Kelso*), Scott Hastings (*Watsonians*), Roger Baird (*Kelso*); Richard Cramb (*Harlequins*) Roy Laidlaw (*Jed-Forest*); David Sole (*Edinburgh Acs*), Gary Callander* (*Kelso*), Norrie Rowan (*Boroughmuir*), Derek White (*Gala*), †Damian Cronin (*Bath*), John Jeffrey (*Kelso*), Finlay Calder (*Stew-Mel FP*), Iain Paxton (*Selkirk*)

IRELAND Philip Danaher (*Lansdowne*); Trevor Ringland (*Ballymena*), Brendan Mullin (*Blackrock Coll*), Michael Kiernan (*Dolphin*), Keith Crossan (*Instonians*); Paul Dean (*St Mary's Coll*), Michael Bradley (*Cork Const*); John Fitzgerald (*Young Munster*), Terry Kingston (*Dolphin*), Des Fitzgerald (*Lansdowne*), Donal Lenihan* (*Cork Const*), Willie Anderson (*Dungannon*), Philip Matthews (*Wdrs*), Willie Sexton (*Garryowen*), Michael Gibson (*London Irish*) ... Replacement: Hugo MacNeill (*London Irish*) for Ringland (5)

REFEREE Roger Quittenton (*England*)

SCORING Mullin, try (0–4); MacNeill, try (0–8); Kiernan, con (0–10); Laidlaw, try (4–10);
G Hastings, con (6–10) (half-time) Kiernan, pen (6–13); Kiernan, drop (6–16); G Hastings, pen
(9–16); Bradley, try (9–20); Kiernan, con (9–22); G Hastings, pen (12–22); S Hastings, try (16–22);
G Hastings, con (18–22)

Several players were unavailable and John Rutherford announced his retirement shortly
after this match. Roger Baird was a surprise recall on the left wing and Damian
Cronin, who was also qualified to play for England and Ireland, won his first cap.
Ireland were more decisive winners than the final score suggests. The Irish forwards
were much sharper and controlled the lineout, and in general Ireland had better
teamwork. Scotland played well enough at times, but made a lot of errors and kicked
away too much possession. Mullin and MacNeill scored early tries for Ireland and
just before the interval Laidlaw pounced on a loose ball at an Irish scrum to score his
sixth try against the men in green. In the second half, Kiernan kicked a penalty and
dropped a goal before Gavin Hastings replied with a penalty. Then from an Irish
scrum, Gibson fed Bradley who twisted through a tackle and over the line. Scotland
rallied towards the end and Scott Hastings scored a late consolation try after a good
handling movement. Gavin Hastings converted at the second attempt after the Irish
charged prematurely.

390 INTERNATIONAL CHAMPIONSHIP 1988 FRANCE

Murrayfield · Saturday 6 February 1988 · Won 23–12

SCOTLAND Gavin Hastings (*Watsonians*); Matt Duncan (*W of Scot*), Alan Tait (*Kelso*),
Scott Hastings (*Watsonians*), Iwan Tukalo (*Selkirk*); Richard Cramb (*Harlequins*), Roy Laidlaw
(*Jed-Forest*); David Sole (*Edinburgh Acs*), Gary Callander* (*Kelso*), Norrie Rowan (*Boroughmuir*),
Alister Campbell (*Hawick*), Damian Cronin (*Bath*), Finlay Calder (*Stew-Mel FP*), Derek Turnbull
(*Hawick*), Derek White (*Gala*)

FRANCE Serge Blanco (*Biarritz*); Phillipe Bérot (*Agen*), Philippe Sella (*Agen*), Marc Andrieu
(*Nîmes*) Patrice Lagisquet (*Bayonne*); Jean-Patrick Lescarboura (*Dax*), Pierre Berbizier (*Agen*);
Louis Armary (*Lourdes*), Daniel Dubroca* (*Agen*), Jean-Pierre Garuet (*Lourdes*), Alain Lorieux
(*Aix-les-Bains*), Jean Condom (*Biarritz*), Eric Champ (*Toulon*), Dominique Erbani (*Agen*), Laurent
Rodriguez (*Montferrand*)

REFEREE Frans Muller (*South Africa*)

SCORING Lescarboura, drop (0–3); Cramb, drop (3–3); Bérot, pen (3–6); G Hastings, try (7–6);
Tukalo, try (11–6) (half-time) Hastings, pen (14–6); Hastings, pen (17–6); Hastings, pen (20–6);
Hastings, pen (23–6); Lagisquet, try (23–10); Bérot, con (23–12)

Iwan Tukalo was recalled in place of Roger Baird and Hawick duo Alister Campbell
and Derek Turnbull came in to strengthen the pack. Lescarboura gave France an early
lead with a drop goal and a few minutes later Cramb replied in kind, grinning broadly
as his kick went over. Bérot missed three penalty attempts, but landed a fourth and
then came the extraordinary turning point. From a lineout, France passed wide to
Lagisquet who tried to chip over the head of Gavin Hastings. Instead, the Scottish
full-back caught the ball and raced away up the touchline before kicking ahead. The
covering Berbezier tried to hack the bouncing ball into touch, but missed it completely

Stand-off Richard Cramb celebrates as Gavin Hastings scores a dramatic kick-and-chase
try against France in 1988.
Scotsman Publications Ltd

and Hastings followed-up to touch down. Just before the interval, Calder grabbed a loose ball and found Turnbull. The explosive flanker handed-off several defenders before giving out a perfect spin-pass to Tukalo who powered over at the left corner. With the wind behind them in the second half, the Scots pressurised their opponents into errors and Gavin Hastings kicked four penalties. Towards the finish, Lagisquet scored a consolation try for the visitors. This was a good team performance by Scotland and they were worthy winners. Richard Cramb, who had been heavily criticised after Dublin, showed growing confidence and good all-round skills. Derek Turnbull made some thundering tackles and won a lot of ball at the end of the lineout.

391 INTERNATIONAL CHAMPIONSHIP 1988 WALES

Cardiff Arms Park · Saturday 20 February 1988 · Lost 20–25

SCOTLAND Gavin Hastings (*Watsonians*); Matt Duncan (*W of Scot*), Alan Tait (*Kelso*), Scott Hastings (*Watsonians*), Iwan Tukalo (*Selkirk*); †Andrew Ker (*Kelso*), Roy Laidlaw (*Jed-Forest*); David Sole (*Edinburgh Acs*), Gary Callander* (*Kelso*), Norrie Rowan (*Boroughmuir*), Alister Campbell (*Hawick*), Damian Cronin (*Bath*), John Jeffrey (*Kelso*), Finlay Calder (*Stew-Mel FP*), Derek White (*Gala*)

WALES Paul Thorburn (*Neath*); Ieuan Evans (*Llanelli*), Mark Ring (*Pontypool*), Bleddyn Bowen* (*South Wales Police*), Adrian Hadley (*Cardiff*); Jonathan Davies (*Llanelli*), Robert Jones (*Swansea*); Staff Jones (*Pontypool*), Ian Watkins (*Ebbw Vale*), David Young (*Swansea*), Phil May (*Llanelli*),

Robert Norster (*Cardiff*), Roland Phillips (*Neath*), Richie Collins (*South Wales Police*), Paul Moriarty (*Swansea*) ... Replacement: Jeremy Pugh (*Neath*) for S Jones (13)

REFEREE Yves Bressy (*France*)

SCORING Calder, try (0–4); G Hastings, pen (7–0); Davies, try (7–4); Evans, try (7–8); Thorburn, con (7–10); Duncan, try (11–10); G Hastings, pen (14–10); G Hastings, pen (17–10) (half-time) G Hastings, pen (20–10); Watkins, try (20–14); Thorburn, con (20–16); Thorburn, pen (20–19); Davies, drop (20–22); Davies, drop (20–25)

Andrew Ker, a brilliant sevens player and Scottish cricket international, came in for the injured Richard Cramb to win his first cap at 33-years-old. This was a classic encounter and Scotland might have won if it had not been for the individual brilliance of Welsh winger Ieuan Evans and stand-off Jonathan Davies. Scotland made a terrific start and Scott Hastings seemed to have scored in the opening seconds, but was ruled to have been in touch. From the ensuing lineout, the ball was tapped back over the tryline and Calder pounced on it for an easy try. Gavin Hastings missed the conversion, but a few minutes later kicked a penalty. On the 20th minute, Jonathan Davies conjured a superb try when he kicked past the defence and used his flaring acceleration to win the race to the touch down. Next came a magical score by Evans who cut inside five defenders on an unstoppable run to the line. Scotland responded when Calder and Tait made incisive runs before Duncan held onto a pass one-handed at his side and thundered over. Hastings missed the conversion, but then kicked two penalties and early in the second half landed an enormous goal from inside his own half. Scotland had the platform for victory, but slowly the Welsh forwards began to take control. Watkins scored a well-worked try, albeit with a pass that looked forward, and Thorburn kicked a penalty to reduce Scotland's lead to a single point. Towards the finish, Davies crowned a great personal display with two drop goals in quick succession to win the match.

---

392   INTERNATIONAL CHAMPIONSHIP 1988   ENGLAND

Murrayfield · Saturday 5 March 1988 · Lost 6–9

SCOTLAND Gavin Hastings (*Watsonians*); Matt Duncan (*W of Scot*), Alan Tait (*Kelso*), Keith Robertson (*Melrose*), Iwan Tukalo (*Selkirk*); Andrew Ker (*Kelso*), Roy Laidlaw (*Jed-Forest*); David Sole (*Edinburgh Acs*), Gary Callander* (*Kelso*), Norrie Rowan (*Boroughmuir*), Derek White (*Gala*), Damian Cronin (*Bath*), Derek Turnbull (*Hawick*), Finlay Calder (*Stew-Mel FP*), Iain Paxton (*Selkirk*)

ENGLAND Jon Webb (*Bristol*); Rory Underwood (*Leicester*), Will Carling (*Harlequins*), Simon Halliday (*Bath*), Chris Oti (*Nottingham*); Rob Andrew (*Wasps*), Nigel Melville* (*Wasps*); Paul Rendall (*Wasps*), Brian Moore (*Nottingham*), Jeff Probyn (*Wasps*), John Orwin (*Bedford*), Wade Dooley (*Fylde*), Micky Skinner (*Harlequins*), Peter Winterbottom (*Headingley*), Dean Richards (*Leicester*) ... Replacement: Gary Rees (*Nottingham*) for Winterbottom (4)

REFEREE Winstone Jones (*Wales*)

SCORING No scoring in the first half. G Hastings, pen (3–0); Andrew, drop (3–3); Webb, pen (3–6); G Hastings, pen (6–6); Webb, pen (6–9)

In stark contrast to the previous match, this was a dreadful encounter that stood comparison with the infamous Welsh game in 1963. Scotland struggled to win possession against the big English forwards, but the visitors did not create any scoring opportunities or do anything imaginative or even interesting. The first half was largely a series of collapsed scrums and missed penalties. The second half was little better, but did produce some points. Gavin Hastings kicked a penalty which was cancelled out by an Andrew drop goal. Webb and Hastings exchanged further kicks and a second Webb penalty completed the scoring. Towards the end, the Scots had a great chance to snatch the game. Duncan made a break and a swift handling took play almost to the English line, but the defence managed to hold out. There was considerable ill-feeling after the game as both sides blamed the other for the lack of spectacle. To make matters worse, the Calcutta Cup was badly damaged in the post-match revelries which led to disciplinary action against replacement John Jeffrey and England No8 Dean Richards. This was Roy Laidlaw's last international match and a sad ending to a distinguished career.

TOUR OF ZIMBABWE 1988 ZIMBABWE

Hartsfield Sports Ground, Bulawayo · Saturday 21 May 1988

Won 31–10

SCOTLAND XV Peter Dods* (*Gala*); Matt Duncan (*W of Scot*), Ruari Maclean (*Gloucester*), Douglas Wyllie (*Stew-Mel FP*), Alex Moore (*Edinburgh Acs*); Craig Chalmers (*Melrose*), Greig Oliver (*Hawick*); David Butcher (*Harlequins*), Jim Hay (*Hawick*), Paul Burnell (*London Scot*), Chris Gray (*Nottingham*), Damian Cronin (*Bath*), Kevin Rafferty (*Heriot's FP*), Derek Turnbull (*Hawick*), Hugh Parker (*Kilmarnock*) ... Replacement: Stewart McAslan (*Heriot's FP*) for Maclean (66)

ZIMBABWE Martiens Grobler (*Old Hararians*); William Schultz (*Karoi*), Mark Letcher (*Karoi*), Rolf Khun (*Harare SC*), Peter Kaulbach (*Old Hararians*); Craig Brown (*Harare SC*), Andrew Ferreira* (*OG*); D Watson (*Queens*), Pieter Albasini (*Zisco*), N Valdal (*Zisco*), Grant Davidson (*Harare SC*), A Macintosh (*Zisco*), Dirk Buitendag (*Harare SC*), Brendon Dawson (*Old Miltonians*), M Carrabott (*Bindura*)

REFEREE S Turnock (*Zimbabwe*)

SCORING Duncan, try (4–0); Grobler, pen (4–3); Oliver, try (8–3); Dods, con (10–3); Butcher, try (14–3); Dods, con (16–3); Oliver, try (20–3); Dods, con (22–3) (half-time) Dods, pen (25–3); Grobler, pen (25–6); Oliver, try (29–6); Dods, con (31–6); Khun, try (31–10)

In May 1988, an under-strength Scotland made a five match tour of Zimbabwe, including two non-cap tests. The first of these was played in very hot conditions, but Scotland won comfortably and scored five tries to one. After only seven minutes, Duncan beat several tacklers on a long run up the touchline for the opening score. The Zimbabwean fringe defence was weak at times and scrum-half Greig Oliver poached three tries from scrums. Scotland's other try was scored by uncapped prop David Butcher after sustained pressure near the line. Uncapped Heriot's flanker Kevin Rafferty was in great form and named man-of-the-match.

Harare Police Ground · Saturday 28 May 1988 · Won 34–7

SCOTLAND XV Peter Dods* (*Gala*); Matt Duncan (*W of Scot*), Ruari Maclean (*Gloucester*), Douglas Wyllie (*Stew-Mel FP*), Alex Moore (*Edinburgh Acs*); Craig Chalmers (*Melrose*), Greig Oliver (*Hawick*); David Butcher (*Harlequins*), Jim Hay (*Hawick*), Paul Burnell (*London Scot*), Chris Gray (*Nottingham*), Jeremy Richardson (*Edinburgh Acs*), Derek Turnbull (*Hawick*), Kevin Rafferty (*Heriot's FP*), Hugh Parker (*Kilmarnock*)

ZIMBABWE Martiens Grobler (*Old Hararians*); William Schultz (*Karoi*), Mark Letcher (*Karoi*), Rolf Kuhn (*Harare SC*), Julian Kamba; Craig Brown (*Harare SC*), Malcolm Jellicoe*; D Watson (*Queens*), Pieter Albasini (*Zisco*), N Valdal (*Zisco*), A Macintosh (*Zisco*), Grant Davidson (*Harare SC*), Brendon Dawson (*Old Miltonians*), Dirk Buitendag (*Harare SC*), M Carrabott (*Bindura*)

REFEREE Kingsley Went (*Zimbabwe*)

SCORING Chalmers, drop (3–0); Dods, pen (6–0); Parker, try (10–0); Dods, con (12–0); Grobler, pen (12–3); Dods, pen (15–3) (half-time) Dods, pen (18–3); Rafferty, try (22–3); Dods, con (24–3); Dods, try (28–3); Dods, con (30–3); Kamba, try (30–7); Moore, try (34–7)

After a midweek victory over Mashonaland Country Districts (53–6), Scotland completed their tour with another comfortable win. The Zimbabweans defended better than the previous weekend, but the Scottish forwards were always in control and won plenty of possession. Scotland scored four tries, the best around the hour mark. From a lineout on halfway, Dods intruded at top speed, cut inside the defence and powered all the way to the line. Kamba scored a consolation try for Zimbabwe and Alex Moore rounded things off nicely with a score in injury-time.

---

393   TOUR MATCH   AUSTRALIA

Murrayfield · Saturday 19 November 1988 · Lost 13–32

SCOTLAND Gavin Hastings (*London Scot*); Matt Duncan (*W of Scot*), Scott Hastings (*Watsonians*), Keith Robertson (*Melrose*), Iwan Tukalo (*Selkirk*); Richard Cramb (*Harlequins*), †Gary Armstrong (*Jed-Forest*); David Sole (*Edinburgh Acs*), Gary Callander* (*Kelso*), Iain Milne (*Heriot's FP*), Alister Campbell (*Hawick*), Damian Cronin (*Bath*), Derek White (*Gala*), John Jeffrey (*Kelso*), Ian Paxton (*Selkirk*) … Replacement: †Graham Marshall (*Selkirk*) for White (40)

AUSTRALIA Andrew Leeds (*NSW*); Acura Niuqila (*NSW*), Michael Cook (*Queensland*), Lloyd Walker (*NSW*), David Campese (*NSW*); Michael Lynagh (*Queensland*), Nick Farr-Jones* (*NSW*); Rob Lawton (*Queensland*), Tom Lawton (*Queensland*), Andy McIntyre (*Queensland*), Steve Cutler (*NSW*), Damien Frawley (*NSW*), Jeff Miller (*Queensland*), Scott Gourlay (*NSW*), Tim Gavin (*NSW*) … Replacement: Brad Burke (*NSW*) for Farr-Jones

REFEREE Dave Bishop (*New Zealand*) · ATTENDANCE 51,245

SCORING Campese, try (0–4); Lynagh, con (0–6); Lynagh, pen (0–9); G Hastings, pen (3–9); Lawton, try (3–13); Lynagh, con (3–15) (half-time) Campese, try (3–19); Lynagh, con (3–21); Robertson, try (7–21); Gourlay, try (7–25); Lynagh, pen (7–28); G Hastings, try (11–28); G Hastings, con (13–28); Lawton, try (13–32)

In autumn 1988, the Australians returned to the British Isles for a 13 match tour. After mixed fortunes in England, the Wallabies found their true form north of the

Border where they swept aside three Scottish district teams, including an emphatic victory over the South of Scotland (29–4) who had beaten them four years earlier. It was a similar story in the test match which the Australians won at a canter. Their forwards dominated possession and Michael Lynagh and Nick Farr-Jones, their world class half-backs, controlled proceedings imperiously. The Scottish kicking was too inaccurate and their defence was often weak although the forwards did well enough at the lineout. Scrum-half Gary Armstrong had a promising debut and John Jeffrey made some vital tackles and was involved in both of Scotland's tries. The first came from a towering kick by Gavin Hastings and after some quick recycling Robertson side-stepped over the line. Then from a tap-penalty and a Jeffrey thrust, Armstrong put Gavin Hastings away to the posts.

394 INTERNATIONAL CHAMPIONSHIP 1989 WALES

Murrayfield · Saturday 21 January 1989 · Won 23–7

SCOTLAND Peter Dods (*Gala*); Matt Duncan (*W of Scot*), Scott Hastings (*Watsonians*), †Sean Lineen (*Boroughmuir*), Iwan Tukalo (*Selkirk*); †Craig Chalmers (*Melrose*), Gary Armstrong (*Jed-Forest*); David Sole (*Edinburgh Acs*), †Kenny Milne (*Heriot's FP*), Iain Milne (*Heriot's FP*), †Chris Gray (*Nottingham*), Damian Cronin (*Bath*), John Jeffrey (*Kelso*), Finlay Calder* (*Stew-Mel FP*), Derek White (*Gala*)

WALES Paul Thorburn* (*Neath*); Mike Hall (*Cambridge U & Bridgend*), Nigel Davies (*Llanelli*), John Devereux (*Bridgend*), Carwyn Davies (*Llanelli*); Bleddyn Bowen (*Swansea*), Jonathan Griffiths (*Llanelli*); Mike Griffiths (*Bridgend*), Ian Watkins (*Ebbw Vale*); David Young (*Cardiff*), Kevin Moseley (*Pontypool*), Phil Davies (*Llanelli*), Roland Phillips (*Neath*), David Bryant (*Bridgend*), Mark Jones (*Neath*) ... Replacement: Hugh Williams-Jones (*South Wales Police*) for Young (51)

REFEREE Jean-Claude Doulcet (*France*)

SCORING Dods, pen (3–0); Dods, pen (6–0); Armstrong, try (10–0); White, try (14–0); Dods, con (16–0); Chalmers, drop (19–0) (half-time) Hall, try (19–4); Bowen, pen (19–7); Chalmers, try (23–7)

Finlay Calder was captain for the first time and Peter Dods returned after an absence of four years in place of the injured Gavin Hastings. There were first caps for New Zealand-born Sean Lineen, Craig Chalmers, Kenny Milne and Chris Gray. The Scottish forwards took a tight grip from the start and their driving and support play was exemplary throughout. The Scots had the game won by the interval although Wales, who at times showed a lack of confidence and experience, staged a mini-recovery in the second half. After two penalties by Dods, Scotland made a superb attack from midfield and Armstrong squeezed over at the corner. White scored a try from a pushover scrum and Chalmers dropped a goal to give the home side a commanding lead at the interval. In the second half, Wales came back with a snap try by Hall and a penalty by Bowen. The visitors had a lot of pressure, but the Scots defended tenaciously and they finished the game with a thrilling try. From a lineout, Lineen created space before giving a short pass to Dods. As he was tackled, the full-back managed to find Chalmers who juggled with the ball before crossing the line.

Gary Armstrong scores the opening try in Scotland's emphatic win over Wales in 1989.
Scotsman Publications Ltd

Twickenham · Saturday 4 February 1989 · Drawn 12–12

SCOTLAND Peter Dods (*Gala*); Keith Robertson (*Melrose*), Scott Hastings (*Watsonians*), Sean Lineen (*Boroughmuir*), Iwan Tukalo (*Selkirk*); Craig Chalmers (*Melrose*), Gary Armstrong (*Jed-Forest*); David Sole (*Edinburgh Acs*), Kenny Milne (*Heriot's FP*), †Paul Burnell (*London Scot*), Chris Gray (*Nottingham*), Damian Cronin (*Bath*), John Jeffrey (*Kelso*), Finlay Calder* (*Stew-Mel FP*), Derek White (*Gala*)

ENGLAND Jonathan Webb (*Bristol*); Rory Underwood (*Leicester*), Will Carling* (*Harlequins*), Simon Halliday (*Bath*), Chris Oti (*Wasps*); Rob Andrew (*Wasps*), Dewi Morris (*Liverpool St Helens*); Paul Rendall (*Wasps*), Brian Moore (*Nottingham*), Jeff Probyn (*Wasps*), Wade Dooley (*Preston Grasshoppers*), Paul Ackford (*Harlequins*), Mike Teague (*Gloucester*), Andy Robinson (*Bath*), Dean Richards (*Leicester*)

REFEREE Guy Maurette (*France*)

SCORING Andrew, pen (0–3); Dods, pen (3–3); Andrew, pen (3–6); Jeffrey, try (7–6); Dods, con (9–6) (half-time) Dods, pen (12–6); Andrew, pen (12–9); Andrew, pen (12–12)

Paul Burnell won his first cap in place of the injured Iain Milne. England had beaten Australia in the autumn and were supremely confident, but they were made to look an ordinary side and Scotland deserved at least a draw. The big English forwards won a lot of ball, but their backs were meandering and could not penetrate some fierce Scottish tackling. Both English kickers, Rob Andrew and Jonathan Webb, were badly off form and missed seven penalty attempts between them. In a tense and sometimes fractious encounter, Scotland led 9–6 at the interval. The only try of the match came when Webb spilled a high ball under pressure, and Jeffrey hacked on and won the race to the touch down. In the second half, Dods extended Scotland's lead with a second penalty, but England came back strongly and Webb levelled with two penalties. Andrew had a chance to win the game right at the end, but he hooked his penalty attempt wide. Scotland could take heart from a good team performance. Burnell was solid in the scrums and the half-backs played confidently. There was some rancour after the match when England coach Geoff Cooke dismissed the Scots as 'scavengers' who were intent on killing the ball and doing nothing constructive. The truth was that he was frustrated that the much-heralded renaissance of English rugby had once again failed to materialise.

---

396 INTERNATIONAL CHAMPIONSHIP 1989 IRELAND

Murrayfield · Saturday 4 March 1989 · Won 37–21

SCOTLAND Peter Dods (*Gala*); Keith Robertson (*Melrose*), Scott Hastings (*Watsonians*), Sean Lineen (*Boroughmuir*), Iwan Tukalo (*Selkirk*); Craig Chalmers (*Melrose*), Gary Armstrong (*Jed-Forest*); David Sole (*Edinburgh Acs*), Kenny Milne (*Heriot's FP*), Paul Burnell (*London Scot*), Chris Gray (*Nottingham*), Damian Cronin (*Bath*), John Jeffrey (*Kelso*), Finlay Calder* (*Stew-Mel FP*), Derek White (*Gala*)

IRELAND Fergus Dunlea (*Lansdowne*); Michael Kiernan (*Dolphin*), Brendan Mullin (*London Irish*), David Irwin (*Instonians*), Keith Crossan (*Instonians*); Paul Dean (*St Mary's Coll*), Fergus Aherne (*Lansdowne*); Tom Clancy (*Lansdowne*), Steve Smith (*Ballymena*), Jimmy McCoy (*Bangor*), Donal Lenihan (*Cork Const*), Neil Francis (*London Irish*), Philip Matthews* (*Wdrs*), Des McBride (*Malone*), Noel Mannion (*Corinthians*)

REFEREE Kerry Fitzgerald (*Australia*)

Damian Cronin breaks away to score against Ireland in 1989. He is well supported by David Sole, Kenny Milne, Finlay Calder, Chris Grey and John Jeffrey.
Scotsman Publications Ltd

SCORING Dods, pen (3–0); Tukalo, try (7–0); Mullin, try (7–4); Kiernan, con (7–6); Jeffrey, try (11–6); Dods, con (13–6); Tukalo, try (17–6); Dods, con (19–6); Kiernan, pen (19–9); Dunlea, try (19–13); Kiernan, con (19–15); Crossan, try (19–19); Kiernan, con (19–21) (half-time) Dods, pen (22–21); Dods, pen (25–21); Cronin, try (29–21); Dods, con (31–21); Tukalo, try (35–21); Dods, con (37–21)

The 100th meeting between the two sides produced a glorious celebration of open rugby. Both sides played expansively and the enraptured crowd were treated to eight spectacular tries. It was ironic that both sides had been criticised earlier in the season for their negative tactics. In the first half, Scotland raced to a comfortable lead only to see it rapidly overtaken in a storming Irish comeback. Despite this, the Scots always looked the more capable side and in the second half Dods restored Scotland's lead with two penalties. Then the Scottish forwards made a series of drives and Cronin accelerated out of a tackle and powered away to the line. Later, Dods intruded into an attack and flicked the ball onto Tukalo who danced inside the defence to complete his hat-trick of tries. The Scottish forwards were in superb form throughout, and their driving play and quick rucking were exemplary. David Sole showed great mobility and Finlay Calder was an inspirational leader. The whole team combined well and there was some great interplay between backs and forwards. Peter Dods fielded impeccably and his touch-kicking was long and accurate. Ireland also played their part in a memorable encounter.

---

397   INTERNATIONAL CHAMPIONSHIP 1989   FRANCE

Parc des Princes, Paris · Saturday 18 March 1989 · Lost 3–19

SCOTLAND Peter Dods (*Gala*); Keith Robertson (*Melrose*), Scott Hastings (*Watsonians*), Sean Lineen (*Boroughmuir*), Iwan Tukalo (*Selkirk*); Craig Chalmers (*Melrose*), Gary Armstrong (*Jed-Forest*); David Sole (*Edinburgh Acs*), Kenny Milne (*Heriot's FP*), Paul Burnell (*London Scot*), Chris Gray (*Nottingham*), Damian Cronin (*Bath*), John Jeffrey (*Kelso*), Finlay Calder* (*Stew-Mel FP*), Derek White (*Gala*)

FRANCE Serge Blanco (*Biarritz*); Philippe Bérot (*Agen*), Philippe Sella (*Agen*), Marc Andrieu (*Nîmes*), Patrice Lagisquet (*Bayonne*); Franck Mesnel (*RCF*), Pierre Berbizier* (*Agen*); Louis Armary (*Lourdes*), Philippe Dintrans (*Tarbes*), Jean-Pierre Garuet (*Lourdes*), Dominique Erbani (*Agen*), Jean Condom (*Biarritz*), Eric Champ (*Toulon*), Alain Carminati (*Béziers*), Laurent Rodriguez (*Dax*)

REFEREE Owen Doyle (*Ireland*)

SCORING Dods, pen (3–0); Berbizier, try (3–4); Bérot, con (3–6) (half-time) Blanco, try (3–10) Bérot, pen (3–13); Lagisquet, try (3–17); Bérot, con (3–19)

This game was something of a let-down after the excitement of the Irish match. The Scots had an outside chance of winning the championship, but they were hammered into submission by a powerful French side. The home forwards were remorseless at the scrums and in their driving play, usually with hooker Dintrans to the fore. Deprived of a steady platform, the Scottish half-backs were under constant pressure and the back-row was made to work extremely hard. Dods kicked an early penalty, but thereafter Scotland barely looked like scoring again and France slowly tightened their grip. The decisive breakthrough came just before the break. From a scrum near the Scottish posts, Rodriguez fed Berbizier who burst through the defence and all the way to the line. Further tries by Blanco and Lagisquet gave France a comfortable victory and perhaps the home side should have won by more. This was an extremely hard match and the Scottish players looked very tired towards the end, but they fought bravely to prevent any further scoring.

 TOUR OF JAPAN 1989 JAPAN

Prince Chichibu Memorial Stadium, Tokyo · Sunday 28 May 1989
Lost 24–28

SCOTLAND XV Cameron Glasgow (*Cambridge U*); Matt Duncan (*W of Scot*), Ruari Maclean (*Gloucester*), Sean Lineen (*Boroughmuir*), Iwan Tukalo (*Selkirk*); Douglas Wyllie (*Stew-Mel FP*), Greig Oliver (*Hawick*); Alex Brewster* (*Stew-Mel FP*), Jim Hay (*Hawick*), Grant Wilson (*Boroughmuir*), Chris Gray (*Nottingham*), Damian Cronin (*Bath*), Derek Turnbull (*Hawick*), Graham Marshall (*Selkirk*), Iain Paxton (*Selkirk*)

JAPAN Toshitsugu Yamamoto; Nofomuli Taumoefolau, Eiji Kutsuki, Seiji Hirao*, Yoshihito Yoshida; Shinobu Aoki, Masami Horikoshi; Osamu Ota, Tsuyoshi Fujita, Masanori Takura, Toshiyuki Hayashi, Atsushi Oyagi, Hiroyuki Kajihara, Shuji Nakashima, Sinali-Tui Latu

REFEREE Les Peard (*Wales*)

SCORING Yamamoto, pen (0–3); Yamamoto, pen (0–6); Yoshida, try (0–10); Oliver, pen (3–10); Hyashi, try (3–14); Kutsuki, try (3–18); Yamamoto, con (3–20); Oliver, pen (6–20) (half-time) Hay, try (10–20); Oliver, con (12–20); Oliver, pen (15–20); Oliver, pen (18–20); Yamamoto, try (18–24); Oliver, pen (21–24); Nofomuli, try (21–28); Wyllie, drop (24–28)

In May 1989, an under-strength Scotland squad made a five match tour of Japan. The Scots recorded some big scores in their provincial matches, including a 91–8 opener against Kanto, but they slipped-up in the test match for which Scotland did not award caps. The tourists were clearly affected by the humidity and they underestimated their opponents. The Japanese put together some good moves and they scored five tries, but they were surprisingly cynical in defence and killed the ball at every opportunity. The Scots were unable to profit because Cameron Glasgow, who had been in excellent kicking form on tour, missed five penalty attempts that would have given Scotland some momentum. Eventually, Greig Oliver took over the kicking duties with greater success. As usual, the Japanese were smaller and lighter than the Scots, but they were skilful enough to build-up a good lead by the interval. Scotland managed to claw back to within two points, but ultimately the gap proved too much. The Scots scored their only try of the game in the 13th minute of the second half. From a lineout, the ball was worked up-field, Turnbull charged to the line and Hay was on hand to gather and score.

Murrayfield · Saturday 28 October 1989 · Won 38–17

SCOTLAND Gavin Hastings (*London Scot*); †Tony Stanger (*Hawick*), Scott Hastings (*Watsonians*), Sean Lineen (*Boroughmuir*), Iwan Tukalo (*Selkirk*); Craig Chalmers (*Melrose*), Gary Armstrong (*Jed-Forest*); David Sole* (*Edinburgh Acs*), Kenny Milne (*Heriot's FP*), Paul Burnell (*London Scot*), Chris Gray (*Nottingham*), Damian Cronin (*Bath*), John Jeffrey (*Kelso*), Graham Marshall (*Selkirk*), Derek White (*London Scot*) ... Replacement: †Adam Buchanan-Smith (*London Scot*) for Marshall

FIJI Severo Koroduadua (*Police & Suva*); Tomasi Lovo (*QVSOB & Suva*), Luke Erenavula (*Hyatt & Nadroga*), Noa Nadruku (*Hyatt & Nadroga*), Isikeli Waqavatu (*Army & Suva*); Waisale Serevi (*Nasinu & Rewa*), Lekima Vasuvulagi (*Baravi & Nadroga*); Mosese Taga (*QVSOB & Suva*), Salacieli Naivilawasa (*Police & Suva*), Sairusi Naituku (*Lomaiviti & Suva*), Ilaitia Savai (*QVSOB & Suva*), Mesake Rasari (*Army & Suva*), Pita Naruma (*Army & Suva*), Alivereti Dere (*Army & Suva*), Esala Teleni* (*Army & Suva*)

REFEREE Patrick Robin (*France*)

SCORING G Hastings, pen (3–0); Koroduadua, pen (3–3); G Hastings, pen (6–3); Milne, try (10–3); G Hastings, con (12–3); Stanger, try (16–3); G Hastings, con (18–3); Koroduadua, pen (18–6) (half-time) Stanger, try (22–6); Serevi, pen (22–9); Gray, try (26–9); G Hastings, con (28–9); G Hastings, try (32–9); G Hastings, con (34–9); Lovo, try (34–13); Rasari, try (34–17); Tukalo, try (38–17)

The popular Fijians were making an eight match tour of Europe and the previous Wednesday had lost to Glasgow (22–11). David Sole took over the captaincy, and Tony Stanger and substitute Adam Buchanan-Smith won their first caps. A little piece of history was made before the start of the match when 'The Flower of Scotland' was used as the Scottish anthem for the first time. Playing in perfect conditions, Scotland were comfortable winners of a highly entertaining game. They largely dictated the pace and direction of play, showed plenty of enterprise and scored six tries, including a brace for newcomer Stanger. The scrum was solid and the team combined well. Several of the Scotland's tries came directly from set-pieces, including the best score of the match. From a scrum inside the Fijian 22, Armstrong fired a long pass to Gavin Hastings who burst between several defenders for a perfect score straight off the training ground. The Fijians showed occasional flashes of adventure, but they were starved of possession and never really in contention, apart from two late consolation tries.

399   1989   ROMANIA

Murrayfield · Saturday 9 December 1989 · Won 32–0

SCOTLAND Gavin Hastings (*London Scot*); Tony Stanger (*Hawick*), Scott Hastings (*Watsonians*), Sean Lineen (*Boroughmuir*), †Lindsay Renwick (*London Scot*); Douglas Wyllie (*Stew-Mel FP*), Gary Armstrong (*Jed-Forest*); David Sole* (*Edinburgh Acs*), Kenny Milne (Heriot's FP), Paul Burnell (*London Scot*), Chris Gray (*Nottingham*), Damian Cronin (*Bath*), John Jeffrey (*Kelso*), Finlay Calder (*Stew-Mel FP*), Derek White (*London Scot*)

ROMANIA Marcel Toader (*Dinamo*); Stefan Chirila (*Politechnica Iasi*), Adrian Lungu (*Dinamo*), George Sava (*Baia Mare*), Bogdan Serban (*Steaua*); Gelu Ignat (*Steaua*), Daniel Neaga (*Dinamo*);

Gheorghe Leonte (*Steaua*), Gheorghe Ion (*Dinamo*), George Dumitrescu (*Steaua*), Sandu Ciorascu (*Baia Mare*), Christian Raducanu (*Dinamo*), Ovidiu Sugar (*Baia Mare*), Ioan Doja (*Dinamo*), Haralambie Dumitras* (*Contactoare Buzau*) ... Replacement: M Motoc (*Steaua*) for Sugar

REFEREE Stephen Hilditch (*Ireland*)

SCORING G Hastings, pen (3–0); Stanger, try (7–0); G Hastings, con (9–0) (half-time) White, try (13–0); G Hastings, con (15–0); Stanger, try (19–0); G Hastings, con (21–0); Stanger, try (25–0); G Hastings, pen (28–0); Sole, try (32–0)

Craig Chalmers and Iwan Tukalo were unavailable because of injury and their places were taken by Douglas Wyllie and new cap Lindsay Renwick. Scotland scored five tries, including three for Tony Stanger, raising his total to five in only two matches. The Scottish forwards dominated possession and the scrum held-up well against some burly opponents. There was never any doubt that Scotland would win, but it was only late in the first half that they scored their first try. After a charge by Gavin Hastings, Wyllie flipped on to Scott Hastings who in turn fed Stanger. The big wing was tackled short, but quickly got back on his feet and threw himself over at the corner. A few minutes after the interval, White picked-up from a scrum and powered away to the line. Stanger then completed his hat-trick before Sole burrowed over from a tap-penalty. Romania were unimaginative and drab, but deserved some sympathy. They had endured a tortuous journey just to get to the game and their country was in the throes of political turmoil. Following the match, one of their players, Cristian Raducanu, escaped from an Edinburgh pub and sought political asylum.

---

400 INTERNATIONAL CHAMPIONSHIP 1990 IRELAND

Lansdowne Road, Dublin · Saturday 3 February 1990 · Won 13–10

SCOTLAND Gavin Hastings (*London Scot*); Tony Stanger (*Hawick*), Scott Hastings (*Watsonians*), Sean Lineen (*Boroughmuir*), Iwan Tukalo (*Selkirk*); Craig Chalmers (*Melrose*), Gary Armstrong (*Jed-Forest*); David Sole* (*Edinburgh Acs*), Kenny Milne (*Heriot's FP*), Paul Burnell (*London Scot*), Chris Gray (*Nottingham*), Damian Cronin (*Bath*), John Jeffrey (*Kelso*), Finlay Calder (*Stew-Mel FP*), Derek White (*London Scot*)

IRELAND Kenny Murphy (*Cork Const*); Michael Kiernan (*Dolphin*), Brendan Mullin (*Blackrock Coll*), David Irwin (*Instonians*), Keith Crossan (*Instonians*); Brian Smith (*Oxford U*), Fergus Aherne (*Lansdowne*); John Fitzgerald (*Young Munster*), John McDonald (*Malone*), Des Fitzgerald (*Lansdowne*), Donal Lenihan (*Cork Const*), Willie Anderson* (*Dungannon*), Philip Matthews (*Wdrs*), Pat O'Hara (*Sunday's Well*), Noel Mannion (*Corinthians*) ... Replacement: Paul Collins (*London Irish*) for O'Hara (38)

REFEREE Clive Norling (*Wales*)

SCORING Kiernan, pen (0–3); Fitzgerald, try (0–7) (half-time) White, try (4–7); Chalmers, con (6–7); Kiernan, pen (6–10); Chalmers, pen (9–10); White, try (13–10)

No 8 Derek White was in great form and scored two tries, but otherwise this was an untidy and forgettable game, and there was little to suggest that it was the first leg of a Grand Slam. The Scots deserved to win for their composure and excellent support play, but in truth neither side was very impressive. Kiernan opened the scoring with a penalty and close to the interval prop John Fitzgerald forced his way over from a lineout. Scotland wasted several try-scoring opportunities and Gavin Hastings missed three penalty attempts before handing over the kicking duties to Craig Chalmers who would go on to be first-choice kicker for the rest of the season. The Scots reverted to a driving game in the second half. After a bout of erratic passing and a miscued up-and-under, Lineen made an incisive break and linked with Jeffrey to set-up White's first try. Chalmers converted and then Kiernan and Chalmers exchanged penalties. Towards the end White picked-up from a scrum inside the Irish 22 and charged all the way to the line with defenders hanging onto him. Kiernan missed a late penalty attempt and Scotland escaped with a rare away win. The Scottish players were rather despondent after the game, knowing that there was plenty of room for improvement.

401   INTERNATIONAL CHAMPIONSHIP 1990   FRANCE

Murrayfield · Saturday 17 February 1990 · Won 21–0

SCOTLAND Gavin Hastings (*London Scot*); Tony Stanger (*Hawick*), Scott Hastings (*Watsonians*), Sean Lineen (*Boroughmuir*), Iwan Tukalo (*Selkirk*); Craig Chalmers (*Melrose*), Gary Armstrong (*Jed-Forest*); David Sole* (*Edinburgh Acs*), Kenny Milne (*Heriot's FP*), Paul Burnell (*London Scot*), Chris Gray (*Nottingham*), Damian Cronin (*Bath*), John Jeffrey (*Kelso*), Finlay Calder (*Stew-Mel FP*), Derek White (*London Scot*)

FRANCE Serge Blanco (*Biarritz*); Pierre Hontas (*Biarritz*), Philippe Sella (*Agen*), Franck Mesnel (*RCF*), Patrice Lagisquet (*Bayonne*); Didier Camberabero (*Béziers*), Henri Sanz (*Narbonne*); Marc Pujolle (*Nice*), Louis Armary (*Lourdes*), Pascal Ondarts (*Biarritz*), Thierry Devergie (*Nîmes*), Olivier Roumat (*Dax*), Jean-Marc Lhermet (*Montferrand*), Alain Carminati (*Béziers*), Laurent Rodriguez* (*Dax*)

REFEREE Fred Howard (*England*)

SCORING G Hastings, pen (3–0) (half-time) Chalmers, pen (6–0); Calder, try (10–0); Chalmers, con (12–0); Tukalo, try (16–0); Chalmers, con (18–0); Chalmers, pen (21–0)

Scotland played with an unruly wind behind them in the first half and led by a solitary penalty at the interval. Soon after the restart, French flanker Alain Carminati was sent-off for illegally stamping on John Jeffrey. He became only the second player to be dismissed in an international at Murrayfield and followed the distant footsteps of New Zealander Colin Meads. Chalmers kicked the resultant penalty and from then on the dishevelled French seemed to lose heart and the Scots eased away. Both of Scotland's tries were exciting kick-and-chase efforts. From a French fumble, the ball was shipped to Iwan Tukalo who kicked ahead and followed up fast to hound the defence. Lineen hacked on and Calder won the race for the touchdown. Then French full-back Serge Blanco, who had an unhappy afternoon, missed a towering up-and-under. The Scots recycled and fed Tukalo in space on the left. The Selkirk winger broke out of one tackle and twirled past another to reach the line. Chalmers converted both tries and added a late penalty. Some of the Scottish driving and loose forward play was first class and Chris Gray had a superb game in the lineout. Meanwhile at Twickenham, England had trounced Wales (34–6) and would be heading to Murrayfield in four weeks time to play for the Grand Slam.

Cardiff Arms Park · Saturday 3 March 1990 · Won 13–9

SCOTLAND Gavin Hastings (*London Scot*); Tony Stanger (*Hawick*), Scott Hastings (*Watsonians*), Sean Lineen (*Boroughmuir*), Iwan Tukalo (*Selkirk*); Craig Chalmers (*Melrose*), Gary Armstrong (*Jed-Forest*); David Sole* (*Edinburgh Acs*), Kenny Milne (*Heriot's FP*), Paul Burnell (*London Scot*), Chris Gray (*Nottingham*), Damian Cronin (*Bath*), John Jeffrey (*Kelso*), Finlay Calder (*Stew-Mel FP*), Derek White (*London Scot*)

WALES Paul Thorburn (*Neath*); Mike Hall (*Cardiff*), Mark Ring (*Cardiff*), Alan Bateman (*Neath*), Arthur Emyr (*Swansea*); David Evans (*Cardiff*), Robert Jones* (*Swansea*); Brian Williams (*Neath*), Kevin Phillips (*Neath*), Jeremy Pugh (*Neath*), Phil Davies (*Llanelli*), Gareth Llewellyn (*Neath*), Mark Perego (*Llanelli*), Richie Collins (*Cardiff*), Mark Jones (*Neath*) ... Replacement: Tony Clement (*Swansea*) for Evans

REFEREE René Hourquet (*France*)

SCORING Cronin, try (4–0); Thorburn, pen (4–3); Chalmers, pen (7–3); Chalmers, pen (10–3) (half-time) Emyr, try (10–7); Thorburn, con (10–9); Chalmers, pen (13–9)

After their heavy defeat by England, Wales appointed a new coach in Ron Waldron and selected seven players from Neath, including the entire front row. This was not a match of any great quality and the tension seemed to inhibit both teams. The Scots successfully exploited Welsh weaknesses at the scrums, but the backs did not create much. Similarly, traditional Welsh passion and defiance could not disguise their limitations. Scotland took the lead when Armstrong broke from the front of a lineout and after an untidy exchange of passes Cronin scored in the corner. Thorburn replied with a penalty and Chalmers kicked two penalties to make the score 10–3 at the break. Early in the second half, Wales scored a gloriously worked try by Emyr and soon after Chalmers kicked his third penalty after a deliberate knock-on had ruined a promising Scottish attack. Wales had two long periods of pressure, but they could not make it count. For Scotland, John Jeffrey had a superb all-round display.

Murrayfield · Saturday 17 March 1990 · Won 13–7

SCOTLAND Gavin Hastings (*London Scot*); Tony Stanger (*Hawick*), Scott Hastings (*Watsonians*), Sean Lineen (*Boroughmuir*), Iwan Tukalo (*Selkirk*); Craig Chalmers (*Melrose*), Gary Armstrong (*Jed-Forest*); David Sole* (*Edinburgh Acs*), Kenny Milne (*Heriot's FP*), Paul Burnell (*London Scot*), Chris Gray (*Nottingham*), Damian Cronin (*Bath*), John Jeffrey (*Kelso*), Finlay Calder (*Stew-Mel FP*), Derek White (*London Scot*) ... Replacement: Derek Turnbull (*Hawick*) for White (28)

ENGLAND Simon Hodgkinson (*Nottingham*); Simon Halliday (*Bath*), Will Carling* (*Harlequins*), Jeremy Guscott (*Bath*), Rory Underwood (*Leicester*); Rob Andrew (*Wasps*), Richard Hill (*Bath*); Paul Rendall (*Wasps*), Brian Moore (*Nottingham*), Jeff Probyn (*Wasps*), Wade Dooley (*Preston Grasshoppers*), Paul Ackford (*Harlequins*), Mick Skinner (*Harlequins*), Peter Winterbottom (*Harlequins*), Mike Teague (*Gloucester*) ... Replacement: Mark Bailey (*Wasps*) for Guscott (65)

REFEREE David Bishop (*New Zealand*)

SCORING Chalmers, pen (3–0); Chalmers, pen (6–0); Guscott, try (6–4); Chalmers, pen (9–4) (half-time) Stanger, try (13–4); Hodgkinson, pen (13–7)

The events surrounding this game have become so familiar that it is difficult to recapture their initial impact. Both sides were unbeaten in the championship and were playing for the Grand Slam, Triple Crown and the Calcutta Cup, the first time that this had ever happened between rugby's oldest international rivals. After years of under-achievement, England finally seemed to be reaching their potential. They had been in imperious form, brushing aside Ireland (23–0) and Wales (34–6) at Twickenham and also winning handsomely in Paris (26–7). With a hugely talented back division and awesome forwards, the white juggernaut seemed unstoppable. Meanwhile, Scotland had been less convincing. They had done well enough against a depleted France, but only scraped narrow wins against Ireland and Wales. Interest in the match reached unprecedented levels and there were reports of tickets selling for many times their face value. It has been suggested that there was a political undercurrent that reflected wider tensions between the two countries although players on both sides have always denied this. Scotland selected the same team as the three previous games, the first time that this had ever happened. Their build-up was deliberately low-key and full of praise for England. Played in an explosive atmosphere, the match was a titanic struggle with both sides unrelenting in their efforts. Famously the Scots made their intentions clear when they *walked* onto the pitch with slow determined steps and steely eyes, laying down the gauntlet to the English challenge. A passionate and full bloodied rendition of 'The Flower of Scotland' made grown men and women weep. With the blustery wind in their favour, the Scots tore into their opponents straight away and never let them settle into their stride. Chalmers missed an early penalty before one of the defining moments of the match. From a tap penalty, Finlay Calder, with his socks rolled down to his ankles and legs pumping, thundered into the heart of the English defence. He was halted momentarily, but the Scottish forwards arrived *en masse* and drove him forwards. Chalmers kicked two penalties to give Scotland an early lead, but after a quarter of an hour England responded with an excellent try. From a scrum just inside the Scottish half, England created an overlap as the defence drifted blind and Carling made a break to set-up Guscott who dummied his way to the line. Towards the end of the first half, England had a series of scrums near the Scottish line. The Scots were repeatedly penalised, but England seemed to be in two minds what to do and they let their opportunity slip away. The siege was eventually lifted to an uproarious cheer and on the stroke of half-time Chalmers kicked his third penalty to make it 9–4 to Scotland at the interval. Gavin Hastings kicked the restart out on the full, but England knocked-on at the ensuing scrum, giving possession back to Scotland. Gary Armstrong drew in the defence before improvising an overhead pass to Gavin Hastings who kicked ahead just before being bundled into touch. Stanger and Underwood raced for the ball and a kind bounce allowed the Scotland wing to grab it with both hands and touch it down. Chalmers missed the conversion, but the Scots had landed an important psychological blow. On the 54th minute, Hodgkinson kicked a penalty to set-up a heart-stopping conclusion. England had most of the pressure and launched waves of attacks, but, try as they might, they could not break the Scottish defence. In another defining moment, Scott Hastings made a superb tackle from behind on Underwood to prevent an almost certain try. The match ended with England encamped in the Scottish 22, but bereft of ideas or inspiration. Scotland were worthy winners of this remarkable match. They kept their momentum throughout and never allowed the bigger English side to impose themselves or develop continuity. The Scots showed great passion, determination and intelligence, varying their tactics when required and scoring at just the right moments. Their defence was very strong, especially the back-row and the midfield. England did not play badly and accepted their defeat in good grace, but it was Scotland who had the greater thirst for victory.

404　TOUR OF NEW ZEALAND 1990　NEW ZEALAND

Carisbrook, Dunedin · Saturday 16 June 1990 · Lost 16–31

SCOTLAND Gavin Hastings (*London Scot*); Tony Stanger (*Hawick*), Scott Hastings (*Watsonians*), Sean Lineen (*Boroughmuir*), Iwan Tukalo (*Selkirk*); Craig Chalmers (*Melrose*), Gary Armstrong (*Jed-Forest*); David Sole* (*Edinburgh Acs*), †John Allan (*Edinburgh Acs*), Iain Milne (*Heriot's FP*), Chris Gray (*Nottingham*), Damian Cronin (*Bath*), John Jeffrey (*Kelso*), Finlay Calder (*Stew-Mel FP*), Derek White (*London Scot*)

NEW ZEALAND Kieran Crowley (*Taranaki*); John Kirwan (*Auckland*), Joe Stanley (*Auckland*), Walter Little (*North Harbour*), Terry Wright (*Auckland*); Grant Fox (*Auckland*), Graeme Bachop (*Canterbury*); Steve McDowell (*Auckland*), Sean Fitzpatrick (*Auckland*), Richard Loe (*Waikato*), Ian Jones (*North Auckland*), Gary Whetton (*Auckland*), Alan Whetton (*Auckland*), Mike Brewer (*Otago*), Wayne Shelford* (*North Harbour*)

REFEREE Colin High (*England*)

SCORING Fox, pen (0–3); Lineen, try (4–3); G Hastings, con (6–3); Crowley, try (6–7); Fox, con (6–9); Gray, try (10–9); Fox, try (10–13); Fox, con (10–15) (half-time) Jones, try (10–19); Fox, con (10–21); Kirwan, try (10–25); Kirwan, try (10–29); Fox, con (10–31); Sole, try (14–31); G Hastings, con (16–31)

In the early summer of 1990, Scotland made an eight match tour of New Zealand. The Scots were successful in their provincial matches, winning five out of six and drawing the other against Wellington (16–16). For the First Test at Dunedin, there were two changes from the side that had beaten England in March, both in the front row. Iain Milne returned in place of Paul Burnell and John Allan, the Edinburgh Accies hooker, took over from Kenny Milne. A controversial choice, Allan was born in Glasgow but raised in South Africa. He went on to make nine appearances for Scotland before returning to South Africa where he won 13 caps for the Springboks. Scotland played some good attacking rugby and scored three tries, but they gave away several soft scores and struggled in the scrums and, in particular, in the middle of the lineouts. The result flattered New Zealand, but they deserved to win by virtue of taking their chances. Scotland scored their first try after only five minutes. From a tap penalty near the line, New Zealand-born Sean Lineen made a looping run around Scott Hastings and raced through a gap to dive over at the posts. Gavin Hastings converted and two minutes later Crowley scored a try when he chipped over the defence and caught the ball on the full. Scotland's second try came when Gavin Hastings made a strong run into the 22 and Stanger linked with Gray who thundered over from close-range. Once again Scotland's lead was short-lived. From a scrum Fox kicked over the defence, Tukalo fumbled the ball and the New Zealand stand-off pounced for a soft try. The All Blacks raised their game in the second half and Jones scored a try when the Scots were temporarily reduced to 13 men because of injury. A brace of tries by Kirwan put the result beyond doubt. Scotland made a strong finish and from a tap penalty David Sole brushed Fox out of the way to score under the posts.

404   TOUR OF NEW ZEALAND 1990   NEW ZEALAND

Eden Park, Auckland · Saturday 23 June 1990 · Lost 18–21

SCOTLAND Gavin Hastings (*London Scot*); Tony Stanger (*Hawick*), Scott Hastings (*Watsonians*), Sean Lineen (*Boroughmuir*), †Alex Moore (*Edinburgh Acs*); Craig Chalmers (*Melrose*), Gary Armstrong (*Jed-Forest*); David Sole* (*Edinburgh Acs*), Kenny Milne (*Heriot's FP*), Iain Milne (*Heriot's FP*), Chris Gray (*Nottingham*), Damian Cronin (*Bath*), John Jeffrey (*Kelso*), Finlay Calder (*Stew-Mel FP*), Derek White (*London Scot*) ... Replacement: Greig Oliver (*Hawick*) for Armstrong (73)

NEW ZEALAND Kieran Crowley (*Taranaki*); John Kirwan (*Auckland*), Joe Stanley (*Auckland*), Walter Little (*North Harbour*), Terry Wright (*Auckland*); Grant Fox (*Auckland*), Graeme Bachop (*Canterbury*); Steve McDowell (*Auckland*), Sean Fitzpatrick (*Auckland*), Richard Loe (*Waikato*), Ian Jones (*North Auckland*), Gary Whetton (*Auckland*), Alan Whetton (*Auckland*), Mike Brewer (*Otago*), Wayne Shelford* (*North Harbour*)

REFEREE Derek Bevan (*Wales*)

SCORING G Hastings, pen (3–0); G Hastings, pen (6–0); Fox, pen (6–3); Stanger, try (10–3); G Hastings, con (12–3); Loe, try (12–7); Fox, con (12–9); Moore, try (16–9); G Hastings, con (18–9); Fox, pen (18–12) (half-time) Fox, pen (18–15); Fox, pen (18–18); Fox, pen (18–21)

Alex Moore won his first cap and Kenny Milne returned to strengthen the front row. Scotland won the try count and came agonisingly close to a first-ever win over New Zealand only to fall to the relentless kicking of Grant Fox who scored five penalties and a conversion of his side's only try. Conditions were awkward with a strong wind and heavy showers. Scotland played with the elements in the first half and Gavin Hastings landed two huge penalties before Fox replied with his first penalty. Then from a scrum near the line, White picked-up and fed Stanger who had enough strength to batter his way over. A few minutes later, the New Zealand forwards drove to the Scottish line and Loe twisted over for a try. Scotland replied with a brilliantly constructed score. After a charge by Gray, Gavin Hastings punted obliquely to the left corner and the quick-thinking Moore beat the cover to the touchdown. Hastings converted from the touchline, but a late Fox penalty reduced Scotland's lead to six points at the interval. Early in the second half, Fox kicked another penalty and Hastings narrowly missed two attempts, both of which were held up in the wind. With about 15 minutes left New Zealand controversially levelled the scores. Crowley made a high kick into the Scottish 22 which was fielded by Gavin Hastings. The Scottish full-back made to reply but changed direction only to be confronted by Brewer who seemed to have appeared from nowhere. Hastings lost his footing as Brewer caught him and conceded a penalty for not releasing the ball. But had Brewer been in an offside position when he made the tackle? Brewer was definitely in front of Crowley when he kicked and should have been at least ten metres away from

Hastings or the place where the ball landed. In addition, Hastings should have been allowed to run five metres before he was tackled. Referee Derek Bevan ruled that Brewer had acted legitimately, one of several marginal decisions that went against the Scots. Fox, inevitably, kicked the penalty and close to the finish he landed the winning goal after Calder was caught offside at a scrum. Despite a gallant late effort the Scots were unable to score again and the match was lost.

406   TOUR MATCH   ARGENTINA

Murrayfield · Saturday 10 November 1990 · Won 49–3

SCOTLAND Gavin Hastings (*Watsonians*); Tony Stanger (*Hawick*), Scott Hastings (*Watsonians*), Sean Lineen (*Boroughmuir*), Alex Moore (Edinburgh Acs); Craig Chalmers (*Melrose*), Gary Armstrong (*Jed-Forest*); David Sole* (*Edinburgh Acs*), Kenny Milne (*Heriot's FP*), Paul Burnell (*London Scot*), Chris Gray (*Nottingham*), †Doddie Weir (*Melrose*), John Jeffrey (*Kelso*), Adam Buchanan-Smith (*Heriot's FP*), Graham Marshall (*Selkirk*)

ARGENTINA Guillermo Angaut (*La Plata*); Diego Cuesta Silva (*San Isidro*), Lisandro Arbizu (*Belgrano*), Santiago Meson (*Tucuman*), Matias Allen (*San Isidro*); Hugo Porta* (*Banco Nación*), Rodrigo Crexell (*Jockey Club Rosario*); Manuel Aguirre (*Alumni*), Alejandro Cubelli (*Belgrano*), Diego Cash (*San Isidro*), Germán Llanes (*La Plata*), Pedro Sporleder (*Curupayti*), Pablo Garreton (*Tucuman U*), Emilio Ezcurra (*Newman*), Miguel Bertranou (*Los Tordos*) ... Replacement: Alejandro Scolni (*Alumni*) for Porta (16)

REFEREE Freek Burger (*South Africa*)

SCORING Stanger, try (4–0); G Hastings, pen (7–0); Moore, try (11–0); G Hastings, con (13–0); Milne, try (17–0) (half-time) Meson, pen (17–3); Stanger, try (21–3); G Hastings, con (23–3); Armstrong, try (27–3); Gray, try (31–3); G Hastings, con (33–3); G Hastings, try (37–3); Milne, try (41–3); G Hastings, con (43–3); Chalmers, try (47–3); G Hastings, con (49–3)

Scotland awarded caps against Argentina for the first time. Doddie Weir, the beanpole Melrose second row, made his debut. On a gloomy afternoon, Scotland enjoyed a comfortable victory although they were made to work hard by rugged opponents. The Scots scored nine tries in total, the first by Tony Stanger after only a few minutes. Their play was slightly ragged in the first half although they had a comfortable lead by the interval. They dominated the rest of the game and put together some nice tries. Gray and Weir did well at the lineout and Jeffrey was prominent in the loose. Gavin Hastings scored a great solo try when he chased his own kick into the Argentinean goal area and leapt high to snatch the ball from the defence and touchdown. The visitors were unimaginative in attack although they were hampered by the loss of their talismanic stand-off Hugo Porta early on. Meson was unlucky to hit a post three times in succession with penalty attempts.

407   INTERNATIONAL CHAMPIONSHIP 1991   FRANCE

Parc des Princes, Paris · Saturday 19 January 1991 · Lost 9–15

SCOTLAND Gavin Hastings (*Watsonians*); Tony Stanger (*Hawick*), Scott Hastings (*Watsonians*), Sean Lineen (*Boroughmuir*), Alex Moore (*Edinburgh Acs*); Craig Chalmers (*Melrose*), Gary Armstrong (*Jed-Forest*); David Sole* (*Edinburgh Acs*), Kenny Milne (*Heriot's FP*),

Paul Burnell (*London Scot*), Chris Gray (*Nottingham*), Damian Cronin (*Bath*), Derek Turnbull (*Hawick*), John Jeffrey (*Kelso*), Derek White (*London Scot*)

FRANCE   Serge Blanco* (*Biarritz*); Jean-Baptiste Lafond (*RCF*), Franck Mesnel (*RCF*), Denis Charvet (*RCF*), Patrice Lagisquet (*Bayonne*); Didier Camberabero (*Béziers*), Pierre Berbizier (*Agen*); Grégoire Lascube (*Agen*), Philippe Marocco (*Montferrand*), Pascal Ondarts (*Biarritz*), Michel Tachdjian (*RCF*), Olivier Roumat (*Dax*), Xavier Blond (*RCF*), Laurent Cabannes (*RCF*), Marc Cécillon (*Bourgoin*)

REFEREE   Ed Morrison (*England*)

SCORING   Camberabero, pen (0–3); Chalmers, drop (3–3); Blanco, drop (3–6); Camberabero, pen (3–9) (half-time) Chalmers, pen (6–9); Chalmers, pen (9–9); Camberabero, drop (9–12); Camberabero, drop (9–15)

The Scottish playing shirts bore a subtle but historic change with the traditional thistle replaced by a new corporate design. France were deserved winners of an undistinguished match bereft of tries and Scotland never recaptured the dynamism of the previous season. At times the Scots won a lot of possession but their play lacked momentum and they made too many errors. The French backs ran powerfully and stand-off Camberabero kicked astutely, including two match-winning drop goals. Experienced full-back Serge Blanco showed excellent positional play and Roumat exploited Scottish shortcomings in the lineout.

---

408   INTERNATIONAL CHAMPIONSHIP 1991   WALES

Murrayfield · Saturday 2 February 1991 · Won 32–12

SCOTLAND   Gavin Hastings (*Watsonians*); Tony Stanger (*Hawick*), Scott Hastings (*Watsonians*), Sean Lineen (*Boroughmuir*), Alex Moore (*Edinburgh Acs*); Craig Chalmers (*Melrose*), Gary Armstrong (*Jed-Forest*); David Sole* (*Edinburgh Acs*), John Allan (*Edinburgh Acs*), Paul Burnell (*London Scot*), Chris Gray (*Nottingham*), Damian Cronin (*Bath*), Derek Turnbull (*Hawick*), John Jeffrey (*Kelso*), Derek White (*London Scot*) ... Replacement: Kenny Milne (*Heriot's FP*) for Allan (47)

WALES   Paul Thorburn* (*Neath*); Ieuan Evans (*Llanelli*), Mark Ring (*Cardiff*), Scott Gibbs (*Neath*), Steve Ford (*Cardiff*); Neil Jenkins (*Pontypridd*), Robert Jones (*Swansea*); Brian Williams (*Neath*), Kevin Phillips (*Neath*), Paul Knight (*Pontypridd*), Glyn Llewellyn (*Neath*), Gareth Llewellyn (*Neath*), Alun Carter (*Newport*), Glen George (*Newport*), Paul Arnold (*Swansea*) ... Replacement: Tony Clement (*Swansea*) for Thorburn (67)

REFEREE   David Bishop (*New Zealand*)

SCORING   Chalmers, pen (3–0); Thorburn, pen (3–3); White, try (7–3); Armstrong, try (11–3); Chalmers, con (13–3); Thorburn, pen (13–6); Chalmers, drop (16–6) (half-time) Chalmers, try (20–6); Ford, try (20–10); Thorburn, con (20–12); G Hastings, pen (23–12); G Hastings, pen (26–12); White, try (30–12); G Hastings, con (32–12)

Scotland bounced back from their defeat in Paris with a comprehensive win over a poor Welsh side. The Scots were in rampant form and better in all aspects. The scrum was solid, the back-row foraged effectively in the loose, the half-backs combined well and the wings were eager to get involved. Scotland controlled the first half to such an extent that Wales did not reach the Scottish 22 until three minutes before the interval.

Scotland's first try came after 19 minutes when Derek White thundered over following a lineout and ruck near the Welsh line. Five minutes later, Armstrong showed great alertness when he dived into a retreating Welsh scrum and touched down under the noses of the Welsh forwards. Armstrong was at it again in the second half when he pinched the ball from a Welsh scrum and broke away up the touchline. Turnbull and Jeffrey gave support and Chalmers finished off with a sublime dummy. Wales made a short revival with a try by Ford before Gavin Hastings kicked two penalties to put the issue beyond doubt. Shortly before the end, White scored a pushover try against a demoralised Welsh scrum.

409　INTERNATIONAL CHAMPIONSHIP 1991　ENGLAND

Twickenham · Saturday 16 February 1991 · Lost 12–21

SCOTLAND Gavin Hastings (*Watsonians*); Tony Stanger (*Hawick*), Scott Hastings (*Watsonians*), Sean Lineen (*Boroughmuir*), Alex Moore (*Edinburgh Acs*); Craig Chalmers (*Melrose*), Gary Armstrong (*Jed-Forest*); David Sole* (*Edinburgh Acs*), Kenny Milne (*Heriot's FP*), Paul Burnell (*London Scot*), Chris Gray (*Nottingham*), Damian Cronin (*Bath*), Derek Turnbull (*Hawick*), John Jeffrey (*Kelso*), Derek White (*London Scot*)

ENGLAND Simon Hodgkinson (*Nottingham*); Nigel Heslop (*Orrell*), Will Carling* (*Harlequins*), Jeremy Guscott (*Bath*), Rory Underwood (*Leicester*); Rob Andrew (*Wasps*), Richard Hill (*Bath*); Jason Leonard (*Harlequins*), Brian Moore (*Harlequins*), Jeff Probyn (*Wasps*), Peter Ackford (*Harlequins*), Wade Dooley (*Preston Grasshoppers*), Mike Teague (*Gloucester*), Peter Winterbottom (*Harlequins*), Dean Richards (*Leicester*)

REFEREE Stephen Hilditch (*Ireland*)

SCORING Hodgkinson, pen (0–3); Hodgkinson, pen (0–6); Chalmers, pen (3–6); Chalmers, pen (6–6); Hodgkinson, pen (6–9) (half-time) Heslop, try (6–13); Hodgkinson, con (6–15); Chalmers, pen (9–15); Chalmers, pen (12–15); Hodgkinson, pen (12–18); Hodgkinson, pen (12–21)

England had a score to settle and used their powerful forwards and Hodgkinson's prodigious kicking to assuage the traumas of 1990. Scotland fought hard and were never entirely out of contention, but England were much stronger and never looked like losing. The English forwards maintained a stranglehold throughout, especially in the lineout and Scotland were reduced to deliberately missing touch with their clearing kicks. The killer blow came shortly after the interval. From a lineout deep inside Scottish territory, the English back-row pulled in the defence and ball was whipped along the line to Heslop who rounded Moore to score wide out. Once again Gary Armstrong battled superbly behind a beaten pack.

410　INTERNATIONAL CHAMPIONSHIP 1991　IRELAND

Murrayfield · Saturday 16 March 1991 · Won 28–25

SCOTLAND Gavin Hastings (*Watsonians*); Tony Stanger (*Hawick*), Scott Hastings (*Watsonians*), Sean Lineen (*Boroughmuir*), Iwan Tukalo (*Selkirk*); Craig Chalmers (*Melrose*), Gary Armstrong (*Jed-Forest*); David Sole* (*Edinburgh Acs*), John Allan (*Edinburgh Acs*), Paul Burnell (*London Scot*), Chris Gray (*Nottingham*), Damian Cronin (*Bath*), Derek Turnbull (*Hawick*),

John Jeffrey (*Kelso*), Derek White (*London Scot*) ... Replacement: Peter Dods (*Gala*) for Tukalo (39)

IRELAND Jim Staples (*London Irish*); Simon Geoghegan (*London Irish*), Brendan Mullin (*Blackrock Coll*), David Curtis (*London Irish*), Keith Crossan (Instonians); Brian Smith (*Leicester*), Rob Saunders* (*London Irish*); John Fitzgerald (*Young Munster*), Steve Smith (*Ballymena*), Des Fitzgerald (*Lansdowne*), Brian Rigney (*Greystones*), Neil Francis (*Blackrock Coll*), Philip Matthew (*Wdrs*), Gordon Hamilton (*NIFC*), Brian Robinson (*Ballymena*) ... Replacement: Kenny Murphy (*Cork Const*) for Staples (70)

REFEREE Kerry Fitzgerald (*Australia*)

SCORING Chalmers, pen (3–0); Chalmers, pen (6–0); Crossan, try (6–4); B Smith, con (6–6); B Smith, drop (6–9); G Hastings, pen (9–9); Robinson, try (9–13); B Smith, con (9–15); G Hastings, try (13–15); Chalmers, con (15–15) (half-time) Geoghegan, try (15–19); Stanger, try (19–19); Chalmers, con (21–19); Chalmers, pen (24–19); S Hastings, try (28–19); Mullin, try (28–23); B Smith, con (28–25)

Scotland had to dig deep to win this exhilarating festival of running rugby. The youthful Irish backs were full of brilliant running, in particular the mercurial blonde wing Simon Geoghegan. At times the Scots looked hesitant and slow, but they showed plenty of resilience to twice come from behind and narrowly win the game. They paced themselves better than their rather frantic opponents and had just enough skill and self-belief to pull through. The forward exchanges were fairly even and the Scottish pack had plenty of drive and cohesion. Scotland scored their best try around the hour mark. Scott Hastings kicked on near halfway and Jeffrey, using his legendary sevens prowess, gathered the ball and improvised a reverse pass back to Hastings for a great score. Ireland made a series of late attacks, but Scotland managed to hold out.

 XV TOUR OF NORTH AMERICA 1991 USA

Dillon Stadium, Hartford, Connecticut · Saturday 18 May 1991 Won 41–12

SCOTLAND XV Peter Dods (Gala); Tony Stanger (*Hawick*), Douglas Wyllie* (*Stew-Mel FP*), Graham Shiel (*Melrose*), Mark Moncrieff (*Gala*); Craig Chalmers (*Melrose*), Greig Oliver (*Hawick*); David Milne (*Heriot's FP*), John Allan (*Edinburgh Acs*), Alan Watt (*GH-K*), Andy Macdonald (*Heriot's FP*), Doddie Weir (*Melrose*), Derek Turnbull (*Hawick*), Graham Marshall (*Selkirk*), Stuart Reid (*Boroughmuir*)

USA Ray Nelson (*Belmont Shore*); Rory Lewis (*Washington*), Kevin Higgins (*Old Blues*), Joe Burke (*Albany Knicks*), Chris Williams (*Old Blues*); Mike De Jong (*Denver Barbarians*), Barry Daily (*San Hose Seahawks*); Chris Lippert (*OMBAC*), Tony Flay (*Old Puget Sound*), Norm Mottram (*Boulder*), Kevin Swords (*Beacon Hill*), Bill Leversee (*OMBAC*), Tony Ridnell (*Old Puget Sound*), Rob Farley (*Philadelphia-Whitemarsh*), Brian Vizard* (*OMBAC*) ... Replacement: Chris O'Brien (*Old Blues*) for Williams (71)

REFEREE G Gadjovich (*Canada*)

SCORING De Jong, pen (0–3); De Jong, pen (0–6); Dods, pen (3–6); Dods, pen (6–6); Dods, pen (9–6); Dods, pen (12–6); De Jong, pen (12–9); De Jong, pen (12–12); Dods, pen (15–12) (half-time) Macdonald, try (19–12); Reid, try (23–12); Stanger, try (27–12); Dods, con (29–12); Stanger, try (33–12); Dods, con (35–12); Reid, try (39–12); Dods, con (41–12)

In May 1991, an under-strength Scotland made a six match tour of North America, including two non-cap tests. In the inaugural meeting between the sides, the Scottish forwards were solid in the set-pieces and made some thunderous drives in the loose. Four of their five tries came from scrum moves, an area that had been targeted by the astute Scottish coaches. No 8 Stuart Reid made an encouraging debut and Chalmers and Oliver, the half-backs, combined well and kicked effectively. Scotland always looked like winning, but they had wait until the hour mark for their first try which was scored by new lock Andy Macdonald from a scrum. The tourists took a firm grip thereafter and scored four more tries, two each for Reid and Stanger. The United States, incidentally, had two players with strong Scottish connections: ex-Glasgow High School prop Norm Mottram, who was listed at 18st 3lbs, and Ray Nelson, a former Scottish Schools full-back.

 XV TOUR OF NORTH AMERICA 1991 CANADA

Canada Games Stadium, Saint John, New Brunswick

Saturday 25 May 1991 · Lost 19–24

SCOTLAND XV Peter Dods (*Gala*); Tony Stanger (*Hawick*), Douglas Wyllie* (*Stew-Mel FP*), Graham Shiel (*Melrose*), Mark Moncrieff (*Gala*); Craig Chalmers (*Melrose*), Greig Oliver (*Hawick*); David Milne (*Heriot's FP*), John Allan (*Edinburgh Acs*), Alan Watt (*GH-K*), Andy Macdonald (*Heriot's FP*), Doddie Weir (*Melrose*), Derek Turnbull (*Hawick*), Ronnie Kirkpatrick (*Jed-Forest*), Stuart Reid (*Boroughmuir*)

CANADA Mark Wyatt* (*Valhallians*); Steve Gray (*Kats*), Christian Stewart (*Meraloma*), John Lecky (*Meraloma*), Tom Woods (*James Bay*); Gareth Rees (*Oak Bay Castaways*), John Graf (*UBC OB*); Eddie Evans (*UBC OB*), Mark Cardinal (*James Bay*), Dan Jackart (*UBC OB*), Alan Charron (*Ottawa Irish*), Norm Hadley (*UBC OB*), Gord MacKinnon (*Britannia Lions*), Bruce Breen (*Meraloma*), Glen Ennis (*Kats*) ... Replacement: Ian Gordon (*Kats*) for Charron (76)

REFEREE Steve Griffiths (*England*)

SCORING Dods and Wyatt kicked two penalties each (6–6) (half-time) Wyatt, pen (6–9); Wyatt, pen (6–12); Wyatt, pen (6–15); Wyatt, pen (6–18); Dods, pen (9–18); Reid, try (13–18); Dods, con (15–18); Wyatt, pen (15–21); Wyatt, pen (15–24); Stanger, try (19–24)

Fielding only seven capped players, Scotland ended their North American tour with a disappointing defeat to a lively and aggressive Canadian side. The burly Canadian forwards were very powerful and regularly stole possession in loose play. Veteran Canadian captain Mark Wyatt punished Scottish indiscipline by kicking eight penalty goals. Scotland made little use of their wind advantage in the first half and the sides turned around on level terms. In the second half, Wyatt kicked a series of four penalties before Dods replied with a single penalty. Reid scored a try from a scrum move and Dods converted, but Scotland carelessly gave away two penalties for foul play and Wyatt landed the vital goals. A late try by Stanger could not detract from a historic day for the Canadians.

23 August Stadium, Bucharest · Saturday 31 August 1991

Lost 12–18

SCOTLAND Peter Dods (*Gala*); Tony Stanger (*Hawick*), Sean Lineen (*Boroughmuir*), Douglas Wyllie (*Stew-Mel FP*), Iwan Tukalo (*Selkirk*); Craig Chalmers (*Melrose*), Gary Armstrong (*Jed-Forest*); David Sole (*Edinburgh Acs*), John Allan (*Edinburgh Acs*), Paul Burnell (*London Scot*), Doddie Weir (*Melrose*), Damian Cronin (*Bath*), Derek Turnbull (*Hawick*), Finlay Calder (*Stew-Mel FP*), Derek White (*London Scot*)

ROMANIA Dorel Piti (*Farul Constanta*); Catalin Sasu (*Farul Constanta*), George Sava (*Baia Mare*), Adrian Lungu (*Dinamo*), Lucian Colceriu (*Steaua*); Florian Ion (*Dinamo*), Daniel Neaga (*Dinamo*); Gheorghe Leonte (*Mielan*), Gheorghe Ion (*Dinamo*), Constantin Stan (*Contactoare Buzau*), Constantin Cojocariu (*Dinamo*), Sandu Ciorascu (*Angoulême*), Gheorghe Dinu (*Grivita*), Andrei Guranescu (*Dinamo*), Haralambie Dumitras* (*Pau*)

REFEREE Alain Ceccon (*France*)

SCORING Dods, pen (3–0); Cioascu, try (3–4); Ion, con (3–6); Dods, pen (6–6); Ion, pen (6–9) (half-time) Sasu, try (6–13); Ion, con (6–15); Ion, pen (6–18); Tukalo, try (10–18); Dods, con (12–18)

In a disappointing and scrappy encounter, Scotland were clearly short of match practice as they continued their build-up to the World Cup. The Scottish set-piece was solid enough, but they struggled at the breakdowns and their defence and discipline were lacklustre. The big Romanian forwards were physically imposing and adept at killing the ball on the ground. Scotland scored their only try about 15 minutes before the finish. Chalmers charged down a clearance and after a quick bout of handling Tukalo ran over. Scotland's best performer by far was the towering Doddie Weir who did well at the set-pieces and the restarts.

Murrayfield · Saturday 7 September 1991 · Drew 16–16

SCOTLAND XV Gavin Hastings (*Watsonians*); Tony Stanger (*Hawick*), Scott Hastings (*Watsonians*), Graham Shiel (*Melrose*), Mark Moncrieff (*Gala*); Craig Chalmers (*Melrose*), Greig Oliver (*Hawick*); David Sole* (*Edinburgh Acs*), Kenny Milne (*Heriot's FP*), Paul Burnell (*London Scot*), Damian Cronin (*Bath*), Doddie Weir (*Melrose*), John Jeffrey (*Kelso*), Finlay Calder (*Stew-Mel FP*), Graham Marshall (*Selkirk*) … Replacement: Derek White (*London Scot*) for Marshall (75)

BARBARIANS André Joubert (*Old Greys & SA*); Andrew Harriman (*Harlequins & England*), Scott Pierce (*North Shore*), Eric Blanc (*RCF*), Tony Underwood (*Cambridge U*); Stuart Barnes* (*Bath & England*), Pierre Berbizier (*Agen & France*); Guy Kebble (*Durban Collegians*), Tom Lawton (*Durban HSOB & Australia*), Enrique Rodriguez (*Warringah & Australia*), Andy Macdonald (*Heriot's FP*), Tony Copsey (*Llanelli*), Wahl Bartmann (*Durban Harlequins & SA*), Eric Rush (*Otahuhu*), Kari Tapper (*Enkoping & Sweden*) … Replacements: Quintin Daniels (*Cape Town Police*) for Underwood (65), Colin Stephens (*Llanelli*) for Joubert (77)

REFEREE Fred Howard (*England*)

SCORING Rush, try (0–4); Chalmers, pen (3–4); Rush, try (3–8); Barnes, con (3–10); Chalmers, pen (6–10) (half-time) Milne, try (10–10); Calder, try (14–10); Chalmers, con (16–10); Daniels, try (16–14); Barnes, con (16–16)

This non-cap international was part of the Barbarians' centenary celebrations and further preparation for Scotland towards the 1991 World Cup. The Barbarians drew players from eight countries, including Swedish No 8 Kari Tapper. On a sunny afternoon, the Scottish forwards stood-up well against heavier opponents and in general Scotland were a big improvement from the previous weekend against Romania. Scotland's first try came after 45 minutes when Jeffrey pounced on a loose tap at a lineout before giving a scoring pass to Milne. A few minutes later, Gavin Hastings charged down a clearance and after a frantic downfield chase Calder lunged over for a try. Towards the finish, the Barbarians launched a daring attack from behind their own line. After quick passing and a kick ahead, Daniels scooped-up the ball and beat the last of the defence for a classic Barbarians' score. Barnes converted to draw the match which probably was a fair result.

Rugby World Cup 1991

The second Rugby World Cup was hosted by England with matches around the British Isles and France. The tournament was an enormous success and did much to bring rugby to the attention of new audiences. Unlike the inaugural event, which was dominated by the mighty All Blacks, the 1991 World Cup was more open and unpredictable. Large crowds saw some thrilling games, many of which were shown on prime-time television, and there were encouraging performances from some of the newcomers such as Western Samoa and Canada. Sixteen teams took part in four pools of four. Scotland were drawn in Pool 2 with their old rivals Ireland, whom they had beaten earlier in the year, plus Japan and Zimbabwe. The draw was very kind to Scotland because they would enjoy home advantage all the way to the final at Twickenham, assuming that they kept winning. Their aspirations were given a further boost when former captain Finlay Calder came out of retirement to join the squad.

412　　　RUGBY WORLD CUP 1991　　　JAPAN

Murrayfield · Saturday 5 October 1991 · Won 47–9

SCOTLAND Gavin Hastings (*Watsonians*); Tony Stanger (*Hawick*), Scott Hastings (*Watsonians*), Sean Lineen (*Boroughmuir*), Iwan Tukalo (*Selkirk*); Craig Chalmers (*Melrose*), Gary Armstrong (*Jed-Forest*); David Sole* (*Edinburgh Acs*), John Allan (*Edinburgh Acs*), Paul Burnell (*London Scot*), Chris Gray (*Nottingham*), Doddie Weir (*Melrose*), John Jeffrey (*Kelso*), Finlay Calder (*Stew-Mel FP*), Derek White (*London Scot*) ... Replacements: Douglas Wyllie (*Stew-Mel FP*) for Chalmers (68), †David Milne (*Heriot's FP*) for Sole (73)

JAPAN Takahiro Hosokawa (*Kobe Steel*); Terunori Masuho (*Waseda U*), Eiji Kutsuki (*Toyota*), Seiji Hirao* (*Kobe Steel*), Yoshihito Yoshida (*Isetan*); Katsuhiro Matsuo (*World*), Wataru Murata (*Toshiba Fuchu*); Osama Ota (*Nihon Denki*), Masahiro Kunda (*Toshiba Fuchu*), Masanori Takura (*Mitsubishi Jiko Kyoto*), Toshiyuki Hayashi (*Kobe Steel*), Ekeroma Tifaga (*Niko Niko Do*), Hiroyuki Kajihara (*Toshiba Fuchu*), Shuji Nakashima (*Nihon Denki*), Sinali Latu (*Sanyo*)

SCORING S Hastings, try (4–0); Chalmers, pen (7–0); Hosokawa, drop (7–3); Stanger, try (11–3); Chalmers, try (15–3); G Hastings, con (17–3); Hosokawa, try (17–7); Hosokawa, con (17–9) (half-time) Penalty try (21–9); G Hastings, con (23–9); G Hastings, pen (26–9); G Hastings, pen (29–9); White, try (33–9); G Hastings, con (35–9); Tukalo, try (39–9); G Hastings, con (41–9); G Hastings, try (45–9); G Hastings, con (47–9)

Fielding their strongest side, Scotland opened their campaign with a convincing win over an enterprising Japanese team who competed well but who were eventually swept away on a wave of Scottish attacks. This was a hugely encouraging display by Scotland. Their handling and support play was very good, the set-piece was solid and they were outstanding in the loose. Weir made some great two-handed catches in the lineout, Allan had a strike against the head and Armstrong tested the defence with his teasing high kicks. The Scots were nervous in the opening stages, but gradually they found their game and the tries started to flow. There was never much danger of Scotland losing, but Japan, although outgunned, played positively and never gave in. Their whole-hearted approach was demonstrated towards the end of the game when Kutsuki hammered Scott Hastings into touch with an uncompromising shoulder-charge. In the closing stages, replacement prop David Milne won his first cap to complete a remarkable hat-trick for the Milne family, his brothers Iain and Kenny having previously played in the front-row for Scotland.

---

413   RUGBY WORLD CUP 1991   ZIMBABWE

Murrayfield · Wednesday 9 October 1991 · Won 51–12

SCOTLAND Peter Dods* (*Gala*); Tony Stanger (*Hawick*), Scott Hastings (*Watsonians*), Sean Lineen (*Boroughmuir*), Iwan Tukalo (*Selkirk*); Douglas Wyllie (*Stew-Mel FP*), Greig Oliver (*Hawick*); Paul Burnell (*London Scot*), Kenny Milne (*Heriot's FP*), †Alan Watt (*GH-K*), Damian Cronin (*Bath*), Doddie Weir (*Melrose*), Derek Turnbull (*Hawick*), Graham Marshall (*Selkirk*), Derek White (*London Scot*) ... Replacement: Craig Chalmers (*Melrose*) for Stanger (78)

ZIMBABWE Brian Currin* (*Old Hararians*); William Schultz (*Karoi*), Richard Tsimba (*Old Hararians*), Mark Letcher (*Karoi*), David Walters (*Karoi*); Craig Brown (*Harare SC*), Ewan MacMillan (*Old Hararians*); Alex Nicholls (*Old Hararians*), Brian Beattie (*Old Miltonians*), Adrian Garvey (*Old Miltonians*), Michael Martin (*Harare SC),* Honeywell Nguruve (*Old Georgians*), Darren Muirhead (*Old Miltonians*), Brendan Dawson (*Old Miltonians*), Brenton Catterall (*Old Hararians*) ... Replacements: Robin Hunter (*Old Miltonians*) for Garvey (46), Elimon Chimbima (*Old Hararians*) for Walters (56), Chippy Roberts (*Harare SC*) for Hunter (78)

REFEREE Don Reordan (*USA*)

SCORING Tukalo, try (4–0); Dods, con (6–0); Garvie, try (6–4); Currin, con (6–6); Dods, pen (9–6); Turnbull, try (13–6); Dods, con (15–6); Garvie, try (15–10); Currin, con (15–12); Hastings, try (19–12); Dods, con (21–12) (half-time) Stanger, try (25–12); Wyllie, drop (28–12); Dods, pen (31–12); Tukalo, try (35–12); Dods, con (37–12); Tukalo, try (41–12); Dods, con (43–12); Weir, try (47–12); White, try (51–12)

Scotland made nine changes, including a first cap for Alan Watt, the enormous

Glasgow High forward. Playing into a strong wind in the first half, the Scots made a lot of errors and were unable to impose themselves on their spirited opponents. For a short period it seemed that the Zimbabweans might be capable of causing an upset, but eventually Scotland's greater fitness and technique were decisive. The Scots scored eight tries in total, three in the last ten minutes, to clinch their place in the knock-out stages. Iwan Tukalo ran in a hat-trick of tries and Sean Linen was at the heart of many of Scotland's moves. The Zimbabweans were physically imposing and ran their hearts out, but they were too individualistic and struggled to secure good possession.

Murrayfield · Saturday 12 October 1991 · Won 24–15

SCOTLAND Gavin Hastings (*Watsonians*); Tony Stanger (*Hawick*), Scott Hastings (*Watsonians*), Sean Lineen (*Boroughmuir*), Iwan Tukalo (*Selkirk*); Craig Chalmers (Melrose), Gary Armstrong (*Jed-Forest*); David Sole* (*Edinburgh Acs*), John Allan (*Edinburgh Acs*), Paul Burnell (*London Scot*), Chris Gray (*Nottingham*), Doddie Weir (*Melrose*), John Jeffrey (*Kelso*), Finlay Calder (*Stew-Mel FP*), Derek White (*London Scot*) ... Replacement: †Graham Shiel (*Melrose*) for Chalmers (42)

IRELAND Jim Staples (*London Irish*); Simon Geoghegan (*London Irish*), Brendan Mullin (*Blackrock Coll*), David Curtis (*London Irish*), Keith Crossan (*Instonians*); Ralph Keyes (*Cork Const*), Rob Saunders (*London Irish*); Nick Popplewell (*Greystones*), Steve Smith (*Ballymena*), Des Fitzgerald (*DLSP*), Donal Lenihan (*Cork Const*), Neil Francis (*Blackrock Coll*), Philip Matthews* (*Wdrs*), Gordon Hamilton (*Ballymena*), Brian Robinson (*Ballymena*)

REFEREE Fred Howard (*England*)

SCORING Keyes, pen (0–3); G Hastings, pen (3–3); Keyes, pen (3–6); Chalmers, drop (6–6); G Hastings, pen (9–6); Keyes, pen (9–9); Keyes, drop (9–12) (half-time) Keyes, pen (9–15); Shiel, try (13–15); G Hastings, con (15–15); G Hastings, pen (18–15); Armstrong, try (22–15); G Hastings, con (24–15)

This was the crunch match of Pool Two. The winners would stay at Murrayfield and the losers would have to travel to Dublin to face Australia, one of the tournament favourites. Scotland had to draw deep on their reserves of courage and determination to come through a pulsating encounter. Ireland were very aggressive and dominated for long periods, but they made the mistake of keeping the ball tight rather than using their talented back division. They were in a strong position early in the second half when they held a six-point lead and Scotland had lost Craig Chalmers, their main playmaker, to injury. Scotland's comeback started controversially. From an Armstrong up-and-under, Jim Staples, the Irish full-back, was caught in a double challenge by Stanger and Calder. From some angles it looked as if Calder had hit the Irishman with an illegal stiff-arm tackle, but play was allowed to continue. A minute later, Staples failed to deal with another high kick and Stanger snatched the ball and fed Shiel for a debut try. This was the turning point in the match and Scotland's superior fitness started to tell as the game wore on. Gavin Hastings kicked a penalty and towards the finish Armstrong looped around Stanger and scored a try. The winning margin would have been greater if the referee had not disallowed a late Scottish pushover try and then claims for a penalty try after Ireland collapsed a scrum on their own line.

Murrayfield · Saturday 15 October 1991 · Won 28–6

SCOTLAND Gavin Hastings (*Watsonians*); Tony Stanger (*Hawick*), Scott Hastings (*Watsonians*), Graham Shiel (*Melrose*), Iwan Tukalo (*Selkirk*); Craig Chalmers (*Melrose*), Gary Armstrong (*Jed-Forest*); David Sole* (*Edinburgh Acs*), John Allan (*Edinburgh Acs*), Paul Burnell (*London Scot*), Chris Gray (*Nottingham*), Doddie Weir (*Melrose*), John Jeffrey (*Kelso*), Finlay Calder (*Stew-Mel FP*), Derek White (*London Scot*)

WESTERN SAMOA Andrew Aiolupo (*Moata'a*); Brian Lima (*Marist St Joseph*), To'o Vaega (*Suburbs*), Frank Bunce (*Helensville*), Timo Tagaloa (*Wellington*); Steven Bachop (*Linwood*), Matthew Vaea (*Marist St Joseph*); Peter Fatialofa* (*Ponsonby*), Stan To'omalatai (*Vaiala*), Vili Alalatoa (*Manly*), Mark Birtwhistle (*Hutt OB*), Eddie Ioane (*Ponsonby*), Sila Viafale (*Marist St Joseph*), Apolo Perelini (*Ponsonby*), Pat Lam (*Marist*)

REFEREE Derek Bevan (*Wales*)

SCORING Vaega, pen (0–3); G Hastings, pen (3–3); Stanger, try (7–3); Jeffrey, try (11–3); G Hastings, con (13–3) (half-time) G Hastings, pen (16–3); Bachop, drop (16–6); G Hastings, pen (19–9); Jeffrey, try (23–9); G Hastings, con (25–9); G Hastings, pen (28–9)

Western Samoa had been the surprise packet of the World Cup and were very capable of further progression, but Scotland met their challenge head-on. This was an outstanding performance by the Scots who were determined and tactically astute. They kept the ball close around the fringes and avoided isolated runners in open space, something that the physical Samoans liked to prey upon. Gary Armstrong and the back-row were in tremendous form and Gavin Hastings thundered his big frame into the Samoans like an auxiliary flanker. Scotland's first try came after 28 minutes when a high kick by Chalmers caught the Samoan defence in disarray and Stanger collected the ball to score. Just before the interval Jeffrey crossed after a quick tap penalty. Samoa were a little unfortunate not to score in the second half, but Scotland were worthy winners. Towards the finish, Jeffrey scored his second try and Gavin Hastings kicked a late penalty to bring his personal tally to 16 points. The Samoans took their defeat in good spirit and at the end of the game they made a lap of honour to the cheers of appreciative crowd.

Murrayfield · Saturday 26 October 1991 · Lost 6–9

SCOTLAND Gavin Hastings (*Watsonians*); Tony Stanger (*Hawick*), Scott Hastings (*Watsonians*), Sean Lineen (*Boroughmuir*), Iwan Tukalo (*Selkirk*); Craig Chalmers (*Melrose*), Gary Armstrong (*Jed-Forest*); David Sole* (*Edinburgh Acs*), John Allan (*Edinburgh Acs*), Paul Burnell (*London Scot*), Chris Gray (*Nottingham*), Doddie Weir (*Melrose*), John Jeffrey (*Kelso*), Finlay Calder (*Stew-Mel FP*) Derek White (*London Scot*)

ENGLAND Jonathan Webb (*Northampton*); Simon Halliday (*Harlequins*), Will Carling* (*Harlequins*), Jeremy Guscott (*Bath*), Rory Underwood (*Leicester*); Rob Andrew (*Wasps*), Richard Hill (*Bath*); Jason Leonard (*Harlequins*), Brian Moore (*Harlequins*), Jeff Probyn (*Wasps*), Paul Ackford (*Harlequins*), Wade Dooley (*Preston Grasshoppers*), Mick Skinner (*Harlequins*), Peter Winterbottom (*Harlequins*), Mike Teague (*Gloucester*)

SCORING G Hastings, pen (3–0); G Hastings, pen (6–0); Webb, pen (6–3) (half-time) Webb, pen (6–6); Andrew, drop (6–9)

In a titanic encounter, England gained revenge for their defeat at Murrayfield in 1990. After a week of feverish anticipation, the match was far from spectacular and had little open play, but there was plenty of drama. The big English forward slowly squeezed the life out of the lighter Scots and the English defence was calm and well organised. In fact the final score flattered Scotland and the visitors might have won by more if they had made greater use of their back division instead of keeping the game tight. In the closing stages, Gavin Hastings, who was later revealed to be suffering from concussion, missed a simple penalty chance that would have put Scotland into the lead. Probably it would not have made any difference because England were always stronger and more capable, although they had to rely on a late drop goal by Rob Andrew to see them through. Scotland made a courageous last rally, but they could not escape from the English stranglehold. At the end Scotland made a lap of honour to their broken-hearted supporters.

417   RUGBY WORLD CUP 1991   NEW ZEALAND

Cardiff Arms Park · Wednesday 30 October 1991 · Lost 6–13

SCOTLAND Gavin Hastings (*Watsonians*); Tony Stanger (*Hawick*), Scott Hastings (*Watsonians*), Sean Lineen (*Boroughmuir*), Iwan Tukalo (*Selkirk*); Craig Chalmers (*Melrose*), Gary Armstrong (*Jed-Forest*); David Sole* (*Edinburgh Acs*), John Allan (*Edinburgh Acs*), Paul Burnell (*London Scot*), Chris Gray (*Nottingham*), Doddie Weir (*Melrose*), John Jeffrey (*Kelso*), Finlay Calder (*Stew-Mel FP*), Derek White (*London Scot*)

NEW ZEALAND Terry Wright (*Auckland*); John Kirwan (*Auckland*), Craig Innes (*Auckland*), Walter Little (*North Harbour*), Va'aiga Tuigamala (*Auckland*); Jon Preston (*Canterbury*), Graeme Bachop (*Canterbury*); Steve McDowell (*Auckland*), Sean Fitzpatrick (*Auckland*), Richard Loe (*Waikato*), Ian Jones (*North Auckland*), Gary Whetton* (*Auckland*), Andrew Earl (*Canterbury*), Michael Jones (*Auckland*), Zinzan Brooke (*Auckland*) ... Replacement: Shayne Philpott (*Canterbury*) for Tuigamala (40)

REFEREE Stephen Hilditch (*Ireland*)

SCORING G Hastings, pen (3–0); Preston, pen (3–3); Preston, pen (3–6) (half-time) Preston, pen (3–9); G Hastings, pen (6–9); Little, try (6–13)

The tournament favourites New Zealand had lost to Australia in the second semi-final at Lansdowne Road. Both Scotland and New Zealand might have treated this play-off match as meaningless, but instead both showed great commitment and this was a rugged and full-blooded encounter. The attitude was typified in the game's best incident. In the second half, Gavin Hastings, angry at himself for having just missed a simple penalty, thundered into the All Black prop Richard Loe and sent him flying onto the seat of his pants. New Zealand dominated possession and deserved to win, but the outcome was in doubt almost until the final whistle. The Scottish defence stood-up courageously and in the second half Scotland had several promising positions, but could not make the best of them. In injury-time, Scotland tried to run from inside their own 22, but the move broke down and Little scored the game's only try. The Scots were disappointed at their defeat, but not too despondent. Scott Hastings playfully tried to swipe the World Cup when he collected his medal, and Finlay Calder and John Jeffrey, who had both announced their retirements, left the dressing-room brandishing old men's walking sticks.

418   INTERNATIONAL CHAMPIONSHIP 1992   ENGLAND

Murrayfield · Saturday 18 January 1992 · Lost 7–25

SCOTLAND Gavin Hastings (*Watsonians*); Tony Stanger (*Hawick*), Scott Hastings (*Watsonians*), Sean Lineen (*Boroughmuir*), Iwan Tukalo (*Selkirk*); Craig Chalmers (*Melrose*), †Andy Nicol (*Dundee HSFP*); David Sole* (*Edinburgh Acs*), Kenny Milne (*Heriot's FP*), Paul Burnell (*London Scot*), †Neil Edwards (*Harlequins*), Doddie Weir (*Melrose*), †Dave McIvor (*Edinburgh Acs*), †Ian Smith (*Gloucester*), Derek White (*London Scot*)

ENGLAND Jonathan Webb (*Bath*); Simon Halliday (*Harlequins*), Will Carling* (*Harlequins*), Jeremy Guscott (*Bath*), Rory Underwood (*Leicester*); Rob Andrew (*Toulouse*), Dewi Morris (*Orrell*); Jason Leonard (*Harlequins*), Brian Moore (*Harlequins*), Jeff Probyn (*Wasps*), Martin Bayfield (*Northampton*), Wade Dooley (*Preston Grasshoppers*), Mick Skinner (*Harlequins*), Peter Winterbottom (*Harlequins*), Tim Rodber (*Northampton*) ... Replacement: Dean Richards (*Leicester*) for Rodber (62)

REFEREE Derek Bevan (*Wales*)

SCORING G Hastings, pen (3–0); Webb, pen (3–3); Webb, pen (3–6); Underwood, try (3–10); White, try (7–10) (half-time) Webb, pen (7–13); Webb, pen (7–16); Guscott, drop (7–19); Morris, try (7–23); Webb, con (7–25)

David Sole, 44 caps 1986–1992.
George Herringshaw/Sporting-Heroes.net

Retirements and injuries meant that Scotland fielded four new caps. Legendary flankers Jeffrey and Calder had gone to be replaced by the Gloucester captain Ian Smith and the grey-haired Dave MacIvor. Anglo-Scot Neil Edwards came in at lock and scrum-half Andy Nicol was plucked from the Scottish Second Division in place of Gary Armstrong who was injured. Nicol's grandfather, George Ritchie, a prop, had played in the same fixture back in 1932. Following the excitement and novelty of the World Cup, this match, and the 1992 championship, had a sense of anti-climax about it. Many of the players, who were still amateurs at this time, were clearly jaded after months of rugby. The final score flattered England, but they took their chances well and were worthy winners. The Scottish forwards were outstanding in the first half and even managed a pushover try against the heavier English pack – a collector's item indeed! England scored two spectacular, long-range tries during the game. The first came from a Scottish handling error and the flying Underwood raced away from his own half. After the interval, Guscott dropped a swaggering goal and then Halliday made a long mazy run before feeding Morris who romped over at the posts. Scotland were never out of contention, but somehow England just eased away.

419   INTERNATIONAL CHAMPIONSHIP 1992   IRELAND

Lansdowne Road, Dublin · Saturday 15 February 1992 · Won 18–10

SCOTLAND Gavin Hastings (*Watsonians*); Tony Stanger (*Hawick*), Scott Hastings (*Watsonians*), Sean Lineen (*Boroughmuir*), Iwan Tukalo (*Selkirk*); Craig Chalmers (*Melrose*), Andy Nicol (*Dundee HSFP*); David Sole* (*Edinburgh Acs*), Kenny Milne (*Heriot's FP*), Paul Burnell (*London Scot*), Neil Edwards (*Harlequins*), Doddie Weir (*Melrose*), Dave McIvor (*Edinburgh Acs*), Ian Smith (*Gloucester*), Derek White (*London Scot*) … Replacement: †Rob Wainwright (*Edinburgh Acs*) for Edwards (77)

IRELAND Kenny Murphy (*Cork Const*); Richard Wallace (*Garryowen*), Brendan Mullin (*Blackrock Coll*), Philip Danaher (*Garryowen*), Simon Geoghegan (*London Irish*); Ralph Keyes (*Cork Const*), Fergus Aherne (*Lansdowne*); Nick Popplewell (*Greystones*), Steve Smith (*Ballymena*), Garrett Halpin (*London Irish*), Mick Galway (*Shannon*), Neil Francis (*Blackrock Coll*), Philip Matthews* (*Wdrs*), Michael Fitzgibbon (*Shannon*), Brian Robinson (*Ballymena*) … Replacements: Des Fitzgerald (*DLSP*) for Halpin (29), David Curtis (*London Irish*) for Geoghegan (40)

REFEREE Tony Spreadbury (*England*)

SCORING Keyes, pen (0–3); Stanger, try (4–3); G Hastings, con (6–3); G Hastings, pen (9–3) (half-time) Nicol, try (13–3); G Hastings, con (15–3); Wallace, try (15–7); Keyes, pen (15–10); G Hastings, pen (18–10)

Billed in some quarters as a contest to avoid the wooden spoon, the outcome might have been different if an early try by Ireland had been allowed to stand. Geoghegan raced onto a kick over the Scottish line, but was adjudged to have been in an offside position. That incident summed-up a miserable afternoon for Ireland and in particular for stand-off Ralph Keyes who was barracked by his own supporters for his poor kicking. Meanwhile, Scotland played with efficiency and discipline without doing anything spectacular. They scored their first try after 26 minutes when Stanger dived over in the left corner after a good sweeping movement. Early in the second half, Derek White, who was in great form, took out two defenders with a sublime pass to create a try for Nichol. Gavin Hastings converted from the touchline into a fierce wind. Shortly before the end, Rob Wainwright, an army doctor, replaced Edwards to win his first cap.

420   INTERNATIONAL CHAMPIONSHIP 1992   FRANCE

Murrayfield · Saturday 7 March 1992 · Won 10–6

SCOTLAND Gavin Hastings (*Watsonians*); Tony Stanger (*Hawick*), Scott Hastings (*Watsonians*),

Sean Lineen (*Boroughmuir*), Iwan Tukalo (*Selkirk*); Craig Chalmers (*Melrose*), Andy Nicol (*Dundee HSFP*); David Sole* (*Edinburgh Acs*), Kenny Milne (*Heriot's FP*), Paul Burnell (*London Scot*), Neil Edwards (*Harlequins*), Doddie Weir (*Melrose*), Dave McIvor (*Edinburgh Acs*), Rob Wainwright (*Edinburgh Acs*), Derek White (*London Scot*)

FRANCE Jean-Luc Sadourny (*Colomiers*); Jean-Baptists Lafond (*RCF*), Philippe Sella* (*Agen*), Franck Mesnel (*RCF*), Philippe Saint-André (*Montferrand*); Alain Penaud (*Brive*), Fabien Galthie (*Colomiers*); Louis Almary (*Lourdes*), Jean-Pierre Genet (*RCF*), Philippe Gallart (*Béziers*), Marc Cecillon (*Bourgoin*), Olivier Roumat (*Dax*), Jean-François Tordo (*Nice*), Laurent Cabannes (*RCF*), Andries van Heerden (*Tarbes*)

REFEREE Freek Burger (*South Africa*)

SCORING Edwards, try (4–0); Lafond, pen (4–3) (half-time) Lafond, pen (4–6); G Hastings, pen (7–6); G Hastings, pen (10–6)

Unlike some previous encounters between the two sides, this was an uninspiring encounter lacking in spectacle. Three weeks earlier, France had lost an ugly match against England and on this occasion they were much more cautious and inhibited than usual. Played on a murky wet day, France had most of the possession, but could not break a strong Scottish defence. The best moment of the game came when the veteran Derek White made a brilliant try-saving tackle on Mesnel who was just getting into his stride. The only try was scored after four minutes when Neil Edwards took a clean catch at a lineout and was driven over the French line.

---

421 INTERNATIONAL CHAMPIONSHIP 1992 WALES

Cardiff Arms Park · Saturday 21 March 1992 · Lost 12–15

SCOTLAND Gavin Hastings (*Watsonians*); Tony Stanger (*Hawick*), Scott Hastings (*Watsonians*), Sean Lineen (*Boroughmuir*), Iwan Tukalo (*Selkirk*); Craig Chalmers (*Melrose*), Andy Nicol (*Dundee HSFP*); David Sole* (*Edinburgh Acs*), Kenny Milne (*Heriot's FP*), Paul Burnell (*London Scot*), Neil Edwards (*Harlequins*), Doddie Weir (*Melrose*), Dave McIvor (*Edinburgh Acs*), Ian Smith (*Gloucester*), Derek White (*London Scot*) ... Replacement: †Peter Jones (*Gloucester*) for Burnell (53)

WALES Tony Clement (*Swansea*); Ieuan Evans* (*Llanelli*), Roger Bidgood (*Newport*), Scott Gibbs (*Swansea*), Mike Hall (*Cardiff*); Neil Jenkins (*Pontypridd*), Robert Jones (*Swansea*); Mike Griffiths (*Cardiff*), Garin Jenkins (*Swansea*), Hugh Williams-Jones (*South Wales Police*), Gareth Llewellyn (*Neath*), Tony Copsey (*Llanelli*), Emyr Lewis (*Llanelli*), Richard Webster (*Swansea*), Stuart Davies (*Swansea*)

REFEREE Marc Desclaux (*France*)

SCORING N Jenkins, pen (0–3); G Hastings, pen (3–3); Chalmers, drop (6–3); Webster, try (6–7); N Jenkins, con (6–9) (half-time) N Jenkins, pen (6–12); Chalmers, pen (9–12); N Jenkins, pen (9–15); Chalmers, pen (12–15)

Scotland ended their campaign by failing to score a try against Wales for the first time in 17 years. They had spells of pressure, but much of their play lacked continuity and they missed too many kicks at goal. In fact this was a poor and forgettable match between two very ordinary sides. The only try of the game was scored after 21 minutes. Evans gathered a loose kick and beat several defenders, Williams-Jones made a powerful burst and Webster finished off. Scotland came closest on the hour mark when Tukalo charged down a clearance and dived on the ball, but was adjudged to have knocked on.

---

422 TOUR OF AUSTRALIA 1992 AUSTRALIA

Sydney Football Stadium · Saturday 13 June 1992 · Lost 12–27

SCOTLAND Gavin Hastings (*Watsonians*); Tony Stanger (*Hawick*), Scott Hastings (*Watsonians*), Sean Lineen (*Boroughmuir*), Iwan Tukalo (*Selkirk*); Craig Chalmers (*Melrose*), Andy Nicol (*Dundee HSFP*); David Sole* (*Edinburgh Acs*), Kenny Milne (*Heriot's FP*), †Peter Wright (*Boroughmuir*), Doddie Weir (*Melrose*), Neil Edwards (*Harlequins*), †Carl Hogg (*Melrose*), Ian Smith (*Gloucester*), Rob Wainwright (*Edinburgh Acs*) ... Replacement: †Ian Corcoran (*Gala*) for Milne (10)

AUSTRALIA Marty Roebuck (*NSW*); David Campese (*NSW*), Richard Tombs (*NSW*), Tim Horan (*Queensland*), Paul Carozza (*Queensland*); Michael Lynagh (*Queensland*), Nick Farr-Jones* (*NSW*); Tony Daly (*NSW*), Phil Kearns (*NSW*), Ewen MacKenzie (*NSW*), Rod McCall (*Queensland*), John Eales (*Queensland*), Willie Ofahengaue (*NSW*), David Wilson (*Queensland*), Tim Gavin (NSW) ... Replacement: Peter Jorgensen (*NSW*) for Carozza (70)

REFEREE L McLachlan (*New Zealand*) · ATTENDANCE 35,535

SCORING G Hastings, pen (3–0); Lynagh, pen (3–3); Campese, try (3–7); Wainwright, try (7–7); G Hastings, con (9–7) (half-time) Carozza, try (9–11); Lynagh, pen (9–14); Lynagh, pen (9–17); G Hastings, pen (12–17); Lynagh, try (12–21); Campese, try (12–25); Lynagh, con (12–27)

In May and June 1992, Scotland made an eight-match tour of Australia, including two test matches against the World Cup winners. Coming at the end of a long season, this was a demanding tour that took its toll on the players. The Scots had mixed fortunes in their provincial games and managed only two wins against lowly Country XVs, but they did well to draw against Queensland (15–15) and the Emerging Wallabies (24–24). For the test match at Sydney, first caps were awarded to Peter Wright and Carl Hogg, and also to Ian Corcoran when he came on after ten minutes. Scotland led 9–7 at half-time and for a while they seemed capable of creating an upset. Their first half try came when Chalmers put up a high kick, Lineen gathered the ball and drove to the line, and Wainwright was in support to finish the move. The game turned Australia's way at the start of the second half. The inimitable David Campese took a loose kick and from the ensuing play Lynagh hacked on for Carozza to score. Lynagh kicked two penalties and further tries by Lynagh and Campese sealed the game for the Wallabies.

---

423 TOUR OF AUSTRALIA 1992 AUSTRALIA

Ballymore, Brisbane · Sunday 21 June 1992 · Lost 13–37

SCOTLAND †Kenny Logan (*Stirling Co*); Tony Stanger (*Hawick*), Scott Hastings (*Watsonians*), Sean Lineen (*Boroughmuir*), Iwan Tukalo (*Selkirk*); Craig Chalmers (*Melrose*), Andy Nicol (*Dundee HSFP*); David Sole* (*Edinburgh Acs*), †Martin Scott (*Dunfermline*), Peter Wright

---

(*Boroughmuir*), Damian Cronin (*London Scot*), Doddie Weir (*Melrose*), Carl Hogg (*Melrose*), Ian Smith (*Gloucester*), Rob Wainwright (*Edinburgh Acs*)

AUSTRALIA Marty Roebuck (*NSW*); David Campese (*NSW*), Richard Tombs (*NSW*), Tim Horan (*Queensland*), Paul Carozza (*Queensland*); Michael Lynagh (*Queensland*), Nick Farr-Jones* (*NSW*); Tony Daly (*NSW*), Phil Kearns (*NSW*), Ewen MacKenzie (*NSW*), Rod McCall (*Queensland*), John Eales (*Queensland*), Willie Ofahengaue (*NSW*), David Wilson (*Queensland*), Tim Gavin (*NSW*) … Replacement: Peter Jorgensen (*NSW*) for Campese (79)

REFEREE Colin Hawke (*New Zealand*)

SCORING Lynagh, pen (0–3); Lynagh, pen (0–6); Lynagh, pen (0–9); Lynagh, pen (0–12); Chalmers, pen (3–12); Carozza, try (3–16) (half-time) Horan, try (3–20); Lynagh, pen (3–23); Horan, try (3–27); Lineen, try (7–27); Chalmers, con (9–27); Carozza, try (9–31); Eales, try (9–35); Lynagh, con (9–37); Sole, try (13–37)

Gavin Hastings withdrew because of injury and Kenny Logan became the first player to be capped from Stirling County. Dunfermline hooker Martin Scott won his only cap having just arrived as a tour replacement. Scotland fought hard, but they were outclassed by the reigning world champions. The first half was marred by a whistle-happy referee and Scotland were fortunate to be only 13 points adrift at the interval. They made several lapses in defence and conceded too many penalties. In the second half, Horan scored a brace of tries and Lynagh kicked a penalty. It seemed that Scotland would be completely swamped, but they made a brave late rally and scored close-range tries by Sean Lineen and David Sole, both of whom retired from international rugby after this game.

424 INTERNATIONAL CHAMPIONSHIP 1993 IRELAND

Murrayfield · Saturday 16 January 1993 · Won 15–3

SCOTLAND Gavin Hastings* (*Watsonians*); Tony Stanger (*Hawick*), Scott Hastings (*Watsonians*), Graham Shiel (*Melrose*), †Derek Stark (*Boroughmuir*); Craig Chalmers (*Melrose*), Gary Armstrong (*Jed-Forest*); Alan Walt (*GH-K*), Kenny Milne (*Heriot's FP*), Paul Burnell (*London Scot*), †Andy Reed (*Bath*), Damian Cronin (*London Scot*), Derek Turnbull (*Hawick*), †Iain Morrison (*London Scot*), Doddie Weir (*Melrose*)

IRELAND Colin Wilkinson (*Malone*); Simon Geoghegan (*London Irish*), Vincent Cunningham (*St Mary's Coll*), Philip Danaher (*Garryowen*), Richard Wallace (*Garryowen*); Niall Malone (*Oxford U*), Michael Bradley* (*Cork Const*); Nick Popplewell (*Greystones*), Steve Smith (*Ballymena*), Paul McCarthy (*Cork Const*), Paddy Johns (*Dungannon*), Richard Costello (*Garryowen*), Philip Lawlor (*Bective Rgrs*), Denis McBride (*Malone*), Noel Mannion (*Lansdowne*)

REFEREE Ed Morrison (*England*)

SCORING G Hastings, pen (3–0); Stark, try (8–0); G Hastings, con (10–0); Stanger, try (15–0) (half-time) Malone, pen (15–3)

This match was the beginning of a new era for Scottish rugby. It was the first all-seated international at Murrayfield, the old terraces having been replaced by the towering north and south stands. Gavin Hastings had been appointed as captain for the season and Derek Stark, Andy Reed and Iain Morrison won their first caps. Another newcomer Alan Sharp had to drop out before the match and he was replaced by Alan Watt. Playing in a strong gusty wind, Scotland enjoyed a comfortable win against a limited Irish side. After an early Hastings penalty, Stark was released down the left and he veered back inside some fragile defence for an excellent debut score. Towards the interval, the Scottish backs put together a good handling movement and Stark made an angled run before lobbing out a pass to Stanger who beat the defence to score at the corner. Gavin Hastings missed the conversion, but the game was as good as won. It was disappointing that Scotland did not score in the second half, but they were never in any danger. The lineout was effective and there were good individual performances by Gary Armstrong and Gavin Hastings.

425　INTERNATIONAL CHAMPIONSHIP 1993　　　FRANCE

Parc des Princes, Paris · Saturday 6 February 1993 · Lost 3–11

SCOTLAND Gavin Hastings* (*Watsonians*); Tony Stanger (*Hawick*), Scott Hastings (*Watsonians*), Graham Shiel (*Melrose*), Derek Stark (*Boroughmuir*); Craig Chalmers (*Melrose*), Gary Armstrong (*Jed-Forest*); Peter Wright (*Boroughmuir*), Kenny Milne (*Heriot's FP*), Paul Burnell (*London Scot*), Andy Reed (*Bath*), Damian Cronin (London Scot), Derek Turnbull (*Hawick*), Iain Morrison (*London Scot*), Doddie Weir (*Melrose*)

FRANCE Jean-Baptiste Lafond (*RCF*); Philippe Saint-André (*Montferrand*), Philippe Sella (*Agen*), Thierry Lacroix (*Dax*), Pierre Hontas (*Biarritz*); Didier Camberabero (*Béziers*), Aubin Hueber (*Toulon*); Louis Armary (*Lourdes*), Jean-François Tordo* (*Nice*), Laurent Seigne (*Mérignac*), Abdelatif Benazzi (*Agen*), Olivier Roumat (*Dax*), Philippe Benetton (*Agen*), Laurent Cabannes (*RCF*), Marc Cecillon (*Bourgoin*)

REFEREE Derek Bevan (*Wales*)

SCORING Camberabero, pen (0–3); G Hastings, pen (3–3) (half-time) Camberabero, pen (3–6); Lacroix, try (3–11)

Scotland's woeful run at the Parc des Princes continued although they might easily have registered their first win at the stadium. The Scottish forwards played very well for the first hour, but the backs wasted a lot of possession and Gavin Hastings landed only one kick out of six. On the 63rd minute Benazzi broke through and after some slick handling Lacroix squeezed over at the right corner. Thereafter France recaptured some of their old self-belief and control. Towards the finish Stark looked to have scored an interception try only to be called back for offside. Gary Armstrong gave another inspirational display and Andy Reed showed his prowess at the lineout.

426　INTERNATIONAL CHAMPIONSHIP 1993　　　WALES

Murrayfield · Saturday 20 February 1993 · Won 20–0

SCOTLAND Gavin Hastings* (*Watsonians*); Tony Stanger (*Hawick*), Scott Hastings (*Watsonians*), Graham Shiel (*Melrose*), Derek Stark (*Boroughmuir*); Craig Chalmers (*Melrose*), Gary Armstrong (*Jed-Forest*); Peter Wright (*Boroughmuir*), Kenny Milne (*Heriot's FP*), Paul Burnell (*London Scot*), Andy Reed (*Bath*), Damian Cronin (*London Scot*), Derek Turnbull (*Hawick*), Iain Morrison (*London Scot*), Doddie Weir (*Melrose*)

WALES Mike Rayer (*Cardiff*); Ieuan Evans* (*Llanelli*), Mike Hall (*Cardiff*), Scott Gibbs

(*Swansea*), Wayne Procter (*Llanelli*); Neil Jenkins (*Pontypridd*), Robert Jones (*Swansea*); Ricky Evans (*Llanelli*), Nigel Meek (*Pontypool*), Hugh Williams-Jones (*South Wales Police*), Gareth Llewellyn (*Neath*), Tony Copsey (*Llanelli*), Emyr Lewis (*Llanelli*), Richard Webster (*Swansea*), Stuart Davies (*Swansea*)

REFEREE   Joel Dume (*France*)

SCORING   G Hastings, pen (3–0); G Hastings, pen (6–0); G Hastings, pen (9–0); Turnbull, try (14–0) (half-time) G Hastings, pen (17–0); G Hastings, pen (20–0)

On a clear afternoon, Scotland gave a near perfect performance to demolish a lifeless Welsh side. The final score and solitary try did not reflect Scotland's domination and the winning margin should have been much greater. The Scottish forwards controlled possession and Wales never threatened the Scottish line. After his erratic display in Paris, Gavin Hastings recaptured his best kicking form and thumped over penalties at regular intervals despite a strong wind. Scotland's only try, which was scored just before the interval, came when Turnbull was driven over from a short-range lineout. The referee waited a long time for the bodies to unravel before he awarded the score, but it was well deserved for Turnbull who had a splendid match, especially at the front of the lineout. Scotland made intelligent use of the conditions and early in the second half Armstrong kicked a huge touch-finder from one 22 to the other which seemed to knock a lot of the fight out of the Welshmen. Towards the finish Scotland made some stirring attempts to score, but could not penetrate the Welsh defence. This was an uplifting win for the Scots who now headed to Twickenham to play for the Triple Crown.

427   INTERNATIONAL CHAMPIONSHIP 1993   ENGLAND

Twickenham · Saturday 6 March 1993 · Lost 12–26

SCOTLAND   Gavin Hastings* (*Watsonians*); Tony Stanger (*Hawick*), Scott Hastings (*Watsonians*), Graham Shiel (*Melrose*), Derek Stark (*Boroughmuir*); Craig Chalmers (*Melrose*), Gary Armstrong (*Jed-Forest*); Peter Wright (*Boroughmuir*), Kenny Milne (*Heriot's FP*), Paul Burnell (*London Scot*), Andy Reed (*Bath*), Damian Cronin (*London Scot*), Derek Turnbull (*Hawick*), Iain Morrison (*London Scot*), Doddie Weir (*Melrose*) ... Replacements: †Gregor Townsend (*Gala*) for Chalmers (22), Kenny Logan (*Stirling Co*) for S Hastings

ENGLAND   Jonathan Webb (*Bath*); Tony Underwood (*Leicester*), Will Carling* (*Harlequins*), Jeremy Guscott (*Bath*), Rory Underwood (*Leicester*); Stuart Barnes (*Bath*), Dewi Morris (*Orrell*); Jason Leonard (*Harlequins*), Brian Moore (*Harlequins*), Jeff Probyn (*Wasps*), Martin Bayfield (*Northampton*), Wade Dooley (*Preston Grasshoppers*), Mike Teague (*Moseley*), Peter Winterbottom (*Harlequins*), Ben Clarke (*Bath*)

REFEREE   Brian Stirling (*Ireland*)

SCORING   G Hastings, pen (3–0); Webb, pen (3–3); Chalmers, drop (6–3); Guscott, try (6–8); Webb, pen (6–11) (half-time) R Underwood, try (6–16); T Underwood, try (6–21); Webb, con (6–23); G Hastings, pen (9–23); Webb, pen (9–26); G Hastings, pen (12–26)

Once again Scotland's hopes of winning the Triple Crown were dashed at Twickenham. The Scots started confidently and took an early lead before losing their playmaker Craig Chalmers with a broken arm after only 24 minutes. Gregor Townsend came on to win his first cap and Graham Shiel moved to the pivotal position. The injury unsettled the Scots, but it was doubtful if it made much difference in the long run. Stuart Barnes, the rotund Bath stand-off, had been recalled to spark some life into the English back division which he did with considerable panache. Shortly after Chalmers' departure, Guscott glided over from a ruck in front of the Scottish posts and early in the second half England scored two spectacular tries from deep. Barnes seemed to be pinned down near his 22, but he sidestepped the cover and found Guscott who accelerated away before releasing Rory Underwood on a run to the line. A few minutes later, Underwood drew the defence with an angled run before passing to his brother Tony who cruised around behind the posts. From then on Scotland did well to avoid a total collapse and restore some of their pride, but this was another black day at the Twickenham graveyard.

 TOUR OF THE SOUTH PACIFIC 1993   FIJI

Commonwealth Stadium, Suva · Saturday 29 May 1993 · Won 21–10

SCOTLAND XV Kenny Logan (*Stirling Co*); Nick Grecian (*London Scot*), Scott Nichol (*Selkirk*), Ian Jardine (*Stirling Co*), Mark Moncrieff (*Gala*); Ally Donaldson (*Currie*), Andy Nicol* (*Dundee HSFP*); Gary Isaac (*Gala*), Jim Hay (*Hawick*), Steve Ferguson (*Peebles*), Chris Gray (*Nottingham*), Robb Scott (*London Scot*), Dave McIvor (*Edinburgh Acs*), Ian Smith (*Gloucester*), Doddie Weir (*Melrose*)

FIJI Tevita Vonolagi; Waisea Komaitai, Viliame Rauluni, Esala Nauga, Tomasi Lovo; Elia Rokowailoa, Waisale Serevi; Mosese Taga*, Alipate Rabitu, Ilisoni Naituku, Pita Naruma, Aisake Nadolo, Ifereimi Tawake, Sakeasi Vonolagi, Eparama Tuvunivono

REFEREE BM Kinsey (*Australia*)

SCORING Hay, try (5–0); Donaldson, con (7–0); Donaldson, pen (10–0) (half-time) Rokowailoa, try (10–5); Serevi, con (10–7); Serevi, pen (10–10); Logan, try (15–10); Donaldson, pen (18–10); Donaldson, pen (21–10)

In May and June 1993, Scotland made a seven-match tour of the South Pacific Islands. Many first-choice players were unavailable, but the tour introduced some promising newcomers and was a useful development exercise. The tour started with victories over Fiji B (14–7) and Fiji Juniors (51–3) before a non-cap test against Fiji at Suva. Played before a sparse crowd and in a gusting wind, Scotland were comfortable winners despite fielding nine uncapped players. The Scottish forwards combined well and some of their driving mauls were exemplary. Centre Ian Jardine was prominent in defence. On the 19th minute, Nicol stole the ball at a scrum and after several drives Hay was shoved over the line. Donaldson, who had a mixed day with the boot, converted and later kicked a penalty. In the second half, Fiji drew level with a try by Rokowailoa which was converted by Serevi who also landed a penalty. Scotland had greater stamina and discipline and they finished strongly. Nicol took a quick tap-penalty and Donaldson put Logan over for a try. Donaldson kicked two further penalties to clinch a satisfactory win.

Teufaiva Stadium, Nuku'alofa · Saturday 5 June 1993 · Won 23–5

SCOTLAND XV Craig Redpath (*Melrose*); Mark Moncrieff (*Gala*), Scott Nichol (*Selkirk*), Ian Jardine (*Stirling Co*), Kenny Logan (*Stirling Co*); Gregor Townsend (*Gala*), Andy Nicol* (*Dundee HSFP*); Gary Isaac (*Gala*), Jim Hay (*Hawick*), Steve Ferguson (*Peebles*), Chris Gray (*Nottingham*), Rob Scott (*London Scot*), Dave McIvor (*Edinburgh Acs*), Ian Smith (*Gloucester*), Doddie Weir (*Melrose*) ... Replacement: Carl Hogg (*Melrose*) for Scott (53)

TONGA Isi Tapueluelu (*Kolomotu'a*); Afu Uasi (*Fua'amotu*), Tavake Tu'ineau (*Fasi & Ma'ufanga*), Manu Lavaka (*Toa-ko-Ma'afu*), Tevita Va'enuku (*Police*); Elisi Vunipola (*Toa-ko-Ma'afu*), Avery Tulikaki; Valita Moa (*Hihifo*), Fololisi Masila (*Kolomotu'a*), Etuini Talakai (*Suburbs*), Teutau Loto'ahea (*Police*), Isi Fatani (*Toa-ko-Ma'afu*), Ipolito Fenukitau (*Kolomotua'a*), Feleti Fakaongo (Vava'u), Martin Manukia* (*Kerikeri*) ... Replacements: Leha'uli Fotu (*Hihifo*) for Tapueluelu, Tevita Lavaki (Kolofo'ou) for Moa, Manu Vunipola (*Toa-ko-Ma'afu*) for Tulikaka

REFEREE Lindsay McLachlan (*New Zealand*)

SCORING Weir, try (5–0); Lavaka, try (5–5); Townsend, pen (8–5) (half-time) Penalty try (13–5); Townsend, con (15–5); Townsend, pen (18–5); Logan, try (23–5)

After a good win in mid-week over a Tongan President's XV (21–5), Scotland continued their winning ways against the Tongan national side. The Scots were lethargic at times and seemed to be affected by the humid conditions, but they did enough for victory and scored three tries to one. The forwards held a definite edge and the scrum was solid thanks to the sterling efforts of uncapped Border props Gary Isaac and Steve Fergusson. The backs tackled well and Ian Jardine gave another competitive performance. Gregor Townsend kicked astutely and kept the Scots going forwards. The highlight of an otherwise mediocre game was the solitary Tongan try. After a charge-down on the Scottish 22, Vunipola kicked past the rushing defence, Fenukitau gathered the ball and charged to the line, and Lavaka dived over for a good impulse score.

Apia Park Stadium · Saturday 12 June 1993 · Lost 11–28

SCOTLAND XV Nick Grecian (*London Scot*); Mark Moncrieff (Gala), Scott Nichol (*Selkirk*), Ian Jardine (*Stirling Co*), Kenny Logan (*Stirling Co*); Gregor Townsend (*Gala*), Andy Nicol* (*Dundee HSFP*); Gary Isaac (*Gala*), Jim Hay (*Hawick*), Steve Ferguson (*Peebles*), Shade Munro (*GH-K*), Rob Scott (*London Scot*), Dave McIvor (*Edinburgh Acs*), Ian Smith (*Gloucester*), Doddie Weir (Melrose) ... Replacements: Andy Macdonald (*Heriot's FP*) for Scott (24), Ian Corcoran (*Gala*) for Hay (78)

WESTERN SAMOA Anitelea Aiolupo (*Moataa*); Lolani Koko (*Wellington*), To'o Vaega (*Moataa*), Alama Ieremia (*Scopa*), Brian Lima (*Marist-St Josephs*); Darren Kellett (*Ponsonby*), Junior Tonu'u (*Apia*); Peter Fatialofa* (*Manukau*), Tala Leasamaivao (*Moataa*), Afa Leu'u (*Papakura*), Potu Leavasa (*Apia*), Lio Falaniko (*Marist-St Josephs*), Sila Vaifale, Malaki Iupeli (*Marist-St Josephs*), Danny Kaleopa (*Moataa*) ... Replacements: Stan To'omalatai (*Vaiala*) for Leu'u (76), Harry Schuster (*Apia*) for Vaifale (76)

SCORING Vaega, try (0–5); Kellett, con (0–7); A Nicol, try (5–7); Kaleopa, try (5–12); Townsend, pen (8–12) (half-time) Kellett, pen (8–15); Kellett, pen (8–18); Kellett, pen (8–21); Townsend, pen (11–21); Lima, try (11–26); Kellett, con (11–28)

On the most testing leg of their South Pacific odyssey, the Scots defeated a Samoan President's XV in midweek (33–8), but were unable to finish their tour on a high against Western Samoa. The Scots struggled in the tropical heat and several of the players looked jaded. The burly Samoan forwards largely held the upper-hand, especially in the lineout, and the home side played with passion and imagination. Samoan stand-off Darren Kellet had an excellent match and varied his tactics effectively. For Scotland Ian Jardine tackled powerfully and Dave McIvor was prominent in the loose. Scotland's only try came from a good scrum on the Samoan line and Nicol reacted quickly to touch down. Afterwards, Nicol was called upon as an emergency scrum-half to join the British Lions on tour in New Zealand.

---

428 TOUR MATCH NEW ZEALAND

Murrayfield · Saturday 20 November 1993 · Lost 15–51

SCOTLAND Gavin Hastings* (*Watsonians*); Tony Stanger (*Hawick*), †Ian Jardine (*Stirling Co*), Graham Shiel (*Melrose*), Scott Hastings (*Watsonians*); Craig Chalmers (*Melrose*), Andy Nicol (*Dundee HSFP*); Alan Watt (*GH-K*), Kenny Milne (*Heriot's FP*), Paul Burnell (*London Scot*), Damian Cronin (*London Scot*), †Andy MacDonald (*Heriot's FP*), Dave McIvor (*Edinburgh Acs*), Rob Wainwright (*Edinburgh Acs*), Doddie Weir (*Melrose*) ... Replacements: †Bryan Redpath (*Melrose*) for Nicol (7-8), Kenny Logan (*Stirling Co*) for G Hastings (35-40), Douglas Wyllie (*Stew-Mel FP*) for Chalmers (56), Carl Hogg (*Melrose*) for Cronin (61)

NEW ZEALAND John Timu (*Otago*); Jeff Wilson (*Otago*), Frank Bunce (*North Harbour*), Matthew Cooper (*Waikato*), Va'aiga Tuigamala (*Auckland*); Marc Ellis (*Otago*), Stu Forster (*Otago*); Craig Dowd (*Auckland*), Sean Fitzgerald (*Auckland*), Olo Brown (*Auckland*), Ian Jones (*North Auckland*), Steve Gordon (*Waikato*), Jamie Joseph (*Otago*), Zinzan Brooke (*Auckland*), Arran Pene (*Otago*) ... Replacement: Eroni Clarke (*Auckland*) for Cooper (75)

REFEREE Frik Burger (*South Africa*)

SCORING Cooper, pen (0–3); Ellis, try (0–8); G Hastings, pen (3–8); Wilson, try (3–13); Cooper, con (3–15); G Hastings, pen (6–15); Brooke, try (6–20); Cooper, con (6–22); Chalmers, pen (9–22) (half-time) Bunce, try (9–27); G Hastings, pen (12–27); Cooper, pen (9–30); G Hastings, pen (15–30); Wilson, try (15–35); Cooper, con (15–37); Ellis, try (15–42); Cooper, con (15–44); Wilson, try (15–49); Wilson, con (15–51)

Ian Jardine and Andy Macdonald won their first caps. Five players graduated from the Scotland A team that had done well against New Zealand the previous weekend at Old Anniesland (9–20). However, the main talking point was the bizarre selection of Scott Hastings, an outstanding centre, on the left wing. The west stand at Murrayfield was being rebuilt so the players changed in temporary accommodation. This match was as one-sided as the final score suggests and New Zealand gave their hosts a master-class in the arts of the modern game. Cooper kicked a penalty in the opening minutes and the New Zealanders never relinquished their iron grip on proceedings. Ellis,

Wilson and Brooke scored tries in the first half and Cooper converted two of them. After the break, Bunce and Ellis added further tries, but the real star was new wing Jeff Wilson who scored a hat-trick and nonchalantly converted his final try with a magnificent kick. Long before the finish, Scotland were a thoroughly bedraggled side. Some of the Scottish players did not look fully fit and the experiment of playing Scott Hastings on the wing backfired horribly, his lack of experience being ruthlessly exposed in two of Wilson's tries.

429 INTERNATIONAL CHAMPIONSHIP 1994 WALES

Cardiff Arms Park · Saturday 15 January 1994 · Lost 6–29

SCOTLAND Gavin Hastings* (*Watsonians*); Tony Stanger (*Hawick*), Gregor Townsend (*Gala*), Ian Jardine (*Stirling Co*), Kenny Logan (*Stirling Co*); Craig Chalmers (*Melrose*), Andy Nicol (*Dundee HSFP*); Peter Wright (*Boroughmuir*), Kenny Milne (*Heriot's FP*), Paul Burnell (*London Scot*), Neil Edwards (*Northampton*), †Shade Munro (*GH-K*), Derek Turnbull (*Hawick*), Iain Morrison (*London Scot*), Rob Wainwright (*Edin Acs*) ... Replacements: Doddie Weir (*Melrose*) for Morrison (18), Douglas Wyllie (*Stew-Mel FP*) for Chalmers (55)

WALES Tony Clement (*Swansea*); Ieuan Evans* (*Llanelli*), Mike Hall (*Cardiff*), Nigel Davies (*Llanelli*), Nigel Walker (*Cardiff*); Neil Jenkins (*Pontypridd*), Rupert Moon (*Llanelli*); Ricky Evans (*Llanelli*), Garin Jenkins (*Swansea*), John Davies (*Neath*), Phil Davies (*Llanelli*), Gareth Llewellyn (*Neath*), Emyr Lewis (*Llanelli*), Mark Perego (*Llanelli*), Scott Quinnell (*Llanelli*) ... Replacement: Mike Rayer (*Cardiff*) for Walker (11)

REFEREE Patrick Robin (*France*)

SCORING N Jenkins, pen (0–3); G Hastings, pen (3–3); N Jenkins, pen (3–6); N Jenkins, pen (3–9) (half-time) N Jenkins, pen (3–12); Rayer, try (3–17); G Hastings, pen (6–17); Rayer, try (6–22); N Jenkins, con (6–24); I Evans, try (6–29)

Shade Munro, the grandson of the great John Bannerman, won his first cap. Still reeling from their heavy defeat by the All Blacks, this was another ghastly afternoon for the Scots and nothing went right for them. It rained heavily throughout the game and they lost Morrison with a broken leg after only 18 minutes. Earlier, Welsh hooker Garin Jenkins should have been sent-off for repeated punching in full view of the touch judge. In the second half, Gregor Townsend had a drop goal disallowed although television replays seemed to show that it was perfectly good. Then Phil Davies sabotaged a promising Scottish attack when he pinched the ball from a position so far offside that it was almost comical. However, Scotland's demise was not all down to bad luck and Welsh skulduggery. The forwards were desperately poor, the backs lacked invention and sharpness, and they conceded too many turnovers. The only compensation was a promising display by youthful Gregor Townsend making his first full start.

430 INTERNATIONAL CHAMPIONSHIP 1994 ENGLAND

Murrayfield · Saturday 5 February 1994 · Lost 14–15

SCOTLAND Gavin Hastings* (*Watsonians*); Tony Stanger (*Hawick*), Scott Hastings

(*Watsonians*), Douglas Wyllie (*Stew-Mel FP*), Kenny Logan (*Stirling Co*); Gregor Townsend (*Gala*), Gary Armstrong (*Jed-Forest*); †Alan Sharp (*Bristol*), Kenny Milne (*Heriot's FP*), Paul Burnell (*London Scot*), Shade Munro (*GH-K*), Andy Reed (*Bath*), †Peter Walton (*Northampton*), Rob Wainwright (*Edin Acs*), Doddie Weir (*Melrose*) ... Replacements: Bryan Redpath (*Melrose*) for Armstrong (49-51), Ian Smith (*Gloucester*) for Wainwright (67), Ian Jardine (*Stirling Co*) for S Hastings (72)

ENGLAND Jonathan Callard (*Bath*); Tony Underwood (*Leicester*), Will Carling* (*Harlequins*) Phil de Glanville (*Bath*), Rory Underwood (*Leicester*); Rob Andrew (*Wasps*), Kyran Bracken (*Bristol*); Jason Leonard (*Harlequins*), Brian Moore (*Harlequins*), Victor Obogu (*Bath*), Martin Bayfield (*Northampton*), Martin Johnson (*Leicester*), John Hall (*Bath*), Neil Back (*Leicester*), Ben Clarke (*Bath*)

REFEREE Lindsay McLachlan (*New Zealand*)

SCORING Callard, pen (0-3); Wainwright, try (5-3) (half-time) G Hastings, pen (8-3); Callard, pen (8-6); Callard, pen (8-9); G Hastings, pen (11-9); Callard, pen (11-12); Townsend, drop (14-12); Callard, pen (14-15)

There were seven changes to the side that started in Wales, including first caps for Peter Walton and Alan Sharp. The big news was the return of Gary Armstrong after a year out because of injury. England were clear favourites, but the Scots played above themselves only to be deprived of victory in the cruellest way. The Scottish forwards were a big improvement and the defence was very strong. Armstrong played like a hungry wolf and narrowly missed a try in the first half because of a strong cover tackle by Hall. A score was not long delayed however and a few minutes later Reed collected the ball from a high kick and passed to Stanger. The big wing evaded a couple of tackles before feeding Wainwright who sprinted over from the English 22. The try capped an excellent performance by Wainwright who was the best forward on view although he fractured his cheekbone towards the end. Scotland's downfall was their failure to kick their goals and Gavin Hastings managed only two from seven attempts. On the 73rd minute, Callard kicked his fourth penalty to give England a one-point lead and set-up a dramatic conclusion. Moving into injury-time, Townsend dropped a towering goal that seemed to have won the game for Scotland, but from the restart they were penalised, perhaps mistakenly, for handling at a ruck. From around 40 metres, Callard made no mistake and the final whistle went. In a television interview after the match, Gavin Hastings was reduced to tears of frustration and disappointment, his feelings being shared by Scots everywhere.

---

431 INTERNATIONAL CHAMPIONSHIP 1994 **IRELAND**

Lansdowne Road, Dublin · Saturday 5 March 1994 · Drawn 6-6

SCOTLAND Gavin Hastings* (*Watsonians*); Tony Stanger (*Hawick*), Scott Hastings (*Watsonians*), Douglas Wyllie (*Stew-Mel FP*), Kenny Logan (*Stirling Co*); Gregor Townsend (*Gala*), Gary Armstrong (*Jed-Forest*); Alan Sharp (*Bristol*), Kenny Milne (*Heriot's FP*), Paul Burnell (*London Scot*), Shade Munro (*GH-K*), Andy Reed (*Bath*), Peter Walton (*Northampton*), Ian Smith (*Gloucester*), Doddie Weir (*Melrose*) ... Replacement: †Michael Dods (*Gala*) for G Hastings (39-40)

IRELAND Conor O'Shea (*Lansdowne*); Richard Wallace (*Garryowen*), Maurice Field (*Malone*),

Philip Danaher (*Garryowen*), Simon Geoghegan (*London Irish*); Eric Elwood (*Lansdowne*), Michael Bradley* (*Cork Const*); Nick Popplewell (*Greystones*), Terry Kingston (*Dolphin*), Peter Clohessy (*Young Munster*), Mick Galwey (*Shannon*), Neil Francis (*Old Belvedere*), Brian Robinson (*Ballymena*), Denis McBride (*Malone*), Paddy Johns (*Dungannon*)

REFEREE Ed Morrison (*England*)

SCORING Elwood, pen (0–3) (half-time) G Hastings, pen (3–3); G Hastings, pen (6–3); Elwood, pen (6–6)

Scotland could easily have beaten a mediocre Irish side, but they lacked enough of a killer instinct and the match ended in stalemate. Scotland faced into a very strong wind in the first half and managed to restrict Ireland to only a six-point lead at the interval. Early in the second half, Gavin Hastings kicked two penalties which should have given Scotland a winning platform, but instead they lost some of their composure and were unable to finish the job. This was a frustrating outcome for the Scots although they could take some compensation from a solid display by the forwards and good all-round defence. Townsend showed flashes of his acceleration and Armstrong was in brilliant form despite playing for some of the time with a hand injury that ruled him out of the next game. One curiosity of this match was the fleeting appearance of Michael Dods, the brother of Peter, as a temporary replacement for Gavin Hastings on the stroke of half-time. It was estimated that Dods was on the field for less than ten seconds before the referee blew for the interval and Hastings returned. It seemed that Dods was destined to have the shortest international career on record until he won his first full cap in the summer.

432 INTERNATIONAL CHAMPIONSHIP 1994 FRANCE

Murrayfield · Saturday 19 March 1994 · Lost 12–20

SCOTLAND Gavin Hastings* (*Watsonians*); Tony Stanger (*Hawick*), Scott Hastings (*Watsonians*), Douglas Wyllie (*Stew-Mel FP*), Kenny Logan (*Stirling Co*); Gregor Townsend (*Gala*), Bryan Redpath (*Melrose*); Alan Sharp (*Bristol*), Kenny Milne (*Heriot's FP*), Paul Burnell (*London Scot*), Shade Munro (*GH-K*), Andy Reed (*Bath*), Peter Walton (*Northampton*), Ian Smith (*Gloucester*), Doddie Weir (*Melrose*)

FRANCE Jean-Luc Sadourny (*Colomiers*); Philippe Saint-André* (*Montferrand*), Philippe Sella (*Agen*), Yanne Delaigue (*Toulon*), William Techoueyres (*Bordeaux U*); Thierry Lacroix (*Dax*), Alain Macabiau (*Perpignan*); Laurent Benezech (*RCF*), Jean-Michel Gonzalez (*Bayonne*), Laurent Seigne (*Merignac*), Olivier Brouzet (*Grenoble*), Olivier Merle (*Grenoble*), Philippe Benetton (*Agen*), Laurent Cabannes (*RCF*), Abdelatif Benazzi (*Agen*) ... Replacement: Pierre Montlaur (*Agen*) for Lacroix (52)

REFEREE Derek Bevan (*Wales*)

SCORING Lacroix, pen (0–3); Sadourny, try (0–8); Lacroix, con (0–10); G Hastings, pen (3–10); G Hastings, pen (6–10); G Hastings, pen (9–10); Lacroix, pen (9–13) (half-time) Saint-André, try (9–18); Montlaur, con (9–20); G Hastings, pen (12–20)

The Hastings brothers, Gavin and Scott, both won their 50th caps and Bryan Redpath made his first full start at scrum-half. France won at Murrayfield for the first time in 16 years and consigned Scotland to the wooden spoon. The Scottish forwards did well enough in the lineout and had some good drives, but the backs lacked genuine pace and creativity. France dominated the opening quarter and after some 18 minutes Delaigue burst between the Scottish centres and chipped ahead for Sadourny to race on and score. Gavin Hastings pulled Scotland back into contention with three penalties, but Lacroix consolidated the French lead with a penalty before half-time. The decisive moment of the match came on the 54th minute when Saint-André intercepted a pass and gleefully ran away to the line. Hastings kicked another penalty, but there was no way back for the Scots. This defeat ended a disappointing championship for Scotland who managed only one try in four matches.

---

433   TOUR OF ARGENTINA 1994   ARGENTINA

Ferro Carril Oeste Stadium, Buenos Aires · Saturday 4 June 1994

Lost 15–16

SCOTLAND Michael Dods (*Gala*); †Craig Joiner (*Melrose*), Ian Jardine (Stirling Co), Graham Shiel (*Melrose*), Kenny Logan (*Stirling Co*); Gregor Townsend (*Gala*), Bryan Redpath (*Melrose*); Alan Sharp (*Bristol*), †Kevin McKenzie (*Stirling Co*), Paul Burnell (*London Scot*), Shade Munro (*GH-K*), Andy Reed* (*Bath*), Peter Walton (*Northampton*), Ian Smith (*Gloucester*), Carl Hogg (*Melrose*)

ARGENTINA Santiago Meson (*Tucumán*); Martin Teran (*Tucumán*), Diego Cuesta Silva (*San Isidro*), Marcelo Loffreda* (*San Isidro*), Gustavo Jorge (*Pucara*); Guillermo del Castillo (*Jockey Club Rosario*), Nicolas Fernandez Miranda (*Hindu*); Matias Corral (*San Isidro*), Juan Angelillo (*San Isidro*), Patricio Noriega (*Hindu*), German Llanes (*La Plata*), Pedro Sporleder (*Curupayti*), Rolando Martin (*San Isidro*), Pablo Camerlinckx (*Regatas*), Cristian Viel Temperley (*Newman*)

REFEREE Wayne Erickson (*Australia*)

SCORING Meson, pen (0–3); Dods, pen (3–3); Meson, pen (3–6) (half-time) Teran, try (3–11); Meson, con (3–13); Meson, pen (3–16); Dods, pen (6–16); Dods, pen (9–16); Dods, pen (12–16); Dods, pen (15–16)

In May and June 1994, Scotland made a six-match tour of Argentina, their first visit since 1969. Several senior players were unavailable and consequently the results were disappointing. The Scots won only one of their provincial games, against Cordoba, and lost both test matches, albeit narrowly each time. The first test was an unattractive and disjointed encounter, mainly a tedious series of set-pieces interrupted by the occasional penalty. Scotland might easily have won if they had played with more adventure and made fewer errors. Some of the players were not at their best and Michael Dods, the first-choice placekicker, missed five penalty attempts. The only try of the game was scored immediately after the interval when Dods spilled a high kick under his own posts and Argentinean winger Teran was up quickly to pounce on the loose ball.

Ferro Carril Oeste Stadium, Buenos Aires · Saturday 11 June 1994

Lost 17–19

SCOTLAND Michael Dods (*Gala*); Craig Joiner (*Melrose*), Ian Jardine (*Stirling Co*), Graham Shiel (*Melrose*), Kenny Logan (*Stirling Co*); Gregor Townsend (*Gala*), Bryan Redpath (*Melrose*); Alan Sharp (*Bristol*), Kevin McKenzie (*Stirling Co*), Paul Burnell (*London Scot*), Shade Munro (*GH-K*), Andy Reed* (*Bath*), Peter Walton (*Northampton*), Ian Smith (*Gloucester*), Carl Hogg (*Melrose*) ... Replacements: Alan Watt (*GH-K*) for Munro (64–71) and Sharp (74), †Scott Nichol (*Selkirk*) for Logan (70)

ARGENTINA Santiago Meson (*Tucumán*); Martin Teran (*Tucumán*), Diego Cuesta Silva (*San Isidro*), Marcelo Loffreda* (*San Isidro*), Gustavo Jorge (*Pucara*); Guillermo del Castillo (*Jockey Club Rosario*), Nicolas Fernandez Miranda (*Hindu*); Federico Mendez (*Tucumán*), Juan Angelillo (*San Isidro*), Patricio Noriega (*Hindu*), German Llanes (*La Plata*), Pedro Sporleder (*Curupayti*), Rolando Martin (*San Isidro*), Cristian Viel Temperley (*Newman*), Jose Santamarina (*Tucumán*)

REFEREE Wayne Erickson (*Australia*)

SCORING Shiel, pen (3–0); Shiel, pen (6–0); Martin, try (6–5); Meson, con (6–7); Meson, pen (6–10); Meson, pen (6–13) (half-time) Meson, pen (6–16); Townsend, drop (9–16); Logan, try (14–16); Dods, pen (17–16); del Castillo, drop (17–19)

Scotland were a big improvement on the previous weekend, but once again they lacked a reliable placekicker. Graham Shiel put over two early penalties, but missed several other attempts during the game. Scotland also spurned some drop goal efforts, including an unlikely one from hooker Kevin Mackenzie. The Argentineans were big and physical, and at times Scotland had to cling on desperately in the face of the onslaught, but the tourists showed great self-belief to recapture the lead after going ten-points down early in the second-half. Townsend started the comeback with a drop goal and on the 54th minute Jardine made a midfield thrust before passing to Logan who was tackled short of the line but stretched over for his first international try. Dods then kicked a penalty to put Scotland into the lead, but immediately del Castillo dropped a goal. In a frantic conclusion, Dods had the chance to snatch victory with a long range penalty but his kick fell short.

---

435 TOUR MATCH SOUTH AFRICA

Murrayfield · Saturday 19 November 1994 · Lost 10–34

SCOTLAND Gavin Hastings* (*Watsonians*); Tony Stanger (*Hawick*), Scott Hastings (*Watsonians*), Graham Shiel (*Melrose*), Kenny Logan (*Stirling Co*); Craig Chalmers (*Melrose*), †Derrick Patterson (*West Hartlepool*); Alan Sharp (*Bristol*), Kenny Milne (*Heriot's FP*), Paul Burnell (*London Scot*), †Jeremy Richardson (*Edinburgh Acs*), Andy Reed (*Bath*), Dave McIvor (*Edinburgh Acs*), Iain Morrison (*London Scot*), Doddie Weir (*Melrose*)

SOUTH AFRICA André Joubert (*Natal*); Pieter Hendriks (*Transvaal*), Pieter Muller (*Natal*), Japie Mulder (*Transvaal*), Chester Williams (*W Province*); Hennie le Roux (*Transvaal*), Joost van der Westhuizen (*N Transvaal*); Os du Randt (*OFS*), Uli Schmidt (*Transvaal*), Tommie Laubscher (*W Province*), Mark Andrews (*Natal*), Phillip Schutte (*Transvaal*), Francois Pienaar* (*Transvaal*), Ruben Kruger (*N Transvaal*), Rudi Straeuli (*Transvaal*)

SCORING Joubert, pen (0–3); van der Westhuizen, try (0–8) (half-time) van der Westhuizen, try (0–13); Joubert, con (0–15); Williams, try (0–20); Joubert, con (0–22); Straeuli, try (0–27); G Hastings, pen (3–27); Mulder, try (3–32); Joubert, con (3–34); Stanger, try (8–34); G Hastings, con (10–34)

South Africa were making a 13 match tour of the British Isles, including four games north of the Border. Ten days earlier, they had lost to Scotland A at Melrose (17–15) which gave Scotland some cause for optimism. Derrick Patterson and Jeremy Richardson won their first caps. Played in front of the Princess Royal, this match marked the opening of the new Murrayfield stadium after an ambitious £44 million redevelopment. Before kick-off some famous Scottish players were introduced to the crowd, including members of the side that had beaten South Africa in 1969, Scotland's last encounter with the Springboks. On an immaculate surface, Scotland started brightly, but it was soon apparent that the South Africans had raised their game for the big occasion. Joubert kicked a penalty after 28 minutes and then from a scrum on the Scottish 22 van der Westhuizen caught the Scottish back-row napping and escaped down the blindside for a classic scrum-half's try. This was just a prelude to a scoring blitz by South Africa in the second half. First, van der Westhuizen danced through several weak tackles to score at the posts. Four minutes later, Joubert intruded into the line and slick passing put Williams over. Then Straeuli finished off a great movement with another try and on the hour mark Mulder broke away after good play by Le Roux. It looked like the floodgates would open, but the South Africans lost some of their concentration and in the closing minutes Stanger rescued a faltering move when he plunged over for a try. The South Africans had given their best performance since their readmission to the international scene in 1992 and produced some vintage rugby that at times had the Scots reeling. This was an important milestone for South Africa on the way to the 1995 World Cup, but a disappointing afternoon for Scotland.

---

436 | **1995** | **CANADA**

Murrayfield · Saturday 21 January 1995 · Won 22–6

SCOTLAND Gavin Hastings* (*Watsonians*); Craig Joiner (*Melrose*), Gregor Townsend (*Gala*), Ian Jardine (*Stirling Co*), Kenny Logan (*Stirling Co*); Craig Chalmers (*Melrose*), Bryan Redpath (*Melrose*); †David Hilton (*Bath*), Kenny Milne (*Heriot's FP*), Peter Wright (*Boroughmuir*), Damian Cronin (*Bourges*), †Stewart Campbell (*Dundee HSFP*), Rob Wainwright (*West Hartlepool*), Iain Morrison (*London Scot*), †Eric Peters (*Bath*)

CANADA Scott Stewart (*UBC OB*); Winston Stanley (*UBC*), Christian Stewart (*W Province & Rovigo*), Steve Gray (*Kats*), Ron Toews (*Meralomas*); Gareth Rees* (*Oak Bay Castaways & Newport*), John Graf (*UBC OB*); Eddie Evans (*UBC OB & IBM Tokoyo*), Mark Cardinal (*James Bay*), Dan Jackart (*UBC OB*), Mike James (*Burnaby*), Kevin Whitley (*Capilano*), Ian Gordon (*James Bay*), Gord Mackinnon (*ex-Brittania Lions*), Colin McKenzie (*UBC OB*) … Replacement: John Hutchinson (*UBC OB*) for Whitley (40)

REFEREE Clayton Thomas (*Wales*)

SCORING Rees, pen (0–3); Hastings, pen (3–3); Rees, pen (3–6); Hastings, pen (6–6); Hastings, pen (9–6); Hastings, pen (12–6) (half-time) Cronin, try (17–6); Hastings, con (19–6); Hastings, pen (22–6)

Scotland made ten changes from the side that had lost to South Africa, including first caps for Stewart Campbell and Eric Peters, who had previously played for England U21. Prop Alan Sharp pulled out through injury and his place was taken by another newcomer David Hilton. Played in bitterly cold weather and on a sodden pitch, Scotland put an end to their miserable sequence of nine matches without a win. The Scottish forwards held the upper-hand throughout and were solid at the set-pieces against some big opponents. Once again there was a lack of penetration amongst the backs although at times Logan threatened with his mazy running. The only try of the match came after some good combined work and a delayed pass from Chalmers to Cronin who made a short run and aquaplaned over the line. Stewart and Rees were excellent for Canada in a losing cause.

437　INTERNATIONAL CHAMPIONSHIP 1995　IRELAND

Murrayfield · Saturday 4 February 1995 · Won 26–13

SCOTLAND Gavin Hastings* (*Watsonians*); Craig Joiner (*Melrose*), Gregor Townsend (*Gala*), Ian Jardine (*Stirling Co*), Kenny Logan (*Stirling Co*); Craig Chalmers (*Melrose*), Bryan Redpath (*Melrose*); David Hilton (*Bath*), Kenny Milne (*Heriot's FP*), Peter Wright (*Boroughmuir*), Damian Cronin (*Bourges*), Stewart Campbell (*Dundee HSFP*), Rob Wainwright (*West Hartlepool*), Iain Morrison (*London Scot*), Eric Peters (*Bath*)

IRELAND Conor O'Shea (*Lansdowne*); Simon Geoghegan (*Bath*), Brendan Mullin (*Blackrock Coll*), Philip Danaher (*Garryowen*), Jonathan Bell (*Ballymena*); Paul Burke (*Cork Const*), Michael Bradley* (*Cork Const*); Nick Popplewell (*Wasps*), Keith Wood (*Garryowen*), Peter Clohessy (*Young Munster*), Paddy Johns (*Dungannon*), Gabriel Fulcher (*Cork Const*), Anthony Foley (*Shannon*), Denis McBride (*Malone*), Ben Cronin (*Garryowen*)

REFEREE Derek Bevan (*Wales*)

SCORING Hastings, pen (3–0); Burke, pen (3–3); Mullin, try (3–8); Hastings, pen (6–8); Hastings, pen (9–8) (half-time) Bell, try (9–13); Joiner, try (14–13); Hastings, con (16–13); Hastings, pen (19–13); Cronin, try (24–13); Hastings, con (26–13)

Gavin Hastings won his 53rd cap to break the Scottish record held jointly by Jim Renwick and Colin Deans. The big full-back was in inspirational form and drove his side to their first win in the championship since 1993. He was well supported by his forwards who dominated at the lineout and stood-up well against the much-vaunted Irish scrum. Scotland were fortunate to be ahead at the interval. Ireland had monopolised most of the play and Mullin scored a well-taken try after 31 minutes. Early in the second half, Ireland recaptured the lead with a fine debut try by Bell. Then Scotland began a magnificent fight-back. Hastings chipped ahead, Logan managed to redirect the ball over the line and Joiner appeared from nowhere to touch down. Hastings converted and a few minutes later kicked a penalty. The match swung towards Scotland and on the 65th minute Cronin scored after heavy pressure on the Irish line. Hastings converted to bring his personal tally to 16 points.

Parc des Princes, Paris · Saturday 18 February 1995 · Won 23–21

SCOTLAND Gavin Hastings* (*Watsonians*); Craig Joiner (*Melrose*), Gregor Townsend (*Gala*), Ian Jardine (*Stirling Co*), Kenny Logan (*Stirling Co*); Craig Chalmers (*Melrose*), Bryan Redpath (*Melrose*); David Hilton (*Bath*), Kenny Milne (*Heriot's FP*), Peter Wright (*Boroughmuir*), Damian Cronin (*Bourges*), Stewart Campbell (*Dundee HSFP*), Rob Wainwright (*West Hartlepool*), Iain Morrison (*London Scot*), Eric Peters (*Bath*) ... Replacement: Doddie Weir (*Melrose*) for Cronin (40)

FRANCE Jean-Luc Sadourny (*Colomiers*); Philippe Bernat-Salles (*Pau*), Philippe Sella (*Agen*), Thierry Lacroix (*Dax*), Philippe Saint-André* (*Montferrand*); Christophe Deylaud (*Toulouse*), Guy Accoceberry (*Bègles*); Christian Califano (*Toulouse*), Jean-Michel Gonzalez (*Bayonne*), Laurent Seigne (*Brive*), Olivier Brouzet (*Grenoble*), Olivier Roumat (*Dax*), Abdelatif Benazzi (*Agen*), Laurent Cabbanes (*RCF*), Philippe Benetton (*Agen*)

REFEREE David Hugh (*Ireland*)

SCORING Saint-André, try (0–5); Hastings, pen (3–5); Townsend, try (8–5); Hastings, con (10–5); Hastings, pen (13–5) (half-time) Lacroix, pen, (13–8); Deylaud, drop (13–11); Hastings, pen (16–11); Sadourny, try (16–16); Saint-André, try (16–21); Hastings, try (21–21); Hastings, con (23-21)

In a memorable encounter, Scotland won in Paris for the first time in 26 years and for the first time ever at the Parc des Princes. They showed great strength of character to come back from two hammer blows at either end of the match and snatch victory in the most dramatic circumstances. Once again Gavin Hastings was inspirational. He scored 18 points, including the match-winning try, and was a tower of strength from first to last. Credit was also due to the Scottish pack who gave an immense display, especially Damian Cronin and Rob Wainwright. France made a great start and within two minutes Saint-André scored a simple try when he raced onto a chip ahead. The Scots had their backs to the wall in the opening stages, but the French failed to capitalise and on the 21st minute Hastings kicked an enormous penalty from inside his own half to settle Scottish nerves. Straight from the restart the Scots made a sweeping move up the field, Jardine fed out a long pass on the French 22 and a lucky ricochet went to Townsend who dummied the defence and scored at the posts, Scotland's first try in Paris for eight years. Hastings converted and kicked a second penalty to put Scotland 13–5 ahead at half-time. The excitement continued in the second half as Lacroix and Hastings traded penalties, Deylaud dropped a goal and Sadourny scored a blind-side try to level the scores. With only eight minutes left Saint-André scored a giveaway try after taking a poor clearance by Townsend. It seemed that the Parisian jinx would strike again, but right at the finish Scotland ran a penalty near halfway and Chalmers fed Townsend who in turn made a deft 'Toony flip' pass to Hastings. Belying his veteran status, the big full-back raced through the startled defence to score under the posts. The conversion was a formality and the Scots held out a nervous last few moments for a sensational victory. *Vive L'Ecosse!*

Murrayfield · Saturday 4 March 1995 · Won 26–13

SCOTLAND Gavin Hastings* (*Watsonians*); Craig Joiner (*Melrose*), Gregor Townsend (*Gala*), Scott Hastings (*Watsonians*), Kenny Logan (*Stirling Co*); Craig Chalmers (*Melrose*), Bryan Redpath (*Melrose*); David Hilton (*Bath*), Kenny Milne (*Heriot's FP*), Peter Wright (*Boroughmuir*), Doddie Weir (*Melrose*), Stewart Campbell (*Dundee HSFP*), Rob Wainwright (*West Hartlepool*), Iain Morrison (*London Scot*), Eric Peters (*Bath*)

WALES Matthew Black (*Bridgend*); Ieuan Evans* (*Llanelli*), Mike Hall (*Cardiff*), Nigel Davies (*Llanelli*), Mark Proctor (*Llanelli*); Neil Jenkins (*Pontypridd*), Robert Jones (*Swansea*); Mike Griffiths (*Cardiff*), Garin Jenkins (*Swansea*), Spencer John (*Llanelli*), Derwyn Jones (*Cardiff*), Gareth Llewellyn (*Neath*), Hemi Taylor (*Cardiff*), Richie Collins (*Pontypridd*), Emyr Lewis (*Cardiff*)

REFEREE Steve Lander (*England*)

SCORING Jones, try (0–5); Jenkins, con (0–7); G Hastings, pen (3–7); G Hastings, pen (6–7); Peters, try (11–7); G Hastings, con (13–7); Hilton, try (18–7); G Hastings, con (20–7) (half-time) G Hastings, pen (23–7); Jenkins, pen (23–10); Jenkins, pen (23–13); G Hastings, pen (26–13)

Scotland made a dreadful start and conceded a soft try after only two minutes. Gavin Hastings landed two penalties and soon the Scottish forwards took a firm grip. Towards the end of the first half the Scots scored two tries within six minutes of each other, the first a real classic. Running from his own 22, Gavin Hastings passed to Weir who found Logan on the left. The wing made a thrilling long run up the touchline before feeding Peters on the switch and the big No 8 romped home. Soon after the Scottish forwards applied heavy pressure on the Welsh line and Hilton was driven over. The highlight of the second half, which took place in intermittent snow showers, was an enormous penalty by Hastings. Jenkins kicked two penalties to reduce Scotland's lead to ten points, but Hastings had the final say with a penalty after 68 minutes. This was a great team performance by Scotland who played simple rugby with exemplary commitment and determination. Thus the Scots, who had been written off before the championship, headed to Twickenham for a Grand Slam shoot-out with England.

Twickenham · Saturday 18 March 1995 · Lost 12–24

SCOTLAND Gavin Hastings* (*Watsonians*); Craig Joiner (*Melrose*), Gregor Townsend (*Gala*), Scott Hastings (*Watsonians*), Kenny Logan (*Stirling Co*); Craig Chalmers (*Melrose*), Bryan Redpath (*Melrose*); David Hilton (*Bath*), Kenny Milne (*Heriot's FP*), Peter Wright (*Boroughmuir*), Doddie Weir (*Melrose*), Stewart Campbell (*Dundee HSFP*), Rob Wainwright (*West Hartlepool*), Iain Morrison (*London Scot*), Eric Peters (*Bath*) ... Replacement: †John Manson (*Dundee HSFP*) for Hilton (44)

ENGLAND Mike Catt (*Bristol*); Tony Underwood (*Leicester*), Will Carling* (*Harlequins*), Jeremy Guscott (*Bath*), Rory Underwood (*Leicester*); Rob Andrew (*Wasps*), Kyran Bracken (*Bristol*); Jason Leonard (*Harlequins*), Brian Moore (*Harlequins*), Victor Ubogu (*Bath*), Martin Johnson (*Leicester*), Martin Bayfield (*Leicester*), Tim Rodber (*Northampton*), Ben Clarke (*Bath*), Dean Richards (*Leicester*) ... Replacements: Dewi Morris (*Orrell*) for Bracken (16–23), Steve Ojomoh (*Bath*) for Richards (50), Graham Rowntree (*Leicester*) for Leonard (66–78)

REFEREE Brian Stirling (*Ireland*)

SCORING Chalmers, drop (3–0); Andrew, pen
(3–3); Andrew, pen (3–6); Chalmers, drop (6–6);
Andrew, pen (6–9); Andrew, pen (6–12) (half-time)
Andrew, pen (6–15); G Hastings, pen (9–15);
Andrew, pen (9–18); G Hastings, pen (12–18);
Andrew, drop (12–21); Andrew, pen (12–24)

With both sides playing for the Grand Slam
there was huge expectation surrounding
this match, but it was a disappointing and
unspectacular encounter decided solely by
kicks. England were strong favourites and
dominated possession, but Scotland gave
them a lot to think about and were by no
means disgraced. The two stand-offs, Rob
Andrew and Craig Chalmers, were both in
excellent form. Andrew dictated much of
the play and scored all of his side's points
whilst Chalmers had one of his best games
for Scotland and dropped two goals under
great pressure. Doddie Weir was a towering
presence in the lineout and prominent in the

Gregor Townsend, 82 caps 1993–2003
George Herringshaw/Sporting-Heroes.net

loose. Scotland had a few try-scoring opportunities, but could not make the vital
breakthrough. Their cause was not helped by some erratic decisions by the referee,
including a harsh yellow card for Peter Wright who became the first Scottish player
to be sent to the sin-bin in an international match. In a television interview immediately after the match, England hooker Brian Moore did himself no favours when
he complained about what he saw as the spoiling tactics of the Scots. More accurately
he summed-up England's frustration that they had not had everything their own way.
The Scots, by contrast, were disappointed but far from despondent and could look
forward confidently to the World Cup.

---

441 WORLD CUP WARM-UP MATCH ROMANIA

Murrayfield · Saturday 22 April 1995 · Won 49–16

SCOTLAND Gavin Hastings* (*Watsonians*); Craig Joiner (*Melrose*), Tony Stanger (*Hawick*),
Graham Shiel (*Melrose*), Kenny Logan (*Stirling Co*); Craig Chalmers (*Melrose*), Bryan Redpath
(*Melrose*); David Hilton (*Bath*), Kevin McKenzie (*Stirling Co*), Peter Wright (*Boroughmuir*),
Doddie Weir (*Melrose*), Stewart Campbell (*Dundee HSFP*), Rob Wainwright (*West Hartlepool*),
Iain Morrison (*London Scot*), Eric Peters (*Bath*) … Replacement: Scott Hastings (*Watsonians*) for
Hastings (78)

ROMANIA Vasile Brici (*Farul Constanta*); Robert Cioca (*Dinamo*), Nicolae Racean (*Cluj U*),
Romeo Gontineac (*Cluj U*), Gheorghe Solomie (*Timisoara U*); Neculai Nichitean (*Cluj U*),
Daniel Nega (*Dinamo*); Gheorghe Leonte (*Vienne*), Valere Tufa (*Dinamo*), Leodor Costea (*Steaua*),
Sandor Ciorascu (*Auch*), Constantin Cojocariu (*Bayonne*), Traian Oroian (*Steaua*),

Alexandru Gealapu (*Steaua*), Tiberiu Brinza* (*Cluj U*) ... Replacement: Catalin Draguceanu (*Steaua*) for Gealapu (48)

REFEREE Nicolas Lasaga (*France*)

SCORING G Hastings, try (5–0); Stanger, try (10–0); G Hastings, con (12–0); Nichitean, pen (12–3); Nichitean, pen (12–6); Shiel, try (17–6); G Hastings, con (19–6); Racean, try (19–11); Nichitean, con (19–13) (half-time) Nichetean, pen (19–16); G Hastings, pen (22–16); Peters, try (27–16); G Hastings, pen (30–16); Joiner, try (35–16); G Hastings, con (37–16); Stanger, try (42–16); Logan, try (47–16); G Hastings, con (49–16)

This was a warm-up match for the 1995 World Cup and the last appearance of Gavin Hastings at Murrayfield in a Scottish jersey (he later returned for the Barbarians). In typical storybook fashion, Hastings scored the opening try after only two minutes and ended the day with a total of 19 points. Overall this was a satisfactory outing for Scotland who played confidently and put together some nice moves. They scored seven tries and each member of the three-quarter line scored at least once. Probably the best try came on the 69th minute. Hastings ran from behind his own line and found support; Shiel broke the defence with a dummy and gave a perfect pass to Stanger who powered away from inside his own half. Just before the end Gavin Hastings was replaced by his younger brother Scott, but he reappeared at the final whistle to take a standing ovation from the crowd.

| XV | WORLD CUP WARM-UP MATCH | SPAIN |

Madrid University Stadium · Saturday 6 May 1995 · Won 62–7

SCOTLAND XV Gavin Hastings* (*Watsonians*); Craig Joiner (*Melrose*), Tony Stanger (*Hawick*), Graham Shiel (*Melrose*), Kenny Logan (*Stirling Co*); Craig Chalmers (*Melrose*), Bryan Redpath (*Melrose*); David Hilton (*Bath*), Kevin McKenzie (*Stirling Co*), Peter Wright (*Boroughmuir*), Damian Cronin (*Bourges*), Doddie Weir (*Melrose*), Rob Wainwright (*West Hartlepool*), Iain Morrison (*London Scot*), Eric Peters (*Bath*) ... Replacements: Stewart Campbell (*Dundee HSFP*) for Cronin (27), Ian Jardine (*Stirling Co*) for Shiel (65), Scott Hastings (*Watsonians*) for Stanger (65), Martin Scott (*Orrell*) for Morrison (73)

SPAIN Francisco Puertas (*Bayona*); Daniel Saenz (*Xerox Arquitectura*), Javier Fernández (*Atlético Portuense*), Alejandro Miño (*El Monte*), Pablo Gutiérrez (*Xerox Arquitectura*); Xabier Gerediaga (*Oviedo*), Jerónimo Hernández-Gil (*Xerox Arquitectura*); Julio Alvarez (*Dulciora El Salvador*), Fernando de la Calle (*Quesos Entrepinares*), Jonadab Díez (*Xerox Getxo*), José Villau (*Seville U*), Juan Escobar (*El Monte*), Alberto Malo (*Santobiana Cicsa*), Jon Etxebarría (*Xerox Getxo*), Jaime Gutiérrez* (*Xerox Arquitectura*) ... Replacements: Iñaki Laskurain (*Xerox Getxo*) for Escobar (40), Pablo Calderón (*Xerox Arquitectura*) for Miño (40), Jorge Torres Morote (*El Monte*) for Hernández-Gil (60), Ignacio de Lázaro (*Xerox Getxo*) for Díez (65)

REFEREE Joel Dumé (*France*)

SCORING G Hastings, try (5–0); G Hastings, con (7–0); Joiner, try (12–0); G Hastings, try (17–0); Wainwright, try (22–0); G Hastings, con (24–0) Morrison, try (29–0); Logan, try (34–0); G Hastings, con (36–0) (half-time) Gutiérrez, try (36–5); Gerediaga, con (36–7); Joiner, try (41–7); Wainwright, try (46–7); G Hastings, con (48–7); Chalmers, try (53–7); G Hastings, con (55–7); Joiner, try (60–7); G Hastings, con (62–7)

In May 1995, Scotland continued their preparations for the World Cup with a two match tour of Spain. In the first match against a Madrid XV, the Scots struggled in the stifling humidity and had to come from behind before eventually winning 27–16. They had fewer problems in the non-cap test match against the Spanish national side where they had a routine victory and scored ten tries. Scotland cruised to a 36–0 lead by the interval, but then wilted in the heat. Spain scored the best try of the game when wing Pablo Gutiérrez finished off a handling movement that had begun near the Spanish line. Scotland's superior fitness told towards the end and they finished in complete control. Thus, in the Gavin Hastings' words, Scotland headed to the World Cup in 'very great heart'.

Rugby World Cup 1995

South Africa had been readmitted to international sport after the ending of apartheid in the early nineties and in 1995 the new Rainbow Nation hosted the third Rugby World Cup. The tournament was a great success and helped unite the formerly divided country as never before. In a 16 team tournament, Scotland were drawn in Pool D along with France, Tonga and the Ivory Coast, the tournament minnows. Scotland were expected to qualify from the pool without too much trouble, but it was important to win the group to ensure an easier route in the knock-out stages.

| 442 | RUGBY WORLD CUP 1995 | IVORY COAST |

Olympia Park Stadium, Rustenburg · Friday 26 May 1995

Won 89–0

SCOTLAND Gavin Hastings* (*Watsonians*); Craig Joiner (*Melrose*), Tony Stanger (*Hawick*), Graham Shiel (*Melrose*), Kenny Logan (*Stirling Co*); Craig Chalmers (*Melrose*), Bryan Redpath (*Melrose*); Paul Burnell (*London Scot*), Kevin McKenzie (*Stirling Co*), Peter Wright (*Boroughmuir*), Doddie Weir (*Melrose*), Stewart Campbell (*Dundee HSFP*), Peter Walton (*Northampton*), Ian Smith (*Gloucester*), Rob Wainwright (*West Hartlepool*)

IVORY COAST Victor Kouassi (*Burotic*); Paulin Bouazo (*Burotic*), Jean Sathicq (*GASG*), Lucien Niakou (*Niort*), Celestin N'Gbala (*Cahors*); Athanase Dali* (*Clamart*), Frederic Dupont (*Nîmes*); Ernest Bley (*Aspaa*), Eduard Angoran (*Rodez*), Toussaint Djehi (*Millau*), Amidou Kone (*Soustons*), Gilbert Bado (*Cognac*), Patrice Pere (*AC Boulogne*), Isimaila Lassissi (*Burotic*), Djakaria Sanoko (*Biarritz*) ... Replacements: Abubacar Camara (*Aspaa*) for Dali (28), Max Brito (*Biscarosse*) for N'Gbala (40), Alfred Okou (*Poitiers*) for Bado (71)

REFEREE F Vito (*Western Samoa*)

SCORING Hastings, try (5–0); Hastings, con (7–0); Hastings, pen (10–0); Hastings, pen (13–0); Hastings, try (18–0); Hastings, con (20–0); Hastings, try (25–0); Hastings, con (27–0); Walton, try (32–0); Hastings, con (34–0) (half-time) Logan, try (39–0); Chalmers, try (44–0); Logan, try (49–0); Hastings, con (51–0); Stanger, try (56–0); Burnell, try (61–0); Hastings, con (63–0); Walton, try (68–0); Hastings, con (70–0); Wright, try (75–0); Hastings, try (80–0); Hastings, con (82–0); Shiel, try (87–0); Hastings, con (89–0)

After weeks of anticipation, Scotland opened their World Cup campaign with an easy win against the plucky Ivorians. The Scots looked nervous in the opening stages of the game and it took a piece of good fortune to settle them down. Gavin Hastings made a speculative kick ahead and the ball bounced wickedly for the defence straight into his arms for him to run over. In a one-sided encounter, the Scots scored another three tries in the first half, including two for Hastings, and nine after the break. This was a good team performance by Scotland in which centre Graham Shiel played very well and Gavin Hastings was immense once again. The Ivory Coast were completely outclassed, but they never stopped trying and kept their discipline throughout. A sad footnote to the match was that Ivorian replacement Max Brito was later permanently paralysed after an injury in his side's game against Tonga.

443   RUGBY WORLD CUP 1995   TONGA

Loftus Versveld Stadium, Pretoria · Tuesday 30 May 1995
Won 41–5

SCOTLAND Gavin Hastings* (*Watsonians*); Craig Joiner (*Melrose*), Scott Hastings (*Watsonians*), Ian Jardine (*Stirling Co*), Kenny Logan (*Stirling Co*); Craig Chalmers (*Melrose*), Derrick Patterson (*West Hartlepool*); David Hilton (*Bath*), Kenny Milne (*Heriot's FP*), Peter Wright (*Boroughmuir*), Damian Cronin (*Bourges*), Doddie Weir (*Melrose*), Rob Wainwright (*West Hartlepool*), Iain Morrison (*London Scot*), Eric Peters (*Bath*) ... Replacement: Paul Burnell (*London Scot*) for Wright (76)

TONGA Sateki Tu'ipulotu (*Manly*); Alaska Taufa (*Wellington*), Unoi Va'enuku (*Toloa OB*), Penieli Latu (*Vaheloto*), Tevita Va'enuku (*Police*); 'Elisi Vunipola (*Toako Ma'afu*), Manu Vunipola (*Toako Ma'afu*); Sa'ili Fe'ao (*Queensland*), Fe'ao Vunipola (*Toako Ma'afu*), Tu'akalau Fukofuka (*Grammar OB*), Willie Lose (*North Harbour*), Pouvalu Latukefu (*Canberra Royals*), 'Inoke Afeaki (*Wellington*), Ipolito Fenukitau (*ACT*), Mana 'Otai* (*Manawatu*)

Replacements: Nafe Tufui (*Kolomotu'a*) for M Vunipola (57), Etuini Talakai (*Siutaka*) for Fe'ao (75)

REFEREE B Leask (*Australia*)

SCORING G Hastings, pen (3–0); G Hastings, pen (6–0); G Hastings, pen (9–0); Fenukitau, try (9–5); G Hastings, pen (12–5); G Hastings, pen (15–5); G Hastings, pen (18–5) (half-time) G Hastings, pen (21–5); G Hastings, pen (24–5); Peters, try (29–5); G Hastings, try (34–5); S Hastings, try (39–5); G Hastings, con (41–5)

Scotland secured their place in the knock-out stages in a scrappy and at times bruising encounter. Once again Gavin Hastings led from the front and scored a personal tally of 31 points. Scotland played a tight game and forced the fiery Tongans to give away a rash of penalties which Hastings duly punished. The Tongans showed occasional flashes of adventure and scored the game's opening try, but the Scottish defence was pretty solid. Scotland's first try came on the hour mark when Joiner tied-in three defenders and Peters surged over the line. Good play by Jardine created a try for Gavin Hastings and towards the finish Jardine hacked on a loose pass for Scott Hastings to swallow dive and score.

Loftus Versveld Stadium, Pretoria · Saturday 3 June 1995

Lost 19–22

SCOTLAND Gavin Hastings* (*Watsonians*); Craig Joiner (*Melrose*), Scott Hastings (*Watsonians*), Graham Shiel (*Melrose*), Kenny Logan (*Stirling Co*); Craig Chalmers (*Melrose*), Bryan Redpath (*Melrose*); David Hilton (*Bath*), Kenny Milne (*Heriot's FP*), Peter Wright (*Boroughmuir*), Damian Cronin (*Bourges*), Doddie Weir (*Melrose*), Rob Wainwright (*West Hartlepool*), Iain Morrison (*London Scot*), Eric Peters (*Bath*) … Replacements: Ian Jardine (*Stirling Co*) for Shiel (temp and 44mins), Paul Burnell (*London Scot*) for Wright (70)

FRANCE Jean-Luc Sadourny (*Colomiers*); Émile Ntamack (*Toulouse*), Philippe Sella (*Agen*), Thierry Lacroix (*Dax*), Philippe Saint-André (*Montferrand*); Christophe Deylaud (*Toulouse*), Guy Accoceberry (*Bordeaux Bègles*); Laurent Benezech (*RCF*), Jean-Michel Gonzalez (*Bayonne*), Christian Califano (*Toulouse*), Olivier Merle (*Montferrand*), Olivier Roumat (*Dax*), Abdelatif Benazzi (*Agen*), Laurent Cabannes (*RCF*), Philippe Benetton (*Agen*) … Replacements: Marc Cecillon (*Bourgoin*) for Benetton (19), Aubin Hueber (*Toulon*) for Accoceberry (33)

REFEREE Wayne Erickson (*Australia*)

SCORING G Hastings, pen (3–0); Lacroix, pen (3–3); G Hastings, pen (6–3); Wainwright, try (11–3); G Hastings, con (13–3) (half-time) Lacroix, pen (13–6); Lacroix, pen (13–9); G Hastings, pen (16–9); Lacroix, pen (16–12); G Hastings, pen (19–12); Lacroix, pen (19–15); Ntamack, try (19–20); Lacroix, con (19–22)

This was the decisive game in Pool Four. The winner would go on to play either Ireland or Wales and the loser would have the unenviable task of facing New Zealand. In a tense and hard-fought encounter, Scotland dominated for long periods only to lose out in the final seconds. The Scots played very well in the first half, in particular the back-row, and fully deserved to be in front at the interval. Their solitary try came just before the turnaround when Redpath caught a loose kick and switched to Gavin Hastings. The Scottish captain thundered up the touchline before despatching Wainwright who broke through two tackles to score. Scotland's fatal mistake was their failure to consolidate a winning position and early in the second half Gavin Hastings missed two penalty attempts that might have killed off the French challenge. By contrast, Lacroix landed two penalties and the momentum started to swing towards France. In a nail-biting conclusion, the French made a series of attacks and with the last move of the game Ntamack broke a despairing tackle to score the winning try. Lacroix rubbed in the salt with a touchline conversion. Scotland had given everything and did not deserve to lose. Some of the Scottish players left the field close to tears.

Loftus Versfeld Stadium, Pretoria · Sunday 11 June 1995

Lost 30–48

SCOTLAND Gavin Hastings* (*Watsonians*); Craig Joiner (*Melrose*), Scott Hastings (*Watsonians*), Graham Shiel (*Melrose*), Kenny Logan (*Stirling Co*); Craig Chalmers (*Melrose*), Bryan Redpath

(*Melrose*); David Hilton (*Bath*), Kenny Milne (*Heriot's FP*), Peter Wright (*Boroughmuir*), Damian Cronin (*Bourges*), Doddie Weir (*Melrose*), Rob Wainwright (*West Hartlepool*), Iain Morrison (*London Scot*), Eric Peters (*Bath*) ... Replacements: Ian Jardine (*Stirling Co*) for Chalmers (40), Stewart Campbell (*Dundee HSFP*) for Cronin (63)

NEW ZEALAND Jeff Wilson (*Otago*); Marc Ellis (*Otago*), Frank Bunce (*North Harbour*), Walter Little (*North Harbour*), Jonah Lomu (*Counties*); Andrew Mehrtens (*Canterbury*), Graeme Bachop (*Canterbury*); Richard Loe (*Canterbury*), Sean Fitzpatrick* (*Auckland*), Olo Brown (*Auckland*), Ian Jones (*North Harbour*), Robin Brooke (*Auckland*), Mike Brewer (*Canterbury*), Josh Kronfield (*Otago*), Zinzan Brooke (*Auckland*)

REFEREE Derek Bevan (*Wales*)

SCORING Little, try (0–5); Mehrtens, con (0–7); G Hastings, pen (3–7); G Hastings, pen (6–7); Lomu, try (6–12); Mehrtens, con (6–14); Mehrtens, pen (6–17); G Hastings, pen (9–17) (half-time) Little, try (9–22); Mehrtens, con (9–24); Mehrtens, try (9–29); Mehrtens, con (9–31); Weir, try (14–31); G Hastings, con (16–31); Bunce, try (16–36); Mehrtens, con (16–38); Fitzpatrick, try (16–43); Mehrtens, con (16–45); Weir, try (21–45); G Hastings, con (23–45); Mehrtens, pen (23–48); S Hastings, try (28–48); G Hastings, con (30–48)

This match marked the end of an era with Gavin Hastings, Kenny Milne and Iain Morrison making their final appearances. Scotland never looked like winning, but they were defiant to the end. After only four minutes, the mighty Jonah Lomu thundered away leaving several defenders in his wake. He was dragged down near the line, but Little was in support for an easy try. Lomu added a try of his own and Scotland were still in the game at the break. Early in the second half, Gavin Hastings dropped a high ball straight into the path of Little who collected and meandered over the line. Then Mehrtens pounced on a loose pass and sprinted away for a great solo score. Scotland made a spirited response and Doddie Weir scored a brace of tries, but in between these Bunce and Fitzpatrick crossed for New Zealand. A few minutes before the end, Gavin Hastings powered through the defence and from the ensuing ruck his brother Scott scored a well-worked try. Scotland weren't good enough to cause an upset and they made too many errors, but in a peculiarly Scottish way they were moral victors. They had scored 30 points against New Zealand which equalled the most that anybody had ever scored against the All Blacks to date. At the finish, Gavin Hastings and the team made a lap of honour in a sea of flag-waving supporters. Thus Scotland ended the 1995 World Cup with mixed emotions: pride that they had done so well, but also regret that they could have gone a stage further.

The Professional Era 1995–2013

It was clear that the huge demands on international players in the 1980s and 1990s were pushing the game towards professionalism, but the announcement of the end of amateurism in August 1995 came as a big surprise. In Scotland, the transition from the amateur game to full-blooded professionalism was traumatic and at times threatened to tear the sport apart. The basic problem was that nobody knew how professional rugby should be organised or how to bridge the gap between the club and international game. There was a lengthy and at times acrimonious debate between those who favoured the creation of professional clubs and others who argued for districts. Clubs were loved by their supporters but few, if any Scottish clubs could afford to pay their players or generate enough income to make professionalism work. Districts lacked a sense of identity and rarely aroused passions, but they were the only realistic option if Scottish teams were to compete in the new European competitions and Scottish rugby was to keep pace with the rest of the world.

In 1996, around 100 leading players were contracted to the Scottish Rugby Union and distributed amongst the four Scottish districts. They represented their districts in Europe and in the District Championship, and played for their clubs the rest of the time. The new set-up was hugely expensive to run and pretty soon the SRU was forced to cut the districts down from four to two just to save costs. Two horrible amalgams were created, pushing ancient rivals together into shotgun marriages: Glasgow Caledonian Reds (Glasgow and the North and Midlands) and the Edinburgh Reivers (Edinburgh and the South of Scotland). Predictably enough, the two sides were unpopular amongst players and supporters. They generated little interest or enthusiasm and their results were mostly poor. A third professional side was established in the Borders, the traditional heartland of Scottish rugby, in 2003, but it also failed to attract enough support and was disbanded after a few years. This left Scotland with only two professional teams, Glasgow Warriors and Edinburgh Rugby. But who were these new sides going to play? Other countries faced similar dilemmas and their only option was to invest in cross-Border competitions. This led to the development of a Celtic League involving professional teams from Scotland, Ireland and Wales, and later Italy. The new league took a long time to establish itself and at the time of writing is still seen by many as only a temporary solution and lacking credibility. There was no relegation from the league so there were a lot of meaningless fixtures and clubs did not always field their strongest sides. In addition, the huge distances between clubs meant that there was little or no travelling support to encourage visiting teams or to create atmosphere. Some leading Scottish players switched to the lucrative English or French leagues and consequently became very distant from the Scottish public, only to be seen on television or at international time. The result of all this upheaval was that many traditional supporters, having seen their historic and much cherished clubs pushed to the margins, became disillusioned with the game and simply walked away.

On the field the professional era has seen plenty of disappointment and frustration for Scotland, but it should be remembered that this often happened in the past as well.

Over the years Scotland enjoyed some famous wins and the odd period of ascendancy, but these were the exception rather than the rule. For much of the time results were only mediocre at best and Scotland have struggled to compete with other countries. The crucial difference in the professional era is that the players, coaching staff and administrators are paid to perform and to deliver success. Winning is everything and good results are not just expected but demanded. There is no hiding place when things go wrong.

Curiously in terms of what followed, Scotland made quite a good start to the new age. They won three games in the 1996 Championship and came close to a Grand Slam. Again in 1999, they won three matches, including an astonishing victory in Paris, and unexpectedly became the last-ever champions of the Five Nations. Indeed, they would have won a Grand Slam if only they been equipped with a better place-kicker. Italy joined the Championship in 2000 and since then Scotland have rarely been serious contenders for the title. Often the Italian match has degenerated into an annual slogging contest just to avoid the wooden spoon. Scotland's best Six Nations to date was in 2006 when they beat France and England at home and also won in Rome. Currently, this is the only time when Scotland have won more than two games in a single season.

The Scots may have lacked consistency and the ability to create winning momentum, but at times they have raised their game, especially at home. They beat England at Murrayfield in 2000, 2006 and 2008, South Africa in 2002 and 2010, and Australia in 2009, their first win over the Wallabies for 27 years. As always, winning away from home has been much harder. Since 2000, Scotland have won twice in Italy and once each in Wales and Ireland, hardly a great record but no worse than the 1970s. They have also struggled on their summer tours and have gone down to some heavy defeats in New Zealand and Australia. On a brighter note, in 2010 Scotland won a test series in Argentina for the first time and two years later they were unbeaten on a three match tour of Australasia. In the Rugby World Cup, Scotland scraped into the quarter-finals in 2003 and 2007, but in 2011 they failed to qualify for the knock-out stages for the first time, admittedly from a very tough group. The conclusion from all this is that test matches are harder to win than ever before. Other countries, including some of the traditional minnows, have adapted to professionalism much more successfully than Scotland. Tougher competition means the Scots have to run even harder just to stand still.

One consequence of professionalism is that there are now many more international matches than previously and test rugby, once something of a rarity, has become commonplace. In the professional age, Scotland play five games in the International Championship, make a summer tour and then have several Autumn Internationals, a minimum of ten games each year and often more. In 2004, Scotland played Australia no less than four times in only a few months, twice at home and twice away. In addition, the Rugby World Cup takes place every four years and may include some warm-up games. This glut of international rugby has meant that established players win a lot more caps than they used to and more players than ever before win international honours. Over the course of the amateur era, from 1871 to 1995, just over 900 players were capped for Scotland. Since 1995, there have been more than 130, roughly seven new men per season. This number has been further inflated by the use of tactical substitutions which were first permitted in 1997. It is not uncommon for around half a team to be replaced during a match, sometimes players coming on for only a few minutes before the end and barely touching the ball. Whether any of this has improved international rugby as a spectacle is a matter for debate.

The two outstanding Scottish players of the professional era were both products of Netherdale. Gregor Townsend was blessed with an abundance of talent and natural flair. A teenage prodigy, he won his first cap at only 19 and went on to make 82 appearances at stand-off, full-back and centre. He was a great reader of a game who had extraordinary pace off the mark and the ability to find a gap. Sometimes it seemed that he was a few steps ahead of his colleagues and he was at his best when he was surrounded by players of a similar calibre to himself. 'Toonie' was a key player on the successful Lions tour of South Africa in 1997 and when Scotland won the championship in 1999. His Gala colleague Chris Paterson, who was five years his junior, won his first cap against Spain in the World Cup in 1999 and was the face of Scottish rugby in the 2000s. He became the first Scotsman to reach the milestone of 100 caps and ended his career with a total of 109 appearances at stand-off, wing and full-back. 'Mossy' was a consummate professional who worked hard to develop his skills. Standing around six foot tall, he was solid in defence and an elusive runner in open play. At one point, it was calculated that he was the most reliable place-kicker in world rugby and at times he seemed to be the only thing standing between Scotland and total disaster. Between them, Townsend and Paterson occupied every position in the back division apart from scrum-half. Both of them played at a time of great uncertainty in Scottish rugby and even at the end of their careers there was still debate about their best positions. Many felt that Paterson, in particular, should have been given an extended run at stand-off where his mercurial talents might have ignited a backline that often lacked enterprise or initiative. Instead, Paterson spent most of his time at full-back. Two players who preceded him there were the fair-haired Aucklander Glenn Metcalfe, who won 40 caps between 1998 and 2003, and the big-booted Hugo Southwell who also turned out at centre.

The advent of professionalism meant that the old hostility towards rugby league vanished overnight and league players were able to move freely back into union. Centre Alan Tait won his first (union) cap at the World Cup in 1987 and the following year he switched codes. A powerfully built player and a strong runner, he had a successful career with Widnes and Leeds as well as representing Scotland and Great Britain. In 1996, at the advanced age of 32, he returned to union with Newcastle and then with Scotland and the British Lions. Tait brought a wealth of experience to the Scottish game, including greater tactical awareness and mental toughness, all learned in the unforgiving world of league. He had a winning attitude and formed a dynamic partnership with New Zealand-born centre John Leslie, one of a new band of professional rugby players, often from the southern hemisphere, who travelled the world to ply their trade. Leslie, Tait and Townsend formed an effective midfield triumvirate which was at the heart of Scotland's championship success in 1999.

Rugby became a much harder game in the professional era and the three-quarters needed to be bigger and more powerful than ever before. Sadly, the days of the smaller, lighter man who had dancing feet and quick wits were largely at an end, at least at international level. Instead there was an increasing emphasis on sheer physical presence and weighty players who could tie in defenders and smash their way through. Scotland had a succession of well-built, strong-running backs such as James McLaren, Andy Henderson, Simon Danielli, Sean Lamont, Nikki Walker and Graeme Morrison. They were all very big men who combined athleticism with power and pace. Simon Webster, who played both at wing and centre, was more in the traditional mould of a fleet-footed runner with a devastating sidestep.

Apart from Gregor Townsend, Scotland struggled to find a world class stand-off in the new era. Australian-born Dan Parks, who won 67 caps over eight years, the first in 2004, was steady rather than spectacular. He had an unusual laid-back style of kicking and was an expert at the snap drop goal, but it took a long time for the Scottish support to warm to him. If stand-off was a problem then scrum-half produced an embarrassment of riches. Following Gary Armstrong and Andy Nichol there was Bryan Redpath of Melrose who 60 caps over ten years and captained Scotland numerous times. Known as 'Basil' after the television character Basil Brush, Redpath was a down-to-earth character and a competent performer rather than a showman. He retired after the World Cup in 2003 and was succeeded by Mike Blair and Chris Cusiter, two scrum-halves of outstanding ability who battled each other for possession of the number nine jersey over several years. At one point, in 2009, both of them were too good to leave out of the side and they became joint captains. Latterly, Greig Laidlaw, the nephew of 1980s star Roy Laidlaw, played both at stand-off and scrum-half, and his reliable goal-kicking saved Scotland on several occasions.

At the coal-face, David Hilton, Mattie Stewart, Bruce Douglas, Gavin Kerr and Euan Murray continued the tradition of long-serving prop forwards, all of them winning over 30 caps each. Loose-head Tom Smith made 61 appearances between 1997 and 2005 as well as playing in six tests for the British Lions. Although not especially big or heavy, he was immensely powerful and developed into one of the best props in the world. Later, the barrel-shaped Alan 'Chunk' Jacobsen won 65 caps over ten years and was a cult figure with the Scottish supporters. He was a great servant of his club Edinburgh and at the end of his career in 2013 it was announced that the club would award a trophy named in his honour to its most dedicated player each season. The trophy was fashioned from a cast of Jacobsen's cauliflower ear. Scotland produced two outstanding hookers in this period. West of Scotland's Gordon Bulloch won 75 caps between 1997 and 2005 and was the only Scot to appear in a test match on the 2005 Lions tour of New Zealand. He was followed by Kelso's Ross Ford, a burly individual who started out at flanker before switching to the front-row. Rob Russell and Dougie Hall were also good hookers who won most of their caps off the bench. In the second-row, Scott Murray, Stuart Grimes, Australian-born Nathan Hines and Alastair Kellock all won over 50 caps each. Swindon-born Jim Hamilton, who was known as 'Big Jim' for his enormous stature, became the one thousandth Scottish international player when he made his debut against Romania in November 2006. Latterly, Richie Gray has been the most recognisable Scottish player of his generation thanks to his towering height and great shock of blonde hair. The back-row continued to be an area of great strength for Scotland with such players as Budge Pountney, who qualified by virtue of a grandmother born in the Channel Islands, and New Zealander Martin Leslie, the younger brother of John. The fair-haired Simon Taylor amassed 66 caps despite a career disrupted by injury. Ally Hogg was a popular, hard-working player who at his peak was rated one of the best back-rowers in the game. Jason White, who won 77 caps between 2000 and 2009, including appearances at lock, was renowned for his uncompromising defence. He was an inspirational captain and led Scotland to famous wins over France and England in 2006. Lastly, the darkly eye-browed Kelly Brown had a long and successful career with the Border Reivers, Glasgow and Saracens, and captained Scotland in the 2013 Six Nations.

| **446** | TOUR MATCH | WESTERN SAMOA |

Murrayfield · Saturday 18 November 1995 · Drawn 15–15

SCOTLAND †Rowen Shepherd (*Melrose*); Michael Dods (*Northampton*), Gregor Townsend (*Northampton*), Graham Shiel (*Melrose*), Kenny Logan (*Stirling Co*); Craig Chalmers (*Melrose*), Bryan Redpath (*Melrose*); David Hilton (*Bath*), †Jim Hay (*Hawick*), Paul Burnell (*London Scot*), Doddie Weir (*Melrose*), Damian Cronin (*Bourges*), Rob Wainwright* (*West Hartlepool*), Ian Smith (*Gloucester*), †Stuart Reid (*Boroughmuir*) ... Replacement: Stewart Campbell (*Dundee HSFP*) for Smith (18-21) and for Reid (57-8)

WESTERN SAMOA Veli Patu (*Vaiala*); Brian Lima (*Marist*), Too Vaega (*Te Atatu & Moataa*), George Leaupepe (*Te Atatu*), Alex Telea (*Petone*); Darren Kellett (*Ponsonby & Marist*), Joe Filemu (*Wellington*); Mike Mika (*Otago U*), Tala Leiasamaiva'o (*Wellington & Moataa*), Peter Fatialofa (*Manukau & Marist*), Lio Falaniko (*Marist*), Potu Leavasa (*Apia*), Sam Kaleta (*Ponsonby*), Sila Vaifale (*Marist*), Pat Lam* (*Auckland & Marist*) ... Replacements: Mathew Vaea (*Marist*) for Filemu (83), Stephen Smith (*Helensville*) for Leavasa (83)

REFEREE Tappa Henning (*South Africa*)

ATTENDANCE 42,744

SCORING Dods, pen (3–0); Dods, pen (6–0); Kellett, pen (6–3); Dods, pen (9–3); Dods, pen (12–3) (half-time) Leaupepe, try (12–8); Dods, pen (15–8); Kaleta, try (15–13), Kellett, con (15–15)

This was Scotland's first international in the new professional era and the first game after the retirement of the inspirational Gavin Hastings. His successor Rowen Shepherd had played his early rugby in Thurso before switching to Edinburgh Accies and then to Melrose. Two other newcomers were hooker Jim Hay, a Hawick stalwart who previously had played in six non-cap tests, and No 8 Stuart Reid, an Edinburgh police officer. Rob Wainwright took over the captaincy. The Samoans were making a 12 match tour of Scotland and England, and had already beaten Edinburgh (35–22) and Scotland A (26–9), but lost to the North and Midlands (9–43). In a scrappy match, the Scots were lucky to escape with a draw, the visitors outscoring them by two tries to nil and winning a moral victory. The Samoans played with great commitment and were much quicker and sharper around the field. They tackled resolutely but were let down by some poor discipline. Michael Dods kicked five out of seven penalty attempts, but otherwise the Scots offered little in attack. The first Samoan try came from a powerful run by centre Leaupepe, who took the ball from a scrum and crashed over. Kellett hooked the simple conversion wide of the post. Scotland held a seven point lead in the closing stages until Filemu took a quick tap-penalty and Kaleta drove through for a try. Kellett converted to give the Samoans a creditable draw.

Lansdowne Road, Dublin · Saturday 20 January 1996 · Won 16–10

SCOTLAND Rowen Shepherd (*Melrose*), Craig Joiner (*Melrose*), Scott Hastings (*Watsonians*), Ian Jardine (*Stirling Co*), Michael Dods (*Northampton*); Gregor Townsend (*Northampton*), Bryan Redpath (*Melrose*); David Hilton (*Bath*), Kevin McKenzie (*Stirling Co*), Peter Wright (*Boroughmuir*), Stewart Campbell (*Dundee HSFP*), Doddie Weir (*Melrose*), Rob Wainwright* (*West Hartlepool*), Ian Smith (*Gloucester*), Eric Peters (*Bath*)

IRELAND Jim Staples* (*Harlequins*); Richard Wallace (*Garryowen*), Jonathan Bell (*Northampton*), Kurt McQuilkin (*Bective Rgrs*), Simon Geoghegan (*Bath*); Eric Elwood (*Lansdowne*), Chris Saverimutto (*Sale*); Nick Popplewell (*Newcastle*), Terry Kingston (*Dolphin*), Peter Clohessy (*Young Munster*), Gabriel Fulcher (*Cork Const*), Neil Francis (*Old Belvedere*), Jeremy Davidson (*Dungannon*), David Corkery (*Cork Const*), Paddy Johns (*Dungannon*)

REFEREE Brian Campsall (*England*)

SCORING McKenzie, try (5–0); Elwood, pen (5–3); Dods, try (10–3); Dods, pen (13–3); Townsend, drop (16–3); Clohessy, try (16–8); Elwood, con (16–10) (half-time)

There was worse to come after the lacklustre draw against Western Samoa. In early January 1996, Scotland A – the full national team in all but name – were beaten 29–17 by Italy in Rieti. Yet two weeks later, with only three changes in the team, Scotland opened their international campaign with an unexpected victory in a wind-swept Dublin. Playing with the elements in their favour, the Scots opened the scoring after 11 minutes when hooker Kevin McKenzie pounced on loose line-out ball for a soft try. Elwood replied with a penalty, but on the 21st minute Townsend made a sniping incision and from quick possession Dods slipped over at the corner. Dods also kicked a penalty after Townsend had been impeded, and then Townsend dropped a goal to give the Scots a comfortable cushion. On the stroke of half-time, Ireland put together a fine move and prop Clohessy crossed for a try converted by Elwood. In the second half, Scotland threatened the Irish line with a series of attacks, and Geoghegan just beat Joiner to a touchdown following a Townsend kick ahead. In a nail-biting conclusion, Ireland had a series of scrums on the Scottish line but could not break the defence. This was an encouraging win for the Scots for whom half-backs Gregor Townsend and Bryan Redpath were in great form and captain Rob Wainwright gave an inspiring lead.

Murrayfield · Saturday 3 February 1996 · Won 19–14

SCOTLAND Rowen Shepherd (*Melrose*), Craig Joiner (*Melrose*), Scott Hastings (*Watsonians*), Ian Jardine (*Stirling Co*), Michael Dods (*Northampton*); Gregor Townsend (*Northampton*), Bryan Redpath (*Melrose*); David Hilton (*Bath*), Kevin McKenzie (*Stirling Co*), Peter Wright (*Boroughmuir*), Stewart Campbell (*Dundee HSFP*), Doddie Weir (*Melrose*), Rob Wainwright* (*West Hartlepool*), Ian Smith (*Gloucester*), Eric Peters (*Bath*)

FRANCE Jean-Luc Sadourny (*Colomiers*); Émile Ntamack (*Toulouse*), Alain Penaud (*Brive*), Thomas Castaignède (*Toulouse*), Philippe Saint-André* (*Montferrand*); Thierry Lacroix (*Dax*),

Philippe Carbonneau (*Toulouse*); Michel Périé (*Toulon*), Jean-Michel Gonzalez (*Bayonne*), Christian Califano (*Toulouse*), Olivier Merle (*Montferrand*), Olivier Roumat (*Dax*), Laurent Cabannes (*RCF*), Abdelatif Benazzi (*Agen*), Fabien Pelous (*Dax*) ... Replacement: Stéphane Glas (*Bourgoin-Jallieu*) for Lacroix (1–13)

REFEREE Clayton Thomas (*Wales*)

SCORING Dods, try (5–0); Castaignède, pen (5–3); Dods, pen (8–3); Dods, pen (11–3); Benazzi, try (11–8) (half-time) Dods, try (16–8); Lacroix, pen (16–11); Lacroix, pen (16–14); Dods, pen (19–14)

From the first whistle, Scotland played with exhilarating, unshackled ambition, running the ball from deep and stretching their opponents across the field. In a delightful, free-flowing match, their impulsive French-style of rugby subdued the visitors and their victory was more emphatic than the final score suggests. Michael Dods scored all 19 points, an individual record for this fixture, although he missed six kicks out of nine. Dods's first try came after seven minutes when he raced onto a delicate kick-through by Bryan Redpath. The Melrose scrum-half had a fine game and triggered the bulk of the Scottish attacks. But for all of Scotland's daring and vigour, they led only 11–8 at the interval. Dods kicked two penalties to one by Castaignède and Benazzi scored a try from a lineout drive. Scotland's second try came after a penetrating run by Joiner and a long pass from Redpath to Dods who juggled with the ball before going over. Lacroix pulled France back with two penalties but Dods sealed a memorable Scottish victory with his third penalty goal a few minutes from time.

449 INTERNATIONAL CHAMPIONSHIP 1996 WALES

Cardiff Arms Park · Saturday 17 February 1996 · Won 16–14

SCOTLAND Rowen Shepherd (*Melrose*); Craig Joiner (*Melrose*), Scott Hastings (*Watsonians*), Ian Jardine (*Stirling Co*), Michael Dods (*Northampton*); Gregor Townsend (*Northampton*), Bryan Redpath (*Melrose*); David Hilton (*Bath*), Kevin McKenzie (*Stirling Co*), Peter Wright (*Boroughmuir*), Stewart Campbell (*Dundee HSFP*), Doddie Weir (*Melrose*), Rob Wainwright* (*West Hartlepool*), Ian Smith (*Gloucester*), Eric Peters (*Bath*) ... Replacement: Kenny Logan (*Stirling Co*) for Joiner (39)

WALES Justin Thomas (*Llanelli*); Ieuan Evans (*Llanelli*), Leigh Davies (*Neath*), Nigel Davies (*Llanelli*), Wayne Proctor (*Llanelli*); Arwel Thomas (*Bristol*), Robert Howley (*Bridgend*); Andrew Lewis (*Cardiff*), Jonathan Humphreys* (*Cardiff*), John Davies (*Neath*), Gareth Llewellyn (*Neath*), Derwyn Jones (*Cardiff*), Emyr Lewis (*Cardiff*), Gwyn Jones (*Llanelli*), Hemi Taylor (*Cardiff*)

REFEREE Joel Dumé (*France*)

SCORING Dods, pen (3–0); A Thomas, pen (3–3); A Thomas, pen (3–6); Dods, pen (6–6) (half-time) Dods, pen (9–6); A Thomas, pen (9–9); Townsend, try (14–9); Dods, con (16–9); Proctor, try (16–14)

In the 100th meeting of the two sides, Scotland played a tighter game than against France and just managed to snatch victory in an exciting, hard-fought encounter. Wales created the better chances but the Scots were more resilient and resourceful, showing impressive self-belief and discipline, and the ability to withstand pressure at crucial moments. Scotland's 73rd minute try came after a superb break by Logan which took play to the Welsh line. From the ensuing scrum Redpath and Smith combined for Townsend to jink and then power through a tackle to score. In a tight finish Wayne Proctor scored in the corner, but Thomas's attempted conversion drifted fractionally wide. Thus for the second time in two years the holy grail of the Grand Slam beckoned for the Scots.

450 INTERNATIONAL CHAMPIONSHIP 1996 ENGLAND

Murrayfield · Saturday 2 March 1996 · Lost 9–18

SCOTLAND Rowen Shepherd (*Melrose*), Craig Joiner (*Melrose*), Scott Hastings (*Watsonians*), Ian Jardine (*Stirling Co*), Michael Dods (*Northampton*); Gregor Townsend (*Northampton*), Bryan Redpath (*Melrose*); David Hilton (*Bath*), Kevin McKenzie (*Stirling Co*), Peter Wright (*Boroughmuir*), Stewart Campbell (*Dundee HSFP*), Doddie Weir (*Melrose*), Rob Wainwright* (*Watsonians*), Ian Smith (*Gloucester*), Eric Peters (*Bath*)

ENGLAND Mike Catt (*Bath*); Jon Sleightholme (*Bath*), Will Carling* (*Harlequins*), Jeremy Guscott (*Bath*), Rory Underwood (*Leicester*); Paul Grayson (*Northampton*), Matt Dawson (*Northampton*); Graham Rowntree (*Leicester*), Mark Regan (*Bristol*), Jason Leonard (*Harlequins*), Martin Johnson (*Leicester*), Garath Archer (*Bristol*), Ben Clarke (*Bath*), Lawrence Dallagio (*Wasps*), Dean Richards (*Leicester*) … Replacements: Tim Rodber (*Northampton*) for Richards (77)

REFEREE Derek Bevan (*Wales*)

SCORING Grayson, pen (0–3); Grayson, pen (0–6); Dods, pen (3–6); Grayson, pen (3–9); Grayson, pen (3–12) (half-time) Dods, pen (6–12); Dods, pen (9–12); Grayson, pen (9–15); Grayson, pen (9–18)

Scotland fielded the same starting line-up as the previous three matches, the only other time that this had happened was in 1990 when they won the Grand Slam. Expectation was high that they could win their third Slam in 12 years, but the bulkier English side maintained a stranglehold on the game that the Scots were unable to break. The match was a personal triumph for Leicester No 8 Dean Richards who controlled the pedestrian pace of the game, preventing the Scots from playing their looser, faster style. England led 12–3 at the interval, Grayson landing four kicks to one from Dods. The Northampton full-back had a variable afternoon, missing three attempts out of six. Neither side looked like scoring a try apart from a lone 60-metre breakout by Townsend early in the second half. Scotland closed to 12–9 in the 57th minute but Grayson kicked two further penalties towards the end to seal England's win. This was a disappointing spectacle and a huge anti-climax for Scotland although there was some comfort that they had been the most entertaining side of the season.

451 TOUR OF NEW ZEALAND 1996 NEW ZEALAND

Carisbrook, Dunedin · Saturday 15 June 1996 · Lost 31–62

SCOTLAND Rowen Shepherd (*Melrose*); Craig Joiner (*Melrose*), Ian Jardine (*Stirling Co*), †Ronnie Eriksson (*London Scottish*), Kenny Logan (*Stirling Co*); Gregor Townsend

(*Northampton*), Gary Armstrong (*Newcastle*); David Hilton (*Bath*), Kevin McKenzie (*Stirling Co*), Peter Wright (*Boroughmuir*), Doddie Weir (*Melrose*), Damian Cronin (*Bourges*), Rob Wainwright* (*Watsonians*), Ian Smith (*Gloucester*), Eric Peters (*Bath*)

NEW ZEALAND Christian Cullen (*Manawatu*); Jeff Wilson (*Otago*), Frank Bunce (*North Harbour*), Scott McLeod (*Waikato*), Jonah Lomu (*Counties*); Andrew Mehrtens (*Canterbury*), Justin Marshall (*Canterbury*); Craig Dowd (*Auckland*), Sean Fitzpatrick* (*Auckland*), Olo Brown (*Auckland*), Ian Jones (*North Harbour*), Robin Brooke (*Auckland*), Michael Jones (*Auckland*), Josh Cronfield (*Otago*), Zinzan Brooke (*Auckland*) ...
Replacement: Eric Rush (*North Harbour*) for Lomu (67)

REFEREE Wayne Erickson (*Australia*) · ATTENDANCE 35,695

SCORING Shepherd, pen (3–0); Jones, try (3–5); Shepherd, drop (6–5); Lomu, try (6–10); Mehrtens, con (6–12); Cullen, try (6–17); Mehrtens, con (6–19); Z Brooke, try (6–24); Peters, try (11–24); Shepherd, con (13–24); Shepherd, pen (16–24); Mehrtens, try (16–29); Mehrtens, con (16–31); Shepherd, pen (19–31) (half-time) Mehrtens, pen (19–34); Cullen, try (19–39); Mehrtens, con (19–41); Joiner, try (24–41); Shepherd, con (26–41); Cullen, try (26–46); Mehrtens, con (26–48); Cullen, try (26–53); Mehrtens, con (26–55); Marshall, try (26–60); Mehrtens, con (26–62); Townsend, try (31–62)

In May and June 1996, Scotland made an eight match tour of New Zealand including two tests. Gary Armstrong returned to the colours and burly centre Ronnie Erikson won his first cap. In a free-flowing game, Scotland suffered another heavy defeat to New Zealand and conceded nine tries, the most since the infamous Springbok massacre way back in 1951. The irony was that the Scots did not play too badly. They scored three tries of their own and the forwards won a decent share of possession, but much of their play was too laboured. By contrast, the New Zealanders did everything at lightning speed and looked like scoring every time they had the ball. Full-back Christian Cullen ran in four tries and personified his side's finishing abilities. Scotland showed plenty of courage and good skills at times, but some of their tackling was fatally weak. Gary Armstrong was back to his best and hooker Kevin Mackenzie, Stirling's wee hard man, played with total commitment.

---

452   TOUR OF NEW ZEALAND 1996   NEW ZEALAND

Eden Park, Auckland · Saturday 22 June 1996 · Lost 12–36

SCOTLAND Rowen Shepherd (*Melrose*); Tony Stanger (*Hawick*), Scott Hastings (*Watsonians*), Ian Jardine (*Stirling Co*), Kenny Logan (*Stirling Co*); Gregor Townsend (*Northampton*), Gary Armstrong (*Newcastle*); David Hilton (*Bath*), Kevin McKenzie (*Stirling Co*), †Barry Stewart (*Edinburgh Acads*), Doddie Weir (*Melrose*), Damian Cronin (*Bourges*), Rob Wainwright* (*Watsonians*), Ian Smith (*Gloucester*), Eric Peters (*Bath*) ... Replacement: Derek Stark (*Melrose*) for Jardine (25)

NEW ZEALAND Christian Cullen (*Manawatu*); Jeff Wilson (*Otago*), Frank Bunce (*North Harbour*), Walter Little (*North Harbour*), Eric Rush (*North Harbour*); Andrew Mehrtens (*Canterbury*), Justin Marshall (*Canterbury*); Craig Dowd (*Auckland*), Sean Fitzpatrick* (*Auckland*), Olo Brown (*Auckland*), Ian Jones (*North Harbour*), Robin Brooke (*Auckland*), Michael Jones (*Auckland*), Josh Cronfield (*Otago*), Zinzan Brooke (*Auckland*) ... Replacements: Adrian Cashmore (*Auckland*) for Wilson (63), Blair Larsen (*North Harbour*) for M Jones (temp), Bull Allen (*Taranaki*) for Dowd (temp)

SCORING penalty try (0–5); Mehrtens, con (0–7); Z Brooke, try (0–12); Mehrtens, con (0–14); Shepherd, try (5–14); Shepherd, con (7–14); Mehrtens, pen (7–17) (half-time) Kronfeld, try (7–22); Mehrtens, con (7–24); M Jones, try (7–29); Peters, try (12–29); Kronfeld, try (12–34); Mehrtens, con (12–36)

Scott Hastings returned to win his 62nd cap and set a new Scottish cap record, Tony Stanger made his first appearance in over a year and prop Barry Stewart won his first cap on a nightmare day for the front-rows. Like the infamous Water Polo Test in 1975, there were doubts whether this game should have been played. Conditions were dreadful with a swirling wind and heavy tropical rain leaving deep puddles on the field. Once again Scotland made an immense effort but could not make it count on the scoreboard, especially in the second half when they had the advantage of the wind. Their cause was not helped by referee Wayne Erikson who awarded a succession of baffling penalties against them. Scotland's first try came on the 36th minute when Rowan Shepherd hoisted a well-placed up-and-under and ran onto the ball as the defence hesitated. Scotland might have had a second try around the hour mark when Townsend raced onto a chip ahead, but he was adjudged to have knocked the ball forwards in the act of scoring. In the dying minutes, Eric Peters went over in the corner after a series of mauls near the New Zealand line.

XV   THE DUNBLANE INTERNATIONAL   BARBARIANS

Murrayfield · Saturday 17 August 1996 · Lost 45–48

SCOTLAND XV Rowen Shepherd (*Melrose*); Derek Stark (*Melrose*), Scott Hastings (*Watsonians*), Ronnie Eriksson (*London Scot*), Kenny Logan (*Stirling Co*); Gregor Townsend* (*Northampton*), Gary Armstrong (*Newcastle*); David Hilton (*Bath*), Graham Ellis (*Currie*), Peter Wright (*Melrose*), Damian Cronin (*Wasps*), Doddie Weir (*Newcastle*), Brian Renwick (*Hawick*), Ian Smith (*Gloucester*), Eric Peters (*Bath*) ... Replacements: Scott Murray (*Edinburgh Acs*) for Renwick (14-20 and 27), Tony Stanger (*Hawick*) for Eriksson (40), Tom Smith (*Watsonians*) for Hilton (74), Craig Chalmers (*Melrose*) for Logan (81)

BARBARIANS Gavin Hastings* (*Watsonians & Scotland*); Aparama Bose (*Mana*), Yukio Motoki (*Kobe Steel & Japan*), Andy McCormack (*Toshiba & Japan*), Tony Underwood (*Newcastle & England*); Pat Howard (*Queensland & Australia*), Augustin Pichot (*San Isidro & Argentina*); Graham Rowntree (*Leicester & England*), Richard Cockrill (*Leicester*), Darren Garforth (*Leicester*), Paddy Johns (*Saracens & Ireland*), Rod McCall (*Queensland & Australia*), Marika Gasuna (*Mana*), Iain Morrison (*London Scot & Scotland*), Arran Pene (*Kaneka & New Zealand*) ... Replacements: Dave McIvor (*Glenrothes & Scotland*) for Gasuna (43), Cameron Glasgow (*Heriot's FP*) for Underwood (58), Duncan Hodge (*Watsonians*) for G Hastings (75), Kenny Milne (*Heriot's FP & Scotland*) for Morrison (79)

REFEREE G Black (*Ireland*) · ATTENDANCE 32,002

SCORING Pene, try (0–5); Cronin, try (5–5); Shepherd, con (7–5); S Hastings, try (12–5); Shepherd, con (14–5); G Hastings, try (14–10); Underwood, try (14–15); G Hastings, con (14–17); Stark, try (19–17); G Hastings, try (19–22); Armstrong, try (24–22); Shepherd, con (26–22) (half-time) Pichot, try (26–27); G Hastings, con (26–29); Townsend, try (31–29); Shepherd, con (33–29); McCall, try (33–34); G Hastings, con (33–36); Stark, try (38–36); S Hastings, try (43–36); Shepherd, con (45–36); Morrison, try (45–41); G Hastings, con (45–43); Johns, try (45–48)

This match was played in support of the community of Dunblane and to raise money for the Dunblane Fund. The Barbarians drew players from eight different countries and managed to coax Gavin Hastings out of retirement to lead the side. For Scotland Gregor Townsend assumed the captaincy in place of the injured Rob Wainwright. On a sunny afternoon of mixed emotions, Murrayfield was treated to an entertaining and rather slapdash encounter in the best traditions of Barbarians rugby. Both sides took every chance to move the ball wide, there were 15 tries in total and the lead swung back and forward before Irish lock Paddy Johns won the game with an injury-time try. At stand-off Gregor Townsend was in wonderfully effervescent form and created several Scottish tries with his mazy incisive running.

---

453   TOUR MATCH   AUSTRALIA

Murrayfield · Saturday 9 November 1996 · Lost 19–29

SCOTLAND Rowen Shepherd (*Melrose*); Tony Stanger (*Hawick*), Gregor Townsend* (*Northampton*), Ronnie Eriksson (*London Scottish*), Kenny Logan (*Stirling Co*); Craig Chalmers (*Melrose*), Gray Armstrong (*Newcastle*); David Hilton (*Bath*), Kevin McKenzie (*Stirling Co*), Barry Stewart (*Edinburgh Acs*), Damian Cronin (*Wasps*), Doddie Weir (*Newcastle*), †Murray Wallace (*GH-K*), Ian Smith (*Gloucester*), Eric Peters (*Bath*) ... Substitute: Bryan Redpath (*Melrose*) for Armstrong (76)

AUSTRALIA Matthew Burke (*NSW*); Tim Horan (*Queensland*), Daniel Herbert (*Queensland*), Pat Howard (*ACT*), Joe Roff (*ACT*); David Knox (*ACT*), Sam Payne (*NSW*); Richard Harry (*NSW*), Michael Foley (*Queensland*), Andrew Blades (*NSW*), Warwick Waugh (*NSW*), John Eales* (*Queensland*), Owen Finegan (*ACT*), David Wilson (*Queensland*), Daniel Manu (*NSW*) ... Substitute: Brett Robinson (*ACT*) for Finegan (65)

REFEREE Patrick Thomas (*France*)

SCORING Shepherd, pen (3–0); Burke, pen (3–3); Waugh, try (3–8); Burke, con (3–10); Shepherd, pen (6–10); Burke, pen (6–13); Burke, pen (6–16); Burke, pen (6–19) (half time) Shepherd, pen (9–19); Burke, pen (9–22); Logan, try (14–22); Herbert, try (14–27); Burke, con (14–29); Stanger, try (19–29)

Glasgow High-Kelvinside flanker Murray Wallace was awarded his first cap. The Australians were making a 12 match tour of Europe, including four games in Scotland and had already beaten Scotland A (47–20), the Combined Cities (37–19) and a Scottish Districts XV (25–9). In a low-key encounter, Scotland competed well but could not match the superior strength and athleticism of the visitors who in truth never looked like losing. The bulky Australian forwards always held an edge and their versatile captain John Eales dominated the lineout and restarts. Scotland's first try came after around the hour mark when Townsend sent out a floated pass to Logan, but a few minutes later the clinical Australians killed the game with a try by Herbert. Tony Stanger scored a late consolation try when he collected a chip ahead by Townsend. A historical footnote of this game was that Australia's Brett Robinson became the first tactical substitute in international rugby when he replaced Owen Finegan.

Murrayfield · Saturday 14 December 1996 · Won 29–22

SCOTLAND Rowen Shepherd (*Melrose*); Tony Stanger (*Hawick*), Scott Hastings (*Watsonians*), Gregor Townsend* (*Northampton*), Kenny Logan (*Stirling Co*); Craig Chalmers (*Melrose*), Bryan Redpath (*Melrose*); David Hilton (*Bath*), Kevin McKenzie (*Stirling Co*), †Mattie Stewart (*Northampton*), Damian Cronin (*Wasps*), Andy Reed (*Wasps*), Murray Wallace (*GH-K*), Ian Smith (*Gloucester*), Eric Peters (*Bath*) ... Substitutes: Derek Stark (*Melrose*) for Shepherd (42), Doddie Weir (*Newcastle*) for Cronin (53)

ITALY Javier Pertile (*Roma*); Nicola Mazzucato (*Padova*), Paolo Vaccari (*Calvisano*), Ivan Francescato (*Treviso*), Marcello Cuttitta (*Milan*); Diego Dominguez (*Milan*), Alessandro Troncon (*Treviso*); Massimo Cuttitta (*Milan*), Carlo Orlandi (*Milan*), Andrea Castellani (*Treviso*), Walter Cristoletto (*Treviso*), Giambattista Croci (*Milan*), Massimo Giovanelli* (*PUC*), Andrea Sgorlon (*Treviso*), Orazio Arancio (*Milan*) ... Substitutes: Alessandro Moscardi (*Treviso*) for Orlandi (40), Leonardo Manteri (*Treviso*) for Mazzucato (65)

REFEREE Daniel Gillet (*France*)

SCORING Dominguez, pen (0–3); Shepherd, pen (3–3); Dominguez, drop (3–6); Dominguez, pen (3–9); Stanger, try (8–9); Dominguez, pen (8–12) (half-time) Logan, try (13–12); Chalmers, con (15–12); Logan, try (20–12); Chalmers, con (22–12); Dominguez, pen (22–15); Penalty try, (22–20); Dominguez, con (22–22); Stark, try (27–22); Chalmers, con (29–22)

Scotland awarded caps against Italy for the first time. Both sides started nervously and Italy took an early lead before Shepherd chipped past the defence and Stanger raced onto score. A few minutes into the second half Cronin made a great pick-up and pass from which Logan scored a try and Chalmers converted. Shortly afterwards Doddie Weir became Scotland's first-ever tactical substitution when he came on for Cronin. Scott Hastings made a half-break before sending out a perfectly-weighted pass to Logan who scored his second try. The Italians fought back to level the scores with a Dominguez penalty and a penalty try which was awarded after the Scottish defence had illegally killed the ball. The winning try started when Hastings, who was in great form, made a crunching tackle before recovering the ball and kicking ahead. Dominguez completely missed his clearance and the Scots recycled to Stark who raced away to the line. This was a solid performance by Scotland who showed plenty of enterprise and scored four well-taken tries. At times the Italians showed their inexperience, but without doubt they had pressed their claims to be admitted to the International Championship.

455 INTERNATIONAL CHAMPIONSHIP 1997 WALES

Murrayfield · Saturday 18 January 1997 · Lost 19–34

SCOTLAND Rowen Shepherd (*Melrose*); Tony Stanger (*Hawick*), Scott Hastings (*Watsonians*), Gregor Townsend (*Northampton*), Kenny Logan (*Stirling Co*); Craig Chalmers (*Melrose*), Gary Armstrong (*Newcastle*); David Hilton (*Bath*), †Graham Ellis (*Currie*), Mattie Stewart (*Northampton*), Doddie Weir (*Newcastle*), Andy Reed (*Wasps*), Peter Walton (*Newcastle*), Murray Wallace (*GH-K*), Rob Wainwright* (*Watsonians*) ... Substitutes: Shade Munro (*GH-K*) for Reed (55), Derek Stark (*Melrose*) for Chalmers (77)

WALES Neil Jenkins (*Pontypridd*); Ieuan Evans (*Llanelli*), Allan Bateman (*Richmond*), Scott Gibbs (*Swansea*), Gareth Thomas (*Bridgend*); Arwel Thomas (*Swansea*), Rob Howley (*Cardiff*); Chris Loader (*Swansea*), Jonathan Humphreys* (*Cardiff*), David Young (*Cardiff*), Gareth Llewellyn (*Harlequins*), Mark Rowley (*Pontypridd*), Steve Williams (*Neath*), Colin Charvis (*Swansea*), Scott Quinnell (*Richmond*) ... Substitutes: Craig Quinnell (*Richmond*) for Rowley (66), Gwyn Jones (*Cardiff*) for Charvis (75), Jonathan Davies (*Cardiff*) for Gibbs (79)

REFEREE Bertie Smith (*Ireland*)

SCORING Jenkins, pen (0–3); Shepherd, pen (3–3); Hastings, try (8–3); Shepherd, con (10–3); Quinnell, try (10–8); Jenkins, con (10–10); Chalmers, drop (13–10) (half-time) Shepherd, pen (16–10); Jenkins, try (16–15); Jenkins, con (16–17); Thomas, try (16–22); Jenkins, con (16–24); Evans, try (16–29); Jenkins, con (16–31); Shepherd, pen (19–31); Jenkins, pen (19–34)

Hawick-born hooker Graham Ellis replaced the injured Kevin McKenzie in the original selection and became the first player to be capped from Currie. Craig Chalmers made his 50th appearance. This was the match of the infamous 'Five Minutes of Madness'. Early in the second half the Scots unaccountably lost their concentration and composure, and gave away three tries in quick succession. Until then the game had been fairly evenly balanced although Wales had looked more confident and inventive. On the 27th minute Scotland made a slick passing movement and Scott Hastings dived joyously over the line. Wales responded a few minutes later when Scott Quinnell was unstoppable from 15 metres. A drop goal and a penalty either side of the interval restored Scotland's lead, but then the match was turned on its head. First, Ieuan Evans made a devastating break which Jenkins finished and a few minutes later Thomas latched onto a loose ball and raced away to the line, almost going out of play in his excitement. Then Jenkins chipped over the defence, Evans plucked the ball out of the air and glided over. Jenkins converted all three tries and added a late penalty to bring his personal tally to 19 points. Try as they might, there was no way back for the startled Scots.

---

456   INTERNATIONAL CHAMPIONSHIP 1997   ENGLAND

Twickenham · Saturday 1 February 1997 · Lost 13–41

SCOTLAND Rowen Shepherd (*Melrose*); Derek Stark (*Melrose*), Tony Stanger (*Hawick*), Ronnie Eriksson (*London Scottish*), Kenny Logan (*Stirling Co*); Gregor Townsend (*Northampton*), Bryan Redpath (*Melrose*); †Tom Smith (*Watsonians*), Graham Ellis (*Currie*), Mattie Stewart (*Northampton*), Doddie Weir (*Newcastle*), Andy Reed (*Wasps*), Peter Walton (*Newcastle*), Ian Smith (*Gloucester*), Rob Wainwright* (*Watsonians*) ... Substitute: Scott Hastings (*Watsonians*) for Eriksson (70)

ENGLAND Tim Stimpson (*Newcastle*); Jon Sleightholme (*Bath*), Will Carling (*Harlequins*), Phil de Glanville* (*Bath*), Tony Underwood (*Newcastle*); Paul Grayson (*Northampton*), Andy Gomarsall (*Wasps*); Graham Rowntree (*Leicester*), Mark Regan (*Bristol*), Jason Leonard (*Harlequins*), Martin Johnson (*Leicester*), Simon Shaw (*Bath*), Lawrence Dallaglio (*Wasps*), Richard Hill (*Saracens*), Tim Rodber (*Northampton*)

REFEREE Paddy O'Brien (*New Zealand*) · **ATTENDANCE** 75,012

SCORING Grayson, pen (0–3); penalty try (0–8); Grayson, con (0–10); Eriksson, try (5–10); Shepherd, con (7–10); Grayson, pen (7–13); Shepherd, pen (10–13); Grayson, pen (10–16) (half-time) Shepherd, pen (13–16); Grayson, pen (13–19); Grayson, pen (13–22); Gomarsall, try (13–27); Grayson, con (13–29); Carling, try (13–34); De Glanville, try (13–39); Grayson, con (13–41)

Loose-head prop Tom Smith was awarded his first cap and Gregor Townsend was switched to stand-off. Once again Scotland conceded three tries in the space of a few minutes although in this case their opponents were already comfortably ahead. The Scots were a little unlucky in the first half when Wainwright was only a fingertip away from an early try and when England were awarded a debatable penalty try for persistent infringement. On the 24th minute Logan corkscrewed through the defence and Eriksson scored. In theory Scotland were still in the hunt around the hour mark but the forwards had been slowly pulverised by the heavyweight English pack. The floodgates opened on the 67th minute when Johnston made a great burst before finding Gomarsall with a deft pass. Two minutes later Carling added a second and then De Glanville surged over the line for a captain's encore. The battered Scots almost scored a late consolation try, but Ellis could not take an overhead pass with the line at his mercy.

457   INTERNATIONAL CHAMPIONSHIP 1997   IRELAND

Murrayfield · Saturday 1 March 1997 · Won 38–10

SCOTLAND Rowen Shepherd (*Melrose*); Tony Stanger (*Hawick*), Alan Tait (*Newcastle*), Gregor Townsend (*Northampton*), Kenny Logan (*Stirling Co*); Craig Chalmers (*Melrose*), Bryan Redpath (*Melrose*); Tom Smith (*Watsonians*), Graham Ellis (*Currie*), Mattie Stewart (*Northampton*), Doddie Weir (*Newcastle*), Andy Reed (*Wasps*), Rob Wainwright* (*Watsonians*), Ian Smith (*Moseley*), Peter Walton (*Newcastle*)

IRELAND Jim Staples* (*Harlequins*); Denis Hickie (*St Mary's Coll*), Maurice Field (*Malone*), Kurt McQuilkin (*Lansdowne*); Jonathan Bell (*Northampton*); David Humphries (*London Irish*), Brian O'Meara (*Cork Const*); Paul Flavin (*Blackrock Coll*), Ross Nesdale (*Newcastle*), Paul Wallace (*Saracens*), Paddy Johns (*Saracens*), Jeremy Davidson (*London Irish*), David Corkery (*Bristol*), Denis McBride (*Malone*), Ben Cronin (*Garryowen*) ... Substitutes: Conor O'Shea (*London Irish*) for Staples (25), Paul Burke (*Bristol*) for McQuilkin (65), Stephen McIvor (*Garryowen*) for O'Meara (67)

REFEREE Gareth Simmonds (*Wales*)

SCORING Hickie, try (0–5); Humphreys, con (0–7); Tait, try (5–7); Shepherd, con (7–7) (half-time) Shepherd, pen (10–7); Walton, try (15–7); Shepherd, con (17–7); Humphreys, pen (17–10); Weir, try (22–10); Shepherd, con (24–10); Townsend, try (29–10); Shepherd, con (31–10); Stanger, try (36–10); Shepherd, con (38–10)

Ten years after winning his first cap, Newcastle centre Alan Tait became the first rugby league player to return to play rugby union for Scotland. A consummate professional, Tait had a fine match and opened Scotland's account on the 30th minute when he latched onto a lovely dummy pass from Craig Chalmers. Played in wet and windy conditions, the first-half was an evenly balanced contest, but after the interval Scotland produced an exhilarating exhibition of attacking rugby that blew their Celtic cousins away. The Scottish forwards were in superb form and stand-off Craig Chalmers controlled play with supreme confidence. On the 56th minute No 8 Peter

Walton powered off the back of a scrum and broke through several weak tackles to score. Ten minutes later Weir completed a Newcastle hat-trick when he spun out of a tackle and dived over the line. The Scottish backs were full of adventure and Townsend scored after a superb sweeping movement. On the stroke of time good handling and teamwork created a simple overlap for Stanger to finish off a heady display.

Parc des Princes, Paris · Saturday 15 March 1997 · Lost 20–47

SCOTLAND Rowen Shepherd (*Melrose*); Tony Stanger (*Hawick*), Alan Tait (*Newcastle*), Gregor Townsend (*Northampton*), Kenny Logan (*Stirling Co*); Craig Chalmers (*Melrose*), Bryan Redpath (*Melrose*); Tom Smith (*Watsonians*), Graham Ellis (*Currie*), Mattie Stewart (*Northampton*), Doddie Weir (*Newcastle*), Andy Reed (*Wasps*), Rob Wainwright* (*Watsonians*), Ian Smith (*Moseley*), Peter Walton (*Newcastle*) ... Substitutes: Damian Cronin (*Wasps*) for Walton (20), †Duncan Hodge (*Watsonians*) for Chalmers (54), †Cameron Glasgow (*Heriot's FP*) for Tait (74)

FRANCE Jean-Luc Sadourny (*Colomiers*); Laurent Leflamand (*Bourgoin*), Christophe Lamaison (*Brive*), Stéphane Glas (*Bourgoin*), David Venditti (*Brive*); David Aucagne (*Pau*), Guy Accoceberry (*Bordeaux Bègles*); Didier Casadei (*Brive*), Marc Dalmaso (*Agen*), Franck Tournaire (*Narbonne*), Hugues Miorin (*Toulouse*), Olivier Merle (*Montferrand*), Abdelatif Benazzi* (*Agen*), Olivier Magne (*Dax*), Fabien Pelous (*Dax*) ... Substitutes: Richard Castel (*Béziers*) for Miorin (55), Marc de Rougemont (*Toulon*) for Dalmaso (73), Jean-Louis Jordana (*Toulouse*) for Tournaire (75), Pierre Bondouy (*Narbonne*) for Venditti (75), Philippe Carbonneau (*Brive*) for Accoceberry (75), Ugo Mola (*Dax*) for Leflamand (75)

REFEREE Ed Morrison (*England*)

SCORING Lamaison, pen (0–3); Shepherd, pen (3–3); Lamaison, pen (3–6); Lamaison, pen (3–9); Benazzi, try (3–14); Lamaison, con (3–16); Shepherd, pen (6–16); Leflamand, try (6–21); Lamaison, con (6–23); Sadourny, drop (6–26); Tait, try (11–26); Shepherd, con (13–26) (half-time) Lamaison, pen (13–29); Lamaison, pen (13–32); Tait, try (18–32); Shepherd, con (20–32); Lamasion, pen (20–35); Tournaire, try (20–40); Lamaison, con (20–42); Magne, try (20–47)

It was party time in Paris as the French said a championship farewell to their beloved Parc des Princes. In the process they scored four glorious tries and completed their fifth Grand Slam. Scotland tried their best and defended well at times, but they were outclassed and lacked sufficient resources to cause an upset. There was some compensation with a brace of tries by Alan Tait, the find of the season for Scotland. Near the interval the French defence mishandled a towering up-and-under by Chalmers and Tait was on hand to grab the loose ball and score. In the second half, Tait used all of his raw power to crash through the defence and cross at the posts. Chalmers was stretchered off after a reckless tackle and Duncan Hodge came on to make his test debut. Towards the finish Cameron Glasgow, the son of 1960s flanker Ron, won his first, and only, cap.

Old Hararians Club, Harare · Tuesday 17 June 1997 · Won 55–10

SCOTLAND XV Derrick Lee (*London Scot*); Craig Joiner (*Leicester*), Scott Nichol (*Melrose*), Ronnie Eriksson (*London Scot*), Hugh Gilmour (*Heriot's FP*); Duncan Hodge (*Watsonians*), Andy Nicol* (*Bath*); George Graham (*Newcastle*), Gordon Bulloch (*W of Scot*), Barry Stewart (*Edinburgh Acs*), Stewart Campbell (*Melrose*), Scott Murray (*Bedford*), Eric Peters (*Bath*), Simon Holmes (*London Scot*), Carl Hogg (*Melrose*) ... Substitutes: Stuart Grimes (*Watsonians*) for Holmes (temp) and for Campbell (h-t), Graeme Burns (*Watsonians*) for Nicol (48), Shaun Longstaff (*Dundee HSFP*) for Eriksson (50), Rowen Shepherd (*Melrose*) for Lee (60)

ZIMBABWE Douglas Trevalla; Campbell Graham, Tafadzwa Manyimo, John Ewing, Aaron Jani; Kennedy Tsimba, Isaac Mberko; Roger Moore, Andrew Knight, Peter Staak, Brenton Catterill, Tendayi Tabuuma, David Kirkman*, Brendan Dawson, John Du Rand ... Substitute: Gary Synder for Staak (46)

REFEREE M Wiles (*Zimbabwe*)

SCORING Scotland's tries were scored by Joiner (3), Nichol (3), Gilmour (2) and Peters. Hodge kicked five conversions. Mberko scored a try for Zimbabwe which was converted by Tsimba who also kicked a penalty. The half-time score was 31–10.

In June 1997, Scotland made a six match tour of Southern Africa beginning with a non-cap test match against Zimbabwe. Played before a crowd of about 1,000 spectators and on a ground without a grandstand, the Scots cruised to an easy victory over the amateur Zimbabweans. The tourists opened the scoring after only a minute when wing Craig Joiner scored the first of his three tries. Centre Scott Nicol also scored a hat-trick in a comprehensive victory. Scotland showed good finishing throughout and their fitness was impressive despite having had little time to acclimatise to the African heat and humidity. In a good all-round team performance, George Graham showed great mobility for a prop, Scott Murray dominated at the lineouts and Simon Holmes was prominent in the loose.

459   TOUR MATCH   AUSTRALIA

Murrayfield · Saturday 22 November 1997 · Lost 8–37

SCOTLAND Duncan Hodge (*Watsonians & Edinburgh*); †James Craig (*W of Scot & Glasgow*), Tony Stanger (*Hawick & Scot Borders*), Alan Tait (*Newcastle F*), Kenny Logan (*Wasps*); Gregor Townsend (*Northampton*), Andy Nicol* (*Bath*); David Hilton (*Bath*), †Grant McKelvey (*Watsonians & Edinburgh*), Mattie Stewart (*Northampton*), Stewart Campbell (*Dundee HSFP & Caledonia*), †Scott Murray (*Bedford*), †Adam Roxburgh (*Kelso & Scot Borders*), Ian Smith (*Moseley*), Eric Peters (*Bath*) ... Substitutes: †Stuart Grimes (*Watsonians & Caledonia*) for Smith (20-28) and for Roxburgh (40), †George Graham (*Newcastle F*) for Stewart (65), Craig Chalmers (*Melrose & Scot Borders*) for Stanger (75), Stewart for Hilton (83)

AUSTRALIA Stephen Larkham (*ACT*); Ben Tune (*Queensland*), Tim Horan (*Queensland*), Pat Howard (*ACT*), Joe Roff (*ACT*); Elton Flatley (*Queensland*), George Gregan (*ACT*); Richard Harry (*NSW*), Michael Foley (*Queensland*), Andrew Blades (*Queensland*), John Langford (*ACT*), John Eales* (*Queensland*), Owen Finegan (*ACT*), Brett Robinson (*ACT*), Willie Ofahengaue (*NSW*) ... Substitute: David Wilson (*Queensland*) for Robinson (40)

SCORING Eales, pen (0–3); Hodge, pen (3–3); Murray, try (8–3); Roff, try (8–8) (half-time)
Larkham, try (8–13); Eales, con (8–15); Eales, pen (8–18); Larkham, try (8–23); Eales, con (8–25);
Gregan, try (8–30); Ofahengaue, try (8–35); Eales, con (8–37)

Scotland fielded four new caps: wing James Craig, the son of Celtic legend Jim;
Zambian-born hooker Grant McKelvey; lock Scott Murray, who had played for
Scotland at every level; and flanker Adam Roxburgh who continued the great tradition of Kelso back-rowers. The Scotland shirt bore a sponsor's logo for the first time
and the players were listed in the match programme by district as well as club.
Australia were making a seven match tour of Argentina, England and Scotland, and
the previous weekend had drawn with England (15–15). This was a disappointing,
one-sided game that lacked any sense of occasion. The opening stages were error
strewn, but on the 28th minute Tait made a strong run and Craig was bundled out at
the corner. From the ensuing lineout Murray gathered a loose throw and dived over
for a debut try. That was as good as it got for Scotland. Close to the interval, the
Australians laid siege to the line and Roff levelled the scores with a try. The second
half opened with a sensational solo score by Australian full-back Stephen Larkham
who showed great footwork to dribble past the defence and win the race to the
touchdown. Larkham, who won the man of the match award, scored again when he
collected a poor clearance and jinked his way through the static defence. Gregan and
Ofahengaue added further tries to complete the rout. Australia were not a great side
by any means, but they won this match with plenty to spare.

---

460 TOUR MATCH SOUTH AFRICA

Murrayfield · Saturday 6 December 1997 · Lost 10–68

SCOTLAND Rowen Shepherd (*Melrose & Caledonia*); Craig Joiner (*Leicester*), Tony Stanger
(*Hawick & Scot Borders*), Craig Chalmers (*Melrose & Scot Borders*), Derek Stark
(*Glasgow Hawks & Glasgow*); Gregor Townsend (*Northampton*), Andy Nicol (*Bath*);
David Hilton (*Bath*), †Gordon Bulloch (*W of Scot & Glasgow*), Mattie Stewart (*Northampton*),
Stewart Campbell (*Dundee HSFP & Caledonia*), Scott Murray (*Bedford*), Rob Wainwright*
(*Dundee HSFP & Caledonia*), Ian Smith (*Moseley*), Eric Peters (*Bath*) ... Substitutes: Duncan
Hodge (*Watsonians & Edinburgh*) for Stanger (21-29) and for Chalmers (51); Gary Armstrong
(*Newcastle F*) for Nicol (63); Peter Walton (*Newcastle Falcons*) for Peters (72); George Graham
(*Newcastle F*) for Hilton (73)

SOUTH AFRICA Percy Montgomery (*W Province*); James Small (*W Province*), André Snyman
(*N Transvaal*), Dick Muir (*W Province*), Pieter Rossouw (*W Province*); Jannie de Beer (*Free State*),
Werner Swanepoel (*Free State*); Os du Randt (*Free State*), James Dalton (*Gauteng Lions*),
Adrian Garvey (*Natal*), Krynauw Otto (*N Transvaal*), Mark Andrews (*Natal*), Johan Erasmus
(*Free State*), André Venter (*Free State*), Gary Teichmann* (*Natal*) ... Substitutes: Franco Smith
(*Griqualand West*) for de Beer (35); Justin Swart (*W Province*) for Small (71); Willie Meyer
(*Free State*) for du Randt (71)

REFEREE Patrick Thomas (*France*)

SCORING Shepherd, pen (3–0); Montgomery, try (3–5); de Beer, con (3–7); Erasmus, try (3–12);
Montgomery, con (3–14) (half-time) Small, try (3–19); Montgomery, con (3–21); Rossouw, try

(3–26); Montgomery, con (3–28); Teichmann, try (3–33); Montgomery, con (3–35); Venter, try (3–40); Montgomery, con (3–42); Stark, try (8–42); Shepherd, con (10–42); Small, try (10–47); Montgomery, try (10–52); Montgomery, con (10–54); Snyman, try (10–59); Montgomery, con (10–61); Smith, try (10–66); Montgomery, con (10–68)

Scotland made six changes, including a first cap for hooker Gordon Bulloch. World Champions South Africa were on a seven match tour of Europe and had already beaten Italy, France (twice) and England. This match was as one-sided as the final score suggests and drew comparisons with the infamous Murrayfield massacre in 1951. Scotland were outclassed by opponents who were stronger, faster, more athletic and utterly ruthless at exploiting Scottish errors and weaknesses. Scotland made an encouraging start and Shepherd kicked a penalty after 15 minutes. Tony Stanger left the field temporarily with a cut head and in his absence Montgomery, who was in brilliant form, scored a try. Jannie de Beer converted and ten minutes later made a half-break from a scrum before feeding Erasmus for the second try. Montgomery converted to put the visitors 14–3 ahead at the interval. Three minutes after half-time, Small scored a try and thereafter the match became a procession. The South Africans scored a further seven tries and full-back Percy Montgomery ended the day with a personal tally of 26 points. Scotland snatched a late consolation try by Derek Stark but their lack of basic skills had been dreadfully exposed. This result set a number of records including Scotland's heaviest defeat in over 125 years of international rugby.

| 461 | 1998 | ITALY |

Stadio Comunale Monigo, Treviso · Saturday 24 January 1998

Lost 21–25

SCOTLAND Rowen Shepherd (*Melrose & Caledonia*); Tony Stanger (*Hawick & Scot Borders*), Alan Tait (*Newcastle F*), Craig Chalmers (*Melrose & Scot Borders*), Craig Joiner (*Leicester*); Gregor Townsend (*Northampton*), Gary Armstrong (*Newcastle F*); David Hilton (*Bath*), Gordon Bulloch (*W of Scot & Glasgow*), Mattie Stewart (*Northampton*), Doddie Weir (*Newcastle F*), Scott Murray (*Bedford*), Rob Wainwright* (*Dundee HSFP & Caledonia*), †Simon Holmes (*London Scot*), Adam Roxburgh (*Kelso & Scot Borders*)

ITALY Corrado Pilat (*Treviso*); Paolo Vaccari (*Calvisano*), Cristian Stoica (*Narbonne*), Luca Martin (*Padova*), Marcello Cuttitta (*Milan*); Diego Dominguez (*Stade Français*), Alessandro Troncon (*Treviso*); Giampiero De Carli (*Roma*), Carlo Orlandi (*Milan*), Andrea Castellani (*L'Aquila*), Giambattista Croci (*Milan*), Walter Cristofoletto (*Treviso*), Massimo Giovanelli* (*Narbonne*), Andrea Sgorlon (*Treviso*), Julian Gardner (*Treviso*) ... Substitute: Orazio Arancio (*Toulon*) for Sgorlon (78)

REFEREE DR Davies (*Wales*)

SCORING Shepherd, pen (3–0); Dominguez, pen (3–3); Shepherd, try (8–3); Dominguez, pen (8–6); Tait, try (13–6); Shepherd, con (15–6); Dominguez, pen (15–9); Shepherd, pen (18–9) (half-time) Dominguez, pen (18–12); Shepherd, pen (21–12); Dominguez, pen (21–15); Vaccari, try (21–20); Dominguez, con (21–22); Dominguez, pen (21–25)

Gary Armstrong made his first start for a year and Simon Holmes, a former captain of Cambridge University, won his first cap. The gloom surrounding Scottish rugby deepened even further with this defeat to international newcomers Italy. Scotland were well beaten and had to rely on two fortuitous interceptions for their tries. The first came on the 21st minute when Shepherd took an attempted chip ahead and raced 80 metres to the corner. Ten minutes later Tait snatched an ambitious pass from Dominguez and ran away to the posts. The Italians never let their heads drop, even when several decisions went against them. Dominguez's steady kicking kept them in contention and they finished very strongly. Troncon was denied a try after the intervention of a touch judge and then from a determined attack Vaccari beat off a weak tackle to score at the posts. Dominguez kicked the conversion and a late penalty to see his side home. In the wake of this defeat, the tenth in 12 matches, the Scottish coaches Richie Dixon and David Johnson resigned their posts to be replaced by a new team of head coach Jim Telfer, assistants Roy Laidlaw and David Leslie, and coaching consultant Ian McGeechan.

462   INTERNATIONAL CHAMPIONSHIP 1998   IRELAND

Lansdowne Road, Dublin · Saturday 7 February 1998 · Won 17–16

SCOTLAND Rowen Shepherd (*Melrose & Caledonia*); Craig Joiner (*Leicester*), Alan Tait (*Newcastle F*), Gregor Townsend (*Northampton*), Kenny Logan (*Wasps*); Craig Chalmers (*Melrose & Scot Borders*), Gary Armstrong* (*Newcastle F*); George Graham (*Newcastle F*), Gordon Bulloch (*W of Scot & Glasgow*), Mattie Stewart (*Northampton*), Damian Cronin (*Wasps*), Doddie Weir (*Newcastle F*), Rob Wainwright (*Dundee HSFP & Caledonia*), Simon Holmes (*London Scot*), Peter Walton (*Newcastle F*) ... Substitutes: Tony Stanger (*Hawick & Scot Borders*) for Joiner (15), David Hilton (*Bath*) for Graham (61), Stuart Grimes (*Watsonians & Caledonia*) for Cronin (63), Derrick Lee (*London Scot*) for Shepherd (77)

IRELAND Conor O'Shea (*London Irish*); Richard Wallace (*Saracens*), Kevin Maggs (*Bristol*), Mark McCall (*London Irish*), Denis Hickie (*St Mary's Coll*); David Humphreys (*London Irish*), Brian O'Meara (*Cork Const*); Reggie Corrigan (*Greystones*), Keith Wood* (*Harlequins*), Paul Wallace (*Saracens*), Paddy Johns (*Saracens*), Malcolm O'Kelly (*London Irish*), David Corkery (*Bristol*), Kieron Dawson (*London Irish*), Eric Miller (*Leicester*) ... Substitutes: Nick Popplewell (*Newcastle F*) for Wallace (62–4), Victor Costello (*St Mary's Coll*) for Dawson (69)

REFEREE André Watson (*South Africa*)

SCORING Humphreys, pen (0–3); Shepherd, pen (3–3); Shepherd, pen (6–3); Penalty try (6–8); Humphreys, con (6–10); Tait, try (11–10) (half-time) Humphreys, pen (11–13); Humphreys, drop (11–16); Chalmers, pen (14–16); Chalmers, pen (17–16)

Gary Armstrong took over the captaincy and Craig Chalmers was restored at stand-off. Under their new coaching regime, Scotland played with improved confidence and determination but in truth this was a forgettable match ruined by a strong wind. On a difficult day for the kickers, Shepherd landed two first-half penalties against one from Humphreys. Nearing the interval Ireland were awarded a controversial penalty try after a series of collapsed scrums on the Scottish line. Then Shepherd drew the Irish defence and slipped an inside pass to Tait who twisted his way over. In the second half, Humphreys kicked a penalty and a drop goal but Ireland did not make enough of their chances. On the hour mark David Hilton replaced Graham at loose-head and his arrival shored up the creaking Scottish scrum. The momentum swung towards the

Scots and Chalmers, showing admirable coolness, kicked two late penalties to win the game.

Murrayfield · Saturday 21 February 1998 · Lost 16–51

SCOTLAND †Derrick Lee (*London Scot*); Tony Stanger (*Hawick & Scot Borders*), Gregor Townsend (*Northampton*), Kenny Logan (*Wasps*); Craig Chalmers (*Melrose & Scot Borders*), Gary Armstrong* (*Newcastle F*); David Hilton (*Bath*), Gordon Bulloch (*W of Scot & Glasgow*), Mattie Stewart (*Northampton*), Damian Cronin (*Wasps*), Doddie Weir (*Newcastle F*), Rob Wainwright (*Dundee HSFP & Caledonia*), Simon Holmes (*London Scot*), Peter Walton (*Newcastle F*) ... Substitutes: Stuart Grimes (*Watsonians & Caledonia*) for Cronin (19), George Graham (*Newcastle F*) for Hilton (64), Adam Roxburgh (*Kelso & Scot Borders*) for Walton (64), †Shaun Longstaff (*Dundee HSFP & Caledonia*) for Chalmers (78)

FRANCE Jean-Luc Sadourny (*Colomiers*); Philippe Bernat-Salles (*Pau*), Christophe Lamaison (*Brive*), Stephane Glas (*Bourgoin*), Christophe Dominici (*Stade Français*); Thomas Castaignède (*Castres*), Philippe Carbonneau (*Brive*); Christian Califano (*Toulouse*), Raphaël Ibañez* (*Dax*), Franck Tournaire (*Toulouse*), Fabien Pelous (*Toulouse*), Olivier Brouzet (*Bordeaux Bègles*), Marc Lièvremont (*Stade Français*), Olivier Magne (*Brive*), Thomas Lièvremont (*Perpignan*) ... Substitutes: David Aucagne (*Pau*) for Lamaison (40), Philippe Benetton (*Agen*) for T Lièvremont (77), Cedric Soulette (*Béziers*) for Tournaire (77), Thierry Cléda (*Pau*) for Pelous (81)

REFEREE Paddy O'Brien (*New Zealand*)

SCORING Chalmers, pen (3–0); Chalmers, pen (6–0); M Lièvremont, try (6–5); Lamaison, con (6–7); M Lièvremont, try (6–12); Lamaison, con (6–14); Chalmers, pen (9–14); Lamaison, pen (9–17); Bernat-Salles, try (9–22) (half-time) Califano, try (9–27); Castaignède, pen (9–30); Bernat-Salles, try (9–35); Castaignède, con (9–37); Stanger, try (14–37); Chalmers, con (16–37); Carbonneau, try (16–42); Castaignède, con (16–44); Castaignède, try (16–49); Castaignède, con (16–51)

Scotland had no shortage of spirit and purpose but there was a huge gulf in quality between the sides. France were stronger and faster in all aspects, combining their traditional exuberance with a new found sense of control and discipline. Some of the French attacks were devastating and they scored seven well-constructed tries. In a team of stars, flanker Olivier Magne had a brilliant game. Scotland started brightly with two early penalties by Chalmers but then came the French onslaught. Bernat-Salles almost made it to the line and after quick recycling Lièvremont ploughed over. Five minutes later the same player finished off a flowing movement with his second try. Chalmers and Lamaison exchanged penalties, and then Magne broke through and gave a long pass to Bernat-Salles who raced away. Early in the second half, Magne took an awkward pass and sent Califano over in the corner. Castaignède added a penalty before Magne made a deft chip ahead for Bernat-Salles to collect and score. Towards the finish, the Scots pounced on a rare French mistake and Stanger managed a consolation try to celebrate his 50th cap. In injury time, Carbonnaeu and Castaignède scored soft tries against some weary defence to finish off a great afternoon for the French.

Wembley Stadium · Saturday 7 March 1998 · Lost 13–19

SCOTLAND Derrick Lee (*London Scot*); Tony Stanger (*Hawick & Scot Borders*), Gregor Townsend (*Northampton*), Alan Tait (*Newcastle F*), Shaun Longstaff (*Dundee HSFP & Caledonia*); Craig Chalmers (*Melrose & Scot Borders*), Gary Armstrong* (*Newcastle F*); David Hilton (*Bath*), Gordon Bulloch (*W of Scot & Glasgow*), Mattie Stewart (*Northampton*), Damian Cronin (*Wasps*), Doddie Weir (*Newcastle F*), Rob Wainwright (*Dundee HSFP & Caledonia*), Adam Roxburgh (*Kelso & Scot Borders*), Eric Peters (*Bath*) ... Substitutes: Rowen Shepherd (*Melrose & Caledonia*) for Lee (28), Stuart Grimes (*Watsonians & Caledonia*) for Cronin (51), George Graham (*Newcastle F*) for Stewart (65)

WALES Kevin Morgan (*Pontypridd*); Wayne Proctor (*Llanelli*), Allan Bateman (*Richmond*), Scott Gibbs (*Swansea*), Gareth Thomas (*Cardiff*); Neil Jenkins (*Pontypridd*), Rob Howley* (*Cardiff*); Andrew Lewis (*Cardiff*), Garin Jenkins (*Swansea*), David Young (*Cardiff*), Mike Voyle (*Llanelli*), Andy Moore (*Swansea*), Rob Appleyard (*Swansea*), Kingsley Jones (*Ebbw Vale*), Colin Charvis (*Swansea*) ... Substitutes: Arwell Thomas (*Swansea*) for N Jenkins (18), Scott Quinnell (*Richmond*) for Appleyard (59), Jonathan Humphreys (*Cardiff*) for G Jenkins (65)

REFEREE Joel Dumé (*France*)

SCORING Townsend, try (5–0); N Jenkins, pen (5–3); Chalmers, pen (8–3); Cronin, try (13–3); A Thomas, (13–6); A Thomas, pen (13–9) (half-time) Proctor, try (13–14); A Thomas, con (13–16), A Thomas, pen (13–19)

Cardiff Arms Park was being redeveloped for the 1999 World Cup and Wales had temporarily decamped to Wembley Stadium. Two weeks previously they had lost at Twickenham (60–26) and Scotland went south with some optimism. Scotland could easily have won this match but they wasted numerous chances, including four kicks at goal, and Wales grew stronger as the game went on. Scotland began purposefully and after only seven minutes Longstaff made a long mazy run through the defence before linking with Townsend who sprinted away to the line. Scotland's second try, which was scored after 34 minutes, was less spectacular: Cronin forcing his way over after some sustained pressure on the Welsh line. Scotland should have consolidated their lead but instead they conceded two soft penalties to keep Wales in the hunt. In the second half, the Welsh forwards lifted their game and Proctor scored an early try after an error by Townsend. Substitute Arwell Thomas converted from the touchline and added a late penalty to seal a hard-fought win. As so often at Wembley, the Scots were left to ponder what-might-have-been.

Murrayfield · Sunday 22 March 1998 · Lost 20–34

SCOTLAND Derrick Lee (*London Scot*); Tony Stanger (*Hawick & Scot Borders*), Alan Tait (*Newcastle F*), Gregor Townsend (*Northampton*), Shaun Longstaff (*Dundee HSFP & Caledonia*); Craig Chalmers (*Melrose & Scot Borders*), Gary Armstrong* (*Newcastle F*); David Hilton (*Bath*), Gordon Bulloch (*W of Scot & Glasgow*), Paul Burnell (*London Scot*), Damian Cronin (*Wasps*), Doddie Weir (*Newcastle F*), Rob Wainwright (*Dundee HSFP & Caledonia*), Adam Roxburgh (*Kelso & Scot Borders*), Eric Peters (*Bath*) ... Substitutes: Stuart Grimes (*Watsonians & Caledonia*) for Cronin (53), †Cameron Murray (*Hawick & Scot Borders*) for Chalmers (72)

ENGLAND Matt Perry (*Bath*); Austin Healey (*Leicester*), Will Greenwood (*Leicester*), Jeremy Guscott (*Bath*), Adedayo Adebayo (*Bath*); Paul Grayson (*Northampton*), Matt Dawson (*Northampton*); Jason Leonard (*Harlequins*), Richard Cockerill (*Leicester*), Darren Garforth (*Leicester*), Martin Johnson (*Leicester*), Garath Archer (*Newcastle F*), Lawrence Dallaglio* (*Wasps*), Neil Back (*Leicester*), Dean Ryan (*Newcastle F*) ... Substitutes: Tony Diprose (*Saracens*) for Ryan (68), Phil de Glanville (*Bath*) for Healey (71), Danny Grewcock (*Saracens*) for Johnson (74), Dorian West (*Leicester*) for Cockerill (83)

REFEREE Clayton Thomas (*Wales*)

SCORING Grayson, pen (0–3); Chalmers, pen (3–3); Grayson, drop (3–6); Chalmers, pen (6–6) (half-time) Penalty try (6–11); Grayson, con (6–13); Dawson, try (6–18); Grayson, con (6–20); Healey, try (6–25); Grayson, con (6–27); Grayson, try (6–32); Grayson, con (6–34); Stanger, try (11–34); Lee, con (13–34); Longstaff, try (18–34); Lee, con (20–34)

A championship match was played on a Sunday for the first time. This was a one-sided encounter and the result was never in much doubt. Scotland fought hard and played some good rugby at times, but England were bigger and stronger and gradually wore them down. The first-half was rather uneventful and England made many errors as they tried to force the game. However, it was not long into the second period that the pressure began to tell on the lighter Scottish pack. After a series of collapsed scrums on the Scottish line, the visitors were awarded a penalty try. Scotland lost their concentration temporarily and the visitors ran in tries by Dawson, Healey and Grayson, who converted all three. Scotland made a late recovery and scored two tries, both involving dynamic bursts by flanker Adam Roxburgh who had an excellent game. Tony Stanger's try in injury-time equalled the Scottish record of 24 set by Ian Smith. Amongst several good individual performances, Gary Armstrong gave an inspiring lead, Derrick Lee was strong in attack and Damian Cronin was at his extrovert best, urging the crowd on and producing one delicate chip ahead to the corner flag.

---

446   TOUR OF FIJI & AUSTRALIA 1998   FIJI

National Stadium, Suva · Tuesday 26 May 1998 · Lost 26–51

SCOTLAND Derrick Lee (*London Scot*); †Hugh Gilmour (*Heriot's FP*), Cameron Murray (*Hawick*), Ian Jardine (*Stirling Co*), Shaun Longstaff (*Dundee HSFP*); Gregor Townsend (*Brive*), Bryan Redpath (*Melrose*); †Gordon McIlwham (*Glasgow Hawks*), Gordon Bulloch (*W of Scot*), †Matthew Proudfoot (*Melrose*), Stuart Grimes (*Watsonians*), Scott Murray (*Bedford*), Rob Wainwright* (*Dundee HSFP*), Adam Roxburgh (*Kelso*), Eric Peters (*Bath*) ... Substitutes: Rowen Shepherd (*Melrose*) for Jardine (22-32), Mattie Stewart (*Northampton*) for Proudfoot (59), Stewart Campbell (*Dundee HSFP*) for Murray (70)

FIJI Jonetani Waqa; Fero Lasagavibau, Sale Sorovaki*, Lawrence Little, Aisea Tuilevu; Nicky Little, Samisoni Rabaka; Joeli Veitayaki, Isaia Rasila, Mosese Taga, Saimoni Raiwalui, Emori Katalau, Apisai Naevo, Meli Tamanitoakula, Alifereti Mocelutu ... Substitutes: Waisale Serevi for N Little (50), Samu Saumaisue for Tamanitoakula (50), Ifereimi Tawake for Mocelutu (62), Jacob Rauluni for Rabaka (79)

REFEREE Paul Hiniss (*New Zealand*)

SCORING Lee, pen (3–0); Lee, pen (6–0); N Little, pen (6–3); Lee, pen (9–3); Lasagavibau, try (9–8); Lee, pen (12–8); Tuilevi, try (12–13) (half-time) Naevo, try (12–18); N Little, con (12–20);

Gilmour, try (17–20); Lee, con (19–20); Waqabitu, try (19–25); Serevi, con (19–27); Serevi, pen (19–30); Tuilevi Kurimudu, try (19–35); Serevi, con (19–37); Tuilevi, try (19–42), Serevi, con (19–44); Bulloch, try (24–44); Lee, con (26–44); Veitayaki, try (26–49); Serevi, con (26–51)

In May and June 1998, an under-strength Scotland made an eight match tour of Fiji and Australia beginning with a test match against Fiji. Scotland's lack of preparation was ruthlessly exposed by the Fijians, who played with all of their traditional exuberance and scored seven lovely tries. Scotland were very ordinary by comparison and made too many errors, including a spate of missed tackles and aimless kicks, that played straight into Fijian hands. Scotland took an early lead with three penalties by Derrick Lee but an interception try by Lasagavibau and a try by Tuilevi gave the Islanders a single point advantage at the interval. Early in the second half, Naevo burst around the front of a lineout and forced his way over in the corner. Scotland finally managed to bring some continuity to their play and Gilmour scored a debut try after a fine movement down the right. This should have encouraged the tourists but instead they collapsed. Fijian substitute and national hero Waisale Serevi made a devastating break before floating out a scoring pass to Waqa. Serevi converted and kicked a penalty, and towards the end Tuilevi scored a brace of tries to put the issue beyond doubt. Bulloch restored some pride with a late consolation try, but with the last move of the game massive Fijian prop Joe Veitayaki thundered over the line for the most popular score of the day. After Serevi's conversion the ecstatic crowd invaded the field and mobbed their smiling heroes. Scottish captain Rob Wainwright described the match as 'one of the most demoralising I've played in. It was humiliating.'

467   TOUR OF FIJI & AUSTRALIA 1998   AUSTRALIA

Sydney Football Stadium · Saturday 13 June 1998 · Lost 3–45

SCOTLAND †Glenn Metcalfe (*Glasgow Hawks*); Derrick Lee (*London Scot*), Cameron Murray (*Hawick*), Rowen Shepherd (*Melrose*), Shaun Longstaff (*Dundee HSFP*); Gregor Townsend (*Brive*), Bryan Redpath (*Melrose*); David Hilton (*Bath*), Gordon Bulloch (*W of Scot*), Matthew Proudfoot (*Melrose*), Scott Murray (*Bedford*), Stuart Grimes (*Watsonians*), Rob Wainwright* (*Dundee HSFP*), †Gordon Simpson (*Kirkcaldy*), Eric Peters (*Bath*) ... Substitutes: Kevin McKenzie (*Stirling Co*) for Bulloch (5), Adam Roxburgh (*Kelso*) for Simpson (77)

AUSTRALIA Matt Burke (*NSW*); Ben Tune (*Queensland*), Daniel Herbert (*Queensland*), Tim Horan (*Queensland*), Joe Roff (*ACT*); Stephen Larkham (*ACT*), George Gregan (*ACT*); Richard Harry (*NSW*), Phil Kearns (*NSW*), Andrew Blades (*NSW*), Tom Bowman (*NSW*), John Eales* (*Queensland*), Matt Cockbain (*Queensland*), David Wilson (*Queensland*), Toutai Kefu (*Queensland*) ... Substitutes: Willie Ofahengaue (*NSW*) for Kefu (49), Owen Finegan (*ACT*) for Cockbain (53), Dan Crowley (*Queensland*) for Harry (66), Jeremy Paul (*ACT*) for Kearns (71)

REFEREE Andre Watson (*South Africa*) · ATTENDANCE 36,263

SCORING Burke, pen (0–3); Burke, pen (0–6); Horan, try (0–11); Burke, con (0–13); Lee, pen (3–13) (half-time) Burke, pen (3–16); Roff, try (3–21); Burke, pen (3–24); Tune, try (3–29); Burke, con (3–31); Tune, try (3–36); Burke, con (3–38); Wilson, try (3–43); Burke, con (3–45)

After their humiliation in Fiji, the Scots got their tour back on course with some encouraging results in their provincial games, including a good win over New South

Wales (34–10). For the First Test at Sydney, Scotland fielded two new caps, both with New Zealand backgrounds: full-back Glenn Metcalfe and flanker Gordon Simpson. In a typical Southern Hemisphere encounter, Scotland did well in parts and never stopped trying, but they made too many errors and could not match the speed and inventiveness of the Australian attack. Scotland suffered an early setback when they lost Gordon Bulloch with a shoulder injury after only five minutes. The Australians scored their first try when Burke fielded a miscued kick and gave a long pass to Herbert who made a break before putting Horan in for a simple score. On the stroke of half-time, Derrick Lee kicked a long penalty for Scotland's only points of the game. In the second-half, Roth chipped over the defence and re-gathered to score a fine solo try. Tune scored a brace of tries against a rapidly tiring defence and one minute from time Wilson pounced on a loose pass inside the Scottish 22 for the final score.

---

468   TOUR OF FIJI & AUSTRALIA 1998   AUSTRALIA

Ballymore, Brisbane · Saturday 20 June 1998 · Lost 11–33

SCOTLAND Glenn Metcalfe (*Glasgow Hawks*); Derrick Lee (*London Scot*), Cameron Murray (*Hawick*), Rowen Shepherd (*Melrose*), Shaun Longstaff (*Dundee HSFP*); Gregor Townsend (*Brive*), Bryan Redpath (*Melrose*); David Hilton (*Bath*), Kevin McKenzie (*Stirling Co*), Matthew Proudfoot (*Melrose*), Scott Murray (*Bedford*), Stuart Grimes (*Watsonians*), Rob Wainwright* (*Dundee HSFP*), Gordon Simpson (*Kirkcaldy*), Eric Peters (*Bath*) ... Substitutes: Craig Joiner (*Leicester*) for C Murray (59), Gordon McIlwham (*Glasgow Hawks*) for Hilton (62), Duncan Hodge (*Watsonians*) for Metcalfe (66), Stewart Campbell (*Dundee HSFP*) for Grimes (75), Adam Roxburgh (*Kelso*) for Simpson (75)

AUSTRALIA Matt Burke (*NSW*); Ben Tune (*Queensland*), Daniel Herbert (*Queensland*), Tim Horan (*Queensland*), Joe Roff (*ACT*); Stephen Larkham (*ACT*), George Gregan (*ACT*); Richard Harry (*NSW*), Phil Kearns (*NSW*), Andrew Blades (*NSW*), Tom Bowman (*NSW*), John Eales* (*Queensland*), Matt Cockbain (*Queensland*), David Wilson (*Queensland*), Toutai Kefu (*Queensland*) ... Substitutes: Owen Finegan (*ACT*) for Cockbain (23–31 and 71), Willie Ofahengaue (*NSW*) for Kefu (40), Dan Crowley (*Queensland*) for Blades (60), Jason Little (*Queensland*) for Tune (62), Nathan Grey (*NSW*) for Horan (74)

REFEREE Brian Campsall (*England*) · **ATTENDANCE** 24,136

SCORING Tune, try (0–5); Lee, pen (3–5); Burke, pen (3–8); Lee, pen (6–8); Larkham, try (6–13) (half-time) Burke, pen (6–16); Burke, pen (6–19); Ofahengaue, try (6–24); Burke, con (6–26); Hodge, try (11–26); Grey, try (11–31); Burke, con (11–33)

In a tough and rugged encounter, Scotland battled courageously but once again Australia had greater speed and resourcefulness. The Scots defended well at times and their set-piece was solid but the Australians always held the upper-hand and scored four well-taken tries. After only five minutes Burke raced onto a chip ahead and after a quick bout of passing Tune had an easy run-in. Two penalties by Lee kept Scotland in contention, but just before the interval Larkham scored a crucial try that sapped some of Scotland's morale. On the hour mark Ofahengaue powered over from close range. Scotland had some consolation towards the end when Shepherd made a break and Hodge forced his way over the line, but Grey ended the match with a try in injury-time. Scotland's captain Rob Wainwright summed up the two tests: 'We were playing against a side that who were better than us. But I would never fault the team for effort.'

 XV   TOUR MATCH   NEW ZEALAND MAORI

Murrayfield · Saturday 14 November 1998 · Lost 8–24

SCOTLAND XV Derrick Lee (*London Scot*); Tony Stanger (*Edinburgh Rvrs*), Jamie Meyer (*Edinburgh Rvrs*), Rowen Shepherd (*Glasgow Cal*), Cameron Murray (*Edinburgh Rvrs*); Gregor Townsend (*Brive*), Bryan Redpath* (*Edinburgh Rvrs*); Tom Smith (*Glasgow Cal*), Gordon Bulloch (*Glasgow Cal*), Paul Burnell (*London Scot*), Scott Murray (*Bedford*), Stuart Grimes (*Glasgow Cal*), Rob Wainwright (*Glasgow Cal*), Budge Pountney (*Northampton Sts*), Eric Peters (*Bath*) ... Substitutes: Doddie Weir (*Newcastle F*) for Grimes (56), Martin Leslie (*Edinburgh Rvrs*) for Wainwright (61), Duncan Hodge (*Edinburgh Rvrs*) for Townsend (61), David Hilton (*Bath*) for Burnell (67), Alan Tait (*Edinburgh Rvrs*) for Shepherd (73)

NEW ZEALAND MAORI Adrian Cashmore (*Auckland*); Bruce Reihana (*Waikato*), Caleb Ralph (*Auckland*), Daryl Gibson (*Canterbury*), Norm Berryman (*Northland*); Tony Brown (*Otago*), Rhys Duggan (*Waikato*); Lee Lidropard (*Counties-Manukau*), Slade McFarland (*North Harbour*), Kees Meeuws (*Otago*), Norman Maxwell (*Canterbury*), Jim Coe (*Counties-Manukau*), Troy Flavell (*North Harbour*), Glen Marsh (*Counties-Manukau*), Deon Muir* (*Waikato*) ... Substitutes: John Akurangi (*Counties-Manukau*) for McFarland (58), Greg Feek (*Taranaki*) for Lidropard (58), Ron Cribb (*North Harbour*) for Coe (74), Leon MacDonald (*Canterbury*) for Gibson (74), Glen Osborne (*North Harbour*) for MacDonald (79), Hare Makiri (*Counties-Manukau*) for Maxwell (79)

REFEREE Steve Lander (*England*) · **ATTENDANCE** 19,200

SCORING Lee, pen (3–0); Cashmore, pen (3–3); Cashmore, pen (3–6); Cashmore, pen (3–9) (half-time) Cashmore, pen (3–12); Marsh, try (3–17); Cashmore, con (3–19); Cashmore, try (3–24); Lee, try (8–24)

In November 1998 New Zealand Maori made a three match tour of Scotland, including this non-cap international against a full strength Scotland XV. Scotland played in their controversial new change strip of mandarin shirts and navy blue shorts. This was a scrappy match played in wet and windy conditions. Scotland worked tirelessly against physically imposing opponents, but the backs looked nervous and did little in attack. On the hour mark the gigantic Maori wing Norm Berryman crashed through the defence to set-up a try for Marsh. A few minutes later Cashmore, who had an outstanding game, added a second try after a sything run from the Scottish 22. Scotland finished strongly and Lee scored a late consolation try after taking a slip pass from Tait.

469   TOUR MATCH   SOUTH AFRICA

Murrayfield · Saturday 21 November 1998 · Lost 10–35

SCOTLAND Derrick Lee (*London Scot*); Alan Tait (*Edinburgh Rvrs*), †Jamie Mayer (*Edinburgh Rvrs*), †John Leslie (*Glasgow Cal*), Cameron Murray (*Edinburgh Rvrs*); Duncan Hodge (*Edinburgh Rvrs*), Bryan Redpath* (*Edinburgh Rvrs*); Tom Smith (*Glasgow Cal*), Gordon Bulloch (*Glasgow Cal*), Paul Burnell (*London Scot*), Scott Murray (*Bedford*), Doddie Weir (*Newcastle F*), Peter Walton (*Newcastle F*), †Budge Poutney (*Northampton Sts*), Eric Peters (*Bath*)

... Substitutes: Gregor Townsend (*Brive*) for Lee (15), †Martin Leslie (*Edinburgh Rvrs*) for Walton (50), David Hilton (*Bath*) for Burnell (57), Kenny Logan (*Wasps*) for Tait (70); Gary Armstrong (*Newcastle F*) for Redpath (76)

SOUTH AFRICA Percy Montgomery (*W Province*); Stefan Terblanche (*Boland Cavaliers*), Andre Snyman (*Blue Bulls*), Christian Stewart (*W Province*), Pieter Rossouw (*W Province*); Henry Honiball (*Natal Sharks*), Joost van der Westhuizen (*Blue Bulls*); Robbie Kempson (*Natal Sharks*), James Dalton (*Golden Lions*), Adrian Garvey (*Natal Sharks*), Krynauw Otto (*Blue Bulls*), Mark Andrews (*Natal Sharks*), Johan Erasmus (*Free State Cheetahs*), Bobby Skinstad (*W Province*), Gary Teichmann* (*Natal Sharks*) ... Substitutes: Ollie le Roux (*Natal Sharks*) for Garvey (50), Andre Venter (*Free State Cheetahs*) for Otto (57)

REFEREE Chris White (England)

SCORING Montgomery, pen (0–3); Hodge, try (5–3); Hodge, con (7–3); Montgomery, pen (7–6); Terblanche, try (7–11) (half-time) van der Westhuizen, try (7–16); Snyman, try (7–21); Montgomery, con (7–23); Hodge, pen (10–23); Rossouw, try (10–28); Skinstad, try (10–33); Montgomery (10–35)

Scotland made five changes, including a first cap for centre John Leslie. One of a band of 'kilted kiwis', Leslie and his younger brother Martin, who was one of the Scottish substitutes, had only arrived in Scotland three weeks earlier. Their father Andy had captained New Zealand against Scotland in 1975, but the sons qualified for Scotland thanks to a grandfather born in Linlithgow. South Africa were making an eight match tour of the British Isles, including three games in Scotland. The two sides were due to meet again in the World Cup and this match, although important in itself, was something of a dress-rehearsal for the big event. In front of a smallish crowd, Scotland were always competitive and the match never degenerated into a rout but South Africa were good enough to win comfortably without being at their best. After an early penalty by Montgomery, the Scottish forwards won a lineout inside the South African 22 and drove to the line where Hodge scored a try. Montgomery kicked a second penalty and just before the interval Terblanche scored South Africa's first try after a superb handling movement. The visitors opened the second half purposefully and within a few minutes Joost van der Westhuizen pilfered the ball and raced almost 60 metres for a great opportunistic score. A try by Snyman ten minutes later effectively ended the contest. Hodge kicked a penalty on the hour mark but Rossouw and Skinstad, who had a tremendous match, scored late tries for the visitors.

 XV   RUGBY WORLD CUP QUALIFIER   PORTUGAL

Murrayfield · Saturday 28 November 1998 · Won 85–11

SCOTLAND XV Gregor Townsend (*Brive*); Kenny Logan (*Wasps*), Jamie Mayer (*Edinburgh Rvrs*), John Leslie (*Glasgow Cal*), Cameron Murray (*Edinburgh Rvrs*); Duncan Hodge (*Edinburgh Rvrs*), Bryan Redpath* (*Edinburgh Rvrs*); Tom Smith (*Glasgow Cal*), Gordon Bulloch (*Glasgow Cal*), David Hilton (*Bath*), Scott Murray (*Bedford*), Doddie Weir (*Newcastle F*), Martin Leslie (*Edinburgh Rvrs*), Budge Pountney (*Northampton Sts*), Eric Peters (*Bath*) ... Substitutes: Gary Armstrong (*Newcastle F*) for Redpath (55), Alan Tait (*Edinburgh Rvrs*) for J Leslie (58), Steve Brotherstone (*Edinburgh Rvrs*) for Bulloch (62), Stuart Grimes (*Glasgow Cal*) for Weir (66), Shaun Longstaff (*Glasgow Cal*) for C Murray (72), Paul Burnell (*London Scot*) for Hilton (72), Rob Wainwright (*Glasgow Cal*) for Peters (79)

PORTUGAL Joao Gomes (*CDUP*); Felipe Saldanha (*Lisboa*), Rohan Hoffmann (*CR Tecnico*), Salvador Amaral (*CDUL*), Luis Lamas (*AEIS*); Nuno Mourao (*CR Tecnico*), Francisco Rocha (*CDUP*); Paulo Marques (*CR Tecnico*), Paulo Silva (*CR Tecnico*), Joaquim Ferreira* (*CDUP*), Manuel Melo (*GD Direito*), Manuel Ribeiro (*CDUL*), Miguel Barbosa (*Os Belenenses*), Miguel Portela (*Grupo DD*), Melo Castro (*CDUL*) ... Substitutes: Joao Mota (*GD Direito*) for Amaral (47), Alcino Silva (*AA Coimbra*) for Marques (56), Rui Gomes (*GD Direito*) for Gomes (60)

REFEREE Giovanni Morandin (*Italy*) · ATTENDANCE 5,691

SCORING J Leslie, try (5–0); J Leslie, try (10–0); Hodge, con (12–0); Peters, try (17–0); Hodge, con (19–0); Townsend, try (24–0); Townsend, try (29–0); Hodge, con (31–0); Mayer, try (36–0); Hodge, con (38–0); Logan, try (43–0); Hodge, con (45–0); Mayer, try (50–0); Hodge, con (52–0) (half-time) Mayer, try (57–0); Hodge, con (59–0); C Murray, try (64–0); Hodge, con (66–0); Bulloch, try (71–0); Hodge, con (73–0); Mourao, pen (73–3); Logan, try (78–3); Hoffman, drop (78–6); Pountney, try (83–6); Hodge, con (85–6); Hoffman, try (85–11)

In November and December 1998, Scotland, Portugal and Spain played each other in a qualifying tournament for the 1999 World Cup. Scotland, in contrast to the other Home Unions, did not award caps for either of these matches. Playing against amateurs, there was never any doubt that Scotland would win both matches handsomely. Indeed the Portuguese rested several of their first choice players in preparation for their mid-week meeting with Spain. Scotland romped to an easy victory and scored 13 tries in a ruthless and highly professional display. Any thoughts of an upset were dispelled after only 75 seconds when centre John Leslie cut through the defence for the opening score. Thereafter the Scottish tries came at regular intervals. Jamie Meyer registered a hat-trick and Duncan Hodge kicked ten conversions. Only the introduction of a raft of substitutes in the second half disrupted the team's rhythm and prevented a higher score. Although hopelessly outclassed, the Portugese stuck to their task and showed plenty of character and some nice touches. Their moment of glory came in injury-time when centre Rohan Hoffmann, who was qualified to play for Scotland, collected a chip ahead, sped off down the left wing and evaded a couple of tackles for the most popular try of the afternoon.

 RUGBY WORLD CUP QUALIFIER   **SPAIN**

Murrayfield · Saturday 5 December 1998 · Won 85–3

SCOTLAND XV Gregor Townsend (*Brive*); Cameron Murray (*Edinburgh Rvrs*), Jamie Meyer (*Edinburgh Rvrs*), John Leslie (*Glasgow Cal*), Kenny Logan (*Wasps*); Duncan Hodge (*Edinburgh Rvrs*), Bryan Redpath* (*Edinburgh Rvrs*); Tom Smith (*Glasgow Cal*), Gordon Bulloch (*Glasgow Cal*), Willie Anderson (*Glasgow Cal*), Scott Murray (*Bedford*), Doddie Weir (*Newcastle F*), Cameron Mather (*Edinburgh Rvrs*), Martin Leslie (*Edinburgh Rvrs*), Eric Peters (*Bath*) ... Substitutes: Stuart Grimes (*Glasgow Cal*) for S Murray (66), Shaun Longstaff (*Glasgow Cal*) for Logan (79)

SPAIN Miguel Angel Frechilla (*Valladolid RAC*); Daniel Garcia (*Licco Frances*), Alvar Encisco (*CC El Salvador*), Fernando Diez (*Licco Frances*), Alberto Socias (*Valencia RC*); Andrei Kovalenco (*Real Canoe RC*), Aratz Gallastegui (*Getzo RT*); Jordi Camps (*UE Santboiana*), Fernando de la Calle (*Valladolid RAC*), Asier Altuna (*Dax*), Luis Javier Martinez (*Oviedo RC*), Steve Tuineau (*UE Santboiana*), Alberto Malo* (*UE Santboiana*), Oscar Astarloa (*Bayona*), Alfonso Mata

(*Dulciora El Salvador*) ... Substitutes: Rafael Bastide (*Colomiers*) for Diez (40), Carlos Souto (*Oviedo RC*) for Malo (56), Jorge Torres-Morote (*Ciencias Sevilla*) for Gallastegui (56 mins), Victor Torres (*UE Santboiana*) for Camps (56), Antonio Socias (*Valencia*) for Garcia (64), Oriol Ripol (*UE Santboiana*) for Encisco (70), Diego Zarzosa (*CD El Salvador*) for Tuineau (79)

REFEREE Scott Young (*Australia*) · ATTENDANCE 6,524

SCORING Logan, try (5–0); Hodge, con (7–0); J Leslie, try (12–0); Hodge, con (14–0); Kovalenko, pen (14–3); M Leslie, try (19–3); Hodge, con (21–3); Smith, try (26–3); Redpath, try (31–3); Hodge, con (33–3); Townsend, try (38–3); Hodge, con (40–3) (half-time) Logan, try (45–3); Hodge, con (47–3); Logan, try (52–3); Hodge, con (54–3); C Murray, try (59–3); Hodge, con (61–3); Weir, try (66–3); Hodge, con (68–3); Logan, try (73–3); Logan, try (78–3); Hodge, con (80–3); Longstaff, try (85–3)

In the middle of the week Spain defeated Portugal at Murrayfield (21–17) to secure their place in the World Cup, despite having had a player sent off and conceeding two tries to nil. Back home, news of Spain's qualification was momentous enough to interrupt television coverage of a Real Madrid football match. Scotland made two changes from the side that had defeated Portugal: tight-head prop Willie Anderson, a stalwart of the Kirkcaldy club, and Auckland-born flanker Cameron Mather, both uncapped at the time. In a repeat of the previous weekend, Scotland had no problems recording another big score against weak opposition. A rejuvenated Kenny Logan scored five tries and Duncan Hodge kicked ten conversions for the second successive week. The Scottish forwards looked hungry and aggressive, and on the whole the team played with great self-belief and confidence.

470 FIVE NATIONS CHAMPIONSHIP 1999 WALES

Murrayfield · Saturday 6 February 1999 · Won 33–20

SCOTLAND Glenn Metcalfe (*Glasgow Cal*); Cameron Murray (*Edinburgh Rvrs*), Gregor Townsend (*Brive*), John Leslie (*Glasgow Cal*), Kenny Logan (*Wasps*); Duncan Hodge (*Edinburgh Rvrs*), Gary Armstrong* (*Newcastle F*); Tom Smith (*Glasgow Cal*), Gordon Bulloch (*Glasgow Cal*), Paul Burnell (*London Scot*), Scott Murray (*Bedford*), Doddie Weir (*Newcastle F*), Peter Walton (*Newcastle F*), Martin Leslie (*Edinburgh Rvrs*), Eric Peters (*Bath*) ... Substitutes: Budge Pountney (*Northampton Sts*) for M Leslie (21-29) and for Walton (67), Stuart Grimes (*Glasgow Cal*) for Weir (40), Alan Tait (*Edinburgh Rvrs*) for Hodge (48), David Hilton (*Bath*) for Burnell (73)

WALES Shane Howarth (*Sale*); Matthew Robinson (*Swansea*), Allan Bateman (*Richmond*), Scott Gibbs (*Swansea*), Dafydd James (*Pontypridd*); Neil Jenkins (*Pontypridd*), Robert Howley* (*Cardiff*); Darren Morris (*Swansea*), Jonathan Humphreys (*Cardiff*), Chris Anthony (*Swansea*), Ian Gough (*Pontypridd*), Chris Wyatt (*Llanelli*), Colin Charvis (*Swansea*), Martyn Williams (*Pontypridd*), Scott Quinnell (*Llanelli*) ... Substitutes: Barry Williams (*Richmond*) for Humpreys (56), Mike Voyle (*Llanelli*) for Gough (66)

REFEREE Ed Morrison (*England*)

SCORING J Leslie, try (5–0); Jenkins, pen (5–3); James, try (5–8); Jenkins, con (5–10); Hodge, pen (8–10); Jenkins, pen (8–13) (half-time) Townsend, try (13–13); Logan, con (15–13); Gibbs, try (15–18); Jenkins, con (15–20); Tait, try (20–20); Logan, pen (23–20); S Murray, try (28–20); Logan, con (30–20); Logan, pen (33–20)

This was a tumultuous and thrilling match where the lead changed hands several times before Scotland finally took control in the last quarter of an hour. Scotland made a sensational start when John Leslie collected Hodge's kick-off and ran away to score within the opening ten seconds. Wales fought back with a Jenkins penalty after seven minutes. Play was fast and furious with both sides missing chances. In the 34th minute, Howley took a quick tap, chipped and re-gathered before feeding James for a try. Hodge and Jenkins exchanged penalties to put the visitors 13–8 ahead at the interval. Early in the second half Duncan Hodge was stretchered off with a leg injury. He was replaced by Alan Tait with Gregor Townsend moving to his preferred position of stand-off. Immediately the Scots enjoyed a piece of good fortune that helped turn the game their way. Howley tried to run a penalty in midfield but Townsend snapped up a loose pass and raced away to score under the posts. Wales recaptured the lead on the 63rd minute when Gibbs crossed after great build-up work by Wyatt. Five minutes later, from a ruck inside the Welsh 22, Townsend drew the defence before passing to Tait, who ran at a perfect angle to score. Logan missed the simple conversion but kicked a penalty to put Scotland into the lead. Near the finish Scott Murray, playing in his first championship match, drove low over the line for the clinching try. Logan's conversion and a late penalty rounded off a stirring win.

471 FIVE NATIONS CHAMPIONSHIP 1999 ENGLAND

Twickenham · Saturday 20 February 1999 · Lost 21–24

SCOTLAND Glenn Metcalfe (*Glasgow Cal*); Cameron Murray (*Edinburgh Rvrs*), Alan Tait (*Edinburgh Rvrs*), John Leslie (*Glasgow Cal*), Kenny Logan (*Wasps*); Gregor Townsend (*Brive*), Gary Armstrong* (*Newcastle F*); Tom Smith (*Glasgow Cal*), Gordon Bulloch (*Glasgow Cal*), Paul Burnell (*London Scot*), Scott Murray (*Bedford*), Stuart Grimes (*Glasgow Cal*), Peter Walton (*Newcastle F*), Martin Leslie (*Edinburgh Rvrs*), Eric Peters (*Bath*) ... Substitutes: Budge Pountney (*Northampton Sts*) for Walton (53), David Hilton (*Bath*) for Burnell (68)

ENGLAND Nick Beal (*Northampton Sts*); David Rees (*Sale*), Jonny Wilkinson (*Newcastle F*), Jeremy Guscott (*Bath*), Dan Luger (*Harlequins*); Mike Catt (*Bath*), Matt Dawson (*Northampton Sts*); Jason Leonard (*Harlequins*), Richard Cockerill (*Leicester Tgrs*), Darren Garforth (*Leicester Tgrs*), Martin Johnson (*Leicester Tgrs*), Tim Rodber (*Northampton Sts*), Lawrence Dallaglio* (*Wasps*), Neil Back (*Leicester Tgrs*), Richard Hill (*Saracens*) ... Substitutes: Danny Grewcock (*Saracens*) for Johnson (67), Kyran Bracken (*Saracens*) for Dawson (69)

REFEREE David McHugh (*Ireland*)

SCORING Rodber, try (0–5); Wilkinson, con (0–7); Luger, try (0–12); Wilkinson, con (0–14); Tait, try (5–14); Logan, con (7–14); Wilkinson, pen (7–17) (half-time) Tait, try (12–17); Logan, con (14–17); Beal, try (14–22); Wilkinson, con (14–24); Townsend, try (19–24); Logan, con (21–24)

The Scots confounded their critics and came desperately close to their first win at Twickenham since 1983. Only a Jonny Wilkinson penalty separated the two sides at the end and if Kenny Logan had not missed three fairly routine kicks at goal Scotland would probably have won. England opened purposely with two tries in the first quarter. The Scots refused to surrender and gradually worked their way into the game. On the

26th minute Peters disrupted an English lineout, Townsend made a half-break and found support to put Tait over at the posts. In the second half, Tait completed his brace when he made a scything run up the middle before stepping past a defender and barging over the line. Logan's conversion brought Scotland back to within three points, but on the 67th minute Beal made a strong run and scored a try. The Scots continued to press and for the second successive match Townsend intercepted a loose pass and ran away to score under the posts. Scotland finished the stronger side but could not produce the vital score. One sour note from an otherwise exciting match was that English lock Martin Johnson made a vicious stamp on John Leslie's neck and was lucky to escape with only a yellow card.

Scott Murray, 87 caps 1997-2007.
George Herringshaw/Sporting-Heroes.net

---

472   1999   ITALY

Murrayfield · Saturday 6 March 1999 · Won 30–12

SCOTLAND Glenn Metcalfe (*Glasgow Cal*); Cameron Murray (*Edinburgh Rvrs*), Alan Tait (*Edinburgh Rvrs*), John Leslie (*Glasgow Cal*), Kenny Logan (*Wasps*); Gregor Townsend (*Brive*), †Iain Fairley (*Edinburgh Rvrs*); Tom Smith (*Glasgow Cal*), Gordon Bulloch (*Glasgow Cal*), Paul Burnell (*London Scot*), Scott Murray (*Bedford*), Stuart Grimes (*Glasgow Cal*), Peter Walton (*Newcastle F*), Martin Leslie (*Edinburgh Rvrs*), Eric Peters* (*Bath*) ... Substitutes: Budge Pountney (*Northampton Sts*) for M Leslie (28–37) and for Peters (73), †Graeme Burns (*Edinburgh Rvrs*) for Fairley (42), Shaun Longstaff (*Glasgow Cal*) for Tait (73), Andy Reed (*Wasps*) for Grimes (79), David Hilton (*Bath*) for Smith (81)

ITALY Javier Pertile (*Roma*); Fabio Roselli (*Roma*), Cristian Stoica (*Narbonne*), Luca Martin (*Padova*), Denis Dallan (*Treviso*); Diego Dominguez (*Stade Français*), Alessandro Troncon (*Treviso*); Massimo Cuttitta (*Calvisano*), Alessandro Moscardi (*Treviso*), Franco Properzi-Curti (*Treviso*), Mark Giacheri (*West Hartlepool*), Valter Cristofoletto (*Treviso*), Massimo Giovanelli* (*Narbonne*), Andrea Sgorlon (*Treviso*), Carlo Checchinato (*Treviso*) ... Substitutes: Carlo Caione (*Roma*) for Checchinato (46), Simone Stocco (*Padova*) for Cristofoletto (76)

REFEREE Robert Davies (*Wales*) · **ATTENDANCE** 26,756

SCORING Logan, try (5–0); Logan, con (7–0); Martin, try (7–5); Dominguez, con (7–7); C Murray, try (12–7); Logan, con (14–7); Logan, con (17–7); Martin, try (17–12); Logan, pen (20–12) (half-time) Townsend, try (25–12), Logan, con (27–12); Logan, pen (30–12)

Gary Armstrong was injured so Kelso's Iain Fairley won his first cap and Eric Peters took over the captaincy. In a low-key encounter, Scotland took the lead within a minute. Italian full-back Pertile lost an up-and-under and the ball was passed quickly to Kenny Logan who scored and converted. Soon afterwards Martin took a crash-ball in midfield and was driven over the line. On the tenth minute Logan, who was in fine form, ran a poor clearance and Metcalfe intruded to give a scoring pass to Cameron Murray. Logan kicked a penalty before Martin scored his second try and just before the interval Logan kicked another penalty. Early in the second half, Graeme Burns replaced Fairley to win his first cap. The Italians had plenty of possession in the third quarter but were unable to break a well-organised Scottish defence. On the 62nd minute, from a scrum near the Italian line, Townsend broke a tackle and twisted over the line. Logan's conversion and another penalty gave Scotland a satisfactory win. Five minutes from time Massimo Giovanelli, the Italian captain, was sent off but the Scots were unable to add further points.

473   FIVE NATIONS CHAMPIONSHIP 1999   IRELAND

Murrayfield · Saturday 20 March 1999 · Won 30–13

SCOTLAND Glenn Metcalfe (*Glasgow Cal*); Cameron Murray (*Edinburgh Rvrs*), Alan Tait (*Edinburgh Rvrs*), John Leslie (*Glasgow Cal*), Kenny Logan (*Wasps*); Gregor Townsend (*Brive*), Gary Armstrong* (*Newcastle F*); Tom Smith (*Glasgow Cal*), Gordon Bulloch (*Glasgow Cal*), Paul Burnell (*London Scot*), Scott Murray (*Bedford*), Stuart Grimes (*Glasgow Cal*), Peter Walton (*Newcastle F*), Martin Leslie (*Edinburgh Rvrs*), Eric Peters (*Bath*) … Substitutes: David Hilton (*Bath*) for Smith (39), Budge Pountney (*Northampton Sts*) for Walton (66), Shaun Longstaff (*Glasgow Cal*) for C Murray (76), †Steven Brotherstone (*Edinburgh Rvrs*) for Bulloch (77), Iain Fairley (*Edinburgh Rvrs*) for Armstrong (79)

IRELAND Conor O'Shea (*London Irish*); Justin Bishop (*London Irish*), Kevin Maggs (*Bath*), Jonathan Bell (*Dungannon*), Girvan Dempsey (*Terenure Coll*); David Humphreys (*Dungannon*), Conor McGuinness (*St Mary's Coll*); Peter Clohessy (*Young Munster*), Keith Wood (*Harlequins*), Paul Wallace (*Saracens*), Paddy Johns* (*Saracens*), Jeremy Davidson (*Castres*), Dion O'Cuinneagain (*Sale*), Andy Ward (*Ballynahinch*), Eric Miller (*Terenure Coll*) … Substitutes: Victor Costello (*St Mary's Coll*) for Miller (16), Trevor Brennan (*St Mary's Coll*) for Ward (60), Rob Henderson (*Wasps*) for Bell (63), Cieran Scally (*UC Dublin*) for McGuinness (75)

REFEREE Derek Bevan (*Wales*)

SCORING penalty try (0–5); Humphreys, con (0–7); C Murray, try (5–7); Logan, pen (8–7); Townsend, try (13–7); Logan, con (15–7); Humphreys, pen (15–10) (half-time) Humphreys, pen (15–13); C Murray, try (20–13); Logan, con (22–13); Grimes, try (27–13); Logan, pen (30–13)

In a free-flowing encounter, Scotland produced a vintage display to overwhelm a disappointing and disjointed Ireland. Stand-off Gregor Townsend showed the range of his mercurial talents with some accurate kicking, clever angles of attack and solid defence. The Scottish forwards gradually subdued a fiery Irish pack and Gary Armstrong was an inspirational link. Ireland were awarded an early penalty try when Dempsey was tackled without the ball. Scotland responded on the eighth minute when John Leslie floated a delightful pass to Cameron Murray who squeezed in at the corner. Logan kicked a penalty and from a lineout near the Irish line John Leslie made a break and Townsend beat off a tackle to score. Ireland pulled back to 15–13 in the second-half, but then came two brilliant tries by Scotland in quick succession. Good combined play by the backs created an overlap for Cameron Murray who joyously rounded the defence for his second try. Two minutes later Townsend stole possession and raced away from his own 22. Tait and Metcalfe were in support before Cameron Murray gave a scoring pass to Grimes who finished off a breathtaking score. Towards the end Steve Brotherstone replaced Bulloch to win his first cap. This was a great victory for the Scots who played some exhilarating open rugby. They could now head to Paris with optimism and an outside chance of winning the last Five Nations Championship.

| 474 | FIVE NATIONS CHAMPIONSHIP 1999 | FRANCE |

Stade de France, Paris · Saturday 10 April 1999 · Won 36–22

SCOTLAND Glenn Metcalfe (*Glasgow Cal*); Cameron Murray (*Edinburgh Rvrs*), Alan Tait (*Edinburgh Rvrs*), John Leslie (*Glasgow Cal*), Kenny Logan (*Wasps*); Gregor Townsend (*Brive*), Gary Armstrong* (*Newcastle F*); Tom Smith (*Glasgow Cal*), Gordon Bulloch (*Glasgow Cal*), Paul Burnell (*London Scottish*), Scott Murray (*Bedford*), Stuart Grimes (*Glasgow Cal*), Peter Walton (*Newcastle F*), Martin Leslie (*Edinburgh Rvrs*), Stuart Reid (*Leeds*) ... Substitutes: George Graham (*Newcastle F*) for Hilton (66), Peter Walton (*Newcastle F*) for Pountney (73), Andy Reed (*Wasps*) for S Murray (79)

FRANCE Émile Ntamack (*Toulouse*); Xavier Garbajosa (*Toulouse*), Pascal Giordani (*Dax*), Franck Comba (*Stade Français*), Christophe Dominici (*Stade Français*); Thomas Castaignède (*Castres*), Philippe Carbonneau (*Brive*); Christian Califano (*Toulouse*), Raphaël Ibañez* (*Perpignan*), Franck Tournaire (*Toulouse*), Olivier Brouzet (*Bordeaux Bègles*), Thierry Cléda (*Pau*), Richard Castel (*Béziers*), Christian Labit (*Toulouse*), Christophe Juillet (*Stade Français*) ... Substitutes: David Aucagne (*Pau*) for Castaignède (4), Christophe Laussucq (*Stade Français*) for Carbonneau (38), Sylvain Marconnet (*Stade Français*) for Califano (55), David Auradou (*Stade Français*) for Cléda (55), Philippe Benetton (*Agen*) for Castel (55), Thomas Lombard (*Stade Français*) for Giordani (62)

REFEREE Clayton Thomas (*Wales*)

SCORING Ntamack, try (0–5); M Leslie, try (5–5); Logan, con (7–5); Tait, try (12–5); Logan, con (14–5); Townsend, try (19–5); Logan, con (21–5); Juillet, try (21–10); Aucagne, con (21–12); Tait, try (26–12); M Leslie, try (31–12); Logan, con (33–12); Dominici, try (33–17); Aucagne, con (33–19); Aucagne, pen (33–22) (half-time) Logan, pen (36–22)

The first 40 minutes of this remarkable match ranks amongst the greatest ever played by Scotland. So often Paris had been their graveyard but this time it was the Scots who produced the champagne rugby. In sunny conditions, they scored five tries in an exhilarating first-half, and played with such adventure and confidence that their long-suffering supporters had to rub their eyes in disbelief. Curiously the Scots made a terrible start and conceded a try within two minutes. Stand-off Thomas Castaignède made a long run to the Scottish line and two phases later Ntamack was over. Castaignède was injured in the process and had to leave the field, depriving France of their main playmaker. For a few moments the Scots were on the ropes but then began an extraordinary recovery. On the eighth minute Logan broke deep into French territory and from the ensuing play Tait passed inside to Martin Leslie who raced away to score. Straight from the restart Metcalfe made a long run to the French line to create a try for Tait. A few minutes later Townsend took a pass on the French 22 and split the defence with a simple show of the ball. It was a moment of history for Townsend who became only the fifth player to score a try in all four Championship matches in a single season, the first Scot to do so since Johnny Wallace way back in 1925. The shell-shocked French replied with a converted try by Juillet, but Scotland's response was instant. Metcalfe made another long run into French territory before slipping an inside pass to Tait who galloped away to the posts. Logan missed the easy conversion and a few minutes later Martin Leslie scored a try after his brother John had made a break and Townsend had taken play up to the line. Incredibly the Scots had scored five tries in under 30 minutes. Scotland played a much tighter game in the second-half and a great defensive effort prevented any further scoring by an increasingly frustrated French side. The only score of the second-half was a penalty goal by Logan and fittingly the game ended with the Scottish forwards hammering on the French line. This was a brilliant team effort by Scotland who showed real quality, especially in midfield. Scotland's victory in Paris meant that they would win the Championship if Wales could beat Grand Slam-chasing England the following afternoon at Wembley Stadium. Against all expectations, the Welshmen did so thanks to dramatic late try by Scott Gibbs and conversion by Neil Jenkins (32–31). On the Monday evening the Scottish team were presented with the Championship trophy in front of thousands of their ecstatic supporters at Murrayfield. It represented a great achievement for the Scots who had been written-off after the traumas of the previous year but who had come through in spectacular fashion. If it had not been for a couple of missed kicks against England then they would have won the Grand Slam. Much of the credit went to coach Jim Telfer who developed a fast rucking style that gave quick ball for the backs to exploit. John Leslie, whose selection had caused much controversy, had helped to transform the back division and brought the best out of players like Alan Tait and Gregor Townsend. Kenny Logan had his finest season in international rugby and full-back Glenn Metcalfe, another New Zealand import, was always dangerous in attack. The forwards were impressive in every game and lock Scott Murray was one of the stars of the Championship.

---

475   WORLD CUP WARM-UP MATCH   ARGENTINA

Murrayfield · Saturday 21 August 1999 · Lost 22–31

SCOTLAND Glenn Metcalfe (*Glasgow Cal*); Cameron Murray (*Edinburgh Rvrs*), Alan Tait (*Edinburgh Rvrs*), †James McLaren (*Bourgoin-Jallieu*), Kenny Logan (*London Wasps*); Duncan Hodge (*Edinburgh Rvrs*), Gary Armstrong* (*Newcastle F*), Tom Smith (*Glasgow Cal*), Gordon Bulloch (*Glasgow Cal*), Paul Burnell (*Montferrand*), Scott Murray (*Saracens*), Stuart Grimes (*Glasgow Cal*), Peter Walton (*Newcastle F*), Budge Pountney (*Northampton*), Stuart Reid (*Narbonne*) ... Substitutes: George Graham (*Newcastle F*) for Burnell (51), Shaun Longstaff (*Glasgow Cal*) for C Murray (58), Gordon Simpson (*Glasgow Cal*) for Walton (61), Doddie Weir (*Newcastle F*) for Grimes (67), Craig Chalmers (*Glasgow Cal*) for McLaren (79)

ARGENTINA Manuel Contepomi (*Newman*); Diego Albanese (*San Isidro*), Eduardo Simone (*Bristol*), Lisandro Arbizu* (*Brive*), Octavio Bartolucci (*Rosario*); Gonzalo Quesada (*Hindu*), Agustin Pichot (*Bristol*); Roberto Grau (*Saracens*), Agustin Canalda (*Newman*), Mauricio Reggiardo (*Castres*), Carlos Fernandez Lobbe (*Liceo Naval*), Alejandro Allub (*JC Rosario*),

Rolando Martin (*San Isidro*), Lucas Ostiglia (*Hindu*), Gonzalo Longo Elia (*San Isidro*) ...
Substitutes: Omar Hasan (*Agen*) for Reggiardo (h-t), Felipe Contepomi (*Newman*) for Simone
(65), Santiago Phelan (*San Isidro*) for Martin (65)

REFEREE Joel Dume (*France*) · ATTENDANCE 11,471

SCORING Quesada, pen (0–3); Quesada, pen (0–6); Albanese, try (0–11); Quesada, con (0–13);
Walton, try (5–13); Quesada, drop (5–16); Logan, pen (8–16) (half-time) Bartolucci, try (8–21);
Quesada, con (8–23); Bartolucci, try (8–28); Quesada, pen (8–31); Metcalfe, try (13–31); Logan,
con (15–31); Tait, try (17–31); Logan, con (19–31)

After a short summer tour of South Africa, where they played only provincial matches,
Scotland continued their preparations for the World Cup with two tests against
Argentina and Romania. Playing in glorious summer sunshine, Scotland were strangely
lethargic and Argentina, who were coached by former All Black Alex Wyllie, recorded
their first-ever international win in the British Isles. The visitors were superior in all
aspects without doing anything spectacular. The Scottish forwards struggled to
contain bigger and stronger opponents and the backs made little impression. It was
only late tries by Metcalfe and Tait that brought some respectability to the final score.
Newcomer James McLaren, who played his club rugby in France, made territory
whenever he had the ball and tackled soundly.

---

476 WORLD CUP WARM-UP MATCH ROMANIA

Hampden Park, Glasgow · Saturday 28 August 1999 · Won 60–19

SCOTLAND Glenn Metcalfe (*Glasgow Cal*); Shaun Longstaff (*Glasgow Cal*), Alan Tait
(*Edinburgh Rvrs*), James McLaren (*Bourgoin-Jallieu*), Kenny Logan (*London Wasps*);
Duncan Hodge (*Edinburgh Rvrs*), Gary Armstrong* (*Newcastle F*); Tom Smith (*Glasgow Cal*),
†Rob Russell (*Edinburgh Rvrs*), George Graham (*Newcastle F*), Scott Murray (*Saracens*),
Stuart Grimes (*Glasgow Cal*), Peter Walton (*Newcastle F*), Martin Leslie (*Edinburgh Rvrs*),
Gordon Simpson (*Glasgow Cal*) ... Substitutes: †Cameron Mather (*Edinburgh Rvrs*) for
Walton (63), Bryan Redpath (*Narbonne*) for Armstrong (63), David Hilton (*Glasgow Cal*)
for Graham (69), Craig Joiner (*Leicester*) for McLaren (74), Doddie Weir (*Newcastle F*) for
Simpson (80)

ROMANIA Mihai Vioreanu (*Timisoara U*); Radu Fugigi (*Caen*), Gabriel Brezoianu
(*Timisoara U*), Romeo Gontineac (*Aurillac*), Cristian Sauan (*Cluj U*); Roland Vusec (*Strasbourg*),
Petre Mitu (*Steaua*); Dragos Niculae (*Aurillac*), Petru Balan (*Dinamo*), Constantin Stan (*Dinamo*),
Catalin Draguceanu (*Steaua*), Daniel Chiriac (*Farul Constanta*), Florin Corodeanu (*Steaua*),
Erdinci Septar (*Farul Constanta*), Alin Petrache* (*Steaua*) ... Substitutes: Ovidiu Slusariuc
(*Dinamo*) for Chiriac (53), Gheorghe Solomie (*Aurillac*) for Brezoianu (53), Marius Iacob
(*Dinamo*) for Sauan (57-79), Vasile Cerces (*Cluj U*) for Niculae (78), Dan Tudosa (*Steaua*) for
Stan (78)

REFEREE Chris White (*England*) · ATTENDANCE 6,802

SCORING Tait, try (5–0); Logan, con (7–0); Mitu, pen (7–3); Logan, pen (10–3); Logan, pen
(13–3); Mitu, pen (13–6); Grimes, try (18–6); Logan, con (20–6); Logan, try (25–6); Logan, con
(27–6); Mitu, pen (27–9) (half-time) McLaren, try (32–9); Logan, con (34–9); Mitu, pen (34–12);
Logan, try (39–12); Logan, con (41–12); Leslie, try (46–12); Logan, con (48–12); Mitu, try
(48–17); Mitu, con (48–19); Smith, try (53–19); penalty try (58–19); Hodge, con (60–19)

Scotland played their first international at Hampden Park since their famous victory over the Springboks way back in 1906. In front of a disappointing crowd, the Scots were a huge improvement on the previous weekend. They scored eight tries and played with much greater urgency and cohesion. Romania gave them a hard workout but were only a limited side. Amongst several good performances, Tom Smith and Gordon Simpson were prominent in the loose and a rejuvenated Kenny Logan scored a personal tally of 26 points. On the 63rd minute, Cameron Mather came on to win his first cap, which meant that Scotland had five New Zealand-born players on the field (Metcalfe, Longstaff, Leslie, Simpson and Mather) as well as one Australian (Russell, also winning his first cap).

The 1999 World Cup

The 1999 World Cup was hosted by Wales with pool matches held around the British Isles and France. The format was expanded to 20 teams playing in five pools of four teams each. The winners of each pool went straight into the quarter-finals, but the second-placed teams and one other had to play an extra round of qualifiers. Scotland were drawn in Pool A with the defending champions South Africa and newcomers Spain and Uruguay. Matches were held at Murrayfield, Netherdale and Hampden Park. In Scotland at least, the World Cup was not a great success and largely failed to capture the public imagination as it had done in 1991. The tournament was poorly organised and promoted, and as result some of the attendances were pathetically small. Rumour had it that the organisers were reduced to playing piped crowd noises in an attempt to create some atmosphere. There was a big gulf in quality between the amateur and professional teams, and the public were unwilling to pay hefty ticket prices for matches that were foregone conclusions.

477 RUGBY WORLD CUP 1999 SOUTH AFRICA

Murrayfield · Saturday 3 October 1999 · Lost 29–46

SCOTLAND Glenn Metcalfe (*Glasgow Cal*); Cameron Murray (*Edinburgh Rvrs*), Alan Tait (*Edinburgh Rvrs*), John Leslie (*Sanix*), Kenny Logan (*London Wasps*); Gregor Townsend (*Brive*), Gary Armstrong* (*Newcastle F*); Tom Smith (*Glasgow Cal*), Gordon Bulloch (*Glasgow Cal*), George Graham (*Newcastle F*), Scott Murray (*Saracens*), Stuart Grimes (*Glasgow Cal*), Martin Leslie (*Edinburgh Rvrs*), Budge Pountney (*Northampton Sts*), Gordon Simpson (*Glasgow Cal*) ... Substitutes: Jamie Mayer (*Edinburgh Rvrs*) for J Leslie (54), Peter Walton (*Newcastle F*) for Simpson (61), Doddie Weir (*Newcastle F*) for S Murray (72), David Hilton (*Glasgow Cal*) for Graham (73)

SOUTH AFRICA Percy Montgomery (*W Province*); Deon Kayser (*E Province*), Robbie Fleck (*W Province*), Brendan Venter (*Free State Cheetahs*), Pieter Rossouw (*W Province*); Jannie De Beer (*Free State Cheetahs*), Joost van der Westhuizen* (*Blue Bulls*); Os du Randt (*Free State Cheetahs*), Naka Drotske (*Free State Cheetahs*), Cobus Visagie (*W Province*), Albert van den Berg (*W Province*), Mark Andrews (*Natal Sharks*), Rassie Erasmus (*Golden Lions*), André Venter (*Free State Cheetahs*), Bobbie Skinstad (*W Province*) ... Substitutes: Ollie le Roux (*Natal Sharks*) for du Randt (47), Krynauw Otto (*Blue Bulls*) for Andrews (47), Breyton Paulse (*W Province*) for Kayser (70), André Vos (*Golden Lions*) for Erasmus (81)

SCORING Logan, pen (3–0); De Beer, pen (3–3); Logan, pen (6–3); Venter, try (6–8); De Beer, con (6–10); De Beer, pen (6–13); Logan, pen (9–13); M Leslie, try (14–13); Logan, con (16–13) (half-time) Fleck, try (16–18); Logan, pen (19–18); Le Roux, try (19–23); De Beer, con (19–25); Kayser, try (19–30); De Beer, con (19–32); Tait, try (24–32); Logan, con (26–32); Venter, try (26–37); De Beer, con (26–39); Townsend, drop (29–39); Van der Westhuizen, try (29–41); De Beer, con (29–43)

This was the crunch match of Pool A, the winner heading to the quarter-finals whilst the loser would have to play an extra qualifying match before probably facing New Zealand, the side that everybody wanted to avoid. The big crowd saw a pulsating display of end-to-end rugby where the lead changed hands five times before South Africa finally ran away with it. The Scots gave their all and at times they had the World Champions under real pressure. In a tight first-half, Kenny Logan kicked three penalties and converted Martin Leslie's 35th minute try which came after some rousing drives by the forwards and a sniping run by Gary Armstrong. The match became more open in the second-half and Scotland were hampered when John Leslie was injured in the act of scoring and had to leave the field. Thereafter, without his steadying influence, Scotland's World Cup plans started to unravel. Another Logan penalty gave Scotland a one-point lead going into final quarter, but two South African tries in quick succession ended the contest. A late try by Alan Tait restored some hopes, but the ruthless South Africans scored two further tries in injury-time. Scotland had worked hard but made too many errors, especially in the lineout and defence. Amongst several heroic performances, the Scottish scrum was solid and prop George Graham battled valiantly against the beast-like Os du Randt.

---

478 RUGBY WORLD CUP 1999 URUGUAY

Murrayfield · Friday 16 October 1999 · Won 43–12

SCOTLAND Glenn Metcalfe (*Glasgow Cal*); Cameron Murray (*Edinburgh Rvrs*), Alan Tait (*Edinburgh Rvrs*), Jamie Mayer (*Edinburgh Rvrs*), Kenny Logan (*London Wasps*); Gregor Townsend (*Brive*), Gary Armstrong* (*Newcastle F*); Tom Smith (*Glasgow Cal*), Gordon Bulloch (*Glasgow Cal*), George Graham (*Newcastle F*), Scott Murray (*Saracens*), Stuart Grimes (*Glasgow Cal*), Martin Leslie (*Edinburgh Rvrs*), Budge Pountney (*Northampton Sts*), Gordon Simpson (*Glasgow Cal*) ... Substitutes: Bryan Redpath (*Narbonne*) for Armstrong (58), David Hilton (*Glasgow Cal*) for Graham (64), Rob Russell (*Edinburgh Rvrs*) for Bulloch (70), Peter Walton (*Newcastle F*) for Leslie (75), Shaun Longstaff (*Glasgow Cal*) for C Murray (78)

URUGUAY Alfonso Cardoso (*Old Boys Club*); Juan Menchaca (*Carrasco Polo*), Pedro Vecino (*Carrasco Polo*), Martín Mendaro (*Carrasco Polo*), Pablo Costábile (*Carrasco Polo*); Diego Aguirre (*Carrasco Polo*), Federico Sciarra (*Carrasco Polo*); Rodrigo Sanchez (*Carrasco Polo*), Diego Lamelas (*Champagnat*), Pablo Lemoine (*Bristol*), Juan Carlos Bado (*Old Boys Club*), Mario Lamé (*Carrasca Polo*), Nicolás Brignoni (*Montevideo CC*), Martín Panizza (*Carrasco Polo*), Diego Ormaechea* (*Carrasco Polo*) ... Substitutes: Fernando Sosa Díaz (*Carrasco Polo*) for Sciarra (40), Nicolás Grille (*Trébol Paysandú*) for Brignoni (60), Eduardo Berruti (*Old Christians*) for Sanchez (63), Agustín Ponce de Léon (*Carrasco Polo*) for Lamé (66), Guillermo Storace (*Old Christians*) for Lemoine (70), Francisco de los Santos (*Carrasco Polo*) for Lamelas (70), José Viana (*Old Boys Club*) for Aguirre (78)

REFEREE Stuart Dickinson (*Australia*) · ATTENDANCE 9,463

SCORING Logan, pen (3–0); Aguirre, pen (3–3); Leslie, try (8–3); Logan, con (10–3); Armstrong, try (15–3); Logan, con (17–3); Sciarra, pen (17–6); Simpson, try (22–6); Logan, con (24–6); Metcalfe, try (29–6) (half-time) Aguirre, pen (29–9); Aguirre, pen (29–12); Townsend, try (34–12); Logan, con (36–12); Russell, try (41–12); Logan, con (43–12)

Scotland returned to winning ways with a routine but unconvincing victory over the amateurs from Uruguay. Playing in front of a small crowd, Scotland scored four tries in the first-half but thereafter struggled to break down a passionate Uruguayan defence. It was only 11 minutes from regulation time that Gregor Townsend slipped through for a fifth try and shortly before the finish substitute Rob Russell forced his way over from close range. Uruguay had no hope of winning, but they were physically imposing and adept at slowing the game down. For Scotland, No 8 Gordon Simpson drove powerfully from the base of the scrum, full-back Glenn Metcalfe was always lively and Gregor Townsend found touch was unerring accuracy.

479 RUGBY WORLD CUP 1999 SPAIN

Murrayfield · Saturday 16 October 1999 · Won 48–0

SCOTLAND †Chris Paterson (*Edinburgh Rvrs*); Cameron Murray (*Edinburgh Rvrs*), Jamie Mayer (*Edinburgh Rvrs*), James McLaren (*Bourgoin-Jallieu*), Shaun Longstaff (*Glasgow Cal*); Duncan Hodge (*Edinburgh Rvrs*), Bryan Redpath* (*Narbonne*); David Hilton (*Glasgow Cal*), Rob Russell (*Edinburgh Rvrs*), Paul Burnell (*Montferrand*), Doddie Weir (*Newcastle F*), Andy Reed (*London Wasps*), Peter Walton (*Newcastle F*), Cameron Mather (*Edinburgh Rvrs*), Stuart Reid (*Narbonne*) ... Substitutes: Gregor Townsend (*Brive*) for McLaren (76), Iain Fairley (*Edinburgh Rvrs*) for Redpath (76)

SPAIN Francisco Puertas (*Saint Jean de Luz*); José Inchausti (*Alcobendas*), Alvar Enciso* (*Dulciora El Salvador*), Sebastian Loubsens (*Bordeaux Bègles*), Miguel Frechilla (*Quesos Entrepinares*); Andrei Kovalenco (*Real Canoe NC*), Aratz Gallastegui (*Getxo Artea*); Victor Torres (*UE Santboiana*), Diego Zarzosa (*Dulciora El Salvador*), José Ignacio Zapatero (*Dulciora El Salvador*), José Villaú (*Stade Montois*), Oskar Astarloa (*Bayonne*), José Diaz (*Castres*), Carlos Souto (*Oviedo*), Alfonso Mata (*Dulciora El Salvador*) ... Substitutes: Alberto Socias (*Valencia*) for Inchausti (48), Ferrán Velazco (*UE Santboiana*) for Puertas (49), Steve Tuineau (*UE Santboiana*) for Astarloa (56), Luis Martínez (*Oviedo*) for Torres (62), Agustín Malet (*Seville U*) for Souto (69), Fernando de la Calle (*Quesos Entrepinares*) for Zarzosa (76)

REFEREE Clayton Thomas (*Wales*) · ATTENDANCE 17,593

SCORING Hodge, pen (3–0); penalty try (8–0); Hodge, con (10–0); Mather, try (15–0); Hodge, con (17–0); Longstaff, try (22–0) (half-time) McLaren, try (27–0); Mather, try (32–0); Hodge, con (34–0); Murray, try (39–0); Hodge, con (41–0); Hodge, try (46–0); Hodge, con (48–0)

Paul Burnell won his 50th cap and Chris Paterson made his debut. Scotland sailed into the knock-out stages of the World Cup with an efficient and highly professional display. In a one-sided encounter, their simple, direct approach kept Spain largely on the back foot, especially in the scrums. Scotland asserted themselves straightaway and after an early penalty goal by Duncan Hodge they were awarded a penalty try when Spain collapsed a retreating scrum on their own line. Further tries by Mather and Longstaff effectively finished the contest after only 30 minutes, even before Spain had reached the Scottish 22. Scotland scored four tries in the second half, but to their credit the Spanish finished strongly and the Scots had to defend well to keep a clean sheet.

480   RUGBY WORLD CUP 1999   SAMOA

Murrayfield · Wednesday 20 October 1999 · Won 35–20

SCOTLAND Glenn Metcalfe (*Glasgow Cal*); Cameron Murray (*Edinburgh Rvrs*), Jamie Mayer (*Edinburgh Rvrs*), James McLaren (*Bourgoin-Jallieu*), Kenny Logan (*London Wasps*); Gregor Townsend (*Brive*), Gary Armstrong* (*Newcastle F*); Tom Smith (*Glasgow Cal*), Gordon Bulloch (*Glasgow Cal*), George Graham (*Newcastle F*), Scott Murray (*Saracens*), Doddie Weir (*Newcastle F*), Martin Leslie (*Edinburgh Rvrs*), Budge Pountney (*Northampton Sts*), Gordon Simpson (*Glasgow Cal*) ... Substitutes: Cameron Mather (*Edinburgh Rvrs*) for Pountney (58), Stuart Grimes (*Glasgow Cal*) for S Murray (71), Duncan Hodge (*Edinburgh Rvrs*) for Townsend (75), Paul Burnell (*Montferrand*) for Graham (79), Rob Russell (*Edinburgh Rvrs*) for Leslie (80)

SAMOA Silao Leaega (*Waitakere City*); Brian Lima (*Ponsonby*), To'o Vaega (*Rugby Lions*), Terry Fanolua (*Gloucester*), Va'aiga Tuigamala (*Newcastle F*); Stephen Bachop (*London Irish*), Steven So'oialo (*Western Suburbs*); Brendan Reidy (*unattached*), Trevor Leota (*London Wasps*), Polo Asi (*Moataa*), Lio Falaniko (*North Harbour*), Lama Tone (*Manurewa*), Semo Sititi (*Marist*), Craig Glendinning (*Marist*), Pat Lam* (*Northampton Sts*) ... Substitutes: Onehunga Matauiau (*Moataa*) for Leota (37), Sene Ta'ala (*Johnsonville*) for Falaniko (59), Robbie Ale (*Johnsonville*) for Asi (66), Earl Va'a (*unattached*) for Bachop (72), Filipo Toala (*Ponsonby*) for Terry Fanolua (75)

REFEREE David McHugh (*Ireland*) · **ATTENDANCE** 15,661

SCORING penalty try (5–0); Logan, con (7–0); Leaega, pen (7–3); Leslie, try (12–3); Logan, pen (15–3); Leaega, pen (15–6) (half-time) Logan, pen (18–6); Logan, pen (21–6); Logan, pen (24–6); Townsend, drop (27–6); Sititi, try (27–11); Leaega, con (27–13); Logan, pen (30–13); C Murray, try (35–13); Lima, try (35–18); Leaega, con (35–20)

Played on a Wednesday afternoon in front of another small crowd, Scotland moved into the quarter-finals of the World Cup with a controlled and effective performance against the burly Samoans. Scotland were the better side and had greater discipline and creativity without doing anything spectacular. The Scottish forwards were able to exert a lot of pressure on the Samoan set-piece and they were prominent in the loose. The Samoans always looked dangerous but they were forced into making costly errors. Scotland started strongly and were awarded an early penalty try after a series of collapsed scrums near the Samoan line. Logan converted and went on to kick five penalties during the match. Close to the interval Martin Leslie scored a try and in the second half Scotland built an unassailable lead thanks to Logan's boot, a Townsend drop goal and a try by Cameron Murray in the corner.

481   RUGBY WORLD CUP 1999   NEW ZEALAND

Murrayfield · Sunday 24 October 1999 · Lost 18–30

SCOTLAND Glenn Metcalfe (*Glasgow Cal*); Cameron Murray (*Edinburgh Rvrs*), Alan Tait

(*Edinburgh Rvrs*), Jamie Mayer (*Edinburgh Rvrs*), Kenny Logan (*London Wasps*); Gregor Townsend (*Brive*), Gary Armstrong* (*Newcastle F*); Tom Smith (*Glasgow Cal*), Gordon Bulloch (*Glasgow Cal*), Paul Burnell (*Montferrand*), Scott Murray (*Saracens*), Doddie Weir (*Newcastle F*), Martin Leslie (*Edinburgh Rvrs*), Budge Pountney (*Northampton Sts*), Gordon Simpson (*Glasgow Cal*) ... Substitutes: Stuart Grimes (*Glasgow Cal*) for Weir (54), George Graham (*Newcastle F*) for Burnell (54), Rob Russell (*Edinburgh Rvrs*) for Bulloch (70)

NEW ZEALAND Jeff Wilson (*Otago*); Tana Umaga (*Wellington*), Christian Cullen (*Wellington*), Alama Ieremia (*Wellington*), Jonah Lomu (*Counties Manukau*); Andrew Mehrtens (*Canterbury*), Justin Marshall (*Canterbury*); Carl Hoeft (*Otago*), Anton Oliver (*Otago*), Craig Dowd (*Auckland*), Norm Maxwell (*Canterbury*), Robin Brooke (*Auckland*), Reuben Thorne (*Canterbury*), Josh Kronfield (*Otago*), Taine Randell* (*Otago*) ... Substitutes: Tony Brown (*Otago*) for Mehrtens (40), Mark Hammett (*Canterbury*) for Oliver (60), Ian Jones (*North Harbour*) for Maxwell (62)

REFEREE Ed Morrison (*England*) · **ATTENDANCE** 59,757

SCORING Mehrtens, pen (0–3); Umaga, try (0–8); Mehrtens, con (0–10); Wilson, try (0–15); Mehrtens, con (0–17); Logan, pen (3–17); Mehrtens, pen (3–20); Umaga, try (3–25) (half-time) Townsend, drop (6–25); Lomu, try (6–30); Pountney, try (11–30); Logan, con (13–30); C Murray, try (18–30)

The World Cup finally came alive with an atmospheric match played under floodlights and in damp conditions. Scotland showed great passion and determination but never looked capable of upsetting New Zealand, the tournament favourites. The All Blacks made a powerful start with a penalty goal and two converted tries before the Scots forced their way into the game. Logan and Mehrtens exchanged penalties and Scotland had a spell of pressure only to be denied by a knock-on. Just before the interval, New Zealand made a slick passing movement and Umaga scored his second try to effectively kill the contest. In the second-half, Scotland fought hard and Townsend dropped a goal but the massive Johan Lomu responded with an unconverted try. The Scots were at their best in the closing stages. On the 67th minute Budge Pountney was bundled over the line and Logan converted, but despite making a great effort Scotland were unable to score again until the final minute. Leslie intercepted a pass and made a long run before feeding Cameron Murray who dummied past the defence for a consolation try. This match marked the end of the careers of Paul Burnell, Alan Tait and Gary Armstrong, all great servants of the game. The iconic Armstrong was one of the most popular and respected players of the 1990s and he left the field in tears.

---

482 SIX NATIONS CHAMPIONSIP 2000 ITALY

Stadio Flaminio, Rome · Saturday 5 February 2000 · Lost 20–34

SCOTLAND Glenn Metcalfe (*Glasgow Cal*); Shaun Longstaff (*Glasgow Cal*), Jamie Mayer (*Bristol*), John Leslie* (*Newcastle F*), Kenny Logan (*London Wasps*); Gregor Townsend (*Brive*), Bryan Redpath (*Narbonne*); Tom Smith (*Glasgow Cal*), Gordon Bulloch (*Glasgow Cal*), Mattie Stewart (*Northampton Sts*), Scott Murray (*Saracens*), Stuart Grimes (*Newcastle F*), Martin Leslie (*Edinburgh Rvrs*), Budge Pountney (*Northampton Sts*), Gordon Simpson (*Glasgow Cal*) ... Substitutes: James McLaren (*Bourgoin-Jallieu*) for J Leslie (14), Stuart Reid (*Narbonne*) for Simpson (20–31), David Hilton (*Glasgow Cal*) for Stewart (70), Doddie Weir (*Newcastle F*) for Murray (72)

ITALY Matthew Pini (*Narbonne*); Denis Dallan (*Treviso*), Manuel Dallan (*Treviso*), Luca Martin

(*Bordeaux Bègles*), Cristian Stoica (*Narbonne*); Diego Dominguez (*Stade Français*), Alessandro Troncon* (*Montferrand*); Massimo Cuttitta (*Calvisano*), Alessandro Moscardi (*Treviso*), Tino Paoletti (*Piacenza*), Carlo Checchinato (*Treviso*), Andrea Gritti (*Treviso*), Massimo Giovanelli (*Rovigo*), Mauro Bergamasco (*Padova*), Wilhelmus Visser (*Treviso*) ... Substitutes: Giuseppe Lanzi (*Calvisano*) for Visser (20-33), Marco Rivaro (*London Irish*) for D Dallan (44), Aaron Persico (*Viadana*) for Bergamasco (62), Giampiero de Carli (*Stade Français*) for Paoletti (67), Matteo Mazzantini (*L'Aquila*) for Troncon (79)

REFEREE Jonathan Kaplan (*South Africa*) · ATTENDANCE 22,155

SCORING Townsend, drop (3–0); Dominguez, pen (3–3); Dominguez, pen (3–6); Bulloch, try (8–6); Logan, con (10–6); Dominguez, pen (10–9); Dominguez, pen (10–12) (half-time) Dominguez, drop (10–15); Domingeuz, drop (10–18); Dominguez, pen (10–21); Townsend, pen (13–21); Dominguez, pen (13–24); Domingeuz, drop (13–27); de Carli, try (13–32); Dominguez, con (13–34); M Leslie, try (18–34); Townsend, con (20–34)

Scotland were the fall guys as Italy made their debut in the International Championship and the Five Nations became Six. The reigning champions were expected to record a routine win but Italy thoroughly deserved their moment of history. Making the best use of their limited resources, the Italians played simple and passionate rugby, and the sluggish Scots fell away badly in the second-half. Flankers Giovanelli and Bergamasco were immense in the loose and the half-backs Troncon and Dominguez controlled the game throughout. Dominguez, in particular, gave an exemplary display. He kicked a total of 29 points, kept his side going forwards and teased the Scottish defence with his accurate punting. Scotland made a purposeful start but unluckily lost captain John Leslie with an ankle injury early on. His absence was keenly felt as Scotland lacked a cutting edge in midfield and a leader capable of lifting the side out of its collective malaise. The Italians rarely threatened to score a try but they kept play in the Scottish half and their score mounted as Scotland gave away needless penalties. By contrast Logan missed several kicks and Italy grew in confidence as the game moved on. De Carli's try three minutes from the end sealed an outcome that had never been in doubt since the early stages of the second-half. A black day for Scotland but a great one for rugby.

483 SIX NATIONS CHAMPIONSHIP 2000 IRELAND

Lansdowne Road, Dublin · Saturday 19 February 2000 · Lost 22–44

SCOTLAND Glenn Metcalfe (*Glasgow Cal*); Shaun Longstaff (*Glasgow Cal*), Jamie Mayer (*Bristol*), Graham Shiel (*Edinburgh Rvrs*), Kenny Logan (*London Wasps*); Gregor Townsend (*Brive*), Bryan Redpath* (*Narbonne*); Tom Smith (*Glasgow Cal*), Gordon Bulloch (*Glasgow Cal*), Mattie Stewart (*Northampton Sts*), Scott Murray (*Saracens*), Stuart Grimes (*Newcastle F*), Martin Leslie (*Edinburgh Rvrs*), Budge Pountney (*Northampton Sts*), Gordon Simpson (*Glasgow Cal*) ... Substitutes: Doddie Weir (*Newcastle Falcons*) for Murray (51), Andy Nicol (*Glasgow Cal*) for Redpath (64), George Graham (*Newcastle F*) for Stewart (64), Rob Russell (*Saracens*) for Bulloch (67), Stewart for Graham (80)

IRELAND Girvan Dempsey (*Terenure Coll*); Shane Horgan (*Lansdowne*), Brian O'Driscoll (*Blackrock Coll*), Mike Mullins (*Young Munster*), Denis Hickie (*St Mary's Coll*); Ronan O'Gara (*Cork Const*), Peter Stringer (*Shannon*); Peter Clohessy (*Young Munster*), Keith Wood* (*Garryowen*), John Hayes (*Shannon*), Mick Galwey (*Shannon*), Malcolm O'Kelly (*St Mary's Coll*),

Simon Easterby (*Llanelli*), Kieron Dawson (*London Irish*), Anthony Foley (*Shannon*) ...
Substitutes: Rob Henderson (*London Wasps*) for Dempsey (38), David Humphreys (*Dungannon*) for O'Gara (50), Jeremy Davidson (*Castres*) for Galwey (56), Justin Fitzpatrick (*Dungannon*) for Hayes (67)

REFEREE Joel Dume (*France*) · ATTENDANCE 49,250

SCORING Logan, pen (3–0); Logan, try (8–0); Logan, con (10–0); O'Kelly, try (10–5); O'Gara, con (10–7); O'Gara, pen (10–10); O'Gara, pen (10–13) (half-time) Horgan, try (10–18); O'Gara, con (10–20); O'Driscoll, try (10–25); Humphreys, con (10–27); Humphreys, pen (10–30); Humphreys, try (10–35); Humphreys, con (10–37); Wood, try (10–42); Humphreys, con (10–44); Metcalfe, try (15–44); Logan, con (17–44); Graham, try (22–44)

Despite the loss in Italy, there was only one change in the starting line-up with Graham Shiel being recalled after an absence of five years. Scotland made a promising start before going down to a calamitous defeat, their first loss to Ireland since 1988. As in Rome, the Scots controlled the opening 20 minutes and Kenny Logan kicked an early penalty. Metcalfe made a penetrative run and from the ensuing play Townsend fired a miss-pass to Logan who steamed in at the corner. Then, unaccountably, the Scots lost direction and completely fell apart. By half-time Ireland had taken a three-point lead and in total the home side scored an astonishing 44 points without reply before the bedraggled Scots made a late rally. It was nothing less than a debacle and worryingly Scotland still had to face the three best sides in the championship.

484   SIX NATIONS CHAMPIONSHIP 2000   FRANCE

Murrayfield · Saturday 4 March 2000 · Lost 16–28

SCOTLAND Chris Paterson (*Edinburgh Rvrs*); Glenn Metcalfe (*Glasgow Cal*), James McLaren (*Bourgoin-Jallieu*), John Leslie* (*Newcastle F*), Kenny Logan (*London Wasps*); Gregor Townsend (*Brive*), Andy Nicol (*Glasgow Cal*); Tom Smith (*Brive*), Steve Brotherstone (*Brive*), Mattie Stewart (*Northampton Sts*), Scott Murray (*Saracens*), Doddie Weir (*Newcastle F*), Martin Leslie (*Edinburgh Rvrs*), Budge Pountney (*Northampton Sts*), Stuart Reid (*Narbonne*) ... Substitutes: Cameron Mather (*Edinburgh Rvrs*) for Reid (15-20), David Hilton (*Glasgow Cal*) for Stewart (69), Stuart Grimes (*Newcastle F*) for Weir (69), Duncan Hodge (*Edinburgh Rvrs*) for McLaren (74)

FRANCE Thomas Castaignède (*Castres*); Émile Ntamack (*Toulouse*), David Venditti (*Brive*), Thomas Lombard (*Stade Français*), Christophe Dominici (*Stade Français*); Gerald Merceron (*Montferrand*), Christophe Laussucq (*Stade Français*); Christian Califano (*Toulouse*), Marc dal Maso (*Colomiers*), Franck Tournaire (*Toulouse*), Jean Daude (*Bourgoin-Jallieu*), Olivier Brouzet (*Bordeaux Bègles*), Sebastien Chabal (*Bourgoin-Jallieu*), Olivier Magne (*Montferrand*), Fabien Pelous* (*Toulouse*) ... Substitutes: Thomas Lievremont (*Perpignan*) for Daude (51), Arnaud Costes (*Montferrand*) for Chabal (53), Raphaël Ibañez (*Perpignan*) for dal Maso (55), Pieter de Villiers (*Stade Français*) for Tournaire (55), Jean-Baptiste Ellisalde (*La Rochelle*) for Pelous (80)

REFEREE Steve Lander (*England*)

SCORING Castaignède, try (0–5); Merceron, con (0–7); Logan, pen (3–7); Melrceron, pen (3–10); Paterson, pen (6–10) (half-time) Nicol, try (11–10); Paterson, con (13–10); Merceron, pen (13–13); Magne, try (13–18); Paterson, pen (16–18); Magne, try (16–23); Merceron, con (16–25); Merceron, pen (16–28)

A brilliant display by Olivier Magne illuminated an otherwise mediocre match. The big French flanker showed his exceptional ball skills and athleticism, and scored two great support tries that clinched the game. Scotland gave an improved performance and the outcome was in doubt until the closing stages, but once again they lost a game that they could have won. Shortly before half-time France lost Ntamack and Daude to the sin-bin. Andy Nicol scored a converted try straight after the restart, but Scotland failed to press their advantage. On the 69th minute Laussucq deftly chipped behind the defence and Ntamack gathered a lucky bounce before passing to Magne who cantered over the line. Paterson kicked a penalty to reduce the margin to two points, but then Ntamack collected a poor clearance and burst through to give Magne his second try. Merceron converted and kicked a late penalty to seal the game. For Scotland, John Leslie marshalled the midfield well, Andy Nicol was steady at scrum-half and kicked astutely, and Chris Paterson, making his first Championship start, showed considerable maturity and some fine positional play and line-kicking.

485 SIX NATIONS CHAMPIONSHIP 2000 WALES

Saturday 18 March 2000 · Millennium Stadium, Cardiff · Lost 18–26

SCOTLAND Chris Paterson (*Edinburgh Rvrs*); Craig Moir (*Northampton Sts*), Gregor Townsend (*Brive*), John Leslie* (*Newcastle F*), Glenn Metcalfe (*Glasgow Cal*), Duncan Hodge (*Edinburgh Rvrs*), Andy Nicol (*Glasgow Cal*); Tom Smith (*Brive*), Steve Brotherstone (*Brive*), Mattie Stewart (*Northampton Sts*), Scott Murray (*Saracens*), Stuart Grimes (*Newcastle F*), Martin Leslie (*Edinburgh Rvrs*), Budge Pountney (*Northampton Sts*), Stuart Reid (*Narbonne*) ... Substitutes: Gordon Bulloch (*Glasgow Cal*) for Brotherstone (50), David Hilton (*Glasgow Cal*) for Stewart (83)

WALES Matt Cardey (*Llanelli*); Gareth Thomas (*Cardiff*), Allan Bateman (*Northampton Sts*), Mark Taylor (*Swansea*), Shane Williams (*Neath*); Stephen Jones (*Llanelli*), Rupert Moon (*Llanelli*); Peter Rogers (*Newport*), Garin Jenkins (*Swansea*), David Young* (*Cardiff*), Ian Gough (*Pontypridd*), Andy Moore (*Swansea*), Nathan Budgett (*Ebbw Vale*), Colin Charvis (*Swansea*), Geraint Lewis (*Pontypridd*)

REFEREE David McHugh (*Ireland*)

SCORING Jones, pen (0–3); Hodge, pen (3–3); Williams, try (3–8); Jones, con (3–10); Jones, pen (3–13) (half-time) M Leslie, try (8–13); Hodge, con (10–13); Jones, pen (10–16); Hodge, pen (13–16); Jones, pen (13–19); Williams, try (13–24); Jones, con (13–26); Townsend, try (18–26)

Scotland made their first appearance at the Millennium Stadium which had been built to host the 1999 World Cup. The visitors had the bulk of territory and possession, especially in the lineout, but failed to capitalise and Wales grew in confidence as the game went on. After an undistinguished opening, the match burst into life when Paterson was caught out of position and Williams hacked on to touch down. Stephen Jones converted and kicked a penalty at the interval. After the restart, Martin Leslie was inexplicably denied a try after a drive from a lineout, but a few minutes later he was barrelled over the line. Wales finished strongly and a second try by Williams sealed their win. Scotland left their best rugby until it was too late and Townsend scored a consolation try in injury-time.

Murrayfield · Sunday 2 April 2000 · Won 19–13

SCOTLAND Chris Paterson (*Edinburgh Rvrs*); †Craig Moir (*Northampton Sts*), Gregor Townsend (*Brive*), James McLaren (*Bourgoin-Jallieu*), Glenn Metcalfe (*Glasgow Cal*); Duncan Hodge (*Edinburgh Rvrs*), Andy Nicol* (*Glasgow Cal*); Tom Smith (*Brive*), Steve Brotherstone (*Brive*), Mattie Stewart (*Northampton Sts*), Scott Murray (*Saracens*), †Richard Metcalfe (*Northampton Sts*), †Jason White (*Glasgow Cal*), Budge Pountney (*Northampton Sts*), Martin Leslie (*Edinburgh Rvrs*) ... Substitutes: Stuart Reid (*Narbonne*) for Leslie (39-40), Gordon McIllwham (*Glasgow Cal*) for Stewart (69)

ENGLAND Matt Perry (*Bath*); Austin Healey (*Leicester Tgrs*), Mike Tindall (*Bath*), Mike Catt (*Bath*), Ben Cohen (*Northampton Sts*); Jonny Wilkinson (*Newcastle F*), Matt Dawson* (*Northampton Sts*); Jason Leonard (*Harlequins*), Phil Greening (*London Wasps*), Phil Vickery (*Gloucester*), Garath Archer (*Bristol*), Simon Shaw (*London Wasps*), Richard Hill (*Saracens*), Neil Back (*Leicester Tgrs*), Lawrence Dallaglio (*London Wasps*) ... Substitutes: Iain Balshaw (*Bath*) for Cohen (58), Martin Corry (*Leicester Tgrs*) for Archer (65), Joe Worsley (*Leicester Tgrs*) for Hill (80)

REFEREE Clayton Thomas (*Wales*)

SCORING Hodge, pen (3–0); Dallaglio, try (3–5); Wilkinson, con (3–7); Wilkinson, pen (3–10); Hodge, pen (6–10); Hodge, pen (9–10) (half-time) Hodge, pen (12–10); Hodge, try (17–10); Hodge, con (19–10); Wilkinson, pen (19–13)

Lock Richard Metcalfe, who stood at seven foot tall, and flanker Jason White won their first caps. Against expectations, Scotland won their first victory over England for ten years with a magnificent team effort that combined skill, intelligence and raw courage. The Scots made an encouraging start and after 20 minutes Hodge kicked a

Duncan Hodge scores the winning try against England at a rain soaked Murrayfield in 2000.
Scotsman Publications Ltd

penalty. The lead was short-lived however and three minutes later Dallaglio picked-up from a scrum near the Scottish line, darted round the blind and scored a try that looked ominously simple. Wilkinson converted and added a penalty. It seemed that the English juggernaut was about to crank into gear but the Scots stuck manfully to their task and Hodge kicked two penalties. The conditions deteriorated during the break and the second-half was played in torrential rain with deep pools of water lying across the pitch. The Scots adapted much better, showing admirable ball retention and sure-footedness. Their confidence grew as the match went on and England looked increasingly uncomfortable and indecisive. On the hour mark Hodge kicked his fourth penalty, but the decisive moment did not come until the 74th minute. Several waves of Scottish attacks were repulsed from the English line until the ball squirted out of the side of a ruck. It seemed that Scotland's chance had gone but Gordon McIlwham reacted quickly and Hodge grabbed the ball and dived over to score. Hodge converted to bring his personal tally to 19 points. In a nervous conclusion, which included an agonisingly long injury time, Wilkinson kicked a penalty but the Scots managed to hold out. Amongst many heroic performances, Andy Nicol gave an inspirational lead and showed great steadiness under pressure. It was fitting that Nicol, with blood seeping from a chin wound and visibly shaking from cold, should have the honour of lifting the Calcutta Cup in front of an ecstatic stadium.

 XV   **2000**   **BARBARIANS**

Murrayfield · Wednesday 31 May 2000 · Lost 42–45

SCOTLAND XV Chris Paterson (*Edinburgh Rvrs*); Glenn Metcalfe (*Glasgow Cal*), Graham Shiel* (*Edinburgh Rvrs*), James McLaren (*Bourgoin-Jallieu*), Alan Bulloch (*Glasgow Cal*); Duncan Hodge (*Edinburgh Rvrs*), Graeme Beveridge (*Glasgow Cal*); Allan Jacobsen (*Edinburgh Rvrs*), Gordon Bulloch (*Glasgow Cal*), Gordon McIlwham (*Glasgow Cal*), Richard Metcalfe (*Northampton Sts*), Iain Fullerton (*Edinburgh Rvrs*), Jason White (*Glasgow Cal*), Gordon Simpson (*Glasgow Cal*), Ross Beattie (*Newcastle F*) ... Substitutes: Derrick Lee (*Edinburgh Rvrs*) for McLaren (27), Steve Scott (*Edinburgh Rvrs*) for Bulloch (57), Barry Stewart (*Edinburgh Rvrs*) for McIlwham (57), Graeme Burns (*Edinburgh Rvrs*) for Beveridge (57), Stewart Campbell (*Glasgow Cal*) for R Metcalfe (65), Jon Petrie (*Glasgow Cal*) for Beattie, Roland Reid (*Glasgow Cal*) for White (74)

BARBARIANS Matt Perry (*England*); Joeli Vidiri (*New Zealand*), Viliame Satala (*Fiji*), Scott Gibbs (*Wales*), Dan Luger (*England*); Neil Jenkins (*Wales*), Rob Howley (*Wales*); Jason Leonard (*England*), Richard Cockerill (*England*), Adrian Garvey (*South Africa*), Robin Brooke (*New Zealand*), John Langford (*Australia*), Lawrence Dallaglio (*England*), Ruben Kruger (*South Africa*), Zinzan Brooke* (*New Zealand*) ... Substitutes: Os du Randt (*South Africa*) for Leonard (47), Jon Preston (*New Zealand*) for Howley (55), Waisale Serevi (*Fiji*) for Jenkins (55), Barry Williams (*Wales*) for Cockerill (55), Walter Little (*New Zealand*) for Luger (66), Dan Lyle (*USA*) for Z Brooke (68), Howley for Preston (75)

REFEREE Didier Mené (*France*) · **ATTENDANCE** 28,375

SCORING Luger, try (0–5); Hodge, pen (3–5); Perry, try (3–10); Jenkins, con (3–12); R Metcalfe, try (8–12); Hodge, con (10–12); Vidiri, try (10–17); Jenkins, con (10–19); Hodge, pen (13–19); Luger, try (13–24); Jenkins, con (13–26); Vidiri, try (13–31); Jenkins, con (13–33); Hodge, pen (16–33) (half-time) G Bulloch, try (21–33); Hodge, con (23–33); Langford, try (23–38); Jenkins, con (23–40); Shiel, try (28–40); Hodge, con (30–40); Hodge, try (35–40); Hodge, con (37–40); Vidiri, try (37–45); Shiel, try (42–45)

Played to celebrate the 75th anniversary of Murrayfield and as preparation for the tour of New Zealand, this exciting match lived up to all of the best traditions of Barbarians rugby. The visitors fielded a strong and skilful side drawing top quality players from eight countries, including the legendary Welsh half-backs Neil Jenkins and Rob Howley, and All Blacks Robin and Zinzan Brooke. Showing their intentions straightaway, the Barbarians attacked from the kick-off; New Zealand wing Joeli Vidri broke away from deep inside his own 22 and beat the defence before feeding Luger for a classic try. The Barbarians scored seven tries, including a hat-trick for Vidiri, and they never relinquished their lead. Scotland entered into the spirit of the game and refused to be intimidated. The home side scored five tries and came close to snatching a win with a heroic late comeback. The three uncapped players, Allan Jacobsen, Iain Fullerton and Ross Beattie, all showed up well.

487 TOUR OF NEW ZEALAND 2000   NEW ZEALAND

Carisbrook, Dunedin · Saturday 24 June 2000 · Lost 20–69

SCOTLAND Chris Paterson (*Edinburgh Rvrs*); Craig Moir (*Northampton Sts*), Gregor Townsend (*Brive*), James McLaren (*Bourgoin-Jaillieu*), Shaun Longstaff (*Glasgow Cal*); Duncan Hodge (*Edinburgh Rvrs*), Andy Nicol* (*Glasgow Cal*); Tom Smith (*Brive*), Gordon Bulloch (*Glasgow Cal*), Barry Stewart (*Edinburgh Rvrs*), Scott Murray (*Saracens*), Richard Metcalfe (*Northampton Sts*), Jason White (*Glasgow Wrs*), Martin Leslie (*Edinburgh Rvrs*), †Ross Beattie (*Newcastle F*) ... Substitutes: †Iain Fullerton (*Edinburgh Rvrs*) for Murray (35), Graham Shiel (*Edinburgh Rvrs*) for Townsend (56), Craig Joiner (*Leicester Tgrs*) for McLaren (62), Gordon Simpson (*Glasgow Wrs*) for Leslie (62), Mattie Stewart (*Northampton Sts*) for B Stewart (70)

NEW ZEALAND Christian Cullen (*Wellington*); Tana Umaga (*Wellington*), Alama Ieremia (*Wellington*), Pita Alatini (*Otago*), Jonah Lomu (*Wellington*); Andrew Mehrtens (*Canterbury*), Byron Kelleher (*Otago*); Carl Hoeft (*Otago*), Anton Oliver (*Otago*), Greg Somerville (*Canterbury*), Todd Blackadder* (*Canterbury*), Norm Maxwell (*Canterbury*), Taine Randell (*Otago*), Scott Robertson (*Canterbury*), Ron Cribb (*North Harbour*) ... Substitutes: Leon MacDonald (*Canterbury*) for Cullen (51), Josh Kronfield (*Otago*) for Randell (51), Craig Dowd (*Auckland*) for Somerville (60), Troy Flavell (*North Harbour*) for Maxwell (65), Mark Hammett (*Canterbury*) for Oliver (65)

REFEREE SM Young (*Australia*) · **ATTENDANCE** 26,128

SCORING Oliver, try (0–5); Mehrtens, con (0–7); Hodge, pen (3–7); Hodge, pen (6–7); Cribb, try (6–12); Mehrtens, con (6–14); Lomu, try (6–19); Umaga, try (6–24); Mehrtens, con (6–26) (half-time) Oliver, try (6–31); Mehrtens, con (6–33); Cullen, try (6–38); Mehrtens, con (6–40); Lomu, try (6–45); Alatini, try (6–50); Mehrtens, con (6–52); Lomu, try (6–57); Mehrtens, con (6–59); Umaga, try (6–64); Metcalfe, try (11–64); Hodge, con (13–64); Flavell, try (13–69); Simpson, try (18–69); Hodge, con (20–69)

In June 2000, Scotland made a seven match tour of New Zealand, including two tests. Carisbrook in Dunedin lived up to its reputation as the 'House of Pain' as Scotland were torn apart by a rampant New Zealand side that scored 11 tries, including a hat-trick by the mighty Jonah Lomu and two by Tana Umaga who had an outstanding match. Scotland started well and had no shortage of ambition, but they could not match the greater speed of the New Zealanders who were miles better in all aspects. The Scots gave away several soft scores and in truth the All Blacks were in a different class, effortlessly brushing aside the best that Scottish rugby had to offer. Scotland salvaged some pride with a brave late rally and Metcalfe and Simpson scored consolation tries, both diving over from short-range.

Eden Park, Auckland · Saturday 1 July 2000 · Lost 14–48

SCOTLAND Chris Paterson (*Edinburgh Rvrs*); Cameron Murray (*Edinburgh Rvrs*), Gregor Townsend (*Brive*), Graham Shiel (*Edinburgh Rvrs*), Craig Joiner (*Leicester Tgrs*); Duncan Hodge (*Edinburgh Rvrs*), Andy Nicol* (*Glasgow Cal*); Tom Smith (*Brive*), Gordon Bulloch (*Glasgow Wrs*), Barry Stewart (*Edinburgh Rvrs*), Iain Fullerton (*Edinburgh Rvrs*), Richard Metcalfe (*Northampton Sts*), Jason White (*Glasgow Cal*), Martin Leslie (*Edinburgh Rvrs*), †Jon Petrie (*Glasgow Cal*) ... Substitutes: Gordon McIlwham (*Glasgow Cal*) for Stewart (53), †Nathan Hines (*Edinburgh Rvrs*) for Metcalfe (64), Ross Beattie (*Newcastle F*) for Petrie (67), †Graeme Beveridge (*Glasgow Wrs*) for Nicol (73), †Steve Scott (*Edinburgh Rvrs*) for Bulloch (74)

NEW ZEALAND Christian Cullen (*Wellington*); Tana Umaga (*Wellington*), Mark Robinson (*Canterbury*), Alama Ieremia (*Wellington*), Jonah Lomu (*Wellington*); Andrew Mehrtens (*Canterbury*), Justin Marshall (*Canterbury*); Carl Hoeft (*Otago*), Anton Oliver (*Otago*), Kees Meeuws (*Otago*), Todd Blackadder* (*Canterbury*), Norm Maxwell (*Canterbury*), Reuben Thorne (*Canterbury*), Josh Kronfield (*Otago*), Ron Cribb (*North Harbour*) ... Substitutes: Mark Hammett (*Canterbury*) for Oliver (53-60 and 74), Scott Robertson (*Canterbury*) for Kronfield (56), Craig Dowd (*Auckland*) for Hoeft (56), Tony Brown (*Otago*) for Mehrtens (62), Leon MacDonald (*Canterbury*) for Umaga (69), Taine Randell (*Otago*) for Maxwell (71)

REFEREE Wayne Erickson (*Australia*)

SCORING Kronfield, try (0–5); Cribb, try (0–10); Mehrtens, con (0–12); Umaga, try (0–17); Mehrtens, con (0–19); Umaga, try (0–24) (half-time) Paterson, try (5–24); Hodge, con (7–24); Ieremia, try (7–29); Mehrtens, con (7–31); Murray, try (12–31); Hodge, con (14–31); Robinson, try (14–36); Marshall, try (14–41); Brown, con (14–43); Cullen, try (14–48)

After the horror show at Carisbrook, the Scots made five changes including a first cap for No 8 Jon Petrie. Played in torrential rain, New Zealand were comfortable winners, but Scotland were more competitive than the previous weekend and restored some of their self-respect. The Scottish defence was much tighter, and the forwards won plenty of possession and kept the ball well in contact. However, the backs lacked real penetration and at times their opponents looked almost unstoppable with their brilliant handling and counter-attacking skills. Scotland scored their first try soon after the interval when Paterson caught a chip ahead by Mehrtens and raced away to the line unopposed. Soon afterwards Townsend kicked past the defence and Cameron Murray, who was in great form, hacked the ball on and touched down.

Murrayfield · Saturday 4 November 2000 · Won 53–6

SCOTLAND Chris Paterson (*Edinburgh Rvrs*); Cameron Murray (*Edinburgh Rvrs*),
†Alan Bulloch (*Glasgow Cal*), John Leslie (*Newcastle F*), †Jon Steel (*Glasgow Cal*);
Gregor Townsend (*Castres*), Bryan Redpath (*Sale Sharks*); Tom Smith (*Brive*), Steve Brotherstone
(*Northampton Sts*), George Graham (*Newcastle F*), Scott Murray (*Saracens*), Stuart Grimes
(*Newcastle F*), Jon Petrie (*Glasgow Cal*), Budge Pountney* (*Northampton Sts*), †Simon Taylor
(*Edinburgh Rvrs*) ... Substitutes: Steve Scott (*Edinburgh Rvrs*) for Brotherstone (37–40 and 64),
Gordon McIlwham (*Glasgow Cal*) for Graham (57), Jason White (*Glasgow Cal*) for Petrie (64),
Craig Joiner (*Edinburgh Rvrs*) for C Murray (68), Richard Metcalfe (*Edinburgh Rvrs*) for
S Murray (71), Graeme Beveridge (*Glasgow Cal*) for Redpath (79), Duncan Hodge
(*Edinburgh Rvrs*) for Townsend (79)

USA Kurt Shuman (*New York AC*); Jovesa Naivalu (*San Mateo*), Phillip Eloff (*Chicago Lions*),
Juan Grobler (*Denver Barbarians*), Malakai Delai (*OMBAC*); Grant Wells (*Golden Gate*),
Kevin Dalzell (*Clermont Ferrand*); Joe Clayton (*Old Blues*), Kirk Khasigian (*Sydney U*), Paul Still
(*Golden Gate*), Luke Gross (*Roma*), Philippe Farner (*Roma*), Dave Hodges* (*OMBAC*),
Oloseti Fifita (*Hayward Griffins*), Dan Lyle (*Bath Rugby*)

REFEREE Pablo Deluca (*Argentina*) · **ATTENDANCE** 35,638

SCORING Townsend, pen (3–0); Townsend, pen (6–0); Townsend, pen (9–0); Townsend, pen
(12–0); Wells, pen (12–3); Townsend, pen (15–3) (half-time) Pountney, try (20–3); Leslie, try
(25–3); Townsend, con (27–3); Paterson, try (32–3); Townsend, con (34–3); Wells, pen (34–6);
Townsend, try (39–6); Townsend, con (41–6); Leslie, try (46–6); Townsend, con (48–6);
Townsend, try (53–6)

Scotland awarded caps against the United States for the first time. Played under floodlights, the early evening kick-off was delayed by 15 minutes because of crowd
congestion. Scotland were always in control and gradually wore down their burly
opponents although it was not until the 50th minute that they scored their first try.
John Leslie intercepted a pass on the half-way, and Cameron Murray and Redpath
carried on for Pountney to touch down. Scotland maintained a fast pace and scored
five more tries, Chris Paterson finishing off the best after a great sweeping movement.
This was a mature and professional display by Scotland who stuck to their task and
never allowed frustration to get the better of them. The largely amateur Americans
had plenty of defiance and defended aggressively, but offered little in attack. Subsequently, they lost to a Scotland Development xv (49–17) at Aberdeen before playing
three games in Wales.

Murrayfield · Saturday 11 November 2000 · Lost 9–30

SCOTLAND Chris Paterson (*Edinburgh Rvrs*); Cameron Murray (*Edinburgh Rvrs*), Alan Bulloch
(*Glasgow Cal*), John Leslie (*Newcastle F*), Jon Steel (*Glasgow Cal*); Gregor Townsend (*Castres*),
Bryan Redpath (*Sale Sharks*); Tom Smith (*Brive*), Steve Brotherstone (*Northampton Sts*),
George Graham (*Newcastle F*), Scott Murray (*Saracens*), Stuart Grimes (*Newcastle F*), Jon Petrie
(*Glasgow Cal*), Budge Pountney* (*Northampton Sts*), Simon Taylor (*Edinburgh Rvrs*) ...
Substitutes: Gordon Bulloch (*Glasgow Cal*) for Brotherstone (51), Gordon McIlwham

(*Glasgow Cal*) for Graham (53), Richard Metcalfe (*Edinburgh Rvrs*) for Grimes (64), Jason White (*Glasgow Cal*) for Petrie (64), Graham for White (79)

AUSTRALIA Chris Latham (*Queensland*); Matt Burke (*NSW*), Daniel Herbert (*Queensland*), Stirling Mortlock (*ACT*), Joe Roff (*ACT*); Rod Kafer (*ACT*), Sam Cordingley (*Queensland*); Bill Young (*ACT*), Michael Foley (*Queensland*), Fletcher Dyson (*Queensland*), David Giffin (*ACT*), John Eales* (*Queensland*), Matt Cockbain (*Queensland*), George Smith (*ACT*), Toutai Kefu (*Queensland*) ... Substitutes: Jeremy Paul (*ACT*) for Foley (40), Jim Williams (*ACT*) for Cockbain (40), Glenn Panoho (*Queensland*) for Dyson (47), Elton Flatley (*Queensland*) for Kafer (55), Mark Connors (*Queensland*) for Kefu (68), Nathan Grey (*NSW*) for Mortlock (73), Chris Whitaker (*NSW*) for Cordingley (76)

REFEREE Chris White (*England*) · ATTENDANCE 64,103

SCORING Burke, pen (0–3); Townsend, pen (3–3); Townsend, pen (6–3); Burke, pen (6–6); Burke, pen (6–9); Townsend, pen (9–9) (half-time) Latham, try (9–14); Burke, con (9–16); Roff, try (9–21); Burke, con (9–23); Burke, try (9–28); Burke, con (9–30)

Scotland were optimistic that they could seriously challenge an Australian side that was in a state of transition. They did well enough for the first hour or so, but eventually the Wallabies scored three tries and cruised home. The visitors had more precision and pace, and their support play was exemplary. Scotland never stopped trying, but they lacked real penetration and never looked like scoring a try. The sides were level at the interval, but the Australians found an extra gear in the second period and simply eased away, scoring three tries. For Scotland, Scott Murray was disruptive in the lineouts, Simon Taylor made a lot of ground and Gregor Townsend played heroically. Otherwise, this was yet another disappointing encounter against a giant from the Southern Hemisphere.

491 AUTUMN TEST 2000 SAMOA

Murrayfield · Saturday 18 November 2000 · Won 31–8

SCOTLAND Chris Paterson (*Edinburgh Rvrs*); Cameron Murray (*Edinburgh Rvrs*), Alan Bulloch (*Glasgow Cal*), John Leslie (*Newcastle F*), Kenny Logan (*London Wasps*); Gregor Townsend (*Castres*), Bryan Redpath (*Sale Sharks*); Tom Smith (*Brive*), Steve Brotherstone (*Northampton Sts*), George Graham (*Newcastle Falcons*), Scott Murray (*Saracens*), Richard Metcalfe (*Edinburgh Rvrs*), Jason White (*Glasgow Cal*), Budge Pountney* (*Northampton Sts*), Jon Petrie (*Glasgow Cal*) ... Substitutes: Ross Beattie (*Newcastle F*) for White (23-25 and 75), Gordon McIlwham (*Glasgow Cal*) for Graham (51), Stuart Grimes (*Newcastle F*) for Metcalfe (56), Gordon Bulloch (*Glasgow Cal*) for Brotherstone (68), Graeme Beveridge (*Glasgow Cal*) for Redpath (75), Duncan Hodge (*Edinburgh Rvrs*) for Alan Bulloch (75)

SAMOA Happy Valley Patu (*Vaiala*); Mussolini Schuster (*Otahuhu*), Faapulou So'olefai (*Taranaki*), Fereti Tuilagi (*Leicester Tgrs*), Filipo Toala (*La Rochelle*); Quintan Sanft (*Kirkcaldy*), Steve So'oialo (*Western Suburbs*); Dan Tafeamali'i (*Vaiala*), Onehunga Matauiau* (*Hawkes Bay*), Polo Asi (*Moataa*), Setefano Tone (*Manurewa*), Sika Poching (*Otahuhu*), Alfie Vaeluaga (*Otahuhu*), Luke Mealamu (*Otahuhu*), Junior Maligi (*Marist St Joseph's*) ... Substitutes: Pula Misa (*Apia*) for Schuster (27), Aleki Toleafoa (*Parma*) for Sanft (55), Mahonri Schwalger (*Taradale*) for Tafaemali'i (63), Joe Mamea (*Apia*) for Maligi (66), Tuaifuaina Veiru (*West Harbour*) for Vaeluaga (75), Anthony Mika (*Apia*) for Mealamu (78)

REFEREE Ian Hyde-Lay (*Canada*) · ATTENDANCE 43,447

Sanft, pen (0–3); Townsend, pen (3–3); Petrie, try (8–3); Patu, try (8–8);
Townsend, pen (11–8); Townsend, pen (14–8) (half-time) Logan, try (19–8); Smith, try (24–8);
A Bulloch, try (29–8); Townsend, con (31–8)

The Samoans, who included Kirkcaldy's Quintan Sanft at stand-off, were on a short
tour of Wales and Scotland, and had already lost to Wales (50–6) and Scotland A
(37–24) at Perth. Playing in constant drizzle, Scotland were unconvincing in the first
half which was marred by handling errors and a lack of cohesion. The Scots
dominated possession and after some 15 minutes John Leslie made a superb dummy
to create a try for Petrie. In the second-half, Scotland played a much tighter game
based on forward control and eventually their greater experience and efficiency was
decisive. The crucial score came on the 55th minute when Kenny Logan was driven
over at the corner. Thirteen minutes later the Scots won a lineout near the Samoan
line and from the ensuing surge Tom Smith was credited with the try. Soon afterwards
a rare Samoan attack broke down inside the Scottish 22, Cameron Murray made a
kick-and-chase that exposed the defence and Alan Bulloch collected the ball for an
easy run-in.

---

492   SIX NATIONS CHAMPIONSHIP 2001   FRANCE

Stade de France, Paris · Sunday 4 February 2001 · Lost 6–16

SCOTLAND Chris Paterson (*Edinburgh Rvrs*); Cameron Murray (*Edinburgh Rvrs*),
James McLaren (*Glasgow Cal*), John Leslie (*Newcastle F*), Kenny Logan (*London Wasps*);
Gregor Townsend (*Castres*), Andy Nicol* (*Glasgow Cal*); Tom Smith (*Brive*), Gordon Bulloch
(*Glasgow Cal*), Mattie Stewart (*Northampton Sts*), Scott Murray (*Saracens*), Richard Metcalfe
(*Edinburgh Rvrs*), Martin Leslie (*Edinburgh Rvrs*), Budge Pountney (*Northampton Sts*), Jon Petrie
(*Northampton Sts*) ... Substitutes: Duncan Hodge (*Edinburgh Rvrs*) for Townsend (4),
Stuart Grimes (*Newcastle F*) for Metcalfe (22), Alan Bulloch (*Glasgow Cal*) for J Leslie (27–33)
and for McLaren (68), Gordon McIlwham (*Glasgow Cal*) for Stewart (53), Robbie Russell
(*Saracens*) for G Bulloch (66), Bryan Redpath (*Sale Sharks*) for Nicol (67), Jason White
(*Glasgow Cal*) for Petrie (74)

FRANCE Xavier Garbajosa (*Toulouse*); Philippe Bernat-Salles (*Biarritz*), Richard Dourthe
(*Béziers*), Franck Comba (*Stade Français*), David Bory (*Montferrand*); Christophe Lamaison
(*Agen*), Fabien Galthié (*Colomiers*); Sylvain Marconnet (*Stade Français*), Raphaël Ibañez (*Castres*),
Pieter de Villiers (*Stade Français*), David Auradou (*Stade Français*), Fabien Pelous* (*Toulouse*),
Christophe Moni (*Stade Français*), Olivier Magne (*Montferrand*), Christophe Juillet (*Stade
Français*) ... Substitutes: Christain Califano (*Toulouse*) for Marconnet (50), Abdelatif Benazzi
(*Agen*) for Auradou (50), Serge Betsen (*Biarritz*) for Moni (50), Gérald Merceron (*Montferrand*)
for Dourthe (71)

REFEREE Stuart Dickinson (*Australia*)

SCORING Logan, pen (3–0); Lamaison, pen (3–3); Logan, pen (6–3); Lamaison, pen (6–6)
(half-time) Bernat-Salles, try (6–11); Lamaison, con (6–13); Lamaison, pen (6–16)

Kenny Logan won his 50th cap. Scotland created enough chances to repeat their
famous Parisian wins of the 1990s, but they could not match the French flair in attack
and the game slipped away from them. The Scots unluckily lost their main playmaker
Gregor Townsend in the opening minutes with a knee injury. Undeterred they made

a promising start and dominated early proceedings, but France grew stronger as the match went on. On the 34th minute Bernat-Salles was denied a try by video evidence and shortly afterwards Martin Leslie was sent to the sin-bin for making a high tackle. On the resumption, with the Scots a man down, France launched a series of attacks and Comba made space for Bernat-Salles who easily rounded Logan before stepping past two defenders for the only try of the match. Scotland defended well for the rest of the game and France made several errors so that the visitors were never out of contention. Towards the finish Paterson made an electrifying run that might have brought a try if Petrie had been able to hold his pass. Lamaison sealed the game for France with a late penalty. Another frustrating defeat for Scotland but a good team performance in which Andy Nicol had two sniping runs, John Leslie showed a welcome return to form and Chris Paterson made two great try-saving tackles.

493　　SIX NATIONS CHAMPIONSHIP 2001　　　　　WALES

Murrayfield · Saturday 17 February 2001 · Drawn 28–28

SCOTLAND Chris Paterson (*Edinburgh Rvrs*); Cameron Murray (*Edinburgh Rvrs*), James McLaren (*Glasgow Cal*), John Leslie (*Northampton Sts*), Kenny Logan (*London Wasps*); Duncan Hodge (*Edinburgh Rvrs*), Andy Nicol* (*Glasgow Cal*); Tom Smith (*Brive*), Gordon Bulloch (*Glasgow Cal*), Mattie Stewart (*Northampton Sts*), Scott Murray (*Saracens*), Richard Metcalfe (*Edinburgh Rvrs*), Martin Leslie (*Edinburgh Rvrs*), Budge Pountney (*Northampton Sts*), Jon Petrie (*Glasgow Cal*) … Substitutes: Gordon McIlwham (*Glasgow Cal*) for Stewart (49), Stuart Grimes (*Newcastle F*) for Metcalfe (66), James Craig (*Glasgow Cal*) for C Murray (68)

WALES Rhys Williams (*Cardiff*); Mark Jones (*Llanelli*), Mark Taylor (*Swansea*), Scott Gibbs (*Swansea*), Dafydd James (*Llanelli*); Neil Jenkins (*Cardiff*), Robert Howley (*Cardiff*); Darren Morris (*Swansea*), Robin McBryde (*Llanelli*), David Young* (*Cardiff*), Ian Gough (*Newport*), Andrew Moore (*Swansea*), Colin Charvis (*Swansea*), Martyn Williams (*Cardiff*), Scott Quinnell (*Llanelli*) … Substitutes: Rupert Moon (*Llanelli*) for Howley (62), Craig Quinnell (*Cardiff*) for Gough (62), Spencer John (*Cardiff*) for Young (80)

REFEREE Steve Lander (*England*)

SCORING Jenkins, drop (0–3); Jenkins, pen (0–6); Logan, pen (3–6); Jenkins, drop (3–9); Jenkins, pen (3–12); Jenkins, drop (3–15); Jenkins, pen (3–18); Logan, pen (6–18) (half-time) Taylor, try (6–23); Jenkins, con (6–25); Paterson, try (11–25); Logan, con (13–25); Logan, pen (16–25); Jenkins, pen (16–28); McLaren, try (21–28); Smith, try (26–28); Hodge, con (28–28)

In a frenetic encounter, Scotland showed great strength of character to snatch a draw after being 19 points down. In the second-half, they played some of their best rugby since their famous win in Paris in 1999 and they probably would have won if Kenny Logan, a controversial choice as kicker, had not missed four shots at goal, including a routine conversion of McLaren's try. By contrast Welsh kicking-machine Neil Jenkins scored a personal tally of 23 points from his boot. Scotland made too many errors in the first-half and found themselves 18–6 down at the break. Straight after the restart Taylor intercepted a careless pass and raced away for a try and Jenkins converted. Scotland responded immediately and Paterson made a long run down the touchline before beating the defence with an outrageous sidestep for a great solo try. Logan and

Jenkins exchanged penalties to set-up a tumultuous conclusion. In a training ground move, Hodge released McLaren on an unstoppable charge to the line. With a minute remaining Hodge gave a quick pass to Smith who beat two defenders with a dummy before sprinting over. Hodge kicked a great pressure goal to level the scores but his last-gasp drop goal attempt was charged down and the honours were shared, the first draw between the countries since 1922.

---

494   SIX NATIONS CHAMPIONSHIP 2001   ENGLAND

Twickenham · Saturday 3 March 2001 · Lost 3–43

SCOTLAND Chris Paterson (*Edinburgh Rvrs*); Cameron Murray (*Edinburgh Rvrs*), Alan Bulloch (*Glasgow Cal*), John Leslie (*Northampton Sts*), Kenny Logan (*London Wasps*); Duncan Hodge (*Edinburgh Rvrs*), Andy Nicol* (*Glasgow Cal*); Tom Smith (*Brive*), Gordon Bulloch (*Glasgow Cal*), Mattie Stewart (*Northampton Sts*), Scott Murray (*Saracens*), Richard Metcalfe (*Edinburgh Rvrs*), Martin Leslie (*Edinburgh Rvrs*), Budge Pountney (*Northampton Sts*), Simon Taylor (*Edinburgh Rvrs*) ... Substitutes: Gordon McIlwham (*Glasgow Cal*) for Stewart (45), Stuart Grimes (*Newcastle F*) for Metcalfe (46), Bryan Redpath (*Sale Sharks*) for Nicol (60), James Craig (*Glasgow Cal*) for C Murray (70), James McLaren (*Glasgow Cal*) for A Bulloch (75)

ENGLAND Iain Balshaw (*Bath*); Austin Healey (*Leicester Tgrs*), Will Greenwood (*Harlequins*), Mike Catt (*Bath*), Ben Cohen (*Northampton Sts*); Jonny Wilkinson (*Newcastle F*), Matt Dawson (*Northampton Sts*); Jason Leonard (*Harlequins*), Dorian West (*Leicester Tgrs*), Phil Vickery (*Gloucester*), Martin Johnson* (*Leicester Tgrs*), Danny Grewcock (*Saracens*), Richard Hill (*Saracens*), Neil Back (*Leicester Tgrs*), Lawrence Dallaglio (*London Wasps*) ... Substitutes: Mark Regan (*Bath*) for West (40), Jason Robinson (*Sale Sharks*) for Catt (62), Joe Worsley (*London Wasps*) for Back (68), Kyran Bracken (*Saracens*) for Dawson (73)

REFEREE Robert Davies (*Wales*)

SCORING Dallaglio, try (0–5); Wilkinson, pen (0–8); Hodge, pen (3–8); Hill, try (3–13); Wilkinson, con (3–15); Dallaglio, try (3–20); Wilkinson, con (3–22) (half-time) Balshaw, try (3–27); Wilkinson, con (3–29); Balshaw, try (3–34); Wilkinson, con (3–36); Greenwood, try (3–41); Wilkinson, con (3–43)

This was not a bad performance by Scotland, but they were no match for a skilful English side that was better in every aspect. The Scots defended tirelessly and never disintegrated, but England played some sublime 15-man rugby and scored six lovely tries. The English forwards were on top throughout and the backs were full of dangerous running. The home side led 22–3 at the interval, including a brace of tries by No 8 Dallaglio who was at his rampaging best. Early in the second half, Greenwood gave a neat behind-the-back pass to Balshaw who swept through the defence to score. Balshaw added his second try when he took a simple cross-field kick from Catt that caught the defence napping. Towards the finish Robinson, the former rugby league star, showed his unique footwork when he broke from his own half to create an easy run-in for Greenwood.

Murrayfield · Saturday 17 March 2001 · Won 23–19

SCOTLAND Chris Paterson (*Edinburgh Rvrs*); James Craig (*Glasgow Cal*), Gregor Townsend (*Castres*), John Leslie (*Northampton Sts*), Kenny Logan (*London Wasps*); Duncan Hodge (*Edinburgh Rvrs*), Bryan Redpath (*Sale Sharks*); Tom Smith (*Brive*), Gordon Bulloch (*Glasgow Cal*), Mattie Stewart (*Northampton Sts*), Scott Murray (*Saracens*), Stuart Grimes (*Newcastle F*), Martin Leslie (*Edinburgh Rvrs*), Budge Pountney* (*Northampton Sts*), Simon Taylor (*Edinburgh Rvrs*) ... Substitutes: Gordon McIlwham (*Glasgow Cal*) for Stewart (40), Cameron Murray (*Edinburgh Rvrs*) for Craig (45), Jon Petrie (*Glasgow Cal*) for Taylor (74), Steve Scott (*Edinburgh Rvrs*) for Bulloch (77)

ITALY Cristian Stoica (*Narbonne*); Massimiliano Perziano (*Treviso*), Walter Pozzebon (*Treviso*), Manuel Dallan (*Treviso*), Luca Martin (*Northampton Sts*); Diego Dominguez (*Stade Français*), Filippo Frati (*Parma*); Andrea Lo Cicero (*Roma*), Alessandro Moscardi* (*Treviso*), Franco Properzi Curti (*Treviso*), Wilhelmus Visser (*Treviso*), Andrea Gritti (*Treviso*), Aaron Persico (*Viadana*), Mauro Bergamasco (*Treviso*), Carlo Checchinato (*Treviso*) ... Substitutes: Matteo Mazzantini (*Treviso*) for Frati (30), Salvatore Perugini (*L'Aquila*) for Properzi Curti (40), Giovanni Raineri (*Roma*) for Dallan (46), Carlo Caione (*Roma*) for Gritti (59)

REFEREE Joel Dumé (*France*)

SCORING Hodge, drop (3–0); Hodge, pen (6–0); Bergamasco, try (6–5); Dominguez, con (6–7); Dominguez, pen (6–10) (half-time) Hodge, pen (9–10); Dominguez, pen (9–13); Hodge, pen (12–13); Smith, try (17–13); Dominguez, pen (17–16); Dominguez, pen (17–19); Hodge, pen (20–19); Hodge, pen (23–19)

Scotland gained revenge for their humiliation in Rome the previous year, but otherwise this was a disappointing encounter. The Scottish forwards stood up well against heavier opponents, but the backs made too many errors and most of their attacks simply fizzled out. The highlight of the match was a brilliant solo try by Italian flanker Mauro Bergamasco. On the 27th minute he took a pass deep inside his own territory, ran away up the left touchline and nobody could catch him as he raced over for a great score. Scotland's only try of the match was less spectacular. From a penalty, Hodge kicked to the corner, Martin Leslie led the charge from the lineout, and Tom Smith finished off by spinning around in a tackle and forcing the ball down. The Italians defended well and took their chances, but they conceded too many penalties. On the 64th minute, a Dominguez penalty gave Italy a narrow lead, but Scotland always looked the better of two mediocre sides and two late penalties by Hodge saw them home.

XV 2001 BARBARIANS

Murrayfield · Thursday 24 May 2001 · Lost 31–74

SCOTLAND XV Chris Paterson (*Edinburgh Rvrs*); Cameron Murray (*Edinburgh Rvrs*), Marcus Di Rollo (*Edinburgh Rvrs*), John Leslie (*Northampton Sts*), James McLaren (*Glasgow Cal*); Duncan Hodge (*Edinburgh Rvrs*), Bryan Redpath* (*Sale Sharks*); Allan Jacobsen (*Edinburgh Rvrs*), Gordon Bulloch (*Glasgow Cal*), Gordon McIlwham (*Glasgow Cal*), Stuart Grimes (*Newcastle F*), Doddie Weir (*Newcastle F*), Gordon Simpson (*Glasgow Cal*),

Andrew Mower (*Newcastle F*), Jon Petrie (*Glasgow Cal*) ... Substitutes: Donnie Macfadyen (*Glasgow Cal*) for Mower (12), Iain Fullerton (*Edinburgh Rvrs*) for Weir (40), Craig Smith (*Edinburgh Rvrs*) for Jacobsen (52), Andrew Henderson (*Glasgow Cal*) for Murray (64), Alan Bulloch (*Glasgow Cal*) for Leslie (64), Graeme Burns (*Edinburgh Rvrs*) for Redpath (72), Steve Scott (*Edinburgh Rvrs*) for Bulloch (75)

BARBARIANS Geordan Murphy (*Leicester Tgrs & Ireland*); Friedrich Lombard (*Blue Bulls*), Tim Horan* (*Saracens & Australia*), Kevin Maggs (*Bath & Ireland*), Jonah Lomu (*Hurricanes & NZ*); Percy Montgomery (*W Stormers & SA*), Joost van der Westhuizen (*Blue Bulls & SA*); Kevin Yates (*Hurricanes & England*), Richard Cockerill (*Leicester Tgrs & England*), Adrian Garvey (*Newport & SA*), Robin Brooke (*Auckland Blues & NZ*), John Langford (*Munster & Australia*), Ben Clarke (*Bath & England*), Angus Gardiner (*Bath*), Pat Lam (*Newcastle F & Samoa*) ... Substitutes: Tom Bowman (*NSW Waratahs & Australia*) for Langford (17), Pat Howard (*Leicester Tgrs & Australia*) for Horan (20-6 and 27), Josh Kronfield (*Leicester Tgrs & NZ*) for Gardiner (46), Philippe Carbonneau (*Pau & France*) for van der Westhuizen (54), Braam van Straaten (*W Stormers & SA*) for Lomu (59), Naka Drotske (*Blue Bulls & SA*) for Cockerill (60), Craig Dowd (*Auckland Blues & NZ*) for Gravey (68)

REFEREE Jim Fleming (*Scotland*) · **ATTENDANCE** 28,626

SCORING Lomu, try (0–5); Lomu, try (0–10); Lombard, try (0–15); Di Rollo, try (5–15); Hodge, con (7–15); Petrie, try (12–15); Hodge, con (14–15); Paterson, try (19–15); Hodge, con (21–15); Lomu, try (21–20); Montgomery, con (21–22); Cockerill, try (21–27); Montgomery, con (21–29); Lomu, try (21–34); McLaren, try (26–34); Lombard, try (26–39); Montgomery, con (26–41) (half-time) van der Westhuizen, try (26–46); Montgomery, con (26–48); Maggs, try (26–53); Montgomery, con (26–55); Bowman, try (26–60); Montgomery, con (26–62); Macfadyen, try (31–62); Clarke, try (31–67); Lam, try (31–72); van Straaten, con (31–74)

The Scottish Rugby Union dedicated this match to the memory of Gordon Brown, the popular Scotland and British Lions lock forward of the 1970s who died earlier in the year. Brown's son Rory and grandson Zac had the honour of leading the teams onto the field. In the sixth encounter between the two sides, New Zealand winger Jonah Lomu bestrode the field like a colossus. The biggest star in world rugby used his awesome frame to brush off tackles and leave defenders flailing in his wake. He scored four tries in the first half, the first two in the opening five minutes, and created several more. When he left the pitch after an hour, he was given a heart-felt standing ovation by the crowd. Lomu's contribution summed-up the gulf in quality between the star-studded Barbarians and a workman-like Scotland side that was missing its small clutch of British Lions. The Scots played with their usual spirit and had their moments, but they conceded too many turnovers and gave the Barbarians too much time and space on the ball. Scotland did manage to score five tries and newcomers Marcus Di Rillo and Donnie Macfadyen gave encouraging displays. Di Rollo showed great alertness and speed when he scored an early interception try and then he made a cleverly angled run to put Jon Petrie in. Likewise, Macfadyen put on a superb turn of pace when he raced away for Scotland's only score of the second-half.

496   SIX NATIONS CHAMPIONSHIP 2001   IRELAND

Murrayfield · Saturday 22 September 2001 · Won 32–10

SCOTLAND Glenn Metcalfe (*Glasgow*); Jon Steel (*Glasgow*), James McLaren (*Glasgow*),

John Leslie (*Northampton Sts*), Chris Paterson (*Edinburgh*); Gregor Townsend (*Castres*), Bryan Redpath (*Sale Sharks*); Tom Smith (*Northampton Sts*), Gordon Bulloch (*Glasgow*), Mattie Stewart (*Northampton Sts*), Jason White (*Glasgow*), Scott Murray (*Saracens*), Gordon Simpson (*Glasgow*), Budge Pountney* (*Northampton Sts*), Simon Taylor (*Edinburgh*) ... Substitutes: George Graham (*Newcastle F*) for Stewart (63), †Andrew Henderson (*Glasgow*) for Leslie (63), Stuart Grimes (*Newcastle F*) for White (71), Jon Petrie (*Glasgow*) for Simpson (75), Steve Scott (*Edinburgh*) for Bulloch (79), Duncan Hodge (*Edinburgh*) for Townsend (79), Andy Nicol (*Glasgow*) for Redpath (79)

IRELAND Girvan Dempsey (*Leinster*); Geordan Murphy (*Leicester Tgrs*), Brian O'Driscoll (*Leinster*), Shane Horgan (*Leinster*), Denis Hickie (*Leinster*); Ronan O'Gara (*Munster*), Guy Easterby (*Llanelli*); Peter Clohessy (*Munster*), Keith Wood* (*Harlequins*), John Hayes (*Munster*), Jeremy Davidson (*Ulster*), Malcolm O'Kelly (*Leinster*), Simon Easterby (*Llanelli*), Kieron Dawson (*London Irish*), Anthony Foley (*Munster*) ... Substitutes: Kevin Maggs (*Bath*) for Murphy (22), Emmett Byrne (*Leinster*) for Hayes (34), Peter Stringer (*Munster*) for G Easterby (53), David Humphreys (*Ulster*) for O'Gara (63), Paul Wallace (*Munster*) for Foley (63), Gary Longwell (*Ulster*) for Davidson (73)

REFEREE Chris White (*England*)

SCORING Pountney, try (5–0); Townsend, con (7–0); Paterson, pen (10–0); Smith, try (15–0); Paterson, con (17–0) (half-time) O'Gara, pen (17–3); Leslie, try (22–3); Paterson, con (24–3); Paterson, pen (27–3); Henderson, try (32–3); Dempsey, try (32–8); Humphreys, con (32–10)

This match was postponed from 7 April because of an outbreak of foot-and-mouth disease in Britain. Ireland had been tipped for a possible Grand Slam, but they were soundly beaten by a rampant Scottish side that played their best 15-man rugby for some time. The Scots were eager in attack and fully committed in defence. The back-row, in particular, were well organised and highly disruptive. Both sides started nervously and the opening stages were full of errors. On the 23rd minute John Leslie made a midfield break and fed Chris Paterson who went on a mazy run before passing to Pountney who scored under the posts. Townsend converted, Paterson kicked a penalty and shortly before half-time Tom Smith muscled over from close range for his third try of the Championship. Scotland kept their momentum in the second-half and stand-off Gregor Townsend played with growing confidence and control. On the hour mark he beat several defenders to set-up a try for John Leslie. Towards the finish substitute Andy Henderson scored a debutant try. In a fine team performance Chris Paterson rarely put a foot wrong in his new role as a wing, Glenn Metcalfe was dangerous when running from deep, Gregor Townsend overcame a shaky start to give a commanding performance and Budge Pountney proved an inspirational captain.

497   AUTUMN TEST 2001   TONGA

Murrayfield · Saturday 10 November 2001 · Won 43–20

SCOTLAND Glenn Metcalfe (*Glasgow*); Jon Steel (*Glasgow*), James McLaren (*Glasgow*), John Leslie (*Northampton Sts*), Cameron Murray (*Edinburgh*); †Gordon Ross (*Edinburgh*), Andy Nicol (*Glasgow*); Tom Smith* (*Northampton Sts*), Gordon Bulloch (*Glasgow*), Mattie Stewart (*Northampton Sts*), Scott Murray (*Saracens*), Stuart Grimes (*Newcastle F*), Jason White (*Glasgow*), †Andrew Mower (*Newcastle F*), Jon Petrie (*Glasgow*) ... Substitutes: Gordon Simpson (*Glasgow*) for Mower (51), George Graham (*Newcastle F*) for Stewart (53),

†Roland Reid (*Glasgow*) for C Murray (66), Andrew Henderson (*Glasgow*) for McLaren (78), Graeme Burns (*Edinburgh*) for Nicol (78), Steve Scott (*Edinburgh*) for Bulloch (78)

TONGA Sateki Tu'ipulotu (*Worcester*); Tevita Tiueti (*Neath*), Siua Taumalolo (*Bridgend*), Gus Leger (*Manukau*), Epeli Taione (*Newcastle F*); Elisi Vunipola (*Coventry*), Silio Martens (*Swansea*); John Pale (*Wellington Hurricanes*), Aleki Lutui (*Bay of Plenty*); Tevita Taumoepeau (*Auckland Blues*), Feleti Fakaongo (*North Harbour*), Viliami Vaki (*Lavengamalie*), Maama Molitika (*Bridgend*), Inoke Afeaki* (*Hurricanes*), Matt Te Pou (*Limerick*) ... Substitutes: Viliami Ma'asi (*Fasi Ma'ufanga*) for Molitika (35–40), Fakataha Molitika (*Whitland*) for Vaki (57), Tony Alatini (*North Harbour*) for Martens (70), Taumo Holo Taufahema (*Caerphilly*) for Tu'ipulotu (75), Taufa'ao Filise (*Bay of Plenty*) for Pale (75), Salesi Finau (*Llanelli*) for Leger (75)

REFEREE Nigel Whitehouse (*Wales*) · **ATTENDANCE** 44,649

SCORING Ross, pen (3–0); Ross, pen (6–0); Vaki, try (6–5); Ross, pen (9–5); Tu'ipulotu, pen (9–8); McLaren, try (14–8); Ross, con (16–8); Ross, pen (19–8); Tu'ipulotu, pen (19–11); Ross, pen (22–11) (half-time) Tu'ipulotu, pen (22–14); Tu'ipulotu, pen (22–17); Metcalfe, try (27–17); Ross, con (29–17); Reid, try (34–17); Ross, con (36–17); Simpson, try (41–17); Ross, con (43–17); Taumalolo, pen (43–20)

Scotland were comfortable winners against a rather lukewarm Tonga who had plenty of heart and muscle but whose play often lacked cohesion. The Scottish forwards could do little damage against a heavy Tongan scrum, but in the lineouts Scott Murray and Stuart Grimes stole around half of the Tongan throw-ins. The Scots made plenty of unforced errors but were always ready to move the ball out wide. For once Scotland took their chances well. James McLaren scored a timely try in the first-half, just when the Tongans were at their most threatening, and after the interval the Scots added three more, one by substitute Roland Reid, a South African-born flanker-turned-winger, who scored with his first touch of the ball. New cap Gordon Ross played with great authority, kicked a total of 23 points and won the man-of-the-match award. His reward was to be left out for the next game!

498   AUTUMN TEST 2001   ARGENTINA

Murrayfield · Sunday 18 November 2001 · Lost 16–25

SCOTLAND Derrick Lee (*Edinburgh*); Cameron Murray (*Edinburgh*), James McLaren (*Glasgow*), John Leslie (*Northampton Sts*), Roland Reid (*Glasgow*); Gregor Townsend (*Castres*), Andy Nicol (*Glasgow*); Tom Smith* (*Northampton Sts*), Gordon Bulloch (*Glasgow*), Mattie Stewart (*Northampton Sts*), Scott Murray (*Saracens*), Stuart Grimes (*Newcastle F*), Jason White (*Glasgow*), Andrew Mower (*Newcastle F*), Jon Petrie (*Glasgow*) ... Substitutes: Gordon Simpson (*Glasgow*) for Petrie (55), George Graham (*Newcastle F*) for Stewart (61)

ARGENTINA Ignacio Corleto (*Narbonne*); Gonzalo Camardón (*Roma*), José Orengo (*Perpignan*), Lisandro Arbizu* (*Bordeaux Bègles*), Diego Albanese (*Gloucester*); Felipe Contepomi (*Bristol*), Agustín Pichot (*Bristol*); Mauricio Reggiardo (*Castres*), Federico Méndez (*Mendoza*), Omar Hasan (*Agen*), Ignacio Fernández Lobbe (*Castres*), Rimas Alvarez (*Perpignan*), Santiago Phelan (*San Isidro*), Rolando Martin (*SIC*), Gonzalo Longo (*Narbonne*) ... Substitutes: Roberto Grau (*Liceo*) for Reggiardo (64), Lucas Ostiglia (*Hindú*) for Phelan (65)

REFEREE Joel Jutge (France) · **ATTENDANCE** 45,113

SCORING Townsend, pen (3–0); Contepomi, pen (3–3); Townsend, try (8–3); Contepomi, pen

(8–6) (half-time) Contepomi, pen (8–9); Townsend, pen (11–9); Corleto, try (11–14); Contepomi, con (11–16); Lee, try (16–16); Contepomi, pen (16–19); Contepomi, pen (16–22); Contepomi, pen (16–25)

Played in wet conditions, Scotland were unable to impose themselves on a big Argentinean side or to disrupt their slow-moving, forward-dominated game in favour of a faster, more expansive style. Similarly, Argentina, who had beaten Wales eight days earlier, never managed to wear down the lighter Scots or to take control. The result was a tight and unspectacular match that could have gone either way. Scotland made a lot of errors but defended well and excelled at the lineouts. Scotland's first try came after 25 minutes when Andy Nicol harassed his opposite number Pichot into a hurried clearance straight into the welcoming arms of Gregor Townsend who ran over for a soft score. Scotland's second was the best move of the game. The forwards made a surge from a lineout inside the Argentinean 22, Leslie and Cameron Murray tied in the defence and Lee made an angled run to surge over the line. In an untidy conclusion Contepomi kicked his side to victory with three penalties.

---

499   AUTUMN TEST 2001   NEW ZEALAND

Murrayfield · Saturday 24 November 2001 · Lost 6–37

SCOTLAND †Brendan Laney (*Edinburgh*); Jon Steel (*Glasgow*), James McLaren (*Glasgow*), John Leslie (*Northampton Sts*), Chris Paterson (*Edinburgh*); Gregor Townsend (*Castres*), Andy Nicol (*Glasgow*); Tom Smith* (*Northampton Sts*), Gordon Bulloch (*Glasgow*), Mattie Stewart (*Northampton Sts*), Scott Murray (*Saracens*), Stuart Grimes (*Newcastle F*), Jason White (*Glasgow*), Andrew Mower (*Newcastle F*), Gordon Simpson (*Glasgow*) ... Substitutes: Simon Taylor (*Edinburgh*) for Simpson (48), George Graham (*Newcastle F*) for Stewart (48), Graeme Burns (*Edinburgh*) for Nicol (60), Andrew Henderson (*Glasgow*) for Leslie (70), Steve Scott (*Edinburgh*) for Bulloch (75), Iain Fullerton (*Sale Sharks*) for Murray (79)

NEW ZEALAND Leon MacDonald (*Crusaders*); Doug Howlett (*Blues*), Tana Umaga (*Hurricanes*), Aaron Mauger (*Crusaders*), Jonah Lomu (*Hurricanes*); Andrew Mehrtens (*Crusaders*), Byron Kelleher (*Highlanders*); Greg Feek (*Crusaders*), Anton Oliver* (*Highlanders*), Greg Somerville (*Crusaders*), Chris Jack (*Crusaders*), Norm Maxwell (*Crusaders*), Reuben Thorne (*Crusaders*), Richie McCaw (*Crusaders*), Scott Robinson (*Crusaders*) ... Substitutes: Mark Robinson (*Blues*) for Kelleher (33), Ben Blair (*Crusaders*) for MacDonald (60), Dave Hewett (*Crusaders*) for Feek (60)

REFEREE Pablo Cesar Deluca (*Argentina*) · ATTENDANCE 67,456

SCORING Paterson, pen (3–0); Mehrtens, pen (3–3); Paterson, pen (6–3); Mehrtens, pen (6–6); Mehrtens, pen (6–9) (half-time) Mehrtens, pen (6–12); Mehrtens, pen (6–15); Mehrtens, pen (6–18); Umaga, try (6–23); Mehrtens, con (6–25); Robinson, try (6–30); Mehrtens, con (6–32); Lomu, try (6–37)

The main talking point was the controversial selection of Brendan Laney at full-back. Born in Invercargill, Laney was parachuted into the side having only arrived in Scotland the previous week and without having played for Edinburgh, his new club. Under new coach John Mitchell, New Zealand were making a short tour of Ireland, Scotland and Argentina, and the previous Tuesday had defeated Scotland A at McDiarmid Park (35–13). Scotland played with plenty of spirit but lacked enough composure and inventiveness to cause an upset. They wasted several opportunities whilst the New Zealand tally steadily mounted thanks to the unerring boot of Andrew Mehrtens, who kicked a total of 22 points. Scotland were still within striking distance inside the final quarter, but the New Zealanders stretched away with a late scoring blitz. Their first try came when Umaga broke a tackle and ran half the length of the field. Substitute Robinson slipped through for the second try and after a break by McCaw the mighty Jonah Lomu brought down the curtain in injury-time. The result flattered the visitors, who played well within themselves, although there was a sense of inevitability about the outcome.

---

500   SIX NATIONS CHAMPIONSHIP 2002   ENGLAND

Murrayfield · Saturday 2 February 2002 · Lost 3–29

SCOTLAND Glenn Metcalfe (*Glasgow*); Brendan Laney (*Edinburgh*), James McLaren (*Glasgow*), Gregor Townsend (*Castres*), Chris Paterson (*Edinburgh*); Duncan Hodge (*Edinburgh*), Bryan Redpath (*Sale Sharks*); Tom Smith (*Northampton Sts*), Gordon Bulloch (*Glasgow*), Mattie Stewart (*Northampton Sts*), Scott Murray (*Saracens*), Stuart Grimes (*Newcastle F*), Jason White (*Glasgow*), Budge Pountney* (*Northampton Sts*), Simon Taylor (*Edinburgh*) ... Substitute: George Graham (*Newcastle F*) for Smith (63)

ENGLAND Jason Robinson (*Sale Sharks*); Austin Healey (*Leicester Tgrs*), Will Greenwood (*Leicester Tgrs*), Mike Tindall (*Bath*), Ben Cohen (*Northampton Sts*); Jonny Wilkinson (*Newcastle F*), Kyran Bracken (*Saracens*); Graham Rowntree (*Leicester Tgrs*), Steve Thompson (*Northampton Sts*), Julian White (*Bristol*), Martin Johnson* (*Leicester Tgrs*), Ben Kay (*Leicester Tgrs*), Richard Hill (*Saracens*), Neil Back (*Leicester Tgrs*), Joe Worsley (*London Wasps*) ... Substitutes: Nick Duncombe (*Harlequins*) for Bracken (40), Danny Grewcock (*Bath*) for Kay (69), Iain Balshaw (*Bath*) for Tindall (72), Jason Leonard (*Harlequins*) for White (75), Charlie Hodgson (*Sale Sharks*) for Wilkinson (83)

REFEREE Steve Walsh (*New Zealand*)

SCORING Robinson, try (0–5); Robinson, try (0–10); Wilkinson, con (0–12); Hodge, pen (3–12) (half-time) Tindall, try (3–17); Wilkinson, con (3–19); Wilkinson, pen (3–22); Cohen, try (3–27); Hodgson, con (3–29)

In their 500th cap international, Scotland dreamed of repeating their great win two years earlier, but they were rudely awakened by a powerful England side who won the match easily and without playing all that well. The Scots worked hard, especially the front-row, but failed to make the best of their opportunities. They won slightly more possession and territory, but their ball was often slow and scrappy whilst England's was more controlled. Likewise, Scotland's attacks were laboured and made little headway against a well-organised defence. England, by contrast, showed lethal finishing, plenty of pace, fast hands and good support running. The visitors started strongly and within 15 minutes the mercurial Jason Robinson had soared over for a brace of tries. The first came from a quick tap penalty and deft handling, the second after Greenwood broke a tackle and Tindall dummied the defence before releasing his full-back. Duncan Hodge kicked a penalty, but on the 51st minute England sealed the match when Tindall chipped ahead and the ball broke kindly for him. Deep into injury-time, Cohen scored a well-taken try after a clearing kick had been charged down. Substitute Charlie Hodgson rubbed in the salt with a touchline conversion.

Stadio Flaminio, Rome · Saturday 16 February 2002 · Won 29–12

SCOTLAND Brendan Laney (*Edinburgh*); Glenn Metcalfe (*Glasgow*), James McLaren (*Glasgow*), Andrew Henderson (*Glasgow*), Chris Paterson (*Edinburgh*); Gregor Townsend (*Castres*), Bryan Redpath* (*Sale Sharks*); Tom Smith (*Northampton Sts*), Gordon Bulloch (*Glasgow*), Mattie Stewart (*Northampton Sts*), Scott Murray (*Saracens*), Stuart Grimes (*Newcastle F*), Jason White (*Glasgow*), Andrew Mower (*Newcastle F*), Simon Taylor (*Edinburgh*) ... Substitutes: George Graham (*Newcastle F*) for Stewart (60), Martin Leslie (*Edinburgh*) for Mower (70)

ITALY Paolo Vaccari (*Calvisano*); Roberto Pedrazzi (*Viadana*), Mirco Bergamasco (*Padova*), Cristian Stoica (*Castres*), Denis Dallan (*Treviso*); Diego Dominguez (*Stade Français*), Alessandro Troncon (*Montferrand*); Giampiero De Carli (*Calvisano*), Alessandro Moscardi* (*Treviso*), Federico Pucciariello (*Gloucester*), Carlo Checchinato (*Treviso*), Santiago Dellapè (*Viadana*), Marco Bortolami (*Padova*), Mauro Bergamasco (*Padova*), Matthew Phillips (*Viadana*) ... Substitutes: Alejandro Moreno (*Agen*) for Pucciariello (52), Andrea Lo Cicero (*Toulouse*) for De Carli (60), Mark Giacheri (*Sale Sharks*) for Delappe (62), Luca Martin (*Northampton Sts*) for Vaccari (68), Ramiro Pez (*Rotherham*) for Dominguez (80), Aaron Ronald Persico (*Viadana*) for Phillips (80)

REFEREE KM Deaker (*New Zealand*)

SCORING Dominguez, pen (0–3); Laney, pen (3–3); Dominguez, pen (3–6); Laney, pen (6–6); Laney, pen (9–6); Dominguez, pen (9–9) (half-time) Dominguez, pen (9–12); Laney, pen (12–12); Laney, pen (15–12); Townsend, try (20–12); Laney, con (22–12); Laney, try (27–12); Laney, con (29–12)

Scotland buried the ghosts of 2000 with a heartening performance that restored some of their self-belief and pride. Although they did not score their first try until the final ten minutes, they always looked likely winners. They were well-organised, strong in defence and disciplined, giving their old nemisis Diego Dominguez few opportunities. The much-maligned Brendan Laney took over the kicking duties after an early injury to Chris Paterson. He silenced his critics by kicking 19 points and he also scored a try near the finish when he sold an outrageous dummy to beat the weary defence. Scotland's other try was scored by Gregor Townsend, back in the stand-off position, who intercepted a careless pass and raced 40 metres unopposed. The Italians were typically robust and committed, but their play lacked enough cohesion to pull off another upset. In a bizarre incident, Laney was slapped on the face by an irate Italian spectator when the players left the field at the end. To his credit, Laney shrugged his shoulders and walked away bemused.

Lansdowne Road, Dublin · Saturday 2 March 2002 · Lost 22–43

SCOTLAND Brendan Laney (*Edinburgh*); Glenn Metcalfe (*Glasgow*), James McLaren (*Glasgow*), Andrew Henderson (*Glasgow*), Chris Paterson (*Edinburgh*); Gregor Townsend (*Castres*), Bryan Redpath* (*Sale Sharks*); Tom Smith (*Northampton Sts*), Gordon Bulloch (*Glasgow*), Mattie Stewart (*Northampton Sts*), Scott Murray (*Saracens*), Stuart Grimes (*Newcastle F*), Jason White (*Glasgow*), Budge Pountney (*Northampton Sts*), Simon Taylor (*Edinburgh*) ...

Substitutes: Martin Leslie (*Edinburgh*) for White (56), George Graham (*Newcastle F*) for Stewart (60), Kenny Logan (*London Wasps*) for Metcalfe (71)

IRELAND Girvan Dempsey (*Leinster*); Shane Horgan (*Leinster*), Brian O'Driscoll (*Leinster*), Kevin Maggs (*Bath*), Denis Hickie (*Leinster*); David Humphreys (*Ulster*), Peter Stringer (*Munster*); Peter Clohessy (*Munster*), Frank Sheahan (*Munster*), John Hayes (*Munster*), Mick Galwey* (*Munster*), Malcolm O'Kelly (*Leinster*), Eric Miller (*Leinster*), David Wallace (*Munster*), Anthony Foley (*Munster*) ... Substitutes: Shane Byrne (*Leinster*) for Sheahan (34), Simon Easterby (*Llanelli*) for Miller (46), Gary Longwell (*Ulster*) for Galwey (71), Ronan O'Gara (*Munster*) for Humphreys (77), Paul Wallace (*Leinster*) for Clohessy (78), Guy Easterby (*Llanelli*) for Stringer (80)

REFEREE Nigel Whitehouse (*Wales*) · ATTENDANCE 48,898

SCORING Humphreys, pen (0–3); Laney, pen (3–3); Laney, pen (6–3); Laney, pen (9–3); O'Driscoll, try (9–8); Horgan, try (9–13); Humphreys, con (9–15); O'Driscoll, try (9–20); Humphreys, con (9–22); Laney, pen (12–22) (half-time) Laney, pen (15–22); Humphreys, pen (15–25); Humpreys, pen (15–28); Humphreys, pen (15–31); S Easterby, try (15–36); Leslie, try (20–36); Laney, con (22–36); O'Driscoll, try (19–41); O'Gara, con (22–43)

Despite high scoring and six tries, this was not a game of any great quality. Scotland made a huge number of errors that the opportunistic Irish were quick to exploit. Ireland's sublimely talented centre Brian O'Driscoll scored a hat-trick of tries, and his speed of thought and blistering pace made his hapless opponents look very ordinary in comparison. His second try summed up the story of the day. A ponderous Scottish attack broke down; O'Driscoll seized on a loose pass and then raced 80 metres to score. The match began promisingly for the Scots, but their early lead evaporated with three tries by Ireland in quick succession, all resulting from Scottish errors. Scotland managed to claw back to within seven points early in the second-half, but three penalties by David Humphreys and a try by Simon Easterby, which came from another dropped pass by the Scots, put the home side comfortably ahead. At times, the visitors were very ill-disciplined and Budge Pountney was yellow-carded at a crucial stage in the second half. Scotland battled hard towards the end and substitute Martin Leslie scored after a driving maul, but O'Driscoll's third try sealed Scotland's fate.

503 SIX NATIONS CHAMPIONSHIP 2002 FRANCE

Murrayfield · Saturday 23 March 2002 · Lost 10–22

SCOTLAND Brendan Laney (*Edinburgh*); Glenn Metcalfe (*Glasgow*), James McLaren (*Glasgow*), John Leslie (*Northampton Sts*), Chris Paterson (*Edinburgh*); Gregor Townsend (*Castres*), Bryan Redpath* (*Sale Sharks*); Tom Smith (*Northampton Sts*), Gordon Bulloch (*Glasgow*), Mattie Stewart (*Northampton Sts*), Scott Murray (*Saracens*), Jason White (*Glasgow*), Martin Leslie (*Edinburgh*), Budge Pountney (*Northampton Sts*), Simon Taylor (*Edinburgh*) ... Substitutes: Jon Petrie (*Glasgow*) for M Leslie (28), George Graham (*Newcastle F*) for Stewart (61), Stuart Grimes (*Newcastle F*) for Murray (62), Rob Russell (*Saracens*) for Bulloch (76), Kenny Logan (*London Wasps*) for McLaren (78)

FRANCE Nicolas Brusque (*Biarritz*); Aurélien Rougerie (*Montferrand*), Tony Marsh (*Montferrand*), Damien Traille (*Pau*), David Bory (*Montferrand*); Gérald Merceron (*Montferrand*), Fabien Galthié* (*Stade Français*); Jean-Jacques Crenca (*Agen*), Raphaël Ibañez (*Castres*), Jean-Baptiste Poux (*Narbonne*), Fabien Pelous (*Toulouse*), Olivier Brouzet (*Northampton Sts*),

Serge Betsen (*Biarritz*), Olivier Magne (*Montferrand*), Imanol Harinordoquy (*Pau*) ... Substitutes: Jimmy Marlu (*Montferrand*) for Brusque (49), Sylvain Marconnet (*Stade Français*) for Poux (62), Thibault Privat (*Béziers*) for Pelous (66), Remy Martin (*Stade Français*) for Betsen (77)

REFEREE Alain Roland (*Ireland*)

SCORING Laney, pen (3–0); Marsh, try (3–5); Merceron, con (3–7); Merceron, pen (3–10) (half-time) Marsh, try (3–15); Galthié, try (3–20); Merceron, con (3–22); Redpath, try (8–22); Laney, con (10–22)

The Scots were an improvement on the Irish humiliation, but once again they made too many errors to threaten a talented French side who in turn played well below their best but still had enough quality to win, the fourth leg of their Grand Slam. Scotland were lively at times and worked hard, and were only seven points adrift at the interval. They wasted several half chances in the opening exchanges and could only muster a penalty goal by Laney. France replied with a try by New Zealand-born centre Tony Marsh which was converted by Merceron who later added a penalty. The match ran away from Scotland in the opening minutes of the second-half. Marsh scored his second try and then veteran scrum-half and French captain Fabien Galthié stole away from a ruck 30 metres out and rushed over at the corner, exposing a lack of pace and sharpness in the Scottish defence. The Scots, as usual, battled valiantly and were rewarded when Laney made a jinking run to create a try for Redpath. The Scottish scrum-half had an outstanding match and lock Scott Murray also gave a rousing display.

---

504 LLOYDS TSB SIX NATIONS CHAMPIONSHIP 2002   WALES

Millennium Stadium, Cardiff · Saturday 6 April 2002 · Won 27–22

SCOTLAND Brendan Laney (*Edinburgh*); Kenny Logan (*London Wasps*), James McLaren (*Glasgow*), John Leslie (*Northampton Sts*), Chris Paterson (*Edinburgh*); Gregor Townsend (*Castres*), Bryan Redpath* (*Sale Sharks*); Tom Smith (*Northampton Sts*), Gordon Bulloch (*Glasgow*), Mattie Stewart (*Northampton Sts*), Scott Murray (*Saracens*), Jason White (*Glasgow*), Martin Leslie (*Edinburgh*), Budge Pountney (*Northampton Sts*), Simon Taylor (*Edinburgh*) ... Substitutes: George Graham (*Newcastle F*) for Stewart (40), Stuart Grimes (*Newcastle F*) for White (57), Glenn Metcalfe (*Glasgow*) for Logan (60), Jon Petrie (*Glasgow*) for M Leslie (71), Rob Russell (*Saracens*) for Bulloch (75), Duncan Hodge (*Edinburgh*) for Laney (84)

WALES Kevin Morgan (*Swansea*); Rhys Williams (*Cardiff*), Mark Taylor (*Swansea*), Andy Marinos (*Newport*), Craig Morgan (*Cardiff*); Stephen Jones (*Llanelli*), Rob Howley (*Cardiff*); Iestyn Thomas (*Ebbw Vale*), Barry Williams (*Neath*), Chris Anthony (*Newport*), Ian Gough (*Newport*), Andy Moore (*Swansea*), Nathan Budgett (*Bridgend*), Martyn Williams (*Cardiff*), Colin Charvis* (*Swansea*) ... Substitutes: Chris Wyatt (*Llanelli*) for Moore (12), Gavin Thomas (*Bath*) for Budgett (40), Robin McBryde (*Llanelli*) for B Williams (43), Iestyn Harris (*Cardiff*) for Marinos (43), Spencer John (*Cardiff*) for Thomas (57), Dwayne Peel (*Llanelli*) for Howley (66), Dafydd James (*Bridgend*) for C Morgan (75)

REFEREE Joel Jutge (*France*)

SCORING Jones, pen (0–3); Jones, pen (0–6); Jones, pen (0–9); Bulloch, try (5–9); Bulloch, try (10–9); Laney, con (12–9); Laney, pen (15–9) (half-time) R Williams, try (15–14); Jones, con (15–16); Laney, pen (18–16); Jones, pen (18–19); Laney, pen (21–19); Jones, pen (21–22); Laney, pen (24–22); Hodge, pen (27–22)

Bill McLaren, the celebrated television commentator, bade farewell to the championship with this match. The Scots recorded a rare away victory and their first at the Millennium Stadium, but otherwise there was little to get excited about. The Scottish forwards were a better unit, Gordon Bulloch scored a brace of tries and Brendan Laney kept his side in contention with his steady kicking. Three penalties by Stephen Jones gave Wales an early lead but the Scots held their composure and made a recovery. Man-of-the-match Scott Murray won a lineout near the Welsh line and after sustained pressure Bulloch twisted under the defence to touch down. Eight minutes later, Bulloch scored again with an almost identical move. Laney added a touchline conversion and kicked a penalty to put Scotland 13–9 ahead at the break. Early in the second half, Rhys Williams scored a fine try which was converted by Jones. The match then degenerated into a see-saw battle between the kickers and the lead changed hands five times. Wales held a one-point advantage going into injury time, but Laney and substitute Duncan Hodge kicked late penalties to see out the game.

 XV | **2002** | **BARBARIANS**

Murrayfield · Saturday 1 June 2002 · Lost 27–47

SCOTLAND XV Glenn Metcalfe (*Glasgow*); Rory Kerr (*Glasgow*), Andy Craig (*Orrell*), Brendan Laney (*Edinburgh*), Chris Paterson (*Edinburgh*); Duncan Hodge (*Edinburgh*), Mike Blair (*Edinburgh*); Craig Smith (*Edinburgh*), Gordon Bulloch (*Glasgow*), Allan Jacobsen (*Edinburgh*), Jason White (*Glasgow*), Stuart Grimes* (*Newcastle F*), Simon Taylor (*Edinburgh*), Martin Leslie (*Edinburgh*), Jon Petrie (*Glasgow*) ... Substitutes: Steve Scott (*Borders*) for Bulloch (53), Joel Brannigan (*Edinburgh*) for Jacobsen (53), Allister Hogg (*Edinburgh*) for Leslie (53), Nathan Hines (*Edinburgh*) for Petrie (60), Marcus Di Rollo (*Edinburgh*) for Meltcalfe (65), Andrew Henderson (*Glasgow*) for Kerr (70), Graeme Burns (*Edinburgh*) for Blair (74)

BARBARIANS Percy Montgomery (*W Stormers & SA*); Thinus Delport (*Natal Sharks & SA*), Pieter Muller (*Cardiff & SA*), Pita Alatini (*Hurricanes & NZ*), Pieter Rossouw (*W Stormers & SA*); Braam van Straaten (*Leeds Tykes & SA*), Mark Robinson (*Auckland Blues & NZ*); Craig Dowd (*London Wasps & NZ*), Mario Ledesma (*Narbonne & Argentina*), Mauricio Reggiardo (*Narbonne & Argentina*), Ian Jones* (*London Wasps & NZ*), Ryan Strudwick (*London Irish*), Kris Chesney (*Saracens*), Josh Kronfeld (*Leicester Tgrs & NZ*), Jim Williams (*Munster & Australia*) ... Substitutes: Paul Gustard (*London Irish*) for Chesney (55), Adrian Garvey (*Newport & SA*) for Dowd (60), Barry Everitt (*London Irish*) for van Stratten (67), Raphaël Ibañez (*Castres & France*) for Ledesma (70), Junior Tonu'u (*Newport & NZ*) for Robinson (70), Kieran Roche (*Saracens*) for Kronfeld (77), Liam Botham (*Newcastle F*) for Rossouw (79)

REFEREE Tony Spreadbury (*England*) · **ATTENDANCE** 35,646

SCORING Hodge, pen (3–0); Chesney, try (3–5); van Straaten, con (3–7); Williams, try (3–12); van Straaten, con (3–14); Alatini, try (3–19); van Straaten, con (3–21); Laney, try (8–21); Laney, con (10–21); Hodge, pen (13–21); Kronfeld, try (13–26); van Straaten, con (13–28) (half-time) Robinson, try (13–33); van Straaten, con (13–35); Blair, try (18–35); Laney, con (20–35); Jones, try (20–40); Muller, try (20–45); Everitt, con (20–47); Paterson, try (25–47); Laney, con (27–47)

Played in warm conditions, the star-studded Barbarians were too good for a new-look Scotland side that had several uncapped players. The visitors played with their traditional flair and were largely in control throughout, winning the try-count 7–3. The experimental Scottish scrum was always under pressure and as a result the back-row lacked a sold attacking platform. New scrum-half Mike Blair had a promising debut, including a great solo try when he outran the cover on a long dash to the line. Scotland's other tries were scored by Brendan Laney, playing at inside centre, and Chris Paterson, who showed good strength to burrow through several tackles and make the line. There were also encouraging displays by newcomers Andy Craig and Rory Kerr, the latter making a weaving run that almost brought a score in the opening minutes.

---

505   TOUR OF NORTH AMERICA 2002   CANADA

Thunderbird Stadium, Vancouver · Saturday 15 June 2002
Lost 23–26

SCOTLAND Glenn Metcalfe (*Glasgow*); †Rory Kerr (*Glasgow*), †Andy Craig (*Orrell*), Brendan Laney (*Edinburgh*), Chris Paterson (*Edinburgh*); Duncan Hodge (*Edinburgh*), †Mike Blair (*Edinburgh*); Mattie Stewart (*Northampton Sts*), Gordon Bulloch (*Glasgow*), †Craig Smith (*Edinburgh*), Nathan Hines (*Edinburgh*), Stuart Grimes* (*Newcastle F*), Jason White (*Glasgow*), Simon Taylor (*Edinburgh*), Jon Petrie (*Glasgow*) ... Substitutes: †Donnie Macfadyen (*Glasgow*) for Petrie (51), †Allan Jacobsen (*Edinburgh*) for Stewart (68), †Ben Hinshelwood (*Worcester*) for Metcalfe (76), Steve Brotherstone (*Newcastle F*) for Bulloch (76)

CANADA Winston Stanley (*Worcester*); Fred Asselin (*James Bay*), Nik Witkowski (*Swansea*), John Cannon (*Rotherham*), Sean Fauth (*Castaway Wdrs*); Jared Barker (*James Bay*), Morgan Williams (*Stade Français*); Rod Show (*Newport*), Pat Dunkley (*Swansea*), Jon Thiel (*Bridgend*), Alan Charron* (*Dax*), Mike James (*Stade Français*), Ryan Banks (*Burnaby Lake*), Dan Baugh (*Cardiff*), Phil Murphy (*Perpignan*)

Substitutes: Colin Yukes (*Druids*) for Murphy (45), Ed Knaggs (*Castaway Wdrs*) for Banks (66), Kyle Nichols (*Balmy Beach*) for Asselin (68), Kevin Wirachowski (*UBC Old Boys*) for Thiel (76)

REFEREE David McHugh (*Ireland*) · **ATTENDANCE** 5,274

SCORING Barker, pen (0–3); Paterson, try (5–3); Laney, con (7–3); Murphy, try (7–8); Barker, con (7–10); Barker, pen (7–13); Laney, pen (10–13); Blair, try (15–13) (half-time) Taylor, try (20–13); Laney, pen (23–13); Barker, pen (23–16); Thiel, try (23–21); Barker, con (23–23); Barker, pen (23–26)

In June 2002, Scotland made a six-match tour of North America, including test matches against Canada and the United States. Some senior players, such as Scott Murray, Tom Smith and Budge Pountney, stayed at home, allowing several newcomers their chance to step-up. After three wins in their provincial matches, Scotland faced the full Canadian national side in the summer sunshine at Vancouver. Scotland fielded four new caps in the starting line-up and another three from the bench. They were expected to win but the Canadians, who included several amateurs, were passionate, physically imposing and very determined. Scotland held a ten-point lead early in the second-half which should have been the springboard for victory, but they fell away badly in the closing stages and the game ended in ignominious defeat. The Scots conceded too many turnovers, lacked control at the breakdown and passed-up several scoring opportunities. The only consolation was that they won the try-count 3–2. Chris Paterson scored the first after the Canadians bungled a quick lineout inside their own 22. Near the interval, Duncan Hodge made a searing break and after several phases debutant Mike Blair scored from close range. On the 42nd minute, Simon Taylor barged over the line after a superb break by Brendan Laney, and a few minutes later Laney added a penalty goal. The Scots seemed to have the match under control, but Canadian stand-off Jared Barker kicked two penalty goals and converted a try by prop John Thiel to snatch a historic win. Only Mike Blair and Simon Taylor stood out in a tepid Scottish display.

506   TOUR OF NORTH AMERICA 2002   USA

Balboa Park, San Francisco · Saturday 22 June 2002 · Won 65–23

SCOTLAND Glenn Metcalfe (*Glasgow*); Rory Kerr (*Glasgow*), Andy Craig (*Orrell*), Brendan Laney (*Edinburgh*), Chris Paterson (*Edinburgh*); Duncan Hodge (*Edinburgh*), Mike Blair (*Edinburgh*); Allan Jacobsen (*Edinburgh*), Gordon Bulloch (*Glasgow*), Mattie Stewart (*Northampton Sts*), Nathan Hines (*Edinburgh*), Stuart Grimes* (*Newcastle F*), Jason White (*Glasgow*), Donnie Macfadyen (*Glasgow*), Simon Taylor (*Edinburgh*) ... Substitutes: Andrew Henderson (*Glasgow*) for Metcalfe (30), Craig Smith (*Edinburgh*) for Jacobsen (39), †Marcus Di Rollo (*Edinburgh*) for Kerr (68), Graeme Burns (*Edinburgh*) for Blair (72), Steve Scott (*Borders*) for Bulloch (75), †Andy Hall (*Glasgow*) for White (77)

USA John Buchholz (*Olympic*); Mose Timoteo (*Golden Gate*), Phillip Eloff (*Chicago Lions*), Link Wilfley (*Rotherham*), Jason Keyter (*Rotherham*); Mike Hercus (*Belmont*), Kevin Dalzell (*Bath*); Mike MacDonald (*U California*), Kirk Khasigian (*Olympic*), Dan Dorsey (*Bath*), Eric Reed (*Chicago Lions*), Luke Gross (*Llanelli*), Aaron Satchwell (*Golden Gate*), Kort Schubert (*U California*), Dave Hodges* (*Llanelli*) ... Substitutes: Conrad Hodgson (*OMBAC*) for Hodges (29-40) and for Satchwell (67), Dan Anderson (*Chicago Griffins*) for Satchwell (37 to 40), Johnny Naqica (*Denver Barbarians*) for Eloff (41), John Tarpoff (*Aberavon*) for Satchwell (57-67) and for Dorsey (67), Kimball Kjar (*BYU*) for Dalzell (67), Andy McGarry (*Chicago Lions*) for MacDonald (70)

REFEREE Pablo Delucca (*Argentina*)

SCORING Timoteo, try (0–5); Wilfley, con (0–7); Laney, try (5–7); Laney, con (7–7); Laney, pen (10–7); Kerr, try (15–7); Wilfley, pen (15–10); Hines, try (20–10); Laney, con (22–10); Hodge, try (27–10); Laney, con (29–10); Wilfley, pen (29–13) (half-time) Paterson, try (34–13); Wilfley, pen (34–16); Henderson, try (39–16); Laney, con (41–16); Hodge, try (46–16); Laney, con (48–16); Craig, try (53–16); Paterson, try (58–16); Laney, con (60–16); White, try (65–16); Keyter, try (65–21); Wilfley, con (65–23)

After a good win in mid-week against United States A (24–8), the Scots completed their North American tour by demolishing the United States in San Francisco. The only blemish was that Nathan Hines was sent off for punching near the end of the first half and became the first Scotsman to be dismissed in a test match. Despite having to play over half of the game with a man short, the Scots kept their composure and were comfortable winners. They were a complete transformation from the hapless side that had lost to Canada the previous weekend and played with great continuity and confidence. Some of their attacking play and running was quite devastating and they scored a total of ten tries. The USA opened with an early try by wing Mosse Timoteo but overall they were a very mediocre team. They were outplayed in the forwards and had serious weaknesses in midfield where several missed tackles cost them dear. For Scotland, Brendan Laney had a fine match, Mike Blair showed pace and inventiveness, and Simon Taylor was always prominent.

Murrayfield · Saturday 9 November 2002 · Won 37–10

SCOTLAND †Stuart Moffat (*Glasgow*); †Nikki Walker (*Borders*), Andy Craig (*Orrell*), Brendan Laney (*Edinburgh*), Chris Paterson (*Edinburgh*); Gordon Ross (*Leeds Tykes*), Bryan Redpath* (*Sale Sharks*); Tom Smith (*Northampton Sts*), Gordon Bulloch (*Glasgow*), †Bruce Douglas (*Borders*), Scott Murray (*Edinburgh*), Stuart Grimes (*Newcastle F*), Martin Leslie (*Edinburgh*), Budge Pountney (*Northampton Sts*), Simon Taylor (*Edinburgh*) ... Substitutes: Mattie Stewart (*Northampton Sts*) for Smith (63), Nathan Hines (*Edinburgh*) for Murray (64), Jon Petrie (*Glasgow*) for Taylor (72), Gregor Townsend (*Borders*) for Ross (72), Ben Hinshelwood (*Worcester*) for Craig (74), Smith for Stewart (77), Steve Scott (*Borders*) for Leslie (79)

ROMANIA Gabriel Brezoianu (*Bordeaux Bègles*); Ioan Teodorescu (*U Cluj*), Valentin Maftei (*Valence*), Romeo Gontineac* (*Aurillac*), Vasile Ghioc (*Dinamo Bucuresti*); Ionut Tofan (*RCF*), Petre Mitu (*Grenoble*); Petru Balan (*Grenoble*), Marius Tincu (*Pau*), Dragos Dima (*Toulouse*), Augustin Petrichei (*Bourgoin-Jallieu*), Cristian Petre (*RCF*), Florin Corodeanu (*Grenoble*), George Chiriac (*Farul Constanta*), Alin Petrache (*Toulon*) ... Substitutes: Petrisor Toderasc (*Farul Constanta*) for Petrichei (40), Stefen Dragnea (*Valence*) for Dima (40), Lucian Sirbu (*RCF*) for Mitu (52), Costica Mersoiu (*Steaua Bucuresti*) for Petrache (60), Marcel Socaciu (*Rovigo*) for Balan (63)

REFEREE Andy Turner (*South Africa*) · ATTENDANCE 34,413

SCORING Grimes, try (5–0); Laney, con (7–0); Tofan, pen (7–3); Laney, pen (10–3); Laney, pen (13–3); Paterson, try (18–3); Laney, con (20–3) (half-time) Leslie, try (25–3); Pountney, try (30–3); Laney, con (32–3); Tofan, try (32–8); Tofan, con (32–10); Moffat, try (37–10)

Played in front of a surpisiringly large crowd, the Scots started their autumn test series with a comfortable five-tries-to-one victory over a drab and unambitious Romanian side, many of whom played their club rugby in France. Scotland had to work hard and did nothing spectacular, but they never looked seriously threatened by opponents renowned for their ability to spoil rather than create. The Scottish forwards met the challenge of a heavy Romanian pack head-on and dominated possession and territory. The three new caps, Stuart Moffat, Nikki Walker and Brice Douglas, showed promise, especially the latter in the scrums. Full-back Moffat was strong and enterprising, and scored a debut try a minute from the end.

Murrayfield · Saturday 16 November 2002 · Won 21–6

SCOTLAND Stuart Moffat (*Glasgow*); Nikki Walker (*Borders*), Andy Craig (*Orrell*), Brendan Laney (*Edinburgh*), Chris Paterson (*Edinburgh*); Gordon Ross (*Leeds Tykes*), Bryan Redpath* (*Sale Sharks*); Tom Smith (*Northampton Sts*), Gordon Bulloch (*Glasgow*), Bruce Douglas (*Borders*), Scott Murray (*Edinburgh*), Stuart Grimes (*Newcastle F*), Martin Leslie (*Edinburgh*), Budge Pountney (*Northampton Sts*), Simon Taylor (*Edinburgh*) ... Substitutes: Gregor Townsend (*Borders*) for Ross (62), Jason White (*Glasgow*) for Grimes (72), Ben Hinshelwood (*Worcester*) for Walker (77), David Hilton (*Glasgow*) for Smith (78), Nathan Hines (*Edinburgh*) for Murray (80)

SOUTH AFRICA Werner Greeff (*W Province*); Breyton Paulse (*W Province*), Adrian Jacobs

(*Falcons*), Robbie Fleck (*W Province*), Friedrich Lombard (*Cheetahs*); Butch James (*Natal Sharks*), Bolla Conradie (*W Province*); Wessel Roux (*Blue Bulls*), Lukas Van Biljon (*Natal Sharks*), Deon Carstens (*Natal Sharks*), Marco Wentzel (*Pumas*), Jannes Labuschagne (*Lions*), Corné Krige* (*W Province*), Pierre Uys (*Pumas*), Joe Van Niekerk (*Lions*) ... Substitutes: André Pretorius (*Lions*) for Jacobs (56), AJ Venter (*Natal Sharks*) for Wentzel (66), CJ van der Linde (*Cheetahs*) for Carstens (77)

REFEREE Nigel Williams (*Wales*) · ATTENDANCE 58,225

SCORING Laney, pen (3–0); Laney, pen (6–0); James, pen (6–3); James, pen (6–6) (half-time) Laney, pen (9–6); Pountney, try (14–6); Laney, con (16–6); Walker, try (21–6)

At long last Scotland managed to down one of the southern giants, their first win since Australia in 1982 and their first over South Africa since 1969. The South Africans were not at their best and both Scottish tries were fortuitous, but nothing could detract from a comprehensive and satisfying display. Playing in almost constant drizzle, the Scots combined determination, aggression and intelligence. The forwards were unstinting in their efforts, the half-backs kicked astutely, and the backs fielded safely and tackled well. The Scots began at great pace and Laney kicked two early penalties. It was only towards the end of the half that the South Africans started to find their game. Stand-off Butch James levelled the scores with two penalties, Chris Paterson made a great tackle on Breyton Paulse to prevent him from scoring under the posts, and the match was finely balanced at the interval. Early in the second-half, Laney kicked another penalty and Scottish self-belief started to grow. A few minutes later, Scott Murray won a lineout in the South African 22 and the forwards drove over the line in an untidy mêlée. After consulting video evidence, which was still inconclusive, the referee awarded a try which was credited to Pountney. Laney converted and the Scots never looked back. They kept up the pressure but it was only towards the end that they sealed the game with another contentious try. Under pressure from Redpath, substitute Andre Pretorius spilled the ball behind his own line and Nikki Walker managed to get the thinnest of touches on it, although it was debatable if he had applied downward pressure. However, there were no arguments about Scotland's victory which was richly deserved. The team was well prepared and every player did what was required of them. Hooker Gordon Bulloch had an outstanding match and the back-row outplayed their illustrious opponents.

---

509 AUTMN TEST 2002 FIJI

AUTUMN TEST 2002

Murrayfield · Sunday 24 November 2002 · Won 36–22

SCOTLAND Ben Hinshelwood (*Worcester*); Nikki Walker (*Borders*), Andy Craig (*Orrell*), Brendan Laney (*Edinburgh*), Chris Paterson (*Edinburgh*); Gregor Townsend (*Borders*), Bryan Redpath* (*Sale Sharks*); Tom Smith (*Northampton Sts*), Gordon Bulloch (*Glasgow*), Bruce Douglas (*Borders*), Jason White (*Glasgow*), Stuart Grimes (*Newcastle F*), Simon Taylor (*Edinburgh*), Budge Pountney (*Northampton Sts*), Jon Petrie (*Glasgow*) ... Substitutes: Nathan Hines (*Edinburgh*) for White (25), Stuart Moffat (*Edinburgh*) for Paterson (41), Martin Leslie (*Edinburgh*) for Petrie (55), Steve Scott (*Borders*) for Bulloch (68), Gorodn Ross (*Leeds Tykes*) for Townsend (69), Graeme Beveridge (*Glasgow*) for Redpath (76)

FIJI Atonio Nariva (*Namosi*); Fero Lasagavibau (*Northland*), Epeli Ruivadra (*Dravo*),

Seremaia Bai (*Southland*), Norman Ligairi (*Southland*); Joseph Narruhn (*Hino Motors*), Jacob Rauluni (*Rotherham*); Isaia Rasila (*Nadroga*), Greg Smith* (*Waikato*), Bill Cavubati (*Wellington*), Apinisa Naevo (*Kaneka*), Simon Raiwalui (*Newport*), Sisa Koyamaibole (*Toyota Shokki*), Alifereti Mocelutu (*Neath*), Setareki Tawake (*Suva*) ... Substitutes: Viliame Satala (*Harlequins*) for Bai (49), Senikavika Leawere (*East Coast*) for Naevo (54), Emori Katalau (*Narberth*) for Tawake (69), Waisale Serevi (*Mont-de-Marsan*) for Rauluni (70), Viliame Gadolo (*Suva*) for Mocelutu (73–9)

REFEREE Mark Lawrence (*South Africa*) · ATTENDANCE 37,351

SCORING Craig, try (5–0); Laney, con (7–0); Narruhn, pen (7–3); Narruhn, pen (7–6); Laney, pen (10–6); Laney, pen (13–6); Craig, try (18–6); Narruhn, pen (18–9); Narruhn, pen (18–12) (half-time) Naevo, try (18–17); Laney, pen (21–17); Laney, try (26–17); Craig, try (31–17); Ligairi, try (31–22); Grimes, try (36–22)

Coach Ian McGeechan made several changes, including a starting place for Gregor Townsend at stand-off. Following the historic win over the Springboks, this scrappy match was something of an anti-climax but Scotland completed a clean sweep of an autumn test series for the first time. They made plenty of errors but they produced some good moves, defended well and denied their opponents space and time on the ball. The burly Fijians were very phsyical and several Scots were on the wrong end of some hefty challenges, especially Jason White who had to be taken to hospital suffering from concussion. Former rugby league player Andy Craig scored three tries and showed good skills and opportunism. He scored his first try after only nine minutes and Scotland led 18–6 after half an hour. Narruhn replied with two penalties and early in the second half lock Naevo scored a kick-and-chase try to reduce the leeway to one point. Fijian winger Norman Ligairi was denied a score by an unlucky bounce of the ball and then the visitors gave away a cheap three points when they sent on a substitute too quickly. Scotland finished strongly and the best try of the match came when Laney took a looped pass from Townsend and powered around the defence to the corner. In a frantic conclusion, Craig completed his hat-trick, Ligairi scored a late consolation try for Fiji, and Stuart Grimes finished off a good movement with an injury-time try.

---

510 RBS SIX NATIONS CHAMPIONSHIP 2003 IRELAND

Murrayfield · Sunday 16 February 2003 · Lost 6–36

SCOTLAND Glenn Metcalfe (*Glasgow*); Kenny Logan (*London Wasps*), Andy Craig (*Orrell*), Brendan Laney (*Edinburgh*), Chris Paterson (*Edinburgh*); Gordon Ross (*Leeds Tykes*), Bryan Redpath* (*Sale Sharks*); Tom Smith (*Northampton Sts*), Gordon Bulloch (*Glasgow*), Bruce Douglas (*Borders*), Scott Murray (*Edinburgh*), Stuart Grimes (*Newcastle F*), Martin Leslie (*Edinburgh*), Andrew Mower (*Newcastle F*), Simon Taylor (*Edinburgh*) ... Substitutes: Gavin Kerr (*Leeds Tykes*) for Douglas (62), Gregor Townsend (*Borders*) for Ross (66)

IRELAND Girvan Dempsey (*Leinster*); Shane Horgan (*Leinster*), Brian O'Driscoll (*Leinster*), Kevin Maggs (*Bath*), Denis Hickie* (*Leinster*); David Humphreys (*Ulster*), Peter Stringer (*Munster*); Reggie Corrigan (*Leinster*), Shane Byrne (*Leinster*), John Hayes (*Munster*), Gary Longwell (*Ulster*), Malcolm O'Kelly (*Leinster*), Victor Costello (*Leinster*), Keith Gleeson (*Leinster*), Anthony Foley (*Munster*) ... Substitutes: Geordan Murphy (*Leicester Tgrs*) for Horgan (25), Leo Cullen (*Leinster*) for Longwell (66), Alan Quinlan (*Munster*) for Costello (69),

Marcus Horan (*Munster*) for Corrigan (73), Guy Easterby (*Llanelli*) for Stringer (76), Frank Sheehan (*Munster*) for Byrne (76), Paul Burke (*Harlequins*) for O'Driscoll (78)

REFEREE Andrew Cole (*Australia*)

SCORING Humphreys, pen (0–3); Hickie, try (0–8); Humphreys, con (0–10); Humphreys, pen (0–13) (half-time) Humphreys, pen (0–16); Ross, pen (3–16); Ross, pen (6–16); Humphreys, pen (6–19); Murphy, try (6–24); Humphreys, con (6–26); Humphreys, try (6–31); Humphreys, con (6–33); Humphreys, pen (6–36)

The optimism generated by a successful autumn all but evaporated as Ireland won at Murrayfield for the first time since 1985. The Scots fought hard but made a lot of errors and gradually their opponents drew away from them and ran out emphatic winners. The Irish forwards played with greater cohesion and conviction, especially flanker Victor Costello who had a fine match. Behind them, Brian O'Driscoll was always dangerous, stand-off David Humphreys kicked very effectively and winger Denis Hickie exposed the lack of pace in the Scottish line. The Scots had their best spell of pressure after the interval, but the Irish defence was firm and the home side could only muster two penalties by Gordon Ross.

---

511   RBS SIX NATIONS CHAMPIONSHIP 2003   FRANCE

Stade de France, Paris · Sunday 23 February 2003 · Lost 3–38

SCOTLAND Glenn Metcalfe (*Glasgow*); Chris Paterson (*Edinburgh*), Gregor Townsend (*Borders*), †Kevin Utterson (*Borders*), Kenny Logan (*London Wasps*); Brendan Laney (*Edinburgh*), Bryan Redpath* (*Sale Sharks*); Tom Smith (*Northampton Sts*), Gordon Bulloch (*Glasgow*), Bruce Douglas (*Borders*), Scott Murray (*Edinburgh*), Stuart Grimes (*Newcastle F*), Martin Leslie (*Edinburgh*), Andrew Mower (*Newcastle F*), Simon Taylor (*Edinburgh*) ... Substitutes: Mike Blair (*Edinburgh*) for Redpath (25–37 and 69), Jon Petrie (*Glasgow*) for Mower (39–40 and 69), Jason White (*Sale Sharks*) for Murray (54), Andy Craig (*Orrell*) for Laney (61), Gavin Kerr (*Leeds Tykes*) for Douglas (62), Douglas for Kerr (69)

FRANCE Clément Poitrenaud (*Toulouse*); Aurélien Rougerie (*Montferrand*), Xavier Garbajosa (*Toulouse*), Damien Traille (*Pau*), Vincent Clerc (*Toulouse*); François Gelez (*Agen*), Fabien Galthié* (*Stade Français*); Jean-Jacques Crenca (*Agen*), Raphaël Ibañez (*Castres*), Sylvain Marconnet (*Stade Français*), Fabien Pelous (*Toulouse*), Olivier Brouzet (*Montferrand*), Serge Betsen (*Biarritz*), Olivier Magne (*Montferrand*), Imanol Harinordoquy (*Pau*) ... Substitutes: Christian Califano (*Saracens*) for Marconnet (66), David Auradou (*Stade Français*) for Brouzet (66), Thomas Castaignède (*Saracens*) for Clerc (67), Sébastien Chabal (*Bourgoin-Jallieu*) for Harinordoquy (73), Dimitri Yachvili (*Biarritz*) for Galthié (73), Jean-Baptiste Rué (*Agen*) for Ibañez (79)

REFEREE Peter Marshall (*Australia*) · ATTENDANCE 78,692

SCORING Gelez, pen (0–3); Paterson, pen (3–3); Pelous, try (3–8); Gelez, pen (3–11); Gelez, pen (3–14); Gelez, pen (3–17) (half-time) Poitrenaud, try (3–22); Gelez, con (3–24); Traille, try (3–29); Gelez, con (3–31); Rougerie, try (3–36); Gelez, con (3–38)

Scotland experimented by moving Brendan Laney to stand-off, his fourth position since his arrival in 2001, and a first cap for Kevin Utterson at inside centre. In a disjointed match, the Scots showed some signs of improvement, but also a lack of confidence and basic skills. They had periods of territorial domination and made several incisive runs, but once again they failed to turn their opportunities into points. By contrast, the French, although playing a long way short of their best, easily outclassed their opponents and scored four tries to nil. The best came around the hour mark when centre Damien Traille made a perfectly-timed leap-and-catch to take a high kick by Gelez before crashing over the line. For Scotland, Glenn Metcalfe and Chris Paterson, making his first start on the right wing, were always dangerous in open play and Utterson had a sound debut. Laney was uncertain at stand-off and was replaced by Gregor Townsend for the final quarter.

512　　RBS SIX NATIONS CHAMPIONSHIP 2003　　WALES

Murrayfield · Saturday 8 March 2003 · Won 30–22

SCOTLAND Glenn Metcalfe (*Glasgow*); Chris Paterson (*Edinburgh*), James McLaren (*Bordeaux Bègles*), Kevin Utterson (*Borders*), Kenny Logan (*London Wasps*); Gregor Townsend (*Borders*), Bryan Redpath* (*Sale Sharks*); Tom Smith (*Northampton Sts*), Gordon Bulloch (*Glasgow*), Bruce Douglas (*Borders*), Scott Murray (*Edinburgh*), Stuart Grimes (*Newcastle F*), Jason White (*Glasgow*), Andrew Mower (*Newcastle F*), Simon Taylor (*Edinburgh*) ... Substitutes: Andy Craig (*Orrell*) for Utterson (51), Gavin Kerr (*Leeds Tykes*) for Douglas (60), Mike Blair (*Edinburgh*) for Redpath (72), Nathan Hines (*Edinburgh*) for Grimes (74), Rob Russell (*Saracens*) for Bulloch (76), Jon Petrie (*Glasgow*) for White (83), Gordon Ross (*Leeds Tykes*) for Townsend (83)

WALES Kevin Morgan (*Swansea*); Rhys Williams (*Cardiff*), Mark Taylor (*Swansea*), Tom Shanklin (*Saracens*), Gareth Thomas (*Bridgend*); Stephen Jones (*Llanelli*), Gareth Cooper (*Bath*); Iestyn Thomas (*Llanelli*), Gareth Williams (*Bridgend*), Ben Evans (*Swansea*), Robert Sidoli (*Pontypridd*), Steve Williams (*Northampton Sts*), Daffyd Jones (*Llanelli*), Martyn Williams* (*Cardiff*), Gavin Thomas (*Bath*) ... Substitutes: Gethin Jenkins (*Pontypridd*) for Evans (44), Gareth Llewellyn (*Neath*) for S Williams (58), Colin Charvis (*Swansea*) for Gavin Thomas (58), Matthew Watkins (*Llanelli*) for Morgan (62), Dwayne Peel (*Llanelli*) for Cooper (71), Iestyn Harris (*Cardiff*) for Shanklin (71), Mefin Davies (*Pontypridd*) for G Williams (71)

REFEREE Pablo Deluca (*Argentina*) replaced by Tony Spreadbury (*England*) at half-time

SCORING Paterson, pen (3–0); Douglas, try (8–0); Paterson, con (10–0); S Jones, pen (10–3); Taylor, try (15–3); Paterson, con (17–3); Cooper, try (17–8); S Jones, con (17–10); Paterson, pen (20–10) (half-time) Paterson, pen (23–10); Paterson, try (28–10); Paterson, con (30–10); Taylor, try (30–15); R Williams, try (30–20); S Jones, con (30–22)

Gregor Townsend returned to his favoured position of stand-off and Jason White was restored at blind-side flanker. Both players were pivotal in a much improved Scottish performance that combined pace, invention, good ball retention and far fewer errors than the previous two matches. Scotland had the game won before half-time. Chris Paterson kicked an early penalty and on the 14th minute tight-head prop Bruce Douglas blasted over from a lineout near the Welsh line, which was Scotland's first try of the championship. Seven minutes later, a floated pass from Townsend was picked-up by Simon Taylor on the left and the No8 dived over for a try. The visitors grabbed a foothold with a try by scrum-half Gareth Cooper, but Paterson, who kicked flawlessly all afternoon, landed two penalties either side of half-time. During the interval, Argentine referee Pablo Deluca retired with a pulled muscle to be replaced by England's Tony Spreadbury. Scotland lost the initiative in the later stages and Wales made a spirited fight-back. However, the Scottish defence was firm and well-organised, even when James McLaren was sin-binned for deliberately killing the ball. Towards the end of an entertaining match, prop Tom Smith grubber kicked behind the Welsh defence and Paterson touched down, the try being awarded after video evidence. The only disappointment was that the Scots lost concentration during an extended period of injury time and Wales scored two late tries. Overall this was an encouraging performance by Scotland, especially man-of-the-match Jason White whose powerful driving play was outstanding.

513   RBS SIX NATIONS CHAMPIONSHIP 2003   ENGLAND

Twickenham · Saturday 22 March 2003 · Lost 9–40

SCOTLAND Glenn Metcalfe (*Glasgow*); Chris Paterson (*Edinburgh*), James McLaren (*Bordeaux Bègles*), Andy Craig (*Orrell*), Kenny Logan (*London Wasps*); Gregor Townsend (*Borders*), Bryan Redpath* (*Sale Sharks*); Tom Smith (*Northampton Sts*), Gordon Bulloch (*Glasgow*), Bruce Douglas (*Borders*), Scott Murray (*Edinburgh*), Nathan Hines (*Edinburgh*), Jason White (*Glasgow*), Andrew Mower (*Newcastle F*), Simon Taylor (*Edinburgh*) ... Substitutes: Stuart Grimes (*Newcastle F*) for Murray (51), Kevin Utterson (*Borders*) for McLaren (56), Ross Beattie (*Bristol*) for Mower (67), Gavin Kerr (*Leeds Tykes*) for Douglas (72) ... Yellows cards: Mower (12–22), Taylor (14–24)

ENGLAND Josh Lewsey (*London Wasps*); Jason Robinson (*Sale Sharks*), Will Greenwood (*Harlequins*), Mike Tindall (*Bath*), Ben Cohen (*Northampton Sts*); Jonny Wilkinson (*Newcastle F*), Matt Dawson (*Northampton Sts*); Graham Rowntree (*Leicester Tgrs*), Steve Thompson (*Northampton Sts*), Jason Leonard (*Harlequins*), Martin Johnson* (*Leicester Tgrs*), Ben Kay (*Leicester Tgrs*), Richard Hill (*Saracens*), Neil Back (*Leicester Tgrs*), Lawrence Dallaglio (*London Wasps*) ... Substitutes: Dan Luger (*Harlequins*) for Tindall (56), Danny Grewcock (*Bath*) for Kay (62), Paul Grayson (*Northampton Sts*) for Wilkinson (66), Trevor Woodman (*Gloucester*) for Rowntree (66), Joe Worsley (*London Wasps*) for Dallaglio (74) ... Yellow card: Robinson (19-29)

REFEREE Alan Lewis (*Ireland*)

SCORING Wilkinson, pen (0–3); Wilkinson, pen (0–6); Paterson, pen (3–6); Paterson, pen (6–6); Lewsey, try (6–11); Wilkinson, con (6–13); Paterson, pen (9–13); Wilkinson, pen (9–16) (half-time) Cohen, try (9–21); Wilkinson, con (9–23); Wilkinson, pen (9–26); Robinson, try (9–31); Wilkinson, con (9–33); Robinson, try (9–38); Grayson, con (9–40)

Scotland took the fight to their opponents and worked hard, especially in the tackle, but eventually they were outgunned by a powerful and direct England side chasing the Grand Slam. The Scots showed lots of passion and guile, but they lacked any sort of cutting edge and contributed to their own downfall with some careless errors. They did well to keep their composure early on when they lost Mower and Taylor to the sin bin, but they never looked capable of upsetting the English juggernaut. The home side ran in four tries, the decisive score coming around the 50th minute. From a scrum near the Scottish line, Matt Dawson, who had a superb game for England, caught Bryan Redpath's kicking foot as the Scot lined up a clearance and Cohen gleefully dived on the loose ball for a try. The highlight of the match was a superb try by the electrifying Jason Robinson, who broke through at top speed and easily rounded Metcalfe. Dour Scottish resistance kept the floodgates from opening until three minutes from time when Dawson popped a short pass to Robinson who skated in under the posts. This was a gutsy effort by Scotland but the gulf in quality between the two sides was only too obvious.

514   RBS SIX NATIONS CHAMPIONSHIP 2003   ITALY

Murrayfield · Saturday 29 March 2003 · Won 33–25

SCOTLAND Glenn Metcalfe (*Glasgow*); Chris Paterson (*Edinburgh*), James McLaren (*Bordeaux Bègles*), Andy Craig (*Orrell*), Kenny Logan (*London Wasps*); Gregor Townsend (*Borders*), Bryan Redpath* (*Sale Sharks*); Tom Smith (*Northampton Sts*), Gordon Bulloch (*Glasgow*), Bruce Douglas (*Borders*), Scott Murray (*Edinburgh*), Nathan Hines (*Edinburgh*), Jason White (*Glasgow*), Andrew Mower (*Newcastle F*), Simon Taylor (*Edinburgh*) ... Substitutes: Ross Beattie (*Bristol*) for White (42), Stuart Grimes (*Newcastle F*) for Murray (59), Rob Russell (*Saracens*) for Bulloch (76)

ITALY Mirco Bergamasco (*Padova*); Paolo Vaccari (*Calvisano*), Andrea Masi (*L'Aquila*), Giovanni Raineri (*Calvisano*), Denis Dallan (*Treviso*); Ramiro Pez (*Rotherham*), Alessandro Troncon* (*Treviso*); Andrea Lo Cicero (*Lazio*), Carlo Festuccia (*Gran Parma*), Ramiro Martinez (*Treviso*), Cristian Bezzi (*Viadana*), Mark Giacheri (*Rotherham*), Andrea De Rossi (*Calvisano*), Aaron Persico (*Viadana*), Matt Phillips (*Viadana*) ... Substitutes: Gert Peens (*Parma*) for Vaccari (40), Leandro Castrogiovanni (*Calvisano*) for Martinez (53), Scott Palmer (*Treviso*) for Phillips (57–70) and for De Rossi (70), Santiago Dellapè (*Treviso*) for Giacheri (76)

REFEREE David McHugh (*Ireland*) · **ATTENDANCE** 45,739

SCORING Bergamasco, try (0–5); Paterson, pen (3–5); Pez, pen (3–8); White, try (8–8); McLaren, try (13–8); Paterson, pen (16–8); Pez, try (16–13); Pez, con (16–15); Logan, try (21–15); Paterson, con (23–15) (half-time) Pez, pen (23–18); Paterson, try (28–18); Paterson, con (30–18); Palmer, try (30–23); Pez, con (30–25); Paterson, pen (33–25)

In an entertaining encounter played in spring sunshine, Scotland salvaged their championship with a deserved victory against a persistent Italian side. The Scots scored four tries and did many things well although at times they looked nervous and uncertain. This match followed a similar pattern to the Welsh game three weeks earlier. The Scots were in control at the interval but spent much of the second half stuck inside their own half before scoring a decisive try against the run of play. Italy opened with an early try by full-back Mirco Bergamasco and then Paterson and Pez exchanged penalties. On the 12th minute, a quickly-taken free kick by Andrew Mower sent Jason White crashing through tackles to score. Three minutes later, Kenny Logan made a lively run, Townsend threw a long pass to James McLaren and the big centre was unstoppable from 20 metres. Paterson kicked a second penalty, but Italian stand-off Ramiro Pez scored and converted a try to reduce the lead to a single point. Shortly before the interval, the enterprising Logan, who had one of his best games for Scotland, took a quick tap-penalty and charged over the line. The Italians dominated territory for a long period in the second half but their only reward was another penalty by Pez. Around the hour mark, Simon Taylor exploded from the base of scrum, rounded the defence and sent Paterson away down the touchline. The winger chipped the defence, gathered the bouncing ball whilst going at full speed and ran in for a superb try. The Italians responded with a converted try by Scott Palmer to set-up a tense conclusion, but Paterson eased the Scots home with a long penalty in injury-time. This was a heartening win for the Scots for whom the back three of Metcalfe, Paterson and Logan were in excellent form.

| | 2003 | BARBARIANS |

Murrayfield · Wednesday 28 May 2003 · Lost 15–24

SCOTLAND XV Glenn Metcalfe (*Glasgow*); Simon Webster (*Edinburgh*), Brendan Laney (*Edinburgh*), Gregor Townsend* (*Borders*), James McLaren (*Bordeaux Bègles*); Chris Paterson (*Edinburgh*), Mike Blair (*Edinburgh*); Gavin Kerr (*Leeds Tykes*), Gordon Bulloch (*Glasgow*), Bruce Douglas (*Borders*), Scott Murray (*Edinburgh*), Nathan Hines (*Edinburgh*), Martin Leslie (*Edinburgh*), Jon Petrie (*Glasgow*), Simon Taylor (*Edinburgh*) ... Substitutes: Jason White (*Sale Sharks*) for Leslie (58), Gordon McIlwham (*Bordeaux Bègles*) for Kerr (63), Andrew Dall (*Edinburgh*) for Murray (67), Rory Kerr (*Glasgow*) for McLaren (70), Dougie Hall (*Edinburgh*) for Bulloch (73), Andrew Henderson (*Glasgow*) for Metcalfe (75)

BARBARIANS Conrad Jantjes (*Bulls & SA*); Scott Staniforth (*Waratahs & Australia*), De Wet Barry (*Stormers & SA*), Daryl Gibson (*Bristol & NZ*), Aurélien Rougerie (*Montferrand & France*); Felipe Contepomi (*Bristol & Argentina*), Darren Edwards (*London Irish*); Ollie Le Roux (*Sharks & SA*), Raphaël Ibañez (*Castres & France*), Adrian Garvey (*Newport & SA*), Mick Galwey* (*Munster & Ireland*), Hottie Louw (*Stormers & SA*), Troy Flavell (*Blues & NZ*), Santiago Phelan (*San Isidro & Argentina*), AJ Venter (*Sharks & SA*) ... Substitutes: Ryan Strudwick (*London Irish*) for Louw (10), Franck Tournaire (*Leicester Tgrs & France*) for Garvey (50), Matt Perry (*Bath & England*) for Jantjes (54), Olivier Magne (*Montferrand & France*) for Galwey (58), Cristian Stoica (*Castres & Italy*) for Contepomi (62 to 64), Matt Sexton (*Ulster*) for Ibañez (67)

REFEREE Nigel Whitehouse (*Wales*) · **ATTENDANCE** 27,526

SCORING Staniforth, try (0–5); Contepomi, con (0–7); Edwards, try (0–12); McLaren, try (5–12); Paterson, pen (8–12); Le Roux, try (8–17); Contepomi, con (8–19); Rougerie, try (8–24) (half-time) Metcalfe, try (13–24); Paterson, con (15–24)

Chris Paterson made his first start at stand-off, which many felt was his best position. Playing with typical adventure, the Barbarians scored almost immediately. South African centre De Wet Barry created space and Australian wing Scott Staniforth ghosted through several tackles. A few minutes later, the visitors set up a rolling maul inside the Scottish 22 before releasing scrum-half Darren Edwards who crossed the line unopposed. The Scots responded on the 22nd minute when wing James McLaren crashed over in the corner after a slick handling move. Paterson missed the conversion but kicked a long penalty to cut the leeway to 12–8. Towards the end of the half, the Barbarians scored further tries by South African prop Ollie Le Roux and French wing Aurelien Rougerie. Scotland improved as the game went on, but they made too many errors to really threaten. They had a lot of territory in the second half and stopped the Barbarians from scoring again. On the 65th minute, full-back Glenn Metcalfe made a quick dart for the line and was strong enough to force his way over. Despite another defeat, the Scots could take many good things from this game. The forwards were always competitive and the backs showed invention and daring. Paterson shone in his new role and formed an effective partnership with Mike Blair.

515   TOUR OF SOUTH AFRICA 2003   SOUTH AFRICA

ABSA Stadium, King's Park, Durban · Saturday 7 June 2003
Lost 25–29

SCOTLAND Glenn Metcalfe (*Glasgow*); Chris Paterson (*Edinburgh*), Andy Craig (*Orrell*), Andrew Henderson (*Glasgow*), Kenny Logan (*London Wasps*); Gregor Townsend (*Borders*), Bryan Redpath* (*Sale Sharks*); Gavin Kerr (*Leeds Tykes*), Gordon Bulloch (*Glasgow*), Bruce Douglas (*Borders*), Scott Murray (*Edinburgh*), Nathan Hines (*Edinburgh*), Jason White (*Sale Sharks*), Andrew Mower (*Newcastle F*), Simon Taylor (*Edinburgh*) ... Substitutes: Martin Leslie (*Edinburgh*) for White (62), Jon Petrie (*Glasgow*) for Mower (72), Rob Russell (*Saracens*) for Bulloch (72), James McLaren (*Bordeaux Bègles*) for Henderson (76)

SOUTH AFRICA Ricardo Loubscher (*Sharks*); Stefan Terblanche (*Sharks*), Andre Snyman (*Sharks*), Trevor Halstead (*Sharks*), Ashwin Willemse (*Lions*); Louis Koen (*Lions*), Joost van der Westhuizen* (*Bulls*); Lawrence Sephaka (*Lions*), Danie Coetzee (*Bulls*), Richard Bands (*Bulls*), Bakkies Botha (*Bulls*), Victor Matfield (*Bulls*), Hendrik Gerber (*Stormers*), Wikus van Heerden (*Lions*), Pedrie Wannenburg (*Bulls*) ... Substitutes: Selborne Boome (*Stormers*) for Botha (68), Juan Smith (*Cats*) for Wannenburg (69), Robbie Kempson (*Stormers*) for Sephaka (71), Cobus Visagie (*Stormers*) for Bands (75), Jaco van der Westhuyzen (*Bulls*) for Loubscher (78)

REFEREE Joel Jutge (*France*) · ATTENDANCE 37,528

SCORING White, try (5–0); Paterson, con (7–0); Koen, pen (7–3); Craig, try (12–3); Koen, pen (12–6) (half-time) Koen, pen (12–9); Paterson, try (17–9); Paterson, con (19–9); Koen, pen (19–12); Paterson, pen (22–12); Paterson, pen (25–12); Terblanche, try (25–17); Koen, con (25–19); Koen, pen (25–22); Halstead, try (25–27); Koen, con (25–29)

In June 2003, Scotland made a two-match tour of South Africa, their first visit to the country since 1960. In the first test at Durban, the Scots were close to a famous victory only to be thwarted right at the end. They played some lovely free-flowing rugby, won the try-count 3-2 and at one stage seemed to have the game under control only for the South Africans to make a late comeback and snatch a win. Scotland opened purposefully and after 13 minutes Jason White scored a try which Paterson converted from the touchline. Thier second try came after some 30 minutes when Logan drew the defence before flicking a pass inside to Craig who joyously romped over the line. Early in the second half, Logan broke away from his own 22 and after some good handling Paterson jinked past the defence for a superb score, later voted International Try of the Year. Paterson converted and kicked two penalties to give Scotland a thirteen point advantage. This should have been enough for victory but instead the South African scored a converted try and penalty, and the game was back in the balance. Scotland were unlucky when Koen hit the post with a penalty and the ball fell straight to Gerber who seemed to knock it forwards. Play was allowed to continue and after quick passing to the left Halstead handed-off Metcalfe and raced in behind the posts. Koen converted to give the South Africans a four point lead. The Scots fought back courageously and in the last move of the game Nathan Hines had the ball knocked out of his grasp, inches from the try-line as he attempted to touch it down one-handed. Scotland had produced one of their best performances for some time and were unfortunate to lose the game, but in the end they had let a chance to make history slip from their grasp.

 TOUR OF SOUTH AFRICA 2003   **SOUTH AFRICA**

Ellis Park, Johannesburg · Saturday 14 June 2003 · Lost 19–28

SCOTLAND Glenn Metcalfe (*Glasgow*); Chris Paterson (*Edinburgh*), Andy Craig (*Orrell*), Andrew Henderson (*Glasgow*), Kenny Logan (*London Wasps*); Gregor Townsend (*Borders*), Bryan Redpath* (*Sale Sharks*); Gavin Kerr (*Leeds Tykes*), Gordon Bulloch (*Glasgow*), Bruce Douglas (*Borders*), Scott Murray (*Edinburgh*), Nathan Hines (*Edinburgh*), Jason White (*Sale Sharks*), Andrew Mower (*Newcastle F*), Simon Taylor (*Edinburgh*) … Substitutes: Martin Leslie (*Edinburgh*) for Hines (45), Rob Russell (*Saracens*) for Bulloch (59), Gordon McIlwham (*Bordeaux Bègles*) for Kerr (59), Gordon Ross (*Leeds Tykes*) for Townsend (61), Jon Petrie (*Glasgow*) for Mower (64), Mike Blair (*Edinburgh*) for Redpath (68), Brendan Laney (*Edinburgh*) for Henderson (74)

SOUTH AFRICA Jaco van der Westhuyzen (*Bulls*); Stefan Terblanche (*Sharks*), Marius Joubert (*Stormers*), Trevor Halstead (*Sharks*), Ashwin Willemse (*Lions*); Louis Koen (*Lions*), Joost van der Westhuizen* (*Bulls*); Lawrence Sephaka (*Lions*), Danie Coetzee (*Bulls*), Richard Bands (*Bulls*), Bakkies Botha (*Bulls*), Victor Matfield (*Bulls*), Hendrik Gerber (*Stormers*), Wikus van Heerden (*Lions*), Pedrie Wannenburg (*Bulls*) … Substitutes: Robbie Kempson (*Stormers*) for Sephaka (48), Cobus Visagie (*Stormers*) for Bands (48), Gcobani Bobo (*Cats*) for Halstead (56), Juan Smith (*Cats*) for Gerber (61), Selborne Boome (*Stormers*) for Botha (68)

REFEREE Scott Young (*Australia*)

SCORING Craig, try (5–0); Paterson, con (7–0); Paterson, pen (10–0); Koen, pen (10–3); Koen, drop (10–6); Paterson, pen (13–6); Koen, pen (13–9); Paterson, pen (16–9); Koen, pen (16–12) (half-time) Terblanche, try (16–17); Koen, con (16–19); Koen, pen (16–22); Paterson, pen (19–22); Koen, pen (19–25); Koen, pen (19–28)

Playing in the high altitude of Johannesburg, Scotland gave another satisfactory display but they did not recapture their dynamism in attack and they wasted a lot of possession. The South Africans were an improved side from the previous weekend and won more comfortably than the score suggests. Scotland had a great start when Andy Craig intercepted a loose pass and made a long run to score under the posts. Paterson converted and his steady kicking gave the Scots a 16–12 lead at the interval. Almost immediately after the restart, the South Africans scored a converted try from Terblanche. A penalty exchange between Paterson and Koen made it 22–19 in South Africa's favour, but Scotland faded in the closing stages despite a raft of substitutions. Koen kicked two further penalties to clinch the match and the series.

517   **RUGBY WORLD CUP WARM-UP MATCH**   **ITALY**

Murrayfield · Saturday 23 August 2003 · Won 47–15

SCOTLAND Ben Hinshelwood (*Worcester*); †Simon Danielli (*Bath*), James McLaren (*Bayonne*),

Andrew Henderson (*Glasgow*), Kenny Logan (*London Wasps*); Gordon Ross (*Leeds Tykes*), Mike Blair (*Edinburgh*); Tom Smith (*Northampton Sts*), Rob Russell (*Saracens*), Bruce Douglas (*Borders*), Scott Murray* (*Edinburgh*), Nathan Hines (*Edinburgh*), Jason White (*Sale Sharks*), Jon Petrie (*Glasgow*), Simon Taylor (*Edinburgh*) ... Substitutes: Chris Paterson (*Edinburgh*) for Logan (2), Gordon Bulloch (*Glasgow*) for Russell (34), Brendan Laney (*Edinburgh*) for Henderson (61), Martin Leslie (*Edinburgh*) for White (61), Gordon McIlwham (*unattached*) for Douglas (68), Iain Fullerton (*Sale Sharks*) for Hines (68)

ITALY Gert Peens (*Parma*); Nicola Mazzucato (*Calvisano*), Andrea Masi (*Viadana*), Cristian Stoica (*Montpellier*), Mirco Bergamasco (*Stade Français*); Ramiro Pez (*Leicester Tgrs*), Allesandro Troncon* (*Treviso*); Andrea Lo Cicero (*Lazio*), Carlo Festuccia (*Gran Parma*), Salvatore Perugini (*Calvisano*), Santiago Dellape (*Treviso*), Marco Bortolami (*Padova*), Maurizio Zaffiri (*Calvisano*), Scott Palmer (*Treviso*), Matt Phillips (*Viadana*) ... Substitutes: Gonzalo Canale (*Treviso*) for Peens (22-28 and 58), Sergio Parisse (*Treviso*) for Zaffiri (50), Mauro Bergamasco (*Stade Français*) for Phillips (51), Fabio Ongaro (*Treviso*) for Festuccia (65), Ramiro Martinez (*Treviso*) for Perugini (65), Francesco Mazzariol (*Gran Parma*) for Mazzucato (65)

REFEREE Donal Courtney (*Ireland*) · **ATTENDANCE** 25,304

SCORING Ross, pen (3–0); Pez, pen (3–3); Ross, pen (6–3); White, try (11–3); Palmer, try (11–8); Ross, pen (14–8); McLaren, try (19–8); Ross, con (21–8); Blair, try (26–8); Ross, con (28–8) (half-time) Mazzucato, try (28–13); Pez, con (28–15); Ross, try (33–15); Danielli, try (38–15); Paterson, con (40–15); Laney, try (45–15); Paterson, con (47–15)

Preparations for the 2003 World Cup continued with a series of warm-up matches against Six Nations opposition, beginning with Italy. Scott Murray won his 50th cap and wing Simon Danielli made his debut. On a sunny afternoon, an understrength Scotland scored six tries and showed plenty of adventure against limited opposition. The Scottish handling, tackling and fitness levels were very good and the newcomers fitted effortlessly into the side. The half-backs combined well and scrum-half Mike Blair enhanced his growing reputation with some slick passing and excellent awareness. It was Blair's speed of thought and opportunism that created the best try of the match. Shortly before the interval, he took a quick tap-penalty inside his own half and fed Chris Paterson who raced away almost to the Italian 22. Blair was in support to take a perfectly-timed pass for a great score.

518   RUGBY WORLD CUP WARM-UP MATCH   WALES

Millennium Stadium, Cardiff · Saturday 30 August 2003 · Lost 9–23

SCOTLAND Glenn Metcalfe (*Glasgow*); Rory Kerr (*Glasgow*), Andy Craig (*Orrell*), Brendan Laney (*Edinburgh*), Simon Danielli (*Bath*); Gregor Townsend (*Borders*), Graeme Beveridge (*Glasgow*); Gavin Kerr (*Leeds Tykes*), Gordon Bulloch (*Glasgow*), Bruce Douglas (*Borders*), Scott Murray* (*Edinburgh*), Stuart Grimes (*Newcastle F*), Martin Leslie (*Edinburgh*), Andrew Mower (*Newcastle F*), Jon Petrie (*Glasgow*) ... Substitutes: Nathan Hines (*Edinburgh*) for Murray (31), Gordon McIlwham (*unattached*) for Douglas (40), †Andrew Dall (*Edinburgh*) for Leslie (61), Chris Paterson (*Edinburgh*) for Laney (72), †Dougie Hall (*Edinburgh*) for Bulloch (74)

WALES Garan Evans (*Llanelli Scarlets*); Jamie Robinson (*Cardiff Blues*), Tom Shanklin (*Cardiff Blues*), Iestyn Harris (*Cardiff Blues*), Matthew Watkins (*Llanelli Scarlets*); Ceri Sweeney

(*Celtic Wrs*), Dwayne Peel (*Llanelli Scarlets*); Duncan Jones (*NS Ospreys*), Robin McBryde (*Llanelli Scarlets*), Adam Jones (*NS Ospreys*), Vernon Cooper (*Llanelli Scarlets*), Michael Owen (*NG Dragons*), Colin Charvis* (*unattached*), Richard Parks (*Celtic Wrs*), Alix Popham (*Leeds Tykes*) ... Substitutes: Rhys Oakley (*NG Dragons*) for Popham (25), Gareth Llewellyn (*NS Ospreys*) for Cooper (51), Huw Bennett (*NS Ospreys*) for McBryde (78), Hal Luscombe (*NG Dragons*) for Watkins (80)

REFEREE Chris White (*England*) · ATTENDANCE 24,740

SCORING Laney, pen (3–0); Harris, pen (3–3); Harris, pen (3–6); Harris, pen (3–9); Harris, pen (3–12); Laney, pen (6–12) (half-time) Harris, pen (6–15); Laney, pen (9–15); Owen, try (9–20); Sweeney, drop (9–23)

The Scots were brought back to earth in a poor match that was littered with errors and ineptitude from both sides. Playing in a half-empty stadium, the Scots showed none of their usual determination or commitment and were too hesitant in attack. They spent a lot of time in the Welsh half but made little impact against a spirited defence. Typically, the only try of the match came from a mistake. After about ten minutes of the second half, the Welsh pounced on a loose pass and took play to the Scottish line where lock Michael Owen stretched over to score. Towards the end of a forgettable encounter, Scotland introduced two new caps in flanker Andrew Dall and hooker Dougie Hall.

519 RUGBY WORLD CUP WARM-UP MATCH IRELAND

Murrayfield · Saturday 6 September 2003 · Lost 10–29

SCOTLAND Glenn Metcalfe (*Glasgow*); Chris Paterson (*Edinburgh*), Andy Craig (*Orrell*), Andrew Henderson (*Glasgow*), Kenny Logan (*London Wasps*); Gordon Ross (*Leeds Tykes*), Mike Blair (*Edinburgh*); Allan Jacobsen (*Edinburgh*), Gordon Bulloch* (*Glasgow*), Gordon McIlwham (*unattached*), Stuart Grimes (*Newcastle F*), Nathan Hines (*Edinburgh*), Ross Beattie (*NG Dragons*), Andrew Mower (*Newcastle F*), Simon Taylor (*Edinburgh*) ... Substitutes: †Simon Webster (*Edinburgh*) for Metcalfe (h-t), Iain Fullerton (*Sale Sharks*) for Grimes (53-65), Jon Petrie (*Glasgow*) for Beattie (62), Matthew Proudfoot (*Glasgow*) for McIlwham (62), James McLaren (*Bayonne*) for Henderson (62), Rob Russell (*Saracens*) for Bulloch (67)

IRELAND Geordan Murphy (*Leicester Tgrs*); Anthony Horgan (*Munster*), Brian O'Driscoll (*Leinster*), Kevin Maggs (*Bath*), Denis Hickie (*Leinster*); Ronan O'Gara (*Munster*), Peter Stringer (*Munster*); Marcus Horan (*Munster*), Keith Wood* (*unattached*), Reggie Corrigan (*Leinster*), Malcolm O'Kelly (*Leinster*), Paul O'Connell (*Munster*), Eric Miller (*Leinster*), David Wallace (*Munster*), Victor Costello (*Leinster*) ... Substitutes: Girvan Dempsey (*Leinster*) for Murphy (21), Simon Easterby (*Llanelli Scarlets*) for Costello (51-55) and for O'Connell (75), Kieron Dawson (*London Irish*) for Miller (69), Guy Easterby (*Rotherham*) for Stringer (75), David Humphreys (*Ulster*) for O'Driscoll (75), Simon Best (*Ulster*) for Corrigan (75), Shane Byrne (*Leinster*) for Wood (77)

REFEREE Nigel Whitehouse (*Wales*) · ATTENDANCE 35,264

SCORING Paterson, pen (3–0); O'Gara, pen (3–3); Maggs, try (3–8); O'Gara, con (3–10) (half-time) Hickie, try (3–15); Horgan, try (3–20); O'Gara, con (3–22); Wallace, try (3–27); O'Gara, con (3–29); Webster, try (8–29); Paterson, con (10–29)

Ireland were comfortable winners but their victory was overshadowed by a serious leg break to their gifted full-back Geordan Murphy which ruled him out of the World Cup. Scotland improved on the previous weekend and won a lot of possession but lacked Ireland's ability to finish. The visitors won the try count 4–1 and showed excellent continuity and strong running. The first half was evenly balanced until Nathan Hines was sin-binned for handling in a ruck. Just before the interval, the Irish forwards made several drives near the Scottish line before the ball was moved left and bustling centre Kevin Maggs powered his way over. Scotland might have been awarded a try soon afterwards when Andrew Mower looked to have touched down but the referee ruled that he had knocked-on. Ireland stretched away in the second half and scored three good tries. Edinburgh winger Simon Webster came on at half-time for his first cap and he scored a late consolation try which Paterson converted.

Rugby World Cup 2003

The 2003 Rugby World Cup was held in Australia and was the most successful tournament to date. The sports-mad Australian public took the World Cup to their hearts and thanks to good marketing the games were well attended, including those with the smaller nations. Scotland were drawn in Pool B alongside their old rivals France, Fiji, Japan and the United States of America. France were clear favourites to win the group, leaving the Scots to battle out second place against some potentially tricky opponents. Scotland suffered a serious blow just before the tournament when Andrew Mower, their only genuine openside, suffered a knee injury which ended his career. The 2003 World Cup was largely disappointing for Scotland. They did well enough to reach the knockout stages, but in truth they were never wholly convincing. Several players were in the twilight of their careers and the team was unable to recapture the promise and dynamism of the summer tour to South Africa.

520   RUGBY WORLD CUP 2003   JAPAN

Dairy Farmers Stadium, Townsville · Sunday 12 October 2003
Won 32–11

SCOTLAND Ben Hinshelwood (*Worcester*); Chris Paterson (*Edinburgh*), Andy Craig (*Orrell*), James McLaren (*Castres*), Kenny Logan (*London Wasps*); Gordon Ross (*Leeds Tykes*), Bryan Redpath* (*Sale Sharks*); Tom Smith (*Northampton Sts*), Rob Russell (*Saracens*), Bruce Douglas (*Borders*), Scott Murray (*Edinburgh*), Stuart Grimes (*Newcastle F*), Jason White (*Sale Sharks*), Jon Petrie (*Glasgow*), Simon Taylor (*Edinburgh*) ... Substitutes: Martin Leslie (*Edinburgh*) for Petrie (57), Ross Beattie (*Bristol*) for Murray (66), Gregor Townsend (*Borders*) for Ross (66), Gavin Kerr (*Leeds Tykes*) for Douglas (73), Simon Danielli (*Bath*) for Paterson (79)

JAPAN Tsutomu Matsuda (*Toshiba Fuchu*); Daisuke Ohata (*Montferrand*), Ruben Parkinson (*Sanix*), Yukio Motoki (*Kobe Steel*), Hirotoki Onozawa (*Suntory*); Keiji Hirose (*Toyota Motors*), Takashi Tsuji (*NEC*); Shin Hasegawa (*Suntory*), Masao Amino (*NEC*), Masahiko Toyoyama (*Toyota Motors*), Hajime Kiso (*Yamaha*), Adam Parker (*Toshiba Fuchu*), Naoya Okubo (*Suntory*), Takuro Miuchi* (*NEC*), Takeomi Ito (*Kobe Steel*) ... Substitutes: Masaaki Sakata (*Suntory*) for Amino (40), Yuji Sonoda (*Kobe Steel*) for Tsuji (51), Andrew Miller (*Kobe Steel*) for Hirose (51), Yasunori Watanabe (*Toshiba Fuchu*) for Okubo (67), Toru Kurihara (*Suntory*) for Matsuda (71)

SCORING Paterson, try (5–0); Paterson, con (7–0); Hirose, pen (7–3); Grimes, try (12–3); Paterson, pen (15–3); Hirose, pen (15–6) (half-time) Onozawa, try (15–11); Paterson, try (20–11); Taylor, try (25–11); Danielli, try (30–11); Townsend, con (32–11)

Scotland started their World Cup with a patchy win over a hard-working Japan. Scotland opened purposefully with two early tries but then they unaccountably lost their way. Encouraged by the majority of the crowd, the Japanese showed great fighting spirit and in the 54th minute they closed to within four points with a try by winger Onozawa. Briefly, it seemed that there might be a shock result but Scotland made a heartening revival in the closing stages. Logan was denied a try by the video official who correctly ruled that the wing had lost the ball when sliding over the line. On the 65th minute, Taylor broke up the right touchline and Paterson grasped a bobbling ball from Japanese hands for the decisive score. Taylor and Townsend added late tries and Scotland breathed a sigh of relief.

521   RUGBY WORLD CUP 2003   USA

Suncorp Stadium, Brisbane · Monday 20 October 2003 · Won 39–15

SCOTLAND Glenn Metcalfe (*Glasgow*); Simon Danielli (*Bath*), Andy Craig (*Orrell*), Andrew Henderson (*Glasgow*), Chris Paterson (*Edinburgh*); Gregor Townsend (*Borders*), Mike Blair (*Edinburgh*); Tom Smith (*Northampton Sts*), Gordon Bulloch* (*Glasgow*), Gavin Kerr (*Leeds Tykes*), Nathan Hines (*Edinburgh*), Stuart Grimes (*Newcastle F*), Ross Beattie (*Bristol*), Jon Petrie (*Glasgow*), Simon Taylor (*Edinburgh*) ... Substitutes: Martin Leslie (*Edinburgh*) for Petrie (53), Brian Redpath (*Sale Sharks*) for Blair (60), Jason White (*Sale Sharks*) for Beattie (66), Ben Hinshelwood (*Worcester Wrs*) for Craig (72), Bruce Douglas (*Borders*) for Smith (73), Kenny Logan (*London Wasps*) for Townsend (77) ... Yellow card: Smith

USA Paul Emerick (*Chicago Lions*); David Fee (*Chicago Lions*), Phillip Eloff (*Chicago Lions*), Kain Cross (*Santa Monica*), Riaan Van Zyl (*Old Puget Sound*); Mike Hercus (*Belmont Shore*), Kevin Dalzell (*Old Mission Beach*); Mike MacDonald (*California U*), Kirk Khasigian (*Belmont Shore*), Dan Dorsey (*Swansea*), Alec Parker (*Gentlemen of Aspen*), Luke Gross (*Rotherham*), Kort Schubert (*Olympic Club*), Dave Hodges* (*Llanelli Scarlets*), Dan Lyle (*Bath*) ... Substitutes: Jurie Gouws (*Santa Monica*) for Hodges (30–38) and Parker (54), Jason Keyter (*Rotherham*) for Cross (43), Kimball Kjar (*Brigham YU*) for Dalzell (66), Richard Liddington (*Stade Français*) for Dorsey (66), Oloseti Fifita (Hayward Griffins) for Hodges (69), Link Wilfley (Rotherham) for van Zyl (80) ... Yellow card: Emerick (64)

REFEREE Jonathan Kaplan (South Africa) · ATTENDANCE 46,796

SCORING Paterson, pen (3–0); Hercus, pen (3–3); Hercus, pen (3–6); Danielli, try (8–6); Paterson, con (10–6); Danielli, try (15–6); Paterson, con (17–6); Kerr, try (22–6); Paterson, con (24–6); Hercus, pen (24–9) (half-time) Hercus, pen (24–12); Paterson, pen (27–12); Hercus, pen (27–15); Townsend, try (32–15); Paterson, try (37–15); Paterson, con (39–15)

Playing in front of a large and vociferous support, the Scots were much livelier than the previous game and won comfortably. The forwards secured some quality posse-ssion and the backs were always enterprising. Scotland looked nervous in the opening stages, but on the 20th minute Danielli made a powerful run around the defence for a great solo try. Shortly afterwards, he scored again and Paterson converted from the touchline. Prop Gavin Kerr charged down a clearance and raced to the line for Scotland's third try which effectively ended the contest. The Scots lost some of their momentum in the second half, but they were never in any danger. Following an elusive run by Paterson, Gregor Townsend made a sublime dummy pass and dived over for the bonus-point try. Near the finish, Paterson moved to stand-off and capped a fine display with a late try and conversion. This was an encouraging result for Scotland who were far from perfect but at least heading in the right direction. After the match, substitute Martin Leslie was cited for deliberately kneeing an opponent on the head and suspended for the rest of the tournament.

---

522   RUGBY WORLD CUP 2003   FRANCE

Telstra Stadium, Sydney · Saturday 25 October 2003 · Lost 9–51

SCOTLAND Glenn Metcalfe (*Glasgow*); Chris Paterson (*Edinburgh*), Andy Craig (*Orrell*), Andrew Henderson (*Glasgow*), Kenny Logan (*London Wasps*); Gregor Townsend (*Borders*), Bryan Redpath* (*Sale Sharks*); Tom Smith (*Northampton Sts*), Gordon Bulloch (*Glasgow*), Gavin Kerr (*Leeds Tykes*), Scott Murray (*Edinburgh*), Stuart Grimes (*Newcastle F*), Cameron Mather (*Glasgow*), Simon Taylor (*Edinburgh*) ... Substitutes: Jon Petrie (*Glasgow*) for Mather (36-40) and Taylor (68), Bruce Douglas (*Borders*) for Kerr (40), Nathan Hines (*Edinburgh*) for Murray (60), James McLaren (*Castres*) for Henderson (66), Rob Russell (*Saracens*) for Bulloch (73)

FRANCE Nicolas Brusque (*Biarritz*); Aurelien Rougerie (*Montferrand*), Tony Marsh (*Montferrand*), Yannick Jauzion (*Toulouse*), Christophe Dominici (*Stade Français*); Frederic Michalak (*Toulouse*), Fabien Galthié* (*Stade Français*); Jean Jacques Crenca (*Agen*), Raphaël Ibañez (*Saracens*), Sylvain Marconnet (*Stade Français*), Fabien Pelous (*Toulouse*), Jerome Thion (*Biarritz*), Serge Betsen (*Biarritz*), Olivier Magne (*Montferrand*), Imanol Harinordoquy (*Pau*) ... Substitutes: Olivier Milloud (*Bourgoin-Jallieu*) for Marconnet (66), Yannick Bru (*Toulouse*) for Ibañez (66), Patrick Tabacco (*Stade Français*) for Magne (67), Damien Traille (*Pau*) for Marsh (74), Gerald Merceron (*Montferrand*) for Galthié (77), Olivier Brouzet (*Montferrand*) for Harinordoquy (80)

REFEREE David McHugh (*Ireland*) · ATTENDANCE 78,974

SCORING Michalak, pen (0–3); Paterson, pen (3–3); Michalak, drop (3–6); Michalak, pen (3–9); Betsen, try (3–14); Michalak, con (3–16); Paterson, pen (6–16); Michalak, pen (6–19) (half-time) Brusque, drop (6–22); Harinordoquy, try (6–27); Michalak, con (6–29); Paterson, pen (9–29); Michalak, try (9–34); Michalak, con (9–36); Galthié, try (9–41); Michalak, pen (9–44); Brusque, try (9–49); Michalak, con (9–51)

Played before almost 80,000 people in Sydney's Olympic Stadium, Scotland were swept aside by a talented French side which scored five unanswered tries. France were superior in all aspects, especially their superb half-backs Fabien Galthié and Frederic Michalak. The latter gave a consummate performance and scored 28 points, including a 'full-house'. The French scrum never conceded an inch and the back-row was simply outstanding. Their first try came from a well-worked movement when Magne drove into the 22 and No 8 Harinordoquy linked with Betsen who scored at the posts. Early in the second-half, the French forwards made an unstoppable drive from a lineout and Harinordinquy scored a try. Thereafter it was largely one-way traffic. Michalak danced through some half-hearted defence for a try under the posts, Galthié scored from a close-range scrum, and near the finish Brusque made a perfect chip over the cover and re-gathered to touchdown at the corner. Michalak brought down the curtain with a brilliant conversion to take France over the 50 points mark. The Frenchmen had been hugely impressive and seemed to be serious challengers for the title. By contrast, the Scots were hopelessly outclassed and on the road to an early exit.

Aussie Stadium, Sydney · Saturday 1 November 2003 · Won 22–20

SCOTLAND Glenn Metcalfe (*Glasgow*); Simon Danielli (*Bath*), Gregor Townsend (*Borders*), Andrew Henderson (*Glasgow*), Kenny Logan (*London Wasps*); Chris Paterson (*Edinburgh*), Bryan Redpath* (*Sale Sharks*); Tom Smith (*Northampton Sts*), Gordon Bulloch (*Glasgow*), Bruce Douglas (*Borders*), Nathan Hines (*Edinburgh*), Stuart Grimes (*Newcastle F*), Ross Beattie (*Bristol*), Cameron Mather (*Glasgow*), Simon Taylor (*Edinburgh*) ... Substitutes: James McLaren (*Castres*) for Danielli (32-8 and 41), Rob Russell (*Saracens*) for Bulloch (40-1), Jason White (*Sale Sharks*) for Beattie (45), Ben Hinshelwood (*Worcester Wrs*) for Metcalfe (73)

FIJI Norman Ligairi (*Yamaha*); Aisea Tuilevu (*Otago*), Epeli Ruivadra (*Dravuni*), Seru Rabeni (*Alambra*), Rupeni Caucaunibuca (*Auckland*); Nicky Little (*Saracens*), Moses Rauluni (*Easts*); Isaia Rasila (*Gaunavou*), Greg Smith (*Waikato*), Joeli Veitayaki (*Calton*), Ifereimi Rawaqa (*Vuda*), Api Naevo (*Calton*), Vula Maimuri (*Auckland*), Koli Sewabu (*Yamaha*), Alifereti Doviverata* (*Yamaha*) ... Substitutes: Nacanieli Seru (*Lomaiviti*) for Smith (32), Sisa Koyamaibole (*Nadroga*) for Maimuri (50), Jacob Rauluni (*Easts*) for Rauluni (67), Kitione Salawa (*Nadi*) for Sewabu (69), Isikeli Nacewa (*Auckland*) for Rabeni (78), Vilimoni Delasu (*Yamaha*) for Ruivadra (79) ... Yellow card: Naevo (76)

REFEREE Tony Spreadbury (*England*) · ATTENDANCE 38,137

SCORING Caucaunibuca, try (0–5); Little, con (0–7); Paterson, pen (3–7); Paterson, pen (6–7); Caucuanibuca, try (6–12); Little, con (6–14) (half-time) Paterson, pen (9–14); Paterson, pen (12–14); Paterson, pen (15–14); Little, pen (15–17); Little, pen (15–20); Smith, try (20–20); Paterson, con (22–20)

Both sides were able to qualify for the next phase of the World Cup so the result was not a foregone conclusion. Scotland left it late but just managed to escape with a win. Fiji had the best of the first-half and on the twelve minute their dynamic wing Rupeni Caucau flew down the left touchline to score in the corner. Paterson replied with two penalties and towards the end of the first half Caucau made a fantastic run from deep inside his own territory for a brilliant solo try. In the second half, Scotland's superior fitness started to tell and Paterson kicked three penalties for a narrow lead. The Scots should have eased away but instead they made a series of errors and Fiji regained the advantage with two penalties by stand-off Nicky Little. With their World Cup dreams slipping away from them, Scotland were thrown a lifeline when Fijian lock Naevo was sent to the sin bin with less than five minutes remaining. The Scots set-up a rolling maul near the Fijian line and prop Tom Smith was pushed over for a vital try. Paterson held his nerve and kicked the winning conversion. It had been a close thing, but Scotland had shown enough patience and discipline to slowly wear their opponents down and come through. Full-back Glenn Metcalfe made two superb try-saving tackles, both centres were strong in defence and Paterson's kicking was almost fault-less. Kenny Logan switched to the right wing in the second-half and did a great job of containing the threat of Caucau. Scotland's reward was a quarter-final meeting with the World Cup hosts and reigning champions Australia.

Saturday 8 November 2003 · Suncorp Stadium, Brisbane
Lost 16–33

SCOTLAND Glenn Metcalfe (*Glasgow*); Simon Danielli (*Bath*), Gregor Townsend (*Borders*), Andrew Henderson (*Glasgow*), Kenny Logan (*London Wasps*); Chris Paterson (*Edinburgh*), Bryan Redpath* (*Sale Sharks*); Tom Smith (*Northampton Sts*), Gordon Bulloch (*Glasgow*), Bruce Douglas (*Borders*), Nathan Hines (*Edinburgh*), Stuart Grimes (*Newcastle F*), Jason White (*Sale Sharks*), Cameron Mather (*Glasgow*), Simon Taylor (*Edinburgh*) ... Substitutes: Ben Hinshelwood (*Worcester Wrs*) for Metcalfe (47), Scott Murray (*Edinburgh*) for Grimes (62), Jon Petrie (*Glasgow*) for White (65), Gordon McIlwham (*Bordeaux Bègles*) for Douglas (69), Rob Russell (*Saracens*) for Bulloch (73), James McLaren (*Castres*) for Townsend (76)

AUSTRALIA Matt Rogers (*S Districts*); Wendell Sailor (*Gold Coast*), Stirling Mortlock (*Gordon*), Elton Flatley (*Brothers*), Lote Tuqiri (*W Harbour*); Stephen Larkham (*ACT*), George Gregan* (*Randwick*), Bill Young (*Eastwood*), Brendan Cannon (*Sydney U*), Ben Darwin (*N Suburbs*), Justin Harrison (*Eastwood*), Nathan Sharpe (*University*), George Smith (*Manly*), Phil Waugh (*Sydney U*), David Lyons (*Sydney U*) ... Substitutes: Matt Cockbain (*GPS*) for Smith (40), Matt Giteau (*Canberra*) for Larkham (54), Joe Roff (*Canberra*) for Rogers (60), Jeremy Paul (*Eastwood*) for Cannon (62), Al Baxter (*N Suburbs*) for Darwin (65), Chris Whitaker (*Randwick*) for Gregan (66), Daniel Vickerman (*Sydney U*) for Giteau (74), Cannon for Waugh (76–7)

REFEREE Steve Walsh (*New Zealand*) · ATTENDANCE 45,412

SCORING Flatley, pen (0–3); Paterson, pen (3–3); Flatley, pen (3–6); Paterson, pen (6–6); Flatley, pen (6–9); Paterson, drop (9–9) (half-time) Mortlock, try (9–14); Flatley, con (9–16); Flatley, pen (9–19); Gregan, try (9–24); Flatley, con (9–26); Lyons, try (9–31); Flatley, con (9–33); Russell, try (14–33); Paterson, con (16–33)

In the first-half, Scotland produced their best rugby of the World Cup, playing with their customary pride and passion and making Australia look an ordinary side. A few minutes before the interval, Chris Paterson kicked an enormous drop goal from around halfway. Paterson's effort was doubly remarkable because in the warm-up before the match he had been knocked senseless by a stray kick and there was some doubt whether he would be able to play. Predictably, the Australians showed greater urgency in the second half although they had a lucky break when they scored their first try five minutes after the restart. Flanker Phil Waugh seemed to be an offside position when he plundered the ball from a ruck. The Scots claimed a penalty but play was allowed to continue and Mortlock slipped a tackle inside his own half and sprinted all the way to the line. Flately converted and kicked a penalty and suddenly the Australians had a ten point lead. On the 58th minute, Tuqiri made a long run to the Scottish posts and from the ensuing ruck Gregan kicked through and won the race to the touchdown. Flately converted to effectively end the contest. Five minutes later, No8 David Lyons powered over from a scrum. Scotland managed a late consolation try when substitute hooker Rob Russell was driven over from a lineout. Scotland had given their all and restored some of their self-respect, but the Australians were just too good for them. This was the final match for some legendery Scottish players, including Kenny Logan, Gregor Townsend and Bryan Redpath.

525   RBS SIX NATIONS CHAMPIONSHIP 2004   WALES

Millennium Stadium, Cardiff · Sunday 14 February 2004

Lost 10–23

SCOTLAND Ben Hinshelwood (*Worcester*); Simon Danielli (*Bath*), †Tom Philip (*Edinburgh*), Brendan Laney (*Edinburgh*), Andrew Henderson (*Glasgow*); Chris Paterson* (*Edinburgh*), †Chris Cusiter (*Borders*); Tom Smith (*Northampton Sts*), Gordon Bulloch (*Glasgow*), Bruce Douglas (*Borders*), Scott Murray (*Edinburgh*), Stuart Grimes (*Newcastle F*), Cameron Mather (*Glasgow*), †Allister Hogg (*Edinburgh*), Simon Taylor (*Edinburgh*) ... Substitutes: †Dan Parks (*Glasgow*) for Laney (45), Gavin Kerr (*Leeds Tykes*) for Douglas (50), Jason White (*Sale Sharks*) for Hogg (50), Simon Webster (*Edinburgh*) for Hinshelwood (64), Mike Blair (*Edinburgh*) for Cusiter (75), Robbie Russell (*Saracens*) for Bulloch (80)

WALES Gareth Thomas (*Celtic Wrs*); Rhys Williams (*Cardiff Blues*), Sonny Parker (*Celtic Wrs*), Iestyn Harris (*Cardiff Blues*), Shane Williams (*NS Ospreys*); Stephen Jones (*Llanelli Scarlets*), Gareth Cooper (*Celtic Wrs*); Duncan Jones (*NS Ospreys*), Mefin Davies (*Celtic Wrs*), Adam Jones (*NS Ospreys*), Brent Cockbain (*Celtic Wrs*), Gareth Llewellyn (*NS Ospreys*), Colin Charvis* (*Tarbes*), Martyn Williams (*Cardiff Blues*), Dafydd Jones (*Llanelli Scarlets*) ... Substitutes: Gethin Jenkins (*Celtic Wrs*) for A Jones (32), Michael Owen (*NG Dragons*) for Llewellyn (53), Jonathan Thomas (*NS Ospreys*) for D Jones (62), Huw Bennett (*Ospreys*) for Davies (69), D Jones for Charvis (76), Dwayne Peel (*Llanelli Scarlets*) for Cooper (80)

REFEREE Donal Courtney (*Ireland*) · **ATTENDANCE** 73,913

SCORING R Williams, try (0–5); S Jones, con (0–7); Paterson, drop (3–7); S Jones, pen (3–10); A Jones, try (3–15); S Jones, pen (3–18) (half-time) R Williams, try (3–23); Taylor, try (8–23); Paterson, con (10–23)

This game marked the start of a new era for Scotland under head coach Matt Williams and former All Black and Edinburgh captain Todd Blackadder. The Scots fielded three new caps: Edinburgh's Tom Philip and Ally Hogg, and Borders scrum-half Chris Cusiter. Australian-born stand-off Dan Parks made his debut off the substitutes' bench. Scottish optimism was brushed aside by a confident and passionate Welsh team building on a successful World Cup. The home side played with a spirited sense of adventure, scored three lovely tries and created lots of opportunities. By contrast, Scotland never looked like scoring in open play. Wales showed their intentions right away with a try by wing Rhys Williams after only three minutes. Chris Paterson replied with a drop goal and Stephen Jones kicked a penalty before the unlikely figure of prop Adam Jones trundled over for a try, much to the delight of the home crowd. Wales came close several times only to be denied by frantic Scottish defence and Stephen Jones finished the half with his second penalty. Wales continued to pressurise in the second period and after several close calls Williams completed his brace, Jones's conversion attempt hitting a post. With the game won, the home side relaxed and in injury time flanker Simon Taylor forced his way over after sustained work by the Scottish forwards on the Welsh line.

Murrayfield · Saturday 21 February 2004 · Lost 13–35

SCOTLAND Ben Hinshelwood (*Worcester*); Simon Danielli (*Bath*), Tom Philip (*Edinburgh*), Brendan Laney (*Edinburgh*), Simon Webster (*Edinburgh*); Chris Paterson* (*Edinburgh*), Chris Cusiter (*Borders*); Tom Smith (*Northampton Sts*), Gordon Bulloch (*Glasgow*), Bruce Douglas (*Borders*), Scott Murray (*Edinburgh*), Stuart Grimes (*Newcastle F*), Jason White (*Sale Sharks*), Cameron Mather (*Glasgow*), Simon Taylor (*Edinburgh*) ... Substitutes: Allister Hogg (*Edinburgh*) for White (18), Andrew Henderson (*Glasgow*) for Philip (15–22) and for Hinshelwood (40), Gavin Kerr (*Edinburgh*) for Douglas (46), Mike Blair (*Edinburgh*) for Cusiter (52), Nathan Hines (*Edinburgh*) for Grimes (54), Robbie Russell (*Saracens*) for Bulloch (64), Dan Parks (*Glasgow*) for Danielli (75) ... Yellow card: Taylor

ENGLAND Ian Balshaw (*Bath*); Josh Lewsey (*London Wasps*), Will Greenwood (*Leicester Tgrs*), Jason Robinson (*Sale Sharks*), Ben Cohen (*Northampton Sts*); Paul Grayson (*Northampton Sts*), Andy Gomersall (*Gloucester*); Trevor Woodman (*Gloucester*), Steve Thompson (*Northampton Sts*), Phil Vickery (*Gloucester*), Danny Grewcock (*Bath*), Ben Kay (*Leicester Tgrs*), Chris Jones (*Sale Sharks*), Richard Hill (*Saracens*), Lawrence Dallaglio* (*London Wasps*) ... Substitutes: Matt Dawson (*Northampton Sts*) for Gomersall (54), Simon Shaw (*London Wasps*) for Kay (56), Henry Paul (*Gloucester*) for Greenwood (75)

REFEREE David McHugh (*Ireland*)

SCORING Paterson, pen (3–0); Cohen, try (3–5); Grayson, con (3–7); Grayson, pen (3–10); Paterson, pen (6–10); Grayson, pen (6–13); Balshaw, try (6–18); Grayson, con (6–20) (half-time); Lewsey, try (6–25); Danielli, try (11–25); Paterson, con (13–25); Grayson, pen (13–28); Grewcock, try (13–33); Grayson, con (13–35)

World Champions England were without the talismanic Jonny Wilkinson but his replacement Paul Grayson was a more-than-able deputy. There was some controversy before the start when the visitors were made to wait a long time until the Scots took the field. Like many recent encounters between these sides, this game had a sense of grinding inevitably about it. Scotland played their hearts out but ultimately the white juggernaut had too much for them. England clocked up their biggest score at Murrayfield to date although they had to rely on a series of Scottish errors for three of their tries. In the first half, Jason Robinson made a speculative chip to the corner and a horrible bounce gave Cohen the simplest of scores. England's second try also came out of nothing. A clearance kick was charged down, Balshaw hacked the ball on, the bounce beat the cover and the England full-back was left on his own to gather and score. Grayson converted to give England a 20–6 lead at the break. Scotland started the second half promisingly only to be undone by another mistake. Lewsey charged down a Paterson clearance and fell on the ball for a gift try. The Scots had their own stroke of luck when a chip ahead by Danielli was fumbled by Balshaw straight into the arms of the onrushing wing. Scotland were reduced to 14 men when Simon Taylor was sin binned and Grayson ended any hopes of a comeback when he kicked his third penalty. Near the finish, Grewcock picked-up from a ruck inside the Scottish 22 and sprinted over without anyone getting near him.

Stadio Flaminio, Rome · Saturday 6 March 2004 · Lost 14–20

SCOTLAND Ben Hinshelwood (*Worcester*); Simon Danielli (*Bath*), Tom Philip (*Edinburgh*), Brendan Laney (*Edinburgh*), Simon Webster (*Edinburgh*); Chris Paterson* (*Edinburgh*), Chris Cusiter (*Borders*); Allan Jacobsen (*Edinburgh*), Gordon Bulloch (*Glasgow*), Bruce Douglas (*Borders*), Scott Murray (*Edinburgh*), Stuart Grimes (*Newcastle F*), Jason White (*Sale Sharks*), Allister Hogg (*Edinburgh*), Simon Taylor (*Edinburgh*) ... Substitutes: Mike Blair (*Edinburgh*) for Cusiter (40), Gavin Kerr (*Leeds Tykes*) for Jacobsen (40), Nathan Hines (*Edinburgh*) for Grimes (65), Jacobsen for Douglas (65), Derek Lee (*Edinburgh*) for Danielli 74, Andrew Henderson (*Glasgow*) for Laney (78), Jon Petrie (*Glasgow*) for White (78)

ITALY Gonzalo Canale (*Treviso*); Nicola Mazzucato (*Calvisano*), Cristian Stoica (*Montpellier*), Manuel Dallan (*Treviso*), Denis Dallan (*Treviso*); Roland De Marigny (*Parma*), Paul Griffen (*Calvisano*); Andrea Lo Cicero (Lazio), Fabio Ongaro (*Treviso*), Martin Castrogiovanni (*Calvisano*), Santiago Dellape (*Treviso*), Marco Bortolami (Padova), Andrea De Rossi* (*Calvisano*), Aaron Persico (Leeds Tykes), Sergio Parisse (*Treviso*) ... Substitutes: Rima Wakarua (*Brescia*) for M Dallan (47), Silvio Orlando (*Treviso*) for Parisse (61), Carlo Festuccia (*Parma*) for Ongaro (74), Mirco Bergamasco (*Stade Français*) for Canale (74)

REFEREE Nigel Whitehouse (Wales) · **ATTENDANCE** 21,340

SCORING De Marigny, pen (0–3); Paterson, pen (3–3); De Marigny, pen (3–6); Paterson, pen (6–6); Paterson, pen (9–6); De Marigny, pen (9–9) (half-time) Ongaro, try (9–14); De Marigny, pen (9–17); De Marigny, pen (9–20); Webster, try (14–20)

Scotland lost in Rome for the second time in three visits. The Scots worked tirelessly but they made too many errors, their play lacked direction and their discipline was often poor. The first half was an uninspiring tactical battle and there was nothing between the sides at the break. Chris Paterson kicked three penalties and South African-born Roland De Marigny replied in kind for Italy. A couple of minutes after the restart, Fabio Ongaro, the Italian hooker, grabbed an untidy lineout ball near the Scottish line and dived over in the corner, although television replays seemed to show that he had knocked on before scoring. De Marigny hit a post with his conversion but later kicked two penalties to see his side home. Simon Webster scored a late consolation try but this could not disguise an unhappy afternoon for Scotland.

Murrayfield · Sunday 21 March 2004 · Lost 0–31

SCOTLAND Derek Lee (*Edinburgh*); Simon Danielli (*Bath*), Tom Philip (*Edinburgh*), Andrew Henderson (*Glasgow*), Simon Webster (*Edinburgh*); Chris Paterson* (*Edinburgh*), Chris Cusiter (*Borders*); Allan Jacobsen (*Edinburgh*), Gordon Bulloch (*Glasgow*), Bruce Douglas (*Borders*), Scott Murray (*Edinburgh*), Stuart Grimes (*Newcastle F*), Jason White (*Sale Sharks*), Cameron Mather (*Glasgow*), Simon Taylor (*Edinburgh*) ... Substitutes: Gavin Kerr (*Leeds Tykes*) for Jacobsen (39), Mike Blair (*Edinburgh*) for Cusiter (40), Allister Hogg (*Edinburgh*) for Mather (40), Nathan Hines (*Edinburgh*) for Grimes (52), Dan Parks (Glasgow) for Lee (62), Rob Russell (*Saracens*) for Bulloch (70), Jacobsen for Douglas (80) ... Yellow card: Lee (15–25)

FRANCE Nicolas Brusque (*Biarritz*); Pepito Elhorga (*Agen*), Yannick Jauzion (*Toulouse*),

Damien Traille (*Pau*); Frederick Michalak (*Toulouse*), Dimitri Yachvili (*Biarritz*); Sylvain Marconnet (*Stade Français*), William Servat (*Toulouse*), Pieter de Villiers (*Stade Français*), Fabien Pelous* (*Toulouse*), Pascal Pape (*Bourgoin-Jallieu*), Serge Betsen (*Biarritz*), Olivier Magne (*Montferrand*), Thomas Lievremont (*Biarritz*) ... Substitutes: Julien Bonnaire (*Bourgoin-Jallieu*) for Betsen (20-21) and Lievremont (49), Julien Peyrelongue (*Biarritz*) for Michalak (40), Yannick Bru (*Toulouse*) for Servat (52), Jean-Jacques Crenca (*Agen*) for Marconnet (62), David Auradou (*Stade Français*) for Pape (71)

REFEREE Scott Young (*Australia*) · ATTENDANCE 66,324

SCORING Magne, try (0–5); Yachvili, pen (0–8); Yachvili, pen (0–11) (half-time) Yachvili, pen (0–14); Yachvili, pen (0–17); Jauzion, try (0–22); Yachvili, con (0–24); Jauzion, try (0–29); Yachvili, con (0–31)

Scotland's miserable championship continued as they failed to score a single point at Murrayfield for the first time since 1978. The Scots played with their usual commitment and determination but they made too many errors and clearly lacked confidence. France scored with their first meaningful attack of the game when Magne finished off a flowing attack down the left of the field. Yachvili kicked a brace of penalties in each half and gradually the Frenchmen drew clear. Scotland were hampered by several injuries and also when Derrick Lee, making his first start for over two years, was sin-binned for a dangerous tackle. Two tries in the closing stages by centre Yannick Jauzion, who deservedly won the man-of-the-match award, underlined French superiority. In truth, the visitors were never really troubled and headed to Paris for the Grand Slam whilst the hapless Scots seemed to be going nowhere.

---

529 RBS SIX NATIONS CHAMPIONSHIP 2004 IRELAND

Lansdowne Road, Dublin · Saturday 27 March 2004 · Lost 16–37

SCOTLAND Chris Paterson* (*Edinburgh*); Simon Danielli (*Bath*), Tom Philip (*Edinburgh*), Andrew Henderson (*Glasgow*), Simon Webster (*Edinburgh*); Dan Parks (*Glasgow*); Chris Cusiter (*Borders*); Allan Jacobsen (*Edinburgh*), Gordon Bulloch (*Glasgow*), Bruce Douglas (*Borders*), Scott Murray (*Edinburgh*), Stuart Grimes (*Newcastle F*), Jason White (*Sale Sharks*), Allister Hogg (*Edinburgh*), Simon Taylor (*Edinburgh*) ... Substitutes: Gavin Kerr (*Leeds Tykes*) for Jacobsen (40), Jon Petrie (*Glasgow*) for Taylor (42), Mike Blair (*Edinburgh*) for Cusiter (59), Nathan Hines (*Edinburgh*) for Grimes (59), Brendan Laney (*Edinburgh*) for Henderson (68), Rob Russell (*Saracens*) for Bulloch (77), Derrick Lee (*Edinburgh*) for Danielli (80)

IRELAND Girvan Dempsey (*Leinster*); Shane Horgan (*Leinster*), Brian O'Driscoll* (*Leinster*), Gordon D'Arcy (*Leinster*), Geordan Murphy (*Leicester Tgrs*); Ronan O'Gara (*Munster*), Peter Stringer (*Munster*); Reggie Corrigan (*Leinster*), Shane Byrne (*Leinster*), John Hayes (*Munster*), Malcolm O'Kelly (*Leinster*), Paul O'Connell (*Munster*), Simon Easterby (*Llanelli Scarlets*), David Wallace (*Munster*), Anthony Foley (*Munster*) ... Substitutes: Marcus Horan (*Munster*) for Corrigan (60), Victor Costello (*Leinster*) for Wallace (80), Guy Easterby (*Rotherham*) for Stringer (80), David Humphreys (*Ulster*) for O'Gara (80), Kevin Maggs (*Bath*) for D'Arcy (80), Donnacha O'Callaghan (*Munster*) for O'Kelly (80), Frank Sheahan (*Munster*) for Byrne (80)

REFEREE Nigel Williams (*Wales*) · ATTENDANCE 42,750

SCORING Paterson, pen (3–0); O'Gara, pen (3–3); D'Arcy, try (3–8); Paterson, pen (6–8);

O'Gara, pen (6–11; Parks, drop (9–11); Murphy, try (9–16) (half-time) Hogg, try (14–16); Paterson, con (16–16); Wallace, try (16–21); O'Gara, con (16–23); Stringer, try (16–28); O'Gara, con (16–30); D'Arcy, try (16–35); O'Gara, con (16–37)

Ireland won their first Triple Crown since 1985 and consigned Scotland to a championship whitewash, but the visitors played better than the score suggests. The Scottish forwards were much improved from recent games and stand-off Dan Parks kicked astutely and made good tactical decisions. However, Scotland lacked any real attacking threat and struggled to contain Irish centres O'Driscoll and D'Arcy. Ireland scored two tries in the first half but Scotland stayed in touch with two penalties by Paterson and a huge drop goal by Parks. Shortly after the restart, the Scots worked through numerous phases before flanker Ally Hogg dived over from a ruck near the posts. Paterson converted to level the scores, but Ireland responded strongly with three converted tries and ran out handsome winners.

  2004　　　　　　　　　　　　　　　　**BARBARIANS**

Murrayfield · Saturday 22 May 2004 · Lost 33–40

SCOTLAND XV Chris Paterson (*Edinburgh*); Stephen Cranston (*Borders*), Tom Philip (*Edinburgh*), Andrew Henderson (*Glasgow*), Simon Webster (*Edinburgh*); Dan Parks (*Glasgow*), Chris Cusiter (*Borders*); Allan Jacobsen (*Edinburgh*), Gordon Bulloch (*Glasgow*), Bruce Douglas (*Borders*), Scott Murray* (*Edinburgh*), Iain Fullarton (*Sale Sharks*), Cameron Mather (*Glasgow*), Scott Gray (*Bath*), Allister Hogg (*Edinburgh*) … Substitutes: Scott MacLeod (*Borders*) for Fullerton (57), Gareth Morton (*Borders*) for Paterson (67), Graeme Beveridge (*Glasgow*) for Cusiter (75)

BARBARIANS Christian Cullen (*Munster & NZ*); Shane Horgan (*Leinster & Ireland*), Thomas Castaignède (*Saracens & France*), Brian O'Driscoll (*Leinster & Ireland*), Vilimoni Delasau (*Canterbury & Fiji*); David Humphreys (*Ulster & Ireland*), Mark Robinson (*Northampton Sts & NZ*); Greg Feek (*Auckland Blues & NZ*), Anton Oliver (*Otago Highlanders & NZ*), Cobus Visage (*Saracens & SA*), Mark Andrews (*Newcastle F & SA*), Malcom O'Kelly (*Leinster & Ireland*), Aaron Persico (*Leeds Tykes & Italy*), Taine Randell* (*Saracens & NZ*), Bobby Skinstad (*NG Dragons & SA*) … Substitutes: Stefan Terblanche (*Ospreys & SA*) for Delasau (40), Eric Miller (*Leinster & Ireland*) for Skinstad (49), Brad Mika (*Auckland Blues & NZ*) for Andrews (53), Neil de Kock (*W Stormers & SA*) for Robinson (63), Matthew Burke (*NSW Waratahs & Australia*) for Terblanche (80)

REFEREE Joel Jutge (*France*) · **ATTENDANCE** 24,441

SCORING Delasau, try (0–5); Humphreys, con (0–7); Robinson, try (0–12); Humphreys, con (0–14) Parks, try (5–14); Parks, con (7–14); Horgan, try (7–19); Humphreys, con (7–21); Horgan, try (7–26); Humphreys, con (7–28) (half-time) Hogg, try (12–28); Parks, con (14–28); Cullen, try (14–33); Paterson, try (19–33); Jacobsen, try (24–33); Parks, con (26–33); Randall, try (26–38); Humphreys, con (26–40); Hogg, try (31–40); Parks, con (33–40)

This exhibition match was a perfect advert for summer rugby. It was full of exciting play and featured eleven tries. Scotland came close to their first victory against the Barbarians, but they could not make enough of their chances. They had a lot of possession and finished well at times but their illustrious opponents always looked more capable. The Barbarians raced to an early lead with tries by Fijian winger

Delasau and All Black scrum-half Robinson. Scotland responded when Dan Parks intercepted a loose pass to score. The Scots had a spell of superiority towards the end of the half, but Irish wing Horgan scored twice before the interval leaving the home side with too much to do. The Scots never gave in and scored four tries in the second half, including a brace by No 8 Ally Hogg who had a fine all-round display.

---

530 TOUR OF THE SOUTHERN HEMISPHERE 2004 SAMOA

Westpac Stadium, Wellington · Friday 4 June 2004 · Won 38–3

SCOTLAND Chris Paterson (*Edinburgh*); †Sean Lamont (*Glasgow*), Ben Hinshelwood (*Worcester*), Andrew Henderson (*Glasgow*), Simon Webster (*Edinburgh*); Gordon Ross (*Leeds Tykes*), Chris Cusiter (*Borders*); Tom Smith (*Northamton Sts*), Gordon Bulloch (*Glasgow*), Bruce Douglas (*Borders*), Scott Murray* (*Edinburgh*), Stuart Grimes (*Newcastle F*), Jason White (*Sale Sharks*), Donnie Macfadyen (*Glasgow*), Allister Hogg (*Edinburgh*) ... Substitutes: Hugo Southwell (*Edinburgh*) for Webster (15-18 and 36-40) and for Paterson (68), Dan Parks (*Glasgow*) for Ross (35-40 and 73), Craig Smith (*Edinburgh*) for Smith (49-52 and 79), Jon Petrie (*Glasgow*) for Macfadyen (79), Mike Blair (*Edinburgh*) for Cusiter (80), Iain Fullerton (*Saracens*) for Grimes (80), Steve Scott (*Borders*) for Bulloch (80)

SAMOA Tanner Vili (*Borders*); Lome Fa'atau (*Marist St Patrick's*), Dale Rasmussen (*Exeter Chiefs*), Brian Lima (*Secom*), Sailosi Tagicakibau (*Clifton*); Roger Warren (*Marist St Joseph's*), Steve So'oialo (*Orrell*); Kas Lealalamu'a (*Marist St Patrick's*), Jonathan Meredith (*Ponsonby*), Tamato Leupolu (*Suburbs*), Leo Lafaiali'i (*Sanyo*), Opeta Palepoi (*Exeter Chiefs*), Siaosi Vaili (*Exeter Chiefs*), Ulia Ulia (*Afega*), Semo Sititi* (*Newcastle F*) ... Substitutes: Michael von Dincklage (*Waitemata*) for Palepoi (42), Simon Lemalu (*Marist Northland*) for Leupolu (58), David Lemi (*Marist St Joseph's*) for Tagicakibau (58), Kitiona Viliamu (*Manchester*) for Ulia (58), Mussolini Schuster (*Warringah*) for Rasmussen (68), John Senio (*Ponsonby*) for Warren (73), Loleni Tafunai (*Vaiala*) for Meredith (79), Leupolu for Lealalamu'a (80)

REFEREE Kelvin Deaker (*New Zealand*) · ATTENDANCE 11,665

SCORING Warren, pen (0–3); Paterson, pen (3–3); Paterson, pen (6–3); Ross, try (11–3) (half-time) Hinshelwood, try (16–3); Paterson, pen (19–3); Hogg, try (24–3); Paterson, con (26–3); Webster, try (31–3); Parks, con (33–3); Blair, try (38–3)

In June 2004, Scotland made a six match tour of the southern hemisphere. The tour started with provincial matches against Queensland (5–41) and New South Wales Country (48–10) before moving onto a test match against Samoa at the neutral Westpac Stadium in Wellington, New Zealand, which the Samoans had chosen as their home venue. Sean Lamont and substitute full-back Hugo Southwell made their debuts. On a wet and windy evening, Scotland won their first victory in eight months and their first under coach Matt Williams. They weathered the early Samoan storm before gradually imposing themselves. They scored five tries and their defence withheld some ferocious attacks. Coached by legendary All Black Michael Jones, the Samoans had the better of the opening exchanges and took an early lead with a penalty by Roger Warren. Chris Paterson replied with two penalties and just before the interval Gordon Ross, who had a fine game, dummied through the defence for the first try. The Scots made sure of victory within a minute of the restart. Scott Murray, the captain, won the ball from the kick-off and began a move which led to a try for Hinshelwood. Paterson kicked a third penalty and Hogg, Webster and Blair added further tries. Towards the finish, Chris Paterson suffered a serious facial injury which ruled him out of the rest of the tour.

531   TOUR OF THE SOUTHERN HEMISPHERE   AUSTRALIA

Telstra Dome, Melbourne · Sunday 13 June 2004 · Lost 15–35

SCOTLAND †Hugo Southwell (*Edinburgh*); Sean Lamont (*Glasgow*), Ben Hinshelwood (*Worcester*), Andrew Henderson (*Glasgow*), Simon Webster (*Edinburgh*); Dan Parks (*Glasgow*), Chris Cusiter (*Borders*); Tom Smith (*Northampton Sts*), Gordon Bulloch (*Glasgow*), Bruce Douglas (*Borders*), Scott Murray* (*Edinburgh*), Stuart Grimes (*Newcastle F*), Jason White (*Sale Sharks*), Donnie Macfadyen (*Glasgow*), Allister Hogg (*Edinburgh*) ... Substitutes: Iain Fullerton (*Saracens*) for Murray (59), Jon Petrie (*Glasgow*) for Macfadyen (66), Craig Smith (*Edinburgh*) for Douglas (66), Mike Blair (*Edinburgh*) for Cusiter (72), Gordon Ross (*Leeds Tykes*) for Parks (72), †Graeme Morrison (*Glasgow*) for Henderson (76), Steve Scott (*Borders*) for Bulloch (76)

AUSTRALIA Joe Roff (*Brumbies*); Wendell Sailor (*Reds*), Clyde Rathbone (*Brumbies*), Matt Giteau (*Brumbies*), Lote Tuqiri (*Waratahs*); Stephen Larkham (*Brumbies*), George Gregan* (*Brumbies*); Bill Young (*Brumbies*), Brendan Cannon (*Waratahs*), Alastair Baxter (*Waratahs*), Justin Harrison (*Waratahs*), Nathan Sharpe (*Reds*), Radike Samo (*Brumbies*), George Smith (*Brumbies*), David Lyons (*Waratahs*) ... Substitutes: Phil Waugh (*Waratahs*) for Smith (53), Jeremy Paul (*Brumbies*) for Cannon (63), Morgan Turinui (*Waratahs*) for Larkham (65), Matt Burke (*Waratahs*) for Rathbone (65), Chris Latham (*Reds*) for Tuqiri (69), Dan Vickerman (*Waratahs*) for Lyons (75), Matt Dunning (*Waratahs*) for Young (78)

REFEREE Paul Honiss (*New Zealand*) · ATTENDANCE 38,222

SCORING Roff, pen (0–3); Roff, pen (0–6); Giteau, try (0–11); Roff, con (0–13); Parks, pen (3–13); Parks, pen (6–13); Parks, pen (9–13); Parks, pen (12–13) (half-time) Tuqiri, try (12–18); Parks, pen (15–18); Roff, pen (15–21); Tuqiri, try (15–26); Roff, con (15–28); Sailor, try (15–33); Roff, con (15–35)

Scotland continued their summer tour with a two test series against World Cup finalists Australia. Encouraged by their solid display against Samoa, the Scots put up a courageous performance but in the end the Australians were too good for them. The Wallabies raced to a 13 point lead before Dan Parks kicked a quartet of penalties to reduce the leeway to a single point at the interval. Scotland never stopped trying but the Australians eased away in the second half. Wing Lote Tuqiri scored a brace of tries, the second just after the hour mark to put the result beyond doubt. Sailor added a late score when he snatched a chip ahead by Webster and raced away un-opposed. A few minutes before time, Glasgow centre Graeme Morrison won his first cap when he replaced Andy Henderson.

532   TOUR OF THE SOUTHERN HEMISPHERE   AUSTRALIA

Telstra Stadium, Sydney · Saturday 19 June 2004 · Lost 13–34

SCOTLAND Hugo Southwell (*Edinburgh*); Sean Lamont (*Glasgow*), Ben Hinshelwood

(*Worcester*), Andrew Henderson (*Glasgow*), Simon Webster (*Edinburgh*); Dan Parks (*Glasgow*), Chris Cusiter (*Borders*); Tom Smith (*Northampton Sts*), Gordon Bulloch (*Glasgow*), Bruce Douglas (*Borders*), Scott Murray (*Edinburgh*), Iain Fullerton (*Saracens*), Jason White (*Sale Sharks*), Donnie Macfadyen (*Glasgow*), Allister Hogg (*Edinburgh*) ... Substitutes: †Craig Hamilton (*Newcastle F*) for Fullerton (49), Craig Smith (*Edinburgh*) for Douglas (59), Gordon Ross (*Leeds Tykes*) for Parks (69), Jon Petrie (*Glasgow*) for Murray (70), Graeme Morrison (*Glasgow*) for Henderson (77)

AUSTRALIA Joe Roff (*Brumbies*); Wendell Sailor (*Reds*), Stirling Mortlock (*Brumbies*), Morgan Turinui (*Waratahs*), Lote Tuqiri (*Waratahs*); Stephen Larkham (*Brumbies*), George Gregan (*Brumbies*); Bill Young (*Brumbies*), Brendan Cannon (*Waratahs*), Alastair Baxter (*Waratahs*), Justin Harrison (*Waratahs*), Nathan Sharpe (*Reds*), Radike Samo (*Brumbies*), Phil Waugh (*Waratahs*), David Lyons (*Waratahs*) ... Substitutes: Matt Dunning (*Waratahs*) for Baxter (55), Clyde Rathbone (*Brumbies*) for Mortlock (57), Dan Vickerman (*Waratahs*) for Harrison (57), Jeremy Paul (*Brumbies*) for Cannon (59), George Smith (*Brumbies*) for Samo (62), Chris Latham (*Reds*) for Sailor (68)

REFEREE Mark Lawrence (*South Africa*) · ATTENDANCE 56,143

SCORING Parks, pen (3–0); Roff, pen (3–3); Sailor, try (3–8); Roff, con (3–10); Tuqiri, try (3–15); Roff, con (3–17); Cusiter, try (8–17); Parks, con (10–17) (half-time) Tuqiri, try (10–22); Parks, pen (13–22); Turinui, try (13–27); Roff, con (13–29); Roff, try (13–34)

Australia were deserved winners but they were flattered by two late tries. Scotland showed plenty of self-belief and enterprise only to be undone by a series of errors and a failure to take their chances. Sydney-born Dan Parks gave Scotland an early lead with a penalty. Roff responded in kind, and Sailor and Tuqiri, the Australian wingers, each scored a try converted by Roth. The Wallabies looked set to run riot but Scotland made a spirited response. Henderson had a clear try disallowed because Gregan, his would-be tackler, had accidently crashed into the referee. A couple of rucks later, Cusiter dived through a narrow gap for a score. Scotland were only seven points adrift at the interval but a few minutes after the restart Turinui created an opening for Tuqiri to score. Scotland continued to battle hard but missed several opportunities and the Wallabies were quick to exploit some missed tackles with tries by Turinui and Roff in the last quarter.

533 AUTUMN TEST 2004 AUSTRALIA

Murrayfield · Saturday 6 November 2004 · Lost 14–31

SCOTLAND Stuart Moffat (*Borders*); Sean Lamont (*Glasgow*), Graeme Morrison (*Glasgow*), Andrew Henderson (*Glasgow*), Chris Paterson (*Edinburgh*); Dan Parks (*Glasgow*), Chris Cusiter (*Borders*); Allan Jacobsen (*Edinburgh*), Gordon Bulloch* (*Glasgow*), Bruce Douglas (*Borders*), Nathan Hines (*Edinburgh*), †Scott MacLeod (*Borders*), †Scott Gray (*Borders*), Allister Hogg (*Edinburgh*), Donnie Macfadyen (*Glasgow*) ... Substitutes: Jon Petrie (*Glasgow*) for Gray (40), Hugo Southwell (*Edinburgh*) for Moffat (40), †Alastair Kellock (*Edinburgh*) for MacLeod (51–62 and 70), Andy Craig (*Glasgow*) for Morrison (66), Craig Smith (*Edinburgh*) for Douglas (66), Mike Blair (*Edinburgh*) for Cusiter (76), †Ross Ford (*Borders*) for Bulloch (77)

AUSTRALIA Chris Latham (*Reds*); Clyde Rathbone (*Brumbies*), Stirling Mortlock (*Brumbies*), Matt Giteau (*Brumbies*), Lote Tuqiri (*Waratahs*); Stephen Larkham (*Brumbies*), George Gregan* (*Brumbies*); Bill Young (*Brumbies*), Jeremy Paul (*Brumbies*), Al Baxter (*Waratahs*), Justin Harrison

(*Waratahs*), Dan Vickerman (*Waratahs*), George Smith (*Brumbies*), John Roe (*Reds*), Phil Waugh (*Waratahs*) ... Substitutes: David Lyons (*Waratahs*) for Waugh (43), Wendell Sailor (*Reds*) for Rathbone (55), Matt Dunning (*Waratahs*) for Young (70), Elton Flatley (*Reds*) for Larkham (72), Mat Rogers (*Waratahs*) for Mortlock (72), Mark Chisholm (*Brumbies*) for Vickerman (76), Brendan Cannon (*Waratahs*) for Paul (80)

REFEREE Steve Walsh (*New Zealand*) · ATTENDANCE 41,234

SCORING Mortlock, try (0–5); Giteau, con (0–7); Rathbone, try (0–12); Giteau, con (0–14); Rathbone, try (0–19); Giteau, con (0–21); Tuqiri, try (0–26); Giteau, con (0–28) (half-time) Lamont, try (5–28); Paterson, con (7–28); Southwell, try (12–28); Paterson, con (14–28); Giteau, pen (14–31)

Scotland started their 2004 autumn series with the first of two games against the touring Australians. Playing in wet conditions, the Scots had a torrid first-half and conceded four brilliant tries. They strated well enough but on the 13th minute Australian winger Rathbone broke through the defence and fed Mortlock who slid in under the posts. Rathbone then scored a brace of tries, Tuqiri added another and Giteau converted all four to give the Australians an astonishing 28–0 lead at the interval. In the second-half, and with the game well beyond them, the Scots made a minor recovery and scored two tries of their own. From a lineout, the forwards muscled to the Australian line and Lamont slipped through a couple of tackles to score. Paterson converted and a few minutes later Southwell finished off a sweeping move after Lamont had created space. The Australians could only score a penalty in the second half although they always looked capable of more if the need arose.

---

534   AUTUMN TEST SERIES 2004   JAPAN

McDiarmid Park, Perth · Saturday 13 November 2004 · Won 100–8

SCOTLAND Hugo Southwell (*Edinburgh*); Chris Paterson (*Edinburgh*), Ben Hinshelwood (*Worcester*), Andrew Henderson (*Glasgow*), Sean Lamont (*Glasgow*); Dan Parks (*Glasgow*), Chris Cusiter (*Borders*); Allan Jacobsen (*Edinburgh*), Gordon Bulloch* (*Glasgow*), Gavin Kerr (*Leeds Tykes*), Stuart Grimes (*Newcastle F*), Nathan Hines (*Edinburgh*), Allister Hogg (*Edinburgh*), Donnie Macfadyen (*Glasgow*), Jon Petrie (*Glasgow*) ... Substitutes: Mike Blair (*Edinburgh*) for Cusiter (40), Rob Russell (*London Irish*) for Bulloch (40), Graeme Morrison (*Glasgow*) for Hinshelwood (55), Gordon Ross (*Leeds Tykes*) for Parks (58), Jason White (*Sale Sharks*) for Hogg (58), Scott MacLeod (*Borders*) for Grimes (64), Craig Smith (*Edinburgh*) for Jacobsen (67),

JAPAN Ryohei Miki (*World Fighting Bulls*); Koichiro Kubota (*NEC*), Seiichi Shimomura (*Sanyo*), Yukio Motoki (*Kobe Steel*), Hayato Daimon (*Kobe Steel*); Keisuke Sawaki (*Suntory*), Wataru Ikeda (*Sanyo*); Yuichi Hisadomi (*NEC*), Takashi Yamaoka (*Suntory*), Ryo Yamamura (*Yamaha*), Takanori Kumagae (*NEC*), Hitoshi Ono (*Toshiba*), Naoya Okubu (*Southland*), Hajime Kiso (*Yamaha*), Takuro Miuchi (*NEC*) ... Substitutes: Feletiliki Mau (*World Fighting Bulls*) for Ono (40), Hideyuki Yoshida (*Kubota*) for Miki (48), Masatoshi Mukoyama (*NEC*) for Motoki (56), Mitsugu Yamamoto (*Sanyo*) for Hisadomi (66), Takatoyo Yamaguchi (*Kubota*) for Okubo (68), Kiyonori Tanaka (*Suntory*) for Ikeda (72), Masahito Yamamoto (*Toyota*) for Yamaoka (77)

REFEREE Andrew Cole (*Australia*) · ATTENDANCE 10,278

SCORING Hogg, try (5–0); Paterson, con (7–0); Daimon, try (7–5); Southwell, try (12–5);

Paterson, con (14–5); Paterson, pen (17–5); Paterson, try (22–5); Paterson, con (24–5); Ikeda, pen (24–8); Parks, try (29–8); Paterson, con (31–8); Petrie, try (36–8) (half-time) Paterson, try (41–8); Blair, try (46–8); Paterson, con (48–8); Henderson, try (53–8); Paterson, con (55–8); Paterson, try (60–8); Morrison, try (65–8); Paterson, con (67–8); S Lamont, try (72–8); Paterson, con (74–8); Macfadyen, try (79–8); Paterson, con (81–8); Russell, try (86–8); Southwell, try (91–8); Paterson, con (93–8); Russell, try (98–8); Paterson, con (100–8)

An enthusiastic crowd created a splendid atmosphere for Scotland's debut at MacDiarmid Park in Perth, the home of St Johnstone FC. As the score suggests, this was a hopelessly one-sided encounter. The Scots ran in 15 tries and reached a century of points in a test match for the first time. Chris Paterson collected a personal tally of 40 points from three tries, 11 conversions and a penalty. Japan were without many of their best players and were a shadow of the side that had done well against Scotland the previous year. The Scots scored within two minutes, Ally Hogg finishing off a slick move after good work by Jacobsen and Cusiter. Japan replied a few minutes later with a well worked try by winger Daimon. For a time, the Scots tried to force the game and they made some errors but eventually Southwell scored a try from which they never looked back. They led 36–8 at the interval and completely dominated the second half. With the last move of the game, hooker Rob Russell was driven over near the posts. Paterson brought up the century with his final kick.

535   AUTUMN TEST SERIES 2004   AUSTRALIA

Hampden Park, Glasgow · Saturday 20 November 2004 · Lost 17–31

SCOTLAND   Hugo Southwell (*Edinburgh*); Chris Paterson (*Edinburgh*), Ben Hinshelwood (*Worcester*), Andrew Henderson (*Glasgow*), Sean Lamont (*Glasgow*); Dan Parks (*Glasgow*), Chris Cusiter (*Borders*); Allan Jacobsen (*Edinburgh*), Gordon Bulloch* (*Glasgow*), Gavin Kerr (*Leeds Tykes*), Stuart Grimes (*Newcastle F*), Nathan Hines (*Edinburgh*), Allister Hogg (*Edinburgh*), Donnie Macfadyen (*Glasgow*), Jon Petrie (*Glasgow*) ... Substitutes: Bruce Douglas (*Borders*) for Kerr (59), Jason White (*Sale Sharks*) for Petrie (59), Graeme Morrison (*Glasgow*) for Henderson (72), Scott MacLeod (*Borders*) for Hines (72), Mike Blair (*Edinburgh*) for Cusiter (77), Rob Russell (*London Irish*) for Bulloch (77)

AUSTRALIA   Chris Latham (*Reds*); Clyde Rathbone (*Brumbies*), Stirling Mortlock (*Brumbies*), Matt Giteau (*Brumbies*), Lote Tuqiri (*Waratahs*); Stephen Larkham (*Brumbies*), George Gregan* (*Brumbies*); Bill Young (*Brumbies*), Jeremy Paul (*Brumbies*), Al Baxter (*Waratahs*), Justin Harrison (*Waratahs*), Dan Vickerman (*Waratahs*), George Smith (*Brumbies*), Phil Waugh (*Waratahs*), David Lyons (*Waratahs*) ... Substitutes: Wendell Sailor (*Reds*) for Mortlock (3), Elton Flatley (*Reds*) for Larkham (40), Mat Rogers (*Waratahs*) for Rathbone (40), Matt Dunning (*Waratahs*) for Young (59), Brendan Cannon (*Waratahs*) for Paul (67), Stephen Hoiles (*Waratahs*) for Lyons (75), Radike Samo (*Brumbies*) for Vickerman (80), Young for Baxter (80)

REFEREE   Alan Lewis (*Ireland*) · ATTENDANCE   28,400

SCORING   Giteau, pen (0–3); Paterson, pen (3–3); Paterson, pen (6–3); Tuquri, try (6–8); Giteau, con (6–10); Paterson, pen (9–10); Waugh, try (9–15); Giteau, con (9–17) (half-time) Paterson, pen (12–17); Giteau, try (12–22); Giteau, con (12–24); Hogg, try (17–24); Gregan, try (17–29); Flatley, con (17–31)

Scotland returned to Hampden Park for this hastily arranged match, the fourth meeting between the two sides in a little over five months. Led from the front by Gordon

Bulloch, the Scots showed plenty of determination and passion, but once again they made unforced errors and could not match the powerful and direct running of the Australian backs. Scotland were 6–3 in front when the visitors scored their controversial opening try. Flanker George Smith seemed to knock the ball forwards in a tackle but the game was allowed to continue and after a couple of moves Tuqiri crossed the line. The Wallabies struck a further blow when Waugh scored a converted try right at the interval. Scotland ralled strongly after the restart and Cusiter, the man-of-the-match, made two scything breaks, the second almost the length of the field, but the Scots were unable to make their pressure count. Then against the run of play Paul made a break and Giteau rounded the defence for a try under the posts. There was excitement when Hogg charged down a clearance, gathered the ball and raced to the corner for an opportunist score. Scotland were only seven points adrift going into the closing stages but a late try by Gregan sealed the game for the visitors.

---

536   AUTUMN TEST SERIES 2004   SOUTH AFRICA

Murrayfield · Saturday 27 November 2004 · Lost 10–45

SCOTLAND Hugo Southwell (*Edinburgh*); Chris Paterson (*Edinburgh*), Ben Hinshelwood (*Worcester*), Andrew Henderson (*Glasgow*), Sean Lamont (*Glasgow*); Dan Parks (*Glasgow*), Chris Cusiter (*Borders*); Allan Jacobsen (*Edinburgh*), Gordon Bulloch* (*Glasgow*), Gavin Kerr (*Leeds Tykes*), Stuart Grimes (*Newcastle F*), Nathan Hines (*Edinburgh*), Jason White (*Sale Sharks*), Donnie Macfadyen (*Glasgow*), Allister Hogg (*Edinburgh*) ... Substitutes: Mike Blair (*Edinburgh*) for Cusiter (15), Scott MacLeod (*Borders*) for Hines (21), Jon Petrie (*Glasgow*) for White (58), Gordon Ross (*Leeds Tykes*) for Parks (58), Bruce Douglas (*Borders*) for Kerr (61), Graeme Morrison (*Glasgow*) for Southwell (77), Rob Russell (*London Irish*) for Bulloch (77)

SOUTH AFRICA Percy Montgomery (*NG Dragons*); Jaque Fourie (*Cats*), Marius Joubert (*Stormers*), Wayne Julies (*Stormers*), Bryan Habana (*Cats*); Jaco van der Westhuyzen (*Bulls*), Fourie du Preez (*Bulls*); Gurthro Steenkamp (*Cats*), John Smit* (*Sharks*), CJ van der Linde (*Stormers*), Bakkies Botha (*Sharks*), Victor Matfield (*Bulls*), Solly Tyibilika (*Lions*), Danie Rossouw (*Bulls*), Joe van Niekerk (*Stormers*) ... Substitutes: Jacques Cronje (*Bulls*) for Rossouw (21–31) and van Niekerk (55), Gerrie Britz (*Bulls*) for van Niekerk (30–32) and Matfield (66), Os du Randt (*Cats*) for Steenkamp (58), Michael Claassens (*Cats*) for Du Preez (75), Gaffie du Toit (*Sharks*) for Joubert (75), Danie Coetzee (*Bulls*) for Van der Linde (78), Gcobani Bobo (*Cats*) for Julies (80)

REFEREE Nigel Williams (*Wales*) · **ATTENDANCE** 44,237

SCORING Fourie, try (0–5); Montgomery, con (0–7); Tyibilika, try (0–12); van der Westhuyzen, drop (0–15); Paterson, pen (3–15); van der Westhuyzen, drop (3–18); Habana, try (3–23); Montgomery, con (3–25); penalty try (8–25); Paterson, con (10–25); Habana, try (10–30); Montgomery, con (10–32) (half-time) Montgomery, pen (10–35); van der Westhuyzen, drop (10–38); van der Westhuyzen, try (10–43); Montgomery, con (10–45)

Chris Paterson won his 50th cap. In their 12th match of 2004, the Scots were cautiously optimistic that they could upset the South Africans, the reigning Tri-Nations champions, but they gave an abject performance and the visitors won at a canter. The Scots were unlucky to lose the talismanic Chris Cusiter and Nathan Hines in the opening stages, but their play was strewn with errors and defensive frailties which were ruthlessly exposed by faster and more efficient opponents. Playing in wet conditions, the South Africans raced to a 25–3 lead with tries by wing Jaques Fourie, debutant flanker Solly Tyibilika and wing Bryan Habana, who intercepting a careless pass on his own ten metre line and sprinted away to the posts. Towards the end of the half, Scotland were thrown a lifeline when both South African locks were sent to the sin bin. The Scots won a penalty try from a five metre scrum against six men, but then conceded a second interception try to Habana and the match was as good as done. The second half was much less eventful and the South Africans seemed happy to sit on their lead. Stand-off Jaco van der Westhuyzen dropped a nonchalant goal, his third of the match, and scored a try after good work by reserve scrum-half Claassens. The Scots played with their usual passion, but the South Africans were better in every respect.

---

537   RBS SIX NATIONS CHAMPIONSHIP 2005   FRANCE

Stade de France, Paris · Saturday 5 February 2005 · Lost 9–16

SCOTLAND Chris Paterson (*Edinburgh*); Simon Danielli (*Borders*), Andy Craig (*Glasgow*), Hugo Southwell (*Edinburgh*), Sean Lamont (*Glasgow*); Dan Parks (*Glasgow*), Chris Cusiter (*Borders*); Tom Smith (*Northampton Sts*), Gordon Bulloch* (*Glasgow*), Gavin Kerr (*Leeds Tykes*), Stuart Grimes (*Newcastle F*), Scott Murray (*Edinburgh*), Jason White (*Sale Sharks*), Jon Petrie (*Glasgow*), Allister Hogg (*Edinburgh*) ... Substitutes: Bruce Douglas (*Borders*) for Kerr (55), Nathan Hines (*Edinburgh*) for Murray (65), Kerr for Smith (74), †Jon Dunbar (*Leeds Tykes*) for Grimes (79)

FRANCE Pépito Elhorga (*Agen*); Aurélien Rougerie (*Clermont Auv*), Brian Liebenberg (*Stade Français*), Damien Traille (*Biarritz*), Christophe Dominici (*Stade Français*); Yann Delaigue (*Castres*), Pierre Mignoni (*Clermont Auv*); Sylvain Marconnet (*Stade Français*), William Servat (*Toulouse*), Pieter de Villiers (*Stade Français*), Fabien Pelous* (*Toulouse*), Jérôme Thion (*Biarritz*), Julien Bonnaire (*Bourgoin-Jallieu*), Sébastien Chabal (*Sale Sharks*), Patrick Tabacco (*Pau*) ... Substitutes: Ludovic Valbon (*Brive*) for Rougerie (17), Olivier Milloud (*Bourgoin-Jallieu*) for de Villiers (52), Yannick Nyanga (*Béziers*) for Tabacco (66), Grégory Lamboley (*Toulouse*) for Thion (69), Frédéric Mihalak (*Toulouse*) for Delaigue (74), Sébastien Bruno (*Sale Sharks*) for Servat (78), Dimitri Yachvili (*Biarritz*) for Valbon (78)

REFEREE Nigel Williams (*Wales*)

SCORING Paterson, pen (3–0); Paterson, pen (6–0) (half-time) Paterson, pen (9–0); Delaigue, pen (9–3); Delaigue, pen (9–6); Delaigue, drop (9–9); Traille, try (9–14); Michalak, con (9–16)

Scotland were completely written-off before this game, but they came agonisingly close to an unexpected win. On the 68th minute and with the Scots holding a three-point lead, No 8 Ally Hogg burst away up the touchline and looked to have scored in the corner. A try at this stage would probably have been decisive, but Simon McDowell, the touch-judge, ruled that Hogg's foot had brushed the line at the start of his run and play was brought back. Television replays suggested that McDowell, who hesitated before making his decision, had been mistaken and the try should have awarded. Then Delaigue dropped a goal to tie the scores and a few minutes before the end France scored the winning try. Taking a high kick, Simon Danielli tried to keep the ball alive, but he was caught and swiftly isolated. Although the Scots won the ensuing ruck, Hugo Southwell's clearance kick was charged down and centre Damien Traille collected the ball for a simple run-in. It was hard lines on Scotland who played with great passion and determination, and certainly deserved at least a draw. Their defence was heroic, but once again they were too indecisive in attack. Amongst several good performances, Hugo Southwell played well in his first game at centre and scrum-half Chris Cusiter was voted man-of-the match for a typically gutsy display.

538   RBS SIX NATIONS CHAMPIONSHIP 2005   IRELAND

Murrayfield · Saturday 12 February 2005 · Lost 13–40

SCOTLAND Chris Paterson (*Edinburgh*); Simon Danielli (*Borders*), Andy Craig (*Glasgow*), Hugo Southwell (*Edinburgh*), Sean Lamont (*Glasgow*); Dan Parks (*Glasgow*), Chris Cusiter (*Borders*); Tom Smith (*Northampton Sts*), Gordon Bulloch* (*Glasgow*), Gavin Kerr (*Leeds Tykes*), Stuart Grimes (*Newcastle F*), Scott Murray (*Edinburgh*), Jason White (*Sale Sharks*), Jon Petrie (*Glasgow*), Allister Hogg (*Edinburgh*) ... Substitutes: Mike Blair (*Edinburgh*) for Cusiter (7–16 & 71), Bruce Douglas (*Borders*) for Kerr (71), Nathan Hines (*Edinburgh*) for Murray (71)

IRELAND Geordan Murphy (*Leicester Tgrs*); Girvan Dempsey (*Leinster*), Shane Horgan (*Leinster*), Kevin Maggs (*Ulster*), Denis Hickie (*Leinster*); Ronan O'Gara (*Munster*), Peter Stringer (*Munster*); Reggie Corrigan (*Leinster*), Shane Byrne (*Leinster*), John Hayes (*Munster*), Malcolm O'Kelly (*Leinster*), Paul O'Connell* (*Munster*), Simon Easterby (*Llanelli Scarlets*), Johnny O'Connor (*London Wasps*), Anthony Foley (*Munster*) ... Substitutes: Eric Miller (*Leinster*) for O'Connor (66), Frankie Sheahan (*Munster*) for Byrne (72), Marcus Horan (*Munster*) for Corrigan (72), Gavin Duffy (*Harlequins*) for Hickie (76), Guy Easterby (*Leinster*) for Stringer (76), Donncha O'Callaghan (*Munster*) for O'Kelly (76), David Humphreys (*Ulster*) for O'Gara (76)

REFEREE Joel Jutge (*France*)

SCORING Paterson, pen (3–0); Southwell, try (8–0); O'Gara, pen (8–3); O'Kelly, try (8–8); O'Gara, con (8–10); O'Gara, pen (8–13); O'Connell, try (8–18) (half-time) Hickie, try (8–23); O'Gara, con (8–25); O'Gara, pen (8–28); Petrie, try (13–28); Hayes, try (13–33); Duffy, try (13–38); Humphreys, con (13–40)

Scotland opened with great promise and after an early penalty by Paterson they conjured a brilliant try out of nothing. Taking a kick inside his own half, Paterson beat several defenders and raced up the field. He found support from Andy Craig who fed Hugo Southwell and the big centre just reached the corner. The try set Murrayfield alight but Ireland had enough skill and composure to turn the game around after their bad start, eventually scoring five tries to two. The Irish forwards used the rolling maul to great effect, and they were quick to the breakdowns and forced many turnovers. Ronan O'Gara kicked astutely and Paul O'Connell proved an inspiring leader. Scotland never stopped trying and Jon Petrie scored a consolation try from a well-executed lineout manoeuvre. Late tries by Hayes and Duffy sealed a record Irish win.

539   RBS SIX NATIONS CHAMPIONSHIP 2005   ITALY

Murrayfield · Saturday 26 February 2005 · Won 18–10

SCOTLAND Chris Paterson (*Edinburgh*); Simon Webster (*Edinburgh*), Andy Craig (*Glasgow*), Hugo Southwell (*Edinburgh*), Sean Lamont (*Glasgow*); Dan Parks (*Glasgow*), Chris Cusiter (*Borders*); Tom Smith (*Northampton Sts*), Gordon Bulloch* (*Glasgow*), Gavin Kerr (*Leeds Tykes*),

Stuart Grimes (*Newcastle F*), Scott Murray (*Edinburgh*), Simon Taylor (*Edinburgh*), Jon Petrie (*Glasgow*), Allister Hogg (*Edinburgh*) ... Substitutes: Ben Hinshelwood (*Worcester*) for Southwell (70), Bruce Douglas (*Borders*) for Kerr (72), Jon Dunbar (*Leeds Tykes*) for Taylor (75), Nathan Hines (*Edinburgh*) for Murray (75), Mike Blair (*Edinburgh*) for Cusiter (78), Gordon Ross (*Leeds Tykes*) for Parks (78), Rob Russell (*London Irish*) for Bulloch (78)

ITALY Roland De Marigny (*Parma*); Mirco Bergamasco (*Stade Français*), Cristian Stoica (*Montpellier*), Andrea Masi (*Viadana*), Ludovico Nitoglia (*Calvisano*); Luciano Orquero (*Padova*), Alessandro Troncon (*Treviso*); Andrea Lo Cicero (*L'Aquila*), Fabio Ongaro (*Treviso*), Leandro Castrogiovanni (*Calvisano*), Santiago Dellape (*Agen*), Marco Bortolami* (*Narbonne*), Aaraon Persico (*Agen*), David Dal Maso (*Treviso*), Sergio Parisse (*Treviso*) ... Substitutes: Roberto Pedrazzi (*Viadana*) for Stoica (57), Carlo Del Fava (*Parma*) for Dellape (63), Salvatore Perugini (*Calvisano*) for Castrogiovanni (63), Paul Griffen (*Calvisano*) for Orquero (68), Kaine Robertson (*Viadana*) for Bergamasco (72)

REFEREE Stuart Dickinson (*Australia*) · ATTENDANCE 48,145

SCORING Paterson, pen (3–0); De Marigny, pen (3–3); Paterson, pen (6–3) (half-time) Paterson, pen (9–3); Paterson, pen (12–3); Paterson, pen (15–3); Paterson, pen (18–3); Masi, try (18–8); De Marigny, con (18–10)

Both sides had lost their opening two matches and the result was a featureless encounter that had little to recommend it. Scotland managed to grind out a victory but only by adopting unexciting tactics: kick deep into the Italian half and let Chris Paterson take advantage of any infringements. The Scotland full-back duly obliged with six penalties and the Scots got their win, but there was little entertainment on view. Italy scored a late consolation try when Andrea Masi latched onto a charge-down, but by this stage most onlookers had lost interest.

540 RBS SIX NATIONS CHAMPIONSHIP 2005 WALES

Murrayfield · Sunday 13 March 2005 · Lost 22–46

SCOTLAND Chris Paterson (*Edinburgh*); †Rory Lamont (*Glasgow*), Andy Craig (*Glasgow*), Hugo Southwell (*Edinburgh*), Sean Lamont (*Glasgow*); Dan Parks (*Glasgow*), Chris Cusiter (*Borders*); Tom Smith (*Northampton Sts*), Gordon Bulloch* (*Glasgow*), Gavin Kerr (*Leeds Tykes*), Stuart Grimes (*Newcastle F*), Scott Murray (*Edinburgh*), Simon Taylor (*Edinburgh*), Jon Petrie (*Glasgow*), Allister Hogg (*Edinburgh*) ... Substitutes: Bruce Douglas (*Borders*) for Kerr (h-t), Nathan Hines (*Edinburgh*) for Grimes (h-t), Gordon Ross (*Leeds Tykes*) for Parks (h-t), Mike Blair (*Edinburgh*) for Cusiter (44), Andrew Henderson (*Glasgow*) for Craig (73)

WALES Kevin Morgan (*NG Dragons*); Rhys Williams (*Cardiff Blues*), Tom Shanklin (*Cardiff Blues*), Gavin Henson (*NS Ospreys*), Shane Williams (*NS Ospreys*); Stephen Jones (*Clermont Auv*), Dwayne Peel (*Llanelli Scarlets*); Gethin Jenkins (*Cardiff Blues*), Methin Davies (*Gloucester*), Adam Jones (*NS Ospreys*), Brent Cockbain (*NS Ospreys*), Robert Sidoli (*Cardiff Blues*), Ryan Jones (*NS Ospreys*), Martyn Williams (*Cardiff Blues*), Michael Owen* (*NG Dragons*) ... Substitutes: Robin McBride (*Llanelli Scarlets*) for Davies (49), John Yapp (*Cardiff Blues*) for D Jones (63), Hal Luscombe (*NG Dragons*) for R Williams (68), Jonathan Thomas (*NS Ospreys*) for Cockbain (71), Ceri Sweeney (*NG Dragons*) for Henson (73)

REFEREE Jonathan Kaplan (*South Africa*) · ATTENDANCE 63,431

SCORING R Jones, try (0–5); S Jones, con (0–7); R Williams, try (0–12); S Jones, con (0–14);

S Williams, try (0–19); S Jones, con (0–21); S Jones, pen (0–24); Paterson, pen (3–24); Morgan, try (3–29); S Jones, con (3–31); Morgan, try (3–36); S Jones, con (3–38) (half-time) R Williams, try (3–43); Craig, try (8–43); Paterson, con (10–43); R Lamont, try (15–43); Paterson, try (20–43); Paterson, con (22–43); S Jones, pen (22–46)

This record defeat was the nadir of the Matt Williams era. A resurgent Welsh side were on the trail of their first Grand Slam for 27 years. In a devastating first-half, they brushed aside an incompetent Scottish side that at times didn't seem to know what it was doing. The visitors streaked into a 24–0 lead after just 18 minutes and had the match in the bag before the interval. Scotland's basic skills were sorely lacking, especially in defence which was often woeful. Wales set the tone early on when winger Ryan Jones scored a try after a poor Scottish clearance kick. On the tenth minute, Scotland created a promising overlap on the Welsh 22, but Dan Parks threw out an ambitious long pass which was intercepted by Rhys Williams who raced away to the posts and break Scots hearts. Three minutes later, Stephen Jones found a big gap in the defence and a simple draw-and-pass created a try for winger Shane Williams. Although Chris Paterson kicked a penalty, a brace of Welsh tries by full-back Kevin Morgan ended the match as a contest. The Scots made three substitutions at the interval, including Gordon Ross for Parks, who had been very inconsistent, and this led to greater fluency in the Scottish attack. After another Welsh try, Scotland made a courageous revival and scored three well-worked tries of their own, although by this stage the visitors were already thinking about their next game.

541   RBS SIX NATIONS CHAMPIONSHIP 2005   ENGLAND

Twickenham · Saturday 19 March 2005 · Lost 22–43

SCOTLAND Chris Paterson (*Edinburgh*); Rory Lamont (*Glasgow*), Andy Craig (*Glasgow*), Hugo Southwell (*Edinburgh*), Sean Lamont (*Glasgow*); Gordon Ross (*Leeds Tykes*), Mike Blair (*Edinburgh*); Tom Smith (*Northampton Sts*), Gordon Bulloch* (*Glasgow*), Gavin Kerr (*Leeds Tykes*), Nathan Hines (*Edinburgh*), Scott Murray (*Edinburgh*), Jason White (*Sale Sharks*), Allister Hogg (*Edinburgh*), Simon Taylor (*Edinburgh*) ... Substitutes: Bruce Douglas (*Borders*) for Smith (23), Stuart Grimes (*Newcastle F*) Murray (32), Jon Petrie (*Glasgow*) for Hogg (65)

ENGLAND Iain Balshaw (*Leeds Tykes*); Mark Cueto (*Sale Sharks*), Jamie Noon (*Newcastle F*), Olly Barkley (*Bath*), Josh Lewsey (*London Wasps*); Charlie Hodgson (*Sale Sharks*), Harry Ellis (*Leicester Tgrs*); Matt Stevens (*Bath*), Steve Thompson (*Northampton Sts*), Duncan Bell (*Bath*), Danny Grewcock (*Bath*), Ben Kay (*Leicester Tgrs*), Joe Worsley (*London Wasps*), Lewis Moody (*Leicester Tgrs*), Martin Corry* (*Leicester Tgrs*) ... Substitutes: Steve Borthwick (*Bath*) for Kay (17), Ollie Smith (*Leicester Tgrs*) for Balshaw (30), Andy Hazell (*Gloucester*) for Moody (40), Mike Worsley (*Harlequins*) for Bell (51), Matt Dawson (*London Wasps*) for Ellis (64), Andy Titterell (*Sale Sharks*) for Thompson (71), Andy Goode (*Leicester Tgrs*) for Hodgson (75)

REFEREE Alain Rolland (*Ireland*)

SCORING Noon, try (0–5); Hodgson, con (0–7); Paterson, pen (3–7); Noon, try (3–12); Hodgson, con (3–14); Worsley, try (3–19); Lewsey, try (3–24); Hodgson, con (3–26); S Lamont, try (8–26); Paterson, con (10–26) (half-time) Craig, try (15–26); Paterson, con (17–26); Ellis, try (17–31); Hodgson, con (17–33); Taylor, try (22–33); Noon, try (22–38); Cueto, try (22–43)

Both sides were out of contention for the Championship so this match had an end-of-season feel about it. Spectators were treated to a fast and entertaining encounter

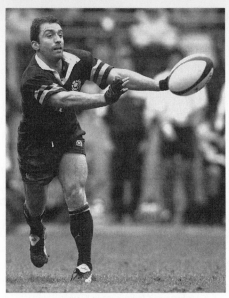

that had plenty of open rugby and ten tries in total. Scotland never looked like winning but they made a spirited revival in the second half and scored three good tries. At one point, they reduced England's lead to only nine points, but immediately conceded a soft try and any hope of a miraculous comeback evaporated. Scotland's tackling was weak at times and several scores should have been prevented. However, they were comfortable with the ball in hand, the back row was prominent, the half-backs combined effectively and Paterson was always dangerous in attack. Soon after this match, head coach Matt Williams and some of his assistants were dismissed after a disastrous record of only three wins in two years from 17 matches.

Bryan Redpath, 60 caps 1993–2003.
George Herringshaw/Sporting-Heroes.net)

| XV | 2005 | BARABRIANS |

Pittodrie Stadium, Aberdeen · Tuesday 24 May 2005 · Won 38–7

SCOTLAND XV Chris Paterson (*Edinburgh*); Rory Lamont (*Glasgow*), Marcus Di Rollo (*Edinburgh*), Andrew Henderson (*Glasgow*), Sean Lamont (*Glasgow*); Gordon Ross (*Leeds Tykes*), Mike Blair (*Edinburgh*); Allan Jacobsen (*Edinburgh*), Scott Lawson (*Glasgow*), Bruce Douglas (*Borders*), Stuart Grimes (*Newcastle F*), Scott Murray (*Edinburgh*), Kelly Brown (*Borders*), Allister Hogg (*Edinburgh*), Jon Petrie* (*Glasgow*) … Substitutes: Dougie Hall (*Edinburgh*) for Lawson (50), Euan Murray (*Glasgow*) for Jacobsen (50), Dan Parks (*Glasgow*) for Ross (63), Andrew Wilson (*Glasgow*) for Hogg (63), Jacobsen for Douglas (66), Hugo Southwell (*Edinburgh*) for R Lamont (72), Graeme Beveridge (*Glasgow*) for Blair (72), Craig Hamilton (*Newcastle F*) for Grimes (80)

BARBARIANS Girvan Dempsey (*Ireland*); Brian Lima (*Samoa*), Matt Burke (*Australia*), Kevin Maggs (*Ireland*), Sireli Bobo (*Fiji*); David Humphreys* (*Ireland*), Bryan Redpath (*Scotland*); Andrea Lo Cicero (*Italy*), Frankie Sheahan (*Ireland*), Darren Morris (*Wales*), Gary Longwell (*Ireland*), AJ Venter (*South Africa*), Owen Finegan (*Australia*), Semo Sititi (*Samoa*), Eric Miller (*Ireland*) … Substitutes: Kenny Logan (*Scotland*) for Lima (48), Thomas Castaignede (*France*) for Burke (57), Mark Robinson (*New Zealand*) for Redpath (60), Raphaël Ibañez (*France*) for Sheahan (65), Selborne Boome (*South Africa*) for Finegan (65), Johnny O'Connor (*Ireland*) for Sititi (65), Sititi for Logan (78), Redpath for Bobo (80)

REFEREE Nigel Owens (*Wales*) · **ATTENDANCE** 20,228

SCORING Henderson, try (5–0); Paterson, con (7–0); Lo Cicero, try (7–5); Humphreys, con (7–7); Paterson, pen (10–7) (half-time) Hall, try (15–7); Paterson, con (17–7); S Lamont, try (22–7); Paterson, con (24–7); Jacobsen, try (29–7); Paterson, con (31–7); Southwell, try (36–7); Paterson, con (38–7)

Under the interim guidance of coach Frank Hadden and in the unusual setting of Pittodrie Stadium, Aberdeen, Scotland won their first-ever victory over the Barbarians. The visitors had players from nine countries, including former Scotland favourites Bryan Redpath and Kenny Logan. Scotland gave a solid team performance and gradually wore down their opponents to secure a convincing win. Andy Henderson scored an early try and the Scots led 10-7 at the interval. They took a firm grip in the second period and added four further tries without reply. The best came around the hour mark when Sean Lamont took a high kick and fed Mike Blair who beat several defenders on a long run before giving Dougie Hall the easiest of chances. Cheered on by an appreciative crowd, this was an uplifting display by Scotland at the end of a long and depressing season. The forwards were solid in the scrums and produced some dynamic driving play whilst the backs were always eager in attack.

---

542   2005   ROMANIA

Dinamo Stadium, Bucharest · Sunday 5 June 2005 · Won 39–19

SCOTLAND   Chris Paterson (*Edinburgh*); Rory Lamont (*Glasgow*), Marcus Di Rollo (*Edinburgh*), Andrew Henderson (*Glasgow*), Sean Lamont (*Glasgow*); Dan Parks (*Glasgow*), Mike Blair (*Edinburgh*); Allan Jacobsen (*Edinburgh*), †Scott Lawson (*Glasgow*), Bruce Douglas (*Borders*), Craig Hamilton (*Newcastle F*), Scott Murray (*Edinburgh*), †Kelly Brown (*Borders*), Allister Hogg (*Edinburgh*), Jon Petrie* (*Glasgow*)... Substitutes: †Andrew Wilson (*Glasgow*) for Petrie (25), Dougie Hall (*Edinburgh*) for Lawson (53), †Euan Murray (*Glasgow*) for Jacobsen (53), Graeme Beveridge (*Glasgow*) for Blair (66), Hugo Southwell (*Edinburgh*) for R Lamont (66), Jacobsen for Douglas (77), †Phil Godman (*Edinburgh*) for Parks (79), Alastair Kellock (*Edinburgh*) for Murray (79)

ROMANIA   Danut Dumbrava (*Steaua*); Cristian Savan (*Rovigo*), Gabriel Brezoianu (*Dax*), Dan Vlad (*Steaua*), Ioan Teodorescu (*Cluj U*); Darie Curea (*Steaua*), Iulian Andrei (*Steaua*); Cezar Popescu (*Agen*), Razvan Mavrodin* (*Tarbes*), Petrisor Toderasc (*Brive*), Valentin Ursache (*Arad*), Cristian Petre (*Tarbes*), Florin Corodeanu (*Grenoble*), Alexandru Tudori (*Perigueux*), Cosmin Ratiu (*Dinamo*) ... Substitutes: Valetin Oprisor (*Perpignan*) for Ursache (37), Stefan Dumitru (*Steaua*) for Vlad (39), Paulica Ion (*Steaua*) for Popescu (53), Bogdan Balan (*Montauban*) for Toderasc (53), Bogdan Zebega (*Steaua*) for Mavrodin (78)

REFEREE   Dave Pearson (*England*)

SCORING   Savan, try (0–5); Dumbrava, con (0–7); Dumbrava, pen (0–10); Murray, try (5–10); Paterson, con (7–10); Henderson, try (12–10); Paterson, con (14–10); Paterson, try (19–10); Dumbrava, pen (19–13) (half-time) Paterson, pen (22–13); Dumbrava, pen (22–16); Lawson, try (27–16); Dumbrava, pen (27–19); Parks, try (32–19); Paterson, con (34–19); Brown, try (19–19)

Scotland did not tour in the summer of 2005 but they did play this one-off match against Romania. The Scots introduced five new caps: hooker Scott Lawson and flanker Kelly Brown, plus Andrew Wilson, Euan Murray and Phil Godman off the bench. Playing in oppressive heat and on a hard ground, Scotland leaked ten points in the first few minutes. Dan Parks gave out a floated pass that was scooped-up by Romanian wing Savan who had a clear run to the line. Dumbrava converted and then kicked a penalty. Scotland slowly settled down and Murray and Henderson scored tries. Paterson converted both and then added a try of his own after an excellent

Scottish movement. The Romanians were typically big and stubborn and they put up a good fight, but after their early scare the Scots were always in control. In the second half, Lawson, Parks and Brown scored tries to complete a highly efficient display.

543   AUTUMN TEST 2005   ARGENTINA

Murrayfield · Saturday 12 November 2005 · Lost 19–23

SCOTLAND Chris Paterson (*Edinburgh Gnrs*); Rory Lamont (*Glasgow Wrs*), Marcus Di Rollo (*Edinburgh Gnrs*), Andrew Henderson (*Glasgow Wrs*), Sean Lamont (*Northampton Sts*); Dan Parks (*Glasgow Wrs*), Mike Blair (*Edinburgh Gnrs*); Gavin Kerr (*Leeds Tykes*), Dougie Hall (*Edinburgh Gnrs*), Bruce Douglas (*Border Rvrs*), Craig Hamilton (*Glasgow Wrs*), Scott Murray (*Edinburgh Gnrs*), Jason White* (*Sale Sharks*), Allister Hogg (*Edinburgh Gnrs*), Simon Taylor (*Edinburgh Gnrs*) … Substitutes: Craig Smith (*Edinburgh Gnrs*) for Douglas (59), Allan Jacobsen (*Edinburgh Gnrs*) for Kerr (59), Chris Cusiter (*Border Rvrs*) for Blair (61), Scott Lawson (*Glasgow Wrs*) for Hall (63), Alastair Kellock (*Edinburgh Gnrs*) for Hamilton (63), Hugo Southwell (*Edinburgh Gnrs*) for R Lamont (74)

ARGENTINA Juan Martin Hernandez (*Stade Français*); Federico Martin Aramburu (*Biarritz*), Manuel Contepomi (*Bristol*), Felipe Contepomi (*Leinster*), Francisco Leonelli (*Edinburgh Gnrs*); Federico Todeschini (*Béziers*), Agustin Pichot* (*Stade Français*); Rodrigo Roncero (*Stade Français*), Mario Ledesma (*Montferrand*), Omar Hassan (*Toulouse*), Ignacio Fernandez Lobbe (*Sale Sharks*), Pablo Bouza (*Harlequins*), Martin Durand (*Montpellier*), Martin Schusterman (*Plymouth Alb*), Juan Fernandez Lobbe (*Liceo Naval*) … Substitutes: Lucas Borges (*Stade Français*) for M Contepomi (12), Manuel Carizza (*Biarritz*) for Bouza (60), Juan Manuel Leguizamon (*London Irish*) for Durand (60), Martin Scelzo (*Montferrand*) for Hasan (74), Bernardo Stortoni (*Bristol*) for Lobbe (77)

REFEREE Kelvin Deaker (*New Zealand*) · **ATTENDANCE** 14,491

SCORING Todeschini, pen (0–3); Parks, drop (3–3); Parks, try (8–3); Paterson, con (10–3); Paterson, pen (13–3); Todeschini, pen (13–6) (half-time) Paterson, pen (16–6); Leonelli, try (16–11); Todeschini, con (16–13); Paterson, pen (19–13); Todeschini, pen (19–16); penalty try (19–21); Todeschini, con (19–23)

Under new captain Jason White, Scotland kicked-off their autumn test series with this disappointing defeat to the touring Argentineans. Scotland dominated for long periods and could easily have won the game. Their set-piece play was solid, they defended well and showed adventure in attack, but once again they wasted too many scoring opportunities. Todeschini kicked an early penalty for the visitors and Parks replied with a trademark drop goal. On the 25th minute, Sean Lamont made a long run from his own half before passing to Hogg who was caught just short of the line. The ball was recycled to Parks who chipped past the defence and won the race to the touchdown. Paterson converted and kicked a penalty, and Scotland led 13–6 at the break, Todeschini having added a second penalty for Argentina. Scotland had a lot of play early in the second half but could only register another Paterson penalty. On the 52nd minute, Francisco Leonelli, the Edinburgh winger, slipped the defence to squeeze in at the corner. Todeschini kicked a great conversion and the game turned in Argentina's favour. Inside the final quarter, Simon Taylor was sin binned for persistent infringement and a few minutes later Argentina were awarded a penalty try after illegal interference at a scrum near the Scottish line. Despite their best efforts, Scotland were unable to produce a late score to save the game.

544   AUTUMN TEST 2005   SAMOA

Murrayfield · Sunday 20 November 2005 · Won 18–11

SCOTLAND Chris Paterson (*Edinburgh Gnrs*); Rory Lamont (*Glasgow Wrs*), Marcus Di Rollo (*Edinburgh Gnrs*), Andrew Henderson (*Glasgow Wrs*), Sean Lamont (*Northampton Sts*); Dan Parks (*Glasgow Wrs*), Chris Cusiter (*Border Rvrs*); Allan Jacobsen (*Edinburgh Gnrs*), Scott Lawson (*Glasgow Wrs*), Craig Smith (*Edinburgh Gnrs*), Craig Hamilton (*Glasgow Wrs*), Scott Murray (*Edinburgh Gnrs*), Jason White* (*Sale Sharks*), Allister Hogg (*Edinburgh Gnrs*), Simon Taylor (*Edinburgh Gnrs*) ... Substitutes: Alastair Kellock (*Edinburgh Gnrs*) for Hamilton (h-t), Gavin Kerr (*Leeds Tykes*) for Smith (47), Hugo Southwell (*Edinburgh Gnrs*) for R Lamont (47), Mike Blair (*Edinburgh Gnrs*) for Cusiter (60), Phil Godman (*Edinburgh Gnrs*) for Parks (60), Dougie Hall (*Edinburgh Gnrs*) for Lawson (64), Kelly Brown (*Border Rvrs*) for White (70)

SAMOA Roger Warren (*Cardiff Blues*); Lome Fa'atau (*Marist St Pats*), Andy Tuilagi (*Leicester Tgrs*), Eliota Fuimaono-Sapolu (*Auckland U*), Alex Tuilagi (*Leicester Tgrs*); Tanner Vili (*Kintetsu Liners*), Garrick Cowley (*Bay of Plenty*); Juston Va'a (*Upper Hut*), Mahonri Schwalger (*Wellington*), Cencus Johnston (*Eltham-Kaponga*), Daniel Leo (*Sunny Bay*), Jonny Fa'amatuainu (*Auckland*), Semo Sititi* (*Border Rvrs*), Iosefa Taina (*Vaimoso*), Daniel Farani (*Petone*) ... Substitutes: Leo Lafaialai'i (*Bayonne*) for Fa'amatuainu (h-t), Paul Tupai (*Rangarui Tupoke*) for Taina (47), Kas Lealamanua (*Biarritz*) for Va'a (56), Notise Tauafao (*Maile Sharks*) for Cowley (64), Aukuso Collins (*Petone*) for Andy Tuiagi (65), Sailosi Tagicakibau (*Chiefs*) for Fa'atau (65), Loleni Tafunai (*Vaiala*) for Warren (75) ... Yellow card: Taina (31)

REFEREE Alain Rolland (*Ireland*) · ATTENDANCE 14,718

SCORING Tuilagi, try (0–5); Hogg, try (5–5); Warren, pen (5–8); Paterson, pen (8–8) (half-time) Paterson, pen (11–8); Warren, pen (11–11); Di Rollo, try (16–11); Paterson, con (18–11)

Scotland won a rather turgid encounter but they were less than convincing and it was largely their superior fitness that saw them through. The Scots dominated the set-pieces and territory but again lacked a cutting edge in attack. Captained by Semo Setiti of the Border Reivers, the burly Samoans defended well, were quick at the break-downs and were never out of contention. In front of a small crowd, Samoa opened the scoring after six minutes with a try by Leicester wing Alex Tuilagi. The Scots replied with a try by Hogg from a lineout manouevre. Warren and Paterson exchanged penalties to tie the scores at the interval. In the second-half, Rory Lamont crossed after a slick passing movement only to be recalled for a forward pass. Another promising attack saw Hogg just denied at the left corner. A Paterson penalty put Scotland ahead after 55 minutes but later Warren equalised. With a few minutes remaining, Scotland took play into the Samoan 22 and Marcus Di Rollo burst through a tackle for the winning score.

545   AUTUMN TEST 2005   NEW ZEALAND

Murrayfield · Saturday 26 November 2005 · Lost 10–29

SCOTLAND Hugo Southwell (*Edinburgh Gnrs*); Chris Paterson (*Edinburgh Gnrs*),

Marcus Di Rollo (*Edinburgh Gnrs*), Andrew Henderson (*Glasgow Wrs*), Sean Lamont (*Northampton Sts*); Dan Parks (*Glasgow Wrs*), Chris Cusiter (*Border Rvrs*); Gavin Kerr (*Leeds Tykes*), Scott Lawson (*Glasgow Wrs*), Bruce Douglas (*Border Rvrs*), Craig Hamilton (*Glasgow Wrs*), Scott Murray (*Edinburgh Gnrs*), Jason White* (*Sale Sharks*), Allister Hogg (*Edinburgh Gnrs*), Simon Taylor (*Edinburgh Gnrs*) ... Substitutes: Mike Blair (*Edinburgh Gnrs*) for Cusiter (25), Alastair Kellock (*Edinburgh Gnrs*) for Hamilton (40), Simon Webster (*Edinburgh Gnrs*) for Di Rollo (56), Craig Smith (*Edinburgh Gnrs*) for Douglas (58), Dougie Hall (*Edinburgh Gnrs*) for Lawson (58), Kelly Brown (*Border Rvrs*) for Hogg (67), Phil Godman (*Edinburgh Gnrs*) for Parks (67)

NEW ZEALAND Isaia Toeava (*Auckland*); Rico Gear (*Crusaders*), Conrad Smith (*Hurricanes*), Tana Umaga* (*Hurricanes*), Joe Rokocoko (*Blues*); Nick Evans (*Highlanders*), Piri Weepu (*Hurricanes*); Saimone Taumoepeau (*Blues*), Anton Oliver (*Highlanders*), John Afoa (*Blues*), Chris Jack (*Crusaders*), James Ryan (*Highlanders*), Angus MacDonald (*Blues*), Richie McCaw (*Crusaders*), Sione Lauaki (*Chiefs*) ... Substitutes: Ma'a Nonu (*Hurricanes*) for Smith (40), Mose Tuiali'i (*Crusaders*) for McCaw (44), Andrew Hoare (*Hurricanes*) for Oliver (48), Jimmy Cowan (*Highlanders*) for Weepu (63), Jason Eaton (*Taranaki*) for Ryan (63), Neemia Tialata (*Hurricanes*) for Taumoepeau (68), Leon MacDonald (*Crusaders*) for Evans (68)

REFEREE Nigel Whitehouse (*Wales*) · **ATTENDANCE** 47,678

SCORING Paterson, pen (3–0); Gear, try (3–5); Evans, try (3–10); Evans, con (3–12); Evans, pen (3–15); Lauaki, try (3–20); Evans, con (3–22) (half-time) Gear, try (3–27); MacDonald, con (3–29); Webster, try (8–29); Paterson, con (10–29)

New Zealand made 13 changes after beating England the previous weekend and were still comfortable winners of this game, the 25th meeting between the two sides. Scotland competed well but they could not match the greater speed, continuity and support play of the All Blacks. Played in drizzling rain, both New Zealand wings tested the Scottish defence early on before Chris Paterson kicked a penalty after five minutes. New Zealand responded immediately, and from a scrum near the Scottish line Weepu chipped past the defence and Gear dived onto the ball for a simple try. Soon afterwards, the Scottish forwards drove over but the grounding of the ball was uncertain. Evans scored and converted a try and then kicked a penalty. Shortly before the interval, Toeava took a cross-field kick and popped the wet ball inside to Ryan. The big lock juggled with it before flicking it back to Lauaki who stretched over to score. Evans converted to put New Zealand 22–3 ahead at the break. Scotland raised their game in the second half and had spells of pressure but could not make it count. Sean Lamont made a thrilling run from his own half but stopped to look for support when he should have kept going. On the 68th minute, the visitors sealed the match with a typical breakout and Gear scored his second try. The Scots managed a late consolation try when Godman chipped through and Webster raced on to score.

546　　RBS SIX NATIONS CHAMPIONSHIP 2006　　　　FRANCE

Murrayfield · Sunday 5 February 2006 · Won 20–16

SCOTLAND Hugo Southwell (*Edinburgh Gnrs*); Chris Paterson (*Edinburgh Gnrs*), Marcus Di Rollo (*Edinburgh Gnrs*), Andrew Henderson (*Glasgow Wrs*), Sean Lamont (*Northampton Sts*); Dan Parks (*Glasgow Wrs*), Mike Blair (*Edinburgh Gnrs*); Gavin Kerr (*Leeds Tykes*), Dougie Hall (*Edinburgh Gnrs*), Bruce Douglas (*Border Rvrs*), Alastair Kellock

(*Edinburgh Gnrs*), Scott Murray (*Edinburgh Gnrs*), Jason White* (*Sale Sharks*), Allister Hogg (*Edinburgh Gnrs*), Simon Taylor (*Edinburgh Gnrs*) ... Substitutes: Simon Webster (*Edinburgh Gnrs*) for Di Rollo (28), Craig Smith (*Edinburgh Gnrs*) for Douglas (41), Chris Cusiter (*Border Rvrs*) for Blair (55), Gordon Ross (*Leeds Tykes*) for Parks (62), Scott Lawson (*Glasgow Wrs*) for Hall (62), Jon Petrie (*Glasgow Wrs*) for White (70), Scott MacLeod (*Border Rvrs*) for Kellock (71)

FRANCE Nicolas Brusque (*Biarritz*); Cedric Heymans (*Toulouse*), Florian Fritz (*Toulouse*), Ludovic Valbon (*Brive*), Christophe Dominici (*Stade Français*); Frederic Michalak (*Toulouse*), Jean-Baptiste Elissalde (*Toulouse*); Sylvain Marconnet (*Stade Français*), Dimitri Szarzewski (*Stade Français*), Pieter De Villiers (*Stade Français*), Fabien Pelous* (*Toulouse*), Jerome Thion (*Biarritz*), Yannick Nyanga (*Toulouse*), Remy Martin (*Stade Français*), Julien Bonnaire (*Bourgoin-Jallieu*) ... Substitutes: Olivier Milloud (*Bourgoin-Jallieu*) for De Villiers (64), Sebastien Bruno (*Sale Sharks*) for Szarzewski (64), Thomas Lièvremont (*Biarritz*) for Bonnaire (70), Guilliaume Bousses (*Bourgoin-Jallieu*) for Brusque (73), Dimitri Yachvili (*Biarritz*) for Elissalde (79)

REFEREE Jonathan Kaplan (*South Africa*) · ATTENDANCE 50,060

SCORING Lamont, try (5–0); Paterson, con (7–0); Paterson, pen (10–0); Paterson, pen (13–0); Elissalde, pen (13–3) (half-time) Lamont, try (18–3); Paterson, con (20–3); Bonnaire, try (20–8); Elissalde, pen (20–11); Bruno, try (20–16)

Jason White won his 50th cap. For the first time, Scotland opened a Six Nations campaign with a win. This was a close and exciting encounter with both teams committed to attacking rugby. Scotland rediscovered some of their old spirit and never allowed the French to settle. The Scottish defence was very strong and the forwards largely outplayed a powerful French pack. After some ten minutes, the Scots took a tap penalty inside the French half and worked play to the line. The ball was spun into midfield, and Sean Lamont stepped back off his left foot and thundered over at the posts. Paterson converted and then added two penalties. Five minutes into the second half, the Scots scored another memorable try. From a lineout on the French 22, the forwards slowly mauled the ball to the line and Lamont, who had joined the maul a few metres out, dived over. Paterson converted to put Scotland 20–3 in front. Five minutes later, France, who played with much greater width in the second half, made a flowing attack and No 8 Julien Bonnaire scored in the left hand corner. Elissalde missed the conversion but later kicked a penalty to reduce the gap to nine points. The furious pace of the game took its toll and some of the players looked very tired in the closing stages. With a couple of minutes to go, substitute hooker Sebastien Bruno scored an unconverted try to set up a nervous ending but Scotland held on for a deserved victory.

547   RBS SIX NATIONS CHAMPIONSHIP 2006   WALES

Millennium Stadium, Cardiff · Sunday 12 February 2006
Lost 18–28

SCOTLAND Hugo Southwell (*Edinburgh Gnrs*); Chris Paterson (*Edinburgh Gnrs*), †Ben MacDougall (*Border Rvrs*), Andrew Henderson (*Glasgow Wrs*), Sean Lamont (*Northampton Sts*); Dan Parks (*Glasgow Wrs*), Mike Blair (*Edinburgh Gnrs*); Gavin Kerr

(*Leeds Tykes*), Scott Lawson (*Glasgow Wrs*), Bruce Douglas (*Border Rvrs*), Alastair Kellock (*Edinburgh Gnrs*), Scott Murray (*Edinburgh Gnrs*), Jason White* (*Sale Sharks*), Allister Hogg (*Edinburgh Gnrs*), Simon Taylor (*Edinburgh Gnrs*) ... Substitutes: Craig Smith (*Edinburgh Gnrs*) for Kerr (54), Ross Ford (*Border Rvrs*) for Lawson (54), Chris Cusiter (*Border Rvrs*) for Blair (60), Gordon Ross (*Leeds Tykes*) for Parks (60), Jon Petrie (*Glasgow Wrs*) for Hogg (66), Scott MacLeod (*Border Rvrs*) for Kellock (66), Simon Webster (*Edinburgh Gnrs*) for MacDougall (77)

WALES Gareth Thomas* (*Toulouse*); Mark Jones (*Llanelli Scarlets*), Hal Luscombe (*NG Dragons*), Matthew Watkins (*Llanelli Scarlets*), Shane Williams (*Ospreys*); Stephen Jones (*Clermont Auv*), Dwayne Peel (*Llanelli Scarlets*); Duncan Jones (*Ospreys*), Rhys Thomas (*Cardiff Blues*), Adam Jones (*Ospreys*), Ian Gough (*NG Dragons*), Robert Sidoli (*Cardiff Blues*), Colin Charvis (*Newcastle F*), Martyn Williams (*Cardiff Blues*), Michael Owen (*NG Dragons*) ... Substitutes: Lee Byrne (*Llanelli Scarlets*) for Luscombe (29-40) and for S Williams (69), Gareth Delve (*Bath*) for Charvis (66), Gethin Jenkins (*Cardiff Blues*) for A Jones (68), Michael Phillips (*Cardiff Blues*) for Peel (69), Nicky Robinson (*Cardiff Blues*) for Watkins (74), Mefin Davies (*Gloucester*) for R Thomas (76), Adam Jones (*Llanelli Scarlets*) for Sidoli (77)

REFEREE Steve Walsh (*New Zealand*)

SCORING penalty try (0–5); S Jones, con (0–7); Paterson, pen (3–7); G Thomas, try (3–12); S Jones, con (3–14); Paterson, pen (6–14) (half-time) Sidoli, try (6–19); S Jones, con (6–21); G Thomas, try (6–26); S Jones, con (6–28); Southwell, try (11–28); Paterson, try (16–28); Paterson, con (18–28)

Scotland were quietly confident but their dreams were shattered in the 23rd minute when lock Scott Murray was sent off for retaliation, effectively ending the match as a contest. Whilst referee Steve Walsh was correct within the rules of the game, Murray's dismissal seemed unduly harsh. He was tackled late by Welsh lock Ian Gough and lashed out with his feet to free himself, accidentally catching Gough in the face. Gough, the perpetrator of the incident, escaped with only a yellow card. Murray became only the second Scot to be sent off in a test match following the dismissal of Nathan Hines against the United States in 2002. Wales made a fiery start and were awarded a penalty try after only six minutes when the Scottish forwards tried illegally to halt a powerful drive on their own line. Paterson kicked a penalty but then came the Murray incident which sapped Scottish confidence and enthusiasm. The Scots defended well until just before the interval when Welsh captain Gareth Thomas chipped ahead and collected the ball to score, leaving Scotland with a mountain to climb. In the second half, Sidoli and Thomas added further tries, both converted by Stephen Jones, but in the closing stages Scotland showed great spirit and salvaged some pride with two late tries. Hugo Southwell squeezed over after heavy pressure on the Welsh line, and in the last action of the day Paterson intercepted a pass inside his own half and raced away to the posts. It wasn't enough to save the game and Wales deserved to win because of their superior scrummaging and finishing. The Scots were left to ponder what might have been.

548   RBS SIX NATIONS CHAMPIONSHIP 2006   ENGLAND

Murrayfield · Saturday 25 February 2006 · Won 18–12

SCOTLAND Hugo Southwell (*Edinburgh Gnrs*); Chris Paterson (*Edinburgh Gnrs*),

Marcus Di Rollo (*Edinburgh Gnrs*), Andrew Henderson (*Glasgow Wrs*), Sean Lamont (*Northampton Sts*); Dan Parks (*Glasgow Wrs*), Mike Blair (*Edinburgh Gnrs*); Gavin Kerr (*Leeds Tykes*), Dougie Hall (*Edinburgh Gnrs*), Bruce Douglas (*Border Rvrs*), Alastair Kellock (*Edinburgh Gnrs*), Scott MacLeod (*Border Rvrs*), Jason White* (*Sale Sharks*), Allister Hogg (*Edinburgh Gnrs*), Simon Taylor (*Edinburgh Gnrs*) ... Substitutes: Nathan Hines (*Perpignan*) for MacLeod (51), Ross Ford (*Border Rvrs*) for Hall (58), Craig Smith (*Edinburgh Gnrs*) for Douglas (60), Chris Cusiter (*Border Rvrs*) for Blair (63), Gordon Ross (*Leeds Tykes*) for Parks (63)

ENGLAND Josh Lewsey (*London Wasps*); Mark Cueto (*Sale Sharks*), Jamie Noon (*Newcastle F*), Mike Tindall (*Gloucester*), Ben Cohen (*Northampton Sts*); Charlie Hodgson (*Sale Sharks*), Harry Ellis (*Leicester Tgrs*); Andy Sheridan (*Sale Sharks*), Steve Thompson (*Northampton Sts*), Julian White (*Leicester Tgrs*), Steve Borthwick (*Bath*); Danny Grewcock (*Bath*), Joe Worsley (*London Wasps*), Lewis Moody (*Leicester Tgrs*), Martin Corry* (*Leicester Tgrs*) ... Substitutes: Perry Freshwater (*Perpignan*) for Sheridan (38–40 & 72), Matt Dawson (*London Wasps*) for Ellis (50–62 & 72), Lawrence Dallaglio (*London Wasps*) for Corry (63), Simon Shaw (*London Wasps*) for Grewcock (66)

REFEREE Alan Lewis (*Ireland*)

SCORING Paterson, pen (3–0); Hodgson, pen (3–3) (half-time) Hodgson, pen (3–6); Paterson, pen (6–6); Paterson, pen (9–6); Parks, drop (12–6); Hodgson, pen (12–9); Paterson, pen (15–9); Hodgson, pen (15–12); Paterson, pen (18–12)

In a dramatic and tense match played under floodlights, Scotland won their second great victory of the 2006 championship with a hugely passionate and courageous display. England were strong favourites and had a big weight advantage in the forwards. Starved of possession, the Scots were unable to play much expansive rugby and hardly ever looked like scoring a try. Instead, they were absolutely resolute in defence, fearlessly standing-up to heavier opponents and knocking them backwards. The Scottish scrum creaked at times but successfully withstood intense pressure just before the interval when an English try looked inevitable. Stand-off Dan Parks had an excellent match with his astute tactical kicking and organisational play. It was his snap drop goal in the 56th minute that helped to tip the game in Scotland's favour. In a nail-biting conclusion, Hodgson and Paterson kicked two penalties each and right at the end England stole a Scottish lineout and launched a frantic attack but knocked on. From the ensuing scrum, the ball was hoofed into the East Stand and Murrayfield erupted.

549   RBS SIX NATIONS CHAMPIONSHIP 2006   IRELAND

Lansdowne Road, Dublin · Saturday 11 March 2006 · Lost 9–15

SCOTLAND Hugo Southwell (*Edinburgh Gnrs*); Chris Paterson (*Edinburgh Gnrs*), Marcus Di Rollo (*Edinburgh Gnrs*), Andrew Henderson (*Glasgow Wrs*), Sean Lamont (*Northampton Sts*); Dan Parks (*Glasgow Wrs*), Mike Blair (*Edinburgh Gnrs*); Gavin Kerr (*Leeds Tykes*), Dougie Hall (*Edinburgh Gnrs*), Bruce Douglas (*Border Rvrs*), Nathan Hines (*Perpignan*), Scott Murray (*Edinburgh Gnrs*), Jason White* (*Sale Sharks*), Allister Hogg (*Edinburgh Gnrs*), Simon Taylor (*Edinburgh Gnrs*) ... Substitutes: Craig Smith (*Edinburgh Gnrs*) for Douglas (56), Chris Cusiter (*Border Rvrs*) for Blair (57), Gordon Ross (*Leeds Tykes*) for Parks (57), Scott Lawson (*Glasgow Wrs*) for Hall (62), Douglas for Smith (62–69), Simon Webster (*Edinburgh Gnrs*) for Paterson (69), Jon Petrie (*Glasgow Wrs*) for White (71)

IRELAND Geordan Murphy (*Leicester Tgrs*); Shane Horgan (*Leinster*), Brian O'Driscoll*
(*Leinster*), Gordon D'Arcy (*Leinster*), Andrew Trimble (*Ulster*); Ronan O'Gara (*Munster*),
Peter Stringer (*Munster*); Marcus Horan (*Munster*), Jerry Flannery (*Munster*), John Hayes
(*Munster*), Malcolm O'Kelly (*Leinster*), Paul O'Connell (*Munster*), Simon Easterby
(*Llanelli Scarlets*), David Wallace (*Munster*), Denis Leamy (*Munster*) ... Replacement:
Donncha O'Callaghan (*Munster*) for O'Connell (64)

REFEREE Stuart Dickinson (*Australia*)

SCORING O'Gara, pen (0–3); O'Gara, pen (0–6); Paterson, pen (3–6); Paterson, pen (6–6);
O'Gara, pen (6–9); Paterson, pen (9–9); O'Gara, pen (9–12) (half-time) O'Gara, pen (9–15)

In the final championship game at the old Lansdowne Road, Scotland were always
competitive and the result was in doubt right to the end, but Ireland deserved to win
because they had greater skill and guile. This match was played in heavy rain which
ruined it as a spectacle and neither side was able to score a try. Chris Paterson kicked
three penalties for Scotland but it was not enough to overhaul Ronan O'Gara's five
for Ireland. The Scots showed plenty of spirit and their defensive effort was magnificent, but once again they were limited in attack. The lineout was poor at times and
their play lacked the intensity they had shown against France and England.

---

550   RBS SIX NATIONS CHAMPIONSHIP 2006   ITALY

Stadio Flaminio, Rome · Saturday 18 March 2006 · Won 13–10

SCOTLAND Hugo Southwell (*Edinburgh Gnrs*); Chris Paterson (*Edinburgh Gnrs*),
Marcus Di Rollo (*Edinburgh Gnrs*), Andrew Henderson (*Glasgow Wrs*), Sean Lamont
(*Northampton Sts*); Gordon Ross (*Leeds Tykes*), Chris Cusiter (*Border Rvrs*); Gavin Kerr
(*Leeds Tykes*), Scott Lawson (*Glasgow Wrs*), Bruce Douglas (*Border Rvrs*), Nathan Hines
(*Perpignan*), Scott Murray (*Edinburgh Gnrs*), Jason White* (*Sale Sharks*), Allister Hogg
(*Edinburgh Gnrs*), Simon Taylor (*Edinburgh Gnrs*) ... Substitutes: Mike Blair (*Edinburgh Gnrs*)
for Cusiter (8), Craig Smith (*Edinburgh Gnrs*) for Douglas (54), Dan Parks (*Glasgow Wrs*) for
Ross (61), Alastair Kellock (*Edinburgh Gnrs*) for Murray (67), Simon Webster (*Edinburgh Gnrs*)
for Lamont (71), Dougie Hall (*Edinburgh Gnrs*) for Lawson (75)

ITALY Cristian Stoica (*Montpellier*); Pablo Canavosio (*Calvisano*), Gonzalo Canale
(*Clermont Auv*), Mirco Bergamasco (*Stade Français*), Ludovico Nitoglia (*Calvisano*); Ramiro Pez
(*Perpignan*), Paul Griffen (*Calvisano*); Salvatore Perugini (*Calvisano*), Fabio Ongaro (*Treviso*),
Martin Castrogiovanni (*Calvisano*), Santiago Dellapè (*Agen*), Marco Bortolami* (*Narbonne*),
Sergio Parisse (*Stade Français*), Maurizio Zaffiri (*Calvisano*), Josh Sole (*Viadana*) ... Substitutes:
Simon Picone (*Treviso*) for Griffen (9-19), Ezio Galon (*Parma*) for Stoica (22), Alessandro Zanni
(*Calvisano*) for Zaffiri (53), Andrea Lo Cicero (*L'Aquila*) for Castrogiovanni (54), Carlo Festuccia
(*Gran Parma*) for Ongaro (61), Carlo Del Flava (*Bourgoin*) for Dellape (66)

REFEREE Alain Rolland (*Ireland*) · ATTENDANCE 24,973

SCORING Bergamasco, try (0–5); Pez, con (0–7); Paterson, try (5–7); Paterson, con (7–7); Ross,
drop (10–7) (half-time) Pez, pen (10–10); Paterson, pen (13–10)

In a hard fought encounter, Scotland just managed to scrape past a stuffy Italian side.
The Scots showed great self-belief after two early setbacks. Italy scored a try after
only five minutes when centre Mirco Bergamasco raced onto a chip ahead by Pez. The

Scots then lost scrum-half Chris Cusiter through injury, but on the tenth minute Paterson scored a try after good play by the forwards. Gordon Ross dropped a goal before the interval and on the 57th minute Pez kicked a penalty to tie the scores. Inside the final five minutes, Italy launched an attack from their half but Jason White made a thundering tackle on prop Lo Cicero to force a penalty. Paterson coolly kicked the goal from around 45 metres to snatch victory. Amongst several good performances, Gordon Ross kicked effectively and Mike Blair made several try-saving tackles. This was Scotland's first away win in the championship for four years and they ended their campaign with three wins out of five.

XV	2006	BABARIANS

Murrayfield · Wednesday 31 May 2006 · Won 66–19

SCOTLAND XV Hugo Southwell (*Edinburgh Gnrs*); Chris Paterson (*Edinburgh Gnrs*), Marcus Di Rollo (*Edinburgh Gnrs*), Andrew Henderson (*Glasgow Wrs*), Sean Lamont (*Northampton Sts*); Dan Parks (*Glasgow Wrs*), Mike Blair (*Edinburgh Gnrs*); Gavin Kerr (*Leeds Tykes*), Scott Lawson (*Glasgow Wrs*), Craig Smith (*Edinburgh Gnrs*), Alastair Kellock (*Edinburgh Gnrs*), Scott Murray (*Edinburgh Gnrs*), Jason White* (*Sale Sharks*), Kelly Bown (*Border Rvrs*), Allister Hogg (*Edinburgh Gnrs*) ... Substitutes: Dougie Hall (*Edinburgh Gnrs*) for Lawson (40), Bruce Douglas (*Border Rvrs*) for Kerr (40), Donnie Macfadyen (*Glasgow Wrs*) for White (40), Simon Webster (*Edinburgh Gnrs*) for Southwell (40), Scott MacLeod (*Border Rvrs*) for Murray (47), Sam Pinder (*Glasgow Wrs*) for Blair (55), Gordon Ross (*Leeds Tykes*) for Parks (55), Blair for Di Rollo (60), Kerr for Smith (63)

BARBARIANS Steve Hanley (*Sale Sharks & England*); Leon Lloyd (*Leicester Tgrs & England*), Will Greenwood* (*Harlequins & England*), Sonny Parker (*Ospreys & Wales*), Lee Robinson (*Bristol*); Chris Malone (*Bath*), Jason Spice (*Ospreys*); Kevin Tkachuk (*Glasgow Wrs & Canada*), Pieter Dixon (*Bath & SA*), John Davies (*Llanelli Scarlets & Wales*), Jim Hamilton (*Leicester Tgrs*), Hottie Louw (*Llanelli Scarlets & SA*), Keiron Dawson (*London Irish & Ireland*), Jason Forster (*NG Dragons & Wales*), Daniel Browne (*Northampton Sts*) ... Substitutes: Jacob Rauluni (*Bristol & Fiji*) for Spice (38), Ugo Monye (*Harlequins*) for Hanley (45), Bobby Skinstad (*Richmond & SA*) for Forster (51), Olivier Azam (*Gloucester & France*) for Dixon (59), Darren Crompton (*Bristol*) for Tkachuk (59), Kevin Maggs (*Ulster & Ireland*) for Greenwood (62), Tony Marsh (*Clermont Auv & France*) for Parker (62), Parker for Lloyd (70)

REFEREE Wayne Barnes (*England*) · ATTENDANCE 28,607

SCORING Paterson, pen (3–0); Dawson, try (3–5); Malone, con (3–7); Blair, try (8–7); Paterson, con (10–7); Henderson, try (15–7); Paterson, con (17–7); Hanley, try (17–12); Paterson, try (22–12); Paterson, con (24–12) (half-time) Di Rollo, try (29–12); Paterson, con (31–12); Hall, try (36–12); Paterson, con (38–12); Pinder, try (43–12); Paterson, con (45–12); Marsh, try (45–17); Malone, con (45–19); Blair, try (50–19); Paterson, con (52–19); Henderson, try (57–19); Paterson, con (59–19); Paterson, try (64–19); Paterson, con (66–19)

On a sunny evening, the Scots warmed-up for their summer tour of South Africa with a nine try romp against a rag-tag Barbarians side. Captained by the former England centre Will Greenwood, the Barbarians were not quite as strong as usual and fielded five uncapped players in their starting line-up, including future Scotland lock Jim Hamilton. The visitors tried hard to play their traditional brand of free-flowing rugby, but they struggled to find cohesion and made a lot of errors. Scotland, by comparison, showed good decision-making and teamwork. There was plenty of entertainment for the big crowd to enjoy, but as usual the match lacked a real competitive edge (although several players had to leave the field with injuries). Scotland finished strongly and scored three tries in the last ten minutes by which time the Barbarians looked a bedraggled side. Chris Paterson gave another perfect kicking display with nine conversions and a penalty, and also two tries.

551　　　TOUR OF SOUTH AFRICA 2006　　SOUTH AFRICA

King's Park Stadium, Durban · Saturday 10 June 2006 · Lost 16–36

SCOTLAND Hugo Southwell (*Edinburgh Gnrs*); Chris Paterson (*Edinburgh Gnrs*), Marcus Di Rollo (*Edinburgh Gnrs*), Andrew Henderson (*Glasgow Wrs*), Sean Lamont (*Northampton Sts*); Dan Parks (*Glasgow Wrs*), Mike Blair (*Edinburgh Gnrs*); Gavin Kerr (*Leeds Tykes*), Scott Lawson (*Glasgow Wrs*), Bruce Douglas (*Border Rvrs*), Nathan Hines (*Perpignan*), Scott Murray (*Edinburgh Gnrs*), Jason White* (*Sale Sharks*), Donnie Macfadyen (*Glasgow Wrs*), Allister Hogg (*Edinburgh Gnrs*) … Substitutes: Simon Webster (*Edinburgh Gnrs*) for Lamont (38), Dougie Hall (*Edinburgh Gnrs*) for Lawson (41), Craig Smith (*Edinburgh Gnrs*) for Douglas (41), Alastair Kellock (*Edinburgh Gnrs*) for Murray (60), Gordon Ross (*Leeds Tykes*) for Parks (62), Kelly Brown (*Border Rvrs*) for Hogg (67), †Sam Pinder (*Glasgow Wrs*) for Blair (71)

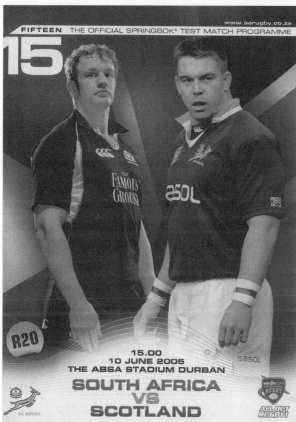

Scottish captain Jason White on the front cover of the programme for the First Test against South Africa in 2006.
Dave Fox

SOUTH AFRICA Percy Montgomery (*Sharks*); Breyton Paulse (*Clermont Auv*), Jacque Fourie (*Cats*), Jean de Villiers (*Stormers*), Andre Snyman (*Leeds Tykes*); Jaco van der Westhuyzen (*Bulls*), Fourie du Preez (*Bulls*); Os du Randt (*Cheetahs*), John Smit* (*Sharks*), Eddie Andrews (*Stormers*), Danie Rossouw (*Bulls*), Victor Matfield (*Bulls*), Schalk Burger (*Stormers*), Juan Smith (*Cheetahs*), Joe van Niekerk (*Stormers*) … Substitutes: Wynand Olivier (*Bulls*) for de Villiers (54), Lawrence Sephaka (*Cats*) for du Randt (56), Ricky Januarie (*Cats*) for du Preez (61), Pedrie Wannenburg (*Sharks*) for van Niekerk (61), Gaffie du Toit (*Cheetahs*) for Paulse (62), Johann Muller (*Sharks*) for Matfield (70), Hanyani Shimange (*Stormers*) for Smit (75)

REFEREE DG Courtney (*Ireland*) · ATTENDANCE 36,088

SCORING Montgomery, pen (0–3); Paterson, pen (3–3); Burger, try (3–8); Montgomery, con (3–10); Paulse, try (3–15); Paterson, pen (6–15); Montgomery, pen (6–18) (half-time) Paterson, pen (9–18); Snyman, try (9–23); Montgomery, con (9–25); Montgomery, pen (9–28); Montgomery, try (9–33); Montgomery, pen (9–36); Webster, try (14–36); Paterson, con (16–36)

Under the captaincy of Jason White, Scotland made a two match tour of South Africa in June 2006. The Scots were cautiously optimistic after their good showing in the Six Nations, but they were well beaten in the first test in Durban. South Africa scored four tries to one and might easily have won by more if they had taken their chances. The abrasive South African pack dominated in all respects and the Scots had little more than a battle for survival. The Scottish defence was weak at times and some of their kicking was too loose. South Africa scored two tries in the first half and never looked threatened. Chris Paterson's third penalty closed the gap to nine points early in the second period, but further tries by Snyman and Montgomery underlined home superiority. Simon Webster bagged a late consolation try for the battered tourists.

---

552   TOUR OF SOUTH AFRICA 2006   SOUTH AFRICA

EPFRU Stadium, Port Elizabeth · Saturday 17 June 2006 · Lost 15–29

SCOTLAND Hugo Southwell (*Edinburgh Gnrs*); Chris Paterson (*Edinburgh Gnrs*), Marcus Di Rollo (*Edinburgh Gnrs*), Andrew Henderson (*Glasgow Wrs*), Simon Webster (*Edinburgh Gnrs*); Gordon Ross (*Leeds Tykes*), Mike Blair (*Edinburgh Gnrs*); Gavin Kerr (*Leeds Tykes*), Dougie Hall (*Edinburgh Gnrs*), Craig Smith (*Edinburgh Gnrs*), Nathan Hines (*Perpignan*), Alastair Kellock (*Edinburgh Gnrs*), Jason White* (*Sale Sharks*), Allister Hogg (*Edinburgh Gnrs*), Jon Petrie (*Glasgow Wrs*) ... Substitutes: Kelly Brown (*Border Rvrs*) for Petrie (55), Bruce Douglas (*Border Rvrs*) for Smith (55), Scott Lawson (*Glasgow Wrs*) for Hall (67), Ben MacDougall (*Border Rvrs*) for Henderson (70), Donnie Macfadyen (*Glasgow Wrs*) for Hogg (70), Scott MacLeod (*Border Rvrs*) for Kellock (70), Sam Pinder (*Glasgow Wrs*) for Blair (72)

SOUTH AFRICA Percy Montgomery (*Sharks*); Breyton Paulse (*Clermont Auv*), Andre Snyman (*Leeds Tykes*), Wynand Olivier (*Bulls*), Bryan Habana (*Bulls*); Jaco van der Westhuyzen (*Bulls*), Fourie du Preez (*Bulls*); Os du Randt (*Cheetahs*), John Smit* (*Sharks*), Eddie Andrews (*Stormers*), Danie Rossouw (*Bulls*), Victor Matfield (*Bulls*), Schalk Burger (*Stormers*), Juan Smith (*Cheetahs*), Joe van Niekerk (*Stormers*) ... Substitutes: CJ van der Linde (*Cheetahs*) for Andrews (51), Jacques Cronje (*Bulls*) for van Niekerk (65), Gaffie du Toit (*Cheetahs*) for Paulse (75), Ricky Januarie (*Cats*) for du Preez (78), Albert van den Berg (*Sharks*) for Matfield (80)

REFEREE Tony Spreadbury (*England*) · ATTENDANCE 25,844

SCORING Montgomery, pen (0–3); Montgomery, pen (0–6); Webster, try (5–6); Montgomery, pen (5–9); van der Westhuyzen, pen (5–12) (half-time) Montgomery, pen (5–15); Paterson, pen (8–15); Montgomery, pen (8–18); Du Preez, try (8–23); Macfadyen, try (13–23); Paterson, con (15–23); Montgomery, pen (15–26); Montgomery, pen (15–29)

Scotland made six changes and were a big improvement on the previous weekend. They were more competitive and decisive, and might have done even better if some marginal decisions had gone their way. After two Montgomery penalties, the Scottish forwards drove into the home 22, Gordon Ross chipped neatly behind the defence and the ball sat up nicely for Simon Webster to score out wide. Just before the interval, Webster was denied a second try when the video referee ruled that he had knocked on in the act of scoring. The game turned on a crucial decision around the hour mark. Chris Paterson intercepted a pass inside his own half and raced away to the line, but was pulled back for a previous infringement by Webster. Momentarily, the Scots lost their concentration and from the next scrum Fourie du Preez darted over in the corner. Inside the last ten minutes, Macfadyen pounced on a dropped pass behind the South African line for an opportunist try which Paterson converted, but two late penalties by Montgomery saw the South Africans safely home.

---

553   AUTUMN TEST 2006   ROMANIA

Murrayfield · Saturday 11 November 2006 · Won 48–6

SCOTLAND Hugo Southwell (*Edinburgh*); Simon Webster (*Edinburgh*), Marcus Di Rollo (*Edinburgh*), †Rob Dewey (*Edinburgh*), Sean Lamont (*Northampton Sts*); Phil Godman (*Edinburgh*), Mike Blair (*Edinburgh*); Gavin Kerr (*Border Rvrs*), Dougie Hall (*Edinburgh*), Euan Murray (*Glasgow Wrs*), Nathan Hines (*Perpignan*), Scott Murray (*Edinburgh*), Jason White* (*Sale Sharks*), Kelly Brown (*Border Rvrs*), †Johnnie Beattie (*Glasgow Wrs*) ... Substitutes: †David Callam (*Edinburgh*) for White (38), Allan Jacobsen (*Edinburgh*) for Kerr (50), Craig Smith (*Edinburgh*) for E Murray (54), †Jim Hamilton (*Leicester Tgrs*) for Hines (54), Chris Cusiter (*Border Rvrs*) for Blair (60), Chris Paterson (*Edinburgh*) for Southwell (66), Scott Lawson (*Glasgow Wrs*) for Hall (70)

ROMANIA Florin Vlaicu (*Steaua*); Gabriel Brezoianu (*Racing Métro*), Catalin Dascalu (*Steaua*), Romeo Gontineac (*Aurillac*), Ioan Teodorescu (*Arad*); Ionut Dimofte (*Arad*), Vali Calafeteanu (*Dinamo*); Petru Balan (*Biarritz*), Marius Tincu (*Perpignan*), Bogdan Balan (*Montauban*), Sorin Socol* (*Agen*), Cristian Petre (*Brive*), Florin Corodeanu (*Grenoble*), Cosmin Ratiu (*Dinamo*), Ovidiu Tonita (*Perpignan*) ... Substitutes: Paulica Ion (*Steaua*) for B Balan (45), Csaba Gal (*U Cluj*) for Dascalu (53), Valentin Ursache (*Arad*) for Corodeanu (62), Cezar Popescu (*Agen*) for P Balan (64), Ionut Tofan (*Limoges*) for Gontineac (69), Razvan Mavrodin (*Pau*) for Tincu (71), Alexandru Lupu (*Steaua*) for Calafeteanu (72)

REFEREE Matt Goddard (*Australia*) · **ATTENDANCE** 12,128

SCORING Beattie, try (5–0); Godman, con (7–0); Vlaicu, pen (7–3); Southwell, try (12–3); Godman, pen (15–3); Southwell, try (20–3) (half-time) Dewey, try (25–3); Godman, con (27–3); Vlaicu, pen (27–6); Godman, try (32–6); Godman, con (34–6); Hall, try (39–6); Godman, con (41–6); Cusiter, try (46–6); Godman, con (48–6)

Scotland opened their 2006 autumn series with a comfortable victory over a Romanian side that was typically stuffy and dogged but limited in attack. There were two new caps in the starting line-up: centre Rob Dewey and No 8 Johnnie Beattie, son of 1980s star John who was commentating on the match for television. Beattie opened the scoring with a well-worked back-row try and later Dewey also scored a debut try. Fullback Hugo Southwell added a first-half brace and used his powerful kicking, defensive and positional play to great effect. The heavyweight Romanian pack was a handful at times, but the visitors posed little threat behind the scrum and some of their first-time tackling was suspect. Sadly, Scotland's inspirational captain Jason White was stretchered off with a knee injury which ruled him out of the rest of the season. White was replaced by another newcomer David Callam and later the enormous Leicester lock Jim Hamilton became the 1000th Scottish international player when he came on for Nathan Hines.

554 AUTUMN TEST 2006 PACIFIC ISLANDERS

Murrayfield · Saturday 18 November 2006 · Won 34–22

SCOTLAND Chris Paterson* (*Edinburgh*); Sean Lamont (*Northampton Sts*), Marcus Di Rollo (*Edinburgh*), Andrew Henderson (*Glasgow Wrs*), Simon Webster (*Edinburgh*); Dan Parks (*Glasgow Wrs*), Chris Cusiter (*Border Rvrs*); Gavin Kerr (*Border Rvrs*), Dougie Hall (*Edinburgh*), Euan Murray (*Glasgow Wrs*), Nathan Hines (*Perpignan*), Scott Murray (*Edinburgh*), Simon Taylor (*Edinburgh*), Kelly Brown (*Border Rvrs*), Johnnie Beattie (*Glasgow Wrs*) ... Substitutes: David Callam (*Edinburgh*) for Beattie (6), Mike Blair (*Edinburgh*) for Cusiter (11), Ross Ford (*Glasgow Wrs*) for Hall (57), Allan Jacobsen (*Edinburgh*) for Kerr (57), Alastair Kellock (*Glasgow Wrs*) for Taylor (65), Hugo Southwell (*Edinburgh*) for Lamont (temp 62-4) and for Paterson (77), Phil Godman (*Edinburgh*) for Parks (73)

PACIFIC ISLANDERS Norman Ligairi (*Fiji*); Lome Fa'atau (*Samoa*), Kameli Ratuvou (*Fiji*), Elvis Seveali'i (*Samoa*), Rupeni Caucaunibuca (*Fiji*); Tusi Pisi (*Samoa*), Moses Rauluni (*Fiji*); Taufa'ao Felise (*Tonga*), Mo Schwalger (*Samoa*), Tevita Taumoepeau (*Tonga*), Simon Raiwalui* (*Fiji*), Daniel Leo (*Samoa*), Viliami Vaki (*Tonga*), Nili Latu (*Tonga*), Epi Taione (*Tonga*) ... Substitutes: Aleki Lutui (*Tonga*) for Schwalger (30), Seru Rabeni (*Fiji*) for Caucaunibuca (53), Ma'ama Molitika (*Tonga*) for Vaki (53), Semo Sititi (*Samoa*) for Taione (53), Justin Va'a (*Samoa*) for Felise (65), Seremaia Bai (*Fiji*) for Seveali'i (65)

REFEREE Bryce Lawrence (*New Zealand*) · **ATTENDANCE** 19,055

SCORING Di Rollo, try (5–0); Paterson, con (7–0); Callam, try (12–0); Paterson, con (14–0); Brown, try (19–0); Paterson, con (21–0); Henderson, try (26–0); Paterson, con (28–0); Caucaunibuca, try (28–5); Paterson, pen (31–5) (half-time) Ratovou, try (31–10); Leo, try (31–15); Di Rollo, drop (34–15); Ratovou, try (34–20); Pisi, con (34–22)

The Pacific Islanders presented a strong physical challenge, but Scotland made a devastating start and raced to a 28–0 lead within the first 30 minutes despite suffering early injuries to Johnnie Beattie and Chris Cusiter. The Islanders scored their first try just before the break and added three more in the second half, but their place-kicking was very poor. Scotland's only points after their early scoring blitz were a Paterson penalty and a late drop goal by Di Rollo but they were never in any danger. The Scottish forwards played well against burly opponents and the half-backs combined effectively.

555 AUTUMN TEST 2006 AUSTRALIA

Murrayfield · Saturday 25 November 2006 · Lost 15–44

SCOTLAND Chris Paterson* (*Edinburgh*); Sean Lamont (*Northampton Sts*), Marcus Di Rollo (*Edinburgh*), Andrew Henderson (*Glasgow Wrs*), Simon Webster (*Edinburgh*); Dan Parks (*Glasgow Wrs*), Mike Blair (*Edinburgh*); Gavin Kerr (*Border Rvrs*), Dougie Hall (*Edinburgh*), Euan Murray (*Glasgow Wrs*), Nathan Hines (*Perpignan*), Scott Murray (*Edinburgh*), Simon Taylor

(*Edinburgh*), Kelly Brown (*Border Rvrs*), David Callam (*Edinburgh*) … Substitutes:
Hugo Southwell (*Edinburgh*) for Webster (8), Phil Godman (*Edinburgh*) for Di Rollo (47–56) and
for Parks (56), Allan Jacobsen (*Edinburgh*) for Kerr (48), Ross Ford (*Border Rvrs*) for Hall (56),
†Alasdair Strokosch (*Edinburgh*) for Brown (68), Jim Hamilton (*Leicester Tgrs*) for S Murray (68),
†Rory Lawson (*Gloucester*) for Blair (70)

AUSTRALIA   Chris Latham (*Reds*); Mark Gerrard (*Brumbies*), Stirling Mortlock* (*Brumbies*),
Scott Staniforth (*Western Force*), Lote Tuqiri (*Waratahs*); Stephen Larkham (*Brumbies*),
Matt Giteau (*Western Force*); Benn Robinson (*Waratahs*), Stephen Moore (*Reds*),
Guy Shepherdson (*Brumbies*), Nathan Sharpe (*Western Force*), Alister Campbell (*Brumbies*),
Rocky Elsom (*Waratahs*), George Smith (*Brumbies*), David Lyons (*Waratahs*) … Substitutes:
Phil Waugh (*Waratahs*) for Smith (59), Wycliffe Palu (*Waratahs*) for Lyons (59), Mark Chisholm
(*Brumbies*) for Elsom (67–75) and for Campbell (75), Tatafu Polota-Nau (*Waratahs*) for
Moore (73), Mat Rogers (*Waratahs*) for Staniforth (73), Al Baxter (*Waratahs*) for Robinson (75),
Josh Valentine (*Reds*) for Larkham (79)

REFEREE   Donal Courtney (*Ireland*)   ·   ATTENDANCE   64,120

SCORING   Paterson, pen (3–0); Webster, try (8–0); Paterson, con (10–0); Mortlock, pen (10–3);
Larkham, try (10–8); Mortlock, con (10–10); Mortlock, pen (10–13); Mortlock, pen (10–16)
(half-time) Gerrard, try (10–21); Mortlock, con (10–23); Gerrard, try (10–28); Mortlock, con
(10–30); Lamont, try (15–30); Moore, try (15–35); Mortlock, con (15–37); Latham, try (15–42);
Mortlock, con (15–44)

Scotland were optimistic that they could record their first victory over Australia since
1982, but they were well beaten by a better side. Scotland made a lively start and after
an early penalty Simon Webster danced through the defence for a great solo try. The
Australians hit back immediately with a Mortlock penalty and then Larkham broke
a weak tackle for a try at the posts. Scotland were only six points adrift at the start
of the second half, but two quick tries by Gerrard put the Australians out of reach.
On the 54th minute, Sean Lamont raised some hopes when he scored a try after the
defence failed to deal with a crosskick. Scotland tried hard, but the visitors ended
firmly in control and scored two late tries in typical opportunistic style. This was a
sobering defeat for Scotland who were easily outclassed by their fleet-footed opponents.

---

556   RBS SIX NATIONS CHAMPIONSHIP 2007   ENGLAND

Twickenham   ·   Saturday 3 February 2007   ·   Lost 20–42

SCOTLAND   Hugo Southwell (*Edinburgh*); Sean Lamont (*Northampton Sts*), Marcus Di Rollo
(*Edinburgh*), Andrew Henderson (*Glasgow Wrs*), Chris Paterson* (*Edinburgh*); Dan Parks
(*Glasgow Wrs*), Chris Cusiter (*Border Rvrs*); Gavin Kerr (*Border Rvrs*), Dougie Hall (*Edinburgh*),
Euan Murray (*Glasgow Wrs*), Jim Hamilton (*Leicester Tgrs*), Alastair Kellock (*Glasgow Wrs*),
Simon Taylor (*Edinburgh*), Kelly Brown (*Border Rvrs*), David Callam (*Edinburgh*) … Substitutes:
Scott Murray (*Edinburgh*) for Kellock (52-61) and for Hamilton (61), Allan Jacobsen (*Edinburgh*)
for Kerr (55), Allister Hogg (*Edinburgh*) for Brown (61), Rob Dewey (*Edinburgh*) for Henderson
(61), Ross Ford (*Border Rvrs*) for Hall (63), Rory Lawson (*Gloucester*) for Cusiter (66),
Rory Lamont (*Glasgow Wrs*) for Parks (68), Kerr for E Murray (73)

ENGLAND   Olly Morgan (*Gloucester*); Josh Lewsey (*London Wasps*), Mike Tindall (*Gloucester*),
Andy Farrell (*Saracens*), Jason Robinson (*Sale Sharks*); Jonny Wilkinson (*Newcastle F*), Harry Ellis
(*Leicester Tgrs*); Perry Freshwater (*Perpignan*), George Chutter (*Leicester Tgrs*), Phil Vickery*

(*London Wasps*), Louis Deacon (*Leicester Tgrs*), Danny Grewcock (*Bath*), Joe Worsley (*London Wasps*), Magnus Lund (*Sale Sharks*), Martin Corry (*Leicester Tgrs*) ... Substitutes: Tom Rees (*London Wasps*) for Worsley (61), Lee Mears (*Bath*) for Chuter (73), Julian White (*Leicester Tgrs*) for Vickery (73), Toby Flood (*Newcastle F*) for Wilkinson (73)

REFEREE Marius Jonker (*South Africa*)

SCORING Wilkinson, pen (0–3); Paterson, pen (3–3); Wilkinson, drop (3–6); Taylor, try (8–6); Paterson, con (10–6); Wilkinson, pen (10–9); Wilkinson, pen (10–12); Robinson, try (10–17) (half-time) Paterson, pen (13–17); Wilkinson, pen (13–20); Wilkinson, pen (13–23); Robinson, try (13–28); Wilkinson, con (13–30); Wilkinson, try (13–35); Wilkinson, con (13–37); Lund, try (13–42); Dewey, try (18–42); Paterson, con (20–42)

England stand-off and national treasure Jonny Wilkinson was the Hammer of the Scots. Playing in his first international since the Rugby World Cup final in 2003, he displayed all his old confidence and control, landing a personal haul of 27 points. Jason Robinson, another man on the comeback trail, scored two tries, but the real star was scrum-half Harry Ellis whose sniping runs caused havoc in the Scottish defence. Ellis created two crucial tries in the second-half that put the result beyond doubt. On the 55th minute, he sent a clever grubber kick down the left touchline that flummoxed Sean Lamont and Robinson was on hand to touch down. Four minutes later, Ellis made a terrific break from a scrum before switching with Wilkinson who dived over at the right corner. Television replays suggested that Wilkinson's foot had been in touch before he grounded the ball, but the try was awarded and Wilkinson added insult to injury with a touchline conversion. Towards the end, Lund scored a soft try from close range to take England over 40 points. Scotland showed plenty of purpose and scored an early try when Simon Taylor snatched a loose ball from a lineout and dived over. The Scots were only four points adrift early in the second-half, but then the big English forwards took control. Scotland went down fighting and Rob Dewey scored a late consolation try.

557 RBS SIX NATIONS CHAMPIONSHIP 2007 WALES

Murrayfield · Saturday 10 February 2007 · Won 21–9

SCOTLAND Hugo Southwell (*Edinburgh*); Sean Lamont (*Northampton Sts*), Marcus Di Rollo (*Edinburgh*), Rob Dewey (*Edinburgh*), Chris Paterson* (*Edinburgh*); Phil Godman (*Edinburgh*), Chris Cusiter (*Border Rvrs*); Gavin Kerr (*Border Rvrs*), Dougie Hall (*Edinburgh*), Euan Murray (*Glasgow Wrs*), Jim Hamilton (*Leicester Tgrs*), Scott Murray (*Edinburgh*), Simon Taylor (*Edinburgh*), Kelly Brown (*Border Rvrs*), David Callam (*Edinburgh*) ... Substitutes: Nathan Hines (*Perpignan*) for Hamilton (48), Allan Jacobsen (*Edinburgh*) for Kerr (55), Allister Hogg (*Edinburgh*) for Brown (55), Ross Ford (*Border Rvrs*) for Hall (67), Simon Webster (*Edinburgh*) for Godman (69), Nikki Walker (*Ospreys*) for Lamont (69), Rory Lawson (*Gloucester*) for Cusiter (74)

WALES Kevin Morgan (*NG Dragons*); Mark Jones (*Llanelli Scarlets*), Jamie Robinson (*Cardiff Blues*), James Hook (*Ospreys*), Chris Czekaj (*Cardiff Blues*); Stephen Jones* (*Llanelli Scarlets*), Dwayne Peel (*Llanelli Scarlets*); Duncan Jones (*Ospreys*), Rhys Thomas (*Cardiff Blues*), Adam Jones (*Ospreys*), Robert Sidoli (*Ospreys*), Alun-Wyn Jones (*Cardiff Blues*), Alix Popham (*Llanelli Scarlets*), Martyn Williams (*Cardiff Blues*), Ryan Jones (*Ospreys*) ... Substitutes: Tom Shanklin (*Cardiff Blues*) for Hook (40), Ceri Sweeney (*NG Dragons*) for Morgan

(45–52), Ian Gough (*NG Dragons*) for Sidoli (52), Gethin Jenkins (*Cardiff Blues*) for D Jones (58), Matthew Rees (*Llanelli Scarlets*) for Williams (58-66) and for Thomas (66), Jonathan Thomas (*Ospreys*) for Williams (67)

REFEREE Alan Lewis (*Ireland*)

SCORING Paterson, pen (3–0); Paterson, pen (6–0); S Jones, pen (6–3); Paterson, pen (9–3); S Jones, pen (9–6) (half-time) Paterson, pen (12–6); Paterson, pen (15–6); S Jones, pen (15–9); Paterson, pen (18–9); Paterson, pen (21–9)

Simon Taylor won his 50th cap. Scotland were unable to score a try and all of their points came from Chris Paterson's boot, but their victory was more convincing than the score suggests. Both sides were anxious to avoid defeat and the result was a scrappy match that was played in persistent drizzle and a swirling wind. The Scottish forwards provided a solid platform with the veteran Scott Murray dominating the lineouts and leading from the front. Stand-off Phil Godman was very steady, and Dewey and Lamont, two big men, brought power and threat to the backs. Scotland's best chance of a try came around the hour mark. Paterson made a neat chip-and-chase, but he had to slow down to collect the bouncing ball and was caught just short. Wales defended well, especially when they were reduced to 14 men in the second half, but they offered little in attack.

---

558   RBS SIX NATIONS CHAMPIONSHIP 2007   ITALY

Murrayfield · Saturday 24 February 2007 · Lost 17–37

SCOTLAND Hugo Southwell (*Edinburgh*); Sean Lamont (*Northampton Sts*), Marcus Di Rollo (*Edinburgh*), Rob Dewey (*Edinburgh*), Chris Paterson* (*Edinburgh*); Phil Godman (*Edinburgh*), Chris Cusiter (*Border Rvrs*); Gavin Kerr (*Border Rvrs*), Dougie Hall (*Edinburgh*), Euan Murray (*Glasgow Wrs*), Nathan Hines (*Perpignan*), Scott Murray (*Edinburgh*), Simon Taylor (*Edinburgh*), Kelly Brown (*Border Rvrs*), David Callam (*Edinburgh*) ... Substitutes: Allan Jacobsen (*Edinburgh*) for E Murray (38-40) and for Kerr (49), Allister Hogg (*Edinburgh*) for Callam (49), Nikki Walker (*Ospreys*) for Godman (58), Ross Ford (*Border Rvrs*) for Hall (58), Rory Lawson (*Gloucester*) for Cusiter (66), Jim Hamilton (*Leicester Tgrs*) for S Murray (73), Andrew Henderson (*Glasgow Wrs*) for Dewey (75)

ITALY Roland De Marigny (*Calvisano*); Kaine Robertson (*Viadana*), Gonzalo Canale (*Clermont Auv*), Mirco Bergamasco (*Stade Français*), Andrea Masi (*Biarritz*); Andrea Scanavacca (*Calvisano*), Alessandro Troncon (*Clermont Auv*); Andrea Lo Cicero (*L'Aquila*), Carlo Festuccia (*Gran Parma*), Martin Castrogiovanni (*Leicester Tgrs*), Marco Bortolami* (*Gloucester*), Alessandro Zanni (*Calvisano*), Mauro Bergamasco (*Stade Français*), Sergio Parisse (*Stade Français*) ... Substitutes: Carlos Nieto (*Gloucester*) for Castrogiovanni (16), Maurizio Zaffiri (*Calvisano*) for Masi (33), Fabio Ongaro (*Saracens*) for Festuccia (58), Salvatore Perugini (*Toulouse*) for Lo Cicero (58), Valerio Bernabo (*Calvisano*) for Dellape (63), Ramiro Pez (*Bayonne*) for Scanavacca (79)

REFEREE Donal Courtney (*Ireland*) · ATTENDANCE 50,284

SCORING Mauro Bergamasco, try (0–5); Scanavacca, con (0–7); Scanavacca, try (0–12); Scanavacca, con (0–14); Robertson, try (0–19); Scanavacca, con (0–21); Dewey, try (5–21); Paterson, con (10–21); Scanavacca, pen (7–24); Paterson, pen (10–24) (half-time) Paterson, try (15–24); Paterson, con (17–24); Scanavacca, pen (17–27); Scanavacca, pen (17–30); Troncon, try (17–35); Scanavacca, con (17–37)

Italy won a Championship match away from home for the first time. This game had one of the most bizarre openings ever seen at Murrayfield as the visitors scored three tries in the first six minutes, all from Scottish errors. The match had barely begun when flanker Mauro Bergamasco charged down a clearing kick and gathered the ball to score. A few minutes later, Scanavacca intercepted and raced away to the posts, and then Robertson did exactly the same. Scanavacca converted all three tries leaving the shell-shocked Scots with a mountain to climb. In the second half, Scotland managed to pull back to within seven points when Paterson sped through the defence for a brilliant solo try, but ultimately the gap was too wide. In the closing stages, the Italians held their nerve and their big forwards kept the Scots pinned down. Scanavacca kicked two penalties and Troncon sealed a historic win when he was driven over after heavy pressure on the Scottish line.

---

559 RBS SIX NATIONS CHAMPIONSHIP 2007　　　　IRELAND

Murrayfield · Saturday 10 March 2007 · Lost 18–19

SCOTLAND Hugo Southwell (*Edinburgh*); Chris Paterson* (*Edinburgh*), Marcus Di Rollo (*Edinburgh*), Rob Dewey (*Edinburgh*), Sean Lamont (*Northampton Sts*); Dan Parks (*Glasgow Wrs*), Chris Cusiter (*Border Rvrs*); Gavin Kerr (*Border Rvrs*), Dougie Hall (*Edinburgh*), Euan Murray (*Glasgow Wrs*), Nathan Hines (*Perpignan*), Scott Murray (*Edinburgh*), Simon Taylor (*Edinburgh*), Kelly Brown (*Border Rvrs*), David Callam (*Edinburgh*) ... Substitutes: Rory Lamont (*Glasgow Wrs*) for Southwell (40), Allister Hogg (*Edinburgh*) for Callam (53), Rory Lawson (*Gloucester*) for Cusiter (57), Allan Jacobsen (*Edinburgh*) for Kerr (60), Ross Ford (*Border Rvrs*) for Hall (60), Andrew Henderson (*Glasgow Wrs*) for Di Rollo (65), Jim Hamilton (*Leicester Tgrs*) for S Murray (77) ... Yellow card: Hines (41)

IRELAND Girvan Dempsey (*Leinster*); Shane Horgan (*Leinster*), Brian O'Driscoll* (*Leinster*), Gordon D'Arcy (*Leinster*), Denis Hickie (*Leinster*); Ronan O'Gara (*Munster*), Peter Stringer (*Munster*); Simon Best (*Ulster*), Rory Best (*Ulster*), John Hayes (*Munster*), Donncha O'Callaghan (*Munster*), Paul O'Connell (*Munster*), Simon Easterby (*Llanelli Scarlets*), David Wallace (*Munster*), Denis Leamy (*Munster*) ... Substitutes: Jerry Flannery (*Munster*) for R Best (60), Neil Best (*Ulster*) for Easterby (67)

REFEREE Dave Pearson (*England*)

SCORING O'Gara, pen (0–3); Paterson, pen (3–3); O'Gara, try (3–8); O'Gara, con (3–10); Paterson, pen (6–10); O'Gara, pen (6–13); Paterson, pen (9–13) (half-time) Paterson, pen (12–13); Paterson, pen (15–13); Paterson, pen (18–13); O'Gara, pen (18–16); O'Gara, pen (18–19)

In a tense encounter, Scotland battled all the way and the result was in doubt until the finish. The Scottish forwards were good at the set-pieces and Murray and Hines were disruptive in the lineouts, but once again the side lacked the ability to finish and had to rely on Chris Paterson's metronomic goal-kicking for all their points. Their best chance came on the 24th minute when Sean Lamont ran from deep inside his own half and carved his way through the scattered Irish defence. Paterson carried on and looked certain to score until he was caught inside the 22. A few minutes later, O'Gara charged down a clearance and after quick hands he was under the posts. Scotland won a lot of possession in the second half and held a five point lead in the closing stages, but two late penalties by O'Gara saw Ireland home. In a strange incident at the end, O'Gara was left prostrate on the turf for several minutes receiving urgent medical attention. It was claimed that one of the Scottish players had tried to choke him but television replays were inconclusive.

RBS SIX NATIONS CHAMPIONSHIP 2007   FRANCE

Stade de France, Paris · Saturday 17 March 2007 · Lost 19–46

SCOTLAND Chris Paterson* (*Edinburgh*); Sean Lamont (*Northampton Sts*), Rob Dewey (*Edinburgh*), Andrew Henderson (*Glasgow Wrs*), Nikki Walker (*Ospreys*); Dan Parks (*Glasgow Wrs*), Rory Lawson (*Gloucester*); Gavin Kerr (*Border Rvrs*), Ross Ford (*Border Rvrs*), Euan Murray (*Glasgow Wrs*), Nathan Hines (*Perpignan*), Scott Murray (*Edinburgh*), Simon Taylor (*Edinburgh*), Johnnie Beattie (*Glasgow Wrs*), Allister Hogg (*Edinburgh*) ... Substitutes: Jim Hamilton (*Leicester Tgrs*) for S Murray (47), David Callam (*Edinburgh*) for Beattie (52), Rory Lamont (*Glasgow Wrs*) for Parks (52), Chris Cusiter (*Border Rvrs*) for Lawson (61), Allan Jacobsen (*Edinburgh*) for Kerr (64), Dougie Hall (*Edinburgh*) for Ford (64), Marcus Di Rollo (*Edinburgh*) for Henderson (77) ... Yellow card: S Lamont (61–71)

FRANCE Clément Poitrenaud (*Toulouse*); Vincent Clerc (*Toulouse*), David Marty (*Perpignan*), Yannick Jauzion (*Toulouse*), Cédric Heymans (*Toulouse*); David Skrela (*Stade Français*), Pierre Mignoni (*Clermont Auv*); Olivier Milloud (*Bourgoin-Jallieu*), Raphaël Ibañez* (*London Wasps*), Pieter de Villiers (*Stade Français*), Lionel Nallet (*Castres*), Jérôme Thion (*Biarritz*), Serge Betsen (*Biarritz*), Julien Bonnaire (*Bourgoin-Jallieu*), Imanol Harindoroquy (*Biarritz*) ... Substitutes: Pascal Papé (*Castres*) for Nallet (55), Damien Traille (*Biarritz*) for Poitrenaud (73), Elvis Vermeulen (*Clermont Auv*) for Harindoroquy (77), Christophe Dominici (*Stade Français*) for Clerc (77)

REFEREE Craig Joubert (*South Africa*)

SCORING Walker, try (5–0); Paterson, con (7–0); Beauxis, pen (7–3); Harinordoquy, try (7–8); Beauxis, con (7–10); Jauzion, try (7–15); Beauxis, con (7–17); Beauxis, pen (7–20); S Lamont, try (12–20); Paterson, con (14–20) (half-time) Marty, try (14–25); Beauxis, con (14–27); Heymans, try (14–32); Milloud, try (14–37); Beauxis, con (14–39); Murray, try (19–39); Vermeulen, try (19–44); Beauxis, con (19–46)

On a fine Parisian afternoon, the destiny of the 2007 championship was not decided until the last move of this exciting game. France had to win by a margin of 24 points or more to snatch the title from Ireland. They held a big enough advantage until a few minutes from the end when Scotland prop Euan Murray scored from a long miss-pass by Paterson. France had time for one last attack and after a succession of forward drives substitute No 8 Elvis Vermeulen powered over the line. There was a lengthy delay for video evidence but eventually the try was awarded and France could start their celebrations. Earlier, Scotland scored a try after only seven minutes. Parks kicked across the field to Walker who rose above the defence to catch the ball and dive over for the line. France responded with tries by Harinordoquy and Jauzion, and just before the interval Sean Lamont took a quick tap-penalty and ran over un-opposed. The French forwards were well on top in the second half and the home side scored three tries in a dazzling 20 minute burst. Between these, Sean Lamont was mistakenly sent to the sin bin for an offence committed by his brother Rory. Murray's late score threatened to spoil the party until the dramatic finale. There was a big gulf in quality between the sides and Scotland never looked like winning but they defended well and were never overwhelmed.

561   WORLD CUP WARM-UP MATCH   IRELAND

Murrayfield · Saturday 11 August 2007 · Won 31–21

SCOTLAND Rory Lamont (*Sale Sharks*); Sean Lamont (*Northampton Sts*), Rob Dewey (*Ulster*), Andrew Henderson (*Glasgow Wrs*), Simon Webster (*Edinburgh*); Chris Paterson (*Gloucester*), Mike Blair (*Edinburgh*); Allan Jacobsen (*Edinburgh*), Ross Ford (*Glasgow Wrs*), Euan Murray (*Northampton Sts*), Nathan Hines (*Perpignan*), Jim Hamilton (*Leicester Tgrs*), Jason White* (*Sale Sharks*), Allister Hogg (*Edinburgh*), Simon Taylor (*Stade Français*) … Substitutes: †Fergus Thomson (*Glasgow Wrs*) for Ford (39-43 and 67-78) and for Hamilton (78), Kelly Brown (*Glasgow Wrs*) for Taylor (38), Scott MacLeod (*Llanelli Scarlets*) for White (56), Craig Smith (*Edinburgh*) for Murray (56), Nikki Walker (*Ospreys*) for Dewey (59), Chris Cusiter (*Perpignan*) for Blair (60), Dan Parks (*Glasgow Wrs*) for Paterson (60)

IRELAND Geordan Murphy (*Leicester Tgrs*); Brian Carney (*Munster*), Brian O'Driscoll* (*Leinster*), Gavin Duffy (*Connacht*), Tommy Bowe (*Ulster*); Paddy Wallace (*Ulster*), Isaac Boss (*Ulster*); Bryan Young (*Ulster*), Jerry Flannery (*Munster*), Simon Best (*Ulster*), Malcolm O'Kelly (*Leinster*), Paul O'Connell (*Munster*), Neil Best (*Ulster*), Stephen Ferris (*Ulster*), Jamie Heaslip (*Leinster*) … Substitutes: Alan Quinlan (*Munster*) for O'Kelly (8–11, 23–32 and 40), Andrew Trimble (*Ulster*) for Duffy (26), Keith Gleeson (*Leinster*) for N Best (60), Ronan O'Gara (*Munster*) for O'Driscoll (66), John Hayes (*Munster*) for Young (70), Rory Best (*Ulster*) for Flannery (74), Eoin Reddan (*London Wasps*) for Boss (74)

REFEREE Tony Spreadbury (*England*) · **ATTENDANCE** 25,127

SCORING Hogg, try (5–0); Paterson, con (7–0); Wallace, pen (7–3); Henderson, try (12–3); Paterson, con (14–3); Murphy, pen (14–6); Murray, try (19–6) (half-time) Henderson, try (24–6); Boss, try (24–11); Wallace, con (24–13); Trimble, try (24–18); Wallace, pen (24–21); Henderson (29–21); Parks, con (31–21)

Scotland did not tour in the summer of 2007, but in August they played two World Cup warm-up matches at Murrayfield against Ireland and South Africa. In the first of these, the Scots gave an encouraging display and recorded their first win over Ireland since 2001. The visitors were not at full strength and the game lacked its usual intensity, but Scotland showed plenty of eagerness and were worthy winners. The Scottish forwards drove well and the backs were full of running, especially centre Andy Henderson who scored three tries. Scotland opened the scoring after only three minutes when Hogg was shoved over from short-range. They held a comfortable lead after Henderson scored his second try early in the second half, but Ireland made a revival and pulled back to within three points. Scotland sealed the match when Parks made a half-break and Henderson was on hand to complete his hat-trick.

562   WORLD CUP WARM-UP MATCH   SOUTH AFRICA

Murrayfield · Saturday 25 August 2007 · Lost 3–27

SCOTLAND Rory Lamont (*Sale Sharks*); Nikki Walker (*Ospreys*), Rob Dewey (*Ulster*), Andrew Henderson (*Glasgow Wrs*), Simon Webster (*Edinburgh*); Chris Paterson (*Gloucester*),

Mike Blair (*Edinburgh*); Gavin Kerr (*unattached*), Ross Ford (*Glasgow Wrs*), Euan Murray (*Northampton Sts*), Nathan Hines (*Perpignan*), Jim Hamilton (*Leicester Tgrs*), Jason White* (*Sale Sharks*), Kelly Brown (*Glasgow Wrs*), Dave Callam (*Edinburgh*) ... Substitutes: Allan Jacobsen (*Edinburgh*) for Kerr (28), Allister Hogg (*Edinburgh*) for White (30-40) and for Callam (62), Hugo Southwell (*Edinburgh*) for Henderson (43), Scott Murray (*Montauban*) for Hamilton (45), Dan Parks (*Glasgow Wrs*) for Paterson (54), Fergus Thomson (*Glasgow Wrs*) for Ford (66), Rory Lawson (*Gloucester*) for Blair (66)

SOUTH AFRICA Percy Montgomery (*Sharks*); JP Pietersen (*Sharks*), Jaque Fourie (*Lions*), Frans Steyn (*Sharks*), Bryan Habana (*Bulls*); Butch James (*Sharks*), Fourie du Preez (*Bulls*); Os Du Randt (*Cheetahs*), Gary Botha (*Bulls*), CJ van der Linde (*Cheetahs*), Bakkies Botha (*Bulls*), Victor Matfield (*Bulls*), Schalk Burger (*Stormers*), Juan Smith (*Cheetahs*), Danie Rossouw (*Bulls*) ... Substitutes: BJ Botha (*Sharks*) for du Randt (30-40 and 61), Wikus van Heerden (*Bulls*) for Rossouw (55), Andre Pretorius (*Lions*) for Steyn (55), Ruan Pienaar (*Sharks*) for Montgomery (61), Bis du Plessis (*Sharks*) for G Botha (61), Albert van den Berg (*Sharks*) for B Botha (61), Ashwin Willemse (*Lions*) for Pietersen (72)

REFEREE Christophe Berdos (*France*) · ATTENDANCE 30,342

SCORING Paterson, pen (3–0); Montgomery, pen (3–3); Habana, try (3–8); Montgomery, con (3–10); Fourie, try (3–15); Montgomery, con (3–17); du Preez, try (3–22); Montgomery, con (3–24) (half-time) Montgomery, pen (3–27)

In this second warm-up match, Scotland were well beaten by a quality South African side. Playing in summer sunshine, the Scots dominated the opening stages, but could only score a Paterson penalty after nine minutes. Montgomery equalised for the visitors who then scored three converted tries in quick succession to end the contest before the interval. Both sides seemed drained of energy after an intense first half and the only score in the second period was a Montgomery penalty. Scotland were always competitive in this match, but clearly were some way behind the best of the southern hemisphere.

Rugby World Cup 2007

In 2007, the Rugby World Cup was hosted by France with some matches played in Scotland and Wales. Twenty teams took part in four pools of five. Scotland were drawn in Pool C along with tournament favourites New Zealand, Italy, Romania and Portugal, the tournament minnows. The Scots started with a match in Saint-Étienne before two matches at Murrayfield and then returning to France. New Zealand were confidently expected to win the pool leaving Scotland and Italy to battle it out for the second qualifying place.

| **563** | RUGBY WORLD CUP 2007 | PORTUGAL |

Geoffrey Guichard Stadium, Saint-Étienne · Sunday 9 September 2007
Won 56–10

SCOTLAND Rory Lamont (*Sale Sharks*); Sean Lamont (*Northampton Sts*), Marcus Di Rollo (*Edinburgh*), Rob Dewey (*Ulster*), Simon Webster (*Edinburgh*); Dan Parks (*Glasgow Wrs*),

Mike Blair (*Edinburgh*); Allan Jacobsen (*Edinburgh*), Scott Lawson (*Sale Sharks*), Euan Murray (*Northampton Sts*), Nathan Hines (*Perpignan*), Scott Murray (*Edinburgh*), Jason White* (*Sale Sharks*), Allister Hogg (*Edinburgh*), Simon Taylor (*Stade Français*) ... Substitutes: Gavin Kerr (*Glasgow Wrs*) for Jacobsen (35), Hugo Southwell (*Edinburgh*) for Di Rollo (51), Chris Paterson (*Gloucester*) for Parks (57), Kelly Brown (*Glasgow Wrs*) for White (61), Scott MacLeod (*Llanelli Scarlets*) for S Murray (61), Rory Lawson (*Gloucester*) for Blair (65), Ross Ford (*Glasgow Wrs*) for S Lawson (68)

PORTUGAL Pedro Leal (*GD Direito*); David Mateus (*CF Belenenses*), Frederico Sousa (*GD Direito*), Diogo Mateus (*CF Belenenses*), Pedro Carvalho (*GD Direito*); Duarte Cardoso Pinto (*AEIS Agronomia*), José Pinto (*GD Direito*); Rui Cordeiro (*Coimbra*), Joaquim Ferreira (*Centro Desportivo UDP*), Ruben Spachuck (*CF Belenenses*), Gonçalo Uva (*Montpellier*), David Penalva (*Blagnac SCR*), Juan Severino Somoza (*AEIS Agronomia*), João Uva (*CF Belenenses*), Vasco Uva* (*GD Direito*) ... Substitutes: Miguel Portela (*GD Direito*) for Sousa (37), João Correia (*GD Direito*) for Ferreira (51), Paulo Murinello (*GDS Casais*) for Penalva (51), Juan Manuel Muré (*CF Belenenses*) for Cordeiro (59), Pedro Cabral (*Centro Desportivo UDL*) for D Pinto (61), Diogo Coutinho (*GD Direito*) for Uva (63), Luis Pissarra (*AEIS Agronomia*) for J Pinto (65)

REFEREE Steve Walsh (*New Zealand*) · ATTENDANCE 34,162

SCORING R Lamont, try (5–0); Parks, con (7–0); R Lamont, try (12–0); Parks, con (14–0); Lawson, try (19–0); Parks, con (21–0); Carvalho, try (21–5); D Pinto, con (21–7); Dewey, try (26–7); Parks, con (28–7); D Pinto, pen (28–10) (half-time) Parks, try (33–10); Parks, con (35–10); Southwell, try (40–10); Paterson, con (42–10); Brown, try (47–10); Paterson, try (49–10); Ford, try (54–10); Paterson, try (56–10)

Playing in sunny conditions, Scotland eased into the World Cup with this straight-forward win over tournament minnows Portugal. The Scots scored eight tries and were never in any danger although there was plenty of room for improvement. Rory Lamont scored an early brace to settle the nerves and from then on the Scots had few problems. Their third try came when a crosskick by Parks landed perfectly into the arms of hooker Scott Lawson who then only had to flop over the line. The largely amateur Portuguese were making their World Cup debut and they rose to the occasion magnificently. On the 27th minute, winger Carvalho delighted the crowd when he scored a try in the corner after a series of rucks near the Scottish line. Carvalho might have completed his double in the second-half when he intercepted a pass and ran the length of the field only to be recalled for an infringement.

564   RUGBY WORLD CUP 2007   ROMANIA

Murrayfield · Tuesday 18 September 2007 · Won 42–0

SCOTLAND Rory Lamont (*Sale Sharks*); Sean Lamont (*Northampton Sts*), Simon Webster (*Edinburgh*), Rob Dewey (*Ulster*), Chris Paterson (*Gloucester*); Dan Parks (*Glasgow Wrs*), Mike Blair (*Edinburgh*); Gavin Kerr (*Glasgow Wrs*), Ross Ford (*Glasgow Wrs*), Euan Murray (*Northampton Sts*), Nathan Hines (*Perpignan*), Jim Hamilton (*Leicester Tgrs*), Jason White* (*Sale Sharks*), Allister Hogg (*Edinburgh*), Simon Taylor (*Stade Français*) ... Substitutes: Craig Smith (*Edinburgh*) for Kerr (50), Scott MacLeod (*Llanelli Scarlets*) for Hines (50), Chris Cusiter (*Perpignan*) for Blair (58), Hugo Southwell (*Edinburgh*) for Dewey (58), Kelly Brown (*Glasgow Wrs*) for Hogg (64), Nikki Walker (*Ospreys*) for Parks (67), Kerr for Murray (67)

ROMANIA Iulian Dumitras (*Pau*); Catalin Fercu (*Arad*), Csaba Gal (*Steaua Bucuresti*), Romeo Gontineac (*Aurillac*), Gabriel Brezoianu (*unattached*); Ionut Dimofte (*Arad*), Lucian Sirbu (*Béziers*); Petrisor Toderasc (*Brive*), Marius Tincu (*Perpignan*), Bogdan Balan (*Biarritz*), Sorin Socol* (*Pau*), Cristian Petre (*Béziers*), Florin Corodeanu (*Grenoble*), Alexandru Manta (*Castres*), Ovidiu Tonita (*Perpignan*) ... Substitutes: Razvan Mavrodin (*Pau*) for Tincu (40), Ionut Tofan (*Limoges*) for Dimofte (44), Valentin Calafeteanu (*Dinamo Bucuresti*) for Sirbu (44), Alexandru Tudori (*Dinamo Bucuresti*) for Manta (53), Cosmin Ratiu (*Dinamo Bucuresti*) for Corodeanu (60), Silviu Florea (*Béziers*) for Balan (68), Florin Vlaicu (*Steaua Bucuresti*) for Gontineac (72)

REFEREE Nigel Owens (*Wales*) · ATTENDANCE 31,222

SCORING Paterson, try (5–0); Paterson, con (7–0); Hogg, try (12–0); Paterson, con (14–0); R Lamont, try (19–0); Paterson, con (21–0) (half-time) Hogg, try (26–0); Paterson, con (28–0); Hogg, try (33–0); Paterson, con (35–0); R Lamont, try (40–0); Paterson, con (42–0)

Scotland returned to Murrayfield for their next two pool matches. On paper, Romania looked tougher opponents than Portugal, but Scotland gave another good team performance and were comfortable winners. The Scots scored six tries, including a hat-trick for flanker Ally Hogg, and Chris Paterson converted all six. Scotland opened the scoring immediately. The Romanians failed to deal with a high kick and Paterson chipped ahead and won the race to the touchdown. There were a lot of handling errors in the wet conditions and this was often a messy encounter, but the Scots were well satisfied with their win. Curiously, the Romanians, who played in all-blue strips, were given the luxury of the Scotland dressing room as they were deemed to be the home team. They had some strapping forwards but they played without ambition and seemed intent just to keep the score down.

---

565   RUGBY WORLD CUP 2007   NEW ZEALAND

Murrayfield · Sunday 23 September 2007 · Lost 0–40

SCOTLAND Hugo Southwell (*Edinburgh*); Nikki Walker (*Ospreys*), Marcus Di Rollo (*Edinburgh*), Andrew Henderson (*Glasgow Wrs*), Simon Webster (*Edinburgh*); Chris Paterson (*Gloucester*), Chris Cusiter (*Perpignan*); †Alasdair Dickinson (*Gloucester*), Scott Lawson (*Sale Sharks*), Craig Smith (*Edinburgh*), Scott MacLeod (*Llanelli Scarlets*), Scott Murray* (*Montauban*), Kelly Brown (*Glasgow Wrs*), †John Barclay (*Glasgow Wrs*), Dave Callam (*Edinburgh*) ... Substitutes: Dan Parks (*Glasgow Wrs*) for Paterson (20), Gavin Kerr (*Glasgow Wrs*) for Smith (50), Fergus Thomson (*Glasgow Wrs*) for Lawson (57), Rory Lawson (*Gloucester*) for Cusiter (58), Smith for Dickinson (65), Rob Dewey (*Ulster*) for Henderson (68), Jim Hamilton (*Leicester Tgrs*) for MacLeod (68)

NEW ZEALAND Leon MacDonald (*Crusaders*); Doug Howlett (*Blues*), Conrad Smith (*Hurricanes*), Luke McAlister (*Blues*), Sitiveni Sivivatu (*Chiefs*); Dan Carter (*Crusaders*), Byron Kelleher (*Chiefs*); Tony Woodcock (*Blues*), Anton Oliver (*Highlanders*), Carl Hayman (*Highlanders*), Reuben Thorne (*Crusaders*), Ali Williams (*Blues*), Chris Masoe (*Hurricanes*), Richie McCaw* (*Crusaders*), Rodney So'oialo (*Hurricanes*) ... Substitutes: Nick Evans (*Highlanders*) for MacDonald (20), Andrew Hore (*Hurricanes*) for Oliver (58), Brendon Leonard (*Chiefs*) for Kelleher (58), Sione Lauaki (*Chiefs*) for McCaw (60), Neemia Tialata (*Hurricanes*) for Hayman (65), Chris Jack (*Crusaders*) for Williams (65), Isaia Toeava (*Blues*) for Smith (65)

REFEREE Marius Jonker (*South Africa*) · ATTENDANCE 64,558

SCORING McCaw, try (0–5); Carter, con (0–7); Howlett, try (0–12); Carter, pen (0–15); Kelleher, try (0–20) (half-time) Carter, pen (0–23); Williams, try (0–28); Carter, try (0–33); Carter, con (0–35); Howlett, try (0–40)

Controversially, Scotland fielded a largely reserve side, keeping their first-choice players for the crunch match against Italy in six days' time. This was a shrewd decision by the coaching staff but hardly in the spirit of the World Cup and betrayed a lack of ambition and self-belief. It was also an insult to spectators who had paid for expensive tickets only to be given an insipid match that lacked real passion. Playing in their unattractive silver-grey strip, New Zealand won easily and scored six tries without reply, the first after only six minutes. The truth was that both sides were only going through the motions and their thoughts were elsewhere. For Scotland, Alasdair Dickinson and John Barclay made encouraging debuts against the toughest of all opposition.

566   RUGBY WORLD CUP 2007   ITALY

Geoffrey Guichard Stadium, Saint-Étienne · Saturday 29 September 2007
Won 18–16

SCOTLAND Rory Lamont (*Sale Sharks*); Sean Lamont (*Northampton Sts*), Simon Webster (*Edinburgh*), Rob Dewey (*Ulster*), Chris Paterson (*Gloucester*); Dan Parks (*Glasgow Wrs*), Mike Blair (*Edinburgh*); Gavin Kerr (*Glasgow Wrs*), Ross Ford (*Glasgow Wrs*), Euan Murray (*Northampton Sts*), Nathan Hines (*Perpignan*), Jim Hamilton (*Leicester Tgrs*), Jason White* (*Sale Sharks*), Allister Hogg (*Edinburgh*), Simon Taylor (*Stade Français*) ... Substitutes: Hugo Southwell (*Edinburgh*) for R Lamont (25), Andrew Henderson (*Glasgow Wrs*) for Dewey (60), Craig Smith (*Edinburgh*) for Kerr (65), Kelly Brown (*Glasgow Wrs*) for Hogg (70), Scott MacLeod (*Llanelli Scarlets*) for Hamilton (72), Chris Cusiter (*Perpignan*) for Blair (72)

ITALY David Bortolussi (*Montpellier Herault*); Kaine Robertson (*Viadana*), Gonzalo Canale (*Clermont Auv*), Mirco Bergamasco (*Stade Français*), Andrea Masi (*Biarritz*); Ramiro Pez (*Bayonne*), Alessandro Troncon* (*Clermont Auv*); Salvatore Perugini (*Toulouse*), Carlo Festuccia (*Gran Parma*), Martin Castrogiovanni (*Leicester Tgrs*), Santiago Dellapè (*Biarritz*), Carlo Del Fava (*Ulster*), Josh Sole (*Viadana*), Mauro Bergamasco (*Stade Français*), Sergio Parisse (*Stade Français*) ... Substitutes: Andrea Lo Cicero (*L'Aquila*) for Perugini (49), Fabio Ongaro (*Saracens*) for Festuccia (54), Perugini for Castrogiovanni (75), Ezio Galon (*Parma*) for Masi (79)

REFEREE Jonathan Kaplan (*South Africa*) · ATTENDANCE 34,701

SCORING Paterson, pen (3–0); Paterson, pen (6–0); Troncon, try (6–5); Bortolussi, con (6–7); Bortolussi, pen (6–10); Paterson, pen (9–10); Paterson, pen (12–10) (half-time) Paterson, pen (15–10); Paterson, pen (18–10); Bortolussi, pen (18–13); Bortolussi, pen (18–16)

On a wet evening, both sides looked happier without the ball and this was largely a kicking duel. Chris Paterson landed six penalties out of six which was just enough to edge out the stuffy Italians. Scotland started well and Paterson kicked two goals in the first five minutes. Italy were reduced to fourteen when Mauro Bergamasco was sent to the sin bin, but then they scored the game's only try. Pez hoisted a kick towards the posts, the Scots were caught in possession and from the ensuing ruck Troncon sold a dummy and dived over. Bortolussi converted and added a penalty, but Paterson restored the lead with two penalties. In the second half, Paterson and Bortolussi kicked two penalties each to set-up a nail-biting conclusion. A few minutes from time, Bortolussi had a long-range effort to win the match, but the ball stayed to the right of the posts. The result could have gone either way but Scotland had a little more composure and maturity. The forwards were solid in the set-piece, Jason White led from the front and Dan Parks won the man-of-the-match award for his superb kicking under intense pressure.

---

567   RUGBY WORLD CUP 2007   ARGENTINA

Stade de France, Paris · Sunday 7 October 2007 · Lost 13–19

SCOTLAND Rory Lamont (*Sale Sharks*); Sean Lamont (*Northampton Sts*), Simon Webster (*Edinburgh*), Rob Dewey (*Ulster*), Chris Paterson (*Gloucester*); Dan Parks (*Glasgow Wrs*), Mike Blair (*Edinburgh*); Gavin Kerr (*Glasgow Wrs*), Ross Ford (*Glasgow Wrs*), Euan Murray (*Northampton Sts*), Nathan Hines (*Perpignan*), Jim Hamilton (*Leicester Tgrs*), Jason White* (*Sale Sharks*), Allister Hogg (*Edinburgh*), Simon Taylor (*Stade Français*) ... Substitutes: Andrew Henderson (*Glasgow Wrs*) for Dewey (40), Craig Smith (*Edinburgh*) for Kerr (56), Kelly Brown (*Glasgow Wrs*) for Hogg (56), Scott MacLeod (*Llanelli Scarlets*) for Hamilton (56), Chris Cusiter (*Perpignan*) for Blair (56), Scott Lawson (*Gloucester*) for Ford (67), Hugo Southwell (*Edinburgh*) for R Lamont (67)

ARGENTINA Ignacio Corleto (*Stade Français*); Lucas Borges (*Stade Français*), Manuel Contepomi (*Newman*), Felipe Contepomi (*Leinster*), Horacio Agulla (*Hindu*); Juan-Martín Hernández (*Stade Français*), Agustín Pichot* (*Stade Français*); Rodrigo Roncero (*Stade Français*), Mario Ledesma (*Clermont Auv*), Martí Scelzo (*Clermont Auv*), Ignacio Fernández Lobbe (*Sale Sharks*), Patricio Albacete (*Toulouse*), Lucas Ostiglia (*Agen*), Juan Fernández Lobbe (*Sale Sharks*), Gonzalo Longo (*Clermont Auv*) ... Substitutes: Rimas Álvarez Kairelas (*Perpignan*) for I Fernández Lobbe (50), Juan-Manuel Leguizamón (*London Irish*) for Ostiglia (54), Omar Hassan (*Toulouse*) for Scelzo (56), Hernán Senillosa (*Hindu*) for M Contepomi (66)

REFEREE Joel Jutge (*France*) · **ATTENDANCE** 76,866

SCORING Parks, pen (3–0); F Contepomi, pen (3–3); F Contepomi, pen (3–6); Longo, try (3–11); F Contepomi, con (3–13); Paterson, pen (6–13) (half-time) F Contepomi, pen (6–16); Hernández, drop (6–19); Cusiter, try (11–19); Paterson, con (13–19)

Argentina were the surprise packet of the World Cup and had beaten the hosts France to win Pool D. Played under floodlights in front of a passionate crowd, this match was not a free-flowing spectacle but it was hugely compelling. Scotland might have won with a little more confidence and good fortune. Dan Parks kicked a long-range penalty after 16 minutes and Felipe Contepomi, one of the stars of the tournament, replied with a brace. Play was cagey, both sides waiting for the other to make a mistake. On the 33rd minute, Longo charged down a clearance and gathered a wicked bounce to score. Contepomi added the conversion and Paterson kicked an angled penalty. In the second half, the Argentineans stretched their lead to 13 points, but as the game wore on Scotland's superior fitness started to tell. On the 67th minute, a powerful run by Sean Lamont took play into the Argentinean 22 and after slick passing Cusiter squeezed over at the corner flag. Paterson kicked a brilliant touchline conversion but try as they might Scotland were unable to score again. Right at the finish, Parks hoisted a hanging kick into the corner but the ball drifted out-of-play taking with it Scotland's dreams.

Murrayfield · Sunday 3 February 2008 · Lost 6–27

SCOTLAND Rory Lamont (*Sale Sharks*); Nikki Walker (*Ospreys*), †Nick De Luca (*Edinburgh*), Andrew Henderson (*Glasgow Wrs*), Simon Webster (*Edinburgh*); Dan Parks (*Glasgow Wrs*), Mike Blair (*Edinburgh*); Allan Jacobsen (*Edinburgh*), Ross Ford (*Edinburgh*), Euan Murray (*Northampton Sts*), Nathan Hines (*Perpignan*), Jim Hamilton (*Leicester Tgrs*), Jason White* (*Sale Sharks*), John Barclay (*Glasgow Wrs*), Dave Callam (*Edinburgh*) ... Substitutes: Kelly Brown (*Glasgow Wrs*) for Callam (49), Scott MacLeod (*Llanelli Scarlets*) for Hamilton (54), Gavin Kerr (*Edinburgh*) for Murray (58), Chris Paterson (*Gloucester*) for Parks (60), Hugo Southwell (*Edinburgh*) for Lamont (60), Chris Cusiter (*Perpignan*) for Blair (65), Fergus Thomson (*Glasgow Wrs*) for Ford (73)

FRANCE Cédric Heymans (*Toulouse*); Vincent Clerc (*Toulouse*), David Marty (*Perpignan*), Damien Traille (*Biarritz*), Julien Malzieu (*Clermont Auv*); François Trinh-Duc (*Montpellier*), Jean Baptiste Elissalde (*Toulouse*); Lionel Faure (*Sale Sharks*), William Servat (*Toulouse*), Julien Brugnaut (*Dax*), Loic Jacquet (*Clermont Auv*), Lionel Nallet* (*Castres*), Thierry Dusautoir (*Toulouse*), Fulgence Ouedraogo (*Montpellier*), Elvis Vermeulen (*Clermont Auv*) ... Substitutes: Nicolas Mas (*Perpignan*) for Brugnaut (49), Dimitri Szarzewski (*Stade Français*) for Servat (49), Julien Bonnaire (*Clermont Auv*) for Vermeulen (54), David Skrela (*Stade Français*) for Trinh-Duc (58), Arnaud Mela (*Albi*) for Jacquet (60), Morgan Parra (*Bourgoin*) for Elissalde (65), Aurelien Rougerie (*Clermont Auv*) for Clerc (72)

REFEREE Alain Rolland (*Ireland*) · ATTENDANCE 67,788

SCORING Parks, drop (3–0); Clerc, try (3–5); Elissalde, con (3–7); Traille, pen (3–10); Malzieu, try (3–15); Elissalde, con (3–17); Parks, pen (6–17) (half-time) Traille, pen (6–20); Clerc, try (6–25); Skrela, con (6–27)

Andrew Henderson won his 50th cap. A new-look French side swept to victory with a vibrant display of instinctive rugby that made Scotland look pedestrian and lacking in ideas. There was some degree of luck about the three French tries, but the visitors were superior in all respects and were never really threatened. Scotland made a lot of errors, gave their opponents too much time on the ball and could not penetrate the French defence. Scotland started brightly enough and Parks dropped an early goal. France responded with a try by Clerc although there was a hint of a forward pass in the movement leading up to it. Elissalde converted and then Traille kicked a penalty from long range. New French wing Malzieu made a speculative kick ahead and the ball bounced kindly to give him an easy run to the posts. Earlier, Parks had missed a simple shot at goal but pulled back three points with a penalty on the half-hour mark. The Scottish forwards made one great shove in a scrum and the unlikely figure of prop Allan Jacobsen had a storming run up the middle of the field, but Scotland's attacks came to nothing. The French forwards were firmly in control in the second half and Traille kicked a penalty after a series of collapsed scrums. In another moment of French brilliance, Clerc took a long pass, kicked past the defence and gathered a favourable bounce to score. With the match beyond them, Scotland came closest to a try when Paterson hacked through but was caught inches short. From the ensuing play, Cusiter had the ball knocked out of his hands when diving over the line, which just about summed-up Scotland's day.

---

569   RBS SIX NATIONS CHAMPIONSHIP 2008   WALES

Millennium Stadium, Cardiff · Saturday 9 February 2008

Lost 15–30

SCOTLAND Hugo Southwell (*Edinburgh*); Nikki Walker (*Ospreys*), Nick De Luca (*Edinburgh*), Andrew Henderson (*Glasgow Wrs*), Chris Paterson (*Gloucester*); Dan Parks (*Glasgow Wrs*), Mike Blair (*Edinburgh*); Allan Jacobsen (*Edinburgh*), Ross Ford (*Edinburgh*), Euan Murray (*Northampton Sts*), Nathan Hines (*Perpignan*), Jim Hamilton (*Leicester Tgrs*), Jason White* (*Sale Sharks*), John Barclay (*Glasgow Wrs*), Kelly Brown (*Glasgow Wrs*) ... Substitutes: Allister Hogg (*Edinburgh*) for White (32); Scott MacLeod (*Llanelli Scarlets*) for Hines (61); Simon Danielli (*Ulster*) for Parks (67); Gavin Kerr (*Edinburgh*) for Murray (67); Graeme Morrison (*Glasgow Wrs*) for De Luca (70); Chris Cusiter (*Perpignan*) for Blair (72); Fergus Thomson (*Glasgow Wrs*) for Ford (72)

WALES Lee Byrne (*Ospreys*); Jamie Roberts (*Cardiff Blues*), Tom Shanklin (*Cardiff Blues*), Gavin Henson (*Ospreys*), Shane Williams (*Ospreys*); James Hook (*Ospreys*), Mike Phillips (*Ospreys*); Duncan Jones (*Ospreys*), Huw Bennett (*Ospreys*), Adam Jones (*Ospreys*), Ian Gough (*Ospreys*), Ian Evans (*Ospreys*), Jonathan Thomas (*Ospreys*), Martyn Williams (*Cardiff Blues*), Ryan Jones* (*Ospreys*) ... Substitutes: Gethin Jenkins (*Cardiff Blues*) for D Jones (53); Stephen Jones (*Llanelli Scarlets*) for Hook (57); Dwayne Peel (*Llanelli Scarlets*) for Philips (57); Matthew Rees (*Llanelli Scarlets*) for Bennett (57); Sonny Parker (*Ospreys*) for Shanklin (72)

REFEREE Bryce Lawrence (*New Zealand*) · **ATTENDANCE** 74,576

SCORING Paterson, pen (3–0); S Williams, try (3–5); Hook, con (3–7); Hook, pen (3–10); Paterson, pen (6–10) (half-time) Paterson, pen (9–10); Hook, try (9–15); Hook, con (9–17); Paterson, pen (12–17); Paterson, pen (15–17); S Jones, pen (15–20); S Williams, try (15–25); S Jones, con (15–27); S Jones, pen (15–30)

Nathan Hines won his 50th cap and led Scotland onto the field. The previous weekend, Wales had won at Twickenham for the first time in 20 years and were firm favourites. Scotland produced another error-strewn performance that lacked passion or serious threat. The Scots never looked like scoring a try and it was only Chris Paterson's unerring boot that kept them within striking distance until the closing stages. The Welsh backs were always dangerous and scored three excellent tries, although there was some controversy about the third. After a scintillating run, diminutive wing Shane Williams dived in at the corner. Television replays seemed to show that his foot had been in touch before he grounded the ball, but the try was awarded after video evidence. Mike Blair fielded impeccably and Kelly Brown was very energetic, but otherwise this was a woeful afternoon for Scottish rugby.

Croke Park, Dublin · Saturday 23 February 2008 · Lost 13–34

SCOTLAND Hugo Southwell (*Edinburgh*); Rory Lamont (*Sale Sharks*), Simon Webster (*Edinburgh*), Andrew Henderson (*Glasgow Wrs*), Nikki Walker (*Ospreys*); Chris Paterson (*Gloucester*), Mike Blair* (*Edinburgh*); Allan Jacobsen (*Edinburgh*), Ross Ford (*Edinburgh*), Euan Murray (*Northampton Sts*), Nathan Hines (*Perpignan*), Scott MacLeod (*Llanelli Scarlets*), Alasdair Strokosch (*Gloucester*), Allister Hogg (*Edinburgh*), Kelly Brown (*Glasgow Wrs*) ... Substitutes: †Ross Rennie (*Edinburgh*) for Brown (45), Jim Hamilton (*Leicester Tgrs*) for Hines (64), Nick De Luca (*Edinburgh*) for Walker (61-67) and for Henderson (69), Dan Parks (*Glasgow Wrs*) for Southwell (66), Fergus Thomson (*Glasgow Wrs*) for Ford (69), Chris Cusiter (*Perpignan*) for Blair (71), Gavin Kerr (*Edinburgh*) for Jacobsen (71), Ford for Murray (75)

IRELAND Geordan Murphy (*Leicester Tgrs*); Tommy Bowe (*Ulster*), Brian O'Driscoll* (*Leinster*), Andrew Trimble (*Ulster*), Robert Kearney (*Leinster*); Ronan O'Gara (*Munster*), Eoin Reddan (*London Wasps*); Marcus Horan (*Munster*), Bernard Jackman (*Leinster*), John Hayes (*Munster*), Donncha O'Callaghan (*Munster*), Mick O'Driscoll (*Munster*), Denis Leamy (*Munster*), David Wallace (*Munster*), Jamie Heaslip (*Leinster*) ... Substitutes: Rory Best (*Ulster*) for Jackman (44), Paul O'Connell (*Munster*) for M O'Driscoll (52), Simon Easterby (*Llanelli Scarlets*) for Heaslip (69), Shane Horgan (*Leinster*) for B O'Driscoll (69), Peter Stringer (*Munster*) for Reddan (72), Tony Buckley (*Munster*) for Hayes (73), Paddy Wallace (*Ulster*) for O'Gara (77)

REFEREE Christophe Berdos (*France*) · **ATTENDANCE** 74,234

SCORING Heaslip, try (0–5); O'Gara, con (0–7); Paterson, pen (3–7); Kearney, try (3–12); O'Gara, con (3–14); Paterson, pen (6–14) (half-time) Horan, try (6–19); O'Gara, pen (6–22); Webster, try (11–22); Paterson, con (13–22); Bowe, try (13–27); O'Gara, con (13–29); Bowe, try (13-24)

Lansdowne Road was being redeveloped so this match was held at Croke Park, the home of Gaelic football. Scotland showed signs of improvement but once again failed to take their chances and made some fatal errors that Ireland were quick to exploit. The home side opened the scoring on the 21st minute against the run of play. From a scrum near the Scottish line, a back-row move worked perfectly and Heaslip had a simple score which O'Gara converted. Paterson drew back three points with a penalty, but a few minutes later Irish wing Kearney scored in the corner. Paterson kicked his second penalty and Scotland wasted a great chance just before interval when a penalty on the Irish line was reversed because of foul play. Early in the second half, O'Gara kicked across field straight into the arms of prop Marcus Horan who trundled over from close range. O'Gara added a penalty before the Scots scored their first try of the Championship. Hogg made a strong run and quick passing allowed Webster to fly over. Paterson converted but any hopes of a miraculous comeback were quashed by two late Irish tries, the second in injury time after a Scottish defensive fumble. A series of injuries meant that scrums were uncontested in the closing stages. Prop Gavin Kerr came off the bench to win his 50th cap near the finish.

Murrayfield · Saturday 8 March 2008 · Won 15–9

SCOTLAND Hugo Southwell (*Edinburgh*); Rory Lamont (*Sale Sharks*), Simon Webster (*Edinburgh*), Graeme Morrison (*Glasgow Wrs*), Nikki Walker (*Ospreys*); Chris Paterson (*Gloucester*), Mike Blair* (*Edinburgh*); Allan Jacobsen (*Edinburgh*), Ross Ford (*Edinburgh*), Euan Murray (*Northampton Sts*), Nathan Hines (*Perpignan*), Scott MacLeod (*Llanelli Scarlets*), Alasdair Strokosch (*Gloucester*), Allister Hogg (*Edinburgh*), Simon Taylor (*Stade Français*) ... Substitutes: Dan Parks (*Glasgow Wrs*) for Lamont (20), Fergus Thomson (*Glasgow Wrs*) for Ford (25), Jason White (*Sale Sharks*) for MacLeod (62), Alasdair Dickinson (*Gloucester*) for Jacobsen (64), Craig Smith (*Edinburgh*) for Murray (69), Kelly Brown (*Glasgow Wrs*) for Hogg (71), Rory Lawson (*Gloucester*) for Blair (76)

ENGLAND Iain Balshaw (*Gloucester*); Paul Sackey (*London Wasps*), Jamie Noon (*Newcastle F*), Toby Flood (*Newcastle F*), Lesley Vainikolo (*Gloucester*); Jonny Wilkinson (*Newcastle F*), Richard Wigglesworth (*Sale Sharks*); Andrew Sheridan (*Sale Sharks*), Lee Mears (*Bath*), Phil Vickery* (*London Wasps*), Simon Shaw (*London Wasps*), Steve Borthwick (*Bath*), Tom Croft (*Leicester Tgrs*), Michael Lipman (*Bath*), Nick Easter (*Harlequins*) ... Substitutes: Matthew Tait (*Newcastle F*) for Flood (66), George Chuter (*Leicester Tgrs*) for Mears (67), Ben Kay (*Leicester Tgrs*) for Shaw (67), Matt Stevens (*Bath*) for Vickery (70), Charlie Hodropson (*Sale Sharks*) for Wilkinson (73), Luke Narraway (*Gloucester*) for Lipman (74)

REFEREE Jonathan Kaplan (*South Africa*) · **ATTENDANCE** 67,987

SCORING Paterson, pen (3–0); Wilkinson, pen (3–3); Paterson, pen (6–3); Paterson, pen (9–3) (half-time) Paterson, pen (12–3); Parks, pen (15–3); Wilkinson, pen (15–6); Wilkinson, pen (15–9)

History repeated itself as Scotland pulled off another famous and unexpected victory over a much fancied English side. This was not a great free-flowing spectacle and neither team looked like scoring a try, but for sheer drama it was a classic. Both teams played the squally, wet conditions and the match was largely a series of testing high kicks. After three demoralising defeats, Scotland rose to the occasion and played with passion, intelligence and self-belief. They made good decisions under the keenest of pressure and showed commendable teamwork and spirit. Scotland made a promising start and Paterson kicked an early penalty after a string of English errors. A few minutes later, Rory Lamont was knocked unconscious in an accidental collision. Dan Parks took over at stand-off and Paterson moved onto the wing. England had an ominous spell of pressure, but

Mike Blair lifts the Calcutta Cup after victory over England in 2008. The Princess Royal, a great supporter of Scottish rugby, shows her approval.
SRU

could only score a Wilkinson penalty. Paterson kicked two penalties and Scotland led 9–3 at the interval. Straight from the restart, Paterson added another goal and a few minutes later Parks struck a fine effort from long range. Wilkinson swiftly replied with two penalties to set-up a nail-biting ending. Jason White came on and immediately made a thunderous driving tackle on Sackey. The closing stages were played in a tremendous atmosphere with the home crowd roaring Scotland onto victory. Lion-hearted Scottish defence kept the visitors safely penned inside their own half until the final whistle. The Princess Royal presented the Calcutta Cup to Mike Blair following which the Scottish players enjoyed a well-deserved lap of honour in front of a joyous stadium.

572 RBS SIX NATIONS CHAMPIONSHIP 2008 ITALY

Stadio Flaminio, Rome · Saturday 15 March 2008 · Lost 20–23

SCOTLAND Hugo Southwell (*Edinburgh*); Simon Danielli (*Ulster*), Simon Webster (*Edinburgh*), Graeme Morrison (*Glasgow Wrs*), Chris Paterson (*Gloucester*); Dan Parks (*Glasgow Wrs*), Mike Blair* (*Edinburgh*); Allan Jacobsen (*Edinburgh*), Fergus Thomson (*Glasgow Wrs*), Euan Murray (*Northampton Sts*), Nathan Hines (*Perpignan*), Scott MacLeod (*Llanelli Scarlets*), Alasdair Strokosch (*Gloucester*), Allister Hogg (*Edinburgh*), Simon Taylor (*Stade Français*) ... Substitutes: Andrew Henderson (*Glasgow Wrs*) for Danielli (5), Scott Lawson (*Sale Sharks*) for Thomson (52), Jason White (*Sale Sharks*) for MacLeod (52), Alasdair Dickinson (*Gloucester*) for Jacobsen (58), Craig Smith (*Edinburgh*) for Murray (58), Kelly Brown (*Glasgow Wrs*) for Hogg (72)

ITALY Andrea Marcato (*Treviso*); Kaine Robertson (*Viadana*), Gonzalo Canale (*Clermont Auv*), Mirco Bergamasco (*Stade Français*), Ezio Galon (*Parma*); Andrea Masi (*Biarritz*), Simon Picone (*Treviso*); Andrea Lo Cicero (*Racing Métro*), Leonardo Ghiraldini (*Calvisano*), Martin Castrogiovanni (*Leicester Tgrs*), Carlo Antonio Del Fava (*Ulster*), Marco Bortolami (*Gloucester*), Josh Sole (*Viadana*), Alessandro Zanni (*Calvisano*), Sergio Parisse* (*Stade Français*) ... Substitutes: Jaco Erasmus (*Viadana*) for Del Fava (48-55), Salvatore Perugini (*Toulouse)* for Lo Cicero (58), Carlos Nieto (*Gloucester*) for Castrogiovanni (59), Pietro Travagli (*Parma*) for Masi (60), Enrico Patrizio (*Padova*) for Picone (63), Fabio Ongaro (*Saracens*) for Ghiraldini (70)

REFEREE Nigel Owens (*Wales*)

SCORING Penalty try (0–5); Marcato, con (0–7); Hogg, try (5–7); Paterson, con (7–7); Parks, pen (10–7); Marcato, pen (10–10); Blair, try (15–10); Paterson, con (17–10) (half-time) Canale, try (17–15); Marcato, con (17–17); Marcato, pen (20–17); Paterson, pen (20–20); Marcato, drop (20–23)

Played in bright sunlight in front of a voluble and passionate crowd, Scotland played their best rugby of the Championship but still came away empty-handed. After a poor start, they dominated play for some 50 minutes before giving away a careless interception try that turned the game. Scotland were forced into an early reorganisation when Danielli was stretchered off. Simon Webster moved to the wing and Andrew Henderson came into midfield. A few minutes later, Italy were awarded a penalty try after a collapsed scrum on the Scottish line. The Scots worked their way back and on the 20th minute Hogg scored a try. Parks and Marcato exchanged penalties and just before the interval Blair took quick ball and dashed through the sleeping defence for a brilliant solo try. Scotland were in the ascendency until disaster struck near the hour mark. Parks floated a pass to his left which was plucked out of the air by No 8 Parisse who raced into the Scottish half. He threw a pass inside which bounced kindly for Canale who ran to the posts, but television replays clearly showed that Parisse's pass was several metres forward. Marcato and Paterson exchanged penalties, and in the last minute a cool-headed Marcato dropped the winning goal to send the Italian supporters into raptures.

---

573 TOUR OF ARGENTINA 2008 ARGENTINA

Estadio Rosario Central, Rosario · Saturday 7 June 2008
Lost 15–21

SCOTLAND Chris Paterson (*Gloucester*); Simon Danielli (*Ulster*), †Ben Cairns (*Edinburgh*), Graeme Morrison (*Glasgow Wrs*), †Thom Evans (*Glasgow Wrs*); Dan Parks (*Glasgow Wrs*), Mike Blair* (*Edinburgh*); Allan Jacobsen (*Edinburgh*), Ross Ford (*Edinburgh*), Euan Murray (*Northampton Sts*), †Matt Mustchin (*Edinburgh*), Scott MacLeod (*Llanelli Scarlets*), Alasdair Strokosch (*Gloucester*), Allister Hogg (*Edinburgh*), John Beattie (*Glasgow Wrs*) ... Substitutes: Kelly Brown (*Glasgow Wrs*) for Beattie (57), Alasdair Dickinson (*Gloucester*) for Jacobsen (67), Alastair Kellock (*Glasgow Wrs*) for MacLeod (67-71) and for Mustchin (71), Simon Webster (*Edinburgh*) for Evans (71), Rory Lawson (*Gloucester*) for Blair (76)

ARGENTINA Bernardo Stortoni (*Glasgow Wrs*); José Nuñez Piossek (*Huirapuca*), Gonzalo Tiesi (*Harlequins*), Felipe Contepomi* (*Leinster*), Tomás De Vedia (*London Irish*); Federico Todeschini (*Montpellier*), Nicolás Vergallo (*JC Rosario*); Marcos Ayerza (*Leicester Tgrs*), Alvaro Tejeda (*Parma*), Santiago González Bonorino (*Capitolina*), Ignacio Fernández Lobbe (*Northampton Sts*), Esteban Lozada (*Toulon*), Martín Durand (*Champagnat*), Juan Martin Fernandez Lobbe (*Sale Sharks*), Juan Manuel Leguizamón (*London Irish*) ... Substitutes: Pablo Gambarini (*San Isidro*) for Tejeda (67), Juan Gómez (*Leinster*) for Bonorino (67), Alejandro Campos (*Pueyrredón*) for Durand (74)

REFEREE Alan Lewis (*Ireland*)

SCORING Paterson, pen (3–0); Todeschini, pen (3–3); Tejeda, try (3–8); Todeschini, con (3–10); Paterson, pen (6–10); Paterson, pen (9–10) (half-time) Paterson, pen (12–10); Paterson, pen (15–10); Todeschini, pen (15–13); Todeschini, pen (15–16); Tiesi, try (15–21)

Eight months after their fateful encounter in the World Cup quarter-final, the sides met again in a two match series in Argentina. Both teams were missing some of their first-choice players because of injury or club commitments. Scotland fielded three new caps: Ben Cairns, Thom Evans and Matt Mustchin, a New Zealander who qualified on residency. Scotland fought bravely against bigger opponents, but they were limited in attack and all of their points came from the steady boot of Chris Paterson. They held a five point lead going into the closing stages but then gave away two late penalty goals and a turnover try in injury-time. This was another frustrating defeat for Scotland. They worked hard and defended heroically but paid heavily for their inability to score tries.

Vélez Sársfield, Buenos Aires · Saturday 14 June 2008 · Won 26–14

SCOTLAND Hugo Southwell (*Edinburgh*); Chris Paterson (*Gloucester*), Ben Cairns (*Edinburgh*), Graeme Morrison (*Glasgow Wrs*), Simon Webster (*Edinburgh*); Phil Godman (*Edinburgh*), Mike Blair* (*Edinburgh*); Allan Jacobsen (*Edinburgh*), Ross Ford (*Edinburgh*), Euan Murray (*Northampton Sts*), Matt Mustchin (*Edinburgh*), Scott MacLeod (*Llanelli Scarlets*), Alasdair Strokosch (*Gloucester*), John Barclay (*Glasgow Wrs*), Allister Hogg (*Edinburgh*) ... Substitutes: Alasdair Dickinson (*Gloucester*) for Barclay (58-68) and for Jacobsen (68), Alastair Kellock (*Glasgow Wrs*) for MacLeod (60), Kelly Brown (*Glasgow Wrs*) for Hogg (65), Dougie Hall (*Glasgow Wrs*) for Ford (68), Dan Parks (*Glasgow Wrs*) for Godman (68), Nick De Luca (*Edinburgh*) for Morrison (71), Rory Lawson (*Gloucester*) for Blair (71)

ARGENTINA Bernardo Stortoni (*Glasgow Wrs*); Lucas Borges (*Treviso*), Gonzalo Tiesi (*Harlequins*), Felipe Contepomi* (*Leinster*), Horacio Agulla (*Dax*); Federico Todeschini (*Montpellier*), Nicolás Vergallo (*JC Rosario*); Marcos Ayerza (*Leicester Tgrs*), Alvaro Tejeda (*Parma*), Santiago González Bonorino (*Capitolina*), Ignacio Fernández Lobbe (*Northampton Sts*), Esteban Lozada (*Toulon*), Martín Durand (*Champagnat*), Juan Martin Fernandez Lobbe (*Sale Sharks*), Juan Manuel Leguizamón (*London Irish*) ... Substitutes: Federico Martin Aramburu (*Perpignan*) for Tiesi (13), Juan Gomez (*Leinster*) for Bonorino (45), James Stuart (*San Isidro*) for Lozada (58), Alvaro Galindo (*Béziers*) for Durand (58), Federico Serra (*San Isidro*) for Aramburu (76)

REFEREE Alain Rolland (*Ireland*)

SCORING Paterson, pen (3–0); Paterson, pen (6–0); Ford, try (11–0); Paterson, con (13–0); Paterson, pen (16–0) (half-time) Paterson, pen (19–0); Fernández Lobbe, try (19–5); Todeschini, con (19–7); Morrison, try (24–7); Paterson, con (26–7); Agullo, try (26–12); Todeschini, con (26–14)

Phil Godman was recalled at stand-off and Mike Blair won his 50th cap. Scotland surprised the rugby world by winning in Argentina for the first time. Playing with a stiff wind behind them, the Scots roared to a 16-0 lead by the interval. Chris Paterson put over two early penalties and then kicked a touchline conversion of a Ross Ford try. Two further Paterson penalties either side of the break gave the Scots a commanding lead. Argentina fought back and on the hour mark Fernández Lobbe bludgeoned his way over after sustained pressure on the Scottish line. With the match in the balance, Scotland had a piece of good luck that took them to victory. Parks intercepted a pass deep inside the Scottish half and raced away. He found support from Morrison who had enough speed to reach the posts, ensuring a simple conversion for Paterson. The only downside of this notable win was that Argentina scored a late try and conversion, and the points differential between the sides denied Scotland eighth place in the IRB world rankings, meaning that they had a much tougher draw for the 2011 World Cup.

575 AUTUMN TEST 2008 NEW ZEALAND

Murrayfield · Saturday 8 November 2008 · Lost 6–32

SCOTLAND Chris Paterson (*Edinburgh*); Thom Evans (*Glasgow Wrs*), Ben Cairns (*Edinburgh*),

Nick De Luca (*Edinburgh*), Sean Lamont (*Northampton Sts*); Phil Godman (*Edinburgh*), Mike Blair* (*Edinburgh*); Allan Jacobsen (*Edinburgh*), Ross Ford (*Edinburgh*), Euan Murray (*Northampton Sts*), Nathan Hines (*Perpignan*), Jim Hamilton (*Edinburgh*), Jason White (*Sale Sharks*), John Barclay (*Glasgow Wrs*), Allister Hogg (*Edinburgh*) ... Substitutes: Hugo Southwell (*Edinburgh*) for Lamont (42), Alasdair Dickinson (*Gloucester*) for Murray (55); Matt Mustchin (*Edinburgh*) for Hines (55), Scott Gray (*Northampton Sts*) for White (61), Dougie Hall (*Glasgow Wrs*) for Ford (63), Murray for Jacobsen (64), Dan Parks (*Glasgow Wrs*) for Godman (70), Rory Lawson (*Gloucester*) for Blair (70)

NEW ZEALAND Isaia Toeava (*Blues*); Anthony Tuitavake (*Blues*), Richard Kahui (*Chiefs*), Ma'a Nonu (*Hurricanes*), Josevata Rokocoko (*Blues*); Stephen Donald (*Chiefs*), Piri Weepu (*Hurricanes*); Jamie Mackintosh (*Highlanders*), Keven Mealamu* (*Blues*), John Afoa (*Blues*), Anthony Boric (*Blues*), Ali Williams (*Blues*), Kieran Read (*Crusaders*), Adam Thomson (*Highlanders*), Liam Messam (*Chiefs*) ... Substitutes: Corey Jane (*Hurricanes*) for Toeva (40), Andy Ellis (*Crusaders*) for Weepu (52), Neemia Tialata (*Wellington*) for Mackintosh (54), Corey Flynn (*Crusaders*) for Mealamu (59), Richie McCaw (*Crusaders*) for Thomson (59), Ross Filipo (*Crusaders*) for Williams (65), Dan Carter (*Crusaders*) for Ellis (70)

REFEREE Wayne Barnes (*England*) · ATTENDANCE 51,511

SCORING Paterson, pen (3–0); Donald, pen (3–3); Tuitavake, try (3–8); Donald, con (3–10); Donald, pen (3–13); Paterson, pen (6–13); Weepu, try (6–18) (half-time) Kahui, try (6–23); Donald, con (6–25); Boric, try (6–30); Carter, con (6–32)

The 27th encounter between the two sides followed a wearily familiar script. Scotland played with plenty of spirit, but they could not turn their pressure into points and made some fatal lapses of concentration that the All Blacks were quick to exploit. In an atmospheric match under floodlights, Chris Paterson kicked an early penalty but Scotland lost the initiative when Nick de Luca was sin binned after only three minutes. Donaldson levelled the scores and then punted across field to Tuitavake for a simple try at the corner. Weepu added a second score when he gathered a chip ahead by Kahui. Towards the end of the half, Boric was sent to the sin bin and Scotland had a series of scrums on the New Zealand line, but they were unable to make their advantage count. New Zealand effectively finished the game within a minute of the restart. A speculative high ball by Jane bounced neatly into the hands of Kahui who sprinted away to the posts. The match then degenerated into a series of messy scrums and fruitless attacks. Scotland tried hard but with the game won New Zealand coasted along to another routine victory. Seven minutes from time Boric took a pop pass and cantered away for the final try. There was a big gulf in quality between the two sides and Scotland never looked like winning despite their best efforts. On the plus side, Mike Blair had some sniping breaks and led from the front, Euan Murray scrummaged solidly, and Thom Evans showed glimpses of his electrifying pace.

---

576 AUTUMN TEST 2008 SOUTH AFRICA

Murrayfield · Saturday 15 November 2008 · Lost 10–14

SCOTLAND Chris Paterson (*Edinburgh*); Thom Evans (*Glasgow Wrs*), Ben Cairns (*Edinburgh*), Nick De Luca (*Edinburgh*), Rory Lamont (*Sale Sharks*); Phil Godman (*Edinburgh*), Mike Blair* (*Edinburgh*); Allan Jacobsen (*Edinburgh*), Ross Ford (*Edinburgh*), Euan Murray (*Northampton Sts*), Nathan Hines (*Perpignan*), Jim Hamilton (*Edinburgh*), Jason White

(*Sale Sharks*), John Barclay (*Glasgow Wrs*), Allister Hogg (*Edinburgh*) ... Substitutes: Hugo Southwell (*Edinburgh*) for Paterson (10), Scott Gray (*Northampton Sts*) for White (58), Alasdair Dickinson (*Gloucester*) for Jacobsen (65), Rory Lawson (*Gloucester*) for Evans (73), Matt Mustchin (*Edinburgh*) for Hines (74)

SOUTH AFRICA Conrad Jantjes (*Stormers*); JP Pietersen (*Sharks*), Adi Jacobs (*Sharks*), Jean de Villiers (*Stormers*), Bryan Habana (*Bulls*); Ruan Pienaar (*Sharks*), Ricky Januarie (*Stormers*); Tendai Mtawarira (*Sharks*), Bismarck du Plessis (*Sharks*), John Smit* (*Sharks*), Bakkies Botha (*Bulls*), Victor Matfield (*Bulls*), Schalk Burger (*Stormers*), Juanne Smith (*Cheetahs*), Pierre Spies (*Bulls*) ... Substitutes: Brian Mujati (*Stormers*) for du Plessis (7), Jaque Fourie (*Lions*) for Habana (54), Andries Bekker (*Stormers*) for Botha (60), Frans Steyn (*Sharks*) for de Villiers (65), Gurthro Steenkamp (*Bulls*) for Mtawarira (74), Danie Rossouw (*Bulls*) for Burger (74), Ryan Kankowski (*Sharks*) for Spies (74)

REFEREE Dave Pearson (*England*) · ATTENDANCE 36,037

SCORING Godman, pen (3–0); Hines, try (8–0); Godman, con (10–0) (half-time) Pienaar, pen (10–3); Pienaar, pen (10–6); Fourie, try (10–11); Pienaar, pen (10–14)

In one of the great 'if only' matches, Scotland were agonisingly close to beating the world champions. The Scots showed plenty of enterprise and dominated for long periods, but like the previous weekend their opponents were quick to take any chances that came their way. Scotland were unlucky to lose the talismanic Chris Paterson after only ten minutes with a facial injury. His absence was keenly felt as the Scots missed four penalty attempts during the match, but they did manage to score their first try at home for over a year. A few minutes before half-time, Blair broke away from a ruck, Godman carried onto the line and after a couple of drives Hines crashed over at the posts. Wiping away blood from a head wound, Godman converted to give Scotland a 10–0 lead at the interval. The game turned in South Africa's favour in the third quarter. The Scots lost their concentration and intensity, and Pienaar kicked three penalties and Fourie scored a try after a slick attack. Scotland regained control in the closing stages and made some ambitious attacks, including one from behind their own line. Godman, who played very well, missed a simple late penalty that would have narrowed the gap to one point. In an exciting conclusion, the Scots threw everything at the South Africans but could not make the decisive breakthrough.

577 AUTUMN TEST 2008 CANADA

Pittodrie Stadium, Aberdeen · Saturday 22 November 2008
Won 41–0

SCOTLAND Rory Lamont (*Sale Sharks*); Simon Webster (*Edinburgh*), Ben Cairns (*Edinburgh*), Nick De Luca (*Edinburgh*), Nikki Walker (*Ospreys*); Phil Godman (*Edinburgh*), Mike Blair* (*Edinburgh*); Allan Jacobsen (*Edinburgh*), Ross Ford (*Edinburgh*), Euan Murray (*Northampton Sts*), Nathan Hines (*Perpignan*), Jim Hamilton (*Edinburgh*), Alasdair Strokosch (*Gloucester*), John Barclay (*Glasgow Wrs*), Simon Taylor (*Stade Français*) ... Substitutes: Alasdair Dickinson (*Gloucester*) for Jacobsen (51), Scott Gray (*Northampton Sts*) for Barclay (51), Dan Parks (*Glasgow Wrs*) for Godman (59), Rory Lawson (*Gloucester*) for Blair (59), †Max Evans (*Glasgow Wrs*) for Webster (64), Dougie Hall (*Glasgow Wrs*) for Ford (64), Matt Mustchin (*Edinburgh*) for Hines (75)

CANADA James Pritchard (*Bedford*); Sean Duke (*Victoria U*), Ciaran Hearn (*Castaway Wdrs*), Ryan Smith (*Calgary Irish*), Justin Mensah-Coker (*Plymouth Alb*); Matt Evans (*Hartpury Coll*), Ed Fairhurst* (*Cornish Pirates*); Kevin Tkachuk (*Glasgow Wrs*), Mike Pletch (*Velox Valhallians*), Scott Franklin (*Cornish Pirates*), Tyler Hotson (*Northern Suburbs*), Josh Jackson (*Bordeaux Bègles*), Jebb Sinclair (*Castaway Wdrs*), Adam Kleeburger (*Victoria U*), Aaron Carpenter (*Brantford Harlequins*) ... Substitutes: Nathan Hirayama (*Victoria U*) for Evans (47), Bryn Keys (*Velox Valhallians*) for Hearn (64), Mike Burak (*Cornish Pirates*) for Jackson (64), Frank Walsh (*Vandals*) for Tkachuk (67), Jason Marshall (*Capilano*) for Kleeburger (67), Morgan Williams (*James Bay*) for Fairhurst (70)

REFEREE George Clancy (*Ireland*) · ATTENDANCE 17,651

SCORING Walker, try (5–0); Godman, pen (8–0); Cairns, try (13–0); Godman, con (15–0) (half-time) Barclay, try (20–0); Godman, con (22–0); Strokosch, try (27–0); Godman, con (29–0); Walker, try (34–0); Parks, con (36–0); Lamont, try (41–0)

On a bitterly cold afternoon and a snow speckled pitch, Scotland ended their autumn series with a much-needed win over lowly Canada. The Scots were in always in control and scored six well-taken tries. Scotland made the perfect start when Aberdeen-born Nikki Walker slid over in the corner after only two minutes. The Scots tried to force the game at times and the Canadians defended well, but shortly before the interval De Luca made a break before giving Cairns a simple run-in. Soon after the restart, Barclay powered over for his first international try and 15 minutes later Stokosch dived over from close-range. The game went rather flat for a while, but Scotland finished strongly with tries by Walker and Lamont. On the 64th minute, Max Evans, elder brother of Thom, replaced Simon Webster to win his first cap.

---

578   RBS SIX NATIONS CHAMPIONSHIP 2009   WALES

Murrayfield · Sunday 8 February 2009 · Lost 13–26

SCOTLAND Hugo Southwell (*Edinburgh*); Simon Webster (*Edinburgh*), Ben Cairns (*Edinburgh*), Graeme Morrison (*Glasgow Wrs*), Sean Lamont (*Northampton Sts*); Phil Godman (*Edinburgh*), Mike Blair* (*Edinburgh*); Allan Jacobsen (*Edinburgh*), Ross Ford (*Edinburgh*), †Geoff Cross (*Edinburgh*), Jason White (*Sale Sharks*), Jim Hamilton (*Edinburgh*), Allister Hogg (*Edinburgh*), John Barclay (*Glasgow Wrs*), Simon Taylor (*Stade Français*) ... Substitutes: Alasdair Dickinson (*Glasgow Wrs*) for White (26-30) and Cross (30), Chris Paterson (*Edinburgh*) for Webster (21), Max Evans (*Glasgow Wrs*) for Cairns (52), Scott Gray (*Northampton Sts*) for Barclay (56), Dougie Hall (*Glasgow Wrs*) for Ford (62), Chris Cusiter (*Perpignan*) for Blair (62), Kelly Brown (*Glasgow Wrs*) for Hogg (73)

WALES Lee Byrne (*Ospreys*); Leigh Halfpenny (*Cardiff Blues*), Tom Shanklin (*Cardiff Blues*), Jamie Roberts (*Cardiff Blues*), Shane Williams (*Ospreys*); Stephen Jones (*Scarlets*), Michael Philips (*Ospreys*); Gethin Jenkins (*Cardiff Blues*), Matthew Rees (*Scarlets*), Adam Rhys Jones (*Ospreys*), Ian Gough (*Ospreys*), Alun-Wyn Jones (*Ospreys*), Daffyd Jones (*Scarlets*), Martyn Williams* (*Cardiff Blues*), Andy Powell (*Cardiff Blues*) ... Substitutes: Dwayne Peel (*Sale Sharks*) for Phillips (62), Andrew Bishop (*Ospreys*) for Jamie Roberts (65), Huw Bennett (*Ospreys*) for Rees (65), John Yapp (*Cardiff Blues*) for Jenkins (65), Luke Charteris (*NG Dragons*) for Gough (65), James Hook (*Ospreys*) for S Jones (65), Bradley Davies (*Cardiff Blues*) for S Williams (74)

REFEREE Alain Rolland (*Ireland*) · ATTENDANCE 65,586

SCORING S Jones, pen (0–3); Shanklin, try (0–8); A-W Jones, try (0–13); Paterson, pen (3–13); S Jones, pen (3–16) (half-time) Halfpenny, try (3–21); Paterson, pen (6–21); S Williams, try (6–26); M Evans, try (11–26); Paterson, con (13–26)

Geoff Cross, a qualified doctor who had combined his medical studies with his rugby career, won his first cap at tight-head prop. On a bitterly cold and snowy day, Scotland were outclassed by a talented Welsh side. The visitors scored four tries to one but missed all of their conversions and a penalty attempt which would have given a truer reflection on the difference between the sides. In the first-half, Wales played some confident, attractive rugby and the match was as good as won by the interval. The Welsh backs were fast and penetrative, especially centre Jamie Roberts who made some searing runs, and their defence was well-organised. Scotland never really got into the game until it was too late. They made countless errors and their attacking play was ponderous and predictable. The first-half was marred by injuries to Simon Webster and Geoff Cross, who was stretchered-off after colliding with an airborne Lee Byrne, an action for which Cross received a yellow card. It was during this period that Wales scored their first two tries. Shane Williams and Byrne combined to send Shanklin over and then Alun-Wyn Jones handed-off Southwell after a scrum turnover in the Scottish 22. A penalty by Stephen Jones and second-half tries by Halfpenny and Shane Williams put the result beyond doubt. Scotland made a late rally and substitute Max Evans used his pace to round the defence for a superb solo score. Near the end, Paterson almost snatched a chip-and-chase try that would have set-up a grandstand finish, but nothing could detract from a fine Welsh performance.

---

579 RBS SIX NATIONS CHAMPIONSHIP 2009 FRANCE

Stade de France, Paris · Saturday 14 February 2009 · Lost 13–22

SCOTLAND Hugo Southwell (*Edinburgh*); Simon Danielli (*Ulster*), Max Evans (*Glasgow Wrs*), Graeme Morrison (*Glasgow Wrs*), Thom Evans (*Glasgow Wrs*); Phil Godman (*Edinburgh*), Mike Blair* (*Edinburgh*); Allan Jacobsen (*Edinburgh*), Ross Ford (*Edinburgh*), Alasdair Dickinson (*Gloucester*), Jason White (*Sale Sharks*), Jim Hamilton (*Edinburgh*), Alasdair Strokosch (*Gloucester*), John Barclay (*Glasgow Wrs*), Simon Taylor (*Stade Français*) ... Substitutes: Kelly Brown (*Glasgow Wrs*) for Hamilton (17), †Murray Low (*Glasgow Wrs*) for Dickinson (46), Dougie Hall (*Glasgow Wrs*) for Ford (65), Chris Paterson (*Edinburgh*) for Danielli (65), Dickinson for Jacobsen (70), Chris Cusiter (*Perpignan*) for Blair (72), Nick De Luca (*Edinburgh*) for Morrison (72)

FRANCE Clémont Poitrenaud (*Toulouse*); Maxime Medard (*Toulouse*), Yannick Jauzion (*Toulouse*), Benoit Baby (*Clermont Auv*), Cédric Heymans (*Toulouse*); Lionel Beauxis (*Stade Français*), Sébastien Tillous-Borde (*Castres*); Fabien Barcella (*Biarritz*), Dimitri Szarzewski (*Stade Français*), Nicolas Mas (*Perpignan*), Lionel Nallet* (*Castres*), Romain Millo-Chluski (*Toulouse*), Thierry Dusatoir (*Toulouse*), Fulgence Ouedraogo (*Montpellier*), Imanol Harinordoquy (*Biarritz*) ... Substitutes: Benjamin Kayser (*Leicester Tgrs*) for Szarzewski (55), Sébastien Chabel (*Sale Sharks*) for Millo-Chulsky (60), Maxime Mermoz (*Perpignan*) for Baby (60), Morgan Parra (*Bourgoin-Jailleu*) for Tillous-Borde (66), Louis Picamoles (*Montpellier*) for Harinordoquy (70), Julien Malzieu (*Clermont Auv*) for Medard (79)

REFEREE George Clancy (*Ireland*)

SCORING Beauxis, pen (0–3); Godman, pen (3–3); Beauxis, pen (3–6) (half-time) Ouedraogo, try (3–11); Beauxis, con (3–13); Godman, pen (6–13); Beauxis, pen (6–16); Beauxis, pen (6–19); T Evans, try (11–19); Paterson, con (13–19); Beauxis, pen (13–22)

Scotland showed real signs of improvement and played with much greater ambition and threat, but still made too many errors to pull-off a surprise win. France produced nothing spectacular but did just enough to stay in front. The first half was tight and undistinguished, and Scotland lost Jim Hamilton with a shoulder injury. Shortly after the restart, France scored a controversial try which was judged fair by touch-judge Wayne Barnes after the referee had been accidentally bowled over. Television replays suggested a hint of crossing and that the final pass from Medard to Ouedraogo was forward. As play opened out, Scotland made some promising attacks and on the 68th minute Godman flipped an inside pass to Thom Evans who scored at the posts. Paterson's conversion reduced the leeway to six points, but a late penalty by Beauxis put the game beyond reach.

---

580   RBS SIX NATIONS CHAMPIONSHIP 2009   ITALY

Murrayfield · Saturday 28 February 2009 · Won 26–6

SCOTLAND Hugo Southwell (*Edinburgh*); Simon Danielli (*Ulster*), Max Evans (*Glasgow Wrs*), Graeme Morrison (*Glasgow Wrs*), Thom Evans (*Glasgow Wrs*); Phil Godman (*Edinburgh*), Mike Blair* (*Edinburgh*); Allan Jacobsen (*Edinburgh*), Ross Ford (*Edinburgh*), Euan Murray (*Northampton Sts*), Jason White (*Sale Sharks*), Alastair Kellock (*Glasgow Wrs*), Alasdair Strokosch (*Gloucester*), John Barclay (*Glasgow Wrs*), Simon Taylor (*Stade Français*) ... Substitutes: Chris Paterson (*Edinburgh*) for Godman (3–12) and for Southwell (47), Dougie Hall (*Glasgow Wrs*) for Ford (52), Chris Cusiter (*Perpignan*) for Blair (56), Scott Gray (*Northampton Sts*) for Barclay (56), Alasdair Dickinson (*Gloucester*) for Jacobsen (63), Jacobsen for Murray (64), Nick De Luca (*Edinburgh*) for Morrison (67), Kelly Brown (*Glasgow Wrs*) for Jacobsen (67)

ITALY Andrea Marcato (*Treviso*); Mirco Bergamasco (*Stade Français*), Gonzalo Canale (*Clermont Auv*), Gonzalo Garcia (*Calvisano*), Matteo Pratichetti (*Calvisano*); Luke McLean (*Calvisano*), Paul Griffen (*Calvisano*); Salvatore Perugini (*Toulouse*), Leonardo Ghiraldini (*Calvisano*), Martin Castrogiovanni (*Leicester Tgrs*), Santiago Dellape (*Toulon*), Marco Bortolami (*Gloucester*), Alessandro Zanni (*Calvisano*), Mauro Bergamasco (*Stade Français*), Sergio Parisse* (*Stade Français*) ... Substitutes: Andrea Bacchetti (*Rovigo*) for Garcia (3), Giulio Rubini (*Parma*) for Marcato (47), Pablo Canavosio (*Viadana*) for Griffen (56), Carlo Del Fava (*Ulster*) for Dellape (57), Franco Sbaraglini (*Treviso*) for Ghiraldini (58), Carlos Nieto (*Gloucester*) for Castrogiovanni (58), Josh Sole (*Viadana*) for Bortolami (76)

REFEREE Nigel Owens (*Wales*) · ATTENDANCE 51,309

SCORING Paterson, pen (3–0); Paterson, pen (6–0); Parisse, drop (6–3); Godman, pen (9–3); Danielli, try (14–3); Godman, con (16–3) (half-time) McLean, pen (16–6); Gray, try (21–6); Paterson, con (23–6); Paterson, pen (26–6)

Scotland scored two exciting tries and were won their first victory of 2009, but otherwise this was an unmemorable encounter and clearly both sides were lacking in confidence. The highlight was Scotland's first try which was scored on the 35th minute. From a lineout just inside the Italian half, Godman and Morrison combined to put Danielli through a gap and the big wing swerved through the remaining defence before diving over at the posts. Scotland played a tightly controlled game and they finished the match strongly. On the 62nd minute, Tom Evans sprinted to the Italian line and Scott Gray was on hand to score. Paterson converted and kicked a penalty to see Scotland home. The match wound down with uncontested scrums and flanker Kelly Brown acted as an emergency prop.

581   RBS SIX NATIONS CHAMPIONSHIP 2009   IRELAND

Murrayfield · Saturday 14 March 2009 · Lost 15–22

SCOTLAND Chris Paterson (*Edinburgh*); Simon Danielli (*Ulster*), Max Evans (*Glasgow Wrs*), Graeme Morrison (*Glasgow Wrs*), Thom Evans (*Glasgow Wrs*); Phil Godman (*Edinburgh*), Mike Blair* (*Edinburgh*); Alasdair Dickinson (*Gloucester*), Ross Ford (*Edinburgh*), Euan Murray (*Northampton Sts*), Jason White (*Sale Sharks*), Jim Hamilton (*Edinburgh*), Alasdair Strokosch (*Gloucester*), John Barclay (*Glasgow Wrs*), Simon Taylor (*Stade Français*) … Substitutes: Nathan Hines (*Perpignan*) for White (50), Chris Cusiter (*Perpignan*) for Blair (51), Dougie Hall (*Glasgow Wrs*) for Ford (57), Scott Gray (*Northampton Sts*) for Barclay (67), Nick De Luca (*Edinburgh*) for Morrison (70)

IRELAND Robert Kearney (*Leinster*); Tommy Bowe (*Ospreys*), Brian O'Driscoll* (*Leinster*), Gordon D'Arcy (*Leinster*), Luke Fitzgerald (*Leinster*); Ronan O'Gara (*Munster*), Peter Stringer (*Munster*); Marcus Horan (*Munster*), Rory Best (*Ulster*), John Hayes (*Munster*), Donncha O'Callaghan (*Munster*), Paul O'Connell (*Munster*), Stephen Ferris (*Ulster*), David Wallace (*Munster*), Denis Leamy (*Munster*) … Substitutes: Jamie Heaslip (*Leinster*) for Leamy (30), Jerry Flannery (*Munster*) for Best (61), Tomas O'Leary (*Munster*) for Stringer (65), Geordan Murphy (*Leicester Tgrs*) for Kearney (75)

REFEREE Jonathan Kaplan (*South Africa*)

SCORING Paterson, pen (3–0); O'Gara, pen (3–3); Paterson, pen (6–3); Paterson, pen (9–3); O'Gara, pen (9–6); Paterson, pen (12–6); O'Gara, pen (12–9) (half-time) Heaslip, try (12–14); O'Gara, con (12–16); O'Gara, drop (12–19); Paterson, pen (15–19); O'Gara, pen (15–22)

Ireland were seeking their first Grand Slam since 1948 and had just enough quality to ease past a competitive Scotland. Once again the Scots showed plenty of promise and determination only to be undone by unforced errors and a failure to take their chances. Scotland had the better of the first half and missed two great chances at either end of it. After a couple of minutes, Danielli burst into the line and almost made it to the corner before being tap-tackled by Fitzgerald. Just before the interval, Thom Evans collected his own chip ahead and rounded the defence before being tackled. He slipped the ball to Godman who looked set to score, but a last-ditch tackle by O'Driscoll sent him crashing into touch. Crucially Scotland gave away several cheap penalties which O'Gara converted, leaving the door open for the visitors. In the second half, Ireland played with much greater purpose and cohesion, and their 50th minute try, which effectively won the match, was a thing of beautiful simplicity. Stringer found a huge gap at the back of the lineout and made a mazy run into the Scottish 22 before slipping the ball to Heaslip who romped joyously to the line. O'Gara converted and then stretched the Irish lead with a drop goal. Paterson revived hopes his fifth penalty but Ireland kept a tight grip and O'Gara sealed victory with a penalty nine minutes from time.

Twickenham · Saturday 21 March 2009 · Lost 12–26

SCOTLAND **Scotland:** Chris Paterson (*Edinburgh*); Simon Danielli (*Ulster*), Max Evans (*Glasgow Wrs*), Graeme Morrison (*Glasgow Wrs*), Thom Evans (*Glasgow Wrs*); Phil Godman (*Edinburgh*), Mike Blair* (*Edinburgh*); Alasdair Dickinson (*Gloucester*), Ross Ford (*Edinburgh*), Euan Murray (*Northampton Sts*), Jason White (*Sale Sharks*), Jim Hamilton (*Edinburgh*), Alasdair Strokosch (*Gloucester*), Scott Gray (*Northampton Sts*), Simon Taylor (*Stade Français*) ... Substitutes: Kelly Brown (*Glasgow Wrs*) for Taylor (40), Nick De Luca (*Edinburgh*) for T Evans (44), Nathan Hines (*Perpignan*) for White (57), Dougie Hall (*Glasgow Wrs*) for Ford (57), Chris Cusiter (*Perpignan*) for Blair (67), Hugo Southwell (*Edinburgh*) for Danielli (76), Moray Low (*Glasgow Wrs*) for Dickinson (76)

ENGLAND Delon Armitage (*London Irish*); Mark Cueto (*Sale Sharks*), Mike Tindall (*Gloucester*), Riki Flutey (*London Wasps*), Ugo Monye (*Harlequins*); Toby Flood (*Leicester Tgrs*), Harry Ellis (*Leicester Tgrs*); Andrew Sheridan (*Leicester Tgrs*), Lee Mears (*Bath*), Phil Vickery (*London Wasps*), Steve Borthwick* (*Saracens*), Simon Shaw (*London Wasps*), Tom Croft (*Leicester Tgrs*), Joe Worsley (*London Wasps*), Nick Easter (*Harlequins*) ... Substitutes: Julian White (*Leicester Tgrs*) for Vickery (13), Danny Care (*Harlequins*) for Ellis (19), Matthew Tait (*Sale Sharks*) for Monye (48), Nick Kennedy (*London Irish*) for Shaw (60), James Haskell (*London Wasps*) for Croft (76), Dylan Hartley (*Northampton Sts*) for Mears (76), Andy Goode (*Brive*) for Flood (77)

REFEREE Marius Jonker (*South Africa*)

SCORING Paterson, pen (3–0); Monye, try (3–5); Flutey, try (3–10); Flood, con (3–12); Flood, pen (3–15) (half-time) Flood, pen (3–18); Paterson, pen (6–18); Godman, pen (9–18); Paterson, pen (12–18); Care, drop (12–21); Tait, try (12–26)

After an early Paterson penalty, Scotland had a great chance when Thom Evans made an electrifying break down the left touchline only to be caught by a last gasp tackle by Monye. Later, Mike Blair sprinted deep into English territory but the support was too slow. These incidents aside, England dominated the first half and scored well-worked tries by Monye and Flutey, the latter literally with his fingertips. At half-time it seemed that England would run away with it but the Scots stayed competitive and made some promising attacks. On the 65th minute Paterson's third penalty reduced the deficit to six points, but Scotland never looked like winning and a Danny Care drop goal put the game beyond them. England were reduced to 14 men when prop Julian White limped off and the match wound down with uncontested scrums. From one of these Tait scored a simple try against a rapidly tiring defence. This was an intense physical contest and there were lengthy delays in both halves when Ellis and Southwell were stretchered off with injuries.

Murrayfield · Saturday 14 November 2009 · Won 23–10

SCOTLAND Rory Lamont (*Toulon*); Sean Lamont (*Scarlets*), †Alex Grove (*Worcester Wrs*), Graeme Morrison (*Glasgow Wrs*), Simon Danielli (*Ulster*); Phil Godman (*Edinburgh*), Chris Cusiter* (*Glasgow Wrs*); Allan Jacobsen (*Edinburgh*), Ross Ford (*Edinburgh*), Moray Low

(*Glasgow Wrs*), Nathan Hines (*Leinster*), Alastair Kellock (*Glasgow Wrs*), Alasdair Strokosch (*Gloucester*), John Barclay (*Glasgow Wrs*), Johnnie Beattie (*Glasgow Wrs*) ... Substitutes: Chris Paterson (*Edinburgh*) for R Lamont (63), Mike Blair (*Edinburgh*) for Cusiter (63), †Kyle Traynor (*Edinburgh*) for Jacobsen (63), Jason White (*Clermont Auv*) for Strokosch (65), Dougie Hall (*Glasgow Wrs*) for Ford (69), Nick De Luca (*Edinburgh*) for Blair (77), †Richie Vernon (*Glasgow Wrs*) for Beattie (77)

FIJI Josh Matavesi (*Exeter Chiefs*); Vereniki Goneva (*Vaturu*), Gabirieli Lovobalavu (*Toulon*), Seremaia Bai* (*Clermont Auv*), Napolioni Nalaga (*Clermont Auv*); Nicky Little (*Bath*), Moses Rauluni (*Saracens*); Alefoso Yalayalatabua (*Navy*), Vili Veikoso (*Mavoci*), Deacon Manu (*Scarlets*), Wame Lewaravu (*London Welsh*), Ifereimi Rawaqa (*World Fighting Bulls*), Josefa Domolailai (*Lomavata*), Akapusi Qera (*Gloucester*), Asaeli Boko (*Tau*) ... Substitutes: Samu Bola (*Police*) for Domolailai (23), Graham Dewes (*Esher*) for Yalayalatabua (40), Sereli Ledua (*FTG*) for Veikoso (70), Waisale Vatuvoka (*Duavata*) for Rauluni (70), Jonetani Ratu (*Cagimaira*) for Matavesi (74), Nasoni Roko (*Yokogawa*) for Goneva (75)

REFEREE Chris White (*England*) · ATTENDANCE 21,826

SCORING Godman, pen (3–0); Beattie, try (8–0); Godman, con (10–0); Godman, pen (13–0); Godman, pen (16–0); Goneva, try (16–5); Little, con (16–7) (half-time) Morrison, try (21–7); Godman, con (23–7); Little, pen (23–10)

The start of another new era as former England flanker Andy Robinson, who had played against Scotland in 1989, took over as head coach. In an innovative selection, and with two outstanding scrum-halves at his disposal, Robinson appointed Chris Cusiter and Mike Blair as joint captains, the former in the starting line-up. After an early Godman penalty, Cusiter darted through a gap at a lineout before giving a scoring pass to Beattie. Godman converted and kicked two penalties, and then Goneva scored a simple try after the Scottish defence was caught out of position. Ten minutes into the second half Morrison scored from a close-range scrum. The rest of the game was rather uninspiring and Fiji finished strongly but they could only score a penalty. Scotland still had plenty of work to do but this was a satisfactory win. The forwards were solid at the set-pieces and prop Moray Low won the man-of-the-match award. Amongst the backs, the Lamont brothers and Simon Danielli ran well and were eager to be involved.

584 AUTUMN TEST 2009 AUSTRALIA

Murrayfield · Saturday 21 November 2009 · Won 9–8

SCOTLAND Rory Lamont (*Toulon*); Sean Lamont (*Scarlets*), Alex Grove (*Worcester Wrs*), Graeme Morrison (*Glasgow Wrs*), Simon Danielli (*Ulster*); Phil Godman (*Edinburgh*), Chris Cusiter* (*Glasgow Wrs*); Allan Jacobsen (*Edinburgh*), Ross Ford (*Edinburgh*), Moray Low (*Glasgow Wrs*), Nathan Hines (*Leinster*), Alastair Kellock (*Glasgow Wrs*), Alasdair Strokosch (*Gloucester*), John Barclay (*Glasgow Wrs*), Johnnie Beattie (*Glasgow Wrs*) ... Substitutes: Rory Lawson (*Gloucester*) for Cusiter (21), Nick De Luca (*Edinburgh*) for Morrison (40), Jason White (*Clermont Auv*) for Strokosch (48), Kyle Traynor (*Edinburgh*) for Low (56), Chris Paterson (*Edinburgh*) for Danielli (63), Richie Vernon (*Glasgow Wrs*) for Beattie (63), Dougie Hall (*Glasgow Wrs*) for Ford (77)

AUSTRALIA Adam Ashley-Cooper (*Brumbies*); Peter Hynes (*Reds*), Ryan Cross (*Reds*), Quade Cooper (*Reds*), Drew Mitchell (*Waratahs*); Matt Giteau (*Brumbies*), Will Genia (*Reds*);

Ben Robinson (*Waratahs*), Stephen Moore (*Brumbies*), Ben Alexander (*Brumbies*), James Horwill (*Reds*), Mark Chisholm (*Brumbies*), Racky Elsom* (*Brumbies*), George Smith (*Brumbies*), Wycliff Palu (*Waratahs*) ... Substitutes: Sekope Kepu (*Waratahs*) for Robinson (17), Tataku Polota-Nau (*Waratahs*) for Moore (45), Dean Mumm (*Waratahs*) for Chisholm (50), Luke Burgess (*Waratahs*) for Genia (62), Richard Brown (*Western Force*) for Palu (65), James O'Connor (*Western Force*) for Cooper (74)

REFEREE Romain Poite (*France*) · ATTENDANCE 44,762

SCORING Giteau, pen (0–3); Godman, pen (3–3) (half-time) Godman, pen (6–3); Paterson, drop (9–3); Cross, try (9–8)

Played under floodlights in heavy squally showers, Scotland stunned the rugby world by defeating Australia for the first time since 1982. The result was a minor miracle because the Australians dominated in all aspects and ought to have won comfortably. The Scots produced little in attack but their defence was superb and the Australians could not find a way through until the very end. Scotland had an early setback when Chris Cusiter went off with a head injury. He was replaced by Rory Lawson, who had a fine match, and Alastair Kellock took over the captaincy. Starved of possession, Scotland barely reaching the Australian 22 in the first-half, but the score was tied 3–3 at the interval and the visitors left the field scratching their heads in disbelief. Early in the second half, Elsom twisted under a pile of bodies on the Scottish line but video evidence was inconclusive and the try was not awarded. Then Godman kicked a long penalty and suddenly the Scots had a sense of self-belief. Scotland continued to defend like lions and in the closing stages they made their only sustained attack of the day and Paterson calmly dropped a goal. In a frantic ending, the Australians hammered on the Scottish line and went through numerous phases before Cross muscled over from short-range. With time up and amidst a chorus of jeers, Giteau sliced the vital conversion past the left post and Scotland, somehow, had won the unlikeliest of victories. Head coach Andy Robinson said afterwards: 'That was the most courageous performance that I have ever been involved in.'

---

585   AUTUMN TEST 2009   ARGENTINA

Murrayfield · Saturday 28 November 2009 · Lost 6–9

SCOTLAND Rory Lamont (*Toulon*); Sean Lamont (*Scarlets*), Ben Cairns (*Edinburgh*), Alex Grove (*Worcester Wrs*), Thom Evans (*Glasgow Wrs*); Phil Godman (*Edinburgh*), Chris Cusiter* (*Glasgow Wrs*); Allan Jacobsen (*Edinburgh*), Ross Ford (*Edinburgh*), Moray Low (*Glasgow Wrs*), Nathan Hines (*Leinster*), Alastair Kellock (*Glasgow Wrs*), Alasdair Strokosch (*Gloucester*), †Alan MacDonald (*Edinburgh*), Johnnie Beattie (*Glasgow Wrs*) ... Substitutes: Chris Paterson (*Edinburgh*) for R Lamont (49), N De Luca (*Edinburgh*) for Cairns (55), Jason White (*Clermont Auv*) for Hines (59), Kyle Traynor (*Edinburgh*) for Jacobsen (63), Dougie Hall (*Glasgow Wrs*) for Ford (63), Richie Vernon (*Glasgow Wrs*) for Strokosch (71), Rory Lawson (*Gloucester*) for Cusiter (73)

ARGENTINA Horacio Agulla (*Brive*); Lucas Borges (*Albi*), Gonzalo Tiesi (*Harlequins*), Martín Rodríguez (*Atlético del Rosario*), Federico Martín Aramburu (*Dax*); Santiago Fernández (*Hindú*), Alfredo Lalanne (*London Irish*); Marcos Ayerza (*Leicester Tgrs*), Alberto Vernet Basualdo (*Toulouse*), Martín Scelzo (*Clermont Auv*), Manuel Carizza (*Biarritz*), Patricio Albacete

(*Toulouse*), Alejandro Campos (*Montauban*), Alejandro Abadie (*Rovigo*), Juan Fernández Lobbe* (*Toulon*) ... Substitutes: Agustín Creevy (*San Luis*) for Vernet Basualdo (38), Rodrigo Roncero (*Stade Français*) for Scelzo (53), Tomás Leonardi (*San Isidro*) for Abadie (68), Agustín Figuerola (*CASI*) for Lalanne (68), Horacio San Martín (*Tala*) for Martín Aramburu (71)

REFEREE Alan Lewis (*Ireland*) · ATTENDANCE 28,292

SCORING Godman, pen (3–0); Godman, pen (6–0) (half-time) Rodríguez, pen (6–3); Rodríguez, pen (6–6); Rodríguez, drop (6–9)

Andy Robinson made three changes, including a first cap for Edinburgh flanker Alan MacDonald. This was a stern, hard-fought encounter and the result was an anti-climax after the heroics against Australia. Scotland dominated the first-half and ought to have had the game under control by the interval. They showed plenty of enterprise and kept their opponents under pressure, but once again they failed to take their chances and many of their old faults re-emerged. The forwards struggled to supply quick ball and the attacks were too lateral and predictable. Scotland faded away in the second half, perhaps of their exertions the previous weekend. On the 48th minute Rory Lamont was stretchered off with an ankle injury and then Nathan Hines was sent to the sin bin for making a dangerous tackle, which helped to lift the Argentineans. Rodríguez kicked two penalties and from then on Argentina mostly held the upper-hand. With a few minutes left, the Argentineans stole two line-outs in quick succession and Rodríguez dropped the winning goal.

586 RBS SIX NATIONS CHAMPIONSHIP 2010 FRANCE

Murrayfield · Sunday 7 February 2010 · Lost 9–18

SCOTLAND Chris Paterson (*Edinburgh*); Thom Evans (*Glasgow Wrs*), Max Evans (*Glasgow Wrs*), Graeme Morrison (*Glasgow Wrs*), Sean Lamont (*Scarlets*); Phil Godman (*Edinburgh*), Chris Cusiter* (*Glasgow Wrs*); Alasdair Dickinson (*Gloucester*), Ross Ford (*Edinburgh*), Moray Lowe (*Glasgow Wrs*), Nathan Hines (*Leinster*), Alastair Kellock (*Glasgow Wrs*), Kelly Brown (*Glasgow Wrs*), John Barclay (*Glasgow Wrs*), Johnnie Beattie (*Glasgow Wrs*) ... Substitutes: Allan Jacobsen (*Edinburgh*) for Lowe (52), Hugo Southwell (*Stade Français*) for Godman (52), Scott Lawson (*Gloucester*) for Ford (66), †Richie Gray (*Glasgow Wrs*) for Hines (68), Lowe for Dickinson (69)

FRANCE Clément Poitrenaud (*Toulouse*); Benjamin Fall (*Bayonne*), Mathieu Bastareaud (*Stade Français*), Yannick Jauzion (*Toulouse*), Aurelien Rougerie (*Clermont Auv*); Francois Trinh-Duc (*Montpellier*), Morgan Parra (*Clermont Auv*); Thomas Domingo (*Clermont Auv*), William Servat (*Toulouse*), Nicolas Mas (*Perpignan*), Lionel Nallet (*Racing Métro*), Pascal Pape (*Stade Français*), Thierry Dusautoir* (*Toulouse*), Fulgence Ouedraogo (*Montpellier*), Imanol Harinordoquy (*Biarritz*) ... Substitutes: Vincent Clerc (*Toulouse*) for Rougerie (5), Luc Ducalcon (*Castres*) for Mas (45), Dimitri Swarzewski (*Stade Français*) for Servat (50), Julien Pierre (*Bourgoin*) for Pape (65), Julien Bonnaire (*Clermont Auv*) for Dusautoir (66), Frederic Michalak (*Toulouse*) for Parra (70), David Marty (*Perpignan*) for Bastareaud (70)

REFEREE Nigel Owens (*Wales*) · ATTENDANCE 61,584

SCORING Paterson, pen (3–0); Bastareaud, try (3–5); Parra, pen (3–8); Paterson, pen (6–8); Bastareaud, try (6–13); Parra, con (6–15) (half-time) Parra, pen (6–18); Paterson, pen (9–18)

The match was preceded by a minute's silence in honour of television commentator Bill McLaren, who died the previous month. Scotland fielded nine players from Glasgow Warriors and there was an air of cautious optimism in the camp, but ultimately it proved another false dawn. Encouraged by a large and vociferous travelling support, the French were largely in control of the match and were comfortable winners. They had a powerful scrum and lineout which gave their talented back division a solid attacking platform and their human wrecking-ball in the centre, Mathieu Bastareaud, scored a brace of tries in the first-half. Scotland showed lots of determination and eagerness, often running the ball from deep, but they were unable to break a well-organised defence or to make their opportunities count. They stuck to their task and never let France get out of sight completely, but they never looked capable of overhauling them.

---

587   RBS SIX NATIONS CHAMPIONSHIP 2010   WALES

Millennium Stadium, Cardiff · Saturday 13 February 2010

Lost 24–31

SCOTLAND Chris Paterson (*Edinburgh*); Thom Evans (*Glasgow Wrs*), Sean Lamont (*Scarlets*), Graeme Morrison (*Glasgow Wrs*), Rory Lamont (*Toulon*); Dan Parks (*Glasgow Wrs*), Chris Cusiter* (*Glasgow Wrs*); Alasdair Dickinson (*Gloucester*), Ross Ford (*Edinburgh*), Euan Murray (*Northampton Sts*), Jim Hamilton (*Edinburgh*), Alastair Kellock (*Glasgow Wrs*), Kelly Brown (*Glasgow Wrs*), John Barclay (*Glasgow Wrs*), Johnnie Beattie (*Glasgow Wrs*) ... Substitutes: Max Evans (*Glasgow Wrs*) for Evans (13-26) and for Paterson (31), Mike Blair (*Edinburgh*) for T Evans (35), Alan MacDonald (*Edinburgh*) for Brown (49-56) and for Parks (77), Allan Jacobsen (*Edinburgh*) for Dickinson (56), Scott Lawson (*Gloucester*) for Ford (56), Phil Godman (*Edinburgh*) for R Lamont (66), Richie Gray (*Glasgow Wrs*) for Hamilton (77) ... Yellow cards: Lawson (73), Godman (78)

WALES Lee Byrne (*Ospreys*); Leigh Halfpenny (*Cardiff Blues*), James Hook (*Ospreys*), Jamie Roberts (*Cardiff Blues*), Shane Williams (*Ospreys*); Stephen Jones (*Scarlets*), Gareth Cooper (*Cardiff Blues*); Paul James (*Ospreys*), Gareth Williams (*Cardiff Blues*), Adam Jones (*Ospreys*), Jonathan Thomas (*Ospreys*), Alun Wyn Jones (*Ospreys*), Andy Powell (*Cardiff Blues*), Martyn Williams (*Cardiff Blues*), Ryan Jones* (*Ospreys*) ... Substitutes: Richie Rees (*Cardiff Blues*) for Cooper (40), Huw Bennett (*Ospreys*) for G Williams (49), Bradley Davies (*Cardiff Blues*) for Powell (49), Gethin Jenkins (*Cardiff Blues*) for James (49), James for Jenkins (59), Sam Warburton (*Cardiff Blues*) for M Williams (67)

REFEREE George Clancy (*Ireland*) · ATTENDANCE 74,173

SCORING Barclay, try (5–0); Paterson, con (7–0); S Jones, pen (7–3); Parks, drop (10–3); M Evans, try (15–3); S Jones, pen (15–6); Parks, pen (18–6); S Jones, pen (18–9) (half-time) Parks, pen (21–9); Byrne, try (21–14); Parks, drop (24–14); Halfpenny, try (24–19); S Jones, con (24–21); S Jones, pen (24–24); S Williams, try (24–29); S Jones, con (24–31)

There were four changes after the French match, including a recall for Dan Parks. Chris Paterson became the first Scotsman to reach the milestone of 100 caps and led the team onto the field to generous applause. This was a classic encounter that was full of incident and had an extraordinary finale. Scotland let a great opportunity for a famous win slip through their fingers. They held a healthy lead going into the last five minutes but then conceded 17 points, including the winning try with the last move of the game. Scotland were very impressive in the first-half and ended their try famine. On the ninth minute Barclay broke through some weak defence inside the Welsh 22 and ran to the line. Scotland scored their second when Parks chipped exquisitely behind the defence for Max Evans to race through and dive on the ball. Paterson missed the touchline conversion and then had to leave the field with a bruised kidney. Meanwhile Jones and Parks exchanged penalties before Thom Evans was injured crashing into Lee Byrne, the Wales full-back. Evans was given lengthy treatment on the field before being taken to hospital for neck surgery. It was later revealed that prompt action by the Scottish medical team had probably saved Evans's life and that his rugby career was finished. Just before the interval, Jones kicked his third penalty and soon after the restart Parks replied in kind. Scotland wasted a great chance to kill the game when Cusiter and Sean Lamont put Kelly Brown away to the line but the try was chalked off for a forward pass. Gradually the momentum began to shift in the Welsh favour and their backs started to find a lot of space. Byrne scored a good try on the 56th minute and diminutive winger Shane Williams saved a certain Scottish try when he took an athletic catch on his own line with two attackers snapping at his heels. Dan Parks, who won the man-of-the-match award, kicked an enormous drop goal on the 65th minute and then Scotland's world collapsed. Substitute Scott Lawson was stupidly sin binned and a rejuvenated Wales laid siege to the Scottish line. With three minutes remaining Shane Williams beat the Scottish defence and set-up Halfpenny down the touchline for a converted try. Then Byrne chipped the ball into space but was tripped by Godman who was sent to the sin bin. Stephen Jones kicked the simple penalty to tie the scores. Blair kicked the restart downfield when he should have put the ball dead and settled for a draw. Wales fought their way into the Scottish 22 and with the Scottish defence in tatters Shane Williams dived under the posts for the winning score. Sometimes this game can break your heart.

588   RBS SIX NATIONS CHAMPIONSHIP 2010   ITALY

Stadio Flaminio, Rome · Saturday 27 February 2010 · Lost 12–16

SCOTLAND Hugo Southwell (*Stade Français*); Simon Danielli (*Ulster*), Max Evans (*Glasgow Wrs*), Graeme Morrison (*Glasgow Wrs*), Sean Lamont (*Scarlets*); Dan Parks (*Glasgow Wrs*), Chris Cusiter* (*Glasgow Wrs*); Allan Jacobsen (*Edinburgh*), Ross Ford (*Edinburgh*), Euan Murray (*Northampton Sts*), Jim Hamilton (*Edinburgh*), Alastair Kellock (*Glasgow Wrs*), Kelly Brown (*Glasgow Wrs*), John Barclay (*Glasgow Wrs*), Johnnie Beattie (*Glasgow Wrs*) ... Substitutes: Mike Blair (*Edinburgh*) for Cusiter (54), Alasdair Strokosch (*Gloucester*) for Beattie (54), Nick De Luca (*Edinburgh*) for Danielli (65), Alasdair Dickinson (*Gloucester*) for Murray (69), Nathan Hines (*Leinster*) for Hamilton (69), Murray for Jacobsen (73)

ITALY Luke McLean (*Treviso*); Andrea Masi (*Racing Métro*), Gonzalo Canale (*Clermont Auv*), Gonzalo Garcia (*Treviso*), Mirco Bergamasco (*Stade Français*); Craig Gower (*Bayonne*), Tito Tebaldi (*Gran Parma*); Salvatore Perugini (*Bayonne*), Leonardo Ghiraldini* (*Treviso*), Martin Castrogiovanni (*Leicester Tgrs*), Quintin Geldenhuys (*Viadana*), Marco Bortolami (*Gloucester*), Josh Sole (*Viadana*), Mauro Bergamasco (*Stade Français*), Alessandro Zanni (*Treviso*) ... Substitutes: Pablo Canavosio (*Viadana*) for Tebaldi (51), Matias Aguero (*Saracens*) for Perugini (69), Kaine Robertson (*Viadana*) for Garcia (69), Carlo Antonio Del Flava (*Viadana*) for Bortolami (69), Fabio Ongarao (*Saracens*) for Ghiraldini (73)

REFEREE Dave Pearson (*England*)

SCORING Mirco Bergamasco, pen (0–3); Mirco Bergamasco, pen (0–6); Parks, pen (3–6); Parks, pen (6–6) (half-time) Mirco Bergamasco, pen (6–9); Parks, drop (9–9); Parks, pen (12–9); Canavosio, try (12–14); Mirco Bergamasco, con (12–16)

Hugo Southwell and Chris Cusiter won their 50th caps. With the wooden spoon beckoning for the loser, this was a tense and unattractive match that only came to life in the closing stages. Playing in spring sunshine, Scotland competed well but once again failed to take their chances. They were unlucky in the first half when Sean Lamont took a quick tap-penalty and raced away to the line only to be recalled because the referee was distracted. In the second half, Jacobsen was twice driven over but video evidence was inconclusive both times. Italy did little in attack until the 66th minute when Canale made a searing break into the 22 and passed to Canavosio who cut-in to the posts and dived over. The Italian defence was firm throughout and easily held out against Scotland's late attempts to save the game. Another disappointing defeat for the Scots for whom the back-row worked tirelessly and Dan Parks again won the man-of-the-match award for his superb kicking and tactical play.

589   RBS SIX NATIONS CHAMPIONSHIP 2010   ENGLAND

Murrayfield · Saturday 13 March 2010 · Drawn 15–15

SCOTLAND Hugo Southwell (*Stade Français*); Sean Lamont (*Scarlets*), Nick De Luca (*Edinburgh*), Graeme Morrison (*Glasgow Wrs*), Max Evans (*Glasgow Wrs*); Dan Parks (*Glasgow Wrs*), Chris Cusiter* (*Glasgow Wrs*); Allan Jacobsen (*Edinburgh*), Ross Ford (*Edinburgh*), Euan Murray (*Northampton Sts*), Jim Hamilton (*Edinburgh*), Alastair Kellock (*Glasgow Wrs*), Kelly Brown (*Glasgow Wrs*), John Barclay (*Glasgow Wrs*), Johnnie Beattie (*Glasgow Wrs*) ... Substitutes: Nathan Hines (*Leinster*) for Hamilton (52), Alan MacDonald (*Edinburgh*) for Brown (55), Rory Lawson (*Gloucester*) for Cusiter (60), Scott Lawson (*Gloucester*) for Ford (65), Simon Danielli (*Ulster*) for Southwell (67), Geoff Cross (*Edinburgh*) for Jacobsen (72), Phil Godman (*Edinburgh*) for Parks (72)

ENGLAND Delon Armitage (*London Irish*); Mark Cueto (*Sale Sharks*), Mathew Tait (*Sale Sharks*), Riki Flutey (*Brive*), Ugo Monye (*Harlequins*); Jonny Wilkinson (Toulon), Danny Care (*Harlequins*); Tim Payne (*London Wasps*), Dylan Hartley (*Northampton Sts*), Dan Cole (*Leicester Tgrs*), Louis Deacon (*Leicester Tgrs*), Steve Borthwick* (*Saracens*), James Haskell (*Stade Français*), Joe Worsley (*London Wasps*), Nick Easter (*Harlequins*) ... Substitutes: Toby Flood (*Leicester Tgrs*) for Wilkinson (44), Ben Foden (*Northampton Sts*) for Armitage (50), Ben Youngs (*Leicester Tgrs*) for Monye (55), Steve Thompson (*Brive*) for Hartley (62), Lewis Moody (*Leicester Tgrs*) for Haskell (62), Courtney Lawes (*Northampton Sts*) for Deacon (74), David Wilson (*Bath*) for Cole (76)

REFEREE Marius Jonker (*South Africa*) · ATTENDANCE 67,114

SCORING Parks, pen (3–0); Wilkinson, pen (3–3); Parks, pen (6–3); Wilkinson, pen (6–6); Parks, drop (9–6) (half-time) Wilkinson, pen (9–9); Flood, pen (9–12); Parks, pen (12–12); Flood, pen (12–15); Parks, pen (15–15)

Dan Parks won his 50th cap, a great achievement for a player who had often struggled for acceptance by the Scottish public and media. Beforehand there was much talk about the anniversary of the famous Grand Slam match in 1990, but in the event this was more like the dour draw in 1989. Play was always interesting and had an enthralling finish, but there was nothing very memorable. Both teams were fully committed and tried to run the ball, but the defences were well on top and neither side looked like scoring a try. Scotland had the better of the first half and should have been further ahead at the interval. In the second half, both sides had spells of pressure but were unable to make the decisive break. Parks twice hit an upright with penalty attempts and in the dying minutes Flood was just short with a long shot at goal. In the final move of the game, Flood attempted a drop goal which was half charged down by Rory Lawson and the ball fell to Morrison who hoofed it into the stand. A draw was probably a fair result. Once again the Scottish back-row was very prominent and Johnnie Beattie was named man-of-the-match for his sterling efforts.

---

590   RBS SIX NATIONS CHAMPIONSHIP 2010   IRELAND

Croke Park, Dublin · Saturday 20 March 2010 · Won 23–20

SCOTLAND Hugo Southwell (*Stade Français*); Sean Lamont (*Scarlets*), Nick De Luca (*Edinburgh*), Graeme Morrison (*Glasgow Wrs*), Max Evans (*Glasgow Wrs*); Dan Parks (*Glasgow Wrs*), Chris Cusiter* (*Glasgow Wrs*); Allan Jacobsen (*Edinburgh*), Ross Ford (*Edinburgh*), Euan Murray (*Northampton Sts*), Jim Hamilton (*Edinburgh*), Alastair Kellock (*Glasgow Wrs*), Kelly Brown (*Glasgow Wrs*), John Barclay (*Glasgow Wrs*), Johnnie Beattie (*Glasgow Wrs*) ... Substitutes: Alan MacDonald (*Edinburgh*) for Brown (26–33, 38–40 & 49–57), Mike Blair (*Edinburgh*) for Cusiter (51), Richie Gray (*Glasgow Wrs*) for Hamilton (52), Alasdair Dickinson (*Gloucester*) for Jacobsen (65), Scott Lawson (*Gloucester*) for Ford (72), Simon Danielli (*Ulster*) for Lamont (73)

IRELAND Geordan Murphy (*Leicester Tgrs*); Tommy Bowe (*Ospreys*), Brian O'Driscoll* (*Leinster*), Gordon D'Arcy (*Leinster*), Keith Earls (*Munster*); Jonathan Sexton (*Leinster*), Tomas O'Leary (*Munster*); Cian Healy (*Leinster*), Rory Best (*Ulster*), John Hayes (*Munster*), Donncha O'Callaghan (*Munster*), Paul O'Connell (*Munster*), Stephen Ferris (*Ulster*), David Wallace (*Munster*), Jamie Heaslip (*Leinster*) ... Substitutes: Rob Kearney (*Leinster*) for Murphy (26), Ronan O'Gara (*Munster*) for Sexton (51), Tony Buckley (*Munster*) for Hayes (79)

REFEREE Jonathan Kaplan (*South Africa*) · ATTENDANCE 80,313

SCORING Parks, pen (3–0); O'Driscoll, try (3–5); Sexton, con (3–7); Beattie, try (8–7); Parks, pen (11–7); Parks, drop (14–7) (half-time) Parks, pen (17–7); Sexton, pen (17–10); Bowe, try (17–15); O'Gara, con (17–17); Parks, pen (20–17); O'Gara, pen (20–20); Parks, pen (23–20)

Played in perfect conditions, this was a vibrant encounter and the outcome was in doubt to the end. Ireland were expected to end their tenure at Croke Park with the Triple Crown, but the Scots spoiled the party. In so doing, Scotland recorded their first win of the 2010 Championship, their first away win in the Championship for four years and their first Championship victory over Ireland since 2001. For once they made the most of their opportunities and had some good fortune along the way. The forwards provided a solid platform and were able to exploit Irish weaknesses at the set-pieces. Dan Parks continued his recent renaissance and once again won the man-of-the-match award. The Scottish stand-off kicked an early penalty before O'Driscoll scored a try for Ireland, albeit with the help of a pass from Sexton that looked forward. Scotland attacked from deep, and Brown and Morrison released Beattie who raced past three defenders to touch down. Parks missed the awkward conversion, but kicked a penalty and a trademark drop goal to give Scotland a 14–7 lead at the interval. Parks added another penalty, but then the match swung towards Ireland and a penalty and a converted try levelled the scores. Parks and O'Gara exchanged penalties to set-up a tense conclusion. A few minutes before the end, Parks sent a long ball deep into the Irish 22 and swift following-up by the Scots forced Kearney to concede a penalty. Parks held his nerve and kicked a magnificent goal from the left touchline, waving his arms in the air as the ball went over. Scotland held on for a famous win that helped compensate for the traumatic finish at Cardiff.

---

591 TOUR OF ARGENTINA 2010 ARGENTINA

Estadio Atletico, Tucuman · Saturday 12 June 2010 · Won 24–16

SCOTLAND Hugo Southwell (*Stade Français*); Max Evans (*Glasgow Wrs*), Nick De Luca (*Edinburgh*), Graeme Morrison (*Glasgow Wrs*), Sean Lamont (*Scarlets*); Dan Parks (*Glasgow Wrs*), Rory Lawson (*Gloucester*); Allan Jacobsen (*Edinburgh*), Ross Ford (*Edinburgh*), Moray Low (*Glasgow Wrs*), Jim Hamilton (*Edinburgh*), Alastair Kellock* (*Glasgow Wrs*), Kelly Brown (*Glasgow Wrs*), John Barclay (*Glasgow Wrs*), Johnnie Beattie (*Glasgow Wrs*) ... Substitutes: Mike Blair (*Edinburgh*) for Lawson (60), Strokosch (*Gloucester*) for Beattie (60), Scott Lawson (*Gloucester*) for Ford (76)

ARGENTINA Martin Rodriguez (*Stade Français*); Lucas Borges (*Albi*), Gonzalo Tiesi (*Harlequins*), Santiago Fernandez (*Montpellier*), Horacio Agulla (*Leicester Tgrs*); Felipe Contepomi*(*Toulon*), Alfredo Lalanne (*London Irish*); Rodrigo Roncero (*Stade Français*), Mario Ledesma (*Clermont Auv*), Martin Scelzo (*Clermont Auv)*, Manuel Carizza (*Biarritz*), Patricio Albacete (*Toulouse*), Genaro Fessia (*Cordoba Ath*), Juan Manuel Leguizamon (*Stade Français*), Juan Martin Fernandez Lobbe (*Toulon*) ... Substitutes: Marcos Ayerza (*Leicester Tgrs*) for Scelzo (44), Lucas Gonzalez-Amorosino (*Leicester Tgrs*) for Borges (47), Mariano Galarza (*La Plata U*) for Carizza (66), Agustin Creevy (*San Luis*) Ledesma (68), Agustin Figuerola (*San Isidro*) for Lalanne (78) ... Yellow card: Leguizamon (39)

REFEREE Dave Pearson (*England*) · **ATTENDANCE** 31,898

SCORING Tiesi, try (0–5); Parks, pen (3–5); Contepomi, pen (3–8); Parks, pen (6–8); Leguizamon, try (6–13); Parks, pen (9–13); Parks, drop (12–13) (half-time) Parks, pen (15–13); Parks, pen (18–13); Parks, drop (21–13); Contepomi, pen (21–16); Parks, pen (24–16)

Following a warm-up match against a Japanese Select xv at Murrayfield, Scotland travelled to Argentina for a two-match series. In the intimidating atmosphere of the Estadio Atletico in Tucuman, where previously Argentina had never lost, the Scots continued where they had left off in Dublin, coming back from early setbacks and onto victory thanks to the steady boot of Dan Parks who scored all of their points. The Scots started poorly and the home side scored early tries by Harlequins centre Gonzalo Tiesi, who finished off a counter-attack from deep, and flanker Juan Manuel Leguizamon, although television replays seemed to show that he had grounded the ball short of the line. The Argentineans looked set to run away with the match, but they conceded a string of penalties which Parks converted to keep Scotland in the hunt. Scotland's best chance to score a try came towards the end of the first-half. After a sweeping move, Sean Lamont dived over at the left corner only for the video referee to rule that he had put his foot in touch. Scotland showed great composure and determination to come through this match and record a win. The forwards battled hard against tough opponents and scrum-half Rory Lawson justified his selection ahead of Mike Blair with an excellent performance.

592   TOUR OF ARGENTINA 2010   ARGENTINA

Estadio Jose Maria Minella, Mar del Plata · Saturday 19 June 2010
Won 13–9

SCOTLAND Hugo Southwell (*Stade Français*); Sean Lamont (*Scarlets*), Max Evans (*Glasgow Wrs*), Graeme Morrison (*Glasgow Wrs*), Simon Danielli (*Ulster*); Dan Parks (*Glasgow Wrs*), Rory Lawson (*Gloucester*); Allan Jacobsen (*Edinburgh*), Ross Ford (*Edinburgh*), Moray Low (*Glasgow Wrs*), Jim Hamilton (*Edinburgh*), Alastair Kellock* (*Glasgow Wrs*), Kelly Brown (*Glasgow Wrs*), John Barclay (*Glasgow Wrs*), Johnnie Beattie (*Glasgow Wrs*) ... Substitutes: Scott MacLeod (*Edinburgh*) for Kellock (50-57 & 65), Alasdair Dickinson (*Gloucester*) for Jacobsen (60), Alasdair Strokosch (*Gloucester*) for Beattie (60), Mike Blair (*Edinburgh*) for R Lawson (67), Scott Lawson (*Gloucester*) for Ford (67), Nick De Luca (*Edinburgh*) for Evans (71)

ARGENTINA Martin Rodriguez (*Stade Français*); Lucas Gonzalez-Amorosino (*Leicester Tgrs*), Gonzalo Tiesi (*Harlequins*), Santiago Fernandez (*Montpellier*), Horacio Agulla (*Leicester Tgrs*); Felipe Contepomi*(*Toulon*), Agustin Figuerola (*San Isidro*); Rodrigo Roncero (*Stade Français*), Mario Ledesma (*Clermont Auv*), Martin Scelzo (*Clermont Auv*), Manuel Carizza (*Biarritz*), Patricio Albacete (*Toulouse*), Genaro Fessia (*Cordoba Ath*), Juan Manuel Leguizamon (*Stade Français*), Juan Martin Fernandez Lobbe (*Toulon*) ... Substitutes: Marcos Ayerza (*Leicester Tgrs*) for Leguizamon (37-47) and Scelzo (74), Alejandro Campos (*Montauban*) for Leguizamon (47), Rafael Carballo (*Bordeaux Begles*) for Contepomi (62), Agustin Creevy (*San Luis*) for Ledesma (65), Santiago Guzman (*Tucuman*) for Carizza (72) ... Yellow card: Roncero (36)

REFEREE Christophe Berdos (*France*) · ATTENDANCE 16,825

SCORING Hamilton, try (5–0); Parks, con (7–0); Contepomi, pen (7–3); Contepomi, pen (7–6); Parks, pen (10–6) (half-time) Rodriguez, pen (10–9); Parks, pen (13–9)

Playing on a sodden pitch and under a grey sky, Scotland created history by winning their first-ever series in the Southern Hemisphere. Argentina had improved from the previous weekend, but the Scots showed plenty of character and resolve. Scotland made a determined start and after only three minutes Jim Hamilton powered over from a lineout near the corner. Argentina hit back with two penalties, but the Scots dominated the first half and would have been further ahead if Parks had not missed several kicks at goal. After the interval, Argentina exerted a lot of pressure but their only reward was a single penalty goal. In a nervous conclusion, the Scots fought out of their own half and five minutes from time Parks kicked a crucial penalty. In the dying moments, Argentina had a lineout near the Scottish line, but substitute Scott MacLeod stole the ball and Blair kicked it away to safety. To put this excellent win into perspective, the following weekend Argentina comprehensively beat France, the Six Nations champions, by a record-breaking 41–13.

Murrayfield · Saturday 13 November 2010 · Lost 3–49

SCOTLAND   Hugo Southwell (*Stade Français*); Rory Lamont (*Toulon*), Max Evans (*Glasgow Wrs*), Graeme Morrison (*Glasgow Wrs*), Sean Lamont (*Scarlets*); Dan Parks (*Cardiff Blues*), Mike Blair* (*Edinburgh*); Allan Jacobsen (*Edinburgh*), Ross Ford (*Edinburgh*), Euan Murray (*Northampton Sts*), Richie Gray (*Glasgow Wrs*), Jim Hamilton (*Gloucester*), Kelly Brown (*Saracens*), John Barclay (*Glasgow Wrs*), Richie Vernon (*Glasgow Wrs*) ... Substitutes: †Greig Laidlaw (*Edinburgh*) for Blair (38), Nathan Hines (*Leinster*) for Hamilton (40), Nikki Walker (*Ospreys*) for R Lamont (40), Alasdair Dickinson (*Gloucester*) for Murray (65), Ross Rennie (*Edinburgh*) for Brown (65), Scott Lawson (*Gloucester*) for Ford (67), †Ruaridh Jackson (*Glasgow Wrs*) for Parks (68)

NEW ZEALAND   Mils Muliaina (*Waikato*); Isaia Toeava (*Auckland*), Conrad Smith (*Wellington*), Sonny Bill Williams (*Canterbury*), Hosea Gear (*Wellington*); Dan Carter (*Canterbury*); Jimmy Cowan (*Southland*); Tony Woodcock (*N Harbour*), Hika Elliot (*Hawkes Bay*), Owen Franks (*Canterbury*), Brad Thorn (*Canterbury*), Sam Whitelock (*Canterbury*), Liam Messam (*Waikato*), Richie McCaw* (*Canterbury*), Kieran Read (*Canterbury*) ... Substitutes: Stephen Donald (*Waikato*) for Carter (50), John Afoa (*Auckland*) for Franks (54), Anthony Boric (*N Harbour*) for Thorn (57), Daniel Braid (Auckland) for McCaw (57), Andy Ellis (*Canterbury*) for Cowan (58), Andrew Hore (*Taranaki*) for Elliot (60)

REFEREE   Dave Pearson (*England*) · ATTENDANCE   56,807

SCORING   Parks, pen (3–0); Gear, try (3–5); Carter, con (3–7); Carter, try (3–12); Carter, con (3–14); Muliaina, try (3–19); Carter, con (3–21); Gear, try (3–26); Carter, con (3–28) (half-time) Muliaina, try (3–33); Carter, con (3–35); Smith, try (3–40); Donald, con (3–42); Ellis, try (3–47); Donald, con (3–49)

The optimism created by the heady wins in Dublin and Argentina disappeared into a black hole. In a one-sided match, Scotland were outclassed by a clinical New Zealand side that scored seven converted tries and posted a record winning margin at Murrayfield. The visitors made everything look deceptively simple with their strong and direct running, and brilliant handling and support play. Scotland worked hard but their attacks were easily contained and at times they were left chasing shadows. Scotland started encouragingly and Parks kicked an early penalty, but New Zealand scored three tries inside the first 20 minutes to effectively end the contest. Winger Hosea Gear scored a fourth when he beat the defence with a simple cutback inside. Just before the interval, Greig Laidlaw, nephew of 1980s scrum-half Roy Laidlaw, replaced Mike Blair to win his first cap. New Zealand scored three more tries in the second half and looked dangerous every time they had the ball. Play ended slightly early when Max Evans was stretchered off the field but his injury was not as serious as first feared. Andy Robinson, Scotland's head coach, pulled no punches: 'We have let the nation down.'

Murrayfield · Saturday 20 November 2010 · Won 21–17

SCOTLAND Hugo Southwell (*Stade Français*); Nikki Walker (*Ospreys*), †Joe Ansbro (*Northampton Sts*), Graeme Morrison (*Glasgow Wrs*), Sean Lamont (*Scarlets*); Dan Parks (*Cardiff Blues*), Rory Lawson* (*Gloucester*); Allan Jacobsen (*Edinburgh*), Ross Ford (*Edinburgh*), Euan Murray (*Northampton Sts*), Scott MacLeod (*Edinburgh*), Richie Gray (*Glasgow Wrs*), Nathan Hines (*Leinster*), John Barclay (*Glasgow Wrs*), Kelly Brown (*Saracens*) ... Substitutes: Richie Vernon (*Glasgow Wrs*) for MacLeod (34), Dougie Hall (*Glasgow Wrs*) for Ford (68), Moray Low (*Glasgow Wrs*) for Murray (68), Chris Paterson (*Edinburgh*) for Walker (73), Ross Rennie (*Edinburgh*) for Brown (78)

SOUTH AFRICA Zane Kirchner (*Blue Bulls*); Gio Apion (*W Province*), Frans Steyn (*Racing Métro*), Jean de Villiers (*W Province*), Lwazi Mvovo (*Sharks*); Morne Steyn (*Blue Bulls*), Francois Hougaard (*Blue Bulls*); Tendai Mtawarira (*Sharks*), Bismarck du Plessis (*Sharks*), Jannie du Plessis (*Sharks*), Bakkies Botha (*Blue Bulls*), Victor Matfield* (*Blue Bulls*), Deon Stegmann (*Blue Bulls*), Juan Smith (*Cheetahs*), Ryan Kankowski (*Sharks*) ... Substitutes: Willem Alberts (*Sharks*) for Smith (20-26) and for Stegman (46), Ruan Pienaar (*Ulster*) for Hougaard (46), Patrick Lambie (*Sharks*) for M Steyn (63), Flip van der Merwe (*Blue Bulls*) for Botha (64), CJ van der Linde (*Cheetahs*) for Mtawarira (71), Adriaan Strauss (*Cheetahs*) for B du Plessis (73)

REFEREE Stuart Dickinson (*Australia*) · **ATTENDANCE** 35,555

SCORING M Steyn, pen (0–3); M Steyn, pen (0–6); Parks, pen (3–6); Parks, drop (6–6); Parks, pen (9–6); Parks, pen (12–6); M Steyn (12–9) (half-time) M Steyn, pen (12–12); Parks, pen (15–12); Parks, pen (18–12); Parks, pen (21–12); Alberts, try (21–17)

Scotland made several changes with Rory Lawson taking over the captaincy and Nathan Hines making his first start at flanker. Northampton centre Joe Ansbro won his first cap as a late replacement for Max Evans. This was a scrappy match played in wet conditions, but Scotland had a point to prove after the All Black humiliation. Despite conceding two early penalties, they led 12-9 at the interval, Dan Parks kicking three penalties and a drop goal. The South Africans tied the scores early in the second half but three more penalties by Parks gave Scotland a nine-point advantage. In the closing stages Alberts scored a simple try from a lineout, but the Scots held onto their narrow lead until the end. Scotland were a transformation from the previous weekend and played with much greater self-belief, tactical awareness and intensity. The forwards gave an immense performance, especially prop Allan Jacobsen, and the defence was well organised. South Africa were unusually error-prone, and looked increasingly frustrated as the weather deteriorated and the crowd got behind the Scots. Amongst several good performances for Scotland, Rory Lawson led by example, Joe Ansbro showed lots of promise, and Richie Vernon was very prominent and had one long run in the second half. The only downside was that Scotland once again failed to score a try. Their best chance came towards the end of the first half when they had a long spell in the South African 22 but were unable to make it count. Not that anybody cared at the final whistle.

Pittodrie Stadium, Aberdeen · Saturday 27 November 2010
Won 19–16

SCOTLAND Hugo Southwell (*Stade Français*); Nikki Walker (*Ospreys*); Joe Ansbro (*Northampton Sts*), Graeme Morrison (*Glasgow Wrs*), Sean Lamont (*Scarlets*); Dan Parks (*Cardiff Blues*), Rory Lawson* (*Gloucester*); Allan Jacobsen (*Edinburgh*), Ross Ford (*Edinburgh*), Euan Murray (*Northampton Sts*), Nathan Hines (*Leinster*), Richie Gray (*Glasgow Wrs*), Kelly Brown (*Saracens*), Richie Vernon (*Glasgow Wrs*), John Barclay (*Glasgow Wrs*) ...
Substitutes: Mike Blair (*Edinburgh*) for Lawson (56), Max Evans (*Glasgow Wrs*) for Ansbro (58), Jim Hamilton (*Gloucester*) for Gray (58), Ruaridh Jackson (*Glasgow Wrs*) for Parks (58), Moray Low (*Glasgow Wrs*) for Murray (58), Dougie Hall (*Glasgow Wrs*) for Ford (74), Ross Rennie (*Edinburgh*) for Vernon (76)

SAMOA Paul Williams (*Sale Sharks*); David Lemi (*London Wasps*), George Pisi (*Taranaki*), Seilala Mapusua (*London Irish*), Alesana Tuilagi (*Leicester Tgrs*); Tasesa Lavea (*Clermont Auv*), Kahn Fotuali'i (*Hawkes Bay*); Sakaria Taulafo (*London Wasps*), Mahonri Schwalger* (*Taranaki*), Cencus Johnston (*Toulouse*), Filipo Levi (*Newcastle F*), Kane Thompson (*Southland*), Ofisa Treviranus (*Malie Sharks*), Manaia Salave's (*Narbonne*), George Stowers (*London Irish*) ...
Substitutes: Anthony Perenise (*Hawkes Bay*) for Johnston (58), Ti'i Paulo (*Clermont Auv*) for Schwalger (60), Joe Tekori (*Castres*) for Thompson (60), Afa Aiono (*Marist*) for Treviranus (66), Fautua Otto (*Scopa*) for Lemi (74), Daniel Leo (*Bordeaux Bègles*) for Salave'a (74)

REFEREE Steve Walsh (*Australia*) · ATTENDANCE 18,290

SCORING Parks, pen (3–0); Fotuali'i, try (3–5); Williams, con (3–7); Walker, try (8–7); Parks, con (10–7); Parks, pen (13–7); Williams, pen (13–10) (half-time) Williams, pen (13–13); Parks, drop (16–13); Williams, pen (16–16); Jackson, pen (19–16)

Sean Lamont and Allan Jacobsen won their 50th caps. On a bitterly cold afternoon with snow lying around the pitch, Scotland were fortunate to escape with a late victory when a draw would have been a fairer result. Dan Parks opened the scoring with an early penalty before Samoan scrum-half Kahn Fotuali'i scored a well-worked try. Scotland replied a few minutes later with a move straight off the training ground. From a scrum near the Samoan line, the ball was whipped into midfield and Nikki Walker ran a perfect angle to score underneath the posts. Parks converted and kicked a penalty to make the score 13–10 at the interval, Williams adding a late penalty for Samoa. In the second half, both sides had periods of pressure, but neither was able to break the defence or maintain any momentum. Parks dropped a goal and Williams kicked two penalties and it seemed that the match would end in stalemate. In the final minute, Scotland won a penalty in the Samoan 22 and substitute Ruaridh Jackson, showing great steadiness, kicked the winning goal.

596   RBS SIX NATIONS CHAMPIONSHIP 2011   FRANCE

Stade de France, Paris · Saturday 5 February 2011 · Lot 21–34

SCOTLAND Hugo Southwell (*Stade Français*); Nikki Walker (*Ospreys*), Joe Ansbro (*Northampton Sts*), Nick De Luca (*Edinburgh*), Max Evans (*Glasgow Wrs*); Dan Parks (*Cardiff Blues*), Rory Lawson (*Gloucester*); Allan Jacobsen (*Edinburgh*), Ross Ford (*Edinburgh*),

Euan Murray (*Newcastle F*), Richie Gray (*Glasgow Wrs*), Alastair Kellock* (*Glasgow Wrs*), Nathan Hines (*Leinster*), John Barclay (*Glasgow Wrs*), Kelly Brown (*Saracens*) ... Substitutes: Mike Blair (*Edinburgh*) for Lawson (h-t), Sean Lamont (*Scarlets*) for De Luca (55), Richie Vernon (*Glasgow Wrs*) for Hines (55), Ross Rennie (*Edinburgh*) for Barclay (62), Ruaridh Jackson (*Glasgow Wrs*) for Parks (69), Moray Low (*Glasgow Wrs*) for Murray (71), Dougie Hall (*Glasgow Wrs*) for Ford (73)

FRANCE Damien Traille (*Biarritz*); Yoann Huget (*Bayonne*), Aurélien Rougerie (*Clermont Auv*), Maxime Mermoz (*Perpignan*), Maxime Médard (*Toulouse*); François Trinh-Duc (*Montpellier*), Morgan Parra (*Clermont Auv*); Thomas Domingo (*Clermont Auv*), William Servat (*Toulouse*), Nicolas Mas (*Perpignan*), Julien Pierre (*Clermont Auv*), Lionel Nallet (*Racing Métro*), Thierry Dusautoir* (*Toulouse*), Julien Bonnaire (*Clermont Auv*), Imanol Harinordoquy (*Biarritz*) ... Substitutes: Clément Poitrenaud (*Toulouse*) for Mermoz (45), Luc Ducalcon (*Castres*) for Mas (52), Dimitri Yachvili (*Biarritz*) for Parra (52), Sébastien Chabal (*Racing Métro*) for Harinordoquy (55), Guilhem Guirado (*Perpignan*) for Servat (58), Jérôme Thion (*Biarritz*) for Nallet (62), Mas for Domingo (69), Vincent Clerc (*Toulouse*) for Médard (74)

REFEREE Wayne Barnes (*England*) · ATTENDANCE 81,337

SCORING Médard, try (0–5); Parra, con (0–7); Trinh-Duc, drop (0–10); Kellock, try (5–10); Parks, con (7–10); penalty try (7–15); Parra, con (7–17) (half-time) Harinordoquy, try (7–22); Yachvili, con (7–24); Brown, try (12–24); Parks, con (14–24); Traille, try (14–29); Parra, con (14–31); Lamont, try (19–31); Jackson, con (21–31); Yachvili, pen (21–34)

In an entertaining encounter, Scotland showed plenty of spirit and competitiveness but they never really looked like overcoming opponents who had more pace and power. The Scottish front-row had a torrid time against a strong French scrum, despite France having the lighter pack. France, the reigning champions, were quick to exploit Scottish errors and three of their tries came from turnovers. It took France only two minutes to open the scoring, Medard running onto a kick ahead after De Luca had been dispossessed near halfway. Parra converted and Trinh-Duc dropped a goal. On the 20th minute, Scotland patiently worked up to the French line and after a couple of drives Kellock burrowed over for a try. Shortly afterwards, France were awarded a penalty try after a series of punishing scrums near the Scottish line. The French showed their sense of adventure when they scored a glorious try on the 54th minute. Taking a slack Scottish kick, Poitrenaud launched a counter-attack from his own 22. Play moved quickly to halfway where Trinh-Duc took a bouncing ball and made an outrageous pass through his legs to Harinordinquy who stepped past two defenders and raced away to the posts. The Scots might easily have let their heads go down, but a few minutes later Kelly Brown burst through some weak defence after a tap-and-go penalty near the French line. Traille responded with a try from a counter-attack and five minutes from the end Sean Lamont broke a tackle and swerved past the defence for a fine solo try. Amongst several good performances, Joe Ansbro had some powerful thrusts in midfield, and Scott Gray was industrious and made two great try-saving tackles in the first half.

Murrayfield · Saturday 12 February 2011 · Lost 6–24

SCOTLAND Hugo Southwell (*Stade Français*); Nikki Walker (*Ospreys*), Joe Ansbro (*Northampton Sts*), Nick De Luca (*Edinburgh*), Max Evans (*Glasgow Wrs*); Dan Parks (*Cardiff Blues*), Rory Lawson (*Gloucester*); Allan Jacobsen (*Edinburgh*), Ross Ford (*Edinburgh*), Euan Murray (*Newcastle F*), Nathan Hines (*Leinster*), Alastair Kellock* (*Glasgow Wrs*), Kelly Brown (*Saracens*), John Barclay (*Glasgow Wrs*), Richie Vernon (*Glasgow Wrs*) ... Substitutes: Sean Lamont (*Scarlets*) for Southwell (20), Mike Blair (*Edinburgh*) for Lawson (47), Moray Low (*Glasgow Wrs*) for Murray (47), Scott Lawson (*Gloucester*) for Ford (67), Ross Rennie (*Edinburgh*) for Barclay (67), Scott MacLeod (*Edinburgh*) for Kellock (71)

WALES Lee Byrne (*Ospreys*); Morgan Stoddart (*Scarlets*), Jamie Roberts (*Cardiff Blues*), Jonathan Davies (*Scarlets*), Shane Williams (*Ospreys*); James Hook (*Ospreys*), Mike Phillips (*Ospreys*); Paul James (*Ospreys*), Matthew Rees* (*Scarlets*), Craig Mitchell (*Ospreys*), Bradley Davies (*Cardiff Blues*), Alun Wyn Jones (*Ospreys*), Dan Lydiate (*NG Dragons*), Sam Warburton (*Cardiff Blues*), Ryan Jones (*Ospreys*) ... Substitutes: Jonathan Thomas (*Ospreys*) for Lydiate (54), Stephen Jones (*Scarlets*) for Hook (66), John Yapp (*Cardiff Blues*) for James (66), Josh Turnbull (*Scarlets*) for Wyn Jones (71), Richard Hibbard (*Ospreys*) for Rees (76), Tavis Knoyle (*Scarlets*) for Phillips (76), Rhys Priestland (*Scarlets*) for Byrne (76) ... Yellow cards: B Davies (23), Byrne (27)

REFEREE George Clancy (*Ireland*) · ATTENDANCE 60,259

SCORING Williams, try (0–5); Hook, con (0–7); Hook, pen (0–10); Hook, pen (0–13); Hook, pen (0–16); Parks, pen (3–16) (half-time) Parks, pen (6–16); Hook, pen (6–19); Williams, try (6–24)

Scotland were a shadow of the side that had done so well in Paris and gave one of their worst performances for some time. Wales made an early flourish and led 16–0 at the end of the first quarter. Scotland lost control of a ball at a scrum inside their own 22, Hook glided through a gap and Williams scored under the posts. Hook converted and then kicked three penalties. The momentum swung to Scotland, but they could only manage two penalties even when Wales were reduced to 13 men. Scotland were desperately poor in attack and made too many errors. The Welshmen took their chances well, but their victory was based largely on a solid defence and their ability to absorb pressure. Towards the finish, Roberts broke away and looked set to score until Lamont cut him down with a superb tackle. Hook added his fourth penalty and then from a Scottish mistake in midfield Jonathan Davies chipped into space for Williams to run on and score his second try unopposed.

Murrayfield · Sunday 27 February 2011 · Lost 18–21

SCOTLAND Chris Paterson (*Edinburgh*); Nikki Walker (*Ospreys*), Nick De Luca (*Edinburgh*), Sean Lamont (*Scarlets*), Max Evans (*Glasgow Wrs*); Ruaridh Jackson (*Glasgow Wrs*), Mike Blair (*Edinburgh*); Allan Jacobsen (*Edinburgh*), Ross Ford (*Edinburgh*), Moray Low (*Glasgow Wrs*), Richie Gray (*Glasgow Wrs*), Alastair Kellock* (*Glasgow Wrs*), Kelly Brown (*Saracens*), John Barclay (*Glasgow Wrs*), Johnnie Beattie (*Glasgow Wrs*) ... Substitutes: Geoff Cross

(Edinburgh) for Beattie (45–54) and for Low (65), Scott Lawson *(Gloucester)* for Ford (54), Dan Parks *(Cardiff Blues)* for Jackson (54), Richie Vernon *(Glasgow Wrs)* for Beattie (54), Rory Lawson *(Gloucester)* for Blair (59), Nathan Hines *(Leinster)* for Barclay (65), Simon Danielli *(Ulster)* for Walker (74) ... Yellow card: Jacobsen (44)

IRELAND   Luke Fitzgerald *(Leinster)*; Tommy Bowe *(Ospreys)*, Brian O'Driscoll* *(Leinster)*, Gordon D'Arcy *(Leinster)*, Keith Earls *(Munster)*; Ronan O'Gara *(Munster)*, Eoin Reddan *(Leinster)*; Cian Healy *(Leinster)*, Rory Best *(Ulster)*, Mike Ross *(Leinster)*, Donncha O'Callaghan *(Munster)*, Paul O'Connell *(Munster)*, Sean O'Brien *(Leinster)*, David Wallace *(Munster)*, Jamie Heaslip *(Leinster)* ... Substitutes: Sean Cronin *(Connacht)* for Best (60), Denis Leamy *(Munster)* for Wallace (60), Peter Stringer *(Munster)* for Reddan (60), Leo Cullen *(Leinster)* for O'Callaghan (65), Jonathan Sexton *(Leinster)* for O'Gara (68), Tom Court *(Ulster)* for Ross (70)

REFEREE   Nigel Owens *(Wales)*   ·   ATTENDANCE 63,082

SCORING Heaslip, try (0–5); O'Gara, con (0–7); Paterson, pen (3–7); Paterson, pen (6–7); Reddan, try (6–12); O'Gara, con (6–14); Paterson, pen (9–14) (half-time) O'Gara, try (9–19); O'Gara, con (9–21); Paterson, pen (12–21); Parks, pen (15–21); Parks, drop (18–21)

There were seven changes after the defeat by Wales, including a first start for Ruaridh Jackson. Playing in perfect conditions, Scotland took the game to their opponents but once again they made too many errors and had no penetration in attack. An experienced Irish side won the try count 3–0 and Scotland only stayed in contention because Ireland gave away too many penalties. The visitors opened the scoring after only six minutes. From a ruck near the Scottish line, hooker Rory Best drew two defenders and passed to Heaslip who jogged over unopposed. O'Gara converted and Chris Paterson replied with two penalties. On the 28th minute, Scotland had to touch down behind their own line and from the ensuing scrum Reddan slipped through for a try at the posts. Paterson reduced the deficit with a penalty but Ireland were in control. Early in the second half, Allan Jacobsen was sin binned for repeated offending at the scrums which gave Ireland a significant boost. After patient build-up play, O'Gara broke a tackle near the line and ran round behind the posts for a try that he also converted. The visitors looked set to run away with it, but slowly Scotland crawled back into contention. Dan Parks replaced Jackson and enlivened the Scottish attack with a succession of accurate kicks. Paterson and Parks kicked penalties, and on the 65th minute Parks dropped a goal to set up a frantic conclusion. Scotland made a rousing effort but Ireland held on for a narrow and deserved victory. For Scotland, Sean Lamont made some powerful thrusts in midfield and a superb try-saving tackle on Tommy Bowe just before the interval. Lock Richie Gray was prominent in the loose and effectively disrupted the Irish lineout.

---

599   RBS SIX NATIONS CHAMPIONSHIP 2011   ENGLAND

Twickenham · Sunday 13 March 2011 · Lost 16–22

SCOTLAND Chris Paterson *(Edinburgh)*; Simon Danielli *(Ulster)*, Joe Ansbro *(Northampton Sts)*, Sean Lamont *(Scarlets)*, Max Evans *(Glasgow Wrs)*; Ruaridh Jackson *(Glasgow Wrs)*, Rory Lawson *(Gloucester)*; Allan Jacobsen *(Edinburgh)*, Ross Ford *(Edinburgh)*, Moray Low *(Glasgow Wrs)*, Richie Gray *(Glasgow Wrs)*, Alastair Kellock* *(Glasgow Wrs)*, Nathan Hines *(Leinster)*, John Barclay *(Glasgow Wrs)*, Kelly Brown *(Saracens)* ... Substitutes: Richie Vernon

(*Glasgow Wrs*) for Brown (43), Geoff Cross (*Edinburgh*) for Low (52), Mike Blair (*Edinburgh*) for Lawson (54), Dan Parks (*Cardiff Blues*) for Jackson (54), Scott Lawson (*Gloucester*) for Ford (65), Alasdair Strokosch (*Gloucester*) for Hines (68), Nick De Luca (*Edinburgh*) for Ansbro (72) ... Yellow card: Barclay (56)

ENGLAND Ben Foden (*Northampton Sts*); Chris Ashton (*Northampton Sts*), Mike Tindall* (*Gloucester*), Shontayne Hape (*Bath*), Mark Cueto (*Sale Sharks*); Toby Flood (*Leicester Tgrs*), Ben Youngs (*Leicester Tgrs*); Alex Corbisiero (*London Irish*), Dylan Hartley (*Northampton Sts*), Dan Cole (*Leicester Tgrs*), Louis Deacon (*Leicester Tgrs*), Tom Palmer (*Stade Français*), Tom Wood (*Northampton Sts*), James Haskell (*Stade Français*), Nick Easter (*Harlequins*) ... Substitutes: Matt Banahan (*Bath*) for Tindall (h-t), Danny Care (*Harlequins*) for Youngs (54), Tom Croft (*Leicester Tgrs*) for Wood (61), Simon Shaw (*London Wasps*) for Deacon (61), Steve Thompson (*Leeds Carnegie*) for Hartley (61), Jonny Wilkinson (*Toulon*) for Flood (61), Paul Doran-Jones (*Gloucester*) for Cole (74)

REFEREE Romain Poite (*France*) replaced by Jérôme Garces (*France*) (58)

ATTENDANCE 82,120

SCORING Paterson, pen (3–0); Flood, pen (3–3); Paterson, pen (6–3); Flood, pen (6–6); Flood, pen (6–9); Jackson, drop (9–9) (half-time) Flood, pen (9–12); Croft, try (9–17); Wilkinson, con (9–19); Evans, try (14–19); Paterson, con (16–19); Wilkinson, pen (16–22)

Scotland had been written-off before this match but they gave a battling performance and made England work hard for their victory. This was an engrossing and physical encounter, and the outcome was never certain. Scotland defended heroically and did not concede a try until the closing 13 minutes. The Scots played with great conviction although the forwards were under a lot of pressure at the set-pieces and England were always dangerous in attack. The sides were locked together 9–9 at half-time. Flood kicked three penalties for England, Paterson two for the Scots and Jackson landed a long drop goal just before the break. Early in the second half, Kelly Brown was stretchered off after being knocked out by England's enormous wing Matt Banahan. Barclay was sent to the sin bin for illegal interference and Flood kicked his fourth penalty. Then referee Romain Poite had to leave the field in obvious agony because of a calf injury. Paterson saved a certain try with a superb tackle of Foden, but on the 67th minute substitute Tom Croft blasted over in the corner for a try converted by Wilkinson. The Scots refused to submit and after some good approach play inside the English 22 Max Evans chipped over the defence, caught the ball on the full and dived over the line. Paterson converted to set up a tense conclusion, but a late penalty by Wilkinson saw England home.

600 RBS SIX NATIONS CHAMPIONSHIP 2011 ITALY

Murrayfield · Saturday 19 March 2011 · Won 21-8

SCOTLAND Chris Paterson (*Edinburgh*); Nikki Walker (*Ospreys*), Joe Ansbro (*Northampton Sts*), Sean Lamont (*Scarlets*), Simon Danielli (*Ulster*); Ruaridh Jackson (*Glasgow Wrs*), Rory Lawson (*Gloucester*); Allan Jacobsen (*Edinburgh*), Ross Ford (*Edinburgh*), Geoff Cross (*Edinburgh*), Richie Gray (*Glasgow Wrs*), Alastair Kellock* (*Glasgow Wrs*), Nathan Hines (*Leinster*), John Barclay (*Glasgow Wrs*), Kelly Brown (*Saracens*) ... Substitutes: Nick De Luca (*Edinburgh*) for Ansbro (19), Alasdair Strokosch (*Gloucester*) for Hines (54),

Mike Blair (*Edinburgh*) for Lawson (64), Scott Lawson (*Gloucester*) for Ford (64), Euan Murray (*Newcastle F*) for Cross (64), Richie Vernon (*Glasgow Wrs*) for Brown (74), Dan Parks (*Cardiff Blues*) for Lamont (78)

ITALY Andrea Masi (*Racing Métro*); Tommaso Benvenuti (*Treviso*), Gonzalo Canale (*Clermont Auv*), Alberto Sgarbi (*Treviso*), Mirco Bergamasco (*Stade Français*); Kristopher Burton (*Treviso*), Fabio Semenzato (*Treviso*); Salvatore Perugini (*Aironi*), Leonardo Ghiraldini (*Treviso*), Martin Castrogiovanni (*Leicester Tgrs*), Carlo Del Fava (*Aironi*), Quintin Geldenhuys (*Aironi*), Alessandro Zanni (*Treviso*), Paul Derbyshire (*Treviso*), Sergio Parisse* (*Stade Français*) ...
Substitutes: Luke McLean (*Treviso*) for Masi (31), Robert Barbieri (*Treviso*) for Derbyshire (54), Valerio Bernabo (*Treviso*) for Del Fava (54), Luciano Orquera (*Brive*) for Burton (54), Andrea Lo Cicero (*Racing Métro*) for Perugini (58), Pablo Canavosio (*Aironi*) for Sgrabi (68), Carlo Festuccia (*Racing Métro*) for Ghiraldini (77)

REFEREE Steve Walsh (*Australia*) · ATTENDANCE 42,464

SCORING Paterson, pen (3–0); Masi, try (3–5); Paterson, pen (6–5); Bergamasco, pen (6–8) (half-time) De Luca, try (11–8); Walker, try (16–8); Paterson, con (18–8); Paterson, pen (21–8)

For once the perennial battle to avoid the wooden spoon provided an entertaining and well contested match that had plenty of enterprise and open play. Italy had unexpectedly beaten France the previous weekend and the two sides were fairly evenly matched, but Scotland deserved to win for their strong showing in the second half. Paterson kicked an early penalty before Italian full-back Andrea Masi hit the line at pace and sprinted over for a fine try. Paterson and Bergamasco exchanged penalties and Italy led 8–6 at the interval. Early in the second half, Scotland managed to score their first try at Murrayfield for 15 months. After some patient build-up play, Nathan Hines gave a perfect offload to substitute Nick De Luca who dived over on the left. Paterson missed the awkward conversion, but a few minutes later he drew the defence to him before unleashing Walker who powered his way to the line. Paterson added the conversion and another penalty to give Scotland a comfortable lead. Italy had a lot of possession in the second half, but the Scottish defence was very sound. Towards the finish, Italian substitute Luke McLean made a superb solo run only to be caught by an equally brilliant cover-tackle by Paterson. In a confident and encouraging display by Scotland, Ruaridh Jackson showed increasing maturity and Richie Gray gave another towering performance in the lineout. Italian No 8 Sergio Parisse also had a fine match.

601　　　　WORLD CUP WARM-UP MATCH　　　　IRELAND

Murrayfield · Saturday 6 August 2011 · Won 10–6

SCOTLAND Chris Paterson (*Edinburgh*); Nikki Walker (*Ospreys*), Joe Ansbro (*London Irish*), Graeme Morrison (*Glasgow Wrs*), Sean Lamont (*Scarlets*); Ruaridh Jackson (*Glasgow Wrs*), Rory Lawson* (*Gloucester*); Allan Jacobsen (*Edinburgh*), Ross Ford (*Edinburgh*), Geoff Cross (*Edinburgh*), Jim Hamilton (*Gloucester*), Richie Gray (*Glasgow Wrs*), Alasdair Strokosch (*Gloucester*), Ross Rennie (*Edinburgh*), Johnnie Beattie (*Glasgow Wrs*) ... Substitutes: †Jack Cuthbert (*Bath*) for Walker (21), †David Denton (*Edinburgh*) for Beattie (58), Alasdair Dickinson (*Sale Sharks*) for Jacobsen (58), Alastair Kellock (*Glasgow Wrs*) for Hamilton (58), Nick De Luca (*Edinburgh*) for Paterson (70), Greig Laidlaw (*Edinburgh*) for Lawson (70), Dougie Hall (*Glasgow Wrs*) for Ford (71)

IRELAND Rob Kearney (*Leinster*); Andrew Trimble (*Ulster*), Fergus McFadden (*Leinster*), Paddy Wallace (*Ulster*), Luke Fitzgerald (*Leinster*); Jonathan Sexton (*Leinster*), Tomas O'Leary (*Munster*); Tom Court (*Ulster*), Sean Cronin (*Leinster*), Tony Buckley (*Sale Sharks*), Donnacha Ryan (*Munster*), Leo Cullen* (*Leinster*), Mike McCarthy (*Connacht*), Niall Ronan (*Munster*), Denis Leamy (*Munster*) ... Substitutes: Kevin McLaughlin (*Leinster*) for Ryan (52), Isaac Boss (*Leinster*) for O'Leary (61), Jerry Flannery (*Munster*) for Cronin (61), John Hayes (*Munster*) for Buckley (61), Marcus Horan (*Munster*) for Court (61), Felix Jones (*Munster*) for Fitzgerald (61), Mick O'Driscoll (*Munster*) for Cullen (61)

REFEREE Wayne Barnes (*England*) · ATTENDANCE 28,288

SCORING Sexton, pen (0–3) (half-time) Paterson, pen (3–3); Sexton, pen (3–6); Ansbro, try (8–6); Jackson, con (10–6)

Kick-off was delayed because of crowd congestion and Scotland wore their new gold-trimmed shirts. This was the first of two warm-up games for the Rugby World Cup and Ireland fielded a largely shadow side. Scotland worked hard and had lots of possession and territory, but once again they failed to make the most of their chances and it was only on the 76th minute that they finally scored a try. From a lineout just inside Irish territory, the ball was moved swiftly right to De Luca who found Ansbro with an exquisite long pass. Going at full tilt, the London Irish centre cut inside the flailing defence for a brilliant score that changed the complexion of the game. Earlier, Jack Cuthbert, the six foot five wing from Bath, and Edinburgh back-rower David Denton won their first caps off the substitutes' bench.

---

602 WORLD CUP WARM-UP MATCH ITALY

Murrayfield · Saturday 20 August 2011 · Won 23–12

SCOTLAND Rory Lamont (*Toulon*); Max Evans (*Castres*), Nick De Luca (*Edinburgh*), Graeme Morrison (*Glasgow Wrs*), Simon Danielli (*Ulster*); Dan Parks (*Cardiff Blues*), Mike Blair (*Edinburgh*); Alasdair Dickinson (*Sale Sharks*), Scott Lawson (*Gloucester*), Moray Low (*Glasgow Wrs*), Nathan Hines (*Clermont Auv*), Alastair Kellock* (*Glasgow Wrs*), Kelly Brown (*Saracens*), John Barclay (*Glasgow Wrs*), Richie Vernon (*Sale Sharks*) ... Substitutes: Euan Murray (*Newcastle F*) for Low (53), Nikki Walker (*Ospreys*) for Danielli (53), Chris Cusiter (*Glasgow Wrs*) for Blair (61), Richie Gray (*Glasgow Wrs*) for Hines (61), Ruaridh Jackson (*Glasgow Wrs*) for Parks (61), Dougie Hall (*Glasgow Wrs*) for Lawson (70), Ross Rennie (*Edinburgh*) for Vernon (75)

ITALY Andrea Masi (*Aironi*); Tommaso Benvenuti (*Treviso*), Gonzalo Canale (*Clermont Auv*), Gonzalo Garcia (*Treviso*), Mirco Bergamasco (*Racing Métro*); Luciano Orquera (*Aironi*), Fabio Semenzato (*Treviso*); Andrea Lo Cicero (*Racing Métro*), Fabio Ongaro (*Aironi*), Martin Castrogiovanni (*Leicester Tgrs*), Carlo del Fava (*Aironi*), Corneilius van Zyl (*Treviso*), Paul Derbyshire (*Treviso*), Robert Barbieri (*Treviso*), Sergio Parisse* (*Stade Français*) ... Substitutes: Tommaso d'Apice (*Aironi*) for Ongaro (40), Joshua Furno (*Aironi*) for Del Fava (50), Riccardo Bocchino (*Aironi*) or Orquera (57), Alessandro Zanni (*Treviso*) for Derbyshire (63), Lorenzo Cittadini (*Treviso*) for Lo Cicero (70), Edoardo Gori (*Treviso*) for Canale (76)

REFEREE D Pearson (*England*) · ATTENDANCE 20,245

SCORING Parks, pen (3–0); Dickinson, try (8–0); Parks, con (10–0); Benvenuti, try (10–5); Bergamasco, con (10–7); Parks, pen (13–7) (half-time) Semenzato, try (13–12); Blair, try (18–12); Parks, con (20–12); Parks, pen (23–12)

Scotland made 14 changes with only centre Graeme Morrison retaining his place in the starting line-up. Playing in the summer sunshine, the Scots were comfortable winners although both teams showed signs of early season rustiness and clearly had work to do before the start of the Rugby World Cup. After an early penalty by Parks, Max Evans made a run to the line and Dickinson was on hand to take the scoring pass. On the 24th minute, Parisse broke from a scrum and the ball was worked to Benvenuti who made an elusive run from his own half for a brilliant solo score. Parks kicked another penalty and early in the second half Semenzato burst through some weak defence to score near the corner. Thoughts of an Italian comeback quickly evaporated when Blair charged down a sloppy clearance and won the race to the touchdown. Parks converted and added a third penalty. The usual raft of substitutions upset the rhythm of the game and there was no further scoring. This was a satisfactory display by Scotland although near the finish Nikki Walker was stretchered off with a knee injury which ruled him out of the World Cup.

Rugby World Cup 2011

In 2011, the Rugby World Cup returned to New Zealand where the inaugural tournament had been held 24 years earlier. The competition was well organised and had some thrilling encounters although it was clear that New Zealand were in a class of their own and probable winners from the start. Once again 20 teams competed in four pools of five. Scotland were drawn in Pool B and faced England, Argentina, Romania and Georgia, a rising power in world rugby and a team that the Scots had never played before. This was a tough group for Scotland and they would have to play at their best to qualify from it.

603   RUGBY WORLD CUP 2011   ROMANIA

Rugby Park Stadium, Invercargill · Saturday 10 September 2011
Won 34–24

SCOTLAND Chris Paterson (*Edinburgh*); Max Evans (*Castres*), Joe Ansbro (*London Irish*), Sean Lamont (*Scarlets*), Simon Danielli (*Ulster*); Ruaridh Jackson (*Glasgow Wrs*), Mike Blair (*Edinburgh*); Allan Jacobsen (*Edinburgh*), Ross Ford (*Edinburgh*), Geoff Cross (*Edinburgh*), Richie Gray (*Glasgow Wrs*), Alastair Kellock* (*Glasgow Wrs*), Kelly Brown (*Saracens*), John Barclay (*Glasgow Wrs*), Richie Vernon (*Sale Sharks*) ... Substitutes: Nathan Hines (*Clermont Auv*) for Gray (52), Dan Parks (*Cardiff Blues*) for Jackson (52), Chris Cusiter (*Glasgow Wrs*) for Blair (61), Alasdair Dickinson (*Sale Sharks*) for Jacobsen (61), Ross Rennie (*Edinburgh*) for Barclay (61), Scott Lawson (*Gloucester*) for Ford (68)

ROMANIA Iulian Dumitras (*Lourdes*); Stefan Ciuntu (*Baia Mare*), Csaba Gal (*Baia Mare*), Ionut Dimofte (*Baia Mare*), Madalin Lemnaru (*Timisoara*); Dan Dumbrava (*Steaua*), Lucian Sirbu (*Millau*); Mihai Lazar (*Aix-en-Provence*), Marius Tincu* (*Perpignan*), Paulica Ion (*London Irish*), Valentin Ursache (*Aix-en-Provence*), Cristian Petre (*Saint-Étienne*), Mihai Macovei (*Baia Mare*), Ovidiu Tonita (*Perpignan*), Daniel Carpo (*Farul Constanta*) ... Substitutes: Ionel Cazan (*Steaua*) for Dumbrava (51), Florin Surugiu (*CSM Bucuresti*) for Sirbu (51), Florin Vlaicu (*Steaua*) for Dumitras (58), Silviu Florea (*Bordeaux Bègles*) for Ion (67), Bodgan Suman (*Steaua*) for

Tincu (67), Stelian Burcea (*Timisoara*) for Macovei (76), Valentin Poparlan (*CSM Bucuresti*) for Petre (78)

REFEREE Dave Pearson (*England*) · **ATTENDANCE** 12,592

SCORING Paterson, pen (3–0); Blair, try (8–0); Dumbrava, pen (8–3); Ansbro, try (13–3); Paterson, con (15–3); Dumbrava, pen (15–6); Paterson, pen (18–6); Lazar, try (18–11) (half-time) Paterson, pen (21–11); Dimofte, pen (21–14); Dimofte, pen (21–17); Carpo, try (21–22); Dimofte, con (21–24); Paterson, pen (24–24); Danielli, try (29–24); Danielli, try (34–24)

Scotland's tournament kicked-off against Romania in Invercargill, one of the southern-most cities in the world. Scotland were expected to win but Romania came dange-rously close to an upset and it was only a late brace of tries by Simon Danielli that decided the issue. Scotland started confidently and after an early Paterson penalty Mike Blair skipped through the defence and ran away to the posts. Strangely Paterson missed the simple conversion as the ball slipped off the kicking tee just as he was about to strike it. Dumbrava kicked a penalty before Ansbro beat four defenders inside the Romanian 22 for a fine solo effort and Paterson converted. The big Romanian forwards started to assert themselves, and just before half-time they made an unstoppable surge to the line and Lazar scored a try. In the second half, Scotland were under a lot of pressure and they made too many errors. With 14 minutes left the Romanians drove a five-metre scrum over the Scottish line and gigantic No 8 Carpo touched down. Scotland kept their composure and Paterson kicked a penalty to level the scores. Towards the finish Vernon made a long run up the left and Danielli was on hand to finish a great try. A few minutes later Danielli scored again after a fine Scottish movement. This was a close shave for Scotland and the Romanians were a lot better than expected. Their forwards were immense and hooker Marius Tincu won the man-of-the-match for an inspiring display.

---

604 RUGBY WORLD CUP 2011 GEORGIA

Rugby Park Stadium, Invercargill · Wednesday 14 September 2011
Won 15–6

SCOTLAND Rory Lamont (*Toulon*); Max Evans (*Castres*), Nick De Luca (*Edinburgh*), Graeme Morrison (*Glasgow Wrs*), Sean Lamont (*Scarlets*); Dan Parks (*Cardiff Blues*), Rory Lawson* (*Gloucester*); Allan Jacobsen (*Edinburgh*), Ross Ford (*Edinburgh*), Euan Murray (*Newcastle F*), Nathan Hines (*Clermont Auv*), Jim Hamilton (*Gloucester*), Alasdair Strokosch (*Gloucester*), Ross Rennie (*Edinburgh*), Kelly Brown (*Saracens*) ... Substitutes: Richie Gray (*Glasgow Wrs*) for Hines (70), Chris Paterson (*Edinburgh*) for R Lamont (70)

GEORGIA Revaz Gigauri (*Figeac*); Irakli Machkhaneli (*Macon*), David Kacharava (*Nice*), Tedo Zibzibadze (*Perigueux*), Sandro Todua (*Lelo*); Merab Kvirikashvili (*Figeac*), Irakli Abuseridze* (*Auxerre*); David Khinchagishvili (*Brive*), Jaba Bregvadze (*Army*), David Zirakashvili (*Clermont Auv*), Levan Datunashvili (*Aurillac*), Vakhtang Maisuradze (*US Seynoise*), Shavla Sutiashvili (*Massy*), Mamuka Gorgodze (*Montpellier*), Dimitri Basilaia (*Aubenas Vals*) ... Substitutes: Giorgi Chkhaidze (*Montpellier*) for Maisuradze (49), David Kubriashvili (*Toulon*) for Zirakashvili (55), Akvsenti Giorgadze (*Castres*) for Bregvadze (64), Viktor Kolelishvili (*Clermont Auv*) for Basilaia (64), Malkhaz Urjukashvili (*Gourdon*) for Todua (66)

SCORING Kvirikashvili, pen (0–3); Parks, pen (3–3); Parks, pen (6–3); Parks, drop (9–3) (half-time) Parks, pen (12–3); Kvirikashvili, pen (12–6); Parks, pen (15–6)

Scotland made ten changes from the side that had struggled against Romania. Georgia were coached by the former Scotland B player Richie Dixon and were expected to provide a formidable physical challenge, but the Scots met them head-on. Played in heavy rain, this was an uncompromising trial of strength between two monstrous forward packs. Neither side came close to scoring a try but Scotland were satisfied with the outcome and were more emphatic winners than the score suggests. The Scottish forwards won the battle up-front and the scrum was very solid. The Scots tackled very well and made several promising breaks. Georgia took an early lead but were never allowed to develop any momentum and they conceded too many penalties. Scotland made plenty of errors in the wet conditions but they always had the game in their hands.

---

605 ## RUGBY WORLD CUP 2011 ARGENTINA

Wellington Regional Stadium · Sunday 25 September 2011

Lost 12–13

SCOTLAND Chris Paterson (*Edinburgh*); Max Evans (*Castres*), Nick De Luca (*Edinburgh*), Graeme Morrison (*Glasgow Wrs*), Sean Lamont (*Scarlets*); Ruaridh Jackson (*Glasgow Wrs*), Rory Lawson* (*Gloucester*); Allan Jacobsen (*Edinburgh*), Ross Ford (*Edinburgh*), Geoff Cross (*Edinburgh*), Richie Gray (*Glasgow Wrs*), Jim Hamilton (*Gloucester*), Alasdair Strokosch (*Gloucester*), John Barclay (*Glasgow Wrs*), Kelly Brown (*Saracens*) ... Substitutes: Nathan Hines (*Clermont Auv*) for Gray (56), Mike Blair (*Edinburgh*) for Lawson (60), Alasdair Dickinson (*Sale Sharks*) for Jacobsen (60), Dougie Hall (*Glasgow Wrs*) for Ford (69), Dan Parks (*Cardiff Blues*) for Jackson (69), Jacobsen for Cross (73), Richie Vernon (*Sale Sharks*) for Brown (78)

ARGENTINA Martín Rodríguez (*Stade Français*); Gonzalo Camacho (*Exeter Chiefs*), Marcelo Bosch (*Biarritz*), Felipe Contepomi* (*Stade Français*), Horacio Agulla (*Leicester Tgrs*); Santiago Fernández (*Montpellier*), Nicolás Vergallo (*Toulouse*); Rodrigo Roncero (*Stade Français*), Mario Ledesma (*Clermont Auv*), Juan Figallo (*Montpellier*), Manu Carizza (*Biarritz*), Pato Albacete (*Toulouse*), Julio Farías Cabello (*Tucumán*), Juan Manuel Leguizamón (*Lyon*), Juan Martín Fernández Lobbe (*Toulon*) ... Substitutes: Genaro Fessia (*Cordoba Ath*) for Fernández Lobbe (30), Martin Scelzo (*Agen*) for Roncero (36), Lucas Amorosino (*Montpellier*) for Rodríguez (68), Agustin Creevy (*Montpellier*) for Ledesma (68)

REFEREE Wayne Barnes (*England*) · ATTENDANCE 26,937

SCORING Contepomi, pen (0–3); Paterson, pen (3–3); Jackson, pen (6–3) (half-time) Contepomi, pen (6–6); Jackson, drop (9–6); Parks, drop (12–6); Amorosino, try (12–11); Contepomi, con (12–13)

England were in a strong position to win Group B and this match was likely to decide who would join them in the knock-out stages. Scotland left out their squad captain Alastair Kellock and played Ruaridh Jackson at stand-off. Prop Euan Murray was unavailable because of his religious convictions. Conditions in the Wellington 'Cake Tin' were difficult with heavy rain starting just after kick-off and turning into a storm at one stage. Although not a free-flowing spectacle, this was an engrossing match that was played on a knife-edge and the outcome was only decided by a piece of individual brilliance towards the end. Scotland's best chance came short after the interval. Max Evans kicked into space and gathered the rebound, Barclay carried on and Lawson made a sniping run, but the ball was lost in contact and the Argentineans cleared. Contepomi kicked a penalty on the 64th minute and then Jackson, who won the man-of-the-match award, dropped a goal. Dan Parks replaced Jackson and within a few minutes he also dropped a goal. Scotland seemed to have built a winning platform, but straight from the restart Argentinean substitute Lucas Amorosino cut inside three defenders for a great solo score. Contepomi held his nerve and kicked the vital conversion to give Argentina a single point lead. Scotland still had time to set up Parks for a drop goal attempt but, under severe pressure from the defence, several of whom had clearly crept offside, his left-footed effort went wide. Scotland could easily have won this match but failed to finish off their opponents when they had the chance. The Argentineans never let their heads go down, despite losing No8 Fernández Lobbe and prop Roncero, two of their most important players, to injury in the first half.

---

606   RUGBY WORLD CUP 2011   ENGLAND

Eden Park, Auckland · Saturday 1 October 2011 · Lost 12–16

SCOTLAND Chris Paterson (*Edinburgh*); Max Evans (*Castres*), Joe Ansbro (*London Irish*), Sean Lamont (*Scarlets*), Simon Danielli (*Ulster*); Ruaridh Jackson (*Glasgow Wrs*), Mike Blair (*Edinburgh*), Allan Jacobsen (*Edinburgh*), Ross Ford (*Edinburgh*), Euan Murray (*Newcastle F*), Richie Gray (*Glasgow Wrs*), Alastair Kellock* (*Glasgow Wrs*), Alasdair Strokosch (*Gloucester*), John Barclay (*Glasgow Wrs*), Richie Vernon (*Sale Sharks*) ... Substitutes: Dan Parks (*Cardiff Blues*) for Jackson (5), Nick De Luca (*Edinburgh*) for Evans (h-t), Nathan Hines (*Clermont Auv*) for Strokosch (62), Ross Rennie (*Edinburgh*) for Barclay (62), Alasdair Dickinson (*Gloucester*) for Jacobsen (66), Chris Cusiter (*Glasgow Wrs*) for Balir (71)

ENGLAND Ben Foden (*Northampton Sts*); Chris Ashton (*Northampton Sts*), Manu Tuilagi (*Leicester Tgrs*), Mike Tindall (*Gloucester*), Delon Armitage (*London Irish*); Jonny Wilkinson (*Toulon*), Ben Youngs (*Gloucester*); Matt Stevens (*Saracens*), Steve Thompson (*London Wasps*), Dan Cole (*Leicester Tgrs*), Louis Deacon (*Leicester Tgrs*), Courtney Lawes (*Northampton Sts*), Tom Croft (*Leicester Tgrs*), Lewis Moody* (*Bath*), James Haskell (*Ricoh Black Rams*) ... Substitutes: Tom Palmer (*Stade Français*) for Lawes (56), Nick Easter (*Harlequins*) for Moody (52-62) and Haskell (62), Dylan Hartley (*Northampton Sts*) for Thompson (66), Toby Flood (*Leicester Tgrs*) for Tindall (70), Alex Corbisiero (*London Irish*) for Stevens (71), Richard Wigglesworth (*Saracens*) for Youngs (72), Matt Banahan (*Bath*) for Wilkinson (74)

REFEREE Craig Joubert (*South Africa*) · ATTENDANCE 58,213

SCORING Paterson, pen (3–0); Parks, pen (6–0); Wilkinson, pen (6–3); Parks, drop (9–3) (half-time) Paterson, pen (12–3); Wilkinson, drop (12–6); Wilkinson, pen (12–9); Ashton, try (12–14); Flood, con (12–16)

Scotland made seven changes from the team that had lost to Argentina. There were numerous permutations about who would qualify from the group but essentially Scotland had to win by more than seven points and deny England a bonus point. Like the previous weekend, the Scots threw in everything and got themselves into a winning position only to have their hearts broken by a dramatic late try. This was not a pretty game but it was completely engrossing and could not have been any closer. Scotland had by far the better of the first half despite losing stand-off Ruaridh Jackson with a pulled muscle inside the opening five minutes. They played with great urgency and intensity, and the forwards held the upper-hand at the set-piece. Paterson and Parks kicked penalties, the second of which, a huge effort by Parks, was referred to the television match official before being awarded. The normally reliable Wilkinson missed three kicks in succession before putting over his fourth attempt and on the stroke of half-time Parks dropped a goal. In the second half, the momentum swung towards England and they were able to bring on some top quality substitutes. The Scots were forced onto the defensive and had only two half-chances to score tries. First, Danielli broke up the left touchline and chipped past the defence, but substitute De Luca, following-up fast, fumbled the ball forward with the line beckoning although the defence probably had him covered. Then a clever cross-kick by Parks landed in the English goal area but Croft just beat the chasing Gray to the touchdown. Paterson kicked a penalty on the 55th minute to put Scotland 12–3 in front, but from the restart Wilkinson responded with a drop goal and five minutes later kicked a penalty to set-up a tense finale. With minutes remaining, Scotland had a promising position and Parks opted for an up-and-under to the English posts, but the defence stood firm. Then England snatched their opportunity. The forwards rumbled towards the line stretching the Scottish defence, the ball was moved right and Flood floated a long pass to Ashton who scored in the corner. Flood converted from the touchline and Scotland had no time to respond. A few hours later, Argentina beat Georgia (25–7) to take second spot in the group and for the first time Scotland had failed to make the knock-out stages of the World Cup. Scotland's passion and commitment could not be faulted and they had come agonisingly close to qualification from a tough group, but they were undone by their perennial inability to consolidate a winning position and to score enough tries.

607 RBS SIX NATIONS CHAMPIONSHIP 2012   ENGLAND

Murrayfield · Saturday 4 February 2012 · Lost 6–13

SCOTLAND Rory Lamont (*Glasgow Wrs*); †Lee Jones (*Edinburgh*), Nick De Luca (*Edinburgh*), Sean Lamont (*Scarlets*), Max Evans (*Castres*); Dan Parks (*Cardiff Blues*), Chris Cusiter (*Glasgow Wrs*); Allan Jacobsen (*Edinburgh*), Ross Ford* (*Edinburgh*), Euan Murray (*Newcastle F*), Richie Gray (*Glasgow Wrs*), Jim Hamilton (*Gloucester*), Alasdair Strokosch (*Gloucester*), Ross Rennie (*Edinburgh*), David Denton (*Edinburgh*) … Substitutes: John Barclay (*Glasgow Wrs*) for Strokosch (58), Mike Blair (*Edinburgh*) for Cusiter (58), Greig Laidlaw (*Edinburgh*) for Parks (58), Alastair Kellock (*Glasgow Wrs*) for Hamilton (58), Geoff Cross (*Edinburgh*) for Jacobsen (75), Scott Lawson (*Gloucester*) for Ford (75)

ENGLAND Ben Foden (*Northampton Sts*); Chris Ashton (*Northampton Sts*), Brad Barritt (*Saracens*), Owen Farrell (*Saracens*), David Strettle (*Saracens*); Charlie Hodgson (*Saracens*), Ben Youngs (*Leicester Tgrs*); Alex Corbisiero (*London Irish*), Dylan Hartley (*Northampton Sts*), Dan Cole (*Leicester Tgrs*), Mouritz Botha (*Saracens*), Tom Palmer (*Stade Français*), Tom Croft (*Leicester Tgrs*), Chris Robshaw* (*Harlequins*), Phil Dowson (*Northampton Sts*) … Substitutes:

Dan Parks, 67 caps 2004–2012. *Scotsman Publications Ltd*

Geoff Parling (*Leicester Tgrs*) for Palmer (57), Lee Dickson (*Northampton Sts*) for Youngs (63), Matt Stevens (*Saracens*) for Corbisiero (63), Jordan Turner-Hall (*Harlequins*) for Hodgson (63), Ben Morgan (*Scarlets*) for Dowson (68), Mike Brown (*Harlequins*) for Barritt (71)

REFEREE George Clancy (*Ireland*) · **ATTENDANCE** 67,144

SCORING Farrell, pen (0–3); Parks, pen (3–3); Parks, pen (6–3) (half-time) Hodgson, try (6–8); Farrell, con (6–10); Farrell, pen (6–13)

With the Rugby World Cup over, there was huge expectation about this match and Scotland fancied their chances against a new-look England. The Scots worked hard and dominated for long periods, but once again they failed to take their chances and lost a game that they should have won. Played under floodlights on a cold evening, Scotland were surprisingly slow to get into their stride and on the 22nd minute Owen Farrell, England's new centre, kicked a penalty after a Scottish defensive mix-up. Scotland responded with two Parks penalties for a 6–3 lead at the interval. A few seconds after the restart, Hodgson charged down a clearance on the Scottish line and scored a giveaway try. From then on Scotland had plenty of possession and territory, but they made too many errors and lacked inventiveness. On the hour mark substitute Greig Laidlaw made a chip-and-chase over the English line, but was just been beaten to the touchdown. A few minutes later, Rennie broke clear with two runners in close support but he delayed his pass fractionally long and it was knocked backwards by Foden. England always looked comfortable in defence and crucially didn't concede penalties when under pressure. They produced little in attack but narrowly missed a second try when Strettle took a cross-field kick only to be caught by Denton who made a superb cover tackle. Both sides grew tired as the game wound down and in the 74th minute Farrell kicked a second penalty. A few days later, Dan Parks, who had experienced many ups-and-downs in his career, announced his retirement from international rugby.

Millennium Stadium, Cardiff · Sunday 12 February 2012
Lost 13–27

SCOTLAND Rory Lamont (*Glasgow Wrs*); Lee Jones (*Edinburgh*), Nick De Luca (*Edinburgh*), Sean Lamont (*Scarlets*), Max Evans (*Castres*); Greig Laidlaw (*Edinburgh*), Chris Cusiter (*Glasgow Wrs*); Allan Jacobsen (*Edinburgh*), Ross Ford* (*Edinburgh*), Geoff Cross (*Edinburgh*), Richie Gray (*Glasgow Wrs*), Jim Hamilton (*Gloucester*), Alasdair Strokosch (*Gloucester*), Ross Rennie (*Edinburgh*), David Denton (*Edinburgh*) ... Substitutes: †Stuart Hogg (*Glasgow Wrs*) for Evans (15), John Barclay (*Glasgow Wrs*) for Strokosch (44), Mike Blair (*Edinburgh*) for Cusiter (48), †Ed Kalman (*Glasgow Wrs*) for Cross (57), Alastair Kellock (*Glasgow Wrs*) for Hamilton (57), Scott Lawson (*Gloucester*) for Ford (71) ... Yellow cards: De Luca (45), R Lamont (54)

WALES Leigh Halfpenny (*Cardiff Blues*); Alex Cuthbert (*Cardiff Blues*), Jonathan Davies (*Scarlets*), Jamie Roberts (*Cardiff Blues*), George North (*Scarlets*); Rhys Priestland (*Scarlets*), Mike Phillips (*Bayonne*); Gethin Jenkins (*Cardiff Blues*), Huw Bennett (*Ospreys*), Adam Jones (*Ospreys*), Ryan Jones* (*Ospreys*), Ian Evans (*Ospreys*), Dan Lydiate (*Dragons*), Aaron Shingler (*Scarlets*), Toby Faletau (*N-G Dragons*) ... Substitutes: Ken Owens (*Scarlets*) for Bennett (9–18 and 41), James Hook (*Perpignan*) for North (39), Paul James (*Ospreys*) for A Jones (72), Andy Powell (*Sale Sharks*) for Lydiate (72), Lou Reed (*Scarlets*) for R Jones (74), Lloyd Williams (*Cardiff Blues*) for Phillips (74), Scott Williams (*Scarlets*) for Roberts (77) ... Yellow card: Jenkins (77)

REFEREE Romain Poite (*France*) · **ATTENDANCE** 73,189

SCORING Laidlaw, pen (3–0); Halfpenny, pen (3–3) (half-time) Cuthbert, try (3–8); Halfpenny, con (3–10); Halfpenny, pen (3–13); Laidlaw, pen (6–13); Halfpenny, try (6–18); Halfpenny, con (6–20); Halfpenny, try (6–25); Halfpenny, con (6–27); Laidlaw, try (11–27); Laidlaw, con (13–27)

Greig Laidlaw made his first start at stand-off. Wales were hot favourites and deserved to win by virtue of their strong-running back line. And yet Scotland outplayed them for much of the game apart from a disastrous spell after the interval when they lost two men in quick succession to the sin bin and conceded 24 points in only 16 minutes. Playing under the Millennium Stadium roof, this was splendid match between two committed sides. The defences were on top in the first half as both teams tried to soften each other up. After 15 minutes, Max Evans was replaced by new cap Stuart Hogg who went on to have an encouraging debut. Scotland had a long spell of pressure just before the interval, but Jacobsen knocked-on near the line and the chance was lost. Scotland made a dreadful start to the second half. The defence was caught napping at the kick-off and Cusiter inadvertently knocked the ball into touch inside the Scottish 22. Wales took the lineout and made a series of charges before Alex Cuthbert, the 16 stone wing, brushed off a tackle to score a try. Worse was to follow when a promising attack broke down, Wales hacked through and De Luca was sent to the sin bin for making an early tackle on his opposite number. Halfpenny and Laidlaw exchanged penalties and then Halfpenny exposed Scotland's weakened defence for a try. A few minutes later, Rory Lamont was yellow-carded for an illegal tackle and Halfpenny score a simple blindside try from a scrum. Halfpenny kicked a fine conversion and in a matter of minutes the game was as good as over. Scotland might easily have collapsed but showed great character to make a comeback. Hogg knocked-on with the line at his mercy and a minute later Laidlaw forced the ball over at close range. There was no further scoring as fatigue took its toll on both sides. For Scotland, David Denton and Ross Rennie were outstanding and newcomer Stuart Hogg had some electrifying runs.

609   RBS SIX NATIONS CHAMPIONSHIP 2012   FRANCE

Murrayfield · Sunday 26 February 2012 · Lost 17–23

SCOTLAND Stuart Hogg (*Glasgow Wrs*); Rory Lamont (*Glasgow Wrs*), Sean Lamont (*Scarlets*), Graeme Morrison (*Glasgow Wrs*), Lee Jones (*Edinburgh*); Greig Laidlaw (*Edinburgh*), Mike Blair (*Edinburgh*); Allan Jacobsen (*Edinburgh*), Ross Ford* (*Edinburgh*), Geoff Cross (*Edinburgh*), Richie Gray (*Glasgow Wrs*), Jim Hamilton (*Gloucester*), John Barclay (*Glasgow Wrs*), Ross Rennie (*Edinburgh*), David Denton (*Edinburgh*) ... Substitutes: Chris Cusiter (*Glasgow Wrs*) for Blair (30), Nick De Luca (*Edinburgh*) for R Lamont (30); †Duncan Weir (*Glasgow Wrs*) for Laidlaw (48), Richie Vernon (*Sale Sharks*) for Denton (53), Ed Kalman (*Glasgow Wrs*) for Cross (62), Alastair Kellock (*Glasgow Wrs*) for Hamilton (68), Scott Lawson (*Gloucester*) for Ford (69)

FRANCE Maxime Médard (*Toulouse*); Vincent Clerc (*Toulouse*), Aurélien Rougerie (*Clermont Auv*), Wesley Fofana (*Clermont Auv*), Julien Malzieu (*Clermont Auv*); François Trinh-Duc (*Montpellier*), Morgan Parra (*Clermont Auv*); Jean-Baptiste Poux (*Toulouse*), Dimitri Szarzewski (*Stade Français*), Nicolas Mas (*Perpignan*), Pascal Papé (*Stade Français*), Yoan Maestri (*Toulouse*), Thierry Dusautoir* (*Toulouse*), Imanol Harinordoquy (*Biarritz*), Louis Picamoles (*Toulouse*) ... Substitutes: Vincent Debaty (*Clermont Auv*) for Poux (51), William Servat (*Toulouse*) for Szarzewski (51), Julien Bonnaire (*Clermont Auv*) for Picamoles (59), Lionel Beauxis (*Toulouse*) for Médard (62), Lionel Nallet (*Racing Métro*) for Maestri (66), Julien Dupuy (*Stade Français*) for Parra (75)

REFEREE Wayne Barnes (*England*) · ATTENDANCE 67,144

SCORING Hogg, try (5–0); Laidlaw, con (7–0); Laidlaw, pen (10–0); Fofana, try (10–5); Parra, con (10–7); Parra, pen (10–10) (half-time) Parra, pen (10–13); Jones, try (15–13); Weir, con (17–13); Médard, try (17–18); Parra, con (17–20); Beauxis, drop (17–23)

In perfect conditions and in front of a full house, this was an entertaining and intense match between two sides that were eager to run the ball. Scotland scored two well-taken tries and showed signs of improvement, but France, the World Cup finalists, did enough to win the match without being at their best. The Scots started in whirlwind fashion and on the seventh minute Hogg dived over in the right-hand corner and Laidlaw converted from the touchline. Both sides had some promising breaks but they were unable to finish them off. Laidlaw kicked a penalty on the 25th minute and three minutes later France scored their first try. From a lineout inside the Scottish 22, Trinh-Duc pushed off a tackle to make an opening for Fofana whose clever angle of running took him over the line. Scotland then lost Rory Lamont and

Mike Blair to leg injuries, and the momentum swung towards the French. Parra kicked a penalty to level the scores and missed a second on the stroke of half-time. Scotland avoided the disastrous restart that had cost them so dearly against England and Wales, but after five minutes Parra kicked a penalty. Scotland were unlucky to lose their playmaker Greig Laidlaw with concussion and Duncan Weir came on for his first cap. On the 55th minute, Barclay stole possession near halfway and fed De Luca who put Vernon away on a sprint to the corner. The big No 8 could probably have scored himself but he passed to Jones who raced over for a try. Scotland needed to consolidate, but two minutes later France attacked from their own half, Malzieu beat a weak tackle and gave Médard a clear run-in from the 22. Hogg raised Scottish hopes with a brilliant step and break but he had the ball knocked out of his hands inside the French 22. The French forwards became more dominant as the game wore on, Beauxis dropped a goal with 12 minutes remaining and the exhausted Scots could not raise themselves for one last effort. France were the better side and gradually had been able to impose themselves, but Scotland had given them plenty to think about. Amongst several good performances, Hogg was a dangerous runner and the back-row were outstanding with Ross Rennie winning the man-of-the-match award. Substitute Nick De Luca had been dropped after the Welsh match and suffered some personal abuse from so-called supporters, but he responded with a fine all-round display that made his critics eat their words.

610   RBS SIX NATIONS CHAMPIONSHIP 2012   IRELAND

Aviva Stadium, Dublin · Saturday 10 March 2012 · Lost 14–32

SCOTLAND Stuart Hogg (*Glasgow Wrs*); Lee Jones (*Edinburgh*), Max Evans (*Castres*), Graeme Morrison (*Glasgow Wrs*), Sean Lamont (*Scarlets*); Greig Laidlaw (*Edinburgh*), Mike Blair (*Edinburgh*); Allan Jacobsen (*Edinburgh*), Ross Ford* (*Edinburgh*), Geoff Cross (*Edinburgh*), Richie Gray (*Glasgow Wrs*), Jim Hamilton (*Gloucester*), John Barclay (*Glasgow Wrs*), Ross Rennie (*Edinburgh*), David Denton (*Edinburgh*) … Substitutes: Euan Murray (*Newcastle F*) for Cross (46), Chris Cusiter (*Glasgow Wrs*) for Blair (50), Ruaridh Jackson (*Glasgow Wrs*) for Laidlaw (56), Alastair Kellock (*Glasgow Wrs*) for Hamilton (59), Richie Vernon (*Sale Sharks*) for Rennie (59), †Matt Scott (*Edinburgh*) for Jones (62) … Yellow card: Evans (73)

IRELAND Rob Kearney (*Leinster*); Tommy Bowe (*Ospreys*), Keith Earls (*Munster*), Gordon D'Arcy (*Leinster*), Andrew Trimble (*Ulster*); Jonathan Sexton (*Leinster*), Eoin Reddan (*Leinster*); Cian Healy (*Leinster*), Rory Best* (*Ulster*), Mike Ross (*Leinster*), Donncha O'Callaghan (*Munster*), Donnacha Ryan (*Munster*), Stephen Ferris (*Ulster*), Peter O'Mahony (*Munster*), Jamie Heaslip (*Leinster*) … Substitutes: Tom Court (*Ulster*) for Healy (51-8) and Ross (78), Sean Cronin (*Leinster*) for Best (54), Ronan O'Gara (*Munster*) for D'Arcy (54), Tomas O'Leary (*Munster*) for Reddan (54), Shane Jennings (*Leinster*) for O'Mahony (62), Fergus McFadden (*Leinster*) for Kearney (73), Mike McCarthy (*Connacht*) for O'Callaghan (78)

REFEREE Chris Pollock (*New Zealand*)

SCORING Laidlaw, pen (3–0); Laidlaw, pen (6–0); Best, try (6–5); Sexton, con (6–7); Sexton, pen (6–10); Laidlaw, pen (9–10); Reddan, try (9–15); Sexton, con (9–17); Gray, try (14–17); Trimble, try (14–22) (half-time) Sexton, pen (14–25); McFadden, try (14–30); Sexton, con (14–32)

Scotland made their first visit to the new Aviva Stadium, the former Lansdowne

Road. Max Evans was a late replacement for Nick De Luca who was injured in the warm-up. Scotland scored one good try and in theory were still in contention until the closing stages, but otherwise this was a step backwards. They worked hard but leaked some soft tries and Ireland ran out convincing winners. Scotland made a flying start with two early penalties, but on the 13th minute Best scored a try in the left corner after a lineout manoeuvre and Sexton converted from the touchline. Sexton and Laidlaw exchanged penalties before Reddan reversed between two tacklers and scuttled over for a try and Sexton kicked another majestic conversion. Close to the interval, Gray showed great athleticism when he burst into the Irish 25 and dummied Kearney for an exciting solo score. Laidlaw's conversion attempt hit one of the posts. Scotland should have been only three points down at the break, but Trimble scored a try in extra-time and the Scots never recovered. After an eventful first half, the second period was rather flat with regular interruptions for re-set scrums, injuries and substitutions. Bowe caught a crosskick and seemed to have scored after a scramble on the ground with Morrison, but the Television Match Official adjudged that he was guilty of a secondary movement and the score was disallowed. Around the hour mark, Jones and Trimble accidentally clashed heads and the Scottish winger was knocked unconscious. There was a long delay whilst he was stretchered off and Matt Scott came on for his first cap. The Irish forwards improved as the match wore on and the Scottish set-piece gradually disintegrated. Sexton kicked a penalty on the 71st minute and a couple of minutes later Max Evans was yellow-carded for illegally tugging back Earls. Ireland took full advantage and after some ferocious attacks McFadden scored underneath the posts to complete Scotland's misery.

611   RBS SIX NATIONS CHAMPIONSHIP 2012   ITALY

Stadio Olimpico, Rome · Saturday 17 March 2012 · Lost 6–13

SCOTLAND Stuart Hogg (*Glasgow Wrs*); Max Evans (*Castres*), Nick De Luca (*Edinburgh*), Graeme Morrison (*Glasgow Wrs*), Sean Lamont (*Scarlets*); Greig Laidlaw (*Edinburgh*), Mike Blair (*Edinburgh*); †Jon Welsh (*Glasgow Wrs*), Ross Ford* (*Edinburgh*), Geoff Cross (*Edinburgh*), Richie Gray (*Glasgow Wrs*), Jim Hamilton (*Gloucester*), John Barclay (*Glasgow Wrs*), Ross Rennie (*Edinburgh*), David Denton (*Edinburgh*) ... Substitutes: Euan Murray (*Newcastle F*) for Cross (52), Alastair Kellock (*Glasgow Wrs*) for Gray (54), Ruaridh Jackson (*Glasgow Wrs*) for Laidlaw (69), Richie Vernon (*Sale Sharks*) for Barclay (69) ... Yellow cards: De Luca (38), Hamilton (54)

ITALY Andrea Masi (*Aironi*); Giovanbattista Venditti (*Aironi*), Tommaso Benvenuti (*Treviso*), Gonzalo Canale (*Clermont Auv*), Mirco Bergamasco (*Racing Métro*), Kris Burton (*Treviso*), Edoardo Gori (*Treviso*); Andrea Lo Cicero (*Racing Métro*), Fabio Ongaro (*Aironi*), Martin Castrogiovanni (*Leicester Tgrs*), Quintin Geldenhuys (*Aironi*), Marco Bortolami (*Aironi*), Alessandro Zanni (*Treviso*), Robert Barbieri (*Treviso*), Sergio Paisse* (*Stade Français*) ... Substitutes: Lorenzo Cittadini (*Treviso*) for Lo Cicero (52), Manoa Vosawai (*Treviso*) for Barbieri (56), Tommaso D'Apice (*Aironi*) for Ongaro (57), Tobias Botes (*Treviso*) for Gori (66), Lo Cicero for Castrogiovanni (67), Giulio Toniolatti (*Aironi*) for Canale (68), Simone Favaro (*Aironi*) for Botes (72), Joshua Furno (*Aironi*) for Geldenhuys (75) ... Yellow card: Zanni (65)

REFEREE Alain Roland (*Ireland*) · ATTENDANCE 72,345

SCORING Bergamasco, pen (0–3); Laidlaw, pen (3–3) (half-time) Venditti, try (3–8); Burton, con (3–10); Laidlaw, pen (6–10); Burton, drop (6–13)

Scotland made their first visit to the Stadio Olimpico, the new home of Italian rugby. Glasgow prop Jon Welsh was a last-second replacement for Allan Jacobsen and turned out to be the only Scotland player to emerge with any credit from a dismal performance. Played in sunshine, this was another forgettable encounter between two mediocre sides trying only to avoid the wooden spoon. Scotland played without any real conviction and conceded too many penalties and turnovers. Their lineout badly malfunctioned and their attacks were slow and unimaginative. The big Italian forwards dominated the first-half, but Scotland defended solidly and the scores were tied 3–3 at the interval. Shortly before the break, De Luca was stupidly sin binned for lashing out at a ball with his foot. Encouraged, Italy launched the second half with great vigour and after a few minutes Venditti brushed aside a weak tackle and ran round behind the posts. Laidlaw kicked a penalty to reduce the margin to four points, but Scotland never looked like scoring even when the Italians were reduced to fourteen men with a quarter of an hour left for play. The home side kept their discipline and Burton dropped a late goal to seal their victory.

612   TOUR OF AUSTRALASIA 2012   AUSTRALIA

Hunter Stadium, Newcastle · Tuesday 5 June 2012 · Won 9-6

SCOTLAND Stuart Hogg (*Glasgow Wrs*); Joe Ansbro (*London Irish*), Nick De Luca (*Edinburgh*), Matt Scott (*Edinburgh*), Sean Lamont (*Scarlets*); Greig Laidlaw (*Edinburgh*), Mike Blair (*Edinburgh*); †Ryan Grant (*Glasgow Wrs*), Ross Ford* (*Edinburgh*), Euan Murray (*Newcastle F*), Alastair Kellock (*Glasgow Wrs*), Richie Gray (*Glasgow Wrs*), Alasdair Strokosch (*Gloucester*), Ross Rennie (*Edinburgh*), John Barclay (*Glasgow Wrs*) … Substitutes: †Tom Brown (*Edinburgh*) for Lamont (36), Chris Cusiter (*Glasgow Wrs*) for Blair (64)

AUSTRALIA Luke Morahan (*Reds*); Joe Tomane (*Brumbies*), Anthony Fainga'a (*Reds*), Mike Harris (*Reds*), Digby Ioane (*Reds*); Berrick Barnes (*Waratahs*), Will Genia (*Reds*); James Slipper (*Reds*), Stephen Moore (*Brumbies*), Dan Palmer (*Brumbies*), Sitaleki Timani (*Waratahs*), Nathan Sharpe (*W Force*), Dave Dennis (*Waratahs*), David Pocock* (*W Force*), Scott Higginbotham (*Reds*) … Substitutes: Rob Simmons (*Reds*) for Timani (55), Michael Hooper (*Brumbies*) for Dennis (65), Ben Alexander (*Brumbies*) for Palmer (70)

REFEREE Jaco Peyper (*South Africa*)

SCORING Laidlaw, pen (3–0); Laidlaw, pen (6–0); Harris, pen (6–3) (half-time) Harris, pen (6–6); Laidlaw, pen (9–6)

In June 2012, Scotland made a three match tour of Australia and the South Pacific (a fourth match against the New South Wales Waratahs was cancelled before the tour). The tour started with a mid-week test match against Australia at the Hunter Stadium in Newcastle, home of the Newcastle Knights rugby league side. Both sides were under-strength and it was indicative of Scotland's lowly status that the Australians treated this match as preparation for their forthcoming series against Wales. Conditions were dreadful with driving rain and storm force winds. Playing with the elements in their favour, Scotland edged into a 6–3 lead at the interval. Greig Laidlaw kicked two penalties against one by Mike Harris. Two minutes after the restart, Harris kicked a penalty to level the scores. The Australians spent most of the second half deep inside Scottish territory, but the visitors defended heroically and held their discipline under enormous pressure. On the hour mark Australian substitute Simmons barged his way over the line, but the Television Match Official was unable to confirm that he had touched down. In the dying seconds Scotland made a rare visit to Australia territory and were awarded a penalty after a collapsed scrum. Facing into a howling gale, Laidlaw kicked the match-winning penalty and Scotland were left singing in the rain. The appalling conditions had been a great leveller and fortune, for once, had favoured Scotland, but nothing could detract from a great team performance and a famous win.

613 TOUR OF AUSTRALASIA 2012 FIJI

Churchill Park, Lautoka · Saturday 16 June 2012 · Won 37–25

SCOTLAND Stuart Hogg (*Glasgow Wrs*); Max Evans (*Castres*), Nick De Luca (*Edinburgh*), Matt Scott (*Edinburgh*), †Tim Visser (*Edinburgh*); Greig Laidlaw (*Edinburgh*), Mike Blair (*Edinburgh*); Ryan Grant (*Glasgow Wrs*), Ross Ford* (*Edinburgh*), Euan Murray (*Newcastle F*), Alastair Kellock (*Glasgow Wrs*), Richie Gray (*Glasgow Wrs*), Alasdair Strokosch (*Gloucester*), Ross Rennie (*Edinburgh*), John Barclay (*Glasgow Wrs*) ... Substitutes: Chris Cusiter (*Glasgow Wrs*) for Blair (55), Richie Vernon (*Sale Sharks*) for Barclay (57), Sean Lamont (*Scarlets*) for Evans (63), Geoff Cross (*Edinburgh*) for Murray (67), Scott Lawson (*Gloucester*) for Ford (75), Duncan Weir (*Glasgow Wrs*) for Laidlaw (78), †Tom Ryder (*Glasgow Wrs*) for Gray (78)

FIJI Simeli Koniferedi (*Gaunavou*); Waisea Nayacalevu (*Uprising*), Vereniki Goneva (*Leicester Tgrs*), Aloisio Buto (*Grenoble*), Watisoni Votu (*Vuda Blues*); Jonetani Ralulu (*Baravi*), Nikola Matawalu (*Navy*); Jerry Yanuyanutawa (*Brumbies*), Viliame Veikoso (*Navoci*), Setefano Samoca (*Sigatoka Bulls*), Api Naikatini (*Hurricanes*), Leone Nakarawa (*Army*), Iliesa Ratuva (*Tovolea*), Mala Ravulo (*North Harbour*), Netani Talei* (*Edinburgh*) ... Substitutes: Josefa Domolailai (*Lomavata*) for Ravulo (17), Kameli Ratuvou (*Saracens*) for Buto (57), Talemaitoga Tuapati (*Woodland*) for Veikoso (57), Metuisela Talebula (*Natabua*) for Koniferedi (59), Waisea Nailago (*Toorak Blues*) for Yanyanutawa (62), Nemia Kenatale (*Highlanders*) for Matawalu (68), Kelepi Ketedromo (*Navoci*) for Ratuva (70)

REFEREE Jaco Peyper (*South Africa*)

SCORING Ralulu, pen (0–3); Ralulu, pen (0–6); Laidlaw, try (5–6); Laidlaw, con (7–6); penalty try (12–6); Laidlaw, con (14–6); Domolailai, try (14–11); Laidlaw, pen (17–11); Visser, try (22–11); Laidlaw, con (24–11) (half-time) Laidlaw, pen (27–11); Nayacalevu, try (27–16); Ralulu, con (27–18); Talebula, try (27–23); Ralulu, con (27–25); Laidlaw, pen (30–25); Visser, try (35–25); Laidlaw, con (37–25)

Dutch-born Tim Visser, who qualified for Scotland on residency, made his long awaited debut and celebrated by scoring a try at the end of each half. Playing in uncomfortably humid conditions, Scotland built a good lead before losing their way after the interval, but then made a late comeback to win the game. Fiji were captained by Edinburgh No 8 Netani Talei and started well with two early penalties. Scotland made a sweeping move down the field and Laidlaw touched down from short range. Laidlaw added the conversion, the first of seven successful goals by the Edinburgh stand-off. From a five-metre scrum, Scotland were awarded a penalty try after a defender illegally kicked the ball away. Fiji quickly responded when Matawalu ran blind from a ruck and Domolailai scored a try. Laidlaw kicked a penalty and a few minutes before the interval De Luca made just enough space to put a delighted Visser over in the corner. Five minutes after the restart Laidlaw kicked another penalty to give Scotland a healthy lead, but then the Fijians hit back with two converted tries to set up a tense conclusion. The turning point was a massive tackle by De Luca which drove his opponent many yards backwards. This lifted the Scots and their superior fitness told in the dying stages. With ten minutes remaining Laidlaw kicked another penalty. Then the Fijian defence made a mess of a high ball and Visser was on hand to collect and jog over for his second try.

614　　　　　TOUR OF AUSTRALASIA 2012　　　　　SAMOA

Apia Park, Apia · Saturday 23 June 2012 · Won 17-16

SCOTLAND Stuart Hogg (*Glasgow Wrs*); Sean Lamont (*Glasgow Wrs*), Joe Ansbro (*London Irish*), Matt Scott (*Edinburgh*), Tim Visser (*Edinburgh*); Greig Laidlaw (*Edinburgh*), Chris Cusiter (*Glasgow Wrs*); Ryan Grant (*Glasgow Wrs*), Ross Ford* (*Edinburgh*), Euan Murray (*Newcastle F*), Richie Gray (*Glasgow Wrs*), Alastair Kellock (*Glasgow Wrs*), Alasdair Strokosch (*Gloucester*), Ross Rennie (*Edinburgh*), Richie Vernon (*Sale Sharks*) ... Substitutes: Mike Blair (*Brive*) for Cusiter (43), Max Evans (*Castres*) for Ansbro (54), Scott Lawson (*London Irish*) for Ford (63), †Rob Harley (*Glasgow Wrs*) for Vernon (63), Tom Ryder (*Glasgow Wrs*) for Kellock (69),

SAMOA Fa'atoina Autagavaia (*Vailoa Palauli*); Paul Perez (*Vaimoso*), Fautua Otto (*Bristol*), Paul Williams (*Stade Français*), David Lemi* (*Glasgow Wrs*); Tusiata Pisi (*Hurricanes*), Kahn Fotuali'I (*Ospreys*); Sakaria Taulafo (*London Wasps*), Ti'i Paulo (*Clermont Auv*), Cencus Johnston (*Toulouse*), Fa'atiga Lemalu (*Papatoetoe*), Daniel Crichton (*Counties*), Ben Masoe (*Papatoetoe*), Maurie Fa'asavalu (*Worcester Wrs*), Kane Thompson (*Waikato Chiefs*) ... Substitutes: Lolo Lui (*Moataa*) for Otto (35), Logovi'i Mulipola (*Leicester Tgrs*) for Johnston (41), Afa Aioni (*Leulumoega*) for Masoe (58), Iosefa Tekori (*Castres*) for Crichton (58), Ole Avei (*Bordeaux Bègles*) for Paulo (64), Johnston for Taulafo (70-5), Jeremy Sua (*Tasman Makos*) for Fotuali'i (79)

REFEREE Jaco Peyper (*South Africa*)

SCORING Pisi, drop (0–3); Ansbro, try (5–3); Laidlaw, con (7–3); Pisi, pen (7–6) (half-time) Pisi, pen (7–9); Laidlaw, pen (10–9); Pisi, try (10–14); Pisi, con (10–16); Harley, try (15–16); Laidlaw, con (17–16)

Joe Ansbro was a last minute replacement for Nick De Luca. Scotland showed great self-belief to score the winning try one minute from time and finish their tour unbeaten. Played in very hot conditions, this was a rather ordinary match that the Samoans ought to have won. They dominated the first hour and would have been comfortable winners if they had taken their chances. Scotland made a lot of errors but they defended heroically and the scrum was very solid against some burly opponents. After 20 minutes, Samoan stand-off Pisi dropped a goal and soon after Matt Scott, who had a great match, made a break to create a try for Ansbro. Laidlaw converted and Pisi kicked a penalty to leave Scotland with a single point advantage at the interval. Early in the second half, Mike Blair came on at scrum-half. He had a big impact on course of the match, especially in the closing stages when he used his vast experience to keep Scotland in contention and the Samoans under pressure. On the hour mark Pisi scored a try that he also converted, but then the Samoans retreated into their shell and Scotland finished strongly. In the last minutes, Blair took a quick tap-penalty near the Samoan line and after a few phases of play he drew-in two defenders to create a gap for Harley to score at the posts. The ever reliable Laidlaw kicked the winning conversion and Scotland escaped with a hard-fought victory.

615   AUTUMN TEST 2012   NEW ZEALAND

Murrayfield · Sunday 11 November 2012 · Lost 22-51

SCOTLAND Stuart Hogg (*Glasgow Wrs*); Sean Lamont (*Glasgow Wrs*), Nick De Luca (*Edinburgh*), Matt Scott (*Edinburgh*), Tim Visser (*Edinburgh*); Greig Laidlaw (*Edinburgh*), Mike Blair (*Brive*); Ryan Grant (*Glasgow Wrs*), Ross Ford (*Edinburgh*), Geoff Cross (*Edinburgh*), Richie Gray (*Sale Sharks*), Jim Hamilton (*Gloucester*), Alasdair Strokosch (*Perpignan*), Ross Rennie (*Edinburgh*), Kelly Brown* (*Saracens*) ... Substitutes: David Denton (*Edinburgh*) for Rennie (19), Alastair Kellock (*Glasgow Wrs*) for Hamilton (58), Max Evans (*Castres*) for De Luca (64), Ruaridh Jackson (*Glasgow Wrs*) for Laidlaw (64), Scott Lawson (*London Irish*) for Ford (64), Allan Jacobsen (*Edinburgh*) for Grant (65), †Henry Pyrgos (*Glasgow Wrs*) for Balir (75)

NEW ZEALAND Israel Dagg (*Crusaders*); Cory Jane (*Hurricanes*), Ben Smith (*Highlanders*), Tamati Ellison (*Highlanders*), Julian Savea (*Hurricanes*); Dan Carter (*Crusaders*), Piri Weepu (*Blues*); Wyatt Crocket (*Crusaders*), Andrew Hore (*Highlanders*), Owen Franks (*Crusaders*), Luke Romano (*Crusaders*), Sam Whitelock (*Crusaders*), Adam Thomson (*Highlanders*), Richie McCaw* (*Crusaders*), Victor Vito (*Hurricanes*) ... Substitutes: Beauden Barrett (*Hurricanes*) for Dagg (25), Dane Coles (*Hurricanes*) for Hore (61), Ben Franks (*Crusaders*) for Franks (61), Tawera Kerr-Barlow (*Chiefs*) for Weepu (61), Ali Williams (*Blues*) for Whitelock (67), Tony Woodcock (*Blues*) for Crockett (72) ... Yellow card: Thomson (44)

REFEREE Jérôme Garcès (*France*) · ATTENDANCE 67,144

SCORING Carter, pen (0–3); Visser, try (5–3); Laidlaw, con (7–3); Dagg, try (7–8); Carter, con (7–10); Laidlaw, pen (10–10); Carter, pen (10–13); Savea, try (10–18); Carter, con (10–20); Jane, try (10–25); Carter, con (10–27); Hore, try (10–32); Carter, con (10–34); Cross, try (15–34); Laidlaw, con (17–34) (half-time) Visser, try (22–34); Carter, pen (22–37); Savea, try (22–42); Carter, con (22–44); Smith, try (22–49); Carter, con (22–51)

Kelly Brown won his 50th cap and took over the captaincy. The match was attended by Scottish Olympians and Paralympians and Sir Chris Hoy presented the match ball to a great ovation. This was an entertaining encounter played before a capacity crowd and in perfect conditions. Scotland in their new saltire change strip were always competitive and scored three tries including a brace by Tim Visser, but they made too many costly errors, especially in defence, which the New Zealanders were quick to punish. Once again the All Blacks were in a different class and much of their play was a delight to watch, in particular their swift and accurate handling, incisive running and brilliant support work. Stand-off Dan Carter controlled the match imperiously and flanker Richie McCaw was always in the right place. New Zealand started with great intent and Carter kicked an early penalty before Scotland scored their first try after 13 minutes. Scott intercepted near halfway and off-loaded to Visser who powered away to the left corner. Scotland were unable to consolidate and five minutes later Carter made a devastating break to create a try for Dagg. A penalty by Laidlaw levelled the scores, but then New Zealand scored three converted tries in a dazzling seven minute spell and their lead was unassailable. Scotland made a late rally and on the stroke of half time Scott was denied a try by the video referee. From the ensuing penalty, Cross drove over from short range and Laidlaw converted. Early in the second-half, Thomson, the New Zealand flanker, was yellow-carded for an illegal stamp. Scotland dominated large parts of the game in terms of possession and territory, but their only reward was a second try by Visser after Laidlaw had cleverly hacked the ball out of a ruck near the New Zealand line. Laidlaw missed the conversion and a couple of minutes later Carter kicked another penalty. Any lingering thoughts of a Scottish comeback were finally killed off on the hour mark when Carter kicked across the field to Savea who gathered a fortunate bounce and cut inside for a superbly worked try. A few minutes before the end, Carter broke through the tired defence and Smith touched down. Scotland had done their best, but there was a big gulf in quality between the sides. The Scottish forwards stood up well and some of their mauling was very good. Richie Gray and Geoff Cross were both prominent in the loose, and veteran scrum-half Mike Blair had another storming match.

616   AUTUMN TEST 2012   SOUTH AFRICA

Murrayfield · Saturday 17 November 2012 · Lost 10–21

SCOTLAND Stuart Hogg (*Glasgow Wrs*); Sean Lamont (*Glasgow Wrs*), Nick De Luca (*Edinburgh*), Matt Scott (*Edinburgh*), Tim Visser (*Edinburgh*); Greig Laidlaw (*Edinburgh*), Mike Blair (*Brive*); Ryan Grant (*Glasgow Wrs*), Ross Ford (*Edinburgh*), Euan Murray (*Agen*), Richie Gray (*Sale Sharks*), Jim Hamilton (*Gloucester*), Kelly Brown* (*Saracens*), John Barclay (*Glasgow Wrs*), David Denton (*Edinburgh*) … Substitutes: Alastair Kellock (*Glasgow Wrs*) for Gray (22), Henry Pyrgos (*Glasgow Wrs*) for Blair (47), Geoff Cross (*Edinburgh*) for Murray (68), Dougie Hall (*Glasgow Wrs*) for Ford (68), Ruaridh Jackson (*Glasgow Wrs*) for Laidlaw (68)

SOUTH AFRICA Zane Kirchner (*Bulls*); JP Pietersen (*Sharks*), Juan de Jongh (*Stormers*), Jean de Villers* (*Stormers*), Francois Hougaard (*Bulls*); Pat Lambie (*Sharks*), Ruan Pienaar (*Ulster*); Gurthrö Steenkamp (*Toulouse*), Adriaan Strauss (*Cheetahs*), Jannie du Plessis (*Sharks*), Eben Etzebeth (*Stormers*), Juandré Kruger (*Bulls*), Francois Louw (*Bath*), Willem Alberts (*Sharks*), Duane Vermeulen (*Stormers*) … Substitutes: Marcell Coetzee (*Sharks*) for Alberts (52), CJ van der Linde (*Lions*) for du Plessis (52), Heinke van der Merwe (*Leinster*) for Steenkamp (62), Flip van der Merwe (*Bulls*) for Kruger (68), Morne Steyn (*Bulls*) for Lambie (73), Schalk Brits (*Saracens*) for Strauss (76) … Yellow card: F van der Merwe (76)

REFEREE George Clancy (*Ireland*) · ATTENDANCE 58,893

SCORING Lambie, pen (0–3); Laidlaw, pen (3–3); Lambie, pen (3–6); Strauss, try (3–11); Lambie, pen (3–14) (half-time) Strauss, try (3–19); Lambie, pen (3–21); Pyrgos, try (8–21); Laidlaw, con (10–21)

The first half was less than inspiring and it took Scotland 32 minutes to reach the South African 22. The Scottish possession was too slow and their attacks easily contained by the well organised South African defence. The visitors scored their first try after 20 minutes. From a shortened lineout inside the Scottish 22, the forwards made an unstoppable drive to the line and hooker Adriann Strauss dived over. Scotland were much more competitive in the second half, but they gave away an early try when Strauss intercepted on the Scottish ten metre line and raced away unopposed. A few minutes later, the Scots kicked a penalty to the corner and from the ensuing lineout the ball was tapped down to substitute Henry Pyrgos who shot through a big gap to score. Scotland dominated the rest of the match and had several spells of pressure on the South African line, but the visiting defence was very strong and time gradually ran out for a frustrated Scotland.

617 AUTUMN TEST 2012 TONGA

Pittodrie Stadium, Aberdeen · Saturday 24 November 2012

Lost 15–21

SCOTLAND Stuart Hogg (*Glasgow Wrs*); Sean Lamont (*Glasgow Wrs*), Max Evans (*Castres*), Matt Scott (*Edinburgh*), Tim Visser (*Edinburgh*); Greig Laidlaw (*Edinburgh*), Henry Pyrgos (*Glasgow Wrs*); Kyle Traynor (*Bristol*), Scott Lawson (*London Irish*), Euan Murray (*Worcester Wrs*), Richie Gray (*Sale Sharks*), Alastair Kellock (*Glasgow Wrs*), Alasdair Strokosch (*Perpignan*), Kelly Brown* (*Saracens*), David Denton (*Edinburgh*) ... Substitutes: Geoff Cross (*Edinburgh*) for Murray (51-53), Dougie Hall (*Glasgow Wrs*) for Lawson (51), John Barclay (*Glasgow Wrs*) for Denton (52), Rory Lawson (*Newcastle F*) for Pyrgos (52), Nick De Luca (*Edinburgh*) for Evans (59), †Tom Heathcote (*Bath*) for Laidlaw (67)

TONGA Vunga Lilo (*Tarbès Pyrenees*); Fetu'u Vainikolo (*Connacht*), Suka Hufanga (*Newcastle F*), Sione Piukala (*Perpignan*), Will Helu (*Fasi M'ufanga*); Fangatapu 'Apikotoa (*Amatori*), Taniela Moa (*Pau*); Alisona Taumalolo (*Perpignan*), Elvis Taione (*W Force*), Halani 'Aulika (*London Irish*), Joe Tu'ineau (*Aix-en-Provence*), Tukulua Lokotui (*Wellington*), Hale T-Pole (*Northland*), Nili Latu* (*NEC Green Rockets*), Viliami Ma'afu (*unattached*) ... Substitutes: Tevita Mailau (*Mont De Marsan*) for 'Aulika (45), Sitiveni Mafi (*Leicester Tgrs*) for T-Pole (51), 'Alipate Fatafehi (*Lyon*) for Hufanga (67), Kama Sakalia (*Marist Tonga*) for Taione (70), Viliame 'Iongi (*Marist Longoteme*) for Helu (75), Sione Timani (*Scarlets*) for Tu'ineau (75) ... Yellow cards: Lokotui (33), Langilangi (68), Mafi (78)

REFEREE Mathieu Raynal (*France*) · ATTENDANCE 20,306

SCORING Apikotoa, pen (0–3); Laidlaw, pen (3–3); Laidlaw, pen (6–3) (half-time) Laidlaw, pen (9–3); Lokotui, try (9–8); Apikotoa, con (9–10); Laidlaw, pen (12–10); Laidlaw, pen (15–10); Apikotoa, pen (15–13); Vainikolo, try (15–18); Apikotoa, pen (15–21)

The result was a big surprise but Tonga were a well-drilled outfit who competed well at the breakdowns, defended solidly and took their chances. Scotland were unconvincing in attack and made too many errors. The Scots dominated possession and territory in the first half, but once again they lacked penetration and composure. They were denied a pushover try on video evidence and Laidlaw made one searing break but could not find support. The momentum swung towards Tonga in the second half and on the 51st minute second row Lokotui burrowed over from short-range. Laidlaw restored the Scottish lead with two penalties before Vainikolo made a long elusive run from halfway for a brilliant solo try. Apikotoa missed the simple conversion but then kicked a penalty and despite losing two men to the sin bin Tonga had few problems holding out for a deserved win. Shortly before the finish, Bath stand-off Tom Heathcote, who had played for England at various age levels, made his debut. Scotland head coach Andy Robinson resigned his post the day after this disappointing defeat.

Twickenham · Saturday 2 February 2013 · Lost 18–38

SCOTLAND Stuart Hogg (*Glasgow Wrs*); †Sean Maitland (*Glasgow Wrs*), Sean Lamont (*Glasgow Wrs*), Matt Scott (*Edinburgh*), Tim Visser (*Edinburgh*); Ruaridh Jackson (*Glasgow Wrs*), Greig Laidlaw (*Edinburgh*); Ryan Grant (*Glasgow Wrs*), Dougie Hall (*Glasgow Wrs*), Euan Murray (*Worcester Wrs*), Richie Gray (*Sale Sharks*), Jim Hamilton (*Gloucester*), Alasdair Strokosch (*Perpignan*), Kelly Brown* (*Saracens*), Johnnie Beattie (*Montpellier*) ... Substitutes: David Denton (*Edinburgh*) for Strokosch (13), Ross Ford (*Edinburgh*) for Hall (47), Alastair Kellock (*Glasgow Wrs*) for Hamilton (55), Henry Pygros (*Glasgow Wrs*) for Laidlaw (73), Max Evans (*Castres*) for Hogg (78)

ENGLAND Alex Goode (*Saracens*); Chris Ashton (*Saracens*), Brad Barritt (*Saracens*), Billy Twelvetrees (*Gloucester*), Mike Brown (*Harlequins*); Owen Farrell (*Saracens*), Ben Youngs (*Leicester Tgrs*); Joe Marler (*Harlequins*), Tom Youngs (*Leicester Tgrs*), Dan Cole (*Leicester Tgrs*), Joe Launchbury (*London Wasps*), Geoff Parling (*Leicester Tgrs*), Tom Wood (*Northampton Sts*), Chris Robshaw* (*Harlequins*), Ben Morgan (*Gloucester*) ... Substitutes: James Haskell (*London Wasps*) for Morgan (45), Dylan Hartley (*Northampton Sts*) for T Youngs (53), Danny Care (*Harlequins*) for B Youngs (57), Mako Vunipola (*Saracens*) for Marler (57), Courtney Lawes (*Northampton Sts*) for Launchbury (64), Toby Flood (*Leicester Tgrs*) for Twelvetrees (67), David Strettle (*Saracens*) for Goode (67), David Wilson (*Bath*) for Cole (73)

REFEREE Alain Rolland (*Ireland*)   ·   **ATTENDANCE** 81,347

SCORING Farrell, pen (0–3); Maitland, try (5–3); Farrell, pen (5–6); Farrell, pen (5–9); Laidlaw, pen (8–9); Ashton, try (8–14); Farrell, con (8–16); Farrell, pen (8–19); Laidlaw, pen (11–19) (half-time) Twelvetrees, try (11–24); Farrell, con (11–26); Parling, try (11–31); Hogg, try (16–31); Laidlaw, con (18–31); Care, try (18–36); Farrell, con (18–38)

Prop Euan Murray won his 50th cap and New Zealand-born wing Sean Maitland, who had previously represented Canterbury and New Zealand Maori, made his debut. Under interim head coach Scott Johnson, Scotland went south more in hope than expectation. This was an entertaining match where the Scots were largely outclassed by a confident English side that scored four tries, had one disallowed and would have had more but for some tremendous Scottish defence. The Scots were unstinting in their efforts and scored two splendid tries of their own, but they were under severe pressure in the scrums, coughed up too much possession at the breakdowns and their ill-discipline allowed England to build momentum. After an early penalty by Farrell, Stuart Hogg made an incisive touchline break from his own half into the England 22 and after a couple of phases Maitland dived over at the right corner. Scotland's lead lasted less than four minutes before Farrell kicked a second penalty. England cont-rolled the rest of the half, Ashton scored a try from close-range and Farrell landed another two penalties. Just before the break, Johnnie Beattie made a powerful run which set up a penalty for Laidlaw. Soon after the restart, England made a good build-up and the superbly named Billy Twelvetrees was unstoppable from a few metres out, albeit with a flat pass that might have been forward. England lock Joe Launchbury was denied a score on the intervention of the touch-judge, but shortly after Farrell took out two defenders with an exquisite overhead pass to Parling who romped over on the left. Scotland might have disintegrated at this point, but with some ten minutes remaining they launched a daring counter-attack from under their own posts. After some quick hands, Maitland and Hogg booted on to the English line and the latter won the race to the touchdown. Laidlaw kicked a superb conversion, but there was little hope of a dramatic comeback and Danny Care scored under the posts in added time. The final outcome was a fair reflection on the course of the game. For Scotland, Stuart Hogg made some penetrating runs from deep, Matt Scott and Richie Gray tackled superbly, and Kelly Brown led from the front, but in truth England were on a higher level.

619   RBS SIX NATIONS CHAMPIONSHIP 2013   ITALY

Murrayfield · Saturday 9 February 2013 · Won 34–10

SCOTLAND Stuart Hogg (*Glasgow Wrs*); Sean Maitland (*Glasgow Wrs*), Sean Lamont (*Glasgow Wrs*), Matt Scott (*Edinburgh*), Tim Visser (*Edinburgh*); Ruaridh Jackson (*Glasgow Wrs*), Greig Laidlaw (*Edinburgh*); Ryan Grant (*Glasgow Wrs*), Ross Ford (*Edinburgh*), Euan Murray (*Worcester Wrs*), Richie Gray (*Sale Sharks*), Jim Hamilton (*Gloucester*), Rob Harley (*Glasgow Wrs*), Kelly Brown* (*Saracens*), Johnnie Beattie (*Montpellier*) ... Substitutes: Moray Low (*Glasgow Wrs*) for Grant (59), Alastair Kellock (*Glasgow Wrs*) for Hamilton (66), Geoff Cross (*Edinburgh*) for Murray (71), David Denton (*Edinburgh*) for Brown (71), Max Evans (*Castres*) for Hogg (72), Henry Pyrgos (*Glasgow Wrs*) for Laidlaw (75), ... Yellow card: Cross (80)

ITALY Andrea Masi (*London Wasps*); Giovanbattista Venditti (*Zebre*), Tommaso Benvenuti (*Treviso*), Gonzalo Canale (*La Rochelle*), Luke McLean (*Treviso*); Luciano Orquera (*Zebre*), Tobias Botes (*Treviso*); Andrea Lo Cicero (*Racing Métro*), Leonardo Ghiraldini (*Treviso*), Martin Castrogiovanni (*Leicester Tgrs*), Quintin Geldenhuys (*Zebre*), Francesco Minto (*Treviso*), Alessandro Zanni (*Treviso*), Simone Favaro (*Treviso*), Sergio Parisse* (*Stade Français*) ... Substitutes: Kris Burton (*Treviso*) for Orquera (48), Eduardo Gori (*Treviso*) for Tobias Botes (48), Davide Giazzon (*Zebre*) for Ghiraldini (60), Alberto de Marchi (*Treviso*) for Lo Cicero (60), Antonio Pavanello (*Treviso*) for Geldenhuys (60), Lorenzo Cittadini (*Treviso*) for Castrogiovanni (64), Paul Derbyshire (*Treviso*) for Favaro (68)

REFEREE Jaco Peyper (*South Africa*) · ATTENDANCE 50,247

SCORING Laidlaw, pen (3–0); Laidlaw, pen (6–0); Visser, try (11–0); Laidlaw, con (13–0); Orquera, pen (13–3) (half-time) Scott, try (18–3); Laidlaw, con (20–3); Hogg, try (25–3); Laidlaw, con (27–3); Lamont, try (32–3); Laidlaw, con (34–3); Zanni, try (34–8); Burton, con (34–10)

Playing in their white and blue saltire strip, Scotland were a big improvement on the previous weekend. They recaptured their traditional aggression and ambition, and showed much greater intensity in defence and at the breakdowns. The backs were lively in attack and they scored four exciting tries. In a high tempo start, Laidlaw kicked to the right-hand corner and Visser was denied a try only by an unkind bounce of the ball. Orquera hit a post with a penalty before Laidlaw landed two goals for the Scots. Near the half hour mark, Botes, the Italian scrum-half, made a great cover tackle on Scott to prevent a certain try. A couple of minutes later, Scotland put together a well-constructed move and Jackson made a smart dummy before giving a one-handed pass to Visser who beat two defenders for the opening try. Shortly after the interval, Maitland intruded from the left wing before feeding Scott near the Italian ten metre line and after juggling with the ball the Edinburgh centre powered away to the line. The decisive score came five minutes later. Italy, who had unexpectedly beaten France the previous week, launched a spirited attack deep into the Scottish 22. Orquera tried to find Benvenuti who was in a scoring position, but Hogg intercepted his pass, weaved his way through the defence and ran the length of the field for a spectacular score. Scott was denied a second try because of a forward pass and on the 68th minute Lamont, who was always in the thick of things, stole a loose ball at a ruck on the Scottish ten metre line and raced away to the posts. The Italians won a lot of possession and territory throughout the game, and from a scrum near the Scottish line Parisse gave a neat inside pass to Zanni for a late consolation score. This was a good team performance by Scotland for whom Hogg and Scott were out-standing. Greig Laidlaw won the man-of-the-match award for an authoritative display, Rob Harley, making his first full start, was very prominent, and Ryan Grant battled on heroically despite an early injury.

620 · RBS SIX NATIONS CHAMPIONSHIP 2013 · IRELAND

Murrayfield · Sunday 24 February 2013 · Won 12–8

SCOTLAND Stuart Hogg (*Glasgow Wrs*); Sean Maitland (*Glasgow Wrs*), Sean Lamont (*Glasgow Wrs*), Matt Scott (*Edinburgh*), Tim Visser (*Edinburgh*); Ruaridh Jackson (*Glasgow Wrs*), Greig Laidlaw (*Edinburgh*); Ryan Grant (*Glasgow Wrs*), Ross Ford (*Edinburgh*), Geoff Cross (*Edinburgh*), Richie Gray (*Sale Sharks*), Jim Hamilton (*Gloucester*), Rob Harley (*Glasgow Wrs*), Kelly Brown* (*Saracens*), Johnnie Beattie (*Montpellier*) ... Substitutes: Moray Low (*Glasgow Wrs*) for Harley (18-25) and for Cross (74), Dougie Hall (*Glasgow Wrs*) for Ford (46), David Denton (*Edinburgh*) for Brown (46-50), Duncan Weir (*Glasgow Wrs*) for Jackson (59), Denton for Beattie (71), Alastair Kellock (*Glasgow Wrs*) for Hamilton (71) ... Yellow card: Grant (15)

IRELAND Rob Kearney (*Leinster*); Craig Gilroy (*Ulster*), Brian O'Driscoll (*Leinster*), Luke Marshall (*Ulster*), Leith Earls (*Munster*); Paddy Jackson (*Ulster*), Conor Murray (*Munster*); Tom Court (*Ulster*), Rory Best (*Ulster*), Mike Ross (*Leinster*), Donncha O'Callaghan (*Munster*), Donnacha Ryan (*Munster*), Peter O'Mahony (*Munster*), Sean O'Brien (*Leinster*), Jamie Heaslip* (*Leinster*) ... Substitutes: David Kilcoyne (*Munster*) for Court (55), Luke Fitzgerald (*Leinster*) for Gilroy (60), Ronan O'Gara (*Munster*) for Jackson (64), Eoin Reddan (*Leinster*) for Murray (68), Devin Toner (*Leinster*) for O'Callaghan (73), Iain Henderson (*Ulster*) for O'Mahony (73)

REFEREE Wayne Barnes (*England*) · **ATTENDANCE** 67,006

SCORING Jackson, pen (0–3) (half-time) Gilroy, try (0–8); Laidlaw, pen (3–8); Laidlaw, pen (6–8); Laidlaw, pen (9–8); Laidlaw, pen (12–8)

Played on a slippery pitch, this was not a pretty match, but it was captivating right to the finish. An under-strength Ireland had the bulk of the territory and possession, and should have won comfortably. In the first half, the Irish backs were lively especially new centre Luke Marshall, but they wasted some clear-cut opportunities because of a lack of precision and a huge defensive effort by Scotland. The Scottish scrum was solid throughout and Jim Hamilton, who won the man-of-the-match award, was disruptive in the lineout. Three minutes into the second half, Ireland finally crossed the try-line. O'Brien broke into the Scottish 22 and after some patient build-up winger Craig Gilroy twisted over from short range. Scotland did not reach the Irish 22 until the 50th minute, but gradually they roused themselves and four penalties by Greig Laidlaw gave them a narrow lead. The closing minutes were unbearably

Greig Laidlaw celebrates victory over Ireland in March 2013.
Scotsman Publications Ltd

exciting as Ireland battered on the line for the winning try, but the defence was impenetrable and Scotland held out for the unlikeliest of victories. Shortly before the end, Alastair Kellock came on to win his 50th cap.

Murrayfield · Saturday 9 March 2013 · Lost 18–28

SCOTLAND Stuart Hogg (*Glasgow Wrs*); Sean Maitland (*Glasgow Wrs*), Sean Lamont (*Glasgow Wrs*), Matt Scott (*Edinburgh*), Tim Visser (*Edinburgh*); Duncan Weir (*Glasgow Wrs*), Greig Laidlaw (*Edinburgh*); Ryan Grant (*Glasgow Wrs*), Ross Ford (*Edinburgh*), Euan Murray (*Worcester Wrs*), Richie Gray (*Sale Sharks*), Jim Hamilton (*Gloucester*), Rob Harley (*Glasgow Wrs*), Kelly Brown* (*Saracens*), Johnnie Beattie (*Montpellier*) ... Substitutes: Alastair Kellock (*Glasgow Wrs*) for Gray (29), †Ryan Wilson (*Glasgow Wrs*) for Beattie (67), Geoff Cross (*Edinburgh*) for Murray (76), Ruaridh Jackson (*Glasgow Wrs*) for Weir (77)

WALES Leigh Halfpenny (*Cardiff Blues*); Alex Cuthbert (*Cardiff Blues*), Jonathan Davies (*Scarlets*), Jamie Roberts (*Cardiff Blues*), George North (*Scarlets*); Dan Biggar (*Ospreys*), Mike Phillips (*Bayonne*); Paul James (*Bath*), Richard Hibbard (*Ospreys*), Adam Jones (*Ospreys*), Alun Wyn Jones (*Ospreys*), Ian Evans (*Ospreys*), Ryan Jones* (*Ospreys*), Sam Warburton (Cardiff Blues), Toby Faletau (*NG Dragons*) ... Substitutes: Justin Tipuric (*Ospreys*) for R Jones (48), Ken Owens (*Scarlets*) for Hibbard (60), Lloyd Williams (*Cardiff Blues*) for Phillips (73), Scott Williams (*Scarlets*) for Roberts (73), Ryan Bevington (*Ospreys*) for Faletau (80) ... Yellow card: James (77)

SCORING Halfpenny, pen (0–3); Laidlaw, pen (3–3); Laidlaw, pen (6–3); Hibbard, try (6–8); Halfpenny, con (6–10); Laidlaw, pen (9–10); Laidlaw, pen (12–10); Halfpenny, pen (12–13) (half-time) Halfpenny, pen (12–16); Laidlaw, pen (15–16); Halfpenny, pen (15–19); Halfpenny, pen (15–22); Laidlaw, pen (18–22); Halfpenny, pen (18–25); Halfpenny, pen (18–28)

Stand-off Duncan Weir made his first start, Sean Lamont won his 75th cap and substitute Ryan Wilson made his debut. This match was desperately close, but it was a fractured and messy encounter ruined by an endless stream of penalties with 18 attempts at goal. South African referee Craig Joubert made several controversial decisions that influenced the course of the game, especially at the scrums, and neither side were able to develop any momentum. Wales were sharper on the ball, more streetwise and they had the upper hand at the breakdowns where flanker Sam Warburton was named man-of-the-match. On the 21st minute, George North made a searing break to the Scottish line and after a series of rucks Richard Hibbard powered over. Denied any sort of set-piece platform, Scotland only threatened in the closing minutes, but even then the Welsh defence was impenetrable. Duncan Weir made one thrilling kick-and-chase in the first half and Greig Laidlaw's long range goal kicking was excellent once again.

622 · RBS SIX NATIONS CHAMPIONSHIP 2013 · FRANCE

Stade de France, Paris · Saturday 16 March 2013 · Lost 16–23

SCOTLAND Stuart Hogg (*Glasgow Wrs*); Sean Maitland (*Glasgow Wrs*), Sean Lamont (*Glasgow Wrs*), Matt Scott (*Edinburgh*), Tim Visser (*Edinburgh*); Duncan Weir (*Glasgow Wrs*), Greig Laidlaw (*Edinburgh*); Ryan Grant (*Glasgow Wrs*), Ross Ford (*Edinburgh*), Euan Murray (*Worcester Wrs*), †Grant Gilchrist (*Edinburgh*), Jim Hamilton (*Gloucester*), Alasdair Strokosch (*Perpignan*), Kelly Brown* (*Saracens*), Johnnie Beattie (*Montpellier*) … Substitutes: Max Evans (*Castres*) for Maitland (30), Alastair Kellock (*Glasgow Wrs*) for Gilchrist (53), Moray Low (*Glasgow Wrs*) for Grant (64), Geoff Cross (*Edinburgh*) for Murray (65), Ruaridh Jackson (*Glasgow Wrs*) for Weir (67), Dougie Hall (*Glasgow Wrs*) for Ford (74), Henry Pyrgos (*Glasgow Wrs*) for Laidlaw (74)

FRANCE Yoann Huget (*Toulouse*); Vincent Clerc (*Toulouse*), Mathieu Bastareaud (*Toulon*), Wesley Fofana (*Clermont Auv*), Maxime Médard (*Toulouse*); Frédéric Michalak (*Toulon*), Morgan Parra (*Clermont Auv*); Thomas Domingo (*Clermont Auv*), Benjamin Kayser (*Clermont Auv*), Nicholas Mas (*Perpignan*), Sébastien Vahaamahina (*Perpignan*), Yoann Maestri (*Toulouse*), Antonie Claassen (*Castres*), Thierry Dusautoir* (*Toulouse*), Louis Picamoles (*Toulouse*) … Substitutes: Maxime Machenaud (*Racing Metro*) for Parra (41), Vincent Debaty (*Clermont Auv*) for Domingo (54), Guilhem Guirado (*Perpignan*) for Kayser (54), Luc Ducalcon (*Racing Metro*) for Mas (63), Yannick Nyanga (*Toulouse*) for Dusautoir (63-7) and Claassen (67), Christophe Samson (*Castres*) for Vahaamahina (70), François Trinh-Duc (*Montpellier*) for Michalak (70), Gaël Fickou (*Toulouse*) for Bastareaud (74)

REFEREE Nigel Owens · ATTENDANCE 81,825

SCORING Laidlaw, pen (3–0); Laidlaw, pen (6–0) (half-time) Michalak, pen (6–3); Michalak, pen (6–6); Michalak, pen (6–9); Laidlaw, pen (9–9); Fofana, try (9–14); Michalak, con (9–16); Médard, try (9–21); Machenaud, con (9–23); Visser, try (14–23); Jackson, con (16–23)

Edinburgh second-row Grant Gilchrist won his first cap. This match had a late evening kick-off and was played in wet conditions on a pitch that cut up badly. Scotland showed plenty of determination, but France, who had yet to win a game in the 2013 Championship, had most of the possession and territory as well as better finishing skills. Scotland did well to hold a narrow lead at the interval. Greig Laidlaw landed two penalties and kicked astutely throughout. Around the half-hour mark France had a lengthy spell hammering on the Scottish line but the visitors' defence was rock solid. The second half was largely one-sided and the French at last rediscovered some of their true form. Michalak gave his side the lead with three penalties and although Laidlaw kicked an equaliser Fofana and Médard scored tries to put the result beyond doubt. There was some compensation for Scotland when they conjured a classic score a few minutes before time. From a lineout deep inside the Scottish half, Scott made a long break and Visser was in support to run under the posts.

623 INCOMING SERIES 2013 SAMOA

King's Park, Durban · Saturday 8 June 2013 · Lost 17-27

SCOTLAND †Greig Tonks (*Edinburgh*); Sean Lamont (*Glasgow Wrs*), †Alex Dunbar (*Glasgow Wrs*), Matt Scott (*Edinburgh*), Tim Visser (*Edinburgh*); Tom Heathcote (*Bath*), Greig Laidlaw (*Edinburgh*); Alasdair Dickinson (*Edinburgh*), †Pat MacArthur (*Glasgow Wrs*), Euan Murray (*Worcester Wrs*), Grant Gilchrist (*Edinburgh*), Alastair Kellock (*Glasgow Wrs*), Alasdair Strokosch (*Perpignan*), Kelly Brown* (*Saracens*), Johnnie Beattie (*Montpellier*) ... Substitutes: †Steven Lawrie (*Edinburgh*) for MacArthur (11), Ryan Wilson (*Glasgow Wrs*) for Brown (h-t), Geoff Cross (*Edinburgh*) for Murray (44), †Peter Horne (*Glasgow Wrs*) for Heathcote (58), Jim Hamilton (*Gloucester*) for Kellock (64), Moray Low (*Glasgow Wrs*) for Dickinson (64), Henry Pyrgos (*Glasgow Wrs*) for Laidlaw (69), †Duncan Taylor (*Saracens*) for Visser (69)

SAMOA James So'oialo (*Castres*); Alapati Leiua (*Hurricanes*), Paul Williams* (*Stade Français*), Johnny Leota (*Sale Sharks*), Alesana Tuilagi (*NTT Shining Arcs*); Tusi Pisi (*Hurricanes*), Jeremy Su'a (*Crusaders*); Logovi'i Mulipola (*Leicester Tgrs*), Ole Avei (*Bordeaux Bègles*), Cencus Johnston (*Toulouse*), Filo Paulo (*Cardiff Blues*), Daniel Leo (*Perpignan*), Ofisa Treviranus (*London Irish*), Jack Lam (*Hurricanes*), Tai Tu'ifua (*Newcastle F*) ... Substitutes: James Johnston (*Harlequins*) for Johnston (54), Manu Leiataua (*North Harbour*) for Avei (54), Fa'atiga Lemalu (*Marist*) for Leo (54), Seilala Mapusua (*Kutoba Spears*) for Leota (73), Zak Taulafo (*Stade Français*) for Mulipola (77), Brando Va'aulu (*Tokyo Gas*) for Leiua (79)

REFEREE John Lacey (*Ireland*) · ATTENDANCE 23,633

SCORING So'oialo, try (0–5); So'oialo, con (0–7); Laidlaw, pen (3–7); Tuilagi, try (3–12); So'oialo, con (3–14); Laidlaw, pen (6–14); Laidlaw, pen (9–14) (half-time) Laidlaw, pen (12–14); Lamont, try (17–14); So'oialo, pen (17–17); Tuilagi, try (17–22); So'oialo, con (17–24); So'oialo, pen (17–27)

In June 2013, Scotland took part in an international quadrangular tournament in South Africa. For their opening match against Samoa they fielded three new caps, including Pretoria-born full-back Greig Tonks, with a further three debutants coming off the bench. They also had to make a change to their original selection when prop Ryan Grant was called-up for the British and Irish Lions tour in Australia. Alasdair

Dickinson took his place for Scotland. Played in perfect sunny conditions, Samoa deservedly beat Scotland for the first time in a cap international. The Scottish set-piece stood up reasonably well against burly opponents and there were some storming runs by the forwards, but the Scots struggled to contain the powerful Samoans in open play and came off second best at the collisions. Samoa started aggressively and scored two well-worked tries in the opening 12 minutes. For the first, they launched an attack from inside their own half and speedy wing Alapati Leiua escaped up the right before giving full-back James So'oialo a simple run-in from the 22. So'oialo kicked the awkward conversion and Laidlaw responded with a penalty. A few minutes later, the Samoans attacked down the left and some slick handling created an overlap for Alesana Tuilagi who romped round to the posts. To their credit, the Scots did not crumble at this point and three penalties by the ever-reliable Greig Laidlaw put them back in the match. Early in second half, Laidlaw kicked a fourth penalty and then heavy pressure by the Scottish forwards forced the Samoans to lose possession near their own line. Scotland moved the ball quickly to the right, Heathcote rescued a loose pass and linked with Dunbar who gave Lamont an easy dive over near the corner. Laidlaw narrowly missed the conversion and So'oialo responded with a penalty to level the scores. Inside the final quarter the formidable Tuilagi, the brother of England and Lions centre Manu, took a pass from a scrum near the Scottish 22 and crashed through three tackles to score at the posts. So'oialo converted and a few minutes later added a penalty. Scotland made a strong effort to save the game but to no avail.

Mbombela Stadium, Nelspruit · Saturday 15 June 2013 · Lost 17–30

SCOTLAND †Peter Murchie (*Glasgow Wrs*); Sean Lamont (*Glasgow Wrs*), Alex Dunbar (*Glasgow Wrs*), Matt Scott (*Edinburgh*), †Tommy Seymour (*Glasgow Wrs*); Ruaridh Jackson (*Glasgow Wrs*), Greig Laidlaw* (*Edinburgh*); Alasdair Dickinson (*Edinburgh*), Scott Lawson (*Newcastle F*), Euan Murray (*Worcester Wrs*), †Tim Swinson (*Glasgow Wrs*), Jim Hamilton (*Gloucester*), Alasdair Strokosch (*Perpignan*), Ryan Wilson (*Glasgow Wrs*), Johnnie Beattie (*Montpellier*) ... Substitutes: Pete Horne (*Glasgow Wrs*) for Jackson (32), David Denton (*Edinburgh*) for Wilson (37), Henry Pyrgos (*Glasgow Wrs*) for Horne (43), Alastair Kellock (*Glasgow Wrs*) for Hamilton (61), Moray Low (*Glasgow Wrs*) for Dickinson (64), Duncan Taylor (*Saracens*) for Murchie (78) ... Yellow card: Hamilton (51)

SOUTH AFRICA Willie le Roux (*Griquas*); Bryan Habana (*W Province*), JJ Engelbrecht (*Blue Bulls*), Jean de Villers* (*W Province*), Bjorn Basson (*Blue Bulls*); Morne Steyn (*Blue Bulls*), Ruan Pienaar (*Ulster*); Tendai Mtawarira (*Sharks*), Adriaan Strauss (*Cheetahs*), Jannie du Plessis (*Sharks*), Eben Etzebeth (*W Province*), Juandre Kruger (*Blue Bulls*), Marcell Coetzee (*Sharks*), Arno Botha (*Blue Bulls*), Pierre Spies (*Blue Bulls*) ... Substitutes: Siya Kolisi (*W Province*) for Botha (4), Flip van der Merwe (*Blue Bulls*) for Etzebeth (66), Coenie Oosthuizen (*Cheetahs*) for Mtawarira (66), Bismarck du Plessis (*Sharks*) for Strauss (66), Jan Serfontein (*Blue Bulls*) for Engelbrecht (68), Pat Lambie (*Sharks*) for Steyn (69), Piet van Zyl (*Cheetahs*) for Pienaar (68), Trevor Nyakane (*Cheetahs*) for du Plessis (76)

REFEREE Romain Poite (*France*) · **ATTENDANCE** 31,056

SCORING Laidlaw, pen (3–0); Steyn, pen (3–3); Steyn, pen (3–6); Scott, try (8–6); Laidlaw, con (10–6) (half-time) Dunbar, try (15–6); Laidlaw, con (17–6); penalty try (17–11); Steyn, con

(17–13); Engelbrecht, try (17–18); Steyn, con (17–20); Lambie, pen (17–23); Serfontein, try (17–28); Lambie, con (17–30)

Scotland were depleted by injuries and fielded a makeshift side, including three new caps. They were completely written off before the match, but they showed great determination and team spirit and restored much of their battered pride. The forwards took the game to their weightier opponents and the defence was aggressive and well organised, especially the back-row who worked tirelessly. Scotland scored two splendid tries and were 17–6 ahead after 48 minutes, but then they lost much of their momentum, in part because of a controversial refereeing decision, and the South Africans finished the stronger side. In an enthralling encounter, Scotland scored their first try on the 21st minute when debutant wing Tommy Seymour chipped into space and re-gathered the ball. He was dragged down just short of the line, but the Scots quickly recycled and Matt Scott, who was superb throughout, scored at the posts. A few minutes after the interval Tim Swinson, another newcomer, made a great burst into the Springbok 22 and slick hands combined to put Alex Dunbar over in the left corner. Greig Laidlaw, who had just switched to stand-off after an injury to substitute Pete Horne, kicked a superb conversion from the touchline. Scotland needed to consolidate, but instead Dunbar gave away a soft penalty for making an illegal obstruction on Habana. From the ensuing kick and lineout the South African forwards made an unstoppable driving maul and were awarded a penalty try when it collapsed on the Scottish line. Then Jim Hamilton made an open-handed shove on Etzebeth after play had stopped on the touchline and he was yellow carded on the advice of the television match official. It was a harsh punishment, but the South Africans seized their opportunity and Engelbrecht scored a try against the depleted Scottish defence. South Africa dominated the rest of the game with Scotland making the occasional breakout and defending heroically. The result was still in the balance until the closing minutes when Lambie kicked a penalty. Then with the last play of the game Serfontein beat several tired defenders to slip over from close-range and add a flattering gloss to the score.

625 · INCOMING SERIES 2013 · ITALY

Loftus Versfeld, Pretoria · Saturday 22 June 2013 · Won 30–29

SCOTLAND Peter Murchie (*Glasgow Wrs*); Tommy Seymour (*Glasgow Wrs*), Alex Dunbar (*Glasgow Wrs*), Matt Scott (*Edinburgh*), Sean Lamont (*Glasgow Wrs*); Tom Heathcote (*Bath*), Greig Laidlaw (*Edinburgh*); Alasdair Dickinson (*Edinburgh*), Scott Lawson (*Newcastle F*), Euan Murray (*Worcester Wrs*), Tim Swinson (*Glasgow Wrs*), Alastair Kellock (*Glasgow Wrs*), David Denton (*Edinburgh*), Alasdair Strokosch (*Perpignan*), Johnnie Beattie (*Montpellier*) ... Substitutes: Tim Visser (*Edinburgh*) for Seymour (43), Henry Pyrgos (*Glasgow Wrs*) for Heathcote (48), Moray Low (*Glasgow Wrs*) for Dickinson (49), Grant Gilchrist (*Edinburgh*) for Swinson (58), Duncan Taylor (*Saracens*) for Murchie (58), Rob Harley (*Glasgow Wrs*) for Beattie (60), †Fraser Brown (*Glasgow Wrs*) for Lawson, Jon Welsh (*Glasgow Wrs*) for Low (72)

ITALY Andrea Masi (*London Wasps*); Leonardo Sarto (*Zebre*), Luca Morisi (*Treviso*), Alberto Sgarbi (*Treviso*), Giovanbattista Venditti (*Zebre*); Alberto Di Bernardo (*Treviso*), Tobias Botes (*Treviso*); Matias Aguero (*Zebre*), Davide Giazzon (*Zebre*), Martin Castrogiovanni (*Toulon*), Leandro Cedaro (*La Rochelle*), Marco Bortolami (*Zebre*), Joshua Furno (*Biarritz*),

Robert Barbieri (Treviso), Sergio Parisse* (*Stade Français*) … Substitutes: Leonardo Ghiraldini (*Treviso*) for Giazzon (47), Alberto de Marchi (*Treviso*) for Aguero (47), Lorenzo Cittadini (*Treviso*) for Castrogiovanni (49), Alessandro Zanni (*Treviso*) for Bortolami (49), Gonzalo Canale (*La Rochelle*) for Morisi (52), Antonio Pavanello (*Treviso*) for Cedaro (52), Luke McLean (*Treviso*) for Sarto (60), Alberto Chillon (*Zebre*) for Botes (69)

REFEREE Leighton Hodges (*Wales*) · ATTENDANCE 5,645

SCORING Sarto, try (0–5); Di Bernardo, con (0–7); Scott, try (5–7); Laidlaw, con (7–7); Di Bernardo, pen (7–10); Lamont, try (12–10); Laidlaw, con (14–10); Laidlaw, pen (17–10); penalty try (17–15); Di Bernardo, con (17–17); Laidlaw, pen (20–17); Di Bernardo, pen (20–20) (half-time) Laidlaw, pen (23–20); Di Bernardo, pen (23–23); Di Bernardo, pen (23–26); Di Bernardo, pen (23–29); Strokosch, try (28–29); Laidlaw, con (30–29)

In this play-off match, Scotland never recaptured the same intensity of the previous weekend but still managed to snatch a dramatic late win. Both sides had periods of ascendency and much of the play had a loose, end-of-season feel about it. Italy made a strong start and within the first minute debutant wing Leonardo Sarto made an angled run through Scottish defence for an early score. Scotland responded five minutes later when David Denton made a midfield burst before off-loading to Matt Scott who weaved around some weak tackles for a try at the posts. Around the 15th minute, Scotland built a good attack and Scott chipped ahead to the Italian line where the bouncing ball just beat the pursuing Denton. Venditti tried to run out of defence but lost possession near his own line and Laidlaw gave a superb pass out of the tackle to Lamont who had a simple run-in. Laidlaw stretched the lead with a penalty before Italy were awarded a penalty try after a series of collapsed scrums near the Scottish line. An exchange of penalties levelled the scores at the interval and early in the second half Laidlaw and Di Bernardo landed further goals. Then Scott, one of the great successes of the tour, had a try chalked-off when the television match official ruled that the final pass from Visser was forward. Two penalties by Di Bernardo gave Italy a six point lead inside the final 15 minutes but Scotland never gave in. Deep into injury time and with some of the Italian squad already celebrating, Scotland won a penalty on the Italian 22. Lamont made a drive before Strokosch found a big hole in the Italian defence and romped all the way to the line. Laidlaw kicked the winning conversion from the right of the posts and Scotland ended their summer tour on a high.

Appendix 1
Scottish International Players

Players are listed here in appearance order. When there was more than one new cap in a game then they are sorted by position. Blank space means not known. Abbreviations: FWD – Forward; HB – Half-back; TQ – Three-quarter; FB – Full-back; W – Wing; C – Centre; SO – Stand-off; SH – Scrum-half; P – Prop; H – Hooker; L – Lock; F – Flanker; 8 – No8; BR – Back-row

Cap No	Name	Known as	Caps	Career	Position	Date of birth	Date of death
1	Brown, *William Davie*		5	1871–75	FB	29.5.1852	24.3.1876
2	Chalmers, *Thomas*	Tom	6	1871–76	FB	19.3.1850	25.5.1926
3	Clunies Ross, *Alfred*	Alfred	1	1871	FB	c.1851	2.1903
4	Marshall, *Thomas Roger*		4	1871–74	Back	26.6.1849	27.6.1913
5	Arthur, *John William*	John	2	1871–72	Back	25.4.1848	15.3.1921
6	Cross, *William*		2	1871–72	Back	10.9.1850	16.10.1890
7	Buchanan, *Angus*	Angus	1	1871	Fwd	15.1.1847	21.2.1927
8	Colville, *Andrew Galbraith*		2	1871–72	Fwd	17.12.1846	17.4.1881
9	Drew, *Daniel*	Daniel	2	1871–76	Fwd	1850	2.2.1914
10	Finlay, *James Fairbairn*	Jim	4	1871–75	Fwd	8.4.1852	25.1.1930
11	Forsyth, *William*		1	1871	Fwd		
12	Irvine, *Robert William*	Robert	13	1871–80	Fwd	19.4.1853	18.4.1897
13	Lyall, *William John Campbell*		1	1871	Fwd	27.1.1848	22.4.1931
14	McFarlane, *John Lisle Hall*	John	3	1871–73	Fwd, HB	19.6.1849	17.3.1874
15	Mein, *James*	James	5	1871–75	Fwd	1.7.1852	2.3.1918
16	Moncreiff, *Francis Jeffrey*	Frank	3	1871–73	Fwd	27.8.1849	30.5.1900
17	Munro, *R*		1	1871	Fwd		
18	Ritchie, *George*	George	1	1871	Fwd	16.4.1848	31.1.1896
19	Robertson, *Alexander Hamilton*		1	1871	Fwd	1.10.1848	12.5.1913
20	Thomson, *John Shaw*		1	1871	Fwd	9.8.1845	22.5.1925
21	Balfour, *Leslie Melville*	Leslie	1	1872	FB	9.3.1854	16.7.1937
22	Maitland, *Reginald Paynter*		1	1872	TQ	6.3.1851	10.4.1926
23	Anderson, *John*	John	1	1872	Fwd	9.5.1849	25.5.1934
24	Bannerman, *Edward Mordaunt*		2	1872–73	Fwd	14.1.1850	
25	Cathcart, *Charles Walker*		3	1872–76	Fwd	16.3.1853	22.2.1932
26	McClure, *James Howe*		1	1872	Fwd	8.7.1851	11.5.1909
27	Marshall, *William*		1	1872	Fwd	22.6.1852	15.10.1907
28	Maxwell, *Frederick Thomson*		1	1872	Fwd	10.1.1849	15.1.1881
29	Renny-Tailyour, *Henry Waugh*		1	1872	Fwd	9.10.1849	15.6.1920
30	Sanderson, *James Lyon Playfair*		1	1873	FB	29.1.1852	1930
31	Grant, *William St Clair*		2	1873–74	TQ	20.7.1853	17.2.1896
32	McClure, *George Buchanan*		1	1873	HB	8.7.1851	11.7.1888
33	Allan, *Henry William*	Henry	1	1873	Fwd	2.4.1850	12.12.1926
34	Anton, *Peter*	Peter	1	1873	Fwd	25.6.1850	10.12.1911
35	Bryce, *Charles Chalmers*		2	1873–74	Fwd	16.4.1848	12.2.1895
36	Davidson, *John Paton*		2	1873–74	Fwd	3.9.1851	21.9.1919
37	Petrie, *Alexander Gordon*	Gordon	11	1873–80	Fwd	14.2.1853	4.2.1909
38	Whittington, *Thomas Price*	Tom	1	1873	Fwd	12.8.1848	7.10.1919
39	Wilson, *Robert Walter*		2	1873–74	Fwd	4.2.1854	6.7.1911
40	Wood, *Alexander Thomson*		3	1873–75	Fwd	30.4.1848	26.10.1905

Cap No	Name	Known as	Caps	Career	Position	Date of birth	Date of death
41	Hamilton, *Hugh Montgomerie*		2	1874–75	TQ	26.6.1854	11.8.1930
42	Kidston, *William Hamilton*		1	1874	TQ	29.4.1852	4.6.1929
43	Stewart, *Alexander Kenneth*		2	1874–76	HB	30.8.1852	13.2.1945
44	Heron, *Gilbert*		2	1874–75	Fwd	6.9.1854	18.3.1876
45	Neilson, *Thomas Paterson*		1	1874	Fwd	22.10.1851	19.1.1909
46	Reid, *James*		5	1874–77	Fwd	24.2.1851	29.7.1908
47	Todd, *John K*		2	1874–75	Fwd	c1853	
48	Young, *Arthur Henderson*	Arthur	1	1874	Fwd	31.10.1854	20.10.1938
49	Cross, *Malcolm*	Malcolm	9	1875–80	TQ	15.6.1856	20.12.1919
50	Finlay, *Ninian Jamieson*	Ninian	9	1875–81	TQ	31.1.1858	7.3.1936
51	Hay, *James Robert* (later Hay-Gordon)		3	1875–77	HB	9.11.1849	15.1.1934
52	Arthur, *Allan*	Allan	2	1875–76	Fwd	3.4.1855	9.10.1923
53	Dunlop, *James William*		1	1875	Fwd	16.10.1854	20.11.1923
54	Finlay, *Alexander Bannatyne*	Alec	1	1875	Fwd	21.4.1854	10.9.1921
55	Fleming, *George Raphael*		2	1875–76	Fwd	5.8.1850	13.12.1909
56	Marshall, *Arthur*		1	1875	Fwd	27.4.1855	9.12.1909
57	Robertson, *Duncan*	Duncan	1	1875	Fwd	30.6.1851	29.9.1907
58	Carrick, *James Stewart*		2	1876–7	FB	4.9.1855	2.1.1923
59	Paterson, *George Quintin*		1	1876	HB	5.3.1855	
60	Bolton, *William Henry*		1	1876	Fwd	15.3.1851	5.12.1896
61	Brewis, *Nathaniel Thomas*	Nat	6	1876–80	Fwd	16.4.1856	21.10.1924
62	Graham, *James Hope Stewart*	'Gussie'	10	1876–81	Fwd	16.4.1856	17.10.1922
63	Junor, *John Elphinstone*		6	1876–81	Fwd	4.11.1855	12.10.1920
64	Lang, *David*		2	1876–77	Fwd	16.8.1852	
65	Villar, *Charles*		3	1876–77	Fwd		
66	Watson, *David Henry*		3	1876–77	Fwd	7.1.1854	3.3.1906
67	Johnston, *Henry Halcro*		2	1877	FB, TQ	13.9.1856	18.10.1939
68	Mackenzie, *Robert Campbell*		4	1877–81	TQ	12.1.1856	26.5.1945
69	Pocock, *Edward Innes*		2	1877	HB	3.12.1855	14.1.1905
70	Napier, *Henry Melville*	Henry	5	1877–79	Fwd	2.5.1854	18.12.1940
71	Smith, *Stewart Henry*		2	1877–78	Fwd	12.4.1855	29.11.1896
72	Torrie, *Thomas Jameson*		1	1877	Fwd	13.4.1857	18.6.1913
73	Maclagan, *William Edward*	Bill	26	1878–90	FB, TQ	5.4.1858	10.10.1926
74	Campbell, *James Alexander*		5	1878–81	HB	1858	20.6.1902
75	Neilson, *John Alexander*		2	1878–79	HB	14.6.1858	16.7.1915
76	Auldjo, *Louis C*	Louis	1	1878	Fwd	6.11.1855	25.6.1943
77	Irvine, *Duncan Robertson*		3	1878–79	Fwd	4.1851	17.3.1914
78	MacLeod, *George William Leslie*		2	1878–82	Fwd	6.5.1858	
79	Masters, *William Hay*		3	1879–80	HB	25.6.1858	2.10.1897
80	Ainslie, *Robert*	Bob	7	1879–82	Fwd	30.1.1858	12.5.1906
81	Brown, *John Blair*		18	1879–86	Fwd	26.5.1856	
82	Smith, *Errol Ross*		1	1879	Fwd	1860	23.3.1902
83	Somerville, *D*		6	1879–84	Fwd		
84	Ewart, *Edward Neil*		3	1879–80	Fwd	2.8.1860	26.4.1935
85	Brown, *William Sorley*		7	1880–83	HB	2.6.1860	15.9.1901
86	McCowan, *David*	David	10	1880–84	Fwd	8.12.1860	15.5.1937
87	Stewart, *Charles Alexander Reid*		2	1880	Fwd		25.2.1890
88	Tait, *John Guthrie*	Jack	2	1880–85	Fwd	24.8.1861	4.10.1945
89	Cassels, *David Young*		7	1880–83	Fwd	4.3.1859	25.1.1923
90	Begbie, *Thomas Allan*		2	1881	FB	1.8.1862	26.2.1896
91	Smeaton, *Patrick Walker*	Pat	3	1881–83	HB	12.11.1857	11.8.1928
92	Allan, *Bryce*	Bryce	1	1881	Fwd	1.3.1859	22.8.1922
93	Reid, *Charles*	Charlie	21	1881–8	Fwd	14.1.1864	25.10.1909

Cap No	Name	Known as	Caps	Career	Position	Date of birth	Date of death
94	Robb, *George Henry*		2	1881–85	Fwd	24.9.1858	15.4.1927
95	Walker, *Archibald*		5	1881–83	Fwd	29.6.1858	10.6.1945
96	Don Wauchope, *Andrew Ramsay*	Andrew 'Bunny'	13	1881–88	HB	29.4.1861	16.1.1948
97	Ainslie, *Thomas*	Tom	12	1881–85	Fwd	18.12.1860	16.3.1926
98	Fraser, *James William*		1	1881	Fwd		21.1.1943
99	Maitland, *Robert James Peebles*		5	1881–85	Fwd	7.1.1862	
100	Peterkin, *William Arthur*		8	1881–85	Fwd	31.12.1857	22.3.1945
101	Anderson, *Thomas*	Tom	1	1882	FB	17.5.1863	17.6.1938
102	Hunter, *Frank*	Frank	1	1882	TQ	26.7.1858	11.10.1930
103	Asher, *Augustus Gordon Grant*		7	1882–86	HB	18.12.1861	15.3.1921
104	Gore, *Arthur Charles Fraser*		1	1882	Fwd	10.7.1857	22.9.1914
105	Veitch, *James Pringle*		8	1882–86	FB	16.9.1862	22.1.1917
106	Philp, *Andrew*		1	1882	TQ		
107	Walker, *James George*		2	1882–83	Fwd	9.10.1859	24.3.1923
108	Walls, *William Andrew*		10	1882–86	Fwd	29.12.1859	19.2.1936
109	Kidston, *David Whitelaw*		2	1883	FB	2.10.1859	27.6.1909
110	MacFarlan, *David James*		8	1883–88	TQ	3.10.1862	2.1.1940
111	Jamieson, *John*		9	1883–85	Fwd		17.11.1921
112	Mowat, *John Gunn*		2	1883	Fwd	22.1.1859	1.1.1935
113	Reid, *Marshall Frederick*		2	1883	TQ	3.8.1864	20.3.1925
114	Aitchison, *George Ritchie*	George	1	1883	HB	19.10.1864	25.1.1895
115	Lindsay, *George Campbell*	George	4	1884–87	TQ	3.1.1863	5.4.1905
116	Tod, *John*	John	9	1884–86	Fwd	9.10.1862	9.9.1935
117	Roland, *Ernest Trousseau*		2	1884	TQ	28.1.1865	16.4.1896
118	Berry, *Charles Walter*		9	1884–88	Fwd	6.9.1863	11.10.1947
119	Harrower, *Patrick Robertson*		1	1885	FB	19.1.1863	6.1936
120	Stephen, *Alexander Edward*		2	1885–86	TQ	21.7.1861	18.8.1942
121	Maitland, *Gardyne*		2	1885	TQ	7.12.1865	
122	Mitchell, *James Gordon*		3	1885	Fwd	26.5.1865	
123	Evans, *Herbert Lavington*		2	1885	TQ	14.12.1859	9.4.1925
124	Don Wauchope, *Patrick Hamilton*		6	1885–87	HB	1.5.1863	9.1.1939
125	Irvine, *Thomas Walter*	Walter	11	1885–89	Fwd	21.10.1865	26.1.1919
126	McIndoe, *James Flowerdew*		2	1886	FB	14.2.1865	11.1.1932
127	Holms, *William Frederick*		6	1886–89	TQ, FB	27.8.1866	30.9.1950
128	Morrison, *Reginald Herbert*	Reggie	3	1886	TQ	24.3.1864	1.5.1941
129	Clay, *Alexander Thomson*		7	1886–88	Fwd	27.9.1863	9.11.1950
130	French, *J*		4	1886–87	Fwd		
131	MacLeod, *William Mackintosh*		2	1886	Fwd	15.6.1861	30.6.1931
132	Milne, *Charles James Barclay*		3	1886	Fwd	15.5.1864	6.5.1892
133	MacLeod, *Duncan Archibald*		2	1886	Fwd	12.6.1866	9.12.1907
134	Wilson, *George Robert*	George	5	1886–91	TQ	12.10.1866	12.3.1908
135	McEwan, *Matthew Clark*		15	1886–92	Fwd	5.10.1865	14.4.1899
136	Woodrow, *Alexander Norie*		3	1887	TQ	13.11.1867	26.2.1916
137	Orr, *Charles Edward*		16	1887–92	HB	21.11.1866	6.4.1935
138	Ker, *Hugh Torrance*	Hugh	7	1887–90	Fwd	23.6.1865	19.3.1938
139	MacMillan, *Robert Gordon*		21	1887–97	Fwd	3.4.1865	3.4.1936
140	Morton, *David Simson*		9	1887–90	Fwd	23.7.1861	7.5.1937
141	Cameron, *Alexander William Cumming*	Alec	3	1887–94	FB	3.3.1866	14.3.1957
142	Chambers, *Henry Francis Townsend*		4	1888–89	FB	22.5.1865	12.2.1934
143	Stevenson, *Henry James*	Harry	15	1888–93	TQ, FB	12.7.1867	8.8.1945
144	Duncan, *Macbeth Moir*		1	1888	Fwd	1.9.1866	2.10.1942
145	Fraser, *Charles Frederick Pollock*		2	1888-89	HB	5.5.1868	10.12.1916
146	Duke, *Alfred*		6	1888-89	Fwd	2.12.1866	11.12.1945

Cap No	Name	Known as	Caps	Career	Position	Date of birth	Date of death
147	Stevenson, *Louis Edgar*		1	1888	Fwd	31.1.1864	19.8.1931
148	White, *Thomas Brown*	Tom	3	1888–89	Fwd	1.3.1866	6.7.1939
149	Malcolm, *Alexander George*		1	1888	Fwd	9.11.1867	18.3.1951
150	Marsh, *James Holt*		2	1889	TQ	1866	1.8.1928
151	Auld, *William*	Bill	2	1889–90	HB	25.4.1868	19.7.1945
152	Boswell, *John Douglas*		15	1889–94	Fwd	16.2.1867	5.1.1948
153	Macdonald, *William A*		3	1889–92	Fwd	c1861	
154	Methuen, *Alfred*		2	1889	Fwd	15.2.1868	5.3.1949
155	Anderson, *Darsie Gordon*	Darsie	8	1889–92	HB	22.2.1868	26.12.1937
156	Aitken, *Alexander Inglis*		1	1889	Fwd	8.1.1869	7.7.1925
157	McKendrick, *JG*		1	1889	Fwd		
158	Orr, *John*	Jack	16	1889–93	Fwd	20.8.1865	5.11.1935
159	MacGregor, *Gregor*	Gregor	13	1890–96	FB, TQ	31.8.1869	20.8.1919
160	Dalgleish, *Adam*	Adam	8	1890–94	Fwd	c1868	14.9.1938
161	Goodhue, *Frederick William Jervis*		9	1890–92	Fwd	26.4.1867	30.12.1940
162	MacIntyre, *Ian*	Ian	6	1890–91	Fwd	27.11.1869	29.6.1946
163	Neilson, *William*	William	14	1891–97	TQ	18.8.1873	16.3.1960
164	Clauss, *Paul Robert Adolph*	Paul	6	1891–95	TQ	22.6.1868	21.4.1945
165	Leggatt, *Herbert Thomas Owen*		9	1891–94	Fwd	26.10.1968	23.5.1945
166	Neilson, *George Thomson*	George	14	1891–96	Fwd	22.1.1872	6.4.1944
167	Wotherspoon, *William*		7	1891–94	HB	2.5.1868	19.8.1942
168	Gibson, *William Ross*		14	1891–95	Fwd	2.1.1865	2.1.1924
169	Campbell, *George Theophilus*		17	1892–1900	TQ	17.10.1872	28.3.1924
170	Millar, *John Neill*		6	1892–95	Fwd	9.3.1873	9.11.1921
171	Woodburn, *James Cowan*		1	1892	TQ	21.4.1870	1.5.1903
172	Henderson, *Nelson Faviell*		1	1892	Fwd	24.9.1865	16.6.1943
173	Robertson, *David Donaldson*		1	1893	TQ	20.3.1869	13.9.1937
174	Gowans, *James J*		8	1893–96	TQ	23.4.1872	1936
175	Greig, *Robert Coventry*		2	1893–97	HB	30.5.1871	10.1.1951
176	Cownie, *William Brodie*		9	1893–95	Fwd	9.3.1871	4.12.1932
177	Hendry, *Thomas Laurie*		4	1893–95	Fwd	25.12.1866	1939
178	Menzies, *Henry Fisher*	Henry	4	1893–94	Fwd	15.6.1867	31.7.1938
179	Donaldson, *William Patrick*		6	1893–99	HB	4.3.1871	27.3.1923
180	Simpson, *John William*		13	1893–99	HB	2.9.1872	11.1.1921
181	Bishop, *James Murray*		1	1893	Fwd	27.12.1867	15.1.1938
182	Fisher, *D*		1	1893	Fwd		
183	Ford, *James R*	Jim	1	1893	Fwd		
184	Davidson, *Roger Stewart*		1	1893	Fwd	17.2.1869	18.2.1955
185	Scott, *Thomas Monro*	Tom	12	1893–1900	Fwd	9.12.1870	19.2.1930
186	Rogerson, *John*		1	1894	FB		
187	Gedge, *Henry Theodore Sidney*		6	1894–99	W, C	19.8.1870	5.12.1943
188	McEwan, *William Maclean Clark*	Willie, Bill	16	1894–1900	Fwd	24.10.1875	4.4.1934
189	Wright, *Hugh Brooks*		1	1894	Fwd	7.11.1875	24.12.1953
190	Anderson, *Alexander Harvie*		1	1894	Fwd	4.11.1873	14.12.1939
191	Neilson, *Walter Gordon*	Gordon	1	1894	Fwd	1.10.1876	29.4.1927
192	Smith, *Allan Ramsay*	Allan	11	1895–1900	FB, W, C	10.1.1875	31.3.1926
193	Welsh, *Robert*	Robin	4	1895–96	W	20.10.1869	21.10.1934
194	Elliot, *Matthew*	Mattha	6	1895–98	HB	14.6.1870	3.12.1945
195	Dods, *John Henry*	Harry	8	1895–97	Fwd	30.9.1875	30.12.1915
196	Smith, *Harry Oswald*	Harry	11	1895–1902	Fwd	1.7.1873	31.7.1957
197	Timms, *Alexander Boswell*	Alec	14	1896–1905	C	2.3.1872	5.5.1922
198	Scott, *Thomas*	Tom	11	1896–1900	C, W	8.3.1875	16.4.1947
199	Patterson, *David*	Davie	1	1896	HB	11.12.1871	21.1.1945
200	Balfour, *Andrew*		4	1896–97	Fwd	21.3.1873	30.1.1931

Cap No	Name	Known as	Caps	Career	Position	Date of birth	Date of death
201	Couper, *James Hammond*		3	1896–99	Fwd	15.9.1873	17.8.1917
202	Morrison, *Mark Coxon*	Mark	23	1896–1904	Fwd	2.4.1877	10.5.1945
203	Fleming, *Charles James Nicol*		3	1896–97	w, c	5.4.1868	13.11.1948
204	Turnbull, *George Oliver*		5	1896–1904	Fwd	21.7.1877	14.1.1970
205	Laidlaw, *Alexander Smith*	Alec	1	1897	Fwd	13.8.1877	12.9.1933
206	Stevenson, *Ronald C*		6	1897–99	Fwd		12.2.1934
207	Bucher, *Alfred Moore*	Alfred	1	1897	w	22.3.1874	20.8.1939
208	Robertson, *Alexander Weir*	Alec	1	1897	w	11.12.1877	28.10.1941
209	Reid, *James Martin*		3	1898–99	FB	17.3.1876	25.5.1967
210	Neilson, *Robert Thomson*	Robbie	6	1898–1900	C, HB	17.11.1878	16.7.1945
211	Spencer, *Edward*		1	1898	C	18.6.1876	10.4.1931
212	Mabon, *John Thomas*	Joe	4	1898–1900	HB	13.2.1874	2.6.1945
213	Dykes, *John Morton*		10	1898–1902	Fwd	15.8.1877	12.10.1955
214	Kerr, *Graham Campbell*		8	1898–1900	Fwd	29.4.1872	18.8.1913
215	MacKinnon, *Andrew*		6	1898–1900	Fwd	30.4.1873	
216	Scott, *Robert*		3	1898–1900	Fwd		
217	Nelson, *Thomas Arthur*	Tommy	1	1898	C	22.9.1876	9.4.1917
218	Monypenny, *Douglas Blackwell*	Douglas	3	1899	C	28.5.1878	22.2.1900
219	Harvey, *Lawrence*		1	1899	Fwd	31.1.1876	30.10.1953
220	Rottenburg, *Heinrich*	Harry	5	1899–1900	FB	6.10.1875	25.3.1955
221	Lamond, *George Alexander Walker*	George	3	1899–1905	C	23.7.1878	25.2.1918
222	Thomson, *William John*		3	1899–1900	Fwd	18.4.1876	10.11.1939
223	Gillespie, *John Imrie*	John	10	1899–1904	HB	16.1.1879	5.12.1943
224	Crabbie, *John Edward*	Jack	6	1900–05	w	11.4.1879	21.8.1937
225	Morrison, *William Henry*		1	1900	C	26.12.1875	9.2.1944
226	Fasson, *Francis Hamilton*		5	1900–02	HB	21.9.1877	23.10.1955
227	Bedell-Sivright, *David Revell*	David	22	1900–08	Fwd	8.12.1880	5.9.1915
228	Henderson, *Frederick William*		2	1900	Fwd	3.1.1879	30.9.1950
229	Welsh, *William Halliday*	Willie	8	1900–02	w	4.9.1879	30.6.1972
230	Campbell, *John Argentine*		1	1900	Fwd	20.10.1877	2.12.1917
231	Greenlees, *James Robertson Campbell*		7	1900–03	Fwd	14.12.1878	16.5.1951
232	Scott, *William Patrick*	Bill	21	1900–07	Fwd	18.3.1880	1.6.1948
233	Bell, *Lewis Hay Irving*	Lewis	3	1900–04	Fwd	23.10.1878	25.6.1924
234	Duncan, *Alexander William*		6	1901–02	FB	19.6.1881	18.11.1934
235	Turnbull, *Phipps*	Phipps	6	1901–02	C	3.4.1878	24.8.1907
236	Fell, *Alfred Nolan*	Nolan	7	1901–03	w	17.1.1878	5.4.1953
237	Bell, *John Arthur*		6	1901–02	Fwd	1882	
238	Flett, *Andrew Binny*		5	1901–02	Fwd	7.12.1875	15.7.1961
239	Frew, *Alexander*		3	1901	Fwd	24.10.1877	4.1947
240	Ross, *James*		5	1901–03	Fwd	15.2.1880	1.11.1914
241	Stronach, *Robert Summers*	Robert	5	1901–05	Fwd	19.5.1882	28.8.1966
242	Dods, *Francis Palliser*		1	1901	Fwd	23.2.1879	29.6.1910
243	Neill, *Robert Miln*		2	1901–02	HB	5.9.1882	14.9.1914
244	Bedell-Sivright, *John Vandaleur*	John	1	1902	Fwd	18.10.1881	21.10.1920
245	Kyle, *William Elliot*	Bill	21	1902–10	Fwd	13.7.1881	11.12.1959
246	Drybrough, *Andrew Stanley*		2	1902–03	C	6.3.1878	12.9.1946
247	Bullmore, *Herbert Henry*		1	1902	Fwd	12.7.1874	28.12.1937
248	Simson, *Ernest David*	Ernest	17	1902–07	HB	13.3.1882	22.7.1910
249	Forrest, *Walter Torrie*	Walter	8	1903–05	FB	14.11.1880	19.4.1917
250	Orr, *Hugh James*		5	1903–04	C, w	21.1.1878	16.5.1946
251	Knox, *John*		3	1903	HB	5.8.1880	20.4.1964
252	Cairns, *Alexander Gordon*		12	1903–06	Fwd	26.4.1878	8.4.1968
253	Kennedy, *Norman*		3	1903	Fwd	17.3.1881	15.1.1960
254	West, *Leonard*		9	1903–06	Fwd	5.1879	26.1.1945

Cap No	Name	Known as	Caps	Career	Position	Date of birth	Date of death
255	France, *Charles*		1	1903	W	11.2.1879	28.10.1946
256	Macdonald, *James Stirling*		5	1903–05	W	15.7.1879	
257	Dallas, *John Dewar*	Jack	1	1903	Fwd	17.6.1878	31.7.1942
258	Crabbie, *George Ernest*	George	1	1904	W	23.7.1882	23.10.1921
259	MacLeod, *Lewis Macdonald*	Lewis	6	1904–05	C	8.6.1885	12.11.1907
260	Bisset, *Alexander Anderson*		1	1904	HB	18.10.1883	14.2.1927
261	Ross, *Edward Johnson*		1	1904	Fwd	2.3.1884	22.6.1943
262	Milne, *William Murray*		4	1904–05	Fwd	27.7.1883	16.12.1982
263	Waters, *Joseph Bow*		2	1904	Fwd	29.4.1882	30.6.1954
264	Fletcher, *Hugh Nethersole*		2	1904–05	Fwd	27.4.1877	29.1.1962
265	Forbes, *John Lockhart*	John	3	1905–06	C	1.1.1883	10.2.1967
266	Munro, *Patrick*	Pat	13	1905–11	HB	9.10.1883	3.5.1942
267	Little, *Andrew Walter*	Ned	1	1905	Fwd	8.12.1880	
268	Ross, *Andrew*		5	1905–09	Fwd	1879	6.4.1916
269	Ritchie, *William Traill*	Bill	2	1905	W	11.3.1882	22.5.1940
270	McCowat, *Robert Harold*		1	1905	W	30.4.1882	20.3.1956
271	Dickson, *Maurice Rhynd*	Maurice	1	1905	Fwd	2.1.1882	10.1.1940
272	Schulze, *Douglas Gordon*	Douglas	13	1905–11	FB	5.3.1881	17.5.1956
273	Elliot, *Thomas*	Tom	1	1905	W	1880	28.11.1948
274	MacCallum, *John Cameron*	John	26	1905–11	Fwd	11.10.1883	29.11.1957
275	Monteith, *Hugh Glencairn*		8	1905–08	Fwd	11.5.1883	10.10.1963
276	Scoular, *John Gladstone*		5	1905–06	FB	17.9.1885	7.9.1953
277	Simson, *John Thomas*		7	1905–11	W	21.10.1884	30.3.1976
278	MacLeod, *Kenneth Grant*	Ken	10	1905–08	C, W	2.2.1888	
279	Sloan, *Tennant*		7	1905–09	W, C	9.11.1884	15.10.1972
280	Greig, *Louis Leisler*	Louis	5	1905–08	HB	17.11.1880	1.3.1953
281	Mackenzie, *James Moir*		9	1905–11	Fwd	17.10.1886	22.1.1963
282	Russell, *William Laing*		4	1905–06	Fwd	31.5.1880	31.10.1933
283	Church, *William Campbell*	Bill	1	1906	W	5.8.1883	28.6.1915
284	Purves, *Alexander Buckholm Haliburton Laidlaw*	Alec	10	1906–08	W	15.8.1886	20.9.1945
285	Walter, *Maurice Winn*	Maurie	8	1906–10	C	4.1.1888	3.9.1910
286	Frew, *George Mitchell*	George	15	1906–11	Fwd	9.9.1883	6.4.1942
287	Geddes, *Irvine Campbell*		6	1906–08	Fwd	9.7.1882	18.5.1962
288	Speirs, *Louis Moritz*	Louis	10	1906–10	Fwd	23.10.1885	21.4.1949
289	Thomson, *WHM*		1	1906	Fwd		
290	MacGregor, *Duncan Grant*		3	1907	C	20.5.1887	5.10.1971
291	Sanderson, *George Alfred*		4	1907–08	Fwd	9.8.1881	23.11.1957
292	Scott, *John Menzies Baillie*	Jock	21	1907–13	Fwd	6.10.1887	14.1.1967
293	Martin, *Hugh*	Hugh	5	1908–09	W	9.4.1888	6.1.1970
294	Cunningham, *George*	George	8	1908–11	HB, C	23.3.1888	8.12.1963
295	Brown, *JA*		2	1908	Fwd		
296	Gowlland, *Geoffrey Cathcart*		7	1908–10	Fwd	27.5.1885	9.10.1980
297	Wilson, *John Skinner*		2	1908–09	Fwd	10.3.1884	31.5.1916
298	Gilray, *Colin Macdonald*	Colin	4	1908–12	C	17.3.1885	15.7.1974
299	Robertson, *James*		1	1908	HB	5.5.1883	
300	Wade, *Albert Luvian*		1	1908	HB	20.9.1884	28.4.1917
301	Robertson, *Lewis*	Lewis	9	1908–13	Fwd	4.8.1883	3.11.1914
302	Angus, *Alexander William*	Gus	18	1909–20	C	11.11.1889	25.3.1947
303	Tennent, *James MacWilliam*	Jim	6	1909–10	HB	7.9.1888	19.3.1955
304	Pearson, *James*	Jimmy	12	1909–13	C, W	24.2.1888	22.5.1915
305	Lindsay-Watson, *Robert Hamilton*	Robert	1	1909	W	4.10.1886	26.1.1956
306	MacGregor, *John Roy*		1	1909	HB	27.8.1885	24.7.1940
307	Lely, *William Gerald*		1	1909	Fwd	15.7.1886	30.1.1972
308	Stuart, *Charles Douglas*		7	1909–11	Fwd	18.5.1887	15.1.1982

Cap No	Name	Known as	Caps	Career	Position	Date of birth	Date of death
309	Moodie, *Alexander Reid*		3	1909–11	Fwd	30.9.1886	21.5.1968
310	Kerr, *James Reid*		1	1909	Fwd	4.12.1883	19.8.1963
311	Buchanan, *Fletcher Gordon*		3	1910–11	FB, C	23.12.1889	1.1967
312	Robertson, *Ian Peter Macintosh*		1	1910	W	3.2.1887	9.5.1949
313	Stevenson, *Robert C*		6	1910–11	Fwd	17.2.1886	1973
314	Sutherland, *Walter Riddell*	Walter	13	1910–14	W, C	19.11.1890	4.10.1918
315	Milroy, *Eric*	Eric 'Puss'	12	1910–14	HB	4.12.1887	18.7.1916
316	Macpherson, *Donald Gregory*		2	1910	W	23.7.1882	26.11.1956
317	Dobson, *James Donald*	Jimmy	1	1910	W	23.11.1888	14.3.1962
318	Lindsay, *Andrew Alexander Bonar*	Andrew	2	1910–11	SH	19.7.1885	15.5.1970
319	Abercrombie, *Cecil Halliday*	Cecil	6	1910–13	Fwd	12.4.1886	31.5.1916
320	Todd, *Hugh Borthwick*	Borth	1	1911	FB	28.10.1888	31.12.1962
321	Young, *Thomas Eric Boswell*		1	1911	C	6.2.1891	12.3.1973
322	Osler, *FL*		2	1911	SH		
323	Fraser, *Rowland*		4	1911	Fwd	10.1.1890	1.7.1916
324	Stevenson, *AM*		1	1911	Fwd		
325	Turner, *Frederick Harding*	Freddie	15	1911–14	Fwd	29.5.1888	10.1.1915
326	Grant, *Donald Macpherson*	Donald	2	1911	W	30.12.1892	8.12.1962
327	Macdonald, *John MacKinnon*		1	1911	W	7.12.1890	1.6.1980
328	Ross, *Andrew Russell*		4	1911–14	Fwd	13.1.1892	21.6.1981
329	Greig, *Andrew*	Andrew	1	1911	FB	27.10.1889	
330	Ogilvy, *Charles*	Carl	3	1911–12	C, FB	13.6.1889	29.8.1958
331	Simson, *Ronald Francis*	Ronald	1	1911	C	6.9.1890	15.9.1914
332	Steyn, *Stephen Sebastian Lombard*	Stephen	2	1911–12	W	10.11.1889	8.12.1917
333	Henderson, *James Young Milne*	James	1	1911	SH	9.3.1891	31.7.1917
334	Bain, *David McLaren*	David	11	1911–14	Fwd	10.9.1891	3.6.1915
335	Dobson, *John*	John	6	1911–12	Fwd	6.9.1886	16.7.1936
336	Hutchison, *William Ramsay*		1	1911	Fwd	16.1.1889	22.3.1918
337	Dickson, *Walter Michael*	Mike	7	1912	FB	23.11.1884	26.9.1915
338	Will, *John George*	George	7	1912–14	W	2.9.1892	25.3.1917
339	Gunn, *Alexander William*	Sandy	5	1912–13	SO, C	16.11.1890	1.4.1980
340	Hume, *John*	'Jenny'	7	1912–22	SH	17.3.1890	20.12.1969
341	Hill, *Colin Cecil Pitcairn*		2	1912	Fwd	17.7.1887	9.6.1953
342	Howie, *David Dickie*	Dave	7	1912–13	Fwd	12.5.1888	19.1.1916
343	Purves, *William Donald Campbell Laidlaw*		6	1912–13	Fwd	4.7.1888	19.9.1964
344	Robertson, *Robert Dalrymple*		1	1912	Fwd	28.7.1891	19.12.1971
345	Burnet, *William Alexander*	Billy	1	1912	C	6.3.1886	25.7.1958
346	Boyd, *James Lawrence*		2	1912	SO	18.8.1891	15.6.1930
347	Usher, *Charles Milne*	Charlie	16	1912–22	Fwd	26.9.1891	21.1.1981
348	Blair, *Patrick Charles Bentley*		5	1912–13	Fwd	18.7.1891	6.7.1915
349	Stewart, *William Allan*	Bill	4	1913–14	W	23.10.1889	29.4.1958
350	Gordon, *Roland Elphinston*	Roland	3	1913	C	22.1.1893	30.8.1918
351	Ledingham, *George Alexander*		1	1913	Fwd	8.3.1890	8.11.1978
352	Macdougall, *John Bowes*		5	1913–21	Fwd	1890	1967
353	Bruce Lockhart, *John Harold*	Rufus	2	1913–20	SO, C	4.3.1889	4.6.1956
354	Bowie, *Thomas Chalmers*		4	1913–14	SO	28.4.1889	28.11.1972
355	Maxwell, *Georgius Henry Hope Patrick*	George	13	1913–22	Fwd	18.10.1892	21.2.1961
356	Wallace, *William Middleton*	Willie	4	1913–14	FB	23.9.1892	22.8.1915
357	Sweet, *John Burton*		2	1913–14	W	26.3.1892	27.2.1943
358	Loudoun-Shand, *Eric Gordon*	Eric	1	1913	C	31.3.1893	8.1972
359	Scobie, *Ronald Mackenzie*		3	1914	C	8.6.1893	23.2.1969
360	Sloan, *Allen Thomson*		9	1914–21	SO, W, C	30.12.1892	2.10.1952
361	Hamilton, *Andrew Steven*		2	1914–20	HB	8.3.1893	3.11.1975

Cap No	Name	Known as	Caps	Career	Position	Date of birth	Date of death
362	Donald, *David Grahame*		2	1914	Fwd	27.7.1891	23.12.1976
363	Laing, *Arthur Douglas*	'Podger'	7	1914–21	Fwd	25.4.1892	24.11.1927
364	Stewart, *Archibald Mathison*		1	1914	Fwd	27.9.1890	18.9.1974
365	Symington, *Archibald William*		2	1914	Fwd	3.1892	8.5.1941
366	Wemyss, *Andrew*	Jock	7	1914–22	Fwd	22.5.1893	21.1.1974
367	Warren, *John Russell*	Jack	1	1914	C	13.8.1889	28.4.1941
368	Huggan, *James Laidlaw*	James	1	1914	W	11.10.1888	16.9.1914
369	Pender, *Ian MacAlister*		1	1914	Fwd	18.8.1894	13.10.1961
370	Young, *Eric Templeton*		1	1914	Fwd	14.4.1892	28.6.1915
371	Pattullo, *George Leonard Shield*		4	1920	FB	9.1892	1966
372	Fahmy, *Ernest Chalmers*		4	1920	C, SO	28.11.1892	25.8.1982
373	Crole, *Gerard Bruce*		4	1920	W	7.6.1894	31.3.1965
374	Kennedy, *Finlay*	Finlay	5	1920–21	P, L	23.1.1892	8.3.1925
375	Gallie, *Robert Arthur*	Bob	8	1920–21	H, P	20.1.1893	25.5.1948
376	Duncan, *Denoon Douglas*		4	1920	Fwd	15.2.1893	20.5.1955
377	Murray, *William Alexander Kininmonth*		3	1920–21	Fwd		3.1985
378	Thom, *George*	George	4	1920	F, 8	1899	27.8.1927
379	MacKay, *Eric Boyle*		2	1920–22	W	1899	23.7.1966
380	Selby, *John Alexander Robertson*	Jake	2	1920	SH	28.7.1900	15.2.1951
381	Macpherson, *Neil Clark*	Neil	7	1920–23	L, F, P	26.9.1892	12.11.1957
382	Browning, *Arthur*	Arthur	7	1920–23	W	2.7.1897	
383	Nimmo, *Charles Stuart*	Charles	1	1920	SH	10.6.1895	20.2.1943
384	Forsayth, *Hector Henry*		7	1921–22	FB	18.12.1899	7.3.1952
385	Kilgour, *Ian James*	Ian	1	1921	W	23.10.1900	20.4.1977
386	Thomson, *Alpin Erroll*		3	1921	C	14.5.1893	6.3.1960
387	Gracie, *Archibald Leslie*	Leslie	13	1921–24	C, W	15.10.1896	2.8.1982
388	Carmichael, *James Howden*	Jimmy	3	1921	W	22.3.1900	22.3.1990
389	Cumming, *Ronald Stuart*		2	1921	P, H	4.4.1900	17.11.1982
390	Bannerman, *John MacDonald*	John	37	1921–29	L	1.9.1901	10.4.1969
391	Donald, *Russell Lindsay Hunter*	Russell	3	1921	SO	9.9.1898	31.12.1932
392	Buchanan, *John Cecil Rankin*	Rankin	16	1921–25	H	18.6.1896	19.2.1976
393	Douglas, *George*		1	1921	L	10.8.1897	26.10.1957
394	Shaw, *James Norrie*	Hamish	2	1921	8	13.9.1896	10.11.1990
395	McCrow, *John William Stuart*		1	1921	W	11.5.1899	25.2.1950
396	Murray, *George Macgibbon*	George	2	1921–26	F, P	6.1900	26.12.1981
397	Stewart, *John Livingstone*	Jock	1	1921	8	6.5.1894	6.8.1971
398	Mackenzie, *Cecil James Granville*		1	1921	C	26.2.1889	7.12.1959
399	Johnston, *William Carstairs*	Bill	1	1922	FB	16.12.1896	6.10.1983
400	Macpherson, *George Philip Stewart*	Phil	26	1922–32	C, SO	12.1903	2.3.1981
401	Liddell, *Eric Henry*	Eric	7	1922–23	W	16.1.1902	21.2.1945
402	Dykes, *James Carroll*	Jimmy	20	1922–29	SO, C	4.7.1901	3.7.1967
403	Bertram, *David Minto*		11	1922–24	H	24.1.1899	10.4.1975
404	Stevenson, *Andrew Kirkwood*		4	1922–23	P	1897	1968
405	Davies, *Douglas S*	Doug	20	1922–27	P, L, F	23.7.1899	9.3.1987
406	Lawrie, *John Ruthven*	Jock	11	1922–24	F	11.9.1900	7.7.1981
407	Warren, *Ronald Crawford*		5	1922–30	C, FB	1900	1992
408	Bryce, *William Erskine*	Willie	11	1922–24	SO	16.1.1901	22.2.1983
409	Dobson, *William Goldie*		3	1922	P	9.2.1894	11.3.1973
410	Tolmie, *James Murdo*	Jimmy	1	1922	W	20.11.1895	9.3.1955
411	Drysdale, *Daniel*	Dan	26	1923–29	FB	18.5.1901	15.10.1987
412	Wallace, *Arthur Cooper*	Johnny	9	1923–26	W	5.10.1900	3.11.1975
413	McLaren, *Edward*	Teddy	5	1923–24	C	28.5.1902	30.3.1950
414	McQueen, *Samuel Brown*		4	1923	SO	27.1.1896	16.9.1983
415	Kerr, *David Simpson*		10	1923–28	P	3.2.1899	6.3.1969

Cap No	Name	Known as	Caps	Career	Position	Date of birth	Date of death
416	Stuart, *Ludovic Mair*	Ludo	8	1923–30	L	22.10.1902	3.3.1957
417	Simpson, *Robert Simpson*		1	1923	F	28.4.1899	16.1.1999
418	Mackintosh, *Charles Ernest Whistler Christopher*		1	1924	W	31.10.1903	12.1.1974
419	Waddell, *Herbert*	Herbert	15	1924–30	SO	19.9.1902	5.1.1988
420	Ross, *Andrew*		2	1924	H, P	8.11.1904	
421	Howie, *Robert*	Bob	7	1924–25	P	11.6.1898	14.5.1992
422	Hendrie, *Kelvin Gladstone Peter*		3	1924	F	2.7.1898	8.12.1953
423	Smith, *Ian Scott*	Ian	32	1924–33	W	31.10.1903	18.9.1972
424	Aitken, *George Gothard*	George	8	1924–29	C	2.7.1898	8.7.1952
425	Gillies, *Alexander Campbell*	Sandy	12	1924–27	8	25.3.1900	22.1.1980
426	Millar, *Robert Kirkpatrick*		1	1924	W	29.6.1901	17.4.1981
427	Henderson, *Robert Gordon*		2	1924	P, L	8.1.1900	24.2.1977
428	Nelson, *James Benzie*	Jimmy	25	1925–31	SO	9.2.1903	26.10.1981
429	Gilchrist, *James*		1	1925	H	8.12.1903	1972
430	Stevenson, *William Hugh*		1	1925	P	3.5.1897	26.8.1972
431	MacMyn, *David James*	David	11	1925–28	L	18.2.1903	16.3.1978
432	Paterson, *John Rimmer*		21	1925–29	F	19.12.1900	25.9.1970
433	Scott, *James William*		18	1925–30	BR, L	24.9.1903	24.8.1949
434	Ireland, *James Cecil Hardin*	Jimmie	11	1925–27	H	10.12.1903	25.10.1998
435	Kinnear, *Roy Muir*	Roy	3	1926	C	3.2.1904	22.9.1942
436	Berkley, *William Vaughan*		4	1926–29	P	14.6.1904	19.5.1973
437	Simmers, *William Maxwell*	Max	28	1926–32	W, C	7.8.1904	14.11.1972
438	Graham, *James*	Jimmie	15	1926–32	F	19.6.1902	5.9.1986
439	Boyd, *GM*		1	1926	W	8.3.1905	1.1.1980
440	Allan, *John White*	Jock	17	1927–34	P	4.6.1905	29.12.1958
441	Taylor, *Edward Graham*		2	1927	W	3.7.1907	13.9.1959
442	Kelly, *Robert Forrest*		4	1927–28	C, W	12.3.1907	23.2.1975
443	Greenlees, *Henry Dickson*	Harry	6	1927–30	SO	31.7.1903	23.5.1969
444	Douty, *Peter Sime*		3	1927–28	SH	26.10.1903	18.7.1948
445	Roughead, *William Nicol*		12	1927–32	H	19.9.1905	22.4.1975
446	Ferguson, *William Gordon*		5	1927–28	P, L	4.3.1904	11.12.1963
447	Welsh, *William Berridge*	Willie	21	1927–33	BR	11.2.1907	27.2.1987
448	Goodfellow, *John*		3	1928	W	24.8.1906	2.4.1951
449	Ferguson, *James Huck*	Jimmy	1	1928	L	19.10.1903	3.4.1992
450	Hume, *John William Gardiner*	Jo	2	1928–30	C	13.6.1906	23.3.1976
451	Lind, *Henry*	Harry	16	1928–36	SO, C	27.3.1906	18.12.1986
452	Brown, *Alexander Henderson*	Alex	3	1928–29	SO	12.5.1905	31.12.1986
453	Mackintosh, *Hugh Stewart*		16	1929–32	P, H	19.1.1903	28.8.1989
454	Smith, *Robert Tait*	Bob	7	1929–30	P	1908	7.4.1958
455	Beattie, *John Armstrong*	Jock	23	1929–36	P, F, L	5.1.1907	10.2.1977
456	Wright, *Kenneth Moncreiff*		4	1929	F, 8	6.9.1905	
457	Aitchison, *Thomas Graham*	Tom	3	1929	FB	8.1.1907	25.12.1977
458	Brown, *Thomas Gow*		1	1929	W	9.2.1902	17.11.1985
459	Brown, *Charles Hogendorf Campbell*	Charlie	1	1929	W	12.11.1909	25.10.1976
460	Langrish, *Reginald Walter*		4	1930–31	FB	1.12.1905	15.3.1986
461	Emslie, *William Duncan*		2	1930–32	SO	3.8.1908	7.8.1969
462	Stewart, *J*	Jack	1	1930	L	2.1905	27.5.1936
463	Waters, *Frank Henry*	Frank	7	1930–32	F, L	2.12.1908	18.10.1954
464	Rowand, *Robert*	Bobby	7	1930–34	8, P	30.8.1906	23.2.1974
465	Hart, *Thomas M*		2	1930	W, SO	1.3.1909	16.2.2001
466	Foster, *Robert Amos*	Jerry	4	1930–32	P	7.12.1907	17.7.1984
467	Agnew, *William Craigie*	Bill	2	1930	F, L	1910	27.3.1961
468	St Clair-Ford, *Drummond*		5	1930–32	W	16.12.1907	12.12.1942
469	Hutton, *James Edward*		2	1930–31	C	8.8.1906	16.10.1985

Cap No	Name	Known as	Caps	Career	Position	Date of birth	Date of death
470	Polson, *Adam Henry*	Henry	1	1930	F	19.11.1907	9.7.1992
471	Wilson, *Alfred William*		3	1931	C, FB	1904	2.5.1985
472	McLaren, *David Alexander*		1	1931	L	29.8.1910	24.2.1974
473	Wilson, *James Stewart*		5	1931–32	F, 8	4.9.1909	30.4.1994
474	Walker, *Alexander William*		5	1931–32	8, L, F	25.10.1908	1976
475	Wood, *George*	Dod	5	1931–32	W, C	19.4.1905	1989
476	Crichton-Miller, *Donald*	Donald	3	1931	F	7.12.1906	5.8.1997
477	Logan, *William Ross*	Ross	20	1931–37	SH	24.11.1909	26.11.1993
478	Lawther, *Thomas Hope Brendan*		2	1932	FB	6.10.1909	12.12.1994
479	Forrest, *James Edminston*		3	1932–35	W	3.2.1907	2.4.1981
480	Stewart, *Mark Sprot*	Mark	9	1932–34	L	7.1.1905	2.3.1993
481	Hutton, *Alexander Harold Miller*	Harry	1	1932	FB	30.12.1907	23.12.1981
482	Dykes, *Andrew S*	Andrew	1	1932	FB	19.6.1904	3.1.1970
483	Macarthur, *John Parlane*		1	1932	SH	12.9.1904	3.1982
484	Wright, *Francis Aitken*		1	1932	L	14.7.1909	14.3.1959
485	Ritchie, *George Fraser*	George	1	1932	8	4.11.1909	7.11.1993
486	Brown, *David Ian*		3	1933	FB	8.2.1909	10.11.1983
487	Lorraine, *Herbert Derrick Bell*	Bertie	3	1933	C	4.1.1913	19.3.1982
488	Fyfe, *Kenneth Carmichael*	Ken	10	1933–39	W	14.4.1914	29.1.1974
489	Jackson, *Kenneth Leslie Tatersall*	Ken	4	1933–34	SO	17.11.1913	21.3.1982
490	Waters, *John Alexander*	Jack	16	1933–37	P, 8	11.11.1908	29.9.1990
491	Ritchie, *James McPhail*	Jim	6	1933–34	H, P	10.7.1907	6.7.1942
492	Thom, *James Robert*		3	1933	P, H	22.11.1910	13.12.1981
493	Henderson, *James McLaren*	Mac	3	1933	F, L	1.5.1907	5.3.2009
494	Gedge, *Peter Maurice Sydney*	Peter	1	1933	W	18.5.1910	27.2.1993
495	Marshall, *Kenneth W*		8	1934–37	FB	23.7.1911	15.10.1992
496	Shaw, *Robert Wilson*	Wilson	19	1934–39	W, SO	11.4.1913	23.7.1979
497	Dick, *Robert Charles Stewart*	Charles	14	1934–38	C	26.7.1913	10.5.2004
498	Park, *J*	Jack	1	1934	W	4.1913	2.10.1992
499	Burnet, *William Alexander*	Bill	8	1934–36	P, L	8.7.1912	19.8.2001
500	Lambie, *Lindsay Barbour*	Lindsay	7	1934–35	H, F	30.5.1910	1996
501	Lowe, *James Douglas*	Douglas	1	1934	L	28.5.1906	7.11.1936
502	Thom, *David Alexander*	David	5	1934–35	F	16.2.1910	1982
503	Crawford, *John Archibald*		1	1934	W	20.11.1910	10.1.1973
504	Cotter, *James Logan*		2	1934	SO	6.1.1907	26.1.1991
505	Cottington, *Gordon Stanley*	Gordon	5	1934–36	H	2.4.1911	7.6.1996
506	Watherston, *Jack Greenshields*	Jack	2	1934	F	24.8.1909	1990
507	Johnston, *William Graham Stuart*		5	1935–37	W	31.5.1913	10.1994
508	Grieve, *Charles Frederick*	Charlie	5	1935–36	SO	1.10.1913	1.6.2000
509	Murray, *Ronald Ormiston*	Ronald	2	1935	P	14.11.1912	5.3.1995
510	Grieve, *Robert George Moir*	Bob	7	1935–36	P	1.2.1911	13.8.2000
511	McNeil, *Alastair Simpson Bell*	Alastair	1	1935	P	28.1.1915	26.1.1944
512	Murdoch, *William Copeland Wood*	Copey	9	1935–48	C, W, FB	3.10.1914	12.10.1987
513	Tait, *Peter Webster*		1	1935	H	19.10.1906	22.4.1980
514	Kerr, *James Mitchell*	Jimmy	5	1935–37	FB	12.5.1910	3.1.1998
515	Gray, *George Leitch*	Dod	4	1935–37	H	12.4.1909	2.9.1975
516	Shaw, *George Duncan*	Duncan	6	1935–39	F	29.5.1915	14.11.1999
517	Murray, *Hugh Martin*		2	1936	C	3.5.1912	1.2003
518	Druitt, *William Arthur Harvey*	Harvey	3	1936	H, P	19.4.1910	6.2.1973
519	Cooper, *Malcolm McGregor*	Mac	2	1936	F	17.8.1910	1.9.1991
520	Duff, *Peter Laurance*		6	1936–39	L	12.11.1912	31.10.2002
521	Whitworth, *Robert John Eve*		1	1936	W	1915	2003
522	Weston, *Vivian George*		2	1936	F	22.5.1914	1979
523	Barrie, *Robert William*	Rob	1	1936	F	7.1911	

Cap No	Name	Known as	Caps	Career	Position	Date of birth	Date of death
524	Macrae, *Duncan James*	Duncan	9	1937–39	C	4.11.1914	15.5.2007
525	Ross, *William Alexander*	Bill	2	1937	SO	15.11.1913	28.9.1941
526	Henderson, *Maurice Michael*	Maurice	3	1937	P	4.4.1913	14.10.1989
527	Inglis, *William Murray*	Joe	6	1937–38	P	20.1.1915	22.4.1988
528	Horsburgh, *George Brown*	George	9	1937–39	L	20.7.1910	1986
529	Melville, *Christian Landale*		3	1937	L	9.12.1913	23.4.1984
530	Young, *William Brewitt*	Bill	10	1937–48	F	7.5.1916	25.4.2013
531	Shaw, *Ian*	Ian	1	1937	C	4.8.1911	
532	Bruce Lockhart, *Rab Brougham*	Rab	3	1937–39	SO	1.12.1916	1.5.1990
533	Dryden, *Robert Hunter*		1	1937	W	10.1.1918	14.3.1996
534	Roberts, *George*	George	5	1938–39	FB	13.2.1914	2.8.1943
535	Drummond, *Archibald Hugh*		2	1938	W	2.4.1915	16.9.1990
536	Forrest, *John Gordon Scott*		3	1938	W	28.4.1917	14.9.1942
537	Dorward, *Thomas Fairgrieve*	Tommy	5	1938–39	SH	27.3.1916	5.3.1941
538	Borthwick, *John Bishop*	Jake	2	1938	P	29.7.1912	25.11.2008
539	Hastie, *John Dickson Hart*	Hart	3	1938	H	16.3.1908	19.1.1965
540	Roy, *Allan*	Allan	6	1938–39	L	13.5.1911	16.4.2011
541	Crawford, *Wilfrid Hornby*	Wilf	5	1938–39	F	24.8.1915	6.6.1993
542	Renwick, *William Norman*		2	1938–39	W	29.11.1914	15.6.1944
543	Blackadder, *William Francis*		1	1938	P	23.1.1913	27.11.1997
544	Craig, *John Binnie*		1	1939	W	7.12.1918	21.7.1976
545	Innes, *John Robert Stephen*	Donny	8	1939–48	C, W	16.9.1917	21.1.2012
546	Brydon, *William Ritchie Crawford*	Willie	1	1939	SH	6.11.1915	11.6.1980
547	Gallie, *George Holmes*		1	1939	P	9.9.1917	16.1.1944
548	Sampson, *Ralph William Fraser*	Sammy	2	1939–47	H	26.9.1913	31.1.2003
549	Purdie, *William Henry*	Bill	3	1939	P	24.6.1910	22.11.1997
550	Penman, *William Mitchell*	Bill	1	1939	FB	12.5.1917	3.10.1943
551	Henderson, *Ian C*		8	1939–48	P, H	31.10.1918	
552	Graham, *Ian Nicoll*		2	1939	H	8.5.1918	2.3.1982
553	Mackenzie, *Donald Kenneth Andrew*		2	1939	8	30.11.1916	12.6.1940
554	Geddes, *Keith Irvine*	Keith	4	1947	FB	25.10.1918	30.3.1991
555	Jackson, *Thomas Graeme Hogarth*	Tom	12	1947–49	W	15.10.1921	21.5.2010
556	Bruce, *Charles Russell*	Russell	8	1947–49	C	25.4.1918	17.4.2009
557	Drummond, *Charles William*	Charlie	11	1947–50	C	26.5.1923	9.5.1985
558	MacLennan, *William Donald*	Bill	2	1947	W	4.4.1921	29.9.2002
559	Lumsden, *Ian James Michael*	Ian	7	1947–49	SO, FB	6.4.1923	
560	Black, *Angus William*	Gus	6	1947–50	SH	6.5.1925	
561	Watt, *Alexander Gordon Mitchell*		6	1947–48	P, 8	19.12.1916	16.4.1982
562	McGlashan, *Thomas Perry Lang*		8	1947–54	P	29.12.1925	
563	Cawkwell, *George Law*	George	1	1947	L	25.10.1919	
564	Hunter, *John Murray*		1	1947	L	10.11.1920	2006
565	Elliot, *William Irving Douglas*	Douglas	29	1947–54	F	18.4.1923	12.5.2005
566	Orr, *John Henry*	John	2	1947	F	13.6.1918	27.9.1995
567	Deas, *David Wallace*		2	1947	8, L	30.3.1919	7.12.2001
568	Mackenzie, *David Douglas*		6	1947–48	W	28.12.1921	4.8.2005
569	Aitken, *Richard*		1	1947	P	29.6.1914	
570	Coutts, *Francis Henderson*	Frank	3	1947	L	8.7.1918	20.10.2008
571	Munro, *William Hutton*	Billy	2	1947	SO, C	28.9.1918	12.9.1970
572	Anderson, *Ernest*	Ernie	2	1947	SH	20.10.1918	27.1.2001
573	Fisher, *Alastair Thomson*	Alastair	2	1947	H	3.9.1916	26.1.1983
574	Campbell, *Howard Hindmarsh*	Howard	4	1947–48	P	10.11.1921	23.2.2012
575	Valentine, *David Donald*	Dave	2	1947	F	12.9.1926	14.8.1976
576	McLean, *Duncan Ian*		2	1947	F, 8	1.5.1923	21.3.1962
577	Lees, *James Blanch*	Jimmy	5	1947–48	8, F	11.8.1919	22.8.2004

Cap No	Name	Known as	Caps	Career	Position	Date of birth	Date of death
578	Wright, *Thomas*	Tommy	1	1947	C	18.12.1924	2.5.1990
579	McDonald, *Charles*	Charlie	1	1947	W	19.4.1919	
580	Hepburn, *Derek Peter*	Peter	9	1947–49	SO, C	15.3.1920	30.4.1996
581	Allardice, *William Dallas*	Dallas	8	1947–49	SH	4.11.1919	4.6.2003
582	Bruce, *Robert Mitchell*		4	1947–48	P, F	19.6.1922	16.6.2001
583	Lyall, *George Gibson*	Doddie	5	1947–48	H	23.5.1921	10.5.1996
584	Currie, *Leslie Robert*		8	1947–49	L, P	25.11.1921	7.8.1983
585	Dawson, *James Cooper*	Hamish	20	1947–53	L, P	29.10.1925	19.10.2007
586	Black, *William Pollock*	Bill	5	1948–51	P, L, 8	27.11.1921	
587	Cameron, *Angus*	Angus	17	1948–56	C, SO, W	24.6.1929	1.4.1991
588	Coltman, *Stewart*	Stewart	5	1948–49	P	27.3.1920	21.7.1999
589	Bruce Lockhart, *Logie*	Logie	5	1948–53	C, SO	12.10.1921	
590	Finlay, *Robert*		1	1948	L	9.4.1923	8.10.1979
591	Gloag, *Lawrence Gjers*		4	1949	C	3.10.1925	28.2.1984
592	Smith, *Douglas William Cumming*	Doug	8	1949–53	W	27.10.1924	22.9.1998
593	Abercrombie, *James Gilbert*	Gibbie	7	1949–50	H	9.5.1928	23.8.1992
594	Wilson, *Graham Alexander*		3	1949	L	23.11.1922	
595	Keller, *Douglas Holcombe*	Doug	7	1949–50	F	18.6.1922	27.3.2004
596	Kininmonth, *Peter Wyatt*	Peter	21	1949–54	8, F	23.6.1924	5.10.2007
597	Thomson, *Alexander McNiven*		1	1949	L	20.2.1921	
598	Wright, *Steven Terence Howard*		1	1949	P	14.2.1927	1965
599	Macphail, *John Alexander Rose*		2	1949–51	H	14.10.1923	2004
600	Burrell, *George*	Dod	4	1950–51	FB	21.1.1921	25.7.2001
601	Macdonald, *Ranald*	Ranald	4	1950	C	18.1.1928	2.10.1999
602	Sloan, *Donald Allen*	Donald	7	1950–53	C	11.5.1926	14.4.2008
603	Dorward, *Arthur Fairgrieve*	Arthur	15	1950–57	SH	3.3.1925	
604	Budge, *Grahame Morris*	Grahame	4	1950	P	7.11.1920	14.11.1979
605	Muir, *Douglas Edgar*		7	1950–52	L	17.3.1925	
606	Gemmill, *Robert*	Bob	7	1950–51	L	20.2.1930	
607	Scott, *Donald Macdonald*	Donald	10	1950–53	W, C	15.4.1928	
608	Gray, *Thomas*	Tommy	3	1950–51	FB	20.1.1917	3.4.2000
609	Scott, *James Stuart*	Hamish	1	1950	F	17.2.1924	12.3.2010
610	Cameron, *Allan Douglas*	Allan	3	1951–54	W, C	4.3.1924	15.10.2009
611	Coutts, *Ian Douglas Freeman*		2	1951–52	C	27.4.1928	
612	Turnbull, *Francis Oliver*	Oliver	2	1951	C	3.6.1919	19.2.2009
613	Rose, *David Macmurray*	David	7	1951–53	W	20.2.1931	
614	Ross, *Iain A*	Iain	4	1951	SH	15.12.1928	
615	Mair, *Norman George Robertson*	Norman	4	1951	H	7.10.1928	
616	Wilson, *Robert Little*	Bob	8	1951–53	P	1.7.1926	
617	Inglis, *Hamish MacFarlan*		7	1951–52	L	3.8.1931	
618	Hegarty, *John Jackson*	Jack	6	1951–55	F, L	13.4.1925	
619	Thomson, *Ian Hosie Munro*		7	1951–53	FB	13.4.1930	
620	Gordon, *Robert*	Bob	6	1951–53	W	25.7.1930	21.3.1995
621	Taylor, *Robert Capel*		4	1951	F	31.8.1924	
622	Dalgleish, *Kenneth James*		4	1951–53	W, C	7.6.1931	1974
623	Hart, *John Garrow Maclachlan*	John	1	1951	W	7.4.1928	10.6.2007
624	Johnston, *James*	Jimmy	5	1951–52	L	17.9.1925	
625	Cordial, *Ian Fergusson*		4	1952	C	14.11.1926	9.2000
626	Allan, *James Leslie*	Les	4	1952–53	C	4.3.1927	
627	Davidson, *James Norman Grieve*	Norman	7	1952–54	SO	28.1.1931	
628	Fulton, *Adam Kelso*	Kelso	2	1952–54	SH	10.4.1929	27.8.1994
629	Munnoch, *Norman McQueen*		3	1952	H	4.1.1929	
630	Fox, *John*	John	4	1952	P, H	30.8.1921	27.9.1999
631	Walker, *Michael*		1	1952	L	11.3.1930	

Cap No	Name	Known as	Caps	Career	Position	Date of birth	Date of death
632	Greenwood, *James Thomson*	Jim	20	1952–59	F, 8	2.12.1928	12.9.2010
633	Cameron, *Neil William*		3	1952–53	FB	2.9.1925	9.1978
634	Weatherstone, *Thomas Grant*	Grant	16	1952–59	W	27.6.1931	
635	Inglis, *James Messer*		1	1952	P	20.3.1928	
636	Friebe, *John P*	Percy	1	1952	8	9.5.1931	
637	Gilbert-Smith, *David Stuart*	David	1	1952	F	3.12.1931	24.3.2003
638	Thomson, *Bruce Ewan*		3	1953	P	19.11.1930	
639	King, *John Hope Fairbairn*	Jock	4	1953–54	H	10.4.1925	8.9.1982
640	Henderson, *John Hamilton*	Chick	9	1953–54	L	9.2.1930	21.11.2006
641	Valentine, *Alexander Richard*	Alec	3	1953	F	5.2.1928	11.5.1997
642	McMillan, *Keith Henry Douglas*	Keith	4	1953	F	13.2.1927	23.5.1998
643	Macdonald, *Donald C*		4	1953–58	F, 8	1931	
644	Cameron, *Donald*	Donald	6	1953–54	C	25.12.1927	15.9.2003
645	Spence, *Kenneth Magnus*	Ken	1	1953	SH	21.11.1929	29.1.1998
646	Millar, *Gurth Christian Hoyer*		1	1953	H	13.12.1929	
647	Wilson, *John Howard*		1	1953	P	3.3.1930	
648	Henriksen, *Edwin Hansen*	Edwin	1	1953	8	14.5.1929	2000
649	Swan, *John Spence*	Ian	17	1953–58	W	14.7.1930	18.9.2004
650	Kerr, *Walter*		1	1953	F	14.9.1930	
651	Cowie, *William Lorn Kerr*		1	1953	8	1.6.1926	
652	Marshall, *John Campbell*		5	1954	5	30.1.1929	26.4.2012
653	MacEwen, *Robert Kenneth Gillespie*	Bob	13	1954–58	H	25.2.1928	29.8.2013
654	McLeod, *Hugh Ferns*	Hugh	40	1954–62	P	8.6.1932	
655	Fergusson, *Ewen Alastair John*		5	1954	L	28.10.1932	
656	Michie, *Ernest James Stewart*	Ernie	15	1954–57	L	7.11.1933	
657	Robson, *Adam*	Adam	22	1954–60	F, 8	16.8.1928	16.3.2007
658	Elgie, *Michael Kelsey*		8	1954–55	C	6.3.1933	
659	Ross, *Graham Tullis*		4	1954	SO	5.7.1928	13.2.2009
660	MacLachlan, *Lachlan Patrick*		4	1954	SH	16.3.1928	
661	Kemp, *James William Young*	Hamish	27	1954–60	L	13.2.1933	5.6.2002
662	Grant, *Malcolm Leith*	Micky	4	1955–57	SO, C	8.11.1927	29.10.1992
663	Docherty, *James Thomas*	Jimmy	8	1955–58	SO, C	5.6.1931	
664	Relph, *William Keith Linford*		4	1955	H	21.11.1928	
665	Hastie, *Ian Robert*	Ian	6	1955–59	P	7.9.1929	6.4.2009
666	Duffy, *Hugh*	Hugh	1	1955	8	1.4.1934	
667	Smith, *Arthur Robert*	Arthur	33	1955–62	W	23.1.1933	3.2.1975
668	Charters, *Robert Gray*	Robin	3	1955	C	29.10.1930	20.5.2013
669	Nichol, *James Alastair*		3	1955	SH	12.2.1932	22.11.2003
670	Elliot, *Thomas*	Tom	14	1956–58	P	6.4.1926	3.5.1998
671	Glen, *William Sutherland*		1	1955	F	13.3.1932	
672	Chisholm, *Robert William Taylor*	Robin	11	1955–60	FB	16.10.1929	2.11.1991
673	MacGregor, *Ian Allan Alexander*		9	1955–57	F	9.8.1931	
674	Macdonald, *Keith Roy*		6	1956–57	C	13.5.1933	
675	Campbell, *Norman MacDonald*		2	1956	SH	23.9.1929	
676	McClung, *Thomas*	Tommy	9	1956–60	C, SO	14.2.1933	
677	Stevenson, *George Drummond*	George	24	1956–65	C, W	30.5.1933	24.10.2012
678	Scotland, *Kenneth James Forbes*	Ken	27	1957–65	FB, SO	29.8.1936	
679	McKeating, *Edward*		6	1957–61	C	1.9.1936	
680	Allan, *John Lewis Forsyth*		2	1957	W	20.8.1934	
681	Maxwell, *James MacMillan*	Jimmy	1	1957	SO	30.4.1931	
682	Smith, *George Kenneth*	Ken	18	1957–61	8, F	2.6.1929	
683	Waddell, *Gordon Herbert*	Gordon	18	1957–62	SO	12.4.1937	13.8.2012
684	Rodd, *John Adrian Tremayne*	Tremayne	14	1958–65	SH	26.8.1935	9.12.2006
685	Bruce, *Norman Scott*	Norman	31	1958–64	H	28.6.1932	28.3.1992

Cap No	Name	Known as	Caps	Career	Position	Date of birth	Date of death
686	Swan, *Malcolm William*		8	1958–59	L	4.12.1934	
687	Robertson, *Michael Alexander*	Mike	1	1958	F	1929	
688	Elliot, *Christopher*	Christie	12	1958–65	W	24.2.1933	
689	Laughland, *Ian Hugh Page*	Ian	31	1959–67	C, SO	29.10.1935	
690	Coughtrie, *Stanley*	Stan	11	1959–63	SH	19.7.1935	
691	Shackleton, *James Alexander Pirie*	Jim	7	1959–65	C	3.4.1940	
692	Rollo, *David Miller Durie*	David	40	1959–68	P	7.7.1934	
693	Bos, *Frans Herman ten*	Frans	17	1959–63	L	21.4.1937	
694	Davidson, *John Alexander*	Jock	3	1959–60	8	6.8.1932	
695	McPartlin, *Joseph James*	Joe	6	1960–62	C	12.6.1938	24.10.2013
696	Sharp, *Gregor*	Gregor	4	1960–64	SO	20.4.1934	27.11.2006
697	Bearne, *Keith Robert Fraser*		2	1960	8	11.3.1937	
698	Stewart, *Charles Edward Bell*	Charlie	2	1960–61	F	23.12.1936	29.11.1998
699	Thomson, *Ronald Hew*	Ronnie	15	1960–64	W	12.10.1936	
700	Shillinglaw, *Robert Brian*	Brian	5	1960–61	SH	24.10.1938	17.10.2007
701	Grant, *Thomas Oliver*	Oliver	6	1960–64	L, 8	5.9.1933	
702	Edwards, *David Baxter*	David	3	1960	F	19.3.1930	8.7.2006
703	Burnet, *Patrick John*		1	1960	C	25.7.1939	
704	Hart, *Walter*	Walter	1	1960	F	30.3.1935	
705	Cowan, *Ronald*	Ronnie	5	1961–62	W	26.11.1941	
706	Campbell-Lamerton, *Michael John*	Mike	23	1961–66	L	1.8.1933	17.3.2005
707	Douglas, *John*	John	12	1961–63	8	18.12.1934	
708	Ross, *Kenneth Innes*	Ken	11	1961-63	F	15.3.1937	
709	Hastie, *Alexander James*	Alec, Eck	18	1961–68	SH	29.7.1935	7.6.2010
710	Brash, *John Craig*		1	1961	F	5.1939	
711	Glasgow, *Ronald James Cunningham*	Ron	10	1962-65	F	5.11.1930	
712	Steven, *Robert*		1	1962	P	19.2.1937	
713	White, *David Mathew*		4	1963	C	21.11.1943	
714	Boyle, *Allan Cameron Wilson*	Cameron	3	1963	P	11.11.1937	19.3.2004
715	Watherston, *William Rory Andrews*		3	1963	F	5.3.1933	
716	Blaikie, *Colin Fraser*	Colin	8	1963-69	FB	21.11.1941	
717	Henderson, *Brian Carlyle*	Brian	12	1963-66	C	31.1.1939	
718	Neill, *John Brian*	Brian, JB	7	1963-65	P	28.7.1937	26.6.2006
719	Fisher, *James Pringle*	Pringle	25	1963-68	BR	17.3.1939	24.4.2009
720	Wilson, *Stewart*	Stewart	22	1964-66	FB	22.10.1942	
721	Hunter, *William John Ferguson*	Billy	7	1964-67	L	5.6.1934	
722	Brown, *Peter Currie*	Peter	27	1964-73	L, 8	16.12.1941	
723	Telfer, *James William*	Jim	25	1964-70	8, F	17.3.1940	
724	Jackson, *William Douglas*	Doug	8	1964-69	W	5.12.1941	
725	Chisholm, *David Hardie*	David	14	1964-68	SO	23.1.1937	27.7.1998
726	Simmers, *Brian Maxwell*	Brian	7	1965-71	SO, C	26.2.1940	
727	Laidlaw, *Francis Andrew Linden*	Frank	32	1965-71	H	20.9.1940	
728	Stagg, *Peter Kinder*	Peter	28	1965-70	L	22.11.1941	
729	Grant, *Derrick*	Derrick	14	1965-68	F	19.4.1938	
730	Whyte, *David James*		13	1965-67	W	21.2.1940	
731	Suddon, *Norman*	Norman	13	1965-70	P	28.6.1943	
732	Hinshelwood, *Alexander James Watt*	Sandy	21	1966-70	W	23.3.1942	
733	Macdonald, *John Donald*		8	1966-67	P	5.4.1938	
734	Turner, *John William Cleet*	Jock	20	1966-71	SO, C	28.9.1943	19.5.1992
735	Boyle, *Alasdair Hugh Wilson*	Alasdair	6	1966-68	8	30.9.1945	
736	Welsh, *Robert Brown*	Rob	2	1967	C	2.2.1943	
737	Carmichael, *Alexander Bennett*	Sandy	50	1967-78	P	2.2.1944	
738	McCrae, *Ian George*	Ian	6	1967-72	SH	19.5.1941	
739	Frame, *John Neil Munro*	John	23	1967-73	C	8.10.1946	

Cap No	Name	Known as	Caps	Career	Position	Date of birth	Date of death
740	Keddie, *Robert Ramsay*		1	1967	W	19.7.1945	
741	Mitchell, *George Willis Earle*	George	3	1967-68	L	23.11.1943	27.1.2003
742	Keith, *George James*	Hamish	2	1968	W	11.9.1939	
743	Elliot, *Thomas Grieve*	Tommy	5	1968-70	F	1.3.1941	
744	Hodgson, *Charles Gordon*	Charlie	2	1968	W	11.5.1938	
745	McHarg, *Alastair Ferguson*	Alastair	44	1968-79	L, 8	17.6.1944	
746	Arneil, *Rodger James*	Rodger	22	1968-72	F	1.5.1944	
747	Robertson, *Ian*	Ian	8	1968-70	SO	17.1.1945	
748	Connell, *Gordon*	Gordon	5	1968-70	SH	3.10.1944	
749	Deans, *Derek Thomas*	Derek	1	1968	H	30.4.1945	
750	Rea, *Christopher William Wallace*	Chris	13	1968-71	C	22.10.1943	
751	Telfer, *Colin McLeod*	Colin	17	1968-76	SO	26.2.1947	
752	Allan, *Richard Campbell*	Dick	1	1969	SH	16.3.1939	
753	Lauder, *Wilson*	Wilson	18	1969-77	F	4.11.1948	
754	Macdonald, *William Gordon*	Gordon	1	1969	FB	30.12.1938	7.2012
755	Steele, *William Charles Common*	Billy	23	1969-77	W	18.4.1947	
756	McLauchlan, *John*	Ian	43	1969-79	P	14.4.1942	
757	Smith, *Ian Sidney Gibson*	Ian	8	1969-71	FB	16.6.1944	
758	Biggar, *Alastair Gourlay*	Alastair	12	1969-72	W	4.8.1946	
759	Paterson, *Duncan Sinclair*	Duncan	10	1969-72	SH	27.3.1943	21.12.2009
760	Brown, *Gordon Lamont*	Gordon	30	1969-76	L	1.11.1947	19.3.2001
761	Smith, *Michael Adam*	Mike	4	1970	W	23.11.1945	
762	Young, *Robert Graham*		1	1970	SH	13.9.1940	
763	Oliver, *George Kenneth*	Ken	1	1970	8	4.3.1946	22.4.2009
764	MacEwan, *Nairn Alexander*	Nairn	20	1971-75	F	12.12.1941	
765	Hannah, *Ronald Scott Murray*	Ronnie	1	1971	W	15.12.1945	
766	Brown, *Arthur Robert*	Arthur	5	1971-72	FB	10.12.1949	
767	Dunlop, *Quintin*	Quintin	2	1971	H	9.3.1943	
768	Turk, *Arthur Stephen*	Stephen	1	1971	C	9.1.1948	
769	Strachan, *Gordon Matthew*	Gordon	5	1971-73	L, 8	16.11.1947	
770	Renwick, *James Menzies*	Jim	52	1972-84	C, W	12.2.1952	
771	Clark, *Robert Lawson*	Bobby	9	1972-73	H	27.1.1944	
772	Lawson, *Alan James Macgregor*	Alan	15	1972-80	SH	19.5.1948	
773	Barnes, *Ian Andrew*	Ian	7	1972-77	L	19.4.1948	
774	Dick, *Lewis Gibson*	Lewis	14	1972-77	W	20.12.1950	
775	Irvine, *Andrew Robertson*	Andy	51	1972-82	FB, W	16.9.1951	
776	Forsyth, *Ian William*	Ian	6	1972-73	C	4.7.1946	
777	Shedden, *David*	David	15	1972-78	W	24.5.1944	
778	McGeechan, *Ian Robert*	Ian	32	1972-79	SO, C	30.10.1946	
779	Wright, *Ronald William James*		1	1973	L	6.5.1949	11.10.1983
780	Morgan, *Douglas Waugh*	Douglas	21	1973-78	SH	9.3.1947	
781	Millican, *John Gilbert*	Jock	3	1973	F	21.8.1951	
782	Bryce, *Robert Donaldson Hamish*	Hamish	1	1973	P	12.11.1941	
783	Gill, *Andrew Davidson*	Drew	5	1973-74	W	30.8.1949	
784	Madsen, *Duncan Frederick*	Duncan	14	1974-78	H	16.4.1947	
785	Watson, *William Sinclair*	Bill	10	1974-79	8, F	7.1.1949	
786	Hunter, *Michael Douglas*		1	1974	C	24.4.1945	
787	Bell, *David Lauder*	David	4	1975	C	28.4.1949	
788	Biggar, *Michael Andrew*	Mike	24	1975-80	F	20.11.1949	
789	Leslie, *David George*	David	32	1975-85	8, F	14.4.1952	
790	Hay, *Bruce Hamilton*	Bruce	23	1975-81	FB, W	23.5.1950	1.10.2007
791	Birkett, *Graham Anthony*	Graham	1	1975	C	2.10.1954	
792	Fisher, *Colin Douglas*	Colin	5	1975-76	H	27.12.1949	
793	Mackie, *George Yuill*	George	4	1975-78	8	19.4.1949	

Cap No	Name	Known as	Caps	Career	Position	Date of birth	Date of death
794	Cranston, *Alastair Gerald*	Alastair	11	1976-81	C	11.12.1949	
795	Wilson, *Ronald*	Ron	9	1976-83	SO	1.7.1954	
796	Tomes, *Alan James*	Alan	48	1976-87	L	6.11.1951	
797	Aitken, *James*	Jim	24	1977-84	P	22.11.1947	
798	Brewster, *Alexander Kinloch*	Alex	6	1977-86	F, P	3.5.1954	
799	Macdonald, *Donald Shaw Mackinnon*	Donald	7	1977-78	8	25.9.1951	
800	Gammell, *William Benjamin Bowring*	Bill	5	1977-78	W	29.12.1952	
801	Pender, *Norman Ewart Ker*	Norman	4	1977-78	P	1.2.1948	
802	Hegarty, *Charles Brian*	Brian	4	1978	F	29.11.1950	
803	Deans, *Colin Thomas*	Colin	52	1978-87	H	3.5.1955	
804	Hogg, *Charles Graham*	Graham	2	1978	W	2.3.1948	
805	Breakey, *Richard William*	Richard	1	1978	SO	14.11.1956	
806	Gray, *David*	David	9	1978-81	L	28.3.1953	2.4.2009
807	Robertson, *Keith William*	Keith	44	1978-1989	W, C	5.12.1954	
808	Cunningham, *Robert Fraser*	Bob	3	1978-79	P	4.1.1953	
809	Dickson, *Gordon*	Gordon	9	1978-82	F	10.12.1954	
810	Lambie, *Iain Kerr*	Iain	4	1978-79	8	13.4.1954	
811	Rutherford, *John Young*	John	42	1979-87	SO	4.10.1955	
812	Milne, *Iain Gordon*	Iain	44	1979-90	P	17.6.1958	
813	Johnston, *David Ian*	David	27	1979-86	C	20.10.1958	
814	Munro, *Stephen*	Steve	10	1980-84	W	11.6.1958	
815	Laidlaw, *Roy James*	Roy	47	1980-88	SH	5.10.1953	
816	Burnett, *James Niven*	Jim	4	1980	P	12.7.1947	
817	Cuthbertson, *William*	Bill	21	1980-84	L	6.12.1949	
818	Beattie, *John Ross*	John	25	1980-87	8	27.11.1957	
819	Lawrie, *Kenneth Graham*	Ken	3	1980	H	31.7.1951	
820	Gossman, *Bryan Murray*	Bryan	3	1980-83	SO	5.5.1951	
821	Rowan, *Norman Arthur*	Norrie	13	1980-88	P	17.9.1951	
822	Gossman, *James Stockbridge*	Jim	1	1980	W	25.9.1955	
823	Calder, *James Hamilton*	Jim	27	1981-85	F	20.8.1957	
824	Paxton, *Iain Angus McLeod*	Iain	36	1981-88	8, L	29.12.1957	
825	Baird, *Gavin Roger Todd*	Roger	27	1981-88	W, C	12.4.1960	
826	Paxton, *Robert Eric*	Eric	2	1982	F	4.4.1957	
827	White, *Derek Bolton*	Derek	41	1982-92	8, L	30.1.1958	
828	Pollock, *James Allan*	Jim	8	1982-85	W	16.11.1958	
829	Gordon, *Richard John*	Rick	2	1982	C	16.3.1958	
830	McGuinness, *Gerald Michael*	Gerry	7	1982-85	P	14.9.1953	
831	Dods, *Peter William*	Peter	23	1983-91	FB	6.1.1958	
832	Smith, *Thomas John*	Tom	4	1983-85	L	31.8.1953	
833	Kennedy, *Alexander Euan*	Euan	4	1983-84	C	30.7.1954	
834	Campbell, *Alister John*	Alister	15	1984-88	L	1.1.1959	
835	Hunter, *Iain Gordon*	Gordon	4	1984-85	SH	7.8.1958	
836	Callander, *Gary James*	Gary	6	1984-88	H	5.7.1959	
837	McGaughey, *Sean Kieran*	Sean	1	1984	F	8.5.1962	
838	Steven, *Peter David*	Peter	4	1984-85	W	4.7.1959	
839	Wyllie, *Douglas Stewart*	Douglas	18	1984-94	SO, C	20.5.1963	
840	Mackenzie, *Alexander David Gregor*	Gregor	1	1984	P	9.7.1956	
841	Jeffrey, *John*	John	40	1984-91	F	25.3.1959	
842	Murray, *Keith Tony*	Keith	3	1985	C	23.3.1962	
843	Tukalo, *Iwan Carmen*	Iwan	37	1985-92	W	5.3.1961	
844	Hastings, *Andrew Gavin*	Gavin	61	1986-95	FB	3.1.1962	
845	Duncan, *Matthew Dominic Fletcher*	Matt	18	1986-89	W	29.8.1959	
846	Hastings, *Scott*	Scott	65	1986-97	C, W	4.12.1964	
847	Sole, *David Michael Barclay*	David	44	1986-92	P	8.5.1962	

Cap No	Name	Known as	Caps	Career	Position	Date of birth	Date of death
848	Campbell-Lamerton, *Jeremy Robert Edward*	Jeremy	3	1986-87	L	21.2.1959	
849	Calder, *Finlay*	Finlay	34	1986-91	F	20.8.1957	
850	Tait, *Alan Victor*	Alan	27	1987-99	C, W	2.7.1964	
851	Oliver, *Greig Hunter*	Greig	3	1987-91	SH	12.9.1964	
852	Cramb, *Richard*	Richard	4	1987-8	SO	7.9.1963	
853	Turnbull, *Derek James*	Derek	15	1987-94	BR	2.10.1961	
854	Cronin, *Damian Francis*	Damian	45	1988-98	L	17.4.1963	
855	Ker, *Andrew Burgher Michael*	Andrew	2	1988	SO	16.10.1954	
856	Armstrong, *Gary*	Gary	51	1988-99	SH	30.9.1966	
857	Marshall, *Graham Robert*	Graham	4	1988-91	BR	23.5.1960	
858	Lineen, *Sean Raymond Patrick*	Sean	29	1989-92	C	25.12.1961	
859	Chalmers, *Craig Minto*	Craig	60	1989-99	SO, C	15.10.1968	
860	Milne, *Kenneth Stuart*	Kenny	39	1989-95	H	1.12.1961	
861	Gray, *Christopher Anthony*	Chris	22	1989-91	L	11.7.1960	
862	Burnell, *Andrew Paul*	Paul	52	1989-99	P	29.9.1965	
863	Stanger, *Anthony George*	Tony	52	1989-98	W, C	14.5.1968	
864	Buchanan-Smith, *George Adam Edward*	Adam	2	1989-90	F	20.7.1964	
865	Renwick, *William Lindsay*	Lindsay	1	1989	W	24.12.1960	
866	Allan, *John*	John	9	1990-91	H	25.11.1963	
867	Moore, *Alexander*	Alex	5	1990-91	W	19.8.1963	
868	Weir, *George Wilson*	Doddie	61	1990-2000	L, 8	4.7.1970	
869	Milne, *David Ferguson*	David	1	1991	P	7.12.1958	
870	Watt, *Alan Gordon James*	Alan	3	1991-93	P	10.7.1967	
871	Shiel, *Andrew Graham*	Graham	18	1991-2000	SO, C	13.8.1970	
872	Nicol, *Andrew Douglas*	Andy	23	1992-2001	SH	12.3.1971	
873	Edwards, *Neil George Barry*	Neil	6	1992-94	L	20.8.1964	
874	McIvor, *David John*	Dave	6	1992-94	F	29.6.1964	
875	Smith, *Ian Richard*	Ian	25	1992-97	F	16.3.1965	
876	Wainwright, *Robert Iain*	Rob	37	1992-98	BR	22.3.1965	
877	Jones, *Peter Martin*	Peter	1	1992	P	28.12.1963	
878	Wright, *Peter Hugh*	Peter	21	1992-96	P	30.12.1967	
879	Hogg, *Carl David*	Carl	5	1992-94	BR	5.7.1969	
880	Corcoran, *Ian*	Ian	1	1992	H	11.5.1963	
881	Logan, *Kenneth McKerrow*	Kenny	70	1992-2003	FB, W	3.4.1972	
882	Scott, *Martin William*	Martin	1	1992	H	5.7.1966	
883	Stark, *Derek Alexander*	Derek	9	1993-97	W	13.4.1966	
884	Reed, *Andrew Ian*	Andy	18	1993-99	L	4.5.1969	
885	Morrison, *Iain Robert*	Iain	15	1993-95	F	14.12.1962	
886	Townsend, *Gregor Peter John*	Gregor	82	1993-2003	SO, C	26.4.1973	
887	Jardine, *Ian Carrick*	Ian	18	1993-98	C	28.5.1965	
888	MacDonald, *Andrew Edward Douglas*	Andy	1	1993	L	17.1.1966	
889	Redpath, *Bryan William*	Bryan	60	1993-2003	SH	2.1.1971	
890	Munro, *Donald Shade*	Shade	7	1994-97	L	19.11.1966	
891	Sharp, *Alan Victor*	Alan	6	1994	P	17.10.1969	
892	Walton, *Peter*	Peter	24	1994-99	BR	3.6.1969	
893	Dods, *Michael*	Michael	8	1994-96	FB, W	30.12.1968	
894	Joiner, *Craig Alexander*	Craig	25	1994-2000	W	21.4.1974	
895	McKenzie, *Kevin Duncan*	Kevin	14	1994-98	H	22.1.1968	
896	Nichol, *Scott Alan*	Scott	1	1994	W	18.6.1970	
897	Patterson, *Derrick William*	Derrick	2	1994-95	SH	6.7.1968	
898	Richardson, *Jeremy Francis*	Jeremy	1	1994	L	7.9.1963	
899	Hilton, *David Ivor Walter*	David	42	1995-2002	P	3.4.1970	

Cap No	Name	Known as	Caps	Career	Position	Date of birth	Date of death
900	Campbell, *Stewart Joseph*	Stewart	17	1995-98	L	25.4.1972	
901	Peters, *Eric William*	Eric	29	1995-99	8	28.1.1969	
902	Manson, *John James*	John	1	1995	P	22.6.1968	
903	Shepherd, *Rowen James Stanley*	Rowen	20	1995-98	FB	25.12.1970	
904	Hay, *James Allan*	Jim	1	1995	H	8.8.1964	
905	Reid, *Stuart James*	Stuart	8	1995-2000	8	31.1.1970	
906	Eriksson, *Bo Ronald Sheehan*	Ronnie	3	1996-97	C	22.4.1972	
907	Stewart, *Barry Douglas*	Barry	4	1996-2000	P	3.6.1975	
908	Wallace, *Murray Ian*	Murray	3	1996-97	F	13.10.1967	
909	Stewart, *Matthew James*	Mattie	34	1996-2002	P	18.5.1973	
910	Ellis, *David Graham*	Graham	4	1997	H	6.4.1965	
911	Smith, *Thomas James*	Tom	61	1997-2005	P	31.10.1971	
912	Hodge, *Duncan William*	Duncan	26	1997-2002	SO, FB, C	18.8.1974	
913	Glasgow, *Iain Cameron*	Cameron	1	1997	W	24.2.1966	
914	Craig, *James Matthew*	James	4	1997-2001	W	2.3.1977	
915	McKelvey, *Grant*	Grant	1	1997	H	28.12.1968	
916	Murray, *Scott*	Scott	87	1997-2007	L	15.1.1976	
917	Roxburgh, *Adam John*	Adam	8	1997-98	BR	14.4.1970	
918	Grimes, *Stuart Brian*	Stuart	71	1997-2005	L	4.4.1974	
919	Graham, *George*	George	25	1997-2002	P	19.1.1966	
920	Bulloch, *Gordon Campbell*	Gordon	75	1997-2005	H	26.3.1975	
921	Holmes, *Simon David*	Simon	3	1998	F	12.12.1966	
922	Lee, *Derrick James*	Derrick	12	1998-2004	FB, W	1.10.1973	
923	Longstaff, *Shaun Louis*	Shaun	15	1998-2000	W	3.1.1972	
924	Murray, *Cameron Andrew*	Cameron	26	1998-2001	C, W	31.3.1975	
925	Gilmour, *Hugh Ross*	Hugh	1	1998	W	13.9.1974	
926	McIlwham, *Gordon Robert*	Gordon	16	1998-2003	P	13.11.1969	
927	Proudfoot, *Matthew Craig*	Matthew	4	1998-2003	P	30.1.1972	
928	Metcalfe, *Glenn Hayden*	Glenn	40	1998-2003	FB	15.4.1970	
929	Simpson, *Gordon Leslie*	Gordon	15	1998-2001	BR	21.9.1971	
930	Mayer, *Michael James Mackenzie*	Jamie	8	1998-2000	C	16.4.1977	
931	Leslie, *John Andrew*	John	23	1998-2002	C	25.11.1970	
932	Pountney, *Anthony Charles*	Budge	31	1998-2002	F	13.11.1973	
933	Leslie, *Martin Donald*	Martin	37	1998-2003	F	25.10.1971	
934	Fairley, *Iain Thomas*	Iain	3	1999	SH	29.8.1973	
935	Burns, *Graeme George*	Graeme	2	1999-2002	SH	29.10.1971	
936	Brotherstone, *Steven James*	Steve	8	1999-2002	H	16.4.1971	
937	McLaren, *James Gerard*	James	30	1999-2003	C	28.6.1972	
938	Russell, *Robert Reid*	Rob	27	1999-2005	H	1.5.1976	
939	Mather, *Cameron George*	Cameron	10	1999-2004	BR	20.8.1972	
940	Paterson, *Christopher Douglas*	Chris	109	1999-2011	SO, W, FB	30.3.1978	
941	Moir, *Craig Calder*	Craig	3	2000	W	25.9.1975	
942	Metcalfe, *Richard*	Richard	9	2000-01	L	21.11.1973	
943	White, *Jason Phillip Randall*	Jason	77	2000-09	F, L	17.4.1978	
944	Beattie, *Ross*	Ross	9	2000-03	F	15.11.1977	
945	Fullarton, *Iain Alexander*	Iain	8	2000-04	L	25.4.1976	
946	Petrie, *Jonathan Michael*	Jon	45	2000-06	BR	19.10.1976	
947	Hines, *Nathan John*	Nathan	77	2000-11	L, F	29.11.1976	
948	Beveridge, *Graeme*	Graeme	6	2000-05	SH	17.2.1976	
949	Scott, *Stephen*	Steve	11	2000-04	H	26.7.1973	
950	Bulloch, *Alan James*	Alan	5	2000-01	C	7.7.1977	
951	Steel, *Jonathan Forbes*	Jon	5	2000-01	W	14.3.1980	
952	Taylor, *Simon Marcus*	Simon	66	2000-09	BR	17.8.1979	
953	Henderson, *Andrew Roger*	Andrew	53	2001-08	C	3.2.1980	

Cap No	Name	Known as	Caps	Career	Position	Date of birth	Date of death
954	Ross, *Gordon*	Gordon	25	2001-06	SO	8.3.1978	
955	Mower, *Andrew Lance*	Andrew	13	2001-03	F	3.9.1975	
956	Reid, *Roland Estcourt*	Roland	2	2001	W	13.9.1978	
957	Laney, *Brendan James*	Brendan	20	2001-04	FB, C, SO	16.11.1973	
958	Kerr, *Rory Campbell*	Rory	3	2002-03	W	20.12.1979	
959	Craig, *Andrew*	Andy	23	2002-05	C, W	16.3.1976	
960	Blair, *Michael Robert Leighton*	Mike	85	2002-12	SH	20.4.1981	
961	Smith, *Craig James*	Craig	25	2002-08	P	30.8.1978	
962	Macfadyen, *Donald John Hunter*	Donnie	11	2002-06	BR	11.10.1979	
963	Jacobsen, *Allan Frederick*	Allan	65	2002-12	P	22.9.1978	
964	Hinshelwood, *Benjamin Gerald*	Ben	19	2002-05	C	22.3.1977	
965	Di Rollo, *Marcus*	Marcus	21	2002-07	C	31.3.1978	
966	Hall, *Andrew John Anderson*	Andrew	1	2002	L	5.6.1979	
967	Moffat, *John Stuart David*	Stuart	4	2002-04	FB	18.8.1977	
968	Walker, *Nikki*	Nikki	24	2002-11	W	5.3.1982	
969	Douglas, *Bruce Andrew Ferguson*	Bruce	43	2002-06	P	10.2.1980	
970	Kerr, *Gavin*	Gavin	50	2003-08	P	3.4.1977	
971	Utterson, *Kevin Norman*	Kevin	3	2003	C	17.7.1976	
972	Danielli, *Simon Charles Jonathan*	Simon	32	2003-11	W	8.9.1979	
973	Dall, *Andrew Keith*	Andrew	1	2003	F	22.7.1977	
974	Hall, *Douglas William Hugh*	Dougie	42	2003-13	H	24.9.1980	
975	Webster, *Simon Lockhart*	Simon	37	2003-09	W, C	8.3.1981	
976	Philip, *Thomas Kenneth*	Tom	5	2004	C	25.6.1983	
977	Cusiter, *Christopher Peter*	Chris	62	2004-12	SH	13.6.1982	
978	Hogg, *Allister*	Allister	48	2004-09	BR	20.1.1983	
979	Parks, *Daniel Arthur*	Dan	67	2004-12	SO	26.5.1978	
980	Lamont, *Sean Fergus*	Sean	79	2004-13	W, C	15.1.1981	
981	Southwell, *Hugo Finlay Grant*	Hugo	59	2004-11	FB, C	14.5.1980	
982	Morrison, *Graeme Alexander*	Graeme	35	2004-12	C	17.10.1982	
983	Hamilton, *Craig Peter*	Craig	5	2004-05	L	1.9.1979	
984	MacLeod, *Scott James*	Scott	24	2004-11	L	3.3.1979	
985	Gray, *Scott Donald*	Scott	8	2004-09	BR	24.2.1978	
986	Kellock, *Alastair David*	Alastair	55	2004-13	L	14.6.1981	
987	Ford, *Ross William*	Ross	68	2004-13	H	23.4.1984	
988	Dunbar, *Jonathan Peter Andrew*	Jon	2	2005	F	4.4.1980	
989	Lamont, *Rory Patrick*	Rory	29	2005-12	W, FB	10.10.1982	
990	Lawson, *Scott*	Scott	38	2005-13	H	28.9.1981	
991	Brown, *Kelly David Robert*	Kelly	58	2005-13	BR	8.6.1982	
992	Wilson, *Andrew William*	Andrew	1	2005	8	9.12.1980	
993	Murray, *Euan Alistair*	Euan	56	2005-13	P	7.8.1980	
994	Godman, *Philip James*	Phil	23	2005-10	SO	20.5.1982	
995	MacDougall, *Benjamin*	Ben	2	2006	C	25.5.1977	
996	Pinder, *Samuel Jared*	Sam	2	2006	SH	15.2.1979	
997	Dewey, *Robert Edward*	Rob	13	2006-07	C	19.10.1983	
998	Beattie, *John William*	Johnnie	24	2006-13	BR	21.11.1985	
999	Callam, *David Alexander*	David	11	2006-08	BR	15.2.1983	
1000	Hamilton, *James Leigh*	Jim	48	2006-13	L	17.11.1982	
1001	Strokosch, *Alasdair Karl*	Alasdair	35	2006-12	BR	21.2.1983	
1002	Lawson, *Rory Gordon MacGregor*	Rory	31	2006-12	SH	12.3.1981	
1003	Thomson, *Fergus Matthew Andrew*	Fergus	8	2007-08	H	18.10.1983	
1004	Dickinson, *Alasdair*	Alasdair	27	2007-13	P	11.9.1983	
1005	Barclay, *John Adam*	John	41	2007-12	BR	24.9.1986	
1006	De Luca, *Nicholas John*	Nick	38	2008-12	C	1.2.1984	
1007	Rennie, *Ross Michael*	Ross	20	2008-12	F	29.3.1986	

Cap No	Name	Known as	Caps	Career	Position	Date of birth	Date of death
1008	Cairns, *Benjamin James*	Ben	7	2008-09	C	29.9.1985	
1009	Evans, *Thom Henry*	Thom	10	2008-10	W	2.4.1985	
1010	Mustchin, *Matthew Lee*	Matt	5	2008	L	2.2.1977	
1011	Evans, *Max Brian*	Max	35	2008-13	W	12.9.1983	
1012	Cross, *Geoffrey Dominic Sebastian*	Geoff	22	2009-13	P	11.12.1982	
1013	Low, *Moray John*	Moray	21	2009-13	P	28.11.1984	
1014	Grove, *Alexander*	Alex	3	2009	C	30.11.1987	
1015	Traynor, *Kyle*	Kyle	4	2009	P	27.2.1986	
1016	Vernon, *Richard John*	Richie	20	2009-12	BR	7.7.1987	
1017	Macdonald, *Alan Robin*	Alan	4	2009-10	F	21.10.1985	
1018	Gray, *Richard James*	Richie	31	2010-13	L	24.8.1989	
1019	Laidlaw, *Greig David*	Grieg	21	2010-13	SH, SO	12.10.1985	
1020	Jackson, *Ruaridh James Howard*	Ruaridh	21	2010-13	SO	12.2.1988	
1021	Ansbro, *Joseph Antony Andrew*	Joe	11	2010-12	C	29.10.1985	
1022	Cuthbert, *Jack Edward*	Jack	1	2011	W	3.9.1987	
1023	Denton, *David Kipling*	David	14	2011-13	BR	5.2.1990	
1024	Jones, *Lee*	Lee	4	2012	W	28.6.1988	
1025	Hogg, *Stuart William*	Stuart	15	2012-13	FB	24.6.1992	
1026	Kalman, *Edward David*	Ed	2	2012	P	7.12.1982	
1027	Weir, *Duncan*	Duncan	5	2012-13	SO	10.5.1991	
1028	Scott, *Matthew Clive McCrimmon*	Matt	15	2012-13	C	30.9.1990	
1029	Welsh, *Jon*	Jon	2	2012-13	P	13.10.1986	
1030	Grant, *Ryan*	Ryan	10	2012-13	P	8.10.1985	
1031	Brown, *Thomas Gordon*	Tom	1	2012	W	30.3.1990	
1032	Visser, *Tim Jan Willem*	Tim	12	2012-13	W	29.5.1987	
1033	Ryder, *Thomas Paul*	Tom	2	2012	L	21.2.1985	
1034	Harley, *Robert John*	Rob	5	2012-13	BR	26.5.1990	/
1035	Pyrgos, *Henry Benjamin*	Henry	9	2012-13	SH	9.7.1989	
1036	Heathcote, *Thomas Alexander*	Tom	3	2012-13	SO	11.2.1992	
1037	Maitland, *Sean Daniel*	Sean	5	2013	W	14.9.1988	
1038	Wilson, *Ryan*	Ryan	4	2013	BR	18.5.1989	
1039	Gilchrist, *Grant Stuart*	Grant	3	2013	L	9.8.1990	
1040	Tonks, *Greig Alexander*	Greig	1	2013	FB	20.5.1989	
1041	Dunbar, *Alexander James*	Alex	3	2013	C	23.4.1990	
1042	MacArthur, *Patrick*	Pat	1	2013	H	27.4.1987	
1043	Lawrie, *Steven*	Steven	1	2013	H	22.2.1984	
1044	Horne, *Peter*	Peter	2	2013	SO	5.10.1989	
1045	Taylor, *Duncan McWilliam*	Duncan	3	2013	W	5.9.1989	
1046	Murchie, *Peter Edward*	Peter	2	2013	FB	7.1.1986	
1047	Seymour, *Thomas Samuel Fenwick*	Tommy	2	2013	W	1.7.1988	
1048	Swinson, *Timothy James*	Tim	2	2013	L	17.2.1987	
1049	Brown, *Fraser James Macgregor*	Fraser	1	2013	H	20.6.1989	

Appendix II
Relatives Capped

Father and Son

Henry Gedge and Peter Gedge
Joseph Waters and Frank Waters
Irvine Geddes and Keith Geddes
John Bruce Lockhart, and Rab Bruce Lockhart and Logie Bruce Lockhart
Allen Sloan and Donald Sloan
Robert and George Gallie
Herbert Waddell and Gordon Waddell
Max Simmers and Brian Simmers
Alastair Fisher and Colin Fisher
Jack Hegarty and Brian Hegarty
Mike Campbell-Lamerton and Jeremy Campbell-Lamerton
Ron Glasgow and Cameron Glasgow
Sandy Hinshelwood and Ben Hinshelwood
John Beattie and Johnnie Beattie
Allan Lawson and Rory Lawson

In addition, Terry Lineen won 12 caps for New Zealand between 1957 and 1960, and his son Sean was capped 29 times for Scotland between 1989 and 1992. Andy Leslie won 10 caps for New Zealand between 1974 and 1976, including one appearance against Scotland, and his two sons Martin and John were both capped for Scotland.

Brothers

John and Allan Arthur
William and Malcolm Cross
James, Ninian and Alec Finlay
Robert and Duncan Irvine
Thomas and William Marshall
James and George McClure (twins)
James and Charles Reid
Bob and Tom Ainslie
Andrew and Patrick Don Wauchope
Robert and Gardyne Maitland
Archibald and James Walker
Matthew and Bill McEwan
Charles and Jack Orr
William, George, Gordon and Robert Neilson
John and Frank Dods
David and John Bedell Sivright

John and George Crabbie
James and Edward Ross
Lewis and Ken MacLeod
Alec and William Purves
Duncan and Ian McGregor
Charles and Ludovic Stuart
James and John Dobson
Dave and Bob Howie
George and Ronald Murray
Jimmy and Andrew Dykes
Mac and Ian Henderson
Wilson and Ian Shaw
Rab and Logie Bruce Lockhart
Tommy and Arthur Dorward
Dave and Alec Valentine
Angus and Donald Cameron
Robin and David Chisholm
Christie and Tom Elliot
Oliver and Derrick Grant
Cameron and Alasdair Boyle
Peter and Gordon Brown
Bryan and Jim Gossman
Jim and Finlay Calder (twins)
Peter and Michael Dods
Iain, Kenny and David Milne
Gavin and Scott Hastings
John and Martin Leslie
Gordon and Alan Bulloch
Sean and Rory Lamont
Thom and Max Evans

In addition, Phipps Turnbull and Gerard Crole were half-brothers. Donald Macdonald won seven caps for Scotland between 1977 and 1978, and his elder brother Dugald won one cap for South Africa in 1974.

Grandfather and grandson

George Ritchie and Andy Nicol
John Bannerman and Shade Munro

Appendix III
Played for more than one country

James Marsh 2 caps for Scotland 1889, 1 cap for England 1892
Bill McEwan 16 caps for Scotland 1894–1900, 2 caps for South Africa 1903
Alec Frew 3 caps for Scotland 1901, 1 cap for South Africa 1903
Colin Gilray 1 cap for New Zealand, 4 caps for Scotland 1908–12
George Aitken 2 caps for New Zealand 1921, 8 caps for Scotland 1924–29
Johnnie Wallace 9 caps for Scotland 1923–26, 8 caps for Australia 1921–28
Doug Keller 6 caps for Australia 6 1947–48, 7 caps for Scotland 1949–50
John Allan 9 caps for Scotland 1990–91, 13 caps for South Africa 1993–96

Appendix IV
Players who did not win a full cap

Players who appeared in Scotland XV internationals but who did not win a full cap

Note: Scotland played three matches against the Netherlands in the 1970s, but the Scottish team was not fully representative. This was also the case for the match against a French XV in 1987 which neither side considered a full international match, even a non-cap one. Also Scotland played two tests on tour in Zimbabwe in 1995, but this was officially the Scotland A team.

Ian Murchie (*W of Scot*) v Argentina (1) 1969
Arthur Orr (*London Scot*) v Argentina (1) 1969
Bruce Laidlaw (*Royal HSFP*) v Argentina (2) 1969
David Ashton (*Ayr*) v Japan 1976
Jim Carswell (*Jordanhill*) v Japan 1976
Colin Mair (*W of Scot*) v Japan 1977
Rob Moffat (*Melrose*) v Japan 1977
Stuart Johnston (*Watsonians*) v Spain 1986
Gary Waite (*Kelso*) v Spain 1986
Ruari Maclean (*Gloucester*) v Zimbabwe 1988 (1 & 2), Japan 1989
David Butcher (*Harlequins*) v Zimbabwe 1988 (1 & 2)
Kevin Rafferty (*Heriot's FP*) v Zimbabwe 1988 (1 & 2)
Hugh Parker (*Kilmarnock*) v Zimbabwe 1988 (1 & 2)
Stewart McAslan (*Heriot's FP*) v Zimbabwe 1988 (1)
Grant Wilson (*Boroughmuir*) v Japan 1989
Mark Moncreiff (*Gala*) v USA 1991, Barbarians 1991, Fiji 1993, Tonga 1993, Western Samoa 1993
Ronnie Kirkpatrick (*Jed-Forest*) v Canada 1991
Brian Renwick (*Hawick*) v Barbarians 1991
Nick Grecian (*London Scot*) v Fiji 1993, Western Samoa 1993
Gary Isaac (*Gala*) v Fiji 1993, Tonga 1993, Western Samoa 1993
Steven Ferguson (*Peebles*) v Fiji 1993, Tonga 1993, Western Samoa 1993
Rob Scott (*London Scot*) v Fiji 1993, Western Samoa 1993
Craig Redpath (*Melrose*) v Tonga 1993
Ally Donaldson (*Currie*) v Fiji 1993
Willie Anderson (*Glasgow Cal*) v Spain 1998
Joel Brannigan (*Edinburgh*) v Barbarians 2002
Stephen Cranston (*Borders*) v Barbarians 2003
Gareth Morton (*Borders*) v Barbarians 2003

Players who appeared in Services Internationals (1942–45) but who did not win a full cap

AL Barcroft (*Heriot's FP*) 2 appearances

WG Biggart (*Army*) 1 appearance
JM Blair (*Army, Edinburgh Acs & Oxford U*) 3 appearances
WWB Buchanan (*London Scot*) 2 appearances
R Cowe (*Army & Melrose*) 3 appearances
MR Dewar (*Fleet Air Arm & Watsonians*) 2 appearances
ECK Douglas (*Army & Edinburgh U*) 4 appearances
E Grant (*RNZAF & RAF*) 4 appearances
SGA Harper (*RNVR & Watsonians*) 1 appearance
JR Henderson (*Glasgow Acs*) 2 appearances
EC Hunter (*RAF & Watsonians*) 2 appearances
MD Kennedy (*Army*) 1 appearance
J Maltman (*Army & Hawick*) 4 appearances
C McClay (*Edinburgh Acs*) 1 appearance
JR McClure (*Army, Ayr & Wasps*) 4 appearances
RM McKenzie (*New Zealand*) 2 appearances
JB McNeil (*Army & Glasgow HSFP*) 2 appearances
EA Melling (*Old Sedberghians*) 1 appearance
AE Murray (*Oxford U*) 1 appearance
JB Nicholls (*RAAF & RAF*) 2 appearances
NW Ramsay (*Army*) 3 appearances
DA Roberts (*Acs-Wdrs*) 1 appearance
JAD Thom (*Hawick & London Scot*) 1 appearance
HG Uren (*Glasgow Acs*) 1 appearance
C Wilhelm (*SA Servs*) 1 appearance

Players who appeared in Victory Internationals (1946) but who did not win a full cap

J Anderson (*London Scot*) 1 appearance
J Kirk (*Acs-Wdrs*) 4 appearances
JR McClure (*Ayr*) 1 appearance
AGM Watt (*Acs-Wdrs*) 5 appearances
KSH Wilson (*Watsonians & London Scot*) 1 appearance

Appendix V
Roll of Honour

Second Lieutenant Douglas Blackwell Monypenny

Douglas Monypenny was educated at Fettes College and played centre for London Scottish and Edinburgh Wanderers. He won three caps in 1899. He served in the Seaforth Highlanders during the Second Anglo-Boer War (1899–1902) and was twice mentioned in dispatches. He died of wounds at the battle of Paardeberg on 19 February 1900.

THE FIRST WORLD WAR

Lieutenant Ronald Francis Simson

Ronnie Simpson was educated at Edinburgh Academy and the Royal Military Academy, Woolwich. A tall player with good hands and a long raking stride, he won one cap against England in 1911. He was a career soldier in the Royal Field Artillery and died at River Aisne on 14 September 1914.

Lieutenant James Laidlaw Huggan

A native of Jedburgh and part educated at George Watson's College, James Huggan played wing for Jed-Forest and Edinburgh University. An army doctor, he won one cap in 1914 when playing for London Scottish. He served in the Royal Army Medical Corps and was recommended for the Victoria Cross two days before his death at the River Aisne on 16 September 1914

Private James Ross

'Jummy' Ross, who was from a Border family and educated at Fettes College, was a sturdily built forward who won five caps between 1901 and 1903. He captained London Scottish for two seasons. He enlisted in the London Scottish Regiment at the outbreak of the war and was killed at Messines on 1 November 1914. His body was never found and he is commemorated on the Menin Gate Memorial to the Missing, Ypres.

Captain Lewis Robertson

A stalwart of London Scottish, Lewis Robertson was a hard and determined forward with a fine physique who won nine caps between 1908 and 1913. A professional soldier, he served in the 1st Cameron Highlanders and died at Ypres on 3 November 1914.

Lieutenant Frederick Harding Turner

Educated at Sedbergh and Oxford University, Fred Turner was a solid and determined forward who won 15 caps between 1911 and 1914. He played in three Varsity matches, captained Oxford in 1910 and also played for Liverpool where he was in business. He enlisted in the 10th Liverpool Scottish and was killed by a sniper near Kemmel in Belgium on 10 January 1915.

Private James Pearson

'Jimmy P' or the 'darling of Myreside' was a fast and elusive centre with a great body-swerve. He was a very slight man who weighed around nine stones, but still managed to win 12 caps between 1909 and 1913. He joined the 9th Royal Scots and died at Hooge, Belgium on 22 May 1915.

Captain David McLaren Bain

Educated at Edinburgh Academy, David Bain played as a forward for Oxford University and won 11 caps between 1911 and 1914. He captained both Oxford and Scotland. He was a medical student and enlisted in the Gordon Highlanders at the outbreak of war. He died on 3 June 1915 at Festubert.

Second Lieutenant William Campbell Church

From a military family, Billy Church was educated at Glasgow Academy, in Switzerland and at Glasgow University. He played wing for Glasgow Academicals and won one cap against Wales in 1906. He served in the 8th Cameronians and died at Gallipoli on 28 June 1915.

Captain Eric Templeton Young

Eric Young was educated at Fettes College and Magdalen College, Oxford. He won a single cap as a forward against England in March 1914. He served in the 8th Cameronians and was killed at Gallipoli on 28 June 1915, the same day as Billy Church.

Second Lieutenant Patrick Charles Bentley Blair

A son of the manse, Blair was educated at Fettes College and at King's College, Cambridge before taking up a post with the Egyptian Civil Service. A big man at over six feet, he was a hard working forward who won five caps in season 1912–13. He served in the 5th Rifle Brigade and was killed by an exploding shell near Ypres on 6 July 1915.

Lieutenant William Middleton Wallace

From a legal family, Willie Wallace was educated at Edinburgh Academy and King's College, Cambridge. He won four caps at full-back in 1913 and 1914. He was still a student when he received a commission in the Rifle Brigade and later transferred to the Royal Flying Corps. He was killed in action near Lille on 22 August 1915.

Surgeon David Revell Bedell-Sivright

One of the hardest and most famous players of his generation, 'Darkie' won 22 caps between 1900 and 1908. He was educated at Fettes and at Cambridge and Edinburgh Universities where he studied medicine. He was commissioned as a surgeon in the Royal Navy and died of blood poisoning near Gallipoli on 5 September 1915.

Second Lieutenant Walter Maurice Dickson

Mike Dickson was educated in South Africa and was a Rhodes Scholar at University College, Oxford. He overcame deafness to win seven caps between 1912 and 1913.

He played full-back with Blackheath and had a good positional sense and powerful left boot although his defence was often weak. He served in the 11th Argyll and Sutherland Highlanders and was killed at the battle of Loos on 26 September 1915.

Lieutenant David Dickie Howie

Dave Howie was educated at Kirkcaldy High School and won seven caps as a forward between 1912 and 1913. A farmer, he enlisted in the Fife and Forfar Yeomanry and was commissioned in the Royal Field Artillery. He fought at Gallipoli and died of pneumonia in Cairo on 19 January 1916.

Private Andrew Ross

Andrew Ross was part educated at The Royal High School and worked as a marine engineer. He was a forward with Royal High School FP and won five caps between 1905 and 1909. He emigrated to Canada and fought with the 29th Canadian Infantry. He was killed in action near Ypres on 6 April 1916.

Lieutenant Cecil Abercrombie

Born in India in 1886, Cecil Abercrombie was a career sailor. He was a forward with London Scottish and the United Services, and played county cricket for Hampshire. He died on HMS *Defence* at the battle of Jutland on 31 May 1916.

Lieutenant Commander John Skinner Wilson

Born in Trinidad, John Wilson won two caps in 1908 and 1909 whilst playing for London Scottish. A hard working forward and a good all-round sportsman, he was a professional sailor and died on HMS *Indefatigable* at the battle of Jutland on 31 May 1916.

Captain Rowland Fraser

Educated at Merchiston Castle and Pembroke College, Cambridge, 'Roley' Fraser captained Cambridge in the Varsity match in 1910 and won four caps at forward in 1911. He was commissioned in the Rifle Brigade and died on 1 July 1916 at the battle of the Somme, less than two weeks after his marriage.

Lieutenant Eric Milroy

Eric Milroy was one of the first specialist scrum-halves in Scotland. An accountant, he played for Watsonians and won 12 caps between 1910 and 1914. He also toured South Africa with the British team in 1910. He joined the Royal Scots and was commissioned in the 8th Black Watch. He was killed in action on 18 July 1916 at the battle of the Somme and is commemorated on the Thiepval Memorial to the Missing.

Lieutenant John George Will

Educated at Merchant Taylors' School and Downing College, Cambridge, George Will was a small and slimly built wing who won seven caps between 1912 and 1914, scoring twice against Wales in 1912. He enlisted early in the war and became a pilot in the Royal Flying Corps. He was killed in a dogfight with German aircraft on 25 March 1917.

Captain Thomas Arthur Nelson

Tommy Nelson was heir to Thomas Nelson Publishers of Edinburgh. He was educated at Edinburgh Academy and Oxford University, and won one cap as a centre in 1898. A Territorial soldier, he served in the Lothian and Border Horse and was thrice mentioned in dispatches. He was killed by artillery fire near Arras on 9 April 1917.

Major Walter Torrie Forrest

Wattie Forrest was born and educated in Kelso where his family ran a fishing tackle business, but he won his seven caps whilst playing for Hawick. He was a solid defensive full-back who liked to take risks. A deeply religious man, he fought at Gallipoli with the King's Own Scottish Borderers and was awarded the Military Cross for conspicuous bravery. He died in Palestine on 19 April 1917.

Lieutenant Albert Luvian Wade

Bertie Wade was educated at Dulwich College and was a scrum-half with London Scottish and Old Alleynians. A solid rather than spectacular player, he won a single cap against England in 1908. He served in the 17th Middlesex Regiment and died at an attack near Arras on 28 April 1917.

Lieutenant James Young Milne Henderson

'JY' Henderson was educated at George Watson's College and played stand-off for Watsonians. He won one cap against England in 1911. He moved to India and then returned to London as works manager for McVittie and Price biscuit manufacturers. He joined the Royal Scots and was commissioned in the Highland Light Infantry. He died near Ypres on 31 July 1917.

Lieutenant John Argentine Campbell

As his middle name suggests, John Campbell was born in Argentina. He was educated at Fettes College and Trinity College, Cambridge where he played in three Varsity matches. A sound and vigorous forward, he won one cap against Ireland in 1900. He returned from Argentina at the outbreak of war and served in the 17th Lancers and the 6th Inniskilling Dragoons. He died of wounds in a German prisoner of war camp on 2 December 1917.

Lieutenant Stephanus Sebastian Lombard Steyn

Stephen 'Beak' Steyn was born in South Africa to a Scottish mother and was a Rhodes Scholar at Oxford University. A long striding wing, he won two caps against England in 1911 and Ireland in 1912. He was studying medicine at Guy's Hospital when war broke out and served in the Royal Field Artillery. He was killed in action near Jerusalem on 8 December 1917.

Lieutenant Colonel George Alexander Walker Lamond

George Lamond was educated at Kelvinside Academy and worked as civil engineer, including time in Egypt. He played at centre for Kelvinside Academicals and Bristol, and won three caps between 1899 and 1905 before giving up rugby for work reasons. He was also a good golfer and a keen fisherman. He enlisted in the Royal Engineers and died of fever in Mesopotamia on 25 February 1918.

Captain William Ramsay Hutchison

A forward, Bill Hutchison played for Glasgow High School FP (where his father was rector) and won a single cap against England in 1911. He returned from Canada to join the Highland Light Infantry and was commissioned in the Royal Scots Fusiliers. He served in France and Salonika, and was killed during the German Spring Offensive on 22 March 1918.

Major Roland Elphinstone Gordon

A strongly built player who was deceptively quick, Roland Gordon was a professional soldier and was educated at King's School, Canterbury and the Royal Military Academy, Sandhurst. He played at centre and won three caps in 1913. He served in the Royal Field Artillery and was awarded the Military Cross. He was severely wounded in 1915, but returned to the Army and died near Amiens on 30 August 1918.

Second Lieutenant Walter Riddell Sutherland

The fair-haired Wattie Sutherland won 13 caps between 1910 and 1914. A wing and centre, he was idolised in Hawick, his home town, and fast enough to become a Scottish sprint champion. He enlisted in the Lothian and Border Horse and was commissioned in the 8th Seaforth Highlanders. He was killed in action near Béthune on 4 October 1918.

In addition, Harry Dods, a forward who won eight caps between 1895 and 1897, was killed with his wife and three children when HMS *Natal* mysteriously exploded in Cromarty harbour on 30 December 1915. Dods, a factor on the Novar estate, was a civilian at the time. The Scottish Football Union lost several committee members in the First World War. Captain James H Lindsay played for Edinburgh Institution FP and served in the Royal Garrison Artillery. He died in June 1915 as a result of a motoring accident and was buried in the Dean Cemetery, Edinburgh. John M Usher played for Edinburgh Wanderers and was the brother of internationalist Charlie Usher. He was a lieutenant in the 9th Gordon Highlanders and died on 25 September 1915 at the battle of Loos. Arthur D Flett was the brother of internationalist Andrew Flett and served as secretary of the SFU in 1914–15. He was a lieutenant in the 16th Royal Scots and was killed in action in France on 9 April 1917, one of three brothers who died in the war.

THE SECOND WORLD WAR

Pilot Officer Donald Kenneth Andrew Mackenzie

Educated at Inverness Royal Academy, Donald Mackenzie was a back-row forward with Edinburgh Wanderers and won two caps in 1939. He was an apprentice chartered accountant before joining the RAF. He died on 12 June 1940 aged 23 and is buried in Colinton Churchyard.

Pilot Officer Thomas Fairgreave Dorward

Tommy Dorward played scrum-half for Gala and won five caps in 1938 and 1939. He was a director of the family tweed mill in Galashiels. A member of the Royal Air Force Volunteer Reserve, he was killed in a flying accident on 5 March 1941, less than two weeks before he was due to be married. He is buried in Eastlands Cemetery, Galashiels.

Sergeant William Alexander Ross

Bill Ross played stand-off for Hillhead High School FP and won two caps in 1937. He was a pilot with the Royal Air Force Volunteer Reserve and died in North Africa on 28 September 1941.

Private Patrick Munro

Pat Munro won 13 caps as a half-back between 1905 and 1911, famously supplying the crosskick for Ken MacLeod's great try against the South Africans in 1906. After Oxford, Munro served in the Sudanese Political Service and in 1931 was elected Unionist MP for Llandaff and Barry, later becoming a Government Whip. He was SRU President in 1939–40. A member of the Home Guard, he died at Westminster during an air raid exercise on 3 May 1942.

Second Lieutenant James McPhail Ritchie

Educated at George Watson's College, Jim Ritchie was a fine all-round athlete who had a powerful physique and colourful personality. A prop forward, he won six caps in 1933 and 1934, and also represented Scotland at water polo. In 1934, he moved to India. He served in the 1st Punjab Regiment and died of enteric fever at Rawalpindi on 6 July 1942.

Flight Sergeant Roy Muir Kinnear

Roy Kinnear played centre with Heriot's FP and won three caps in 1926. Two years earlier, he toured South Africa with the British team in 1924 and played in four tests. In 1927, he turned professional with Wigan. He served as an air gunner and drill instructor in the RAF and died when playing in a rugby match on 22 September 1942.

Lieutenant John Gordon Scott Forrest

A student at Cambridge University, Forrest won three caps as left wing in the Triple Crown winning side in 1938 during which he scored two tries against Ireland. He served in the Royal Naval Volunteer Reserve based at HMS *Blackcap* in Cheshire and died on 14 September 1942.

Lieutenant-Commander Drummond St Clair-Ford

A winger with the Royal Navy and United Services, St Clair-Ford won five caps in the early 1930s. He joined the Royal Navy in 1924. He was in command of the HMS Submarine *Traveller* which was lost in the Mediterranean in early December 1942.

Lieutenant George Roberts

George Roberts played full-back for Watsonians and won five caps between 1938 and 1939. He also represented Scotland at golf. A bank official, he enlisted in the Gordon Highlanders and died in a Japanese prisoner of war camp on 2 August 1943. His younger brother Kenneth was killed on active service in June 1940.

Wing Commander William Mitchell Penman

A former pupil of Royal High School, Bill Penman played full-back for London Scottish and the United Services, and won his only cap against Ireland in 1939. A small and compact man, he was a professional airman and won several awards for gallantry during the war, including the Distinguished Flying Cross. He died during a raid over Germany on 3 October 1943 and is buried in Hanover War Cemetery.

Surgeon Lieutenant Alastair Simpson Bell McNeil

A prop forward, Alastair McNeil won one cap against Ireland in 1935. He also represented Scotland at cricket. He was educated at George Watson's College and Edinburgh University where he read medicine. He served in the Royal Naval Volunteer Reserve and died on 26 January 1944.

Captain William Norman Renwick

Renwick was educated at Loretto, where he was head boy, and University College, Oxford. He won two caps on the wing in 1938 and 1939. He was commissioned in the Royal Field Artillery before being posted to the 1st Royal Horse Artillery. He fought in North Africa and died in Italy on 15 June 1944.

Major George Holmes Gallie

Son of 1920s internationalist Bob, George Gallie won one cap as a prop against Wales in 1939. He was awarded the Military Cross in August 1943. He served in the Royal Artillery and was killed in action in southern Italy on 16 January 1944.

Eric Liddell

Winner of sevens caps and an Olympic gold medal, Eric Liddell was the most popular athlete Scotland has ever produced. He worked as a missionary in China and died on 21 February 1945 in a Japanese internment camp.

In addition, Archie Symington, who was listed in the Roll of Honour in Sandy Thorburn's book, had a distinguished war record. He was educated at Fettes College and Cambridge University, and won two caps as a forward in 1914. He was twice wounded in the First World War and won the Military Cross. He received a commission in the Royal Flying Corps and subsequently entered the Royal Air Force where he promoted to Squadron Leader at the beginning of the Second World War. He was invalided out of the service in early 1944 and died of heart failure during a fishing trip near Oban on 7 May 1944.

Appendix VI
And finally... some unexpected stuff

By far the most common occupation amongst players in the amateur era was medicine. At a rough count, well over 90 players out of about 900 were doctors or medical students, most at the University of Edinburgh. Perhaps they didn't mind inflicting pain or the sight of blood. Amongst several prominent medical careers, Andrew Balfour won four caps in the 1890s and rose to become director of the London School of Tropical Medicine. He was knighted in 1930 and wrote medical textbooks and adventure novels in his spare time. In the current (2013) squad, Geoff Cross has combined a professional rugby career with medical studies. The burly Jock Allan, who won 17 caps between the wars, was a psychiatric nurse at Dingleton hospital in Melrose.

Law has also been a popular career choice. John Dallas won a single cap in 1903, but his greater claim to rugby fame was as referee of Wales v New Zealand in 1905. Controversially, he did not award a late try by All Black Bob Deans which meant that the tourists lost their unbeaten record. The same year Dallas was called to the bar and subsequently became Sheriff of Aberdeenshire for 20 years. Several Scottish players have been members of the prestigious Society of Writers to the Signet, including Leslie Balfour, John Boswell, Patrick Don Wauchope, James Graham, Ninian Finlay, Ian MacIntyre, James Moir Mackenzie, Thomas Marshall, John Scott and Harry Stevenson.

Rugby and religion may not seem obvious bedfellows, but at least ten Scottish players have had careers in the church. Amongst these, Peter Anton, a forward who won one cap in 1873, became Church of Scotland minister at Kilsyth for 30 years and wrote books on theology and local history. Father and son Henry and Peter Gedge both played for Scotland and both were vicars in England, the former for almost 30 years at York Minster where he is remembered by a small plaque. James Cotter won two caps in 1934 and subsequently became minister at Langholm and Dalserf. He published his autobiography *Tackling Life* in 2000. Famously, Eric Liddell became a Christian missionary in China between the wars. John Arthur, one of the 1871 originals, did evangelical work in Glasgow and held weekly Bible classes in Hillhead for over 30 years. In the current (2013) squad, prop Euan Murray chooses not to play on a Sunday because of his religious beliefs.

Eric Liddell won the gold medal for the 400 metres at the Paris Olympics in 1924, but Scottish rugby has other links with the Olympic Games. Robert Lindsay-Watson threw the hammer at London in 1908, CEWC Mackintosh took part in the long jump in 1924 and Bill Stewart ran for Australasia at Stockholm in 1912. Ewan Douglas, a war-time cap, threw the hammer in 1948 and 1952. David Robertson won the bronze medal for golf in 1900. Robin Welsh was a member of the British curling squad that won gold at the Chamonix Winter Olympics in 1924. At the time curing was a demonstration sport, but in 2006 the International Olympic Committee upgraded it and the medals were awarded retrospectively.

John Buchan's famous spy thriller *The Thirty-Nine Steps* is dedicated to a Scottish rugby player. Whilst at Oxford University in the 1890s, Buchan became friends with Tommy Nelson of the famous Edinburgh publishing firm who won a single cap in 1898. Subsequently, Buchan dedicated his novel, which was published in 1915, to his great friend.

Amongst other literary connections, John Boswell, a forward who won 15 caps in the 1890s, was a descendant of James Boswell, the famous biographer. John Guthrie Tait, who won two caps in the 1880s, was an authority on the life and works of Sir Walter Scott and edited an edition of Scott's *Journal* in the 1930s.

Louis Greig, who won five caps between 1905 and 1908, trained as a doctor and became a close friend and adviser to the Duke of York, later King George VI. A biographical study of their complex relationship entitled *Louis and the Prince* was published in 1999.

Henry Halcro Johnston, who won two caps in 1877, was a great man of Orkney. He was a descendant of the Royal Norse family of Halcro and also King Robert the Bruce. He had a distinguished medical career and was an important amateur botanist. He collected samples from all over the world, wrote scientific papers and amassed a huge collection of flora and fauna from Orkney and Shetland.

Peter Kininmonth is famous for his drop goal that beat Wales in 1951. After a career as a financial broker, he made a successful foray into cheese-making using milk from his own herd of pedigree cows. Cranborne Chase Cheeses won several awards and became one of the official cheeses at the Houses of Parliament.

Scottish rugby has produced several politicians. Ian MacIntyre, who won six caps in the 1890s, was Conservative MP for West Edinburgh between 1924 and 1929. Pat Munro was Conservative MP for Llandaff and Barry between 1931 and 1942. Gordon Waddell was a South African MP for Johannesburg North representing the anti-apartheid Progressive Federal Party in the mid-1970s. John Bannerman stood unsuccessfully as a Liberal party candidate at several general elections and in 1967 he became Baron Bannerman of Kildonan so finally entered Parliament. Tremayne Rodd succeeded his uncle as the 3rd Baron Rennell in 1978 and took the Conservative whip in the House of Lords. A great all-rounder, he represented the Lords at cricket, bridge and chess, and played rugby for a Lords and Commons XV well into his fifties.

Several Scottish players have been principals at Border Common Ridings and festivals. Bill Kyle was Hawick Cornet in 1905; Adam Polson, first Braw Lad of Galashiels in 1930; Douglas Lowe, Town Champion at Musselburgh Riding of the Marches in 1935; Jimmy Maxwell, Langholm Cornet in 1955; Eric Paxton, Kelso Laddie in 1976; and Graham Sheil, Melrosian in 1993.

And to play us out, the world's most unlikely orchestra. On piano Joe Inglis; bagpipes, John Boswell; cello, Rufus Bruce Lockhart; guitarists John Beattie and Stewart Campbell; trumpet, Jim Renwick; ukulele, Andy Macdonald; and on vocals Thom Evans, former singer and bassist with boy band Twen2y4se7en. Pass the earplugs and take it away lads.

Luath Press Limited
committed to publishing well written books worth reading

LUATH PRESS takes its name from Robert Burns, whose little collie Luath (*Gael.*, swift or nimble) tripped up Jean Armour at a wedding and gave him the chance to speak to the woman who was to be his wife and the abiding love of his life. Burns called one of 'The Twa Dogs' Luath after Cuchullin's hunting dog in Ossian's *Fingal*. Luath Press was established in 1981 in the heart of Burns country, and now resides a few steps up the road from Burns' first lodgings on Edinburgh's Royal Mile.

Luath offers you distinctive writing with a hint of unexpected pleasures.

Most bookshops in the UK, the US, Canada, Australia, New Zealand and parts of Europe either carry our books in stock or can order them for you. To order direct from us, please send a £sterling cheque, postal order, international money order or your credit card details (number, address of cardholder and expiry date) to us at the address below. Please add post and packing as follows: UK – £1.00 per delivery address; overseas surface mail – £2.50 per delivery address; overseas airmail – £3.50 for the first book to each delivery address, plus £1.00 for each additional book by airmail to the same address. If your order is a gift, we will happily enclose your card or message at no extra charge.

Luath Press Limited
543/2 Castlehill
The Royal Mile
Edinburgh EH1 2ND
Scotland

Telephone: 0131 225 4326 (24 hours)
Fax: 0131 225 4324
email: sales@luath.co.uk
Website: www.luath.co.uk